June 27–30, 2017
Stanford, CA, USA

Association for
Computing Machinery

Advancing Computing as a Science & Profession

IDC 2017

Proceedings of the 2017 ACM Conference on Interaction Design and Children

Sponsored by:

ACM SIGCHI

Supported by:

Google, SRI Education, & Stanford University

Association for
Computing Machinery

Advancing Computing as a Science & Profession

The Association for Computing Machinery
2 Penn Plaza, Suite 701
New York, New York 10121-0701

ISBN: 978-1-4503-4921-5 (Digital)

ISBN: 978-1-4503-5591-9 (Print)

Additional copies may be ordered prepaid from:

ACM Order Department
PO Box 30777
New York, NY 10087-0777, USA

Phone: 1-800-342-6626 (USA and Canada)
+1-212-626-0500 (Global)
Fax: +1-212-944-1318
E-mail: acmhelp@acm.org
Hours of Operation: 8:30 am – 4:30 pm ET

IDC 2017 Chairs' Welcome
Celebrating the 50 years of Logo

Welcome to IDC 2017, the 16th International ACM Conference on Interaction Design & Children, hosted at Stanford University during June 27 – 30, 2017.

The IDC (Interaction Design and Children) conference series began in 2002, when a workshop was held in Eindhoven, NL that brought together researchers and practitioners seeking to study how best to develop and design interactive technologies for children. In 2003, the ChiCI group at UCLan hosted the first 'conference' and the community has since held an annual conference, either in Europe or the USA.

Interaction Design and Children is an interdisciplinary international community focusing on the promises and challenges of leveraging technology so as to enable children to participate in nurturing and empowering experiences and bring children's voice and sentiments into this process. The mission of the IDC conference is to bring together researchers, designers, and educators from the cognitive sciences, human-computer interaction, learning sciences, and the various formal and informal educational settings, to explore new forms of technology, design and engaged learning among children. The annual conference incorporates papers, presentations, speakers, workshops, participatory design experiences and discussions on how to create better interactive experiences for children. IDC 2017 offers a wide-ranging program, supporting and facilitating the exchange of ideas within and between all of these communities.

IDC 2017 theme: "Logo: The Next 50 Years"

2017 marks the 50th anniversary of Logo, the first programming language for children, which materialized a pedagogical vision of empowering children. Logo was created by Wally Feurzeig, Seymour Papert, and Cynthia Solomon. Sadly, 2017 is also the first Logo year without Seymour Papert, who passed away on July 31, 2016. But in 2016 we also lost two crucial figures in the history of Logo: Marvin Minsky and Edith Ackermann. And just recently we lost another visionary: Robert Tinker. And so it now is up to all of us to carry forth the legacies of Marvin, Bob, Edith, and Seymour — indeed an honorable calling for the IDC community. This legacy is greater than turtles, recursion, and coding. It is the legacy of envisioning new resources and bold pedagogies that invite children into previously inaccessible content. More broadly, it is the legacy of creating for children environments where each will find the gears of their childhood, early experiences and engaging practices that are formative of lifelong academic passions, as Seymour wrote back in 1980 in his groundbreaking book, Mindstorms.

The IDC 2017 theme, *Logo: The Next 50 Years*, thus pays homage to Papert's powerful educational ideas in celebration of his achievement — lifelong and beyond. And so, as we now begin the next 50 years of the Logo legacy, how should we proceed? What new opportunities do we foresee ahead, what new challenges? How do Papert's theoretical assertions, design frameworks, and educational vision speak to current turns in the research that inform our collective and varied IDC efforts? What technological innovations better enable us to realize his principles in the form of construction and instruction materials? What is becoming of Papert's quest for epistemological pluralism, global equity, the right for a second chance, gender equality, access, intellectual ownership, and emancipation?

Let us revisit the constructionist vision to reimagine education in the 21st century, where all children engage, own, and enact powerful ideas through a range of expressive media. Many of Papert's futuristic ideas from Mindstorms are now taken for granted, such as the importance of fostering students' computational reasoning, the inherent roles of the body, society, and culture in creative problem solving, and making space for diverse cognitive predilections. Ironically, a mark of Papert's lasting influence is that his "psychedelic" ideas from the 60's and 70's have been assimilated so well into mainstream educational discourse and practice that we just assume those ideas were always here… It has been an epic voyage, and it is far from over. *We are not there yet.*

IDC 2017 has therefore invited scholars, designers, and practitioners to celebrate Logo by sharing their work on technologies that improve all children's opportunities to interact with expressive media, engage in new literacies, and develop powerful ideas. We sought contribution on emerging technologies for children, design, and evaluation of interactive experiences, as well as new methods, approaches, and theoretical perspectives.

The conference theme is instantiated at IDC 2017 in the form of a special panel chaired by Profs. Jeanne Bamberger, Mike Eisenberg, and Richard Noss.

Conference Program

This year, the accepted submissions come from 35 countries: Germany, United States, Sweden, Denmark, Austria, Germany, Israel, Japan, Belgium, Norway, Switzerland, United Kingdom, Portugal, Egypt, Canada, The Netherlands, China, Italy, Brazil, France, Ireland, Seoul, New Zealand, Greece, Finland, Israel, Greece, Madeira, Spain, Scotland, Uganda, Colombia, Korea, Australia, and Thailand. The program committee reviewed a record 118 full paper submissions, 33 notes, 75 work in progress/late breaking, 26 demos, and 13 submissions for the Doctoral Consortium. The full paper acceptance rate was 21.1% (25 full papers accepted). The keyword breakdown is shown in the following table, ranked by their occurrence. The IDC community is still loyal to many of its original themes – education, families, creativity, participatory design, and the acceptance of multiple types of research methods – and we witness the most welcome development of Assistive Technologies as an emerging theme.

Keyword	Primary	Secondary	Score[1]
Education/Learning	24	60	36.0
Children/Parents	13	50	25.3
Empirical studies on a system	6	27	13.0
Creativity and Children	10	15	11.7
Schools/Educational Setting	0	34	11.3
Methods for involving children in design	7	19	11.0
Participatory Design	5	20	10.0
Games/Play	5	19	9.7
Programming kits for children	7	11	8.3
Individuals with Disabilities & Assistive Technologies	7	11	8.3
Design guidelines	3	18	8.0
Interaction Design	1	21	7.7
Qualitative Methods	0	23	7.7
Novel applications for children	3	15	7.0

[1] Each keyword score was calculated by the following formula: (primary keyword * 2 + secondary keyword) / 3

Keynotes

We will have three keynote talks, which will guide us to a better understanding of the future of the field:

- **Andy diSessa (University of California, Berkeley):** What If Your Project's Timeline is a 100 Years?: Reflections on Computational Literacies.
- **Alissa Antle (Simon Fraser University):** Crazy Like Us: Design for Vulnerable Populations.
- **Joshua Miele (The Smith-Kettlewell Rehabilitation Engineering Research Center on Low Vision and Blindness):** Teaching Teachers and Making Makers: What the Maker Movement Can Teach the World About Accessibility and Design.

Panels

Special panel on "50 years of Logo"

Chairs: Jeanne Bamberger (MIT and University of California-Berkeley), Mike Eisenberg (University of Colorado-Boulder), and Richard Noss (University College London)

The panel will offer diverse perspectives on the history of the Logo language as well as the future of constructionist learning environments inspired by the Logo aesthetics and philosophy, where children learn through using computational technologies to build things.

Learning Sciences and Interaction Design for Children

Chairs: Michelle Wilkerson (University of California-Berkeley) and Yasmin Kafai (University of Pennsylvania)

Members of the panel will examine relationships between efforts to develop theory, empirical research, and products that contribute to children's learning. Drawing on perspectives from the Learning Sciences, Human-Computer Interaction, and more, they will evaluate opportunities and challenges in strengthening connections between the Interaction Design for Children and the Learning Sciences communities.

Industry and Interaction Design for Children

Chairs: Jeremy Roschelle (SRI) and Mindy Brooks (Google)

This industry panel will feature members of product design teams from research, public broadcasting, and technology organizations to discuss how collaborations across different disciplines (e.g. learning science, media design, character development, and user experience) can shape large scale products that positively impact the lives of children across diverse settings.

Putting together *IDC 2017* was a team effort. We first thank the authors for providing the content of the program. We are grateful to the Chairs and Program Committee, who worked very hard in reviewing and meta-reviewing submissions and providing feedback for authors, producing almost 700 individual reviews. Finally, we are grateful to Stanford, the hosting university, our sponsor, ACM SIGCHI, and the incredible support of our generous corporate supporters, Google and SRI International.

We hope that you will find this program interesting and thought provoking and that the conference will provide you with a valuable opportunity to share ideas with other researchers and practitioners from institutions around the world.

Paulo Blikstein
Stanford University

Dor Abrahamson
University of California, Berkeley

Citing work in the proceedings:

The entire proceedings:

Blikstein, P., & Abrahamson, D. (Chairs), *"Logo: The Next 50 Years" – Proceedings of the 16th annual Interaction Design and Children conference (IDC 2017).* Stanford University: IDC.

Keynote, Panel:

Smith, J., & Doe, X. (2017). Keynote/Panel name here. In P. Blikstein & D. Abrahamson (Chairs), "Logo: The Next 50 Years" – *Proceedings of the 16th annual Interaction Design and Children conference (IDC 2017)* (pp. xx – yy). Stanford University: IDC.

Full Paper:

Smith, J., & Doe, X. (2017). *Title here.* In P. Blikstein, D. Abrahamson, M. Horn, & B. Zaman (Eds.), *"Logo: The Next 50 Years" – Proceedings of the 16th annual Interaction Design and Children conference (IDC 2017)* (pp. xx – yy). Stanford University: IDC.

Note:

Smith, J., & Doe, X. (2017). *Title here.* In P. Blikstein, D. Abrahamson, K. Fisher, T. Clegg, & K. Ryokai (Eds.), *"Logo: The Next 50 Years" – Proceedings of the 16th annual Interaction Design and Children conference (IDC 2017)* (pp. xx – yy). Stanford University: IDC.

Work in Progress/Late Breaking:

Smith, J., & Doe, X. (2017). *Title here.* In P. Blikstein, D. Abrahamson, N. Holbert, & L. Anthony (Eds.), *"Logo: The Next 50 Years" – Proceedings of the 16th annual Interaction Design and Children conference (IDC 2017)* (pp. xx – yy). Stanford University: IDC.

Demo:

Smith, J., & Doe, X. (2017). *Title here.* In P. Blikstein, D. Abrahamson, M. Worsley, & J. Fails (Eds.), *"Logo: The Next 50 Years" – Proceedings of the 16th annual Interaction Design and Children conference (IDC 2017)* (pp. xx – yy). Stanford University: IDC.

Design Competition:

Smith, J., & Doe, X. (2017). *Title here.* In P. Blikstein, D. Abrahamson, A. Sipitakiat, & R. B. Shapiro (Eds.), *"Logo: The Next 50 Years" – Proceedings of the 16th annual Interaction Design and Children conference (IDC 2017)* (pp. xx – yy). Stanford University: IDC.

Table of Contents

Health, Wellness, and Development (Full Paper Session)

Session Chairs: Michael Horn *(Northwestern University)* & Bieke Zaman *(KU Leuven)*

Coding and Computational Thinking (Full Paper Session)

Session Chairs: Michael Horn *(Northwestern University)* & Bieke Zaman *(KU Leuven)*

Peer & Robot Interactions (Full Paper Session)

Session Chairs: Michael Horn *(Northwestern University)* & Bieke Zaman *(KU Leuven)*

Literacy and Mixed Learning Environments (Full Paper Session)

Session Chairs: Michael Horn *(Northwestern University)* & Bieke Zaman *(KU Leuven)*

Notes (Short Papers)

Session Chairs: Karen Fisher *(University of Washington)*, Tamara Clegg *(University of Maryland)*, Kimiko Ryokai *(University of Califonia, Berkeley)*

Work in Progress/Late Breaking

Session Chairs: Nathan Holbert *(Columbia University)*, Lisa Anthony *(University of Florida)*

Demonstrations

Session Chairs: Marcelo Worsley *(Northwestern University)*, Jerry Alan Fails *(Boise State University)*

Workshops

Session Chairs: Shuli Gilutz *(Tel-Aviv University)*, Tamar Fuhrmann *(Stanford University)*, Bertrand Schneider *(Harvard University)*

Research and Design Competition

Session Chairs: Arnan Sipitakiat *(Chiang Mai University)*, R. Benjamin Shapiro *(University of Colorado – Boulder)*

IDC 2017 Organization

The 16th International Conference on Interaction Design and Children

General Chairs:	Paulo Blikstein *(Stanford University, USA)* Dor Abrahamson *(University of California, Berkeley, USA)*
Consultant Chairs:	Michail Giannakos *(Norwegian University of Science and Technology, Norway)* Janet Read *(University of Central Lancashire, UK)*
Technical Program and Publications Chairs:	Greg Walsh *(University of Baltimore, USA)* Christopher Frauenberger *(TU Wien, Austria)*
Full Papers Chairs:	Michael Horn *(Northwestern University, USA)* Bieke Zaman *(KU Leuven, Belgium)*
Short Paper (Notes) Chairs:	Karen Fisher *(University of Washington, USA)* Tamara Clegg *(University of Maryland, USA)* Kimiko Ryokai *(University of California, Berkeley, USA)*
Demo Chairs:	Marcelo Worsley *(Northwestern University, USA)* Jerry Alan Fails *(Boise State University, USA)*
Workshop / Courses Chair:	Shuli Gilutz *(Tel-Aviv University, Israel)* Tamar Fuhrmann *(Stanford University, USA)* Bertrand Schneider *(Harvard University, USA)*
Work in Progress Chairs:	Nathan Holbert *(Teachers College-Columbia University, USA)* Lisa Anthony *(University of Florida, USA)*
"50 years of Logo" Special Panel chairs	Mike Eisenberg *(University of Colorado, Boulder, USA)* Jeanne Bamberger *(MIT/University of California, Berkeley, USA)* Richard Noss *(University College London, England)*
"Industry and IDC" Panel Chairs:	Jeremy Roschelle *(SRI, USA)* Mindy Brooks *(Google, USA)*
"Learning Sciences and Interaction Design for Children" Panel Chairs	Michelle H. Wilkerson *(University of California, Berkeley, USA)* Yasmin Kafai *(University of Pennsylvania, USA)*
Research and Design Competition Chairs:	Arnan Sipitakiat *(Chiang Mai University, Thailand)* R. Benjamin Shapiro *(University of Colorado, Boulder, USA)*

Doctoral Consortium Chairs: Juan Pablo Hourcade *(University of Iowa, USA)*
Matthew Berland *(University of Wisconsin-Madison, USA)*
Chronis Kynigos *(National and Kapodistrian University of Athens, Greece)*

Student Volunteer Chairs: Richard Davis *(Stanford University, USA)*
Veronica Li *(Stanford University, USA)*

Social Activities Chairs: Kiera Chase *(University of California, Berkeley, USA)*
Engin Bumbacher *(Stanford University, USA)*

Publicity and Social Media Chairs: Anna Weltman *(University of California, Berkeley, USA)*
Ting Siu *(San Francisco State University, USA)*

Associate Paper Chairs: Kylie Peppler *(Indiana University, USA)*
Jasmine Y. Ma *(New York University, USA)*
Iman C. Chahine (*Georgia State University, USA / University of Johannesburg, South Africa)*
Andrew Manches *(University of Edinburgh, UK)*
Sharona T. Levy *(University of Haifa, Israel)*
Yishay Mor (*Levinsky College of Education, Israel)*
Michiel Veldhuis (*Universiteit Utrecht, Netherlands)*
Chronis Kynigos *(National and Kapodistrian University of Athens, Greece)*
Ibrahim Dahlstrom-Hakki *(Landmark College, USA)*
Narcis Pares (*Universitat Pompeu Fabra, Barcelona)*
Michael Tan *(National Institute of Education, Singapore)*
Vince Geiger *(Learning Sciences Institute Australia, Australian Catholic University, Australia)*
Wolmet Barendregt *(University of Gothenburg, Sweden)*
Anna Shvarts *(Lomonosov Moscow State University, Russia)*

Reviewers: Muhammad Haziq Lim Abdullah, Dor Abrahamson, Samir Aknine, Ruthi Aladjem, Alyssa Alcorn, Ma'ayan Alexander, Zachary Alstad, Ragaad AlTarawneh, Valentina Andries, Ling Weay Ang, Michelle Annett, Lisa Anthony, Gabriella Anton, Ahmed Arif, Jodi Asbell-Clarke, Zeina Atrash Leong, Madeline Balaam, Amartya Banerjee, Rahul Banerjee, Wolmet Barendregt, Ankica Barisic, Mary Barreto, Elham Beheshti, Sophia Bender, Laura Benton, Sergi Bermúdez i Badia, Marina Bers, Roos Blankespoor, Paulo Blikstein, Elizabeth Bonsignore, Boudewijn Boon, Federico Botella, Corey Brady, Rick Bryck, Laia Canals, Stefan Carmien, Karina Caro, Elizabeth Carter, Eva Cerezo, Teresa Cerratto Pargman, Iman Chahine, Senthil Chandrasegaran, Timothy Charoenying, Jinghui Cheng, Jundong Cho, Gi Woong Choi, Sharon Lynn Chu, Priscilla Chueng-Nainby, Tamara Clegg, Tamara Clegg, Ashley Colley, Ciera Crowell, Bronwyn Cumbo, Sally Jo Cunningham, Quintin Cutts, Ibrahim Dahlstrom-Hakki, Sayamindu Dasgupta, Richard Davis,

Reviewers (continued): Rahmad Dawood, Luigi de Russis, Kayla DesPortes, Mihaela Dragomir, Carolien Duijzer, Sarah Eagle, Michael Eisenberg, Houda El mimouni, Eva Eriksson, Jerry Fails, Min Fan, Amy Farris, Karen Feder, Rodrigo Fernandes, Gabriele Ferri, Tiare Feuchtner, Deborah Fields, Daniel Fitton, Stéphanie Fleck, Sue Fletcher-Watson, Tom Flint, Angus Forbes, Steve Funke, Dilrukshi Gamage, Franca Garzotto, Vincent Geiger, Eirini Geraniou, Michail Giannakos, Carina Girvan, Keith Green, Jose Gutierrez, Jonna Häkkilä, Alexandria Hansen, Danielle Harlow, Heidi Hartikainen, Bart Hengeveld, Wilko Heuten, Nathan Holbert, Tyler Hollett, Paula Hooper, Michael Horn, Juan Pablo Hourcade, Kate Howland, Shah Rukh Humayoun, Ke Huo, Seray Ibrahim, Netta Iivari, Germaine Irwin, Javier Jaen, Sujin Jang, Tim Jay, Mads Møller Jensen, Priscilla Jimenez Pazmino, Ken Kahn, Bridget Kane, Eva-Sophie Katterfeldt, Saba Kawas, Kevin Keith, Molly Kelton, Anna Keune, Nam Wook Kim, Jeeeun Kim, Marianne Kinnula, Angeliki Kolovou, Tina Kothe, Pei-Yi Kuo, Chronis Kynigos, Jianwei Lai, Monica Landoni, H. Chad Lane, Bokyung Lee, Ju-Hwan Lee, Victor Lee, Jill Lehman, Samantha LeVan, Sharona Levy, Eric Lindsay, Brenda Lopez Silva, Silvia Lovato, Jasmine Ma, Joseph Maguire, Lisa Maione, Katerina Makri, Laura Malinverni, Andrew Manches, Crystle Martin, Manolis Mavrikis, Peter Mckenna, Brenna McNally, Chulhong Min, Robb Mitchell, Mohd Firdaus Mohd Ab Halim, Yishay Mor, Joan Mora-Guiard, Alejandro Moreno, Leonel Morgado, Fabio Morreale, Alexander Muir, Maximilian Müller, Cukurova Mutlu, Hyunjoo Oh, Nancy Otero Ornelas, Mara Otten, Helen Pain, Kyparisia Papanikolaou, Narcis Pares, Sarah Parsons, Roma Patel, Christina (Yu) Pei, Kylie Peppler, Anthony Perritano, Laia Pujol-Tost, Chris Quintana, Sarah Radke, Iulian Radu, Vyshnavi Ramesh, Janet Read, Daniel Rees Lewis, Glenda Revelle, Peter Rich, Kathryn Ringland, Jessica Roberts, Judy Robertson, Guarionex Salivia, Iván Sánchez Milara, Ruth Sancho Huerga, Rafi Santo, Yann Savoye, Marie-Monique Schaper, elina Schepers, Mishael Sedas, Liat Shalev (Biberman), Cyrus Shaoul, Jinjuan She, Roy Shilkrot, Anna Shvarts, Gavin Sim, Yue-Ting Siu, Wouter Sluis-Thiescheffer, Kiley Sobel, Carles Sora, Katharina Spiel, Cristina Sylla, Michael Tan, Monica Tentori, Naomi Thompson, Mike Tissenbaum, Olof Torgersson, Dragan Trninic, A.M. Tsaasan, Tobias Uebbing, Suraj Uttamchandani, Maarten Van Mechelen, S.C. van Veen, Asimina Vasalou, Christina Vasiliou, Michiel Veldhuis, Ilgim Veryeri-Alaca, Krystal Villanosa, Gualtiero Volpe, Aditi Wagh, Torben Wallbaum, Jillian Warren, David Weintrop, Justin Whiting, Michelle Wilkerson, Karen Wohlwend, Paweł Woźniak, Nikoleta Yiannoutsou, Jason Yip, Nicola Yuill, Leah Zhang, Qian Zhao, Zhi Zheng, Ninger Zhou, Kening Zhu

IDC 2017 Sponsor & Supporters

Sponsor: SIGCHI

Supporters: Google

SRI Education™

A DIVISION OF SRI INTERNATIONAL

Stanford University

What If Your Project's Timeline is a 100 Years? Reflections on Computational Literacies

Andrea A diSessa
University of California, Berkeley
Berkeley, CA 94720, USA
disessa@berkeley.edu

IDC '17, June 27-30, 2017, Stanford, CA, USA

ACM ISBN 978-1-4503-4921-5/17/06.
http://dx.doi.org/10.1145/3078072.3078075

Abstract

What could it mean to have a project with goals that take decades or even a century to realize? In this talk, I reflect on my own intention to work toward a genuinely new and deep literacy—computational literacy—which I would place in eventual impact about halfway between algebra/calculus (as a literacy) and the root prototype, mass literacy centered on written text.

I start by explaining what I mean by computational literacy and what experiences have concretized it for me and made it an attractive and plausible goal. Because of its nature as a cultural phenomenon, a literacy can only be achieved by a long and meandering path of social genesis. I illustrate the nature of such development with phenomena—cultural memes, movements, sensitivities, and values (MMSVs)—as they influence development. Example MMSVs include "computational thinking" as construed by the computer science community, and the widespread current popularity of "coding academies." Finally, I position some of the best modern allies in the quest for computational literacy—such as constructionism and computer modeling—in what I take to be the larger frame: the development of a true computational literacy.

Biography

Andrea A diSessa is Corey Professor Emeritus of Education at UC Berkeley. He has an AB from Princeton and a PhD in physics from MIT. He is a member of the National Academy of Education and a Fellow of the American Educational Research Association. Prof. diSessa joined Seymour Papert's Logo group in 1972, and is well known for his early (1981) book on *Turtle Geometry* (with Hal Abelson) and for developing the Boxer computational medium, along with associated ideas about computational literacies. He has written over a hundred articles and chapters, and authored or edited a half dozen books and monographs, including *Changing Minds: Computers, Learning, and Literacy* (MIT Press). Recent work has tilted toward empirical and theoretical study of learning, particularly the role of intuitive knowledge in science learning, as founder of the "knowledge in pieces" approach to conceptual change. Current work includes teaching and studying the learning of dynamical systems theory ("patterns of change and control") by pre-high school students, and writing a sequel to *Turtle Geometry* in physics.

Crazy Like Us: Design for Vulnerable Populations

Alissa Antle
Simon Fraser University
Burnaby, BC V5A 1S6 Canada
aantle@sfu.ca

IDC '17, June 27-30, 2017, Stanford, CA, USA

ACM ISBN 978-1-4503-4921-5/17/06.
http://dx.doi.org/10.1145/3078072.3078074

Abstract

Most ethics boards classify children as a vulnerable population – all children. The reason given for this is that children lack the necessary cognitive capacity to decide whether or not to participate in most research. It may be difficult for them to foresee the risks and potential benefits to their own well-being or to understand how the conditions of research may or may not be in their own best interests. Children who have special challenges, such as those with dyslexia, ADHD, developmental delays, or mental health issues, or children living in poverty, who may be illiterate or repressed, may have even less capacity to understand and give assent to participate in research. Working with and for children, which is the cornerstone of the child-computer interaction community, raises a number of ethical challenges. First, we must present our research to children in ways they can understand. Because if we don't do this then we exclude the children who could benefit the most from the work we do, because they cannot easily give assent or because they may be difficult to access or work with. This raises an even more important issue. We may think that children can benefit from participating in our research or from using the computational systems that result from our research. But is this true? How do we know if the children we study are benefiting from our research? Third, what happens after our research is over? What legacy do we leave behind when our research is complete? And lastly, whether we are aware of it or not, we all make assumptions about what children's development, education and even their lives should look like. Author Ethan Watters wrote a book called, *Crazy Like Us, The Globalization of the American Psyche*. In this book, Watters suggests that mental health professionals from industrialized countries have generated modern theories of the human psyche, created treatments based on these models and then exported them to many of the world's cultures – sometimes with devastating consequences. Can we really take what we know about mental health and well-being and transfer it to other cultures? Does it really apply? The assumption behind this commodification is that everyone is crazy like us! But is this true?

Based on my own experience working with vulnerable children, in both industrialized and non-industrialized countries, I will discuss ethical challenges that deserve our consideration when we conduct research in child-computer interaction. By examining these issues as we plan and conduct our research we can – as a community – take the necessary care to ensure that our work has a positive impact and that we are contributing in ways that are important not just in our own minds, but in the lives of the children our work is intending to serve.

Biography

Dr. Antle is an innovator and scholar. Her research in design and human-computer interaction pushes the boundaries of computation to augment the ways we think and learn. As a designer and builder of interactive technologies, her goal is to explore the ways in which these innovations can improve, augment, and support children's cognitive and emotional development. Her interactive technologies have been deployed to facilitate collaborative learning about aboriginal heritage, sustainability and social justice; improve learning outcomes for dyslexic children; and teach self-regulation to disadvantaged children. In 2015, Dr. Antle was inducted into the Royal Society of Canada's College of New Scholars, Artists and Scientists. This is the highest honour for a scholar in Canada, acknowledging her as one of Canada's intellectual leaders. Dr. Antle began her career receiving dual Bachelor degrees in Systems Design Engineering and Liberal Arts from the University of Waterloo and a Ph.D. from the University of British Columbia. After her graduate studies, Dr. Antle worked in the new media industry as a senior designer and executive producer for companies including CBC Children's Television. Currently, Dr. Antle is a Professor in the School of Interactive Arts + Technology at Simon Fraser University.

Teaching Teachers and Making Makers: What the Maker Movement Can Teach the World about Accessibility and Design

Joshua Miele
The Smith-Kettlewell Rehabilitation Engineering Research Center on Low Vision and Blindness
San Francisco, CA 94115, USA
jam@ski.org

Abstract

Although interactive technologies and the maker movement offer stunning prospects for the next 50 years of educational inclusion and accessibility for learners with visual disabilities, a surprising array of physical, digital, and cultural barriers continue to communicate lessons of exclusion and inequity. Accessibility is a fundamental aspect of digital and physical design which, when present, allows a user with a disability to have an effective and substantively equivalent experience to that of a user without a disability. Here we consider interaction barriers for people with visual disabilities, but the themes readily apply to other disability-specific challenges in universal design and inclusion.

Consider any cross section of exciting instructional technologies, and chances are they are dominated by visual metaphors, graphical user interfaces, data visualizations, and interactive video. Systems that incorporate ostensibly non-visual, multi-modal interactives such as haptics and active manipulation do not necessarily expand access for blind and visually-impaired learners, as such tools are likely also to include key interface elements that are visual.

The same may be said of mainstream information technologies –accessibility is still temperamental and far from complete for such seemingly simple and ubiquitous resources as Google Suite, Facebook, and YouTube, let alone advanced immersive experiences such as Oculus Rift. The iconic tools of the maker movement and experiential learning – 3D design, modeling, and printing – while lauded and

IDC '17, June 27-30, 2017, Stanford, CA, USA

ACM ISBN 978-1-4503-4921-5/17/06.
http://dx.doi.org/10.1145/3078072.3078073

enthusiastically embraced by sighted designers of accessible instructional materials, remain largely unusable by independent blind makers.

Nevertheless, the maker movement and its characteristic openness and creativity is sowing seeds of change for accessibility and inclusion with long-term positive implications for people with visual disabilities in education, employment, and entertainment. This presentation will describe a long-term strategy for leveraging the maker movement and its technologies to:

- Expand inclusion of people with visual disabilities in experiential STEAM learning opportunities
- Actively Involve learners with and without visual disabilities in user-centered design of accessible solutions
- Improve representation of people with visual disabilities in STEM majors and careers

In discussing overlapping themes of user-centered design, metamaking, and Accessibility From First Principles, the presenter will draw on examples and case studies from his career as an accessible-technology researcher, as well as from a lifetime of direct experience as a blind scientist and student. His primary message is that accessibility is far more than the inclusion of non-visual interface elements and adherence to standards – it is a design consideration which, in order to be meaningful and effective, must come from a user-centered culture holistically integrated with other critical factors of design and usability. The next 50 years offers people with visual disabilities the potential for vast improvements in educational and employment equity and inclusion, but not without dedicated engagement and activism by teachers, students, developers, and policy makers.

In this vision we start simply, with blind and sighted teachers and students using the tools of the maker movement to begin building tomorrow's accessible world – together.

Biography

Dr. Joshua Miele is an innovative leader in both the accessible technology and blindness communities whose inventions are characterized by the creative use of low-cost, off-the-shelf technologies to improve information accessibility for the blind in education, employment, and entertainment. As a scientist and Associate Director of The Smith-Kettlewell Rehabilitation Engineering Research Center on Low Vision and Blindness he spends his days designing and developing new tools and techniques for improving information accessibility. As a community leader and founder of the Blind Arduino Project, LightHouse Labs, and the Description Leadership Network, Dr. Miele is a teacher and bridge builder, with an approach to accessibility that integrates community, communication, and self-empowerment with user-centered and universal design principles. His career spans decades, including contributions to screen readers; auditory and tactile displays; tactile maps, models, and graphics; mobile wayfinding; braille input; video description; hobby robotics; and more. Dr. Miele was born in Brooklyn and lives in Berkeley with his wife and two children. He is a graduate of the University of California at Berkeley where he received his BA in physics and his Ph.D. in psychoacoustics.

Intermediate-Level Knowledge in Child-Computer Interaction: A Call for Action

Wolmet Barendregt[1], Olof Torgersson[1], Eva Eriksson[1, 2], Peter Börjesson[1]
[1]University of Gothenburg & Chalmers University of Technology
[2]Aarhus University
olof.torgersson; wolmet.barendregt; peter.borjesson@ait.gu.se, eva.eriksson@chalmers.se

ABSTRACT

Based on an analysis of all papers at IDC from 2003 to 2016 this paper urges the Child-Computer Interaction (CCI) field to start formulating intermediate-level knowledge, in the form of e.g. strong concepts. Our analysis showed that 40% of all papers at the Interaction Design and Children conference presents the design of an artefact accompanied by an evaluation (to which we will refer as 'artefact-centered' papers). While exploring the design space in the form of artefacts is important and valuable, it can be argued that those artefact-centered papers generally make a smaller contribution to the field as a whole, which is also visible in the number of citations to such papers in comparison to the number of citations to other kinds of papers. As a first step towards more intermediate-level knowledge, we have thus attempted to formulate and ground three suggestions for strong concepts in CCI, namely Head-up gaming, Collective storytelling and Remote sensing. We based these concepts on an analysis of a set of relatively often-cited artefact-centered papers from the IDC conference proceedings. The three strong concepts we present here aim to show that the artefact-centered papers presented at the IDC conference over the last 15 years potentially contain useful knowledge that should be capitalized upon. The contribution of this paper is to initiate a discussion in the CCI community on the need for intermediate-level knowledge and how this knowledge, such as strong concepts, should be generated.

Author Keywords
Intermediate-level knowledge; Child-Computer Interaction; strong concepts.

ACM Classification Keywords
H.5.2. User Interfaces: User-centered design.

INTRODUCTION

The IDC conference has existed for 15 years now, and in 2016 Panos Markopoulos held a keynote concerning the development of the CCI field since its inception and up until today. One of the observations in his talk was whether the IDC conference tends to mirror the latest technological developments: e.g., when a new technology is introduced it tends to spur a flow of papers exploring its application to the domain of interaction design and children. When a new technology comes into play, the previous ones fade away and researchers and designers explore the latest trend. The wish to explore the possibilities offered by the latest technological advancements is natural but the recurrent shifts of focus lead to the question whether the exploration of one technological platform can lead to any knowledge specific to the field of CCI that can be applied to the next trend that comes around or if there is a risk that the field falls into to a constant exploration of possibilities where only a small part of the knowledge gained from exploring one trend can be carried over to the next one.

During our visits to several IDC conferences, we have also observed that quite a few of the presentations are rather heavily focused around the design and evaluation of a particular artefact. In short, the presenter gives some background, talks about the design process, describes the artefact and its evaluation, and sometimes also some design considerations or directions for future research. While the particular artefacts are all very nice examples of work within the field of interaction design and children and the researchers demonstrate the value of the artefacts for various groups of children or how they could be inspirational for other researchers, they are still to a large extent unique, stand-alone products occurring as separate points in the vast design space of possible interactive products and systems aimed at children. In the remainder of this paper we will call papers of this kind 'artefact-centered papers'.

The above-mentioned observations relate to ongoing discussions within HCI regarding research through design [72] and how to produce knowledge from design work [14, 26, 36, 42]. Of particular interest for the present paper is the notion of Intermediate-Level Knowledge [36], which consists of representations of knowledge in-between general theories and particular artefacts in terms of abstraction and generalizability. It is our belief that to evolve as a discipline there is a need for the CCI field to look beyond particular artefacts and start developing intermediate-level knowledge, while still acknowledging the value of the artefact-centered paper. In this paper we therefore pose the following research questions:

IDC '17, June 27-30, 2017, Stanford, CA, USA

ACM 978-1-4503-4921-5/17/06… $15.00
http://dx.doi.org/10.1145/3078072.3079719

- Is it true that a large part of the papers presented at the Interaction Design and Children Conference consists of artefact-centered papers?
- Do artefact-centered papers generally have a lower impact than other kinds of papers measured in terms of citations?
- Can Intermediate-Level Knowledge be generated by analyzing the currently available artefact-centered papers?

To answer these research questions we first discuss several of the proposals for what constitutes intermediate-level knowledge, and argue that strong concepts as proposed by [36] are the most relevant when trying to determine what knowledge can be gained from artefact-centered papers. Thereafter, we describe how the literature review was carried out, including a stricter definition of what constitutes an artefact-centered paper, followed by a results section in which we aim to give the answers to our three research questions. The main contribution of this paper is an opening up of the debate on how we can help the CCI field to maturate, for example by looking at the potential to generate strong concepts or other kinds of Intermediate-Level Knowledge.

INTERMEDIATE-LEVEL KNOWLEDGE

According to Höök and Löwgren [36] "In the HCI field, the dominant approach to knowledge construction is to design innovative interaction schemes and to evaluate them empirically through more or less rigorous use studies." This can then be seen has having two major aims (i) to present the actual artefacts developed and (ii) to contribute to a more general understanding of HCI. Our assumption is that the same reasoning can be applied to CCI being a subfield of HCI. Further, Höök and Löwgren argue that HCI research mainly produces knowledge at the level of *instances* and *theories* as illustrated in Figure 1.

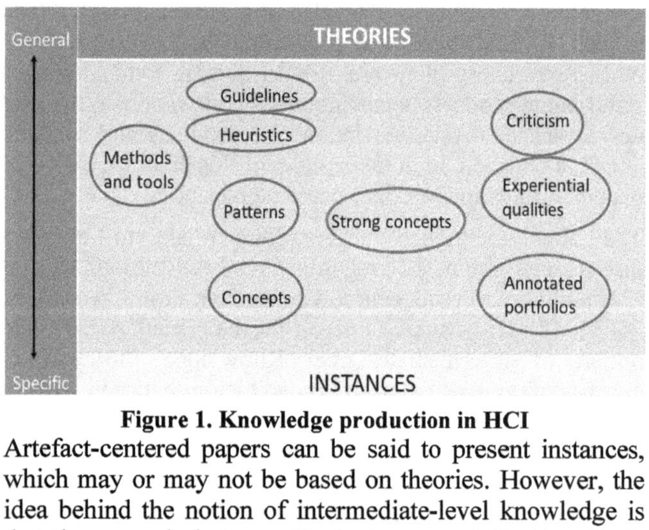

Figure 1. Knowledge production in HCI

Artefact-centered papers can be said to present instances, which may or may not be based on theories. However, the idea behind the notion of intermediate-level knowledge is that the space in-between the instances and the theories is non-empty and can be filled with knowledge constructs that are more general than the particular instances but have a different scope and purpose than general level theories [35, 36, 42]. Some examples are Patterns, Guidelines, Methods and Tools, Strong Concepts, Bridging Concepts, and Annotated Portfolios. While guidelines and methods are well-established notions within both HCI and CCI, other intermediate-level knowledge forms like strong and bridging concepts were introduced rather recently. We therefore provide an overview of Strong concepts, Bridging concepts and Annotated portfolios since they are the most relevant forms of intermediate-level knowledge for approaching our third research question.

Strong Concepts

According to Höök and Löwgren, strong concepts are design elements abstracted beyond particular instances, which have a generative potential. A strong concept has the following characteristics [36]:

- "It concerns the dynamic gestalt of an interaction design, that is, its interactive behavior rather than its static appearance.
- It resides at the interface between technology and people. It is a design element, a potential part of an artifact, and at the same time, it speaks of a use practice and behavior unfolding over time.
- It carries a core design idea which has the potential to cut across particular use situations and perhaps even application domains.
- It resides on an abstraction level above particular instances, which means that it can be realized in many different ways when it comes to interface detailing."

The canonical example of a strong concept is Social Navigation [36] based on the observation that we tend to follow the behavior of others and that this can be used to guide navigation. The construction of strong concepts begins from an instance (or possibly several related instances) by identifying the elements or principles in the instance that could be of value in other design situations within the same genre or domain as the original instance, or transgressing genre/domain boundaries, depending on the abstraction level of the strong concept identified. Artefact-centered papers could thus potentially contain the basis for one or more strong concepts. However, in order to show that strong concepts are contestable and defensible they should be **horizontally and vertically grounded.** Horizontal grounding means that the concept is related to similar concepts, focusing on similarities and differences that can help to understand the range of applicability of the strong concept. Vertical grounding means that the concept is connected to other instances, and/or to relevant theories. Finally, strong concepts need to have generative power.

Bridging Concepts

Bridging concepts [14] are rather similar to strong concepts. The main difference is that while the construction of a strong concept typically starts out from one or more particular instances, a bridging concept can alternatively have its origins in general theory rather than in particular instances.

Bridging concepts reside between abstract theory and design practice, and are distinguished by their ability to facilitate exchange between them. Bridging concepts have three defining constituents; a theoretical foundation, a set of design articulations and a range of instances that demonstrate the scope and potential of their application. One example of a bridging concept is Peepholes, meaning interactive artefacts that provide a limited view into a large space [14], and play on the tension between what is hidden and what is revealed. The theoretical grounding of peepholes builds upon pragmatist philosophy, while design articulations are demonstrated in several cases, e.g. Drift Table [27], Hydroscopes [14], UFOscope [21], see Fig 2a and 2b. Another example of a bridging concept is 'affordances', which is well-established in HCI and also holds a strong theoretical grounding.

Figure 2. a) UFOscope [21] and b) LibPhone [41] as examples of design articulations of peepholes in CCI

Annotated Portfolios

Annotated portfolios are an approach to communicate design research, introduced by Gaver and Bowers [25]. It is basically about gathering a range of design experiments and highlighting the most interesting aspects that run through them. What is often characteristic about the instances in an annotated portfolio is that they are interrelated and partly build on each other, or are different instances of the same concerns. Working with annotated portfolios can be more comfortable for some HCI researchers, rather than having to integrate their work with theoretical constructs that might not motivate or drive their work. An example is the annotated portfolio based on 10 years of work from the Goldsmiths interaction research studio [25]. Annotated portfolios can be a link between design practice and academic research and are located in the body of work in intermediary knowledge practices [42].

The similarities and differences between the different forms of intermediate-level knowledge discussed previously are given in Table 1. Since our aim with this paper is to analyze a set of artefact-centered papers for their potential intermediate-level knowledge it is of particular interest what the primary origins are, that is, if the intermediate-level knowledge construct is based on theory or practice and what the primary intent is. Based on this comparison of the various forms of intermediate-level knowledge we considered Strong concepts the best choice for expressing the potential intermediate-level knowledge found in artefact-centered papers; Bridging concepts have less focus on using the instances as a basis for forming concepts, and Annotated portfolios give fewer possibilities to connect to theories.

	Conceptual constructs	**Strong Concepts**	**Bridging concepts**	**Annotated portfolios**
Primary origins	Theory	Instances	Instances and theory	Instances
Primary intent	Theoretical advancements	Informin g design practice	Facilitating exchange between theory and practice	Communicate design research
Construc tion	Top down	Bottom up	Mediating between top and bottom	Design practice
Example	Dynabook	Social navi-gation	Peepholes	Goldsmiths interaction research studio

Table 1. Comparison of the origins and objectives of different forms of intermediate-level knowledge, inspired by [14]

Examples-of Intermediate-level knowledge in CCI

As mentioned above, different forms of intermediate-level knowledge include Methods and Tools, Patterns, and Guidelines. Within the CCI field there are some rather well-known papers that can be classified as representing intermediate-level knowledge within some of these categories. For instance, the top cited paper from the IDC conference "Using the fun toolkit and other survey methods to gather opinions in child computer interaction" [56] falls into the intermediate-level knowledge category Methods and Tools. Other examples in this category from the top 10 most cited IDC papers are Mission from Mars [18] and Mixing Ideas [29]. An example that can be classified as presenting intermediate-level knowledge in the form of guidelines is given by Resnick and Silverman in the third most cited paper [57] where they present 10 guidelines for designing construction kits for children. However, while those examples clearly show the presence of different forms of intermediate-level knowledge in the CCI field, this paper focuses on artefact-centered papers and the intermediate-level knowledge that may be obtained from them.

RESEARCH METHOD

To answer our research questions we performed an analysis of all full papers from the IDC conference from 2003 to 2016, 260 in total. For each paper, we first determined whether it was an artefact-centered paper or not. We defined an artefact-centered paper as follows:

- The main object of discussion of the paper is a concrete functional artefact developed within a research project
- The creators of the artefact have been involved in writing the paper.
- The paper typically presents a background (including theories, previous work by others inspiring the design

of the artefact etc.), design process (including user-studies, co-design activities, prototypes etc.), the actual artefact, a kind of evaluation, and optionally some generalizations in the form of recommendations or guidelines of directions for future work.

Examples of papers not belonging to this category are design and evaluation methods, pure user-studies, guidelines or heuristics, or papers only dealing with the initial stages of a design project.

In order to determine the clarity of our definition, two coders independently determined for all papers from 2004, 2009 and 2010 whether they were artefact-centered papers or not, by reading the abstracts, and when necessary the full texts. Cohen's kappa for those 49 papers was 0.70, which is satisfactory. Thereafter each paper was analyzed by at least two of the authors, and in case of disagreement, a third author also analyzed the paper and a decision was made after discussion. Papers that were particularly prone to disagreement were papers that described the design and evaluation of an artefact meant to be used with children to support the design process, such as the DisCo tool for asynchronous distributed child and adult design partners [66]. We decided not to classify such papers as artefact-centered papers.

To answer the second research question, we initially noted the number of citations to all papers as indicated in both Google Scholar and the ACM Digital Library. However, while doing this we found out that the number of citations in Google Scholar was generally just a factor higher than in the ACM library, but without showing a different tendency of the relative impact of each paper. Therefore, we decided to base our further analysis on the number of citations indicated in the ACM Digital Library only.

Finally, while all artefact-centered papers can potentially contain strong concepts, we reasoned that artefact-centered papers with unusually many citations would be the strongest candidates to start searching for such concepts. In order to determine which papers had an unusually high number of citations, we first determined the mean and the standard deviation of the number of citations according to the ACM Digital Library for each year. Using these numbers we selected all artefact-centered papers that were cited more often than 1 standard deviation above the mean number of citations for the year it was published. Papers from the 2015 and 2016 conferences were excluded from this analysis since only very few citations were available yet. This procedure resulted in fourteen papers. Each of these papers was then read in detail by one of the authors who noted down in what way the paper was referred to by the citing papers by gathering the abstracts as well as the sentences explicitly referring to the artefact-centered paper. For each paper the analyzing author described a potential strong concept. After this analysis, the authors shared their lists of potential strong concepts and discussed whether there were any overlaps in possible strong concepts between the papers, which would underscore their importance even more. Based on this discussion we chose three possible strong concepts that covered several of the papers, and tried to apply both vertical and horizontal grounding for each of them. The decision to describe only three strong concepts was mainly based on page limitations for this paper, in relation to the need to describe each concept in enough detail.

RESULTS

Percentage of artefact-centered papers

Our first research question was whether it is true that a large part of the papers presented at the IDC conference are artefact-centered. Our analysis of all papers gave the results presented in Figure 3.

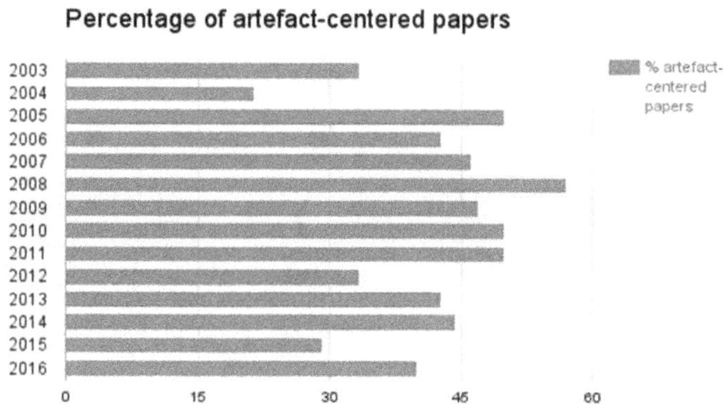

Figure 3. Percentage of artefact-centered papers in CCI between 2003 and 2016

Overall, the percentage of artefact-centered papers was 42%, which shows that a significant part of all papers at the IDC conference indeed focuses on a particular artefact, rather than on more general design knowledge. This is in line with a study by Jensen and Skov [39] that found that much of the research on the design of children's technologies focused on evaluating or engineering purposes, presenting a design solution followed by an evaluation. It is also in line with the finding by Yarosh, et al. [71], that 43% of the papers in the IDC conferences from 2002 to 2010 focused on the design (and often the evaluation) of a novel system for children. Interestingly, while they saw a strong trend towards an increase of this kind of papers in the later years of the conference, our analysis does not indicate that this trend has continued. For the years 2011-2016 the percentage actually decreased to 40%. This may indicate that the field is starting to focus more on intermediate-level forms of knowledge.

Impact of artefact-centered papers

Our second research question focused on the relative impact of the artefact-centered papers. Our hypothesis was that such papers are generally cited less often than other kinds of papers due to their specific scope. An independent-samples t-test was conducted to compare the number of citations for artefact-centered papers and other kinds of papers. There was indeed a significant difference in the scores for artefact-centered papers ($M=7.9$, $SD=9.6$) and other papers ($M=11.2$, $SD=14.9$); $t(258)=2.17$, $p = 0.030$. These results suggest that artefact-centered papers really do have a lower impact than other kinds of papers in terms of how often they are cited.

Strong concepts in artefact-centered papers

We identified 14 artefact-centered papers in the years 2003-2014 with an unusually high number of citations (>1 SD above the mean for the artefact-centered papers of that year):

Year	Title	# Citat.
2003	Case study: the design of CBC4Kids' StoryBuilder [1]	35
2004	Read-It: five-to-seven-year-old children learn to read in a tabletop environment [62]	32
2005	pOwerball: the design of a novel mixed-reality game for children with mixed abilities [9]	38
2006	On the design of Camelot, an outdoor game for children [67]	32
2007	Jabberstamp: embedding sound and voice in traditional drawings [55]	40
2008	Huggy Pajama: a mobile parent and child hugging communication system [65]	27
2009	Developing a media space for remote synchronous parent-child interaction [70]	43
2010	Mobile collaboration: collaboratively reading and creating children's stories on mobile devices [22]	16
2010	Mobile system to motivate teenagers' physical activity [3]	18
2011	Mobile learning in museums: how mobile supports for learning influence student behavior [11]	9
2011	Towards Utopia: designing tangibles for learning [2]	14
2012	CASTOR: learning to create context-sensitive and emotionally engaging narrations in-situ [53]	9
2013	Designing ScratchJr: support for early childhood learning through computer programming [23]	19
2014	Fiabot!: design and evaluation of a mobile storytelling application for schools [59]	5

Table 2. Artefact-centered papers with an unusually high number of citations (according to the ACM Digital Library in December 2016)

By reading the papers, and the papers that cited them we tried to determine if there were any strong concepts that we could describe. In the following paragraphs we will give three examples of such potential strong concepts; Head-up gaming, Remote sensing and Collaborative storytelling. In order to show that these strong concepts have the potential to be *contestable, defensible* and *substantive* we describe their novelty as a concept (contestability) and provide some first steps towards vertical and horizontal grounding (defensibility). Thereafter, we provide an example of how those three concepts could be generative. Note that the particular examples do not aim to cover all intermediate-level knowledge or strong concepts that can be found in the fourteen papers mentioned above. Rather, they show that there is something to gain from revisiting the papers that are already out there.

Head-up Gaming

One re-occurring theme in several of the papers we analyzed is gaming where several children together perform tasks moving around 'in the wild'. Some of these are based on the use of standard mobile devices but one can discern a different strand based on the idea of 'heads up' rather than 'heads down'. Following [63] we refer to this as Head-up gaming.
Head-up gaming is defined as the employment of multi-player games that use simple and reliable technologies that are easy to bring along and play with anywhere, anytime. The purpose is to involve children in rich social interactions and physical outdoors activity. The virtual worlds in these games are imagined rather than visualized using sensors to sense motion, proximity or contact. Social interactions are based on spoken language or body language. Camelot [67] can be seen as the first example of a head-up game and the term was coined by the developers of this game in a later paper [63].

Horizontal grounding: Related concepts are exergaming, intelligent playgrounds, pervasive gaming and persuasive gaming. Exergaming is a term used for video games that are also a form of exercise [8]. Popular examples are Dance Dance Revolution and Wii Fit. An important difference between exergaming and head-up gaming is that the latter is more focused on outdoor use. Intelligent playgrounds [64] are environments with interactive objects that react to the interaction with children and actively encourage children to play. It shares some of the objectives of head-up gaming by stimulating children to move and interact socially. However, a difference is that intelligent playgrounds are location-based, while head-up gaming is location-independent. Pervasive gaming [43] also transfers gaming experiences out into the physical world by mixing technologies with players' real environments, but the aims for doing so are not necessarily social interaction or physical activity. Head-up gaming thus has an explicit goal which is similar to persuasive gaming. Finally, persuasive gaming practices combine the dissemination of information with attempts to engage players in particular behaviors and attitudes (http://persuasivegaming.nl/). However, those behaviors and attitudes are not necessarily of a social or physical nature.

Vertical grounding: There are several instances that use this concept in research prototypes, such as Heartbeat, a gaming platform that uses biofeedback [44] and Stop the Bomb [33]. A commercial product for head-up games is Swinx (http://www.swinx.com), which is a game console focusing on active outdoor and indoor games.
While we have not been able to find any references to particular theories underpinning head-up gaming, one of the citing papers [13] refers to Place Attachments, which contributes to the establishment of identity, sense of belonging and overall well-being of children. Place Attachment [12] is based on psychoanalytic theory, which has considered the role of places and things within their social context; environmental autobiography, which has

evaluated places saved through the sieve of memory; behavior mapping, which has observed where children and adolescents congregate; and favorite place analyses, which have explored the reasons for their preferences. Bakker et al. [4] have also developed an observation scheme for the evaluation of head-up games, determining physical activity, focus, and social interaction between the players.

Remote Sensing

In a science context remote sensing is the science of obtaining information about objects or areas from a distance. Inspired by this and a large amount of work related to communication, awareness and presence we suggest the strong concept *Remote sensing*, where one can make a connection through various senses and media to a remotely located person. The typical scenario investigated in the CCI field is communication between children and remote parents or other close relatives. Indeed, a review of family and design in IDC and HCI found that Distant Family Communication was one of the most common themes at the IDC conference [38]. In terms of our literature review remote sensing has its basis in the particular instances ShareTable [70] and Huggy Pajama [65].

The core design idea in remote sensing is to create artefacts to share sensory impressions or transfer tactile expressions from one person to another to strengthen feelings of connectedness between participants. While it can target any sense, the most common senses are sight, hearing and touch. Remote sensing differs from standard written communication or video conferencing through its focus on creating an experience that can be shared by the participants using complementary or additional means of communication in a shared space, place, activity, or feeling.

Horizontal grounding: There are two major strands of work in CCI related to remote sensing: (i) systems related to supporting sensing through the use of audio and video and (ii) systems taking a tangible and tactile approach supporting sense like touch, heat and pressure. Remote sensing can also be synchronous or asynchronous.

Remote sensing has connections to work in Computer Supported Cooperative Work aimed mostly at supporting distance collaboration. Common technologies in this area are tabletops, video and audio. An important notion in this area is to allow co-workers located in separate places to work together on a shared object of some kind [37]. Remote sensing also has connections to work in tangible interaction and ubiquitous computing where significant effort has gone into experimenting with various kinds of input devices and actuators and where there are many examples of ambient displays aimed at communication using other modes than verbal, e.g. by using interactive pillows to strengthen connectedness [48]. Thus, there exists quite a lot of work on different techniques and approaches that can be used to realize remote sensing. Finally, remote sensing has ties to work on e.g. mediated intimacy and supporting long distance relations carried out within HCI [32, 45, 49].

Vertical grounding: In CCI remote sensing has mostly been applied to strengthen the bond between family members living apart. The importance of parents being involved more or less daily in their children's lives and effects on educational achievements has been observed by for instance [17]. At the same time it has been observed that children have a hard time keeping focused when phone or video chat is used for communication [69]. In the area of CCI mediated intimacy in families has been investigated by Dalsgaard et al [15]. An attempt at creating a general framework for telepresence can be found in [31]. While we cannot say that we have found a specific theoretical base for remote sensing these examples illustrate areas that could be used for creating a more thorough theoretical grounding for the concept and support that there is a need for tools for remote connectedness and also for mediating activities which strengthen the bonds between parties by carrying out joint activities.

Remote sensing through touch and pressure can be found in instances such as Huggy Pajama, which aims to provide a feeling similar to a one-way hug, Bear-with-me [24] which expands this concepts to two-way communication, Kissenger [61] "a physical interface for transmitting a kiss between two remotely connected people" and InTouch [46] which expands remote story-telling with a tool for sharing touches and squeezes. While ShareTable is the most cited exemplar in CCI of a system based on using video for remote sensing, there are many variations. The defining feature of ShareTable is that users can share a common space. Related systems include Family Room [50] based on always-on video, Family Story play [54], which combines an interactive book and a video connection, and Waazam [34], which was designed to support video mediated creative play.

Collective Storytelling

Storytelling is likely to be as old as mankind, and tools supporting narrative activities form one of the dominating themes in the papers analyzed. In many cases the goal is to support children creating stories together and we have chosen to refer to this as Collective Storytelling.

Collective storytelling can be defined as the combination of cooperative technologies with storytelling in order to coordinate several authoring efforts. The authoring efforts can range from providing feedback and peer review to developing a narrative or story. The applications can support different creative media formats such as e.g. text, sketch, video, sound, and the supported interaction is collocated and/or remote, and can consist of serial and/or parallel storytelling. A collective storytelling activity facilitates social interaction, has shared expression forms and is beneficial for all participants.

Storytelling and the creation of narrative support children in shaping, and give structure and significance to the world around them. Storytelling can facilitate pedagogical and psychological development such as children's communication, creative self-expressions, and social skills

[58]. One basic quality of collective storytelling is enriched storytelling experiences, where both teller and listener can experience stories collaboratively. Another basic quality is the existence of a narrating tool that can support various types of stories, e.g., free play type storytelling where the focus is on story creation, more structured storytelling and sharing of the story. A third quality emerges in creating, sharing or performing stories collaboratively. Creating stories consists of both stimulating imagination and creating story elements together. Sharing is here understood as the possibility to present one's own ideas or build on others, and can take place throughout the process or more as presentations at the end. Performing stories can be through full body engagement or various forms of tangible interaction

An early example of a desktop computer application for collective storytelling for children was KidPad, created by Druin et al. in 1997 [20]. Later applications include more tangible and full-body interactions such as Storymat [60], eCell for collaboration in school environments [10], and mobile applications for collective storytelling in situ during field trips [53].

Horizontal grounding: Related concepts are digital storytelling and interactive storytelling. Gillespie defined digital storytelling as a modern prototype of play [28] and interactive storytelling was first introduced by Bers et al. at the CHI conference [7], based on work from 1990 and onward. Work has been done to create interactive storytelling tools to explore personal family narratives [19], theatrical approaches to human-computer interaction [40], traditional literary problems such as point of view and suspension of disbelief [47], emotionally believable agent-based systems [5], and emergent, dynamic, adaptive story creation [16]. Collective storytelling differs from interactive storytelling and digital storytelling in that it puts a focus on the enriched collective authoring experience.

Vertical grounding: Göttel [30] reviewed children's collaboration practices in digital storytelling environments, and found that collaboration and storytelling often appear together in CCI literature, promising to provide creative, social, imaginative, and fun aspects of learning. The instances range from coping with cardiac illness in a hospital setting to learning narration in a formal learning context, while most common are variations of story authoring tools [30]. One example is StoryMat [60] a soft intelligent play mat that records and recalls children's storytelling activities. Its fundamental function is to become a play space where children can collaboratively tell and listen to their own stories. The Klump is a collaborative tool based around an amorphous 3D object that can be stretched, textured and colored and that makes sounds as it changes and is manipulated is one of several examples in [6]. The CBC4Kids' StoryBuilder is a website designed for children ages 8-10 years that enables online collaborative structured writing and provides the child with a collection of settings and images to use in a comic-book style [1]. Göttel [30] recommends to better meet the benefits of traditional storytelling by providing authoring tools that support children's collaboration practices to create, share, and perform stories.

Technologies for collective storytelling are generally based on constructivist theory and experiential learning [52] and constructionism learning theory e.g. [51]. Situated learning theory is also relevant for collective storytelling [10], as well as collective behavior theory and creativity as a process of combining past experiences and reality [68].

Generative power of the strong concepts

The main motivation for working with strong concepts is that they can function as an intermediary knowledge form with a generative power. That is, when we are faced with a new design challenge we can turn to the existing catalogue of strong concepts and use them as a starting point for design. The grounding behind the concept as well as the example applications of the concept by others also give possibilities to function both as inspiration and reference. Although we do not claim to know whether the three examples of strong concepts described here have generative power, we do think they could have been useful for our own work. We have been running a project where the design challenge became to design for helping children to develop their collaborative skills. The solutions we are currently working on are based around the idea of collaborative games using forced interaction and a combination of several mobile devices. This particular focus evolved over time but was not based on any form of intermediary-level knowledge. However, we do think that training of collaborative skills through Collective Storytelling would have been a very sensible alternative path, offering us a new way to look at collaboration. A lot of the existing work forming the basis for the concept already points in this direction and a developed Collective Storytelling concept would have provided both design inspiration and theoretical grounding. The generative power of the strong concepts does not predict a certain outcome or successful design, but points to a likely combination of use behavior and dynamic gestalt that might guide design. In our case, if there would have existed more intermediary knowledge, we would have had a larger set of potential starting points and inputs for our project.

DISCUSSION AND CONCLUSION

In this paper we have shown that currently, a large part of the papers at the IDC conference describe a particular instance of a technology for children, and that such papers generally are cited slightly less frequently. We have therefore argued that the IDC community is in need of intermediate-level knowledge, and that one possible approach to generate this kind of knowledge is to define strong concepts and we have made a first attempt to create this kind of knowledge by looking for strong concepts in artefact-centered papers that have received an unusually high number of citations. By identifying 14 candidate papers and reading all citing papers we have identified three examples of potential strong concepts: Head-up gaming, collective storytelling, and remote sensing. We have tried to describe the vertical and horizontal grounding for those strong concepts, and we think they have the potential to have generative power. However, we do not claim that the suggested concepts in this paper represent all possible strong concepts that can be found through an analysis of the given material for CCI or that the vertical and horizontal grounding we have performed is perfect. Grounding requires a deep and broad knowledge of related concepts, instances and theories, which we probably do not completely possess. There are several other ways to uncover strong concepts that we have not explored in this paper. It is possible that a larger set of papers that only have very few citations each, could contain a strong concept. This would require a collective effort to go through all papers and possibly create annotated portfolios, which could serve as tool for identifying common ideas and patterns, for several related artefacts. Second, it could also be useful to determine whether strong concepts defined within the HCI field at large are applicable for the CCI field, or whether they need to be adapted. Third, we are aware that given the tentative trend of declining numbers of artefact-centered papers in recent years, researchers may have already started to define some strong concepts in the CCI field. Since we have only analyzed artefact-centered papers, we might have missed those strong concepts in the other kinds of papers.

All in all, we argue that we have shown that there is both a need for intermediate level knowledge as well as a potential to create this kind of knowledge, for example in the form of strong concepts. We invite the CCI community to participate in efforts to make the field more mature by organizing forums for this kind of analytical work, for example in the form of workshops at the IDC conference, dedicated paper sessions on this topic, and/or a wiki.

ACKNOWLEDGMENTS

The work presented in this paper is a part of the Touch AT! project funded by the Marcus and Amalia Wallenberg Foundation under grant 2013.0063. We would like to thank Staffan Björk for reminding us of the potential usefulness of the idea of strong concepts.

REFERENCES

1. Alissa N. Antle. 2003. Case study: The design of CBC4Kids' StoryBuilder in *IDC '03*, ACM Press, 59-68.
2. Alissa N. Antle, Alyssa F. Wise and Kristine Nielsen. 2011. Towards Utopia: designing tangibles for learning *IDC '10*, ACM, Ann Arbor, Michigan, 11-20.
3. Sonia M. Arteaga, Mo Kudeki, Adrienne Woodworth and Sri Kurniawan. 2010. Mobile system to motivate teenagers' physical activity *IDC '09*, ACM, Barcelona, Spain, 1-10.
4. Saskia Bakker, Panos Markopoulos and Yvonne de Kort. 2008. OPOS: an observation scheme for evaluating head-up play *NordiCHI '08*, ACM, Lund, Sweden, 33-42.
5. Joseph Bates, Pattie Maes and Barbara Hayes-Roth. 1995. Working Notes: Interactive Story Systems, Plot and Character. in *AAAI Spring Symposium*.
6. Steve Benford, Benjamin B. Bederson, Karl-Petter Åkesson, Victor Bayon, Allison Druin, Pär Hansson, Juan Pablo Hourcade, Rob Ingram, Helen Neale, Claire O'Malley, Kristian T. Simsarian, Danaë Stanton, Yngve Sundblad and Gustav Taxén. 2000. Designing storytelling technologies to encouraging collaboration between young children *CHI '00*, ACM, The Hague, The Netherlands, 556-563.
7. Marina Umaschi Bers, Edith Ackermann, Justine Cassell, Beth Donegan, Joseph Gonzalez-Heydrich, David Ray DeMaso, Carol Strohecker, Sarah Lualdi, Dennis Bromley and Judith Karlin. 1998. Interactive storytelling environments: coping with cardiac illness at Boston's Children's Hospital *CHI '98*, ACM Press/Addison-Wesley Publishing Co., Los Angeles, California, USA, 603-610.
8. Ian Bogost. 2005. The rhetoric of exergaming. *Proceedings of the Digital Arts and Cultures (DAC)*.
9. Bas Brederode, Panos Markopoulos, Mathieu Gielen, Arnold Vermeeren and Huib de Ridder. 2005. pOwerball: the design of a novel mixed-reality game for children with mixed abilities *IDC '05*, ACM, Boulder, Colorado, 32-39.
10. John Seely Brown, Allan Collins and Paul Duguid. 1989. Situated cognition and the culture of learning. *Educational researcher*, 18 (1). 32-42.
11. Clara Cahill, Alex Kuhn, Shannon Schmoll, Wan-Tzu Lo, Brenna McNally and Chris Quintana. 2011. Mobile learning in museums: how mobile supports for learning influence student behavior *IDC '11*, ACM, Ann Arbor, Michigan, 21-28.
12. Louise Chawla. 1992. Childhood Place Attachments. in Altman, I. and Low, S.M. eds. *Place Attachment*, Springer US, Boston, MA, 63-86.
13. Bronwyn J. Cumbo, Jeni Paay, Jesper Kjeldskov and Brent C. Jacobs. 2014. Connecting children to nature with technology: sowing the seeds for proenvironmental behaviour *IDC '14*, ACM, Aarhus, Denmark, 189-192.
14. Peter Dalsgaard and Christian Dindler. 2014. Between theory and practice: bridging concepts in HCI research *CHI '14*, ACM, Toronto, Ontario, Canada, 1635-1644.
15. Thomas Dalsgaard, Mikael B. Skov, Malthe Stougaard and Bo Thomassen. 2006. Mediated intimacy in families: understanding the relation between children and parents *IDC '06*, ACM, 145-152.
16. Glorianna Davenport. 1994. Seeking dynamic, adaptive story environments. *IEEE MultiMedia*, 1 (3). 9-13.
17. Charles Desforges. 2003. *The impact of parental involvement, parental support and family education on pupil achievements and adjustment: A literature review*, London: Department for Education and Skills.
18. Christian Dindler, Eva Eriksson, Ole Sejer Iversen, Andreas Lykke-Olesen and Martin Ludvigsen. 2005. Mission from Mars: a method for exploring user requirements for children in a narrative space *IDC '05*, ACM, Boulder, Colorado, 40-47.
19. Abbe Don. 1990. Narrative and the interface. *The art of human-computer interface design*. 383-391.
20. Allison Druin, Jason Stewart, David Proft, Ben Bederson and Jim Hollan. 1997. KidPad: a design collaboration between children, technologists, and educators *CHI '97*, ACM, Atlanta, Georgia, USA, 463-470.
21. Eva Eriksson. 2010. U.F.O.scope!: families playing together at the public library *DIS '10*, ACM, Aarhus, Denmark, 344-347.
22. Jerry Alan Fails, Allison Druin and Mona Leigh Guha. 2010. Mobile collaboration: collaboratively reading and creating children's stories on mobile devices *IDC '10*, ACM, Barcelona, Spain, 20-29.

23. Louise P. Flannery, Brian Silverman, Elizabeth R. Kazakoff, Marina Umaschi Bers, Paula Bontá and Mitchel Resnick. 2013. Designing ScratchJr: support for early childhood learning through computer programming *IDC '13*, ACM, New York, New York, USA, 1-10.
24. Allan Fong, Zahra Ashktorab and Jon Froehlich. 2013. Bear-with-me: an embodied prototype to explore tangible two-way exchanges of emotional language *Extended Abstracts CHI '13*, ACM, Paris, France, 1011-1016.
25. Bill Gaver and John Bowers. 2012. Annotated portfolios. *interactions*, 19 (4). 40-49. 10.1145/2212877.2212889
26. William Gaver. 2012. What should we expect from research through design? *CHI '12*, ACM, Austin, Texas, USA, 937-946.
27. William W. Gaver, John Bowers, Andrew Boucher, Hans Gellerson, Sarah Pennington, Albrecht Schmidt, Anthony Steed, Nicholas Villars and Brendan Walker. 2004. The drift table: designing for ludic engagement *Extended Abstracts CHI '04*, ACM, Vienna, Austria, 885-900.
28. Thom Gillespie. 1997. Digital storytelling and computer game design *Extended Abstracts CHI '97*, ACM, Atlanta, Georgia, 148-149.
29. Mona Leigh Guha, Allison Druin, Gene Chipman, Jerry Alan Fails, Sante Simms and Allison Farber. 2004. Mixing Ideas: A New Technique for Working with Young Children as Design Partners *IDC '04*, ACM, College Park, Maryland, USA, 35-42.
30. Timo Göttel. 2011. Reviewing children's collaboration practices in storytelling environments *IDC '11*, ACM, Ann Arbor, Michigan, 153-156.
31. Antal Haans and Wijnand A. IJsselsteijn. 2012. Embodiment and telepresence: Toward a comprehensive theoretical framework. *Interacting with Computers*, 24 (4). 211-218. 10.1016/j.intcom.2012.04.010
32. Marc Hassenzahl, Stephanie Heidecker, Kai Eckoldt, Sarah Diefenbach and Uwe Hillmann. 2012. All You Need is Love: Current Strategies of Mediating Intimate Relationships through Technology. *ACM Trans. Comput.-Hum. Interact.*, 19 (4). 1-19. 10.1145/2395131.2395137
33. Koen Hendrix, Guo Yang, Dirk Van De Mortel, Tim Tijs and Panos Markopoulos. 2008. Designing a head-up game for children. in *BCS HCI '08*, British Computer Society, 45-53.
34. Seth E. Hunter, Pattie Maes, Anthony Tang, Kori M. Inkpen and Susan M. Hessey. 2014. WaaZam!: supporting creative play at a distance in customized video environments *CHI '14*, ACM, Toronto, Ontario, Canada, 1197-1206.
35. Kristina Höök, Peter Dalsgaard, Stuart Reeves, Jeffrey Bardzell, Jonas Löwgren, Erik Stolterman and Yvonne Rogers. 2015. Knowledge Production in Interaction Design *Extended Abstracts CHI '15*, ACM, Seoul, Republic of Korea, 2429-2432.
36. Kristina Höök and Jonas Löwgren. 2012. Strong concepts: Intermediate-level knowledge in interaction design research. *ACM Trans. Comput.-Hum. Interact.*, 19 (3). 1-18. 10.1145/2362364.2362371
37. Hiroshi Ishii. 1990. TeamWorkStation: towards a seamless shared workspace *CSCW '90*, ACM, Los Angeles, California, USA, 13-26.
38. Sara Isola and Jerry A. Fails. 2012. Family and design in the IDC and CHI communities. in *IDC '12*, ACM, 40-49.
39. Janne J. Jensen and Mikael B. Skov. 2005. A review of research methods in children's technology design *IDC '05*, ACM, Boulder, Colorado, 80-87.
40. Brenda Laurel. 2013. *Computers as theatre*. Addison-Wesley.
41. Andreas Lykke-Olesen and Jesper Nielsen. 2007. BibPhone: Adding Sound to the Children's Library. in *IDC '07*, 145-148.
42. Jonas Löwgren. 2013. Annotated portfolios and other forms of intermediate-level knowledge. *interactions*, 20 (1). 30-34. 10.1145/2405716.2405725
43. Carsten Magerkurth, Timo Engelke and Maral Memisoglu. 2004. Augmenting the virtual domain with physical and social elements: towards a paradigm shift in computer entertainment technology. *Comput. Entertain.*, 2 (4). 12-12. 10.1145/1037851.1037870
44. Remco Magielse and Panos Markopoulos. 2009. HeartBeat: an outdoor pervasive game for children *CHI'09*, ACM, Boston, MA, USA, 2181-2184.
45. Michael Massimi and Carman Neustaedter. 2014. Moving from talking heads to newlyweds: exploring video chat use during major life events *DIS '14*, ACM, Vancouver, BC, Canada, 43-52.
46. Elaine Massung, Sarah Dickins, James Torbett, James Holmes, Kirsten Cater and Victoria Bates. 2015. InTouch Tactile Tales: Haptic Feedback and Long-Distance Storytelling *Extended Abstracts CHI '15*, ACM, Seoul, Republic of Korea, 1289-1294.
47. Janet Murray. 1991. Anatomy of a New Medium: Literacy and Pedagogic Uses of Advanced Linguistic Computer Structures. *Computers and the Humanities*, 25. 1-14.
48. Frank Nack, Thecla Schiphorst, Zeljko Obrenovic, Michiel KauwATjoe, Simon de Bakker, Angel Perez Rosillio and Lora Aroyo. 2007. Pillows as adaptive interfaces in ambient environments *Proceedings of the international workshop on Human-centered multimedia*, ACM, Augsburg, Bavaria, Germany, 3-12.
49. Carman Neustaedter and Saul Greenberg. 2012. Intimacy in long-distance relationships over video chat *CHI '12*, ACM, Austin, Texas, USA, 753-762.
50. Erick Oduor and Carman Neustaedter. 2014. The family room: a multi-camera, multi-display family media space *Proceedings of the companion publication of the 17th conference on CSCW & social computing*, ACM, Baltimore, Maryland, USA, 289-292.
51. Seymour Papert. 1991. Situating Constructionism. in Harel, I. and Papert, S. eds. *Constructionism*, Ablex Publishing, Norwood NJ.
52. Jean Piaget. 1950. *The Psychology of Intelligence*. Routledge, New York.
53. Fabio Pittarello and Luca Bertani. 2012. CASTOR: learning to create context-sensitive and emotionally engaging narrations in-situ *IDC '12*, ACM, Bremen, Germany, 1-10.
54. Hayes Raffle, Rafael Ballagas, Glenda Revelle, Hiroshi Horii, Sean Follmer, Janet Go, Emily Reardon, Koichi Mori, Joseph Kaye and Mirjana Spasojevic. 2010. Family story play: reading with young children (and elmo) over a distance *CHI '10*, ACM, Atlanta, Georgia, USA, 1583-1592.
55. Hayes Raffle, Cati Vaucelle, Ruibing Wang and Hiroshi Ishii. 2007. Jabberstamp: embedding sound and voice in traditional drawings *ACM SIGGRAPH 2007 educators program*, ACM, San Diego, California, 32.
56. Janet C. Read and S. MacFarlane. 2006. Using the fun toolkit and other survey methods to gather opinions in child computer interaction *IDC '06*.

57. Mitchel Resnick and Brian Silverman. 2005. Some reflections on designing construction kits for kids *IDC '05*, ACM, Boulder, Colorado, 117-122.
58. Elisa Rubegni, Luca Colombo and Monica Landoni. 2013. Design recommendations for the development of a digital storytelling mobile application *BCS HCI '13*, British Computer Society, London, UK, 1-6.
59. Elisa Rubegni and Monica Landoni. 2014. Fiabot!: design and evaluation of a mobile storytelling application for schools *IDC '14*, ACM, Aarhus, Denmark, 165-174.
60. Kimiko Ryokai and Justine Cassell. 1999. StoryMat: a play space for collaborative storytelling *Extended Abstracts CHI '99*, ACM, Pittsburgh, Pennsylvania, 272-273.
61. Hooman Aghaebrahimi Samani, Rahul Parsani, Lenis Tejada Rodriguez, Elham Saadatian, Kumudu Harshadeva Dissanayake and Adrian David Cheok. 2012. Kissenger: design of a kiss transmission device *DIS '12*, ACM, Newcastle Upon Tyne, United Kingdom, 48-57.
62. Wouter Sluis, Ivo Weevers, Claudia van Schijndel, Lyuba Kolos-Mazuryk, Siska Fitrianie and Jean-Bernard Martens. 2004. Read-It: five-to-seven-year-old children learn to read in a tabletop environment *IDC '04*, ACM, Maryland, 73-80.
63. Iris Soute and Panos Markopoulos. 2007. Head up games: the games of the future will look more like the games of the past *11th IFIP TC 13 international conference on Human-computer interaction*, Rio de Janeiro, Brazil.
64. Janienke Sturm, Tilde Bekker, Bas Groenendaal, Rik Wesselink and Berry Eggen. 2008. Key issues for the successful design of an intelligent, interactive playground *IDC '08*, ACM, Chicago, Illinois, 258-265.
65. James Keng Soon Teh, Adrian David Cheok, Roshan L. Peiris, Yongsoon Choi, Vuong Thuong and Sha Lai. 2008. Huggy Pajama: a mobile parent and child hugging communication system *IDC '08*, ACM, Chicago, Illinois, 250-257.
66. Greg Walsh, Allison Druin, Mona Leigh Guha, Elizabeth Bonsignore, Elizabeth Foss, Jason C. Yip, Evan Golub, Tamara Clegg, Quincy Brown, Robin Brewer, Asmi Joshi and Richelle Brown. 2012. DisCo: a co-design online tool for asynchronous distributed child and adult design partners *IDC '12*, ACM, Bremen, Germany, 11-19.
67. Janneke Verhaegh, Iris Soute, Angelique Kessels and Panos Markopoulos. 2006. On the design of Camelot, an outdoor game for children *IDC '06*, ACM, Tampere, Finland, 9-16.
68. Lev Semenovich Vygotsky. 1980. *Mind in society: The development of higher psychological processes*. Harvard university press.
69. Svetlana Yarosh and Gregory D. Abowd. 2011. Mediated parent-child contact in work-separated families *CHI '11*, ACM, Vancouver, BC, Canada, 1185-1194.
70. Svetlana Yarosh, Stephen Cuzzort, Hendrik Müller and Gregory D. Abowd. 2009. Developing a media space for remote synchronous parent-child interaction *IDC '09*, ACM, Como, Italy, 97-105.
71. Svetlana Yarosh, Iulian Radu, Seth Hunter and Eric Rosenbaum. 2011. Examining values: an analysis of nine years of IDC research. in *IDC'11*, ACM, 136-144.
72. John Zimmerman, Jodi Forlizzi and Shelley Evenson. 2007. Research Through Design as a Method for Interaction Design Research in HCI. in *CHI 2007*, San Jose, California, USA, ACM.

Abandoned but Not Forgotten: Providing Access While Protecting Foster Youth from Online Risks

Karla Badillo-Urquiola
University of Central Florida
Orlando, FL, U.S.A
kcurquiola10@knights.ucf.edu

Scott Harpin
University of Colorado
Aurora, CO, U.S.A
Scott.Harpin@ucdenver.edu

Pamela Wisniewski
University of Central Florida
Orlando, FL, U.S.A
pamwis@ucf.edu

ABSTRACT

Teens in the foster care system often have histories that involve severe trauma, such as physical and sexual abuse, substance use, incarceration, and early pregnancy. While studies have investigated foster teens' engagement with high-risk behaviors offline, there is a dearth of information regarding foster teens and their engagement in online activities that may facilitate increased risk behaviors. Moreover, the extent to which technology acts as a positive versus negative influence on foster youth is unclear. We synthesize the current literature on foster youth and online safety to illustrate: 1) the tensions between providing access to networked technologies versus keeping foster youth safe from risks, 2) the lack of empirical research or technology-based interventions to ensure the online safety of foster youth, and 3) the importance of pursuing future research to design solutions that can alleviate some of these tensions. Our goal is to inform researchers, designers, and educators on the importance of keeping in mind the needs of particularly vulnerable populations, such as teens within the foster care system, when designing interactive systems.

Author Keywords

Adolescent Online Safety; Teens; Foster Care; Technology; Participatory Design.

ACM Classification Keywords

K.4.1 Computers and Society: Public Policy Issues.

INTRODUCTION

On a given day, over 400,000 youth reside in the foster care system within the United States, and approximately 30% of these youth are aged 13 to 20 [54]. Many of these youth experience a multitude of traumatic events in their lives. Nearly 80% of foster youth have had at least one adverse experience related to parental divorce, death, domestic violence, or family drug addiction with almost half (48.3%) experiencing four or more of these traumatic events before they reach adulthood [7]. Research has consistently confirmed that youth in foster care are susceptible to higher levels of risk than those who are not in foster care and have more detrimental outcomes due to their risk experiences [39,40]. However, very little research has examined the influence of networked technologies (e.g., social media, mobile smart devices) on foster youths' risk behaviors, adverse experiences, or negative outcomes [3,22].

IDC 2017, June 27–30, 2017, Stanford, CA, USA.
© 2017 ACM ISBN 978-1-4503-4921-5/17/06...$15.00.
http://dx.doi.org/10.1145/3078072.3079724

In terms of adolescents in general, we know that technology currently consumes a large portion of teens' lives. According to Pew Research, more than half of the teens in the United States report going online multiple times a day, if not constantly being connected [1]. The prevalence of technology use has been shown to expose teens to a number of online risks. For instance, one in four teens will unintentionally be exposed to sexually explicit materials online [37]. Understanding these potential risks has motivated researchers in the Interaction Design and Children (IDC) conference and the broader HCI community to study effective methods for keeping teens safe from online risks [2,4,21,29,48]. Some suggestions include building trust through discourse [29], emphasizing teen resilience [48], and moving toward design solutions that promote active parental mediation [34] and teen-self regulation, as opposed to solutions that are privacy invasive and reinforce restrictive parenting practices [47]. However, such recommendations may not be generalizable to foster youth as they are a particular vulnerable population of teens.

In this paper, we draw from existing literature to argue that researchers and designers will likely need to conceptualize different approaches when studying and developing interactive systems so that they meet the unique needs of foster youth. We do this by synthesizing research regarding the high-risk offline behaviors of foster youth, research that pertains to foster youth and technology use, and, more generally, adolescent online safety literature as it relates to other vulnerable teen populations. Overall, we found evidence that foster youth are particularly susceptible to both offline and online risks, though very little research has empirically examined the role technology may play in exacerbating or mitigating such experiences on or offline. Based on our findings, we urge HCI researchers and interaction designers to engage with foster youth and other vulnerable teen populations to find solutions for providing access to networked technologies that can benefit the teens while protecting them from severe online risks. We recommend specific areas for future research on adolescent online safety for foster youth and outline some of the challenges we may face as we engage with foster teens.

BACKGROUND

First, we situate our research within the IDC community, researchers and practitioners focused on designing technology to improve children's well-being, as a response to the call for more interaction design research with adolescent populations. We then relate interaction design for adolescents to online safety research and expand our background literature to discuss two themes that have emerged within this broader subject area: 1) online safety through increased parental mediation and 2) empowering teens to protect themselves online. We discuss how these themes may not translate well to foster youth and show how our work contributes to the existing literature.

Interaction Design for Adolescents

In 2011, Yarosh et al. [53] conducted a nine-year review of articles published at IDC and concluded that more of the research had focused on younger children (ages 6 to 12) than adolescent populations (ages 13 to 17). These researchers recommended that IDC expand its focus to investigate other adolescent populations and their unique needs. As a result, more IDC researchers began examining the special needs of teens [31], as well as the methodological challenges and best practices of conducting interaction design research with adolescents [42]. When discussing interaction design in the context of adolescents, online safety becomes a central concern as we want to allow teens to engage through technology beneficially but also want to protect them from harm [29]. As such, we believe the tension between trying to mediate teens' online behaviors to protect them versus trusting and empowering them to protect themselves should be explicitly addressed when designing interactive systems to achieve such goals.

Adolescents Online Safety through Parental Mediation

Quite a bit of interdisciplinary research has focused on the topic of adolescent online safety and risks. For example, researchers have studied the prevalence and factors that are associated with online sexual solicitations and sexting [37,44], as well as exposure to pornography or other explicit materials online [9]. One common theme within this literature is an emphasis on effective parental mediation strategies for reducing these online risk exposures [4,10,16,47] and understanding adolescent online safety from the perspective of parents. For example, Blackwell et al. [4] found that parents felt frustrated and anxious when they were unaware of the activities in which their children were engaging in from their mobile devices. They recommended parents have open dialogues with their teens to provide a channel for understanding and establishing mutual expectations [4]. Other researchers have also recommended approaches that promote online safety through engaged parental mediation and trust relationships [29,34].

Unfortunately, more recent research has found that many of the current solutions for online safety, particularly in mobile contexts, tend to focus instead on more authoritarian parenting approaches of restriction and monitoring [47]. This may be problematic because overly restrictive parenting practices can suppress positive online experiences their teens have online, as well as the negative ones; more engaged parenting, on the other hand, can empower teens to cope with risks so that they can benefit from being online [49]. Still, family communication regarding teens' negative online experiences is often poor and teens do not feel comfortable discussing their online experiences with their parents [50]. So even within typical family settings, parental mediation approaches for ensuring adolescent online safety are still works-in-progress.

Empowering Teens to Protect Themselves Online

A recent and alternative approach within the adolescent online safety literature involves moving away from parental-focused online safety strategies to ones that empower teens to cope with and be resilient to the online risks they may face [47,48,50,51]. For instance, a two-month long diary study with 13 to 17-year-olds suggested that most of the online risk experiences teens encounter are unintentional, and teens can largely cope with these experiences to resolve them on their own. These risk experiences may actually help teens develop important interpersonal skills, such as conflict resolution and empathy [51]. boyd et al. [6] further explained why teens should be empowered to take control of their safety online. The internet is inherently part of a teen's life and reveals the struggles teens face not just online, but offline as well. Therefore, by providing teens with the proper navigation tools and avenues of communication, they will be able to overcome many of the negative online experiences [5].

As a result, some researchers have attempted to empower teens to meet their own online safety challenges through design. For instance, Ashktorab and Vitak [2] used participatory design techniques with teens to develop solutions to prevent online harassment and cyberbullying. They found that teens appreciated the opportunity to get involved in designing solutions that positively affect their peers and their own well-being, as well as the chance to work with adults as peers. Such research shows the importance of providing teens opportunities to engage with HCI researchers and designers. Having more agency and responsibility in the design process can encourage teens to place more value on engaging online safely.

Adolescent Online Safety of Foster Youth

A literature review on adolescent online safety, also published at IDC 2017, found that the few design-based interventions exist at all, and those that do are focused on promoting more collaborative practices for parent-teen rule-setting behaviors [41]. To date, the main stream literature on adolescent online safety has not examined the unique situations of foster youth as it has predominantly focused on teens in general. Nor has it posed the possibility that promoting parental mediation and teen empowerment may not be generalizable to more vulnerable populations of teens. For instance, youth within the foster care system do not have traditional family units and, consequently, conventional parental mediation strategies, which require a relational bond between the parent and child may not be possible [3]. Further, this subpopulation of teens is already considered high-risk due to their long-standing difficulties.

Foster youth may lack the developmental maturity and resilience to appropriately manage unmediated access to technology [52], much less highly negative online risk experiences [3]. At the same time, foster youth could greatly benefit from the social support and resources provided by having access to internet-connected technologies [27]. The organization iFoster [55] has estimated that less than 21% of foster youth have access to home computers, compared to 90% of the general teen population [1]. Thus, foster youth may require additional support to remain safe online without restricting access to beneficial online resources. With this in mind, we critically examined the current literature around adolescent online safety and foster youth in order to build the case that more research needs to be done in terms of interaction designs to promote the well-being and safety of foster teens. The end goal being to increase their access to networked technologies without putting them at even greater risk. Thus, we make the following research contributions:

- We synthesize interdisciplinary literature related to foster teens and offline risks, the online safety of foster youth, as well as the unique challenges of other vulnerable teen populations as they engage with and through internet-connected platforms.
- We illustrate the lack of research related to the online safety of foster teens, effective strategies for supporting foster parents in mediating technology use, and design-based interventions for promoting online safety.
- We recommend avenues for new research and suggest leveraging participatory design approaches with foster youth to engage them directly in developing practical solutions to provide access to technology while minimizing potential harm.
- We present some of the ethical and legal challenges HCI researchers and designers may face as we move forward with this proposed research agenda.

METHODS

Due to the novelty of our topic, we first chose to conduct a comprehensive review of the literature related to foster teens and their online risks to synthesize themes around three main topics: 1) foster youth's high-risk behaviors and outcomes, 2) foster youths' online safety and technology use, and 3) more generally, online safety of vulnerable populations of teens. To identify relevant research across multiple disciplines, we first searched a diverse set of digital libraries, which included the ACM Digital Library, PsychInfo, ProQuest Education, and ProQuest Sociology. After these searches were exhausted, we used Google Scholar to conduct a broader search to ensure inclusivity and multidisciplinary perspectives. We also cross-referenced the citations of each article to identify any additional articles that should be included. The following search terms were used within the search criteria for each of our three main topics:

1) **Foster youth susceptibility to offline risks:** "foster care," "adolescents," "teen," "youth," "risks," and "challenges."
2) **Foster youth and online risks:** "foster care," "adolescents," "teen," "youth," "technology," "social media," "online safety," and "online risk."
3) **Vulnerable and "at-risk" youth online safety:** "at-risk," "vulnerable," "adolescents," "teen," "youth," "susceptible," "technology," "social media," "internet," and "online safety."

We searched specifically for articles that were peer-reviewed and published between the years of 2006 and 2017. An initial analysis was performed by reading titles and abstracts to identify relevant articles and remove irrelevant sources. Note that we performed the third search on vulnerable youth and online safety after we found so few publications that were related to foster youth and technology use.

SYNTHESIZING THE LITERATURE

Overall, we found extensive research in the areas of foster youth and offline risks, as well as online safety for vulnerable or at-risk adolescents. Of the literature found, we summarize the 20 most relevant sources for these two topics. In contrast, little research was found specifically at the intersection of online safety, technology use, and foster youth (only 5 articles). Therefore, we summarize the findings from all articles we identified within this topic. We summarize the literature related to these three topics below and provide key themes across the literature.

Foster Youth as a Particularly Vulnerable Population

We define vulnerable teens as those that have encountered previous harms and are thus more susceptible to future harm [52]. Research has confirmed that teens within the foster care system report higher levels of risk and harm compared to other teens. As such, researchers have investigated foster youths' extreme vulnerabilities to health, developmental, social, and emotional risks. For instance, foster youth are more susceptible to detrimental outcomes, such as substance use [39], poor health [19,26], and early pregnancy [40]. For example, Gramkowski et al. [26] found that approximately 43% of foster youth reported being sexually active compared to 34% of a comparative teen sample. Oshima et al. [40] used a longitudinal study design and discovered that over 50% of the foster youth became pregnant before the age of 19.

Shpiegel [45] suggests that foster teens are also less resilient to risks when they have a history of physical or sexual abuse, placement instability, and delinquency. Other risk factors that have been found to contribute to negative long-term outcomes include child maltreatment, school transitions, and child welfare factors [38,40,45]. In contrast to studying the high-risk outcome and risk factors of foster youth, some researchers have also studied the protective factors that help these teens succeed and live healthy lives. Salient factors include intellectual ability, educational attainment, religiosity[38,42], social support, extracurricular activities, and types of supportive environments [30,38,40,45]. These protective factors have been shown to counteract negative outcomes, such as teen pregnancy, homelessness, mental illness, substance use, and criminal involvement [18,32,40,45]. Additionally, quite a few studies focused on older teens transitioning into adulthood or "aging out" of the foster care system [19,38–40,45]. These studies emphasized that the risks and problems foster teens faced in their youth follow them into adulthood. Studies suggest that many of these teens lack the proper skills and knowledge to live independently, such as not having a high school diploma [33]. Due to their lack of access to technology, many foster youths lack the ability to perform basic tasks, such as searching for a job online [55].

Benefits vs. Risks of Technology Use by Foster Youth

We identified five articles (recently published between 2015-2017) that discussed youth in foster care in combination with technology use or online safety. An overall trend we identified was that the articles represented a spectrum of perspectives, from the benefits of technology use to the potential risks associated with it. Given the lack of research in this area, we give a detailed summary of the findings from each of these emerging studies below, focusing on the trade-offs between benefits and risks.

Gustavsson and MacEachron [27] were the first to take a digital perspective of foster youths' development by exploring the benefits and potential risks associated with internet use by applying positive youth development theory (PYD). For example, they found that the internet can serve as a means for foster youth to find an immense amount of information on topics of personal importance (e.g., medical health, employment, school work). Access to technology also provides foster youth the ability to build social connections and receive social support. Yet, the internet may also expose them to false, offensive, or threatening information that could cause harm. By implementing the "five Cs" of PYD (i.e., competence, connections, confidence, character, and caring), the researchers offered policy-level suggestions for supporting foster youths' safe internet use. For example, policies should cover ways to mitigate risks and enhance competency of healthy online practices for foster teens. Ultimately, they advocated for involving foster youth in the strategies to combat internet-related risks.

Fitch [20] created a framework for developing privacy guidelines for social media disclosures so that foster youth and their networks (e.g., case workers, foster parents) would not expose them to undue risks. Using Critical Systems Heuristics as a guide, this framework provides twelve guiding questions organized under the following four categories: 1) *motivation* – who the disclosures may benefit, 2) *power* – who has authority or the information, 3) *knowledge* – who is considered the expert on the topic, and 4) *legitimacy* – what is appropriate to disclose? The purpose of utilizing this framework was to include foster teens as stakeholders in developing policies that regulate their social media use. While Fitch advocated foster youths' involvement in policy development, he acknowledged that this approach could open up issues of liability for foster agencies.

Denby et al.'s [12,13] DREAMR project sought to help foster youth develop healthy relationships through the use of smartphones. Using the relational competence framework, they hypothesized that enhanced communication with social service providers would serve as a protective factor against various risk outcomes. The researchers gave teens access to mobile phones paired with a web-based application. Using survey-based and focus group data to triangulate the experience through the eyes of the teens, they found both positive and unintended consequences of the intervention. Most teens found the smartphones to be easy to use, enabling them to develop a closer bond with their social service providers. However, 43% of teens were also frustrated with the program due to the restrictions implemented on the phones (e.g., limited contact lists). This prevented the teens from building a trusting and positive relationship with their caseworkers.

Badillo et al. [3] focused primarily on the unique challenges of foster parents of teens when it came to mediating technology use. They found the first empirical evidence that foster youth may be more susceptible to particularly risky online behaviors and experiences (e.g., sexting, sexual predation, elopement, and sex trafficking) beyond that of typical teens. Foster parents expressed multiple concerns for mediating the teens' technology use with authority and control representing the most major issue. Foster parents felt they often did not have the right or a sufficient trust-relationship with foster youth to place boundaries on the teen's technology use. Additionally, some foster parents tried to overcompensate for teens' previous deprivation, resulting in teens having an attitude of entitlement. Nevertheless, the idea of constructing "normalcy" in the teen's life by providing opportunities to engage with technology was very important for many foster parents, as they are aware that their teens have faced several childhood traumas. Yet, foster parents felt at a loss for how to properly mediate technology use, often taking an all-or-nothing approach by not mediating use at all to revoking technology access altogether.

To compare and contrast the literature summarized above, the first two studies were primarily policy focused, whereas the latter three included empirical evidence from foster youth and foster parents. However, all of the studies illustrated a clear tension between advocating for access to technology so that foster youth could benefit and addressing the need for protecting teens from undue harm from online risk exposure.

Online Safety of Vulnerable and "At-Risk" Youth

Considering the limited research at the intersection of technology use, online safety, and foster youth, we expanded our search to "at-risk" and vulnerable populations of teens. Broadening our search offers evidence for the importance of studying and designing for the unique needs of vulnerable teen populations, which include foster youth. Our search yielded literature on a variety of vulnerable teen populations, including those who are lesbian, gay, bisexual, and transgender (LGBT) [11], struggle with anorexia [24,46], have a diagnosis of attention deficit hyperactivity disorder (ADHD) or Asperger syndrome [35], or are homeless [17,28,43,52]. Similar to foster youth, many of these teens have been marginalized from society and struggle with adversity in their everyday lives.

These vulnerable subpopulations of teens have been found to face very difficult challenges associated with engaging online. Having culturally and societally stigmatized identities often lead teens to search for social support or relationships in online communities that otherwise are not available to them [11,24]. However, teens who suffer from anorexia nervosa, for instance, often fall victim to online threats due to disclosing personal details about themselves in online forums [46]. While online discussion forums have many benefits, researchers have found some community forums to be unhealthy. For example, in a pilot study conducted with patients suffering from eating disorders (ED) and parents, approximately 35.5% of patients used Pro-ED sites, communities that support and guide those that want to maintain their eating disorder activities. Over 70% of teens studied said they used weight loss websites, while 52% of their parents claimed they did not [46]. Similarly, individuals with ADHD, Asperger syndrome, or similar disabilities often find themselves at a higher risk of cyberbullying within online platforms [35]. However, their parents were also unaware or misinformed regarding their online experiences. About 73% of parents indicated their child had never been bullied, even though over 21% of the youth said they had been cyberbullied within the last two months [35].

Arguably, homeless teens may be the most similar population to foster youth for a number of reasons. First, many homeless teens have spent time in the foster care system prior becoming homeless [17]. They are also likely to not have a stable family environment, reporting a history of sexual and physical abuse, as well as family dysfunction [43]. Despite their housing instability, homeless teens still access the internet frequently. Harpin et al. [28] found that over half (55.6%) of teens living on the streets of Denver accessed the internet regularly. Similarly, Rice and Barman [43] found that 72% of homeless youth in Los Angeles accessed the internet within the last two days of participating in their survey. While many homeless youths own their own cell phone (46.7%) [28], they also rely on free internet access, such as from public libraries and youth service agencies [43]. While these studies examined technology-aided interventions for homeless teens, they did not examine the associated risks of providing access.

INDENTIFYING GAPS IN THE LITERATURE

Offline Programs vs. Technology-based Interventions

We identified some potential limitations and gaps in the existing literature to help inform areas of opportunity for future research. First, most of the research on foster teens and offline risks offered solutions that relied on mentoring or relational nurturing to encourage positive psychological and behavioral outcomes among foster youth [36,38]. Unfortunately, many of these programs put in place to support the unique needs and circumstances of teens in foster care are underfunded, poorly monitored, and heavily influenced by politics [25]. This may be why the DREAMR researchers [12,13] have turned to study more technology-based interventions that help create the infrastructure for positive relationship building within foster youths' existing social networks.

Few Empirical Findings related to Technology's Role in Foster Youth Outcomes

The offline risk literature deeply examined the prevalence of and outcomes associated with different risk behaviors, as well as protective factors that helped to mitigate these high-risk outcomes. However, this literature did not examine offline risks in relation to online risks or how technology may influence different risk outcomes. For example, some adolescent online safety literature suggests that teens who have mobile smart devices expose themselves to more sexual-related risks [44]. Yet, this literature makes no mention of technology use and its influence on risk outcomes. Otherwise, the research conducted thus far on online safety and risks of foster youth has been largely theoretical or policy-oriented (i.e., no empirical data from foster youth) [20,27]. For example, focusing on the potential benefits of giving foster youth access to technology [3,12,13,27] or proposing policies for protecting foster youths' privacy while online [20,27]. To date, no research has been conducted related to online safety and/or risks from foster youths' own perspectives.

An Overall Lack of Knowledge regarding How to Ensure the Online Safety of Foster Youth

While foster youth are often identified as stakeholders in the policies designed to keep them safe online, more emphasis seems to be placed on the goals of foster parents or agencies who are charged to protect foster youth [3,12,13]. Researchers who performed a 40 year review of research on out-of-home-care [36] found that priority, from an agency perspective, has typically been placed on increasing authority and control— there is a belief that if we restrict or limit, we are safeguarding teens. Interestingly, this mentality mirrored some of the prevailing perspectives we found in the adolescent online safety literature, which have been shown to be overly restrictive and, likely, ineffective [29,47]. So, then the question becomes: How do we ensure the online safety of foster youth?

Our review has shown that other populations of vulnerable teens face similar adversities as foster youth: yearning for belonging and positive connections; a history of trauma, sometimes in the form of sexual and physical abuse; and unhealthy relationships leading into adulthood [17,24,45]. We found a number of underlying similarities shared by these teens that could inform future research and design regarding online safety and risks for foster teens. For example, engaging in behaviors or communities online that intensify their serious behavior and mental health [24,25]. Suggestions have been made to develop programs that educate parents and teens on internet safety, as well as appropriate reactions and reporting [35]. However, more investigation is needed to understand the online risks of marginalized teen populations and whether such findings are generalizable to foster youth.

RECOMMENDING FUTURE RESEARCH DIRECTIONS

Alleviating the Tension between Access vs. Exposure

Technology can provide benefits and a sense of "normalcy" to foster youth, as well as an opportunity to receive needed social support [27]. However, due to the lack of solutions ensuring foster youths' safety while they engage with others through the use of technology, foster parents are forced to take an "all or nothing" approach [3], which either leaves teens exposed to online risks or precluded from having positive online experiences due to lack of access to technology. More research is needed to understand foster youths' unique online safety needs and explore effective interventions to fill our gaps in knowledge regarding how to best protect foster youth while giving them access to technology. Due to the limited literature on online safety among foster teens, we were not surprised to discover the lack of interventions being developed for keeping foster teens safe while they engage with others through the use of technology.

Some researchers have begun to step away from promoting overly restrictive and control-based approaches to more nurturing ones in offline contexts [38]. Despite these efforts, current intervention strategies have not been successfully implemented [25] for foster parents to receive the proper support to teach their teens effective online strategies, nor to teach foster youth how to protect themselves online. Researchers and designers should prioritize the needs of foster teens to provide avenues for all involved to feel comfortable in giving their foster youth access to technology, while ensuring that teens will use it in a safe manner. To encourage this action, we provide the following research questions as a helpful guide for future investigations related to foster youth and online safety:

- Who are the stakeholders responsible for developing and implementing policies and interventions that support online safety of foster youth?
- What role should foster agencies, caregivers, and other stakeholders play in mediating technology use within a foster home?
- Does technology use facilitate an increase in foster youths' offline risk behaviors? If so, how?
- How can we best design, develop, and implement effective interventions for ensuring the online safety of foster youth?

Engaging Foster Youth to Understand Their Needs

To effectively design solutions for promoting online safety for foster teens, we strongly believe that teens themselves need to have a say in the process. Poole and Peyton [42] emphasize the importance of using teens as primary participants in interaction design for adolescents, rather than adults (in our case, foster parents, case workers, etc.) as proxies. In order to do this, we propose using participatory design techniques [2,34]. This process would involve developing partnerships between researchers and foster youth. Participatory design sessions would encourage teens to envision or offer design ideas that may help reach a solution to the problem at hand [14,15]. Directly involving foster youth in the research design process would enable them to openly share their opinions [42]. By listening to their opinions, researchers and designers would then be able to take a user-centered design approach to understand the specific preferences and needs of foster youth when designing interventions, instead of relying on assumptions.

Participatory design with teens has been successful in previous research related to cyberbullying [2]. However, the population recruited in the previous research were teens from a private high school, suggesting a higher socio-economic status than our foster youth population. Other studies have incorporated a family-oriented participatory design process [31], which may also be applicable for foster youth who are in stable in-home situations. Considering the word "family" can have many different meanings, researchers and designers must also include those individuals involved directly in the foster youths' lives. As the design of online safety interventions affect the entire foster system, it is important to not only involve teens, but individuals who act as their caregivers.

Considering Ethical and Legal Complexities

Even though embarking on research that engages directly with foster youth is recommended, we acknowledge that this research does not come without challenges. We briefly discuss some of these challenges, which include: 1) consent and assent, 2) confidentiality and privacy, and 3) data sensitivity. First, participation of foster teens in research is often governed by federal, state, and local laws and policies. Some of these regulations require the consent of a biological parent [23] and often depends on where the youth is in the adjudication process. Unfortunately, obtaining this consent can prove to be difficult, if not impossible, since many of these teens are not in contact with their biological parents due to a variety of situations (e.g., parental incarceration) [45]. Because foster youth are often considered wards of the state (regulation 21 CFR 50.3(q)) once they are separated from their biological parents, challenges arise when attempting to conduct research with this population. We propose that future research should look into developing clear regulations for the consent and assent process, as well as practice clearly articulating the benefits of research with foster youth.

Second, foster youth are accustomed to repeating their life stories to multiple individuals (e.g., case managers, guardians, local authorities) and may be too forthcoming with researchers about topics even unrelated to the research. This poses unanticipated consequences as subjects might describe reportable situations (e.g., abuse from a caregiver) without understanding the ramifications of their actions. Although respect for confidentiality and privacy is a major principle of research ethics, a researcher must break confidentiality with a participant to report the incident [56]. Clearly disclosing these mandates to participants in the informed consent documents and the onset of data collection can support transparency and honesty between the researcher and participant.

Finally, working with foster teens may involve collecting extremely sensitive data (e.g., sexually explicit material, drug use, criminal behavior). Handling these data can be difficult, especially if the content violates the teen's rights or puts them in jeopardy. For example, we often try to protect a participant's confidentiality and privacy by removing all personally identifiable information and ensuring any publicly available comments, if retrieved from online platforms, are non-searchable [8]. Unfortunately, with large social media data sets that contain photographs, there is limited flexibility for removing all identifiable information. Therefore, a researcher must make a tradeoff between the risks of exposing a teen's identity and conducting research to benefit this specific population of teens.

CONCLUDING REMARKS

Limitations and Future Research

The purpose of this paper was to urge HCI researchers and interaction designers to focus on a subpopulation of teens that may otherwise fall between the cracks. In doing this, we may have missed some articles that would be relevant to our discussion. Yet, in our literature review, we found very little emphasis on protecting the online safety of foster youth, even after multiple searches. Therefore, we feel it is an accurate portrayal of the existing literature. Due to the lack of literature to inform our work, we drew from other relevant research related to foster youths' offline risk proclivity and the online challenges faced by other vulnerable teen populations. We did this to draw similarities and make recommendations, but ultimately, our main conclusion is simply that more research needs to be done on protecting the online safety of foster teens so that they can benefit from having access to networked-technology.

In our future work, we plan to conduct more empirical research involving case workers, foster parents, and, most importantly, foster youth to further understand the complex challenges and possible solutions for designing technology-based interventions to give foster youth the opportunity to engage through and with technology without making them even more vulnerable to risks. Our end goal involves allowing foster youth to engage with technology, just like other teens, but also help provide additional protection and guidance to ensure their safety. Future research should focus on introducing technological solutions and educational programs that empower teens in foster care to learn and practice online safety.

CONCLUSION

There are undoubtedly many benefits associated with technology use by foster teens, but these teens are often denied access as an attempt to protect them from high-risk behaviors and outcomes. To help foster youth engage in positive online interactions, we challenge HCI researchers and interaction designers to help us find more effective solutions that allow foster youth to be connected to others online without being harmed. To do this, researchers and designers of more pervasive sociotechnical and interactive systems, such as social media platforms and smartphones, should also consider the unique needs of vulnerable teen populations. While these teens may represent only a small and marginalized segment of all users, they are also ones who can most greatly benefit from being able to safely gain social and emotional support through digital networks. If we can take even the smallest steps to help foster youth gain a sense of "normalcy" in our technology-filled world, we would be making great strides to help those who are most in need.

ACKNOWLEDGEMENTS

We would like to thank Drs. Lindsay Taliaferro and Mel Stanfill who provided feedback on early versions of this work and acted as collaborators in other capacities related to our work on adolescent online safety and foster youth.

REFERENCES

1. Amanda Lenhart. 2015. Teens, Social Media & Technology Overview 2015. *Pew Research Center: Internet, Science & Tech.* Retrieved September 30, 2016 from http://www.pewinternet.org/2015/04/09/teens-social-media-technology-2015/
2. Zahra Ashktorab and Jessica Vitak. 2016. Designing Cyberbullying Mitigation and Prevention Solutions Through Participatory Design With Teenagers. In

Proceedings of the 2016 CHI Conference on Human Factors in Computing Systems (CHI '16), 3895–3905. https://doi.org/10.1145/2858036.2858548

3. Karla A. Badillo-Urquiola, Arup Kumar Ghosh, and Pamela Wisniewski. 2017. Understanding the Unique Online Challenges Faced by Teens in the Foster Care System.
4. Lindsay Blackwell, Emma Gardiner, and Sarita Schoenebeck. 2016. Managing Expectations: Technology Tensions among Parents and Teens. 1390–1401. https://doi.org/10.1145/2818048.2819928
5. danah boyd. 2014. Let Kids Run Wild Online. *Time*. Retrieved November 20, 2016 from http://time.com/23031/danah-boyd-let-kids-run-wild-online/
6. danah boyd, Alice Marwick, Parry Aftab, and Maeve Koeltl. The Conundrum of Visibility. *Taylor & Francis*. Retrieved January 25, 2017 from http://www-tandfonline-com.ezproxy.net.ucf.edu/doi/full/10.1080/17482790903233465
7. Matthew D. Bramlett and Laura F. Radel. 2014. *Adverse family experiences among children in nonparental care, 2011-2012*. Retrieved from https://www.cdc.gov/nchs/data/nhsr/nhsr074.pdf
8. Amy Bruckman, Kurt Luther, and Casey Fiesler. 2015. When Should We Use Real Names in Published Accounts of Internet Research? In *Digital Research Confidential: The Secrets of Studyig Behavior Online*. 243. Retrieved February 1, 2017 from https://books-google-com.ezproxy.net.ucf.edu/books/about/Digital_Research_Confidential.html?id=d1c1CwAAQBAJ
9. Sahara Byrne, Sherri Jean Katz, Theodore Lee, Daniel Linz, and Mary McIlrath. 2014. Peers, predators, and porn: Predicting parental underestimation of children's risky online experiences. *Journal of Computer-Mediated Communication* 19, 2: 215–231.
10. Alexei Czeskis, Ivayla Dermendjieva, Hussein Yapit, Alan Borning, Batya Friedman, Brian Gill, and Tadayoshi Kohno. 2010. Parenting from the pocket: Value tensions and technical directions for secure and private parent-teen mobile safety. In *Proceedings of the Sixth Symposium on Usable Privacy and Security*, 15. Retrieved September 21, 2016 from http://dl.acm.org.ezproxy.net.ucf.edu/citation.cfm?id=1837130
11. Samantha DeHaan, Laura E. Kuper, Joshua C. Magee, Lou Bigelow, and Brian Mustanski. The Interplay between Online and Offline Explorations of Identity, Relationships, and Sex: A Mixed-Methods Study with LGBT Youth. *Journal of Sex Research*. Retrieved January 19, 2017 from http://www-tandfonline-com.ezproxy.net.ucf.edu/doi/full/10.1080/00224499.2012.661489
12. Ramona Denby, Efren Gomez, and Keith Alford. 2016. Promoting Well-Being Through Relationship Building: The Role of Smartphone Technology in Foster Care. *Journal of Technology in Human Services* 34, 2: 183–208.
13. Ramona Denby Brinson, Efren Gomez, and Keith Alford. 2015. Becoming "Smart" about Relationship Building: Foster Care Youth and the Use of Technology. *Issue Brief Social Services*: 1–12.
14. Allison Druin. 1996. A place called childhood. *interactions* 3, 1: 17–22. https://doi.org/10.1145/223500.223506
15. Allison Druin. 1999. Cooperative inquiry: developing new technologies for children with children. 592–599. https://doi.org/10.1145/302979.303166
16. Matthew S. Eastin, Bradley S. Greenberg, and Linda Hofschire. 2006. Parenting the Internet. *Journal of Communication* 56, 3: 486–504. https://doi.org/10.1111/j.1460-2466.2006.00297.x
17. Jennifer P. Edidin, Zoe Ganim, Scott J. Hunter, and Niranjan S. Karnik. 2012. The mental and physical health of homeless youth: a literature review. *Child Psychiatry & Human Development* 43, 3: 354–375.
18. Tonya Edmond, Wendy Audlander, Diane Elze, and Sharon Bowland. 2006. Signs of Resilience in Sexually Abused Adolescent Girls in the Foster Care System. *Journal of Child Sexual Abuse* 15, 1: 1–28.
19. S. P. Farruggia and D. H. Sorkin. 2009. Health risks for older US adolescents in foster care: the significance of important others' health behaviours on youths' health and health behaviours. *Child: Care, Health and Development* 35, 3: 340–348. https://doi.org/10.1111/j.1365-2214.2009.00960.x
20. Dale Fitch. Youth in Foster Care and Social Media: A Framework for Developing Privacy Guidelines. *Journal of Technology in Human Services*. Retrieved September 30, 2016 from http://www.tandfonline.com.ezproxy.net.ucf.edu/doi/full/10.1080/15228835.2012.700854
21. Elizabeth Foss, Allison Druin, and Mona Leigh Guha. 2013. Recruiting and retaining young participants: strategies from five years of field research. 313–316. https://doi.org/10.1145/2485760.2485798
22. Jesse A. Francomano and Scott B. Harpin. 2015. Utilizing Social Networking Sites to Promote Adolescents' Health: A Pragmatic Review of the Literature. *CIN: Computers, Informatics, Nursing* 33, 1: 10–20. https://doi.org/10.1097/CIN.0000000000000113
23. FSU Office of Research. Florida Law and Human Subjects. Retrieved December 1, 2016 from

https://www.research.fsu.edu/research-offices/human-subjects/florida-law-and-human-subjects/

24. Jeff Gavin, Karen Rodham, and Helen Poyer. 2008. The Presentation of "Pro-Anorexia" in Online Group Interactions. *Qualitative Health Research* 18, 3: 325–333.
25. Jennifer Mullins Geiger and Lisa Ann Schelbe. 2014. Stopping the Cycle of Child Abuse and Neglect: A Call to Action to Focus on Pregnant and Parenting Youth in and Aging Out of the Foster Care System. *Journal of Public Child Welfare* 8, 1: 25–50.
26. Bridget Gramkowski, Susan Kools, Steven Paul, Cherrie Boyer, Erica Monasterio, and Nancy Robbins. 2009. Health Risk Behavior in Foster Youth. *Journal of child and adolescent psychiatric nursing : official publication of the Association of Child and Adolescent Psychiatric Nurses, Inc* 22, 2: 77. https://doi.org/10.1111/j.1744-6171.2009.00176.x
27. Nora Gustavsson and Ann MacEachron. 2015. Positive Youth Development and Foster Care Youth: A Digital Perspective. *Journal of Human Behavior in the Social Environment* 25, 5: 407–415. https://doi.org/10.1080/10911359.2014.966223
28. Scott B. Harpin, Jillian Davis, Hana Low, and Christine Gilroy. Mobile Phone and Social Media Use of Homeless Youth in Denver, Colorado. *Journal of Community Health Nursing*. Retrieved December 4, 2016 from http://www-tandfonline-com.ezproxy.net.ucf.edu/doi/abs/10.1080/07370016.2016.1159440
29. Heidi Hartikainen, Netta Iivari, and Marianne Kinnula. 2016. Should We Design for Control, Trust or Involvement?: A Discourses Survey about Children's Online Safety. 367–378. https://doi.org/10.1145/2930674.2930680
30. Michael Hass, Quaylan Allen, and Michelle Amoah. 2014. Turning points and resilience of academically successful foster youth. *Children and Youth Services Review* 44: 387–392. https://doi.org/10.1016/j.childyouth.2014.07.008
31. Sara Isola and Jerry Alan Fails. 2012. Family and design in the IDC and CHI communities. 40–49. https://doi.org/10.1145/2307096.2307102
32. Loring Jones. 2012. Measuring Resiliency and Its Predictors in Recently Discharged Foster Youth. *Child and Adolescent Social Work Journal* 29, 6: 515–533. https://doi.org/10.1007/s10560-012-0275-z
33. Loring Paul Jones. 2014. The Role of Social Support in the Transition From Foster Care to Emerging Adulthood. *Journal of Family Social Work* 17, 1: 81–96. https://doi.org/10.1080/10522158.2013.865287
34. Minsam Ko, Seungwoo Choi, Subin Yang, Joonwon Lee, and Uichin Lee. 2015. FamiLync: Facilitating Participatory Parental Mediation of Adolescents' Smartphone Use. In *Proceedings of the 2015 ACM International Joint Conference on Pervasive and Ubiquitous Computing* (UbiComp '15), 867–878. https://doi.org/10.1145/2750858.2804283
35. Robin M. Kowalski and Cristin Fedina. 2011. Cyber bullying in ADHD and Asperger Syndrome populations. *Research in Autism Spectrum Disorders* 5, 3: 1201–1208. https://doi.org/10.1016/j.rasd.2011.01.007
36. Jennifer Lehmann and David Vicary. 2015. Out-of-Home Care - Where to Next? *Children Australia* 40, 4: 290–297. https://doi.org/http://dx.doi.org.ezproxy.net.ucf.edu/10.1017/cha.2015.53
37. Kimberly J. Mitchell, Lisa M. Jones, David Finkelhor, and Janis Wolak. 2013. Understanding the decline in unwanted online sexual solicitations for U.S. youth 2000–2010: Findings from three Youth Internet Safety Surveys. *Child Abuse & Neglect* 37: 1225–1236. https://doi.org/10.1016/j.chiabu.2013.07.002
38. Michelle R. Munson and J. Curtis McMillen. 2009. Natural Mentoring and Psychosocial Outcomes among Older Youth Transitioning From Foster Care. *Children and youth services review* 31, 1: 104. https://doi.org/10.1016/j.childyouth.2008.06.003
39. Sarah Carter Narendorf and J. Curtis McMillen. 2010. Substance Use and Substance Use Disorders as Foster Youth Transition to Adulthood. *Children and youth services review* 32, 1: 113–119. https://doi.org/10.1016/j.childyouth.2009.07.021
40. Karen M. Matta Oshima, Sarah Carter Narendorf, and J. Curtis McMillen. 2013. Pregnancy Risk Among Older Youth Transitioning Out Of Foster Care. *Children and Youth Services Review* 35, 10: 1760–1765. https://doi.org/10.1016/j.childyouth.2013.08.001
41. Anthony Pinter, Pamela Wisniewski, Heng Xu, Mary Beth Rosson, and John M. Carroll. 2017. Adolescent Online Safety: Moving Beyond Formative Evaluations to Designing Solutions for the Future.
42. Erika S. Poole and Tamara Peyton. 2013. Interaction design research with adolescents: methodological challenges and best practices. 211–217. https://doi.org/10.1145/2485760.2485766
43. Eric Rice and Anamika Barman-Adhikari. 2014. Internet and Social Media Use as a Resource Among Homeless Youth. *Journal of Computer-Mediated Communication* 19, 2: 232–247. https://doi.org/10.1111/jcc4.12038
44. ric Rice, Hailey Winetrobe, Ian W. Holloway, Jorge Montoya, Aaron Plant, and Timothy Kordic. 2015. Cell Phone Internet Access, Online Sexual Solicitation, Partner Seeking, and Sexual Risk Behavior among

Adolescents. *Archives of sexual behavior* 44, 3: 755–763. https://doi.org/10.1007/s10508-014-0366-3

45. Svetlana Shpiegel. 2015. Resilience Among Older Adolescents in Foster Care: the Impact of Risk and Protective Factors. *International Journal of Mental Health and Addiction* 14, 1: 6–22. https://doi.org/10.1007/s11469-015-9573-y
46. Jenny L. Wilson, Rebecka Peebles, Kristina K. Hardy, and Iris F. Litt. 2006. Surfing for Thinness: A Pilot Study of Pro–Eating Disorder Web Site Usage in Adolescents With Eating Disorders. *Pediatrics* 118, 6: e1635–e1643. https://doi.org/10.1542/peds.2006-1133
47. Pamela Wisniewski, Arup Kumar Ghosh, Mary Beth Rosson, Heng Xu, and John M. Carroll. 2017. Parental Control vs. Teen Self-Regulation: Is there a middle ground for mobile online safety?
48. Pamela Wisniewski, Haiyan Jia, Na Wang, Saijing Zheng, Heng Xu, Mary Beth Rosson, and John M. Carroll. 2015. Resilience Mitigates the Negative Effects of Adolescent Internet Addiction and Online Risk Exposure. In *Proceedings of the 33rd Annual ACM Conference on Human Factors in Computing Systems* (CHI '15), 4029–4038. https://doi.org/10.1145/2702123.2702240
49. Pamela Wisniewski, Haiyan Jia, Heng Xu, Mary Beth Rosson, and John M. Carroll. 2015. Preventative vs. Reactive: How Parental Mediation Influences Teens' Social Media Privacy Behaviors. 302–316. https://doi.org/10.1145/2675133.2675293
50. Pamela Wisniewski, Mary Beth Rosson, Heng Xu, and John M. Carroll. 2017. Parents Just Don't Understand: Why Teens Don't Talk to Parents about Their Online Risk Experiences. In *Proceedings of the 20th ACM Conference on Computer Supported Cooperative Work & Social Computing*.
51. Pamela Wisniewski, Heng Xu, Mary Beth Rosson, Daniel F. Perkins, and John M. Carroll. 2016. Dear Diary: Teens Reflect on Their Weekly Online Risk Experiences. 3919–3930. https://doi.org/10.1145/2858036.2858317
52. Jill Palzkill Woelfer. 2014. Engaging homeless young people in HCI research. *interactions* 21, 1: 54–57. https://doi.org/10.1145/2543580
53. Svetlana Yarosh, Iulian Radu, Seth Hunter, and Eric Rosenbaum. 2011. Examining values: an analysis of nine years of IDC research. 136–144. https://doi.org/10.1145/1999030.1999046
54. AFCARS Report #22, Children's Bureau, Administration for Children and Families. Retrieved September 30, 2016 from http://www.acf.hhs.gov/cb/resource/afcars-report-22
55. iFoster - Life changing resources for children and youth. Retrieved February 2, 2017 from https://www.ifoster.org/iNewsCompDetails.aspx?NewsID=109
56. Mandatory Reporters of Child Abuse and Neglect - Child Welfare Information Gateway. Retrieved January 25, 2017 from https://www.childwelfare.gov/topics/systemwide/laws-policies/statutes/manda/

Child as Protagonist: Expanding the Role of Children in Participatory Design

Ole Sejer Iversen
CAVI
Aarhus University, Denmark
oiversen@cavi.au.dk

Rachel Charlotte Smith
CAVI
Aarhus University, Denmark
rsmith@cavi.au.dk

Christian Dindler
CAVI
Aarhus University, Denmark
dindler@cavi.au.dk

ABSTRACT
We suggest that a commitment to political participatory design defines a new role for children in participatory practices—the role of *protagonist.* The objective here transcends the goal of giving children a voice in design, and addresses more broadly how children can be empowered to shape technological development and critically reflect on the role of technology in their practices. This re-accentuation of political participatory design to formulate the protagonist role is important, because it deepens our understanding of how children may be empowered through design. It is also timely in view of current societal challenges pertaining to training children in twenty-first century skills. Based on a case study, we illustrate how the protagonist role, based on political participatory design, can change the objective, process, and outcome measures of the design process.

Author Keywords
Protagonist; participatory design; political participatory design; design competence; twenty-first century skills.

ACM Classification Keywords
H.5.m. Information interfaces and presentation (e.g., HCI): Miscellaneous.

INTRODUCTION
Children's role in Participatory Design (PD) remains a topic of great interest in Interaction Design and Children (IDC) research. Landoni et al. [25] ask "How many roles can children play?" emphasizing that children are often invited into the early ideation phases of design, but rarely admitted to other aspects of the design process. Read et al. [31] criticize parts of current IDC research for being "fast and furious" or for being a "reduced PD" in which children are engaged only in isolated, short-term design sessions but are left out of the more important decision-making process. This kind of PD is, according to Read et al. [31], better referred to as "crowdsourcing of ideas," as children do not necessarily influence the final outcome here and little emphasis is put on design as a mutual learning process as manifested in PD theory [36]. This concern is further scrutinized by Frauenberger et al. [16], who introduce a methodological framework for critically reflecting on PD projects according to their alignment of values, outcomes, epistemology, and stakeholder participation. They point out that PD involving children needs to be evaluated not just in relation to tangible outcomes, but also in relation to the participants' learning gains, the values of the projects, and their grounding epistemological perspectives.

In this paper, we offer a novel perspective on children's role in PD—the role of *protagonist.* Our suggestion builds on the tradition of political PD to emphasize that the objective of design is not only technological products, but for participants to develop new insights, design abilities, and a critical and reflective stance toward technology through their engagement in design work. We position the role of *protagonist* in relation to existing IDC research, involving children as users, testers, informants, co-designers [12, 17] and co-researchers [10]. Through our case study we also illustrate how the role of protagonist differs from previous approaches in *objective*, *process*, and *outcome measures*.

There are at least two related incentives for re-accentuating political PD and introducing the role of protagonist. First, focusing on the intangible outcomes of design—such as new skills, new insights, and a reflective stance toward technology—contributes to the understanding of how children may be empowered through design. Second, in the European context the societal challenge of preparing children for a digitized society has surfaced very prominently in recent years. The notion of twenty-first century skills is currently high on the European political agenda as an attempt to articulate the skills needed to succeed in a highly globalized and digitally mediated society. Some of these skills are closely related to children's abilities to create with digital materials and also solve complex societal problems [1]. As pointed out by several researchers (e.g. [32]), these competences are not necessarily new. Complex problem-solving has always been a component of human progress. It has also been central in the development of design theory from the beginning, including concerns for digital technology, and has been taught in design schools worldwide for decades

[32]. Promoting twenty-first century skills is currently being investigated through implicit or explicit adaptations of design theory to education from kindergarten to ninth grade to support children's development of competences [34]. Bekker et al. [4] have introduced a design tool kit to support children's design thinking, while Smith et al. [34] provide a framework for understanding children's design competence in their account of design judgment. Blikstein [6] coins the rapidly extending reach of digital fabrication technologies as a "democratization of innovation" that emphasizes the possibilities for including children in the design of new technologies by introducing those technologies into formal education.

The concept of *design protagonist* suggested in the present paper extends the concern to empower children into developing technology, critically reflecting on it, and acting upon it. It also provides an approach to addressing the challenge of twenty-first-century skills training. In the paper we use the term "protagonist" in a dual sense: first, to articulate the idea that in this approach children are the main agents in the design process as they engage with authentic design problems; and second, to suggest that through their engagement in design, children develop skills in designing and reflecting on technology, and that these skills empower them to make more informed decisions about technology in their lives. Both these ideas derive from the tradition of political PD.

Our inquiry into political PD and the role protagonist is structured as follows. In the two following sections we review literature on PD involving children and the political perspective in PD. We then outline the differing conceptions of children's participation reported in the IDC literature and present our protagonist perspective. Our case study demonstrates how the protagonist perspective may play out in practice. Finally, we discuss potentials of the suggested perspective and outline avenues for future work.

PARTICIPATORY DESIGN WITH CHILDREN

PD has always played a significant role in IDC research, dating back to Druin's seminal work on cooperative inquiry [11,12], Read's work on PD for children [28], and the work by Iversen et al. on the Scandinavian and political aspects of PD with children [21, 22]. In recent years, PD methods and techniques within IDC research have expanded and become increasingly sophisticated, as with the development of a framework describing common PD methods and their use [40] bringing PD to special needs (e.g. [15,26]), facilitating distributed PD work [39,41] in game environments [38], in schools [3,35], and under extreme constraints [14]. The sophistication of existing PD methods is also clear in Mechelen's [27] framework for understanding children's group dynamics and underlying values through PD work. Similarly, Read et al. [31] developed the Rapid Analysis of Design Ideas for integrating ethical and inclusive analysis of large sets of data deriving from a PD project. All these endeavors have extended the scope of PD work so as to include the analysis of data—something that was not previously considered to be a PD activity.

As PD is now considered mainstream—and, arguably, has almost become a trademark of IDC research—many different interpretations of this particular design approach coexist. Guha et al. [17] emphasize the intergenerational *co-design* aspects of PD in their revisiting of cooperative inquiry, whereas Yip et al. [42] describe PD as a "method" of enhancing technology for children by designing with children. Citing [13], Read et al. [31] consider PD to be a "philosophy" in which end-users actively engage with designers and developers to collaboratively explore future design solutions. Iivari and Kinnula [19] discuss the challenge of creating "genuine participation." Iversen and Dindler [23] describe participatory "epistemology" in which they point to the intangible outcomes of PD processes, such as "emancipation" through design with and for children. As stressed by [16], the field of PD has expanded and diversified and a broad spectrum of approaches and methodologies have emerged to support the design of children's technology. Despite the diversity of understandings of PD, the ethos at the heart of PD (as suggested by Read et al. [28]) is active engagement of children in the design of new technology in order to both develop better technologies and give children a voice in the design process. This particular interpretation of PD resonates well with Simonsen and Robertson's [36] notion of *pragmatic* PD. Pragmatic PD stresses the need for users and developers to learn together about possible and useful technological solutions ([36], p. 6). Empowerment is obtained by providing participants legitimate access to the entire design process, from project definition to evaluation of the design outcomes.

POLITICAL PARTICIPATORY DESIGN

Historically, PD has always had a strong political component [9, 24]. From a political standpoint, PD has been a struggle for democracy. The overarching goal was to create an emancipatory practice in which users, through their own commitment to the design of new technologies, could become capable of influencing their practice. While tangible technological products were an important part of the early political PD, many of the activities in the projects were aimed at providing practitioners with skills related to IT and creating organizational arrangements that would support local development and influence. As stated by Bansler [2], user organizations such as trade unions "... must carry out their own investigations, independently of management, and raise their own demands regarding the use of new technology in order to establish a basis for negotiations with management" ([2], p.16). The core PD objective was the education and encouragement of users to actively participate in the design of technology through a mutual learning process. Accordingly, much of the material produced during the early PD projects (such as DEMOS, DUE, UTOPIA) was in the form of educational material and reports that documented local experiences with democratizing the introduction of technology (see [5]). The tangible outcome of the process was an IT product, but a more important outcome was the new-won insights, skills, visions, and democratic awareness among users that had been attained through their engagement. To achieve this objective, the design *process* was constructed around making future users and stakeholders active participants in the process. The process aspect of PD is arguably its best - known aspect, and has since been adopted within a range of communities related to technology design, including IDC. The agenda of providing people with the skills needed to shape their own practice and engage in relevant political negotiations continues to play a role in the PD community, but it has arguably been overshadowed by research that focuses on tools and techniques for user–designer cooperation and experiences with involving various user groups in design. Much less documented is the extent to which the ambitions of political PD have actually been achieved. Formal evaluation and *outcome measures* are rarely reported in the PD literature [7]. These have surfaced recently in retrospective studies assessing what people gain from PD projects [7,8] and in frameworks suggesting how such outcomes might be evaluated [16]. But in IDC research, the political agenda now appears all but absent except for a few cases in recent work [18,20,21,22,31] tracing back the underlying political roots of PD in Child–Computer Interaction research.

In this paper we suggest that the focus of political PD—providing people with opportunity and means to shape their own technology and practices—resonates well with IDC's ambition of enhancing children's ability to critically understand, reflect on, and take action in a digitally mediated society through the tools, technology, and dialog provided in the PD process. In order to examine political PD in the context of IDC, we review the various roles played by children in participatory IDC practices and discuss these in terms of *objective*, *process*, and *outcome measure*. We illustrate how political PD differs within each of these categories defining the role of *protagonist.* Through a case, we show how this role may be instantiated in terms of objective, process, and outcome measures.

CHILDREN'S ROLE IN PD

Druin [12] developed a highly influential framework for understanding children's role in PD, known as "the onion model." The model distinguishes between roles in PD processes that engage children as users, testers, informants, and co-designers. Children can be studied as *users* of technology, yielding insight into their practices and the significance of technology. They can also be engaged as *testers* of a new system, and thus engaged in the design process to determine the importance of features and the usability of the system. More proactively, and at an earlier stage in the design process, children can be encouraged to generate ideas for a new system as *informants* in the design process. Here, children act as information providers in relation to expert designers or researchers. Finally, Druin [12] introduces the role of *design partner* to give children a voice throughout the design process by articulating their expertise and real-life experiences. Guha et al. [17] elaborate on this conceptual understanding by stressing the different dimensions of roles in the design process and by specifying how those roles are brought into play in PD projects in relation to the developers, the technology, and the goal of the inquiry. Doorn [10] recently expanded the understanding of children's role in PD by studying how children can act as co-researchers in design by gathering, sharing, and enriching contextual data.

The various different categories of children's roles can be represented by objective, process, and outcome measures (Table 1). Engaging with children as users involves studying children's practice and use of technology with the objective of gaining insights that may aid in designing technology. The outcome measure relates to the amount, validity, and quality of the knowledge obtained. Involving children as testers points to the objective of developing new technology or adjusting new designs so as to better fit children's behavior. In this mode of involvement, the objective is to gain insights into a particular design or prototype by having children try out the proposed design. The outcome is tightly connected to the quality of the new design: outcome measures relate to issues such as usability, utility, and the experiential qualities of the design. While the objective of informant design parallels the "child as tester" perspective, the process in which the objectives are met and the outcomes gained differs significantly. According to Guha et al. [17] and Scaife and Rogers [33], informant design advocates working with children at those specific points during the design process when their input is considered to be most valuable or most needed. The "child as design partner" perspective has its objective in common with informant design, though it emphasizes empowerment by giving children access to the design process [12]. Also, design partnering is often based on a long-term commitment between children and designers, emphasizing a co-design perspective with shared responsibilities and concerns. As stated by Guha et al. [17], informant design is a process of providing feedback to adults. The goal of design partnering, by contrast, is the elaboration and negotiation of all perspectives on design. For a thorough review of these differences, see [33]. Finally, Doorn [10] introduces the co-researcher perspective, which differs significantly from existing roles. In this perspective, children are engaged in the knowledge production that can eventually lead to the design of new artifacts. The objective is to generate context-sensitive and situated knowledge, by allowing children to gather, share, and enrich contextual data from their environment. This process sometimes becomes detached from design work, since the emphasis here is on knowledge production. The outcome of this process is a strong conceptual understanding of children's praxis that can be used to design better products.

These categorizations of children's role in design are of course archetypical, and they draw on some of the same methods and techniques for collaboration. The categorizations could also be criticized for being one-dimensional in relation to the complex matter of child participation. Mechelen [27] argues that children's role is not exclusively determined by the relationship to designers and the design process, but also to group dynamics among the children. Nevertheless, the archetypical roles offer broad categorizations for understanding how, why, and when children are engaged in design.

The contribution of this paper is to offer a sixth category based on principles drawn from political PD, stressing the training and prompting of participants to develop skills to shape technology themselves and accordingly to critically reflect on the role of technology in their practice. We term this sixth category "child as protagonist." While a few IDC authors have touched on ideas closely related to political PD [18,21,22,29], we find the perspective is underdeveloped. This category shares certain traits with "child as design partner" and "child as co-researcher," but we argue that it is distinct, in particular in its objective and its outcome measures. The objective of the "child as protagonist" category is to develop a critical and reflective stance toward technology and to develop skills for designing technology.In terms of process, we suggest that this objective is realized by children engaging in processes through which they develop design competence. This has some similarities in common with, for example, the "child as design partner" approach, in which children also participate in design work. The difference with the "child as protagonist" is that here the process is arranged primarily to help children develop their design competence and ability to reflect on the role of technology, rather than with the primary aim of developing good products. In terms of outcome measures, the "child as protagonist" category will look at the extent to which children have developed insights into the nature of digital technology as well as enhancing their design competence and their ability to reflect on the role of technology in their lives. In the section that follows we illustrate, through a case study, how this category may be used in participatory practices, and we highlight how the objective, process, and outcome measures may be materialized.

	Objective of participation	**Participatory process**	**Outcome measures from participation**
Child as user	Researchers test a general concept that may help inform future technology or provide better understanding of the process of learning which may contribute to future educational practices.	Children are observed, video-taped or tested before and/or after technology use.	Knowledge about children's technology use and learning.
Child as tester	Researchers gain insights into children's use of a particular technology and eventually improve that technology based on these insights.	Children test prototypes of a particular technology.	Knowledge about the usability, utility, and experiential qualities of the proposed technology.
Child as informant	Researchers gain insights to inform the design at various stages of the design process by eliciting and including children's expert knowledge.	Children may be observed with existing technologies, or they may be asked for input throughout the entire design process.	Knowledge provided by children that relates directly to the technology being designed.
Child as design partner	Researchers give children a voice in the design process. Children and researchers co-design new and meaningful technologies by means of partnership.	Children and researchers engage in various design sessions with a shared goal of designing new technology.	Empowerment of children by giving them a voice in design. Development of meaningful technologies.
Child as co-researcher	Researchers and children gain contextual knowledge by jointly studying children's practices.	Children contribute to design by sharing, gathering, and analyzing data from their own use practice.	Knowledge about the design context and the possibility of incorporating this knowledge into new technology.
Child as protagonist	Researchers encourage children to be the main agents in driving the design process and thereby to develop skills to design and reflect on technology and its role in their life.	Children carry out a complete design process in which process and product reflection is a central component.	Children's new insights into design and digital technology and reflective stance toward technology in their life.

Table 1: An overview of children's different roles in the design process adapted from Druin [12], Guha et al. [17] and Doorn [10] and extended by a perspective on child as protagonist.

METHOD

Our case study derives from a research project conducted in Danish public schools (folkeskoler) for children aged six to sixteen. Based on the insights gained over three months of participant observations [37, 34] in design and crafts teaching, the research team developed a research-through-design experiment [43] to examine how we could invite children into design in a protagonist role. The experiment was carried out in collaboration with three seventh-grade classes at N. J. Fjordsgades School in Aarhus, Western Denmark, between October and December 2014. A design researcher acted as the main facilitator of the project, in collaboration with a local teacher, while three design researchers documented the process using video and field notes. The experiment was conducted in the school's makerspace, and the activities were continuously developed, evaluated, and refined by the team in three iterations. In total, 69 students (aged 13–14) were engaged in the research experiment, which ran over the course of six weeks and amounted to two to four lessons per week. The researchers followed selected groups of students throughout the process. They also conducted semi-structured interviews (20 to 30 minutes in duration) with 14 pairs of students about their experiences of and reflections on the design process.

The field notes and video material from the observational studies and the research experiments were logged and analyzed, with a particular focus on the groups of students we followed most closely. This is described in Smith et al. [34] with a focus on the case study and the comparison between actions and experiences in the design process and the students' retrospective reflections. In the present paper, this case study serves to illustrate how the protagonist perspective might be realized in the context of a concrete design experiment. To meet the ethical concerns that arise in PD research involving children [29,30], informed consent for conducting the research was gained from the school principal, teachers, parents, and the students themselves. All 69 students chose to participate for the entire duration of the study. We did refrain from engaging children in the process of framing the design brief and activities, and analyzing the data. This could potentially have strengthened the study and the depth of the children's involvement, but it would have demanded more than the available resources.

The design experiment was conducted as part of the Aarhus University FabLab research project: an ongoing interdisciplinary research project studying how digital fabrication technologies in combination with design thinking can be introduced into formal education. In Smith et al. [34], we presented a thorough account of the design experiment and described how the interventions enhanced the design competence among the participating students. In the present paper, we use the design experiment to illustrate how a political PD perspective supports children's protagonistic role in design. We demonstrate in the following three sections how political PD fundamentally affects and changes the objective, process, and outcome measures compared with more established PD approaches as discussed in the preceding section.

OBJECTIVE: ENCOURAGING CHILDREN TO BECOME PROTAGONISTS

The objective of the research project was to encourage children to be the main actors in driving the design process and in so doing to improve their skills to design and reflect on technology and its role in their everyday life. These aims were articulated throughout the process activities, but perhaps most explicitly in the opening design brief (Table 2).

In accordance with its status as EU Capital of Culture 2017, Aarhus Municipality has received funding from the European Union's Re-designing Urban Spaces Program to redesign Aarhus's city hall park. Frederiks Allé (a local street) will be led through a tunnel under the park so as to open up a whole new park area between the city's concert hall and city hall. Aarhus's vision for the new city park is to create an innovative and engaging public space especially for young people. The city council has therefore asked three school classes to develop a number of design proposals for the Capital of Culture 2017 campaign.

Table 2: The design brief

The design brief challenged the students to redesign a public park in accordance with the city council's aim of developing a more recreational space in the area for everyday leisure and social activities. It was intended to direct the students' attention away from their own personal (arbitrary) ideas and rather toward the opportunities provided by the brief so as to develop relevant concepts for a specific context.. The brief contained two important components to engage the children as protagonists in the design process, namely authenticity and closeness. The design brief was developed from an *authentic* challenge in that Aarhus had just been elected European Capital of Culture in 2017, an honor that had been hyped in the local news as something potentially affecting the cultural identity of the city. It was hoped that the authenticity of the design brief would give the children an intrinsic motivation to engage in the design work. Further, the municipality's involvement as project sponsor allowed the children to feel that they were part of a broad network of professionals exploring future urban environments. The design brief also situated the design challenge in the students' own neighborhood. The *closeness* of the brief was an important aspect of allowing the students to identify with the challenge, while openness of the concrete framing was maintained so as to allow the students to develop their ideas freely. The children were thus faced with a challenge that was complex but within which they could potentially affect a public decision-making process, and, more importantly, change their own physical surroundings for the better.

The design brief and its requirements were regularly revisited through the students' work. As researchers and facilitators of the process, we created the role of design expert. This was intended to distance us from being "teachers" who have predefined answers to the outcome of the process and to support our roles as facilitators who were to guide the students and groups in their own work. After we had introduced the design brief, the urban context, and the planned activities for the students' field studies, the students worked to frame and reframe their unique challenge and plan the execution of their process. Our roles were to support activities and collaboration in the groups and to scaffold the students' sense of ownership and legitimacy in the process.

Rather than developing specific technological artifacts, the design brief emphasized an exploratory process, working with technology as a flexible and creative means. The role of the technology was downplayed in the initial activities and introduced during the ideation phase as students were able to work with and integrate relevant technologies into their projects. The availability of different technologies as flexible tools and materials to be integrated into the process shifted the students' perceptions of technology from something involving fixed objects to something involving digital means for creating their own alternative opportunities and solutions. This strategy was chosen to support the students in developing their own reflective stance toward technology.

PROCESS: SCAFFOLDING AN ITERATIVE AND REFLECTIVE PROCESS

To support the process of children engaging as protagonists, we employed a process model that could support this particular stance throughout the entire design process. The model was based on six main activities. The circular model illustrates design as an iterative process, since all design outcomes eventually lead to new research questions and new problem framings. Moreover, iterations occur within and between each of the activities and with increaasing experience, eventually crisscrossing effects are created that use the model as a framework for navigating through one's own design project. The model contains six main design activities, each including several sub-activities: (1) the design brief, for framing a complex challenge and planning the design process; (2) field studies, to explore and research the context and users; (3) ideation, for the creative development of ideas using various techniques and materials; (4) fabrication, for mock-up and prototyping of concepts using digital technologies; (5) argumentation, for testing a design concept or product and reflecting on the design moves and arguments of the process; and (6) reflection, for reflecting on the learning outcome—or design competence—developed through the entire design process (see Fig. 1). For a description of the process model, see Smith et al. [34].

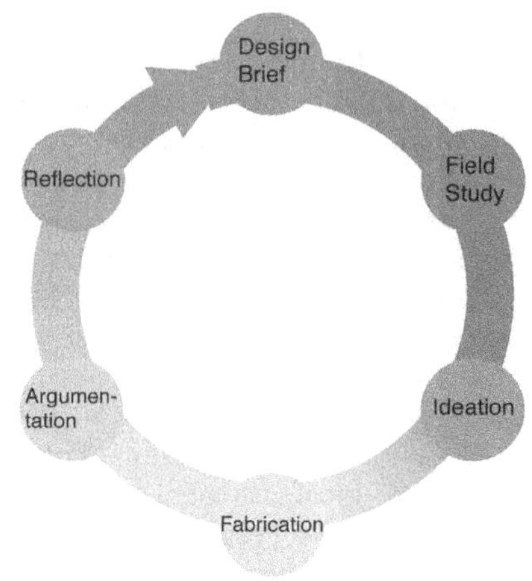

Figure 1: The six main design activities illustrated in an iterative design process model.

We recognize that our process model is one among several suitable design models to illustrate iterative design processes. However, this particular model was designed to embed certain characteristics that support children as protagonists throughout the design process. First, the design model supported an ongoing interplay between divergent and convergent thinking and doing. Divergence and convergence notoriously compel the children to open up their design process and take in new perspectives and subsequently deselect (potentially important) aspects in their efforts to reach a meaningful design solution. The interplay between divergence and convergence demands a high level of commitment, agency, and determination. These in turn sustain the children's role as protagonists in the process. Second, the design model incorporates argumentation and reflection as the closing activities of each iteration. By positioning reflection as the outcome of the design activity, the design process closely ties its aim to the objective of developing a reflecting stance toward technology and design, as described in the "child as protagonist" perspective. Third, the design model does not prescribe either specific actions or project measures. It merely indicates how the design process develops. This is to encourage the children to be mindful about their process, their collaboration, and their choices during the process, rather than focusing solely on the tangible outcome. There are no formal instructions in the model, indicating that there is no correct way for children to proceed through the stages of project framing, research, ideation, and fabrication to the final stages of argumentation and reflection. This lack of authority in the model transfers a high level of self-efficacy and agency to the children. They have to stay in charge of the design process while they gradually explore the design brief and activities provided by the design experts.

In the case study, the process model was carefully introduced and monitored by the design team. An important task for the researchers was to support the alternation between divergent and convergent thinking and thus to keep the process going. The purpose was not to harvest ideas from the students, but to scaffold their process in order to develop their design abilities. Each activity was supported by the general framing, but the real challenge was the leap between the activities. Moving from field studies to ideation, or from ideation to fabrication, demanded the transformation of diverse data, ideas, and materials into a new activity, while at the same time interweaving the design challenge and the constraints posed by analog and digital materials. In order to develop the students' design abilities, we were careful of how we assisted and supported their forward progression. Sometimes the students sought direct instructions, but we emphasized our roles as facilitators of their process and mostly provided new questions rather than solutions. They were not instructed in, for example, how to integrate the Arduino software and hardware with their concept, but were pointed toward ways of finding out what they needed to know. In this way, self-motivation, collaboration, and trial and error rather than predetermined learning goals were the drivers in making decisions.

OUTCOME MEASURES: EVALUATING THE OUTCOME OF A POLITICAL PD PROCESS

Both the evaluation process and the outcome measures were aligned with the political PD agenda. A strong emphasis was put on children's new insights into design and digital technology and their reflective stance toward technology in their everyday life. Consequently, the evaluation targeted not only the intellectual outcomes directly related to the design process, but also the outcomes in terms of student insights and their general perception of technology. The reflection activity and the argumentation activity of the process model were a critical component in ensuring that students gained insights into the nature of the design process and of technology more generally. The students gave a presentation of their design argument to the class as a coherent presentation of their research findings, ideas, and prototype, inviting representatives from the municipality and from the university. Each group made video scenarios of their design idea, as well as oral presentations of their functioning prototypes. Feedback from the panel was given in relation both to the design brief and to the design decisions taken by the group during the process. In addition, the researchers, the teacher and the students had a shared discussion about the learning outcome of the entire design process, reflecting on the activities, the iterative connections between them, and their applicability in other complex issues in which design and technology were relevant. These collaborative assessments of the outcome and of learning from the process were conducted in order to give the students shared experiences of designing—as well as a language and reflections about the quality of design—to strengthen their (collective and individual) design competence. The activities may resemble those of other design processes in which participants collaboratively debrief, except that in this case the reflection activities were positioned as the end goal of the design process.

To further pursue outcome measures related to political PD and the role of protagonist, we also examined the children's personal gains emerging from the process participation. To do this, we inquired into the children learning gains – not only in relation to the specific design outcome, but in relation to the children's general perception of technology and design. To a large extend, the questions we posed resemble the evaluation taxonomy proposed by Bossen et al. [8]. Although the interviews were informal and dialogue-based, they centered around nine fundamental questions. The nine questions (*italic*) and their relation to the taxonomy (**bold**) provided by Bossen et al. [8] are listed in Table 3. The interviews were conducted after the design process. In this project, 14 students were interviewed in rounds of two-and-two. The reason for interviewing the students in pairs was to engage them in conversation around the questions and their prototypes, supporting each other in reflecting on insights from the design process.

It is important to note that engaging children with these nine abstract questions demands a certain expertise: sometimes the questions needed to be simplified and converted into concrete examples and communicated in everyday dialog. Nevertheless, the questions provide a way of learning about what children gain from the design process, as well as how they may transfer knowledge gained in the process to their everyday lives.

Influence on the project and product *How did your personal engagement influence the design process and the design outcome?*
Most satisfying and most frustrating experiences *What were the most important experiences and challenges you remember from the design process?*
Personal gain from participation *Thinking back on the process, what was the most valuable personal insight you gained?*
Extent of new outlook on technology or personal practices *How did your relationship to digital technology develop during the design process (and after the process)?*
New quality of work, new possibilities discovered, or more influence on own work conditions *How would you consider your experiences in relation to other types of school work?*
New areas of competence acquired *Which new competences (research, programming, ideation, reflection) have you gained from the design process?*
Subsequent shifts in career or future training path owing to the project *(How) did your participation change your relation to education and future career plans?*
Overall assessment of participation in project *How would you describe your participation in the process?*
Newly emerged opportunities in general *(How) did your project participation make you consider new opportunities in relation to design of digital technology?*

Table 3: Interview guide for evaluating children's gains.

The questions point to great variation among student gains. Some students do not necessarily internalize knowledge from this kind of participation [34]. In our design experiment, however, some students followed an almost vertical learning curve in terms of their ability not only to participate in design process but also in their understanding of digital technology. As an illustrative example of the interview process and the outcome measures of a political PD process, two girls reflected on the question "Which new competences (research, programming, ideation, reflection) did you gain from the design process?" as follows:

Sarah: *Well, you can design everything. It's not closed. It's completely open, for everything. I really didn't expect to have this result now* [looking at her prototype].

Agnes: *No, I really hadn't expected that either. It seemed hopeless at one point.* [...] *You just have to keep on and on and on, and then you will succeed.*

Researcher: *What did you think design was?*

Sarah: *I thought it was something like...*

Agnes: *Clothes, or something...*

Sarah: *Yes, clothes! That's what you think of when you hear the word design.*

Researcher: *So what do you think design is now?*

Agnes: *I think it's something new; your own imagination that you can think aloud with! You can design many things, like this wall for example* [touching the wall].

Sarah: *Before this, I hadn't even thought about such things. I didn't think, Okay, how can I improve an urban space. But I do now, because we've learned about it here, and you've taught us how to think in this way.* [...] *You begin to think differently, How could I do this, and What if I did it this way. It's a creative way of thinking.*

As this example illustrates, the students managed not only to create coherent products in response to the design challenge. Through their participation, they also managed to develop a design language and a sense of direction that enabled them to engage dynamically in the complex process of using a range of analog and digital materials in iterative movements of reflection and action. Finally, the interview sessions suggested that the process had implications for their general perception of digital technology and design.

The design case study illustrates how the protagonist approach to PD is explicitly embedded in our outcome measures. A protagonist approach includes questions related to the children's new insights both into design and digital technology and into the reflective stance toward technology in their everyday life.

DISCUSSION

As the case study illustrates, a political PD process has many similarities with more conventional PD approaches such as cooperative inquiry [12, 17] in which children are engaged as design partners. Political PD will draw from the same toolbox of methods and techniques [40], and the process will seek empowerment by giving children a voice in the design process. However, adopting the perspective of political PD and framing children as protagonists has both epistemological and practical consequences. In terms of epistemology, it frames the objective of participatory work not as the design or testing of a particular product, but the insights, skills, and reflective stance that children develop through the process. This, in turn, serves the purpose of empowering children to take an active role in developing technology and in making decisions about technology in their lives.

In terms of how this is practiced, our case study exemplifies how the process of participation is reshaped by the protagonist perspective. At first glance, the protagonist role looks similar to that of design partner, since both roles imply that children take an active part in designing. However, there are key differences reflected in the way that objective, process, and outcome measures were realized in our case. As described, an important part of supporting the children in taking on the role of protagonist was to create legitimacy and ownership in the process. We deliberately chose a design challenge connected to the children's everyday life in order to motivate them to take on an active role. Additionally, the open-ended design model was used to invite students to employ their own ideas and reasoning in the process. The process itself reflects that the objective was not to conduct co-design or to elicit ideas and requirements from the children, as typically in design partnering, but to support them in developing their own skills.

In terms of outcome measures, the questions and categories listed in Table 2 differ very distinctly from conventional PD approaches in IDC research. While learning from the process certainly takes place in the design partnering, for example, it is not the explicit objective there, nor will it typically be the measure of evaluation. The nine questions (Table 2) proposed for measuring outcomes resonate well with Fraunberger et al. [16], who argue that PD must display an "internal rigor" by critically reflecting how PD processes and outcomes correspond with its epistemological ground.

The overview in Table 1 portrays the protagonist role as separate from other roles. It is important to stress however that in practice children will likely move between these roles during any given process. This point is also made by Druin [11,12]. Moreover, as the "onion model" suggests, any layer of the model will incorporate the preceding one. Hence in any given process the question may be the extent to which children play a given role rather than having one particular role throughout.

Since the protagonist role in general as well as the example provided in our case study emphasize the skills and competence children acquire through participation, it may be argued that this approach bridges the divide between a design approach and a learning approach. A recent study has looked precisely at the intersection between PD and education [3]. Recognizing this work, we do however see a difference between setting learning goals for design activities and engaging children as protagonists in open-ended inquiries through participatory design.

CONCLUSION

We suggest that political PD provides a new role for children in PD practices—the role of *protagonist.* A protagonist perspective positions the children at the center of the design process as they engage with real-world design problems. The objective is to support their own development of skills in terms of designing and reflecting on technology. Our argument is that these skills empower children to make more informed decisions about technology in their lives. We have illustrated how a political PD epistemology and the understanding of children as protagonists significantly change the objectives, process, and outcome measures of the design process.

ACKNOWLEDGMENTS

This research study was supported by The Danish Industry Foundation as part of the fablab@school.dk. The empirical studies were conducted in collaboration with our colleagues Kasper Skov Christensen and Mikkel Hjorth. We also acknowledge the work of teachers and students from N. J. Fjordsgade School who participated in the study.

REFERENCES

1. Katerina Ananiadou and Magdalena Claro. 2009. 21st century skills and competences for new millennium learners in OECD countries. Paris: Organization for Economic Cooperation and Development.
2. Jørgen Bansler. 1989. System Development Research in Scandinavia: Three Theoretical Schools," in *Scandinavian Journal of Information Systems*: Vol.1(1), 1.
3. Wolmet Barendregt, Tilde M. Bekker, Peter Börjesson, Eva Eriksson, and Olof Torgersson. 2016. Legitimate Participation in the Classroom Context: Adding Learning Goals to Participatory Design. In *Proceedings of the the 15th International Conference on Interaction Design and Children* (IDC '16). ACM, New York, NY, USA, 167–174.
4. Tilde Bekker, Saskia Bakker, Iris Douma, Janneke van der Poel, Koen Scheltenaar. 2015 Teaching children digital literacy through design-based learning with digital toolkits in schools, In *International Journal of Child-Computer Interaction* Volume 5, 29–38.
5. Gro Bjerknes, Pelle Ehn, Morten Kyng, Kristen Nygaard. 1987. Computers and democracy: a Scandinavian challenge, Avebury.
6. Paulo Blikstein. 2013. Digital Fabrication and "Making" in Education: The Democratization of Invention. In J. Walter-Herrmann & C. Büching (Eds.), FabLabs: Of Machines, Makers and Inventors. Bielefeld: Transcript Publishers.
7. Claus Bossen, Christian Dindler, Ole Sejer Iversen. 2016. Evaluation in participatory design: a literature survey. In *Proceedings of the 14th Participatory Design Conference: Full papers—Volume 1* (PDC '16), Vol. 1. ACM, New York, NY, USA, 151–160. DOI: http://dx.doi.org/10.1145/2940299.2940303
8. Claus Bossen, Christian Dindler, Ole Sejer Iversen. 2010. User gains and PD aims: assessment from a participatory design project. In *Proceedings of the 11th Biennial Participatory Design Conference* (PDC '10). ACM, New York, NY, USA, 141–150. DOI=http://dx.doi.org/10.1145/1900441.1900461
9. Susanne Bødker. 2003. A for alternatives. *Scandinavian Journal of Information Systems*. 15(1), 87–89.
10. Fenne Van Doorn. 2016. Children as co-researchers in design: Enabling users to gather, share and enrich contextual data, Doctoral thesis from T/U Delft, NL.
11. Allison Druin.1998.The design of children's technology, Morgan Kaufmann Publishers Inc., San Francisco, CA.
12. Allison Druin. 2002. The Role of Children in the Design of New Technology. In *Behaviour and Information Technology*, Vol. 21(1), 1–25.
13. Pelle Ehn. 1990. Work-Oriented Design of Computer Artifacts. L. Erlbaum Assoc. Inc., Hillsdale, NJ, USA.
14. Karen E. Fisher, Katya Yefimova, and Eiad Yafi. 2016. Future's Butterflies: Co-Designing ICT Wayfaring Technology with Refugee Syrian Youth. In *Proceedings of the The 15th International Conference on Interaction Design and Children* (IDC '16). ACM, New York, NY, USA, 25–36. DOI: https://doi.org/10.1145/2930674.2930701
15. Christopher Frauenberger, Judith Good, Alyssa Alcorn. 2012. Challenges, opportunities and future perspectives in including children with disabilities in the design of interactive technology. In *Proceedings of the 11th International Conference on Interaction Design and Children (IDC '12)*. ACM, New York, NY, USA, 367–370. DOI=http://dx.doi.org/10.1145/2307096.2307171
16. Christopher Frauenberger, Judith Good, Geraldine Fitzpatrick, Ole Sejer Iversen. 2015. In pursuit of rigour and accountability in participatory design. *International Journal of Human–Computer Studies*, 74(0), 93–106.
17. Mona Leigh Guha, Allison Druin, Jerry Alan Fails. 2013 Cooperative Inquiry revisited: Reflections of the past and guidelines for the future of intergenerational co-design, *International Journal of Child–Computer Interaction*, Vol. 1(1), 14–23.
18. Juan Pablo Hourcade. 2008. Interaction Design and Children. In *Foundations and Trends in Human–Computer Interaction*, Vol. 1(4), 277–392.

19. Netta Iivari and Marianne Kinnula. 2016. Inclusive or Inflexible: a Critical Analysis of the School Context in Supporting Children's Genuine Participation. In *Proceedings of the 9th Nordic Conference on Human–Computer Interaction* (NordiCHI '16). ACM, New York, NY, USA,, Article 63, 10 pages. DOI: https://doi.org/10.1145/2971485.2971531

20. Ole Sejer Iversen and Rachel Charlotte Smith. 2012. Scandinavian participatory design: dialogic curation with teenagers. In *Proceedings of the 11th International Conference on Interaction Design and Children* (IDC '12). ACM, New York, NY, USA, 106–115. DOI=http://dx.doi.org/10.1145/2307096.2307109

21. Ole Sejer Iversen, Anne Marie Kanstrup, and Marianne Graves Petersen. 2004. A visit to the "new Utopia": revitalizing democracy, emancipation and quality in co-operative design. In *Proceedings of the Third Nordic Conference on Human–Computer Interaction* (NordiCHI '04). ACM, New York, NY, USA, 171–179. DOI: https://doi.org/10.1145/1028014.1028040

22. Ole Sejer Iversen and Christina Brodersen. 2008. Building a BRIDGE between children and users: a socio-cultural approach to child–computer interaction. *Cogntion, Technology & Work* 10(2), 83–93. DOI=http://dx.doi.org/10.1007/s10111–007–0064–1

23. Ole Sejer Iversen and Christian Dindler. 2013. A Utopian agenda in child-computer interaction, In *International Journal of Child–Computer Interaction*, Volume 1(1), 24–29.

24. Finn Kensing and Jeanette Blomberg. 1998. Participatory Design: Issues and Concerns. *Computer Supported Cooperative Work* 7, 3–4, 167–185. DOI=http://dx.doi.org/10.1023/A:1008689307411

25. Monica Landoni, Elisa Rubegni, Emma Nicol, and Janet Read. 2016. How Many Roles Can Children Play?. In *Proceedings of the 15th International Conference on Interaction Design and Children* (IDC '16). ACM, New York, NY, USA, 720–725. DOI: http://dx.doi.org/10.1145/2930674.2932222

26. Julia Makhaeva, Christopher Frauenberger, and Katharina Spiel. 2016. Creating creative spaces for co-designing with autistic children: the concept of a "Handlungsspielraum." In *Proceedings of the 14th Participatory Design Conference: Full papers—Volume 1* (*PDC '16*), Vol. 1. ACM, New York, NY, USA, 51–60. DOI: http://dx.doi.org/10.1145/2940299.2940306

27. Maarten Van Mechelen, M. (2016). Designing technologies for and with children: Theoretical reflections and a practical inquiry towards a co-design toolkit. Doctoral thesis defended in June 2016, UHasselt—KU Leuven.

28. Janet C. Read, Peggy Gregory, Steward MacFarlane, B. McManus, P. Gray and R. Patel. 2002. An Investigation of Participatory Design with Children: Informant, Balanced and Facilitated Design. Interaction Design and Children, Eindhoven, Shaker Publishing.

29. Janet C. Read, Matthew Horton, Gavin Sim, Peggy Gregory, Daniel Fitton, and Brendan Cassidy. 2013. CHECk: a tool to inform and encourage ethical practice in participatory design with children. In *CHI '13 Extended Abstracts on Human Factors in Computing Systems* (CHI EA '13). ACM, New York, NY, USA, 187–192. DOI: http://dx.doi.org/10.1145/2468356.2468391

30. Janet Read. 2015. Children as participants in design and evaluation. *Interactions* 22, 2 (February 2015), pp. 64–66. DOI=http://dx.doi.org/10.1145/2735710

31. Janet C. Read, Daniel Fitton, Gavin Sim, and Matt Horton. 2016. How Ideas make it through to Designs: Process and Practice. In *Proceedings of the 9th Nordic Conference on Human–Computer Interaction* (NordiCHI '16). ACM, New York, NY, USA, Article 16, 10 pages. DOI: https://doi.org/10.1145/2971485.2971560

32. Andrew J. Rotherham and David.T. Willimgham. 2009. 21st century skills: the challenges ahead. In *Educational Leadership*, 67(1), 17–20.

33. Mikec Scaife and Yvonne Rogers, Y. 1998. Kids as informants: telling us what we didn't know or confirming what we knew already? In A. Druin (ed.) The Design of Children's Technology: How We Design, What We Design, and Why. Morgan Kaufman.

34. Rachel C. Smith, Ole S. Iversen, Mikkel Hjorth. 2015. Design thinking for digital fabrication in education. In *International Journal of Child–Computer Interaction* Volume 5, September 2015, 20–28.

35. Rachel C. Smith, Ole S. Iversen, Thomas Hjermitslev, and Aviaja B. Lynggaard. 2013. Towards an ecological inquiry in child–computer interaction. In *Proceedings of the 12th International Conference on Interaction Design and Children* (IDC '13). ACM, New York, NY, USA, 183–192. DOI=10.1145/2485760.2485780 http://doi.acm.org/10.1145/2485760.2485780

36. Jesper Simonsen and Tony Robertson. 2013. Routledge International Handbook of Participatory Design. New York: Routledge.

37. James Spradley.1980. Participant Observation. Holt, Rinehart and Winston, New York.

38. Greg Walsh, Craig Donahue, and Zachary Pease. 2016. Inclusive Co-Design within a Three-Dimensional Game Environment. In *Proceedings of the 15th International Conference on Interaction Design and Children* (IDC '16). ACM, New York, NY, USA, 1–10. DOI: http://dx.doi.org/10.1145/2930674.2930721

39. Greg Walsh and Elizabeth Foss. 2015. A case for intergenerational distributed co-design: the online kidsteam example. In *Proceedings of the 14th*

International Conference on Interaction Design and Children (IDC '15). ACM, New York, NY, USA, 99–108. DOI=http://dx.doi.org/10.1145/2771839.2771850

40. Greg Walsh, Elizabeth Foss, Jason Yip, and Allison Druin. 2013. FACIT PD: a framework for analysis and creation of intergenerational techniques for participatory design. In *Proceedings of the SIGCHI Conference on Human Factors in Computing Systems* (CHI '13). ACM, New York, NY, USA, 2893–2902. DOI: http://dx.doi.org/10.1145/2470654.2481400

41. Greg Walsh, Craig Donahue, and Zachary Pease. 2016. Inclusive Co-Design within a Three-Dimensional Game Environment. In *Proceedings of the 15th International Conference on Interaction Design and Children* (IDC '16). ACM, New York, NY, USA, 1–10. DOI: http://dx.doi.org/10.1145/2930674.2930721

42. Jason Yip, Tamara Clegg, Elizabeth Bonsignore, Helene Gelderblom, Emily Rhodes, and Allison Druin. 2013. Brownies or bags-of-stuff?: domain expertise in cooperative inquiry with children. In *Proceedings of the 12th International Conference on Interaction Design and Children* (IDC '13). ACM, New York, NY, USA, 201–210.

43. John Zimmerman, Jodi Forlizzi, and Shelley Evenson. 2007. Research through design as a method for interaction design research in HCI. In *Proceedings of the SIGCHI Conference on Human Factors in Computing Systems* (CHI '07). ACM, New York, NY, USA, 493–502. DOI=http://dx.doi.org/10.1145/1240624.1240704

Blending Methods: Developing Participatory Design Sessions for Autistic Children

Christopher Frauenberger, Julia Makhaeva, Katharina Spiel
TU Wien (Vienna University of Technology), Austria
christopher.frauenberger@tuwien.ac.at
julia.makhaeva@tuwien.ac.at
katharina.spiel@tuwien.ac.at

ABSTRACT
Over the past two years, we have engaged autistic children in a participatory design (PD) process to create their own, individual smart object. In this paper, we reflect on our methodological choices and how these came about. Describing the design process with one of our participants as a case, we show how we developed participatory activities by combining, blending, re-interpreting and adapting techniques and tools from a pool of methods on the basis of the characteristics of the child, our own skills as designers and the history and context of our collaboration. Reflecting on this practice retrospectively, we seek to make two contributions: firstly, we distill a repertoire of methodological building blocks which draw on our experience of co-designing with autistic children. Secondly, we present a visual tool that captures the process by which we combined, blended and interpreted these building blocks into coherent design activities with a view to provide systematic guidance for future work. While the work presented here is set within the context of designing with autistic children, we argue that the underlying approach can be applicable and useful in a wider co-design context.

ACM Classification Keywords
H.5.m. Information Interfaces and Presentation (e.g. HCI): Miscellaneous

Author Keywords
participatory design; autism; children

INTRODUCTION
Participatory Design (PD) constitutes an approach and a vision that argues for involving people affected by technologies in their design [10]. Motivations for adopting a participatory approach range from addressing a pragmatic need to increase the fit between features and users' requirements to idealistic agendas related to empower people, democratise innovation and designing alternative futures [18]. Whatever the orientation, the diversification of contexts and goals for which technologies are designed has led PD to become a central theme in the research culture and practice of HCI and particularly in interaction design and children [9].

There is a consensus that PD is particularly powerful when creating technology for groups who are typically marginalised in design and have life-worlds which are far removed from those of designers and researchers. Autistic children[1] are one prime example of such a group and a number of research efforts have sought to co-design technology in this context. While the PD literature is brimming with different methods and techniques on how to engage participants, the rationale for methodological choices and the strategies for translating methods into actual activities are hardly ever reported on, impacting on our collective ability to effectively build on each others work. With certain participant groups, such as autistic children, the significance of this gap becomes particularly apparent as there is a constant need to adapt and re-interpret existing methods to consider needs and abilities of participants in order to find ways of facilitating safe and inspiring engagement.

Thus, in this paper, we reflect on our own methodological choices within OutsideTheBox in which we engaged autistic children in a participatory process to design their own smart object. While our project set out to implement existing PD methods for engagement with autistic children, after two years we found ourselves working in different ways: much more akin to tapping into an extending toolbox or repertoire, we found ourselves blending different smaller, methodological building blocks and tools in a fluid and agile manner, responding to how the design process unfolded. Retrospectively, we now reflect on our practice and investigate what we have done in which way and why.

Below we describe in detail the design case of Mia, an 8 year old autistic girl, who worked with us over the course of one school year. We focus on the sequence of participatory activities we designed for the work with Mia and show how we took elements of methods, appropriated, mixed and blended them to iteratively develop a coherent string of activities for meetings. In doing so, we not only continuously extended our own repertoire of building blocks, but also a child-specific

[1] We are aware about the complex discussions surrounding person-first vs. label-first language; we opt for the latter, due to it being the predominantly self-chosen form of people on the spectrum [16].

IDC '17, June 27-30, 2017, Stanford, CA, USA

ISBN 978-1-4503-4921-5/17/06...$15.00
DOI: http://dx.doi.org/10.1145/3078072.3079727

repertoire of proven and working elements that we could tap into for future sessions. With the aim to capture this way of working, and provide systematic guidance for future work and others, we here present a visual tool that resulted from analysing our processes after the fact.

The contribution this paper seeks to make is twofold: firstly, we present and discuss this visual tool for designers and demonstrate its possible use. Secondly, we revisit all our processes in OutsideTheBox and distill an overall repertoire of techniques and tools for participatory design with autistic children from the experiences we have made over the last two years.

In the following, we review related work, both on frameworks to make methodological choices as well as concerning the adaptation of methods to particular contexts. We then introduce OutsideTheBox to set the scene for our design case. From this description, we draw out the concept for the visual tool for designers and exemplify its potential use by describing how it could have supported the systematic transition from one session to another.

Finally, we take a step back and collect all methodological building blocks we used across the whole project. We close by discussing how we intend to use this process in our future work and how it might be useful in other contexts.

RELEVANT WORK

Autism is a neuro-developmental condition which manifests itself in impaired social and communication skills, and repetitive and monotropic thought patterns or behaviours. While these manifestations comprise the diagnostic criteria, the way they play out make autistic people an extremely heterogeneous group with very diverse life-worlds. The spectrum of abilities ranges from people who never develop language to people who's autism has only minor impact on their life. The prevalence of Autism-Spectrum Conditions (ASCs) is estimated to be above 1% [1].

Many autistic people have an affinity to technology, as they appreciate the structure and predictability of the medium [5]. This has sparked research interest in computer-based learning interventions [22], as well as the development of technologies which target every-day routines and functional support (see [17] for a recent survey of interactive technologies for autism).

It is widely acknowledged that participatory approaches to designing technology are particularly valuable in an autism context, not only in terms of creating meaningful technology, but also for the enriching and empowering experiences of participants in the design process [15, 28, 3, 21]. However, the typical traits in autism also make facilitating participation in design work particularly challenging. Special interests, rigidity and perfectionism as well as design's features as a socially demanding activity are all considerations to be taken into account [11].

Consequently, methods for engagement and design work require careful adaptation and re-interpretation when working with autistic children. IDEAS, for example, is a participatory design approach that builds on the widely used TEACCH intervention programme [20] to provide specific structures and supports to involve autistic children [2]. The same authors have aimed to widen the applicability of their approach and have proposed the D4D framework (Designing for Diversity) which consists of two main strategies to adapt participatory design activities for a neuro-diverse population: structuring the environment and providing additional supports [4]. With respect to both elements, they highlight how "understanding the culture" can help adapting the activities to the general characteristics of a neuro-diverse population and how "tailoring to the individual" requires designers to respond to the particular needs of the participants.

The CiC framework (Children in the Centre) provides a way of structuring collaboration in multi-discplinary PD projects with special needs children through nested layers of influence [14]. At its core, it is concerned about the interests, strengths and needs of the child. At the outer levels, it includes teachers and parents, before moving on to child-centred technologies, everyday environments and inclusion in society as a whole. The authors acknowledge that while CiC provides valuable perspectives on the arenas of participation, it does not provide a systematic way of developing actual activities.

Gaudion et al., discuss a designer's approach to involving autistic adults in co-creation processes [13]. They describe their methodology as being driven by their designerly, empathic understanding, rather than by preselected methods. As a lens for reflection on their activities, they used the framework for organising techniques and tools in PD proposed by Sanders et al. [23].

Summarising, with our paper we build on Benton's work [2], the CiC framework [14] and Gaudion et al. [13] who all highlighted the need to adapt methods to the children and their environment, in order to be able to engage them in design processes. However, we argue that we lack a more holistic view that transparently and systematically incorporates the designer's expertise and experiences as well as a historical perspective that reflects the course of the collaboration and previous results to develop a coherent series of design activities. Additionally, we see value in building repertoires of method elements that designers can readily tap into and appropriate as the collaboration unfolds. With this paper we aim to address precisely this gap.

OUTSIDETHEBOX

OutsideTheBox - Rethinking Assistive Technologies with Children with Autism[2] is a three year research project, exploring alternative roles for technologies in the lives of autistic children. We argue that traditional assistive technologies have predominately focused on mitigating functional limitations and have consequently ignored a rich and versatile design space for creating technology that is driven by desires and ideas beyond those related to the disability. While limitations certainly are one part of the disabled experience, we argue that they should not narrowly determine the kinds of technologies designed in this space. Consequently, OutsideTheBox takes a

[2] `http://ousidethebox.at`

Figure 1. Mia's alarm clock (right) and several impressions from its development

different approach and engages autistic children in a participatory design process which has two simple requirements in its brief: firstly, the resulting artefact should afford meaningful and positive experiences and secondly, the design should scaffold the child in sharing these experiences with others.

Children we work with are between 6 and 8 years old and are diagnosed with an Autism Spectrum Condition. All children attend an integrative mainstream school and we collaborate with the education department of the City of Vienna for recruiting. We meet children approximately every fortnight for a co-design session, which results in 12-16 meetings over the school year. In these sessions, two researchers are present which have distinct roles: one is the Play Partner of the child who teams up with the child to work through the planned activity; the other is the Active Observer who sets tasks, keeps the time, provides materials and collects observational data. The technological opportunity space this project chooses to explore is ubiquitous computing and the collaboration spans all across ideation, conceptualisation, prototyping and evaluation. At the end, each child owns their smart object.

The outcome of the project is threefold: firstly, we explore different participatory methods to engage autistic children and enable them to lead the design process with their ideas [19, 27]. Secondly, we create a series of design case studies through which we seek to demonstrate that such an approach leads to very different kinds of technologies, opening a design space that would be inaccessible to neuro-typical, adult designers [12, 26]. Thirdly, we work on novel ways of evaluating the experience children have with these novel kinds of technologies [24, 25].

In the following, we introduce a case study from the second year. Overall, we worked with 9 children and we have chosen to present Mia's[3] case here because of the variety of methods we used and the high degree of their appropriation, making it a rich and fitting example for our argument. In the second year, we also had established our design practice in a more systematic way and Mia's case in particular helped us to reflect on our strategies in developing a coherent string of workshop activities. All processes were thoroughly documented using audio, video, pictures, artefacts and research diaries.

[3]We altered all names to protect the privacy of participants.

CASE STUDY

At the time of our collaboration, Mia was 8 years old. She had been diagnosed with Autism Spectrum Condition two years earlier. Before we met her for the first time, we conducted contextual interviews with Mia's mother, her teacher, and her mentor, who described Mia's difficulties to follow teaching lessons, but emphasised her imaginative skills. Mia became easily overwhelmed by pressure during lessons and subsequently quickly lost her motivation to try new things. As we got to know Mia, we encountered her great drawing skills and her highly focused interest on the Super Mario Universe. She also told us about her difficulties to get up early in the morning and that she linked this to her low motivation and bad mood at school.

Our co-design process stretched over an entire school year, during which we met Mia approximately every fortnight - 16 sessions in total. At the beginning our collaboration took place primarily at school, in a separate room next to her classroom. The room allowed us to freely arrange tables and seats, assigning different areas for brainstorming, role playing or prototyping. Her teacher was not present in the sessions, but available at any time. In particular, the teacher helped to initiate sessions by handing Mia her project folder when the researchers picked her up and Mia insisted on reporting back to the teacher immediately after each session about what she worked on. Towards the end of the design process we also met Mia repeatedly at our research lab to make use of digital fabrication tools.

Based on the initial information from the interviews and our first meetings, we started developing a repertoire of appropriate techniques and tools. Mia's great imagination and interest in pretend play with her toys from the Super Mario Universe, led us to reinterpret techniques from drama based methods (c.f., [6]). We combined those with different common design techniques e.g. brainstorming, mind mapping, research diaries for idea generation and low-tech prototyping for conceptualisation. When ideas became more concrete, we added techniques around collaborative making and digital fabrication.

During the whole co-design process we consistently tailored elements of the techniques to fit Mia's individual characteristics, her particular needs and the ideas generated in previous sessions. For example, since Mia always brought her favourite toys from the Super Mario Universe to our meetings,

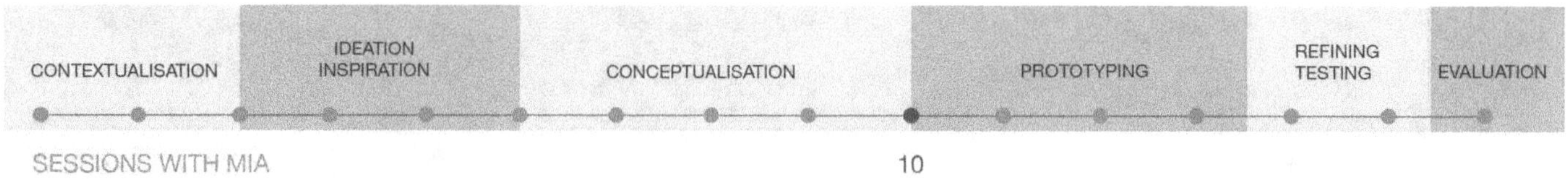

Figure 2. An overview of the design process with Mia

Method Element	Rationale	Child	Adapted Element
Warm up	comfortable working atmosphere	preference for routines and rituals	schedule of reflecting on the last session, ritual of grimacing at the beginning
Technology immersion	novel interaction possibilities	strong need for structure, overwhelmed by too many options	step by step introduction of materials
Prototyping	converging on technology	low motivation to work with technologies	prototyping as prop design for established role play
Role play	motivation, novel ideas	pretend play with toys	incorporating toys as characters in role play
Scenario building	motivation, proof of concept	difficulty of wake up in the morning	wake up scenario
Mapping	specification of materials	toys	involving toys in brainstorming activities

Table 1. Summary of planned methodological elements for session 10, the rationale for including them and how they were adapted to the child. Elements listed here also became part of the repertoire as described further below

we started to give them a role in the process and would ask their opinion about ideas. The toys were also involved in role play activities, intended to enable us to test first prototypes in specific scenarios. Working with Mia meant to be mindful of her attention spans and to include a sufficient number of breaks to play soccer or talk about other things on her mind. To "warm up" at the beginning of each session the Play Partner and Mia established a routine of grimacing and posing for the pictures the Active Observer took for the research diary, before reflecting on the last session. During the collaboration it also emerged that she regularly produces short pieces of text and pictures, that she assembles for her newspaper for her class mates. We picked up on this idea in the evaluation of the object for which she produced an advertisement and wrote an article about our collaboration. For this she also conducted a couple of interviews with her family and our research team about the final prototype (see also [27] for a more detailed account).

Based on Mia's desire "to start her day in a good mood" and her current difficulties to get up in the morning, we developed the idea of a personalised alarm clock which consists of three components: 1) the alarm clock itself showing the time and providing a mechanism to set an alarm; 2) a pillow that starts shaking once the alarm goes off and 3) a floor mat that is used to turn the alarm off. The alarm clock plays Mia's favourite tune of the Super Mario Universe followed by a short melody that provides a "mood-forecast" for the day, inspired by her fascination of reading the daily horoscope. There is no traditional clock-face or digital display on the main device. Instead, its form is inspired by a Super Mario figure and includes several LEDs and buttons that are used to indicate the time and set an alarm. Figure 1 provides pictures from design sessions and the final object.

To be able to illustrate the process we went through to develop a particular session, we now provide a detailed account of the build-up to our 10th meeting. As figure 2 shows, we have chosen a session that marks the transition from conceptualisation towards prototyping, i.e. we were aiming to converge on a specific concept that could be taken further into the development of a smart object. This phase within the design process offers a good example as we had already worked with the child for some time, had established a trusting relationship with Mia and had explored her interests and ideas in various directions. We illustrate how we developed the subsequent session that would build on this experience *and* would push the design process into the next phase. We first describe our planning of the session and then how the session unfolded in practice.

Planning a session

In previous work with Mia we identified a strong preference for routines and concise tasks as new, unknown materials or topics were overwhelming. Mia enjoyed our rituals and routines at the beginning and the end of our sessions: a short review of today's schedule, grimacing and posing, involving her toys in role-play activities, and presenting the outcomes of the session to her teacher. During the conceptualisation activities, we established a consistent scenario of a "wake up" situation to test various ideas. In the 9th session, Mia developed the concept of her own smart alarm clock and built the first card board prototype. It combined basic functions of an alarm clock she had at home with new ideas, such as Super Mario Music and a shaking pillow. We built these prototypes out of a necessity for props in acting out the "wake up" scenario.

Since these ideas were rooted in very classical aesthetic and functional expectations, our 10th session had the aim to carefully open up the design space. To explore more potential forms and functions of the whole alarm system we chose to combine elements of technology immersion (as in [8]) with our established role-play activities to develop hybrid, semi-functional prototypes. To this end we planned to introduce LittleBits[4], an easy to use electronic tool kit that allows creating simple sensor-actuator systems by combining ready-made building blocks.

Next to the established routines (reviewing pictures from the last session and documenting what we have done in the end), we created a space for discussing the previous 'research exercise' and tasks Mia might have completed in between sessions, if she wanted to.

We planned to introduce LittleBits, since they offer a large choice of inputs and outputs and could broaden Mia's understanding of the interactive potential of her alarm system. However, we expected that introducing them all at once would have overwhelmed Mia and have an intimidating effect on her contrary to the empowering and inspiring effect we desired. Hence, engaging with the LittleBits was facilitated in two distinct phases: First, an exploration of possibilities and second, the determined use of LittleBits as design material. This would ensure that Mia would feel comfortable with the material when using it in her own creation. We planned to hand out a subset of sensors and actuators along a set of tasks with increasing complexity. At the start, we would first show different sensors and let her choose any except buttons to encourage her to step out of well-known interaction paradigms. Then, she would have to combine two input modes until she was free to explore different combinations on her own. When she would feel comfortable in that exploration, we would suggest thinking about the LittleBits together with the cardboard prototypes from the last session in order to create hybrid prototypes that were also semi-functional.

These hybrid prototypes would then function as props for another play-through of the "wake-up" scenario. Mia could explore how the semi-functional props took up some of the pretend play and we could observe how well these worked. Additionally, we could see how she would integrate potentially new interaction paradigms in her play and subsequent morning routine. These play-throughs would also help to iteratively test the generated ideas in a well-known scenario. We would then assemble a list of materials required to build the system. This would tell us more about Mia's mental model of the important parts of the alarm clock and the vibrating cushion. Through the discussion of components at this level, we would learn more about how Mia specified her invention and make decisions that are often made implicitly by designers explicit, which opens them up for collaboration.

Table 1 summarises the elements that we planned on using, alongside with the basic rationale and how they were adapted.

How the session unfolded

At the beginning of the actual session Mia was tired and in a bad mood. The Active Observer gave her space to talk about her concerns and only then presented her with the photographs of the last session. Mia and her Play Partner started to laugh and grimaced again. This warm up routine not only helped Mia to feel comfortable, but it also sparked her enthusiasm to work with us.

The Active Observer first gave a systematic overview over the diverse electronic features the LittleBits offer. Then Mia tested each component one by one along given tasks, increasing in complexity according to our plan. She then was asked to choose four different sensors or buttons as appropriate functions for the designed alarm clock. At first, she was confused about this task and did not know how to make an informed decision. Encouraged by her design team, formed by her Play Partner and her toys, Yoshi and Toad from the Super Mario Universe, they made a decision. She enthusiastically played out how Yoshi and Toad offer their opinions on the different features of the various electronic components, giving her a vehicle to structurally debate advantages and disadvantages of each single component.

However, afterwards she refused to create props including the chosen components. Mia wanted to skip the prototyping activities and move directly to the next activity on the schedule, her favourite task of acting out of the "wake up" scenario. The Active Observer decided to move on and suggested to act out this well known scenario and then continue to make new props for it.

In preparing the scene, Mia and her Play Partner chose cardboard, cloths and bubble wrap as materials for the alarm clock. The Active Observer offered them on a separate table. Prototyping with electronic components merged with role-play and the known scenario framed our activities, offering Mia more structure to feel safe while being confronted with a variety of materials and the unknown complexity of LittleBits. Acting happily in the known role, Mia came up with new ideas for her alarm system that resulted from her exposure to simple electronics and the interaction with the resulting hybrid prototypes.

For example, while she danced to the alarm music, she decided to turn off the alarm clock by stepping onto a mat. This was inspired by the haptic affordances of the bubble wrap placed under a cardboard. We could then establish together that we would need a sensor under that mat that recognises her standing on it. While she set an alarm at six o'clock in the morning, Mia showed that she preferred having one button that she would press six times. At the end of the session she was very excited to present her new ideas to the teacher.

Describing the session in practice gives a detailed impression on how our preparations addressed Mia's specific needs and how ad-hoc changes to our plans stemmed from previous experiences, the separation of our own roles, our expertise and the existing methodological repertoire.

A VISUAL SESSION PLANNING TOOL

Reflecting on our own process of how we planned sessions, we created a visual tool intended to support designers in developing participatory design activities in a similar manner. The tool allows to systematically blend methodological building blocks and appropriate them from five main perspectives: the child, the designers, the context, previous work and available

[4] `http://littlebits.cc`

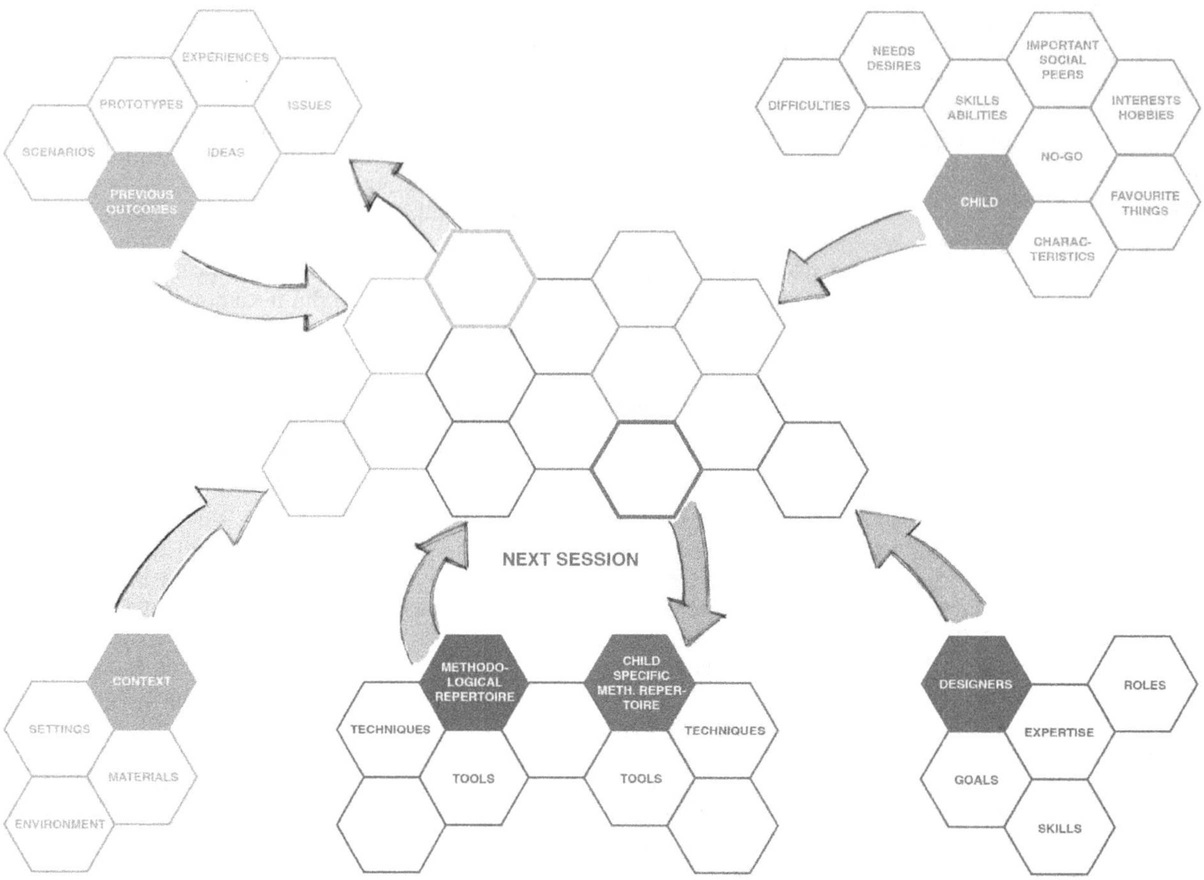

Figure 3. Blueprint of the visual tool

methodological repertoires. The format of the tool is inspired by a board game with hexagonal cards of different colours which can be arranged and re-arranged on a grid to guide designers in constructing a holistic picture of diverse perspectives of considerations that influence planning. The cards themselves can be re-used and adapted to fit other contexts. Figure 3 presents the blue print of the tool.

The playing field at the centre of Figure 3 is where cards from the five perspectives can be combined. There exist two distinct **methodological repertoires** from which designers can take techniques and tools to start planning: one is the general repertoire which is filled by techniques and tools the designers are familiar with or that exist in literature. The second is a repertoire that is built up over the time of collaboration with this specific child. It consists of techniques and tools that already were interpreted for this child and the context. **Child cards** describe specific characteristics of the child. The majority of child cards gets generated at the begin of a collaboration, based on the profile and contextual enquiry. However, new cards can be added as the collaboration unfolds and designers foster a stronger relationship with the child. Cards that capture **previous outcomes** represent ideas, issues, prototypes or scenarios that can be referred to or built upon. **Context cards** describe the physical setting in which the work takes place, the available range of raw materials and more broadly the relevant context in which the work is being conducted (project structure, schools etc). The final group of cards describes the perspective of the **designers**. In particular, this includes their goals, expertise, skills and the different roles they assume in the collaboration.

In planning a session, designers start choosing tools and techniques from the methodological repertoires that support the overall aim of the next session. Next, cards from the remaining four categories are brought in to describe the ways in which the methodological building blocks need to be merged, adapted or re-interpreted. This can lead to the creation of new cards representing child-specific techniques or tools, which are derived from those in the generic pool. Such new cards can also emerge through post-hoc reflection on the actual session. As our example above shows, designers often need to fluidly change their initial plans and respond to the situation in-situ. In these cases, new cards can describe an emergent technique or tool, or a characteristic of the child that became apparent, or a contextual feature that shifted the process. All these cards are fed back into the five pools of cards which form the basis for subsequent planning. Importantly, this includes cards that describe the outcomes of the session, e.g., ideas and concepts generated.

The planning tool in use

We now retrospectively apply the tool to the planning of the session we described above, and demonstrate how it would

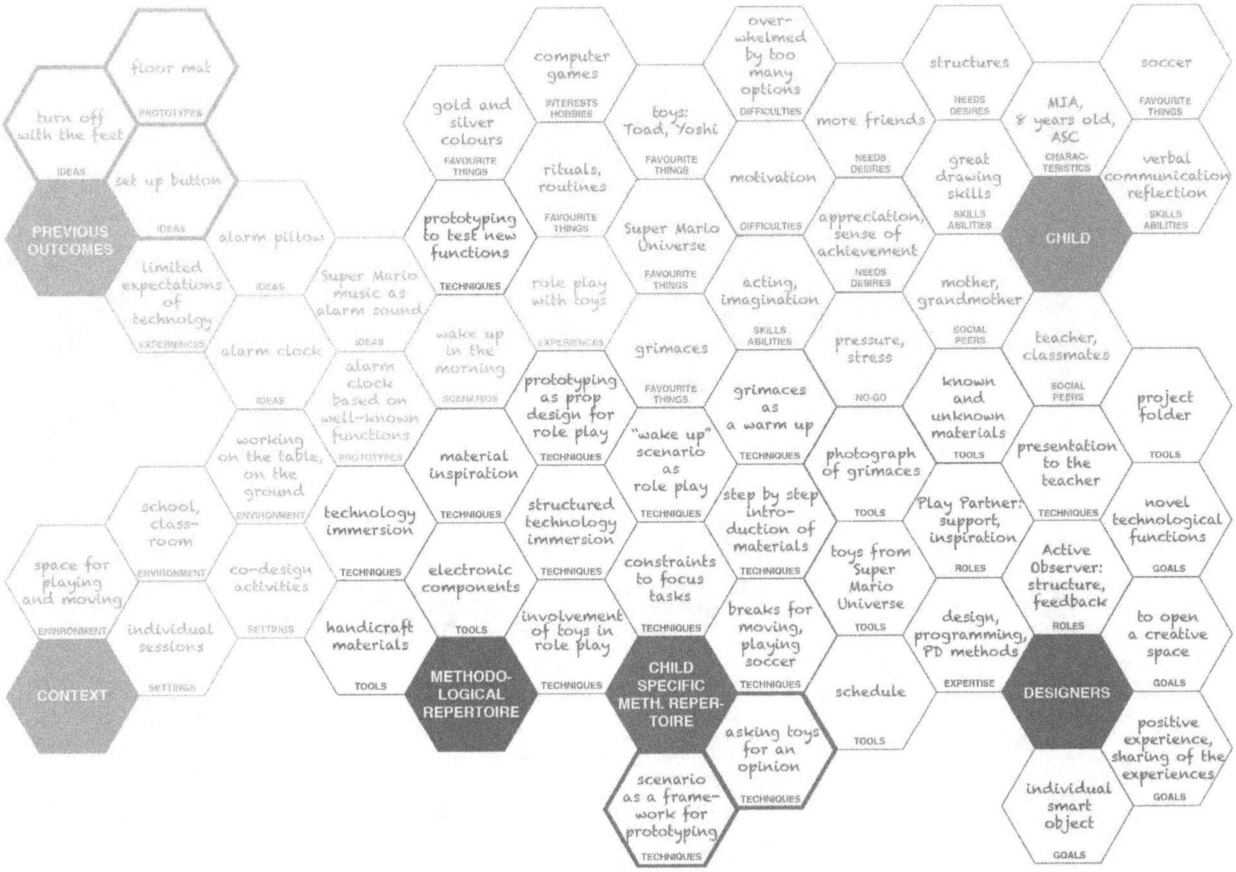

Figure 4. Applying the visual tool to design a session with Mia

have allowed us to systematically develop the next session - figure 4.

An initial set of cards describes aspects from each of the five perspectives. These cards have been created during the collaboration with the child, for example informed by the contextual enquiry phase in the beginning of the work. At this point in the process, we already have a wealth of cards describing Mia, her interests, her no-go's and characteristics. We also can build on previous outcomes, such as the card board prototypes and the basic concept of an alarm system. The child specific methodological repertoire is already populated with techniques that have been previously effective for engaging Mia, for example the warm-up routine and the role-play scenario. Context and the designers' perspectives have remained stable over the course of the collaboration.

The initial selection of techniques and tools is guided by our overall goal for the 10th session of opening a creative space for novel technological functions. From our general methodological repertoire, we chose the techniques of *technology immersion* and *material inspiration* as well as different tools like *electronic components* and *handicraft materials*.

Interpreting generic techniques and tools for this session leads to the creation of new, child specific techniques, e.g., structured technology immersion or prototyping as a prop for role play. These are developed considering the larger network of considerations from the four remaining perspectives: the child, previous outcomes, context and designers. For example, structured technology immersion considered that Mia required time and structure to be introduced to new materials, particularly if they offered many options. Some of that structure comes from previous outcomes and experiences in the design process. Additional structural support comes from the well-known roles the designers play and the usual physical setting in which the session is conducted. We also tailor the selected tools to specific requirements to reduce potential confusion. For example, we balance novel with well-known handicraft materials and include her favourite colours.

We blend prototyping with role-play and Mia's preference for acting out scenarios. Prototypes then become props for role play, constituting a new, child-specific technique. We embed newly introduced materials in the wake-up scenario, with already ritualised role play activities to quickly test the prototypes created. We supplement Mia's need for structure through well-known components, such as the visual schedule and the presentation of outcomes to the teacher after the session.

After the session we replenish the sets of cards with new ones describing outcomes and child specific techniques and tools, e.g. the concept of a floor mat to switch the alarm off and the ideas around setting an alarm with a single button. While not planned, two child specific techniques emerge upon reflection:

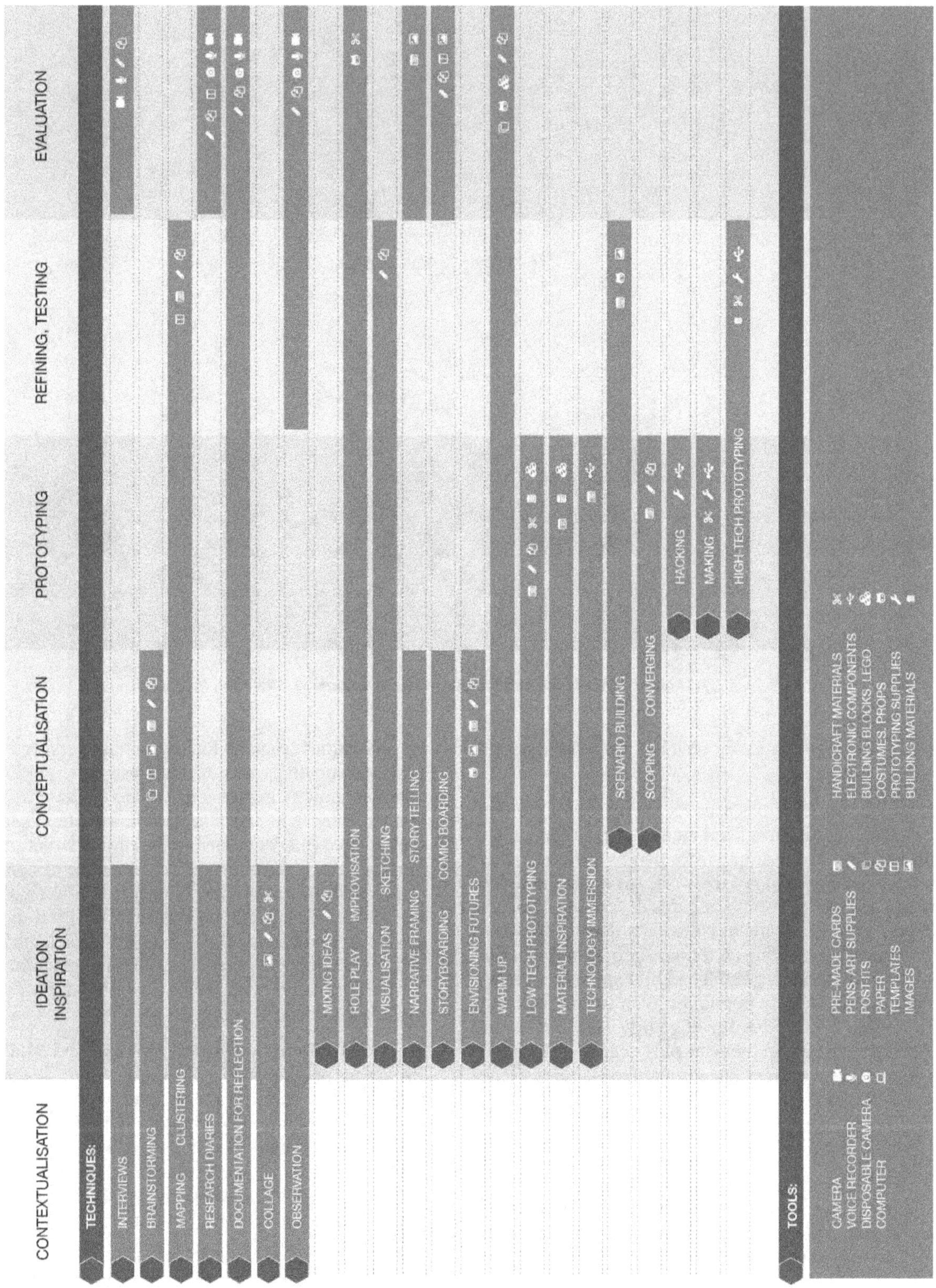

Figure 5. Tools and Techniques in OutsideTheBox

Firstly, *to ask Mia's toys for an opinion* is a technique that could be useful in situations in which direct questions will socially overwhelm her. Secondly, using the *"wake up" scenario as a narrative frame for creating prototypes*, rather than for testing prototypes became a powerful technique to give Mia more inherent motivation to build things.

REPERTOIRE OF BUILDING BLOCKS

The above detailed the design case of Mia and exemplified the use of our visual tool for planning sessions. Looking across *all* our collaborations, we have identified a wider range of building blocks that formed our overall repertoire of tools and techniques in OutsideTheBox. Figure 5 presents these, organised along their intended use time in the design process: contextualisation, ideation & inspiration, conceptualisation, prototyping, refining & testing, and evaluation.

We deliberately use the same terminology as Sanders et al. [23] to distinguish between approaches, methods, techniques and tools. While approaches reflect broad strategies, methods are structured activities which may be comprised of different techniques that are purposefully combined and supported by tools. Other than our collection of building blocks, the framework by Sanders et al. proposed to categorise techniques along their intended purpose to distinguish between probing, priming, understanding and generating. While these categories also resonate with our building blocks, we have found many techniques working across them. Hence, we decided to organise them along the time they have been used in the design process.

The techniques included here are components of other methods that appear in various forms in existing literature, for example, in Fictional Inquiry [7], Co-operative Inquiry [8] or Contextual Mapping [29]. Others are general techniques, widespread in design, such as brainstorming, interviews or collages. They all are conceptually not fully fledged PD methods in their own right, but can be purposefully combined to make up activities that form a coherent method.

Our methods are supported by a multitude of tools. The variety reflects not only the diverse expertise and background of the research team, but also the diversity of needs and abilities of the children we work with. As such, their visualisation represents the physical suitcase full with prototyping materials, electrical components and other tools (some of which are depicted in Figure 5), we bring to every session. Having such a large fund of tools available during the sessions enables us to be flexible according to a child's specific needs in a specific moment.

Techniques and tools combined represent the building blocks we blended and combined at various stages in our design process. The range of techniques presented here, thus, reflects the particular work we do - participatory design with autistic children. They also serve as a snapshot of our current repertoire. Visualising the techniques and tools we have used so far also lets us reflect on our choices and provides options for expansion. When encountering a child with needs and abilities not yet reflected in our repertoire, we can expand it appropriately. In that, the visualisation comprises a summary of the diverse range of needs and abilities researchers and children bring together in OutsideTheBox.

CONCLUSION

In this paper we have argued for making methodological choices and appropriations in participatory design processes more transparent. While others have repeatedly made the case that PD methods are not meant to be off-the-shelf components [23], the process of choosing, re-interpreting, adapting and blending techniques and tools is often left un-reported. To fill this gap, we have proposed a visual tool for designers to plan PD activities and sessions. It is informed by a critical reflection on our own practises in designing smart objects with autistic children, where we found ourselves fluidly tapping into a repertoire of techniques and tools to develop a series of PD activities that were tailored to the child, the context and our own expertise. Importantly, we also found ourselves flexibly responding to the outcomes of previous sessions which significantly shaped the planning of the next activity.

To reflect this process and to increase the transparency of the judgements involved, our visual tool takes the form of a board game on which designers can combine cards from the different perspectives we identified above. It allows designers to systematically plan PD activities and become aware of the multi-faceted considerations that are required. It also makes designers aware of their continuously growing repertoire of methodological building blocks they can tap into. We demonstrate how this tool might work by retrospectively applying it to the planning of a session in our design case.

We argue such a tool has the potential to make contributions in at least three ways: firstly in facilitating the planning, but also the constructive reflection on design processes. Secondly, it provides a systematic and transparent means to document processes and finally, it can facilitate the communication within and outside the design team.

Taking a step back, we also sought to identify the building blocks of our own repertoire within this project. These building blocks are *not* full fledged methods, but techniques and tools that are meant to be combined and blended to lead to a coherent and situated participatory approach. While the selection we present is limited in scope, we argue that it can nevertheless be useful for others in search for their own repertoire of methodological building blocks.

As with the selection of tools and techniques, the arguments in this paper are made from within the context of participatory design with autistic children. However, we argue that they hold true for a wide range of participatory work, which will benefit from increased transparency in the development of their methodological approach.

ACKNOWLEDGEMENTS

This research is funded by the Austrian Science Fund (FWF): [P26281-N23] "OutsideTheBox - Rethinking Assistive Technologies with Children with Autism" project. We would also like to thank our participating children, families, schools and the local government.

REFERENCES

1. Simon Baron-Cohen, Fiona J. Scott, Carrie Allison, Joanna Williams, Patrick Bolton, Fiona E. Matthews, and Carol Brayne. 2009. Prevalence of Autism-Spectrum Conditions: UK School-Based Population Study. *The British Journal of Psychiatry* 194 (2009), 500–509. DOI: http://dx.doi.org/10.1192/bjp.bp.108.059345

2. Laura Benton and Hilary Johnson. 2014. Structured approaches to participatory design for children: can targeting the needs of children with autism provide benefits for a broader child population? *Instructional Science* 42, 1 (Jan. 2014), 47–65. DOI: http://dx.doi.org/10.1007/s11251-013-9297-y

3. Laura Benton and Hilary Johnson. 2015. Widening participation in technology design: A review of the involvement of children with special educational needs and disabilities. *International Journal of Child-Computer Interaction* 3, 4 (2015), 23–40. DOI: http://dx.doi.org/10.1016/j.ijcci.2015.07.001

4. Laura Benton, Asimina Vasalou, Rilla Khaled, Hilary Johnson, and Daniel Gooch. 2014. Diversity for Design: A Framework for Involving Neurodiverse Children in the Technology Design Process. In *Proceedings of the 32Nd Annual ACM Conference on Human Factors in Computing Systems (CHI '14)*. ACM, New York, NY, USA, 3747–3756. DOI: http://dx.doi.org/10.1145/2556288.2557244

5. Sven Bölte, Ofer Golan, Matthew S. Goodwin, and Lonnie Zwaigenbaum. 2010. What can innovative technologies do for Autism Spectrum Disorders? *Autism* 14, 3 (May 2010), 155–159. DOI: http://dx.doi.org/10.1177/1362361310365028

6. E. Brandt and C. Grunnet. 2000. Evoking the future: Drama and props in user centered design. In *Proceedings of the 6th Biennial Participatory Design Conference*. ACM, New York, NY, USA, 11–20.

7. Christian Dindler and Ole Sejer Iversen. 2007. Fictional Inquiry - design collaboration in a shared narrative space. *CoDesign* 3, 4 (Dec. 2007), 213–234. DOI: http://dx.doi.org/doi:10.1080/15710880701500187

8. Allison Druin. 1999. Cooperative Inquiry: Developing New Technologies for Children with Children. In *Proceedings of the SIGCHI Conference on Human Factors in Computing Systems (CHI '99)*. ACM, New York, NY, USA, 592–599. DOI: http://dx.doi.org/10.1145/302979.303166

9. Allison Druin. 2002. The Role of Children in the Design of New Technology. *Behaviour and Information Technology* 21, 1 (2002), 1–25. http://hcil.cs.umd.edu/trs/99-23/99-23.html

10. Pelle Ehn. 1989. *Work-oriented design of computer artifacts*. Ph.D. Dissertation. Arbetslivscentrum.

11. Christopher Frauenberger, Judith Good, Alyssa Alcorn, and Helen Pain. 2013. Conversing through and about technologies: Design critique as an opportunity to engage children with autism and broaden research(er) perspectives. *International Journal of Child-Computer Interaction* 1, 2 (May 2013), 38–49. DOI: http://dx.doi.org/10.1016/j.ijcci.2013.02.001

12. Christopher Frauenberger, Julia Makhaeva, and Katharina Spiel. 2016. Designing Smart Objects with Autistic Children: Four Design Exposès. In *Proceedings of the 2016 CHI Conference on Human Factors in Computing Systems (CHI '16)*. ACM, New York, NY, USA, 130–139. DOI:http://dx.doi.org/10.1145/2858036.2858050

13. Katie Gaudion, Ashley Hall, Jeremy Myerson, and Liz Pellicano. 2015. A designer's approach how can autistic adults with learning disabilities be involved in the design process? *CoDesign* 0, 0 (2015), 1–21. DOI: http://dx.doi.org/10.1080/15710882.2014.997829

14. Eija Kärnä, Jussi Nuutinen, Kaisa Pihlainen-Bednarik, and Virpi Vellonen. 2010. Designing Technologies with Children with Special Needs: Children in the Centre (CiC) Framework. In *Proceedings of the 9th International Conference on Interaction Design and Children (IDC '10)*. ACM, New York, NY, USA, 218–221. DOI: http://dx.doi.org/10.1145/1810543.1810575

15. Wendy E. Keay-Bright. 2007. The Reactive Colours Project: Demonstrating Participatory and Collaborative Design Methods for the Creation of Software for Autistic Children. *Digital Creativity* 1, 2 (June 2007), 7–16. http://ijg.cgpublisher.com/product/pub.154/prod.17

16. Lorcan Kenny, Caroline Hattersley, Bonnie Molins, Carole Buckley, Carol Povey, and Elizabeth Pellicano. 2015. Which terms should be used to describe autism? Perspectives from the UK autism community. *Autism* 20, 4 (2015), 1362361315588200. DOI: http://dx.doi.org/10.1177/1362361315588200

17. Julie A. Kientz, Matthew S. Goodwin, Gillian R. Hayes, and Gregory D. Abowd. 2013. Interactive Technologies for Autism. *Synthesis Lectures on Assistive, Rehabilitative, and Health-Preserving Technologies* 2, 2 (2013), 1–177. DOI: http://dx.doi.org/10.2200/S00533ED1V01Y201309ARH004

18. Morten Kyng. 2010. Bridging the Gap Between Politics and Techniques: On the next practices of participatory design. *Scandinavian Journal of Information Systems* 22, 1 (2010), 49–68.

19. Julia Makhaeva, Christopher Frauenberger, and Katharina Spiel. 2016. Creating Creative Spaces for Co-designing with Autistic Children: The Concept of a "Handlungsspielraum". In *Proceedings of the 14th Participatory Design Conference: Full Papers - Volume 1 (PDC '16)*. ACM, New York, NY, USA, 51–60. DOI: http://dx.doi.org/10.1145/2940299.2940306

20. Gary B. Mesibov, Victoria Shea, and Eric Schopler. 2005. *The TEACCH Approach to Autism Spectrum Disorders*. Springer Science & Business Media, Heidelberg.

21. Sarah Parsons, Nicola Yuill, Mark Brosnan, and Judith Good. 2015. Innovative technologies for autism: critical reflections on digital bubbles. *Journal of Assistive Technologies* 9, 2 (April 2015), 116–121. DOI: http://dx.doi.org/10.1108/JAT-03-2015-0005

22. Sathiyaprakash Ramdoss, Wendy Machalicek, Mandy Rispoli, Austin Mulloy, Russell Lang, and Mark O'Reilly. 2012. Computer-based interventions to improve social and emotional skills in individuals with autism spectrum disorders: A systematic review. *Developmental Neurorehabilitation* 15, 2 (2012), 119–135. DOI: http://dx.doi.org/10.3109/17518423.2011.651655

23. Elizabeth B.-N. Sanders, Eva Brandt, and Thomas Binder. 2010. A Framework for Organizing the Tools and Techniques of Participatory Design. In *Proceedings of the 11th Biennial Participatory Design Conference (PDC '10)*. ACM, New York, NY, USA, 195–198. DOI: http://dx.doi.org/10.1145/1900441.1900476

24. Katharina Spiel, Christopher Frauenberger, and Geraldine Fitzpatrick. 2017a. Experiences of autistic children with technologies. *International Journal of Child-Computer Interaction* 11 (Jan. 2017), 50–61. DOI: http://dx.doi.org/10.1016/j.ijcci.2016.10.007

25. Katharina Spiel, Christopher Frauenberger, Eva Hornecker, and Geraldine Fitzpatrick. 2017b. When Empathy Is Not Enough: Assessing the Experiences of Autistic Children with Technologies. In *Proceedings of the 2017 CHI Conference on Human Factors in Computing Systems (CHI '17)*. ACM, New York, NY, USA. DOI:http://dx.doi.org/10.1145/3025453.3025785 Honorable Mention (best 4% of submissions).

26. Katharina Spiel, Julia Makhaeva, and Christopher Frauenberger. 2016. Embodied Companion Technologies for Autistic Children. In *Proceedings of the TEI '16: Tenth International Conference on Tangible, Embedded, and Embodied Interaction (TEI '16)*. ACM, New York, NY, USA, 245–252. DOI: http://dx.doi.org/10.1145/2839462.2839495

27. Katharina Spiel, Laura Malinverni, Judith Good, and Christopher Frauenberger. 2017. Participatory Evaluation with Autistic Children. In *Proceedings of the 2017 CHI Conference on Human Factors in Computing Systems (CHI '17)*. ACM, New York, NY, USA. DOI: http://dx.doi.org/10.1145/3025453.3025851 Honorable Mention (best 4% of submissions).

28. H. van Rijn, F. Sleeswijk Visser, and P.J. Stappers. 2009. Connecting through interacting: Toys that help designers learn from children with autism by playing with them. In *International Association of Societies of Design Research 2009: Rigor and Relevance in Design*. Korean Society of Design Science, Seoul, South Korea, 2055–2064.

29. Helma van Rijn and Pieter Jan Stappers. 2008. Expressions of Ownership: Motivating Users in a Co-design Process. In *Proceedings of the Tenth Anniversary Conference on Participatory Design 2008 (PDC '08)*. Indiana University, Indianapolis, IN, USA, 178–181. http://dl.acm.org/citation.cfm?id=1795234.1795266

The Haptic Bridge: Towards a Theory for Haptic-Supported Learning

Richard Lee Davis
Graduate School of Education
Stanford University
rldavis@stanford.edu

Melisa Orta Martinez
Mechanical Engineering
Stanford University
melisao@stanford.edu

Oliver Schneider
Hasso Plattner Institute and
University of British Columbia
oliver.schneider@hpi.de

Karon E. MacLean
Computer Science
University of British Columbia
maclean@cs.ubc.ca

Allison M. Okamura
Mechanical Engineering
Stanford University
aokamura@stanford.edu

Paulo Blikstein
Graduate School of Education
Stanford University
paulob@stanford.edu

ABSTRACT
Haptic force feedback systems are unique in their ability to dynamically render physical representations. Although haptic devices have shown promise for supporting learning, prior work mainly describes results of haptic-supported learning without identifying underlying learning mechanisms. To this end, we designed a haptic-supported learning environment and analyzed four students who used it to make connections between two different mathematical representations of sine and cosine: the unit circle, and their graph on the Cartesian plane. We highlight moments where students made connections between the representations, and identify how the haptic feedback supported these moments of insight. We use this evidence in support of a proposed theoretical and design framework for educational haptics. This framework captures four types of haptic representations, and focuses on one – the haptic bridge – that effectively scaffolds sense-making with multiple representations.

ACM Classification Keywords
H.5.2. Information interfaces and presentation: User Interfaces – Theory and Methods, User-Centered Design; K.3.m. Computers and Education: Miscellaneous

Author Keywords
Haptic-Feedback Devices; Dynamic Visualizations; Constructivism; Guided Discovery

INTRODUCTION
Within the last 10 years, new standards in science and mathematics education in several countries have shifted their focus from long lists of content topics to fewer, central ideas in a discipline, with methodological emphasis on active learning practices such as conducting experiments, testing hypotheses, and building engineering devices (e.g., NGSS [27], British Columbia curriculum). These practices have rekindled interest in constructivist approaches to learning, which advocate for sense-making processes and learning environments that include and facilitate active learning activities. Further, technologies designed to create or support constructivist learning experiences can make it easier to scale such experiences to a broader population of students, while expanding possible learning activities. Constructivist learning environments are successful when they lead learners to (and through) moments of cognitive conflict, by providing them with opportunities to restructure their knowledge and achieve deeper understanding, either by interacting with the world, making things, or doing empirical work [9,19]. Effective constructivist learning environments result from intentional and precise design.

Two particularly effective technologies in the constructivist educator's toolbox are dynamic visualizations (e.g., computer simulations, visualizations, animations) and physical manipulatives. Dynamic visualizations have found widespread use in science and mathematics education due to their low cost, accessibility, and flexibility [30]. Physical manipulatives – like the large, cut-out letters used in Montessori schools – have been used in education for the better part of a century [6]. Well-designed dynamic visualizations and physical manipulatives are both capable of providing students with powerful, effective learning experiences [4,28].

Haptic feedback devices can function at the intersection of dynamic visualization and physical manipulatives. Most commonly, these devices are used to supply an additional sensory modality (touch) to more traditional computer simulations and dynamic visualizations, creating opportunities for students to touch and feel virtual objects that would normally be manipulated with a mouse and keyboard. The haptic device's sensors send positional information to the computer controller where they are incorporated into the virtual model. Thus, when you push on a virtual wall the virtual wall can "push back".

IDC 2017, June 27–30, 2017, Stanford, CA, USA.

ACM ISBN 978-1-4503-4921-5/17/06 ...$15.00.
http://dx.doi.org/10.1145/3078072.3079755

As haptic feedback devices become mainstream, they are seeing more use in educational settings. There is little doubt that these haptic experiences are novel, engaging, and potentially useful for education; however, their role in and impact on learning processes involving haptic devices has not been well characterized. In some situations, like motor training simulations for surgery, the learning process seems relatively straightforward. However, learning *abstractions* goes beyond familiarization or sensorimotor memory. Here, there is a critical need for a clear, explicit theory of how haptic feedback impacts learning.

The study reported in this paper was designed to provide insight into how haptic feedback supports learning, and suggest a framework for haptic-supported learning experiences that would inform our future designs. We designed and developed haptic-supported software for learning mathematics called Trigonometry Explorer. We recorded video and audio of a small sample (n=4) of students learning in this environment, and performed two related analyses of the data. The first, a microgenetic analysis of the collected video, provided us with a picture of how the haptic feedback influenced students' abilities to make connections between different mathematical representations. Second, with thematic analysis [21] we developed a novel framework for categorizing haptic learning experiences, wherein haptic representations are broken into two dimensions: the number of corresponding dynamic visualizations, and their resemblance to forces that exist in the physical world.

BACKGROUND

The opportunities explored in this research are newly possible due to the convergence of several technologies and practices with high relevance to education: *dynamic visualizations, physical manipulatives* such as *tangible interfaces*; and *haptic (force feedback) devices.*

Dynamic visualizations are increasingly common in educational settings across disciplines and age ranges. Physics simulations, virtual labs, and mathematical visualizations all aim to promote understanding of concepts using widely available and multi-use hardware (e.g., computers and tablets). Because of their wide availability, low cost, and ability to support open-ended discovery, these types of computational media are a potentially effective way of scaling constructivist learning experiences to a broader population of learners [5].

There is considerable evidence that dynamic visualizations can lead to deeper learning when carefully designed. A particularly effective use is in combining multiple representations in a single interface. Different representations can provide learners with multiple pathways to the core concepts [11, 18], or help manage the "epistemological complexity" of an idea through selective foregrounding and backgrounding [17]. However, there is a danger of overloading the learner's working memory, leaving fewer cognitive resources for sense making, building connections, or constructing mental models [13]. Appropriate supports can address these concerns [3, 28].

Physical manipulatives are three-dimensional, physical objects manipulated with learners' bodies, while dynamic visualizations are two-dimensional, virtual constructs accessed with a mouse and keyboard. Both can be successfully used as building blocks in constructivist learning technologies. In a meta-analysis involving over 7000 students, Carbonneau et. al found consistent, significant results in favor of concrete manipulatives in mathematics education [4].

Theoretical explanations for the effectiveness of physical manipulatives resemble those for dynamic visualizations. When discussing manipulatives, Post writes that "Manipulative materials may now be viewed simply as isomorphic structures that represent... abstract mathematical notions we wish to have children learn... When exposed to a number of seemingly different tasks that are identical in structure, children will tend to abstract the similar elements from their experiences" [20]. Like dynamic visualizations, physical manipulatives are effective in part because they provide learners with multiple perspectives.

In recent years, new learning technologies are emerging at the intersection of dynamic visualizations, tangible interfaces, and physical manipulatives. Haptic feedback devices are one, and have been used as building blocks of many technology-based learning tools and environments: like tangible interfaces, they can support physical manipulation of virtual objects, but also render forces to create the illusion of feeling those objects.

Much of the work on haptic feedback in education is concerned with creating more realistic simulations, including surgical simulators [2], dental simulators [29], and vehicle simulators [1]. All of these aim to create more realistic virtual experiences that better prepare learners to perform tasks in the physical world. Haptic devices have also found use in mathematics and science education, where students can feel mathematical functions and concepts [7, 26], forces generated by objects in virtual laboratories [10], and even molecular forces on the macro scale [22, 23].

Another body of haptic research relates to its use in representing abstractions, as opposed to literal simulations, as laid out in [12]. Recently, a framework describing how users employ multiple interpretive facets in their cognitive sense-making of artificial vibrotactile stimuli underlies navigation of a stimulus library using linked visual representations of those facets [24]. This group previously examined how the addition of force feedback compares to dynamic visualization alone in students' understanding of Newtonian spring forces, finding subtle differences in strategy [14]. Here, we took the next step of looking more deeply into a haptic-facilitated strategy with a qualitative approach.

RESEARCH OBJECTIVES

This study is part of an ongoing program to understand the impact of haptics in education, in which we have developed software and hardware (e.g., [14, 15]), and conducted studies in and out of schools. For more nuanced understanding of how haptic feedback impacts learning, we needed:

1. Deeper understanding of how haptic feedback impacts cognition and learning;

2. A framework to inform the design of future haptic learning experiences.

We determined that these research questions required a different methodological approach than those more commonly used in haptics research (e.g., quantitative comparative studies, or pre/post interviews). We used both microgenetic analysis [25] of video collected during the study to address RQ1 and grounded theory [8] to address RQ2. We present the results of these analyses to illustrate the value of this approach when applied to haptics in learning environments.

METHODS

Participants and Approach

We recruited four high-school seniors (two girls, two boys, aged 17 to 19) from a charter school in the San Francisco Bay Area serving one of the lowest-income communities in California, USA. These students had previously studied trigonometry, but lacked an understanding of the relationship between the unit circle and the graph of sine/cosine on the Cartesian plane. None of them had seen or used a haptic device before the study.

Students worked in pairs to promote discussion and collaboration. We chose to focus on one particular pair (referred to as Manuel and Juan) in our qualitative analysis. While both pairs informed our findings, we focused analysis and reporting on one pair of students for clearer illustration.

This single case study offered insight into the nuances of how haptic feedback and learning can interact, with no attempt to be to be broadly representative. With a qualitative approach, we aimed to capture and analyze the full process of learning with a haptic-supported dynamic visualization, and to use this description and analysis to characterize, design, and assess a haptic learning experience.

Data Collection and Analysis

We collected three primary sources of data. We captured (1) students' interactions with the software by recording screen and webcam video from the interaction computer, (2) audio and video of student interactions with the haptic device and one another with a tripod-mounted camera; and (3) student drawings of the graphs of sine and cosine (Study Phases 2-3).

Our analysis had two components. First, microgenetic analysis [25] of video collected during haptic-supported lessons on trigonometry provided us with key insights into the unique ways that haptic feedback can support students' understanding. Secondly, we employed grounded theory [8] to identify a framework to encompass our observations.

Technological Materials

Haptic Feedback Device: Hapkit

Hapkit [16] (Figure 1) is a one-degree-of-freedom (1-DOF) haptic device. It can be programmed to output forces based on the position of the handle, thus rendering 1-DOF virtual environments based on physical concepts, such as springs and dampers. It is designed as an open-source kit, meant to be accessible and assembled by students and educators, with a cost of approximately US $50, using parts obtained through

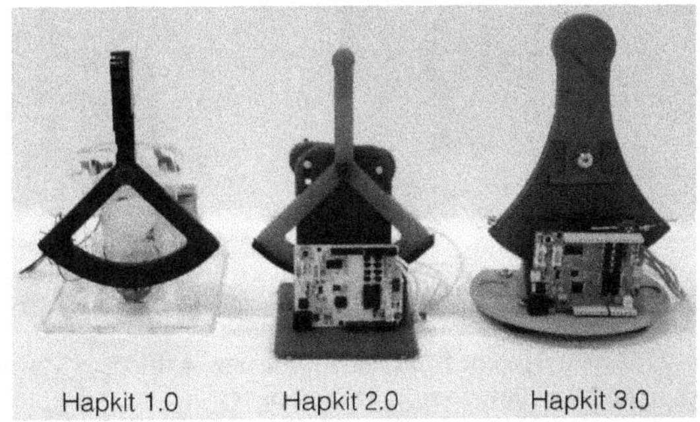

Figure 1. Three versions of low-cost, single-degree-of-freedom, open-source haptic devices for education: Hapkit 1.0 was designed in 2013 and uses laser-cut acrylic structural elements. Hapkit 2.0 was designed in 2014 and a combination of acrylic and 3-D printed plastic structural elements. Hapkit 3.0 was designed in 2015 and uses 3-D printed plastic structural elements.

online purchasing and structural components from digital fabrication tools such as laser cutting or 3-D printing. Hapkit's electronics board allows students to program their Hapkits using any computer, without the need for specialized laboratory equipment. Open-source Hapkit designs are available at `http://hapkit.standford.edu`.

Software Interface: Trigonometry Explorer

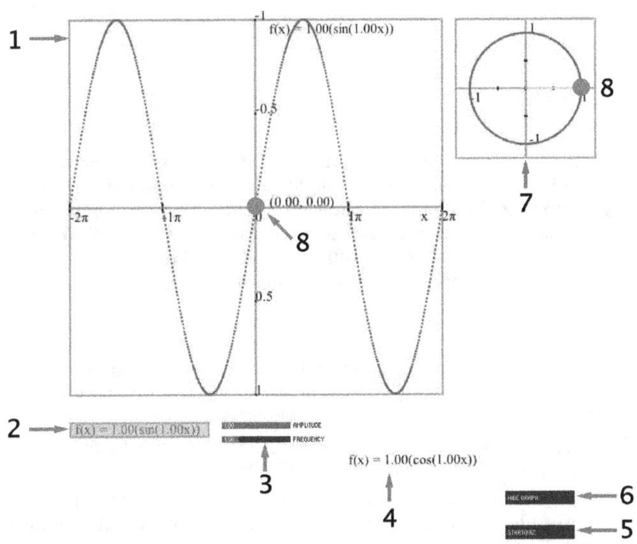

Figure 2. Initial screen of Trigonometry Explorer's Graphical User Interface with labels for each of its 3 components: 1) Graph Box 2) Function Drop Target 3) Amplitude and Frequency Sliders 4) Draggable Functions 5) Quiz Button 6) Hide Graph Button 7) Unit Circle Box 8) User Marker

Trigonometry Explorer (Figures 2, 4) illustrates the relationship between the graph of the trigonometric functions of sine(x) and cosine(x) and the unit circle. The program has two parts: the graphical user interface (GUI), programmed in Processing to run on any personal computer, and the Arduino-based software on the Hapkit Board, which renders haptic feedback and sends position data to the computer. Figure 2 shows Trigonometry Explorer's graphical user interface (GUI)'s eight components:

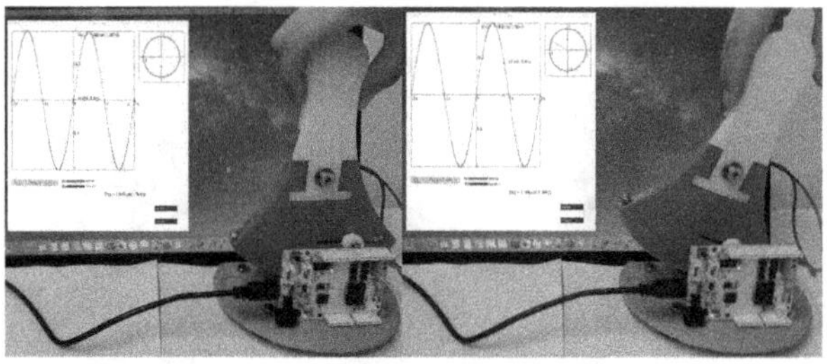

Figure 3. Moving Hapkit from side to side moves the User Marker along the graph and the unit circle in Trigonometry.

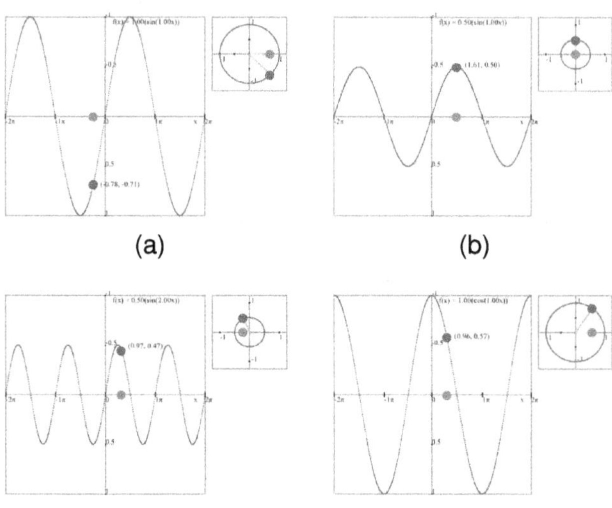

Figure 4. Four different use cases for Trigonometry Explorer. (a) Sine Function selected with Amplitude 1 and Hapkit at -0.78 rad position. (b) Sine Function selected with amplitude 0.5 and Hapkit at 1.61 rad position. (c) Sine Function selected with amplitude 0.5, frequency of 2 and Hapkit at 0.47 rad position. (d) Cosine Function selected with amplitude 1 and Hapkit at 0.96 rad position.

1. *Graph Box:* Shows graph of the function chosen by the user, and the point in the graph the user is currently on using the User Marker.
2. *Function Drop Box:* The user "drops" the function he or she wants displayed in the Graph Box into this box.
3. *Amplitude and Frequency Sliders:* Allow the user to change the amplitude and frequency of the graph chosen via the Function Drop Box.
4. *Functions:* The functions the user can choose to display and feel.
5. *Start Quiz Button:* The software supports a "quiz" modality that was not used for this work.
6. *Hide Graph Button:* Hide the graph from the user. The user can still explore the chosen graph using Hapkit, but will not see it in the graph box.
7. *Unit Circle Box:* Always displays the unit circle and the value of the graph the user is currently on.
8. *User Marker:* Represents the value of the current graph on the Graph Box and the Unit Circle Box.

A student then uses Hapkit as a joystick to move across a graph of a trigonometric function, and "feel" it. Hapkit translates the position the user is at in the graph to a force which the user can feel using the equations $F = A * \sin(f * x)$ or $F = A * \cos(f * x)$, depending on the function chosen. x is the horizontal position of the user in the graph, f is the frequency of the function, and A is the amplitude of the function. The student can change the function's amplitude and frequency using the GUI and see and feel the effects of those changes, while observing the relationship between the graph and the unit circle (Figure 4). When moving the handle, one feels the forces computed from the equations above as either resisting or assisting the motion. The higher above the x-axis, the more force force pushing the handle to the right. The lower below the x-axis, the more force pushing to the left (Figure 5).

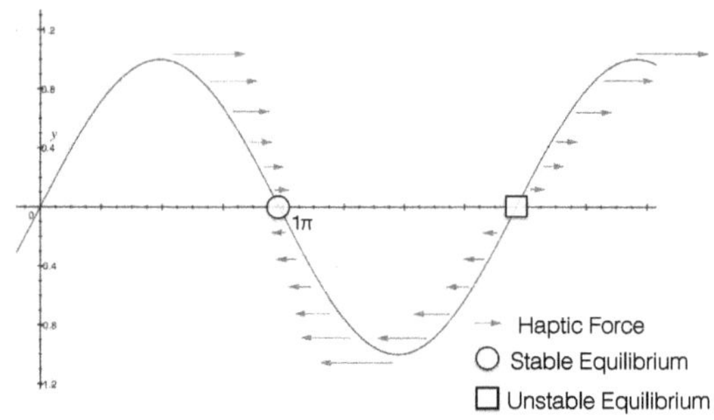

Figure 5. Displacement of the Hapkit handle represents the input to the sine function, and the forces rendered by the Hapkit represent the output.

Procedure

Participants were involved in an hour-long lesson about the relationship between the unit circle and the trigonometric functions sine and cosine. The lesson was designed for students who had studied some trigonometry and were familiar with sine and cosine, but did not fully grasp the relationship between the unit circle and these trigonometric functions. The lesson's learning goal was to help students create the conceptual links necessary to move fluidly between the unit circle and the graph of sine and cosine on the Cartesian plane.

The lesson consisted of four 15-minute phases. The first was a traditional lecture on sine, cosine, and the unit circle. The second and third phases guided students through a haptic-supported, guided-discovery activity: deriving and drawing the graphs of sine and cosine using a dynamic visualization of the unit circle. In the final phase, students guessed the frequency and amplitude of hidden graphs with varying frequencies and amplitudes. We describe these phases in more detail below, along with their intended learning goals and the research questions they were designed to answer.

Phase 1: The Initial Lecture

The first phase was designed to (re)introduce the students to the trigonometric concepts, representations, and methods used to coordinate between them. It did not directly address any research questions, but ensured that the students were familiar with the concepts in the study.

The instructor (an author) led the student pair through a lesson on the unit circle, sine, and cosine. The instructor lectured with PowerPoint slides, asked the students questions, and occasionally moved to the whiteboard to elaborate on specific concepts. The Hapkit was not used.

To determine students' prior knowledge, the instructor asked them if they had learned about sine and cosine in school, if they remembered the "soh-cah-toa" formula, and to draw angles of 45 and −45 degrees, convert from degrees to radians, and use the unit circle to find the sine or cosine of a given angle. The instructor then explicitly showed them how to use the unit circle to find the sine and cosine of a given angle.

Phase 2: Derive the Graph of Sine

The second and third phases of the study were designed to expose the ways in which the haptic feedback impacted the students' understanding of the connections between the two different trigonometric representations. As the students worked through the tasks in these phases, we were able to observe the impact of the haptic feedback through the students' actions, their discussions with each other, and their questions to the experimenters.

In Phase 2, students were asked to derive and draw the graph of $\sin(x)$ using the Hapkit and the unit-circle software. At this time, the actual graph of $\sin(x)$ was not displayed in the central window. The students were given a piece of paper with the central window's coordinates printed out and derive and draw the graph.

Phase 3: Derive the Graph of Cosine

The third phase was identical to the second, except that students were asked to derive and draw the graph of $\cos(x)$. This was more difficult than deriving and drawing $\sin(x)$, because it required students to translate the horizontal position of the point rotating around the unit circle to the vertical position on the graph.

Phase 4: Determine the Unknown Frequency and Amplitude

The fourth phase of the study served to check robustness of the students' interpretation of the haptic feedback. Since the students had not been taught about frequency and amplitude in the initial lecture, their ability to correctly guess the unknown frequency and amplitude would depend on their ability to correctly interpret the haptic feedback and unit-circle animation.

The instructor increased task difficulty by changing frequency and amplitude. Before this, frequency and amplitude of sine and cosine were both fixed at 1. Now, the unit circle radius changed with amplitude, while the rate at which the point moved around the circumference changed with frequency (Figure 6). Students could not see the adjusted values of frequency and amplitude. Then students were asked to determine the frequency and amplitude by viewing the "unit circle" representation and feeling the forces rendered by Hapkit.

FINDINGS

Our first research objective was to arrive at a deeper understanding of how haptic feedback might impact learning. We present this microgenetic analysis under Theme 1, below. Our second research objective, a framework for organizing haptic learning experiences, is addressed under Theme 2.

We offer these findings to illustrate the kinds of data and analyses that are possible using this methodology. Based on a single case study, they should be considered exploratory; further work must determine whether successful interpretation

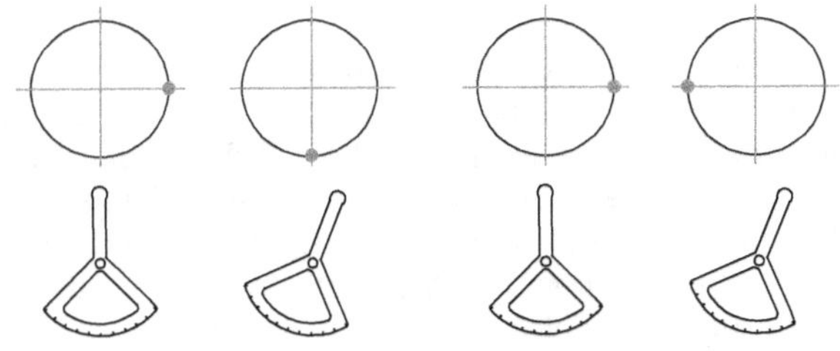

(a) (b)

Figure 6. (a) With a frequency of 1Hz, 2cm movement of the Hapkit handle moves the User Marker $\frac{\pi}{2}$ radians. (b) With a frequency of 2Hz, 2cm movement of the Hapkit handle moves the User Marker π radians.

of the haptic representation scaffolds the process of making connections between multiple representations of a single core concept.

Theme 1: A Microgenetic Analysis of Learning with Haptics

In the following, we present an analysis of the students' utterances, actions, and artifacts from their sessions. Findings are presented in chronological order, and grouped into sections that reflect themes that emerged during the analysis. The first section shows that before working with the Hapkit and Trigonometry Explorer, our featured student pair was unable to make the connection between the unit-circle representation of sine and cosine and the functions' graphs on the Cartesian plane. The second section details how the students learned to make this connection with the support of the haptic representation rendered by the Hapkit and Trigonometry Explorer software. For both students, the haptic representation was initially confusing; however, over the course of the study both students learned to correctly interpret the haptic representation. In the second section, we detail how the students' understanding of the connection between the two different trigonometric representations changed in tandem with their ability to correctly interpret the haptic representation.

Phase 1: Understanding the Pieces but Missing the Connection with Graphics Alone

At the beginning of their session, the students confirmed that they were familiar with sine and cosine, that they understood the relationship between the side lengths of a right triangle and the sine and cosine of its angles ("soh-cah-toa"), and that they had worked with the unit circle. However, in the first phase of the study they struggled to demonstrate this knowledge. For example, when asked to draw a 45-degree angle, one of the students drew a -45-degree angle instead. After a few minutes of help, both students were able to draw both positive and negative angles, but another concept in particular proved more difficult: neither were able to demonstrate how the unit circle could be used to find the sine/cosine of a given angle.

Instructor: *"So we draw a unit circle, and we put an angle there."* Manuel: *"I know one of these has to be sine and one has to be cosine."* Instructor: *"Do you remember which is which?"* Both students: *"No."*

After this exchange, the instructor worked with the students for five minutes to explain how the unit circle could be used to determine the sine and cosine of an angle. During this phase, the instructor explicitly showed the students how to use the unit circle to find the sine and cosine of a given angle. Following this, when the students were given a unit circle and a point of intersection, they were able to correctly determine the sine and cosine of the angle.

This is important because in the second and third phases, the students' task was to use the unit circle to determine the graph of sine and cosine on the Cartesian plane. However, despite the instructor's explicit explanation and their demonstrating their ability to do so in Phase 1, the students were initially unable to use the information from the interactive, dynamic visualization of the unit circle to derive the graph of sine in phase two. At first, the students tried simply remembering the graph of sine, but were unsuccessful. The instructor urged them to use the unit circle representation to re-derive the graph.

Manuel: *"I'm trying to remember which one this is; is it middle-up-middle?"* Instructor: *"You could figure it out right now. You don't even have to remember it."*

Although initially unable to use the unit-circle representation to help them draw the graph of sine, they were eventually able to solve the problem.

Phase 2: Juan Learns to Interpret the Haptic Representation

A primary research goal was to capture the act of student learning with a haptic device – not to determine if haptic feedback could support learning (though we did find evidence of this), but to better understand the *process* of learning with it. Both of the students in our case study utilized the haptic feedback to problem-solve in Phases 2, 3 and 4. Our analysis indicated that haptic feedback helped the students make connections between the different representations for sine and cosine, and that the effectiveness of haptic feedback on learning was tied to the students' ability to interpret it.

At the beginning of the second phase, Juan and Manuel were unclear on how to proceed. After several minutes of re-explaining the concepts from Phase 1, the instructor prompted the students use the Hapkit and software to try and figure out the graph of $\sin(x)$; Juan pulled the Hapkit closer and began to move the handle back and forth. He spent most of Phase 2 systematically manipulating the Hapkit and trying to make sense of what he was feeling and seeing. As he moved it back and forth, he whispered to himself *"middle, up, middle, down."* Each time Juan said a word, the Hapkit visibly rendered a different force. Juan was giving names to the different haptic sensations as he manipulated the handle.

Juan then proposed a hypothesis for how the haptic feedback related to the sine graph: *"So when it's doing this and it gets harder then you're going up higher and higher; then you start getting here and it starts getting easier as it's going down; then you start getting around here again and it starts getting a little harder; at that point you're going up again."*

In this description, Juan refers to "this," "around here," and "at this point." All of these utterances corresponded to a unique Hapkit position. Juan's description of the graph of sine was perfectly synchronized with his movement of the Hapkit. Furthermore, he was correct; the minima and maxima of the graph were located at the two points where the force generated by the Hapkit was highest. The instructor asked Juan to draw the graph. During the one minute and 17 seconds it took Juan to do this, he returned to the Hapkit three times before putting pen to paper. He then drew the graph of sine correctly on the first try.

Phase 3: Manuel's Struggles Lead to a Moment of Insight

At the start of Phase 3, Juan and Manuel traded the Hapkit back and forth to feel the new haptic representation. After a few moments with the Hapkit, Juan announced that he had figured out the graph. While moving the Hapkit, Juan said, *"It starts here at middle, goes up here,... middle again here, I think... down here, and middle here."* As before, Juan's utterances were correctly synchronized with his movements of the Hapkit. When asked by the instructor if the Hapkit helped him figure out the graph, Juan said *"I feel like it helped me figure out exactly what I was looking at."*

Manuel had a harder time than Juan in interpreting the haptic feedback. When Manuel took a turn with the Hapkit, he moved the handle back and forth and exclaimed *"it feels weird... it doesn't stay. [It feels weird] when it changes, [and feels good] at the middle, when it hits the one."* The "one" referred to is labeled 1π in Figure 2, and is the place where the sine wave intersects the x-axis. This is a point of stable equilibrium for the Hapkit; in other words, it is a point where the Hapkit naturally comes to rest. Juan and Manuel agreed that the Hapkit felt "right" when it was in a stable equilibrium, and felt "weird" in other places.

Manuel then moved the handle back and forth while giving verbal labels to the different Hapkit positions. However, unlike Juan, Manuel did not appear to be making the connection between the haptic feedback and the graph of cosine, saying *"I don't know... I know how it looks, cosine, I'm just seeing how can this gonna help it, how's it going to help a person understand how cosine works."*

At this point, the instructor went back to the whiteboard to re-explain how the graph of cosine could be figured out through use of the unit circle. While the explanation was nearly identical to the one presented at the start of the lesson, the result of the explanation couldn't have been more different. After the brief exposition, Manuel had a moment of insight: *"Ohhh, yeah, that's why!"* He then reached for the pen and paper and sketched out his graph of cosine. However, unlike Juan with the graph of sine, Manuel did not return to the Hapkit before putting pen to paper. And also unlike Juan, Manuel failed to get the graph of cosine correct. Although he got the amplitude and point of intersection with the y-axis correct, the frequency was too low (Figure 7, left).

The instructor asked Manuel to try using the Hapkit to improve on his drawing. Manuel took over the Hapkit from Juan, and for the next two minutes, sat quietly using it. Eventually, he grabbed another piece of paper and made a second attempt at drawing the graph of cosine. This drawing was improved

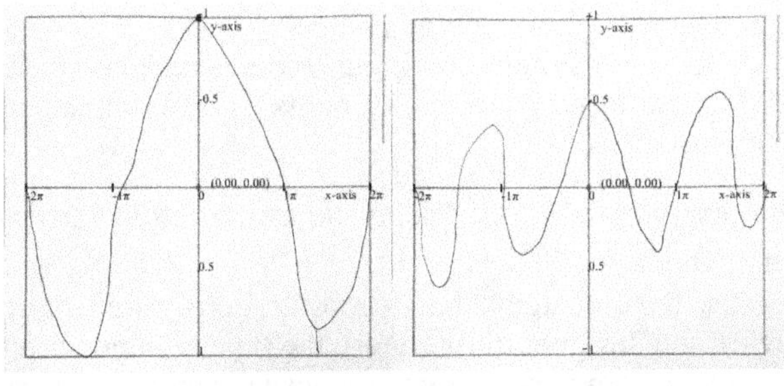

Figure 7. Manuel's first and second attempts at drawing cosine;

(the frequency was much closer to the true graph) but still contained errors (Figure 7, right). When the instructor pointed out what Manuel had gotten wrong, Juan announced that he had seen what was wrong in the drawing but did not reveal it.

Phase 4: Juan and Manuel Work Together to Develop a Complete Understanding

In the fourth and final phase, the instructor secretly varied both the frequency and amplitude of the hidden graph and asked the students to guess them using the Hapkit and Trigonometry Explorer. Instead of drawing the graph each time, the students verbally reported the values of amplitude and frequency to the instructor.

For the first few minutes, the instructor oriented the students to the changes. Both the amplitude and frequency of the function could be changed by moving two sliders on the GUI. As amplitude was decreased, the radius of the unit circle as rendered graphically decreased accordingly. The range of forces rendered by the Hapkit (from minima to maxima) decreased as well (and vice versa). As frequency increased, moving the Hapkit handle resulted in the User Marker moving more rapidly around the circumference of the unit circle (and vice versa).

The instructor asked Juan and Manuel to vary the frequency and amplitude sliders to explore how the unit circle animation and haptic feedback changed. After a few moments, Juan and Manuel guessed at their relationship. Manuel pointed to the amplitude slider and said, *"I know this one is how high it is."* Juan pointed to the frequency slider and said, *"This one is how many loops are in this thing."*

The instructor then set amplitude to 1 and frequency to $\frac{2}{3}$. Both values were hidden from the students; the only way they could determine the new frequency and amplitude was by using the unit circle visualization and the haptic feedback. Juan immediately determined the correct frequency, but was unable to figure out the exact amplitude, saying *"I think it's going to be pretty high... I know the frequency is 3, I just don't know what the amplitude is."* Manuel then reached over and pointed to the unit circle, saying *"You can pretty much tell. Remember that... the x, y would be 1."*

The instructor changed the frequency to $\frac{4}{3}$ and the amplitude to 1. Again, Juan figured out frequency immediately but was unable to determine amplitude, while Manuel was able to determine amplitude by looking at the unit circle. When asked how he was figuring out the frequency, Juan said, *"[I count] the number of times this thing goes in a circle from 0 up to 2π."* Manuel confirmed that he was determining amplitude by looking at the length of the radius of the unit circle.

For the second exercise in a row, Juan determined the correct frequency while Manuel determined the correct amplitude. The instructor then asked Juan to teach Manuel how to determine the frequency, which resulted in the following exchange.

Juan: *"Start here in the middle. Then one full rotation, two, three, four... so four."* Manuel: *"So every time it just clicks, right?"* Juan: *"The number of rotations made in a circle up until 2π."* Manuel: *"You know it's a rotation every time you feel that little... pressure it gives you, whatever you call that."*

Finally, the instructor changed the amplitude and frequency again. This time, the amplitude was set to 0.5 and the frequency was set to $\frac{3}{2}$. Manuel determined the correct amplitude immediately, but got the frequency off by 0.5. The instructor explained that the frequency might not be an integer, and Manuel said *"I know it takes two little stumbles... Ooh! It goes off! Is it 1.5?"* At this point, with little time remaining, the instructor ended the lesson.

In this final phase of the study, Manuel relied on aspects of both the unit-circle representation and the haptic representation when trying to determine the unknown frequency and amplitude. Manuel began this phase unable to determine the unknown frequency. Juan instructed Manuel to *"count the number of times this thing goes in a circle from 0 up to 2π."* Instead of relying only on the graphical, unit-circle representation, Manuel used the haptic feedback to help him identify the phenomenon of interest: *"You know it's a rotation every time you feel that little... pressure it gives you."* As Manuel learned to correctly interpret the haptic representation, he also gained the ability to determine the unknown frequency.

Theme 2: A Proposed Categorization of Haptic Learning Experiences

Here we describe the two major categories we found in our analysis, then use these to identify and describe two important types of haptic representations, each with its own distinct set of learning outcomes. We call these two types of haptic learning experiences "mirror" and "bridge."

Isolated and Connected Haptic Representations

Although haptic representations can be designed to be experienced without a visual component, more often they are designed to accompany dynamic visualizations. A common way of categorizing dynamic visualizations is according to the number of representations present simultaneously. There is evidence that multiple, connected representations are better at helping learners make connections between different aspects of the same concept [11, 18], while individual, isolated representations may be provide other benefits (e.g., lower cognitive load). We extend this categorization to the haptic representations that typically accompany dynamic visualizations, provide examples of existing haptic environments that fit into these categories, and identify the different learning goals that examples in each category best achieve.

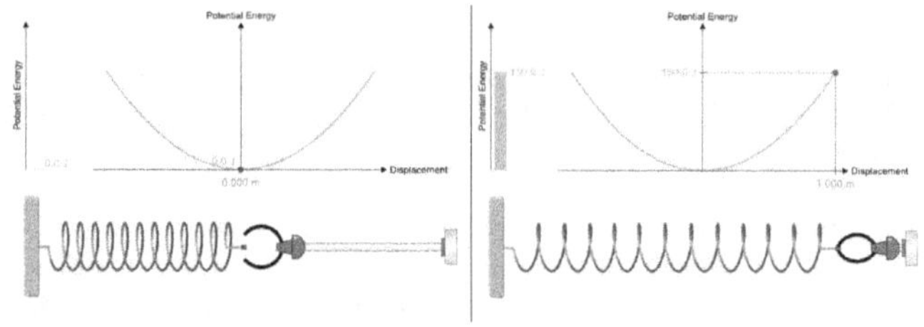

Figure 8. An example simulation that provides a dynamic visualization, but does not contain haptic feedback.

Isolated haptic representations are physical simulations that accompany a single, non-haptic dynamic visualization. As the user manipulates the haptic controller, the visual aspects of the virtual object update accordingly. When a single dynamic visualization is combined with a single haptic representation, often the goal is to create a realistic simulation of interacting with an object in the physical world. For example, isolated haptic representations can render physical simulations of objects including springs, walls, viscous fluids, bodies being operated upon, magnets, and atoms. These types of haptic representations can also provide haptic feedback for virtual objects that are too small or too large to physically manipulate (e.g., atoms, planets) or for objects that are impossible to manipulate directly in the physical world (e.g., mathematical functions, physical quantities like potential energy).

Connected haptic representations are physical simulations that accompany multiple non-haptic, dynamically-linked representations. To help explain these types of representations, we created an example simulation that does not contain haptic feedback (Figure 8). This simulation shows two distinct, dynamic representations: a spring that can be moved using a mouse, and a graph that shows the relationship between spring displacement and potential energy on the Cartesian coordinates. When the user clicks on the spring and drags to the right, both representations respond: the virtual spring stretches and the graph changes to represent the increase in potential energy. These types of dynamic visualizations are designed to help students make links between multiple representations and can lead to deeper conceptual understanding. However, without appropriate pedagogical support, students may struggle to understand the relations between the different representations. This example was modified to contain a connected haptic representation using a haptic device. The forces the user feels when manipulating the haptic device is a connected haptic representation. In our example, the haptic representation connects two visualizations: a spring being stretched and a graph changing in real time.

Isolated and connected haptic representations are similar in that they both provide additional support for students' learning with dynamic visualizations. We hypothesize that each supports a different learning outcome. Because isolated haptic representations combine a dynamic, physical representation with a single dynamic visualization, they seem well-suited to supporting learning about a single, focused concept or single aspect of a complex concept. In contrast, because connected haptic representations combine a dynamic, physical representation with multiple, dynamically-linked visualizations, they seem best suited to helping students make connections between multiple concepts, or between different aspects of complex concepts.

The Semiotics of Haptic Feedback: Iconic and Symbolic Representations

Because the rendered haptic feedback is programmed into the device, the designer must choose the type of haptic representation to accompany the dynamic visualization. In the spring simulation example, a natural choice is to program the haptic feedback device to mimic a spring, so that as the user moves the controller to the right, the user feels a linearly increasing force. Another choice would be to have the haptic device represent the graph of potential energy, so that as the controller was moved to the right, the user feels a quadratically increasing force. We refer to the first type of representation, in which the haptic feedback is designed to mimic a physical object, as an iconic representation, and the second type of representation as a symbolic representation.

When working with an iconic haptic representation, the forces the user feels while manipulating the virtual object are designed to mimic the actual forces that a user would feel when manipulating the corresponding physical object. Symbolic haptic representations make no attempts to mimic physical objects by accurately rendering forces that would be found in the physical world. Instead, these haptic representations are linked to dynamic visualizations in a way that requires interpretation. In our spring example, when the student displaces the virtual spring, she will feel a quadratically increasing force. This haptic representation symbolizes the relationship between displacement and potential energy. If the student correctly interprets the haptic representation, this could aid her in making the conceptual link between displacement and potential energy. However, since there is no way to directly feel the potential energy stored in a displaced spring in the physical world, the student will not be able to draw on analogous experiences in the physical world when trying to correctly interpret the haptic representation. Thus, the student may need additional guidance and support before being able to understand symbolic haptic representations.

Haptic Mirrors and Haptic Bridges

The framework that we have developed allows us to separate haptic learning experiences into four different categories: isolated, iconic haptic representations; isolated, symbolic haptic representations; connected, iconic haptic representations; and connected, symbolic haptic representations. Here, we highlight two of the four categories: haptic mirrors (isolated, iconic representations) and haptic bridges (connected, symbolic representations) (Figure 9). The goal of a haptic mirror is to accurately mimic a physical experience. Examples of haptic mirrors are surgical simulators, vehicle simulators, and physics simulators. Haptic mirrors are useful for simulating situations that are dangerous, expensive, or rarely encountered. Since haptic mirrors are typically used as stand-ins for physical situations, their effectiveness can be measured by comparing students who learn with the haptic mirror to students who learn in the actual physical situation. In most cases, we hypothesize

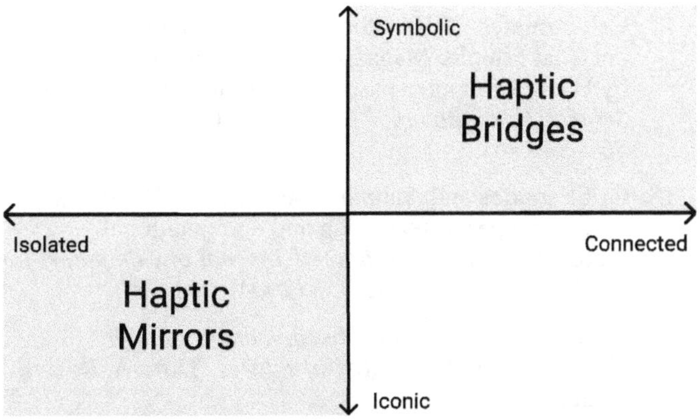

Figure 9. Illustration of our proposed framework. Haptic bridges (e.g., Trigonometry Explorer) occupy the connected & symbolic quadrant, and haptic mirrors (e.g., dental simulators) occupy the isolated & iconic quadrant.

that the more accurately haptic mirrors can reflect the physical world, the better the learning outcomes.

Haptic bridges connect multiple dynamic visualizations with a haptic representation that requires some degree of interpretation. The Trigonometry Explorer is an example of a haptic bridge: one of the dynamic visualizations is the unit circle, and the other is the (hidden) graph of the function on the Cartesian plane. Manipulating the haptic device causes both dynamic visualizations to update, and the haptic representation symbolizes the function's output value. In our analysis, we detailed how interpreting the haptic representation correctly required sustained effort, and how each student's performance was related to his ability to correctly interpret the haptic feedback.

Unlike Haptic Mirrors, the haptic representation of a Haptic Bridge is not necessarily meant to be learned. Once the student has made the connection between the different visual representations, the Haptic Bridge may no longer be needed. This makes it a form of scaffolding; a Haptic Bridge supports students as they learn to make connections between concepts, and once those connections are made it can be removed or forgotten. This is in contrast to the examples of haptic mirrors provided above, where the haptic representation is often meant to be learned.

DISCUSSION

Making sense of the haptic representation required interpretation. That this can be difficult is well known to haptic practitioners; more surprising was that its successful interpretation appeared to be related to the students' ability to solve the problems in each of the phases. Juan learned to correctly interpret the haptic feedback early in the study, and encountered little resistance while working through the remaining problems. In contrast, Manuel failed to interpret the haptic feedback in Phase 2, struggled with the interpretation in Phase 3, and then, with the help of Juan, learned to correctly interpret it in Phase 4. Once Manuel learned to correctly interpret the haptic representation in the final phase—evidenced by his statment that *"you know it's a rotation every time you feel that little... pressure it gives you"*—he gained the ability to determine the unknown frequency.

To those who are not haptic designers, the idea of interpreting haptic feedback may seem strange. Many haptic devices are programmed to mimic reality, so that when manipulating a virtual object it feels the same as manipulating a physical object. In these cases, the ability to make sense of the haptic feedback is automatic, bootstrapped by our ability to use our sense of touch to incorporate information about the physical world. However, the haptic feedback incorporated into Trigonometry Explorer is different: the forces rendered by the Hapkit have no real-world analogue. That is, it is impossible to go into the physical world, find a sine wave, and learn how it feels by touching it. In cases like this, the haptic feedback becomes symbolic, which means (in this case) that the students' ability to use the Hapkit to help them imagine the hidden graphs of sine and cosine is dependent on their ability to make meaning of, or interpret, the haptic feedback.

We propose a framework consisting of two dimensions—iconic-symbolic and isolated-connected—for organizing haptic experiences (Figure 9). These dimensions were chosen to organize haptic experiences according to their different learning outcomes. Haptic mirrors are iconic, isolated haptic representations, and are often used for motor training (e.g., learning to drill a tooth). Most examples of educational haptics would be categorized as haptic mirrors. However, when the goal is to improve or achieve conceptual understanding, haptic mirrors are less appropriate. Haptic bridges are connected, symbolic representations that combine a symbolic haptic representation with a dynamic visualization consisting of multiple representations. de Jong et. al write that "It is worthwhile to further investigate the effects of different types of support when offering learners multiple representations. Integrating representations looks promising, but... additional support is probably needed to let learners have mindful interaction with the representations" [28]. Although our results are preliminary, there is evidence that the students working with the Trigonometry Explorer—a haptic bridge—were aided in their ability to make sense of the multiple representations by the haptic feedback.

ACKNOWLEDGEMENTS

This material is based upon work supported by the National Science Foundation under grant no. 1441358. We also thank the Lemann Center for Entrepreneurship and Educational Innovation in Brazil for its support for this research.

REFERENCES

1. M. Angerilli, A. Frisoli, F. Salsedo, S. Marcheschi, and M. Bergamasco. 2001. Haptic simulation of an automotive manual gearshift. In *Proceedings 10th IEEE International Workshop on Robot and Human Interactive Communication. ROMAN 2001 (Cat. No.01TH8591).* 170–175.
2. C. Basdogan, S. De, J. Kim, Manivannan Muniyandi, H. Kim, and M. A. Srinivasan. 2004. Haptics in minimally invasive surgical simulation and training. *IEEE Computer Graphics and Applications* 24, 2 (March 2004), 56–64.
3. Daniel Bodemer, Rolf Ploetzner, Inge Feuerlein, and Hans Spada. 2004. The active integration of information

during learning with dynamic and interactive visualisations. *Learning and Instruction* 14, 3 (June 2004), 325–341.

4. Kira J. Carbonneau, Scott C. Marley, and James P. Selig. 2013. A meta-analysis of the efficacy of teaching mathematics with concrete manipulatives. *Journal of Educational Psychology* 105, 2 (2013), 380–400.
5. Ton De Jong and Wouter R. Van Joolingen. 1998. Scientific discovery learning with computer simulations of conceptual domains. *Review of educational research* 68, 2 (1998), 179–201.
6. F. Froebel. 1887. The education of man.(WN Hailmann, Trans.) New York: Appleton. (1887).
7. S. Gerofsky, M. Savage, and K E MacLean. 2009. 'Being the graph': Using haptic and kinesthetic interfaces to engage students learning about functions. In *the 9th Int'l Conf on Technology in Mathematics Teaching (ICTMT '09)*. Metz, France, 5 pages.
8. Barney G. Glaser and Anselm L. Strauss. 2009. *The discovery of grounded theory: Strategies for qualitative research.* Transaction publishers.
9. E. von Glasersfeld. 2005. Thirty years constructivism. *Constructivist Foundations* 1, 1 (2005), 9–12.
10. Majid H. Koul, Subir K. Saha, and M. Manivannan. 2013. Teaching Mechanism Dynamics using a Haptic Device. In *Proceedings of the 1st International and 16th National Conference on Machines and Mechanisms (iNaCoMM2013), IIT Roorkee, India.*
11. Jill H. Larkin and Herbert A. Simon. 1987. Why a diagram is (sometimes) worth ten thousand words. *Cognitive science* 11, 1 (1987), 65–100.
12. K E MacLean. 2008. Foundations of Transparency in Tactile Information Design. *IEEE Trans on Haptics* 1, 2 (2008), 84–95.
13. Richard E. Mayer, Roxana Moreno, Michelle Boire, and Shannon Vagge. 1999. Maximizing constructivist learning from multimedia communications by minimizing cognitive load. *Journal of educational psychology* 91, 4 (1999), 638.
14. Gordon Minaker, Oliver Schneider, Richard Davis, and Karon E. MacLean. 2016. HandsOn: Enabling Embodied, Creative STEM e-learning with Programming-Free Force Feedback. In *EuroHaptics Conference*. 427–437.
15. M. Orta Martinez, J. Campion, T. Gholami, M. K. Rittikaidachar, A. C. Barron, and A. M. Okamura. 2017. Open Source, Modular, Customizable, 3-D Printed Kinesthetic Haptic Devices. In *IEEE World Haptics Conference*. In Press.
16. Melisa Orta Martinez, Tania K. Morimoto, Annalisa T. Taylor, Aaron C. Barron, J. D. Akzl Pultorak, Jeanny Wang, Agnes Calasanz-Kaiser, Richard Lee Davis, Paulo Blikstein, and Allison M. Okamura. 2016. 3-D Printed Haptic Devices for Educational Applications. In *IEEE Haptics Symposium*. 126–133.
17. Orit Parnafes. 2010. When Simple Harmonic Motion is not That Simple: Managing Epistemological Complexity by Using Computer-based Representations. *Journal of Science Education and Technology* 19, 6 (Dec. 2010), 565–579.
18. Orit Parnafes and Andrea Disessa. 2004. Relations between types of reasoning and computational representations. *International Journal of Computers for Mathematical Learning* 9, 3 (2004), 251–280.
19. Jean Piaget. 1977. *The development of thought: Equilibration of cognitive structures.(Trans A. Rosin).* Viking.
20. Thomas Post. 1981. The role of manipulative materials in the learning of mathematical concepts. *Selected issues in mathematics education* (1981), 109–131.
21. Gery W. Ryan and H. Russell Bernard. 2003. Techniques to identify themes. *Field methods* 15, 1 (2003), 85–109.
22. G. Sankaranarayanan, S. Weghorst, M. Sanner, A. Gillet, and A. Olson. 2003. Role of haptics in teaching structural molecular biology. In *11th Symposium on Haptic Interfaces for Virtual Environment and Teleoperator Systems, 2003. HAPTICS 2003. Proceedings.* 363–366.
23. Makoto Sato, Xiangning Liu, Jun Murayama, Katsuhito Akahane, and Masaharu Isshiki. 2008. A haptic virtual environment for molecular chemistry education. In *Transactions on edutainment I.* Springer, 28–39.
24. Hasti Seifi and Karon E MacLean. 2017. Haptic Facets: exploiting users' sensemaking schemas as a path to design and personalization. *IJHCS* (2017), 12.
25. Robert S. Siegler. 2006. Microgenetic analyses of learning. (2006).
26. Alexei Sourin and Lei Wei. 2009. Visual immersive haptic mathematics. *Virtual Reality* 13, 4 (Sept. 2009), 221–234.
27. NGSS Lead States. 2013. *Next generation science standards: For states, by states.* National Academies Press.
28. Jan van der Meij and Ton de Jong. 2006. Supporting students' learning with multiple representations in a dynamic simulation-based learning environment. *Learning and Instruction* 16, 3 (June 2006), 199–212.
29. D. Wang, Yuru Zhang, Yuhui Wang, Y. S. Lee, Peijun Lu, and Yong Wang. 2005. Cutting on triangle mesh: local model-based haptic display for dental preparation surgery simulation. *IEEE Transactions on Visualization and Computer Graphics* 11, 6 (Nov. 2005), 671–683.
30. Carl E. Wieman, Wendy K. Adams, and Katherine K. Perkins. 2008. PhET: Simulations that enhance learning. *Science* 322, 5902 (2008), 682–683.

Not my Gumdrop Buttons! Youth Tool Use in Designing an Electronic Shrek-themed Bean Bag Toss

Jasmine K. McBeath
Gevirtz Graduate
School of Education
UC Santa Barbara
Santa Barbara, CA
kmcbeath@education.ucsb.edu

Richard P. Durán
Gevirtz Graduate
School of Education
UC Santa Barbara
Santa Barbara, CA
duran@education.ucsb.edu

Danielle B. Harlow
Gevirtz Graduate
School of Education
UC Santa Barbara
Santa Barbara, CA
dharlow@education.ucsb.edu

ABSTRACT

The Maker Movement, with a novel approach to learning and conceptualizing science, could potentially increase representation from groups traditionally alienated by mainstream science. However, only a few studies have been conducted on underrepresented groups' participation in Maker projects. In this paper, we explore how a group of Latina youths, who initially expressed an aversion to STEM and had limited knowledge about circuits, created an electronic bean bag toss. Cultural Historical Activity Theory (CHAT) provided insight into how the girls delegated and accomplished Maker tasks, used or repurposed tools, and developed expertise. Analyzing video data, student work, and group exit interviews revealed the use of non-technical terms or "insider labels" for tools described within the group. The girls were aware of their switch to more scientific language when posting online and preparing for presentations. Similarly, the young women demonstrated distinct forms of comprehension within the group when creating the project (functional understanding) versus explaining to others beyond the group (conceptual understanding).

Author Keywords

Gender; girls in STEM; Latino; art; Making; digital fabrication; design-based research; engineering education; technology; craft; tool use; cultural historical activity theory

ACM Classification Keywords

J.2. Physical Sciences and Engineering [Electronics];
J.5. Arts and Humanities;
K.3.2. Computer and Information Science Education [Computer Uses in Education, Literacy]

IDC 2017, June 27–30, 2017, Stanford, CA, USA.

ACM ISBN 978-1-4503-4921-5/17/06...$15.00.
DOI: http://dx.doi.org/10.1145/3078072.3079721

INTRODUCTION

The Maker Movement could offer STEM-underrepresented groups, including minorities and women, a route to engage with science in a non-traditional way. With the key tenets of playful experimentation, creation of artifacts, social learning and community participation, Making offers opportunities for hands-on learning and broadening perceptions of STEM [32]. However, the inclusive ethos of Making might not be enough to increase access. The Maker Movement could perpetuate the same inequities within conventional science if programs and activities are not carefully framed and enacted [9]. The few studies on underrepresented groups in Making reach similar conclusions on the importance of intentional framing and design, including diverse activities and levels to target a variety of interests and abilities [1, 29]. Deliberate planning with respect to people and place is also crucial, including role models and mentorship [1, 29, 38], and an accessible site and welcoming community [1, 20, 29].

Barely any studies have considered tool use within a program encouraging participation from STEM-underrepresented groups, despite tool appropriation providing insight into participation patterns. If tool oriented, the focus tends to be on developing the Maker Mindset of creative problem-solving and productive response to failure [12]. Martin, Dixon, and Hagood's research considers a problem-solving approach but also tool use with their concept of "adaptive resourcefulness" [23]. They examined how students and mentors used tools creatively and drew from social networks to solve specific problems in the design process [23]. Developing conceptual tools and applying knowledge to new situations can be challenging, and others have documented novice Makers struggling to conceptualize project goals and finding communicating, negotiating, and externalizing their ideas very challenging [36]. Grounding projects in a real-life, social context can provide structure and motivation, helping students better understand their projects and the design process [36]. In particular, young women appear motivated by creating for others rather than themselves [20], and other underrepresented groups benefit from collaborative, community-oriented designs and projects [9]. Therefore, it is important to consider both how students use tools to invent new things and how they understand their creations in relation to their group and broader community.

In this paper, we investigate the role of tool use in the context of an afterschool Maker program working with low-income immigrant Latina teens. We explore how a group of 7 Latina girls delegated and accomplished tasks, used or repurposed tools, and developed expertise when designing and creating an electronic game for a family festival. The project, with a blend of art and science, allowed for different types of participation and provided insight into youth development. We focus on how this group of novice Makers developed expertise using new tools. We examine conceptual tool use throughout the project, considering Smagorinsky's five degrees of appropriation for conceptual tools: lack of appropriation, appropriating a label, surface features, conceptual underpinnings, and reaching mastery [17, 35]. Building from Smagorinsky's work, we identify three levels of conceptual tool use in the Bean Bag Project: *Familiarizing, Labeling, and Understanding.* We argue that communicating about the products and process plays an important role in tool use and understanding beyond the creation process.

RELEVANT LITERATURE

Women in STEM and Making

There is evidence that traditional learning environments have a strong effect on girls, and over time, can reinforce stereotypes, lowering girls' ambitions towards science and engineering careers [19]. Boys and girls are now taking the same number of math and science classes in K-12, and leave high school equally ready to study science and engineering [19]. However, that has not translated into equal career trajectories for women and men in science. Women earn less than 40% of undergraduate degrees in physics and technological sciences and less than 20% in computer science and engineering [37]. Women are actually *less* likely to pursue a computer science bachelors now than they were fifteen years ago [26]. Women are also graduating to a pay gap, and are more likely to face underemployment or unemployment. These results are worse for female minority scientists, who encounter unemployment rates around 7%, compared to white men at less than 4% [26]. The gap is even more dramatic if we focus on Latina women in STEM disciplines [11].

There is a large body of research on women in science documenting that women tend to move away from the physical sciences and engineering due to the competitive and impersonal culture of academic science [5]. However, the Maker Movement could offer women a route to engage with science in a non-traditional way. With the key tenets of playful experimentation, creation of artifacts, social learning and community participation, the Maker Movement offers opportunities for hands-on learning and broadening perceptions of STEM [33]. Makers create with a variety of materials including digital tools in a learning community, resulting in a process that is both learner-centered and project-based [28, 30]. Making benefits from both the do-it-yourself empowerment of individuals and community sharing of tools, designs, and products. A playful, collaborative mindset and a positive response to overcoming failure are also key components [22]. In addition to collaboration and creativity, the Maker ethos includes resourcefulness, ideation, and problem-solving [28]. There is also a blurring of the bounds between informal and formal spaces for learning, as Making processes, practices, and tools are dynamic, multidisciplinary, and multimodal [18]. The Makerspace environment encourages "re-authoring and re-mixing practices from a wide range of experiences, both in and out of school" [9]. People use a variety of tools and traditional crafts as well as electronics and new technologies such as 3D printing [21, 22, 28].

Making also draws from other disciplines and hobbies, as Makers range "from traditional artisans to computer hackers, and encompass crafters, musicians, artists, cooks, students, welders, scientists, engineers, software developers, and circuit benders" [38]. Leah Buechley, advocate for girls in Making and inventor of LilyPad, a line of sewable electronics products, explains that Making allows people to explore science in new, appealing contexts. Her designs blend art with technology, allowing for "alternative cultures" within STEM. According to Buechley, "The best way to increase diversity in STEM is to seed new subcultures where STEM can happen and a person can keep her own identity—as artsy, outdoorsy, a people-person, or feminine" [38].

Including girls in Making does not mean restricting activities to traditionally gendered activities such as jewelry-making or fashion design [20]. Presenting a variety of activities at multiple levels is helpful for increasing accessibility [29]. Perhaps more important than activity choice is the program or project framing. Girls appear to benefit from the collaborative and community-oriented aspects of Making [38]. Girls cite helping or giving as their biggest motivation for Making, and tend to pursue projects that benefit the community [38]. For example, young women designing toys for younger children were more motivated and confronted challenges more effectively when Making and related practices were presented as supporting their community [20]. Bridging student-centered and community-oriented learning, Maker alternatives to traditional science could potentially appeal to many types of students alienated by mainstream STEM disciplines.

STEM-Underrepresented Groups and Making

Proponents advocate that the Maker Movement has the potential to "democratize access to the discourses of power that accompany becoming a producer of artifacts" [18]. However, there has been criticism of the Maker Movement as primarily "an adult, white, middle-class pursuit, led by those with the leisure time, technical knowledge, and resources to make" [8]. Make Magazine and the Maker Movement have also been criticized for promoting expensive high-tech devices and excluding Makers who are inventive despite limited resources. For example, until recently Make Magazine had not featured diverse Maker topics such as lowrider car mechanics or geometric patterns in knitting, even though these traditions include many valuable and complex STEM practices [6].

A handful of researchers have explored how Maker activities can purposely encourage participation in STEM fields by under-represented populations, including women but also ethnic minorities and people with disabilities. Intentional program design and framing appears crucial to increasing accessibility and encouraging participation [1, 9, 20, 29]. To enable youth to "remake the world around them, we must rethink how we frame making so that it more directly aligns with the interests and goals of the communities and people we hope to engage" [20]. Through intentional design, Maker programs for youth can encourage subcultures within STEM and legitimize participation. Program framing can define "not only what counts as authentic 'making' but also youth identities as makers, participants, collaborators, community-members, youth people *who legitimately belong in this makerspace*" [9].

Part of this framing includes diverse format and varying difficulty levels or tracks for participation. One university-community partnership program stressed the importance of providing diverse program formats including afterschool, workshops, and outreach events [29]. They also offered different levels and made sure to always include a level for students without previous experience. "Mixed-ability makerspaces" such as DIYAbility and Assistive Design Center at the Perkins School for the Blind recommend projects be easy to start but include increasing complexity and multiple pathways for self-expression to empower youth with disabilities [1]. Alper argues, "Mixed-ability maker culture recognizes that different bodies produce different types of knowledge" [1]. Valuing different abilities and skillsets is important, allowing students to learn with and from each other about science, technology, and art [29].

The content and rigor vary significantly from program to program, from one day workshops to a four-year math preparation and engineering program [39]. The pre-engineering program, operating for over twenty years, has had great success at providing a "jump-start to college," improving high school and college retention for low income inner city students. However, this program enrolls students with high grades that are nominated by their teachers and persist through a four-year summer program. In comparison, other programs try to reach students alienated by school science. A university-community partnership program in Amherst offers curriculum especially for those "with no previous experience or interest" in STEM [29]. They ask, "Can makerspaces help to both stop leaks and open doors along the STEM pipeline for all students, but in particular for women and multicultural students?"

For stopping leaks and opening doors, many programs emphasize the importance of role models and mentorship. Some programs present mentors as "ambassadors" for participating in STEM fields, arguing that through discussions with college students, youth learn about the culture of the field and imagine themselves participating in the future [29]. Role models and mentors promote creativity and problem-solving in Making as well as improve recruitment and retention for women in STEM fields [38]. When working with students with disabilities, mentorship can be crucial for both tackling Maker projects and feeling welcome in the Makerspace [1].

Youth-oriented Makerspaces and Maker Faires should be welcoming not only for students but also their family and others, such as therapists or aids for students with disabilities [1]. One way to increase accessibility and make spaces more welcoming is "to bring maker kits and tools to places where these underrepresented groups gather" [20]. Calabrese-Barton described the benefits of running a Maker program out of two Boys and Girls Clubs in the Midwest [9]. Students could easily interact with others at the club not participating in the Maker program, and youth brought their funds of knowledge from home, school, peers, online, etc. into the Makerspace and vice versa [9]. In these youth-oriented Makerspaces, students problem-solved based on youth histories, connected to their networks to engage with social issues, and promoted collective aims [9]. Leveraging the knowledge and community concerns of youth Makers can help redefine traditional yet undervalued practices in ways that are empowering for the individual and community [3] and challenge normative views on Making and STEM participation [9].

The Maker Movement offers various ways to learn and conceptualize science, and could provide alternative or additional ways to engage in STEM for underrepresented groups. However, the educational side of the Maker Movement is still in its infancy, and educators and researchers are struggling with how to best implement and assess these learning practices [18, 28]. Substantial research is needed to prepare educators to lead Maker-type activities [28], maximize resource use to engender deep rather than superficial understanding [4], and draw from underrepresented groups' funds of knowledge [9]. Much more remains to be explored in relation to underrepresented groups in Making. In particular, there is very little research on Latina young women and their ways of speaking and acting associated with engaging in collective, artistic, community-oriented Maker projects. How do these novice Makers adopt and adapt tools, and in doing so position themselves in relation to Making or science?

PARTICIPANTS AND CONTEXT

The Study

This research is part of a larger NSF fellowship project to develop a Makerspace program at a youth center in Southern California near a major research university. The youth-oriented Makerspace was developed from an initiative to strengthen university-community ties, given longstanding disparities in income, formal education, and social services [7]. Our intentional stance is that Maker projects promote deeper connections and opportunities for social and educational development when they arise from authentic activities in the teens' everyday lives as community members. Notably, activities can still provide grounding in STEM content and literacies necessary to implement Maker projects.

Research Site

The Teen Center provides bilingual after-school programs for 100 youth in grades 6-12 and their families. Over 90 percent of the teen participants are Latino and come from low income immigrant families. Their programs address issues of youth safety and risky behaviors, low test scores and high dropout rates among Latino youth. Teens participate daily in tutoring programs, homework groups, and recreation and enrichment activities. Youth benefit from mentoring relationships, counseling, and community service or leadership opportunities. In addition to program activities, the site provides access to technology for homework and entertainment. Desktop computers provide a base for interfacing with other kinds of digital devices, such as microprocessors, and the Internet.

Participants

The group of participants were members of the all-female leadership group at the Teen Center. According to their volunteer contract, being a part of the group meant being "a Leader in your community and the voice of your peers in order to improve your Teen Center." Most of the leadership girls initially expressed a low regard for STEM subjects in school. However, they agreed to do Maker projects as part of their commitment to the leadership group. These joint Maker-leadership projects were often geared toward younger kids. According to Irene (one of the teen participants), "We usually make [things] for kids in the community." Sophie valued how the group would "tell people 'oh there's really cool stuff in science [for] little kids, inform them like 'this is what we did and this is how we did it,' let them know what's behind it." The group's participation in the Children's Day family festival demonstrates the blend between the leadership and Makerspace teams. Every spring the leadership group designs and leads booths related to Teen Center activities at Children's Day. Last year they designed and created the Bean Bag Toss as a faire game to engage families and to encourage younger children to join the Makerspace.

Figure 1. Inside and outside of the Teen Center.

Figure 2. Participating in the university Maker Faire.

At the time of the study, Irene, Esperanza, Malia, Isabel, and Sophie were 7th graders while Valentina and Alexa were freshman. (All participant names are pseudonyms). Irene, Isabel, Valentina, Esperanza, and Alexa were more interested in the art and design aspects of most projects while Malia and Sophie were more technology and science oriented. Sophie and Malia were considered "smart" and "good at Math and Science" by their peers while the other girls admitted more difficulty in these subjects at school and said they were not known for their science or math abilities.

At the beginning of the year, the girls had limited or no knowledge about circuits and capacitive touch sensing. None of them had ever used electronic tools such as a Touchboard microprocessor, or associated materials of conductive paint or copper tape. Only Irene and Sophie had previously used a power drill, and only once before. They were comfortable searching for sounds on Google and browsing YouTube but were inexperienced in the process of downloading sounds and converting between different formats. When they created the poster and posted online about their project, they were already familiar with Google docs and compiling information but the "how-to" site Instructables.com was new.

THEORETICAL FRAMEWORK

Cultural Historical Activity Theory

Employing Cultural Historical Activity Theory (CHAT) allowed us to examine how the young women talked about their project, delegated tasks, and used tools to develop expertise and achieved goals over time. In this framework, identity is conceptualized through the performance of subjects, as agents who learn how to engage with others to attain goals. This requires that subjects adhere to rules or norms for how to interact, and that they position themselves by dividing their labor or roles according to group objectives and desired outcomes. More proximally, subjects author their experiences through conceptual and physical tools to achieve immediate objectives that eventually lead to more transformative outcomes. Identity is a complex and

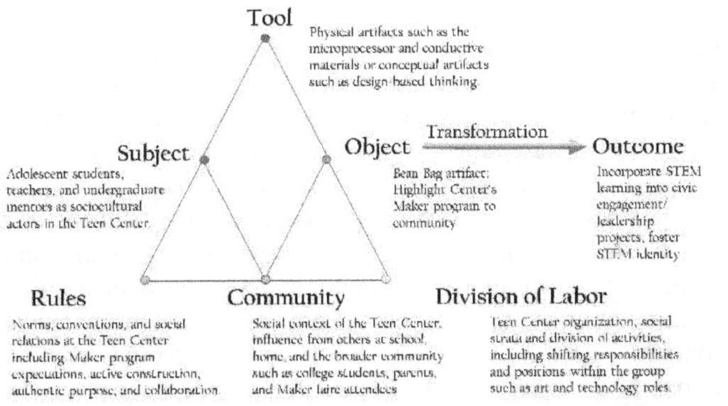

Figure 3. Representation of the components of the activity system within the Bean Bag Project at the Teen Center.

ever-changing trajectory constructed by discourse and practices, while constructing them as well [27]. From a CHAT perspective, collaboration among participants requires developing an awareness of each other's contributions to ensure successful teamwork. This collaboration is also an opportunity for team members to learn other members' roles, thus allowing for the transfer of skills and roles across participants.

Figure 4 summarizes this notion of an activity system [14] constituting our Makerspace. Accordingly, we considered the young women participants, undergraduate facilitators, graduate researchers, and staff as socio-cultural actors in the transformative activity system of the Teen Center. We explored how students built an electronically-mediated object and how conceptual and physical tools interacted with norms, division of labor, and community relationships to generate a new and enduring social space for STEM identity development.

In particular, tool use in fabricating bean bag artifacts provides insight into project development and the young women's enactment as novice Makers. Appropriation, or the ways people take up and modify tools, is key to understanding the learning process and how people develop social practices [35]. Active participation allows students "to reconstruct the knowledge they learn, thus transforming both their conception of the knowledge and in turn that knowledge

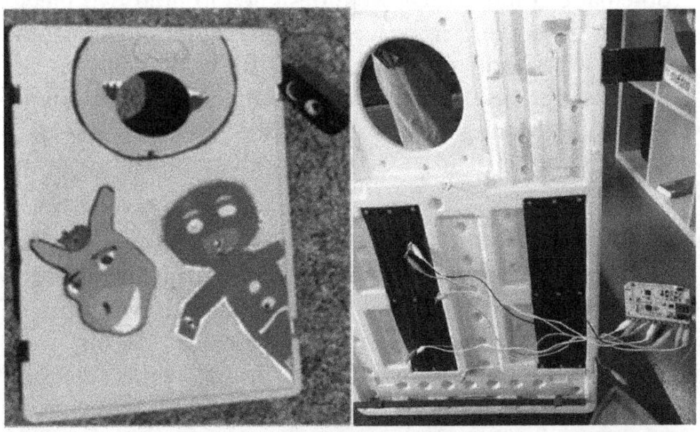

Figure 4. Front and back of Bean Bag Stand, painted with conductive ink and connected to Touchboard microprocessor.

as it is construed and used by others" [35]. We examined conceptual tool use throughout the project, considering Smagorinsky's five degrees of appropriation for conceptual tools: lack of appropriation, appropriating a label, surface features, conceptual underpinnings, and reaching mastery [17, 35].

Sense, Analyze, and Act

We also considered tool use in relation to a "sense, analyze, and act" framework which explains how electronic entities sense cues, process information, and respond [25]. Even simple robot hardware and an electronic circuit can interpret electronic signals. Electronically controlled devices chemically, electrically, and physically sense environmental information, process and analyze sensory information, and actuate, creating an output that makes something happen in the real world [25]. This type of framing can help students develop an understanding of tools such as microprocessors and associated concepts such as capacitive touch sensing.

METHODS

We observed 7 Latina students (aged 13-15) in the bean bag project activity, collecting ethnographic notes on the young women's design process during the project. We traced dialogic exchanges and multimodal practices across time [16], to examine how youths worked collaboratively. We studied how participants adopted tools and scientific practices tied to their unique and shared group experiences, and to their emerging technical expertise as Makers working with electronics and fabrication.

This paper addresses the following research questions: How did this group of novice Makers develop expertise using new tools? How did the young women use conceptual tools in relation to the physical Maker tools?

Data Sources

The data sources are from a yearlong ethnographic study, with particular focus on the quarter-long Bean Bag Project. For the Bean Bag Project we examined 7 hours of video data, recorded on 10 days, spanning 3 months. The videotaped sessions provided an account of interactions and project development. Reviewing the video data "allowed us to revisit salient episodes of students/teacher interaction that were essential to how scientific meaning was discursively constructed" [31].

We also collected digital photographs of final student products (Bean Bag Stand), as well as products throughout the process (sketches, notes from brainstorming, lists of roles, web posts). Other data sources include undergraduate field notes, analytic memos, and focus group exit interviews with the youth participants.

Qualitative Analysis

We first performed descriptive coding [32], transcribing video segments and then constructing representations of events to consider chains of actions [2]. We created transcripts to depict micro-level communication and event maps to illustrate larger scale activity [16]. An overall event map was created to reveal the progression of different projects, as well as a minute by minute event map for sessions to indicate patterns of activity and roles. In our findings, we provided examples of transcript dialogue and descriptions as evidence of student use of internalized conceptual tools, of appropriated ways of talking and acting that demonstrate scientific practices and ways of thinking [31]. These examples illustrate the ways participants articulated their projects and employed scientific sensemaking by "appropriating collectively co-constructed practices that they had a part in defining" [31].

After descriptive coding, we used MaxQDA12 software to direct code the video. We performed emergent coding in alignment with CHAT to designate themes [32]. The preliminary coding scheme was refined through group discussion. Next pattern coding was used to organize codes into smaller sets [32]. A second researcher went through one session's video and coded independently for calibrating purposes. Disparities prompted discussion which helped to refine codes. Then the second researcher independently coded randomly selected video segments. Researchers agreed on over 80% of codes, providing a satisfactory degree of inter-coder reliability. After coding all 6 videos, we returned to the earliest videos and checked codes to account for a potential "definitional drift in coding" [15]. The codes from the videos were triangulated with text from the analytic memos, field notes, and student focus group transcript to verify across sources and warrant claims about outcomes [13].

RESULTS

Building from Smagorinsky's degrees of appropriation [17], we identified three levels of conceptual tool use in the Bean Bag Project: *Familiarizing, Labeling, and Understanding.* Familiarizing included everyday connections and innovative applications to capture how the young women applied what they knew from other contexts in both conventional and unconventional ways. Carrying out the project and communicating about it revealed both internal and external components. Internal to the group, the girls used non-technical terms or "insider labels" for materials and tools, while switching to more scientific language when posting online and preparing for presentations. Similarly, the girls demonstrated distinct forms of understanding when creating the project within the group versus explaining to others beyond the group.

Conceptual Tool Use	Sublevels
Familiarizing	Everyday connections Innovative applications
Labeling	Insider labels Scientific labels
Understanding	Functional understanding Conceptual understanding

Table 1. Levels and sublevels of conceptual tool use.

Familiarizing

In this section we describe *Familiarizing*, or becoming acquainted with new tools and applying, repurposing, or remixing associated practices. The two sub-constructs of familiarizing are *everyday connections* and *innovating applications*. In everyday connections, we present examples of the young women realizing commonalities between the Maker tools which initially seemed very foreign and sometimes intimidating. We also describe how they applied existing knowledge to new contexts in similar ways. Innovative applications illustrated how the young women transposed what they knew to novel contexts in unconventional or unexpected ways.

Everyday Connections

Even though the concepts of "engineering design" and "Making" and the related electronic tools were new, the young women often found similarities between the new materials and their everyday experiences. For example, when the teacher introduced the lithium ion battery, Sophie and Irene realized that they had seen it before in "cheapy phones...when they're falling and the battery comes out." Often the young women applied this everyday knowledge to use new materials in conventional ways. For example, the girls with the most artistic experience, Alexa and Irene, applied what they knew about acrylic painting on posters to using conductive paint within the new context of the bean bag stand. Even though they had no experience doing a Maker project that integrated technology with art, they were able to leverage their art abilities (perspective, design elements) to develop new types of expertise and share them with others.

Innovative Applications

Other times the lack of experience with the new materials or tools led to alternative or unconventional solutions. The use of the drill was unconventional, where the screws did not serve the typical interlocking purpose. Instead, the girls inserted screws to link the painted front of the stand to the wires and Touchboard on the back. Also, after Sophie accidently broke the pilot-hole drill bit, the girls decided to use screws and a hammer to make the pilot holes. This resulted in some crooked screws, which might have been problematic if the screws were designed to hold two pieces together. However, it proved a good solution since the screws were only used to link the wires from the Touchboard's electrode terminals to the front of the stand. The young women innovated based on their budding understanding of hand tools, to solve the problem given the constraints.

Labeling

Labeling represented how the young women and the facilitator referred to tools and materials. The two types of labels were *insider* and *scientific*. Insider labels were informal and only used within the group, while scientific labels were more formal and only used for outside the group purposes such as posting online.

Insider Labels

After gaining familiarity with the new tools, the young women would often devise their own labels. While the facilitator referred to the materials and tools by the official label of "alligator clips" or "Touchboard" the girls used more familiar labels. For example, they referred to the alligator clips as "wires" or jokingly called them "los cables." They called the conductive paint and fabric as "special" rather than "conductive." They referred to the Touchboard and other parts interchangeably as "thingy." Many of the girls continued to refer to the Touchboard as "Makey Thing" or "Makey" even though the group had transitioned away from using the MakeyMakey brand version after the first day. After the facilitator pointed out it was not a MakeyMakey, but a Touchboard, they referred to it as the "board thing" or "touchpad." The young women were connecting the physical tools correctly, but using a modified vocabulary to refer to these tools that was easier to understand and more accepted by the group than their technical terms. It wasn't until they needed to make their materials and process visible to others that they referred to the microprocessor more consistently as the Touchboard, and the fabric and paint as conductive.

Scientific Labels

The appropriation of the more "scientific labels" didn't happen until the girls were expected to explain how the project worked to other people. They understood that others would not understand their terms, even though these terms made it easier to communicate and built up a sense of group membership during the project. When Irene and Sophie practiced explaining for Children's Day or the Maker Faire, the facilitator introduced more scientific labels, and the girls were focused on using terms others could understand. The girls also worried about their audience and language when writing the online tutorial. Sophie worried that "They'll be like 'This sucks!...They'll be like 'More description!'" She wanted to be accurate and communicate in a way that was clear to others outside the group. Therefore, she listed out the "supplies" using formal labels rarely used while constructing the bean bag toss. Alexa, Sophie, Irene, and Malia asked the facilitator questions or looked up details about tools and materials to include more information in the tutorial. For example, including "Lipo Battery (3.7v)", or "acrylic" and "conductive" as the paint labels. Some names were negotiated at that point, such as "Plastic Bean Bag Stand." These labels were designed to clarify parts and steps for others to replicate the project, but also helped the young women realize they were part of a bigger community using these labels. When Sophie switched from "special" to "conductive" and searched for "conductive paint" on Google, she realized that other people were using and talking about the same materials. She exclaimed, "That's *our* paint!" and noted that they were part of a bigger group of Makers sharing their ideas and creations.

Understanding

In this section, we discuss the different types of understanding the young women demonstrated throughout the process of building the artifact. We divided understanding into *functional* and *conceptual* components.

Functional understanding refers to a more limited understanding of a tool, developed from the concept of "surface feature appropriation." In this type of learning, the student "is making some effort to grasp the official conception, yet is succeeding in doing so only at the surface level" [17]. The learner might not fully understand part-whole connections between different features of the tool or project but is able to appropriate tools to create a functional product. In contrast, conceptual understanding requires a theoretical grasp of the tool's purpose. Conceptual understanding is more abstract and equips learners with the ability to apply what they've learned to new contexts.

To connect the components and produce a working game, the girls needed some degree of functional understanding, but not necessarily any of the conceptual understanding. However, they did need an understanding of the science behind their project (e.g. capacitive touch sensing) to explain to children and parents how the project worked. While functional understanding was important throughout, it was foregrounded during the construction process. Traces of conceptual understanding appeared during building, but most evidence occurred after construction was complete when the young women were practicing their presentations or creating informational displays.

Functional Understanding

Functional understanding, or grasping how the project worked as a whole and how the pieces fit together, was most prominent in the middle of the project. At this point, the young women had finished downloading sounds and were adding conductive materials and connecting the Touchboard. During these sessions, the discussion was often about how to make the project work, which included what certain tools did, and their role in the project. First, the young women needed to understand the cause and effect of placing screws in key areas, then painting around them to broaden the conductive area. In the Instructables entry that Sophie and Malia wrote to describe how to create their project, they wrote "We drilled holes on the places we wanted to hear a sound. We put screws into the holes. for example we put three screws in Shrek's face." They did not explain the science behind the process, but they made a connection between where they drilled and the sound effect. They further instructed: "The screws and the touch board were connected by alligator clips. Don't forget to test it out before to make sure the sounds are right for each character" illustrating the connection between the screws in the bean bag stand and the Touchboard with the sounds. They also stressed the importance of this step, checking which points trigger which sound, or attaching the wires from the desired electrode terminal on the Touchboard to the correct screws to pair up correctly. They then explained the purpose of using conductive materials and painting around the screws to broaden the electrically conducting area that the bean bag could strike:

> we also used conductive paint on the top side of the screws. we used conductive paint so that all of the board makes a sound when anything conductive touches it. you have to use conductive fabric wrapped around the beanbag so that it worked when it touches the conductive paint.

This explanation of the conductive paint and conductive bean bags as creating bigger targets and triggers demonstrated understanding of the interaction between components, and the beginnings of conceptual underpinnings of conductivity and touch capacitance. Adding the conductive paint was a key step in the project, where the girls juggled including the conductive paint in a way that increased each electrode's trigger area, did not interfere with surrounding trigger points, and looked aesthetically pleasing. Alexa, Isabel, and Irene were part of the art group outlining the figures with electrically conductive materials, and had the longest discussions about how to outline figures without crossing paint or copper tape lines. Irene called this, "the hardest job." The facilitator explained the design constraints in a few different ways, including explaining the science behind the process, but Irene and Isabel did not understand until Sophie presented a more straightforward explanation that focused on concrete steps. The facilitator started by explaining:

> What you don't want is for these two to touch each other, so if you're going around that's good but don't do it going around and to each one. {Gesturing, pointing at Shrek}...So, when you're going around you want it to touch one of them but not all of them. Cause if you touch two, it's going to short circuit so electricity is not going to go where you want it to. {Pointing to gingerbread man}

Though the concept of electricity and short circuit was alluded to by the facilitator, there was not further explanation about what a short circuit means electrically, or why it would not allow an electrical circuit to operate as intended. After Isabel expressed confusion, the facilitator focused on the specific process needed to complete the section rather than further explaining concepts:

FACILITATOR: So you don't want this, that's going around, it can touch one of these and then have (a) break and touch another one but you just don't want it to be touching the same (screw) {Isabel looks confused}
Sophie: Okay, so you want to outline this and touch that, okay? But if you like outline it again with the same color and it touches this it won't work.
Irene: I still don't get you there.
Isabel: Oh, so this one, while touching this one can't touch this one. Okay I get it.

Ultimately, it was Sophie who helped the others understand this crucial part of the project. After this discussion, the girls finished adding the conductive materials and began to test their product. While creating a working electronic bean bag stand demonstrated functional understanding and conceptual underpinnings, deeper conceptual understanding wasn't made explicit until they were asked to explain their project to others.

Conceptual Understanding

Conceptual understanding goes beyond the *how* of making the project and includes *why* the tool and project worked, or a scientific or theoretical understanding of the tool. Awareness of certain scientific processes can emerge from understanding how electronic devices sense cues, process information, and actuate [25]. In this section, we examine the progression of dialogue and expression of different parts of the "sense, analyze, and act" process. The conversations revealed gradual understanding of the functioning of the Touchboard microprocessor and the basic science behind electricity, circuits, capacitance, and permittivity. In particular, Sophie and Irene's participation illustrated distinct ways of understanding the "sense, analyze, act" process. Sophie focused on conductive material sensors while Irene honed in on the analyze step, making connections between the Touchboard and other touch sensing devices.

Sense, Analyze, and Act

When the young women first started, they were new to most of the materials and tools. Though they expressed the general concept of *actuate* by saying, "We're making Shrek have a sound," they did not have the conceptual understanding of how that happened and voiced dissatisfaction with their own explanation. When the site coordinator questioned how the Shrek-themed bean bag toss could attract new participants to the Makerspace, Malia demonstrated dropping the bean bag into the hole, "Look, when it goes in, it's going to say something, yah. And they're going to go, 'That's cool!' And we're going to go, 'Join [the program]!'" At this point the site coordinator lacked confidence in their ability to explain the project to children because the girls were solely focused on the *actuate* part of the process, or triggering the sound.

A week before their demonstration at Children's Day, Irene and Sophie were still unable to explain what was happening on a conceptual level. The site coordinator stressed the importance of explaining the project and Sophie flippantly responded that she would tell children and families, "What's up homey-g?" Irene was terse in her explanation, "It's a project that we did, okay?" Others expressed dissatisfaction with Irene and Sophie's explanation and suggested that Malia or Alexa man the booth instead because they were more articulate. However, with prompting from the facilitator, Sophie and Irene were able to explain what *senses* and *analyzes* in order to produce the sound and why certain materials were used:

FACILITATOR: But beyond the conductive fabric, what's happening when --you touch it?
Sophie: --Um, it has the special paint.
FACILITATOR: Yah, it has conductive paint, conductive fabric and conductive paint.
Sophie: And they pair up and it makes noise.

Sophie demonstrated an understanding of capacitive touch sensing and needing a certain type of object, which is "special" in order to produce a response. The "special paint" acted as a *sensor* and the noise, or *actuation*, didn't happen unless there was an interaction. She stated that a person's finger or the bean bag "pair up" with the conductive paint to make noise. The Touchboard *analyzed* this incoming information, which was part of the "pair up" necessary to act, or produce a sound. The facilitator continued along this line of logic:

FACILITATOR: Remember how it works like your phone, with the --touch sensing?
Irene: --You mean like the touchable, itouch, --iphone
FACILITATOR: --So you can tell people it works like your phone, it senses your finger is interrupting the electric field.
Sophie: Except with this thing it's conductive stuff.
FACILITATOR: Yes, yah, that's it. Conductive, but your finger also works, right? {Sets off Gingy sound: *Tell me! Not my gumdrop buttons!*} So your finger you're interrupting the electric field around the electrode on the board or this is, anything that conducts electricity will also interrupt the electric field. Just like your phone, if you try to do it with the fabric gloves on it doesn't work because your finger isn't interrupting or --making issues with the electric field.
Sophie: --With the frabric. Fabric.

Afterward Sophie asked about a material that hadn't yet been mentioned, showing she was digging deeper and making connections about the sensing process beyond what was discussed:

Sophie: What are we going to tell them about the tape?
FACILITATOR: So, what do you think?
Sophie: It's like the same thing as the paint.
FACILITATOR: Yah, so it's made of copper, the metal conducts. You could have done it with steel, iron, any metal, but copper is easy to make into tape. That's a good thing to show them too, that it's not just the paint but also the screw is made out of metal, the copper tape is made out of metal.
Sophie: So basically it has to have like a metal something?
FACILITATOR: Yah it has to conduct and metal is a really good conductor. But you also conduct electricity. There's a lot of things that conduct but metal conducts really well.

These conversations revealed applications to other materials and contexts, such as that all metals conduct electricity well, or that other touch screens use capacitive touch sensing. When further prompted, Sophie proceeded to explain how touch capacitance worked in her own words:

FACILITATOR: Okay, so what do you guys say when someone says, "How does this work?"
Sophie: "You have conductive fraaabic…Fabric. And then the conductive paint thingy and when you hit it, it makes a noise with the touchpad, and the touchpad is like your phone that gets it but instead with your finger works with the conductive stuff. BOOM. {high fives Irene}

Sophie related the Touchboard to a phone with a processor that "gets it," or *analyzes* after the screen *senses* someone's finger. She specified that a finger can trigger the response, but so does "conductive stuff." Conductive materials "work with" with the Touchboard, where the conductive paint is the sensor set off by the conductive bean bag. As she stated earlier, the conductive elements "pair up." After *sensing* and *analyzing* the change in permittivity, the Touchboard *acts* by producing the sound effect. That's where the magic happens, hence the "BOOM." After further discussion that emphasized the vocabulary of "capacitive touch sensing" Irene wrote on the poster: "The sensor senses objects that change the electric field. It can sense anything that is conductive or that has a significantly different permittivity than air. Any touchscreen device also works with capacitive sensing."

Although the process is complicated, the young women demonstrated an understanding of the Touchboard as a processor within a family of devices that all sense a change and process this information. Their understanding of a capacitive touch sensor as "sensing a change in the electric field" might seem surface level, but they articulated that the paint and copper tape acted as a sensor, and that a conductive material triggered a response from the Touchboard.

These conversations about the Touchboard and capacitive touch sensing were considered conceptual underpinnings rather than deep understanding or mastery since it was the young women's first Maker project and they were missing more in-depth and nuanced understanding about electricity, circuits, capacitance, and permittivity. But this project provided an entry point, and the expectation that they could explain the project to others provided rationale and encouragement to understand on a deeper level beyond making the project work.

Beyond the Project

Since conceptual understanding helps learners apply what they have learned to new contexts, we briefly considered applications outside the construction of the Bean Bag Toss.

In the exit interview, two of the girls mentioned learning about circuits in Physics, and most of the young women expressed increased confidence in their abilities to operate the Touchboard. Valentina stated that she felt differently about herself as a Maker at the end because "cause I know how to use the Touchboard" to which Alexa responded, "Yeah so now like if we're working on it at school be like I know how to do that." The facilitator validated their experiences and competence with the tool by stating, "Yeah you guys can be the experts in that." The facilitator positioned the teens as experts in relation to other classmates, and on their way to developing a deeper understanding in future projects. However, despite developing confidence with the Touchboard, most of the young women expressed in the exit interview that they needed to master more tools to have the skillset of "hundred percent" Makers. They embraced their understanding and skillset, while realizing that claiming an identity or mastering something is a long-term endeavor. Still, it is worth noting that the young women have continued to participate in long-term Maker projects and three of the five eligible girls were accepted this year to an elite engineering academy within a local high school.

DISCUSSION

This study provided insight into how a group of young women adapted and adopted new Maker practices and tools while positioning themselves in a collaborative, artistic project. Whether working with paint, power tools, or microprocessors, the girls applied their existing knowledge to develop familiarity with new tools. Sometimes the young women superimposed an existing framework to apply to another domain with similar applications, while other times they repurposed tools to suit their needs. The variety of project materials and tools allowed for various ways of engaging and personalizing the project. Drawing and painting were tasks the girls had more experience with, and using materials such as conductive paint provided an entry point to new digital fabrication tools. The girls shared art-oriented advice related to design and perspective while referencing art in daily life such as painting nails, putting on makeup, or building furniture with relatives. Incorporating drawing and painting to the digital fabrication process appeared to leverage "'women-centric knowledge' without an overreliance upon women-dominated activities" [20]. Overall, the artistic and collaborative elements helped the young women relate to and feel more comfortable with new materials, demonstrate their design skills, and gain expertise in areas previously unfamiliar to them.

Various forms of expertise also helped to expand the definition of Maker and provide "alternative cultures" within STEM for young women [38]. The girls were performing as Makers and science people when considering different uses for materials, operating and connecting components, creating instructional guides, and explaining how the tool or project worked to others. They negotiated and made visible their competence by engaging in scientific practice and discourse. They were recognized by their peers and people outside the group as Makers, which some researchers consider as important as mastering STEM content [12]. In alignment with other studies, identifying as Makers helped our youth integrate diverse learning experiences [24] and positioned them as technologically and scientifically capable of creating things for themselves or others [12].

Successfully producing a functional bean bag stand was also important because it fostered a sense of pride and motivation to share. Sharing was crucial to developing a deeper level of understanding that went beyond the surface features of the tools and how they worked together. On its own, creating the project allowed for engagement, innovation, and the understanding necessary to produce a functional bean bag stand. However, the context of the final faire demonstration as a learning experience shared with younger children appeared to be the largest motivator for developing scientific understanding and communication. Girls in other Maker projects have expressed a preference to make for others rather than themselves, and tend to find the community orientation motivating and sustaining [20, 38]. Our research supports this motivational aspect for young women when designing and completing their project, and adds the importance of dialogue with community for deepening learning and improving scientific understanding. The girls were motivated by the need to accurately communicate to others outside the group how the project worked. They realized that the terms used in their working group would not make sense to outsiders, and adjusted their speech and online posts accordingly. Teaching others also positioned the young women as more expert Makers and mentors for younger children and family members who attended the Children's Day or Maker Faire festivals.

Other researchers have documented increased dedication and learning from children teaching others in comparison to learning for their own benefit [10]. Referred to as the "Protégé effect," the phenomenon has even been demonstrated with middle school students instructing online "teachable agents" such as a computer program called Betty's Brain [10]. The researchers hypothesized that guiding the teachable agent Betty motivated learning by promoting responsibility, encouraging revision, and protecting against failure [10]. The idea of increased responsibility is especially relevant in our project, where the young women realized they represented their group and the Makerspace as a whole when trying to recruit younger children. Multiple times the girls presenting the information were scrutinized by their peers to present an explanation that everyone felt comfortable with. Being held responsible to others was a motivating and guiding influence, and the site coordinator often provided criticism by asking the group to consider how others would understand their design. These discussions helped avoid the issue mentioned in other Maker projects where teachers were unable to assess relevance and worried about hampering creativity by providing feedback. When presenting their final products, those students "were unable to discuss the complexity of the context, the qualities of their output, or their choices during the process" [36]. In contrast, in our project the outside audience helped structure feedback from staff, mentors, and other students. The audience provided a context to reflect on decisions and to practice and refine explanations. In general, the specific audience could help mitigate the "process-related challenges" in Maker education, including delineating the project scope, communicating and negotiating ideas, and expressing and critiquing designs [36]. Productive failure and redesign are well-known learning devices in Maker programs, but it is also important to consider failure and revision in relation to *communicating* about the products and process. In this sense, the communication process can be considered a conceptual tool to tinker with and ultimately better understand the science beyond making a functional end product.

CONCLUSION

In this article, we presented the three levels of conceptual tool use, *Familiarizing*, *Labeling*, and *Understanding*, as important processes for both creating the electronic bean bag game and explaining functional and conceptual components to others. Building on previous knowledge resulted in both conventional and innovative applications and allowed for engagement in relation to artistic, technical, and scientific factors throughout the project. The program framing drew from a body of research on alternative approaches to include women in science [5] and a handful of recent studies on engaging underrepresented groups in Making [1, 20, 29, 38].

Our program included intentional framing and design and targeted a variety of interests and abilities, improving accessibility to novices [1, 20, 29]. Undergraduate and graduate student mentors provided project-related guidance and general STEM-related mentorship [29, 38]. Also, like the Makerspaces developed in Boys and Girls Clubs, our program occurred at an afterschool Teen Center, a place the young women considered accessible and welcoming [9]. We drew from students' individual and collective interests and embedded cognitive program goals while still allowing the students to maintain control and ownership. This combination led the students to develop the functional and conceptual understanding required to build the project and explain the science behind it to others. The community audience embedded a challenge and yet clearer teaching and learning goals.

Maker education, especially in afterschool settings, can be portrayed as student-centered with minimal guidance. However, we presented an example of a successful collaborative project guided by adult mentorship and framed by a community audience. We fostered student engagement and ownership while offering intellectually useful tools to carry out goals. Although our study was limited in generalizability due to only looking at one site and 7 Latina young women participating in the project, our findings could apply to Maker projects both in afterschool sites and schools, especially when working with girls and other underrepresented groups. Regardless of the site, we advocate for projects that include an authentic audience and time dedicated to practicing and revising communication with this audience.

Still more research is needed to understand how underrepresented groups adapt and adopt new Maker practices and tools. In particular, we should consider how groups traditionally excluded from STEM position themselves in community-oriented Maker projects, and how participation could increase accessibility and ultimately equity in STEM fields.

ACKNOWLEDGEMENTS

We would like to thank the participating students, facilitators, and Teen Center staff involved in this research.

This material is based upon work supported by the National Science Foundation Graduate Research Fellowship under Grant No. DGE 1144085. Any opinion, findings, and conclusions or recommendations expressed in this material are those of the authors(s) and do not necessarily reflect the views of the National Science Foundation.

REFERENCES

1. Meryl Alper. 2013. Making space in the makerspace: Building a mixed-ability maker culture. In *Proceedings of the ACM Conference on Interaction Design and Children* (IDC 2013).
2. Douglas Baker, Judith L. Green, and Audra Skukauskaite. 2008. Video-enabled ethnographic research: A microethnographic perspective. *How to Do Educational Research*: 77–114.
3. Paulo Blikstein. 2008. Travels in Troy with Freire: technology as an agent for emancipation. In *Social Justice Education for Teachers: Paulo Freire and the Possible Dream,* P. Noguera & C. A. Torres (eds.). Sense, Rotterdam, Netherlands, 205-244.
4. Paulo Blikstein and Marcelo Worsley. 2016. Children are not hackers: Building a culture of powerful ideas, deep learning, and equity in the maker movement. In *Makeology: Makerspaces as learning environments*, Kylie Peppler, Erica Rosenfeld Halverson and Yasmin B. Kafai (eds.). Taylor & Francis, New York, NY, 64–79.
5. Nancy W. Brickhouse, Patricia Lowery, & Katherine Schultz. 2000. What kind of a girl does science? The construction of school science identities. *J R Sci Teach*, 37, 5: 441–458.
6. Leah Buechley. 2016. Inclusive Maker Ed: STEM is everywhere. Keynote speech presented at FabLearn '16. Retrieved November 2, 2016 from https://edstream.stanford.edu/Video/Play/a33992cc9fb2496488c1afa9b6204a571d
7. Melinda Burns. 2016. Is Isla Vista Growing Up? Retrieved June 20, 2016 from http://www.independent.com/news/2016/mar/03/isla-vista-growing/
8. Angela Calabrese Barton and Edna Tan. 2015. Designing equity-oriented Makerspaces Part II: Responding to the equity challenges. Retrieved October 1, 2015 from http://invincibility.us/?p=238
9. Angela Calabrese Barton, Edna Tan, and Day Greenberg. 2016. The Makerspace Movement: Sites of possibilities for equitable opportunities to engage underrepresented youth in STEM. *Teachers College Record.* To appear.
10. Catherine Chase, Doris Chin, Marily Oppezzo, and Daniel Schwartz. 2009. Teachable agents and the protégé effect: increasing the effort towards learning. *Journal of Science Education and Technology* 18, 4: 334-352.
11. Gloria Crisp and Amaury Nora. *Overview of Hispanics in Science, Mathematics, Engineering and Technology (STEM): K-16 representation, preparation and participation*. Hispanic Association of Colleges and Universities, 2006.
12. Sharon Chu, Francis Quek, Sourabh Bhangaonkar, Amy Ging, and Kumar Sridharamurthy. 2015. Making the Maker: A Means-to-an-Ends approach to nurturing the Maker mindset in elementary-aged children. *International Journal of Child-Computer Interaction*, 5, 11–19. http://doi.org/10.1016/j.ijcci.2015.08.002
13. Design-Based Research Collective. 2003. Design-based research: An emerging paradigm for educational inquiry. *Educational Researcher* 32, 1: 5–8.

14. Yrjö Engeström. 1987. *Learning by Expanding: An Activity-Theoretical Approach to Developmental Research.* Orienta-Konsultit.

15. Graham R. Gibbs. 2007. *Analyzing Qualitative Data.* Sage.

16. Judith L. Green, Audra Skukauskaite, and Douglas Baker. 2012. Ethnography as Epistemology. In *Research Methodologies and Methods in Education,* James Arthur, Michael Waring, Robert Coe and Larry V. Hedges (eds.). Sage, London, UK, 309-321.

17. Pam Grossman, Peter Smagorinsky, and Shelia Valenica. 1999. Appropriating tools for teaching English: A theoretical framework for research on learning to teach. *American Journal of Education* 108, 1: 1–29.

18. Erica Halverson and Kimberly Sheridan. 2014. The maker movement in education. *Harvard Educational Review* 84, 4: 495–505.

19. Catherine Hill, Christianne Corbett, and Andresse St. Rose. *Why so few? Women in Science, Technology, Engineering, and Mathematics.* American Association of University Women, 2010.

20. Nathan Holbert. 2016. Bots for tots : building inclusive makerspaces by leveraging "ways of knowing ." In *Proceedings of the ACM Conference on Interaction Design and Children* (IDC 2016), 79–88. http://doi.org/10.1145/2930674.2930718

21. Margaret Honey and David E. Kanter (eds.). 2013. *Design, Make, Play: Growing the Next Generation of STEM Innovators.* Routledge.

22. Lee Martin. 2015. The promise of the Maker Movement for education. *Journal of Pre-College Engineering Education Research* 5, 1: 30-39.

23. Lee Martin, Colin Dixon, and Danielle Hagood. 2014. Distributed adaptations in youth making. In *Proceedings of the ACM FabLearn Conference on Creativity and Fabrication in Education.*

24. Lee Martin and Colin Dixon. 2013. Youth conceptions of Making and the Maker Movement. In *Proceedings of the ACM Conference on Interaction Design and Children* (IDC 2013).

25. Modular Robotics. *Using Cubelets to Explore Behavior.* 2012. Retrieved January 5, 2017 from https://www.modrobotics.com/education/lesson-plans/elementary-school/a-b-3-using-cubelets-to-explore-behavior/

26. National Science Foundation, National Center for Science and Engineering Statistics. *Women, minorities, and persons with disabilities in science and engineering: 2013.* Special Report NSF 13-304, 2013.

27. William R. Penuel and James Wertsch. 1995. Vygotsky and identity formation: A sociocultural approach. *Educational Psychologist* 30, 2: 83-92.

28. Kylie Peppler, Erica Rosenfeld Halverson and Yasmin B. Kafai. 2016. *Makeology: Makerspaces as learning environments.* Taylor & Francis, New York, NY, 64–79.

29. Paula Rees, Christine Olson, Charles Schweik, and Steven Brewer. 2015. Exploring the role of makerspaces and flipped learning in a town-gown effort to engage K12 students in STEAM. *In Proceedings of the ASEE Annual Conference & Exposition.*

30. Mitchel Resnick and Eric Rosenbaum. 2013. Designing for tinkerability. In *Design, make, play: Growing the next generation of STEM innovators*, Margaret Honey and David E. Kanter (eds.). Routledge, New York, NY, 163–181.

31. John M. Reveles, Gregory J. Kelly, and Richard P. Durán. 2007. A sociocultural perspective on mediated activity in third grade science. *Cultural Studies of Science Education* 1, 3: 467–495.

32. Johnny Saldaña. 2009. *The Coding Manual for Qualitative Researchers.* Sage Publications.

33. Mike Sharples, Patrick McAndrew, Martin Weller, Rebecca Ferguson, Elizabeth FitzGerald, Tony Hirst, and Mark Gaved. *Innovating Pedagogy 2013.* The Open University, 2013.

34. Kimberly Sheridan, Erica Rosenfeld Halverson, Breanne Litts, Lisa Brahms, Lynette Jacobs-Priebe, and Trevor Owens. 2014. Learning in the making: A comparative case study of three makerspaces. *Harvard Educational Review* 84, 4: 505-531.

35. Peter Smagorinsky. 2011. *Vygotsky and Literacy Research: A Methodological Framework.* Sense Publishers.

36. Rachel Charlotte Smith, Ole Sejer Iversen, and Mikkel Hjorth. 2015. Design thinking for digital fabrication in education. *Int J Child Comput Interact,* 5: 20–28. http://doi.org/10.1016/j.ijcci.2015.10.002

37. Ming-Te Wang and Jessica Degol. 2016. Gender gap in Science, Technology, Engineering, and Mathematics (STEM): Current knowledge, implications for practice, policy and future directions. *Educ. Psychology Review.* 1-22.

38. Renee Wittemyer et al. *MakeHers: Engaging girls and women in technology through making, creating, and inventing.* Intel Global Girls and Women Initiative, 2014.

39. Kumar Yelamarthi and Ruby Mawasha. 2008. A pre-engineering program for the under-represented, low-income and/or first generation college students to pursue higher education. *J STEM Educ*, 9, 3: 5–15.

Design Guidelines for Parent-School Technologies to Support the Ecology of Parental Engagement

Marisol Wong-Villacres *
Georgia Institute of Technology
Atlanta, USA
lvillacr@gatech.edu

Escuela Superior Politecnica del Litoral
Guayaquil, Ecuador
lvillacr@espol.edu.ec

Upol Ehsan *
Georgia Institute of Technology
Atlanta, USA
ehsanu@gatech.edu

Amber Solomon
Georgia Institute of Technology
Atlanta, USA
asolomon30@gatech.edu

Mercedes Pozo Buil
Georgia Institute of Technology
Atlanta, USA
mercedes.pozo@eas.gatech.edu

Betsy DiSalvo
Georgia Institute of Technology
Atlanta, USA
bdisalvo@cc.gatech.edu

ABSTRACT
Parents' engagement in their children's education is key to children's academic success and social development. For many parents in the U.S., engagement is still a struggle partly due to a lack of communication and community-building tools that support the broader ecology of parenting, or parental ecology. Although current technologies have the potential to create opportunities to improve parental engagement, little is known about the impact of existing technology's design on the parental ecology. We present findings from 63 interviews with parents and an observation of existing technologies that support parent-school interactions. We found four critical issues that the design of current technologies need to address: (1) inflexibility in the boundaries of digital spaces, (2) inequality, (3) fragmentation and inconsistency of information, and (4) lack of relevant non-academic information. As a result, we propose design guidelines for technologies to support the parental ecology, and reflect on design issues that require further research.

ACM Classification Keywords
H.5.3 Group and Organization Interfaces: Computer-supported cooperative work

Author Keywords
Social Network; Parental Engagement; Schools and Teachers; Community Building; Meaningful Interactions

*Both authors equally contributed to this work

IDC '17, June 27-30, 2017, Stanford, CA, USA

DOI: http://dx.doi.org/10.1145/3078072.3079748

INTRODUCTION
Parental engagement in their children's education is key to the academic success and social development of their children [3, 6, 16]. However, for many parents in the United States, this engagement is challenging [26, 23, 15] in part because of a lack of communication and community-building tools that support the broader ecology of parenting [24, 11]. We refer to the broader ecology of parenting, or parental ecology, as the many influences on how one acts as a parent [7, 1, 5]. Our focus is to understand how digital technologies can support the parental ecology so as to augment opportunities for children to reach educational outcomes.

Schools have traditionally provided some digital communication tools, but these tools have been limited to supporting official interactions with parents, such as electronic grade reports, digital newsletters, and websites or parent portals where teachers post information [15, 8, 19]. This traditional communication tends to disenfranchise parents' ability to act outside school-created channels of communication. In addition, it ignores the engagement that happens between parents or others in the community (e.g., other parents or their children's former teachers) [15, 21]. Previous research suggests that parents have been leveraging other information technology tools to connect and interact in meaningful ways with other individuals in the parenting ecology [9]. These tools enable parents to create and maintain spaces in their parenting ecology, where they can communicate with other parents. However, we argue that these tools do not provide every parent the same opportunity to contribute their voice equitably and influence the ecology.

Regardless, technology can be a way to support more accessible, meaningful, and equitable communication to improve parental engagement. It can also open new channels of communication with schools, teachers, and other parents [13, 25]. However, there have been few studies exploring how parent-school communication technologies support community engagement [14] and how should be designed to support the parental ecology [29, 28].

To address these issues, we expand existing work on parents and technology by studying technologies' ability to facilitate meaningful interactions in the parental ecology. Based on the work of Hughes et al. [17], we define *meaningful interactions* as the communicative activities in which all parties can express their experiences and interests, and make sense of others' expressions in terms of their own particular purposes and agendas. To better understand the structures and resources that support the interactions amongst members of the ecology, we use the concept of *space* described by Barton et al. [1]. They define a *space* as a setting in which people come together to pursuit desirable outcomes. Looking at the digital and non-digital spaces of the parenting ecology allows us to identify social norms for participating in those spaces, the tools they use to support the shared participation, and the types of interactions the spaces support.

In this paper, we present the findings from 63 interviews with parents as well as observations of parents and schools/teachers interactions in existing digital spaces. This study focuses on parents as a response to parents' lack of voice in the existing communications technologies hosted by schools. We recognize that teachers and schools may have different needs and agendas for communications and are important actors in the parenting ecology. However, our findings and previous research suggest that existing technologies do not support meaningful interactions amongst individuals of the parenting ecology. Instead, these technologies tend to reinforce power and equity issues between schools and parents, as well as amongst parents.

We contribute in three ways to the growing body of research on the design of parent-school communication technologies. First, we examine existing parent-school communication technologies beyond the operational issues of their integration in schools and homes. We provide a rich description of the issues and opportunities of improvement in these technologies in terms of parental engagement within the parenting ecology. Second, drawing from our findings and inspired by previous work on parents, technology, and education [9, 2], we derive design guidelines for digital interaction spaces that support parents' engagement with their children's education. Third, we identify a research agenda for the creation of such digital interaction spaces.

We begin this paper by reviewing previous research on the notion of parental engagement and the impact of technology in parent-school relationships. Next, we describe the methods and findings from our study, focusing on the role of technologies in supporting spaces of interaction within a parenting ecology. Finally, we conclude by proposing design guidelines for interaction spaces and reflect on design issues that require further research such as privacy and community management.

RELATED WORK

In this section we provide a rationale for focusing on parental *engagement* instead of the traditional concept of parental *involvement*. We then explain the relevance of meaningful interactions for the parenting ecology. Finally, we establish differences between our work and previous work on technology and parental engagement.

From Parental Involvement to Parental Engagement

Educational research has traditionally used the term *parental involvement* to define activities and ways for parents to interact with the school environment [16, 12, 3]. These activities are determined to be extremely relevant to the growth and development of children [27, 16, 12]. However, the term parental involvement does not adequately portray the dynamic nature of parents' participation in schools [1, 7]. Thus, in our study we chose to use the term *engagement* as defined by Barton et al.'s [1]. They conceptualize parental *engagement* as the dynamic, distributed, and interactive process that parents go through to navigate barriers between home and school. They propose parental engagement as a relational phenomenon among parents, teachers, and communities framed by the spaces in which the engagement happens. Such spaces are the underlying structures and resources where parents can engage in meaningful exchanges to establish their presence at school and influence it in nontraditional and informal ways.

Exploring technology-mediated parent-school interactions through the lens of engagement enables us to move beyond describing how parents use or complain about technologies imposed by schools. Furthermore, it allows us to identify gaps and opportunities in existing technologies to foster the creation of spaces where parents can interact in the parental ecology.

Meaningful Interactions

Interactions amongst parents and schools is an issue of concern for educational researchers. Parent-school interactions entail mostly the delivery of school-directed information (e.g., parent-teacher conferences where teachers inform parents about their child's progress and activities, an email with a newsletter, etc.) [11]. However, these restricted types of exchanges tend to hinder parental agency to impact the school environment [15, 21, 17]. Teachers tend to interact with parents as if they are visitors [20]. Thus, feeling unwelcomed, parents tend to perceive that their interests and ideas for improvement are not considered valuable.

For these reasons, many researchers have argued that parent-school interactions need to go beyond the exchange of depersonalized information, and instead, focus on building real connections between all individuals of the parenting ecology and be meaningful for all parties [15, 2, 17, 14]. These interactions need to be meaningful for all parties [17, 14]. *Meaningful interactions* enable all parties to represent their practices (e.g., home practices, school practices, teacher's and parents' practices) and interests to impact the schooling environment. Moreover, meaningful interactions allow participants to interpret others' shared information in terms of their own particular purposes and agendas. To better understand technology's role in the parent-school relationship, we analyze parent-school physical and digital interactions through the lens of meaningful interactions.

Parental Engagement and Technology Use

Research on the role of technology in parental engagement has mostly focused on assessing parents' and teachers' perceptions of how useful technologies are. For example, previous work has established that parents perceive parent portals and electronic progress to be useful for being more aware of their children's academic performance [10, 8]. Nelms [22] found that many parents appreciate email-based communication and feel that technology allows them to ask questions and voice concerns. Grujanac [15] demonstrated that schools and teachers tend to resist operational procedures introduced by new technology due to lack of adequate training or support to integrate these practices into their routines .

Unlike existing research, our study focuses on identifying and studying the spaces for parental engagement that existing technologies are fostering. Our approach attempts to inform the design of new technologies that foster equitable partnerships between schools and parents.

Parental Engagement and Technology Design

In regards to HCI-related research, parents in children's education are an emergent audience. Research on the topic has proposed the use of existing/new technologies such as videotapes [17], online forums [2], social networking sites [29], and learning suites [28] to help parents, teachers, and children participate in school-based activities. However, no previous studies have focused on the design of parent-school technologies to support parental engagement from a community-based, ecological perspective.

Although prior research has provided some design implications, it has not focused on supporting the parental ecology. For example, work on parents' practices when seeking educational information for their children [9, 18] suggested parent-school communication technology should allow both parents and teachers to have an impact at school, consider parents' reading and writing levels, and facilitate parent-led initiatives rather than school-authored ones as the only way of communication.

We extend HCI-related research on technology design for parental engagement by providing detailed design guidelines for a digital interaction space that supports equitable voices in the parental ecology. Our goal is to harness technology's potential to strengthen social systems related to parenting and education.

METHODS

To understand the impact of existing parent-school technology's design aspects on the parental ecology, we analyzed interviews with parents on the technology they use to communicate with schools and stay informed on their child's progress and observed parents using existing parent-school related technologies.

Parent Interviews

We analyzed 63 semi-structured interviews conducted with parents in the U.S. to understand the types of parent-school interactions that communication technologies currently support. These interviews were from a larger study about parents' strategies for finding learning opportunities for their children [9].

Interviews included questions on the relationship between parents and teachers and the technologies they use to communicate. Participants were from three different audiences: 28 parents were from a low socioeconomic status (SES) from a southern U.S. urban area, 15 parents were from a high-SES in small towns and rural areas in the Midwest of the U.S., and 20 parents were from a high SES in suburban and urban areas across the U.S., mainly concentrated in the southeast. The age of participants' children varied from one to eighteen years old.

Technology Observations

In addition to the 63 interviews, we reached out to 9 parents and 2 teachers from various backgrounds to understand technology's role in supporting parents' creation of online communication spaces. We asked these informants to direct us to the current technologies parents and schools use to interact with each other (e.g., Class Dojo, email, Facebook pages/groups, etc.). We observed one informant using technologies that require private access such as school email, Class Dojo, and closed groups of parents on Facebook. We also interacted with publicly available technologies (school Facebook pages, schools' websites, and teachers' blogs). We took detailed notes of the content managed in these tools, as well as on the existing online interactions taking place.

Data Analysis

Interviews were transcribed, and participants' names were anonymized and replaced with pseudonyms. Using the transcripts and the notes taken during our observations of the technologies, we conducted an inductive approach to data analysis, grounded in coding techniques. We generated a set of codes that described patterns related to technology support for spaces of interaction and meaningful interactions. Then, an iterative analytic process allowed us to generate themes that were reduced over time and that led to the findings we present in this paper.

FINDINGS

We organize our findings based on the concept of *spaces* within the parenting ecology. This focus on spaces allowed us to identify the underlying structures and resources available for parents to engage in meaningful interactions and establish their presence in schools. In this section, we first define the spaces we identified from our investigations. Then, we provide a review of existing parent-school technologies in terms of their role in parents' creation and maintenance of interaction spaces. Last, we describe the issues and opportunities existing technologies entail for supporting the parental ecology.

Interaction Spaces

Based on our findings, we extend Barton et al.'s work [1] and propose a new categorization of spaces based on the ownership of the space. We identify two types of spaces where parents can interact in meaningful ways: *formal* and *informal*. *Formal spaces* are owned by a school or a school endorsed organization, like the Parent Teacher Association (PTA). *Informal spaces* are owned by parents, e.g., parents informal meetings with teachers when they are picking up their children from school, and parent groups on Facebook.

Our findings also show that spaces can be characterized by interactions both in the physical and digital world. Sometimes digital interactions help maintain spaces in the physical-world.

For example, the exchange of text messages and emails between parents and teachers informs parent-teacher informal conversations during pick-up time. Other times, spaces are created and maintained by almost-only digital interactions. This is the case of school's Facebook pages and websites.

Formal Spaces

Both interviews and our observations of digital environments show that most parent-school interactions in formal spaces (e.g., the classroom, science nights, and school's Facebook page) involve the exchange of school-directed information only. These findings are in line with previous work, which found schools often define the terms of home-school relationship [17, 14].

When meaningful interactions occur in formal spaces, it is often the result of two communication mechanisms. The first mechanism is actualized by parents' efforts to connect with a member of the school (e.g., a teacher) and to construct a close relationship with that member. For that purpose, parents and teachers use mostly face-to-face interactions supported by personal communication technologies, such as SMS, email, and cellphone calls. Most parents explained this constant communication allows them to have more agency in the communication.

The second mechanism entails school's and teachers' efforts to suggest information (e.g., about extra curricular activities) instead of imposing it (e.g., progress reports or calls for mandatory school events). In our interviews, parents mentioned they utilized these opportunities to help their children explore new learning experiences according to both their, and their children's purpose.

Informal Spaces

Informal spaces are spaces created by parents inside or outside formal spaces. Many parents shared their stories of creating informal spaces within the school by consistently interacting with teachers or other school actors. In addition, many parents attempt to participate in spaces for meaningful interactions with other parents and teachers outside the school (e.g., cell phone conversations, WhatsApp and Facebook groups). In these spaces, parental voices can flourish– parents can express themselves without potential judgment from teachers or school-based moderators. Parents with access to such spaces are more empowered to make decisions about their child's academic life. For example, Carolina shared how she harnesses these informal spaces to support her daughter's academic success.

> *"Then when she [Mia, Carolina's daughter] adds the AP classes into it, it will be interesting to see how that all kind of plays out. A lot of my friends at church have kids that have already gone through high school, or not gone all the way through but have kids higher than what Mia is. I call them up and say, 'OK. Now what do we do?' Or even just asking about teachers. I mean your child is going to have that teacher but sometimes it's nice to know: Is it a hard teacher? What are the quirks of this teacher? So that you can kind of prepare her to kind of work around."* [Carolina, mother of a high-schooler]

Many parents also described how they capitalize their use of social media, such as Facebook and WhatsApp, to participate in parent-to-parent informal spaces. For example, Renata told us how she used Facebook as an informal space to gain perspectives from other parents' opinions.

> *" I would go on Facebook and post something and see what my friends who have kids the same age might recommend. Yeah. If there's something ...say, 'Hey. My kid needs extra help in history. What do you know that's out there' then I might type something and then with how Facebook works in 30 minutes you've got 10 different ideas come in at you."* [Renata, mother of a middle-schooler]

Parents' accounts on their participation in informal spaces for parent-to-parent interactions strongly suggest these spaces are key for a successful engagement. Next, we describe the current parent-school communication technologies in terms of their role in the creation and maintenance of formal and informal spaces of interaction.

Technologies and Interaction Spaces

In this section, we describe the technologies parent and schools are using to communicate. We have grouped these technologies in the following categories: technologies for classroom management, technologies for community-building, and technologies for personal communications. In contrast to previous work on technology and parental engagement, our descriptions of these technologies focus on the support they provide to the creation of interaction spaces.

Technology for Classroom Management

Classroom management technologies allow schools to create digital *formal spaces*. Schools use these technologies to inform parents on their child's academic progress or behavior. For example, Class Dojo is a cross-platform application for community-building where teachers post photos or videos of moments in the classroom to help parents stay informed on what their child did in class. Parents can also instant message teachers, but not to other parents. Other technologies for classroom management include customized versions of "parent portals" offered by various school districts and schools . These are web-based applications where teachers can post students' grades for parents to see and send messages to parents. Although these technologies allow for parents to communicate with individual teachers, most interviewed parents indicated they would rather use personal technologies such as email and SMS to support their interactions with teachers.

Technology for Community Building

Both interviews and technology observations demonstrated schools and school-related organizations use social media sites to create *formal spaces*. Likewise, these technologies are being used by parents to create *informal spaces* where they can interact with other parents and teachers.

From our observation of school-related digital technology we learned that schools use their Facebook pages as formal spaces for broadcasting school-related information (e.g., events or general weather advice to parents). On Facebook pages, parents can post, but the school ultimately decides what content stays. Organizations associated with the school, like the PTA, often create their own Facebook groups. Schools also use Twitter to communicate with parents on more urgent matters, like a late bus arrival. In addition, many schools ask their teachers to post all classroom related information on school-hosted blogs.

Our interviews, as well as our observations showed how many parents use social tools to self-organize into *informal* communities with other parents and teachers. Miranda, for example, shared how useful a "Mom's Google group" was to her.

> *"A lot of the moms in the class, we're on a Google Group, so we'll all email each other when there's different events coming up, or when there's an educational thing that we want to bring to the school."* [Miranda, mother of a pre-schooler]

We observed that in these spaces parents can share information that represents their interests and experiences, like questions on child-rearing, or children-related social events outside of the school.

Technology for Personal Communication

As a whole, the data we collected highlighted that parents and schools use technologies such as emails, text messages, and phone calls to foster different types of spaces. These technologies support parents' efforts to create *informal spaces* within the schooling environment. On the other hand, schools use such technologies to extend their *formal spaces* outside the school boundaries.

Many parents we interviewed frequently strove to construct strong relationships with school actors, which include teachers and administration staff. These relationships allowed them to create informal spaces of interaction that afford a two-way communication in which parents felt they could influence life in schools. To foster these spaces parents still preferred using opportunities for face-to-face interaction such as stopping by the school, visiting the class, showing up to conferences, and even volunteering to help in class. However, our interviews highlight that communication through personal technologies such as email, text messages, and phone calls are key in helping parents pave the way for creating and maintaining those informal spaces. Tamara, explains how she depends on these technologies to develop a sense of closeness with her daughters' teachers.

> *"All of her teachers, I develop close relationships with them. I even have their cell phone numbers. We email sometimes. I might just stop up to the school to visit the class or check in on her. But a lot of times if I can't get them at the school I always try email first. But I ask them if they don't mind me having their cell phone number, and most of them never mind. So, yeah. I have a lot of access to her teachers."* [Tamara, mother of a middle-schooler]

In addition, parents, such as Pablo and his wife, use these technologies to activate informal spaces of interaction with other parents.

> *"What will happen generally is we don't email her friends' parents a lot, but let's say we hear something from our daughter about a camp that one of her friends went through, we may either wait until we see that parent and talk to them about it or we send them an email. So technology does facilitate that and like I said, I bet my wife emails and stuff more than I know, because she won't copy me on things like that, but she uses word of mouth but she also uses texting and emailing to ask."* [Pablo, father of a middle-schooler]

Our observation of existing technology shows that schools and teachers also use personal technologies, but their purpose is to strengthen the presence and outreach of existing textitformal spaces. For example, teachers use email to inform parents about their child's in-class activities and progress. Schools often use text messages, phone calls, and emails to send mass messages to every parent. Mass messages are read-only and do not allow replies.

Issues to Further Explore

Our analysis of existing technologies revealed four critical issues that the design of current digital tools needs to address: (1) inflexibility in the boundaries of digital spaces, (2) inequality, (3) fragmentation and inconsistency of information, and (4) lack of relevant non-academic information. In this section, we discuss these issues in detail.

Inflexible Boundaries of Digital Spaces

Parent interviews reconfirmed the ecological nature of effective parental engagement. Within this ecology, parents interact with different teachers, parents, friends, and relatives. As a result, the existing formal and informal spaces in the physical world often have ill-defined boundaries. For example, a formal space could entail the whole school (parents, children, all teachers, etc.), or could only entail one parent and one teacher (e.g., parent-teacher conferences). Likewise, parents can have an informal space where they interact with parents and teachers from different grades and schools. For example, Esther explains how she has leveraged the knowledge of other friends who are parents to receive advice on a better school option for her daughter.

> *"I wasn't that thrilled with the [child's school] experience. So, I was kind of looking for stuff on my own, trying to be an advocate for my daughter and just finding what I could find online. Then when this came up again, my friend who is an attorney said, 'Oh, you forgot about the IB Program', because we were looking at alternatives. I said, 'You know what? I had that in the back of my mind, but I kind of forgot it was there."'* [Esther, mother of 2 middle-schoolers]

It is flexibility in terms of space boundaries what allows parents to garner information for making decisions about how to support their children's education. However, our investigation revealed that the design of existing technologies does not fully account for such flexible boundaries. In these regards, the support of technology to the creation and maintenance of spaces is either too spread out or too restrictive.

From our technology observations we learned that, Class Dojo, for example, restricts interactions by only allowing parents to interact with parents of the same classroom. And even then, it constraints possible ways to interact by only allowing parents to communicate with others through comments they can post on school's and teachers' posts. This lack of opportunities for parents to connect with others hinders possibilities for parents to expand their presence within the parenting ecology. Something similar happens with technologies that support informal spaces between parents and teachers, such as email and SMS. These technologies are good at reinforcing a notion of connectedness and closeness. However, they do not support parents ability to engage in meaningful interactions with more members of the parenting ecology.

In contrast, we observed that technologies such as Facebook allow too many individuals of the parenting ecology to come together. This also impacts negatively opportunities for meaningful interactions. For example, a parent-led Facebook group can have up to 200 to 300 members. This suggests that these digital environments can become overwhelming for many parents. In addition, although members from Facebook groups could include teachers from different classes and even parents from different schools, participation is coming often from the same people. Thus, such technologies discourage many parents from connecting with others in meaningful ways.

Issues of Inequality
Our observation of existing technology demonstrates that these tools do not adequately support equitable participation among all members of the ecology. This, unfortunately, prevents parents from establishing their presence in the schooling social system.

Technologies specifically designed for supporting formal spaces assume schools should be in charge of initiating communication with parents. For instance, in Class Dojo, teachers have to first post content before parents can make a response. Likewise, in parent portals, teachers generally have to update the site with assignments and grades so that parents can react accordingly. Consequently, parents' roles in these systems are more reactionary and they have little agency.

Even technologies like Facebook, that have not been explicitly designed for schooling endeavors, reinforce inequities. This tends to happen both in formal and informal spaces, and is the result of different design decisions. For example, the establishment of a page ownership (e.g., whoever creates the page owns it) tends to shape participation in digital formal spaces. In these spaces, posts by parents on a school Facebook page can be dismissed or even deleted by school administrators. Although it could be argued that parents are given some voice by being allowed to post, their voices are vulnerable to strict moderation and censorship by a higher, more powerful authority. This, in turn, can make parents feel like the school does not value their opinions. Informal spaces supported by Facebook groups also raise issues of voice. These groups have the potential of broadening parents' access to members of the school ecosystem. However, the interactions we observed in Facebook pages stress that parents need to be cautious of what they post in these groups. Certain topics, such as complaining about a teacher, could get parents in trouble with teachers or school administrators.

In addition, both formal and informal spaces on Facebook lack mechanisms to foster equitable integration of potentially marginalized parents. We observed that in these online communities a select group of members with privileged voice establishes the etiquette and social norms of the space. Parents who are not aware of these norms could, therefore, feel hesitant to participate because of their lack of knowledge of the type of questions or responses that are appropriate. For example, an immigrant parent may not understand what a potluck means and may feel it is inappropriate to ask teachers to further explain the concept. Tacit knowledge is best learned through peer-to-peer communication. As peer-to-peer communication is either restricted or hard to achieve in these spaces, parents are not given the opportunity to teach or learn some of this knowledge.

Fragmentation and Inconsistency
Both our observations of technology and our interviews revealed that current technology fragments parent-school interactions by distributing information via too many channels of communication. Schools frequently use SMS, Twitter, Facebook, emails, and paper notifications to send information to parents. This issue of fragmentation is worsened by the fact that none of the existing channels can satisfy all the needs of the ecology. For example, Class Dojo allows parents to see what is going on in the classroom, but does not show grades. Parent portals allow parents to see grades, but not what is happening in the classroom. Such high fragmentation can hamper meaningful interactions by overwhelming and preventing parents from making sense of the received information. Parents, such as Monica and Karl, told us how this fragmentation affected their ability to understand the context of the information.

> *"I know [my child's school has been good. They have already invited us to join the Facebook page. If you do Twitter, join this. We got a 16 page newsletter from the PTA in May. I'm like, 'How long is this thing?' But it was great. It gave me so much information. But then because I've never done this before I'm like, 'Is that who I am going to get my information from, the PTA? Or is it going to be from the Facebook page?' How does that work? I don't know."* [Monica, mother of 2 middle-schoolers].

> *"We talk [with teachers], pretty much regularly. For the most part...If I don't get a phone call at least once a week...giving me an update...I get emails. These are the assignments that are due next week, so I hear from them pretty regularly...and it kinda gets a little cumbersome because with one in high school and one in middle school...there are about 8 different teachers that will contact me *snaps fingers* back-to-back, and it seems like they always come at the same time for information. "* [Karl, father of two middle and one high-schooler]

Inconsistency in the way information is managed in some digital formal spaces is also an issue. Parents, such as Marina, told us how this affected their engagement.

Marina (M): " *Because communication is an issue, so we do rely on other parents in the similar grade and we get information about what they are doing in their classrooms and stuff like that, we get information. But some teachers are very good in posting things online so we can go and visit their website and get information and some are not.*"
Interviewer (I): " *So do you wish there was more interaction with his teachers?*"
M: " *I don't ... I don't really wish for that. It's not going to change our life in any way but I do feel that if they had a website set up and there is information updated on a regular basis, it does help the child and the parents to kind of stay ahead and be prepared for it.*" [Marina, mother of a middle-schooler]

This inconsistency forces parents to seek other mechanisms to access relevant information about their children. Anahi shared how she relies more on her child's memory that on the information delivered by digital formal spaces.

"*The teachers, most of them have websites that let you know when things are coming up. Not all of them do or they are just not able to keep it up or whatever. I understand that too. So just kinda a variety of ways between websites and him telling me and most of the time remembering to study. I just keep asking him, 'Do you have anything coming up this week?' He's usually pretty good about remembering. That's probably the most reliable, is him.*" [Anahi, the mother of a middle-schooler]

The information inconsistency of formal spaces negatively affects engagement. It can discourage parental intentions to construct a close relationship with the teacher. This might not be a problem for parents who have already strong connections with other members of the ecology. However, for parents who depend on their relationship with the school and the teacher, inconsistency can impact the entire parent-school relationship.

Lack of Relevant Non-Academic Information

Current technology supports sharing academic information well. Applications like a school district's parent portal, Class Dojo, and even email can easily, and sometimes immediately, update parents on their children's academic progress. Parent interviews, however, confirm that successfully engaged parents strive for access to nonacademic information important to their child's academic success. Engaged parents, like Jaime, are not hesitant to move beyond the information teacher provides to find out how to provide extra-curricular learning opportunities to their children. He describes the mechanisms he uses to select and garner ideas for learning experiences:

"*Usually every summer we have something that I try to plug them into. A lot of times it's art stuff, because that's hard to fit in and I do consider that academic, because involves a lot of the problem-solving. I sort of watch the kids who are moving and shaking in the school. I'm usually friends with the parents. So word-of-mouth as to 'what is your kid doing this summer?' and then you start finding out about opportunities that may be really good. I find good stuff, I bookmark it or stick it in a folder, and I write it down. Is she going to apply this summer for this program, and when does she need to apply next summer for another program? You kind of put them in the back of your mind so that you might know what some of the criteria might be so that your kids can be ready to be a competitive applicant for some of the programs.*" [Jaime, father of 2 high-schoolers]

On the other hand, parents who have issues engaging with the parenting ecology, face a limited access to other members who can share with them opportunities to better assist their children. Their access usually depends on how well they know how to search information or how good their relationship with teachers is. As a result, many of these parents are either not aware of existing opportunities or cannot find opportunities that suites their constraints. For example, Leonor, a working mother of a middle-schooler, shared that her daughter had no regular exposure to non-academic educational support (e.g., out-of-school programs, museum visits, educational books). Her answers suggest this lack of exposure is a result of a lack of interaction with other members of the ecology.

Interviewer: "*What about educational books?*"
Leonor: "*I bought some for her for Christmas.*"
I: "*What books did you buy?*"
L: "*I bought like a math book and some writing books. Those are the ones she needs help with the most, her writing skills and math.*"
I: "*Okay. How did you find those books?*"
L: "*I just looked.*"

Gabriela and Rosa told us how hard it has been for them to look for opportunities on line alone.

"*So, she's interested in everything STEM, you know. I'm challenged with the cost of after-school programs, summer programs. I was online today googling around for affordable programs. There are camps at [local college], they mostly have programs for high school kids. Then I did find something on the Boys and Girls site. Try to get the ball rolling.*" [Gabriela - mother of a middle-schooler]

"*He's brought home some things from school, even on the engineering route, just some of them are really expensive. So it's hard to...you know kind of figure that out. Some of the programs, like at colleges, like [name of a local college] or whatever, some of the programs are, you know, pretty expensive. You know like $3,000 to do something like that. So it's kind of hard to.*" [Rosa - mother of a 16 year-old]

Our findings show that existing technologies hosted by schools are not effectively connecting parents to the rest of the ecology. Moreover, parents who struggle the most with making connections are not tapping into informal spaces to build those connections on their own. Despite technology facilitating some teacher to parent communication, our interviews indicated that this was not enough for parents to be effectively engaged with their child's education. In order to give all parents the opportunity to engage, parent-school technologies need to go

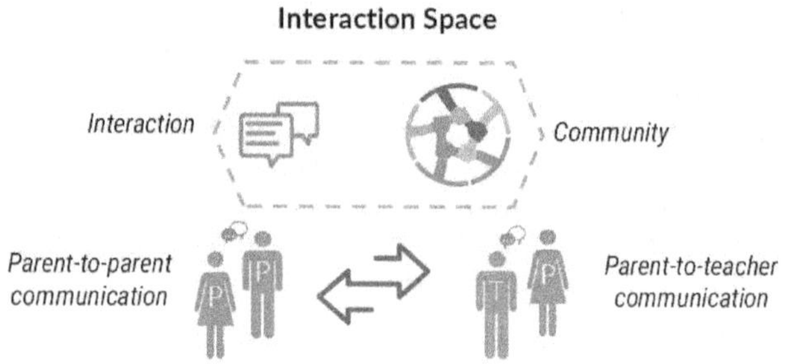

Figure 1. Interaction Space Overview

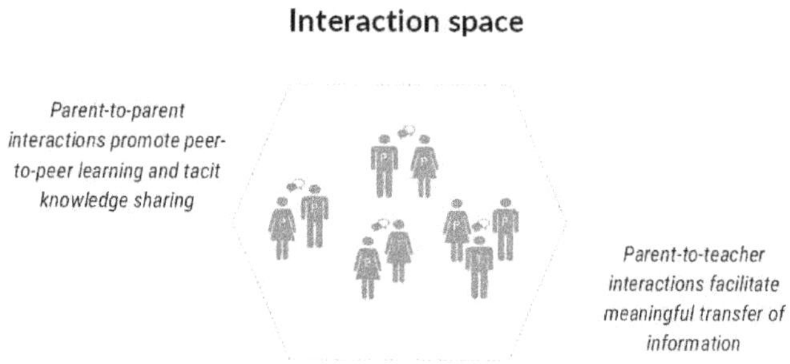

Figure 2. Single Interaction Space

beyond providing academic information in three main ways. They need to: 1) enable parents to engage with teachers and other parents in more equitable and open manner, 2) create connections across groups, and 3) expose enable parents to make the most out of the available learning opportunities.

DESIGN GUIDELINES FOR INTERACTION SPACES

The findings indicate that current technologies do not support community-building amongst members of the parental ecology. Four issues were identified: inflexibility in the boundaries of spaces, fragmentation and inconsistency of information, inequity, and lack of relevant non-academic information. To address these issues, we propose a set of design guidelines for digital interaction spaces. These guidelines will allow parents and school actors (teachers, staff, etc.) to engage in meaningful interactions and come together as an equitable community. (Figure 1). In the following sections, we describe the proposed design guidelines and suggest possible technological approaches that could be used to realize them.

Support Equitable Informal Spaces

Our findings showed that *informal spaces* are key for parental engagement. These spaces allow parents to connect with other members of the ecology and learn from them. Thus, an interaction space that fosters the parenting ecology should offer members (parents and teachers) equal opportunities take the lead in the communication and on forming groups with other members. To enable equitable opportunities for all members of the space to issue their voice, an interaction space must strive to safeguard privacy and security-a balance that is hard to achieve. Different types of conversations require different levels of privacy. For example, in a conversation around teacher performance, there may be a chilling effect if a parent knows a teacher can view the conversation. Utilizing privacy-by-design principles, parents can have conversations with other parents or form groups that allow proper privacy controls.

Allow Members to Define Community's Boundaries

Parents do not always connect with parents or teachers from their children's school. Our findings demonstrated that successfully engaged parents transcend the boundaries of the school. In fact, parents can connect and align themselves along a variety of identities, such as ethnicities (e.g., parents of black students in private schools of Chicago) and special needs (e.g., parents of autistic children in rural areas). In addition, as we learned during our technology observations, extremely large formal and informal spaces tend to hinder meaningful interactions. An interaction space should allow members to define the boundaries that best suit their social and communication needs so as to enable all users to exercise their voices.

Augment Opportunities for Connection

Avenues for information exchanges can maximize resourcefulness of the entire community, increase the diversity of voices and perspectives, and facilitate meaningful interactions. Instead of just a single interaction space, where one community comes together (Figure 2), there can be multiple interaction spaces, each with their own configuration and properties (Figure 3). For example, each space can be a single grade or class. A huge challenge for multiple spaces is the ability to effectively leverage the tacit knowledge of the whole community. This could be addressed by introducing machine intelligence to the system. Approaches such as a generative profile building can allow members across spaces to communicate. For example, a teacher from the third grade, can reach out a teacher from sixth grade to ask a specific question, or a parent (from space A) with some specialized knowledge can help his/her peer (from space B) with a special question.

Provide a Unified and Organized Source of Information

An interaction space that enables meaningful interactions amongst members should also address issues of fragmentation of information. Our findings showed that numerous channels of communication often bombarded parents with information, which hindered their ability to make sense of that information. An interaction space should offer a unified channel of communication that gathers and integrates information from other channels. Members should be able to define the type and frequency of information they receive. In addition, information in this space should be organized and streamlined in a way that is meaningful for parents. Automation mechanisms fed by user preferences could be used to achieve this goal; for instance, the space can leverage options such as crowd-sourced tagging (e.g., similar to online Stackoverflow forums) or automatic-topic tagging (e.g., similar to the question-answering platform Quora) or a combination of these.

An interaction space should avoid becoming yet another tool that parents have to learn to use to keep up-to-date with school. To address this issue, we suggest leveraging parents' existing

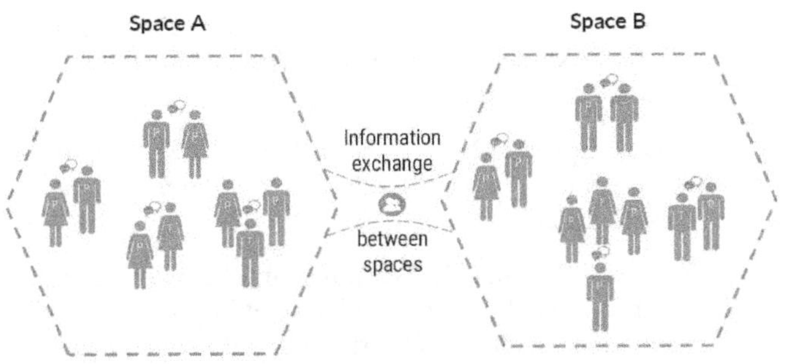

Figure 3. Connected Interaction Spaces

knowledge of current technologies (e.g., parent portals, Facebook, text messages, and emails). Features of the interaction space should be inspired from familiar platforms to reduce the learning curve to increase adoption.

Enable Access to Relevant Information

Access to relevant information, both academic and nonacademic, is vital for parents. We found that successfully engaged parents often resort to a group of teachers and peers as their go-to people for accessing key information. For many other parents, however, effective go-to people are harder to identify. This is especially true for parents who are new to the community or lack social capital or both. Interaction spaces should allow for information to be decentralized and delivered to members of the community in a way that is meaningful to them.

A potential approach for satisfying this guideline is to leverage machine intelligence. The intelligence can match opportunities, parents, events, etc. by indexing the relevant information. Topic modeling techniques can distillate key points in people's interactions. Using the topics most discussed by a user, a profile about that user can be built over time in a generative manner. For example, if the parent of a child engages in a lot of discussions around college opportunities, the system can use natural language understanding and topic modeling techniques to add tags to the said parents profile dimensions. When a new member asks for recommendations on funding opportunities to attend college (a previously indexed topic), the space should have intelligence in the back-end that curates and channels questions to the appropriate parties.

Make it Matter

Understanding and leveraging motivation of parents is important in designing the space. Broadly speaking, we can design the space taking advantage of parental motivation in three areas: benefit to the child, relevant nonacademic information, and peer-based social communities. In terms of benefit to the child, parental engagement (or lack thereof) about the education system impacts the child's education [16, 12, 4]. As a result, there is value in seeking out meaningful engagement with other parents and teachers.

As our findings revealed, parents want to access relevant nonacademic information. This entails information about extracurricular activities, as well as information around social and cultural norms. For instance, issues around how long should a child stay for a sleepover, what to bring to a potluck, how to organize holiday events in a school, etc. Even if a parent is knowledgeable and successfully engaged to the parental ecology, incorporating a diverse perspective can improve the knowledge base and allow for better parental engagement.

There is also a social benefit to parents if they are engaged. Parents can meet other people who are in similar life stages and motivated by a common goal of engagement in their children's education, which can foster membership into a community. Such facilitated interactions become even more important for working or busy parents who may not have many opportunities to engage in communal activities. In an inclusive environment, parents may feel less intimidated to voice their feelings and concerns.

RESEARCH AGENDA

There are areas such as privacy, community management, compliance, and sustainability that require further investigation to make the proposed design guidelines robust. The following sections go over the need to investigate further across those four areas.

- **Privacy-related issues**: Since discussions in the interaction space can involve sensitive information, such as grades or (physical and mental) health related, it is important to establish the right balance between privacy and security. To develop privacy-by-design principles, it is relevant to further investigate topics such as cultural factors and the role of anonymity in parent-school interactions.

- **Community Management**: Stewardship of the community is important. However, mechanisms to establish policies and codes of conduct should be designed considering the need to foster equitable interactions. Exploring infrastructures that allow communities to develop codes of conduct should be investigated, rather than assuming a one-size fits all approach.

- **Analytics**: Assessing the impact of an interaction space on parental engagement is key for its sustainability. There is a range of methods that could gather data related to parenting and schools. For example, data on interaction dynamics such as number of messages, average length, and overall sentiment, could be collected to get a rough sense of user engagement. Computing network dynamics, density of network, and average activity in the network could gauge engagement at a sub-group or group level. Further investigation is needed to determine the most optimal criteria of analysis.

- **Formative research with school actors**: While our study was focused on parents needs, formative research with school actors (teachers, staff, and administrators), is important as they are essential parts of the interaction space. For an interaction space to be successful, it will need to meet the requirements of all actors, including issues such as teacher workloads, and administrative challenges in communicating with parents.

CONCLUSION

Parental engagement should be considered a relational phenomenon that depends on interactive relationships between parents, teachers, and other school actors in the school environment [1]. Our findings reveal critical issues that are not supported by existing technology, restricting meaningful communications within the parenting ecology. To address these issues, we proposed design guidelines for an interaction space and suggest possible technological approaches that could be used to realize them. The interaction spaces in our platform go beyond the communication realm and support parental engagement through community-building. Technology needs to go beyond just facilitating a space for communication. It needs to enhance the inherent dynamic and social component of the communication.

REFERENCES

1. Angela Calabrese Barton, Corey Drake, Jose Gustavo Perez, Kathleen St Louis, and Magnia George. 2004. Ecologies of parental engagement in urban education. *Educational Researcher* 33, 4 (2004), 3–12.
2. Ronald A Beghetto. 2001. Virtually in the middle: Alternative avenues for parental involvement in middle-level schools. *The Clearing House* 75, 1 (2001), 21–25.
3. Aprile D. Benner, Alaina E. Boyle, and Sydney Sadler. 2016. Parental Involvement and Adolescents' Educational Success: The Roles of Prior Achievement and Socioeconomic Status. *Journal of Youth and Adolescence* 45, 6 (2016), 1053–1064.
4. Eugenia Hepworth Berger. 2003. *Parents as partners in education: Families and schools working together.* Prentice Hall.
5. G. P. Carreon, C. Drake, and a. C. Barton. 2005. The Importance of Presence: Immigrant Parents' School Engagement Experiences. *American Educational Research Journal* 42, 3 (2005), 465–498.
6. Rosario Ceballo, Laura K Maurizi, Gloria a Suarez, and Maria T Aretakis. 2014. Gift and sacrifice: parental involvement in Latino adolescents' education. *Cultural diversity & ethnic minority psychology* 20, 1 (2014), 116–27.
7. James P Comer and Norris M Haynes. 1991. Parent involvement in schools: An ecological approach. *The Elementary School Journal* (1991), 271–277.
8. Grace B del Valle. 2011. Using a Web-Based Program to Increase Parental Involvement: Teachers' and Administrators' Perceptions. *ProQuest LLC* (2011).
9. Betsy DiSalvo, Parisa Khanipour Roshan, and Briana Morrison. 2016. Information Seeking Practices of Parents: Exploring Skills, Face Threats and Social Networks. In *Proceedings of the 2016 CHI Conference on Human Factors in Computing Systems (CHI '16).* ACM, New York, NY, USA, 623–634.
10. Shannon D Dries. 2014. *The influence of Parent Portal Access on Student Efficacy and Parental Involvement.* Ph.D. Dissertation.
11. Joyce L Epstein. 2001. *School, family, and community partnerships: Preparing educators and improving schools.* ERIC.
12. Weihua Fan, Cathy M Williams, and Christopher A Wolters. 2012. Parental involvement in predicting school motivation: Similar and differential effects across ethnic groups. *The Journal of Educational Research* 105, 1 (2012), 21–35.
13. Susan Graham-Clay. 2005. Communicating with parents: Strategies for teachers. *School Community Journal* 15, 1 (2005), 117.
14. L Grant. 2011. 'I'm a completely different person at home': using digital technologies to connect learning between home and school. *Journal of Computer Assisted Learning* 27, 4 (2011), 292–302.
15. Mara Paich Grujanac. *How does Internet Facilitated Communication impact teacher and parent partnerships?* Ph.D. Dissertation. Loyola University Chicago. https://www.learntechlib.org/p/124606
16. Nancy E Hill and Diana F Tyson. 2009. Parental involvement in middle school: a meta-analytic assessment of the strategies that promote achievement. *Developmental psychology* 45, 3 (2009), 740.
17. Martin Hughes and Pamela Greenhough. 2006. Boxes, bags and videotape: enhancing home–school communication through knowledge exchange activities. *Educational Review* 58, 4 (2006), 471–487.
18. Parisa Khanipour Roshan, Maia Jacobs, Michaelanne Dye, and Betsy DiSalvo. 2014. Exploring How Parents in Economically Depressed Communities Access Learning Resources. In *Proceedings of the 18th International Conference on Supporting Group Work (GROUP '14).* ACM, New York, NY, USA, 131–141.
19. Jane E Miner. 2011. A Parental Response to Online Progress Reports. (2011).
20. Debra Miretzky. 2004. The communication requirements of democratic schools: Parent-teacher perspectives on their relationships. *Teachers College Record* 106, 4 (2004), 814–851.
21. Jill L Murphy. 2009. *Survey study of the relationship between parents' and teachers' perceptions of what constitutes effective school-to-home communications.* Ph.D. Dissertation. Walden University.
22. Elizabeth L Nelms. 2002. The effects of a teacher-created web page on parent communication: An action research study. *Action Research Exchange* 1, 2 (2002).
23. Zehra Ozcinar and Nihat Ekizoglu. 2013. Evaluation of a blog based parent involvement approach by parents. *Computers and Education* 66 (2013), 1–10.

24. Fred Ramirez. 2001. Technology and parental involvement. *The Clearing House* 75, 1 (2001), 30–31.
25. Bridget Somekh, Diane Mavers, and Cathy Lewin. 2003. Using ICT to enhance home-school links: an evaluation of current practice in England: a report to the DfES. (2003).
26. Susan Sonnenschein, Shari R Metzger, and Joy A Thompson. 2016. Low-Income Parents' Socialization of Their Preschoolers' Early Reading and Math Skills. *Research in Human Development* 13, 3 (2016), 207–224.
27. Matt Villano. 2008. Meet the Parents: Notification Tools Can Do More Than Alert the School Community to an Emergency. New Systems Are Cultivating Parental Involvement by Sending Home Daily Reports on Students' Behavior, Attendance, and Performance. *THE Journal (Technological Horizons In Education)* 35, 4 (2008), 48.
28. Yuhang Zhao, Alexis Hope, Jin Huang, Yoel Sumitro, James A. Landay, and Yuanchun Shi. 2013. Hero: Designing Learning Tools to Increase Parental Involvement in Elementary Education in China. In *CHI '13 Extended Abstracts on Human Factors in Computing Systems (CHI EA '13)*. ACM, New York, NY, USA, 637–642.
29. Jolene Zywica. 2013. *Using social media to connect families and kindergarten classrooms*. Ph.D. Dissertation.

Plan & Play: Supporting Intentional Media Use in Early Childhood

Alexis Hiniker[1,2]
alexisr@uw.edu

Bongshin Lee[1]
bongshin@microsoft.com

Kiley Sobel[1,2]
ksobel@uw.edu

Eun Kyoung Choe[3]
echoe@ist.psu.edu

[1]Microsoft Research, Redmond, WA, USA
[2]Human Centered Design and Engineering, University of Washington, Seattle, WA, USA
[3]College of IST, The Pennsylvania State University, University Park, PA, USA

ABSTRACT

Parental controls allow parents to set limits on children's use of technology, but prior work suggests that controlling children alone is unlikely to foster the development of healthy media habits. We took elements from evidence-based preschool curricula that teach self-regulation and translated them to the digital space by creating a tool for preschoolers and parents to plan their device-based play-time. In an observational lab study with 11 parent-child dyads and follow-up interviews with 14 parents, we found that children demonstrated intentionality and made goal-directed choices as they planned, the mediating factor in developing self-regulation. We observed that parents prompted their child to be intentional and solicited children's input. When children played through their plan, they transitioned to the next activity without intervention 93% of the time. Our results suggest that evidence-based practices for teaching self-regulation in a non-digital context can be applied productively to children's use of technology. As parents supported children in trying the tool for the first time, a further contribution of this work is a hierarchical model of parents' approaches to scaffolding children's use of a novel technology.

Author Keywords

Child-computer interaction; parental mediation; self-determination theory; preschool; screen time; tablets; parental controls.

ACM Classification Keywords

H.5.m. Information interfaces and presentation (e.g., HCI): Miscellaneous.

INTRODUCTION

With technology more embedded in daily life than ever before, concerns about young children's use of digital media abound. Pediatric and child development researchers caution that extensive leisure time with screen-based media and exposure to violent media content in early childhood can each have a negative impact on children's long-term outcomes [35,37]. On the other hand, prior work has demonstrated that watching *Daniel Tiger's Neighborhood* (a television show for preschoolers) can increase empathy [28], while engaging with other specific content predicts gains in literacy [29], creativity [39], and appreciation for racial diversity [5]. Taken together, prior work on the use of digital media in early childhood leaves parents with the challenging role of guiding young children toward healthy media habits by providing opportunities to engage with technology, while also vetting content, setting limits, and engaging in media use together with their child [1,7,36].

A variety of commercial offerings promise to support parents in managing their child's use of digital media. These parental controls offer to filter content, turn off specific functionality, enforce digital time limits, and impose other restrictions. While these tools effectively enforce limits in the moment, they do not attempt to address the larger task of mentoring children in becoming thoughtful, self-regulated consumers [40]. They also do not attempt to support parents in providing this mentorship [40].

The goal of this work was to build on what is already known about how children acquire self-regulation skills, and to examine how technology might play a role in facilitating this process. To do so, we drew on two existing bodies of work. First, we examined the developmental arc of self-regulation and the way in which evidence-based preschool curricula support the development of this skill. Second, we grounded our work in self-determination theory to understand what structures are likely to foster children's long-term intrinsic motivation to self-regulate their use of technology.

Using this foundation, we conducted a participatory design workshop with preschoolers to elicit design insights for a tool for this scenario [19]. We used this design guidance to develop "Plan & Play," a system-level interface for Android devices. Plan & Play supports children and parents in collaboratively planning out their use of apps with intention. We then conducted an observational lab study with 11 parent-child dyads and follow-up interview study with 14

IDC 2017, June 27–30, 2017, Stanford, CA, USA.

ACM ISBN 978-1-4503-4921-5/17/06...$15.00.
DOI: http://dx.doi.org/10.1145/3078072.3079752

parents to understand how preschoolers and their parents use and experience this system.

We found that all children made choices with intention as they created a plan for their play time and that parents used language to highlight children's autonomy and choice-making. We also found that within the context of the lab, children were highly responsive to transition cues from Plan & Play and only required parent intervention 7% of the time. Parents reported that they struggle with the tension between forcing children to make choices they approve of and trusting them with the freedom to make these choices autonomously. For many parents, the Plan & Play interface offers promise as a way of addressing this conflict.

BACKGROUND AND RELATED WORK

Planning and Early Childhood

By the time children are three years old, they are capable of making thoughtful, self-regulated decisions, a skill they refine between the ages of three and six [12]. High-quality, evidence-based preschool curricula provide explicit mechanisms for supporting this development, and one of the most effective mechanisms for doing so is providing opportunities for planning [12]. When children are regularly prompted to thoughtfully plan out their actions in advance, their behavior becomes more intentional and they become more capable of learning across domains [25]. By supporting preschoolers in making plans, parents and teachers help them identify and internalize norms and become more intentional, self-regulated learners [12,15].

Tools of the Mind (TotM) is an evidence-based curriculum for three-to-six-year-old children that provides opportunities for making, executing, and reflecting on plans [4]. A randomized controlled trial of TotM with more than 200 3- and 4-year-old children showed that preschoolers exposed to the curriculum demonstrated improved executive function (the capacity for being goal-oriented) and greater learning gains relative to those who were not [3]. A core component of TotM is making "Play Plans," child-created plans describing how the child intends to play.

The *High/Scope* preschool curriculum also emphasizes the importance of planning and includes a "Plan-Do-Review" sequence for children to engage in activities of their choosing in an intentional way [33]. A longitudinal, randomized controlled trial of the High/Scope curriculum demonstrated that children who experienced this curriculum as preschoolers were higher earners, more likely to have graduated from high school, and dramatically less likely to have an arrest record as adults than peers in traditional preschool classrooms [32]. Researchers attribute these differences in community and social behaviors to High/Scope's emphasis on planning and child initiative.

This prior work demonstrates that providing opportunities to plan is both effective for improving self-regulation and a developmentally appropriate tool for preschoolers. We build on this work in early childhood education by translating the planning steps developed by these curricula to a digital context and explicitly adopt components of these curricula in the design of our system.

Self-Determination Theory

Self-determination theory (SDT) is a well-developed model of the role of internal and external motivation in supporting learning, well-being, and participation [30]. Work in SDT has repeatedly shown that individuals who feel agency and self-direction with respect to a particular activity will be more likely to both: 1) self-regulate their behavior in a way that enables them to perform the activity successfully, and 2) internalize these regulatory processes such that they are intrinsically motivated to enact them [14]. As a result, environmental factors that foster a sense of self-determination improve individuals' intrinsic motivation and self-regulation. For example, adults who are given freedom of choice are more likely to persist in tedious tasks than adults who are told that they are required to complete these exercises [9].

Though the majority of studies on SDT have been conducted with adults, prior work shows that this model is also applicable to children [8,10,13]. Sheehan and colleagues report that children's sense of self-determination predicts their intrinsic motivation to exercise [34], and a series of studies have shown that parenting approaches that are more supportive and less controlling are more effective at facilitating long-term compliance [14]. A field study of first- and second-grade children showed that rules for a painting activity accompanied by controlling language undermined children's creativity and motivation relative to the same rules accompanied by neutral language [22]. Other work has shown that preschoolers with disabilities benefit from support structures that foster self-determination [27].

We build on this work by framing children's ability to self-regulate their use of entertainment media in the context of SDT. It is well-understood that children need autonomy to regulate their behaviors and develop the intrinsic motivation to comply with social norms. It is also well-documented that self-regulating stimulating media experiences is a challenge, even for adults [2,20,21]. Combining this prior knowledge with the fact that existing parental controls emphasize controlling children rather than mentoring them, we set out to investigate how technology might go beyond the lock-out mechanisms that are available today and explicitly foster the autonomy and self-determination children need to self-regulate their screen media use.

Designing for Parental Mediation

Many commercially available technologies include features that allow parents to set limits on their children's media use. A recent review of this design space categorizes existing filters and restrictions, all of which strive to prevent risky situations (such as using digital media for an extended period of time, making in-app purchases, or encountering adult content) [40]. Existing tools do not yet strive to support children in developing resilience to such situations when they do occur [40], despite the fact that internalized resilience has more protective effects than external restrictions [38].

However, the child-computer interaction research community is beginning to explore more nuanced solutions. Hashish and colleagues developed a system called "Kid-in-the-Loop" that provides children and parents with tools to collaboratively set content filters on a device [17], and Hartikainen and colleagues call for tools that work to build trust between parents and children [16]. A value-sensitive design exploration to understand parents' values with respect to parental controls found that parents value being involved and exercising control with respect to their children's use of technology, but they also value children's independence and the development of an internal moral compass that children can use to guide their own decisions [26]. We contribute to this space by exploring the design of parental controls that emphasize children's autonomy, intrinsic motivation, and acquisition of self-regulation. We also examine parents' role in mentoring and supporting their children in forming habits and not just their role as authority figures setting limits.

SYSTEM DESIGN

Using elements from Tools of the Mind, the High/Scope curriculum, and design insights from a workshop we conducted with 7 children age 4–6 [19], we created a set of initial sketches for a system-level app to support planning screen time activities on a phone or tablet. We then iteratively developed and revised storyboards which we used to implement an Android app called *Plan & Play*.

Planning

Plan & Play first takes the user through a series of screens for planning out a session of device-based activity. A cartoon panda narrates the experience and asks the child to first set a total time limit in minutes. On the next screen, the user can select apps to put in the plan by tapping to include or exclude them (Figure 1a). On the next screen, the user sees a numbered list of apps, with the first app in the plan at the top (Figure 1b). Dragging and dropping on this screen allows the user to swap the order of the apps.

On the next screen, the user is presented with a slider with multiple thumbs (Figure 1c). The slider represents the total duration of the plan, and each segment within it represents the duration of a single app. Dragging any thumb in the slider gradually reapportions time. On the last screen, the plan is presented along with a picture of the parent and a picture of the child (Figure 1d). Each picture has a button next to it, and tapping the button turns it into a checkmark. When both buttons have been tapped and display checkmarks, a "play" button appears at the bottom of the screen. Pressing this button begins the plan.

Playing

When the user presses the play button, the first app in the plan launches automatically, and a widget is overlaid above the app content in the top-right corner. This persistent widget displays one of three images: a cheering panda when the currently planned app in the foreground, a sad panda

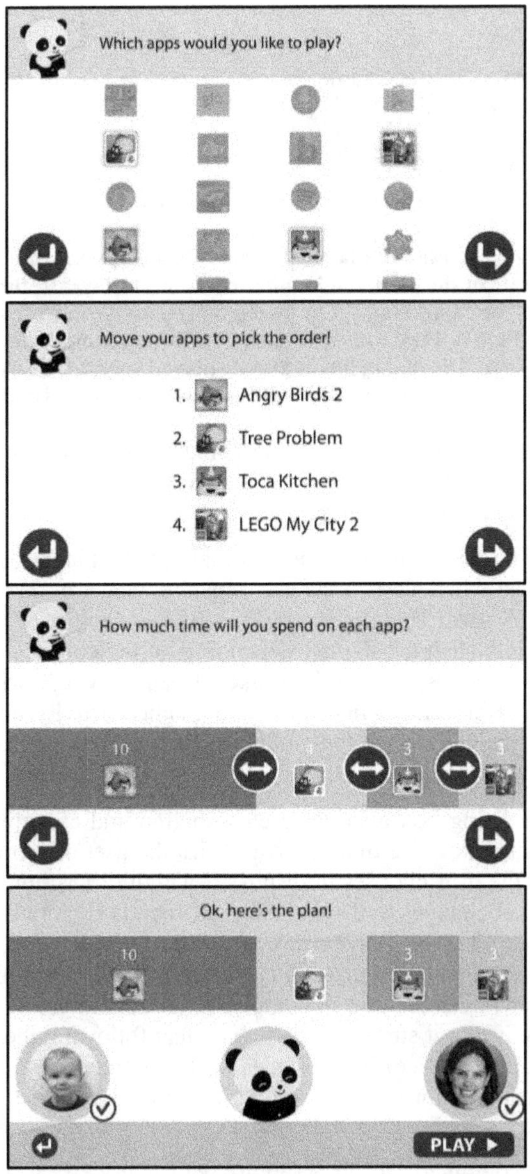

Figure 1. Screens for planning. a) Selecting apps by tapping to select/unselect, b) ordering apps by dragging and dropping, c) changing app duration by sliding thumbs of a slider, d) parent and child agree to the plan by tapping their own buttons; after both agree, play button appears.

Figure 2. Three possible states of the Plan & Play widget that is displayed in the top right corner above all screen content whenever a plan is active. Widget states: the active app is the planned app (left), counting down before a transition (center), the active app is not the planned app (right).

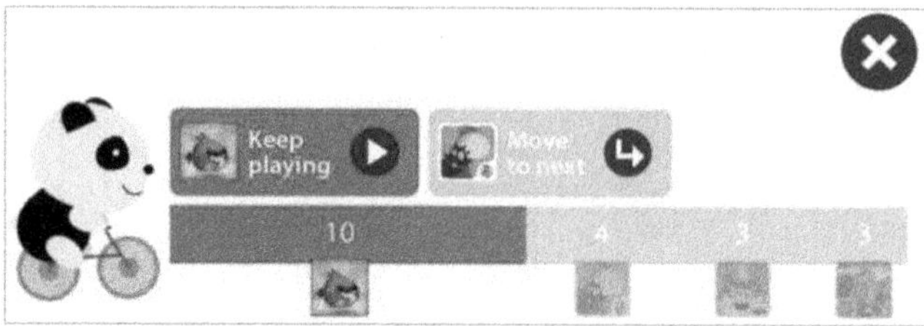

Figure 3. Plan & Play dialog box. Dialog options reflect the state of the plan and in other cases might say, "Return to Plan" or "End Plan." The dialog box opens when the user taps the Plan & Play widget (Figure 2) that floats above all screen content. The dialog box is also displayed spontaneously when it is time to transition. It can always be dismissed.

when a different app in the foreground, or a countdown with the appropriate number of seconds whenever the user is within 30 seconds of a transition (Figure 2).

During the users' play time, a dialog box (Figure 3) is displayed whenever: 1) the user taps the widget or 2) the plan dictates that it is time to transition. The content of the dialog box changes slightly depending on the context. For example, it displays options like "Keep Playing" when the user is currently engaged in the planned activity and "Return to Plan" when the child has deviated from the planned activity.

The dialog box also has a close button and can always be dismissed. If the dialog box notifies the user of a transition and the user chooses to dismiss it without transitioning, the widget changes to display the "sad" panda (Figure 2, right). Thus, Plan & Play always provides visible information about whether the user is currently following the plan but never forces the user to comply. A central feature of Plan & Play is that it surfaces norms (i.e., that following the plan is a valued choice) but provides both the freedom to deviate from these norms, and information about this departure.

METHODS

We combined lab observations with interviews to conduct an initial evaluation of Plan & Play. The goals of this study were to determine how parents and children collaborate to use the system and how parents feel about this approach to mediating their child's use of digital media. Study procedures and materials were reviewed by the Microsoft Research privacy manager assigned to this space.

Participants

Fourteen parent-child dyads participated in our study (11 in the observation portion, as the other three brought incompatible devices to the study session). Our child participants included 4 boys and 10 girls, and our parents included 5 fathers and 9 mothers. Six children were 6-years-old, three children were 5, and five children were 4. Nine children were of Asian or Southeast Asian descent, four children were non-Hispanic White, and one child was Afro-Caribbean. Families were recruited through institutional mailing lists, and mailing lists for local parents' groups and local preschools. Inclusion criteria for participating in the study were that parent and child speak English comfortably throughout the study session and that the child use an Android device to play apps for entertainment at least once a week on average.

Participants were instructed to bring the Android device that their child uses to the study session. Three families enrolled in the study but brought a device to the study session that did not support Plan & Play. In these cases, the family was not included in the observational portion of our study and only participated in the parent interview.

Materials and Procedures

Planning and Playing

All procedures were conducted in a user research laboratory and audio and video recorded. A researcher installed Plan & Play on the family's device and then handed the device to the child. The researcher told the child that she had put a new app on the device and showed the child where to find it. The researcher explained that this app would let the child plan out what to play on the tablet and asked the child to make a plan for 15 minutes of play time. The researcher further said that the child should make the plan, and that mom or dad could help. The researcher then left the room.

The research team then gave the parent and child time to collaboratively create a plan for 15 minutes of play time and for the child to play through the plan. After observing this experience in its entirety, two researchers returned to lab. One researcher stayed in the room with the child to perform a follow-up exercise, and the other escorted the parent to an adjoining room to conduct the parent interview.

Child Follow-up Task

In the follow-up exercise, the researcher asked the child if he or she could show the researcher how to use the Plan & Play app. The child then led a walk-through of Plan & Play by setting up a 3-minute plan while the researcher watched and asked questions about each screen. The child then played through the planned activities.

Parent Interview

While the child completed the follow-up tasks, the parent was interviewed in a separate room by another researcher. The semi-structured protocol included 12 questions and explored the child's typical screen media use, the limits the family sets on these activities, whether the family uses any parental controls, what the parent hopes for the child's future technology use, and feedback about the Plan & Play app.

In addition to these tasks, all participants also completed a separate set of activities as part of a second study outside the scope of this investigation. This data is not analyzed here. As a thank-you for their participation in both studies, each family received one gift card to Amazon for US$150.

Data Analysis

The research team transcribed all parent-child Plan & Play sessions into field notes documenting participants' physical actions, interactions with the screen, and dialogue. This process was repeated for the follow-up session between child and researcher. All parent interviews were transcribed by a professional transcription service and spot-checked by the research team for accuracy.

We performed a holistic open coding of each set of transcripts and used this to develop a code book. After collaboratively narrowing our focus to a subset of the most relevant themes, we conducted a directed coding to identify instances of each theme in each subset of the data. The final code book included codes about children's intentionality, parents' attempts to scaffold children's interactions, statements that children and parents made about the app's authority, parents' statements about the child's authority, children's responses to transition events, children's understanding of the interface, and parents' perspectives on parental controls, child autonomy, child compliance, and children's technology use. One researcher conducted a directed coding of the entire dataset. A second researcher coded a randomly selected subset of the data for comparison. Nearly all codes matched, and disagreements were discussed until consensus was reached.

RESULTS

Children's Intentionality

As children used the app with their parent to construct a plan, they consistently showed evidence of using it with purpose to achieve specific objectives. All children showed this intentionality during the process of selecting the apps they wanted to play. In some cases, children narrated their choices as they made them, saying things like, "*I love these apps! I wanna play this one*" (C7), or "*I want to play...(pause)...this (pointing to app)*" (C10). Many children scrolled slowly through the full list of apps with their index finger hovering over the screen, appearing to search carefully for specific app icons. In one instance, the app crashed after the child had finished selecting her apps to play (C17) and then restarted. The child re-selected the same apps, suggesting she was making choices with intention and not at random.

All children engaged in activities like scrolling past apps without selecting them and saying things like, "*That's not one I want to play*" (C2), and announcing when they had finished making their selections. Many children showed this same intentionality as they ordered apps and specified their duration. These children said things like, "*I wanna do equal time [on each]*" (C11) while specifying each app's duration, and "*So I already played that one... maybe we can do that last, because I played it*" (C9) while ordering the list of apps.

As children described their intentions, they sometimes directed their statements to the adult they were with, saying things like, "*[I want] this one*" (C16). In other instances, children's descriptions of their intentions took the form of private speech [23] and were not directed at any audience, such as, "*I'll spend two on that (pause) I want (pause) no. There we go. I think I'll do (pause) I think I'll do (pause) equal*" (C14). Thus, in a variety of forms, children's statements demonstrated that they were making choices and doing so with intention. All 11 children made statements of this type when constructing their plans.

Parents' Support for Children's Intentionality

During the planning phase, parents' language not only respected children's autonomy but also actively encouraged it. Parents said things like, "*Let's pick the [apps] you really, really want,*" (P1), "*So what would you like to play?*" (P2), "*How much time do you want to play Lego?*" (P10), "*Is that a good order now?*" (P14), and "*Are you happy with this?*" (P3). All 11 parents made statements throughout the planning process prompting their children to identify their own intrinsic interests and take ownership of constructing a plan built with intention.

In addition to encouraging children's agency, parents also played a central role in helping children learn to use the app interface. Though all children were able to construct and execute a plan the first time they used the app, they did not do so in a vacuum, and parents' behaviors were central to children's interactions. A few children mastered all components of the UI spontaneously and without support, but many others looked to their parent for help at least once.

Across all 11 children's encounters with our planning interface, parents collectively provided 96 different facilitation attempts to teach children to use these controls correctly. We coded the ways that parents scaffolded children's understanding and found that their approaches clustered into eight different techniques, such as modeling the correct interaction, asking a question about the purpose of a control, or describing the intended interaction (Table 1).

Further, we observed that parents frequently provided multiple types of scaffolding and that the order in which they engaged in each type of scaffolding was not arbitrary. If a

Intervention	*Mom reaches out and adjusts the time limit immediately to 15 without saying anything to the child.*
Modeling	*Dad reaches over and demonstrates reordering, saying, "Set the order like this, wheep!"*
Purpose Description	*"So you're telling each one how long you're going to play."*
Purpose Question	*"Which one do you want to play first?"*
Purpose Instruction	*"Pick which apps you would like to play."*
UI Description	*"So if you move that it will add more time and take away time from that."*
UI Question	*"Do you think you hit the next [arrow]?"*
UI Instruction	*"Just drag it left to right."*

Table 1: Categories of parent facilitation with examples.

child did not engage in a productive interaction pattern after one attempt at facilitation, the parent would try another approach. We saw that parents tended to move from more open-ended instructions to more explicit ones, ostensibly providing more hands-on support if the child continued to struggle. For example, in the following exchange, the parent supports the child in using the duration control (Figure 1c) correctly but only after increasingly explicit attempts at facilitation:

> ***P9:*** *"So do you want it to be 5 minutes on each one? Or do you want more time on one?"*
> *Child leans in, has her pointing finger out, but hesitates and doesn't seem to have a clear mission.*
> ***C9:*** *"I... want... one." (Doesn't touch the screen)*
> ***P9:*** *"Ok. Which one do you want more time on?"*
> ***C9:*** *"This one." (Points to the first app)*
> ***P9:*** *"The building one? Ok, so if you move that" (pointing to thumb) "it will add more time" (pointing to first app) "and take away time from that" (pointing to second app)*
> *Child taps the thumb.*
> ***P9:*** *"Oh. Drag it."*
> *Child taps in several spots around the thumb and it jumps.*
> ***P9:*** *"Oh, drag it that way" (motions back and forth with her index finger demonstrating the drag).*
> *Child drags it smoothly and allocates more time to the app she had specified that she wanted to play longer.*
> ***P9:*** *"There ya go."*

To better understand the systematic pattern to parents' scaffolding attempts, we coded each instance of support that parents provided to children according to the eight themes we identified. We modeled parents' 96 collective facilitation attempts as a directed graph, with each type of scaffolding (purpose question, model, etc.) as its own node, and each sequential pair of facilitation attempts as a directed edge from the first type of facilitation to the type that followed.

We then ordered the vertices of the graph using the minimum linear arrangement algorithm [6], which assigns an ordering that minimizes the distances among nodes. Because minimum linear arrangement does not account for directionality, we applied the sum back-edge modification [24], which minimizes the amount of error introduced by backward edges. This approach showed that parents systematically applied facilitation strategies that followed the progression in Figure 4, consistent with the impression that parents' facilitation became increasingly more explicit if hands-off attempts failed.

Children's and Parents' Responses to Transitions

After planning out their play time, all children initiated and engaged in their planned play session. Using data from these sessions, we next examined children's interactions with and responses to the cues Plan & Play provided to support the user in sticking to his or her plan. Collectively,

```
1. Purpose Description
2. Purpose Question
3. {UI Description, UI Question}
4. Model
5. Purpose Instruction
6. UI Instruction
7. Intervention
```

Figure 4. Hierarchical order to parents' attempts at facilitating their child's understanding of the interface.

children encountered 41 transition points. In these cases, Plan & Play indicated that it was time to either move on to the next app or stop playing. In 31 instances, the child immediately responded to Plan & Play's cue and transitioned to the next activity without parent input. For example, a child transitioned from one app to the next on schedule as follows:

> *Countdown finishes for the second app and the Plan & Play dialog box appears.*
> ***P14:*** *"Did you finish?"*
> ***C14:*** *"Yeah, I did."*
> ***P14:*** *"Nice."*
> ***C14:*** *"Next is Toca!"*
> *Child taps the "Start Next App" button in the dialog box.*

In an additional five instances, the child did not make the transition immediately and instead spent a brief period of time continuing the current activity, then transitioned without parent intervention. In two instances, the parent did not give the child the opportunity to make this choice; when Plan & Play presented the cue, the parent intervened immediately and moved the child to the next activity before the child had a chance to respond. Finally, in three instances, the child ignored the cue and the parent eventually intervened.

As children played through their plans, both children and parents made comments describing the Plan & Play app as authoritative. Parents said things like, "*So you get 8 minutes with this app*" (P2), "*It looks like your 6 minutes are up,*" (P9), and "*Ok, so now it says 'Start Next App,' so press 'Start Next App'*" (P11), implying that the on-screen prompts should be followed. Children similarly said things like, "*It looks like we're all done*" (C7) and "*I have 28 seconds*" (C14). Some children also made statements tying these directions to their original planning like, (laughing) "*This one's gonna be only one minute, I did one minute for this one!*" (C1), though this was less common.

Usability and Follow-up

Children created a second plan during their follow-up session in which they taught a researcher to use Plan & Play. In their second encounter with these UI elements, children spontaneously performed the correct interaction with no support 88% of the time (53 out of 60 instances). Furthermore, children described their own actions and the controls they were using, saying things like "*[this is] how many minutes I play all the games together*" (C14) to describe the interface for setting the initial time limit, and "*This one you can also, like, move... which one you wanna play first*" (C9) to describe the screen for reordering apps (Figure 2b). Though several children required parent support to use aspects of the interface the first time they tried it, 10 out of 11 children could either explain the purpose of all six controls or use them purposefully during this second encounter.

Parent Perspectives

In addition to our observational data about children's use of our app, we also analyzed parents' responses to Plan & Play and their broader perspectives on their children's media use. As one measure of parents' interest in our approach, we offered to delete the Plan & Play app off the device at the end of each session. All 11 parents who brought a compatible device declined, saying things like, "*Do you need to delete it?*" (P9) and, "*Actually, can you leave it?*" (P1). Two parents spontaneously told their child at the end of the session that they thought they should start using the app at home, saying things like, "*So did you like making a plan to play? Do you think we should do that when you watch a screen?*" (P2). We did not ask parents at any point if they would be interested in trying Plan & Play again or using it at home, but at the end of the study session, several parents spontaneously mentioned that they felt inspired to make planning a part of their screen-time routine, saying things like, "*After seeing this, I am definitely motivated to set that kind of a plan for him.*" (P10). And all 11 parents elected to take Plan & Play home.

We explored parents' perspectives by asking them about topics relevant to Plan & Play. Here, we describe themes that emerged from the parent interview portion of our study.

Inevitability of Technology Use

Across participants, interviewees continually brought up the inevitability of their child's use of digital media now and in the future. Some parents framed this negatively, saying things like, "*I know she's gonna get way too much just because it's gonna be part of her world*" (P7) while others described this neutrally, saying things like, "*I know that as they grow older, since the schools use tablets and things like that, they're going to take notes on that*" (P8). Though their value judgments of the phenomenon varied, parents consistently told us that they expect digital media of all kinds to be deeply embedded in their child's daily life as they grow.

As a result, a recurring concern for parents is the need for their child to eventually become capable of limiting their use of technology to appropriate contexts and quantities. When describing their hopes for their child's future use of technology, parents told us things like, "*I hope that she'll be able to limit herself pretty well on how much time she's spending on screen time or tablet time*" (P9) and that, "*He should know, 'Okay, this is not the time to do it'*" (P10). Across participants, we heard that parents believe technology is going to play an increasingly prominent role in their child's life, and that this prominence is going to require children to develop the discipline and awareness to use it thoughtfully.

Child Compliance vs. Child Autonomy

All 14 parents told us that they set bounds on their child's media use and feel this is important. We pointed out that Plan & Play solicits child input in setting these limits, and we asked parents, "*How would that kind of approach fit with your family's values?*" Though 13 parents explicitly said that it would be a natural fit, as they believe children should be part of the conversation, parents surfaced two different perspectives on how these limits should be enforced.

Some parents felt strongly that children need to be regulated by parents, saying things like, "*You can [try to] rely on kids being good...but they are not. In all honesty, kids will try to push the boundaries wherever they can*" (P2). A nontrivial minority of parents expressed this view, and explained that, while children's voices should be part of the limit-setting process, children cannot be trusted to adhere to limits. However, the more dominant view among our participants was that children need a balance of both oversight and independence. These parents said things like, "*You have to trust a little bit that your kids are gonna make smart choices*" (P7). Of 14 interviewees, 9 said that in addition to soliciting children's input when setting limits, they also want their child to take some agency and responsibility in regulating their behavior.

Despite their proactive interest in giving children control, this second group of parents explained that compliance and self-determination, both of which they value, are in natural conflict. As one parent said:

> "*It's very hard to give her a sense of control in things, because, as a parent, you kind of just want them to do it the right way rather than do it their way in a lotta things. And so when I think about it, I do want her to make her own choices...those are good skills to develop because then it's going to help her become self-disciplined rather than parent-disciplined.*" (P9)

Similarly, another participant described the challenge of valuing both compliance and self-regulation by saying that:

> "*We definitely try to give them choices and let them decide. Sometimes it becomes really difficult because sometimes as parents we think that, 'Okay, we are telling you something. Just do it!'*" (P8)

Despite this tension, these parents felt that it is essential to give children some control over the limits they live by and the opportunity to self-regulate. As another parent explained:

> "*I feel like that's...necessary in this generation. The sooner...he figures out where his limits are and where the boundary is where like, 'Oh, I spent too much time*

and now I feel weird,' or like, 'I really wish I wouldn't' – it's good for him to figure that our earlier." (P4)

While these parents feel it is important for children to have bounds on the time they spent with entertainment media, they also feel that internalizing the ability to set and adhere to those limits is an important skill in the media-rich world that their children will inherit.

Parents surfaced this same theme in response to our open-ended prompt asking for positive and negative feedback about Plan & Play. Parents repeatedly told us that the most useful aspect of the app from their perspective was its ability to give children agency and ownership within defined parameters. As P11 explained:

"I like the idea of us defining the time limit, total, but I like the idea of her deciding, within that time limit, what it is she can do, cause I think that's good for just building up those planning skills and kind of giving her a sense of control."

Others spoke about Plan & Play, telling us that giving their child some input into explicitly setting up limits "*might give her a sense of responsibility*" (P7), or would lead to "*a conversation about it [the limits]. I think he would prefer that*" (P3). Similarly, another parent echoed that the approach would provide a valuable blend of boundaries and freedom, saying, "*I really like the idea... because we can say 'Totally you get this much time. It's now your decision'*" (P10). The majority of our parent participants felt that an experience that both encouraged limits and supported autonomy would align with parents' values and appeal to children as well.

Perspectives on Parental Controls

To further explore families' likelihood of adopting such a tool in daily life, we also asked parents about their interest in and experience with parental controls. Even though our parent participants want their children to use digital media within certain limits, very few currently use technology support to enforce these boundaries. For some parents, parental controls are both unnecessary and insufficient, as they believe children in this age range require supervision. They told us things like, "*Honestly, I don't want him to be using technology at this age without me being around*" (P2), and "*We try to just keep a close eye on what they're doing*" (P17).

For other parents, the idea of using parental controls had appeal, but their past experience with these tools has been too laborious or buggy. These parents described the controls they had tried as "*a hassle*" (P12) and said that they "*don't have time really*" (P1), "*don't know exactly how it's set up*" (P9), and "*don't really use those anymore as much as I did when we first got them*" (P4). They described their lack of useful tools as a problem that they expect to get worse as children grow, saying things like, "*I have no idea how I'm going to be able to control that as he kind of grows up, and to make sure that he's kind of safe by playing these games*" (P3).

While these parents are interested in reinforcement from technology, they reported a generally negative experience with the options that they have tried and a sense that they are not fully aware of the options that are available. Despite their dissatisfying past experiences, seven parents had tried using parental controls and 13 reported that they would like to do so in the future, suggesting that among our participants there is widespread interest in this space.

DISCUSSION

Children's Behaviors When Planning and Playing

Prior work shows that between the ages of 3 and 6, children have the capacity to engage in planning activities, and exercises that explicitly prompt planning are accessible and pedagogically valuable in the development of self-regulation [4,12]. Consistent with these recommendations for non-digital settings, we saw that all 11 children were capable of understanding and using the Plan & Play interface to make intentional choices about their playtime. Children made two different plans over the course of the study; for several participants, their first attempt required notable parent support, but by their second encounter with the interface, children were able to set a time limit, select apps, order them, and set a duration for each. However, the parents in our study provided attentive, hands-on support, and we do not know if children would have been able to navigate the interface or understand its purpose without this aid.

As they planned, all 11 children stated goals out loud and showed instances of initiative, the mediating factor in achieving gains in self-regulation through planning [31]. This evidence of children making self-directed, goal-oriented choices about the structure and content of their play experience is of particular interest, because it demonstrates the possibility for the interface to nudge children toward the autonomous behaviors that foster intrinsic motivation. While we saw that all children displayed purposeful decision making when selecting apps, a few of our participants did not show the same intentionality as they chose app durations, suggesting that their emerging understanding of order and magnitude could be a barrier to developing intentions about these components of their plan.

Finally, we saw that children understood the transition cues that Plan & Plan presented as they played and used these as a guide to adhere with minimal intervention to their self-defined choices. Both parents and children treated the app as a kind of third-party mediator. A few children referenced their own decision-making when they deferred to the authority of the plan.

Parent Perspectives on Child Autonomy

When we asked parents if they want their child to participate in limit-setting, nearly all of our participants told us that they do. The majority of parents further said that they value giving children some autonomy in living up to these limits, and that they feel it is essential for children to practice self-regulating. However, they also reported that giving children the freedom to exercise autonomy and self-regulation is not always straightforward. Even parents who value such opportunities, explain that there is an inherent tension between giving children control and keeping children within bounds. The majority of our parents reported that they value both, and that they struggle with the contradiction between them.

A minority of parents said that, though they want to solicit children's input when setting limits, they do not trust children to adhere to them without parent intervention. These parents reported wanting to maintain control over enforcing limits and did not place the same value on children's autonomy or opportunities for self-regulation. One contribution of this work is to identify these two distinct schools of thought among parents of young children.

Though we designed Plan & Play with the intention that children would have opportunities to proactively choose for themselves whether or not to comply with limits, it is clear from our small set of participants alone that the desire to foster children's self-determination is not universal among parents. We see the potential for Plan & Play to fit the lifestyles of families with diverse perspectives on this topic, and all parents proactively chose to bring the app home. However, future work remains to understand how families with these differing values and mediation styles use our tool in practice.

Parent Support

Independent of our exploration of self-regulation, we saw that parents played a central role in children's mastery of the UI. When children planned for the second time with a member of the research team, they were almost always able to work with all aspects of UI independently, but this was not true when they initially encountered the app with a parent. Many of our child participants' initial interactions were bolstered by support from their parents, and parents' facilitation attempts clustered into a taxonomy of eight techniques which they used hierarchically. Without prompting, parents spontaneously attempted to support their children with indirect techniques first and increasingly became more hands-on.

This progression is consistent with prior work in other domains demonstrating that providing instructions and support in a least-to-most intrusive fashion is an effective way of increasing children's learning [11,18]. Our parent participants' spontaneous use of this hierarchy suggests that adults may have an inherent or learned awareness of how they can best support their children in mastering novel interfaces.

However, other work has shown that scaffolding children's use of digital media can be challenging [36], thus it may be valuable to develop a formal theory to define effective practices for scaffolding child users. The systematic pattern to participants' successful facilitation suggests that this hierarchy is worth exploring as a general-purpose model for supporting novices learning to use new interfaces. Future work remains to determine whether the categories we identified and the progression our participants followed are useful in other contexts.

Limitations and Future Work

We do not yet know what children's experiences with Play & Play will be like in the wild or with repeated use for a longer period of time. While it is likely that children will continue to be capable of using the interface, we do not know whether they will continue to respond to the app's cues or follow their own plans. It is possible that children will habituate to these cues and ignore them, or even that repeated instances of planning without follow-through lead to diminished self-regulation. Through a future field deployment, we intend to evaluate children's media use, autonomy, and self-regulation after extended use of Plan & Play. We hope that these efforts will help us characterize the habits children develop in response to our system, and the role that the family plays in this habit formation.

We conducted our study with a small number of families from a single geographic area, and we recruited from high-tech populations. We saw that the ways in which parents engaged in the interaction together with their children played a central role in the child's experience, and we do not know how different parenting styles, levels of parent involvement, parent familiarity with technology, or parent attitudes toward technology will change children's experience with Plan & Play. While our lab setting gave us the opportunity to perform a close and detailed study of users' interactions with our system, the contribution of these findings is knowledge of these users' values, mental models, and interactions, not a generalizable understanding of the effects of Plan & Play.

CONCLUSIONS

Today's preschoolers will come of age in a world where they have the opportunity to engage with digital media at almost any moment. Technology has the potential to support them in the challenging task of becoming self-regulated individuals who take advantage of all that technology has to offer, but who also proactively disengage from technology as they feel is conducive to their well-being. Current mediation tools are effective in setting and enforcing limits, but this restriction-only approach is unlikely to catalyze development of the regulatory skills children need to become responsible and independent digital citizens.

Here, we present a system called Plan & Play for guiding preschoolers in using digital media purposefully. We show that, in the short-term, this system prompts intentionality and guides children in following through on these intentions. Parents play an integral role in determining the way children use and respond to digital media, and we show that, for most our parents, our system directly addresses the tension they wrestle with as they strive to both set boundaries for their children and give children the opportunity to learn to set boundaries for themselves.

REFERENCES

1. American Academy of Pediatrics. 2014. Where We Stand: TV Viewing Time. *Healthy Children.* Retrieved from http://www.healthychildren.org/English/family-life/Media/Pages/Where-We-Stand-TV-Viewing-Time.aspx
2. Morgan Ames. 2013. Managing mobile multitasking: the culture of iPhones on Stanford campus. *CHI '13*, ACM Press, 1487–1498. http://doi.org/10.1145/2441776.2441945
3. W. Steven Barnett, Kwanghee Jung, Donald J. Yarosz, Jessica Thomas, Amy Hornbeck, Robert Stechuk, Susan Burns. 2008. Educational effects of the Tools of the Mind curriculum: A randomized trial. *Early Childhood Research Quarterly* 23, 3, 299–313. http://doi.org/10.1016/j.ecresq.2008.03.001
4. Elena Bodrova and Deborah J. Leong. 2007. *Tools of the Mind: The Vygotskian Approach to Early Childhood Education.* Pearson Education, Upper Saddle River, NJ.
5. Sherryl Browne Graves. 1999. Television and prejudice reduction: When does television as a vicarious experience make a difference? *Journal of Social Issues* 55, 4, 707–727. http://doi.org/10.1111/0022-4537.00143
6. Moses Charikar, Mohammad Taghi Hajiaghayi, Howard Karloff, and Satish Rao. 2006. l22 spreading metrics for vertex ordering problems. *Proc. SODA '06*. Society for Industrial and Applied Mathematics, 1018–1027.
7. Common Sense Media. 2014. Screen Time. Retrieved August 1, 2015 from https://www.commonsensemedia.org/screen-time
8. Edward L. Deci, Robert E. Driver, Lucinda Hotchkiss, Robert J. Robbins, and Ilona McDougal Wilson. 1993. The relation of mothers' controlling vocalizations to children's intrinsic motivation. *Journal of Experimental Child Psychology* 55, 2, 151–162. http://doi.org/10.1006/jecp.1993.1008
9. Edward L. Deci, Haleh Eghrari, Brian C. Patrick, and Dean R. Leone. 1994. Facilitating internalization: the self-determination theory perspective. *Journal of Personality* 62, 1, 119–142. http://doi.org/10.1111/j.1467-6494.1994.tb00797.x
10. Edward L. Deci, John Nezlek, and Louise Sheinman. 1981. Characteristics of the rewarder and intrinsic motivation of the rewardee. *Journal of Personality and Social Psychology* 40, 1, 1–10. http://doi.org/10.1037/0022-3514.40.1.1
11. Patricia M. Doyle, Mark Wolery, Melinda Jones Ault, and David L. Gast. 1988. System of least prompts: a literature review of procedural parameters. *Research and Practice for Persons with Severe Disabilities* 13, 1, 28–40. http://doi.org/10.1177/154079698801300104
12. Ann S. Epstein. 2003. How planning and reflection develop young children's thinking skills. *Young Children* 58, 5, 28–36.
13. Ann Frodi, Lisa Bridges, and Wendy Grolnick. 1985. Correlates of mastery-related behavior: a short-term longitudinal study of infants in their second year. *Child Development* 56, 5, 1291. http://doi.org/10.2307/1130244
14. Wendy S. Grolnick, Edward L. Deci, and Richard M. Ryan. 1997. *Internalization within the family: The self-determination theory perspective.* John Wiley & Sons Inc.
15. Wendy S. Grolnick and Richard M. Ryan. 1989. Parent styles associated with children's self-regulation and competence in school. *Journal of Educational Psychology* 81, 2, 143–154. http://doi.org/10.1037/0022-0663.81.2.143
16. Heidi Hartikainen, Netta Iivari, and Marianne Kinnula. 2016. Should we design for control, trust or involvement? *Proc. IDC '16*, ACM Press, 367–378. http://doi.org/10.1145/2930674.2930680
17. Yasmeen Hashish, Andrea Bunt, and James E Young. 2014. Involving children in content control: a collaborative and education-oriented content filtering approach. *Proc. CHI '14*, ACM Press, 1797–1806. http://doi.org/10.1145/2556288.2557128
18. Lindsay Hilsen. 2013. *A step-by-step ABA curriculum for young learners with autism spectrum disorders (age 3-10)*. Jessica Kingsley Publishers.
19. Alexis Hiniker, Kiley Sobel, and Bongshin Lee. 2017. Co-designing with preschoolers using fictional inquiry and comicboarding. *Proc. CHI '17*, ACM Press, *to appear*. http://doi.org/http://dx.doi.org/10.1145/3025453.3025588
20. Alexis Hiniker, Kiley Sobel, Hyewon Suh, Yi-Chen Sung, Charlotte P. Lee, and Julie A. Kientz. 2015. Texting while parenting: How adults use mobile phones while caring for children at the playground. *Proc. CHI '15*, ACM Press, 727–736. http://doi.org/10.1145/2702123.2702199
21. Minsam Ko, Subin Yang, Joonwon Lee, Christian Heizmann, Jinyoung Jeong, Uichin Lee, Daehee Shin, Koji Yatani, Junehwa Song, and Kyong-Mee Chung. 2015. NUGU: A group-based intervention app for improving self-regulation of limiting smartphone use. *Proc. CSCW '15*, ACM Press, 1235–1245. http://doi.org/10.1145/2675133.2675244
22. Richard Koestner, Richard M. Ryan, Frank Bernieri, and Kathleen Holt. 1984. Setting limits on children's

behavior: The differential effects of controlling vs. informational styles on intrinsic motivation and creativity. *Journal of Personality* 52, 3, 233–248. http://doi.org/10.1111/j.1467-6494.1984.tb00879.x

23. Lawrence Kohlberg, Judy Yaeger, and Else Hjertholm. 1968. Private speech: Four studies and a review of theories. *Child Development* 39, 3, 691. http://doi.org/10.2307/1126979
24. Laszlo Kozma. 2012. Ordering Cyclic Graphs. *LK Blog*. Retrieved from http://lkozma.net/blog/ordering-cyclic-graphs/
25. Shannon Lockhart. 2010. Play: An important tool for cognitive development. *Extensions Curriculum Newsletter from HighScope* 24, 3, 1–8.
26. Marije Nouwen, Maarten Van Mechelen, and Bieke Zaman. 2015. A value sensitive design approach to parental software for young children. *Proc. IDC '15*, ACM Press, 363–366. http://doi.org/10.1145/2771839.2771917
27. Susan B. Palmer, Jean Ann Summers, Mary Jane Brotherson, Elizabeth J. Erwin, Susan P. Maude, Vera Stroup-Rentier, Hsiang-Yi Wu, Nancy F. Peck, Yuzhu Zheng, Cindy J. Weigel, Szu-Yin Chu, Greg S. McGrath, and Shana J. Haines. 2013. Foundations for self-determination in early childhood: An inclusive model for children with disabilities. *Topics in Early Childhood Special Education* 33, 1, 38–47. http://doi.org/10.1177/0271121412445288
28. Eric E Rasmussen, Autumn Shafer, Malinda J. Colwell, Shawna White, Narissra Punyanunt-Carter, Rebecca L. Densley, and Holly Wright. 2016. Relation between active mediation, exposure to *Daniel Tiger's Neighborhood*, and US preschoolers' social and emotional development. *Journal of Children and Media* 10, 4, 443–461. http://doi.org/10.1080/17482798.2016.1203806
29. Mabel L. Rice, Aletha C. Huston, Rosemarie Truglio, and John C. Wright. 1990. Words from "Sesame Street": Learning vocabulary while viewing. *Developmental Psychology 26*, 421–428.
30. Richard M. Ryan and Edward L. Deci. 2000. Self-determination theory and the facilitation of intrinsic motivation, social development, and well-being. *The American psychologist* 55, 1, 68–78.
31. Lawrence J. Schweinhart and David P. Weikart. 1997. The High/Scope preschool curriculum comparison study through age 23. *Early Childhood Research Quarterly* 12, 2, 117–143. http://doi.org/10.1016/S0885-2006(97)90009-0
32. Lawrence J Schweinhart, Jeanne Montie, Zongping Xiang, William S. Barnett, Clive R. Belfield, and Milagros Nores. 2005. *Lifetime effects: the High/Scope Perry Preschool study through age 40*. High/Scope Press.
33. Lawrence J. Schweinhart and D. P. Weikart. 1988. The High/Scope Perry Preschool. *14 ounces of prevention: A casebook for practitioners*. John Wiley.
34. Dwayne P. Sheehan, Sue Scott, Nadine van Wyk, Cynthia Watson, Kim Nagan, and Miranda MacCallum. 2013. Using self-determination theory to assess the attitudes of children and youth towards physical activity. *Physical & Health Education Journal* 79, 4, 40.
35. Aric Sigman. 2012. Time for a view on screen time. *Archives of disease in childhood* 97, 11, 935–42. http://doi.org/10.1136/archdischild-2012-302196
36. Lori Takeuchi and Reed Stevens. 2011. The new coviewing: Designing for learning through joint media engagement. *New York, NY: The Joan Ganz Cooney Center at Sesame Workshop.*
37. Barbara J. Wilson. 2008. Media and children's aggression, fear, and altruism. *Future of Children* 18, 1, 87–118.
38. Pamela Wisniewski, Haiyan Jia, Na Wang, Saijing Zheng, Heng Xu, Mary Beth Rosson, and John M. Carroll . 2015. Resilience mitigates the negative effects of adolescent Internet addiction and online risk exposure. *Proc. CHI '15*, ACM Press, 4029–4038. http://doi.org/10.1145/2702123.2702240
39. Nicola Yuill, Yvonne Rogers, and Jochen Rick. 2013. Pass the iPad: collaborative creating and sharing in family groups. *Proc. CHI '13*, ACM Press, 941–950. http://doi.org/10.1145/2470654.2466120
40. Bieke Zaman and Marije Nouwen. 2016. Parental controls: advice for parents, researchers and industry. *EU Kids Online*. Retrieved from http://eprints.lse.ac.uk/65388/

Investigating the Effects of Interactive Features for Preschool Television Programming

Elizabeth J. Carter
Disney Research
Pittsburgh, PA, USA
liz.carter@disneyresearch.com

Jennifer Hyde
Disney Research
Pittsburgh, PA, USA
jdtam@cs.cmu.edu

Jessica K. Hodgins
Disney Research
Pittsburgh, PA, USA
jkh@cs.cmu.edu

ABSTRACT
As children begin to watch more television programming on systems that allow for interaction, such as tablets and videogame systems, there are different opportunities to engage them. For example, the traditional pseudo-interactive features that cue young children's participation in television viewing (e.g., asking a question and pausing for two seconds to allow for an answer) can be restructured to include correct response timing by the program or eventually even feedback. We performed three studies to examine the effects of accurate program response times, repeating unanswered questions, and providing feedback on the children's likelihood of response. We find that three- to five-year-old children are more likely to verbally engage with programs that wait for their response and repeat unanswered questions. However, providing feedback did not affect response rates for children in this age range.

ACM Classification Keywords
H.5.m. Information Interfaces and Presentation (e.g. HCI): Miscellaneous

Author Keywords
Child-computer interaction; interactive multimedia for children; children's television; pseudo-interaction.

INTRODUCTION
The introduction of *Blue's Clues* in 1996 ushered in an expansion of pseudo-interaction in children's television, in which characters appear to converse with their viewers directly [5]. These conversational features typically consist of a character asking a question, pausing for a set amount of time, and then responding either in a way that does not acknowledge the child's answer specifically (e.g., presenting the correct answer and then moving on) or responding only positively (e.g., saying, "Great!" and presenting the correct answer, regardless of whether the viewer's response was correct). The massive popularity of shows like *Blue's Clues* and *Dora the Explorer* indicates that children enjoy the pseudo-interactive features and become very engaged with the shows and their characters. Moreover, the format has been shown to have positive effects on viewers (e.g., [3, 9, 16]), helping ensure that this style of programming has remained on the air for two decades.

IDC 2017, June 27–30, 2017, Stanford, CA, USA.

ACM ISBN 978-1-4503-4921-5/17/06 ...$15.00.
http://dx.doi.org/10.1145/3078072.3079717

With the advent of computers and tablets, contingent reactions by the media to children's responses are now possible. Broadcast television is limited by its inability to provide flexible timelines for response, prompt a second time to attempt to get an answer, or contribute feedback. Tablets provide an opportunity to improve upon standard television techniques because they have embedded microphones that can be used to detect user speech. Moreover, children as young as two years old use touchscreen tablets to perform simple tasks [10]. While accurate speech recognition is not yet developed for preschool-aged children, detecting speech (i.e., sound) is possible.

We designed a set of three experiments to investigate the effects of using temporal contingency (i.e., having the character respond quickly after the child finishes rather than after a set amount of time), repeating unanswered questions, and providing feedback on children's engagement. In the first study, we compared an unaltered television episode containing prompts followed by a set amount of silence to a similar episode that we divided into video clips to create a program in which the amount of silence following each prompt was contingent on the child's response. After a prompt, an experimenter waited for the child to provide a verbal response before advancing to the next clip. If no response was given after 10 s, the next clip would automatically play. In the second study, we compared the temporally contingent version to a version that was temporally contingent with "reprompts". In the version with reprompts, the child would be prompted with the same question again if s/he had not responded within 8 s. These two studies mimic the use of a microphone in an app to detect speech. In the third study, we compared the effects of using speech recognition to provide feedback for correct and incorrect answers to doing only basic speech detection. We specifically focused on behaviors reflecting engagement (e.g., answering questions) because they are an important base for more complex research questions.

RELATED WORK
It has long been known that young children engage with television. Much of the previous research on program structure probed pseudo-interactive features and their effects on learning and memory in order to inform the development of educational programming. For example, adding different questions to a televised story determined that learning was facilitated

most by asking personalized, viewer-directed questions, followed by asking rhetorical questions and asking no questions [16]. Long-term viewing of programs with pseudo-interactive features has been found to be positively correlated with vocabulary size and expressive language production in toddlers [9]. Moreover, rates of responsiveness to these features during an episode correlate with story comprehension [2].

In addition to the presence of the pseudo-interactive features themselves, various aspects of the programs can affect the likelihood of response. For example, toddlers were better able to learn a task from a pre-recorded video when it was presented by a familiar, socially meaningful character rather than an unfamiliar character [6, 8]. Additionally, use of a familiar actor (their mother) has been found to help infants and toddlers imitate videorecorded actions [7]. Moreover, multiple viewings of a single episode of a program with pseudo-interactive features elicited increased verbal and nonverbal interactions from preschool children [3]. Program familiarity has also been demonstrated to affect the relationship between pseudo-interactive features and comprehension such that children who are already familiar with programs show greater comprehension benefits from pseudo-interaction cues [13].

Finally, perceived contingency matters. Contingency is a key component of interpersonal interaction. Infants younger than six months of age can distinguish and attend differently to temporally contingent interactions over videoconference than to prerecorded presentations [4]. Truly social interactions are inherently temporally contingent, to the degree that adults are sensitive to audiovisual interaction delays of 500 ms and audio delays of 400 ms when using telecommunication, beyond which conversations are considered unnatural [15]. Even very young children show influences of social contingency. Prior research found that two-year-olds who were given instructions via passive video viewing were not able to follow them as well as those given instructions in person; however, having a brief, contingent interaction over videoconference that demonstrated the instructor's ability to share attentional focus mitigated the effect [17]. Social contingency improves imitation [12], novel verb learning [14], and verbal pattern learning [11]. These results suggest that social familiarity and temporal contingency can affect engagement in and recall of interactions.

EXPERIMENT 1

In our first experiment, we manipulated the timing of a television program to increase perceived contingency and investigated the effects on verbal and nonverbal responses.

Participants

Seventeen children between the ages of 3 and 5 years (10 girls, 7 boys, age range 3.003 to 5.537 years, mean(stdev) age = 4.240(0.833)) participated successfully in this research, which was approved by our Institutional Review Board. We recruited children from the local community via posted advertisements and email lists. An additional boy was enrolled in the study but not included in the analysis due to equipment failure. Participants had normal or corrected-to-normal hearing and vision. Families were compensated for their time.

Episode	Total Prompts	Repeat Phrase	Yes/No	Free Response
Egg	26	7	6	13
Birdhouse	24	7	9	8

Table 1. Number of prompts by episode.

Materials

We selected a television program, *Mickey Mouse Clubhouse*, that was directed at a preschool-aged audience (ages three to five years), contained prompts to elicit verbal responses from the children, and included characters that are familiar to most children in our culture. By using familiar characters, we hoped to maximize the children's verbal responses to the program, similar to previous research (e.g., [6, 8]). We watched several episodes of the program and annotated various categories of prompts (i.e., phrase repetition, yes-or-no questions, and free response questions) to identify two similar episodes. (See Table 1.) In one episode, the characters built a birdhouse ("Goofy the Homemaker", henceforth referred to as Birdhouse episode); in the other, they took care of an egg ("Donald Hatches an Egg", or Egg episode). In both episodes, viewers are asked directly to help the characters select tools to solve problems. The episodes contained 24 and 26 total prompts, 7 of which asked the child to repeat what the character said, with the pauses typically lasting less than 2 s (mean(stdev) = 1.790(0.962), range = 0 to 5.471 s). To make the episodes short enough that a within-subjects design was feasible within one hour, we edited them down from 24 min to approximately 20 min while ensuring that only content irrelevant to the overarching plots was removed (e.g., the theme song) and all prompts were unaltered. The Birdhouse and Egg episodes then lasted 19 min 49 s and 20 min 14 s, respectively.

For each episode, we created two versions. For the Original version, we only edited the episodes for length, so the children saw the episodes in a similar fashion to watching them on television at home. For the Contingent version, we edited the videos into individual clips that ended after each prompt. (See Figure 1.) The clips ranged in length from 3 s to 2 min 34 s, and the two episodes did not differ significantly in clip length (Birdhouse mean(stdev) clip length = 41.4(44.6) s, Egg = 45.9(41.1), $t = 0.553$, $p = 0.583$). We created software that could play the Original and Contingent versions of the episodes. When playing the Contingent versions of the episodes, the program would play a clip until its end and then start a timer for 10 s. A manual command could be sent to interrupt the timer and play the next clip immediately. If no command was sent, the next clip would automatically play at the end of the timer. We used a Wizard-of-Oz method wherein an experimenter listened to the participant and only sent the manual command to play the next clip after each prompt had received a verbal response. (Nonverbal responses were ignored, as they would be by a microphone.) If a participant failed to respond to a prompt, the experimenter let the software advance automatically to the next clip after the waiting period of 10 s. This experimenter remained out of the child's view.

Figure 1. Illustrations of the Original and Contingent conditions.

To assess the children's memory for different characters and events throughout the episodes, we designed a quiz. After each episode, an experimenter asked the participant to put images of four scenes from the episode in chronological order. Additionally, participants were asked five questions to see if they remembered various plot points. The experimenter also asked if they thought the characters could hear them, what their favorite part was, and if they had seen the episode before.

For each participant, a parent completed a survey to assess the child's familiarity with the program: how often the child watched the show; whether the child had watched these episodes; and whether the child was familiar with each character. We also asked whether the child watched similar programs (*Dora the Explorer*, *Blue's Clues*) or used tablet applications that provide responses to prompts (e.g., ToyTalk/PullString^{TM} apps; Disney Junior Appisodes); the child's favorite shows; if the child typically responded to televised prompts; and if the child behaved similarly to how s/he would at home.

Procedure

Each participant came into the laboratory individually for the experiment. While participants viewed the episodes, their parents completed the surveys about media habits. Parents were allowed into the experiment room, but we requested that they remain quiet and at a small distance to ensure that they did not interfere with the children's responses. Participants were recorded while viewing each episode on an Apple 27-inch monitor with an integrated camera and microphone system to ensure corresponding timestamps on the episode and the participant video. Each participant sat on a chair approximately 0.85 m from the monitor, alongside an experimenter.

Each episode of the selected program started with the same scene and two prompts ("Want to come inside my clubhouse?" and "Say the magic words...") prior to the theme song. Thus, the experimenter sitting near the child was able to indicate to children who were not responding at the beginning of either episode that they needed to respond without affecting memory for the unique content of the episode (e.g., "<Character> can't hear you, you need to speak up."). This experimenter also informed participants if they were not speaking loudly enough to be accurately recorded and heard by the wizard experimenter. Other than these instructions, the experimenter kept her own speech to a minimum by not initiating conversation and providing only minimal responses when the child initiated interactions (e.g., saying only yes or no and then attending to the monitor).

A repeated-measures design was performed to maximize statistical power. Each participant viewed two episodes of the program, one each in the Original and Contingent conditions. Episode and condition were both counterbalanced, and combinations were randomly assigned. After each episode, they completed the corresponding quiz.

Analysis

An annotator reviewed the videos for all participants and used ELAN annotation software [1] to denote: the beginning and ending of each utterance made by the child, whether each utterance was or was not a response to a prompt from the TV show, and whether each utterance in response to a prompt was a valid (expected) or unexpected response. Similarly, they denoted the same features for nonverbal behaviors (e.g., pointing or other gestures) and behaviors where the children combined verbal and nonverbal responses (e.g., pointing while saying, "That one!"). Responses including both verbal and nonverbal content were marked as combined. In some cases, children responded to an anticipated prompt before the prompt actually occurred. In cases where this response began more

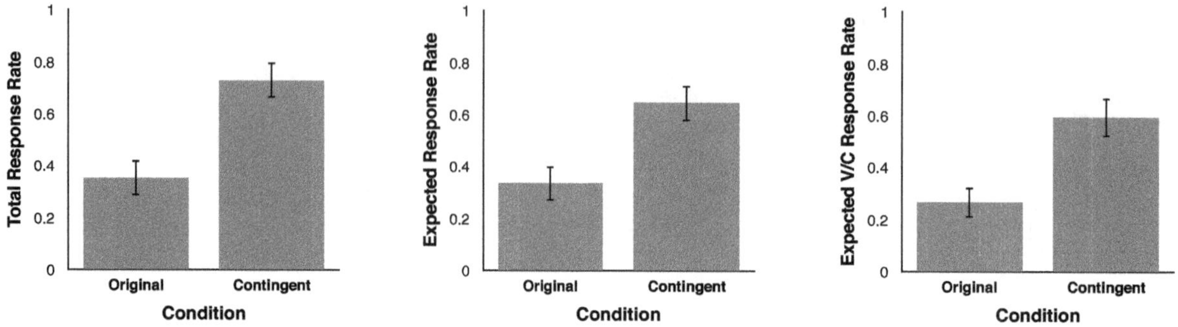

Figure 2. Response rates by condition for (a) all possible responses, (b) expected responses, and (c) expected verbal or combined responses. Error bars represent standard error in all figures.

than 800 ms before the end of the prompt, we classified it as an Early Response and considered it separately in analyses. We did not score whether any answer was correct because we did not want to penalize incorrect but valid answers (e.g., saying no instead of yes, suggesting an incorrect tool to solve a problem when it was also listed as a possibility). Additionally, in cases where a participant pointed at an object on the screen and said, "That one!", it was often impossible for the experimenter or annotator to tell where they were pointing.

We looked at the overall rate of response, rate of expected response, and response time for all categories of behavior (verbal, nonverbal, combined) together. To analyze the combined behaviors, we merged them with verbal behaviors because they included the verbal output required for contingency. This categorization simulated the use of a microphone by an app.

We analyzed the data using the Restricted Maximum Likelihood (REML) approach to ensure proper p-values for multiple comparisons and account for non-normal distribution.

Results

We examined both response rates and response times in our analyses. We omitted data from the first two prompts because they served as practice with experimenter intervention.

Response Rates

First, we examined the overall response rate, calculated as the ratio of prompts that received any response (verbal, nonverbal, or combined; expected or unexpected). The children responded significantly more to the prompts in the Contingent condition (Original mean(stdev) response rate $= 0.354(0.266)$, Contingent $= 0.730(0.272)$; $F = 75.335$, $p < 0.0001$). (See Figure 2 and Table 2.) In fact, higher response rates for the Contingent condition were found for 16 of the 17 children. Additionally, they responded more to the video that they saw second (First $= 0.489(0.382)$, Second $= 0.594(0.261)$; $F = 14.570$, $p = 0.0030$) and more to one episode of the program than the other (Egg $= 0.640(0.300)$, Birdhouse $= 0.444(0.331)$; $F = 15.617$, $p = 0.0023$). There was no significant effect of whether the children reported having seen an episode before (which occurred for 12 children for the Egg episode and 9 for the Birdhouse episode). When we limited our analysis to only expected (verbal, nonverbal, or combined) responses, we found the same pattern of effects with a greater response to Contingent than Original videos (Original mean(stdev) response rate $= 0.336(0.259)$, Contingent $= 0.647(0.279)$; $F = 53.779$, $p < 0.0001$), to the video they saw second (First $= 0.467(0.360)$, Second $= 0.526(0.263)$; $F = 9.401$, $p = 0.0108$), and to the Egg episode than the Birdhouse episode (Egg $= 0.570(0.291)$, Birdhouse $= 0.414(0.314)$; $F = 10.384$, $p = 0.0081$). Again, prior viewing had no significant effect.

	Original	Contingent	F	p
Overall Response Rate	0.354	0.730	75.335	< 0.0001
Expected Response Rate	0.336	0.647	53.779	< 0.0001
Expected V/C Response Rate	0.283	0.595	69.625	< 0.0001
Overall Response Time	0.584	2.243	25.668	0.0004
V/C Response Time	0.673	2.110	18.754	0.0001

Table 2. Response data by condition.

We then looked at effects in the various response categories. For these analyses, the combined responses were analyzed with the verbal responses because they contained verbal content that a microphone could hear in a system similar to current apps doing speech detection. We saw the same pattern in the verbal/combined responses such that the rate was higher for the Contingent condition (Original mean(stdev) response rate $= 0.283(0.245)$, Contingent $= 0.675(0.295)$; $F = 69.625$, $p < 0.0001$), to the video they saw second (First $= 0.450(0.378)$, Second $= 0.508(0.290)$; $F = 7.150$, $p = 0.0222$), and to the Egg episode (Egg $= 0.605(0.307)$, Birdhouse $= 0.353(0.317)$; $F = 24.572$, $p = 0.0005$). Prior viewing had no effect. The same pattern was found for expected verbal/combined responses (Original mean(stdev) response rate $= 0.268(0.236)$, Contingent $= 0.595(0.300)$; $F = 62.462$, $p < 0.0001$; First $= 0.418(0.356)$, Second $= 0.445(0.274)$; $F = 5.816$, $p = 0.0347$; Egg $= 0.534(0.300)$, Birdhouse $= 0.329(0.301)$; $F = 20.347$, $p = 0.0009$).

For the 64 observed nonverbal responses, we did not see a similar pattern. There were no significant effects for condition, order, episode, or prior viewing, but there was a significant interaction between condition and order such that the children responded nonverbally more often when they saw the Contingent version first than second ($F = 6.437$, $p = 0.0282$).

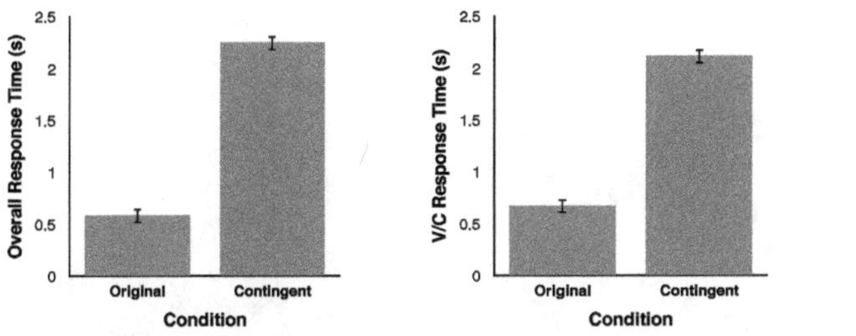

Figure 3. Response times by condition for (a) all responses and (b) verbal and combined responses only.

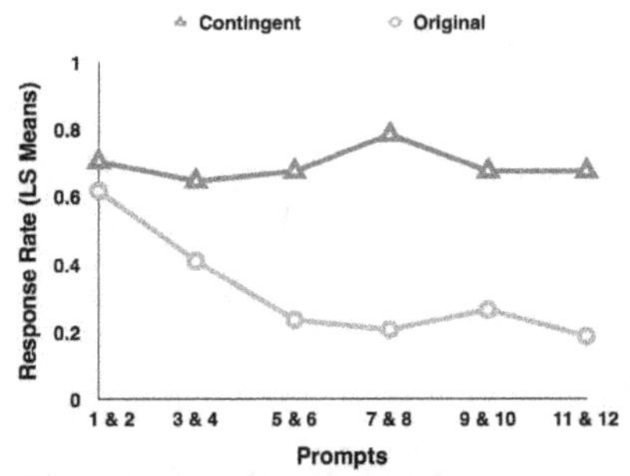

Figure 4. Response rates by prompt for the first twelve prompts in the Contingent and Original conditions.

The rate of Early Response (37 occurrences) was not affected by condition, order, episode, prior viewing, or the interaction between condition and order.

Response Times

When we examined the time that elapsed between the end of a prompt and the beginning of a response, we found a significant effect of condition that indicated slower responses in the Contingent condition (Original mean(stdev) response time (s) $= 0.584(0.305)$, Contingent $= 2.243(0.962)$; $F = 25.668$, $p = 0.0004$). (See Figure 3.) There were no other significant effects. When we examined verbal/combined responses alone, we similarly found only an effect of condition (Original $= 0.673(0.431)$, Contingent $= 2.110(1.053)$; $F = 18.754$, $p = 0.0001$). In the Original condition, the maximum response time to any prompt was 3.667 s. For the Contingent condition, the maximum response time to any prompt was 10.317 s. We found that 94.4% of responses in the Contingent condition occurred in under 8 s. When we compared the response times in the Contingent condition to the pauses provided in the Original condition, we found that 48.9% of the responses in the Contingent condition began after the pause in the Original condition would have ended.

Response Trends

To determine whether the children understood or were aware that the Contingent episode required a verbal response to continue, we examined longitudinal patterns in the children's responses. The response rates to the first two prompts were similar and very high (Original mean response rate $= 0.618$, Contingent $= 0.688$) because the children who did not speak on their own during these two prompts in both conditions were encouraged to do so by the experimenter. We paired the subsequent ten prompts in order to examine approximately half of each episode, assuming that it would take fewer than 12 prompts for children to realize that the video was advancing when they responded. The results are displayed in Figure 4. An analysis of variance (ANOVA) revealed significant main effects of condition ($F = 65.342$, $p < 0.0001$), prompt pair ($F = 2.665$, $p = 0.0240$), episode ($F = 8.300$, $p = 0.0046$), and the interaction between prompt and condition ($F = 2.473$, $p = 0.0343$). This interaction shows that children become significantly less likely to respond to a question in the Original condition as time passes relative to the Contingent condition.

Questionnaire Results

In addition to using the responses on the parent questionnaires and children's quizzes to determine which children were familiar with the episodes, we examined them to put the results in context. Three children provided no expected verbal, nonverbal, or combined responses while viewing either condition. From the parent questionnaires, we learned that two of those children had no prior experience with pseudo-interactive television (or, in one case, any television). The third child was shy and the parent reported that she was not behaving and speaking as she would at home. Additionally, we found no significant correlations between correct answers to the memory questions in the children's quiz (mean(stdev) $= 2.42(1.12)$) and whether the parents or children reported that they had seen the episodes before. Finally, there were no significant differences in the number of correct quiz questions by condition or episode. However, we did find a significant correlation between age and total score ($r = 0.654, p = 0.002$), which may have overwhelmed any other potential effects.

Discussion

Overall, whether children were viewing an episode in the Contingent versus Original condition had many effects. Children had higher response rates, expected response rates, verbal/combined response rates, and expected verbal/combined response rates in the Contingent condition. Additionally, they had longer response times (overall and verbal/combined) during the Contingent condition, nearly half of which occurred after the original pause lengths. Together, these findings suggest that children are far more likely to speak to the television when the episode is waiting for them and they have time to do so. Moreover, they realize that the episode is or is not waiting for their responses within the first several prompts. Additionally, the pauses in typical television programs may preempt responses by providing insufficient time for children to formulate and speak their answers before proceeding, although future research should investigate this question more directly. Typically, the programs wait only up to two seconds for responses. Our findings suggest that even when children answer, it is often not within this time window, and contingent programs should wait up to 8 s.

The children were also more likely to provide any response, expected responses, and verbal/combined responses for the second episode that they saw in the experiment relative to the first. These findings suggest that there may be a warm up period in which children are learning about and adjusting to the technology, after which response rates increase.

Figure 5. An example of what happened if a child did not respond to a prompt in the Reprompt condition.

Our findings also suggest that one episode contained more challenging prompts than the other. The response rate, expected response rate, verbal/combined response rate, and expected verbal/combined response rate were all higher for the Egg episode than the Birdhouse episode. These results suggest that the Birdhouse episode was more difficult.

Finally, some variables had no effect on response types, rates, or timing. Prior viewing of an episode did not seem to be reflected in behavior, and nonverbal behaviors were generally unaffected by experimental manipulations. Given that there was no positive reinforcement for nonverbal behaviors in either condition, the lack of a significant effect was unsurprising and also indicated that the children only adjusted to the reinforced (i.e., verbal) behavior.

EXPERIMENT 2

Our second experiment investigated whether repeating questions that did not originally receive a response affected the likelihood of eliciting verbal responses from children.

Participants

We enrolled 16 children between the ages of 3 and 5 years for this study (9 girls, 7 boys, age range 3.485 to 5.638 years, mean(stdev) age $= 4.583(0.655)$). Five additional children were not included in analyses due to equipment failure. Eleven of the children participated in Experiment 1, and five children previously participated in Experiment 3. Participants waited at least one month between visits (mean(stdev) $= 65(25)$ days, range 37 to 113 days). Recruitment and consent procedures were identical to Experiment 1.

Materials

We used the same selection methodology to choose the two episodes included in Experiment 2, "Pete's Beach Blanket Luau" (referred to as Luau episode) and "Mickey's Roundup" (Roundup episode). These videos were matched on the number and structure of prompts (see Table 3) and had similar clip lengths (Luau $= 37.8(51.769)$ s, Roundup $= 43.8(46.346)$ s, $t = 0.452$, $p = 0.653$). The Contingent condition remained the same; however, we replaced the Original condition with a Reprompt condition that had additional clips. Thus, participants viewed two episodes each, one Contingent and one Reprompt. For the Reprompt condition, the software would replay a clip containing only the prompt from the end of the previous clip if the participant remained silent for 8 s (Figure 5). We decreased this interval from 10 s to 8 s based on the response time results from Experiment 1. The experimenter would play the next clip

Episode	Total Prompts	Repeat Phrase	Yes/No	Free Response
Luau	28	5	5	18
Roundup	27	6	8	13

Table 3. Number of prompts by episode.

as soon as a verbal response was produced; alternatively, the software automatically advanced in the absence of a verbal response after an additional 8 s.

Procedure

We followed the same procedure as in Experiment 1 for viewing. The episodes and conditions were again counterbalanced, and participants completed a similar quiz after each episode. We administered the parent questionnaire to new participants.

Analysis

We used an identical coding scheme, analysis method, and statistical model as in Experiment 1, with the addition of noting which clips consisted of reprompts where the previous prompt was repeated.

Results

In order to get a full picture of the effects of reprompting, we specifically examined individual instances of reprompts after performing our initial analyses.

Response Rates

Across both the Contingent and Reprompt conditions, participants showed a high overall response rate (mean(stdev) $=$ $90.8(0.162)\%$) to the first instances of the prompts. There was a similarly high verbal/combined response rate ($89.1(0.174)\%$) and expected verbal/combined response rate ($85.727(0.177)\%$). We examined the total response rates, verbal/combined response rates, and expected verbal/combined response rates to the prompts that all children saw (i.e., without reprompt clips) and found no significant effects of condition, episode, order, or their interactions (all $p > 0.05$).

Response to Reprompts

Eleven of the 16 participants saw at least one reprompting clip. The other six children provided a verbal response to all of the original prompts during the Reprompt condition. Forty-one instances of reprompting occurred throughout the entire experiment, for which there were 440 opportunities in the Reprompt condition. For the 41 instances, two had an interval

Participant	Instances	Responses	Expected V/C
1	1	1	0
2	5	3	3
3	8	8	8
4	2	2	1
5	4	4	4
6	2	2	2
7	7	4	4
8	2	2	1
9	2	1	0
10	5	5	5
11	1	0	0
Total	39	32	28

Table 4. For the participants who saw at least one reprompt clip, the number they saw (Instances) and the number to which they subsequently responded in any way (Responses) and in an expected verbal or combined way (Expected V/C).

between the reprompt clip and the following clip of under 0.2 s, indicating that they answered during the reprompt clip before it noticeably played. Thus, only 39 reprompt clips were analyzed (Table 4). Of the 11 children who saw reprompts, the number of reprompts ranged from 1 to 8 (mean(stdev) = 3.545(2.423)). In 32 of these cases, the participants responded in the interval following the reprompt clip; 28 times with an expected verbal or combined response. Participants did not respond to the reprompt clip in the remaining six cases. Thus, 32 of 39 (82.1%) of the experienced reprompts elicited responses, 28 (71.8%) of which were appropriate and included verbal input.

Because only a subset of the children ever saw a Reprompt clip, we analyzed their data separately. These 11 children did not show significant differences in their overall response rates, verbal/combined response rates, and expected verbal/combined response rates by condition. However, we note for future research that the means for all response rates were greater in the Reprompt condition than for the Contingent condition (90.693 vs. 85.606, 88.396 vs. 83.297, and 85.750 vs. 78.692).

Questionnaire Results

Because the parent questionnaire and children's quiz responses for Experiment 1 did not affect results, we did not integrate questionnaires into these analyses. We do note that every child in this experiment spoke in both conditions, including the three who had not provided expected responses in Experiment 1.

Discussion

In Experiment 2, we showed the children two video conditions, both of which waited for them to provide a verbal response before continuing. In the Contingent condition, the episode would continue after eight seconds regardless of whether the child provided a response; in the Reprompt condition, the episode would repeat the prompt in the absence of a verbal response and wait up to eight additional seconds for a response before continuing. The overall rates of verbal response were quite high in this experiment, likely because all but two of the children had previously experienced contingent programming in the laboratory. The children who did see reprompts provided

Figure 6. Zoe and Bigbot.

responses to the majority of these instances, and most of those responses were expected verbal or combined responses. These results suggest that building reprompts into pseudo-interactive programming helps maintain engagement.

EXPERIMENT 3

After determining that children are sensitive to temporal contingency, we wanted to examine the effects of providing feedback (as contingency of content) on children's responses. We created a new animated short film with clip playback controlled by a WoZ system. After completing an interactive task with or without feedback, participants took a quiz to assess their memory, generalization of material, and experiences.

Participants

Participants were recruited using online and physical bulletin boards in the local community. Twenty-four children between the ages of four and five years (12 boys, 12 girls, mean (stdev) =4.869(0.488)) successfully completed this experiment, four of whom previously completed Experiment 1 and/or 2. Additional participants were not included in our analyses because of nine technical failures, one case of parent interference, and one behavior issue. This research was approved by our Institutional Review Board, and families were compensated.

Children participated in this study as part of a larger series of studies that additionally included two experiments on interaction with robots and one experiment on storytelling. We chose to combine these studies into a single research session because they were each very brief and one of the child-robot interaction studies required repeated, separate interactions with the robot. The Bigbot activity was not integrated with or similar to any previous experience in the session. Together, the entire session took approximately 50 minutes, up to 10 of which was spent in the Bigbot study.

Animations

In collaboration with a team of animators, we created an animated program for children starring a human character named Zoe and her two robot friends, Smallbot and Bigbot. The program started by showing Zoe, Smallbot, and Bigbot in their treehouse. The viewer had to help Zoe and Smallbot identify a problem with Bigbot (a dead battery) and then get him out of the treehouse, across a river, and up the stairs into a laboratory

Figure 7. The toolbox shown to the children

building so that they could install a new battery. To achieve these goals, children were asked what they believed the original problem was and then selected tools from a virtual toolbox belonging to Smallbot to solve subsequent problems. All children saw the same base clips between the question and answer segments; these clips lasted between 10 and 53 s, totaling 3 min 18 s. The children saw a toolbox with only the four tools they would need during the episode. The questions themselves were therefore phrased such that the children, who only had one item left in their toolbox for the last question, were asked if that specific tool would work to solve the problem instead of being asked which tool would solve that problem. In total, all children saw five prompts, one about identifying Bigbot's problem and four about choosing tools to help him on his way.

No Feedback. For the *No Feedback* condition (11 children), we created a set of short clips that would play after each question was posed to the children. All children in this condition saw the same clips, regardless of their responses. In these clips, Zoe neutrally presented the correct answer to the question (e.g.,"Hmm, I think we should try the pulley."). These clips lasted between 1 and 5 s.

Feedback. For the *Feedback* condition (13 children), we created a larger set of short clips that were played after the children were given the opportunity to respond. This set included four types of responses for Zoe to present:

1. Repeating the question (played if the child did not respond within 8 s)
2. Positive feedback (played for correct answers–e.g., "I think you're right, the see-saw could work if we use it to launch him across.")
3. Negative feedback (played for incorrect answers–e.g., "I think we should try something else. What might work better?")
4. Neutral feedback (played in the absence of a verbal response even after the question was repeated a second time–identical to the clips used in the No Feedback condition).

These clips were 1 to 3 s in length.

Questionnaires

Upon completion of the experiment, the experimenter asked the children ten questions. The children were given a sheet of paper showing the contents of Smallbot's toolbox that they had seen earlier. The first four of these questions were about which tools were used to solve specific problems during the program. The subsequent four questions asked which tool the participants would use to solve new tasks that were similar to those shown in the program. Finally, the participants were asked whether they thought Zoe could hear them and what their favorite part was.

Procedure

Participants entered the lab and were seated on a chair approximately 0.85 m in front of a 27-inch Apple monitor with an integrated camera and microphone system. The camera and microphone were used to record the participants throughout the experiment. An experimenter sat next to the participant and ensured that the child was comfortable and ready before proceeding. The experimenter gave participants the following instructions, "You will be watching a cartoon about Zoe and her robots and you're going to help her. In order to help her, you are going to need to use your big voice. Do you have a big voice? [Pause for response] Great! Let's start."

At that point, the wizard would play the first clip of the cartoon. If the child spoke too quietly for the wizard to hear clearly, the experimenter would remind the child that s/he needed to use a big voice. Otherwise, the experimenter strove not to speak during the cartoon and would direct attention toward the screen if the child looked at her. In cases where speech was unavoidable (e.g., a participant directly asked her a task-related question), she responded as minimally as possible (e.g, supplying a word for an item) and then redirected the child's attention to the screen.

In the *No Feedback* condition, the wizard advanced to the neutral version of the next clip after the child spoke; if no speech occurred, a reprompt occurred after 8 s of silence. For the *Feedback* condition, she selected the appropriate version of the following clip (positive, negative) or let the reprompt and neutral response occur based on the child's reaction. Because the wizard was replacing a speech recognition module, gestures (such as tapping the monitor) were ignored.

After the final clip of the animation, the experimenter administered the questionnaire to the child and displayed the image of the toolbox for all questions.

Analysis

An annotator watched all of the recordings of the children completing the experiment to note the timing and occurrence of multiple features. For verbal features, she transcribed the children's speech, noted to whom it was directed, and marked whether each instance was a correct response to a prompt, an incorrect response to a prompt, or unrelated speech. She also annotated nonverbal behaviors, including gestures (e.g., shrugs, points, etc.), the person or thing at whom they were directed (e.g., Zoe, experimenter), and whether the behavior was an accurate response, an inaccurate response, or unrelated to a prompt. Finally, the annotator tracked when the experimenter spoke and whether the speech was to reiterate instructions.

Additionally, we analyzed the questionnaire data to determine the number of correct answers for the memory questions, the number of correct answers for the generalization questions, and whether the participants thought Zoe could hear them.

Results

We compared the response patterns for the Feedback and No Feedback conditions as well as examining responses within the Feedback condition to determine the effects of feedback.

Response Rates

The response rates were high for both conditions (total mean(stdev) = 99.17%(4.08), Feedback mean(stdev) = 98.33(5.77), No Feedback mean(stdev) = 1.00(0)). REML analysis showed no significant difference in response rates between conditions (p = 0.385). The verbal/combined response rates were also similar across conditions (Feedback mean(stdev) = 88.33(1.80), No Feedback mean(stdev) = 90.00(13.48), $F = 0.021$, $p = 0.886$). Condition also did not impact correct verbal/combined response rates (Feedback mean(stdev) = 68.33(15.86), No Feedback mean(stdev) = 73.33(23.09), $F = 0.328$, $p = 0.573$).

Response to Reprompts

There were 13 instances in which children failed to respond and saw reprompts (mean(stdev) = 0.542(0.588) reprompts per child). Eleven children saw one reprompt, one child saw two reprompts, and the remaining twelve children saw no reprompts. For the 13 instances of reprompts, 12 (92.31 %) garnered responses, 11 (84.62 %) elicited verbal responses, and 5 (38 %) received correct verbal responses. There were no differences between conditions for the number of reprompts seen or the likelihood of a response to a reprompt or a verbal response to a reprompt ($p > 0.20$). All five correct verbal responses to a reprompt were given by children in the Feedback condition; however, the number of instances is too small to be informative.

Reactions to Negative Feedback

The 13 children in the Feedback condition saw a total of 13 instances of Negative Feedback (two saw 0 instances, eight saw 1 instance, one saw 2 instances, and one saw 3 instances). In 10 of 13 instances (76.92%), children verbally provided the correct answer after receiving negative feedback.

Questionnaire Results

On the four recall questions, overall accuracy was high (mean(stdev) = 3.88(0.34)), and a t-test revealed no difference between conditions. Similarly, the responses to generalization questions were largely accurate (mean(stdev) = 3.38(1.05)) and there was no significant difference between conditions.

Discussion

In Experiment 3, temporal contingency elicited high overall, verbal/combined, and correct response rates. These rates were unaffected by whether the children received feedback on the accuracy of their answers. Once again, reprompts elicited high rates of response, although the responses were often incorrect, potentially suggesting that children failed to respond to the first prompt because they did not know the answer. Additionally, children provided accurate responses to quiz questions.

GENERAL DISCUSSION

We performed three Wizard-of-Oz experiments to determine how increasing contingency affects preschool children's responses while viewing pseudo-interactive television programs. In Experiment 1, we found that adding temporal contingency–waiting for the child to provide a response before continuing the episode–approximately doubled the response rates relative to typical viewing, in which the episode moves on automatically after a set amount of time. Our second experiment revealed that repeating a prompt when a child fails to answer elicits a response the majority of the time in a contingent condition. In Experiment 3, the presence or absence of feedback did not affect any response rates, but we confirmed that prompt repetition is effective at eliciting responses.

Design Implications

Our findings inform the design of pseudo-interactive television programs and apps for preschool-aged children. First, we recommend that any available microphone be used to detect the presence or absence of speech. Contingent timing of media increased children's verbal responses, which in turn may increase engagement and enjoyment of programming. This feature could be integrated into tablet applications and apps on video game consoles, such as the XBox Kinect, both of which have access to microphones to capture speech input. Although considering the use of varied devices will introduce a challenge for content producers, the content will likely reach a broader audience. Given that a few children in Experiment 1 who had no previous exposure to pseudo-interactive programming showed low levels of verbal responses even after the experimenter gave introductory instructions, it may also be beneficial to integrate instructions during early exposure to this programming and repeat those instructions as needed so that children learn to respond. Additionally, we recommend repetition of questions in the absence of responses to re-engage children who might be distracted. However, it might be wise to limit this repetition if children persistently do not answer to avoid making the experience unpleasant. It could be limited to only key questions and plot points or a subset of missed responses.

We also recommend the use of this technology in a few specific contexts, specifically for speech elicitation. For example, encouraging young children's speech in a fun, engaging context could be used to improve therapeutic interventions. An app with temporal contingency could be designed to boost rehearsal of specific sounds and words for children in speech therapy. Additionally, adding temporal contingency to interactions could be useful for researchers who need children's speech data, such as by being integrated into prompts to elicit speech to build datasets and train speech recognition technology for this age group. The quantity of data that can be attained in an app far exceeds that recorded in person.

Limitations and Future Work

In this research, we aimed to increase children's responses to pseudo-interactive media by manipulating temporal contingency and media responses. Because prior work demonstrated that children who respond more to educational media have better comprehension in some cases [2], future work should explicitly investigate whether the increased level of response specifically resulting from contingency can also improve comprehension. It is possible that this method of increasing engagement could result in additional learning from and memory for media. Although we assessed memory, we were unable to do so in a way that accounted for prior knowledge (e.g., already knowing what "aloha" means) in this research. Moreover, we likely had a ceiling effect for the quiz results due to a combination of straightforward questions and prior knowledge. Future work should use novel media to which children have not had prior access and unusual content, along with a pre/posttest design, to examine this point.

Future research also could examine other aspects of media that may influence children's responsiveness and engagement. For example, characters in typical pseudo-interactive programs often assume that the viewer answered a question correctly and compliment them, even when this is not the case. This process could result in children being reinforced for incorrect answers and learning inaccurate information. Subsequent experiments could assess whether it is feasible to provide feedback for answers. While speech recognition for very young children currently has very low accuracy rates, it is possible that even occasional feedback (e.g., for a yes/no question where a speech recognizer might plausibly be developed) could positively affect the perception of contingency. Moreover, expectations of accurate understanding by the system could be influenced by age, so a larger age range of children should be examined.

Additionally, we relied on a Wizard-of-Oz procedure because we wanted to quickly determine whether adding these various types of contingency would be a worthwhile endeavor. Future research should test whether technological solutions can provide similar response times and effects as a human listener.

A final issue in the line of research is whether children's behavior in the laboratory is comparable to their behavior at home. Future work could include more in-depth interactions with parents to ascertain this information, and standalone apps developed in the future could be sent home for testing over longer time periods and more naturalistic settings.

ACKNOWLEDGMENTS

We thank our participants. We are grateful to A. Rivera, K. McIntosh, M. Landlord, M. Mahler, J. Krahe, B. Karp, J. Lehman, and I. Leite for their assistance.

REFERENCES

1. Hennie Brugman and Albert Russel. 2004. Annotating Multi-media/Multi-modal Resources with ELAN. In *LREC, Fourth International Conference on Language Resources and Evaluation.*
2. Sandra L Calvert, Bonnie L Strong, Eliza L Jacobs, and Emily E Conger. 2007. Interaction and participation for young Hispanic and Caucasian girls' and boys' learning of media content. *Media Psychology* 9, 2 (2007), 431–445.
3. Alisha M Crawley, Daniel R Anderson, Alice Wilder, Marsha Williams, and Angela Santomero. 1999. Effects of repeated exposures to a single episode of the television program "Blue's Clues" on the viewing behaviors and comprehension of preschool children. *Journal of Educational Psychology* 91, 4 (1999), 630.
4. Sylvia MJ Hains and Darwin W Muir. 1996. Effects of stimulus contingency in infant-adult interactions. *Infant Behavior and Development* 19, 1 (1996), 49–61.
5. Dade Hayes. 2008. *Anytime Playdate: Inside the Preschool Entertainment Boom, or, How Television Became My Baby's Best Friend.* Simon and Schuster.
6. Alice Ann Howard Gola, Melissa N Richards, Alexis R Lauricella, and Sandra L Calvert. 2013. Building meaningful parasocial relationships between toddlers and media characters to teach early mathematical skills. *Media Psychology* 16, 4 (2013), 390–411.
7. Marina Krcmar. 2010. Can social meaningfulness and repeat exposure help infants and toddlers overcome the video deficit? *Media Psychology* 13, 1 (2010), 31–53.
8. Alexis R Lauricella, Alice Ann Howard Gola, and Sandra L Calvert. 2011. Toddlers' learning from socially meaningful video characters. *Media Psychology* 14, 2 (2011), 216–232.
9. Deborah L Linebarger and Dale Walker. 2005. Infants' and toddlers' television viewing and language outcomes. *American Behavioral Scientist* 48, 5 (2005), 624–645.
10. Michael Cohen Group and USDOE. 2011. *Young Children, Apps and iPad.* Michael Cohen Group.
11. Lauren J Myers, Rachel B LeWitt, Renee E Gallo, and Nicole M Maselli. 2016. Baby FaceTime: Can toddlers learn from online video chat? *Developmental Science* (2016).
12. Mark Nielsen, Gabrielle Simcock, and Linda Jenkins. 2008. The effect of social engagement on 24-month-olds' imitation from live and televised models. *Developmental Science* 11, 5 (2008), 722–731.
13. Jessica Taylor Piotrowski. 2014. Participatory cues and program familiarity predict young children's learning from educational television. *Media Psychology* (2014), 311–331.
14. Sarah Roseberry, Kathy Hirsh-Pasek, and Roberta M Golinkoff. 2014. Skype me! Socially contingent interactions help toddlers learn language. *Child Development* 85, 3 (2014), 956–970.
15. Jennifer Tam, Elizbeth Carter, Sara Kiesler, and Jessica Hodgins. 2012. Video increases the perception of naturalness during remote interactions with latency. In *CHI'12 Extended Abstracts on Human Factors in Computing Systems.* ACM, 2045–2050.
16. Ron Tamborini and Dolf Zillmann. 1985. Effects of questions, personalized communication style, and pauses for reflection in children's educational programs. *The Journal of Educational Research* 79, 1 (1985), 19–26.
17. Georgene L Troseth, Megan M Saylor, and Allison H Archer. 2006. Young children's use of video as a source of socially relevant information. *Child Development* 77, 3 (2006), 786–799.

Identifying Patterns in IDC Research: Technologies for Improving Children's Well-being Connected to Overweight Issues

Marikken Høiseth[1]
Department of Design, Faculty of Architecture and Design, Norwegian University of Science and Technology (NTNU)
Trondheim, NO-7491, Norway
Marikken.hoiseth@ntnu.no

Maarten Van Mechelen[1]
Meaningful Interactions Lab
(Mintlab, KU Leuven – imec)
Parkstraat 45 box 3605, 3000 Leuven, Belgium
Maarten.vanmechelen@kuleuven.be

ABSTRACT
How is technology being designed to improve children's well-being? We address this question in connection to childhood overweight issues. On a global level, overweight and obesity among children and youth is recognized to be an alarmingly growing health challenge. We have conducted a literature review to explore how studies from the Interaction design and children (IDC) community frame health challenges related to overweight amongst children and youth. Based on the available IDC research focusing on aspects connected to overweight problems, we identify patterns in type of initiative, ages of children, context of use, kind of solution or technology, focus of the research activities and theoretical frameworks. We discuss the importance of increased research and development efforts in this area within the IDC community and call for a broader approach in terms of initiatives, research focus and application of philosophical paradigms and related theory to address a holistic understanding of children's well-being.

Author Keywords
Childhood overweight; interaction design and children studies; technology; meta-analysis

ACM Classification Keywords
H.5.m. Information interfaces and presentation (e.g., HCI): Miscellaneous.

INTRODUCTION
Humanity is facing a true crisis regarding the development of overweight and connected problems. This concerns people of all ages and from all parts of the world. In fact, most of the world population lives in countries where death is more frequently caused by overweight than underweight [1]. The alarming numbers show that the global obesity prevalence has more than doubled since 1980 [1]. Research on the topic belongs to many different disciplines and includes various perspectives, implying its complexity. With our interest in children and how the designed environment corresponds to their needs and desires, we focus on childhood overweight problems and ask how technologies are being designed to improve children's well-being. Numbers from World Health Organization (WHO) show that in 2014, there were 41 million children aged 5 years or younger who were overweight or obese [1].

In this paper, we review research from the Child Computer Interaction (CCI) community to explore how the community frames studies on health challenges related to overweight amongst children and youth. The CCI community investigates the phenomena surrounding the interaction between children and technologies, relying on inputs and perspectives from multiple scientific disciplines [2]. In the past decade, CCI has become a stable part of the HCI landscape, with its own ACM Sigchi conference on Interaction Design and Children (IDC). For this study, we included all IDC proceedings since the first edition in 2003. Although the CCI community exceeds the IDC conference, for now we limit our scope to IDC research [3]. The authors are fully aware that there exists significant academic work on this topic from other research venues. However, our reason for this limitation is its value for guiding the IDC community in identifying areas of weakness and opportunities for growth.

Within this body of research, we identify patterns concerning the kinds of technologies and solutions that are being offered as well as the theories and research activities that inform the design of technology connected to childhood overweight issues. Our goal is to provide a status quo on the IDC community's contribution in responding to the global crisis which childhood overweight and obesity represent. This is expected to benefit future community debate and research directions. Our aim is to raise

IDC '17, June 27-30, 2017, Stanford, CA, USA

ACM ISBN 978-1-4503-4921-5/17/06…$15.00
http://dx.doi.org/10.1145/3078072.3079739

[1] Both authors contributed equally to this paper.

awareness of how research related to child obesity has been framed in the community and inspire enhanced collaboration between CCI practitioners and related fields to tackle this worldwide epidemic.

Following this introduction, we define terms and present our research method for the review process and subsequent analysis. Next, we present our findings. Finally, we discuss the findings considering their importance for improving children's well-being and suggest opportunities for future IDC research directions.

METHOD

A semi-structured literature review was conducted. Here, a semi-structured approach implies a pre-defined set of tentative, flexible inclusion criteria as opposed to a narrow, closed framework. The review included all proceedings of IDC that are available on the ACM Digital Library and covers the period between 2003 and 2016. The proceedings consist of 870 discrete research contributions in the form of either full paper or short paper.

Review Process

Based on our goal, we started the review process by defining the following set of inclusion criteria:

- Physical activity
- Well-being or health promotion
- Healthy lifestyle
- Overweight or obesity (prevention or treatment)
- Nutrition

For the first round of selection, the papers needed to include at least one of these topics. One author read each of the 870 titles and related abstract. Papers that matched the inclusion criteria were marked as "Yes" (23) and in cases of doubt the papers were marked as "Maybe" (30). Afterwards, the other author checked the entire list with the proposed marking to confirm the initial selection. After a joint discussion, this resulted in a collection of 32 papers. Next, one author read through these papers in their entirety and made summaries. This process revealed that some papers were not suited for our purpose (i.e., did not fit the inclusion criteria after all), and resulted in a final collection of 30 papers of which 11 full papers and 19 short papers. The summaries included the following analysis units:

- Type of initiative, age of children involved and the context of use; e.g., focus on healthy nutrition in primary school.
- Kind of solution or technology proposed by the authors; e.g., a mobile exergame or an interactive playground.
- Focus of the research activities; e.g. description of the design method, UX evaluation, trial study.
- Theoretical framework or orientation of the study; e.g. a constructionist or behaviorist starting point.

Analysis

After all summaries were checked and confirmed by the second researcher, an in-depth qualitative analysis was conducted. This was an interpretative and highly iterative process in which patterns within each of the above-mentioned analysis units were identified and discussed. Through an open, bottom-up process, different aspects, orientations and contextual specificities in the interaction designs (e.g. interaction style, pedagogical design, game elements, technical platform in terms of hardware/software) emerged. These were mapped out on different matrices and spreadsheets to look for meaningful relationships and insights (cf. axial coding).

DEFINING TERMS

In this section, we provide our understanding of the inclusion criteria that resulted in the selection of 30 papers.

Physical activity can be defined as "any bodily movement produced by the muscles that results in an increase in energy expenditure", and accordingly it includes activities on a spectrum from non-vigorous (e.g. light walking) to medium (e.g. jogging) to vigorous (e.g. running) [4]. Hence, physical activity overlaps with activities that are regarded more as exercise [5]. For children, the general perception is that being physically active is an extension of being a child, it is regarded a "natural phenomenon". Moreover, children are expected to be substantially more active than adults [6]. However, research suggests that nowadays children are increasingly less physically active. This is mainly due to a high proportion of sedentary lifestyles, combined with an institutionalization of childhood, both in education and leisure time [4].

Our understanding of **well-being** is holistic by signifying physical, mental and social coherence. This is in line with the WHO definition of health as "a state of complete physical, mental and social well-being and not merely the absence of disease or infirmity" [7]. Defining health from an ecological perspective, rather than from a medical perspective, entails that the broader context is considered and the focus is not merely on the individual.

With this broad understanding, acknowledging the unity of body and mind as well as the impact of the broader context, we argue that the concept of a **healthy lifestyle** should also be holistically understood. Moreover, a healthy lifestyle means different things to different people. From such an interpretivist perspective, a deeper understanding of what is meant by a healthy lifestyle will require investigation into aspects and practices related to time, space and place. Nevertheless, some general agreement is reflected in national legislations and guidelines. In such texts, a healthy lifestyle is usually described in terms of food intake, activity choices and levels, smoking, alcohol and/or substance use [8]. In addition, special rules and guidelines often exist for institutions where children spend much of their time such as daycare centers, schools, and sports and leisure facilities.

WHO defines **overweight and obesity** as “abnormal or excessive fat accumulation that may impair health” and refers to the Body Mass Index (BMI) which is a commonly used index of weight-for-height to grade overweight and obesity of adults and especially useful as a population-level measure [1]. Adults with a BMI index between 25 and 30 are considered overweight or pre-obese, those with an index of 30 or more are considered obese. For children and teens, BMI is age- and sex-specific and is often referred to as BMI-for-age [9]. This is because children's body composition varies as they age and varies between boys and girls. Therefore, BMI levels among children and teens need to be expressed relative to other children of the same age and sex. Overweight for children is defined as a BMI at or above the 85th percentile, and obesity as a BMI at or above the 95th percentile for children and teens of the same age and sex. However, BMI should be considered as a rough guide because it may not correspond to the same body fat percentage in different individuals [9]. In addition, the notion of overweight is culturally and socially determined.

According to WHO, **nutrition** is “the intake of food, considered in relation to the body’s dietary needs”. Whereas a so-called good nutrition is recognized to be a cornerstone of good health through “an adequate, well balanced diet combined with regular physical activity”, poor nutrition can cause “reduced immunity, increased susceptibility to disease, impaired physical and mental development, and reduced productivity” [10]. With regard to child obesity, it has been argued that society has created an environment that promotes unhealthy lifestyles through the advertising of unhealthy nutrition and parental ignorance towards the issue [11].

FINDINGS

A first finding is the actual share of IDC papers corresponding to our defined set of inclusion criteria, we consider 30 out of 870 (3,4%) a relatively low share given the recognized magnitude of problems connected to overweight issues among the global child population. Figure 1 shows how the papers are distributed per year, ranging from zero to five contributions. Whereas the number of overweight and obese children has been steadily growing worldwide (e.g. from 32 million globally in 1990 to 42 million in 2013 for children aged 0 to 5 years according to [1]), this evolution is not reflected in the amount IDC papers. In the following sections, we present identified patterns within each of the selected analysis units.

Type of Initiative, Ages and Contexts

Figure 2 shows a word cloud indicating the distribution of the type of the **initiatives** (e.g. focus on physical activity, healthy nutrition) that are presented in the research. The cloud was made by selecting key words from the paper summaries. Some words clearly stand out although we found considerable overlap between the different initiatives in the papers.

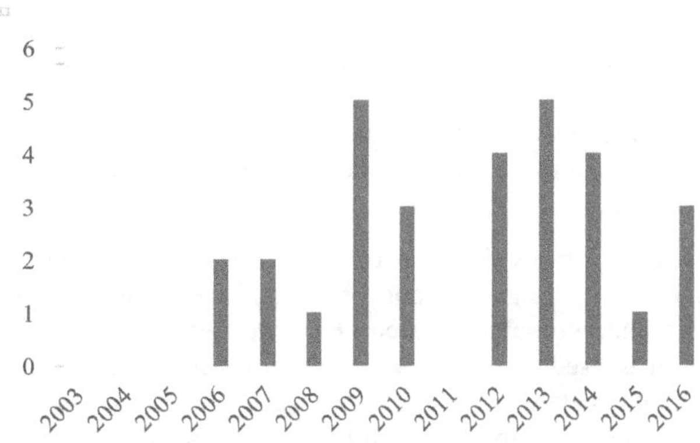

Figure 1. Number of IDC papers corresponding to our inclusion criteria distributed per year.

Most of the research focuses on promoting children’s physical activity (21 out of 30 papers). Play is thereby often considered as a key component, either through so-called physical play or as a condition for entering physical activity. Moreover, in some papers, social aspects are considered in parallel with the aim to increase children’s physical activity. For example, Bekker and Sturm [12], describe a design process on tangible play objects, *ColorFlares*, that stimulate social and physical play. In the user study, children used the objects to collaboratively create various games, stimulating both physical activity and social interactions. In several contributions, encouraging physical activity and promoting a healthy lifestyle are interrelated without a clear distinction between both types of initiatives.

Remarkably, the clear majority of papers concentrates on promoting physical activity as a prevention measure rather than as a treatment for obesity or other health related issues. An exception is provided by Boon et al. [13], who developed playful, open tools that promote unstructured physical play. The tools target hospitalized children undergoing cancer treatment and stimulate the development of motor skills that typically stagnate when children face long-term hospitalization. Hence, facilitating physical play becomes a part of the treatment. However, in general, the studies do not follow a medical trajectory including prevention, diagnostics, treatment and/or disease management. Moreover, no papers directly address children who suffer from overweight or obesity, although some authors use the obesity epidemic as a general frame to stress the relevance of their work [14], [15].

Only three papers address nutrition. Joi et al. [16] developed interactive tableware to encourage children to eat more vegetables and educate them about the health benefits of vegetables. Ptakauskaite et al. [17] developed a game to promote healthy eating behaviors, and De Carolis and Rossano [18] designed an edutainment system focused on healthy nutrition for children.

In terms of **age** distribution, most papers address children between 7 and 15 years with a significant peak at the age of

10 (figure 3). This is in line with findings of Yarosh et al. [3], who conducted a meta-review of all IDC papers published between 2003 and 2011. Similarly, in our study, we found no interest at targeting children under the age of two, and only three papers focus exclusively on teenagers (age 13 – 19).

Context can imply different things, but we refer to context as the places (e.g. outdoor or indoor) or settings (e.g. educational, home) in which the proposed technological solution is used or tested. Most of the technologies can be positioned between leisure/public and education/school, meaning they are applicable in both contexts (see figure 4). For instance, *BrainQuest* developed by Gray et al. [19] is an active smartphone game that aims to enhance executive functions (i.e., a set of cognitive control skills). Thus, stimulating children's physical activity through a game is just a means to an end, although high value is placed on the fun factor of the technological solution. Only a few technologies are explicitly developed for leisure contexts or education/school settings, but this does not necessarily mean that they cannot be used in other contexts through the process of appropriation. A minority of papers (3 out of 30) target a medical or hospital context. These technologies are typically for indoor use only, whereas a slight majority of the technologies for leisure/public and education/school contexts are intended primarily for outdoor use. As for the targeted user, the focus is generally on the individual child or peer groups. Only a few papers address the child within the larger context of the family [14], [16].

Figure 2. Word cloud indicating distribution of initiative types.

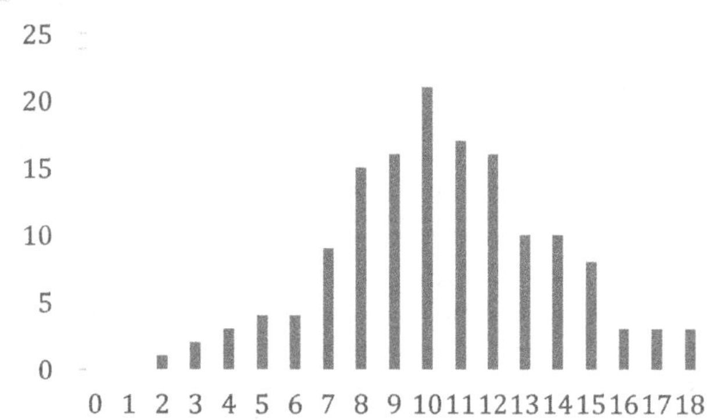

Figure 3. Age distribution, each year in an age range is counted.

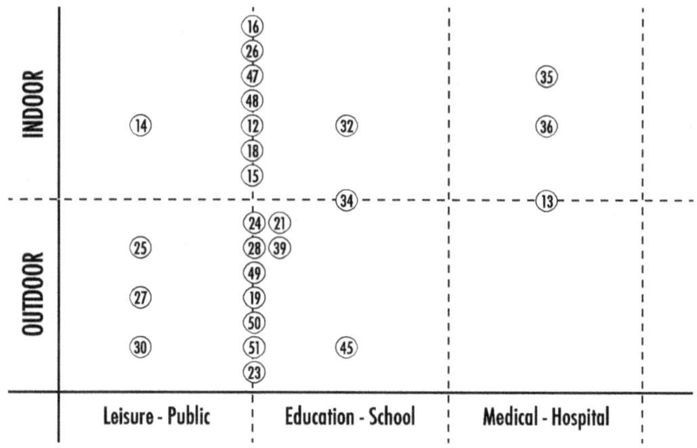

Figure 4. Context distribution (the numbers represent the papers as listed in the references)

Kind of Solution

Regarding the kind of solutions and technologies, our literature review showed that most can be placed on a spectrum ranging from games, over playware and playscapes to non-games. The latter include educational technology (partly) and systems for digital peer support.

Games

Most technologies presented belong to the category identified as games (17 out of 30 papers). In the words of Dennis Wixon, "games are hard to define, but you know one when you see it" [20]. Wixon uses the following definition from Encarta as a starting point for thinking about games concerning design, research, business and pleasure: "Game: an activity that people participate in for fun" and adds to this: 1. In games we don't focus on results or outcomes the way we do for productivity applications; 2. In games we don't use traditional scenarios. The game mechanics, that is the objects and rules, are ideally "easy to learn, difficult to master" (quoting Nolan Bushnell); 3. Many games can chance elements, making uncertainty an inherent game element; and 4. Games are their own reward, meaning that we play games because of the feelings we experience [20].

Within our corpus of papers that propose game-like solutions, we identified mobile games (2 papers), Head Up games (2 papers), outdoor games (3 papers) and exergames (8 papers). There is a lot of overlap, and most of the games are combinations of two or more of these sub-categories. Two papers did not fit in any of these subcategories.

Camelot is an example of a **mobile outdoor game** which is designed to encourage physical activity and social interaction between players – small teams of children aged 7 to 10 years [21]. The game is about collecting virtual resources that lets children earn parts of a physical castle to be constructed. The first team to finish the castle wins. Competition among teams and obstacles such as a virtual ghost that steals makes the game challenging and thrilling. Interviews and observations revealed that children enjoyed a combination of physical activity, excitement, role-play and continuous involvement. In turn, based on focus groups and interviews, Arteaga et al. found that desired game characteristics are those that facilitate socialization and/or competition, are played outdoor, simple to learn and offer a lot of variations [22]. The aim of their study was to understand teenagers' requirements for mobile applications intended to motivate physical activity.

The aspects of "wildly running around" and "rich social interaction" with other players form the fundamental idea for **Head Up games** [23], [24]. As the name suggests, Head Up games distinguish themselves from other interactive outdoor games played with mobile technology in that the technology used should rather support face-to-face interaction and physical activity. An example of Head Up Games is *GameBaker* developed by Avontuur et al. [23]. The application allows children to take control of outdoor game technology by modifying the game rules on the spot.

Exergames, in turn, are a type of serious games that combine digital gaming with physical exercising through technology that tracks body movement and/or reaction [19]. *BunnyBolt* is an interactive exercise game wherein players take on the role of a hero and unlock succeeding storylines through a set of short 10-minute workouts [25].

Playscapes, Playgrounds and Pervasive Technologies

On the continuum from games to non-games, this category represents technologies positioned somewhere in the middle but leaning towards games. Technologies that fit within this category (5 out of 30 papers) facilitate play, but, because of their open, unstructured character (cf. free play), cannot be labeled as 'games'. We identify playscapes, interactive playgrounds and pervasive technologies as sub-categories.

Playscapes (1 paper) can be described as "a design perspective inspired by children's outdoor play in natural environments or 'natural playscapes'" [13]. This design perspective represents a shift in focus from health-related fitness to physical competence. Boon et al. applied playscapes in a hospital environment to enable hospitalized children's physical play at suitable levels of challenge by focusing on three qualities: bodily play, dispersed play and free play [13]. **Interactive playgrounds** (3 papers) are designed to provide children with rich physical and social activity by combining their existing interest in interactive media with playgrounds, for example in the form of interactive slides, poles and balls [26], [27]. For instance, *UbiPlay* is a technology platform that allows children to design, program and play their own games in interactive play spaces [28].

Pervasive technology (1 paper) can, according to Techopedia, be defined as "an emerging trend associated with embedding microprocessors in day-to-day objects, allowing them to communicate information [29]. It is also known as ubiquitous computing. The terms ubiquitous and pervasive signify "existing everywhere." Pervasive computing systems are totally connected and consistently available" [29]. Inspired by the opportunities that pervasive and emerging technologies offer, Cumbo et al. identify opportunities for supporting children's connectedness to nature through digital technologies aiming at encouraging positive environmental attitudes and healthy physical play [30].

Educational Technologies

This category represents technologies that have an educational purpose (7 out of 30 papers). Educational Technologies can be defined as "the study and ethical practice of facilitating learning and improving performance by creating, using, and managing appropriate technological processes and resources" [31]. Within this category, we have identified edutainment, EduWear and data-driven learning as sub-categories.

As an example of **edutainment** (4 papers) (i.e., content designed to both educate and entertain), De Carolis and Rossano present a prototype wherein animated characters (Smurfies) show, explain and provide useful advices about healthy nutrition to children aged 5 and 6 years [18]. Joi et al. present an interactive tableware aimed at encouraging 3 and 4-year-old children to eat vegetables [16]. The tableware is connected to a mobile application which is intended to teach children about the benefits of eating vegetables through a gamification approach. *MunchCrunch* is a health game developed to encourage adolescent's balanced eating habits through an entertaining multiple-choice quiz [15]. Similarly, Ptakauskaite et al. study how the concept of healthy eating can be explored through game-based learning [17].

Dittert and Schelhowe present a different approach to facilitate learning about physical exercise, namely an activity-based approach referred to as **EduWear** (1 paper) [32]. This approach builds on the constructionist learning approach of Seymour Papert and his research group. The core idea here is that hands-on activities enable people to take an active role in their learning processes and thus ideal learning processes occur as people design and create personal meaningful objects themselves. Dittert and Schelhowe explore the idea of combining sports and construction kits through so-called EduWear workshops. For instance, *TechSportiv* combines physical education with ICT construction activities and encourages children to design their own devices, such as a smart soccer shoe, to learn about movement that is relevant in their everyday lives [32].

Data-driven learning (2 papers) is yet another way to encourage health education. Toscos proposes to use health data and ubiquitous computing technologies to educate children with diabetes and their parents for enhanced self-management and as such foster positive parent-child relations [33]. The design efforts of Lee and Drake aim to encourage children to collect and analyze health data from their recess activities to gain more insight into their physical activities [34].

Digital Peer Support

Technologies that fit within this category (2 papers) enable children to support each other in different ways without interference of adults. Lindberg et al. investigate the role of Digital Peer support for bringing together peers with similar backgrounds to help adjusting to a disease and, hence, increases children's well-being [35]. Based on design workshops with children, they propose patterns for designing digital mediation for social interaction. In turn, Nalin et al. discuss how a robotic companion can have a peer-like purpose. It can increase hospitalized children's well-being through a combination of emotional, relational and educational support [36].

Focus of Research Activity

Yarosh et al. propose three categories for distinguishing contributions of IDC papers, namely in the form of a system, a study or a reflection [3]. Even though this is recognized to be a rather rough division, entailing that there is considerable overlap, we find the categories useful for providing an overview of the type of research activities related to health and well-being. Inspired by the work of Yarosh et al., we propose the following categories: system-focus, process-focus and reflexivity-focus. Papers with a **system-focus** primarily present thorough descriptions of novel solutions and technologies. Papers with a **process-focus** have a main emphasis on the quality of methods conducted with users during the design process, be it at an early ideation stage, at development of prototypes and midway investigations or as part of final evaluation and implementation stages. Papers with a **reflexivity-focus** provide exhaustive accounts of ideas and perspectives on a theoretical level beyond the reflection sections that are usually included as part of the conclusions. Reflexivity is a more active form of reflection [37] and involves finding ways to explore attitudes, values, lines of thought and assumptions [38].

Most of the papers, counting 18, were classified to have a system-focus (6 full papers, 12 short papers). Common contributions of system-focus papers are design criteria, design patterns, qualities, dimensions and guidelines for the technologies or solutions. For example, Soler-Adillon et al. describe the physical and digital design of a new approach to sliding – an interactive slide developed to enhance children's physical activity and socialization opportunities [26]. Based on informal observations of large amounts of users (>1000) and ethnographic methods, the researchers gather insights about children's ways of playing and interacting with the slide which allows for further refinement of the system. Lindberg et al. present six design patterns to stimulate children's social interactions [35]. Boon et al. [13] present and test three qualities, namely bodily play, dispersed play and free play, to help interaction designers in encouraging physical competence in a playful manner [13]. Sturm et al. [27] identify key issues for design of interactive playgrounds and present the following five dimensions: Social interaction, simplicity, challenge, goals and feedback.

10 papers were recognized to have a process-focus (5 full papers, 5 short papers). Common contributions of system-focus papers are methodological considerations, practical recommendations regarding applications of methods and facilitation of genuine user participation or evaluations of workshop activities. For example, Gray et al. describe the qualities of their user-centered design approach, an iterative process wherein children and professionals participated in idea conception activities, game storming sessions, and a series of rapid prototyping alternated with user evaluation studies to develop a smart phone game [19]. Verhaegh et al. [21] present several methodological lessons learnt from a case study wherein a mobile outdoor game was deliberately designed as a trial application of various techniques for child involvement. Soute et al. [39] consider the role of prototyping in user-centered processes for design of outdoor games and conclude that testing with hi-fi prototypes gives much better results in terms of play experiences than low-fi prototypes. Ptakauskaite et al. [17] explored children's understandings of the notion of healthy eating through a series of workshop activities. To account for various levels of literacies and provide equal contribution opportunities, the children were encouraged to draw their answers.

We found no papers that belonged to the category of reflexivity-focus. 2 papers were found to not lend themselves to our three categories due to their either general perspective or a more future-oriented research outlook. These were short papers in the form of a workshop summary and a doctoral consortium paper.

Theoretical Framework

Only one third of the papers (9 out of 30) explicitly mention a theoretical framework or refer to a specific theory underlying the study. Broadly speaking, a distinction can be made between behaviorist and interpretivist theoretical frameworks. Both frameworks differ on a fundamental level in terms of ontology (i.e. what is real), epistemology (i.e. what is true) and methodology (i.e. how do I examine what is real). Whereas behaviorist frameworks typically rely on quantitative measures and try to change children's behavior, interpretative frameworks focus on understanding and empowering children, and creating optimal conditions for learning [40].

Behaviorist frameworks are rooted in a positivist paradigm and assume that the learner does not take an active role in discovering his/her environment but is merely reactive to conditions in this environment [41]. Interpretivist frameworks, on the other hand, assume that children actively construct their own knowledge through experiences and that this construction is based on each child's existing knowledge structures [41]. Within the interpretivist framework, different strands can be distinguished including constructivism, constructionism, social constructionism and situated learning. Whereas constructivism emphasizes the active role of the learning child, constructionism goes a step further, arguing that building knowledge structures is most fruitful in contexts where children are consciously engaged in constructing public entities or 'things' [42]. Social constructionism, in turn, focuses on social constructs in meaning making contexts [43], and situated learning looks at the relationship between learning and the surrounding social situation [44].

Whereas 6 papers belong to the behaviorist school of thought, only 2 papers are rooted in the interpretivist paradigm by building on constructivism and constructionism respectively. 1 paper appears to be somewhat ambiguous by referring to "theories from childhood psychology" which can imply an interpretivist or behaviorist paradigm [45].

With the instrumental aim of changing health-related behavior or lifestyle, a behavior change approach is commonly used. According to Tengland, there are different versions of this approach, including behavior-strategies through behaviorist conditioning, communicative persuasion, group pressure and instrumental power [40]. It is difficult to trace each of these strategies within the selected papers. However, specific references to persuasive applications and technologies as well as behavior change interventions are found in [12], [19], [22], [33], [46]. For instance, Bekker and Sturm [12] use theories about behavior change, exercise psychology and developmental psychology. Bec [14], in turn, suggests that behavior change theories can inspire different possibilities and dimensions for game play to enhance children's physical activity.

An interpretivist framework can be found in the work of Dittert and Schelhowe [32] who provide a careful account of constructionism and how this is reflected in the applied method (a series of workshops), the hands-on activities and the resulting tools. They claim that children engage in an active learning process while they create meaningful and personal objects. This learning happens on different levels, including an increased understanding of health topics that might otherwise be perceived as rather abstract. Lee and Drake [34], in turn, refer to constructivism regarding technology enhanced learning.

Even though the clear majority of papers (21 out of 30) lacks a theoretical framework, many show clear tendencies towards either constructivism or behaviorism through the combination of methods used (i.e. qualitative or quantitative), specific phrasings and properties that characterize the solutions. For example, phrasings such as "wanted behaviors", "aim to trigger play behaviors" and "designed to change behaviors in users" indicate leanings toward behavioristic frameworks, whereas "co-construction activities" and "participatory engagements" suggest preferences for an interpretivist approach.

DISCUSSION

The aim of our paper was to raise awareness of how research related to child overweight and obesity has been framed in the CCI community and inspire enhanced collaboration between CCI practitioners and related fields to tackle this worldwide epidemic. Our findings show how research related to child overweight and obesity has been addressed in IDC literature.

IDC research includes a surprisingly low number of papers dealing with physical activity, healthy lifestyle, overweight or obesity, health-promotion/well-being or nutrition. We would have expected these interrelated topics to be high on the research and design agenda. Given that overweight and obesity are global problems, and that the child population is critically affected, this lack of attention is difficult to explain. When looking at how the 30 selected papers are distributed across the last 14 years, we see an alternating distribution without any indication of a clear pattern.

Based on the small amount of research that exists, however, our review provides some valuable findings as to how research related to child overweight and obesity has been framed within the IDC community.

Regarding types of initiatives, ages and contexts our findings show that most research tends to promote physical activity. In connection to physical activity and play, support of social interaction is often explicitly stated to be an equally important goal. This is in line with the findings of Yarosh et al. [3] identifying that support of social interaction and connectedness is a key theme in IDC research. Most papers address children between 7 and 15 years, and the target contexts are equally distributed among leisure and school as well as outdoor and indoor. Only a few papers focus on medical or hospital contexts and no papers directly address childhood overweight or obesity. In fact, the topic of overweight and obesity is merely exploited to set the stage, functioning as a background to contextualize the research.

How do these findings relate to children's well-being? From our perspective, encouraging children's physical activity is very positive. Designing and applying technology to increase movement and exercise is worthwhile and can, besides stimulating pleasurable social experiences, also provide children with an improved relation to their own bodies and health. Our holistic understanding of well-being denotes physical, mental and social coherence. The lack of research focusing on overweight and obesity as well as nutrition in a more direct sense is striking. Research dealing with treatment and how to lose weight in a healthy manner is missing. Moreover, connected problems such as social exclusion and ideas of ideal body images are not addressed. The complexity of these diseases call for a broad and interdisciplinary approach. Given prominent IDC values, such as facilitating for children's active role in design, sensitivity towards diversity and personal growth [3], the community should be well equipped to contribute with important knowledge and solutions. Aspects of food cultures and food joy can for example be important areas to further explore and design for as they strongly relate to healthy lifestyle and well-being in a similarly way as physical activity.

Most of the solutions and technologies represented in our collection of papers belong to the games category which includes mobile games, Head Up games, outdoor games and exergames. Together, the other three categories of education technology, playware/playscapes and pervasive technologies and digital peer support count less than half of the papers. Several papers conclude that the impact of proposed solutions need to be confirmed through more extensive longitudinal studies [16], [19], [39], [45]. Moreover, interactive solutions that go beyond the format of games can be useful entrances for addressing well-being. For example, construction kits that facilitate for children's learning through creating personally meaningful objects have the potential to stimulate important insights regarding own body and health [32].

Most of the selected IDC research is identified to have a system-focus in that they present thorough descriptions of novel solutions and technologies and typically contribute with design criteria and guidelines. One third of the total collection is identified to have a process-focus, that is they present in-depth descriptions of user-centered methods and commonly provide contributions in the form of methodological considerations. None of the papers were identified to have a reflexivity-focus. Reflexivity papers are expected to contribute important knowledge about the complexity surrounding childhood overweight and obesity, such as deeper accounts on social constructs from a cultural and social point of view. For example, taking into consideration how overweight and obesity problems relate to entire ecological systems can redirect the massive one-sided focus on the individual level.

Regarding the applied theoretical frameworks, most papers make no explicit mention of neither philosophical paradigms, postulates or specific theories. Less than one third of the papers provide theoretical accounts beyond a mere description of research method, and most of these belong to the behaviorist school of thought. The quality of the theoretical accounts is generally quite deficient as they often do not provide a clear explanation of what the theoretical framework entails in terms of central foundations and concepts as well as how these relate to data analysis and more tangible solutions. This is confirmed by Little et al. who claim that there tends to be a vague connection between theories and how they are applied to develop, evaluate and deliver solutions [46]. We argue that a conscious awareness and use of theoretical frameworks can result in new lines of thought regarding the available solution space for designing technologies that will benefit the child population.

Overall, our findings suggest that an enhanced research effort on the topic of childhood overweight and obesity is timely. The IDC community has started this work – with emphasis on promoting physical activity through games that support social interaction. However, based on our review we see many more opportunities for IDC researchers to contribute to children's well-being connected to overweight issues. In the following we share some ideas for future IDC research directions:

- The predominance of games can be challenged to pave way for exploration of other kinds of solutions, including educational technologies and digital peer support.
- Longitudinal studies are scarce, but highly necessary to provide better understanding of how children make meaning with proposed technologies.
- Papers with reflexivity-focus can stimulate fruitful debates on how technologies are designed to improve children's well-being connected to overweight issues.
- Dedicated utilization of the interpretivist paradigm (e.g. a social constructionist framework). This implies embracing co-learning processes as a starting point rather than aiming to change behavior.

CONCLUSION

Based on a systematic review of IDC proceedings from 2003 to 2016, we explored how the community has framed studies on health challenges related to overweight and obesity amongst children. Despite the magnitude of the obesity epidemic, only a small amount of IDC papers (3,4%) has addressed issues on overweight or closely related topics. Within the available literature, we identified patterns in type of initiative (e.g. promoting healthy lifestyle, healthy nutrition), characteristics of technologies and proposed solutions, focus of research activities and underlying theoretical frameworks. Most papers focus on promoting a healthy lifestyle and physical play with game-like solutions, and do not take the larger context into account. Moreover, obesity is rarely addressed explicitly and is merely used as an overall frame to contextualize the research.

The literature review presented in this paper will serve as a starting point for further research. To begin, we plan to extend the literature review by mapping how other research venues cover the intersecting topics of technology, well-being and childhood overweight. A connected long-term aim is to contribute to develop technological solutions to combat child obesity. Following a social constructionist and ecological perspective, we will extend the focus beyond the individual child to also include the family, school and larger societal context. Obesity is a gradual process based on unhealthy lifestyle choices and dietary habits that usually begins to develop at a young age. Because of this, the choices that many children make will set the stage for the rest of their lives. Hence, in future work, we will focus on the first 1000 days (i.e., from pregnancy to two years).

Furthermore, we plan to investigate design possibilities related to diversity within children's food cultures and meals practices, e.g. how we can facilitate for sharing and learning. In addition, we hope that our paper will raise debate in the child-computer interaction community about the urgency of child obesity, and will inspire increased interdisciplinary collaboration to address this worldwide epidemic.

REFERENCES

[1] WHO, "Report of the Commission on Ending Childhood Obesity," World Health Organization, Geneva, 2016.

[2] J. C. Read and P. Markopoulos, "Child-computer interaction," *Int. J. Child-Comput. Interact.*, vol. 1, no. 1, pp. 2–6, 2013.

[3] S. Yarosh, I. Radu, S. Hunter, and E. Rosenbaum, "Examining Values: An Analysis of Nine Years of IDC Research," in *Proceedings of the 10th International Conference on Interaction Design and Children*, New York, NY, USA, 2011, pp. 136–144.

[4] P. H. A. of C. Government of Canada, "Healthy Living and Healthy Weight - Public Health Agency of Canada," 10-Mar-2008. [Online]. Available: http://www.phac-aspc.gc.ca/hp-ps/dca-dea/publications/yjc/ch3_51_54-eng.php. [Accessed: 02-Feb-2017].

[5] C. J. Caspersen, K. E. Powell, and G. M. Christenson, "Physical activity, exercise, and physical fitness: definitions and distinctions for health-related research.," *Public Health Rep.*, vol. 100, no. 2, pp. 126–131, 1985.

[6] M. Axelsen, M. Danielsson, M. Norberg, and A. Sjöberg, "Eating habits and physical activity: Health in Sweden: The National Public Health Report 2012. Chapter 8," *Scand. J. Public Health*, vol. 40, no. 9 Suppl, pp. 164–175, Dec. 2012.

[7] WHO, "WHO | Constitution of WHO: principles," *WHO*. [Online]. Available: http://www.who.int/about/mission/en/. [Accessed: 02-Feb-2017].

[8] M. I. K. von Bothmer and B. Fridlund, "Gender differences in health habits and in motivation for a healthy lifestyle among Swedish university students," *Nurs. Health Sci.*, vol. 7, no. 2, pp. 107–118, Jun. 2005.

[9] S. E. Barlow, "Expert Committee Recommendations Regarding the Prevention, Assessment, and Treatment of Child and Adolescent Overweight and Obesity: Summary Report," *Pediatrics*, vol. 120, no. Supplement 4, pp. S164–S192, Dec. 2007.

[10] WHO, "WHO | Nutrition," *World Health Organization*. [Online]. Available: http://www.who.int/topics/nutrition/en/. [Accessed: 02-Feb-2017].

[11] H. Grossklaus and D. Marvicsin, "Parenting efficacy and its relationship to the prevention of childhood obesity," *Pediatr. Nurs.*, vol. 40, no. 2, pp. 69–86, Apr. 2014.

[12] T. Bekker and J. Sturm, "Stimulating Physical and Social Activity Through Open-ended Play," in *Proceedings of the 8th International Conference on Interaction Design and Children*, New York, NY, USA, 2009, pp. 309–312.

[13] B. Boon, M. Rozendaal, M. M. van den Heuvel-Eibrink, J. van der Net, and P. J. Stappers, "Playscapes: A Design Perspective on Young Children's Physical Play," in *Proceedings of the The 15th International Conference on Interaction Design and Children*, New York, NY, USA, 2016, pp. 181–189.

[14] R. Bec, "Creating Physically Active Games for Young Adolescents," in *Proceedings of the 11th International Conference on Interaction Design and Children*, New York, NY, USA, 2012, pp. 331–334.

[15] A. Mansour, M. Barve, S. Bhat, and E. Y.-L. Do, "MunchCrunch: A Game to Learn Healthy-eating Heuristics," in *Proceedings of the 8th International Conference on Interaction Design and Children*, New York, NY, USA, 2009, pp. 166–169.

[16] Y. R. Joi *et al.*, "Interactive and Connected Tableware for Promoting Children's Vegetable-Eating and Family Interaction," in *Proceedings of the The 15th International Conference on Interaction Design and Children*, New York, NY, USA, 2016, pp. 414–420.

[17] N. Ptakauskaite, P. Chueng-Nainby, and H. Pain, "Supporting Social Innovation in Children: Developing a Game to Promote Health Eating," in *Proceedings of the The 15th International Conference on Interaction Design and Children*, New York, NY, USA, 2016, pp. 688–693.

[18] B. De Carolis and V. Rossano, "A Team of Presentation Agents for Edutainment," in *Proceedings of the 8th International Conference on Interaction Design and Children*, New York, NY, USA, 2009, pp. 150–153.

[19] S. Gray, J. Robertson, and G. Rajendran, "BrainQuest: An Active Smart Phone Game to Enhance Executive Function," in *Proceedings of the 14th International Conference on Interaction Design and Children*, New York, NY, USA, 2015, pp. 59–68.

[20] D. Wixon, "What is a Game?," *interactions*, vol. 13, no. 2, p. 37–ff, Mar. 2006.

[21] J. Verhaegh, I. Soute, A. Kessels, and P. Markopoulos, "On the Design of Camelot, an Outdoor Game for Children," in *Proceedings of the 2006 Conference on Interaction Design and Children*, New York, NY, USA, 2006, pp. 9–16.

[22] S. M. Arteaga, M. Kudeki, A. Woodworth, and S. Kurniawan, "Mobile System to Motivate Teenagers' Physical Activity," in *Proceedings of the 9th International Conference on Interaction Design and Children*, New York, NY, USA, 2010, pp. 1–10.

[23] T. Avontuur, R. de Jong, E. Brink, Y. Florack, I. Soute, and P. Markopoulos, "Play It Our Way: Customization of Game Rules in Children's Interactive Outdoor Games," in *Proceedings of the 2014 Conference on Interaction Design and Children*, New York, NY, USA, 2014, pp. 95–104.

[24] I. Soute, S. Lagerström, and P. Markopoulos, "Rapid Prototyping of Outdoor Games for Children in an Iterative Design Process," in *Proceedings of the 12th International Conference on Interaction Design and Children*, New York, NY, USA, 2013, pp. 74–83.

[25] C. Keung, A. Lee, S. Lu, and M. O'Keefe, "BunnyBolt: A Mobile Fitness App for Youth," in *Proceedings of the 12th International Conference on Interaction Design and Children*, New York, NY, USA, 2013, pp. 585–588.

[26] J. Soler-Adillon, J. Ferrer, and N. Parés, "A Novel Approach to Interactive Playgrounds: The Interactive Slide Project," in *Proceedings of the 8th International Conference on Interaction Design and Children*, New York, NY, USA, 2009, pp. 131–139.

[27] J. Sturm, T. Bekker, B. Groenendaal, R. Wesselink, and B. Eggen, "Key Issues for the Successful Design of an Intelligent, Interactive Playground," in *Proceedings of the 7th International Conference on Interaction Design and Children*, New York, NY, USA, 2008, pp. 258–265.

[28] J. Mattila and A. Väätänen, "UbiPlay: An Interactive Playground and Visual Programming Tools for Children," in *Proceedings of the 2006 Conference on Interaction Design and Children*, New York, NY, USA, 2006, pp. 129–136.

[29] Techopedia, "What is Pervasive Computing? - Definition from Techopedia," *Techopedia.com*. [Online]. Available: https://www.techopedia.com/definition/667/pervasive-computing. [Accessed: 02-Feb-2017].

[30] B. J. Cumbo, J. Paay, J. Kjeldskov, and B. C. Jacobs, "Connecting Children to Nature with Technology: Sowing the Seeds for Proenvironmental Behaviour," in *Proceedings of the 2014 Conference on Interaction Design and Children*, New York, NY, USA, 2014, pp. 189–192.

[31] M. Eisenberg, "Tangible Ideas for Children: Materials Sciences As the Future of Educational Technology," in *Proceedings of the 2004 Conference on Interaction Design and Children: Building a Community*, New York, NY, USA, 2004, pp. 19–26.

[32] N. Dittert and H. Schelhowe, "TechSportiv: Using a Smart Textile Toolkit to Approach Young People's Physical Education," in *Proceedings of the 9th International Conference on Interaction Design and Children*, New York, NY, USA, 2010, pp. 186–189.

[33] T. Toscos, "Using Data to Promote Healthy Behavior in Children," in *Proceedings of the 9th International Conference on Interaction Design and Children*, New York, NY, USA, 2010, pp. 344–347.

[34] V. R. Lee and J. Drake, "Quantified Recess: Design of an Activity for Elementary Students Involving Analyses of Their Own Movement Data," in *Proceedings of the 12th International Conference on Interaction Design and Children*, New York, NY, USA, 2013, pp. 273–276.

[35] S. Lindberg, P. Wärnest\a al, J. Nygren, and P. Svedberg, "Designing Digital Peer Support for Children: Design Patterns for Social Interaction," in *Proceedings of the 2014 Conference on Interaction Design and Children*, New York, NY, USA, 2014, pp. 47–56.

[36] M. Nalin, I. Baroni, A. Sanna, and C. Pozzi, "Robotic Companion for Diabetic Children: Emotional and Educational Support to Diabetic Children, Through an Interactive Robot," in *Proceedings of the 11th International Conference on Interaction Design and Children*, New York, NY, USA, 2012, pp. 260–263.

[37] M. Dowling, "Approaches to reflexivity in qualitative research," *Nurse Res.*, vol. 13, no. 3, pp. 7–21, Apr. 2006.

[38] G. Bolton, *Reflective Practice: Writing and Professional Development*, 4th ed. Thousand Oaks: SAGE Publishing, 2014.

[39] I. Soute, M. Kaptein, and P. Markopoulos, "Evaluating Outdoor Play for Children: Virtual vs. Tangible Game Objects in Pervasive Games," in *Proceedings of the 8th International Conference on Interaction Design and Children*, New York, NY, USA, 2009, pp. 250–253.

[40] P.-A. Tengland, "Behavior Change or Empowerment: On the Ethics of Health-Promotion Strategies," *Public Health Ethics*, vol. 5, no. 2, pp. 140–153, Jul. 2012.

[41] J. P. Hourcade, "Interaction Design and Children," in *Foundational Trends in Human-Computer Interaction*, Boston - Delft: NOW Publishers, 2008.

[42] S. Papert, *Constructionism: A New Opportunity for Elementary Science Education*. MIT Press, 1986.

[43] R. A. Young and A. Collin, "Introduction: Constructivism and Social Constructionism in the Career Field," *J. Vocat. Behav.*, vol. 64, no. 3, pp. 373–388, Jun. 2004.

[44] J. Lave and E. Wenger, *Situated Learning: Legitimate Periperal Participation*. Cambridge: Cambridge University Press, 1990.

[45] A. P. Macvean, "Developing Adaptive Exergames for Adolescent Children," in *Proceedings of the 11th International Conference on Interaction Design and Children*, New York, NY, USA, 2012, pp. 339–342.

[46] L. Little, B. Bell, G. Defeyter, J. C. Read, D. Fitton, and M. Horton, "Behaviour Change Interventions: Teenagers, Technology and Design," in *Proceedings of the 12th International Conference on Interaction Design and Children*, New York, NY, USA, 2013, pp. 610–612.

[47] P. Landry *et al.*, "Design Strategy to Stimulate a Diversity of Motor Skills for an Exergame Addressed to Children," in *Proceedings of the 12th International Conference on Interaction Design and Children*, New York, NY, USA, 2013, pp. 84–91.

[48] P. Landry, N. Parés, J. Minsky, and R. Parés, "Participatory Design for Exertion Interfaces for Children," in *Proceedings of the 11th International Conference on Interaction Design and Children*, New York, NY, USA, 2012, pp. 256–259.

[49] M. Bekker, E. van den Hoven, P. Peters, and B. klein Hemmink, "Stimulating Children's Physical Play Through Interactive Games: Two Exploratory Case Studies," in *Proceedings of the 6th International Conference on Interaction Design and Children*, New York, NY, USA, 2007, pp. 163–164.

[50] S. Lagerström, I. Soute, Y. Florack, and P. Markopoulos, "Metadesigning Interactive Outdoor Games for Children: A Case Study.," in *Proceedings of the 2014 Conference on Interaction Design and Children*, New York, NY, USA, 2014, pp. 325–328.

[51] I. Soute, "HUGs: Head-up Games," in *Proceedings of the 6th International Conference on Interaction Design and Children*, New York, NY, USA, 2007, pp. 205–208.

Bicultural: Examining Teenage Latinas' Perspectives on Technologies for Emotional Support

Ralph Vacca
New York University
New York, USA
ralph.vacca@nyu.edu

ABSTRACT
Latina adolescents are one of the fastest growing demographic groups in the United States and have been found to experience higher levels of emotional distress than their non-Latino counterparts. Reliance on emotional support from the teens' social network is a common coping mechanism. While digital media is increasingly used by Latinas to communicate and express themselves, few, if any, studies have explored the perspectives of Latinas on the role of technology in helping the enactment of emotional support. In this paper, we share the perspectives of thirteen Latina adolescents (15-18 years old) that emerged through a series of participation design workshops. Our findings suggest that bicultural aspects of Latina identity can influence perspectives on the role of technology, and provide insights into attitudes towards bicultural conflicts in emotional health. We also share our participatory design technique that incorporated an ecological framework and suggestions for future use of such an approach.

Author Keywords
Latina; social emotional health; biculturalism, participatory design; emotional support

ACM Classification Keywords
H.5.m. Information interfaces and presentation (e.g., HCI): Miscellaneous.

INTRODUCTION
The mental health – the emotional, psychological, and social wellbeing – of adolescent Latinas continues to be a focus for those working with the Latino community [34]. Both the increasing population of Latinos in the United States and the disparity amongst Latina adolescents and other groups in mental health indicators are key drivers for such a focus on mental health [35].

ACM 978-1-4503-4921-5/17/06 $15.00
http://dx.doi.org/10.1145/3078072.3079742

In understanding Latina mental health, researchers have increasingly adopted an ecological perspective that views a young person's development context as a microsystem (e.g., parent, school, peer), and macrosystem (e.g., culture, power) factors based on the social ecology of human development [7,8]. Designing for specific cultural groups can be challenging as there is diversity within a defined group in terms of culture and ecological factors. Because of this variation within groups labeled "Latina", it can be challenging to understand what it means to design for Latinas [19]. However, aspects of the Latina lived experience often involve biculturalism, in which aspects of cultural identity, practices, and language are actively negotiated in ways that go beyond a singular cultural identification and instead entail multiple meaning systems [36,39]. The extent to which ecological factors that influence bicultural aspects of teenage Latina experiences should and can be designed for when tackling emotional support technologies, is not well understood.

The use of participatory design may help address this gap in understanding and help designers situate technical tools in existing cultural identities and practices. Our goal in this explanatory work was to identify new opportunities for technology design by taking a step back to examine the complex interplay of influences on teenage Latina's mental health related practices. Using an ecological framing we conducted an eight-week participatory study to examine teenage Latinas' reflection upon various ways in which multiple levels of influence constrain or enable them to engage in emotional support, and the subsequent implications for the design of technologies that encourage emotional support. Through this work, we gained critical insight into their values, attitudes, and lived experiences. Our findings serve as a useful starting point for designing systems that take into account cultural identity, practices, and reflect the Latina emotional support context.

After discussing experiences around emotional health with participants, we used the Multiracial Feminist Framework [45] to develop generate scenarios around their need for emotional support. In this framework, there are cultural and ecological contexts along different levels that influences one's emotional vulnerability, and in turn influence the role of emotional support. Participants were guided in activities that helped them brainstorm how technology could facilitate emotional support given intrapersonal, family, and community levels of influence.

Our research makes three contributions to the design and research community. First, we characterize a set of adolescent perspectives on the role that technology can have in emotional support for mental health. Second, we describe ways in which biculturalism can play a role in designing for Latina emotional support. Finally, we detail how our methodological approach, which is grounded in a socio-ecological framing, can help guide future research examining cultural groups' perceptions of personal, social, and environmental influences on emotional support and related technologies.

RELATED WORK

Support from one's social network is a key coping strategy used by young adult Latinas [18]. In receiving emotional support from parents, friends, family members, and other adults among others, Latinas can better cope with different mental health challenges they experience [35]. Despite current research that provides insight into the impetus for such support and how such support can be enacted, there has been little published research that provides insights into the increasing role of technology in mediating emotional support and involvement of Latina teens themselves in the design and building of technology to mediate emotional support for emotional health.

Latina Emotional Health and Support

In comparison to other ethnic groups, Latina adolescents frequently report higher levels of depressive symptoms and psychological distress [13]. In 2015, among girls in grades 9–12, over one in four Latinas (26%) reported seriously considering attempting suicide in the 12 months prior to the interview, and had attempted suicide in the prior 12 months (15%) [12].

In understanding the causes, researchers have noted that Latinas also disproportionately experience stressors such as living in poverty and in disadvantaged neighborhoods, including high crime rates, low-quality housing and schools, substance abuse and teen pregnancy [43]. However, increasingly researchers are understanding the significant role of conflict between family obligations and adolescent autonomy in the Latina experience [43]. Familism – the Latino emphasis on family and cultural traditions – can pull in a different direction than American norms in seeking increased autonomy as an adolescent, in turn contributing additional levels of psychological conflict and family tension.

Building on Bronfenbrenner's [7,8] work on adolescent development emerging ecological frameworks highlight the layers of the individual, family, friends, community, and society that interact in ways that influence mental health resiliency, as well as at-risk factors [35]. For instance, in the Multiracial Feminist Framework (MFF) [35:3] used for this study, Latina mental health can be understood as illustrated in Figure 1. At the individual are aspects that have been internalized over time from the meso and macro layers that in turn continue to interact together and on the individual. The MFF is unique in that it recognizes race as a critical factor of power, and gendered experiences as intertwined with race and class [2].

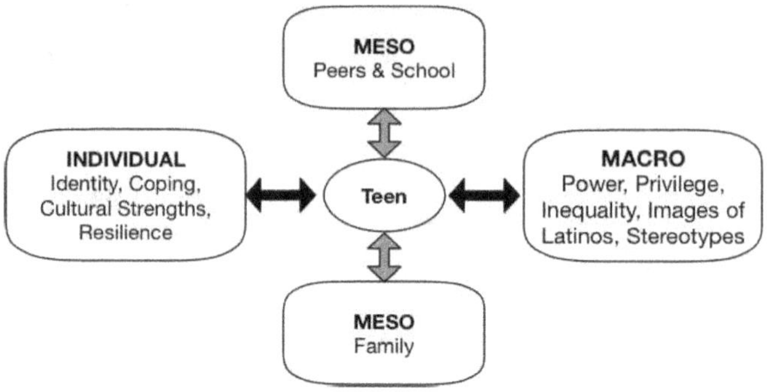

Figure 1: Multiracial Feminist Framework adapted from Romero [35]

Participatory Design with Latina Adolescents

Increasingly, individual expressions, and interactions with peers and family are occurring online [16,17,29,46]. As of now, there has been very little research on the design of technological solutions for Latina mental health. There has been research on the role of digital media in the lives of Latinas, specifically around emotional health [e.g. ,41]. However, participatory design can be a powerful approach to exploring new kinds of design approaches such as work done on cyberbullying in youth [3]. Some research has shown that the process itself of engaging in a form of co-design can given youth a sense of belonging [37]. Participatory design with youth can be seen as a form of "expressing, surfacing, and supporting engagement with youth perspectives in research and design projects" [15]. Currently, participatory approaches with Latinas are more in line with youth participatory action research (YPAR), focusing on youth advocating for change and self-empowerment through the creation process [10,31,38].

METHOD

From Fall 2015 to Spring 2016 a series of participatory design workshops were conducted with thirteen Latina youth (ages 15-18). We recruited participants through social media and local afterschool programs that work with low-income students of color.

Participants

All students were from low-income households, and identified as female. Six of the students were from Caribbean backgrounds; one from mixed Central American/African-American backgrounds; three from South American backgrounds; three from mixed Caribbean/Mexican backgrounds. All but one of the students spoke primarily Spanish at home with their caregiver, and all spoke English in their schools and with peers.

Design Activities

The thirteen participants engaged in a series of eight sessions held once a week for two hours with the lead researcher leading participants through the study activities.

A research assistant helped throughout the process, assisting mainly with note-taking and documenting artifacts. An overview of the participatory design process is outlined in the following subsections.

#	Focus
1	Exploring emotional health
2-3	Scenarios
4-7	Brainstorming and prototypes
8	Reflecting

Table 1: List of sessions

Exploring Emotional Health

The initial session focused on familiarizing participants to the user-centered design process, and exploring emotional health topics. The session was structured using the Multiracial Feminist Framework [35] to prompt discussions that addressed various layers of Latina ecologies. From the discussions the group identified a variety of emotional health challenges such as bullying, friendship, romantic relationships, parental relationships, and social identity.

Scenarios

In these two sessions we focused on the context in which certain challenges presented themselves using scenario-based design [11]. We generated both written scenarios as well as using visual storyboards to draw out scenarios. In addition, we used the Multiracial Feminist Framework [35] in how we framed the scenario, detailing how the scenario touched on meso (e.g., friends, school, family) and macro (e.g., power, privilege) layers of Latina ecologies. Participants were divided into groups and prompted to refine their scenario storyboards as a group using markers and paper templates structured as a comic strip (two rows of three squares). We then shared and discussed the scenarios, attaching assumptions, emotions, and key drivers of behaviors underlying the scenario as post-its.

Brainstorming and Prototypes

We gave each group large paper, markers, and sticky notes and asked them to brainstorm as many technology ideas as they could to address any of the scenarios. Groups were then paired and asked to explain two of their best ideas to one another. After reflecting on the feedback they received, groups chose what they felt was their best idea and iterated on their concepts, mixed ideas, or changed their concepts and repeated the exercise two more times. We then voted on the top idea for each group. In the following sessions, we started to build a paper prototype using materials such as cardboard, stickers, and construction paper. Students later iterated on their prototypes using the critiques provided by other groups. Building a clickable prototype in Balsamiq and role-playing with it helped the students to articulate how they wanted to interact with the technology.

Reflecting

In the final session, we reflected on the process and discussed how youth might experience the prototypes they created. The purpose of the reflection and guided discussion was to understand the extent to which participants viewed their work as being "for Latinas", and what that meant to them in terms of addressing their own personal emotional health challenges.

DATA COLLECTION & ANALYSES

In the study we used multiple data collection methods. Each session was audio-recorded, the group discussions were transcribed, and field notes were compiled. We used open coding to inductively characterize the concepts. The resulting codes were iteratively clustered to arrive at higher-level themes across the various data sources. Following are the five design concepts the groups focused on listed alongside the group abbreviation (Gx) and the participant abbreviation (Px).

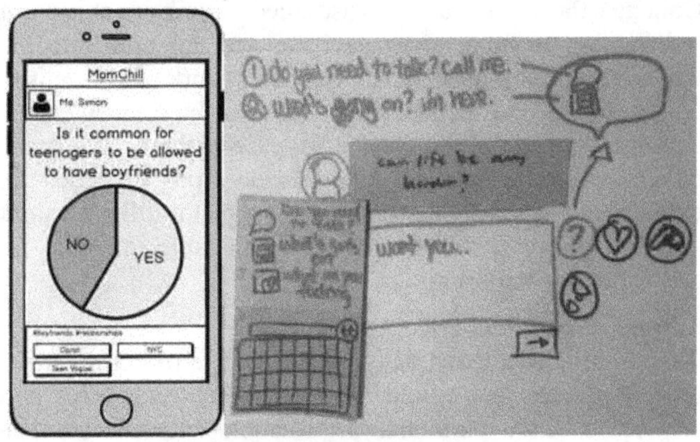

Figure 2. Wireframe of the MomChill (G1) and sketch of the tinktink (G2) design concepts

MomChill (G1; P1-P3)

MomChill is a website/app similar to Instagram that is a series of curated images linked to short articles focused on tackling typical preoccupations mothers have, which the teens felt were warranted but often extreme. The goal of MomChill is to provide mothers with education from trusted sources on topics such as letting their daughters date, how to have conversations about boyfriends, the accepted norms of teens being able to hangout, etc. This design emerged from two core scenarios involving conflict between mother and daughter. In one scenario the conflict revolved around wanting to go hangout and being restricted, while the other scenario was around experiencing a painful social situation involving a close friend and romantic interest, yet feeling unable to talk about the issue with their mother.

tinktink (G2; P4-P5)

tinktink is a design for dialog boxes in social media networks like Facebook and Instagram. The design provides scaffolds to help the user better provide emotional support when someone is sharing their distress or problems online. The design is similar to canned responses and emoticon libraries in chat and email software interfaces. This design emerged from three core scenarios. The first was a scenario on not knowing what to say to a friend that posts a cryptic statement on experiencing emotional distress. Another was a scenario on not knowing how to support a friend that is feeling guilty about focusing on wanting to get an internship instead of taking of their younger sibling. The last scenario was on wanting to craft a way to better express anger at one's parents.

gPower (G3; P6-P8)

gPower is a mod of the Giphy tool where one can easily access memes that speak to common Latina stereotypes. This design emerged from one scenario of providing support to another teen through funny videos, images, and memes. In the scenario the use of icons such as a fist, or a video of someone going crazy was used to reinforce this idea of standing up for oneself in conflict.

College Packs (G4; P9-P11)

College Packs is a crowdsourced knowledgebase of information to help youth navigate and communicate the college process with parents. The tools works as a website where teens and counselors can contribute answers to common questions and concerns parents have about the college process. The design emerged from difficulty in explaining the reasons why going away to college might make sense for students in terms of available financial aid and expanded opportunities.

Screamer (G5; P12-P13)

This is an app or potentially also a feature of commenting user interfaces that would let you collect your vents and choose to share particular information with others. The design allows for sharing different degrees of detail and with varying degrees of privacy. The design has similar features to YikYak, but also serves as a middle layer with existing social media platforms like Facebook. The design emerged from a scenario in which a user spends significant time writing a status update that never ends up getting posted. For instance, with the tool, a user would spend time writing a long rant on Facebook and decide to either post anonymously or keep as part of a private journal. The design acknowledges that much of the private self-reflection inherent in journaling can occur at the point of wanting to engage in social media through a status update.

FINDINGS

Through our inductive analysis, several themes emerged, characterizing how participants felt technology could facilitate emotional support. Our findings highlight that perceptions on the role technology can play in mediating emotional support varied, and that the participants' bicultural aspects of Latina identity influenced the experiences the groups designed.

Role of Technology

Our findings show that students' need for providing coping support to others, managing conflict, and challenging stereotypes were among the most important factors impacting their desire to use technology for emotional support.

Technology as Coping Support

The ability to positively manage emotional stressors can be learned and is often understood as coping. In our analysis of participant designs one role technology assumed was one of supporting the coping process. The tinktink idea originated from participants' desire to be able to better support their friends' coping and be supported by their friends. In this regard, the group described the process of saying something of value to friends in emotional distress as challenging and P2 pointed out that: *"Sometimes I have no clue like what to say. I mean even if we're sitting and talking. I'm like thinking of what I would want someone to say to me. But it's hard. Like I hate when people post something like really like cryptic. And I'm like... does this person want me to ask them about it? Like I don't know what their deal is."*

Participants brainstormed ideas for how technology could help support communication with their friends, with the goal of saying something useful and not annoying. The group expressed their desire for somehow leveraging existing expertise in their communication with friends. One of their ideas was a bot that they could put their friend in contact with –an artificially intelligent helper that they could ask questions. Their final design was a design for dialog boxes in social media networks like Snapchat and Instagram that provided scaffolds for how to respond to certain posts. They felt that the computer could provide templates that would allow posters and responders to better align. Previous research has looked at the role of such scaffolds on problem-based learning. For instance, research has shown that message labels and sentence openers can be effective in encouraging more elaboration and higher cognitive discourse [1]. Systems have been designed in which partial sentences are selected as a way to improve discussions [23]. Additionally, there has been research on how collaborative scripts can support certain kinds of behaviors such as paraphrasing, criticizing, asking meaningful questions, constructing counterarguments, and proposing argument syntheses [32]. The teens wanted to use such templates to help them better understand how to empathize, listen, inquire, and advocate as a means of providing emotional support to their friends.

Technology as Ambassador

The second category of designs stemmed from wanting to use technology to help make their case to others, mainly caregivers. Two of the design concepts – "MomChill" (G1), and "College Packs" (G4) – place technology in the role of helping to communicate with parents. The designs emerged from discussions on conflict with parents. For instance, P5 described a time when here parents would not let her go to a movie with friends, and expressing her frustration with how her older brother was able to do such things when he was her age.

There has been extensive research on the importance of parent-child communication with research supporting the importance of such communication in substance abuse and sexual behavior [e.g. ,24]. Research has shown that girls' communication with parents generally intensifies in middle adolescence, as indicated by increasing parental solicitation, increasing adolescent disclosure, and decreasing adolescent secrecy [26]. However, the role of information in this communication varies. In research on parent-child communication with Mexican heritage youth, researchers found that the kind of messages and information included in the messages made the difference in the effect of communication on perspectives on alcohol consumption [24]. In the participants designs what emerged was technology serving as a surrogate to broach two kinds of topics: (i) hard to discuss, and (ii) complex knowledge.

In MomChill (G1) the participant group scenarios revolved around relationships and sex. Here technology acted as a surrogate to buffer the challenge of having difficult conversations with caregivers about having boyfriends, sexual activity, drug use, etc. In contrast, College Packs (G4) acted as a repository of crowdsourced information serving more as a way of translating lengthy, complicated college access information.

Technology as Advocacy

The third role technology assumed in participant designs is one of serving as an advocate. In this role technology addressed the macro-layer of power and stereotypes. Participants that designed gPower mentioned that they wanted to not feel disempowered by stereotypes, but somehow empowered by them, or to feel they can flat out challenge them. They described scenarios where friends would make general remarks about girls being overly dramatic or how Latinas get very angry. They wanted to be able to either confront or own these stereotypes so they did not feel as threatening to their self-confidence. Their design was based on the idea that one can create memes that poke fun, takes ownership, or challenges prevailing stereotypes that are used by others to make them feel bad about their behaviors, reactions, or feelings.

Role of Being Bicultural

Latinas are commonly understood as a group often navigating between cultural worlds. The term biculturalism describes this non-singular cultural identification and how people with more than one cultural identity manage and experience these multiple meaning systems [5]. Researchers are increasingly connecting bicultural stress to health disparities amongst adolescents – particularly between Latinos and non-Latinos [36]. The notion of bicultural stress is not without critics. Issues with the concept of biculturalism are that culture itself can be a complex construct recreated and experienced differently by individuals, not to mention the immense variation within what we mean by the term Latina to begin with. In addition, critics point to the focus on the deficits of biculturalism such as how prioritization of family or gender norms can hamper Latina autonomy or cause conflict [36]. Scholars have increasingly sought to balance such deficit perspectives with highlighting the advantages of biculturalism and its role as a protective factor in Latina emotional health [5]. In this paper we use the term bicultural to denote the emerging broader multidimensional perspective that views acculturation as complex and operating on multiple dimensions of language, identity, cultural practices, etc., that can interact in ways that are conflicting, concurrent, or synthesized in unique instances (e.g., nuyorican) [39]. In this perspective, Latinas are not seen as having a static acculturation level that denotes the degree to which they are bicultural, but instead as actively negotiating multiple levels of cultural identity, practices, and language. In our analysis we identified three ways in which biculturalism was enacted in designed experiences.

Intergenerational Acculturation Gaps

While participants reflected on the general conflicts that arise with parents amongst their friends, many of their designs revealed a need to manage the impact of intergenerational acculturation gaps on emotional health. Intergenerational acculturation gaps refer to the differences that can emerge between generations over time in language, behavior, attitudes and values, stemming from the degree to which one generation may be particularly acculturated to their heritage culture rather than their new culture [6]. This intergenerational acculturation gap can lead to acculturation stress, particularly in Latina youth [36]. However, researchers have argued that acculturation is not always negative and does not always occur in generational patterns one might expect (i.e., parents are not always more acculturated to heritage culture than their children).

For instance, in MomChill (G1) the design reflected not just the discomfort of broaching subjects like boyfriends with caregivers, but also gender norms around being Latina. As one participant put it, *"Seriously though. I think if I were to bring it up my mom would just think I'm being slutty or am gonna end up pregnant. I mean I don't think she would say that, but she'd think it. You know."* Researchers have highlighted how differences in acculturation level can lead to conflict between parents and their children specifically in the area of gender role expectations [13]. In this way, MomChill served as an ambassador not just for taboo topics, but in topics that also pushed up against cultural norms on what it means to be a "good Latina girl."

Another example is the College Packs (G4) concept that not only reflected the use of technology to serve as an ambassador for complex information, but highlighted the brokering role that Latinas often play for their families [9,25,42]. Brokering often takes place when Latino children help their parents navigate institutions or social systems they are not familiar with or cannot easily interact with due to language challenges. In this way, College Packs served as a platform to support brokering college access information to reduce the emotional stress of having to broker this information to their Latino parents. One participant shared her experience, *"I can't have the conversation about going away [to college] with my mom again. I mean every time we have it she ends up crying and I – I just don't really feel anything. I'm like numb."*

Coping Norms

While research has shown that internalizing emotions may be gender driven, stemming from biological and socialization factors [14], there is research to support that coping strategies used by Latinas may be influenced heavily by cultural norms [27]. Specifically, internalizing has been identified as a maladaptive coping strategy that is thought to emerge from familism – where the family needs are prioritized above any individual needs [27]. In addition for Latinas, the gender norm of serving the family is more pronounced than for males, making the influence of familism on internalizing one's emotions more pronounced.

In Screamer (G5) what emerged was a focus on the challenge of self-concealment and internalizing behaviors. While there is some research [29] that describes how teens do not post information as much as they scan others' posts, there is also research that Latinas have even stronger tendencies to not share or externalize [28]. As one participant shared, *"I feel like there is this idea of keeping it in the circle... you keep it between us [family]."* Similarly tinktink (G2) can be seen as a mechanism for helping teens provide coping support to other teens, and also as a way of helping Latinas pull information from peers that may have hinted at wanting to talk, but is internalizing. In discussions amongst the G2 group that designed tinktink, the scenarios shared the pattern of not knowing how to get the other person sharing in a way that they do not feel judged and shut down. In studies that explore how to decrease internalizing behaviors and related suicidal behaviors, learning to create a bidirectional exchange of feelings and thoughts between mother and daughter was effective [40,44]. tinktink may highlight Latinas' need to learn how to facilitate such bidirectional exchanges with peers.

Stereotypes

The design concepts generated varied in terms of how they challenged stereotypes. Only one final concept focused on stereotypes, gPower (G3), which helps create memes that could be randomly and easily plugged into conversations similar to Giphy. In the group discussions, participants broached gender stereotypes within the context of dealing with peers in school, however cultural stereotypes about Latinas were directed more at themselves as a form of challenging internalized conceptions of what it means to be Latina. One participant said, *"Sometimes the crazy Latina fires me up, but sometimes it makes me feel like I'm way dramatic."* Another participant who shared that most of her schoolmates are Latino said in reference to her experience with stereotypes, *"I feel like there's a whole lot of sex and getting pregnant. I mean, have you every watched those stupid Univision shows? It's like crazy."*

Research has shown that negative stereotypes on ethnicity can add to cultural stress [36]. Particularly, there is Latino/a adolescents demonstrated that the risk of depression was most strongly associated with having experienced discrimination. In using technology as a form of advocacy, the participants chose to target Latinas, using the platform as a way to reclaim stereotypes images, rather than in advocating to non-Latinos. Peña [33] has highlighted the value of reclaiming stereotyped images of Latinos, particularly of Latinas, so as approach mental health from a strength perspective.

In gPower there is this use of the tool to advocate towards Latinas and claim both gender and cultural stereotypes. Through this design, bicultural stress is managed not through distancing oneself from cultural identity, or dealing with conflict with prejudiced groups, but a way of finding empowerment through cohesively reclaiming stereotypes and rewriting them within the both female and Latina group.

Intended Audience

During the reflection session, participants discussed their view that many of their designs would work with any youth, not just Latinas. In addition, many of the participants shared that throughout the process, their intention was not to design for Latinas, but to design for the scenarios they had defined as a group. As one participant phrased it, *"I know we're all... Latinas (air quotes), but I was always thinking, not about, you know, being Latina. I mean the stories we came up with, I think are things my friends would also say. Like my white and black friends, ...whatever."*

DISCUSSION

Our findings characterized our participants' perspectives on digital tools for emotional support and the role that technology can play in enacting that support. Across our findings, the issue of existing in two cultures arose and played out in the designed experiences in different ways. Together these manifestations suggest important directions for future research on Latina adolescent emotional support promotion. We next discuss directions for future work on the design and evaluation of technologies that promote emotional support for Latinas.

Incorporating Ecological Perspectives

In exploring how technology might better facilitate emotional support, the participants conceptualized tools that embedded cultural norms and practices. However, the norms and practices went beyond those of the individual, but traversed layers of Latina ecologies that include interactions between the individual, family, friends, and society. For instance, the designs reflected the meso-layer dynamics between peers and parents that can play into issues of acculturation, and perceived conflict in cultural values of such systems. The scenarios reflected how such dynamics influence emotional vulnerability, and in turn the designs served as a way to better navigate such pulls. As the field of design increasingly explores the role of culture [20], and incorporation of critical race theory and feminism [4], the value of incorporating ecological perspectives into participatory design methods for emotional support can be useful. It can allow for both cross-discipline scholarship and designs that are more systems-oriented rather than focused on behavior change on the part of the Latina teen [30].

Designing for Biculturalism

In designing for biculturalism what emerged was this notion of co-opting or building on existing platforms. Similar to the way in which biculturalism can entail switching or merging of cultural worlds, the designs that emerged were largely experiences that extended existing platforms. Screamer (G5) extended existing sharing affordances of social media platforms, while tintink (G2) sought to extend messaging and commenting interactions on existing social media platforms. MomChill (G1) could easily be implemented through the Instagram platform, while gPower could simply be a new backslash for the Giphy tool. Future work on designing for biculturalism may benefit from focusing on more structured remixing methods as part of the participatory design process, possibly even constraining the designs to focus on plugins, extensions, or mods.

Yet there is also a danger in focusing on biculturalism as a construct that can be designed for. In parallel to cultural psychological research on biculturalism, the construct is complex and cannot easily be attached to such a large and heterogeneous group like Latinas. Increasingly Latino scholars are questioning research that treats Latinos as a single group rather than a complex group that includes widely different heritages and related cultural practices [21]. Emerging work on acculturation and on biculturalism has expanded to be a much more multidimensional construct that allows for complex individual variation [39].

Future Work

Future work may benefit from deeper exploration of the three specific kinds of bicultural stress that were targeted through designs: (i) intergenerational acculturation gaps, (ii) cultural coping norms, and (iii) stereotypes. Particularly the unique ways in which the role of technology sought to facilitate emotional support in ameliorating bicultural stress. In dealing with intergenerational acculturation gaps, technology served as an ambassador buffering against cultural norms that make topics extremely taboo and the need for brokering complex information even more important. In dealing with cultural coping norms, technology served as way to guide certain kinds of inquiry and dialogue, yet also highlighted the challenge of Latina emotional internalization and self-concealment. Lastly, in dealing with stereotypes technology served as an advocate less so towards external groups and more so as an inwardly directed Latina group advocate.

LIMITATIONS

One major limitation to this work is in understanding the ways in which grouping participants by the label Latinas influenced the degree to which they emphasized emotional health challenges related to their Latina identity. While the activities allowed for the participants to identify their own challenges, scenarios, and design concepts, the context of working within a specific group may delineate unconscious design constraints. Despite this limitation, the findings still provide insight into how technology may address biculturalism from the Latina perspective. Along similar lines an additional limitation of the study is the degree to which Latinas can be understood as a cultural group. Cultural psychologists have contested the simplification of ethnicity arguing that it is complex and involves lifeways of individuals in a manner that is more profound than ethnic labels [19,22].

CONCLUSIONS

Our findings highlight the importance of attending to biculturalism as a sociocultural construct in co-design with Latina teens. It raises the issue that for some people emotional support is very much influenced by cultural values and a convergence of differences in emotional support practices, perspectives, and resources. For our participants, biculturalism was evident in their desire to better navigate the differences. In creating space for cultural identity and practices to be considered during co-design, our participants not only seemed to enact their internalized bicultural negotiation through techno artifact design, but also design for a lived experience important to them as teens, Latinas, and individuals existing in complex emotional contexts.

ACKNOWLEDGMENTS

Thank you to our colleagues and to our teen design partners that contributed their time, energy, and perspectives to the study. We would also like to thank VotoLatino for partially funding this study.

REFERENCES

1. Şerife Ak. 2016. The role of technology-based scaffolding in problem-based online asynchronous discussion. *British Journal of Educational Technology* 47, 4: 680–693. https://doi.org/10.1111/bjet.12254
2. Leticia M. Arellano and Christina Ayala-Alcantar. 2004. Multiracial Feminism for Chicano/a Psychology. In *Multiracial feminism for Chicana/o psychology.* 215–230.
3. Zahra Ashktorab and Jessica Vitak. 2016. Designing Cyberbullying Mitigation and Prevention Solutions through Participatory Design With Teenagers. *Proceedings of the 2016 CHI Conference on Human Factors in Computing Systems - CHI '16*: 3956–3969. https://doi.org/10.1145/2858036.2858433
4. Shaowen (Indiana University) Bardzell. 2010. Feminist HCI : Taking Stock and Outlining an Agenda for Design. *Proceedings of the 28th International Conference on Human Factors in Computing Systems*: 1301–1310.

https://doi.org/10.1145/1753326.1753521

5. V. Benet-Martínez, J. Leu, F. Lee, and M. W. Morris. 2002. Negotiating Biculturalism: Cultural Frame Switching in Biculturals with Oppositional Versus Compatible Cultural Identities. *Journal of Cross-Cultural Psychology* 33, 5: 492–516. https://doi.org/10.1177/0022022102033005005
6. D Birman and M Poff. 2011. Intergenerational Differences in Acculturation. *Encyclopedia on Early Childhood Development*: 1–8.
7. Urie Bronfenbrenner. 1986. Ecology of the family as a context for human development: Research perspectives. *Developmental Psychology* 22, 6: 723–742. https://doi.org/10.1037//0012-1649.22.6.723
8. Urie Bronfenbrenner. 2009. *The ecology of human development.*
9. R. Buriel, W. Perez, T. L. de Ment, D. V. Chavez, and V. R. Moran. 1998. The Relationship of Language Brokering to Academic Performance, Biculturalism, and Self-Efficacy among Latino Adolescents. *Hispanic Journal of Behavioral Sciences* 20, August: 283–297. https://doi.org/10.1177/07399863980203001
10. Julio Cammarota. 2016. The praxis of ethnic studies: transforming second sight into critical consciousness. *Race, Ethnicity & Education* 19, 2: 233–251. https://doi.org/10.1080/13613324.2015.1041486
11. John M. Carroll. 1999. Five reasons for scenarios Based Design. 13, c: 43–60.
12. Centers for Disease Control & Prevention. 2015. *Youth online: High school youth risk behavior survey (YRBS).*
13. Yolanda M. Céspedes and Stanley J. Huey. 2008. Depression in Latino adolescents: A cultural discrepancy perspective. *Cultural Diversity and Ethnic Minority Psychology* 14, 2: 168–172. https://doi.org/10.1037/1099-9809.14.2.168
14. Tara M. Chaplin and Amelia Aldao. 2013. Gender differences in emotion expression in children: A meta-analytic review. *Psychological Bulletin* 139, 4: 735–765. https://doi.org/10.1037/a0030737
15. Philippa Collin and Teresa Swist. 2015. From products to publics? The potential of participatory design for research on youth, safety and well-being. *Journal of Youth Studies* 6261, December: 1–14. https://doi.org/10.1080/13676261.2015.1098774
16. Guadalupe Espinoza. 2015. Daily cybervictimization among Latino adolescents: Links with emotional, physical and school adjustment. *Journal of Applied Developmental Psychology* 38: 39–48. https://doi.org/10.1016/j.appdev.2015.04.003
17. Gillian Fergie, Kate Hunt, and Shona Hilton. 2016. Social media as a space for support: Young adults' perspectives on producing and consuming user-generated content about diabetes and mental health. *Social Science & Medicine* 170: 46–54. https://doi.org/10.1016/j.socscimed.2016.10.006
18. Alberta M Gloria, Jeanett Castellanos, and Veronica Orozco. 2005. Perceived Educational Barriers , Cultural Fit , Coping Responses , and Psychological Well-Being of Latina Undergraduates. 27, 2: 161–183. https://doi.org/10.1177/0739986305275097
19. Roger Geertz Gonzalez and Jeaná Morrison. 2016. Culture or No Culture? A Latino Critical Research Analysis of Latino Persistence Research. *Journal of Hispanic Higher Education* 15, 1: 87–108. https://doi.org/10.1177/1538192715579460
20. David Hakken and Paula Maté. 2014. The culture question in participatory design. *Proceedings of the 13th Participatory Design Conference on Short Papers, Industry Cases, Workshop Descriptions, Doctoral Consortium papers, and Keynote abstracts - PDC '14 - volume 2*: 87–91. https://doi.org/10.1145/2662155.2662197
21. D. K. Hatch, N. Mardock Uman, and C. E. Garcia. 2015. Variation Within the "New Latino Diaspora": A Decade of Changes Across the United States in the Equitable Participation of Latina/os in Higher Education. *Journal of Hispanic Higher Education.* https://doi.org/10.1177/1538192715607333
22. Janet E Helms, Maryam Jernigan, and Jackquelyn Mascher. 2005. The meaning of race in psychology and how to change it: A methodological perspective. *The American psychologist* 60, 1: 27–36. https://doi.org/10.1037/0003-066X.60.1.27
23. L. Hirsch, M. Saeedi, J. Cornillon, and L. Litosseliti. 2004. A structured dialogue tool for argumentative learning. *Journal of Computer Assisted Learning* 20, 1: 72–80. https://doi.org/10.1111/j.1365-2729.2004.00068.x
24. Jennifer A. Kam, Bridget Potocki, and Michael L. Hecht. 2014. Encouraging Mexican-Heritage Youth to Intervene When Friends Drink. *Communication Research* 41, 5: 644–664. https://doi.org/10.1177/0093650212446621
25. Vikki S Katz. 2010. How Childen of Immigrants Use Media to Connect their Families to the Community: The case of Latinos in South Los Angeles. *Journal of Childen and Media* 4, 3: 298–315. https://doi.org/10.1080/17482798.2010.486136
26. Loes Keijsers and François Poulin. 2013. Developmental changes in parent-child communication throughout adolescence. *Developmental psychology* 49, 12: 2301–8. https://doi.org/10.1037/a0032217
27. Jill A. Kuhlberg, Juan B. Peña, and Luis H. Zayas. 2010. Familism, parent-adolescent conflict, self-esteem, internalizing behaviors and suicide attempts among adolescent Latinas. *Child Psychiatry and Human Development* 41, 4: 425–440. https://doi.org/10.1007/s10578-010-0179-0
28. Jill a Kuhlberg, Juan B Peña, and Luis H Zayas. 2010. Familism, parent-adolescent conflict, self-esteem, internalizing behaviors and suicide attempts among adolescent Latinas. *Child psychiatry and human development* 41, 4: 425–40. https://doi.org/10.1007/s10578-010-0179-0

29. María E. Len-Ríos, Hilary E. Hughes, Laura G. McKee, and Henry N. Young. 2016. Early adolescents as publics: A national survey of teens with social media accounts, their media use preferences, parental mediation, and perceived Internet literacy. *Public Relations Review* 42, 1: 101–108. https://doi.org/10.1016/j.pubrev.2015.10.003

30. Hazwani Mohd Mohadis and Nazlena Mohamad Ali. 2015. Using Socio-ecological Model to Inform the Design of Persuasive Applications. *Proc. of 33rd Ann ACM Conf Ext Abst on Hum Factors in Comp Sys* 18: 1905–1910. https://doi.org/10.1145/2702613.2732835

31. Joanne Noone, Maggie Sullivan, Nancy Castillo McKinnis, Tiffany L. Allen, Carolina Regalado, and Teresa Esqueda. 2016. Latino youth participation in community-based participatory research to reduce teen pregnancy disparities. *Children and Youth Services Review* 63: 36–39. https://doi.org/10.1016/j.childyouth.2016.02.011

32. Omid Noroozi, Armin Weinberger, Harm J A Biemans, Martin Mulder, and Mohammad Chizari. 2013. Facilitating argumentative knowledge construction through a transactive discussion script in CSCL. *Computers and Education* 61, 1: 59–76. https://doi.org/10.1016/j.compedu.2012.08.013

33. Ezequiel Peña. 2003. Reconfiguring Epistemological Pacts : Creating a Dialogue between Psychoanalysis and Chicano/a Subjectivity, a Cosmopolitan Perspective. *Journal for the Psychoanalysis of Culture and Society* 8, 2: 308–319.

34. Georgina Perez, Pamela Della Valle, Sarah Paraghamian, Rachel Page, Janet Ochoa, Fabiana Palomo, Emilia Suarez, Angela Thrasher, Anh N Tran, and Giselle Corbie-Smith. 2015. A Community-Engaged Research Approach to Improve Mental Health Among Latina Immigrants: ALMA Photovoice. *Health promotion practice*, July: 1524839915593500-. https://doi.org/10.1177/1524839915593500

35. Andrea J. Romero, Lisa M. Edwards, Sheri Bauman, and Marissa K. Ritter. 2014. *Preventing Adolescent Depression and Suicide Among Latinas*. Springer International Publishing, Cham. https://doi.org/10.1007/978-3-319-01381-7

36. Andrea J Romero, Daniel Martinez, and Scott C Carvajal. 2007. Bicultural stress and adolescent risk behaviors in a community sample of Latinos and non-Latino European Americans. *Ethnicity & health* 12, 5: 443–463. https://doi.org/10.1080/13557850701616854

37. Stephanie Ryan, Jason Yip, Mike Stieff, and Allison Druin. 2013. Cooperative Inquiry as a Community of Practice Introduction to Cooperative Inquiry Three Themes in Cooperative Inquiry Participation. In *Computer-Supported Collaborative Learning Conference, CSCL*, 145–148.

38. Patricia Sánchez. 2009. “In Between Oprah and Cristina”: Urban Latina Youth Producing a Countertext with Participatory Action Research. *Social Justice* 36, 4: 54–68.

39. Seth J Schwartz and Jennifer B Unger. 2010. Rethinking the Concept of Acculturation: Implications for Theory and Research. *American Psychologist* 65, 4: 237–251. https://doi.org/10.1037/a0019330.

40. Sandra G Turner, D Ph, Carol P Kaplan, Luis Zayas, and Ruth E Ross. 2002. Suicide Attempts by Adolescent Latinas : An Exploratory Study of Individual and Family Correlates. *Child and Adolescent Social Work Journal* 19, 5: 357–374.

41. Hua Wang and Arvind Singhal. 2016. East Los High:Transmedia edutainment to promote the sexual and reproductive health of young Latina/o Americans. *American Journal of Public Health* 106, 6: 1002–1010. https://doi.org/10.2105/AJPH.2016.303072

42. Holley A. Wilkin, Vikki S. Katz, and Sandra J. Ball-Rokeach. 2009. The role of family interaction in new immigrant Latinos’ civic engagement. *Journal of Communication* 59, 2: 387–406. https://doi.org/10.1111/j.1460-2466.2009.01421.x

43. Luis Zayas, Lauren E. Gulbas, Nicole Fedoravicius, and Leopoldo J. Cabassa. 2010. Patterns of distress, precipitating events, and reflections on suicide attempts by young Latinas. *Social Science & Medicine* 70, 11: 1773–1779. https://doi.org/10.1016/j.socscimed.2010.02.013

44. Luis H Zayas, Charlotte L Bright, Thyria Alvarez-Sánchez, and Leopoldo J Cabassa. 2009. Acculturation, familism and mother-daughter relations among suicidal and non-suicidal adolescent Latinas. *The journal of primary prevention* 30, 3–4: 351–69. https://doi.org/10.1007/s10935-009-0181-0

45. Luis H Zayas, Rebecca J Lester, Leopoldo J Cabassa, and Lisa R Fortuna. 2005. Why do so many latina teens attempt suicide? A conceptual model for research. *The American journal of orthopsychiatry* 75, 2: 275–287. https://doi.org/10.1037/0002-9432.75.2.275

46. Baoshan Zhang, Qianyun Gao, Marjolein Fokkema, Valeria Alterman, and Qian Liu. 2015. Adolescent interpersonal relationships, social support and loneliness in high schools: Mediation effect and gender differences. *Social Science Research* 53: 104–117. https://doi.org/10.1016/j.ssresearch.2015.05.003

Virtual Reality MRI: Playful Reduction of Children's Anxiety in MRI Exams

Stefan Liszio
University of Duisburg-Essen
Entertainment Computing Group
Duisburg, Germany
stefan.liszio@uni-due.de

Maic Masuch
University of Duisburg-Essen
Entertainment Computing Group
Duisburg, Germany
maic.masuch@uni-due.de

ABSTRACT
Many people, especially children, perceive MRI exams as threatening. They experience anxiety and stress during the procedure. Often this results in premature termination of the scan or low image quality. To avoid these adverse effects, it is common to sedate anxious patients. We present a playful virtual reality (VR) application for children (8 - 15 years) to counter anxiety and avoid sedation. Our approach uses a realistic virtual MRI scanner for desensitization and habituation to the MRI exam. To compensate the limited amount of profound knowledge about the design of child-tailored VR applications, we pursued a child-centered design process. Starting with expert interviews, we iterated through several development cycles and carried out focus group testings to evaluate prototypes of the VR application. Then, we conducted a field study with 13 patients under real life clinical conditions. Although results were non-significant, tendencies indicate a drop in the anxiety level after using the application. Furthermore, the application received strong support of the participating children, and medical professionals.

ACM Classification Keywords
H.5.1. Information Interfaces and Presentation (e.g. HCI): Multimedia Information Systems: Artificial, augmented, and virtual realities; K.8.0. Personal Computing: General: Games

Author Keywords
VR gaming; stress; magnetic resonance imaging; child-centered design; sedation; patient preparation; desensitization.

VIRTUAL REALITY IN HEALTHCARE
Today's VR technology is capable of presenting highly realistic simulated experiences while being relatively inexpensive. By providing simulated stereoscopic images and synchronization of head movements, it is possible to elicit high levels of sensory immersion [32]. The higher the level of sensory immersion, the more likely it is for a recipient to experience presence, that is, the feeling of actual being in the virtual world [14]. Thus, VR allows the recipient to experience virtual worlds as if they were real. These worlds represent completely controllable environments, which can be explored safely and independently of time and place. Consequently, VR has been applied in a multitude of domains related to healthcare, such as for graded exposure therapy of anxiety disorders, but also for education, and training of surgical skills [22, 1]. It has been shown that confronting patients with specific feared stimuli in immersive virtual environments is an effective way to reduce anxiety [26]. Thus, virtual reality exposure therapy (VRET) has proven to be suitable for a variety of affective (especially anxiety) disorders like specific phobias (e.g. claustrophobia, fear of heights, fear of flying, PTSD, social phobia) [43, 41]. VRET addresses some of the disadvantages of classical in vivo and imaginal exposure therapy approaches: Unlike in vivo exposure, VRET is independent from time and space, and can be performed in a safe environment without the risk of public embarrassment [43]. In contrast to imaginal exposure, VRET does not require imaginative abilities of the patient to visualize the anxiety-evoking scenario. Furthermore, a remarkable amount of research has been done in applying VR-technology to support distraction therapy in pain management [36]. Hoffman et al. [15], the pioneers of this approach, used a VR game to distract patients from pain during woundcare. With functional magnetic resonance imaging, the authors were able to show that VR as a distraction technique is successful and effective in reducing pain perception. Several follow-up studies have reinforced these findings also for chronic pain [42].

Although some authors have already anticipated the potential of VR as a method for preparing individuals for stressful situations [43, 34], to our knowledge, this is the first attempt to systematically design and use a playful VR application for the reduction of children's anxiety and stress related to magnetic resonance imaging (MRI). We present an approach which combines patient information, play-therapeutic elements, games, and VR exposure in one VR application for desensitization and habituation to both the MRI examination procedure and the MRI scanner itself prior to the actual scan. To design this application in accordance with the needs and preferences of the target group, we followed an iterative child-centered design process.

IDC '17, June 27-30, 2017, Stanford, CA, USA

ISBN 978-1-4503-4921-5/17/06...$15.00

DOI: http://dx.doi.org/10.1145/3078072.3079713

PATIENT'S FEAR OF MRI EXAMS

The number of MRI units and exams is rapidly increasing worldwide [25]. MRI technology has improved diagnosis and treatment and is, in the current state of knowledge, physically less harmful compared to conventional radiography and computed tomography. However, some patients, especially children, experience the MRI exam as threatening. Thus, they react with expressions of anxiety and stress [30]. Some authors report that up to 30% of patients experience high levels of anxiety during the examination [12]. Klonoff, Janata and Kaufman [16] estimate that 20% of the patients undergoing an MRI exam exhibit claustrophobic reactions. The reasons are manifold, some are related to the specific characteristics of the MRI scanning procedure, others relate to internal factors. Fear-inducing factors attributed to the MRI unit and the examination procedure are, among others, spatial narrowness of the scanner tube, unfamiliarity with the surrounding and the medical equipment, the noise, or the duration of the scan and the necessity of lying motionlessly [12, 30]. Among the internal factors are the unfamiliarity with the situation, the anticipation of pain and discomfort, a sense of being not in control of the situation, and worries about the diagnosis [12]. Some patients have reported feeling "buried alive" or "abandoned" [12]. Children are particularly prone to these negative feelings because they lack understanding of the situation and instructions [30]. Thus, it is likely that they respond with sometimes extreme stress reactions. These stress reactions are highly problematic because movements of the patient result in motion artifacts, which impede the diagnosis. Indeed, Malisza et al. [21] reported a failure rate of at least 50% when performing MRI studies with children aged 2 to 5 years, and a failure rate of 35% for children aged 6 to 7 years. Furthermore, the duration of the examination increases with lacking patient compliance and the procedure becomes more unpleasant for the patient [12]. Such negative experiences may also result in procedure-induced traumas and phobias [12]. Stressed patients show increased susceptibility for infections, increased sensation of pain leading to a higher need for analgesics subsequent to the treatment [40] as well as delayed wound healing [24]. Refusal to undergo the scan and premature termination cause adverse health consequences and a serious waste of resources [6]. Sedation or general anesthesia (GA) are commonly applied to improve patient cooperation and thus image quality [7]. However, sedation and GA can have several physiological impacts on the function of heart, lung, and circulatory system as well as a higher risk for patients with accompanying diseases [40]. The aforementioned problems emphasize the advantages of non-pharmacological strategies to help anxious patients to cope with the threatening situation. Such interventions can either be applied prior to the MRI exam as preventive measures or during the scanning procedure, like the performance of relaxation techniques [39], distraction from the fear-inducing stimuli [11], or the presentation of mood enhancing audio-visual cues [5]. Proper patient preparation is considered a well-received preventive measure making the actual examination more comfortable for pediatric and adult patients, and leading to a higher probability of successful scan completion and increased image quality [16, 30, 7].

STRATEGIES FOR PATIENT PREPARATION

Among several non-pharmacological methods to prepare the patient for the MRI exam and to reduce anxiety, the use of information material such as brochures, flyers, or films is the most common. Törnqvist et al. [38] reported that 4% of the MR images of patients receiving information material prior to the examination showed motion artifacts compared to 15.4% of the images of patients not receiving such material. For children there are some books on the topic of MRI exams (e.g. [10], [31]). These books use stories and metaphors commonly used in conventional children's books to explain the process of MRI scans or how MRI machines work. However, books cannot give a real-life impression of the noises and the narrowness of the MRI tube. Even illustrated books cannot address experiential factors of the MRI exam. Hence, books or other informational material is often used supplemental to other strategies for anxiety reduction but has to be edited and presented in a child-tailored manner, for instance as a picture book. Especially young children may have problems in transferring the content of the book to the real life experience, though. However, to our knowledge, there is no empirical validation of the efficacy of children's books in reducing anticipatory or acute anxiety related to MRI exams.

A more sophisticated strategy to prepare young patients is to use elements of play-therapy to help children familiarize with the forthcoming exam. Pressdee et al. [28] showed that a play-therapeutic session prior to the MRI exam reduced the need for sedation or anesthetics. Bharthi et al. [4] were able to replicate these results in a randomized controlled trial with children aged 4 to 10 years. Both studies applied comparable procedures. At first, patients and caregivers received detailed information regarding the MRI exam in easy understandable language from a play-therapist. In a second step, a small model of the MRI unit was used to accustom the child to the visual appearance of the machine. The characteristic sounds and noises of the MRI were played at increasing volume. Subsequently, the children were asked to choose their favorite toy and place it in the scanner. The children were instructed about the importance of being motionless during the scan. They were encouraged to stand as still as possible. If a child was able to stand still for 5 minutes (which is the average time of a single MRI sequence [4]), the training session was considered to be successful. Finally, the children were asked to reenact the MRI examination procedure with the toy to support their sense of control of the situation.

Another promising but far more time-consuming and complex method is to provide young patients with the opportunity to explore the MRI scanner and the examination room itself prior to the actual scan. Therefore, some hospitals own practice or Mock MRI units. Such Mock MRI scanners consist of only the shell of the machine without the magnets or any electronics. Several studies demonstrated that simulations of MRI scans with Mock MRI scanners could reduce anxiety in pediatric patients. Children who otherwise would have received sedation or GA were able to successfully complete the MRI exam after practicing [30, 7, 6]. Barnea-Goraly et al. [2] showed that even a simple and inexpensive toy tunnel can be utilized to simulate an MRI exam and to increase success rates significantly. Play-therapy and practice with Mock MRI scanners provide the most lively and realistic experience to children. Such training sessions allow gradual approximation to the fear inducing stimuli, though they are costly in time and resources. A therapist or medical staff member has to be around to instruct and guide the child. Hospitals need to have the necessary space, materials, and a simulator available.

Due to the limitations of these approaches, Wiederhold and Wiederhold [43] suggest creating a simulated MRI scanner using VR technology. In VR, users can visit and explore places that are not easily accessible in reality. Thus, we assume that a VR application can help patients to experience an MRI scan prior to the actual exam and to become familiar with the process and the medical environment.

VIRTUAL REALITY FOR CHILDREN

Research on the systematic design of child-tailored VR-systems, i.e. the hard- and software for operating VR applications [9], is still limited. The specific developmental characteristics of children have diverse implications for the design of both VR hardware and VR software. Head-mounted displays (HMD) like Oculus Rift or HTC Vive represent state-of-the-art VR hardware and are available for a broad consumer market since 2016. While these HMDs need to be connected with wires to a high-end PC, wireless solutions are preferable for child-tailored VR in terms of safety for the child and the equipment. Google Daydream and Samsung Galaxy VR are prominent examples for a family of smartphone based VR displays. The smartphone is used for processing and displaying the virtual world and is worn in front of the face with a special head-mount. The mobility of such HMDs comes at the expense of processing power, display resolution, field-of-view as well as the need for an internal power supply compared to wired HMDs. With regard to product design and ergonomics, most currently available HMDs target at adult users, ignoring the special physical demands of children [13]. For instance, head circumference is growing with age [35]. Together with the weight of the device, this can be problematic for both comfort and safety reasons [13]. Robinson [29] reports that children experienced the Oculus Rift as being too heavy and felt uncomfortable after wearing the device for a longer period of time. Furthermore, interpupillary distance (IPD), i.e. the distance between the centers of both pupils, varies between individuals and depends on age, gender, and ethnicity [8]. Since IPD is a determining factor for stereoscopic sight, it is necessary that a child-tailored HMD is adjustable even for lower IPD values. Children are more sensitive to restrictions in the field-of-view in HMDs than adults and have difficulties in orienting and navigating in a virtual world [23]. This is due to their inability to abstract the world and gain knowledge about their route. Speaking of immersion and presence, some research indicates that young children are more likely to experience higher levels of presence than adults [13]. Recent research of Baumgartner et al. [3] with children aged 6-11 used functional magnetic resonance imaging technology to analyze activity of certain brain regions while the participants received a fully immersive virtual environment. The results indicate that both left and right dorsolateral prefrontal cortex (DLPFC) moderate the experience of presence in adults, while the authors did not find activity in these structures in children. This is due to the fact that the DLPFC is not fully matured in younger ages. Concerning direct physiological effects of VR consumption in children, i.e. simulator sickness, our observations show that children are less prone to simulator sickness than adults are. However, there is only little scientific research on this topic, but some indications that age is not an indicator for VR related nausea or discomfort [13].

APPROACH

Anxiety and stress are closely related phenomena, where anxiety is the emotional component of a stress response to a stressor (i.e. a stress inducing stimulus) [37]. In order to find a solution to reduce children's anxiety as an outcome of stress, we need to understand how stress arises. According to the transactional model of stress and coping developed by Lazarus [18], stress is a result of reciprocal adjustment processes of the individual to the environment, that is, the individual actively affects the environment and the environment affects the individual's behavior [27]. Hence, the individual is actively involved in the occurrence of stress and the stress reactions. Central to this model is the cognitive appraisal of the stressful event (primary appraisal) and the available resources (secondary appraisal). Thus, whether a stimulus is perceived as stressful depends on its meaning for the individual and the existence of suitable resources to react to or cope with the stimulus. Stress results, if the stimulus is appraised as potentially harmful or threatening and the resources as insufficient. In this case, coping processes are triggered. These coping processes can be either problem-oriented or emotion-oriented. Problem-oriented coping strategies can be applied if the individual is able to control the situation. Otherwise, the individual has to use emotion-oriented strategies. As the name of this model indicates, this process of appraisal and coping is dynamic. After a coping strategy has been applied, a reappraisal of the stimulus happens and the process starts again. Based on these assumptions, interventions to prevent stress – and consequently anxiety – can have two starting points: Either they address the primary cognitive appraisal of the stimulus or they provide suitable coping strategies to the individual. Our approach focuses on a change in the primary cognitive appraisal of the potentially threatening characteristics of MRI exam and its context using child-tailored VR technology. More precisely, we integrate elements of play-therapy and desensitization in a playful VR application incorporating games and narrative components. Hence, we fuse patient preparation methods, which have been proven to be anxiety reducing with the advantages of VR and digital games. The application aims at the prevention of stress and anxiety of children undergoing an MRI exam in general. Additionally, it can be used as an intervention for children who have expressed such reactions in prior MRI exams. As pointed out before, typical potentially stress-inducing stimuli can be divided into two categories, such as unfamiliarity with the environment and the characteristics of the MRI unit (e.g. spatial narrowness, noise, necessity to lie motionlessly) on the one hand, and experiential stress-inducing factors on the other hand. The child's lack of understanding of the procedure, uncertainty, the anticipation of

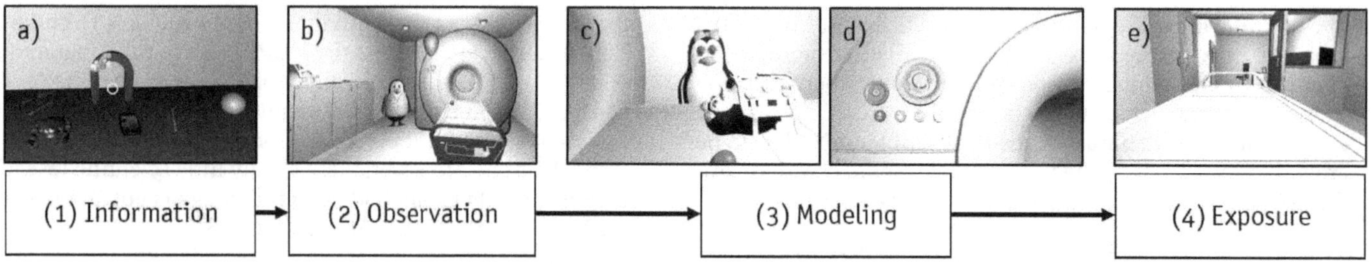

Figure 1. The application is structured according to the phases of play-therapeutic strategies to reduce anxiety prior to MRI exams (lower row). Screenshots from the prototyp in the upper row demonstrate the virtual MRI scanner and the environment as well as the characters (b-c). Pictures a) and b) depict two of the implemented games, while e) shows the view of the user when she is moved into the virtual MRI scanner.

pain, or the feeling of not being in control of the situation are informational factors possibly leading to anxiety and stress.

Experience

A virtual MRI scanner and examination room presented in VR can provide patients with the opportunity to explore the unknown environment in advance. Thanks to the high quality of sensory immersion of modern VR-systems, it is possible to create a natural simulation of an actual MRI scan. The use of a realistic VR MRI scanner and records of the real MRI's characteristic sounds and noises help to make the patient feel present in the virtual scanner. Furthermore, patients can use the application at any time and from any location, at home or even from their hospital bed. If they do feel too anxious, the virtual exploration can be easily interrupted without any organizational limitations. Likewise, it is possible to repeat the exploration as often as desired. Thus, the application can be used for desensitization and training of the whole procedure.

Information

Informational stress factors can further be addressed with the use of VR by presenting information about the MRI exam in a child-tailored and interactive way, interwoven with story-elements. Proceeding through the story, the child learns, for instance, about the purpose of an MRI, how it works, that it is noisy but harmless, and what the coils are for. The story helps the child to gain an understanding of the procedure, while the protagonists demonstrate how to behave, encourage, and motivate the child [19, 13]. Therefore, it is necessary to design characters the child can identify with [20], supporting empathy and involvement.

Games

Besides experience and information, we use the pleasing and motivating effects of games to further educate the children and to elicit positive emotions like fun and joy. As Lazarus and Abramovitz [17] have shown with their emotive imaginary technique, children's fears can be systematically reduced by the induction of positive emotions. Comparable to systematic desensitization, the child is guided to imagine situations which elicit emotions that are incompatible with anxiety. This technique is based on the effect of reciprocal inhibition as described by Wolpe [44], that is, an anxiety reaction is either completely or partly inhibited, if an emotional response incompatible to anxiety (e.g. anger, relaxation) is evoked. According to Lazarus and Abramovitz [17], a rapid and sustainable change of the child's emotional experience can be achieved with this technique.

CONCEPT AND IMPLEMENTATION

The theoretical approach presented in the previous section builds the foundation for the concept of our playful VR application, which aims at the reduction of anxiety and stress of children aged 8 to 15 years who await an MRI exam. Before going into more detail about the elements of the application in the following subsections, we introduce its basic structure. The application follows four steps as in play-therapy: (1) Information, (2) observation,(3) modeling, and (4) exposure. Additionally, it incorporates several methods to desensitize children for the upcoming medical examination using game elements (Figure 1). We created a virtual MRI examination room with a realistic animated MRI scanner as well as a virtual preparation room. After a short introduction to the story and its protagonists follows a tutorial, which teaches the user the controls and the basic interaction concept. (1) Subsequently, information about the MRI exam and the scanner itself are provided by the application's narrative elements and several interactive objects which are common in this domain. Furthermore, a simple game teaches the child which items can be taken into the MRI scanner and which not. (2) Following, in the observation phase, the child enters the virtual MRI room and is acquainted with the virtual MRI unit. The steps of the MRI scanning procedure are explained using the example of the story's protagonists. (3) In the subsequent modeling phase, the child is encouraged to reenact these steps in a second game. (4) In the final exposure phase, the child is invited to experience a virtual MRI scan in VR. A further game challenges the child not to move for five minutes. The application ends with a short conclusion of the story.

Pretest and First Design Lessons

In order to ensure the optimal fit of the application to the needs and preferences of the target group, we followed an iterative child-centered design process [20], that is, the active participation of children as representatives of the target group in the different stages of the application development. Children can provide valuable insights and information to inform the design process and thus should be involved in the development phases as equal partners, informants, and testers [13]. Thus, in a first step, we created a short interactive story a as VR application for Google Cardboard and presented it to two boys (both 7 years old) and three girls (10 years old). We conducted an explorative and unstructured interview, to learn how they react to and think about VR. Furthermore, we gained knowledge about possible usability and ergonomic issues. The most urgent question for us was whether the children would feel present in the virtual world and if the story would be absorbing, even though the used VR hardware does not offer a high level of immersion. The feedback from all young testers was positive. The children were very interested in the technology and wanted to know how it works. While following the story, the testers intuitively looked around in the virtual world and explored every detail actively. They showed positive emotions and expressed joy and amusement in their verbal expressions. Some children highlighted the feeling of being inside the world as what they liked most. Moreover, all children were completely absorbed while playing and did not react to any event or noise in the surrounding. However, in this first test, a standard Playstation 3 game controller was used as input device for movement and action in the VR application. Although all children stated to know the controller, some had problems in finding the right buttons since they were not able to see them. The testers criticized wearing comfort of the Google Cardboard head-mount used in this testing because of its weight and sharp edges. Thus, we decided to use the Mattel View-Master VR viewer for the actual VR application.

Story and Characters

The application tells the story of a little penguin girl (Figure 1c) who visits a doctor with her mother for an MRI exam because she has stomach pains. The story is told by a virtual doctor (Figure 1b), who is also a penguin. The doctor guides the user through the story, gives background information and feedback, explains the games and controls of the application, and performs the simulated MRI exam. All narrative and informational elements are presented in spoken, easy language. At the end of the story, the cause for the patient's pain (a swallowed fishbone) is identified with the MR images and the little penguin is fit again.

Interactive Objects and the Virtual MRI Environment

In order to give the young patients an impression of the MRI environment and the devices they will encounter, we modeled a virtual preparation room and a scanner room including a realistic animated MRI unit with sounds recorded from a real MRI scanner. The user can explore several interactive objects in the two rooms (e.g. a head-coil, the MRI computer terminal with MR images, or the emergency button). If she selects one of these object, the virtual doctors gives explanations about the object. The rooms are connected by a door, which is closed at the beginning of the session. The user starts in the preparation room and can proceed to the scanner room after having succeeded in the first game. Afterwards, the user can change the two rooms as often as she likes.

Games

Playful elements and games are used to induce a positive mood and to increase motivation. Games deliver a feeling of success, self-determination, and can facilitate knowledge transfer and learning. The games in our application are contextually embedded in the story and the process of the MRI exam. It is not possible to lose in these games, as mistakes are not punished. Instead, the virtual doctor gives detailed feedback about what the player did wrong.

Information Phase: Magnet Game

Just like in the real world, the player has to take of all magnetic objects before entering the MRI room. In this game, a variety of magnetic and non-magnetic objects are presented to the player (Figure 1a). The virtual doctor explains the player that the MRI consists of big magnets, which attract any magnetic object. Thus, the player has to identify those objects which are not allowed in the MRI scanner. If the player selects a correct object, it is attracted by a virtual magnet and the doctor gives positive feedback ("Very good! This would have made a mess!"). If the player chooses a non-magnetic object, a short animation of the object is played as well as verbal feedback of the doctor ("Not exactly. You can bring this to an MRI exam!"). After all magnetic objects have been found, the virtual doctor praises the player and tells her that she can now proceed to the scanner room.

Observation and Modeling Phase: Control Game

In the MRI scanner room, the user is first confronted with the virtual MRI (Figure 1b). According to the core assumptions of VRET and play-therapy, a gradual exposure to an anxiety inducing stimulus (the MRI scanner) supports the elimination of fears associated with the stimulus. Hence, we design a game allowing the child to get to know the scanner from the outside first and to gain an understanding about the specific steps of the scanning procedure. Like in play-therapeutic approaches, the child is invited to re-enact these steps. At the beginning of the game, the virtual patient lies down on the table (Figure 1c). With the buttons of a control panel on the virtual MRI scanner (Figure 1d), the MRI table can be moved up and down as well as slit into and out of the tube. Another two buttons start and end the scanning procedure. Realistic sounds recorded from an actual MRI unity are played according to the corresponding steps in the procedure. Thus, the child can listen to these sounds from outside the scanner prior to her own virtual MRI scanning experience. The player has to hit the buttons in the right order. A wrong button is highlighted in red color and a verbal feedback is given. If the player does not remember the right sequence, she can select the virtual doctor who will repeat a shorter version of the initial explanation. When all steps are repeated correctly, the doctor explains that the scan was successful and praises the virtual patient for her patience and bravery and the user for her help. The virtual patient states that the examination was not as bad as she had thought and that she had no fear. Finally, the images of the scan are presented and explained to the player.

Exposure Phase: Target Game

The final step is the experience of a virtual MRI scan. Before the MRI exam starts, the user is asked to remove the HMD and lay down. Afterwards, the child can put on the HMD again and finds herself lying on the simulated MRI table in the scanner room (Figure 1e). She is than slowly transported into the tube. The virtual doctor explains that the virtual scan starts now and that the player can exit the simulation at any time by either clicking the virtual emergency button or just putting down the HMD. Furthermore, the doctor reminds the player, that the scan is accompanied by loud noises but will not be harmful. He encourages the player to think of something positive. For this game, as for the actual scan, it is necessary to be completely motionless. Therefore, a target is displayed at the tube's ceiling. The player has to keep her view fixed on the target, otherwise the doctor tells her not to move in order not to blur the images. A comparable application was developed in a non-scientific student's project in 2015[1]. Following Bharti et al. [4], the duration of this exercise is five minutes. Half way through the virtual scan, the doctor praises the player, shortly before this session ends, telling her that she almost did it. When the child successfully finishes this game, she is told that she is well prepared for the real MRI scan.

VR-Hardware and Interaction Design

The View-Master is an inexpensive smartphone mount comparable to Google Cardboard, but is made of plastic and thus easy to clean, which is important due to the medical context. As a child product, it is very robust and has an extra safety mechanism to protect the smartphone. The mount comes without head-straps, thus the user has to hold it in front of her face. In the present use case, this has the advantage that the HMD can easily be removed if the user feels uncomfortable (e.g. because of simulator sickness or due to the individual health conditions) or if the anxiety level becomes critical during the exposure. The View-Master has a simple lever on the right side of the device, which can be used for simple interaction in the VR. Hence, we dismissed the use of an extra game controller and decided to incorporate a simple point and click interaction design, as this interaction concept is, according to our aforementioned pretest, the most suitable. For this interaction concept, a white dot is displayed in the center of the viewing field, which is comparable to a mouse cursor. If the user focuses an interactive object, that is, it is centered in her view, the dot expands to a bigger white circle to indicate that an action is possible. To perform this action, the user has to pull down and release the lever on the HMD. This is beneficial for several reasons: The children do not need to remember complex controls and do not need to find the right buttons on the game controller while not being able to see them. Further, no extra input device is needed, which makes the whole VR-system less costly and easier to use in the targeted context of medical examinations. Hence, it allows children to understand and execute the necessary steps to navigate through the virtual world. We arranged all objects around the user to avoid that the user gets lost in the virtual world. Reducing player locomotion to a minimum is furthermore advisable because it reduces the risk of causing simulator sickness. However, to give the children an exact overview of the preparation room and the MRI room it is necessary to allow the user to travel from one room to the other. Thus, we decided to use slow autonomous locomotion over teleporting the user from one point in the virtual world to another. Travelpoints as well as the starting positions of the games are indicated by colored balloons (Figure 1b). The user has to click on a balloon in order to move to its position or to start the respective game. Since we followed a child-centered design process, we conducted a focus group testing with children with and without MRI experience as well as with medical staff members as a proof of concept and to ensure the target group's acceptance of our approach (Study 1). Moreover, the testing was used to detect and correct flaws in the application. A revised version of the prototype was then used in a second study in the real clinical setting with children who needed to have an MRI exam (Study 2). This study was carried out to investigate whether the use of our application prior to the MRI exam reduces anxiety and stress related to the procedure.

[1]https://sites.google.com/site/mrisimulator/, last visited on 2017-04-18

STUDY 1

Subsequent to the implementation of a first version of the application, we conducted a focus group testing with five children who underwent one or more MRI scans before and two children who have never been in an MRI scanner before. In addition, we asked four staff members of the radiology department of the Essen University Hospital, Germany for their professional feedback. The participants and the children's caregivers were completely informed about the study's background and goals and gave written consent about their participation in the study. Each participant had the chance to try out the entire application. Afterwards, they were asked if they would answer some questions about their opinion about the application. We used structured interviews in order to gain an understanding of how these three user groups perceive usability, design, and content of our application. The interview included questions about usability issues ("How hard was it for you to navigate in the virtual world?") and user experience ("How did you like wearing the VR glasses?", "Did you feel comfortable while playing?"). While experienced children could give feedback about how close the VR application is to their experience in reality, those children without any previous experience could describe whether they believe the application is helpful and the information provided is easy understandable ("Do you think, the application helps other children not to be frightened of the MRI?"). The staff members helped us to ensure the correctness and completeness of the content.

Results

Overall, we received positive feedback from all participants, the children as well as the staff members, about the VR application and the ideas behind it. The children were fascinated by the VR system and curious in exploring the virtual world. They enjoyed the story and its protagonists. Furthermore, they believed that the application would be helpful to reduce fear during MRI scans. The participants had no problems to orientate and navigate in the virtual world. The pacing of the spoken story and knowledge elements was deemed appropriate. Besides these encouraging results, we identified some issues and shortcomings in our design based on the participants' feedback and our observations. (1) We had to reduce the length of the spoken description of the action sequence in the simulation game, since it exceeded the attention span of some children. (2) The children did not recognize the balloons in the scene as interactive elements. Thus, we added a spoken description and added some balloons in the tutorial, so that the children could practice the interaction concept.

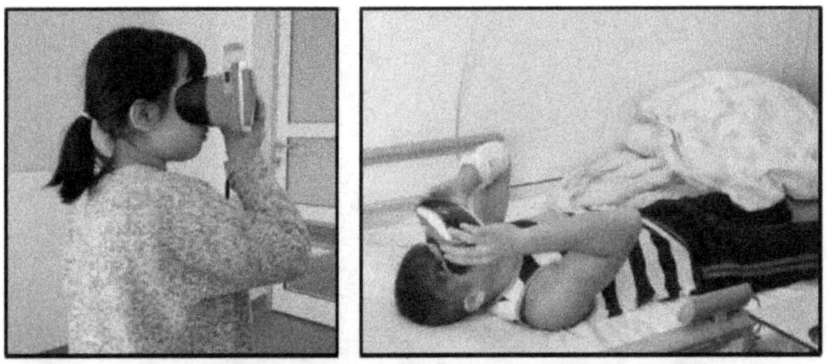

Figure 2. Two participants of study 2 testing the application. Left image: Girl with a peripheral venous catheter inserted into the back of her hand. She was not able to hold the HMD with both hands and to pull the lever.

(3) On the basis of the medical professionals' feedback, we changed some details in the story to make it more accurate and realistic. The most significant change was the introduction of the mother as a representative for a close relative who is usually present during MRI scans of children. (4) In the majority of MRI exams, head or body coils are used. These coils are additional antennas, which detecting the radio frequency signals emitted by the body during the scan. A coil looks like a frame or, in the case of head coils, like a helmet, which fits over the examined body part. Because these coils are commonly used in MRI exams but have a threatening effect on many children, the professionals suggested adding them as interactive objects. Additionally, a body coil is placed on the virtual patient when she is prepared for the examination (Figure 1c).

STUDY 2

We conducted a second study to test the revised prototype in the real clinical setting with children who needed to have an MRI exam. The aim of this study was to investigate whether the use of the VR application prior to the MRI exam reduces the children's perceived stress and anxiety. Furthermore, we wanted to get more insight about whether the target group likes the application. Figure 2 shows two participants testing the VR application during this study.

Method

Participants

Thirteen children aged 8 to 15 years ($M = 11.84$, $SD = 2.41$) participated in the study (4 female, 9 male). Patients fitting the target group were selected from the hospital's central patient database. Additionally, a consulting pediatrician judged whether the participation in the study was reasonable and safe for each child based on the individual health conditions. Only in this case the patients and the caregivers were asked whether they want to participate in the study. Nine patients had a history in MRI exams.

Procedure

All participants and caregivers were completely informed about the study's goals and procedure and gave written informed consent. We received full support of the ethical board of the University of Duisburg-Essen as well as the ethical board of the Essen University Hospital. Patients who were similar concerning age, sex, and previous MRI experience were paired and assigned to either the experimental group (EG; $N = 6$) or a control group (CG; $N = 7$). Participants in the EG used the VR application while they were waiting for the MRI exam. The CG did not receive a special treatment, that is they waited in the waiting room with their parents. All data was assessed using paper-pencil questionnaires. We assessed the current level of anxiety using the State-Trait Anxiety Inventory for Children (STAIC) developed by Spiegelberger [33]. The STAIC is a shortened version of the original STAI questionnaire, adapted in language and extent for children. Participants rated their state anxiety before, after, and during the MRI exam on the STAIC-S subscale. Anxiety during the MRI scan was assessed directly after the exam. In the EG group state anxiety was additionally measured directly after they used the VR application. Furthermore, general anxiousness in terms of a trait characteristic was measured using the T-scale of STAIC. Moreover, children in the EG were asked to rate the application according to several aspects of user experience: fun, story, whether they liked VR and the HMD, problems in orientation, presence and immersion as well as whether they found it helpful and if they would recommend the application to other children.

Group Factor	*Before MRI Scan*	*After Application*	*During MRI Scan*
EG	29.0 (3.95)	27.7 (6.08)	29.8 (7.47)
CG	27.7 (4.07)	–	27.4 (4.61)
Prior exp.	27.6 (4.06)	27.7 (6.08)	28.4 (6.50)
No prior exp.	30.0 (3.37)	–	28.8 (5.38)

Table 1. Mean STAIC-S scores for all points of measurement grouped by condition and prior MRI experience (Standard deviation in brackets).

Results

State Anxiety

The mean STAIC-T scores indicate that general anxiousness in this sample was within the norm [33]. Differences in the mean scores of EG ($M = 29.5$, $SD = 6.80$) and CG ($M = 33.4$, $SD = 5.13$) were non-significant, $t(11) = 1.19$, $p = .260$.

Total STAIC-S values in this sample are rather low in general (Table 1). The mean STAI-S score in the EG before the MRI scan is 29.0 ($SD = 3.95$), while the mean score in the CG was 27.7 ($SD = 4.07$). The EG's mean STAI-S score measured after the usage of the VR application did slightly decrease to 27.7 ($SD = 6.08$). During the MRI scan, an increase of participant's mean anxiety level in the EG to 29.8 ($SD = 7.47$) was measured. Participants in the CG experienced a mean anxiety level of 27.4 ($SD = 4.61$) during the exam. (Figure 3). Differences in the mean STAIC-S scores of all three measure points in the EG group were not significant, as indicated by a multivariate analysis of variance (MANOVA), $F(1,5) = 0.41$, $p = .675$, $\eta_p^2 = .076$. A paired-samples t-test indicated that the STAIC-S scores of the CG did not differ significantly between both points of measurement, $t(12) = 0.24$, $p = .815$, $d = -0.07$. A MANOVA did not show significant differences of the mean STAIC-S scores of both groups before and after the MRI scan, $F(1,11) = 0.12$, $p = .733$, $\eta_p^2 = .011$. Using prior MRI experience as a group factor, mean STAIC-S score before

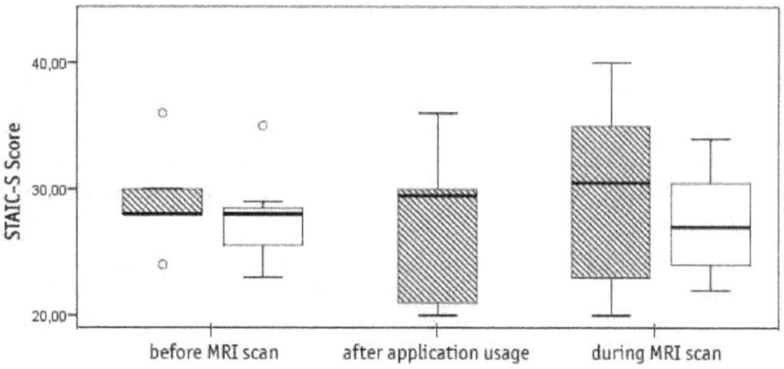

Figure 3. Total state anxiety scores of the EG (shaded boxes) compared to the CG (white boxes) over three points of measurement.

the MRI exam was 30.0 ($SD = 3.37$) for participants without prior MRI experience ($N = 4$) and 27.6 ($SD = 4.06$) for those with prior MRI experience ($N = 9$). There were no patients without prior MRI experience in the EG, thus mean and standard deviation are the same as mentioned above. During the MRI scan, patients without prior MRI experience reached a mean anxiety level of 28.8 ($SD = 5.38$). The mean value for patients with prior MRI experiences was 28.4 ($SD = 6.50$). A MANOVA did not show significant differences either, $F(1, 11) = 0.39$, $p = .544$, $\eta_p^2 = .034$. Furthermore, we did not find significant correlations of the STAIC-S scores with presence, immersion, or age.

User Experience

The six children in the EG were asked to rate several aspects of user experience on a 3-point scale (1 = "little", 2 = "medium", 3 = "much") (Figure 4). Four children answered to the question whether they had fun while using the application with "much", one child answered "medium", and one child answered "little" ($M = 2.50$, $SD = 0.84$). Three children liked the story "much", while the other three children answered "medium" ($M = 2.50.$, $SD = 0.55$). All six participants liked VR in general "much" and five children liked the HMD itself "much". One child liked the HMD with "medium" ($M = 2.83$, $SD = 0.41$). The children had no problems orientating in the virtual world, only one child answered that she had many problems ($M = 1.34$, $SD = 0.82$). Rather low ratings were reached for spatial presence. The children were asked how much they had the feeling that the virtual world was surrounding them. One child answered "much", three children responded "medium". Two children perceived only "little" spatial presence ($M = 1.83$, $SD = 0.75$). Cognitive immersion was operationalized with the question of how much the child was aware of the real world when using the VR application (i.e. high values indicate low levels of cognitive immersion). Two children answered "much", three children answered "medium". Only one child reported that she was not aware of the real world ($M = 2.17$, $SD = 0.75$). The last question to evaluate user experience was how likely the participants would use the application again. Three children answered "very", while the other three answered "medium" ($M = 2.50$, $SD = 0.55$). When asked what they did not like about the application, two of the six children named the sounds played during the virtual MRI scan. All children felt that the application can reduce fear of the MRI exam and would recommend it to other children.

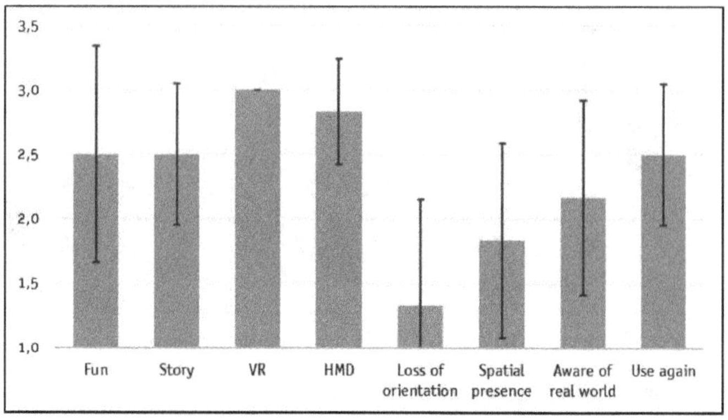

Figure 4. Aspects of user experience were assessed with single questions, which were answered on a 3-point scale.

DISCUSSION

The purpose of the second study was to evaluate the feasibility of our approach to use a playful VR application to reduce stress and fear of children related to the MRI exam. We intended to gain knowledge about how the application is adopted and perceived by the target group, how it could be integrated into the hospital's routines, and whether the application is able to positively affect the emotional state of the children. The descriptive comparison of the mean STAIC-S scores indicates a decline in the anxiety level of the EG directly after using the VR application. During the MRI exam, however, it returns to its initial level again. Although the results were not significant, we found tendencies in the data which underline our assumptions. The anxiety level in the control group remains constant before and during the MRI exam. Even though the anxiety reduction was not persistent over the course of the MRI exam, the observed drop in the anxiety level in the experimental group is a promising result. Note that the application was used only once directly before the MRI exam. We assume that intense and repeated usage of the application, would strengthen the effect and eliminate or lastingly reduce anxiety and stress of the young patients. The small number of participants did not raise hope for significant results. Due to the uncontrollable situational circumstances in the hospital's daily routine, the distribution of participants over the two groups is uneven with regard to individual variables like gender, age, and prior MRI experience. In a field study like this, it is not possible to rule out every influencing external factor. The influence of behavior, worries, and fears of the parents on the child's own emotional experience is not to be underestimated [28]. However, it was our aim to evaluate the application before conducting a large-scale clinical trial, which investigates the application's effects on children.

The results of the user experience evaluation of our prototype are promising. All children enjoyed the application and were fascinated by the VR. The VR-system was able to distract the patients from the real world, even though sensory immersion was limited due to restrictions of the VR-hardware. The most encouraging finding for us is that all participants were convinced that the application would be helpful for other children, since the participants were mostly "experts" in undergoing MRI exams. Thus, we are confident that our approach to use VR for preparing children for the MRI is a suitable alternative to conventional methods. However, the current state of research does not provide information about possible physiological or psychological long-term effects of VR reception, neither for adults nor for children. As for now, it is up to the researcher's and designer's responsibility to carefully design VR-systems and to keep investigating on their impact on humans. In order to enhance the anxiety and stress reducing effect, future implementations of our approach should incorporate elements that teach patients coping strategies to overcome fears before or during the MRI exam. Our proposed application could further be aligned with post-procedural interventions, which address situations in which the child remains frightened after the MRI scan in order to prevent fearful reactions in future hospital visits or MRI exams.

CONCLUSION

An MRI exam can be a lifesaver and sedation can be a risk. Therefore, it is important to help children to cope with this frightening procedure. This paper shows that preparing young patients for the MRI scan with the use of a playful VR application is a promising approach for a medication-free method to reduce anxiety and stress and eventually supports the young patients' well-being.

ACKNOWLEDGMENT

We thank A. Schroeder for her contribution to this project. We also thank Dr. O. Basu and the staff members of the radiology department of the Essen University Hospital for their valuable feedback. Finally, we thank all young patients and their parents for participating in our studies.

REFERENCES

1. Rajesh Aggarwal, Teodor P. Grantcharov, Jens R. Eriksen, Dorthe Blirup, Viggo B. Kristiansen, Peter Funch-Jensen, and Ara Darzi. 2006. An evidence-based virtual reality training program for novice laparoscopic surgeons. *Annals of surgery* 244, 2 (2006), 310–314.
2. Naama Barnea-Goraly, Stuart A. Weinzimer, Katrina J. Ruedy, Nelly Mauras, Roy W. Beck, Matt J. Marzelli, Paul K. Mazaika, Tandy Aye, Neil H. White, Eva Tsalikian, Larry Fox, Craig Kollman, Peiyao Cheng, and Allan L. Reiss. 2014. High success rates of sedation-free brain MRI scanning in young children using simple subject preparation protocols with and without a commercial mock scanner–the Diabetes Research in Children Network (DirecNet) experience. *Pediatric Radiology* 44, 2 (2014), 181–186.
3. Thomas Baumgartner, Dominique Speck, Denise Wettstein, Ornella Masnari, Gian Beeli, and Lutz Jäncke. 2008. Feeling present in arousing virtual reality worlds: Prefrontal brain regions differentially orchestrate presence experience in adults and children. *Frontiers in Human Neuroscience* 2 (2008).
4. Bhavneet Bharti, Prahbhjot Malhi, and N. Khandelwal. 2016. MRI Customized Play Therapy in Children Reduces the Need for Sedation–A Randomized Controlled Trial. *Indian journal of pediatrics* 83, 3 (2016), 209–213.
5. Joke Bradt, Cheryl Dileo, and Minjung Shim. 2013. Music interventions for preoperative anxiety. *The Cochrane database of systematic reviews* 6 (2013).
6. Amanda J. Carter, Mary-Louise C. Greer, Simon E. Gray, and Robert S. Ware. 2010. Mock MRI: reducing the need for anaesthesia in children. *Pediatric Radiology* 40, 8 (2010), 1368–1374.
7. C. J. T. de Amorim e Silva, A. Mackenzie, L. M. Hallowell, S. E. Stewart, and M. R. Ditchfield. 2006. Practice MRI: Reducing the need for sedation and general anaesthesia in children undergoing MRI. *Australasian radiology* 50, 4 (2006), 319–323.
8. Neil A. Dodgson. 2004. Variation and extrema of human interpupillary distance. In *Proc. SPIE 5291 (SPIE Proceedings)*, Andrew J. Woods, John O. Merritt, Stephen A. Benton, and Mark T. Bolas (Eds.), Vol. 36. SPIE, 36–46.
9. Ralf Dörner, Wolfgang Broll, Paul Grimm, and Bernhard Jung (Eds.). 2013. *Virtual und Augmented Reality (VR / AR): Grundlagen und Methoden der Virtuellen und Augmentierten Realität*. Springer Berlin Heidelberg, Berlin, Heidelberg.
10. Ashleigh Frayne. 2015. *Pluto and the MRI Rocket Ship Adventure*. Lulu Press, Inc., Raleigh, NC 27607.
11. Jonathan Gershon, Elana Zimand, Melissa Pickering, Barbara Olasov Rothbaum, and Larry Hodges. 2004. A pilot and feasibility study of virtual reality as a distraction for children with cancer. *Journal of the American Academy of Child and Adolescent Psychiatry* 43, 10 (2004), 1243–1249.
12. Susan J. Grey, Geraint Price, and Andrew Mathews. 2000. Reduction of anxiety during MR imaging: a controlled trial. *Magnetic Resonance Imaging* 18 (2000), 351–355.
13. Libby Hanna. 2008. Designing Electronic Media for Children. In *Ergonomics for Children*, Rani Lueder and Valerie J. Berg Rice (Eds.). CRC Press, Boca Raton, Fla., 754–782.
14. Carrie Heeter. 1992. Being There: The Subjective Experience of Presence. *Presence: Teleoperators and Virtual Environments* 1, 2 (1992), 262–271.
15. Hunter G. Hoffman, Azucena García-Palacios, David R. Patterson, Mark Jensen, Thomas A. Furness, III., and William F. Ammons, Jr. 2001. The Effectiveness of Virtual Reality for Dental Pain Control: A Case Study. *CyberPsychology & Behavior* 4, 4 (2001), 527–535.
16. Elizabeth A. Klonoff, Jeffrey W. Janata, and Benjamin Kaufman. 1986. The use of systematic desensitization to overcome resistance to magnetic resonance imaging (MRI) scanning. *Journal of Behavior Therapy & Experimental Psychiatry* 17, 3 (1986), 189–192.
17. Arnold A. Lazarus and Arnold Abramovitz. 1962. The use of "Emotive Imagery" In the Treatment of Children's Phobias. *The British Journal of Psychiatry* 108, 453 (1962), 191–195.
18. Richard S. Lazarus and Susan Folkman. 1984. *Stress, appraisal, and coping*. Springer publishing company.
19. James C. Lester, Sharolyn A. Converse, Susan E. Kahler, S. Todd Barlow, Brian A. Stone, and Ravinder S. Bhogal. 1997. The Persona Effect: Affective Impact of Animated Pedagogical Agents. In *Proceedings of the ACM SIGCHI Conference on Human factors in computing systems*, Steven Pemberton (Ed.). ACM, New York, NY, 359–366.
20. Janine Liebal and Markus Exner. 2011. *Usability für Kids: Ein Handbuch zur ergonomischen Gestaltung von Software und Websites für Kinder*. Vieweg+Teubner Research, Wiesbaden.
21. Krisztina L. Malisza, Toby Martin, Deborah Shiloff, and Dickie C. T. Yu. 2010. Reactions of young children to the MRI scanner environment. *Magnetic resonance in medicine* 64, 2 (2010), 377–381.
22. Fabrizia Mantovani, Gianluca Castelnuovo, Andrea Gaggioli, and Guiseppe Riva. 2003. Virtual Reality Training for Health-Care Professionals. *CyberPsychology & Behavior* 6, 4 (2003), 389–395.

23. Faith A. McCreary and Robert C. Williges. 1998. Effects of Age and Field-of-View on Spatial Learning in an Immersive Virtual Environment. *Proceedings of the Human Factors and Ergonomics Society Annual Meeting* 42, 21 (1998), 1491–1495.
24. Lynanne McGuire, Kathi Heffner, Ronald Glaser, Bradley Needleman, William Malarkey, Stephanie Dickinson, Stanley Lemeshow, Charles Cook, Peter Muscarella, William Scott Melvin, and others. 2006. Pain and wound healing in surgical patients. *Annals of Behavioral Medicine* 31, 2 (2006), 165–172.
25. OECD. 2015. Medical technologies. In *Health at a Glance 2015*, OECD (Ed.). OECD Publishing, Paris, 102–103.
26. Thomas D. Parsons and Albert A. Rizzo. 2008. Affective outcomes of virtual reality exposure therapy for anxiety and specific phobias: a meta-analysis. *Journal of behavior therapy and experimental psychiatry* 39, 3 (2008), 250–261.
27. Franz Petermann and Dieter Vaitl (Eds.). 2009. *Entspannungsverfahren: Das Praxishandbuch* (4 ed.). Beltz, Weinheim.
28. D. Pressdee, L. May, E. Eastman, and D. Grier. 1997. The use of play therapy in the preparation of children undergoing MR imaging. *Clinical Radiology* 52, 12 (1997), 945–947.
29. Peter Robinson. 2014. Researching Oculus Rift with Kids: What they Really Think of Virtual Reality. (2014). `http://de.slideshare.net/dubit/oculus-rift-virtual-reality-kids-research`
30. D. R. Rosenberg, J. A. Sweeney, J. S. Gillen, J. Kim, M. J. Varanelli, K. M. O'Hearn, P. A. Erb, D. Davis, and K. R. Thulborn. 1997. Magnetic resonance imaging of children without sedation: preparation with simulation. *Journal of the American Academy of Child and Adolescent Psychiatry* 36, 6 (1997), 853–859.
31. Gabriele Salomonowitz. 2000. *Die Geschichte der Magnetmännchen: Für Kinder im Alter von viereinhalb bis hundertzwanzig Jahren.* Facultas.wuv, Wien.
32. Mel Slater. 2003. A Note on Presence Terminology. *Presence Connect* 3, 3 (2003).
33. Charles D. Spiegelberger. *State-Trait Anxiety Inventory for Children: Sampler Set: Manual, Instrument, and Scoring Guide.* Mind Garden, Inc.
34. Melba C. Stetz, Richard I. Ries, and Raymond A. Folen. 2011. Virtual Reality Supporting Psychological Health. In *Advanced Computational Intelligence Paradigms in Healthcare 6*, Sheryl Brahnam and Lakhmi C. Jain (Eds.). Studies in computational intelligence, Vol. 337. Springer Berlin Heidelberg, Berlin and Heidelberg, 13–27.
35. H. Stolzenberg, H. Kahl, and K. E. Bergmann. 2007. Körpermaße bei Kindern und Jugendlichen in Deutschland. *Bundesgesundheitsblatt - Gesundheitsforschung - Gesundheitsschutz* 50, 5-6 (2007), 659–669.
36. Camelia Sulea, Ahmad Soomro, Chelsie Boyd, and Brenda K. Wiederhold. 2014. Pain management in virtual reality: a comprehensive research chart. *Cyberpsychology, behavior and social networking* 17, 6 (2014), 402–413.
37. Werner Tolksdorf. 1985. *Der präoperative Streß.* Springer Berlin Heidelberg, Berlin, Heidelberg.
38. E. Törnqvist, Å. Månsson, E.-M. Larsson, and I. Hallström. 2006. Impact of Extended Written Information on Patient Anxiety and Image Motion Artifacts During Magnetic Resonance Imaging. *Acta Radiologica* 47, 5 (2006), 474–480.
39. Daniela Villani, Francesco Riva, and Giuseppe Riva. 2007. New technologies for relaxation: The role of presence. *International Journal of Stress Management* 14, 3 (2007), 260–274.
40. Dietmar Weixler and Klaus Paulitsch. 2003. *Praxis der Sedierung.* facultas. wuv/maudrich.
41. Brenda K. Wiederhold and Stéphane Bouchard (Eds.). 2014. *Advances in Virtual Reality and Anxiety Disorders.* Springer and Springer US, New York.
42. Brenda K. Wiederhold, Kenneth Gao, Camelia Sulea, and Mark D. Wiederhold. 2014. Virtual reality as a distraction technique in chronic pain patients. *Cyberpsychology, behavior and social networking* 17, 6 (2014), 346–352.
43. B. K. Wiederhold and Mark D. Wiederhold. 2005. *Virtual reality therapy for anxiety disorders: Advances in evaluation and treatment* (1st ed. ed.). American Psychological Association, Washington, DC.
44. Joseph Wolpe. 1968. Psychotherapy by Reciprocal Inhibition. *Conditional reflex: a Pavlovian journal of research & therapy* 3, 4 (1968), 234–240.

Sex Talk: Designing for Sexual Health with Adolescents

Matthew Wood
Open Lab
Newcastle University
Newcastle upon Tyne, UK
m.wood8@ncl.ac.uk

Gavin Wood
Northumbria University
Newcastle upon Tyne, UK
gavin.wood@northumbria.ac.uk

Madeline Balaam
Open Lab
Newcastle University
Newcastle upon Tyne, UK
madeline.balaam@ncl.ac.uk

ABSTRACT
In this paper, we describe a user-centred design process, where we engaged with 58 adolescents over an 18-month period to design and evaluate a multiplayer mobile game which prompts peer-led interactions around sex and sexuality. Engagement with our design process, and response to our game, has been enthusiastic, highlighting the rich opportunities for HCI to contribute constructively to how HCI may contribute to sexual health in adolescents. Based on our experiences we discuss three lessons learnt: lightweight digital approaches can be extremely successful at facilitating talk among young people about sex; sharing control of the conversation between all stakeholders is a fair and achievable approach; even problematic interactions can be opportunities to talk about sex.

Author Keywords
Design, Sexuality, Young People, User-Centered Design

ACM Classification Keywords
H.5.m. Information interfaces and presentation (e.g., HCI): Miscellaneous

INTRODUCTION
Adolescents have emerged as a priority in public health in recent years. In a recent commission on adolescent health and wellbeing, The Lancet [26] reports that although adolescence is often considered the healthiest period in individual's lives, its significance in global health is increasing. Partly, this is because of relative decreases in this population's overall health and wellbeing, but moreover, health amongst this population is a good predictor for health trajectories across the life course [12].

Digital technologies are repeatedly highlighted as holding some of the greatest possibilities in improving health outcomes for adolescents [26]. Mobile content has been identified as one of the primary sources in which young people access health information [22] and, as such, the novel communicational and networking opportunities presented by the digital, particularly in increasing health literacy, have been emphasized as an under considered area for health promotion in adolescents [16].

Sexual and reproductive health is a key priority for this population, particularly through changing patterns in risk in reference to sexually transmitted infections and unplanned pregnancy [4]. Changes in the sociocultural, political and legal contexts have been shown to play a key role within these new vulnerabilities [26], and here digital technologies have also played no small role. Popular representations in new social media are argued to be changing young people's attitudes around sex and sexuality, particularly around casual sex. For example, 'new' public health problems such as young people taking and sending sexually explicit photographs of themselves, or sexting as it has been termed, have been described by some as a new public health 'epidemic' amongst young people [33].

The provision of sexual health information and sex education is seen to come from two countering perspectives. On the one hand, there is a perceived need for access to 'correct' or 'trustworthy' authoritative information, often with the overriding objective of reducing sexual activity amongst young people (sometimes referred to as a 'restrictive' approach to sexual health and sex education). On the other, a 'permissive' approach argues that we should acknowledge young people as sexual beings, and put their needs and perspectives at the fore [1, 13, 14]. In grappling this tension, our paper details our digital response to adolescent sexual and reproductive health, a game we designed in conjunction with young people to promote 'healthy' discussions around sex and sexuality. We detail how, whilst proving popular with our participants, use of the game in youth group settings reproduced many of the tensions characterising this space. We pose these as lessons learnt for IDC, and HCI more broadly, in responding meaningfully to the complex and multifaceted design space of sexual health in adolescents. We propose the benefits of lightweight digital approaches for face-to-face interaction, suggest how all stakeholders can control the level of these communications, and suggest that when problematic interactions arose, these presented opportunities to our agenda of promoting discussion about sex and sexuality.

IDC '17, June 27-30, 2017, Stanford, CA, USA

ACM ISBN 978-1-4503-4921-5/17/06.
http://dx.doi.org/10.1145/3078072.3079747

Sexual and Reproductive Health in Adolescents

Adolescents are defined by the WHO as individuals between 10 and 24 years old. This population poses an important yet also challenging setting for sexual and reproductive health. This age bracket covers a key transitionary period across the life course, particularly from a legal perspective, spanning from official 'childhood' to 'responsible adults'. Furthermore, perspectives from young people within this bracket can vary drastically, with adolescents often maturing sexually at very different times, which is influenced largely by socioeconomic factors [26]. This has resulted in the majority of sexual health interventions focusing the biological 'facts' of reproduction, the risks and dangers of unprotected sex, and often focuses on abstinence [13].

This 'restrictive' approach has been widely denounced by scholars working in critical sexuality [1]. It has been argued that a focus on abstinence reproduces unhelpful constructions surrounding male and female sexuality, for example, the view that men are the active, desiring sexual agents in sexual relationships (see 'the male sex drive discourse' [17]), which by virtue means that (heterosexual) women are required to protect themselves against men's sexual desire. There is also evidence to suggest that a focus on the risks and dangers surrounding sex, such as unwanted pregnancies and STDs, does not reduce sexual activity amongst young people, only that it discourages contraception use when young people come to have sex [21]. Moreover, a focus on the mechanics of 'sexual intercourse' we privilege a 'heteronormative' model of sex education, promoting heterosexual sex as the only legitimate form of sexuality [12]. Therefore, Taylor [28] has argued that by rejecting young people as being sexual beings, we are harming young people's overall sexual health. A preoccupation with the physical 'act' of sex, often reduced to be the insertion of a penis into a vagina [24], also prevents a focus on matters surrounding sex, such as relationships and intimacy [30].

Sex is not a Natural Act

Leanore Tiefer has made the influential claim that contrary to how sex is culturally constructed, that 'sex is not a natural act' [30]. By this she argued against the typical rhetoric of sex as an innate, and the idea that there is a standardized or inbuilt model of sexual response. Instead she argues there is very clear evidence that sexual behavior varies hugely from person to person. In contrast to being an inbuilt biological urge, cross cultural studies have shown us that sex is fundamentally shaped by the social context [21].

To these ends, Tiefer argues that the construction of sex as an inbuilt biological entity has resulted in most cultures simply not talking to young people about sex, with a "history of silence and embarrassment", based on the assumption that nature will simply 'take its course'. In [31] Walker suggests that young people in particular have desires to talk about sex with their elders, yet often find they are not able to have open and frank conversations about sex and sexuality, due to all parties, be it parents, schools or siblings, 'offsetting' responsibility for these conversations to others. She argues that the result of this is that needed conversations simply do not happen, and that the consequences of this are two-fold. Firstly, she argues that this prevents people from having a fulfilled sex life. The literature surrounding couples' sexual difficulties suggests that the major obstacles in couples' sex lives is simply being able to talk about sex - a topic we have been taught is 'embarrassing' or 'dirty' from an early age [20]. But more pressingly, she argues a consequence of embarrassment is people being exploited. By classing sex as a topic we don't talk about, conversations about consent, sexual violence and exploitation are reduced to the margins.

In contrast, cultures where sex is talked about more openly boast better overall sexual health. The Netherlands have some of the lowest rates of teen pregnancy and STIs, with research also suggesting that young people are more likely to delay sexual activity later than those in the US or UK. A cross-cultural study between the UK and the Netherland's sex education materials showed that the Dutch model of sex education taught about sex at a much earlier stage than in the UK [21], and that they also taught about the pleasurable aspects of sex. In response, Fine and McLelland [14] advocate 'a discourse of desire' in relation to young people and sexuality, acknowledging aspects of sexual pleasure, recognizing young people (particularly young women) as sexual agents in their own right, and being inclusive of sexual minorities. To these ends, we suggest that permissive, positive discussions for young people around sex and sexuality is an important goal for improving overall sexual health, and as will now be discussed, an opportunity for HCI.

Sexual Interactions and HCI

Digital technology provides clear opportunities for having conversations about sex. Previous research in HCI has examined the role that digital self-presentation plays in interaction around intimacy and sexuality. This has included how romantic relationships can be supported by technology, from their initiation [23] to their sustainment over time and distance [25]. The anonymity technology offers has been explored by [19] in investigating how explicit talk about 'making love' was expressed in various ways through a dedicated anonymous posting website, whilst [2] has investigated the (often) sexual content on anonymous Facebook 'Confession Boards' [5]. Research examining location based social networks such as Grindr and Tinder argue how self-presentation and anonymity become complicated in these online spaces [7], with [6] arguing that the prominence of these apps should now lead us to consider sex as a significant motivator in of itself for interaction with technology. An examination of these existing systems indicates how technology can create new or distinct ways for people to have interactions around sex, yet despite this HCI has made little way in terms of scoping a design space or response to these identified opportunities.

Sex Education and Technology

"Serious Games" have been one of the few HCI responses to sex education [29], using a computer game, some 20 years ago, to "increase [young people's] skill and self-efficiency", while more recently [3] using a gameshow format to reduce 'risk' of sexual coercion. Design concepts from social gaming may also have good application to the context of young people's sexuality; for example, 'play' has been used extensively in therapy settings to improve wellbeing, through 'playing out' concerns and anxieties [9]. Yet an objective of 'playfulness' has also become a more common focus for HCI research in recent years [8]. Specifically, humour and play have been evidenced as promising strategies for 'taboo' design [10], with Almeida et al. [2] arguing that humour provides an effective tool for designers wishing to diminish social awkwardness around sensitive areas.

This positioning underpinned a perspective for our work. We wished to respond to the design space of young people's sexual health with a playful and permissive approach, orientated around young people's perspectives. Moreover, we wished to explore the opportunities of digital play and humour in this context, in seeking to encourage 'positive' interactions around the topic.

TALKING ABOUT SEX

We therefore identified 'talking about sex' as an agenda for inclusive, permissive sex education, and identified games and play as a suitable mode of response. The development of our design concept was a collaboration between the authors. The first author is a sex and sexuality researcher, with experience in working with young people. The second author is a games designer with interests in designing for improvised play and using games with card-based playful interactions. The third author is an interaction designer who focuses on designing for digital health and wellbeing. The work was informed by the critical literature around sex and sexuality, and 12 design workshops where we workshopped and tested several playful techniques for promoting interaction about sex and sexuality with young people.

As previously mentioned, the WHO defines adolescents as individuals between 10 – 24 years old. Since research around this topic with such a diverse age group would be a considerable ethical challenge, the decision was made, in the first instance, to work alongside local authority led youth groups who work with 13-19 year olds. Although this is a wide age bracket, all the young people in these groups knew each other, and regularly came together to talk about a range of social issues, including sexual health. These groups were also organised age appropriately, with only young people of similar ages participating in the same group as one another. This made them an ideal starting point for this design work, as we sought to develop a design which could be extended for adolescents' discussions about sex and sexuality across a broader context.

Our engagements with the youth groups started with the youth group leaders. We had several meetings where we discussed the nature their engagements with adolescents, and how they ran their sessions. We then conducted 3 design workshops with 4 youth groups, who comprised of adolescents from both urban and rural environments and from a range of socio-economic backgrounds. Altogether we engaged 21 adolescents in these sessions.

Building on the existing activities used by youth workers, we developed a series of design activities to trail with young people, each designed to promote discussions about sex and sexuality. These were (1) a body mapping activity where young people were asked to plot their ideas of sex and sexuality onto inflatable mannequins, (2) an activity where young people were asked to timeline when they learnt about sex and sexuality and where from and (3) an activity using Lego where participants were asked to design some sexual health interventions. These workshops were looked at broadly for the types of interactions we found amongst our participants, and we identified two sensitising concepts: that of *inclusivity* and *digital playfulness*.

Inclusivity

There was a broad diversity of the topics covered by the workshops. Although our sessions were orientated around generating conversation about sex and sexuality, these engagements led to topics, as directed by participants, around body image, appearance concerns and mental health, alongside many other areas. Whilst a design response may not address all these complex matters, it did prompt us to extend our conception of sexuality for young people. While some young people presented themselves as experienced sexual beings, e.g. "I know what I'm doing!", others presented themselves as uninterested by sex, e.g. "Still now, I don't find sex appealing at all". Ideas of sexuality and intimacy often presented themselves in subtler ways, such as talking about the role of friendships or in using social media.

Digital Playfulness

The use of digital technology, particularly social media, was a prominent part of these youth group settings. This was illustrated most strikingly in a visit to one group where first arrivals immediately logged into Facebook on the available computers. Mobile phone use was a prominent part of these workshops, with participants regularly taking pictures on their phones, messaging friends, playing music from their phones and using social media. Although occasionally disruptive e.g. "Youth worker: Come on, get with the programme!", we were particularly interested in how digital technology organically introduced opportunities for social play in these community settings, for example sharing pictures of artefacts they had produced in the workshop on social media. This reinstated the assertion that mobile technologies were a particularly suitable medium in which to focus our prototype.

The Prototype

Building on these insights from the workshops in conjunction with the dialogue in the critical sexuality literature, our prototype was a result of numerous design sessions and discussions, paper based prototyping and body storming. 'Talk About Sex' is a multiplayer game, developed for iOS, designed initially for young people to play together. Using a peer-to-peer network over Wi-Fi or Bluetooth on players' devices, the game begins by instructing all players to turn their phones face down. After a three second pause, one player's phone vibrates and makes a short sound, indicating that it is their turn. Once they turn their phone face up, it presents the player with a task presented in Figure 1. To progress, all must return their phone face down where the process is repeated with the next player. This continues until all tasks have been played through. Figure 2 shows screenshots of how these tasks were presented to players. Further details about our game design can be found in [32].

The set of tasks for our initial prototype were devised by the authors, informed by the above findings of inclusivity and playfulness. Due to the diversity of perspectives presented to us in the workshops it was important that our tasks retained a sense of inclusivity. None of the tasks explicitly referred to sex, instead using more ambiguous terms such as 'moment' (tasks 4, 7) or 'tickly bits' (16). Additionally, it was important that our tasks had an element of playfulness, particularly through digital play, such as using the phone's camera or drawing functionality, but also tasks which explicitly encouraged head up [27] interactions, playing with the social setting of the game.

GAME PLAYING SESSIONS

We conducted two phases of game playing sessions with young people. In phase 1, we presented young people with the game with tasks generated by us, to explore broadly how the game was appropriated and played in youth group settings. Then we conducted phase 2 where, after playing through the tasks as devised by us, and describing our rationale to the young people, we invited participant-led content for the games' tasks.

We have played 'Talk about Sex' with a total of 46 young people across these two phases of game playing sessions. Four groups participated in the first phase (n=24) and three in the second phase (n=22). These sessions have been conducted in the three different locations where we held the initial workshops, and in one additional setting. All young people participating in the design workshops were invited to this gameplay phase, but most players were new to the project. Each of the sessions was audio recorded, and we made field notes around the interactional qualities of the gameplay. After play, all groups were also asked about their experiences of playing the game. This data was then analysed using thematic analysis, which we organised into three 'themes' around the most pertinent interactional elements in these settings: *'physical' play*, arguably *'problematic' play*, and *'exclusion' & a lack of direction.*

Overview

Overall, the game was met by enthusiasm from most participants. At the young people's request, the game was often played multiple times, starting with a different player each turn: "I really want to play the game again!" / "I'd like to do it again". On one occasion, the youth workers had trouble to get young people stop playing the game to move on to the group discussion: "Come on, put it down now!" When we asked how and where this game could be played, one participant told us: "I could imagine all our friendship group at school playing this game", and another: "This would be brilliant cos we have like free periods where we basically should be doing work but instead we get games on our phones that everyone can play". We were particularly pleased by how the young people framed this game as 'not' education, i.e. they "should be doing work", as it was our aim to distance our prototype from the traditional, restrictive discourse of sex education. Youth workers were also positive about the game: "If you could get them to sit that long and do that it says a lot about the resource".

At the same time, some, typically older, participants (16+), were more cautious of the game, responding less enthusiastically than younger players. For instance, in post-game discussions a 17-year-old player commented: "I just think that I wouldn't play it, because (.) I just think I'm a bit old". Similarly, in almost all groups, at least one player suggested that the game "wasn't really talking about sex" or could go further in how 'extreme' it was. Furthermore, some 16+ young people and youth workers appeared somewhat unsure about the 'purpose' of the game, suggesting it should focus more directly on the delivery of information. Here, we consider how the game was experienced by both enthusiastic participants and those more cautious, before indicating some of the challenges and opportunities encountered in our second phase of game playing where we invited participant-led game tasks.

Phase 1: Gameplay

There was almost always a palpable sense of curiosity as the game began, and in the livelier groups participants were often excitable, turning their phones over prematurely to see what might have happened. When the first device indicated a player's turn, there was often a tentative negotiation over whose device had buzzed. Play in all groups began hesitantly, as the players got familiar with the protocol of turning over their phone, completing the task, and then placing it back face down. Players showed signs of anticipation before their go, often showing visible signs of apprehension before turning over their phone, e.g. "oh shit!" / "I'm scared of what it's going to say!" Participants also often non-verbally enacted shock, embarrassment, surprise or confusion as the tasks were revealed. As the game then progressed onto the second and third turn, more

1. Write the name of your first kiss 2. Blow a kiss to another player 3. Read out loud this paragraph: *Alexis brought me close to their neck, and I smiled as I took in the smell of their sweet aroma, once more. I let out a contented sigh as my thoughts irrevocably slipped to my Skye. What would they make of our blossoming relationship?* 4. Mark on Google Maps where you've had a 'moment' 5. Take a photo of a body part 6. Hold your phone and draw a love heart in the air 7. Get everyone to leave the room then describe poignant or daring intimate moment to another player 8. Draw a body part 9. Use google image search to find a photo of a romantic location 10. Shout a pet or slang name for a body part 11. Wink at one of the other players 12. Choose a friend(s) – then place your phones in your pockets and swing together to an imaginary beat	13. Sing, hum or whistle your best sexy theme tune 14. Stop playing the game. Return in 1 minute (timed) 15. Choose a song from your mobile that you associate with someone or romance 16. Draw some tickly bits on your phone 17. Simulate a massage with your phone 18. Draw something to do with sex, intimacy or sexuality NOW and quickly 19. Swap phones with another player and don't give it back to them until the end of the game 20. Take someone else's phone and record a private message for them 21. Take a selfie on someone else's phone 22. Hold hands with another player clasping the phone and swing your arms together 23. Shine the light to illuminate a part of your body 24. Write a message to someone important in your life

Figure 3: The 'final set' of tasks presented in the prototype version of the game

enthusiastic groups relaxed into the rhythm of the game, with rapt attention, and often laughter as each player completed their task. In less enthusiastic groups it took rather more time for participants to 'get comfortable', yet gameplay almost always reached the stage where participants were playfully completing tasks. A notable exception was with one group of 16+ young people, where almost all tasks were hastily passed without completing them, much to their amusement, before playing them through again 'properly'.

Physical Play

Younger groups (under 16) typically displayed enthusiasm when joining in activities together. Although many tasks were individual, often all players wanted to play the turn, such as all shouting names for body parts (task 5) and often players took full opportunity to play in physical space. For instance, when the game asked for all but two players to leave the room (task 7), in one lively group of young men a participant shouted: "Right, everyone out!", while other members of the group attempted playfully to hide under the table. However, in a group of older teenagers this task was met with a 'sigh': "Do we really have to leave the room?", who collectively then changed this task to "two people leave the room" as some players didn't want to get up.

As such, it was the more physical activities such as swaying, dancing and singing that were most often 'passed'. While some participants took to these requests enthusiastically, all joining in singing a popular pop song for example, participants did sometimes skip these or completed them warily, reluctantly humming a nondescript tune as a 'sexy theme tune' for example. On one occasion, a young man repeatedly turned the device face-up and face-down many times (tasks 12 through 16) to find a task that "wasn't rubbish". Our attempts to utilize digital play also had mixed success. Whilst almost all groups were happy and excited to "take a selfie on someone else's phone" (task 21), the task to "mark on Google Maps where you've had a 'moment'" (task 4) noticeably held up the rhythm of the gameplay, as participants navigated to the app and took time in finding a location. For other tasks navigating outside the app was dismissed as "pointless", for instance in the task 'Use a Google image search to find a picture of a romantic location' (task 9), where on two occasions participants changed the task themselves to "just name a place" as that was "easier".

Perhaps one of the most successful tasks was task 2, blow a kiss to another player, played on by most groups as a humorous display of affection, but also introduced a surprising dialogue around sexuality between a young man, who didn't want to complete the task, and the youth worker: "Just cos you're blowing a kiss to someone doesn't mean it always has to be a sexual thing". It was therefore often the simplest tasks which led to the most successful gameplay. Whilst more complex activities using maps (task 4) and image searches (task 9) stalled gameplay, the 'selfie' task (task 21) and 'take a picture of a body part' (task 5) were typically more successful, where the process was less involved.

'Problematic' Play

Our invitations for digital play also led to some difficult scenarios, most prominent in our evaluations with groups of young men. In swapping phones with another player (task 19), one participant repeatedly entered the wrong passcode into his friend's phone, so he was temporarily locked out of his device, resulting in mild upset. In another group of young men, the task to 'take a photo of a body part' (task 5) was met with the suggestion to "take a photo of your penis brah!" As the young men got to their feet, suggesting they may do something inappropriate, slight chaos ensued as the youth workers intervened: "Seriously, not your penis" / "If the police caught you with that".

The conversations and interactions that the game initiated were broad and far ranging, from the sexually explicit to discussions that avoided the topic of sex altogether. For instance, responses to tasks where players were requested to

Figure 2: Screenshots from 'Talk About Sex'

describe a 'moment', varied from subtle, nondescript accounts: "I don't really have one. Lying on the grass. There we go" to very sexually upfront: "The first anal in my life". We witnessed some conversations about participants' first kiss: "I remember mine, it was quite embarrassing", or relationships: "Was that your boyfriend? How long have you been together?" Yet overall, conversations did not extend far beyond the tasks set. Moreover, in some instances our 'ambiguity' resulted in participants going somewhat 'off topic'. The 'pause' we inserted into the game (task 14) intended to prompt reflection on the gameplay often resulted in conversations around other things: "I'm really tired" / "I'm getting my nails done tomorrow". Likewise, when one participant commented that they "don't have a moment" in response to task 4, their conversations occasionally forayed into the obscure: "P1: Just make up one! P2: Right, there was a donkey, it turned into a unicorn before my very eyes".

'Exclusion' and a lack of direction

Some participants had difficulty interpreting some of the language in the game, such as the word 'poignant' (task 7), and although the term 'moment' was intended to "mean anything" as one participant acknowledged, the lack of direction meant some thought the task didn't apply to them: "I don't have one" / "I haven't done anything". Some participants expressed frustration at this lack of direction, with one commenting that task 20 "didn't tell me what kind of message to record". Therefore, the game was sometimes accused of "not talking about sex" or "what to do".

Simultaneously, however, some expressed our game had gone too far. One (older) participant refused to read out the 'bad sex' paragraph (task 3): "Oh gosh! Oh no, I don't want to read it", commenting that the text was "So dirty, how are 14 year olds going to cope with this?" On another occasion, a participant exclaimed "I am not doing that! Take a photo of a body part, as if!" Although another member of the group reflected to the participant the ambiguity of the task: "It could be any body part!", this vagueness, particularly surrounding the taking of photographs, was clearly less than ideal, as our 'problematic' example illustrated earlier. Additionally, the seemingly innocuous task "Write the name of your first kiss" implies some level of experience, and indeed sexuality, which was flagged as potentially difficult by some participants: "[our friend] hasn't had her first kiss yet, it's quite a big deal for her".

Summary

Reflecting on these initial play sessions, the premise of the game appeared to have promising design elements which were interesting and leading to good gameplay. Asking players to interact with each other's phones during gameplay drew on broad ideas of intimacy and trust, flipping the device before revealing tasks added anticipation and momentum, and tasks around physical play were generally received positively, particularly for younger players. Yet there were also several problems with the tasks we drew up. Activities had mixed rates of success when they were perceived to have higher 'barriers to entry', whilst others appeared to legitimize arguably problematic behaviour. Curiously, in taking an indirect approach with the hope participants would mediate these interactions at a pace comfortable to them, we had managed to be simultaneously too tame, with tasks "not talking about sex" or "not telling me what to do", yet also too extreme: "She hasn't had her first kiss yet" / "That's so dirty, how are 14 year olds going to cope with this?" Based on these findings, we felt we could involve our participants more through a second round of gameplay and design sessions.

A further challenge in these play sessions was the unpredictable nature of youth groups, meaning the environment was less than ideal for a multi-device networked game, particularly one played on young people's own phones. Young people often joined and left the game haphazardly, meaning the ad-hoc networking was disturbed and the flow of the game interrupted. Additionally, we had underestimated just how much young people relied on their phones. Notifications came through young people's devices at an often-rapid rate, causing further disruptions, and young people indicated that even ten minutes was a long time to go without access to their phone's functionality. Due to these factors, although gameplay always began on individual devices, often it continued a single device shared by players, using their own devices to complete tasks. Therefore, in this second round of evaluations, we decided to present the game as a single device experience.

Phase 2: Participant Generated Content

This second set of play sessions followed a process where young people played through our set of tasks on a tablet or phone, and used their own devices to complete tasks. After reflecting on the gameplay, the group was then asked for their suggestions. We explained our rationale for creating tasks, that we tried to make them playful, inclusive and use the digital affordances of the mobile phone, but we did not dictate these as conditions for their tasks. We asked participants to imagine playing the game with their friends, and to write down on cards either specific tasks they thought the game could play through, or more general topics/areas they thought the game should address. Where the group was big enough, we split the group in two so that each half could play through the other half's suggestions. The workshops were audio recorded and observational notes were taken. Suggestions from participants resulted in 67 participant-driven tasks, which were collated and analysed thematically into: "Personal sharing", "Playful tasks" and "Health orientated tasks", which we will discuss.

Play on a single device

In comparison to the networked gameplay on individuals own mobile phones, we saw the single device version leading to more flexible gameplay, meaning everyone, no matter what their make of device, could use their own phone to complete tasks. It also meant young people could spend more time on them, such as recording a message for a friend, whilst gameplay continued centrally. This led to hastier, non-disrupted gameplay, and tasks revealed in the centre were seen by everyone, meaning completion of them was more collective. This also resulted in turn-taking negotiation by players, which was typically policed rigidly, and led to instances of players 'trading' tasks: "I did the last one, now it's your go!" In this more 'public' version of the game, young people also often insisted that the youth workers joined in as well.

Playful tasks

A minority of players' suggestions (11) had a 'playful' element. Some were like our task, 'Blow a kiss to another player' (task 2): "Say I love you to a friend" / "Say 'you are beautiful' to someone", whilst others introduced a guessing element: "Get a friend to guess your crush". There were also some suggestions for 'physical' tasks, particularly around movement, such as "Do Gangnam style" / "'Dab' [dance] with your friends". Yet other tasks did start to verge on something that might be inappropriate: "Take off one piece of clothing" / "touch a body part of your choice". The latter task was commented on specifically by a youth worker as something he couldn't do in this setting: "It would have undermined my safeguarding role in the group". Only three tasks suggested use of mobile phones: "Text from another player's phone", "[give a player your] unlocked phone" and "let someone send one message".

Personal sharing tasks

More tasks (21) requested a level of personal sharing. Young people's suggestions were generally more upfront than our 'set'. The use of our word 'moment' was interpreted more specifically to "share an embarrassing moment" or "school moment", and was also extended to a "tell the group a once in a life experience you have had". Requests to share also became more specific to "share something you regret" or to "tell a story about your first kiss", whilst others became more dark, e.g. "Who do you hate?" The 'act' of sex was focused on more specifically by some, typically older, members, such as more vaguely suggesting tasks around "your ideal first time", or perceptions around "first time – hurt?"

Other tasks started to verge into close-ended 'truth or dare' territory, again more especially around the act of sex: "How many times have you had sex?", "have you had sex while drunk?", "what age did you 'lose it'?", "Name one famous person you would have sex with". The topic of 'talking about sex' was also touched on in some tasks, rather than giving more specific suggestions for activities or conversations: "Do you talk about sex? If so, who with?". The tasks which prompted some sense of personal sharing were perhaps the most successful when played through, prompting several conversations around celebrity crushes and regrettable experiences, e.g.: "Oh man I've got so many!" / "You've got to name yours now."

Health orientated tasks

The tasks suggested by youth workers, and some 16+ young people were largely 'health' orientated, or around the provision of information. One youth worker in particular, "Joel" (pseudonym) was seemingly unsatisfied with the game simply being a playful experience, asking, "What is it that the game really supposed to do? [...] I think it should be about misconceptions about sex". Countering our 'playful' approach, Joel suggested two knowledge based tasks: "Explain the C-Card scheme [UK condom distribution scheme]", and "What is the legal age of consent in the UK?". He also suggested that the game could instead be a 'fact or fiction' game around specific statements, a suggestion given by a few youth workers and health professionals in response to seeing our game. This rhetoric was supported by a minority of young people, typically older teenagers, who also suggested some knowledge testing tasks such as "What does STI stand for?", and questions more focused around morality such as "what do you think of teen pregnancy?" Some young people expressed dissatisfaction at these 'health orientated tasks', particularly Joel's suggestions, with one young person suggesting: "That sounds boring!" in response. This dialogue mirrors debates in sex education and, as we will discuss, the game embodied such tensions around what role technology for young people's sexuality 'should' have.

Playing Young Person-Led Tasks

In most workshops, numbers were sufficient to enable us to split the group in half so that young people could play through each other's tasks. Tasks were placed in the centre and participants played through these as if they were a card game. Participants typically took to playing each other's tasks with considerable interest. Sometimes the tasks were questioned by each half of the group, for example: "Can I just ask, boys, who wrote 'remove one item of clothing'?" However, some of the older players who were more hesitant when playing through our initial set of activities took to these 'user-centred' tasks more enthusiastically. This was particularly evident with those that required a level of personal sharing, and in some of the 'moral' questions such as 'What do you think of teen pregnancy?': "I have some serious opinions on that, don't get me started!"

DISCUSSION

We present our process of user-centred design as a successful enquiry between young people, researchers and youth workers on the topic of young people and sexuality. 'Talk About Sex', has resulted in enthusiastic, lively and fun gameplay, particularly from younger participants, with tasks providing a focus for interactions. Nevertheless, we have also encountered ongoing challenges working within this space. Gameplay sessions did at times have a lack of focus, while some tasks led to exclusion and legitimized 'problematic' behaviour. Moreover, the presence of technology in these settings epitomized many of the tensions around young people's sexualities, and the perceived role technology should be having. We present these as lessons learnt, suggesting adolescents' sexuality as a fruitful, if challenging, design space for HCI.

Lesson Learnt: Lightweight Digital Play

'Talk About Sex' began as paper based prototyping, and participant-generated tasks were played through as a card game in the latter stages of our process. Our game is therefore in some ways like analogue-based discussion games, such as 'spin the bottle' or 'truth or dare'. Despite this, we argue there are many benefits to our game as a digital experience. Not insignificantly, the very act of delivering a game through a piece of technology provided a focus for some participants, with one youth worker commenting it said "a lot about the resource" that it "could get them to sit that long" while another jokingly remarked that she'll "do all my sessions on an iPad now!" Moreover, the 'pause and reveal' mechanism provided rhythmic gameplay and a sense of anticipation before each task, which was lacking in our early prototyping sessions. Indeed, one of our early testers commented "it's way better on phones than cards!" This was particularly evident when the game was played uninterrupted on a single device, where the timing of the game provided a fast, but clear, directive pace to these interactions. With the game audibly indicating a player's turn, all players were given the opportunity to share, as directed through the device.

The digital medium also gave novel opportunities for play, such as introducing a timed 'pause' in the middle of the game (task 14), and requests to use the digital functionality of the phone. Tasks using the camera (task 21), messages (task 24), maps (task 3) and image search (task 9) all gave opportunity to explore how uses of mobile technologies intercept with intimacy. Yet we found that digital play was received most successfully when simple and easy to understand. For example, 'take a selfie on someone else's phone' (task 21), or 'shine the light to illuminate a body part' (task 23) were more successful in comparison to tasks which required more involvement, such as 'mark on Google Maps where you've had a 'moment' (task 4). It was also notable that one of our most successful tasks was the non-digital 'blow a kiss to another player'. Therefore, in a game where we were seeking to encourage interaction between players, it was much more important to seek broader ways of promoting 'head up' [26] interaction through the device, rather than focus on more granular digital interactions.

Despite this, a card game also possesses qualities, which we are now looking to explore in a further iteration of this game. The analogue nature of physical games means they are easily reproducible by individuals wishing to use ideas in their own practice, and there are also rules which dictate traditional games which make external facilitation less necessary. In our deployments, the researchers and youth workers very much facilitate play of this game, whereas in a card game play sessions facilitated by young people may be more easily enabled. The tangible quality of cards in a game is also preferred by some. The interrelation of traditional card games and games with digital elements, and utilising the affordances of both effectively, is an aspect we are exploring in further work.

Lesson Learnt: Share Control of the Conversation

We took two different approaches to involving young people in our process of user-centred design, spanning the different levels of involvement Druin highlights in 'The Role of Children in the Design of Technology' [11]. In the first stage of our research we treated young people as 'research informants', whereas in the second stage of our research we treated participants more as 'design partners' by inviting their suggestions for tasks. We found that in each case these approaches had individual benefits and drawbacks.

The initial set of tasks we developed for this game were based around insights interpreted from our initial engagements and our interests in digital play. This resulted in several tasks that were successful, e.g. 'take a selfie on someone else's phone' (task 21), but also tasks that were too fiddly e.g. 'mark on Google Maps where you've had a moment' (task 4), and tasks that had problematic elements, e.g. 'take a photo of a body part' (task 5). Different tasks also had varying degrees of success with different participant groups. While one younger group took enthusiastically to our request for all but two to leave the room (task 7), some older groups were more cautious, i.e. "do we really have to leave the room?" Moreover, in all the groups, one or more players commented that our tasks "weren't really talking about sex", and some of our tasks were interpreted as exclusive - "I don't have a moment" / "[our friend] hasn't had her first kiss yet".

Taking a participant-led approach to the devising of tasks avoided some of these problems. In general, the tasks that participants wrote were more specific and had an element of personal sharing; for example, "share something you regret" and "celebrity crush" resulted in some of the liveliest conversations. Equally however, some of these tasks had problematic aspects. Only a minority of tasks had 'playful elements', and many were closed ended, e.g. 'How many times have you had sex'. In most cases, this resulted in play which was rather more static, lacking an 'energy', and closed-ended tasks which didn't invite further discussion. Moreover, some of the tasks were defined by youth workers as actively problematic within a youth group setting, for example 'touch a body part'.

Many of the youth workers and some older young people often suggested tasks around health promotion, for example: "Explain the C-Card scheme" / "What services could you access?" This reflects arguments within the sex education literature discussed earlier, centred on the debate between a 'restrictive' discourse of sexuality seeking to control young people's sexual activity, or a 'permissive' approach seeking to legitimize and acknowledge sexuality [14]. When Joel, one of the youth workers, explained why he thought the game should have an explicit educative purpose, he said "because that's my job". Yet, this was simultaneously seen as a problem by a young person, stating that his tasks sounded "boring".

This variety of perspective indicates the complexity of young people and sexuality as a design space. None of these approaches is the 'correct' approach to take, rather, we argue the standpoints of these stakeholders needs to be balanced and shared. If we were, as is planned, to hand over control of this game, our users, be it young people or youth workers, are likely to use the game for their own purposes. This could be 'truth or dare' style tasks, closed tasks around specific sexual acts, or being used as testing adolescent's knowledge. It is a benefit that stakeholders are able to utilise the tool for their own purposes, yet in treating young people (and youth workers) as 'design partners', we argue researchers should be aware that in doing this, the outcome of user-centred design may no longer align with the agenda it was originally envisaged with. In this case, the game may no longer possess the playful and inclusive agenda it was designed with.

As discussed, the 'agenda' of our game was broad, in that we wished to open a dialogue about sex and sexuality with young people through the medium of a game. We have discussed the extent to which this was successful, with discussions breaking out in both helpful and perhaps less-helpful ways. Also, the necessity of human facilitation due to the nature of the game meant this inevitably shaped the conversations, such as the power dynamics between youth workers and young people. These are aspects that we are looking to explore in further work.

Lesson Learnt: Problems can be Opportunities to Talk

On several different occasions, our own conceptions of child sexuality, and how young people should behave in these settings, were challenged. One task appeared to legitimize unkindly locking another player out of his phone (task 19), and another prompted a player's threat to produce child pornography (task 5). We were also more than a little alarmed, as our readers may be, for an underage man describe "first anal" as a 'moment'. Yet the fact that these uncomfortable issues were raised enforces them as legitimate areas of enquiry in young people's sexuality, and highlights the importance of talk. Many young people did present themselves as mature sexual beings, and some youth workers reflected that young people's responses to the tasks reflected the complicated reality of sexuality, particularly in relation to technology. Discussing the incident around a player threatening to take a picture of his penis (task 5), one youth leader mentioned "that's a part of their life now, taking photos…so maybe do keep it [the task] in", and with one young man locking a player out of his phone, matters of intimacy and trust were actively played out even more than we were expecting. Therefore, although some of these tasks may appear on the surface problematic, they were perhaps one of the most meaningful sources of conversation with these young people, touching on the self-production of child pornography, and notions of friendship and trust.

CONCLUSION

In this paper, we extend previous work in HCI around sexuality, through suggesting young people, sexuality and technology as an agenda for the field. We have shown how in utilising insights from play and social gaming, and through taking an extended, multi-layered process of user centred design, we were able to produce work that distanced itself from HCI's more traditional, restrictive and problematic discourses around sex and sexuality [19]. Our approach took a 'permissive' approach [14], prioritised young people's perspectives, and respected their sexual agency, regularly lacking from 'interventions' in this area [21], particularly when sexuality is considered in conjunction with technology [29].

Young people's sexuality is a contentious topic, dominated by adult opinion, with conflicting views over how the topic should be approached. This research explored how this might be counteracted through a process of user-centred design. Our findings have highlighted the value of engaging all concerned stakeholders in this process of design, and suggested that even when problems arise in the process, this may be an opportunity to have productive and meaningful opportunities to 'Talk About Sex'.

ACKNOWLEDGEMENTS

This research was funded through the EPSRC Centre for Doctoral Training in Digital Civics (EP/L016176/1). Data supporting this publication is openly available under an 'Open Data Commons Open Database License'. Additional metadata are available at: http://dx.doi.org/10.17634/154300-46. Please contact Newcastle Research Data Service at rdm@ncl.ac.uk for access instructions.

REFERENCES

1. Louisa Allen. 2008. Young People's Suggestions for Improving Sexuality Education Content. Sexualities 11, 5: 573–594.
2. Teresa Almeida, Rob Comber, Gavin Wood, Dean Saraf, and Madeline Balaam. 2016. On Looking at the Vagina Through Labella. In Proc. of CHI'2016. ACM
3. Sylvester Arnab, Katherine Brown, Samantha Clarke, Ian Dunwell, Theodore Lim, Neil Suttie, Sandy Louchart, Maurice Hendrix, and Sara de Freitas. 2013. The development approach of a pedagogically-driven serious game to support Relationship and Sex Education. Computers & Education 69: 15–30.
4. Nathalie Bajos, Michel Bozon, Nathalie Beltzer, Caroline Laborde, Armelle Andro, Michele Ferrand, Veronique Goulet, Anne Laporte, Charlotte Le Van, Henri Leridon, and others. 2010. Changes in sexual behaviours. Aids 24, 8: 1185–1191.
5. Jeremy Birnholtz, Nicholas Aaron Ross Merola, and Arindam Paul. 2015. Is it weird to still be a virgin: Anonymous, locally targeted questions on facebook confession boards. In Proc. of CHI'2015. ACM
6. Jeremy Birnholtz, Irina Shklovski, Mark Handel, and Eran Toch. 2015. Let's Talk About Sex (Apps), CSCW. In Proc. of CSCW'2015. ACM
7. Courtney Blackwell, Jeremy Birnholtz, and Charles Abbott. 2015. Seeing and being seen: Co-situation and impression formation using Grindr, a location-aware gay dating app. New Media & Society 17, 7: 1117–1136.
8. M. A. Blythe, K. Overbeeke, A. F. Monk, and P. C. Wright. 2004. Funology: From Usability to Enjoyment. Springer Science & Business Media.
9. Sue C. Bratton, Dee Ray, Tammy Rhine, and Leslie Jones. 2005. The Efficacy of Play Therapy With Children: A Meta-Analytic Review of Treatment Outcomes. Professional Psychology 36, 4: 376–390.
10. Claire Dormann and Robert Biddle. 2006. Humour in game-based learning. Learning, Media and Technology 31, 4: 411–424.
11. Allison Druin. 2002. The role of children in the design of new technology. Behaviour and information technology 21, 1: 1–25.
12. Lars-Magnus Engström. 2008. Who is physically active? Cultural capital and sports participation from adolescence to middle age—a 38-year follow-up study. Physical education and sport pedagogy 13, 4: 319–343.
13. Debbie Epstein and Richard Johnson. 1998. Schooling sexualities. McGraw-Hill Education (UK).
14. Michelle Fine and Sara McClelland. 2006. Sexuality Education and Desire: Still Missing after All These Years. Harvard Educational Review 76, 3: 297–338.
15. Jayden Garner, Gavin Wood, Sandra Danilovic, Jessica Hammer, and Florian Mueller. 2014. Intangle: Exploring Interpersonal Bodily Interactions Through Sharing Controllers. In Proc. of CHI'2014. ACM
16. Kylene Guse, Deb Levine, Summer Martins, Andrea Lira, Jenna Gaarde, Whitney Westmorland, and Melissa Gilliam. 2012. Interventions using new digital media to improve adolescent sexual health: a systematic review. Journal of Adolescent Health 51, 6: 535–543.
17. Janet Holland, Caroline Ramazanoglu, Sue Sharpe, and Rachel Thomson. 2004. The male in the head: Young people, heterosexuality and power. JSTOR.
18. Gopinaath Kannabiran, Jeffrey Bardzell, and Shaowen Bardzell. 2011. How HCI Talks About Sexuality: Discursive Strategies, Blind Spots, and Opportunities for Future Research. In Proc. of CHI'2011. ACM
19. Gopinaath Kannabiran, Jeffrey Bardzell, and Shaowen Bardzell. 2012. I just made love: the system and the subject of experience. In Proc. of CHI'2012. ACM
20. Ellyn Kaschak and Leonore Tiefer. 2014. A new view of women's sexual problems. Routledge.
21. Jane Lewis and Trudie Knijn. 2003. Sex Education Materials in The Netherlands and in England and Wales: A comparison of content, use and teaching practice. Oxford Review of Education 29, 1: 113–150.
22. Mary Madden, Amanda Lenhart, Maeve Duggan, Sandra Cortesi, and Urs Gasser. 2013. Teens and technology 2013. Pew Internet & American Life Project Washington, DC.
23. Christina Masden and W. Keith Edwards. 2015. Understanding the Role of Community in Online Dating. In Proc. of CHI'2015. ACM
24. Kathryn McPhillips, Virginia Braun, and Nicola Gavey. 2001. Defining (hetero) sex: how imperative is the "coital imperative"? In Women's Studies International Forum, 229–240.
25. Kenton P. O'Hara, Michael Massimi, Richard Harper, Simon Rubens, and Jessica Morris. 2014. Everyday dwelling with WhatsApp. I In Proc. of CSCW'2014. ACM
26. George C. Patton, Susan M. Sawyer, John S. Santelli, David A. Ross, Rima Afifi, Nicholas B. Allen, Monika Arora, Peter Azzopardi, Wendy Baldwin, Christopher Bonell, and others. 2016. Our future: a Lancet commission on adolescent health and wellbeing. The Lancet 387, 10036: 2423–2478.

27. Iris Soute. 2007. HUGs: Head-up Games. In Proc. of IDC'2007. ACM

28. Affrica Taylor. 2010. Troubling Childhood Innocence: Reframing the Debate over the Media Sexualisation of Children. Journal of Early Childhood 35, 1: 48.

29. R. Thomas, J. Cahill, and L. Santilli. 1997. Using an interactive computer game to increase skill and self-efficacy regarding safer sex negotiation: field test results. Health Education & Behavior: The Official Publication of the Society for Public Health Education 24, 1: 71–86.

30. Leonore Tiefer. 1995. Sex is not a natural act and other essays. Westview Press.

31. Joy Walker. 2004. Parents and sex education—looking beyond "the birds and the bees." Sex Ed 4, 3: 239–254.

32. Matthew Wood, Gavin Wood, and Madeline Balaam. 2015. Talk About Sex: Designing Games to Facilitate Healthy Discussions Around Sex. In Proc. of CHIPLAY'2015. ACM

33. Michele L. Ybarra and Kimberly J. Mitchell. 2014. "Sexting" and its relation to sexual activity and sexual risk behavior in a national survey of adolescents. Journal of Adolescent Health 55, 6: 757–764.

SPRING: Customizable, Motivation-Driven Technology for Children with Autism or Neurodevelopmental Differences

Kristina T. Johnson & Rosalind W. Picard
MIT Media Lab
Cambridge, MA, USA
{ktj, picard}@media.mit.edu

ABSTRACT

Current research to understand and enhance the development of children with neurological differences, including Autism Spectrum Disorder (ASD), is often severely limited by small sample sizes of human-gathered data in artificially structured learning environments. SPRING: **S**mart **P**latform for **R**esearch, **I**ntervention, and **N**eurodevelopmental **G**rowth is a new hardware and software system designed to 1) automate quantitative data acquisition, 2) optimize learning progressions through customized, motivating stimuli, and 3) encourage social, cognitive, and motor development in a personalized, child-led play environment. SPRING can also be paired with sensors to probe the physiological underpinnings of motivation, engagement, and cognition.

Here, we present the design principles and methodology for SPRING, as well as two heterogeneous case studies. The first case highlights enhanced attention and accelerated skill development using SPRING, while the second pairs SPRING data with electrodermal activity measurements to identify a possible physiological signature of engagement and challenge in learning.

Author Keywords

Augmentative technology; Children; Autism; ASD; Neurodevelopmental disorders; Physiology; Motivation; Engagement; Learning; Objective outcome measures

ACM Classification Keywords

H.5.2. User Interfaces: User-Centered Design.

INTRODUCTION

Children with complex developmental needs, including many children diagnosed with Autism Spectrum Disorder (ASD), face an array of challenges in cognition, motor planning, emotion regulation, sensory modulation, communication, and social interaction [1, 10, 14]. Traditional approaches to address these difficulties, such as Applied Behavior Analysis (ABA) [4] and Discrete Trial Training [18], typically present activities in a regimented learning environment, using desirable reinforcements to encourage attention and focus. Studies have shown that these frequent, discrete trialing procedures can be effective for skill acquisition, especially for children with significant delays [18]; however, these methods require a trained therapist, often for upwards of 20 hours per week [5], vary highly across therapists [19], and can limit opportunities for child-directed learning [6]. In addition, young children can be difficult to study, particularly in a quantitative manner that produces reliable and reproducible results. New technology to address these shortcomings is essential to advance research and developmental aids for these children.

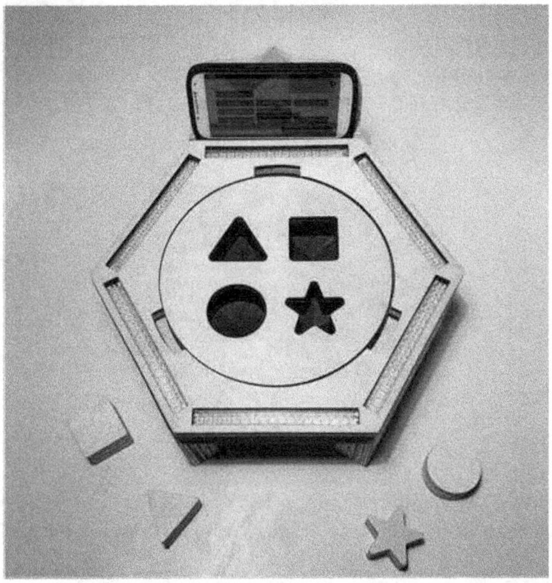

Figure 1. The Smart Platform for Research, Intervention, and Neurodevelopmental Growth (SPRING) with a Shape Sorting Module.

This paper introduces SPRING: **S**mart **P**latform for **R**esearch, **I**ntervention, & **N**euro-developmental **G**rowth, a new hardware and software system designed to 1) automate quantitative data acquisition, 2) optimize learning progressions through customized, motivating stimuli, and 3) encourage social, cognitive, and motor development in a personalized, child-led play environment. SPRING is interdisciplinary, combining methods from psychology, mechanical and electrical engineering, computer science, education theory, and human-computer interaction.

IDC '17, June 27-30, 2017, Stanford, CA, USA

ACM ISBN 978-1-4503-4921-5/17/06...$15.00
http://dx.doi.org/10.1145/3078072.3079718

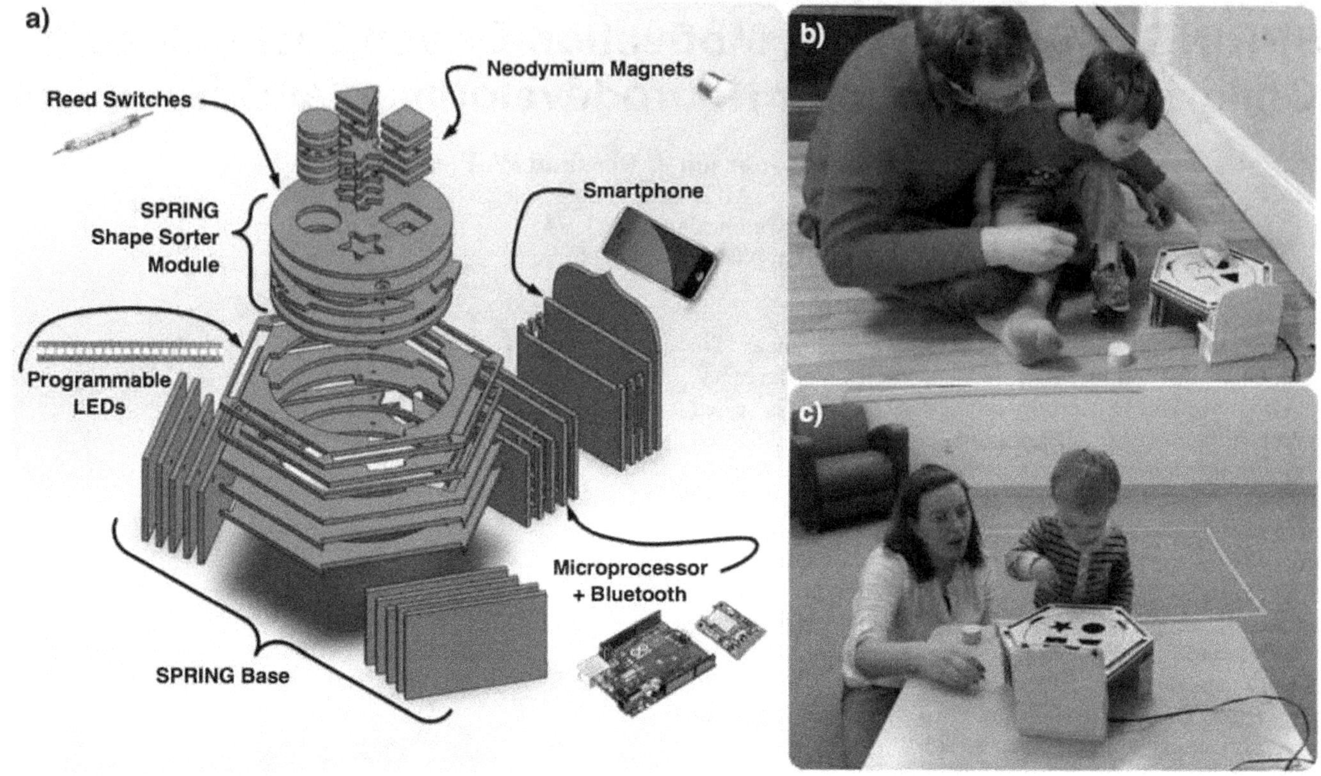

Figure 2. a) Exploded, annotated view of the first SPRING system. b) Video capture of child playing with SPRING during first user case study. c) Video capture of child playing with SPRING during pilot study, showing oscillating blue LED feedback.

SPRING is also a Tangible User Interface [20], fusing its physical-digital inputs and outputs to create new tangible technology for learning [e.g., 12, 15]. In addition, SPRING extends beyond an interactive toy platform to the research domain, enabling not only descriptive models of motivation, engagement, and neurodevelopment, but also possible *predictive* models based on fundamental principles.

In this paper, we first present the design principles of SPRING. Then, we describe SPRING's physical form, scaffolded learning characteristics, and other notable features. We then discuss how it utilizes personalized feedback to motivate learning and how this scalable customization is achieved. Next, we discuss results from two case studies, one from an early user and one from a pilot study that combines SPRING with physiological sensors. Finally, we describe limitations of the current model and improvements for the next-generation SPRING system.

DESIGN PRINCIPLES

SPRING embodies the following design principles:

Smart. Using embedded sensors, a microprocessor, and a smartphone, SPRING records time-stamped digital data and provides real-time sensory feedback in the form of LED light displays, music, videos, and other electronic stimuli (see Figures 1 and 2). These features offer a wide range of input and output stimuli to accommodate the needs, preferences, and developmental levels of each user.

Platform. SPRING is both a learning system and a research device. It supports multiple specially designed modules that can resemble toys, puzzles, or assessment tools. These Modules are designed to be removable and replaceable, allowing the activity to be adjusted to the developmental level of the child. This modularity also places most of the expensive, high-tech components in the reusable Base, making SPRING more economical.

Research. SPRING collects multimodal time-stamped data of a child's interactions during play, including the rate of play, the current activity, and the child's preferred sensory feedback. The data help *quantify* developmental trajectories for non-traditional learners, validate objective models of learning, and establish the role of motivating stimuli in children with and without ASD. We can also pair the time-synchronized data with physiological sensors to measure affective states while learning and playing.

Intervention. SPRING embodies many principles of therapy that are effective for children with ASD and other neurodevelopmental disorders [e.g., 4, 18], but it does so in a child-led, play-based environment. By automating data collection and responsive feedback, we do not require a therapist's constant presence, allowing the child to explore and learn at favorable times (even 5 am) and to pursue self-driven learning. A child's parent or therapist can build a personalized portfolio to match the child's current interests and can track interactions with SPRING over time (see Customization Process section).

Neurodevelopmental Growth. Fundamentally, SPRING is a learning system designed to bolster development in young children, especially those who benefit from highly personalized learning aids.

DEVICE DESCRIPTION

Base. The SPRING Base is hexagonal with a 6-inch edge length, making it 12 inches wide, tip to tip (see Figure 1). With legs situated under three of the edges, SPRING stands 6 inches high, allowing 3 inches of clearance between the Module insert and the tabletop. The Base houses an Arduino microprocessor, Bluetooth adapter, and Android smartphone, plus 108 programmable LEDs (Adafruit Neopixels) embedded along the outer edges of the Base.

Module. The SPRING Module is a circular center component that contains an activity such as shape sorting (current function), block design (in progress; see Future Work), or pretend play (planned). The Module is designed to be removable and replaceable, allowing adjustment to match the developmental level of the child.

In the current prototype's Shape Sorter Module, each shape contains a precise arrangement of neodymium magnets that trigger reed switches embedded within the layers of the Module when the shapes are inserted in their corresponding holes. Note that we have chosen the arrangement and strength of the magnets to only trigger the switches when inserted in the proper hole. These switches connect to the Arduino microcontroller in the Base, which communicates with the smartphone via Bluetooth, which then records the interaction in a data log and tells SPRING to display a personalized response.

Smartphone Interface. The smartphone runs a custom app (Figure 3) that provides prompts for activities, records inputs from the SPRING sensors, and presents dynamic, customized feedback in the form of music, videos, or images. The LEDs also provide feedback through visually engaging light displays. The phone keeps a time-stamped log file of every action – e.g., what prompt was displayed when, what sensors were triggered, what feedback was presented – allowing researchers, teachers, and caregivers to analyze the data of the user's interactions with SPRING and to time-synchronize it with other information, such as data from physiological sensors or video coding.

Scaffolded Learning

Following Vygotsky [21], SPRING Modules incorporate a scaffolded learning approach, whereby Module levels build upon one another (see Figure 3a). For example, the Shape Sorting Module begins with a free play level, where the child receives motivating feedback (e.g., lights, music, videos) for each successfully inserted shape. It then can progress to a series of matching levels, which work on matching, 2D-to-3D generalization, and abstract-to-

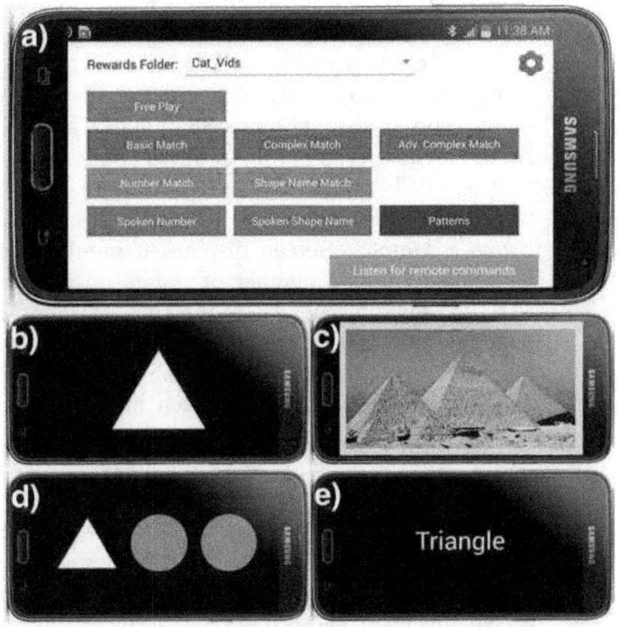

Figure 3. Screenshots of the SPRING Shape Sorter smartphone interface: a) the home screen, depicting the various scaffolded learning levels; b) a triangle prompt from the Basic Match level; c) a triangle prompt from the Complex Match level; d) a triangle-circle-circle prompt from the Patterns level, encouraging left-to-right sequential ordering; and e) a triangle prompt from the Shape Name Match level that encourages early reading skills. The dropdown menu on the home screen allows the user to select a personalized response folder matching the specific interests of the child (e.g., cat videos, rocket ships, Elmo songs). The "Listen for Remote Commands" button allows SPRING to be controlled remotely via wifi, such as by a researcher in a separate room.

concrete generalization. The learning continues to grow with the child, covering concepts such as sequencing, basic word and number recognition, and auditory recognition skills. Many of these concepts can be challenging to teach, so SPRING provides an opportunity for a child to repeatedly develop and hone their knowledge in a highly motivating, responsive environment.

The current prototype of the SPRING Shape Sorter Module includes the following levels:

- *Free Play:* No prompt. Shape play is reinforced with personalized feedback after each insertion.
- *Basic Match:* Screen displays a high-contrast silhouette of a shape (see Figure 3b). Child receives personalized feedback upon inserting the correct corresponding shape. Note that, if the prompt is a triangle, only placing a triangle will elicit feedback. Inserting any other shape will not produce an effect.
- *Complex Match:* Screen displays an abstract representation of a shape (e.g., a basketball, a yield sign, a starfish; see Figure 3c). As before, child receives personalized feedback only upon insertion

of the correct corresponding shape. (Feedback continues in this manner for all subsequent levels, unless otherwise specified.)

- *Advanced Complex Match:* Screen displays a more complex abstract representation of a shape or shape category (e.g., a pile of overlapping coins, a screen filled with gumballs, several boats with triangular sails).
- *Number Match:* Screen displays a number that corresponds to the number of points on a shape (e.g., '5' for the star, '4' for the square). Painting dots on each shape can assist the user. (Note: Because of the ambiguity of the circle's characteristics, this level has seen infrequent use during pilot testing.)
- *Shape Name Match:* Screen displays a word corresponding to a shape name (see Figure 3e).
- *Spoken Number:* Phone audio states a number corresponding to the number of points on a shape (e.g., "The next number is 4," for the square.) As above, this level has seen infrequent use.
- *Spoken Shape Name:* Phone audio states a shape name (e.g., "The next shape is triangle.") This level requires the user to listen closely to the prompt in order to respond.
- *Patterns:* Screen first displays a single high-contrast white-on-black shape as in the matching levels. Then, once this shape has been inserted correctly, the screen displays two shapes. The leftmost shape is white, while the other is shaded gray (see Figure 3d). Once the leftmost shape has been inserted, it turns gray and then next sequential shape becomes white. After completing the two-shape prompt, three shapes are displayed, and so on. Personalized feedback is presented only after the completion of the full sequence of shapes in each prompt. Placing an "incorrect" shape moves the user back a level within this Patterns activity (e.g., from four shapes to three) without presenting feedback.

Because language is challenging for much of our target population, SPRING does not require any verbal instructions for play; although some levels, like Spoken Name Match, work to develop receptive language. In principle, gestures, visual cues, and SPRING's feedback guide the child to advance.

Other Notable Design Features

The wooden construction of SPRING creates an aesthetic similar to classic, non-digital children's toys, placing the emphasis on a physical interaction with SPRING and the surrounding environment instead of a solely screen-based device. Children – and those with ASD, in particular – can become fixated on digital devices (e.g., tablets, phones, video games), often to the exclusion of other activities. The tangible interaction design enhances development of critical motor skills and provides tactile feedback not accessible from screen-based environments [15]. In addition, multi-player SPRING systems are in development (see Future Work) to stimulate social interaction – typically a challenging activity to motivate or teach.

Another feature is that a silicone mat – the same kind often used in baking – has been affixed to the bottom layer of the SPRING Shape Sorter Module (see blue regions in Figure 1). Diagonal slits in the silicone allow the shapes to pass through the holes with gentle pressure (comparable to the force necessary to press an elevator button). This construction serves multiple purposes: First, it ensures a more consistent response from the reed switches embedded inside the Module, which trigger more reliably with a momentary pause in the presence of the magnetic field. Second, it allows multiple shapes to remain in the Module simultaneously (see SPRING in Figure 2b), enabling more extensive opportunities for play. For example, the Module can function equally like a puzzle or a more classic through-hole sorter. Third, the mat provides proprioceptive input in the form of slight resistance. Proprioceptive feedback has been shown to have a positive, calming sensory effect for individuals, including those with ASD [8,9]. Indeed, users with and without ASD have frequently commented on this feature, stating – often with surprise – that it "feels very good" or "satisfying" to push the shapes through their holes.

PERSONALIZED MOTIVATION-DRIVEN LEARNING

In general, typically-developing children are motivated to learn and explore intrinsically, often driven by curiosity or pursuits of mastery and independence [16]. For many children with neuro-differences, however, this intrinsic motivation may be insufficient to overcome environmental distractions, sensory demands, or motor challenges required to focus or complete a task. Yet, children diagnosed with ASD or other developmental disorders often show intense, specific affinities for particular items or topics that can be leveraged to teach skills or ideas [13, 1]. Inspired by these affinities, we have designed SPRING to be easily programmable in order to provide motivating stimuli *tailored to the child.*

Note that the level of specificity SPRING provides is critical for many children with ASD. In our pilot study, we asked parents what interested their children. For neurotypical (NT) children, we were generally given broad categories of topics – cars, Legos, Star Wars, etc. – but for ASD children, the interests were much more precise:

"There are only two highly preferred videos he will attend to on YouTube..."

"He likes watching Peppa Pig... the parts where George cries..."

"He is into songs that have letters and numbers in them..."

The specific interests were also more pivotal to children with ASD compared to NT children. For example, the last mother continued:

"He is very reluctant to do anything if he is not motivated. If you hit that motivation button, you see many skills you thought he did not have."

She also mentioned that *"his reinforcers change,"* so she would let us know if there were any changes right before he came in for the study. Reinforcer variation has also been shown to improve attention and progression [7], so SPRING is rapidly and fully customizable (see Customization Process below).

SPRING also allows teachers and researchers to systematically explore methods to reduce the need for discrete reinforcement and promote intrinsically motivated exploration beyond the given task, particularly as the activities become easier or more familiar.

Customization Process

SPRING is designed to be customizable across three important domains: 1) the activity, 2) the developmental level of the activity, and 3) the feedback.

Activity. The play facilitator (e.g., a teacher, therapist, or caregiver) can change an activity by removing SPRING's central Module and replacing it with a new Module. The current prototype houses a Shape Sorting Module; however, new Modules with different activities are nearing completion (see Future Works), allowing the facilitator to select the most developmentally appropriate activity for the user on that day or play session. The Module twists in and out of the Base like a large screw, making it easy to exchange in a matter of seconds.

Activity Level. As described previously, a facilitator can choose among scaffolded learning activities with a Module. These levels are designed to developmentally build upon one another in order to achieve the "just right" challenge or place the user in the zone of proximal development [17, 21]. While these levels are currently pre-programmed into the smartphone interface, they could be open-sourced to allow individuals to create their own "just right" levels for any Module. (While we intend to open-source this design for broad use, this feature is not currently supported.)

Feedback. SPRING is also customizable in its feedback, producing lights, music, images, or videos of nearly any topic or theme. The programmable LEDs built into the SPRING Base can produce an extensive array of visual displays, from slow glowing lavender lights to multicolor rainbow patters to bright red lights that bounce around like ping pong balls. We have programmed over 25 light shows into the microcontroller and created a Settings screen on the SPRING app that allows the play facilitator to select which light displays to include as feedback options (see Figure 4). This interface allows the facilitator to choose light displays that match the preferences and regulatory needs of the user. For example, if the user finds diffuse glowing lights calming and regulating, they can be selected to the exclusion of other options. Likewise, if lights are aversive

Figure 4. Settings screen of the SPRING smartphone interface. The user can select which LED light shows will appear (check marks) and how often they will be cycled through the reward feedback (40% of the time here). The "Reward % Chance" drop down option allows the user to set the feedback to appear less than 100% of the time, which can be useful when a child is proficient at the skill and does not require consistent, immediate feedback.

stimuli, all options can be deselected. To date, most users prefer the widest range of options and feedback novelty.

The likelihood of seeing LED feedback is also customizable using the drop-down option at the top of the Settings screen (see Figure 4, "Light % Chance"). Choosing 100% will present only LED feedback while 0% will display no LED feedback. Most users seem to prefer pseudo-random lights to appear as feedback about 40% of the time, but this percentage has been set across the full range of options to meet the needs of users during our early testing.

In addition to LED feedback, SPRING can present almost any multimedia file that can be played on a smartphone. Video clips, images, and audio files can be downloaded from the internet or from the user's personal directories and then loaded into a personalized folder on the SPRING smartphone microSD card. Currently, SPRING contains over 2000 "pre-loaded" multimedia references in 50+ categories, ranging from cat videos to pinwheels to princesses. These clips are stored in folders on the phone microSD card and can be accessed via the drop-down menu on the SPRING app home screen (see "Rewards Folder" at top of Figure 3a). A user can also build a personalized folder by copying files into a new folder on the microSD card. As soon as the app is reopened, the new, personalized "reward folder" will appear in the drop-down menu of the home screen. This procedure requires time to source the desired videos, images, or audio files initially, but once the material is saved, the customization process takes less than a minute. Additionally, the folder-based drop-down menu allows a teacher or caregiver to switch between different feedback schemes for different users – or the same user with varying regulatory needs or desires for that day – in a matter of seconds.

In early pilot testing, this feature has proven critical in addressing the user preferences as he or she interacts with SPRING. Some children with ASD love a topic so acutely that still images and short, 3-5 second video chips are the

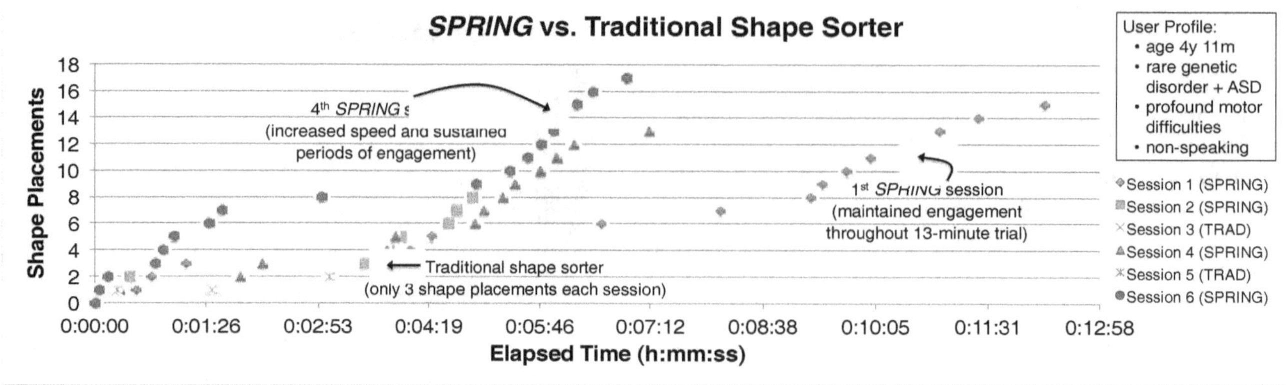

Figure 5. Plot of cumulative shape placements as a function of time for a single user over 6 sessions within an 8-day period. Sessions 1, 2, 4, and 6 used the SPRING Shape Sorter Module while Sessions 3 and 5 used a traditional, non-responsive shape sorter. Each session with a traditional shape sorter resulted in only 3 shape placements. Note the sustained periods of engagement with SPRING and the increasing rate of shape placement with subsequent SPRING sessions. Parental guidance and praise was similar across all trials.

"just right" motivating response. For other children, however, particularly those for whom the activity is a marked developmental challenge, anything less than a 15-second clip of a highly preferred song or scene appears to elicit visible frustration or agitation. These experiences – and their corresponding physiological measurements – are still being collected and analyzed and will be presented in a future paper.

PRELIMINARY RESULTS & DISCUSSION

Case 1: Motivation-driven learning for child with autism

Figure 5 presents the first multi-day case study with SPRING. The user was an almost-5-year-old boy, diagnosed with autism as well as a rare genetic disorder that involves significant difficulties in motor planning (e.g., he was still an early walker and did not use his hands for the first few years of life). As such, shape sorting was still an arduous and ambitious task, demanding his full attention, both cognitively and physically. He could not speak and did not respond to spoken words, though he was highly motivated by "dancing" light shows and musical feedback.

Over the span of eight days, the child played with either SPRING or an off-the-shelf, non-digital Fisher Price shape sorter in his home in a Floortime-style [22] play environment with at least one parent (see Figure 2b). Various LED shows were chosen as reinforcements, and no settings were changed between sessions. Each session was video recorded, and consent/assent was obtained from the parents and child prior to the start of the study.

Note that Figure 5 depicts only complete shape placements. It does not capture incomplete attempts (close to the correct hole, but not all the way in) or incorrect attempts (e.g., placing the triangle sideways in the square hole). Since these attempts are valuable – and often clever – steps in the learning process, modifications to capture them are underway (see Future Work).

During the first session (Figure 5, blue diamond markers), the child and his mother were seated on the floor in front of SPRING. Initially, the child tried to twist away from his mother, but his mother quickly placed a circle in SPRING, causing a red strip of light to race around the Base. As soon as he saw the lights, the child turned himself toward SPRING and calmly watched the light show without moving. He then reached for a shape – independently and without prompting – and attempted to place it in the circle hole. He was unsuccessful, appeared frustrated quickly, and tried to twist away again. With prompting from his mother, he attempted four more shape placements (unsuccessfully) before successfully placing a circle (Figure 5, 00:32). Then, unprompted and unaided, he almost immediately inserted the circle again (00:44). He then tried to place the square in the circle hole. With help from his mother, he was able to place the square in its proper hole (01:11) before needing a short break.

After a few minutes, the child returned to SPRING with his father but did not try any shape sorting until he saw the lights again. Then, with noticeable concentration and only minor assistance, he inserted the circle twice (04:05, 04:22). The child then began to move about the room and chose to place shapes in SPRING intermittently over the next few minutes. Then, for the last four minutes of the session (09:00-13:00), the child played intently and consistently, placing eight shapes without complaint or breaks. He was outwardly regulated and visibly engaged in the task+lights.

The following day (Session 2, orange square markers), the child approached SPRING without complaint and independently inserted the circle twice without prompting or assistance. He then attempted to insert several shapes with no assistance for over a minute (not captured in Figure 5 data), but after failing to elicit any light shows, he walked away. With prompting, he returned to SPRING and independently inserted six pieces. Then the child became fixated on the camera being used to film the session and did not reengage with SPRING.

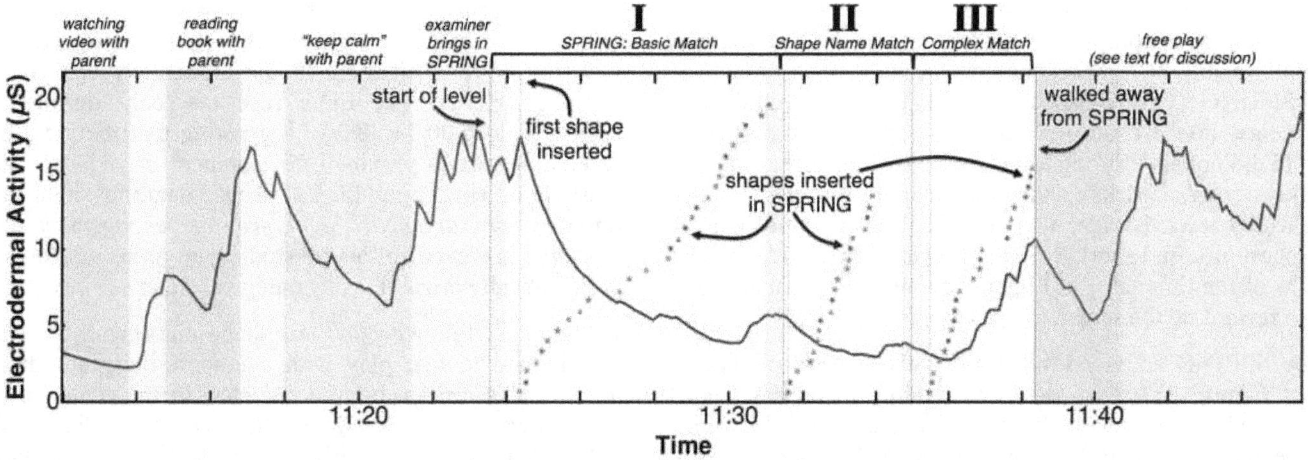

Figure 6. Plot of a child's electrodermal activity (EDA; blue line) as a function of time during a pilot case study with time-synchronized SPRING data overlaid. EDA data were captured via a wrist-worn sensor with wet electrodes at 32 samples per second. These data were filtered by taking a moving median of +/- 3 seconds about each point (i.e., 192 samples per window). Vertical gray dotted lines indicate the start of a new level using the SPRING Shape Sorter Module, while vertical pink dashed lines mark the child's first shape placement for that level. Each colored shape marker denotes placement of that shape in SPRING. Video capture shows that the declines in arousal correspond to the child's deep engagement or boredom in relatively rote activities that were either visibly easy (I; Basic Match) or too challenging (II; Shape Name Match). However, during the last level (III; Complex Match), the child's arousal rose as he strategized the correct shape. These data suggest that SPRING may facilitate measurement of physiological signatures of learning and engagement for children.

The first session with a traditional shape sorter (Session 3, green 'x' markers) was completed on an indoor platform swing in an effort to help regulate and engage the child. The child had not been exposed to a traditional shape sorter in the previous 12 months. With hand-over-hand assistance and extensive prompting, the child was able to insert three shapes. (These placements were manually timed and counted using the video.) The child did not attempt any shape placements without prompting. After four minutes, the child was markedly agitated and repeated attempts to reengage or redirect the child to the activity were unsuccessful, so the session was ended.

In order to determine if the child's agitation was related to the unresponsive shape sorting activity or to something else, the child was offered SPRING less than two minutes after the end of the previous session (Session 4, purple triangle markers). He then calmly and steadily played with SPRING for the next eight minutes. Almost any gap in placements during Session 4 were moments when the child was *attempting* to place the shape. The child remained visibly engaged and outwardly regulated the entire session.

The next session (two days later) with the traditional shape sorter (Session 5, brown 'x' markers) went similarly to Session 3 with three shape placements over seven minutes, each with extensive assistance and prompting. The child again became agitated and repeatedly tried to leave the activity. The father tried singing songs and tickling the child to help calm him and reinterest him in the shapes without success. The session was then ended.

The final session with SPRING (Session 6, red circle markers) began with the child independently inserting seven shapes in under two minutes. After a brief distraction, the child was easily directed back to the toy (without complaint) and proceeded to insert another nine shapes in less than two minutes.

These data show a clear improvement in shape placement and engagement over time, but only with the motivating sensory feedback via SPRING. This result suggests that the feedback was a *necessary* feature for the child to learn and progress in this activity. In addition, it indicates that standard methods to evaluate this child's skills in shape sorting, which typically do not involve responsive feedback, might underestimate his ability and potential.

Case 2: SPRING + physiological sensors

The second case study is part of a larger pilot study with SPRING. Over a dozen children, age 2-5, both with and without ASD have participated, with another 18 planned. As the study is ongoing and the data are heterogeneous, a full description of the methods, results, and analysis will be discussed in a subsequent paper. In Figure 6, we present a single child's data, showing the ability of SPRING to time-synchronize quantitative measures of learning with physiological data and to deliver new insights into engagement, challenge, and motivation.

The child (male, age 2) and his mother were recruited from the Boston metro area and participated in the study in a clinical room at a local university (see Figure 2c). After providing informed consent, the child, parent, and examiner each wore a wireless heart rate monitor with chest electrodes (Actiwave Cardio) and a wireless electrodermal activity (EDA) and accelerometry sensor with wet wrist electrodes (Affectiva Q Sensor) to record their physiology. The study was video and audio recorded.

After watching a video (Figure 6, blue shaded region), reading a book (purple region), and trying to "keep calm" (pink region), all with his mother, the child was introduced to SPRING. (Green shaded regions indicate the examiner's presence in the room.) According to parental report, the child did not have strong affinities for any one topic, but did enjoy "cars, trucks and construction vehicles." The SPRING reward folder was set to a collection of vehicle images, gifs, and short (3-5 second) video clips with sound; 40% of the time, an LED light show would appear instead of a reward on the screen for variety [7].

The SPRING activity level during Stage I (Basic Match; see Figure 3b) was developmentally appropriate and appeared to be relatively easy for the child. He first appeared motivated by the novelty and general shape sorting feature of SPRING, but when he realized – through verbal prompting from his mother (*"Look! It asked for a square and you put in a square and you got a truck!"*) – that placing the shape corresponding to the image on the screen produced an image of a type of vehicle he enjoyed, he appeared to become more deliberate about his shape placements, responding directly to the screen prompts in order to see more vehicles. During this time, the child's EDA steadily declined (Figure 6, blue line, ~11:24-11:30), suggesting calm engagement in a rote activity or potential boredom [3, 10]. Towards the end of Stage I, the child began to rouse himself by shouting out the names of the shapes and prompts (*"Square!" "Car!"*) and bouncing in place while playing. The EDA in Figure 6 reflects these attempts to increase his own arousal with a small rise around 11:30:30.

Given the child's success with basic matching, the next level was set to Shape Name Match (Figure 6, Stage II), where a shape word on the screen prompts the user to insert the corresponding shape (see Figure 3e). This level was developmentally advanced for a two year old, but we were investigating whether the child would be motivated to work out what the words meant in order to continue seeing cars and trucks. Yet, without maximal assistance from his mother, the level was too difficult and the child began playing his own "game" with the shapes – placing all four shapes in SPRING and then pushing them all through the holes. (The silicone mat supports the shapes before they are pushed through the holes.) This approach had the inadvertent effect of producing the desired feedback once out of every four shape placements (since, after inserting all four shapes, one of them would match the word on the screen). Since inserting shapes appeared to be easy for the child, he was effectively doing a much simpler activity than the word reading. His EDA levels continued to decline during this stage, again suggesting rote engagement or possible boredom (Figure 6, blue line, ~11:31:30-11:34) [3, 10].

In Stage III, the child began playing the Complex Match level (see Figure 3c). At first, the child continued playing his newly invented game of placing all four shapes, but then, with prompting from his mother (e.g., *"Look! It's a waffle! What shape is the waffle?"*), he began to reengage with perceived excitement in the moderately challenging learning activity. His EDA rose markedly during this activity (11:36:00-11:38:20), suggesting that the child had entered a zone of proximal development or encountered a "just right" challenge [17, 21]. These data may indicate a possible *physiological signature of engagement and learning*; however, follow-up studies are necessary to more systematically probe this physiological state.

Immediately following his last shape placement, the child was invited to free play with age-appropriate non-digital toys (blocks, trucks, baby dolls, etc.) in the center of the room, away from SPRING. His EDA immediately fell (11:38:28), reaffirming his engagement in the previous moderately challenging activity. After a minute and a half (11:40:00), his EDA rose as he became physically active with the toys (knocking down block towers, carrying boxes across the room, etc.). These results are consistent with previous studies of physiology and child activity [10, 3].

FUTURE WORK

A number of discrete improvements to address limitations of the current design are in progress:

Mapping pre-learning and exploratory strategies

In the current SPRING Shape Sorter Module, binary reed switches detect and timestamp the placement of shapes, limiting our information about the learning strategies or exploratory methods used *before* the shape was inserted. For example, did the child try to place the star in the circle hole before successfully placing it in the star hole? Or did s/he attempt the star hole immediately – indicating cognitive awareness of the shape correspondence – but lacked the motor prowess to ultimately place the star through the hole?

By replacing the reed switches with analog voltage Hall effect sensors, we will be able to track the unique magnetic signature of each shape while it is still on the *surface* of SPRING. Additionally, a piezoelectric microphone situated just below the surface of the Module provides a clear indicator of any movement of the wooden shapes against the wooden surface. These modifications are currently underway.

Proximity detection

By adding a close-range (10-80 cm) proximity detector, we will be able to record when a child approaches SPRING and pair that information with the speed with which s/he engages. For example, if a child approaches but does not engage, it may indicate that the task is too challenging or the feedback is not enticing enough. This modification is in progress.

Linked, "social" SPRING

Eliciting social interactions such as joint attention, turn taking, and cooperative play can be especially challenging for children with ASD, and making SPRING more socially integrated is the most common request we have received regarding the platform. Social skills are difficult to teach and are even harder to objectively assess [e.g., 1]. In response, we are designing and building a linked, multi-user SPRING system that wirelessly pairs multiple SPRING devices. Their smartphones communicate in real-time over an open chat room, providing simultaneous data-logging and feedback from all devices. Then SPRING can provide personalized, motivating feedback after players have collaborated on a playful request. SPRING can scaffold, cueing users to take turns or work cooperatively during SPRING levels.

For example, consider a new Shape Sorter Module with four different shapes (e.g., crescent, heart, cross, hexagon). If a prompt from the SPRING smartphone interface requests a heart, only the player with a heart can elicit the feedback, necessitating cooperation and/or social exchanges between players. Likewise, a teacher or caregiver could do the prompting, further extending the social dynamic. Similar modes of cooperative play have been envisioned for other SPRING Modules within a linked, "multi-player" setting.

New modules

We also have designed Modules that inspire ring stacking (similar to Towers of Hanoi), pretend play (e.g., making meals or shopping), and language skills (e.g., prepositions and spatial relations). Every Module employs the same Base and the same motivation-driven principles discussed earlier in the paper.

Block design module

The next Module for SPRING (in progress) detects the placement and orientation of nine cubes. Similar to the WAIS Block Design cubes (see Figure 7), the blocks have two solid red sides, two solid white sides, and two red/white sides split diagonally. This design allows the user to engage in creative, open-ended play by forming pictures and patterns or more structured play through design prompts. At the same time, by mimicking the WAIS blocks, we are able to compare SPRING data to decades of neuropsychological research. These data may further contribute to building and assessing computational models of cognition, motivation, and problem solving.

Objective outcome measures

A primary motivation to create WAIS-like blocks for the next Module is to explore using SPRING as a TUI neuropsychological assessment tool. Current assessment or outcome measures often lack reproducible objectivity or fail to capture the true potential of non-standard users (e.g., the first case study user whose performance with a classic shape sorter was markedly lower than that with SPRING). Hence, we aim to develop a system that is reliable, reproducible, sensitive to small or subtle changes, and able to detect changes over time (i.e., longitudinal improvement or plateauing). In addition, by making it highly motivating and play-based, we hope that it is easy to administer repeatedly, and fun and engaging for our target population.

Figure 7. Wechsler Adult Intelligence Scale (WAIS) Block Design cubes. Each cube has two sides of solid red, solid white, and half red-half white. The next SPRING Module will create a TUI version of this classic activity.

CONCLUSIONS

We have introduced SPRING: a tangible, customizable, responsive device designed to accelerate learning and skill acquisition for children with neurodevelopmental differences. The design approach and inspiration for SPRING stem from its governing principles of self-motivated, child-led play, but SPRING also records objective data, rendering it a novel scalable system for systematic, long-term studies of motivation and learning behaviors. Two early case studies using the SPRING Shape Sorting Module illustrate SPRING's ability to accelerate development through motivating feedback and provide possible quantifiable physiological signatures of proximal development and engagement. With its extensible modules, personalized motivating feedback, and behavioral data logging, SPRING is well-positioned to provide data-driven insights to advance learning and development for all children.

ACKNOWLEDGEMENTS

We thank Matthew Goodwin, Jillian Sullivan, and Oliver Wilder-Smith for collaborating on the second case study and for the parents and children who participated in both studies. Special thanks to Craig Ferguson for developing the SPRING smartphone interface and for many valuable discussions. We also thank undergraduate students Luis Donatiu, Laura Yenchesky, Conor Kirby, Carly Silvernale, and Luis Torres for their hard work to advance SPRING. This research was supported by a grant from the Simons Foundation to the Simons Center for the Social Brain at MIT and the MIT Media Lab Consortium.

REFERENCES

1. Adamson, L.B., Deckner, D.F. and Bakeman, R., 2010. Early interests and joint engagement in typical development, autism, and Down syndrome. *Journal of Autism and Dev Disorders*, *40*(6), pp.665-676.
2. Association, A.P. 2013. *Diagnostic and Statistical Manual of Mental Disorders (DSM-5).* American Psychiatric Publishing.
3. Boucsein, W., 2012. *Electrodermal activity*. Springer Science & Business Media.
4. Cooper, J., Heron, T., & Heward, W. 2007. *Applied Behavior Analysis*. New Jersey: Pearson Education.
5. Dawson, G., Rogers, S., Munson, J., Smith, M., Winter, J., Greenson, J., Donaldson, A. and Varley, J., 2010. Randomized, controlled trial of an intervention

for toddlers with autism: the Early Start Denver Model. *Pediatrics*, *125*(1), pp.e17-e23.

6. Dawson, M., Mottron, L., & Gernsbacher, M.A. 2008. Learning in autism. *Learning and memory: A comprehensive reference*. New York: Elsevier.
7. Egel, A.L. 1981. Reinforcer variation: Implications for motivating developmentally disabled children. *Journal of Applied Behavior Analysis*, 14(3): 345-350.
8. Esposito, G., Yoshida, S., Ohnishi, R., Tsuneoka, Y., del Carmen Rostagno, M., Yokota, S., Okabe, S., Kamiya, K., Hoshino, M., Shimizu, M. and Venuti, P., 2013. Infant calming responses during maternal carrying in humans and mice. *Current Biology*, *23*(9), pp.739-745.
9. Koomar, J.A. and Bundy, A.C., 1991. In Fisher, A.G., Murray, E.A. and Bundy, A.C. (eds.), *Sensory integration: Theory and practice*. Philadelphia: FA Davis Company.
10. Hedman, E., Miller, L., Schoen, S., Nielsen, D., Goodwin, M. and Picard, R.W., 2012, September. Measuring autonomic arousal during therapy. In *Proc. of Design and Emotion* (pp. 11-14).
11. Iarocci, G. & McDonald, J. 2006. Sensory integration and the perceptual experience of persons with autism. *Journal of Autism and Dev Disorders,* 36(1): 77-90.
12. Marshall, P., Price, S., and Rogers, Y. 2003. Conceptualising tangibles to support learning. *Proc of Interaction Design and Children (IDC'03)*, ACM Press, Preston, UK.
13. Mancil, G.R. & Pearl, C.E. 2008. Restricted interests as motivators: Improving academic engagement and outcomes of children on the Autism Spectrum. *TEACHING Exceptional Children Plus*, 4(6).
14. Piek, J. & Dyck, M. 2004. Sensory-motor deficits in children with developmental coordination disorder, attention deficit hyperactivity disorder and autistic disorder. *Human Movement Science*, 23(3-4): 475-488.
15. Resnick, M., Maryin, F., Berg, R., Borovoy, R., Colella, V., Kramer, K., Silverman, B. 1998. Digital manipulatives: new toys to think with. *Proc of CHI '98*, ACM Press, New York, NY, 281-287.
16. Ryan, R.M. & Deci, E.L. 2000. Self-determination theory and the facilitation of intrinsic motivation, social development, and well-being. *American psychologist*, 55(1): 68.
17. Schaaf, R.C. and Miller, L.J., 2005. Occupational therapy using a sensory integrative approach for children with developmental disabilities. *Developmental Disabilities Research Reviews*, *11*(2), pp.143-148.
18. Smith, T. 2001. Discrete trial training in the treatment of autism. *Focus on autism and other developmental disabilities*, 16(2), 86-92.
19. Symes, M. D., Remington, B., Brown, T., & Hastings, R. P. 2006. Early intensive behavioral intervention for children with autism: Therapists' perspectives on achieving procedural fidelity. *Research in Developmental Disabilities*, 27(1), 30-42.
20. Ullmer, B. & Ishii, H. 2000. Emerging frameworks for tangible user interfaces. *IBM Systems Journal*, 39(3-4), 915-931.
21. Vygotsky, L.S. 1980. *Mind in society: The development of higher psychological processes.* Harvard University Press.
22. Wieder, S. & Greenspan, S.I. 2003. Climbing the symbolic ladder in the DIR model through floor time/interactive play. *Autism*, 7(4): 425-435.

From Smart Homes to Smart Kids: Design Research for CataKit

Aviv Sheriff
Media Innovation Lab
Interdisciplinary Center
Herzliya, Israel
aviv.sheriff@post.idc.ac.il

Rona Sadan
Media Innovation Lab
Interdisciplinary Center
Herzliya, Israel
rona.sadan@idc.ac.il

Yasmin Keats
Media Innovation Lab
Interdisciplinary Center
Herzliya, Israel
yasmin.keats@post.idc.ac.il

Oren Zuckerman
Media Innovation Lab
Interdisciplinary Center
Herzliya, Israel
orenz@idc.ac.il

ABSTRACT

This paper presents the design research process of CataKit, a construction kit for children inspired by catapults, Rube-Goldberg chain reaction machines, and mechanical automata. We set out to promote children's initiative, positive risk-taking, and procedural thinking, all in the context of their bedrooms. Our motivation is to contrast the rising smart home movement in industry, which we fear may decrease children's initiative if children's bedrooms become too automated. We describe our design research process with six children followed by a low fidelity prototype design and evaluation. We present the qualitative analysis of children's reactions to the prototype and show support for our initial goals: encourage systematic exploration of mechanical concepts and initiative over automation. We hope that construction kits like Catakit will empower children to develop curiosity about the mechanical world around them, to think about risk taking as a potentially positive experience, and to think more critically about initiative in the smart home era.

ACM Classification Keywords

K.3.2 Computer and Information Science Education: Computer science education

Author Keywords

Construction Kit; Children; Computational Thinking; Learning; Positive Risk-Taking.

IDC '17, June 27-30, 2017, Stanford, CA, USA

ISBN 978-1-4503-4921-5/17/06...$15.00

DOI: http://dx.doi.org/10.1145/3078072.3079729

Figure 1. Girl looks on intently as she experiments with the CataKit prototype.

INTRODUCTION

In his well-known foreword to Mindstorms, 'Gears of my Childhood', Seymour Papert details his early fascination with gears and how they sparked his love and understanding of math [30]. The gears, says Papert, were models that served as his 'genesis of knowledge' and ultimately led to his theory of Constructionism. In the era of smartphones, smart homes, and upcoming autonomous technologies, children spend increasingly more time with digital devices, playing computer games, and consuming digital media [14], acting as consumers of media rather than creators. We fear that playful exploration of mechanisms in the physical world such as Papert's gears has lost its relevance in today's children culture. Resnick [32] exemplifies playful exploration beautifully with the case of Alexandra, a young girl who took on the project of constructing a "marble machine", a device in which marbles are carried up and down various tracks and pathways, bouncing around and activating devices. The project engaged Alexandra for weeks, as she experimented and iterated her design, working hard but embracing the challenge due to the personal meaning of the project. Complex and meaningful projects such as Alexandra's marble machine engage children in what Papert called procedural thinking [30]. Children who learn and think procedurally connect abstract 'propositional' knowledge, as learned in classrooms, with the real world. Without the procedural and experiential element, learning may become dissociated, such that the learner cannot associate what he knows with personal experience.

Papert believed that children could develop procedural thinking by programming in LOGO [30]. More recently, in her influential 2006 article, Jeannette Wing [43] referred to this type of procedural problem-solving as 'computational thinking' (CT) and said that it "represents a universally applicable attitude and skill set everyone, not just computer scientists, would be eager to learn and use". CT is a creative process that includes iteration, deconstructing problems, debugging, and generalization through patterns [17]. Bundy [9] reports that CT influences 'research in nearly all disciplines' and Wing [44] envisions that it will bring innovation to 'all fields of endeavor'. However, researchers are still looking for methods of instilling CT in children.

Computational thinking is most often associated with programming, but many of its core elements are also relevant to mechanical problem-solving and physical tinkering, such as iteration and debugging. Moreover, it has been shown that children have less knowledge of mechanical operations. One study, conducted with young children (ages 9-10), showed that children were unable to accurately explain mechanical concepts even after a robot building session that covered those concepts [10]. The modern digital lifestyle may not provide enough opportunities for kids to interact with, explore, or invent mechanisms. In a way, the digital world has moved the interiors of machines into what Paulo Blikstein refers to as the background [7], or 'black box' [33]. These trends might have negative implications in various domains. One concern in US college education is the steady decline in the number of engineering freshmen in the United States, with fewer than half of those students obtaining an engineering degree [6]. We hope that playful tinkering with physical mechanisms will promote procedural thinking and CT among children.

Positive Risk-Taking

Little [22] argues that the departure from physical play is depriving children of developmentally significant opportunities for positive risk-taking. Parents and society in general are increasingly overprotective [15, 16], which causes children to miss out on worthwhile risks that provide stimulating experiences [38]. By contrast, positive risk-taking promotes learning but minimizes the chance of injury. In addition, it allows children to learn about risk and risk evaluation, an important skill later on in life [22]. Children who engage in high positive risk-taking are "confident in challenging themselves to complete difficult tasks", whereas children who engage in high negative risk-taking "use equipment in a dangerous or inappropriate manner, contrary to intended uses" [23]. The first definition emphasizes that positive risk-taking experiences have the potential to give children perceptions of self-efficacy [3]. The second definition emphasizes the need to design construction kits in a way that scaffolds away from potential "dangerous or inappropriate" uses, commonly found in negative risk-taking. Finally, the lack of easily accessible urban outdoor play areas for children [39] suggests that indoor opportunities for positive risk-taking are a worthwhile alternative.

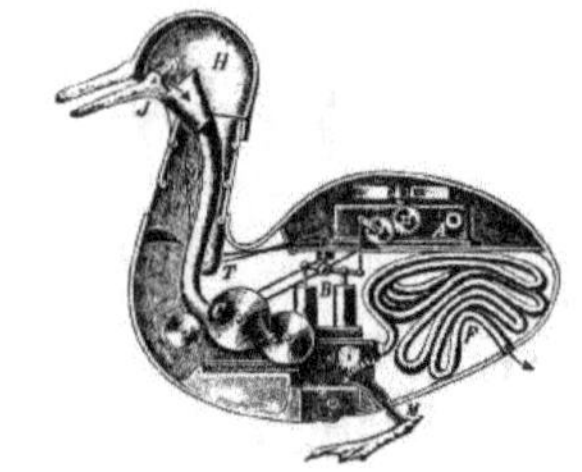

Figure 2. Jacques Vaucanson's mechanical digesting duck as depicted by an observer.

Figure 3. Rube Goldberg's Self-Operating Napkin.

Automata and Rube Goldberg

History is rife with examples of clever and creative mechanical engineering that intrigued children and adults alike. Early hydraulic and pneumatic mechanisms, or automata, have been designed as early as ancient Greece and that early work has inspired extensive creation during the Renaissance [4]. One notable example is Jacques Vaucanson (1709-1782), arguably the most important inventor in the history of automata and a key figure in the history of machine technology. Vaucanson spent his life constructing various novelties such as his first android - a life-sized figure of a musician that played the flute. His most famous creation was "an artificial duck of gilt brass which drinks, eats, flounders in water, digests and excretes like a live duck" (Fig. 2). The creation of automata that produce music has inspired the Academy of Sciences in St. Petersburg to host what may be considered an 'Enlightenment Age Hackathon' in 1779. The contest sought the creation of a speaking head that could utter the five vowels, but no winner was declared, although the contest inspired many to construct speaking heads over the following decades. Modern artists have, around the turn of the previous century, built certain automata as a commentary and satire on the advent of modern technology, namely - Rube Goldberg machines [24]. Rube Goldberg studied engineering but eventually became a newspaper cartoonist [42] who sketched various absurdly complex mechanisms that perform mundane tasks, such as the self-operating napkin with rocket and parrot (Fig. 3; [42]). "An illogical bunch of things that are put in a logical sequence", is how Goldberg once described his inventions in an interview. This quote portrays Goldberg as a proponent of tinkering for its own sake, much like modern Makers.

Kim and Park [20] have advocated the use of Rube Goldberg machines as an exciting means of captivating young minds while promoting important abilities, such as design aptitude, engineering skills, and creativity. O'Connor [27] describes a Rube-Goldberg-based course for fifth graders set to cover math (metric system), science (simple machines), and history (the industrial revolution). The students responded with excitement and recruited their families to assist.

Smart Homes - Friend or Foe?

Chain reaction machines such as Rube Goldberg's present an opportunity for children to actively design their personally meaningful spaces rather than passively use smart technologies. Smart home technology, in particular, is on the rise [2] and is beginning to penetrate the lives of children and adults alike. Personal assistants, automated kitchens, and self-adjusting light bulbs are offering to take over manual tasks. As wonderful as smart homes technology can be, we see a downside in a gradual process that can lead people to decrease in initiative. As our homes become automated, various functions are taken out of our control and we risk becoming passive and sedentary. As Yvonne Rogers stated in her 2006 paper [36], there is a need to be engaged by technology, rather than subdued, and we need to shift 'from proactive computers to proactive people'. We strongly support this agenda. Moreover, kids may be at a particular risk in this context; the more black boxes around them, the fewer opportunities they'll have for exploration and for acquiring an intuitive understanding of the world around them. We believe that the smart homes trend should be leveraged to excite children who are fascinated by such technologies with the possibility of personally designing machines that control their homes and rooms.

CataKit

We present the design research process of a new construction kit, called CataKit (Fig.1), a set of components that allows kids to construct and use catapult-style small machines to design and implement their own smart room experience.

RELATED WORK

In our design of the CataKit, we found inspiration in previous work on automata and the literature on scaffolding. Within the Human Computer Interaction (HCI) literature, we found related work on construction kits, with a specific focus on mechanism construction.

Mechanisms and Automata

Henry T. Brown's 1868 classic technical book "507 Mechanical Movements" is now available online including illustrations and some animations [8, 26]. Modern authors have noted the educational potential and have developed instructional books for children, such as Robert Adam's 'How to Make and Design Automata' [1]. Within the HCI community, important work has recently been published on 'Paper Mechatronics' by the Craft Technology Team at the University of Boulder, Colorado [28]. Their project began with simple paper-based mechanisms and has evolved into a cardboard-based mechanical kit with Arduino circuit boards for designing percussion instruments [29]. The Craft Technology Team has gathered insights from workshops using the kit and note the importance of the mechanisms' physicality in facilitating iterative learning and problem-solving. Some notable commercial kits have also inspired us, such as Lakeshore Learning's 'Create-A-Chain Reaction STEM Kit' that uses a small ball-throwing mechanism as the primary component [21], Learning Resource's various 'Gears! Gears! Gears!' sets [35], and Pathfinder's hydraulic catapults and machines [11].

Guidelines of Construction Kit Design

In our work, we were deeply influenced by the work of the lifelong kindergarten group at MIT Media Lab and the insights gathered there following decades of construction kit design. Specifically, we drew inspiration from the guidelines described by Resnick and Silverman [34], which include: 'Design for Designers', 'Low Floors and Wide Walls', and 'Make Powerful Ideas Salient - Not Forced'. Additional guidelines came from our own previous work; Zuckerman [46] drew a classification from the distinct philosophies of Montessori and Froebel, and described the design principles that underlie their work. In our Catakit, we drew inspiration from the following of those principles: 'An open-ended system with minimal constraints', 'isolation of properties', and 'conceptual manipulation'.

Scaffolding

In his influential sociocultural theory, Lev Vygotsky introduced the concept of the Zone of Proximal Development (ZPD; [41]). The ZPD is the difference between an individual's personal ability and what he can achieve when supported, or scaffolded, by someone else. Vygotsky influenced learning theorists greatly and today the support described in his theory is most commonly termed 'Scaffolding'. The term scaffolding was first coined by Wood, Bruner, and Ross [45] and originally referred strictly to tutoring given to a child by a teacher. The term has since expanded to various contexts of learning support, including in the absence of any social interaction. Podolefsky, Moore, and Perkins [31] have developed interactive simulations based on a framework of implicit scaffolding. Implicit scaffolding is "built into the tool itself - using affordances, constraints, cueing and feedback" and should be seamless, without the explicit attention of the learner to the fact that he or she is being directed. For example, one important idea adopted in their framework is 'framing', in which the construction kit designer answers the question "what sort of activity is this?" and communicates the answer through the design [19, 40]. Hadwin and Winne [18] make a similar distinction between tacit and explicit scaffolding and propose that tacit scaffolds promote self-regulated learning. This may occur because users tend to attribute positive external events to themselves [25], such that a user will self-attribute interface successes and get motivated.

DESIGN RESEARCH

Our goal was to design a construction kit that will encourage children's systematic exploration of mechanical concepts, initiative over automation, and positive risk-taking in a home context. To better understand children's preferences and attitudes on these topics, we defined three components of the kit - a thrower, a catcher, and a pusher. We did not design the components, rather we integrated them into our interviews as a research probe.

Method and Procedure

We obtained institutional review board approval, parental consent, and interviewed three boys and three girls, ages 8-12. The children were recruited through an ad on social media and through personal acquaintance with the researchers. The interviews were conducted in the children's homes, in their rooms. Previous work indicates that collecting data in kids' own environment produces insights that may otherwise be missed [12, 5]. In addition, following Druin's [12] recommendations, one researcher transcribed the interaction while another researcher served as the interactor so that he could talk naturally with the kids. The interviews lasted between 45 minutes and an hour. The interviews followed a semi-structured format. At first, we only gave the children a simple verbal description of the three basic components and sticky papers that represented the various components (with the name of each component printed on the paper), so that the kids could use them to act out their ideas and plans. We also mentioned that the components could connect anywhere in their rooms. As the interview progressed, we showed the kids some pictures that illustrated possible implementations of each component, as well as an inspiration video that shows a Rube-Goldberg type chain reaction machine in a breakfast context.

Findings

We present the qualitative analysis of children's reactions to the concept of CataKit and the components we described. In line with our research goal, we analyzed our interviews with the following questions in mind: whether children envision the kit as more functional or playful, do they see the kit as smart/automated or as requiring manual initiative, and do they have more positive-risk or negative-risk ideas for using the kit.

Functional versus Fun Ideas

We wanted to see whether children desire functional, "smart home", uses for the kit or whether they are more interested in fun and games. Children's ideas were classified into functional/fun and then counted for each child. We also asked them to indicate and detail their preference for functional/fun uses for the kit.

Four out of the six children had notably more functional than fun ideas for using the kit.

> Jim (10): "It can turn the computer on and off, for example. I throw it outside (away from the table) and then back to the computer's button. It saves you the need to bend. (Fig. 4)

Two children had an equal mix of functional and fun ideas:

Figure 4. Depiction of Jim's bedroom and ideas. Blue - closing the door. Green - switching the computer on and off. Red - pulling off the blanket to wake up. Yellow - turning the light on and off

> Jane (8): "It can play catch and you can play piggy in the middle with no friends." (fun); "She (her mother) presses it and it releases the bottle and it flies (to her bed)." (functional)

When asked whether they prefer the functional or the fun ideas, four of the six children firmly supported the functional ideas.

> Bill (12): "I think it would be mainly for practicality and on the way it has some fun."

Two children said they liked both functional and fun uses:

> Jane (8): "Both. Kids need to have fun sometimes. Mostly. The useful stuff can help the parents and help educate the kids. But (with) the fun stuff you can play tricks on them."

Initiative versus Automation

The children referred to buttons, remote controls, robots, and similar automated digital devices when describing the kit. We counted the number of those references to assess the extent to which children envisioned the kit as automated.

Four of the six children mentioned electronics between one and four times, which we define as a low amount of references. The two remaining children mentioned electronics eight and twelve times, which we define as a high amount of references.

Out of the two children with a high amount of references, one of them, a girl, was very much into robotics and mentioned them multiple times. The second of the two, a boy, mentioned all types of technology - sensors, holograms, and electronics.

Four out of the six children mentioned using a remote with the kit at least once.

(How do you make it throw the cup?) Jane (8): "There's a remote control in your pocket."

Positive versus Negative Risk-Taking
We used Little, Wyver, and Gibson's [23] guidelines to classify children's ideas for using the kit as positive or negative risk-taking and as constituting high risk, moderate risk, low risk, or very low/no-risk. In addition, we asked children who is responsible if the kit broke something in the house, in order to assess their risk-awareness.

Most of the children's ideas were very-low/no-risk.

Jim (10): "I want it to push the door."

Bill (12): "Maybe it could sense if someone was coming in."

The second most common type of idea was low-risk positive.

Jane (8): "There's a remote control in your pocket. One hand pressing the remote control. You get ready and then you catch (the glass), and it can have juice inside it. And then you can pretend you didn't know about this and just drink it."

Overall, there were only four negative risk ideas out of about 45 ideas.

Jim (10): "You can come home and it'll toss the lunch food in your face, or upside down on the table."

All of the children were aware of the potential risks of throwing things with the kit, such as interrupting others and breaking things.

Mary (10) suggested throwing a sponge. When asked why, she said "Because it doesn't break anything, it's harmless, it's a sponge."

DESIGN GUIDELINES

In the interviews, the children treated the concept of CataKit with great consideration and thought carefully about their answers. They showed a "tech-mindset" and mentioned several times that the kit should be electronic in nature. Interestingly, their ideas were mostly safe or involved positive low risk. Based on our interview findings and related work, we defined the following design guidelines as a base for our CataKit design process.

1. **Meaningful Connection with the Room**. Kids found their rooms to be fertile soil for ideas. Siblings who were interviewed in joint rooms had ideas that centered around their own personal space - mainly their beds. The guideline we derived from this insight is that CataKit components should attach to as many surfaces as possible within the room.

2. **Perceived Usefulness, Actual Playfulness**. The children expressed a desire for the kit to serve a functional use, or in other words - to serve a real purpose in their daily lives. However, when they acted out their scenarios it was clear that they were quite playful. For instance, shutting down the computer by constructing a complex chain reaction is a playful but inefficient way of turning it off. We decided that the CataKit should balance between 'perceived usefulness' and actual playfulness.

3. **Initiative over Automation**. Children's desire for remote controls and robots strengthened our position that CataKit should be designed primarily with mechanisms. We believe that, with the right design and playful affordances, children would be motivated to design complex mechanisms in order to reach their goal of automation.

4. **Positive Risk-Taking**. In our interviews, we found that kids' ideas were safe or low in risk. The Catakit should encourage them to take more risks but in a safe and playful way.

5. **Low floor, Wide Walls**. Building on Resnick [34], we wish that the kit be easy to start with and require little prior knowledge so that kids can start experimenting right away (low floors). At the same time, it should allow for many diverse creations (wide walls).

6. **Systematic Exploration**. The kit should allow children to explore mechanical ideas through iteration, debugging, problem-solving, and planning. We hope that exploration of mechanical concepts and the relationship between cause and effect will encourage an 'engineer's mindset' of playful design and promote CT skills at an early age.

PROTOTYPE DESIGN AND IMPLEMENTATION

Based on our design guidelines and related work, we designed a low fidelity prototype of one of the CataKit components, the thrower, which is a catapult. In this work, we chose to focus on the catapult component because it resonates with the concept of risk-taking, even to the point of vandalism. We felt that the catapult metaphor captures the imagination of kids and adults alike. Finally, the mechanism of the catapult is not so complex as to obscure the underlying mechanical operations, which corresponds with our goal of encouraging systematic exploration of mechanical concepts.

After iterating several versions of the catapult (Fig. 5), we built a moldable, minimal, and 'simple as possible' [34] prototype. The prototype (Fig. 6) allows for a meaningful connection with the room (guideline 1) via suction mechanisms fitted to the component's sides and bottom (Fig. 6; A) that attach to smooth surfaces. In addition, we minimized the size of the base (Fig. 6; B) so as not to block the view for the child or serve as an obstacle in the room.

To promote systematic exploration (guideline 6), the cup (Fig. 6; C) and the rod (Fig. 6; D) are adjustable. The cup can be moved up and down the rod and little cubes at the top and bottom can be used to fixate its position. The adjustability of the tossing mechanism invites experimentation with different tensions, and as a result different kinetic energy that results in various throwing distances.

We used scrap materials to make the kit accessible and less intimidating. We wanted kids to feel free to modify and even break some of the kit's parts during the testing sessions, as they explored various uses.

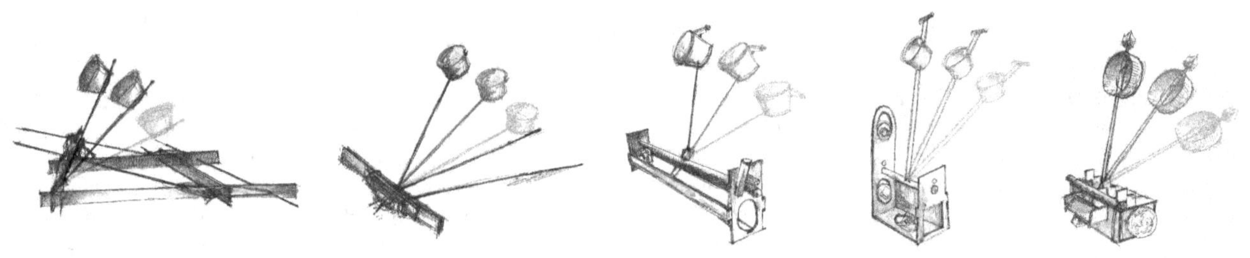

Figure 5. Iterations of the catapult, starting from earliest (left) to latest (right). Model 2 added the adjustability of the cup. Model 3 added connectivity via suction mechanisms. Model 4 condensed the design. Model 5 added vacuums and sturdiness via wood construction.

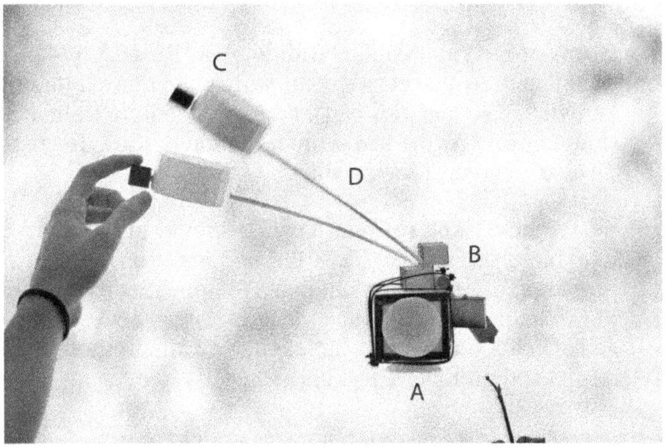

Figure 6. Final catapult prototype.

Figure 7. The arsenal of balls. Hard and heavy ball on the left, followed by rubber yellow ball, sponge soccer ball, styrofoam ball, and fluffy ball.

In order to ensure 'low floor' (guideline 5), we wanted the mechanism to be completely visible. This serves as an affordance for the main operation of pulling and releasing the rod (Fig. 6; D). In addition, the high visibility minimizes the number of black boxes.

To encourage positive risk-taking (guideline 4), the catapult was accompanied by an arsenal of five balls that varied in softness, weight, and size (Fig. 7). The green ball is the hardest, heaviest, and produces a loud sound when it falls on hard surfaces. By contrast, the red ball is the lightest, softest, and fluffiest.

The perceived usefulness (guideline 2) of the kit is contextual, in the sense that connecting it to the environment and using it to activate other objects makes it useful. Without connectivity, the catapult on its own has no purpose.

We intentionally created tension between the immediate association of the catapult as a destructive machine and our desire to create a kit for positive risk-taking within the house. We believe that this tension creates playfulness and adds an element of whimsical humor.

USER STUDY

Using our prototype, we revisited five of the original six children from the design research phase, in their homes. The sixth child was not interviewed for logistical reasons. The interviews took place in the same rooms as the original interviews. We displayed the catapult and the arsenal of balls and asked the kids to explore and use the prototype. As in the design research phase, one interviewer focused on interacting with the child and one was a designated transcriber. We analyzed the interviews according to the themes presented below.

Low Floors and Wide Walls

To evaluate this design guideline, we observed children's activity, especially at the beginning of the activity, to see whether they found the kit accessible and easy to start using (low floor). In addition, we looked for a variety of uses for the kit (wide walls).

Three of the five children did not intuitively understand that the rod needs to be pulled back in order to throw, a design flaw that prevented the children from using the system as planned. At this point, the researcher explained the mechanism so that the user testing could proceed. The two other children understood straight away, without any explanation.

In addition, four of the five children were at first scared to break the kit, either by having it fall from a high place or by pulling the rod too far back.

All five children said the rod wasn't flexible enough. They suggested using alternative materials such as rubber or other tension mechanisms, such as springs.

> Jane (8): "Maybe make it more flexible. So you can bend it and there's a spring you can fold down and it makes it jump up."

In terms of connectivity, all five children intuitively grasped the purpose of the suction mechanisms and successfully connected the catapult to various surfaces in their room, such as windows, cupboards, tables, the floor, their bed, a mirror, a computer, and a computer monitor. This indicates that the connectivity aspect is easy to start using and works with diverse surfaces. When asked to rate "to what extent they would be able to connect the kit wherever they wanted", from 1 (very low) to 5 (very high), three children answered 3 and two children answered 4.

> Jane (8): "3, It needs to be stickier." Jody (11): "3, It can connect to some places and some places it can't." Bill (12): "4, basically there's no place I need to stick it and it can't (connect)."

The children had a diverse range of new ideas for the kit (wide walls), which were also related to their personal interests.

> Jane (8), who likes to draw and paint: "It will throw a ball and it will activate a giant Ferris wheel and it'll pour a little bit of every color to the palette and then I can paint."

> Bill (12): "Oh! It can work like an alarm clock. Sometimes I hit snooze three times... I'll throw and if I hit it'll stop ringing. If it doesn't, I have to get up and so I'm up."

> Jody (11): "Put the dog's ball in (the prototype) and make him go fetch."

> John (10), who plays the violin, said: "This part looks a bit like a flute. Maybe it can play a little tune... The rod can activate something that creates a flow of air or an exploding balloon or something."

We asked the children whether they could build their own prototype, like ours, from 1 (no way) to 5 (absolutely). All five children answered 4.

> Jody (11): "4, because I'm good at building things."

Systematic Exploration

We wanted to see how quickly and extensively the children would engage in a systematic exploration of the kit's uses, as evidenced by adjusting the rod, connecting the kit, firing various objects, implementing their original ideas, iterating, and debugging.

Once we assured the children that it was fine if they broke the kit, they began experimenting freely. Each child made dozens of attempts to throw the various balls around the room freely or to hit specific targets that they conjured up (Fig. 1). Each of the five children made dozens of attempts as they practiced their aim while trying to hit their marks.

> When asked how many times he tried to hit the computer switch, Jim (10) said:, "More than twenty I think. But it was before we got closer. Otherwise, it would take me seven."

> Jane (8), when throwing the ball for the first time: (excited) "That's exactly where I was trying to aim!"

All of the children made use of the rod's adjustability mechanism systematically, in order to help them improve their aim. When asked why, they were able to correctly explain the logic.

> (Why do you take it up and down?) John (10): "If it's longer it can throw harder and better. And higher. If it's shorter it's harder to throw."

> Jody (11): "If you move it closer it changes the force because then it (the rod) goes less backward and if you put it really far it can go more backward and get more leverage."

Two of the children asked for built-in instruments to help them measure distances or adjust the catapult, thus allowing for even greater systematic exploration.

> John (10): "You can create a gauge that will indicate the distances. Here it will say ten and that way you know it's ten meters."

One child had a completely different idea for how the kit would operate. He suggested that the cup would catch a ball, rather than throwing it, which would push the rod down and press a button.

> Bill (12): "You can throw a weight here (into the cup), or something heavy and then it'll drop down (the rod), and then activate something. But then I need the cube to be like a touch (softer).", When asked what ball would do the trick, "A ball that had enough weight to make it drop down. I think it could also help you learn about different weights."

Positive Risk-Taking

As previously stated, the children were initially afraid to break the kit, which is a design flaw because it discouraged risk-taking. Once we alleviated their concerns, they began to take more risks. We presented them with the arsenal of five balls and assessed their risk-taking using Little, Wyver, and Gibson's [23] guidelines of positive or negative risk-taking and as constituting high risk, moderate risk, low risk, or very low/no-risk.

Much like their ideas in the design research stage, most of the children's uses were no-risk/low risk. They mostly used the lighter balls, generally avoided aim at breakable objects, and rarely placed the kit in dangerous places.

The second most common uses were low-risk positive, such as throwing balls at pictures on the wall and connecting the kit to sensitive surfaces such as computer monitors and mirrors.

When they examined the hardest, heaviest ball, three children appropriately expressed risk avoidance - a reluctance to engage in the task with it.

> Jane (8), when asked whether she wants to throw the heavy ball, said "No, it's a little dangerous. It can hurt."

> John (10), when asked why he won't use the heavy ball, said "It's too heavy and it can break something, even the kit itself and something in the room."

Two children attempted to throw the heavy ball on a hard floor, a moderate negative risk that produced considerable noise. One child threw the heavy ball on the carpet, which indicates preparedness and a moderate positive risk.

We asked the children to rate how dangerous the kit was from 1 (not dangerous) to 5 (very dangerous). They rated it 2, 2, 2, 1.5 and 2.5.

> Bill (12): "2.5, if people are stupid and put it in dangerous places then yes, it'll be dangerous." Jane (8): "1.5 You can throw the hard ball by mistake."

We also asked the parents to evaluate how dangerous the kit was. None of them expressed apprehension.

> Mother 1 said "About 2 or 3 out of 5, only the hard ball is dangerous." Mother 2 said "1 in my opinion.", and proceeded to play around with the kit and with the heavy ball.

Automation versus Initiative

We revisited the concept of automation and initiative by asking the children, at the end of the interview, whether they would prefer an electronic or mechanical smart room system. In contrast to the kids' answers in the design research stage, where they expressed an explicit desire for remotes, robots, electronics, and automation, the kids changed their mind. Having played with the kit, all five children were now leaning towards mechanical usage and initiative.

> Jane (8): "To make it more interesting and not boring you want to activate it. If you click on the remote it's pretty boring. In order for it to be interesting, you can use your hands."

> Bill (12): "Personally? I don't know how it would work with something electric. With the alarm clock, the whole idea is that you do it yourself so that you wake up."

> John (10): "I would prefer a string (and not a remote). Or a rubber band. Because that's the most convenient, and to know that you activated it. And it can be fun to try and hit the mark."

> Jody (11): "If everything is robotic, then what is it good for? It's more practical (manually) and instead of a robot doing it and you just sit and watch and get bored."

> Jim (10): "I prefer this one. If it does the same thing anyway then this one is better because you see how everything works. It (automatic) would be more boring, basically."

DISCUSSION

We set out to design a construction kit that will encourage children's systematic exploration of mechanical concepts, initiative, and positive risk-taking. We performed a design research process, defined six design guidelines, and implemented a low fidelity prototype. We tested our prototype in a qualitative study with the same children as in the design research and found encouraging support, detailed below.

Design principle	How it was manifested in the user testing
Ease of Use / Low floor	The children found the mechanism inaccessible at first but were able to use it after a short explanation. The children were afraid to break the kit. The children found the use of the suction mechanisms intuitive and had many diverse ideas for using it.
Systematic Exploration	The children adjusted the rod's length to achieve different trajectories. The children asked for additional tools of systematic exploration, such as distance gauges. The children experimented with throwing the differently weighted balls.
Positive Risk-Taking	Most of the children's ideas were low-risk, rather than positive or negative risk. The children all thought the kit is safe and, on average, rated it 2 (safe) out 5 (risky) on "risk". Children's parents rated the kit as low on risk.
Automation-Initiative	Children progressed from a pro-automation stance in the design interviews to a pro-initiative stance after using the initial prototype.

Table 1. Summary of user testing findings.

Construction Kits in a Meaningful Context

Designing their own smart rooms using chain reaction mechanisms requires that children use their ingenuity and creativity. Indeed, the children we interviewed came up with a variety of ideas that would provide a stimulating challenge for them to execute, such as the chain reaction dog feeder, and the bunk-bed bottle delivery system. The children intuitively grasped the concept of the suction mechanisms and connected the prototype all over their rooms, even requesting additional connectivity with magnets and strings. Traditionally, construction kits are designed as stand-alone and independent of the environment. CataKit contributes in this regard by adding integration with the surrounding as a key affordance, specifically within the child's own meaningful and personal context - his or her room.

Mischievous Scientists

Piaget famously described children as little scientists, who ceaselessly conduct experiments [37]. Some of these experiments, alas, cause mischief and are often viewed with suspicion by parents and adults. We believe that this precise element constitutes excitement and interest for the child - to discover boundaries and have safe fun while doing it. We see CataKit as a catalyst for positive risk-taking in the home, that allows children to expand the repertoire of what is allowed indoors, in a safe and playful way. Our findings are in line with those of previous researchers [23] - children are taking very little risks in their play activities. Designers of construction kits should take this into their attention and create more opportunities for positive risk-taking.

Inspiring the 'Engineer Mindset'

Our construction kit targets important mechanical concepts such as cause-and-effect, tension, force, trajectory, and mechanical advantage - the ratio of the force produced by a mechanism to the force applied to it. Oh et al. [29, 28] have also noted the potential of mechanical automata for construction kits and Exploratorium [13] have developed projects in which kids build both automata and Rube Goldberg chain reaction machines. We contribute by adding, on top of the construction, the systematic exploration of mechanical concepts. The children we interviewed explored various uses. For instance, the children iterated with the tension produced by the catapult's rod in order to vary the force and trajectory of the toss. In addition, they experimented with different payloads, which introduced the interaction of weight. Finally, they explored cause-and-effect as they attempted to create chain reactions. For example, eight-year-old Jim threw the ball well over twenty times at a funnel that he placed over his older brother's computer power switch. Eventually, he succeeded in producing sufficient force and precision to shut down the computer, which resulted in an all-too-familiar sibling ordeal.

From Smart Homes to Smart Kids

Yvonne Rogers [36] makes a strong case for technologies that engage us rather than sedate us. In our paper, we took that approach to the extreme by foregoing the use of electronics in our prototype. Further development and research are required to assess whether this approach has merit or whether digital components are compulsory at one stage or another when designing an ambitious kit. Nonetheless, our findings show that children were captivated by the low-tech, mechanical prototype, despite its simple nature and design shortcomings. Even as we subtly emphasized the advantages of smart appliances in completing the same tasks - efficiency, time, and effort, they countered with their own arguments in favor of manual construction - that passivity is boring, and that "It kind of doesn't make sense. It's like robots took over the world. We have to do things on our own."

Conclusion

Our findings show support for our initial goals: encourage systematic exploration of mechanical concepts, initiative over automation, and positive risk-taking in a home context. In addition, we would like to highlight that most of the children expressed a preference towards usefulness of the kit. As we described in our initial interview analysis, we interpret this finding as 'perceived usefulness' because the children's ideas were, in essence, not really useful. For instance, one child's idea to turn off his personal computer with a chain reaction system is not really useful but was perceived as such by the child. We believe that designers of technology for children should consider perceived usefulness as a design guideline in their work.

The study had several limitations. First, the sample we used was small and we did not utilize random sampling or quantitative research methods. In addition, our decision to design just one component of the kit limited the extent of user-testing. Finally, most of our findings are limited to the context of children's bedrooms.

In sum, we believe that our research brings value to the HCI community and can inform designers and educators. We hope that construction kits like Catakit will empower kids to think more critically about life in an ultra-digital era, to take initiative in their daily lives using technology, to develop curiosity about the mechanical world around them, and to think about risk taking as a potentially positive experience, if done within safe limits.

ACKNOWLEDGMENTS

We thank all the children who participated in this study and shared their creative insights with us. This research was supported by the I-CORE Program of the Planning and Budgeting Committee, the ISF grant #1716/12 and the Sarah Fine Foundation.

REFERENCES

1. Robert Addams. 2003. *How to Design and Make Simple Automata*. Craft Education.
2. Muhammad Raisul Alam, Mamun Bin Ibne Reaz, and Mohd Alauddin Mohd Ali. 2012. A review of smart homes - Past, present, and future. *IEEE Transactions on Systems, Man, and Cybernetics, Part C (Applications and Reviews)* 42, 6 (2012), 1190–1203.
3. Albert Bandura. 1977. Self-efficacy: toward a unifying theory of behavioral change. *Psychological review* 84, 2 (1977), 191.
4. Silvio A Bedini. 1964. The role of automata in the history of technology. *Technology and Culture* 5, 1 (1964), 24–42.
5. Hugh Beyer and Karen Holtzblatt. 1997. *Contextual design: defining customer-centered systems*. Elsevier.
6. Glenn Blauvelt, Michael Eisenberg, and others. 2006. Computer aided design of mechanical automata: Engineering education for children. In *Proceedings of International Conference on Education and Technology*. 61–66.
7. Paulo Blikstein. 2013. Gears of our childhood: constructionist toolkits, robotics, and physical computing, past and future. In *Proceedings of the 12th international conference on interaction design and children*. ACM, 173–182.
8. Henry T Brown. 1881. *Five Hundred and Seven Mechanical Movements: Embracing All Those which are Most Important in Dynamics, Hydraulics, Hydrostatics, Pneumatics, Steam Engines, Mill and Other Gearing, Presses, Horology, and Miscellaneous Machinery; and Including Many Movements Never Before Published, and Several which Have Only Recently Come Into Use*. Brown & Brown.

9. Alan Bundy. 2007. Computational thinking is pervasive. *Journal of Scientific and Practical Computing* 1, 2 (2007), 67–69.
10. Joan M Chambers, Mike Carbonaro, and Hana Murray. 2008. Developing conceptual understanding of mechanical advantage through the use of Lego robotic technology. *Australasian Journal of Educational Technology* 24, 4 (2008).
11. Pathfinders Design and Technology. 2017 (accessed January 31, 2017). http://www.pathfindersdesignandtechnology.com
12. Allison Druin. 1999. Cooperative inquiry: developing new technologies for children with children. In *Proceedings of the SIGCHI conference on Human Factors in Computing Systems*. ACM, 592–599.
13. Exploratorium. 2017 (accessed January 31, 2017). http://tinkering.exploratorium.edu
14. Ingunn Fjørtoft. 2001. The natural environment as a playground for children: The impact of outdoor play activities in pre-primary school children. *Early childhood education journal* 29, 2 (2001), 111–117.
15. Frank Furedi. 2001. *Paranoid parenting: Abandon your anxieties and be a good parent*. Allen Lane.
16. Cheryl Greenfield. 2004. 'Can run, play on bikes, jump the zoom slide, and play on the swings': exploring the value of outdoor play. *Australian Journal of Early Childhood* 29, 2 (2004), 1–6.
17. Shuchi Grover and Roy Pea. 2013. Computational Thinking in K–12 A Review of the State of the Field. *Educational Researcher* 42, 1 (2013), 38–43.
18. Allyson Fiona Hadwin and Philip H Winne. 2001. CoNoteS2: A software tool for promoting self-regulation. *Educational Research and Evaluation* 7, 2-3 (2001), 313–334.
19. David Hammer, Andrew Elby, Rachel E Scherr, and Edward F Redish. 2005. Resources, framing, and transfer. *Transfer of learning from a modern multidisciplinary perspective* 89 (2005).
20. Yilip Kim and Namje Park. 2012. Development and application of STEAM teaching model based on the Rube Goldberg's invention. In *Computer science and its applications*. Springer, 693–698.
21. Lakeshore Learning. 2017 (accessed January 31, 2017). http://www.lakeshorelearning.com
22. Helen Little. 2006. Children's risk-taking behaviour: Implications for early childhood policy and practice. *International Journal of Early Years Education* 14, 2 (2006), 141–154.
23. Helen Little, Shirley Wyver, and Frances Gibson. 2011. The influence of play context and adult attitudes on young children's physical risk-taking during outdoor play. *European Early Childhood Education Research Journal* 19, 1 (2011), 113–131.
24. Peter C Marzio. 1972. Art, Technology and Satire: The Legacy of Rube Goldberg. *Leonardo* (1972), 315–324.
25. Youngme Moon. 2003. Don't blame the computer: When self-disclosure moderates the self-serving bias. *Journal of Consumer Psychology* 13, 1-2 (2003), 125–137.
26. 507 movements. 2017 (accessed January 31, 2017). http://507movements.com/
27. Debra O'Connor. 2003. Application sharing in K-12 education: Teaching and learning with Rube Goldberg. *TechTrends* 47, 5 (2003), 6–13.
28. Hyunjoo Oh, Michael Eisenberg, Mark D Gross, and Sherry Hsi. 2015. Paper mechatronics: a design case study for a young medium. In *Proceedings of the 14th International Conference on Interaction Design and Children*. ACM, 371–374.
29. Hyunjoo Oh, Jiffer Harriman, Abhishek Narula, Mark D Gross, Michael Eisenberg, and Sherry Hsi. 2016. Crafting Mechatronic Percussion with Everyday Materials. In *Proceedings of the TEI'16: Tenth International Conference on Tangible, Embedded, and Embodied Interaction*. ACM, 340–348.
30. Seymour Papert. 1980. *Mindstorms: Children, computers, and powerful ideas*. Basic Books, Inc.
31. Noah S Podolefsky, Emily B Moore, and Katherine K Perkins. 2013. Implicit scaffolding in interactive simulations: Design strategies to support multiple educational goals. *arXiv preprint arXiv:1306.6544* (2013).
32. Mitchel Resnick. 2004. Edutainment? No thanks. I prefer playful learning. *Associazione Civita Report on Edutainment* 14 (2004), 1–4.
33. Mitchel Resnick, Robbie Berg, and Michael Eisenberg. 2000. Beyond black boxes: Bringing transparency and aesthetics back to scientific investigation. *The Journal of the Learning Sciences* 9, 1 (2000), 7–30.
34. Mitchel Resnick and Brian Silverman. 2005. Some reflections on designing construction kits for kids. In *Proceedings of the 2005 conference on Interaction design and children*. ACM, 117–122.
35. Learning Resources. 2017 (accessed January 31, 2017). http://www.learningresources.com
36. Yvonne Rogers. 2006. Moving on from Weiser's vision of calm computing: Engaging ubicomp experiences. In *International conference on Ubiquitous computing*. Springer, 404–421.
37. Robert S Siegler, Judy S DeLoache, and Nancy Eisenberg. 2003. *How children develop*. Macmillan.
38. Alison Stephenson. 2003. Physical risk-taking: dangerous or endangered? *Early Years: An International Journal of Research and Development* 23, 1 (2003), 35–43.

39. Ch A Tandy. 1999. Children's Diminishing Play Space: a Study of Inter-generational Change in Children's Use of their Neighbourhoods. *Australian geographical studies* 37, 2 (1999), 154–164.

40. Deborah Tannen. 1993. *Framing in discourse*. Oxford University Press on Demand.

41. Janneke Van de Pol, Monique Volman, and Jos Beishuizen. 2010. Scaffolding in teacher–student interaction: A decade of research. *Educational Psychology Review* 22, 3 (2010), 271–296.

42. Official Rube Goldberg Website. 2017 (accessed January 31, 2017). `https://www.rubegoldberg.com/`

43. Jeannette M Wing. 2006. Computational thinking. *Commun. ACM* 49, 3 (2006), 33–35.

44. Jeannette M Wing. 2008. Computational thinking and thinking about computing. *Philosophical transactions of the royal society of London A: mathematical, physical and engineering sciences* 366, 1881 (2008), 3717–3725.

45. David Wood, Jerome S Bruner, and Gail Ross. 1976. The role of tutoring in problem solving. *Journal of child psychology and psychiatry* 17, 2 (1976), 89–100.

46. Oren Zuckerman. 2009. Designing digital objects for learning: lessons from Froebel and Montessori. *International Journal of Arts and Technology* 3, 1 (2009), 124–135.

Using Eye-Tracking to Unveil Differences Between Kids and Teens in Coding Activities

Sofia Papavlasopoulou
Norwegian University of Science and Technology
Trondheim, Norway
spapav@ntnu.no

Kshitij Sharma
Faculty of Business and Economics,
University of Lausanne and
École Polytechnique Fédérale de Lausanne
Lausanne, Switzerland
kshitij.sharma@epfl.ch

Michail N. Giannakos
Norwegian University of Science and Technology
Trondheim, Norway
michailg@ntnu.no

Letizia Jaccheri
Norwegian University of Science and Technology
Trondheim, Norway
letizia.jaccheri@ntnu.no

ABSTRACT
Computational thinking and coding is gradually becoming an important part of K-12 education. Most parents, policy makers, teachers, and industrial stakeholders want their children to attain computational thinking and coding competences, since learning how to code is emerging as an important skill for the 21st century. Currently, educators are leveraging a variety of technological tools and programming environments, which can provide challenging and dynamic coding experiences. Despite the growing research on the design of coding experiences for children, it is still difficult to say how children of different ages learn to code, and to cite differences in their task-based behaviour. This study uses eye-tracking data from 44 children (here divided into "kids" [age 8–12] and "teens" [age 13–17]) to understand the learning process of coding in a deeper way, and the role of gaze in the learning gain and the different age groups. The results show that kids are more interested in the appearance of the characters, while teens exhibit more hypothesis-testing behaviour in relation to the code. In terms of collaboration, teens spent more time overall performing the task than did kids (higher similarity gaze). Our results suggest that eye-tracking data can successfully reveal how children of different ages learn to code.

Author Keywords
Eye-tracking; maker movement; coding; teens; kids.

ACM 978-1-4503-4921-5/17/06...$15.00
http://dx.doi.org/10.1145/3078072.3079740

ACM Classification Keywords
K.3.2 Computer Science Education; H.5.m Information interfaces and presentation (e.g., HCI): Miscellaneous

INTRODUCTION
Nowadays, students need to acquire skills and digital competences in accordance with 21st-century needs. Computational thinking, problem-solving, and coding have become an integral part of our world. Most parents want their child's school to offer coding and problem-solving competences [12], and most people believe that learning how to code is as important as reading, writing, and math [28]. In light of this growing recognition, ACM, Code.org, Computer Science Teachers Association, Cyber Innovation Center, and National Math and Science Initiative have developed conceptual guidelines for coding education. The K–12 Computer Science Framework was developed to inform the development of standards and curriculum, build capacity for teaching computer science, and implement computer science pathways (K–12 CS Framework - www.k12cs.org). Many computing platforms and various tools exist to support computational thinking and coding to provide learning experiences [5]. However, despite the apparent growing body of research in the area, there is limited evidence to support the design of appropriate learning experiences to allow children to learn how to code.

Currently, educators are leveraging a variety of technological tools and programming environments – such as Alice, Scratch, Greenfoot, and Kodu – which can set challenging and dynamic learning experiences in educational contexts. Since Papert's [31] constructionist framework was created, different practices, models, and strategies have represented new ways in which computers can be used in student-centred design learning experiences. Construction-based learning has been widely studied over the years in various pedagogical contexts, in both formal and informal education [30]. Coding constitutes a beneficial key aspect that enables students to not only enhance their problem-solving skills but also change their attitudes toward computing by creating computational artefacts with a practical, personal, or societal intent [7].

Several efforts have been made to broaden participation in coding and introduce computational literacy to children. Giannakos and Jaccheri [13] focused on how physical construction with recycled materials can help in designing creative coding activities, while Buechley et al [6] developed LilyPad Arduino to make coding an approachable and natural activity for girls. The importance of teaching coding to everyone from a young age also refers to the use of programmable objects and interactive robots in learning experiences right from kindergarten [10]. Combining physical fabrication and coding results in engagement in programming concepts and practices (e.g., testing and debugging) [7] [23]. Previous research describes various approaches to motivate and engage students with coding through making and constructing in a fun and enjoyable way [40]. Children can learn coding through various construction-based activities and utilize current powerful learning environments [37] such as Alice, Kodu, Scratch, and Scratch Junior, as well as other visual block-based coding environments that can improve children's understanding of concepts like loops and variables [27].

Despite the growing research on the design of construction-based coding experiences for children [30], it is still difficult to say what the main needs of different age groups are. We have seen systems utilizing various affordances to support different age groups (e.g., Scratch and Scratch Junior), but research on how different age groups use those tools is still in its infancy. Current research has been focusing on traditional qualitative and/or quantitative measurements, such as observations, interviews, tests, and surveys, to investigate children's engagement, experience and learning [30]. Nevertheless, further research should also focus on using other measures to better understand the way in which children of different ages learn how to code, along with their task-based behaviour, in order to provide feedback on how to design coding experiences to improve the learning process. To this end, the current study uses physiological (eye-tracking) data to understand the learning process of coding in a deeper way, along with the role of gaze in the learning gain and the different age groups.

In this paper, we provide an overview of our construction-based coding activity, and present an evaluation of the activity carried out by 44 children (here divided into "kids" [age 8–12] and "teens" [age 13–17]). During the coding activity, we recorded the gaze of the children and measured their learning gain in order to answer the following research questions:

- What are the differences between kids' and teens' gaze during coding?
- How is children's gaze associated with their learning gain during coding?

The rest of the paper is structured as follows: the next section provides an overview of the related work; the third section presents the methodology employed in this study; and the fourth session presents the empirical results. The fifth section discusses the results, the limitations of the study, and recommendations for future research.

RELATED WORK

Construction-based coding activities to support children's learning

The constructionist learning approach provides children with freedom to learn by actively engaging in creating meaningful projects. More precisely, constructionist learning is a process of exploring and reflecting with the ultimate goal of learners obtaining their own knowledge and identifying with it, instead of being passive recipients [31]. Nowadays, educational strategies incorporate elements from Papert's constructionism [31], which states that students can learn deeply during activities that require them to apply the knowledge obtained by executing tasks. This form of instruction has been described according to various concepts, such as learning by doing, learning by designing, and project-based learning, to name a few. These concepts are applied both inside and outside of the classroom [21]. In the recent special issue of *Child–Computer Interaction* on digital fabrication in education, Iversen et al. [18] pointed out the importance of design-based activities to teach digital literacy. Computer programming, mainly in relation to game programming, is considered to be another form of constructionist learning environment and promotes coding, problem-solving, critical thinking, computational thinking, and collaborative skills [30; 40].

Coding is not only a fundamental skill within computer science, but is also a demonstration of computational competences [16] – a way to support computational thinking and develop students' high-order thinking skills. Kids as young as 4–6 can build and code simple robot-based projects and learn ideas from engineering, technology, and coding, and thereby enhance their computational thinking skills [3]. Visual programming languages introduce the potential of a broader and younger group of students to learn programming concepts [40]. Nevertheless, construction-based coding activities (e.g., making, modding, hacking) can help students aged 9–10 to engage in more complex programming languages, such as Java. Various studies have proven the importance of combining coding and physical fabrication to engage students with complex programming concepts (e.g., loops, conditionals, events) and practices (e.g., remixing, testing, debugging) [7] [23] [22] found that digital storytelling in a school setting demonstrates competence in several key programming concepts, such as event-driven programming and synchronization. In their project, an early-childhood robotics curriculum, TangibleK, fostered multiple skills, including problem representation, systematic generation and implementation of solutions, debugging, and strategies to approach difficult problems. Denner et al. [7] reported results from an analysis of 108 games created by middle-school girls to show that it is feasible to learn programming concepts when designing and coding activities are seamlessly combined.

There is some variation in the ways in which students handle coding tasks and how they manage concepts and practices. For example, novices tend to approach programs in a line-by-line fashion, rather than in blocks [38], and are not persistent in debugging their programs [11]. In their study on middle-school girls, Denner et al. [7] reported that the students rarely used "variables" to handle coding processes, and faced difficulty in joining pieces of code to successfully complete an operation. Students aged 11 to 12 made their own computer games using software called Adventure [37], spending the most amount of time adding new content to their code, rather than changing what they had already done, and girls spent more time writing the dialogue for their games than did boys. The most popular practices used in projects by students of almost the same age – 11–14 – were reusing and remixing already existing code, and addressing problems in an incremental and iterative way [23]. Kids aged 5–6 either carefully thought about and tried to predict results before trying the commands, or tried out different commands to receive immediate feedback [10].

Capturing children's coding knowledge and learning

Many studies have collected the actual code created in children's projects and then analysed it using Brennan and Resnick's framework for computational thinking [24], Bloom's modified taxonomy or solo taxonomy [4], or other types of deductive coding schemes to evaluate the projects [7] and understand how children learn coding [25]. "Fairy assessment", which is based on Alice's programming environment, requires students to modify and add existing code in order to assess their understanding of algorithm abstraction and code. Other ways of capturing children's progress and understanding include multiple-choice instruments or quizzes that measure the learning of computer science concepts, or even traditional assessments such as tests and grades [8].

Capturing computational thinking skills and the way in which children learn coding is challenging, and more objective mechanisms are needed to illuminate children's understanding and knowledge gain regarding computational concepts and other computational thinking skills, such as debugging and problem decomposition [15]. Assessments utilizing coding blocks (akin to Parson's puzzles), where students have to snap them in correct order are widely used in eBooks [32]. Assessments in which snippets of basic code are used to test whether children can identify the core constructs are widely used as well [9]. Thus, the most common method to capture learning gain in computational thinking and coding is knowledge acquisition tests with combined types of questions [15].

Eye-tracking in coding

Prior research has shown that collaborative eye-tracking has been used to explain the different cognitive mechanisms of coding of adult programmers; however, to the best of our knowledge, collaborative eye-tracking has not been used in explaining children's mechanisms of coding. Existing results using eye-tracking data have examined expertise [20], collaboration quality [43], learning outcome [19], and task-based performance [29].

In the domain of coding activities, Pietinen et al. [34] provided a new metric to measure joint visual attention in a co-located pair-programming setup, using the number of overlapping fixations and the fixation duration of overlapping fixation to assess the quality of collaboration. In a study by Pietinen et al [33], a possible design for an eye-tracking setup was presented for co-located pair-programming, and some of the problems regarding setup, calibration, data collection, validity, and analysis were outlined. Bednarik and Tukiainen [2] examined coordination of different program representations in a program-understanding task. Experts have concentrated more on the source code than on looking at other representations, with the different representations being taken to be different areas of interest (AOIs). Bednarik et al. [1] related the information types posited by Good and Brna [14] to the gaze among the four AOIs (Code, Output, Control Panel, and Animation of program). The authors concluded that the presence of information type (e.g., high-level or low-level) in the comprehension summary does not necessarily confirm that that the target program has been correctly comprehended.

Romero et al. [39] compared the use of different program representation modalities (propositional and diagrammatic) in an expert novice debugging study in which experts had a balanced shift of focus among the different modalities compared to that of the novices. Sharif et al. [42] emphasized the importance of code scan time in a debugging task and concluded that experts perform better and have shorter code scan time compared to non-experts. Hejmady and Narayanan [17] compared the gaze shift between different AOIs in a debugging. The authors concluded that good debuggers were switching between code and the expression evaluation and variable window, rather than code and the control structure and data structure window.

In our study, we collected eye-tracking data to capture the gaze of children while they were accomplishing instructional tasks during our coding activity. In addition, to examine the association between learning gain and gaze, we performed a knowledge acquisition test. The study presented in this paper attempts to fill in the gap regarding use of eye-tracking data to investigate how children learn to code.

METHODOLOGY

Coding activity

We designed and implemented a coding activity in conjunction with an initiative organized at the Norwegian University of Science and Technology (NTNU), in Trondheim, Norway. The workshop activities are based on the constructionist approach, as one of the main principles of this is learning by making. The workshop was conducted in a largely informal setting, as an out-of-school activity, and lasted for four hours in total. Various student groups, ranging from 8–17 years old, were invited in NTNU's specially designed rooms for creative purposes to interact with digital robots and create games using Scratch and the Arduino hardware platform. Specifically, Arduino was attached to the digital robots to connect them with the computer. At that point, an extension of Scratch called Scratch for Arduino (S4A) provided the extra blocks needed to control the robots. Scratch programming language uses colourful blocks grouped into categories (motion, looks, sound, pen, control, sensing, operators, and variables), with which children can develop stories, games, and any type of animation. In general, children who attended the workshop worked collaboratively in triads or dyads (depending on the number of children). The workshop was designed for children without (or with minimum) previous experience in coding. During the workshop, student assistants were the responsible supporting each team as needed. Approximately one assistant observed and helped one or two teams. Three researchers were also present throughout the intervention focusing on observing, writing notes, keeping notes and taking care of the overall execution of the workshop. The workshop had two main sections.

Interacting with the robots: In the first section, the children interacted with digital robots made from an artist (using recycling materials). Each of the different robots was placed next to the computers (one for each team). When the children entered the room, one assistant welcomed them, told them to be seated and briefly presented an overview of the workshop. The assistants then advised the children to pay attention to the paper tutorial and the worksheet placed on the desks (one for each student). First, the children filled in the worksheet to answer questions regarding the exact place and the number of sensors and lights on the robots. The tutorial contained instructions with examples and pictures (Figure 1 up), similar to the robots they were using (Figure 1 down). The examples had little text and more images, and described exactly how the children could interact with the robots. The children accomplished a series of simple loops that controlled the robots and made them react to the environment with visual effects (such as turning on a light when sensors detected that the light was below a certain threshold). Children could touch and play with the robots but not change any parts of them. Although the duration of the session was different for each team, it lasted between 45 minutes and one-and-a-half hours, and ended with a break before the next session.

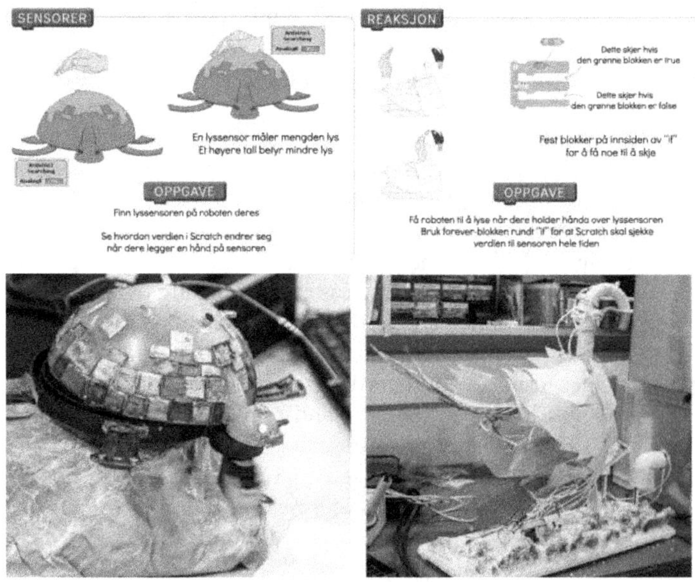

Figure 1. Examples of the tutorial materials (up) and the robots children interacted with (down)

Creating games using Scratch: This session focused on the creative implementation of simple game development concepts using Scratch. All children took another paper-based tutorial containing examples and visualizations to help them ideate their own game. The tutorial comprised simple text explanations and included basic computational thinking concepts and possible loops that the children were supposed to use in their own games (Figure 2 left). First, the assistants advised the children to concentrate on understanding the idea of the game, discuss it with their team members, and then create a draft storyboard. The children then developed their own game by collaboratively designing and coding using Scratch. To accelerate the children's progress, they were given already existing game characters and easy loops. While the children worked on their projects, help was provided whenever they asked for it and complex programming concepts were introduced on an individual level according to the relevance to their project. Children created their games step by step by iteratively coding and testing them. After completing the games, all teams reflected and played each other's games (Figure 2, right image). This section lasted approximately three hours.

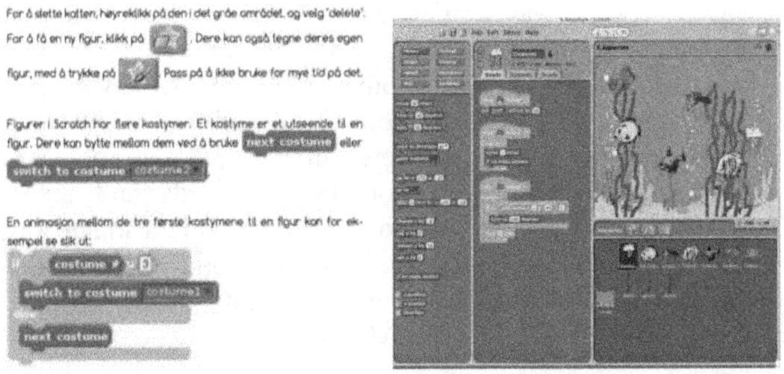

Figure 2. An example of children's paper tutorial (left), and an example of the developed game (right)

Sampling

The study was conducted in a dedicated lab space at the Norwegian University of Science and Technology (NTNU), in Trondheim, Norway. Through a two-week period during Autumn 2016, 44 children from 8th to 12th grade (age 8–17 years old) participated in our coding activity. The sample comprised 12 girls (mean age: 12.64, S.D.: 2.838) and 32 boys (mean age: 12.35, S.D.: 2.773). Five workshops took place over two weeks, following the coding activity described in the previous section. Our activities were organized for kids (8–12 years old) and teens (13–17 years old); the teens were children from local schools whose teachers/schools applied to attend our coding activity, while the kids were recruited from local coding clubs, which are after-school groups in which youngsters can interact and learn how to code. All of the participants were coding novices. When the participants were selected, a researcher contacted their teachers and parents in order to obtain the necessary consent from both the child and the legal guardian for the data collection.

Measures

As noted above, we divided our sample into kids (8-12 years) and teens (13-17 years). The main reason for this categorization is that after the age of 12, children's ability with respect to complex thought improves, and they develop a stronger sense of right and wrong (www.cdc.gov/ncbddd/childdevelopment/facts.html).

The children completed pre- and post-knowledge acquisition tests. These consisted of nine coding questions of increasing difficulty. The questions were adopted from previous study [15] and followed instructors' suggestions. The children took approximately 10 minutes to finish the tests. The tests were paper-based and were manually graded by the researcher. Figure 3 shows two sample questions from the test.

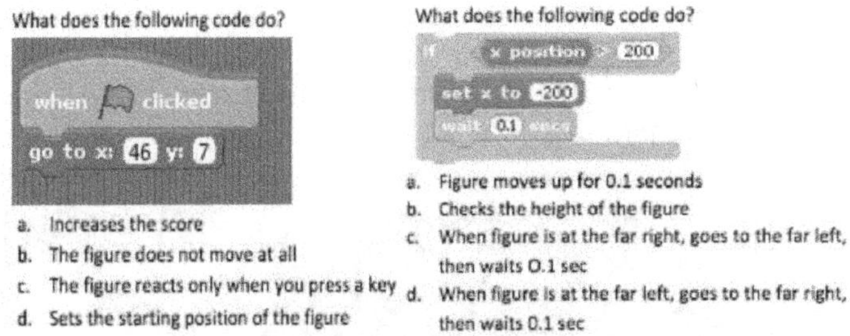

Figure 3. Sample questions used in our post-test

In our study, we calculated the relative learning gain (RLG) as defined from Sangin [41] (see the type below). RLG is more accurate compared to learning gain, since it takes into consideration the difficulty in gaining more knowledge if the learner is already very knowledgeable in a subject. In this work, RLG is considered as the dependent variable.

$$RLG = \begin{cases} \dfrac{Posttest - Pretest}{Max.\,in\,pretest - Pretest}, if\ Posttest \geq Pretest \\ \dfrac{Posttest - Pretest}{Pretest}, if\ Posttest < Pretest \end{cases}$$

During the coding activity, the children worked in triads (or, in some exceptions, in dyads) and wore eye-tracking glasses. Four SMI RED 250 and one TOBII mobile eye-tracker working at 60Hz were used. A sampling rate of 60hz is considered sufficient for usability studies [35]. For this research, we selected the following gaze measures:

Time spent on each AOI: We divided the whole visual field into six AOIs – five on the screen and the sixth as the robot. We used specifically made QR codes to scan the robots and the area around them (Figure 4).

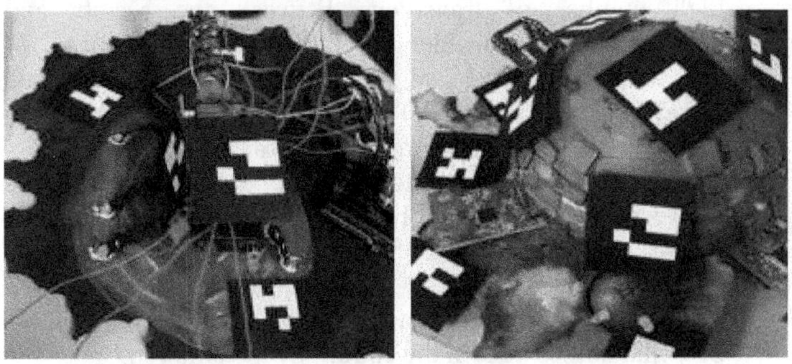

Figure 4: Examples of the robots with the QR codes

The five AOIs on the screen were as follows (see Figure 5):

1. **Tools**: This area of the screen contains a general categorization of the commands available. For example, controlling the motion, looks, sound, and other variables.
2. **Command**: This area contains all available commands within the currently selected tools.
3. **Scripts**: This is the area of the screen in which the coding task is performed.
4. **Output**: This area shows participants the output of their scripts.

5. **Sprites**: This area controls the aesthetic of the program. The participants can change the appearance of the animated character using the characters available in this part of the interface.

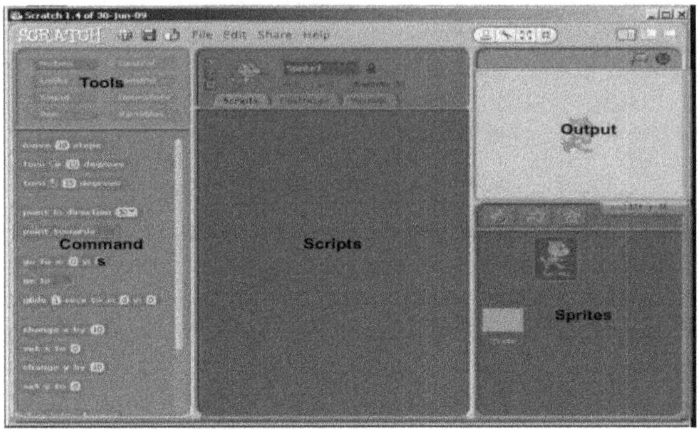

Figure 5. The five AOIs of the Scratch interface

Transitions among AOIs: We also computed the transitions to and from one AOI to another. This helped us to understand the temporal relationship between the children's gaze patterns, and depict the coding process used by the participants. For example, frequent transitions between scripts and output, or script and robot, depict the typical behaviour of hypothesis verification. The participants made a small change in the program based on a certain hypothesis about the output or robot's movement; once they had observed the output/robot's behaviour, either their hypothesis was confirmed and they moved on to the next step in coding, or they modified the program to re-verify their hypothesis. This behaviour would result in a high number of transitions between the scripts and output/robot. We consider only three types of transitions for this analysis based on the literature. Hejmady and Narayanan [17] showed that experts shift their attention more, between the code and the output, than novices do. This is why we chose to compare the gaze transitions between the script and robot/output. The third type of transition we include in our analysis is the transitions between the commands and the script areas. These transitions imply a behaviour that shows a thinking process of "what comes next in the code?" by the children.

Gaze similarity: We computed the gaze similarity as the proportion of time all participants were looking at the same AOI within a time window of 4 seconds. For dyads, this measure is equivalent to the cross-recurrence proposed by Dale et al [36]. For triads, we extend the concept of cross-recurrence (originally defined for two temporal scales) to three-dimensional cross-recurrence.

Data Analysis

To answer our research question in regards to differences between kids and teens, we split the sample using the age of 12 as a threshold. First, we conducted a one-way analysis of variance (ANOVA) to test any potential differences between the children's age and their RLG. Second, a one-way ANOVA was conducted to examine any potential difference in the time spent in the various AOI between kids and teens. Third, another one-way ANOVA was conducted to examine any potential difference in the three AOI transitions (i.e., scripts and output; scripts and commands; script and robot) between kids and teens. Finally, we conducted one more ANOVA to investigate any potential difference between teens' and kids' gaze similarity. We did not assume the equality of the variance across groups for any of the ANOVAs.

In the second group of tests, we wanted to identify any potential correlation between the children's gaze and their learning gain. That is, we wanted to investigate, first, any potential correlation between gaze similarity and RLG; second, any potential correlation between the six AOIs and the RLG; and last, any potential correlation between the three AOI transitions and RLG. Pearson correlation was used for all three of these tests.

RESEARCH FINDINGS

A one-way ANOVA was conducted to compare the kids' RLG (M_1=0.00, SD_1=0.43) and teens' RLG (M_2=0.35, SD_2=0.56). The results showed a statistically significant difference (F[1, 36.13]=4.07, p=.05). This means that teens outperformed kids.

To examine the difference in the time spent in the six AOIs between kids and teens, we conducted a one-way ANOVA with children's age as the independent variable (kids or teens) and the six AOIs as dependent variables (commands, output, robot, scripts, sprites, tools). As can be seen from the outcome data in Table 1, the teens spent more time on scripts, output, and commands compared to the kids, while the kids spent more time on sprites than did the teens. There was no significant difference in the time spent on tools and the robot.

AOIs	Kids Mean (SD)	Teens Mean (SD)	Sig.
Commands	0.13 (0.04)	0.17 (0.06)	**4.20***
Output	0.14 (0.06)	0.18 (0.06)	**4.10***
Robot	0.18 (0.06)	0.17 (0.08)	0.27
Scripts	0.16 (0.06)	0.20 (0.06)	**5.00***
Sprites	0.22 (0.08)	0.13 (0.05)	**14.22*****
Tools	0.16 (0.06)	0.15 (0.08)	0.02

Significance Level, ***p< .001;**p< .01; *p< .05

Table 1. Differences in the proportions of time spent in AOIs between kids and teens using (ANOVA).

From Figure 6, it can be observed that the kids spent most of their time in the sprites area of screen, while the teens focused on scripts. It is also interesting that the teens spent the least amount of time in the sprites area, while the kids focused on the commands area. In general, Figure 6 suggests that when kids become teens their attention will move from the sprites area to other areas more relevant to text-based coding, such as scripts, output, and commands.

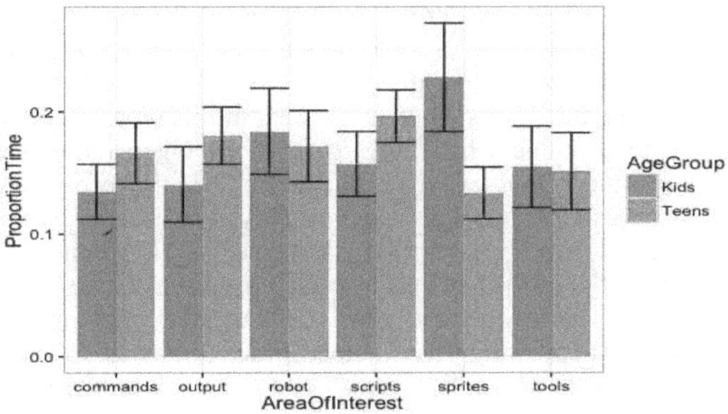

Figure 6. Proportion of time children and teens spent in each of the six AOIs

Transitions from one AOI to another help us to understand the temporal relationship between the gaze patterns of the children. For example, a transition from command to scripts or scripts to command might reflect the thinking process of the student while he or she is trying to figure out how to extend the instruction list in the program or which command to use so that the scripts becomes executable. Moreover, a back-and-forth transition between scripts and output or scripts and robot might reflect the debugging behaviour of the children. In order to examine the difference in the time spent in the three transitions from one AOI to another between children and teens, we conducted a one-way ANOVA with children's age as the independent variable (kids or teens) and the three transitions as the dependent variables (scripts.output, scripts.command, and scripts.robot). As can be seen from the outcome data in Table 2, as well as from Figure 7, the teens had higher proportions of transitions to and from scripts and output, scripts and commands, and scripts and robot compared to the kids.

Transitions	Kids Mean (SD)	Teens Mean (SD)	Sig.
scripts.command	0.09 (0.06)	0.14 (0.07)	**5.85****
scripts.output	0.07 (0.05)	0.12 (0.06)	**6.51****
scripts.robot	0.09 (0.06)	0.15 (0.08)	**6.15****

Significance Level, ***p< .001; **p< .01; *p< .05

Table 2. Differences in the proportions of transitions between AOIs between kids and teens using (ANOVA)

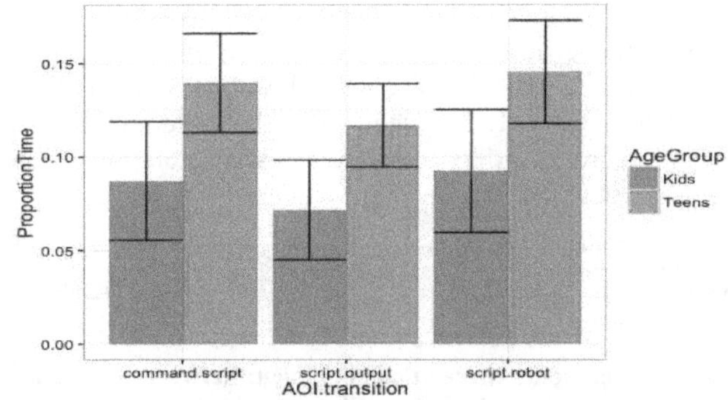

Figure 7. Proportions of time kids and teens spent in the three transitions from one AOI to another

A one-way ANOVA was conducted to compared the kids' gaze similarity (M_1=0.006, SD_1=0.003) and the teens' gaze similarity (M_2=0.026, SD_2=0.02). The results showed a statistically significant difference ($F[1,11.23]=9.90$, $p=.009$). This means that teens have more gaze similarity compared to kids. Regarding the association between gaze similarity and RLG, by applying Pearson's correlation we observed a positive and significant correlation between the gaze similarity and the average RLG for the groups ($r(14)=0.72$, $p=.001$). Thus, the groups with high gaze similarity also had a high average RLG (see also Figure 8).

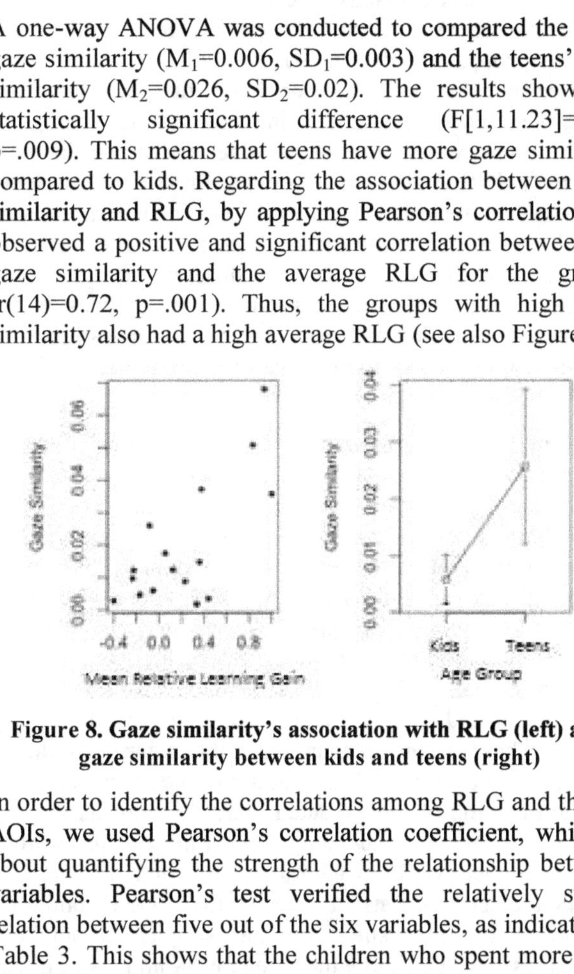

Figure 8. Gaze similarity's association with RLG (left) and gaze similarity between kids and teens (right)

In order to identify the correlations among RLG and the six AOIs, we used Pearson's correlation coefficient, which is about quantifying the strength of the relationship between variables. Pearson's test verified the relatively strong relation between five out of the six variables, as indicated in Table 3. This shows that the children who spent more time on scripts, output, and commands had high RLG. On the other hand, children who spent more time on sprites and tools attained a low RLG.

Scripts	Output	Robot	Sprite	Tools	Commands
0.43**	0.30*	-0.18	-0.35*	-0.31*	0.35*

Significance level: ***p< .001;**p< .01; *p< .05

Table 3. Pearson's correlation coefficient between RLG and the different AOIs (N=44)

In order to identify the correlations between RLG and the three transitions (i.e. scripts and output, scripts and commands, scripts and robot), we again used Pearson's correlation coefficient. Pearson's test verified the relatively strong relation in all the three variables of the transitions, as indicated in Table 4. This shows that the children who had many more scripts.command, scripts.output, and scripts.robot transitions had high RLG.

	scripts.command	scripts.output	scripts.robot
RLG	0.38**	0.37**	0.39**

Significance level: ***p< .001;**p< .01; *p< .05

Table 4. Pearson's correlation coefficient between RLG and the three transitions (N=44)

DISCUSSION AND CONCLUSIONS

In this section, we discuss the results from our study in which children (8–17 years old) performed certain coding tasks in groups (dyads and triads) while their gaze was recorded and their RLG measured. For the purpose of this study, we divided the sample into kids (8–12 years) and teens (13–17 years) to analyse the difference in gaze patterns and RLG across age groups. In general, the teens outperformed the kids in terms of RLG. The key motivation behind our contribution was to establish the relations between gaze, different RLGs, and different age groups. In this study, we established certain key differences in the gaze patterns of kids and teens in order to investigate the reasons why/effects of the fact that teens outperformed kids in the RLG from the coding tasks.

First, one interesting feature of the results is that the teens spent more time looking at the scripts, output, and command AOIs, while kids spent more time on the sprites AOIs. The sprites control the aesthetic part of the problem at hand. For example, what the main animated character or the different costumes look like. Spending more time on the appearance of the output proved to be detrimental to the kids' RLG. On the other hand, the scripts, output, and commands control the actual functionality of the coding environment and the main areas of attention in the coding process. These are the areas in which the coder must choose the appropriate command, then add it to the scripts area and see the outcome of the executed code. Our results showed that teens, who were spending more time on these areas, attained higher RLG. In addition, we found positive and significant correlations between the RLG and the proportion of time spent on the scripts, output, and commands AOIs and the negative and significant correlation between the RLG and the proportion of time spent on the sprites. In a study by Lee et al. [26], all participants aged 10–12 spent significant time on aesthetics; however, the authors identified differences in the time spent on aesthetics in terms of gender. Girls spent more time on aesthetics and also tried harder to balance technical functionality.

Second, the teens had a higher number of transitions among scripts and output/command/robot, compared to the kids. The higher number of transitions between scripts and outputs indicates behaviour that is either caused by a debugging activity or a desire to verify a hypothesis. In addition, a higher number of transitions between script and robot shows similar behaviour. For example, moving back and forth between script and output might result from frequent changes in the code and a need to check the output. Thus, if the output matches the student's hypothesis, after, executing the desired code the student moves on to the next step to continue with a new task. If the output does not match the hypothesis, he or she refines the code and rechecks the output. This is a typical hypothesis verification cycle. Such a cycle is often associated with the novice coding style [44]. Novices who tend to use this style often perform better. Since the teens used this style in coding, it might explain why they outperformed the kids. Young students who are novices usually do not try to debug their code, and thus face the difficult task of solving a poorly executed block of code, or successfully joining pieces of code [7]. The finding of a positive correlation between the RLG and the number of transitions between script and output supports this explanation as well. Moreover, the higher number of transitions between script and command areas shows the process of choosing the appropriate command to follow the current script. The teens spent more time finding the correct command, and trying different ones, than did the kids. Thus, the teens learned more compared to the kids; again, a significant and positive correlation between the RLG and the number of transitions between the script and command AOIs support our explanation. A study involving kids as young as 5–6 showed that it is possible for kids to plan their actions and think two or three commands ahead; those who do so concentrate hard on the screen, do not pay much attention on other's comments, and have more confidence in their actions and knowledge [10].

Finally, we found a relation between the gaze and age groups, since the teens had higher gaze similarity than the kids did. One plausible explanation for this could be that the groups with high gaze similarity were able to reflect together on their progress and deal with the coding tasks by making decisions together. This might have helped them to create a shared understanding of the problem at hand. Having a higher level of shared understanding helped them to attain a higher average RLG [43]. This can also be verified based on observations, and assistants' comments during the activity that the teen teams helped each other more, while the children quarrelled more about who would take the lead role in coding. On the other hand, the groups with low levels of gaze similarity mostly focused on the different parts of the program within the given time frame, and this might have had a detrimental impact on their level of shared understanding, and in turn, their average RLG. The significantly positive correlation between the gaze similarity and the groups' average RLG further strengthens this explanation. This result is in line with several other studies showing high levels of cross-recurrence or gaze similarity being correlated with task-based performance [19] and/or learning gains.

Implications

Scholars, educators, and practitioners should take into consideration the existence of differences between kids' and teens' gaze during coding activities, and realize the impact this has on students' learning. Our findings in this regard highlight the importance of developing age-appropriate learning instructions. For example, the kids focused more on aesthetics and had lower gaze similarity and learning gain, so instructors should ensure that children in the young age bracket of 8–12 receive guidelines on where to pay attention when they code (such as commands and output). The learning environment should support collaboration within teams and good communication, so that all members get the advantage of each other's help.

Limitations

The present study is one of the first to use eye-tracking data to examine the relation between gaze, and children's means of accomplishing coding tasks and their learning gain. However, our study entails several limitations. One of the main challenges the study encountered pertained to the fact that it was difficult to capture the kid's gaze because of their constant head movements during the activity and the fact that the eye-tracking glasses were not really appropriate for kids (8–12), since they were not the perfect size for their faces and caused irritation, meaning that the kids had to take them off frequently. In addition, the collaborative concept of the workshop allowed the children to speak to each other to share their experience and express their enthusiasm, which made difficult to collect high-quality data. We were only able to use 75% of the data in total. Furthermore, the workshops varied in duration because of time constraints related to whether the children had been recruited form schools or local coding clubs. In all workshops, the activities were successfully completed by the children. Moreover, the participants were randomly selected from our region so other sampling methods could have been applied to ensure a more consistent sample was obtained in terms of the children's prior knowledge of coding. Finally, this study lacked structured qualitative data (e.g., observations and interviews), which would be a fruitful opportunity for further research.

Future Research

This study opens up interesting perspectives for future research by introducing the idea of collecting eye-tracking data from coding activities involving children. An opportunity would be to use that type of data to explore gender differences and attitudes within coding activities. Furthermore, since our study showed differences between teens' and kids' coding methods, it could be useful to focus on a specific age group and examine their particular gaze behaviour. Future studies could compare the role of gaze in alternative learning environments, as well as obtaining deeper insights from longitudinal collection of eye-tracking data.

Conclusions

In this paper, we used eye-tracking data to analyse children's learning process in coding and discover any differences in their task-based behaviour according to their age. We implemented a coding activity with 44 children aged 8–17. After collecting their gaze using mobile eye trackers, we measured their learning gain through pre- and post-tests. The teens (13–17 years old) had higher RLG compared to the kids, and tackled coding in a different way. The kids focused more on the appearance of the characters, while teens followed more structured behaviour comprising basic programming practices such as debugging and testing. In addition, the gazes showed that the teen teams collaborated better during the activity, a fact that might have led to their higher learning gain. The paper introduces new means and measures by which to understand how children learn coding.

ACKNOWLEDGMENTS

The authors would like to express their gratitude to all of the children, teachers and parents for volunteering their time. Our very special thanks go to Kristin Susanne Karlsen, Ioannis Leftheriotis, Amanda Jørgine Haug, Lidia Luque Fernandez, Marjeris Sofia Romero, Eline Stenwig, Kristoffer Venæs Monsen. The project has been recommended by the Data Protection Official for Research, Norwegian Social Science Data Services (NSD), following all the regulations and recommendations for research with children.

This work was funded by the Norwegian Research Council under the projects FUTURE LEARNING (number: 255129/H20) and the Centre for Excellent IT Education (ExcITEd -http://www.ntnu.edu/excited)

REFERENCES

1. Roman Bednarik, Niko Myller, Erkki Sutinen, and Markku Tukiainen. 2006. Program visualization: Comparing eye-tracking patterns with comprehension summaries and performance. In *Proceedings of the 18th Annual Psychology of Programming Workshop*, 66-82.
2. Roman Bednarik and Markku Tukiainen, 2006. An eye-tracking methodology for characterizing program comprehension processes. In *Proceedings of the 2006 symposium on Eye tracking research & applications* (ETRA'06), 125-132. http://dx.doi.org/10.1145/1117309.1117356
3. MU Bers. 2008. Blocks, robots and computers: Learning about technology in early childhood. *Teacher's College Press, NY, NY.*
4. John B Biggs and Kevin F Collis. 2014. *Evaluating the quality of learning: The SOLO taxonomy (Structure of the Observed Learning Outcome)*. Academic Press.
5. Paulo Blikstein. 2013. Gears of our childhood: constructionist toolkits, robotics, and physical computing, past and future. In *Proceedings of the 12th*

international conference on interaction design and children (IDC'13), 173-182. http://dx.doi.org/10.1145/2485760.2485786

6. Leah Buechley, Mike Eisenberg, Jaime Catchen, and Ali Crockett. 2008. The LilyPad Arduino: using computational textiles to investigate engagement, aesthetics, and diversity in computer science education. In *Proceedings of the SIGCHI conference on Human factors in computing systems* (CHI'08), 423-432. http://dx.doi.org/10.1145/1357054.1357123
7. Jill Denner, Linda Werner, and Eloy Ortiz. 2012. Computer games created by middle school girls: Can they be used to measure understanding of computer science concepts? *Computers & Education 58*, 1: 240-249. http://dx.doi.org/10.1016/j.compedu.2011.08.006
8. Katelyn Doran, Acey Boyce, Samantha Finkelstein, and Tiffany Barnes. 2012. Outreach for improved student performance: a game design and development curriculum. In *Proceedings of the 17th ACM annual conference on Innovation and technology in computer science education* (ITiCSE '12), 209-214. http://dx.doi.org/10.1145/2325296.2325348
9. Barbara Ericson and Tom McKlin. 2012. Effective and sustainable computing summer camps. In *Proceedings of the 43rd ACM technical symposium on Computer Science Education* (SIGSCE'12), 289-294. http://dx.doi.org/10.1145/2157136.2157223
10. Georgios Fessakis, Evangelia Gouli, and E Mavroudi. 2013. Problem solving by 5–6 years old kindergarten children in a computer programming environment: A case study. *Computers & Education 63*: 87-97. http://dx.doi.org/10.1016/j.compedu.2012.11.016
11. Ann E Fleury. 1993. Student beliefs about Pascal programming. *Journal of Educational Computing Research 9*, 3: 355-371. http://dx.doi.org/10.2190/VECR-P8T6-GB10-MXJ5
12. Google and Gallup. 2015. Searching for computer science: Access and barriers in U.S. K–12 education.
13. Michail N Giannakos and Letizia Jaccheri. 2013. What motivates children to become creators of digital enriched artifacts? In *Proceedings of the 9th ACM Conference on Creativity & Cognition* (C&C'13), 104-113. http://dx.doi.org/10.1145/2466627.2466634
14. Judith Good and Paul Brna. 2004. Program comprehension and authentic measurement:: a scheme for analysing descriptions of programs. *International Journal of Human-Computer Studies 61*, 2: 169-185. http://dx.doi.org/10.1016/j.ijhcs.2003.12.010
15. Shuchi Grover, Stephen Cooper, and Roy Pea. 2014. Assessing computational learning in K-12. In *Proceedings of the 2014 conference on Innovation & technology in computer science education* (ITiCSE'14), 57-62. http://dx.doi.org/10.1145/2591708.2591713
16. Shuchi Grover and Roy Pea. 2013. Computational Thinking in K–12 A Review of the State of the Field. *Educational Researcher 42*, 1: 38-43. http://dx.doi.org/10.3102/0013189X12463051
17. Prateek Hejmady and N Hari Narayanan. 2012. Visual attention patterns during program debugging with an IDE. In *Proceedings of the Symposium on Eye Tracking Research and Applications* (ETRA'12), 197-200. http://dx.doi.org/10.1145/2168556.2168592
18. Ole Sejer Iversen, Rachel Charlotte Smith, Paulo Blikstein, Eva-Sophie Katterfeldt, and Janet C Read. 2016. Digital fabrication in education: Expanding the research towards design and reflective practices. *International Journal of Child-Computer Interaction 5*: 1-2. http://dx.doi.org/10.1016/j.ijcci.2016.01.001
19. Patrick Jermann and Marc-Antoine Nüssli. 2012. Effects of sharing text selections on gaze cross-recurrence and interaction quality in a pair programming task. In *Proceedings of the ACM 2012 conference on Computer Supported Cooperative Work (CSCW'12)*, 1125-1134. http://dx.doi.org/10.1145/2145204.2145371
20. Patrick Jermann, Marc-Antoine Nüssli, and Weifeng Li, 2010. Using dual eye-tracking to unveil coordination and expertise in collaborative Tetris. In *Proceedings of the 24th BCS Interaction Specialist Group Conference* British Computer Society, (BCS'10), 36-44.
21. Larry Johnson, Samantha Adams Becker, Victoria Estrada, and Alex Freeman. 2015. *The NMC Horizon Report: 2015 Museum Edition*. ERIC.
22. Yasmin B Kafai and Quinn Burke. 2015. Constructionist gaming: Understanding the benefits of making games for learning. *Educational psychologist 50*, 4: 313-334. http://dx.doi.org/10.1080/00461520.2015.1124022
23. Yasmin B Kafai and Veena Vasudevan. 2015. Constructionist gaming beyond the screen: Middle school students' crafting and computing of touchpads, board games, and controllers. In *Proceedings of the Workshop in Primary and Secondary Computing Education* (WiPSCE'15), 49-54. http://dx.doi.org/10.1145/2818314.2818334
24. Mitchel Resnick Karen Brennan. 2012. New frameworks for studying society computer science exemplification project. *Paper presented at AERA.*
25. Lieve Laporte and Bieke Zaman. 2016. Informing Content-driven Design of Computer Programming Games: a Problems Analysis and a Game Review. In

Proceedings of the 9th Nordic Conference on Human-Computer Interaction (NordiCHI'16), 61. http://dx.doi.org/10.1145/2971485.2971499

26. Eunkyoung Lee, Yasmin B Kafai, Veena Vasudevan, and Richard Lee Davis. 2014. Playing in the arcade: Designing tangible interfaces with MaKey MaKey for Scratch games. In *Playful User Interfaces* Springer, 277-292. http://dx.doi.org/10.1007/978-981-4560-96-2_13
27. John H Maloney, Kylie Peppler, Yasmin Kafai, Mitchel Resnick, and Natalie Rusk. 2008. *Programming by choice: urban youth learning programming with scratch.* In *Proceedings of the 39th SIGCSE technical symposium on Computer science education* (SIGSCE'08), 367-371. http://dx.doi.org/10.1145/1352135.1352260
28. Horizon Media. 2015. Horizon Media study reveals Americans prioritize STEM subjects over the arts; science is "cool," coding is new literacy. PR Newswire.
29. Marc-Antoine Nüssli, Patrick Jermann, Mirweis Sangin, and Pierre Dillenbourg. 2009. Collaboration and abstract representations: towards predictive models based on raw speech and eye-tracking data. In *Proceedings of the 9th international conference on Computer supported collaborative learning-Volume 1* International Society of the Learning Sciences, (CSCL'09), 78-82.
30. Sofia Papavlasopoulou, Michail N Giannakos, and Letizia Jaccheri. 2017. Empirical studies on the Maker Movement, a promising approach to learning: A literature review. *Entertainment Computing* 18: 57-78. http://dx.doi.org/10.1016/j.entcom.2016.09.002
31. Seymour Papert. 1980. *Mindstorms: Children, computers, and powerful ideas*. Basic Books, Inc.
32. Dale Parsons and Patricia Haden. 2006. Parson's programming puzzles: a fun and effective learning tool for first programming courses. In *Proceedings of the 8th Australasian Conference on Computing Education-Volume 52* (ACE'06), 157-163.
33. Sami Pietinen, Roman Bednarik, Tatiana Glotova, Vesa Tenhunen, and Markku Tukiainen. 2008. A method to study visual attention aspects of collaboration: eye-tracking pair programmers simultaneously. In *Proceedings of the 2008 symposium on Eye tracking research & applications* (ETRA'08), 39-42. http://dx.doi.org/10.1145/1344471.1344480
34. Sami Pietinen, Roman Bednarik, and Markku Tukiainen. 2010. Shared visual attention in collaborative programming: a descriptive analysis. In *proceedings of the 2010 ICSE workshop on cooperative and human aspects of software engineering* (CHASE'10), 21-24. http://dx.doi.org/10.1145/1833310.1833314
35. Alex Poole and Linden J Ball. 2006. Eye tracking in HCI and usability research. *Encyclopedia of human computer interaction 1*, 211-219.
36. Daniel C Richardson, Rick Dale, and Natasha Z Kirkham. 2007. The art of conversation is coordination common ground and the coupling of eye movements during dialogue. *Psychological science 18*, 5: 407-413. http://dx.doi.org/10.1111/j.1467-9280.2007.01914.x
37. Judy Robertson. 2012. Making games in the classroom: Benefits and gender concerns. *Computers & Education 59*, 2: 385-398. http://dx.doi.org/10.1016/j.compedu.2011.12.020
38. Anthony Robins, Janet Rountree, and Nathan Rountree. 2003. Learning and teaching programming: A review and discussion. *Computer science education 13*, 2: 137-172. http://dx.doi.org/10.1076/csed.13.2.137.14200
39. Pablo Romero, Rudi Lutz, Richard Cox, and Benedict du Boulay. 2002. Co-ordination of multiple external representations during Java program debugging. In *Human Centric Computing Languages and Environments, 2002. Proceedings. IEEE 2002 Symposia on* IEEE, 207-214. http://dx.doi.org/10.1109/HCC.2002.1046373
40. José-Manuel Sáez-López, Marcos Román-González, and Esteban Vázquez-Cano. 2016. Visual programming languages integrated across the curriculum in elementary school: A two year case study using "Scratch" in five schools. *Computers & Education 97*: 129-141. http://dx.doi.org/10.1016/j.compedu.2016.03.003
41. Mirweis Sangin, 2009. Peer knowledge modeling in computer supported collaborative learning École Polytechnique Fédérale de Lausanne.
42. Bonita Sharif, Michael Falcone, and Jonathan I Maletic, 2012. An eye-tracking study on the role of scan time in finding source code defects. In *Proceedings of the Symposium on Eye Tracking Research and Applications* (ETRA'12), 381-384. http://dx.doi.org/10.1145/2168556.2168642
43. Kshitij Sharma, Daniela Caballero, Himanshu Verma, Patrick Jermann, and Pierre Dillenbourg, 2015. Looking AT versus looking THROUGH: A dual eye-tracking study in MOOC context. In *Exploring the material conditions of learning: opportunities and challenges for CSCL, " the Proceedings of the Computer Supported Collaborative Learning Conference*, (CSCL'15), 260-267.
44. Elliot Soloway and Kate Ehrlich, 1984. Empirical studies of programming knowledge. *IEEE Transactions on software engineering*, 10, 5: 595-609. http://dx.doi.org/10.1109/TSE.1984.5010283

Between a Block and a Typeface: Designing and Evaluating Hybrid Programming Environments

David Weintrop
UChicago STEM Education
University of Chicago
dweintrop@uchicago.edu

Uri Wilensky
Center for Connected Learning and
Computer-based Modeling
Northwestern University
uri@northwestern.edu

ABSTRACT
The last ten years have seen a proliferation of introductory programming environments designed for learners across the K-12 spectrum. These environments include visual block-based tools, text-based languages designed for novices, and, increasingly, hybrid environments that blend features of block-based and text-based programming. This paper presents results from a quasi-experimental study investigating the affordances of a hybrid block/text programming environment relative to comparable block-based and textual versions in an introductory high school computer science class. The analysis reveals the hybrid environment demonstrates characteristics of both ancestors while outperforming the block-based and text-based versions in certain dimensions. This paper contributes to our understanding of the design of introductory programming environments and the design challenge of creating and evaluating novel representations for learning.

Author Keywords
Block-based programming; K-12 Education; Programming Environments; Design

ACM Classification Keywords
D.1.7 Visual Programming; D.2.2 Design Tools and Techniques; K.3.2 Computer Science Education

INTRODCUTION
The last ten years has seen a proliferation of introductory programming environments. Led by the popularity of tools like Scratch and Alice, visual block-based programming is increasingly becoming the modality of choice for programming environments designed for novices of all ages. A recent review of coding environments for children included 19 drag-and-drop tools among the 24 environments reviewed for learners under the age of eight, and 28 drag-and-drop environments out of the 47 total reviewed environments [10]. Further, we expect this trend to continue as a growing number of libraries are making it easy to develop environments that incorporate a block-based programming interface [12]. This growth in popularity can be seen both in informal environments as well as in classrooms where a growing number of curricula, like Exploring Computer Science [29] and the Beauty and Joy of Computing [13] utilize block-based programming.

Until recently, block-based and text-based programming environments have been distinct. An environment used either one modality or the other. As a result, learners trying to migrate from a block-based environment to a more conventional text-based programming language had few environmental supports to facilitate the transition. Multiple approaches have been developed to mitigate this transition cost. One approach is pedagogical, relying on teachers to assist learners in moving between modalities. An alternative approach sees this challenge as a design question, asking: how can we design programming environments to scaffold learners in moving from block-based to text-based programming? Two strategies have been employed in response to the design solution to this challenge: dual modality environment that support both block-based and text-based programming and hybrid block/text environments that try and blend features of both modality to create a best-of-both world tool. This paper explores one implementation of a hybrid block/text programming environment and answers the following research question:

How does a hybrid block/text programming environment perform compared to isomorphic block-based and text-based environments with respect to the conceptual learning of programming concepts and learners' attitudes and perceptions of the field of computer science?

To answer this question, we conducted a 15 week, quasi-experimental study in which high school students in an introductory computer science classroom used either a block-based, text-based, or hybrid block/text programming environment. Data were collected to understand how these three programming modalities impacted learners' experiences. This paper presents the results of this study, specifically focusing on how students in the hybrid condition performed relative to peers in the block-based and text-based environments.

IDC '17, June 27-30, 2017, Stanford, CA, USA

ACM 978-1-4503-4921-5/17/06…$15.00
http://dx.doi.org/10.1145/3078072.3079715

This paper begins with a review of prior work, specifically looking at empirical and design work related to block-based programming environments. Next, we introduce Pencil.cc, the multi-modality programming environment created to study the stated research question. A methods section follows, which details the study design and provides information on the setting and participants. Findings from the study are then presented, including results on outcomes of attitudinal surveys and content assessments. The paper concludes with a discussion section that presents implications of this work.

PRIOR WORK

Block-based programming

Block-based programming (Figure 1) is a programming modality that is becoming increasingly widespread in introductory computing contexts. We use the term modality to capture the representational infrastructure used to depict the program, as well as the various forms of interactions supported by the representation and its presentation. Block-based programming environments leverage a programming-primitive-as-puzzle-piece metaphor that provides visual cues to the user about how and where commands can be used. Composing programs in these environments takes the form of dragging blocks into a canvas and snapping them together to form scripts. If two blocks cannot be joined to form a valid syntactic statement, the environment prevents them from snapping together, thus preventing syntax errors but retaining the practice of assembling programs instruction-by-instruction. Along with using block shape to denote usage, there are other visual cues to help programmers, including color coding by conceptual use and nesting of blocks to denote scope [20,32]. Early versions of this interlocking blocks approach include LogoBlocks [4] and BridgeTalk [5] which helped formulate the programming approach which has since grown to be used in dozens of applications across a variety of domains [10]. The growing ecosystem of block-based tools speaks to the need for more critical research around the affordances and drawbacks of the modality [30,38].

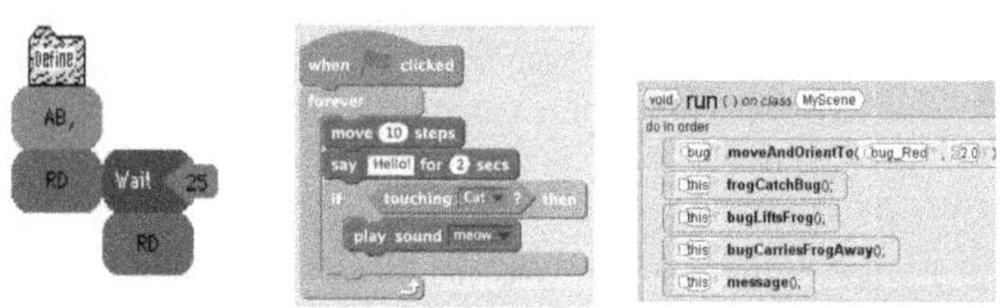

(A) LogoBlocks (B) Scratch (C) Alice

Figure 1. Three examples of block-based programming tools.

Bridging Block-based to Text-based Programming

With the rise in popularity of the block-based approach to programming, a question of growing importance is how well these tools prepare students for future, text-based programming languages. An emerging body of scholarship is exploring the question of transfer of programming knowledge between block-based and text-based programming. For example, as Alice is often used in undergraduate computer science classrooms, the transition from Alice to Java is an active area of research showing mixed results. A number of studies have reported student difficulties in making the transition [7,14,26], with one study stating: "Students do not seem to naturally make a strong connection between the formal coding process and what they are doing with Alice" [25:213]. In contrast, other researchers have found Alice to be an effective way to introduce learners to programming and have had success transition learners to Java [8,9].

A few studies have been conducted looking at the transition from Scratch to other text-based programming languages. While many of these report only anecdotal evidence, Armoni, Merrbaum-Salant & Ben-Ari [1] conducted a longitudinal study looking at whether students who had taken Scratch programming classes in middle school performed better in a high school, text-based programming course. Overall, the researchers found little quantitative difference in performance on assessments between students who had previous worked with Scratch and those who had not, but were able to find some areas where the Scratch students out-performed their peers (specifically on the concept of looping). Additionally, the authors found qualitative differences between the two populations, with students who had prior Scratch experience reporting higher levels of motivation and self-efficacy. A quasi-experimental study investigating students transition from block-based languages to Java found block-based programming, without pedagogical support, provided relatively little benefit for novices in the transition to a text-based language [33].

Scaffolding the Block-to-Text Transition

Block-to-Text Transformations

A growing number of tools are being designed to address the block-to-text gap, either as new stand-alone tools or add-ons to existing tools. One direction programming designers have pursued is giving users the ability to convert block-based programs into equivalent text-based scripts. This includes environments like PicoBlocks, TurtleArt, and the App Inventor Java Bridge [40]. Other tools provide native language translation, for example, the Blockly toolkit comes with built-in language generators that allow you to convert graphical scripts to equivalent JavaScript, Python, or XML files [12]. Additionally, Blockly is architected in such a way as to make it easy to add additional generators to the library making it extensible for future block-to-text transformations. The DrawBridge project is noteworthy in its effort to bridge block-based and text-based programming by introducing pen-and-paper drawing and program-by-demonstration features into its larger pedagogical strategy [31]. Game authoring has also been used as a context to motivate block-to-text programming as demonstrated by the Flip project [17].

Dual Modality Programming Environments

While the environments listed in the previous section provide a one-way transition from a block-based interface to the textual form, a growing number of tools are providing bi-directional support. Pencil Code [3] provides a two-way transition between blocks and CoffeeScript, JavaScript, and HTML, while tools have also been built for Java [21], Python [2], and Grace [16]. In these environments, the user can move back and forth between block-based and text-based representations of their program. Matsuzawa et al. [21] taught an introductory programming course using an environment that allowed users to program with either a block-based or text-based Java interface and found that over the course of the semester, students systematically transitioned from blocks to text on their own. These findings were replicated in another study that investigated the cause of block-to-text transitions, and found students often used the block-based modality when adding commands to their programs for the first time, revealing one specific way dual modality environments are able to scaffold novice programmers [34].

Hybrid environments

The last section of this literature review looks at the types of environments that are the focus of this work: hybrid block/text environments. These environments blend features of block-based interfaces with conventional text-based editors to create a new modality distinct from both blocks and text. One recent example of this type of environment is Greenfoot's Frame-based Editor. As its creators explain, frame-based editing "maintains some of the graphical representation advantages, discoverability and error avoidance of blocks while providing the flexibility, keyboard-entry capabilities, and readability of text" [19:29–30]. A central design goal of the Frame-based editing approach is to keep the atomic unit of operation a valid node in the program's abstract syntax tree (i.e. you add/edit/delete full commands, akin to working in blocks), but that manipulation of these nodes can be completed with the keyboard and the program presentation retains the visual characteristics of a text-based program. Early analysis of frame-based editing shows the promise of this specific hybrid approach [27]. A second example of a hybrid block/text programming tool can be seen with GP, a tool inspired by Scratch that seeks to address the drawbacks of block-based languages as programs become larger and more complicated by incorporated text layouts and keyboard-driven compositional mechanisms [22]. A third hybrid block/text environment is Pencil.cc, which is the focus of this paper and described in detail below.

MEET PENCIL.CC

Pencil.cc is a customized version of the Pencil Code environment [3] that supports block-based, text-based, and hybrid block/text programming, but is designed such that a given user only has access to one of these programming modalities. Pencil.cc's blocks interface (Figure 2a) features many of the defining features of block-based tools, including the drag-and-drop programming mechanism, a palette of blocks for the user to choose from, and visual cues on how and where blocks can be used. The text version of Pencil.cc presents users with a text editor that includes basic programming supports like highlighting, automatic formatting, and syntax checking.

The hybrid form of Pencil.cc retains the block-palette and the ability to drag-and-drop commands into a program, but replaces the blocks canvas with a text editor. When a user drags a block from the palette onto the text canvas, the block turns into the textual equivalent and is inserted into the program in a syntactically valid way. Thus, the hybrid interface supports both drag-and-drop and keyboard-driven composition. Figure 2b and 2c shows Pencil.cc's hybrid interface. This hybrid approach was informed by earlier findings on the design of block-based tools, including features that learners found to be useful as well as perceived drawbacks of block-based programming tools [36]. Specifically, this hybrid design retains features including a browsable blocks library, drag-and-drop composition, and pre-fabricated commands. At the same time, the text-editor interface tries to address some of the drawbacks identified by learners in block-based tools, such as perceived inauthenticity and issues with block-based environment being less powerful or slower than text-based alternatives.

In Pencil Code, users are free to move back-and-forth between the blocks and text modalities. With Pencil.cc, this

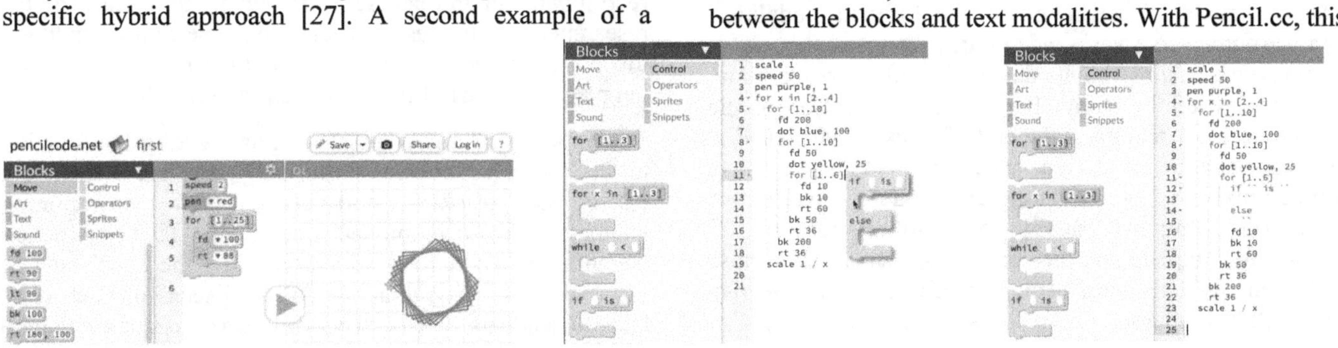

(a) (b) (c)

Figure 2. Pencil.cc's interfaces. (a) shows the blocks interface while (b) and (c) show Pencil.cc's hybrid block/text interface. The middle image (b) shows how learners can drag-drop blocks into the text editor; the right image (b) shows the results of this action.

ability has been removed, instead users see either the block-based interface, the text-based interface, or the hybrid interface. Aside from the programming modality, all other features of the three modes of Pencil.cc are the same, making the three environments isomorphic, meaning the capabilities and expressive power are equivalent across modalities; anything that can be done in one mode can also be achieved in the other two. Pencil.cc was chosen as the environment for this study due to its ability to support all three modalities and because it shares many characteristics with widely used introductory environments such as visual execution of programs and accessible language primitives.

METHODS

In this section, we present details of the study conducted to understand outcomes of hybrid block/text programming environments relative to isomorphic block-based and text alternatives. We begin by detailing the design of the study, then present information about the participants and setting.

Study Design and Data Collection Strategy

This study uses a quasi-experimental setup with three high school introductory programming classes. The study follows each classroom for the first 15 weeks of a yearlong introduction to programming course. The 15 weeks were broken down into two phases, a five-week introductory phase, which was immediately followed by a 10-week Java phase. During the introductory phase, each of the three classes used a different Pencil.cc modality (block-based, text-based, or hybrid). This means students only saw one of the three modalities (so a student in the blocks condition, never saw the text or hybrid interface). These three classes constituted the three conditions of the study: Blocks, Text, and Hybrid. Starting in week six, all three classes transition to Java and followed the same curriculum in the same programming environment for the remaining 10 weeks.

The study began on the first day of school with students in the three classes taking Pre attitudinal surveys and content assessments. The Commutative Assessment [37] was used for the content assessment and a modified version of the attitudinal survey from the Georgia Computes project [6] was used for the attitudinal survey with questions added related to students' perceptions of the different modalities. The attitudinal survey and content assessments were administered at three points during the fifteen-week study: the first day of the study (Pre), at the conclusion of the introductory curriculum at the end of week 5 (Mid), and at the conclusion of the study in week 15 (Post). The surveys were administered online during class time on consecutive days. The attitudinal survey took students around 20 minutes to complete and the content assessment took close to 25 minutes. The assessments were given on the same day across all three classes.

The five-week curriculum for the introductory phase of the study was based on the Beauty and Joy of Computing course [13], along with an assortment of other introductory computing activities grounded in the Constructionist programming tradition and the Logo programming language [15,23]. An emphasis of this design was to allow students creative freedom in each assignment. Over the course of the five-week introductory phase, four major conceptual topics were covered: variables, conditional logic, looping logic, and procedures. Throughout the activities, care was taken to blend visually executing programs (like traditional Logo graphics drawing activities) and text-based activities (like asking for and responding to input from the keyboard). The curriculum was largely designed by the first author but the classroom teacher contributed ideas and customized the activities while teaching them. Full versions of the Commutative Assessment, the attitudinal survey, and the five-week curriculum can be found in the appendices of [33].

Setting and Participants

This study was conducted at a large, urban, public high school in a Midwestern city in the United States of America, serving almost 4,000 students. The school is a selective enrollment institution, meaning students have to take an exam and qualify to attend. In this school district, students are selected based on their performance on the admissions test relative to other students from their school (as opposed to all other applicants). As a result, students attend this school from across the city and there is an equal representation of students from under-resourced schools as from schools in more affluent parts of the city. A majority of the students in the school (58.6%) come from economically disadvantaged households.

The computer science course used for the study is an elective class but historically has attracted students from a variety of racial background and been taken by both male and female students. A total of 90 students participated in the study. The self-reported racial breakdown of the participants was: 41% White, 27% Hispanic, 11% Asian, 11% Multiracial, and 10% Black. The classes comprised of students across all four years of high school, with a reported mean age of 17.1 (SD = 1.1 years). The three classes in the study were comprised of 15 female students and 75 male students. This gender disparity is problematic, but as recruitment for the courses was out of the control of the researchers, there was little that could be done to address this. Of the students participating in the study, 47% speak a language other than English in their households.

The experiment was conducted in an existing Introduction to Programming course. Historically, the class spent the entire year teaching students the Java programming language. To accommodate the study, Java instruction began in the sixth week of school, after the conclusion of the five-week curriculum previously discussed. Each class had 30 students and each student was assigned a laptop which they used every class. Students sat in individual desks that were on wheels, that allowed them to move their desks around. The same teacher taught all three sections of the course, allowing us to control for teacher effects.

FINDINGS

The findings section is broken down into two main sections. First, we look at student performance on the content assessment by modality, then we look at attitudinal and perceptual outcomes from this study. While there is much that can be said about the data presented below, the analysis and discussion in the paper is focuses specifically on the Hybrid condition and understanding how it fared relative to the Blocks and Text conditions. A comparison of the Blocks condition to the Text condition can be found in [35]. Throughout this section, only significant statistics are presented; absent values were not significant.

Content Assessment

We begin our findings section by looking at how students performed on the content assessment at the three time points based on the version of Pencil.cc they used during the introductory five weeks of the study. At the outset of the study, the Hybrid condition was not statistically different than either the Blocks class or the Text condition. This means that the three classes are not different from each other with respect to their incoming programming knowledge. Figure 3 shows cumulative scores for students across the three conditions on the Pre, Mid, and Post Commutative Assessment administrations[1].

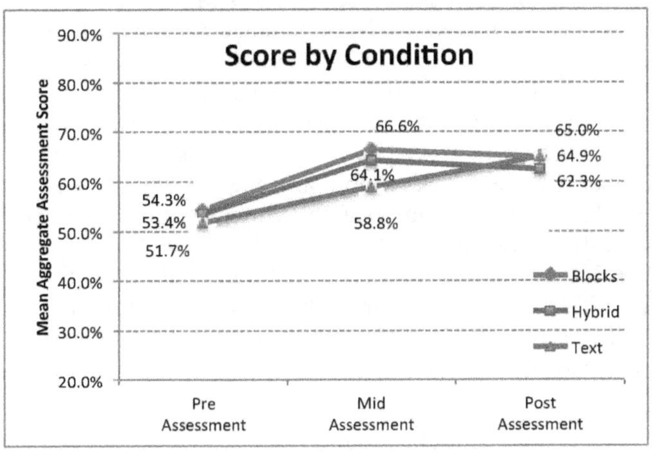

Figure 3. Content scores by condition over time.

The positive slope for all three conditions between the Pre and Mid assessments means that, in aggregate, students in all three classes performed better on the Mid survey than they did on the Pre. Given that this was an introductory class it is not surprising, but still noteworthy and an encouraging sign given that these three conditions cover almost the entirety of the modalities used to introduce learners to programming. For the Hybrid condition, the improvement on test scores from the Pre to the Mid was significant, $t(26) = 6.65$, $p < .001$, $d = .65$. This shows that students in the Hybrid condition did better on the assessment after working in the Hybrid interface of Pencil.cc for five week.

[1] Please note the line charts in this paper to not start at 0.

On the Mid assessment, students' performance in the Hybrid condition was significantly different from the Text condition, albeit with a moderate effect size ($t(52) = 2.03$, p-value = 0.04, d= 0.58), and not different from the Blocks condition. On the Post assessment, the three conditions converge, resulting in the Hybrid condition not being statistically different from the other two conditions. Looking over the three time points in Figure 3 shows a pattern of students in the Hybrid condition performing more similarly to the Blocks condition than to the Text condition over the course of the 15-week study. This trend can be seen by the fact that the change in the score between the Mid and Post administrations for the Hybrid condition was significantly different than the learning gains observed for the Text condition ($t(48) = 2.88$, $p = .01$, $d = .81$), but not the Blocks condition.

Condition by Concept

This section investigates how students in the Hybrid condition performed compared to the Blocks and Text conditions with respect to specific programming concepts. The Commutative Assessment covers six content areas: Algorithms, Code Comprehension, Conditional Logic, Functions, Iterative Logic, and Variables. If we look at how students performed on each of the six content areas on the Mid assessment, we find that students in the Hybrid condition scored between their Block-based and Text-based peers on half of them (Code Comprehension, Conditional Logic, and Functions,). In two concept areas (Iterative logic and Algorithms) the Hybrid condition scored the highest, while they scored the lowest on Variables questions. None of these differences are statistically significant at the $p < .05$ level. This means with this data, we cannot state that students learned specific concepts better in the Hybrid version of Pencil.cc compared to either the Blocks or Text modalities. Where we do see differences emerge is in students' perceived ease-of-use of these concepts. On the Mid attitudinal assessment, students were asked: "How easy was it to use ___ in Pencil.cc?", where ___ was replaced with the concept under question. The mean responses to the 7-point Likert questions are shown in Figure 4. The higher the score, the easier a student thought it was to use the given concept.

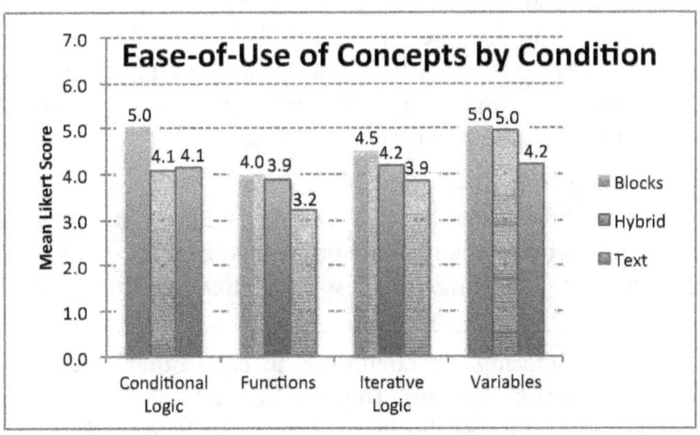

Figure 4. Student reported ease of using concepts in Pencil.cc.

Two of the four concept areas show a significant difference between Hybrid and another modality. interestingly, in one case the Hybrid condition is similar to the Text condition, and in the other, the Hybrid is similar to Blocks. When asked how easy students found it to use conditional logic, students in the Hybrid condition reported a scores that was significantly lower than their Block-based peers ($U = 212$, $p = .01$)[2], and no different from the Text condition. This means, first, the Hybrid condition found conditional statements significantly harder to use than students in the Blocks condition. Second, students working in the Hybrid condition found conditional logic as difficult to use as students in the Text condition. This suggests the drag-and-drop mechanism provided by the Hybrid interface was not successful in providing the same amount of scaffolding as the full Blocks interface provided.

Running the same analysis on the responses to the question of how easy are variables to use, we find the opposite trend. The Hybrid condition is significantly different from the Text condition ($U = 248.5$, $p = .05$) but no different from the Blocks condition. Here, the drag-and-drop composition mechanism provided by the Hybrid programming environment was successful in making students feel like variables were as easy to use as the Blocks condition.

Looking across the data, one explanation for ease-of-use in the Hybrid condition is that the simpler the post-addition modification is, the easier the construct to be used is perceived. Whereas the use of a conditional statement in the Hybrid condition often included non-trivial post addition edits (i.e. defining the test and the commands to be followed after the test is evaluated, as can be seen by the ``s that need to be replaced by the user in Figure 2c), when adding variables to a program via drag-and-drop, only very straightforward edits are necessary, like entering the name or changing the value. In this way, the addition of variable blocks to a program in the Hybrid condition presented a template that required simple replacements. This finding is useful in that it can provide direction in terms of the design of new hybrid environments and how the addition of different programming constructs is accomplished. One other important thing to note from this analysis is the revelation that the effect of a given hybrid block/text implementation does not necessarily have a uniform benefit across the various constructs that constitute a programming language. This highlights the need for nuanced analysis beyond just aggregated assessment scores.

Attitudes and Authenticity

The attitudinal assessment given to students included a series of 10-point Likert scale questions. In this section, we present data looking at how students in the Hybrid condition responded relative to their block-based and text-based peers with respect to confidence, enjoyment, perceived authenticity of the programming environment, and interest in pursuing the field of computer science.

Confidence in Programming Ability

The first attitudinal dimension we present is students' perceived confidence in their own programming ability. Student responses to the following two Likert scale statements: I will be good at programming (or I am good at programming on the Post survey) and I will do well in this course, which were then averaged together. These questions show an acceptable level of correlation, having Cronbach's α scores of .79 (Pre), .80 (Mid), and .88 (Post) on the surveys, all of which are near the .8 threshold commonly used to denote an acceptable level of reliability.

Looking at how students responded on the confidence questions at the Midpoint of the study (i.e. after working in Pencil.cc for five weeks) we find no difference between the Hybrid condition and either the Blocks condition or the Text condition, as all three groups reported roughly the same average level of confidence. However, after students transitioned to Java, a difference between the conditions emerges. At the conclusion of the study, the Hybrid students reported confidence level was $M = 8.3$ ($SD = 1.9$), compared to Blocks students' average of $M = 7.4$ ($SD = 2.3$) and Text students' $M = 8.3$ ($SD = 1.1$). In other words, the Hybrid students and Text students had a higher level of confidence than the Blocks condition. The Hybrid conditions average confidence score is only significantly higher than the Blocks condition at the .10 level ($U = 274$, $p = .10$) and not significantly different than the Text condition. Taken together, this shows, with respect to confidence, at the conclusion of the study, the Hybrid condition was more similar to the Blocks students and their higher reported level of confidence compared to students who had worked in the Text only interface.

Enjoyment of Programming

The second attitudinal dimension is whether or not students' enjoyment of programming differed based on the modality they used. To calculate a measure of enjoyment, responses to the following three Likert statements from the Pre, Mid, and Post surveys were averaged: I like programming, Programming is Fun, and I am excited about this course. These three questions were found to reliably report the same underlying disposition at all three time points (Pre Cronbach's $\alpha = .84$, Mid Cronbach's $\alpha = .84$, Post Cronbach's $\alpha = .89$). Comparing students' scores at the Mid and Post time points, the Hybrid condition was not significantly different from either the Blocks condition or the Text condition. The conclusion here is that the hybrid version of Pencil.cc did not affect students' enjoyment of the act of programming. This is possibly because there are other more salient features of a programming experience that shape enjoyment (like the activities, setting, or runtime environment) or that modality does not affect enjoyment.

[2] When comparing the conditions to each other, we use a Wilcoxon Rank Sum test (reported as a U statistic). This test is appropriate as the two samples are independent and the underlying data is non-parametric and ordinal in nature.

Programming is Hard

The attitudinal survey included the Likert statement: Programming is Hard. On both the Mid survey and the Post survey, students in the Hybrid condition reported scores significantly lower than the Blocks condition (Mid: U = 488, p = .01; Post: U = 481, p = .04) and not different than the Text condition. This mean, that with respect to perceived difficulty of programming, the Hybrid condition was viewed as the same as the Text condition, suggesting that the Hybrid interface did not succeed in making students feel like programming was easier.

Interest in Future Computer Science

The last attitudinal category looks at whether or not the modality used in the introductory programming environment affected students' interest in future computer science courses. More specifically, students were asked to respond to the statement: I plan to take more computer science courses after this one. Figure 5 shows the average response for students grouped by condition.

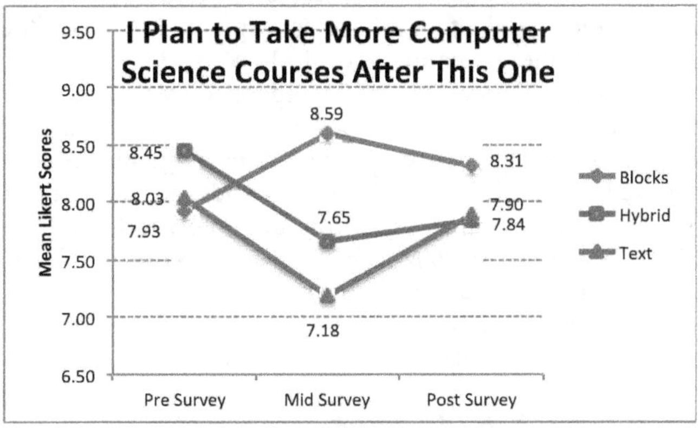

Figure 5. Average responses to the Likert statement: I plan to take more computer science courses after this one.

Like with the other attitudinal findings, these data show student responses in the Hybrid condition being more similar to the Text condition than the Blocks condition. On the Mid survey, the Hybrid condition is significantly different from the Blocks condition (U = 451, p = .05) but not different from the Text condition. On the Post survey, there is no statistically significant difference between the Hybrid group and either the Blocks condition as the reported attitudes converge. Like with the overall scores shown in Figure 3, the three conditions diverge at the midpoint of the study, then converge at its conclusion. However, unlike the content assessments, when asked about interest in future computer science courses, the Hybrid condition's path followed that of the Text condition, rather than the Blocks condition. This is not the desired outcome as the Blocks condition reported a higher level of interest in future computer science learning opportunities.

Perceived Authenticity

One drawback identified in using block-based programming environments with high school-aged learners is the perceived lack of authenticity and a recognized difference between what it looks like to program in block-based languages versus conventional text-based languages [36]. On the Mid and Post attitudinal surveys, students were asked if what they did in the first five weeks of the course was similar to what "real programmers" do. Responses were given on a ten-point Likert scale, with a higher score meaning students agreed more strongly. Figure 6 shows student responses by condition to this prompt.

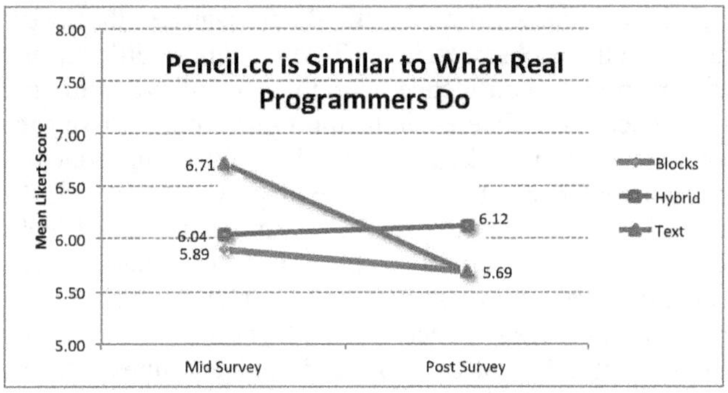

Figure 6. Student responses to the authenticity prompt: Pencil.cc is similar to what real programmers do.

After working in Pencil.cc for five weeks, students in the Text condition viewed the environment as the most similar to what real programmers do, while the Blocks and Hybrid conditions had similar views of the authenticity, which were lower than the Text condition. This suggests that this specific Hybrid implementation was not successful in addressing the authenticity concern previously identified in the literature. However, after spending 10 weeks programming in Java, students' perceptions of the authenticity of Pencil.cc shifted. In both the Text and Blocks conditions, students viewed Pencil.cc as less authentic than they had initially, while the perceived authenticity of Hybrid improved, meaning students thought the Hybrid Pencil.cc environment was slightly more authentic than they had initially. This positive change for the Hybrid condition is significantly different from the negative change for the Text condition (U = 437.5, p = .01) but not the Blocks condition. The Hybrid condition was the only modality with a positive slope, suggesting that after working in Java, students did not see the Hybrid condition as less authentic than they had before. One possible explanation for the Hybrid condition's different outcome stems from the fact that only in that condition do students interact with more than one modality (graphical blocks and text side-by-side), thus possibly suggesting to students that programming is not a uniform activity, but instead, that the act of programming and programming languages and environments can take many shapes and rely on many modalities, interfaces, and technologies.

DISCUSSION

The research question this paper addresses is investigating whether or not it is possible to design a "best-of-both worlds" introductory programming modality that includes features of both block-based and text-based editors. In this section, we summarize the findings, first looking at how the three conditions fared relative to each other during the 5-week comparative portion of the study, then looking at if and how those differences persisted as students transition to Java. Finally, we step back from this specific study and discuss the larger implications of these findings.

The Hybrid Condition: The First Five Weeks

Over the first five weeks of the study, students in the Hybrid condition showed attitudinal changes that were similar to those observed in the Text condition: little change with respect to confidence or enjoyment of programming and a decrease in interest in taking future computer science courses. When asked about how the introductory environment compared to what real programmers do, the Hybrid students gave responses similar to the Blocks students, which were lower than their Text-based peers. Together, these findings show that the Hybrid environment was not particularly successful with respect to cultivating positive attitudes relative to the other modalities. On the Mid administration of the Commutative Assessment, the Hybrid condition scored between the Blocks and Text students overall, but was closer to the higher score of the Blocks condition than to the Text condition. When asked about the perceived ease-of-use of various programming constructs, the Hybrid students reported that variables and functions were as easy to use as the students in the Blocks condition, but found conditional logic more difficult to use, like the Text condition. Taken together, these results highlight how the Hybrid condition has successfully blended the Blocks and Text modalities, however, was not universally successful in achieving a best-of-both-world outcome, as there were instances where the Hybrid condition was closer to the underperforming modality. There were also a few places where the Hybrid condition is distinct from the other two modalities, suggesting that, along some dimensions, the Hybrid modality is more than the sum of the other two modalities.

The Hybrid Condition: Transitioning to Java

Whereas the Hybrid condition did not seem to produce positive outcomes with respect to attitudinal measures during the first five weeks, things changed after the transition to Java. When asked to reflect on their time in the introductory modality, students in the Hybrid condition reported their time in Pencil.cc as being the most similar to what real programmers do. In the four other attitudinal categories evaluated, the Hybrid condition saw relatively little change, having three categories showing slight increases (enjoyment, perceived difficulty, and interest) and a minor decrease the last (confidence). Students' scores on the Commutative Assessment decreased slightly after working in Java for ten weeks, suggesting the modality was not an outlier with respect to preparation for future text-based learning in a different language.

Modality is Malleable

One of the contributions of this work is providing evidence that modality is malleable and showing that its design is consequential. Unlike many other domains, the representations novices use when being introduced to computer science are not set, but instead are part of an active area of design research. Designing novice programming tools is one instantiation of the larger intellectual pursuit of creating new ways of expressing ideas and interacting with representational systems [18,24,39]. Programming languages provide an especially rich context for this work due to what Papert [23] called the *Protean* nature of computers. Computers provide the ability to introduce layers of abstraction between the way a representational infrastructure is presented to the user and the form those instructions must take in order to be executed by the machine upon which they reside. From this relatively blank canvas, a vast design space emerges for the creation of new modalities. Looking at the three modalities used for this work, we can start to see the various dimensions along which computationally situated modalities can be defined. Visual rendering (color, shape, location on the screen, etc.) serves as a first dimension along which modality design can explore. Likewise, the novelty of the modality and if, how, and when other representational systems are incorporated can differ. For example, when comparing Scratch Jr. [11] and its use of glyphs to Scratch [28] where natural language expressions are used, to Pencil Code [3] which provides visual supports on top of programming keywords, and finally to Logo [23], which is a fully text language, we see a spectrum of how textual language can exist within a programming interface. Figure 7 shows the turn right command as it is represented across these four tools.

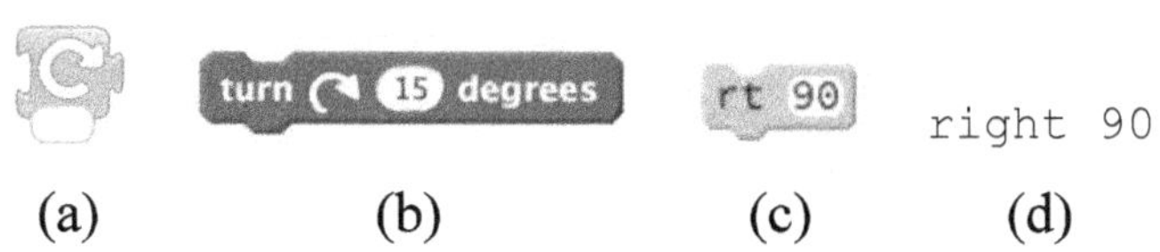

Figure 7. The command to turn right in four modalities: (a) Scratch Jr., (b) Scratch, (c) Pencil Code, and (d) Logo.

These four representations highlight visual differences between modalities. Other design dimensions to be explored in the creation of new modalities include temporal differences (have the representation change over time), auditory components, responsive or interactive modalities where the representation changes based on state or input, or creating tangible dimensions of the modality that are independent or live alongside virtual elements.

As our definition of modality includes interactions, thus designing modalities extends beyond just the visual depiction of the representation. Consideration of modality design also includes various interaction capabilities that influence the mechanics of interaction with and use of the modality. In this work, the difference between dragging-and-dropping blocks on the canvas versus typing commands in character-by-character with the keyboard highlight difference in interaction.

A final important dimension to discuss in terms of the malleability of modalities is to point out that a user need not be pinned to a specific modality. The learners in this study were held to a specific modality for the purpose of the research, not because of design constraints. The growing number of dual modality environments discussed earlier in this paper highlight the potential of this approach. The ability to provide multiple modalities within the same environment further opens the set of possibilities to designers of learning environments and computational tools more broadly. A strength of this approach is that it gives agency to the learner to decide not just how to use the various features of a single modality, but also to choose the modality they want to use.

CONCLUSION

As the presence of programming and computer science in K-12 classrooms grows, it is important that we take time and care to develop and evaluate the environments learners are using. Introductory programming environments that blend features of the block-based and textual modalities are one design approach that is gaining popularity. In this paper, we present one such implementation of a hybrid programming environment and compare it to isomorphic block-based and text-based alternatives to understand the impacts of this approach. In doing so, we have identified places where this hybrid design is effective and other dimensions where more design work needs to be done to better support learners. The hybrid design used in this study shows the potential for this line of work towards the greater goal of developing effective and accessible programming environments. Looking beyond programming environments, the larger contribution of this work is showing how the design choices made in the creation of new modalities and learning environments can produce outcomes similar to either of the source modalities used, as well as unique outcomes distinct from the designs that served as its inspiration. The hope for this work is that by attending to modality and viewing it as a design challenge, we can improve existing and create new ways for learners to engage with the powerful ideas of computing that surround them.

REFERENCES

1. M. Armoni, O. Meerbaum-Salant, and M. Ben-Ari. 2015. From Scratch to "Real" Programming. *ACM Transactions on Computing Education (TOCE)* 14, 4: 25:1-15.
2. A. C. Bart, E. Tilevich, C. A. Shaffer, and D. Kafura. 2015. From interest to usefulness with BlockPy, a block-based, educational environment. In *Blocks and Beyond Workshop, 2015 IEEE*, 87–89.
3. D. Bau, D. A. Bau, M. Dawson, and C. S. Pickens. 2015. Pencil Code: Block Code for a Text World. In *Proceedings of the 14th International Conference on Interaction Design and Children* (IDC '15), 445–448.
4. A. Begel. 1996. LogoBlocks: A graphical programming language for interacting with the world. Electrical Engineering and Computer Science Department. MIT, Cambridge, MA.
5. J. Bonar and B. W. Liffick. 1987. A visual programming language for novices. In *Principles of Visual Programming Systems*, S. K Chang (ed.). Prentice-Hall, Inc.
6. A. Bruckman, M. Biggers, B. Ericson, T. McKlin, J. Dimond, B. DiSalvo, M. Hewner, L. Ni, and S. Yardi. 2009. Georgia computes!: Improving the computing education pipeline. In *ACM SIGCSE Bulletin*, 86–90.
7. D. C. Cliburn. 2008. Student opinions of Alice in CS1. In *Frontiers in Education Conference, 2008. FIE 2008. 38th Annual*, T3B–1.
8. W. Dann, S. Cooper, and B. Ericson. 2009. *Exploring Wonderland: Java Programming Using Alice and Media Computation.* Prentice Hall Press.
9. W. Dann, D. Cosgrove, D. Slater, D. Culyba, and S. Cooper. 2012. Mediated transfer: Alice 3 to Java. In *Proceedings of the 43rd ACM technical symposium on Computer Science Education*, 141–146.
10. C. Duncan, T. Bell, and S. Tanimoto. 2014. Should Your 8-year-old Learn Coding? In *Proceedings of the 9th Workshop in Primary and Secondary Computing Education* (WiPSCE '14), 60–69.
11. L. P. Flannery, B. Silverman, E. R. Kazakoff, M. U. Bers, P. Bontá, and M. Resnick. 2013. Designing ScratchJr: Support for early childhood learning through computer programming. In *Proceedings of the 12th International Conference on Interaction Design and Children*, 1–10.
12. N. Fraser. 2013. *Blockly*. Google, https://developers.google.com/blockly/.
13. D. Garcia, B. Harvey, and T. Barnes. 2015. The Beauty and Joy of Computing. *ACM Inroads* 6, 4: 71–79.
14. R. Garlick and E. C. Cankaya. 2010. Using Alice in CS1: A quantitative experiment. In *Proceedings of the fifteenth annual conference on Innovation and technology in computer science education*, 165–168.
15. B. Harvey. 1997. *Computer science logo style: Beyond programming*. The MIT Press.
16. M. Homer and J. Noble. 2014. Combining Tiled and Textual Views of Code. In *IEEE Working Conference on Software Visualisation (VISSOFT)*, 1–10.
17. K. Howland and J. Good. 2014. Learning to communicate computationally with flip: A bi-modal programming language for game creation. *Computers & Education.*
18. J. Kaput, R. Noss, and C. Hoyles. 2002. Developing new notations for a learnable mathematics in the

computational era. *Handbook of international research in mathematics education*: 51–75.

19. M. Kölling, N. C. C. Brown, and A. Altadmri. 2015. Frame-Based Editing: Easing the Transition from Blocks to Text-Based Programming. In *Proceedings of the Workshop in Primary and Secondary Computing Education* (WiPSCE '15), 29–38.
20. J. H. Maloney, M. Resnick, N. Rusk, B. Silverman, and E. Eastmond. 2010. The scratch programming language and environment. *ACM Transactions on Computing Education (TOCE)* 10, 4: 16.
21. Y. Matsuzawa, T. Ohata, M. Sugiura, and S. Sakai. 2015. Language Migration in non-CS Introductory Programming through Mutual Language Translation Environment. In *Proceedings of the 46th ACM Technical Symposium on Computer Science Education*, 185–190.
22. J. Mönig, Y. Ohshima, and J. Maloney. 2015. Blocks at your fingertips: Blurring the line between blocks and text in GP. In *2015 IEEE Blocks and Beyond Workshop*, 51–53.
23. S. Papert. 1980. *Mindstorms: Children, computers, and powerful ideas*. Basic books, New York.
24. S. Papert. 2006. Afterword: After how comes What. In *The Cambridge Handbook of the Learning Sciences*, R.K. Sawyer (ed.). Cambridge University Press, 581 – 586.
25. D. Parsons and P. Haden. 2007. Programming osmosis: Knowledge transfer from imperative to visual programming environments. In *Procedings of The Twentieth Annual NACCQ Conference*, 209–215.
26. K. Powers, S. Ecott, and L.M. Hirshfield. 2007. Through the looking glass: teaching CS0 with Alice. *ACM SIGCSE Bulletin* 39, 1: 213–217.
27. T. W. Price, N. C. C. Brown, D. Lipovac, T. Barnes, and M. Kölling. 2016. Evaluation of a Frame-based Programming Editor. In *In Proceedings of the 2016 ACM Conference on International Computing Education Research*, 33–42.
28. M. Resnick, B. Silverman, Y. Kafai, J. Maloney, A. Monroy-Hernández, N. Rusk, E. Eastmond, K. Brennan, A. Millner, E. Rosenbaum, and J. Silver. 2009. Scratch: Programming for all. *Communications of the ACM* 52, 11: 60.
29. J. J. Ryoo, J. Margolis, C. H. Lee, C. D. Sandoval, and J. Goode. 2013. Democratizing computer science knowledge: transforming the face of computer science through public high school education. *Learning, Media and Technology* 38, 2: 161–181.
30. R. B. Shapiro and M. Ahrens. 2016. Beyond Blocks: Syntax and Semantics. *Commun. ACM* 59, 5: 39–41.
31. A. Stead and A. F. Blackwell. 2014. Learning Syntax as Notational Expertise when using DrawBridge. In *Proceedings of the Psychology of Programming Interest Group Annual Conference (PPIG 2014)*, 41–52.
32. M. Tempel. 2013. Blocks Programming. *CSTA Voice* 9, 1.
33. D. Weintrop. 2016. Modality Matters: Understanding the Effects of Programming Language Representation in High School Computer Science Classrooms. Northwestern University, Evanston, IL.
34. D. Weintrop and N. Holbert. 2017. From Blocks to Text and Back: Programming Patterns in a Dual-Modality Environment. In *Proceedings of the 2017 ACM SIGCSE Technical Symposium on Computer Science Education* (SIGCSE '17), 633–638.
35. D. Weintrop and U. Wilensky. In Press. Comparing Blocks-based and Text-based Programming in High School Computer Science Classrooms. *ACM Transactions on Computing Education (TOCE).*
36. D. Weintrop and U. Wilensky. 2015. To Block or Not to Block, that is the Question: Students' Perceptions of Blocks-based Programming. In *Proceedings of the 14th International Conference on Interaction Design and Children* (IDC '15), 199–208.
37. D. Weintrop and U. Wilensky. 2015. Using Commutative Assessments to Compare Conceptual Understanding in Blocks-based and Text-based Programs. In *Proceedings of the Eleventh Annual International Conference on International Computing Education Research* (ICER '15), 101–110.
38. D. Weintrop and U. Wilensky. 2015. The challenges of studying blocks-based programming environments. In *2015 IEEE Blocks and Beyond Workshop*, 5–7.
39. U. Wilensky and S. Papert. 2010. Restructurations: Reformulating knowledge disciplines through new representational forms. In *Proceedings of the Constructionism 2010 conference.*
40. 2014. *App Inventory Java Bridge*. Retrieved from https://code.google.com/p/apptomarket/

Tangible and Shared Storytelling: Searching for the Social Dimension of Constructionism

M. Cecília C. Baranauskas
Institute of Computing and NIED,
University of Campinas (UNICAMP)
Campinas, Brazil
cecilia@ic.unicamp.br

Julián E. Gutiérrez Posada
Systems Engineering and Computing,
University of Quindio (UNIQUINDIO)
Armenia, Colombia
jugutier@uniquindio.edu.co

ABSTRACT

To reimagine Logo's ideas in the next years demands imagining ways of reinventing 'programming' in learning environments, making sense in different social contexts. The benefits of storytelling environments built with tangible technologies have shown a successful endeavor favoring the shared construction of the narratives. This article presents a computational environment based on tangible interfaces with the purpose of allowing a group of children and teachers, to create, share and tell stories together. The proposed environment was experimented within an educational context with 9 years old children and their teachers. This environment intends to illustrate the concept of socio-constructionism.

Author Keywords

Socio-constructionism; tangible user interface; narrative construction.

ACM Classification Keywords

H.5.2 User Interfaces (D.2.2, H.1.2, I.3.6)

INTRODUCTION

Constructionism is a concept developed by Seymour Papert [19] in the early 80's, encompassing two fundamental ideas: a view of the relation teaching-learning as a reconstruction rather than as a transmission of knowledge, and the understanding that learning is most effective when the learner experiences the construction of a product meaningful to him/her.

Papert's legacy to those interested in technology design and in children's education is undeniable. The understanding of the learner as a 'bricoleur', one who, having his/her inventiveness, builds knowledge as s/he explores and constructs objects of his/her interest has been the moto for many people interested in the design of technology-based learning environments for children.

IDC '17, June 27-30, 2017, Stanford, CA, USA.
© 2017 ACM ISBN 978-1-4503-4921-5/17/06...15.00
DOI: http://dx.doi.org/10.1145/3078072.3079743

Central to the powerful ideas proposed by Papert is the materialization he provided with the Logo language, which left its marks in other programming languages, Scratch as possibly the most popular inheritor. To reimagine Logo's ideas in the next years means to imagine what would be 'programming' 50 years ahead! Perhaps this should not be a challenge for Papert, who always have been ahead of his time. In this work, we try to revisit and situate constructionist ideas in the design of a programmable storytelling learning environment for children.

We are naming socio-constructionist the (learning) environment which besides encouraging the user to be active, and providing sufficient freedom to the user to create concrete or conceptual objects that are of personal interest to him/her, is socio-situated favouring working together, sharing a common interest and knowledge construction with others (partners).

By working together, we do not mean just having collaborators in the work; while a collaborator may temporarily help with the construction of a part of the job, he/she does not necessarily feel fully committed to the final product. In the socio-constructionist approach, all partners who want to realize their creation share this commitment in co-authorship. To illustrate this, imagine a group of children organized to create a story about a matter of common interest; in the process of story creation, they need help for creating a story element (e.g. a character) and seek the assistance of another child of other group, who is good at drawing. This last child does not necessarily share commitments regarding the history as a whole, although has a real interest in building its character.

In this paper, we take the benefits of the storytelling activity for children and the use of tangible elements such as toys and children's drawings, to illustrate the concept of a socio-constructionist environment. The tangible objects make it easier for children to play, build their ideas, and advance their stories in creative ways [21]. This aspect motivated us to explore the relationship between storytelling and Tangible User Interfaces (TUIs), to design a socio-constructionist environment.

With the idea of facilitating the construction of stories, the environment makes use of children's own designs / pictures and sounds, including their self-projection. As these elements (designs, pictures, sounds) alone do not tell a story, a framework called BME (Beginning, Middle and End) [15] is used to give a dramatic structure to the stories. Moreover, the BME framework allows the use of interactive elements, which in the environment are translated into some events programmed by the user. In addition to the mentioned requirements, the environment should be affordable by school contexts of lower socio-economic levels. Moreover, we have considered the principles of universal design [7] to cope with inclusive environments requirements.

This paper is organized as follows: the next section presents a literature review on storytelling learning environments based on TUI and situate our contribution. Then, we present the CPES a Collaborative Programmable Environment for Storytelling, its design rationale, interaction design model, followed by a section that illustrates the use of the proposed environment with children and adults in an educational space. In the sequence, a discussion summarizes the contributions and the final section concludes pointing out further work.

TUI AND STORYTELLING - RELATED WORK

Tangible User Interfaces may be defined as interfaces allowing to augment the real physical world by coupling digital information to everyday physical objects and environments [12]. The alignment between TUIs and storytelling is also supported by others, in previous works: with TUIs the users can immediately start telling stories without much training or prior knowledge on technology [22] and [8]. TUI-based environments have the potential to engage children along learning activities [24] by evoking strong feelings of joy and motivation [9], especially important in learning processes. TUIs, particularly those constructed with RFID technology, are an alternative to make computers more accessible as they provide a less abstract interface [20]. Moreover, there is also a potential of TUIs for constructing environments that promote an inclusive education.

Previous work on the academic literature review [8] and [4], based on the digital libraries of ACM, Springer, IEEE, Science Direct, identified a set of related works, some of which are summarized in Table 1.

Alessandrini et al. (2014) [1] present a TUI-based tool for working with children with autism, which lets the user assign sounds to sheets of paper. This feature aims to motivate the child to the activity of storytelling. The paper sheets can have drawings created by children, images or photos, becoming a flexible tool that a therapist can easily take ownership.

Alves et al. (2010) [2] as well as Muños et al. (2012) [17], comment about a tool to create stories using a table with tangible objects. The table is used to locate characters and modify some of their properties such as location, inclination and size. By using commands (through buttons, physical objects or cards), the user can create scenes, assign sounds, and more. There are differences between these two proposals mainly in the way different devices are used to increase the possibilities for the user. For example, the second proposal is more open to the user, allowing him/her to create new scenarios and characters, while in the first these elements are predefined.

Juan C. et al. (2008) [13] present a system that uses augmented reality cubes with different markings on their faces, which are captured by a camera, processed by a computer and replaced by images that overlap the marks. By looking at small screen with a Head-Mounted Display HMD, the user manipulates the cubes; each face indicates, for example, a different ending to the story. This system does not create new elements of the story, but let the user to manipulate the development of it.

Reference	Country	Children	Working with partners	New content by the user	User programming
Alessandrini et al. [1]	Italy	8 – 12		✓	
Alves et al. [2]	Brazil	5 – 9	✓	✓	
Juan C. et al. [13]	Spain	5 – 8			
Labrune & Mackay [14]	France	10 - ...		✓	
Muños et al. [17]	Italy	4 – 10	✓	✓ (full)	
Sylla [23]	Portugal	4 – 5	✓		
Vaucelle & Ishii [26]	USA	4 – 10		✓	
Vaucelle & Jehan [25]	USA	5	✓	✓	
Williams [27]	USA	3 – 5	✓		
Willis et al. [28]	USA	-			
Our proposal	Brazil	4 - ...	✓	✓ (full)	✓

Table 1. Summary of TUI related projects

Labrune & Mackay (2005) [14] and Vaucelle & Ishii (2008) [26] carried out two different approaches to the problem of storytelling, but in essence the two projects use different cameras to capture the context of a child, either over a wide area (first project) or restricted to the interaction between two toys. The creative part of children's work is manifested in what and how to film.

Sylla (2013) [23] presents a new device that allows children to combine in many ways, different story elements to create multiple stories. To make this possible, the different elements of the story are previously associated with physical objects (blocks); the device identifies the blocks and sends the information for the stories engine, which is responsible for taking the combination made by children and generating the final story.

Vaucelle & Jehan (2002) [25] and Williams (2010) [27], used puppets with an embedded electrical device to add new capabilities such as recording and playback of dialogues (first project), or use accelerometers for controlling virtual characters that are projected onto a screen (second project).Willis et al. (2013) [28] combine a camera and a mobile projector to create a new device to be targeted by the user (not restricted to children). For example, the pages of a book, which have marks made with a special ink (invisible to the human eye), are interpreted, resulting in the projection of a graphical element, of a certain embodied action of a character.

Without ignoring the contribution that each of these proposals present, and their different approaches, the system proposed by Muñoz gives children complete freedom to create different elements of the history, including their image, as well as the possibility of collective construction of the story, fundamental characteristics to be considered in a socio-constructionist environment. The other proposals constrain the type of story elements that the child can create to a few or none, or limit the possibilities of work with partners to create stories.

Finally, none of the analysed proposals considered the programming of elements of interactivity by children. This feature, which gives the power to the child, not only to create new elements of the story, but also to program interactivities with them, is one of the contributions of our proposal. Besides this difference, there are other characteristics that differentiate our proposal, such as: the design method, the use of low-cost technology, the effort to make inclusive technology and at the same time "invisible", i.e., hiding the complexity of it. The next sections characterize, present the design rationale and illustrate the use of the proposed environment.

A COLLABORATIVE PROGRAMMABLE ENVIRONMENT FOR STORYTELLING – CPES

Design Rationale

The proposed tangible storytelling environment draws on the BME framework for structuring narratives with the use of elements of interactivity, on the concept of Affectibility, and on the Universal Design principles.

The BME framework [15] proposes an organization for the narrative to be constructed in six steps: 1. Define the concept of history as a problem to be solved; 2. Define the problem solution in general; 3. Describe the general solution in three acts (Beginning: Introduction and call to the adventure, Middle: problems / conflicts, and End: problem/ conflict solving); 4. Set the main symbols of the history, as characters and scenarios; 5. Within each act, create micro stories, as many times as desired; 6. Whenever possible, create for each story, interaction elements that describe how the characters will interact in the scenario (with other characters within the same scenario).

The Affectibility concept [11] refers to affective states potentially evoked by the environment. It supported design considerations regarding emotional aspects materialized in six design principles: 1. Allow communication of affective states; 2. Consider the social context of user-values, culture; 3. Allow the user to include his/her content in the story (Tailoring); 4. Promote collaborative construction; 5. Enable the User to perceive the physical presence of others or characters (Awareness); 6. Explore creatively the different media.

Universal Design [7] was our background reference for inclusive environment design. It is summarized in seven principles: 1.Equate the use possibilities for people with different abilities; 2. Make use flexible to meet a wide range of individuals; 3. Set a simple and intuitive use, regardless of the user conditions; 4. Communicate the necessary information effectively, regardless of their sensory capacity or environmental conditions; 5. Minimize the risk and consequences of unintended or unforeseen actions; 6. Minimize physical effort for efficient and comfortable use; 7. Scale the physical space for appropriate use and interaction, regardless of size, posture or mobility of the user.

These 3 conceptual foundations were articulated in the proposition of the Collaborative Programmable Environment for Storytelling CPES. In general, the proposed environment is characterized by:

- Support to multimedia communication, necessary for creating free scenarios, characters, sounds, effects, etc. with the use of Tangible User Interfaces -TUI;
- Invisibility of technology. The focus should be in the story, technology should be in the background;
- Inclusive design. The environment should be accessible, understood and used by the greatest possible extent of people;

- Diving into the story. The user and his/her own physical environment might be elements of a story; the users can share a scene with other real or fictional characters;
- Collaborative construction of narratives. The environment should engage people in creating stories collaboratively with peers, using the BME framework;
- Memory and Reuse. The environment should preserve the stories and their elements maintaining a memory of the created stories and offering the possibility of reusing elements;
- Programming of events. The environment should allow the user to create new interaction elements.

The Narrative Construction Process

The narrative construction using CPES involves three main steps (Figure 1): "Planning a story", "creating the story" and "storytelling". In the first step, the partners meet to define the different elements of the story, and to plan the beginning, middle and end of the story (the story plan) using the BME Framework with levels of detail compatible with the participants abilities. In the second step, the partners create all elements of the story using the available physical resources (e.g. toys, drawings, etc.), and the CPES elements to create the story. Finally, in the last step "the story is told to an audience with the use of CPES features. During this process of telling the story, the tellers and the audience can generate system interactions motivated by some behaviour (e.g. applause), causing the execution of commands programmed by the users themselves in CPES.

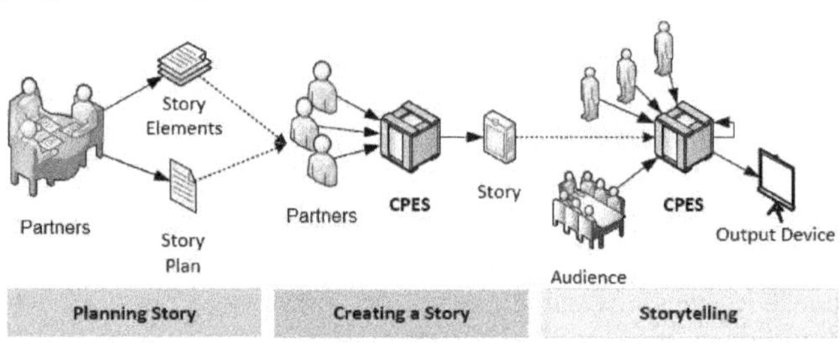

Figure 1. General process of narrative construction with CPES

The CPES Interaction Model

CPES provides different modes of interaction to support the children with different skill levels (different ages, abilities, conditions) in creating and telling the story. This model is used to define the abstract components of CPES and their general responsibilities as well as the relationship among components. This model also provides the definition of usage scenarios with different levels of the technology use (Figure 2).

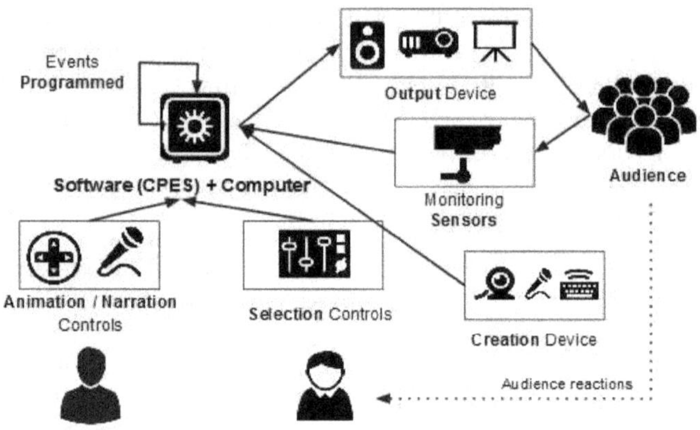

Figure 2. The most complete level of technology use (Mode 4)

Note that the devices in Figure 2 are classified into categories such as Output Devices and Creation Devices. The devices displayed inside the boxes are just examples that can be changed when the model is instantiated. For example, an Output Device can be a TV or an LCD monitor.

CPES supports four modes of interaction (Figure 3); each mode supports the lower modes, creating a system which starts from a basic configuration (lowest level of interactivity), which is ideal for users with less skill. The following modes of interaction, for example, modes 3 and 4 represent the highest levels of interactivity of CPES, but also requires a greater degree of skill from the user.

In **Mode 1 - Presenter**[1] the users can create stories or narratives as in a slideshow added with sounds and narrations. Within CPES, the slides are always created by the users themselves (individually or collaboratively). The creations are built with physical objects of the user environment, such as plasticised models, drawings, figures made of paper or cloth, etc.

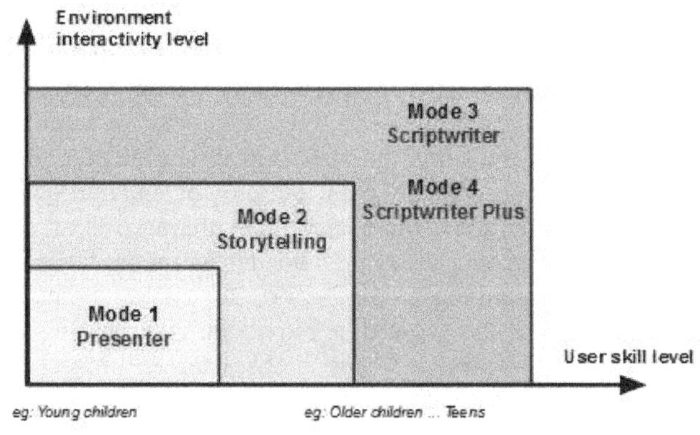

Figure 3. Interaction Modes of CPES

In this mode, the child uses the Selection Controls to indicate the action s/he wants to execute in the instance of CPES, for

[1] Mode 1 was first presented in HCII 2015 [10].

example, create a scene or a story. The creation is made with the devices available in the specific instance of CPES. In this mode, the characters are dependent of the stage created; they may look like cartoon drawings. Note that the audience that is watching/listening the story may express reactions that make the narrator change the course of the story, or add new details. Depending on the restrictions to instantiate the model, a Selection Control can be a traditional keyboard, a barcode reader, a device specially designed to control or a RFID (*Radio-Frequency IDentification*) card reader, among many other alternatives. Of course, there must be a processing unit (Computer) with software control of the instantiated environment.

The stories made in Mode 1 are the least interactive, regarding the technology usage. However, this does not mean that their experience with the environment and the narrative construction is less rich. Children in their everyday life, create several objects with the physical resources available to them (crayons, modelling clay, pieces of cloth or paper, clay, sand, glue, cardboard, among a larger set of resources). All those objects help for the fun, the learning, and the development of skills, while allowing them to express their emotions, their ideas and their dreams. The children can use the Mode 1, for example, to capture each of these objects, and the same children can use CPES to present their creations to an audience (other children, parents or teachers) in the order they wish to show concepts or ideas that are behind these creations, or to tell a story with them.

In **Mode 2 – Storytelling**, the stories can be told on the fly, while the children use the environment, or as planned, for example, following a dramatic structure (BME Framework). In any case, the user has various resources to create the story, such as characters, sound effects, scenes, and animations of the characters made at the time he/she is telling the story. To make this feature possible, the Mode 2 adds the Animation / Narration Controls. These controls allow the user to animate freely the characters. In addition to this, the CPES provides the resources to do a live narration (e.g., character size amplification and / or sound recording).

The type of stories created in Mode 2 is more interactive than the stories created in Mode 1, due to the new features of animation of characters, and the possibility of making specific changes at any moment. For example, through the Selection Controls the users can make changes in the middle of the story regarding the place where the story unfolds, the dress of the characters, among other things. This kind of flexibility allows more interaction with the audience, as they can interact choosing certain aspects of the story, even during the narration itself.

The **Mode 3: Scriptwriter** is, in fact, a combination of Mode 2 - Storytelling with the ability to program actions on CPES, to be executed in response to some external events triggered by the Animation Controls. Some possible events include combining character and scene, animating a character, colliding two characters, colliding a character with an edge of the scene. In response to the events, one or more commands available in CPES can be executed, such as changing scene, changing clothes of a character, replaying a sound effect or narration, altering the size of a character, among others.

The types of stories that can be created in this Mode are similar to those created in Mode 2, except by the ability to program certain actions. Programming actions to certain events, aims to promote the development of logical and creative thinking of the child, making richer narratives.

The Mode 3 can be used, if necessary, to introduce children in the use of a programming language such as Scratch[2]. For example, CPES can do an automatic conversion of a story to the programming language; there, in the Scratch environment, the children can continue the programming process, adding more actions that CPES does not provide.

The last mode, **Mode 4 - Scriptwriter Plus**[3] (Figure 2) adds the use of sensors on the audience to use their reactions as a trigger to execute commands on CPES. This mode aims to increase the experience of the audience to become an active participant in the process of telling the story. In addition, we also seek to enrich the programming process, expanding the possibilities that involve having an active audience. Examples of these sensors could be microphones that capture the level of euphoria (applause, shouts ...) of the public, cameras to identify some expressions on the spectators, sensors to determine the movement of participants, or maybe sensors to measure vital signs of the attendees, through smart watches. The Selection Controls, and Animation / Narration (modes 2, 3 and 4) are categories that may have conventional devices such as a keyboard, or "unconventional" as other physical objects (tangible interfaces).

Regardless of the devices that are used to instantiate the model, the important thing is to define the general responsibilities of the elements and their relationships. In summary, we can say that:

- The software (CPES) is responsible for coordinating all controls and devices, as well as managing the events programmed or generated by the installed sensors (modes 3 and 4).
- The Output Devices should allow to "send" information to the user, which includes visual and auditory information. Other senses might be included such as smell or touch (devices available only experimentally).
- The Creation Devices should allow the user to create new elements for a story, for example, new images, sounds, text.
- The Selection of controls should allow the user to activate certain features such as visual aids and/or sound

[2] http://scratch.mit.edu/

[3] Figure was first presented in HCII 2015 [10].

resources, or they can execute a command or sequence of commands.

The CPES model instantiated

Several technologies could be used to create parts of the CPES model; one possibility is presented here. The selection criteria for the technology is related to Universal Design, and maintaining the lowest possible cost, to be economically viable for a larger number of schools.

In our implementation, the following technological resources were used: a camera with stand and embedded microphone (Figure 4-a); a RFID card reader (Figure 4-b); a set of RFID cards (Figure 4-c); some physical objects with fiducial marks (Figure 4-d); a LCD monitor with a theatre-like decoration (Figure 4-e), which in fact tries to hide the technology ("invisibility of technology"); a computer with speakers and printer (Figure 4-f); a small piece of green material (Figure 4-g); and a large piece of green cloth (Figure 4-h).

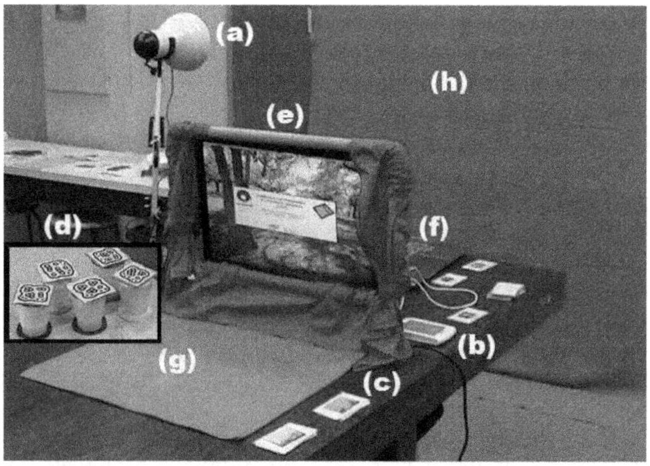

Figure 4. An Instantiation of CPES

Taking Figure 2 as a reference, the technological resources are grouped as follows: **Creation Devices**: camera with stand, small piece of green material, large piece of green cloth, and microphone; **Selection Controls:** RFID card reader with their respective set of cards; **Animation / Narration Controls:** physical objects with fiducial marks, small piece of green material, and microphone; **Output Devices:** LCD monitor, speakers and printer; **Monitoring Sensor:** microphone; **Computer with software** of control of CPES: computer.

Technical Aspects and Choices for CPES

Several development frameworks, tools and techniques were used in the current CPES instantiation. For its GUI implementation, we used the C# Visual Studio.NET 2010 Express, the Microsoft XNA Framework (Games), under Freeware – EULAs (End User License Agreement). The AForge.NET (LGPL v3 Lesser General Public License) was used for operation of the camera. Python 2.7 (GPL General Public License) was used for controlling the environment and providing the communication of TUI elements with Scratch 2.0.

Chroma Key technique was used for the characters creation and the ReacTIVision Framework (GNU Lesser General Public License) was used for the characters animation.

Chroma key compositing, or chroma keying, is a visual effects technique for layering two images together based on colour hues (chroma range). The technique has been used in videogame industries and other fields to remove a background from a photo. The green background (example in Figure 4-h) is used because it differs most distinctly in hue from most human skin colours. This effect allows a static image, for example a photo of a character taken in front of this green background (example in Figure 5-bottom-left) to be inserted into the scene.

The animation controls are used to locate and move the characters in the scene. Each physical object has a character associated that the user can change at will at any time. The controls have fiducial marks (Figure 4-d) on top of them, and the ReacTIVision computer vision framework is used to facilitate the tracking of these marks with a camera (Figure 4-a). Figure 5-bottom-right illustrates the animation operation by a child. In addition to the reference marks (fiducial), the controls have small signs (represented by small circles in relief) to identify by touch the control of each character, allowing its use by people with vision impairments. Another feature of controls is that they may have physical extensions (such as a small stick) for facilitating action of people with mobility problems.

An additional physical element related to accessibility is the green basis, where the control elements are positioned (Figure 4-g). This basis should have a correspondence between its borders and the limits the camera is able to capture, so that if a control is placed on the top right corner of the basis, the character associated with the control will be located on the upper right corner of the screen. Furthermore, the basis thickness facilitates the perception of the screen limits without restricting the movement of the control elements. This correspondence between the position of the physical object and the position of the character on the screen is especially important for visually impaired people to construct a perception of the characters in the scene.

The CPES language, composed by 41 commands, described in BNF (Backus–Naur Form), allows the selection and processing of the RFID cards read by the RFID reader. Within each RFID card, there is a chip and an antenna that captures the radio frequency field that the RFID reader produces. By a physical phenomenon of energy transfer from the reader, the chip inside the card is activated, and transmits, for example, its identification number (unique to each card) to the reader, which sends the information to the computer to be processed. The type of processing depends on the function associated with that particular card.

Some reasons to support the decision of using RFID cards are: the RFID cards allow full customization with drawings of children, and/or embossed marks, especially useful for people with low vision. In addition, to use a RFID card, we only need to put it near the reader without even touching the reader; it enables people with fine motor problems to participate in the narrative construction using CPES. The reader has another important feature regarding accessibility: it beeps and flashes a light every time the users make a correct approach of a card. This element represents important feedback also for visually impaired or hearing problems users.

EXPERIMENTING THE ENVIRONMENT

Context and participants

The CPES project was developed with a partnership of the Division of Children's Complementary Education, which is an educational space inside the University of Campinas, State of São Paulo in Brazil, aiming at the supplementary education of the children of the university employees. The practice of using the CPES environment we are going to illustrate here occurred in the first half of 2015. In the next subsection, we present some results of the workshops with CPES, conducted with both the teachers, and children separately.

We worked with nineteen children between 9 and 10 years old, and with fourteen teachers between 30 to 50 years old. The average age of the group of teachers is 42 years.

Method

Seven (7) workshops were conducted along the semester, with teachers of the educational unit, and with children and their responsible teacher. During this process, the system was being introduced and its design refined. The teachers attended a final workshop to work on semio-participatory practices [3, 5] as a closing activity and conclusion of the proposed work.

We filmed all workshops resulting in 15 hours of recording. All the practices had the written consent of all participants or their respective representatives in the case of children. The videos allowed us to observe the behaviour of the system environment, demands for improvements and for new functionalities along the process.

In addition to filming, at the end of each workshop all participants (children and teachers) filled the SAM (Self-Assessment Manikin) instrument [6]. SAM is a nonverbal instrument of self-assessment of emotions, specifically the level of pleasure, arousal and dominance, associated with the affective reaction of a person to a stimulus, in this case, the CPES environment they were experimenting.

The Workshops

As a strategy for the beginning, the stories created by the teachers in their first workshop were used as an example for children, thus encouraging them to create their own stories. At the end of the presentations, the children had a clearer idea of the possibilities in CPES and showed enthusiasm to make their own stories.

It is worth mentioning how this group of teachers used physical elements of everyday life: sheets of paper and coloured pencils to create the background of the story, clay to create the characters, colour paper to decorate the characters and the use of two brushes to hold a character to simulate a frog jumping. Of course, every story and every group uses the free resources available, but independent of it, all groups showed creativity, motivation and collaboration in each stage of the story creation.

With children, something similar occurred in the three moments of the narratives construction (Figure 1). Each group met to plan the story and follow some simple instructions; each group freely defined the main theme of the story and its moments (plan of story) as well as the characters and their interactions (story elements). After planning, the children used all available physical resources (as happened with the teachers) to create scenes and characters in stories. Finally, the created stories were socialized among the groups (Storytelling). We did an anonymous voting for children to choose the stories they liked the most, rewarding everyone with chocolates.

An example of a particular story tells about the adventures of a girl who goes in a trip (beginning of the story) to various famous places of the world (middle of history) and eventually returns to school to share their experiences with their friends (the end of the history).

It is worth mentioning that none has had the opportunity to visit any place outside Brazil, or even of their town. Also the way the different abilities of the children and their preferences of material were combined in the same story. Regarding the previous example, there are scenes made with a combination of drawing, modelling clay and characters cut; other scenes are just made of modelling clay, others were made using water paints.

In Mode 2, differently from Mode 1, the characters are independent of the background image and can have position, orientation and size changed using tangible commands (RFID cards and physical objects, in this case cups with fiducial marks). These features can be used when creating scenes (background and characters), or when the story is being told.

Regarding the stories created in Mode 2, some teachers used body expressions and different objects like ropes, and spoons in addition to their characters, while other group of teachers decided to create characters using puppets.

In one of the stories created by the teachers in Mode 2, they tell the story of the activities carried by two children in their free time at school: playing in the sandbox, playing soccer, and jumping rope in the park. It is worth noting that each teacher in the scenes are independent characters, and the ball itself is a separate character. Thus, the teachers had to compose scenes using the tangible elements, instead of just taking a photo as happens in Mode 1.

In Mode 2 the children gathered together for several minutes to plan the whole story (even being near the technological environment), discussing and organizing themselves to plan the scenes, the characters, the accessories, the poses. Once planning is done, they create the characters and compose the scenes through tangible objects, creating the story in CPES. Finally, the end result of all groups is socialized by showing their work (storytelling), and, as happened in the Mode 1, the groups were awarded with chocolate after voting for the most popular stories.

Other children's example tells the story of two young girls playing in the forest (beginning of the story), when suddenly it started raining and two friends arrived with umbrellas (middle of history). Then, the snow started to fall and everyone felt very cold; hopefully, other friends arrived with warm clothing for all and so they could play in the snow (end of story). In this story, it is worth noting the use of proper body positions, and the creative use of physical objects like pencils to simulate umbrellas. This point is interesting because for the children, the fact of not having the umbrellas at the moment was not a problem for creating the scenes they wanted, showing creativity and motivation for the activity. Again, the stories created exercise the children's imagination, as none of the children have seen or experimented the snow before, as they live in a tropical country and never had the opportunity to be outside the country.

For Modes 3 and 4, both teachers and children observed five demonstrations of programmed events as a preparation to integrate programming in their stories later. With the end of the class activities in that semester, the involvement with event programming was planned for activities with older children in the following semester. Nevertheless, these groups of children and teachers experimented to program four types of events in Mode 3: a combination character-background to maintain context between characters and background; moving a character to create animations; collision between characters to create interaction between the characters; collision between a character and an edge of the screen to create navigation between scenarios. The fifth type of event (Mode 4), refers to the capture of a loud sound to generate an action, in this example a character can applaud the audience when the audience applauds.

Programming of these five events is made using RFID cards and everyday objects. The CPES software provides the configuration of the events. For example, if the user has three active characters on the screen, and execute the command to program the event of collision, then the CPES software generates all the necessary configuration to detect the collision between those characters. Similar situations occur for other events involving characters.

Figure 5. In the top the 3 moments of narrative construction (planning, creating and telling the story); in the bottom details of creating and animating characters in CPES

Although Modes 3 and 4 were not used to create their own stories, they could create the examples of the demonstrations and used SAM to assess their feelings about it.

Signs of Effectiveness and Affective Responses

A brief analysis of the responses to the SAM (Self-Assessment Manikin) instrument after each workshop, reveals the emotional experience with CPES and narrative construction. Using a scale of 0 to 8, in Mode 1, most of the responses are in the positive half of the scale and the percentages of the value 8 responses are: 78.1%, 37.5%, and 40.6% for Pleasure, Arousal and Dominance respectively. Regarding the results for Mode 2, the percentages regarding choices of value 8 are: 91.7% for Pleasure, 62.5% for Arousal, and 45.8% for Dominance, respectively. This represents an increase of 13.5%, 25.0% and 5.2% respectively for each dimension, compared to Mode 1 results. The responses for Modes 3 and 4, when compared to the responses for Mode 2, drop 7.7%, 10.5%, and 5.8% for Pleasure, Arousal and Dominance, respectively. This last result might be explained by the greater demands of Modes 3 and 4 and less time of practice with them. Nevertheless, the results remain in the positive half of the scale, and are even better than for Mode 1 regarding Pleasure and Arousal, although slightly lower in the Dominance.

At the end of the workshops, the teachers were asked to evaluate their experience with CPES, by writing their opinions on the overall level of acceptance of CPES. As a result, all teachers assigned the highest value for the acceptance of CPES, and agreed that the experience produced greater motivation and cooperation among children, creating more complex and rich stories in emotional and social aspects, when compared to the stories created without the environment.

DISCUSSION

Literature has shown some works on storytelling supported by computational technology, although we could not find evidence of works allowing children to program their own interactive elements. We have proposed an environment that allows children to program events, and all programming is done through tangible objects (with fiducial marks) and RFID cards.

To meet our goal, we had to devise various modes of interaction so that a wider range of users could use the system, balancing user skill with the interactivity level offered by the environment.

The environment that implements all the modes of interaction of the model, meets the four essential properties of digital environments ideal for creating narratives, according Murray [18]: Procedural, Participatory, Spatial and Encyclopaedic. The first property is satisfied with the possibility to program sequences of actions (procedures) associated with the interaction elements of the story (events). The second property is satisfied because the event programming allows the computer to respond to certain actions (events) every time they occur when the story is told; even in Mode 2, the child's ability to animate characters with physical objects, can fulfil this second property. These two features define the environment as interactive. The third characteristic is directly related to the ability to navigate in a space; in this case, scenes that represent places and situations in the narrative create the stories; the scenes can be freely navigable using the already mentioned collision events. The fourth property is satisfied when we recognize the storage capacity of CPES and the power of expression that the child has, accessing all the elements of the story created by him/her or shared by others.

As Murray says, these four characteristics give the writer the opportunity to tell stories from different points of view and build stories intertwined to form a dense network. At this point, we highlight the use of the BME Framework to support children in planning and creating micro-stories that in turn, can be organized into micro-stories forming recursive and complex structures for the general story.

The system design was a result of semio-participatory practices involving the participation of different stakeholders (researchers, teachers, students) in workshops conducted to reflect on and discuss both the design and the use of the system. The development of different workshops with teachers and with children along the different versions of the CPES system evolution, allowed us to incorporate extremely valuable contributions of the different participants (teachers and children) regarding their views on design decisions made and on functions that should be offered. The workshops allowed us to reach a product accepted by teachers and children, and with the possibility to be used by a wide variety of users (children from 4 years old, teachers with 50 years old) aiming to an inclusive school [16].

The workshops also allowed observing the creativity of teachers and children, collaboration between partners and between groups of partners. A possible explanation for this collaboration is that CPES naturally does not restrict users, allowing the use of different resources to create their story elements; the latter feature takes advantage of the ability of children to use the physical elements of classroom and of their daily lives, to create the elements of the story.

We must highlight the importance of using a structure for planning and creating stories (BME Framework), as well as the importance of the having different modes of interaction for different age groups of children.

During the activities of narrative construction through the system, we observed that children appropriated of the environment, independently of having some disability, to participate in the process of storytelling [10]. Thus, the CPES environment has shown that people with disabilities or different degrees of computer skills can be important parties in the process of storytelling.

The designed environment uses low-cost technology easily accessible to public schools in the demanding socio-economic contexts, especially ours. In addition, we selected technologies that allowed to "hide" the formal computer, with the intention of leaving the stories and story elements as the protagonists. Moreover, this invisibility can help face the implicit fear of the computer by some people, allowing the user to focus and enjoy more their creations.

Towards a socio-constructionism

Just as it is incontestable the heritage of Seymour Papert in Mindstorms when reflecting on computational technology and knowledge construction, it is impossible to think about education and social vision without referring to Paulo Freire and his Pedagogy of the Oppressed [29].

Paulo Freire (1921-1997), educator and Brazilian philosopher, is considered one of the most remarkable thinkers in the history of world pedagogy. Currently Patron of the Brazilian Education, stood out for his work in the area of popular education, focusing both on schooling and on the formation of political consciousness. Freire is contrary to the process he named the "banking model of education", that of "filling" the students with "content". Instead, he proposes dialogue as the basis of education [29]: "No one educates anyone, no one educates himself, men educate one another, mediated by the world" (p.78).

Both, Papert and Freire, were together in a remarkable meeting in São Paulo, 1995, documented in video, to discuss the future of the school and the impact of technology on learning. More than discussing the "use of technology in school", the debate showed how they think the School as an institution in the 'contemporary' world, which more and more includes technology.

For Papert, in the education of children we must give them more awareness of the learning process, more control and encourage them to participate in this process. Both agree in this aspect. Regarding technology itself, Freire projects his concern about the lack of access for most (Brazilian) children and recognizes its consequences over time: "What is the repercussion of the technology with these and most of the Brazilian children, today, and in 20-30 years these millions of children will be further away from technology".

The debate is stimulating and ends with the recognition of Freire that there is an identity between them and, up to a certain point of the path, they want the same thing. Their lines of thought differ, for Freire, at the point in which Papert's analysis seems more metaphysical and his own more historical-political.

To project Logo's ideas 50 years ahead, in our view, demands revisiting Papert's constructionism to include the social issues into practical consideration. For this we draw on Freire´s understanding for 'emancipation' to consider ways of supporting children in making sense of technology, from their social contexts. Any wish of transforming educational processes, should not ignore the fundamental and critical discussion that both thinkers put to us about the meaning of a learning space.

Thus, a socio-constructivist approach to the creation of technology-based learning environments demands a socially aware design process [3], which can be summarized in the following principles:

- It should be a design situated in the socio-economic and cultural reality of a social group, without losing its location in the world.
- It should recognize the Other in his/her differences as essential to a systemic view of the design of interactive systems.
- It should recognize design expertise in the interested parties and enable their creative and responsible involvement in design solutions.
- It should recognize communication between the parties as a socially, culturally constructed phenomenon, and propose artefacts for the mediation of such communication that ensure their creative and collaborative use in order to lead to design proposals that make sense to those involved.
- The design of systems in the socially aware perspective demands articulation of meanings of the social group, at their informal and formal levels for the co-construction of the system at the technical level.

The situations promoted along the workshops with children and with teachers give space to this expressive manifestation of the parties along the design of CPES.

CONCLUSION

To project Papert's ideas to the future demands imagining ways of making sense of 'programming' in different social contexts learning environments. In this paper, we have shown that TUIs can be proposed to be a cost effective technology to create an intellectually rich and socially engaging way of involving children in the process of narrative construction with the possibility of programming. We presented the design of a socio-constructionist environment that also draws on other important concepts like affectibility and universal design.

Imagining Logo's ideas projected into wide world scenarios 50 years ahead of our time is an ambitious endeavour. Nevertheless, it should not prevent us of imagining a world everyone would like to be living in; yes, a world full of increasingly ubiquitous technology, but more and more designed for a fairer society.

ACKNOWLEDGMENTS

We thank all the the students, teachers and administrative staff of DEDIC (Division of Child and Supplementary Education), GGBS-UNICAMP, the research group on Human-Digital Artefact Interaction (InterHAD) at UNICAMP, and the University of Quindío. Author 1 gratefully acknowledges the grant from CNPq (#308618/2014-9) and grant #2015/16528-0, São Paulo Research Foundation (FAPESP).

REFERENCES

1. Alessandrini, A., Cappelletti A., Zancanaro M. 2014. Audio-augmented paper for therapy and educational intervention for children with autistic spectrum disorder. *International Journal of Human-Computer Studies* 72, no. 4: 422-430.
2. Alves, A., Lopes, R., Matos, P., Velho, L., Silva, D. 2010. Reactoon: Storytelling in a tangible environment. In *Digital Game and Intelligent Toy Enhanced Learning*, 161-165. IEEE.
3. Baranauskas, M. C. C. 2014. Social awareness in HCI, *Interactions*, Vol. 21, Fac. 4, 66-69, New York, USA.
4. Baranauskas, M. C. C., Gutiérrez Posada, J.E. 2013. Universal access to interaction as revealed by UAHCI words. In *Universal Access in Human-Computer Interaction. Design Methods, Tools, and Interaction Techniques for eInclusion*, 21-30. Springer Berlin.
5. Baranauskas, M.C.C., Martins, M.C., de Assis, R., 2012. XO na escola e fora dela: uma proposta semio-participativa para tecnologia, educação e sociedade. Unicamp.
6. Bradley, Margaret M., and Peter J. Lang. 1994. Measuring emotion: the self-assessment manikin and the semantic

differential. *Journal of behavior therapy and experimental psychiatry* 25, no. 1: 49-59.

7. CEUD. 2014. Principles of Universal Design. Centre for Excellence in Universal Design. Retrieved December 2, 2014 from http://www.universaldesign.ie/exploreampdiscover/the7principles
8. Gutiérrez Posada, J. E., Baranauskas, M.C.C., Maike, V. 2014. Manipulando histórias: uma investigação sobre o uso de interfaces tangíveis e narrativas na escola. In *Proc. of the 13th Brazilian Symposium on Human Factors in Computing Systems*, 160-168. SBC.
9. Gutiérrez Posada, J. E., Hayashi, E., Baranauskas, M.C.C. 2014. On Feelings of Comfort, Motivation and Joy that GUI and TUI Evoke. In *Design, User Experience, and Usability. User Experience Design Practice*: 273-284. Springer International Publishing.
10. Gutiérrez Posada, J. E., Hornung H., Martins, M. C., Baranauskas, M.C.C. 2015. A TUI-Based Storytelling for Promoting Inclusion in the Preschool Classroom - In *Universal Access in Human-Computer Interaction. Access to Learning, Health and Well-Being, 89-100.* Springer International Publishing.
11. Hayashi, E., Baranauskas, M.C.C. 2013. Affectibility in Educational Technologies: A Socio-Technical Perspective for Design. *Journal of Educational Technology & Society* 16.1: 57-68.
12. Ishii, H., and Ullmer, B. 1997. Tangible bits: towards seamless interfaces between people, bits and atoms. In *Proceedings of the ACM SIGCHI Conference on Human factors in computing systems*, 234-241. ACM.
13. Juan, C., Canu,R., Gimenez, M. 2008. Augmented reality interactive storytelling systems using tangible cubes for edutainment. In *Proc. Advanced Learning Technologies*. ICALT'08. 233-235. IEEE.
14. Labrune, J. B., and Mackay,W. 2005. Tangicam: exploring observation tools for children. In *Proceedings of the 2005 Conference on Interaction Design and Children*, 95-102. ACM.
15. Maike, V., Baranauskas, M.C.C. 2013. An Authoring Process for Educational Role Playing Games: From the Paper to the Web. In *Proc. ICCE'13 21st Int. Conference on Computers in Education*. UHAMKA Press.
16. MEC - Ministry of Education - Department of Special Education. 2010. Special Education Mark Political-Legal Perspective on Inclusive Education. (2010). Retrieved May 15, 2014 from http://pfdc.pgr.mpf.mp.br/atuacao-e-conteudos-de-apoio/publicacoes/educacao/marcos-politico-legais.pdf
17. Muñoz, J., Marchesoni, M. and Costa,C. 2012. i-Theatre: Tangible Interactive Storytelling. In *Intelligent Technologies for Interactive Entertainment*, 223-228. Springer Berlin Heidelberg.
18. Murray, J. H. 1997. *Hamlet on the holodeck: The future of narrative in cyberspace*. Simon and Schuster.
19. Papert, S. 1980. *Mindstorms: Children, computers, and powerful ideas*. Basic Books, Inc.
20. Pastel, R., Wallace, C., Heines, J. 2007. RFID cards: a new deal for elderly accessibility. In *Universal Access in Human Computer Interaction. Coping with Diversity*, 990-999. Springer Berlin Heidelberg.
21. Ryokai, K., Jongseon M. L., Breitbart, J.M. 2009. Children's storytelling and programming with robotic characters. In *Proc. 7th ACM conference on Creativity and cognition*, 19-28. ACM.
22. Shen, Y. T., and Mazalek,A. 2010. PuzzleTale: A tangible puzzle game for interactive storytelling. *Computers in Entertainment (CIE)* 8, no. 2: 11.
23. Sylla, C. 2013. Designing a tangible interface for collaborative storytelling to access 'embodiment' and meaning making. In *Proceedings of the 12th International Conference on Interaction Design and Children*, 651-654. ACM.
24. Sylla, C., Branco, P., Coutinho, C., Coquet, E.. 2012. TUIs vs. GUIs: comparing the learning potential with preschoolers. *Personal and Ubiquitous Computing* 16, no. 4: 421-432.
25. Vaucelle, C., and Jehan,T. 2002. Dolltalk: a computational toy to enhance children's creativity. In *CHI'02 Extended Abstracts on Human Factors in Computing Systems*, 776-777. ACM.
26. Vaucelle, C., Ishii, H.. 2008. Picture this!: film assembly using toy gestures. In *Proc. 10th international Conference on Ubiquitous Computing*, 350-359. ACM.
27. Williams, J. M. 2010. Move it! puppetry for creativity. In *Proc. 4th Int. Conference on Tangible, Embedded, and Embodied interaction*, 323-324. ACM.
28. Willis, K. D.D, Shiratori, T., Mahler,M. 2013. HideOut: mobile projector interaction with tangible objects and surfaces. In *Proceedings of the 7th International Conference on Tangible, Embedded and Embodied Interaction*, 331-338. ACM.
29. Freire, P. 1970. *Pedagogy of the Oppressed*, Herder&Herder, New York.

Collaborative Storytelling between Robot and Child: A Feasibility Study

Ming Sun[1], **Iolanda Leite**[1,2], **Jill Fain Lehman**[1], **and Boyang Li**[1]
[1]Disney Research, Pittsburgh PA, USA
[2]KTH Royal Institute of Technology, Stockholm, Sweden
[1]{ming.sun, jill.lehman, albert.li}@disneyresearch.com, [2]iolanda@kth.se

ABSTRACT
Joint storytelling is a common parent-child activity and brings multiple benefits such as improved language learning for children. Most existing storytelling robots offer rigid interaction with children and do not contribute to children's stories. In this paper, we envision a robot that collaborates with a child to create oral stories in a highly interactive manner. We performed a Wizard-of-Oz feasibility study, which involved 78 children between 4 and 10 years old, to compare two collaboration strategies: (1) inserting new story content and relating it to the existing story and (2) inserting content without relating it to the existing story. We hypothesize the first strategy can foster true collaboration and create rapport, whereas the second is a safe strategy when the robot cannot understand the story. We observed that, although the first strategy creates heavier cognitive load, it was as enjoyable as the second. We also observed some indications that the first strategy may mitigate the difficulties in story creation for young children under the age of 7 and encourage children to speak more. This study suggests that a mixture strategy is feasible for robots in collaborative storytelling, providing sufficient cognitive challenge while concealing its shortcomings on natural language understanding.

Author Keywords
conversational agents; conversational storytelling; child-robot interaction

ACM Classification Keywords
H.5.m. Information Interfaces and Presentation (e.g. HCI): Miscellaneous

INTRODUCTION
Storytelling is one of the most common parent-child activities. Modern research finds that it offers substantial benefits to the child, including broadened vocabulary, increased complexity of produced sentences, better narrative comprehension, and accelerated cognitive development [6, 19, 21]. In addition to exposure to new words, conversational storytelling provides an exercise for using language to express concrete meaning with social feedback, which facilitates the acquisition of early literacy [9], which in turn is predictive of later academic success [12]. This fits into the broad pedagogical argument that early intervention at preschool ages can be immensely rewarding [16, 11].

Parents and guardians may not always have the time or energy to engage their children in joint storytelling, despite their best intentions. Recently, interactive, virtual, robotic, and toy characters have emerged as viable play-pals for children [20, 29, 27]. A mixed-initiative storytelling task involves a computational character constructing one or more stories together with a child [3, 24]. Given the benefits of joint storytelling, incorporating storytelling capabilities into interactive characters can bring pedagogical benefits and improve the utility of these characters.

However, traditional storytelling robots or virtual characters interact with children in a rigid and sparse way (e.g., [3, 27]). The robot usually makes little contribution *during* the child's story and waits for the child to completely stop before telling its own story. In contrast, storytelling activities between children and parents or peers tend to contain more interruptions, questions, affirmation, backchanneling behaviors, negotiation over the story content, and so on.

In this paper, we envision a robot capable of performing collaborative storytelling with natural, fluid and fine-grained interaction. For example, when the child experiences difficulty in continuing the story, the robot may encourage further storytelling with questions (e.g., "What happens next?" or "Now your hero has come to a forest. What if a tiger suddenly appears?"), backchanneling, and other social responses, which are known to improve robot-child interaction [5] and argued to be essential for certain types of language learning [15]. Thus, our design goal is to encourage children to tell their own stories by establishing rapport, maintaining engagement, and offering scaffolding, so as to create an experience more entertaining and more engaging than traditional storytelling robots.

Nevertheless, the vision of a collaborative storytelling robot is limited by the current capabilities of artificial intelligence (AI). Despite recent progress, AI remains imperfect in recognizing children's speech and understanding the semantics of natural language. Imperfect speech recognition and natural language understanding imply that the robot may not respond to children in a semantically coherent manner. With these impeding factors, it remains an open question whether fluid

IDC'17, Jun 27–30, 2017, Stanford, CA, USA

ISBN 978-1-4503-4921-5/17/06...$15.00
DOI: http://dx.doi.org/10.1145/3078072.3079714

collaborative child-robot storytelling is feasible or is perceived as valuable by children.

CURRENT WORK

In this paper, we report a Wizard-of-Oz experiment designed to test the feasibility of the envisioned form of collaborative storytelling. Two adult experimenters worked with 78 children in an oral storytelling task. The experimenters took the place of the robot to compare the effects of two story collaboration strategies. The collaboration happened when the experimenters introduce five objects and characters throughout the story. The first, contextual strategy is to relate the inserted object or character to the existing story. The second, non-contextual strategy is to avoid relating to the existing story and use mechanical utterances like "Let's include a kitten in the story." Although the first strategy seems ideal, when the robot does not understand the child's story, it has to use the second strategy.

With this experiment, we aim to answer the following research questions:

- What are the effects of non-contextual and contextual prompts on children's storytelling experience?
- Are those effects in the first question specific to children's age and gender?

The effects were measured in terms of (1) the complexity of children's language and fluency in storytelling, (2) recall of story elements in story retelling, and (3) children's self reports of enjoyment. The reason for studying the effects of age and gender is that these factors are substantially correlated with language development for participants in the age group (4-10 years old) that we are interested in [4, 14].

We find that the self-reported enjoyment remained high across the two conditions with no statistically significant difference. The use of contextual prompts caused slight degradation of short-term language performance. This could be explained as the contextual prompts imposed a high cognitive load on children, which created difficulties for young children and boys. We also observe occasional evidence that the contextual prompts, when used in the right situation, provided scaffolding. We conclude that both strategies can be useful for practical interaction design.

RELATED WORK

Mixed-initiative storytelling with children has been a popular topic in interaction design. As technology progresses, the form of interaction has become more natural over time. In early systems like Rosebud [10], children typed stories into a computer. Later systems begin to recognize speech, but the turn-taking mechanism remains relatively simple and rigid. The most common form is to let the robot tell one story after listening to the child's story. The SAGE system [3], for example, first listened to a child's story and responded with a traditional tale in an effort to impart wisdom. The Sam system [24] was an embodied storytelling virtual character, who was a peer to preschool children and told stories around a figurine and a toy castle. The child was asked to tell his/her own story after Sam had finished. In a similar mode of interaction, the storytelling robot in [27] made use of language that was adaptive to the children's level to facilitate learning. In this paper, we push the boundaries of interaction even further and aim for a highly fluid process of co-storytelling where the computational partner is allowed to contribute new characters and objects during children's storytelling.

Most similar to our work, Tewari and Canny [26] tested the feasibility of interactive virtual character carrying out a question-and-answer conversation with preschool children using a Wizard-of-Oz experiment. Our work is similar in that the collaborative storytelling activity makes use of, but is not limited to, question and answer. The conversation in our experiment revolved around the creation of a story, whereas [26] focused on fact-finding.

Another type of story-based interaction consists of robots participating as actors rather than storytellers. Plaisant *et al* [22] used remotely controlled robots to act out stories written by children in order to help children with rehabilitation. GENTORO [25] utilized a robot controlled by hand-held projectors to perform as a character in the story authored by children.

Existing works also studied other issues related to storytelling with children. Benford *et al.* [2] designed graphical interfaces for encouraging children to collaborate in creating stories. StoryMat [7] recorded children's voices to allow collaborative storytelling across time. KidPad [8] is a collaborative story authoring tool that provides children with the ability to draw, type, and insert hyperlinks. Al Moubayed *et al.* [1] considered the problem of providing proper feedback and backchanelling to human storytellers. Their system relied on analysis of video and audio signals of storytellers to synthesize facial expressions and motion behaviors for a virtual human's head and AIBO, a dog-like robot, but SAIBA did not attempt to understand the semantics of stories. Leite and Lehman [17] studied children's sense of privacy in the presense of a seemingly prescient robot during conversational storytelling.

EXPERIMENT

To test the feasibility of the envisioned form of collaborative storytelling and answer the research questions introduced earlier, we designed a task which contained five steps organized in three phases and involved one child and one experimenter at a time. Figure 1 illustrates a general outline. In the first phase (including 1.1 to 1.3 in Figure 1), the child and the experimenter collaboratively created one oral story. In the second phase, the child rated his or her experience in the storytelling activity. In Phase 3, the child was asked to retell the story to a wizarded robot. Two experimenters experienced in interacting with young children took turns to be assigned to an incoming child. The same experimenter went through all three phases with the assigned child. Details of these three phases are described in subsequent subsections.

We recruited 78 children from 4 to 10 years old through postings in physical and online community bulletin boards. Participants were randomly assigned to two conditions (experimental and control), while maintaining the balance of female and male participants across age groups (See Table 1). In total, we had 40 male children and 38 female children, of which 42 are

Table 1: Demographic information of child participants in the experiments.

Age	Control		Experimental		Total
	M	F	M	F	
4.0 - 6.9	11	9	12	10	42
7.0-10.9	8	9	9	10	36
Total	19	18	21	20	78

between 4.0 and 6.9 years old and 36 are between 7.0 and 10.9 years old.

Among the 78 participants, 7 children did not verbally engage in storytelling activity (some used body movements and vocal sounds to tell the story). One participant's speech could not be understood by the data annotator. Two participants' sessions were not recorded due to a software issue. After careful inspection, experimenters did not use enough correct type of prompts in seven participants (more details later). After discarding those data, the analysis for storytelling (Phase 1) used data from the remaining 61 children. For self-reported post-storytelling evaluations, we recorded 76 responses among the total 78 participants. Among the 61 children who successfully participated in the storytelling, we recorded 60 story retelling sessions. We perform analysis of the experiments based on available data.

Phase 1: Collaborative Storytelling

The main activity of Phase 1 is the collaborative telling of a story involving a hero (*Dragon Lady, Flying Toaster, Windstorm*, or *Red Octopus*), a villain (*Trash Can Guy*), four auxiliary entities (a cat, a fork, a pair of roller skates and a bottle of magic potion) and a scene (forest or marketplace). Storytelling took place inside a room instrumented with microphones and a camera. Figure 2 shows the setup. A tablet app (concealed from the child) was developed to notify the experimenter of the current child's condition (experimental vs. control) and the remaining time before the introduction of the next character or object. In order to ground concepts and establish joint attention, which is believed to improve learning [9], we printed the two scenes on letter-sized paper and presented all characters and entities as small cards on stands. The cards remained hidden from the child until they were introduced into the story.

The experimenter and the child first engaged briefly in small talk to build rapport. Immediately after that, the child was asked to select a super hero from four candidates as the main protagonist of the story, as well as a background scene for the story. After the selection, the child was prompted to begin telling the story. During the storytelling, the experimenter would verbally and physically introduce the villain and the auxiliary entities one by one to the child.

In order to minimize confounding factors, the collaboration in this storytelling activity was limited to the experimenter introducing entities in a fixed sequence into the story — first the villain, *Trash Can Guy*, followed by the cat, the fork, the pair of roller skates, and the potion, in roughly one minute intervals. The corresponding entity card was shown to the

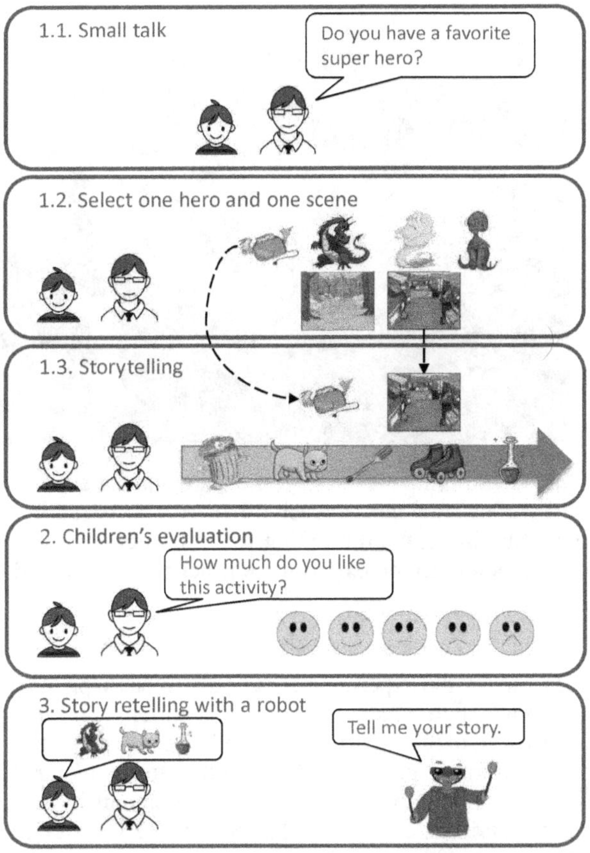

Figure 1: The outline of the procedure. The first phase starts with a small talk (1.1) and the selection of a hero and a scene (1.2). In the main activity (1.3), the experimenter collaborates with the child in telling a story by introducing five entities in roughly one-minute intervals. In the second phase, the child evaluates his or her experience. In the third phase, the child retells the story to a wizarded robot.

child at the same time. After the introduction of a new entity, the child was not restricted to exclusively talk about it. As an effort to maintain consistency across the two experimental arms, we utilized a time window for introducing new entities. The time window was from 50 seconds to 70 seconds (i.e., 1 minute $\pm$ 10 seconds) after the last entity's introduction. This gave the experimenter some flexibility in choosing the best moment to introduce an entity. This time window was displayed on the tablet to the experimenter, but not visible to the child.

In addition to the *introduction* of a new entity, we designed another type of collaborative storytelling: *encouragement*. The experimenter may encourage the child to create more content, if the child stopped his or her story prematurely before the one-minute time limit.

Either type of experimenter utterance may be *contextual* or *non-contextual*. As mentioned earlier, in the control condition, the experimenter was not allowed to refer to the story in her introduction or encouragement utterances. We call these utterances non-contextual. For example, as non-contextual en-

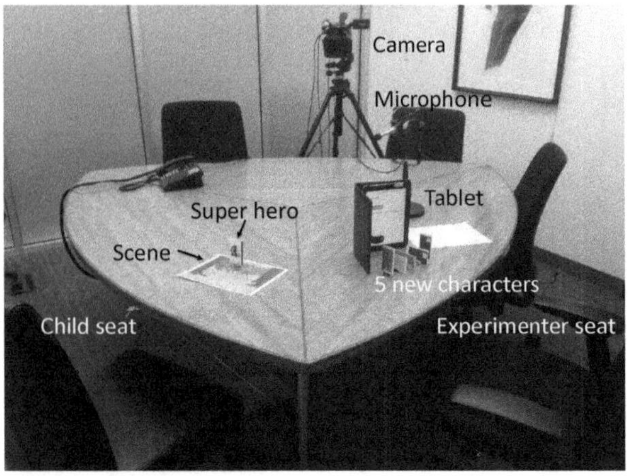

Figure 2: Experimental setting: the child and the experimenter (exp) were seated next to each other. A web-based interface on a tablet indicated the timing for introducing new objects and characters to the experimenter, but was concealed from the child.

couragement, the experimenter can say "What happens next?". As an introduction, she may say "Let's include a kitten." In comparison, in the experimental condition experimenters were instructed to use prompts related to the story thus far. Examples of such utterances include encouragements like "Where did the kitten hide?", "What happened after Trash Can Guy saw the kitten?", or introductions like "Let's say while the kitten was running away from the villain, it found a magic potion in the forest." We call these experimenter utterances contextual. As the experimenters do not always have time to ponder over their utterances in the fast-paced storytelling task, some non-contextual utterances may occasionally occur in the experimental condition.

The rationale for this contextual versus non-contextual dichotomy is to simulate the effect of imperfect natural language understanding and imperfect speech recognition. While a robot can be pre-authored with a set of non-contextual prompts in the control condition, sophisticated comprehension models are needed to generate contextual prompts in the experimental condition. If the robot cannot understand the story well, its best strategy is to avoid referring to the story in order not to make mistakes.

Phase 2: Children's Evaluation of Experience

In this phase, we focus on whether or not children in the control condition (mostly non-contextual prompts) would experience storytelling activity differently from those in the experimental condition (mostly contextual prompts). After the collaborative storytelling activity, participants rated their experience using the Smileyometer instrument [23], which communicates the idea of Likert scale using smiley faces. The children were asked to choose one face for each of the following two questions:

Q1: How much do you like this activity?

Q2: How brave was your superhero?

Prior to the storytelling activity, the children were briefly trained to understand the smiley scale: they were first asked about a few daily events (such as favorite vegetable, the feeling when somebody stepped on their toes). Experimenters helped them associate their feelings with appropriate smiley faces.

Phase 3: Story Retelling

In the third phase of the experiment, the child was led away from the room to interact with a puppeteered robot. The robot asked the child to retell the story. The experimenter stood next to the child and provide assistance as necessary. One type of assistance was explaining what the child was expected to do (e.g., "you can just tell the robot your story"). The second type of assistance happened when the child struggled to remember his/her story. In this case, the experimenter may provide a minimum hint by saying, for example, "I think you have a flying toaster in your story." The interaction among the child, the robot and the experimenter was recorded and transcribed into text. Phase 3 allows us to measure the child's memory of the collaboratively created story, as recall may be related to language learning, which is believed to be a major benefit of storytelling [6, 19, 21]. The design of Phase 3 is part of a larger study. The robot was puppeteered by a researcher experienced with child-robot interaction, who followed a preauthored script. The controls include hand-held controllers and a virtual reality headset connected to two cameras mounted on the robot's head. We refer interested readers to a parallel publication [18] for more details.

Data Annotation

One experienced annotator annotated the storytelling (Phase 1) video with the ELAN software package [28]. Using the display of waveforms, the annotator marked the utterance boundaries with approximately 100ms silence at the beginning and the end. She transcribed each utterance into text and associated each experimenter utterance to indicate (1) whether an utterance referred to some elements in the story (CON vs. NONCON) and (2) whether the utterance introduced a new character into the story or simply encouraged a child to continue (INTRO vs. ENC). See Table 2 for a detailed explanation of these functions. The following conversations were discarded: small talk before the storytelling (i.e., discussion on the child's favorite super hero) and chat after the end of a story, as well as experimenter utterances which served as acknowledgments, empathy or back-channel (e.g., "Red octopus is my favorite too!", "Ok, so the cat is gone.", "++uh-huh++").

For children's self evaluation of the experience (Phase 2), we converted the smiley faces selected by the children to ratings from 1 to 5, where 1 indicates the most negative and 5 indicates the most positive.

We manually analyzed the transcripts of story retelling (Phase 3) to count the characters and objects recalled by the participants. We looked for mentions of the five entities and the protagonist introduced in storytelling (Phase 1) and ignored linguistic variations. For example, we considered the "cat" character as successfully recalled as long as the child mentioned any of the words "cat", "kitten" or "kitty". Table 3

Table 2: Functions of each experimenter utterance.

Function	Explanation	Examples
CON-INTRO	*Contextually* introduce a **new character** to the child.	"What will happen if *the kitten* finds this **fork**?" "But wait. *He lay down* and he found a **fork** underneath him." "But *when he was at the supermarket*, he found the **roller-skate**."
NONCON-INTRO	Non-contextually introduce a **new character** to the child.	"Let's include a **kitten** in the story." "Let me give you a **magic potion** and now you can end your story."
CON-ENC	*Contextually* encourage the child to continue with the story.	"*OK, kitty and dragon are hanging around the forest.* What will happen?" "What happened after *trash can appeared in the market place and flying toaster was all around flying in the market place.* Where did they go next?"
NONCON-ENC	Non-contextually encourage the child to continue with the story.	"Go for it!", "No, no, no. This can't be the end. We still have time." "So what happened next?"

shows an example of this process. The hero character, *Windstorm*, was not considered as a successful recall because it was directly hinted by the experimenter in Turn 5. In Turn 8, the three characters mentioned by the child himself were counted as successful recalls.

RESULTS

In this section, we report our analysis of the experiment. We first examine linguistic measures, followed by enjoyment and story recall.

Linguistic Measures

We define an *exchange* as two turns in the storytelling, in which the experimenter and the child each speak once. Note that both the experimenter's turn (or prompt) and the child's turn in one exchange can contain more than one utterances. The experimenter always initiated the conversation, so her prompt always appeared before the child's turn in an exchange. An example of turn segmentation as well as exchange segmentation is shown in Table 4. The experimenter prompt in one exchange was annotated as either *contextual* or *non-contextual* based on experimenter utterance function — a prompt is considered contextual if at least one of the experimenter utterances in that prompt was annotated as contextual introduction of new character (CON-INTRO) or contextual encouragement (CON-ENC). Otherwise, this prompt is considered non-contextual.

Experimenters were asked to use either contextual or non-contextual prompts according to the experiment condition. However, due to time pressure, experimenters sometimes were not able to meet this requirement and used the wrong type of prompt. For 61 out of the 68 participants, the experimenter used the correct type of prompts more than 70% of the exchanges. In order to keep our experiment strictly between-subject, we used data from these 61 participants and computed the average performance for each individual.

We propose four linguistic measurements of the quality of the children's storytelling. As measures of language complexity, we used the *duration* of the child's entire response in one exchange and the *mean length per utterance* (MLU), which

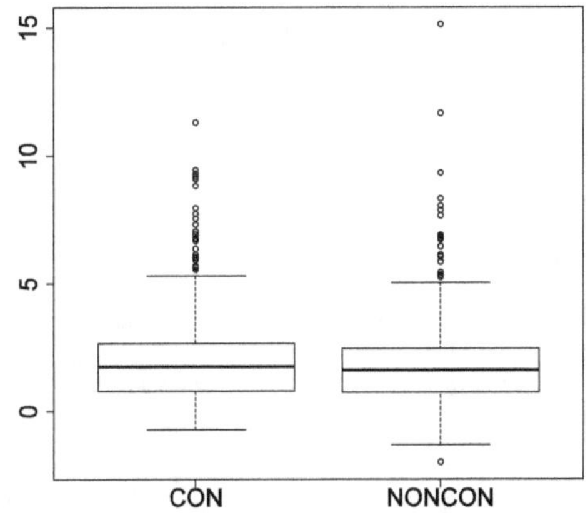

Figure 3: Box-and-whisker plots for experimenter latency across contextual (CON) and non-contextual (NONCON) groups.

is the number of words per utterance. We computed two measures of fluency as follows: *Content speech rate* is defined as the number of words per minute, excluding stopwords (e.g., "the", "that") and fillers. *Response latency* is defined as the time the child spent before responding to an experimenter prompt. These four measures were automatically computed based on the human annotations of the stories.

Experimenter latency is defined as the amount of time the experimenter waited before she started her prompt in an exchange. It may be a confound variable because it indicates whether the experimenter prompt is well timed or not, which may have effects on the storytelling activity. We find this variable to be well controlled across contextual and non-contextual groups, as their distributions are very similar (see Figure 3). To see if values of experimenter latency in the contextual group and the non-contextual group are identically distributed, we first check if they can be described by Gaussian distributions or Log-Normal distributions using the Shapiro-Wilk test, yielding negative answers for both. Using the non-parametric Wilcoxon-Mann-Whitney test and Kolmogorov-

Table 3: A transcript for a story retelling. [unint] indicates unintelligible speech.

Turn ID	Transcription	Recalled objects
1	Robot: "Was storytelling fun?"	[]
2	Child: "Yeah."	[]
3	Robot: "That's great. We like to keep you happy. Tell me your story."	[]
4	Child: "++uh++, so it was long, but one part was that... ++um++ ..." *(Child turned to the experimenter)*	[]
5	Exp: "Who was your, who was your hero? Windstorm."	[]
6	Child: "Yeah."	[]
7	Exp: "One part was windstorm, and what happened?"	[]
8	Child: "**Kitty** came to ... and to scare the **fork** and the ... and the [unint], and **trash can**."	[cat, fork, villain]
9	Robot: "That was a very interesting adventure. Is there time for me to tell a story?"	[]
10	Exp: "No. Sorry about that. We have to go play the next game."	[]

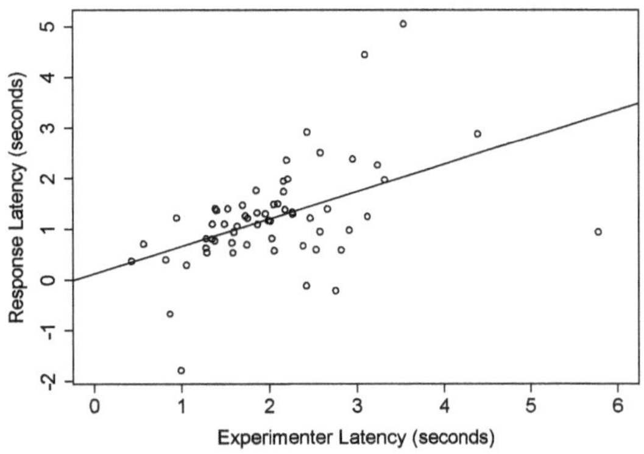

Figure 4: The relationship between experimenter latency and children's response latency.

Smirnov test, we cannot reject the null hypothesis that the two distributions of experimenter latency are the same. Given our reasonably large sample sizes ($N_{contextual} = 385$ exchanges, $N_{non-contextual} = 348$), this suggests the contextual and non-contextual groups are quite similar in this aspect.

We conduct analysis of covariance (ANCOVA) to determine the difference between contextual and non-contextual prompts on children's language performance, controlling for experimenter latency. We do not find significant interaction between contextualization and experimenter latency across our measurements. We find that contextualization significantly impacted the duration of children responses ($F = 8.7$, $p = .005$). Non-contextual prompts yielded longer responses ($M = 11.80$ seconds, $SD = 7.09$) compared to contextual prompts ($M = 6.30$, $SD = 5.91$). For MLU, non-contextual prompts encouraged longer sentences ($M = 9.07$ words/utterance, $SD = 3.14$) compared to contextual ones ($M = 6.89$, $SD = 2.97$).

Experimenter latency is associated with content speech rate ($F = 5.3$, $p = .025$) and children's response latency ($F = 18.1$, $p < .001$). As shown in Figure 4, longer experimenter latency was associated with worsen language performance (e.g., longer children response latency).

Age Effects

We first separate the children into a younger group who are between 4.0 and 6.9 years old and an older group whose ages are between 7.0 and 10.9. After that, we perform a two-way ANCOVA to investigate the impact of contextualization on children's verbal responses controlling experimenter latency.

In the younger age group, we find significant interaction between contextualization and experimenter latency ($F = 8.6$, $p = .007$) on duration. The interaction is shown in Figure 5a. For control group (non-contextual prompts), longer experimenter latency is associated with shorter responses. However, when providing contextualized prompts, this trend can be reversed (see the red dashed line in Figure 5a). We find a main effect of contextualization ($F = 11.9$ $p = .002$) on duration where non-contextual prompts yielded longer responses ($M = 10.39$ seconds, $SD = 7.37$) compared with contextual prompts ($M = 4.06$, $SD = 2.30$). For MLU, non-contextual prompts significantly encouraged longer sentences ($F = 4.6$, $p = .040$). On average, children produced 7.65 ($SD = 2.71$) words per utterance after non-contextual prompts. But after contextual prompts, they produced 5.57 ($SD = 2.39$). For content speech rate, we find that longer experimenter latency is associated with significantly slower yield of meaningful content ($F = 5.3$, $p = .028$). For response latency, we find significant interaction between contextualization and experimenter latency ($F = 6.5$, $p = .016$). As the red dashed line in Figure 5b shows, contextual prompts can help attenuate the negative impact of long response latency.

For older children, we do not find any statistically significant interaction or main effects on duration, MLU, and content speech rate. However, we find experimenter latency to be strongly associated with children response latency. Again, longer experimenter latency co-occurs with longer children response latency.

Gender Effects

We separated participants to boys and girls and conducted Type-II ANCOVA within each group. We first report the results on boys. For duration, there is a statistically significant difference between contextual and non-contextual prompts ($F = 11.8$, $p = .002$). Non-contextual prompts led to children generating longer responses ($M = 11.83$ seconds,

Table 4: A transcript for the three steps in Phase 1. C denotes the child and E denotes the experimenter. Subscripts denote different turns.

Step	Turn	Utterance
1.1 Small Talk	E_1	Do you like superhero stories?
	C_1	Yes.
	E_2	Who is your favorite superhero?
	C_2	Spiderman.
	E_3	Tell me about his adventure.
	C_3	He is ...
		...
1.2 Hero and Scene Selection	E_5	There are red octopus, windstorm, flying toaster, and dragon lady. Who do you want to be the hero of your story?
	C_5	Toaster.
		...
1.3 Storytelling	E_8	One day, flying toaster was in the market when the villain, trash can guy, showed up. What happened?
	C_8	The trash can started to eat all the fruits and vegetables. Or at least all the stuff.
	E_9	And then what happened? (*story continues ...*)
	E_{12}	Alright, well, let's see what will happen if somebody has roller skates. (*story continues ...*)
	E_{24}	Is there anything else that happens?
	C_{24}	[Toaster] brings it [magic potion] to his house and use it the next time he needed to save somebody. The end.

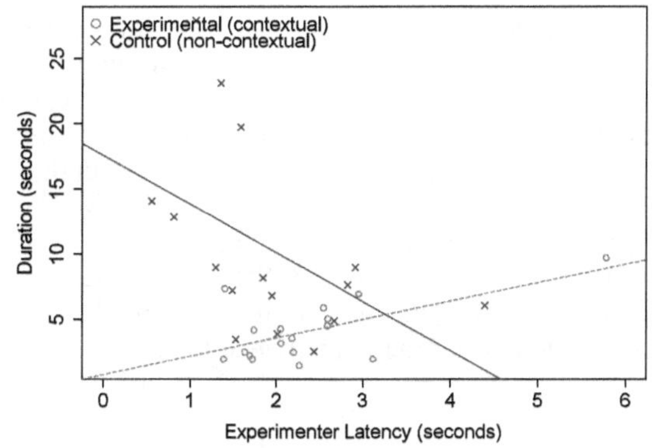

(a) Duration

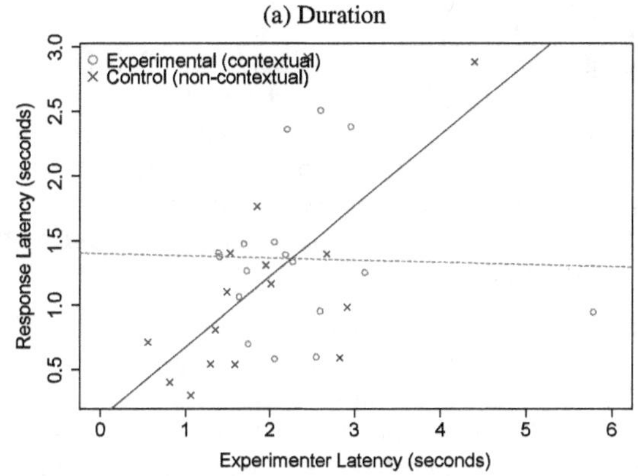

(b) Response Latency

Figure 5: The interaction between contextualization and experimenter latency on young children's language performance.

$SD = 7.55$) compared with contextual prompts ($M = 4.52$, $SD = 2.35$). For MLU, non-contextual prompts are statistically significantly better as well ($F = 4.4$, $p = .046$). On average, children's utterances are 8.74 words long ($SD = 2.48$) after non-contextual prompts. However, they are only 6.50 ($SD = 3.14$) after contextual prompts. For content speech rate and latency, we find a statistically significant main effect of experimeter latency ($F = 4.9$, $p = .037$ for content speech rate; $F = 13.2$, $p = .001$ for children response latency). Longer experimenter latency is associated with slower content speech rate and longer child latency.

For girls, we do not find significant interaction or main effects on duration, MLU, and content speech rate. We find a main effect of experimenter latency ($F = 6.4$, $p = .017$) on child response latency. Again, longer experimenter latency is associated with worsen response latency.

Enjoyment

We collected ratings of enjoyment using the Smileyometer instrument [23]. The data we obtained from this evaluation are skewed; most participants rated the aforementioned two questions with the most positive rating, 5. Given the ordinal nature of the ratings, we use ordinal logistic regression to investigate the impact of gender, age group, condition (experimental or control) as well as their interactions on those ratings. For Q1, there is no significance found. For Q2, younger children rated the braveness of their superheroes significantly higher ($p = 0.04$).

Character/Object Recall

We also measured the recall of the six individual story entities in story retelling. Among the aforementioned 61 children who successfully participated in storytelling in the correct conditions, we lost 1 recording of story retelling due to technical issues. Using Fisher's exact test to compare the control group and the experimental group, we do not find any statistical significance.

Separating the participants into two age groups, we observe that older children (7-10 years old) in general recall more than younger children. For hero characters, children in old group statistically significantly recalled more than children in young group ($p = .021$). For different gender groups, as shown in Figure 7b, girls tended to recall more than boys. The difference is significant for the potion object ($p = .016$). Participants tended to recall earlier characters like heroes and villains than entities introduced later.

We further inspect the total number of entities recalled and the effect of gender, age and contextualization using a three-way type-II ANOVA. We find a marginal contextualization effect ($F(1,53) = 3.9$, $p = .055$). Children in the control group recalled more ($M = 2.69$, $SD = 2.05$) than those in the experimental group ($M = 1.79$, $SD = 1.45$). We also found a marginal gender effect ($F(1,53) = 3.4$, $p = .072$) that girls tended to recall more ($M = 2.68$, $SD = 1.87$) than boys ($M = 1.83$, $SD = 1.73$). We find neither statistically significant effects of age nor interaction between factors.

DISCUSSION

The goal of this experiment is to study the effects of contextual and non-contextual prompts. In the control group, the experimenters were not allowed to refer to the story content when they encouraged the child or introduced new entities into the story. In the experiment group, the experimenters were asked to refer to the story content whenever possible during the two types of utterances.

Measures on language complexity, including response duration and MLU, showed the children spoke less and spoke less fluently when contextual prompts were used. This may be explained by the hypothesis that collaborative storytelling imposes a heavy cognitive load on children. When an adult experimenter proposed a change to the story as a contextual prompt, the child must understand the proposed change to the story and incorporate this change into his or her own idea of the unfolding story. This extra work was absent in the non-contextual condition.

Upon detailed inspection, we note the reduction in response duration and MLU concentrated on children younger than 7 and boys, which are groups that are typically less well developed in speech production and, more generally, language abilities. For instance, Hyde and Lynn's meta-analysis of 165 studies [13] found speech production to be the area with the most female advantage, though the analysis was not limited to children. More recent studies [4, 14] noted young girls exhibit faster language development than young boys in areas like learning new meanings of familiar words and complexity of produced language. This agrees with the hypothesis that contextual prompts imposed heavier cognitive load on children than non-contextual prompts in the collaborative task.

However, we also find that speaking less is not equivalent to using less content words. The fluency measures, especially the content word speech rate, in the two conditions appear rather similar. In addition, the self-reported enjoyment between the two conditions shows no statistically significant difference, so the additional cognitive load is unlikely to discourage children from participation. As long-term participation in a cognitive demanding task may accelerate cognitive development, these results can be considered to corroborate previous findings [6, 19, 21] that storytelling fosters children's cognitive development. Admittedly, the current experiment only measures short-term effects of collaborative storytelling. Further studies are needed to ascertain long-term effects of the proposed interaction paradigm.

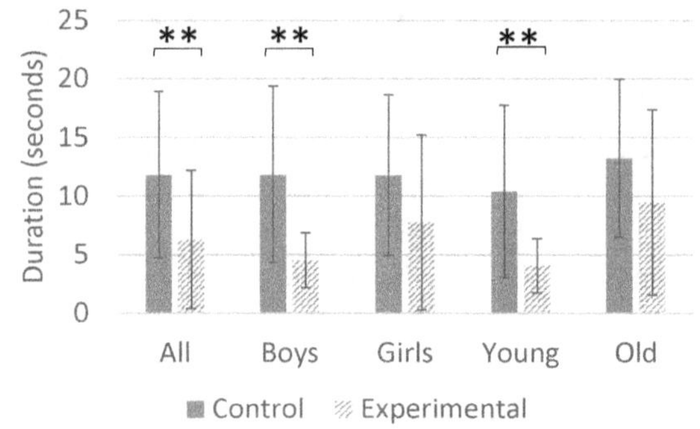

(a) Response Duration

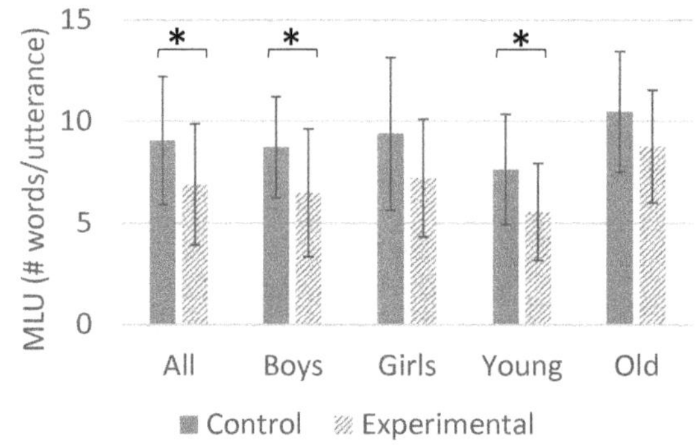

(b) Mean Length of Utterance

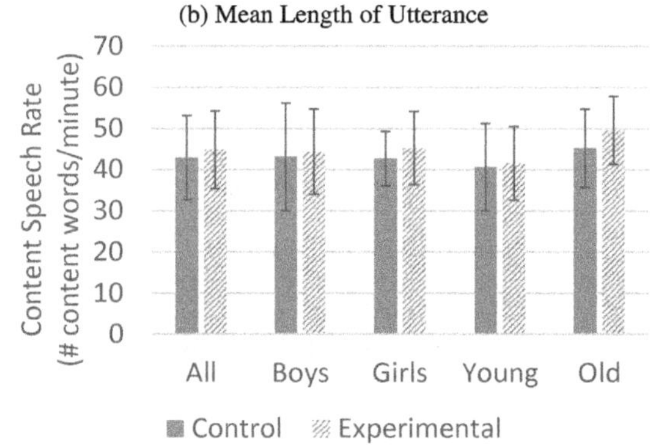

(c) Content Speech Rate

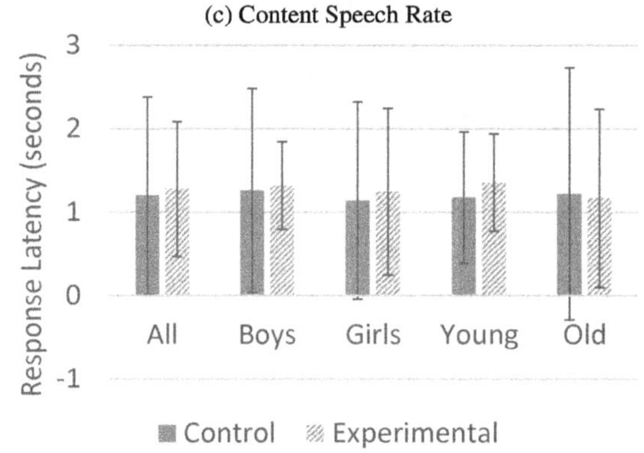

(d) Response Latency

Figure 6: The effects of contextualization on (1) all participants, (2) different age groups, and (3) different gender. ** denotes $p < 0.01$. * denotes $p < 0.05$.

After the effects of individual factors are accounted for, we observe a statistically significant interaction between contextual / non-contextual prompts and experimenter latency among young children. This deserves further discussion. A longer experimenter latency is generally associated with a longer response latency from children (See Figure 4). We provide the hypothesis that this mostly happened when the child ran out of steam and the experimenter waited for the child. That is, a long experimenter latency was likely caused by a pause from the child, rather than a pause from the experimenter who could not find what to say. After receiving the experimenter's prompt, the child likely continued struggling, leading to a short response duration and a long response latency. However, when young children received contextual prompts after a long experimenter latency, the above trend mostly disappeared (See Figure 5). This suggests that a contextual prompt may have given the child something to talk about. We conclude the contexual prompts can provide valuable scaffolding when used in the right situation, such as when the child completely runs out of things to say.

In summary, we found contextual prompts to be cognitively demanding, if occasionally helpful, to children creating stories orally. The participants found the collaborative storytelling task very enjoyable and the two collaboration strategies had statistically insignificant effects on overall enjoyment. This strengthened our confidence in the collaborative storytelling task as an engaging form of interaction for language learning. As a design guideline, we propose that a practical robot should utilize both strategies depending on the child's cognitive development and the robot's ability to understand the story. Contextual prompts should be used to create optimal challenges to accelerate learning. On the other hand, non-contextual prompts can be used when the robot fails to recognize speech or understand the story semantics.

CONCLUSIONS

In this paper, we report a study for social collaborative storytelling between an adult and a child. The adult served as a surrogate for an envisioned storytelling robot, which can contribute new characters and objects to the child's story. Our aim was to investigate the effects of two collaboration techniques, which differ in whether they relate new content to existing story content or not. Relating new content to the existing story intuitively appears to be beneficial. However, it is not applicable when the robot fails to understand the child's story due to imperfect technology.

The experiment finds that both collaboration techniques can create enjoyable storytelling experiences. In general, the contextual technique led to degraded performance on young children and boys in the short term, which can be explained by the high cognitive this technique imposes on children. The experiment also suggests, however, properly positioned contextual prompts can help young children in story creation. Thus, instead of sticking to a single collaboration strategy, we recommend the combined use of two strategies. We believe this would provide the correct amount of cognitive challenge, and also allow a robot to have a smooth interaction even when its understanding of the story may be imperfect. Although further studies are needed to measure long-term effects, this study is a stepping stone toward a natural form of collaborative storytelling between robots and children.

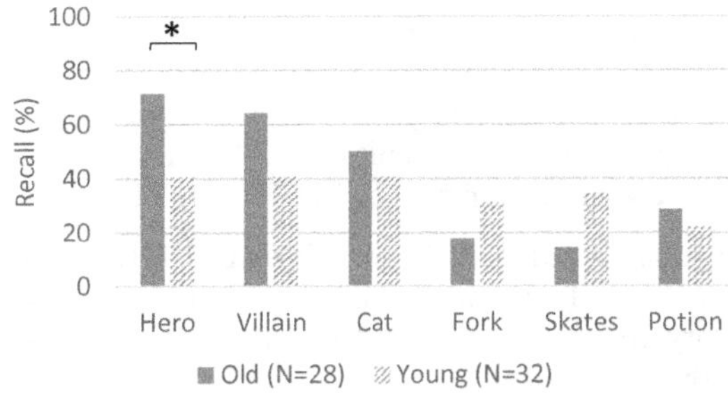

(a) Age

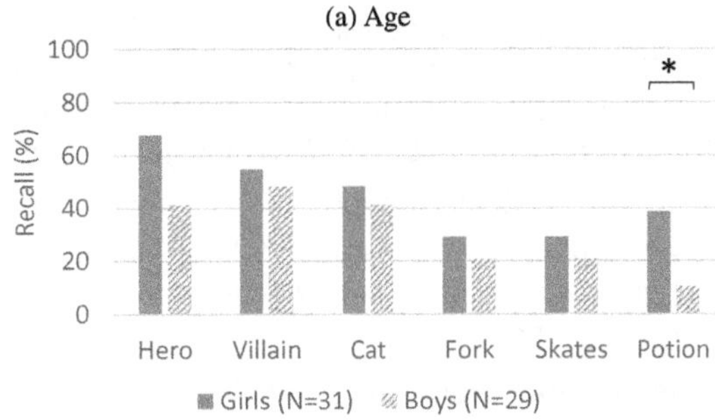

(b) Gender

Figure 7: The effects of experiment conditions, gender and age on recall of story characters. * denotes $p < 0.05$.

REFERENCES

1. S. Al Moubayed, M. Baklouti, M. Chetouani, T. Dutoit, A. Mahdhaoui, J.C. Martin, S. Ondas, C. Pelachaud, J. Urbain, M. Yilmaz, and F. Thalés. 2008. *Multimodal feedback from robots and agents in a storytelling experiment*. Technical Report.
2. Steve Benford, Benjamin B. Bederson, Karl-Petter Akesson, Victor Bayon, Allison Druin, Pär Hansson, Juan Pablo Hourcade, Rob Ingram, Helen Neale, Claire O'Malley, Kristian T. Simsarian, Danaë Stanton, Yngve Sundblad, and Gustav Taxén. 2000. Designing Storytelling Technologies to Encouraging Collaboration Between Young Children. In *Proceedings of the SIGCHI Conference on Human Factors in Computing Systems*. ACM, 556–563.
3. Marina Umaschi Bers and Justine Cassell. 1998. Interactive storytelling systems for children: Using technology to explore language and identity. *Journal of Interactive Learning Research* 9, 2 (1998).
4. Caroline Bouchard, Natacha Trudeau, Ann Sutton, Marie claude Boudreault, and Joane Deneault. 2009. Gender differences in language development in French Canadian children between 8 and 30 months of age. *Applied Psycholinguistics* 30, 4 (2009), 685–707.
5. Cynthia Breazeal, Paul L. Harris, David DeSteno, Jacqueline M. Kory Westlund, Leah Dickens, and Sooyeon Jeong. 2016. Young children treat robots as informants. *Topics in Cognitive Science* (2016), 1–11.

6. Adriana G. Bus, Marinus H. Van Ijzendoorn, and Anthony D. Pellegrini. 1995. Joint book reading makes for success in learning to read: A meta-analysis on intergenerational transmission of literacy. *Review of Educational Research* 65, 1 (1995), 1–21.
7. Justine Cassell and Kimiko Ryokai. 2001. Making space for voice: Technologies to support children's fantasy and storytelling. *Personal and ubiquitous computing* 5, 3 (2001), 169–190.
8. Allison Druin, Jason Stewart, David Proft, Ben Bederson, and Jim Hollan. 1997. KidPad: A Design Collaboration Between Children, Technologists, and Educators. In *Proceedings of the ACM SIGCHI Conference on Human Factors in Computing Systems*. 463–470.
9. A. Duranti and C. Goodwin. 1992. *Rethinking context: Language as an interactive phenomenon*. Cambridge University Press.
10. Jennifer Williamson Glos. 1997. *Digital augmentation of keepsake objects: a place for interaction of memory, story, and self.* Master's thesis. Massachusetts Institute of Technology.
11. Michael J. Guralnick. 2016. Why Early Intervention Works: A Systems Perspective. *Infants and young children* 24, 1 (2016), 6–28.
12. B. Hart and T.R. Risley. 1995. *Meaningful differences in the everyday experience of young American children.* Paul H. Brookes Publishing Co.
13. Janet S. Hyde and Marcia C. Linn. 1988. Gender differences in verbal ability: A meta-analysis. *Psychological Bulletin* 104 (1988), 53–69.
14. Margarita Kaushanskaya, Megan Gross, and Milijana Buac. 2013. Gender differences in child word learning. *Learning and Individual Differences* 27 (2013), 82–89.
15. Patricia K. Kuhl. 2007. Is speech learning gated by the social brain? *Developmental Science* 10, 1 (2007), 110–120.
16. S. H. Landry, K. E. Smith, P. R. Swank, and C. Guttentag. 2008. A Responsive Parenting Intervention: The Optimal Timing Across Early Childhood For Impacting Maternal Behaviors And Child Outcomes. *Developmental Psychology* 44, 5 (2008), 1335–1353.
17. Iolanda Leite and Jill Fain Lehman. 2016. The robot who knew too much: toward understanding the privacy/personalization trade-off in child-robot conversation. In *Proceedings of the 2016 conference on Interaction design and children*. ACM, 379–387.
18. Iolanda Leite, André Pereira, and Jill Fain Lehman. 2017. Persistent memory in repeated child-robot conversations. In *Proceedings of the 16th International Conference on Interaction Design and Children.*
19. Lesley Mandel Morrow. 1985. Retelling Stories: A strategy for improving young children's comprehension, concept of story structure, and oral language complexity. *The Elementary School Journal* 85, 5 (1985), 647–661.
20. Bilge Mutlu, Jodi Forlizzi, and Jessica Hodgins. 2006. A storytelling robot: Modeling and evaluation of human-like gaze behavior. In *Proceedings of the 6th IEEE-RAS International Conference on Humanoid Robots.*
21. Carole Peterson and Allyssa Mccabe. 2004. Echoing our parents: Parental influences on children's narration. In *Family stories and the life course: Across time and generations.* Lawrence Erlbaum, 27–54.
22. Catherine Plaisant, Allison Druin, Corinna Lathan, Kapil Dakhane, Kris Edwards, Jack Maxwell Vice, and Jaime Montemayor. 2000. A storytelling robot for pediatric rehabilitation. In *Proceedings of the fourth international ACM conference on Assistive technologies.* ACM, 50–55.
23. Janet C. Read and Stuart MacFarlane. 2006. Using the fun toolkit and other survey methods to gather opinions in child computer interaction. In *Proceedings of the 2006 conference on Interaction design and children.* ACM, 81–88.
24. Kimiko Ryokai, Cati Vaucelle, and Justine Cassell. 2003. Virtual peers as partners in storytelling and literacy learning. *Journal of computer assisted learning* 19, 2 (2003), 195–208.
25. Masanori Sugimoto, Toshitaka Ito, Tuan Ngoc Nguyen, and Shigenori Inagaki. 2009. GENTORO: A system for supporting children's storytelling using handheld projectors and a robot. In *Proceedings of the 8th International Conference on Interaction Design and Children.* 214–217.
26. Anuj Tewari and John Canny. 2014. What did Spot hide?: A question-answering game for preschool children. In *Proceedings of the 32nd Annual ACM Conference on Human Factors in Computing Systems (CHI '14).* 1807–1816.
27. Jacqueline Kory Westlund and Cynthia Breazeal. 2015. The interplay of robot language level with children's language learning during storytelling. In *Proceedings of the 2015 ACM/IEEE international conference on Human-Robot Interaction (Extended Abstracts).* ACM.
28. Peter Wittenburg, Hennie Brugman, Albert Russel, Alex Klassmann, and Han Sloetjes. 2006. ELAN: A professional framework for multimodality research. In *Proceedings of LREC.*
29. Chun-Cheng Wu, Chih-Wei Chang, Baw-Jhiune Liu, and Gwo-Dong Chen. 2008. Improving vocabulary acquisition by designing a storytelling robot. In *2008 Eighth IEEE International Conference on Advanced Learning Technologies.* 498–500.

Classification of Children's Handwriting Errors for the Design of an Educational Co-Writer Robotic Peer

Shruti Chandra[†,⋆], Pierre Dillenbourg[†] and Ana Paiva[⋆]
[†]CHILI, École Polytechnique Fédérale de Lausanne, Switzerland
[⋆]INESC-ID & Instituto Superior Técnico, Universidade de Lisboa, Portugal
shruti.chandra@tecnico.ulisboa.pt, pierre.dillenbourg@epfl.ch, ana.paiva@inesc-id.pt

ABSTRACT
In this paper, we propose a taxonomy of handwriting errors exhibited by children as a way to build adequate strategies for integration with a co-writing peer. The exploration includes the collection of letters written by children in an initial study, which were then revised in a second study. The second study also analyses the "peer-learning" (PL) and "peer-tutoring" (PT) learning methods in an educational scenario, where a pair of children perform a collaborative writing activity in the presence of a robot facilitator. The data obtained in the first two studies allowed us to create a "taxonomy of handwriting errors". A set of writing errors were selected and implemented in an educational activity for validation. This activity constituted a third study, wherein we systematically induced the errors into a Nao robot's handwriting using the PT method - A teacher-child corrects the handwriting errors of the learner-robot. The preliminary results suggest that the children in general showed awareness to the writing errors and were able to perceive the writing abilities of the robot.

ACM Classification Keywords
K.3.1. Computer Uses in Education: Collaborative learning; K.3.2. Computer and Information Science Education: Information systems education

Author Keywords
Peer assisted learning methods; handwriting difficulties; child-robot-interaction;

INTRODUCTION
Handwriting problems in children affect them negatively with respect to both their academic performance [13] and their motivation and self-esteem [28]. The development of young children's writing ability is not only considered an essential criterion for success in school [32, 35] but also a critical skill that will impact all of us throughout adulthood [15]. A few studies have indicated that handwriting can often be used to judge children in schools; students with poor handwriting are assigned lower grades compared to those with legible handwriting despite similar content [12, 36]. The number of children presenting handwriting problems is estimated to be between 10 and 30% [24], and their consequences include an inability to keep up with the written work required in the class, to obtain high scores in Mathematics, and to achieve sustained attention [31, 26]. Quite often, children with handwriting problems are mislabeled as lazy, which in turn causes additional frustration and behavioral problems [31].

Mastering handwriting involves a complex blend of motor-perceptual abilities, and ineffective motor skills are difficult to change once they are acquired. Hence, special attention should be given to sharpening the motor and cognition skills of preschoolers from the very beginning [30] to prevent problems later on.

Research in educational robotics has proven its significance in different fields such as mathematics, programming, science, games and design[20]. During the past few years, social robots have been used with children to explore new methods of learning in education. For example, Kanda et al. used a humanoid robot as an English peer-tutor for Japanese students [22] in a study. The results showed that the robot encouraged children to improve their English vocabulary and was able to form relationships with them. Furthermore, the EMOTE project[1] addressed the role of empathy in robots [10].

The current work is conducted under the *CoWriter project*[2], which explores the long-term research question of *how to create a social robot that can help children to acquire handwriting skills.* With this vision in mind, we have been investigating the following aspects:

Handling writing difficulties - to explore children's common handwriting errors, which may differ according to their age and motor-perceptual abilities.

Modes of Interaction - to determine the more adequate modes of child-robot interaction to maximise the learning gains of children having different levels of writing skills.

"Peer-learning"(PL) and "peer-tutoring"(PT) are two types of peer-assisted learning methods effectively used in the field of education. In both these methods, the interaction generally occurs between two students. In the PL method,

[1] www.emote-project.eu
[2] http://chili.epfl.ch/cowriter

IDC '17 June 27-30, 2017, Stanford, CA, USA
© 2017 ACM. ISBN 978-1-4503-4921-5/17/06...$15.00
DOI: http://dx.doi.org/10.1145/3078072.3079750

there is an equal alliance between the two students, whereas in the PT method, one student holds responsibility over another student [25].

Learning benefits through child-robot interaction - to use a robot as an agent for enhancing children's learning. In this interaction, it becomes necessary to understand how children perceive the abilities and behavior of a social robot that was endowed with not only writing competence but also writing difficulties.

This article investigates the above-mentioned aspects through a series of three studies. In these studies, we show how a taxonomy of writing difficulties in letters, more specifically, the English alphabet, can be exploited to effectively build a robotic peer to help children. The taxonomy can be used by an automated system, such as a social robot; school teachers; or parents to understand a particular writing issue faced by a child and then help him/her to correct that particular issue.

Section "*Study I*" explains a first study that was conducted with children 4-6 years of age to collect their handwritten letters to identify common handwriting errors and to test learning modes of interactions. Section "*Study II*" presents a second study with children 6-8 years of age to investigate further writing errors to revise the built taxonomy, extend it, and explore the modes of interaction in the presence of a social robot. Finally, section "*Study III*" details the implementation of a set of three writing errors from the taxonomy in a system for the validation and testing of the errors in a third study. The study combined the results of the first and second studies into a version of a robotic peer that has difficulties and needs to learn from the child. When introducing a robotic peer, it is crucial to understand how children perceive the robot's abilities and behavior in a child-robot interaction. Therefore, in this final study, we also explored the children's perception of a "Learning" vs "Non-learning" robot. Finally, the last section concludes by reiterating the contributions of the article.

BACKGROUND

It is believed that the development of handwriting in children begins with early scribbling on paper or other surfaces after they are able to grasp tools for handwriting or drawing. The literature also suggests that writing instructions should be given until a child masters nine shapes, including lines, circle, triangles and oblique crosses [6]. At the ages of 2-3, a child begins to form basic geometric shapes, such as horizontal and vertical lines, followed by being able to imitate a cross, square and triangle between the ages of 4-6 years [6]. The ability to copy the shape of an oblique cross is seen as readiness for handwriting [6, 2]. The research indicates that the typical time period to develop the quality of handwriting lies between primary school grades 1-5 (ages 6-11). Among these years, the level of skill improves more quickly during Grade 1 (ages 6-7) and reaches a plateau by Grade 2 (ages 7-8). Further development during the ages of 8-9 leads to the emergence of more automatic and organised letter formation, which is regarded as a foundation for fluent writing [24, 8].

Handwriting is a complex motor-perceptual ability and includes several components: coordination of visual-motor skills, perceptual and cognitive skills, motor planning, and kinesthetic and tactile sensitivities [27]. In addition, external factors related to environment/biochemical issues, such as sitting position, posture, and chair/desk height, may also influence the handwriting performance [15]. Because handwriting is a combination of forms of letter (orthographic codes), names of letter (phonological codes) and shapes of letters (graphomotor codes) [5], researchers have argued that memory, more specifically the ability to recall the shapes of letters and orthographic processes, is more responsible for handwriting skills rather than motor skills [4].

Simner [33] discussed that the writing errors produced by kindergarten children include additions, deletions and misalignment in parts of a letter. These errors not only influence their academic performance in the kindergarten period but also throughout their first grade. Other common writing errors, due to insufficient motor skills often observed in grade 1 children (ages 6-7 years), are incorrect sizes of letters, placement of letters, and relationships among parts in a letter [34]. The motor skill aspects include isolation, grading and timing of movements. The isolation and grading aspects resulted from the inadequate grasping of the pen. In addition, slow and haphazard writing are associated with the timing of movements affecting the flow of writing [14]. The result of a survey with 169 primary grade teachers indicated that 23% (SD = 14%) of the children in their class faced difficulty with handwriting and that the most common handwriting problems experienced by students are related to overall neatness (76%), spacing between words (66%), letter size (59%), letter formation (57%), alignment of letters (54%), and reversals (52%) [16].

In this article, we focused on classifying the common handwriting errors of children 4-8 years of age because of the lack of extensive details on the writing errors.

In the field of education, researchers have used peer-assisted learning methods either involving an interaction between students or between a robot and a student to support childhood learning. The PL has a reciprocal learning style, where both students act as both teacher and learner [9] without holding power over each other [9, 25]. In a two-month field study, Kanda et al. used Robovie [23], a humanoid robot as a peer-learner/friend, and the results indicated that the robot was able to make friendly relations with children. On the other hand, the PT learning method (also known as the learning-by-teaching method) relies on a one-way learning style: there is an unambiguous distinction between the learning and teaching roles among the students [9]. One student acts as a teacher, while the other one acts as a learner. The research also indicated that when a person teaches someone, knowledge becomes clearer and better organised in his/her mind because of the feedback and communication of ideas [7]. Tanaka et al [37] used the PT method in a study wherein children taught English verbs to a Nao robot[3], which acted as a care receiving interactive agent. The results suggested that the robot was able to enhance the children's spontaneous learning and accelerated their motivation to provide care-taking.

[3] Aldebaran robotics: `https://www.aldebaran.com/en`.

To design better robot-aided learning scenarios for children, it is crucial to understand how children perceive the abilities and behavior of a robot. In a study by T.N. Beran et al., conducted with 168 students, the results have shown that a significant number of students attributed to the robot cognitive and behavioral characteristics [3]. Likewise, another study by Kahn et al., indicated that the majority of children ascribed a robot with mental states and as a social being [21]. In a similar line of research, we explored children's perception of the abilities and behavior of a *Learning* vs. *Non-Learning* robot.

We used the PL and PT learning methods as modes of interaction to explore their effectiveness in the acquisition of handwriting skills. Recent studies have also explored these methods involving a child-robot interaction to improve children's ability in forming shapes and handwriting. For example, Shizuko et al. [29] performed a study with a tele-operated Nao robot whereby children drew some shapes associated with English words. The results suggested that the robot helped children to learn unknown English words. Following a similar line, Hood et al. [18] used the PT method in a learning scenario whereby children taught handwriting skills to the autonomous Nao robot. The results indicated greater engagement with the robot by the children and their improved writing skills. Another long-session study was conducted with children with handwriting difficulty using the PT method, where the Nao robot adapted to the children's handwriting issues. The results indicated the children's increased self-confidence and commitment towards the robot [19].

Because the previous studies have introduced random writing errors, we attempt to provide a classification of errors that will allow them to be approached in a systematic manner. The work presented in the article makes two major contributions: 1) Proposal of a taxonomy of writing issues present in children's handwritten letters in the age group of 4-8 years - which may be suitable for the educational community in evaluating children's handwriting skills. 2) Test of a set of writing errors from the built taxonomy in an educational scenario in a 4-week-long study. The goal of the last study is to understand children's perception towards a robot having writing difficulties and showing two different competencies: *'Learning'* vs. *'Non-Learning'*.

DESIGNING MODES OF INTERACTIONS

In the context of this work, we attempted to develop educational activities that are intended to help children in the acquisition of handwriting skills. Because the research targeted young children, it was crucial to design an activity that was playful, simple to understand, effective and capable of sustaining children's engagement for a certain period of time. We chose the PL and PT learning methods as modes of interactions to understand different aspects of children's behavior and writing skills. The two designed interaction modes were termed as "peer-learner mode" and "teacher-learner mode" and served as two conditions for the first study. Each interaction mode involved a pair of children with a human facilitator, and a collaborative writing activity was performed. The role

Figure 1: Children using: (a) Paper; (b) Tablet

of the facilitator was to provide the instructions to the children during the activity. The modes are explained below:

- ***Peer-learner mode***: In this mode, no role was assigned to the children. The experimenter showed a letter card to both children and asked them to copy the letter onto their respective sheets. After they finished writing, the experimenter prompted them to provide corrections on each other's writing performance. The activity was repeated with other letter cards. For half of the letters, children used a paper sheet, whereas for the other half, they used a tactile device (one per child).
- ***Teacher-learner mode***: In this mode, the experimenter assigned roles to children: one child acted as a learner, and the other acted as a teacher. The experimenter asked the teacher-child to show a letter card to the learner-child so that s/he could copy the letter onto a paper sheet. Then, the experimenter prompted the teacher-child to provide corrective feedback on the learner-child's writing performance. Here, the children again used both paper sheets and tactile devices. After copying half of the letters, the experimenter exchanged their roles, and the activity was repeated with the remaining letters.

STUDY I

Objectives

The overall goal of the study was to form a database of children's handwritten letters to explore the most common handwriting errors. In addition, the other objectives were as follows:

- To identify the common writing errors in the letter samples of the collected data during the study and to build a taxonomy of these errors.
- To assess the effectiveness of both interaction modes.

Methodology

We conducted a first study with 20 English-speaking children in the age group of 4 to 6 years (reception class) in a school. The study followed the ethical norms of privacy and responsibility. As such, only children who assented to the study and whose parents signed the consent form participated. The study consisted of a between-subject design, and out of 20 children, 10 children (5 pairs) participated in the peer-learner mode (M = 4.95, SD = .15; 6 male and 4 female), and the other 10 participated in the teacher-learner mode (M = 4.95, SD = .41; 3 male and 7 female). The materials used in the study were an experimental record sheet, paper sheets, tablets (tactile devices), tablet pens, a camera with a microphone, and target cards with printed letters. For the pre- and post-test, we chose 8 letters, a combination of upper- and lowercase letters (α, π, y, j, S, N, m and Q) printed on 8 separate cards and based on different geometrical shapes. Out of the 8 letters, 6 letters (α, π, y, j, S and Q) were included in the main writing activity. The α and π letters were only included among other English letters to observe the transfer skill, as we knew that children did not have prior knowledge of these Greek letters. For the tactile device, a specific writing app was developed to provide the dual-user interactive feature: when a shape is drawn on one tablet, it can be observed on the other tablet in real time. In addition, an eraser button is provided for children to erase their own writing. This functionality allowed a pair of children to correct each other's writing on their own tablet in real time. The interaction modes were presented as a game to children, and each interaction lasted approximately 10-14 minutes. The study followed the phases detailed below:

Pre-test: In this phase, an experimenter displayed the 8 target letter cards on the table to a pair of children and asked them to write the letters individually on a paper of sheet.

Writing activity: After finishing the pre-test, the experimenter performed the writing activity with 6 target letter cards according to one of the interaction modes selected for the children (see Fig. 1) (explained in section- *Designing modes of interaction*).

Post-test: After finishing the writing activity, the pre-test activity was repeated and also served as a post-test.

Analysis

To analyse the handwriting errors in the letters, we collected the data from the paper sheets as well as from the tablets. The data were analysed by two independent coders, who examined each sample by comparing it with the letter target card (letter presented during the study). Then, the samples were classified based on various factors such as the shapes of the trajectory and sub-trajectory, the number of strokes, and the alignment. Furthermore, a taxonomy of writing issues was built depending on the classification. To capture the communication modalities, two other coders annotated the videos using the ELAN multimedia annotation tool[4]. In terms of the reliability of a participant's writing errors and communication modalities, Cohen's kappa showed agreement values of .65 and .85, indicating a good agreement.

Results

To better understand the interactions among children, we classified the modalities into three main categories: verbal (*e.g.* explanations/short answers), gesture (*e.g.* Pointing), and back channel (*e.g.* facial expressions, nodding etc). Due to the small size of the sample data, the results are discussed in terms of frequency. In terms of corrective feedback, we observed that the children were unable to provide explanations to their peer's writing performance. Most of the time, they preferred short answers (*e.g.* Yes/No) compared to explanations, as shown in Fig. 3. We believe that this may be because of their young age (4-6 years old), and they might not have knowledge

[4]https://tla.mpi.nl/tools/tla-tools/elan/

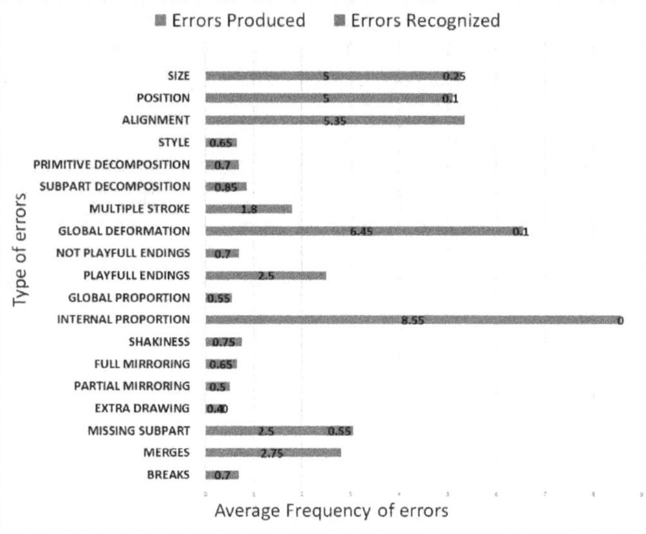

Figure 2: Types of handwriting errors produced and recognised by children

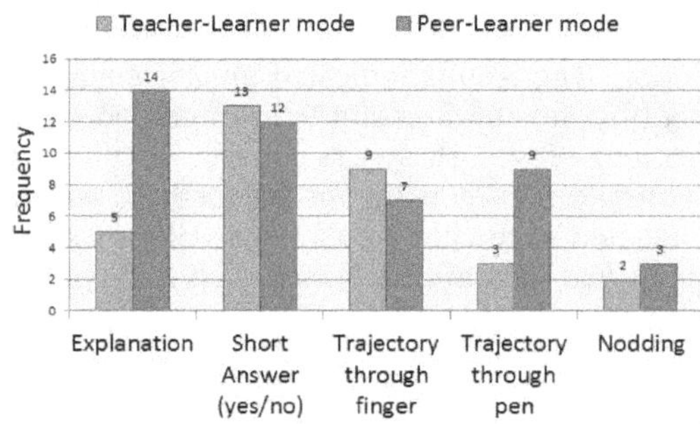

Figure 3: Communication modalities used by children for providing corrective feedback

concerning the shapes of letters. The second most-used communication modality was gestures - demonstrating the correct trajectory of a letter through a finger or a pen (see Fig. 3).

Regarding the difficulties in letter writing, we observed that for most of the children, the letters α and π were difficult to write compared to the other letters. This difficulty might have arisen due to unfamiliarity of these letters. In general, children were able to understand both modes, but from the experimenter's point of view, the children showed more excitement in the "teacher-learner mode" compared to the "peer-learner mode", as they seemed excited to act as a 'teacher'. The built taxonomy was further revised in the second study and detailed in section *Study II*(see Fig. 4). The frequencies of the errors produced and recognised by the children are shown in Fig. 2.

STUDY II

The results of the first study did not present sufficient evidence to differentiate the effectiveness of the two interaction modes. Additionally, we observed that the children were immature in providing corrective feedback on their peers' writing performance due to their young age. Thus, we conducted a second study that consisted of a between-subject design with 40 children in the age group of 6-8 years. We replicated the protocol of the first study but replaced the human facilitator

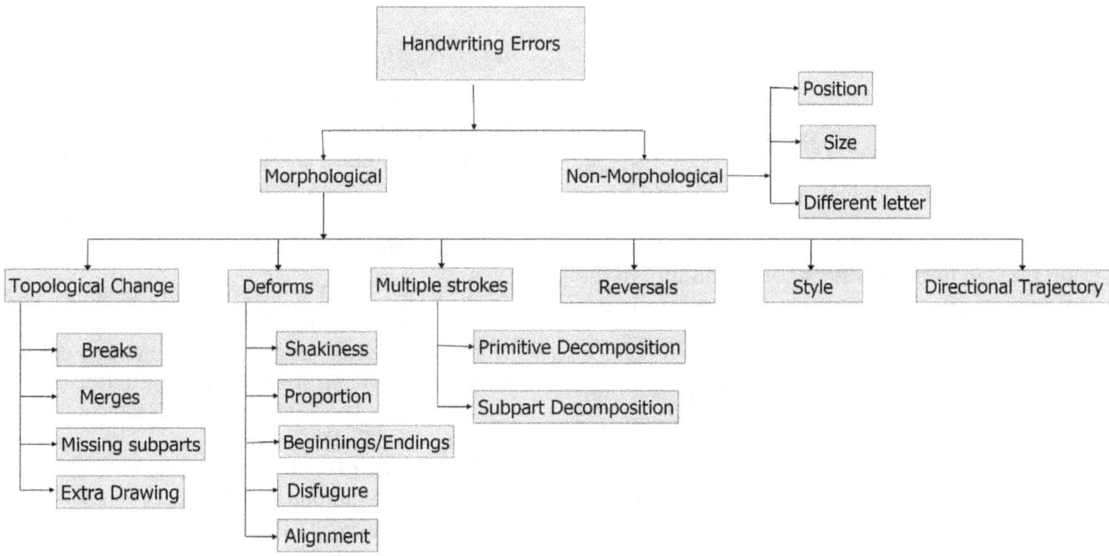

Figure 4: Taxonomy of errors

Figure 5: Children interacting with a robot under the PL/PT conditions

with a robot facilitator. The material in the study included a tablet and a pen for each child, installed with the writing app (used in *Study I*). For the pre-post test, paper sheets with printed letters (j, D, K, y, W, t, α, and π) were used, while for the writing activity, 4 cards were created, and each card had a letter or word written on it: h, Moon, Ice-cream and Rainbow. In addition, we also used cameras, microphones and the Aldebaran's Nao robot (torso part)[5].

Goals

The overall goal of this study was to further investigate the writing errors of children in the age group of 6-8 years, revise the built taxonomy, and explore the PL and PT interaction modes, more precisely, in terms of the assessment of children's behavior with their peers while performing a collaborative writing activity. The research questions of the study include the following:

1) Would children 6-8 years of age perform similar writing errors as children 4-6 years of age?

2) Would children in the age group of 6-8 years be able to provide corrective feedback on the written performance of their peers?

3) How do the two interaction modes differ in terms of corrective feedback? Which type of corrective feedback (short feedback or extended feedback) would children provide?

Methodology

To collect the handwriting samples of children and to explore the impact of introducing a robotic facilitator, the study was performed under two conditions: 1) a pair of children with a robot facilitator, performing a collaborative writing activity based on the PT method, and 2) a pair of children with a robot facilitator, performing a collaborative writing activity based on the PL method. The children were assigned the role of a teacher or a learner according to the learning method used under each condition. The role of the robot-facilitator was to provide instructions and interaction flow during the activity. A Wizard-of-Oz procedure was used to control the robot's behavior. A total of 16 children (8 pairs) participated in Condition 1, and 24 children participated in Condition 2. Each interaction session lasted approximately 10-15 minutes. The study followed these phases:

Pre-test: In this phase, a researcher guided two children in a study room and asked them to copy the letters onto their paper sheets.

Interaction with the robot: After completing the pre-test, the children were guided to a room where the robot facilitator was already placed. The researcher explained the study and left the room. Soon after, the interaction started with the introduction of the robot to the children. Then, the robot explained the features of the writing app and the writing activity. After that, the robot randomly assigned roles to the children according to the conditions (PT or PL). Under the PT condition, the robot asked the tutor-child to pick a card and show it to the learner-child so that he/she could write the letter or word on the tablet application. Then, the facilitator prompted the teacher-child to provide corrective feedback on the learner-child's written performance (see Fig. 5). On the other hand, under the PL

[5]Aldebaran robotics: `https://www.aldebaran.com/en`

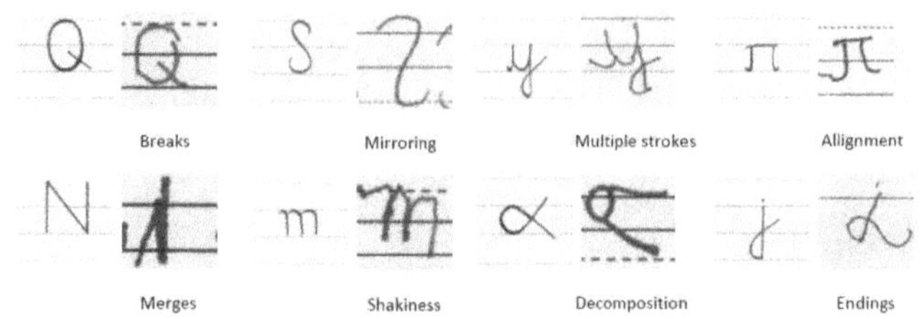

Figure 6: Children's handwritten letters corresponding to the errors. The correct samples of letters are shown on the left side of each letter.

condition, no roles were assigned to the children, and both acted as a teacher and as a learner. The robot alternatingly asked one of the children to pick a card. Both were instructed to write a letter/word on the tablet and prompted to provide feedback on each other's performance (see Fig. 5). Again, the process was repeated for all the letters/words. In the last phase of interaction, the robot thanked the children for their time.
Post-test: After finishing the interaction with the robot, the children were guided to the same room where they had performed the pre-test. The children then repeated the pre-test, which also served as post-test.

Analysis

We collected the data from the tablets and paper sheets and analysed 60% of the data with two independent coders. Furthermore, we performed video analysis of all the groups by annotating the verbal communication between the children and the robot facilitator. We again used the ELAN tool with two independent coders. The agreement value of Cohen's kappa was .58 for the writing errors, which is considered as moderate agreement. The agreement value of Cohen's kappa was .92 for the verbal behaviors and .80 for the pre-/post-test scores. For further analysis, we used the non-parametric Exact Wilcoxon rank-sum (Mann-Whitney U) test, which also seems appropriate for the unequal sample size of the data.

Results

Taxonomy of handwriting errors

After analysing the incorrect letters from the collected database of children 6-8 years of age, we revised the previous taxonomy to incorporate modifications based on the second study. As shown in Fig. 4, the error tree is classified into 17 types of handwriting errors. The classification of the tree is based on the English alphabet, including both uppercase and lowercase letters. However, in the first and second studies, two Greek letters were also included to check the expertise of the children, as they were unfamiliar with the letters. Moreover, the classification included different writing styles, for example, manuscript and cursive.

We classified the writing errors into two broad categories: morphological and non-morphological. These categories are further divided into subcategories (see Fig. 4).

Morphology is defined here as the study of the shapes of letters. The writing issues that show a change in the morphology of a letter belong to this category and are further divided into 6 subcategories: *topology changes*, *deforms*, *multiple strokes*, *reversals*, *directional trajectory*, and *style*.

1- Topology change- Topology is related to the properties of shapes that are preserved under continuous deformations, for example, bending and shrinking without breaking or merging. The writing issues that show a change in the topology of a letter belong to this category. This category contains four more subcategories explained below: [6]

- ***Breaks***- Any discontinuity in the shape of a letter can be observed as a 'hole' in the letter. The writing errors that contains breaks or holes belong to this category (see Fig. 6)
- ***Merges***- When a sub-part of a letter is glued to another sub-part of the same letter, it creates a merging error in the letter (see Fig. 6).
- ***Missing Sub-parts***- Only those letters that have more than one stroke can have this error. A missing stroke in a letter creates this type of error.
- ***Extra drawing***- This type of error refers to when an additional stroke is added (not necessarily touching the letter) to make a letter decorative or exaggerated. However, this is not considered to be a major error, as it generally adds artistic value to a letter.

2- Deforms- When a letter shows any deformation in the shape of the letter while maintaining the topology of the letter, the error belongs to this category. The deformations can be present in a sub-part of the letter (locally) or in all parts of the letter (globally). This category is further divided into 5 subcategories, discussed below:

- ***Shakiness***- This type of error occurs when a letter shows a visible jerk in its trajectory. (see Fig.6).
- ***Proportion***- This type of error occurs when a letter shows an asymmetry or disproportion in its shape, *e.g.* shrinking or stretching in any direction.
- ***Beginnings/Endings***
  This issue is when then beginning or ending is extended (in the shape of a curve or a straight line). This type of error is different from the *extra drawing* error, as it only exaggerates the extensions. This error is further divided into two additional categories, detailed below.
  Playful- When a letter shows a decorative extension and the child who formed this letter is aware of the extension, then the error belongs to this category.
  Non-playful-When a letter shows extensions (not decorative) and a child does not have knowledge of forming the extensions, then the error belongs to this category. However, it is difficult to identify this issue by looking at the final images of letters. It can be easily seen during the formation of a letter.
- ***Distortion***
  This is a general category of errors that do not follow any specific patterns. This type may include, for example, wide, curvy, and snake-style distortions in the shapes of letter and sometimes leads to fully distorted shapes resulting in illegible letters.

[6]https://en.wikipedia.org/wiki/Topology

- ***Alignment***
  This refers to the misalignment or rotation of a letter through some angle (see Fig.6).

3- Multiple strokes- When a letter is formed by decomposing it into parts, this type of error is created (see Fig.6). If the parts are well joined in the final image of the letter, then it is difficult to visualise this error; however, during the formation of a letter, this issue can be easily observed. In addition, the error may or may not change the topology of the letter and can be present locally or globally. This category contains two subcategories, detailed below:

- ***Primitive Decomposition***- This type of issue is when a letter is formed by decomposing it into basic shapes, for example, circles and horizontal/vertical lines (see Fig. 6). In the first study, we observed this error mostly in beginners, and it may occur due to the lack of knowledge about shapes. For example, when writing the letter *alpha*, a few children decomposed it into a circle and straight lines, as the letter was unfamiliar to them (see Fig.6).
- ***Sub-part Decomposition***- This issue refers to when a letter is formed by decomposing a single stroke into several strokes. This is different from the above error, as in this case, the decomposed strokes do not resemble basic shapes such as a circle. Here, a circle can possibly be made with several small strokes.

4- Reversals- This error refers to when a subpart or a full letter is reversed in any of the four directions, left, right, top, or bottom; then, a reversed image is created. This does not affect the topology of the letter.
5- Direction of trajectory- This writing error can only be observed during the formation of a letter, as it concerns the direction of the trajectory of the letter. This issue does not produce a change in the topology of the letter and can be present locally or globally.
6- Style- This issue refers to when a letter is formed with a different style (cursive or manuscript) instead of the required style. However, this is a minor issue and can be present locally or globally. The topology may or may not be changed.

Non-morphological errors do not produce a change in the shape of a letter and therefore are not related to the morphology of a letter. In addition, this error does not affect the topology of the letter. This category is divided into three additional subcategories, discussed below.
1- Position- This issue refers to the correct placement of a letter with respect to base/reference lines present on a writing base where the letter is drawn.
2- Size- As the name suggests, this issue is related to the size of a letter with respect to reference lines or other letters present on a writing base where the letter is drawn.
3- Different letter- This error is related to the misinterpretation of a letter. For example, in both studies, we found two letters, α and π, were misinterpreted as the letters "a" and "r" or "u", respectively. Initially, we did not include this issue in the tree because we thought that this error might occur due to the introduction of unknown letters to the children. However, in the second study, we found that two children misinterpreted the letters "W" and "j" as 'U' and 'G', respectively, which

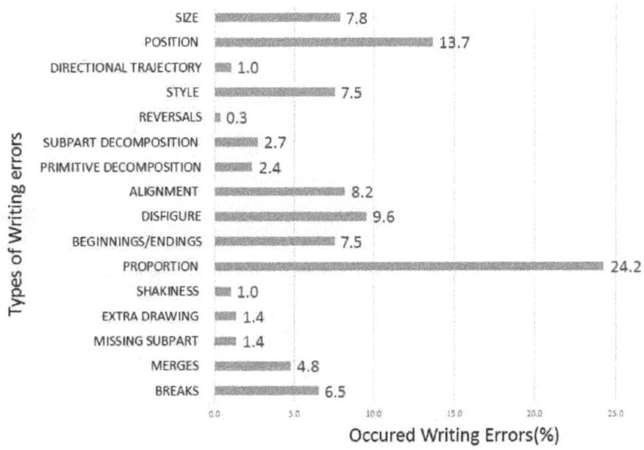

Figure 7: Handwriting errors that occurred (%)

shows that this error may occur, although not often.
The above writing issues were explored by analysing the letter images as well as by observing the formation of letters during both studies. The classification is based on considering the change in shape of the letters and patterns of the writing errors. We revised the taxonomy in the second study and modified it by adding and merging some writing issues. For example, the writing errors *decomposition* and *multiple strokes* were merged, and the error *different letter* was added in the revisions. Although we observed that a few writing errors, such as shakiness, missing subpart and extra drawing, seemed to be less frequent in the second study (see Fig. 7), other errors remained prevalent in both studies. The frequencies of the errors in the second study are shown in Fig. 7, and a few samples of the handwritten letters from the second study are presented in Fig. 8.

Exploration on modes of interaction & Children's assessment on their peers

The two modes of interaction, the PL and PT learning methods, were explored in terms of three variables: 1) self-disclosure, 2) corrective feedback, and 3) learning gains. Regarding self-disclosure, all the tutor-children and learner-children under the PT condition gave significantly more extended self-disclosures to the robot in comparison to the children under the PL condition [11]. Regarding the corrective feedback given by the children, the result of a Man-Whitney U test suggested that all learner-children under the PT condition gave significantly more extended feedback to their peers (Mdn = 5.0) compared to the children under the PL condition (Mdn = 0.0), $U = 57$, $p < 0.05$, $r = .43$, as depicted in Fig. 9(a) [11]. On the other hand, the results showed that all the tutor-children under the PT condition gave significantly more extended corrective feedback to their peers (Mdn = 2.5) in comparison to the children under the PL condition (Mdn = 0.0), $U = 21$, $p < .001$, $r = .73$, as observed in Fig. 9(b) [11]. The results of the children's learning gains under the PT condition suggest a significant improvement in the children's learning gains in the post-test compared to the pre-test. However, no significance differences in pre- /post-test scores were found under the PL condition [11]. Overall, the *PT* method found to be more effective in all three regards.

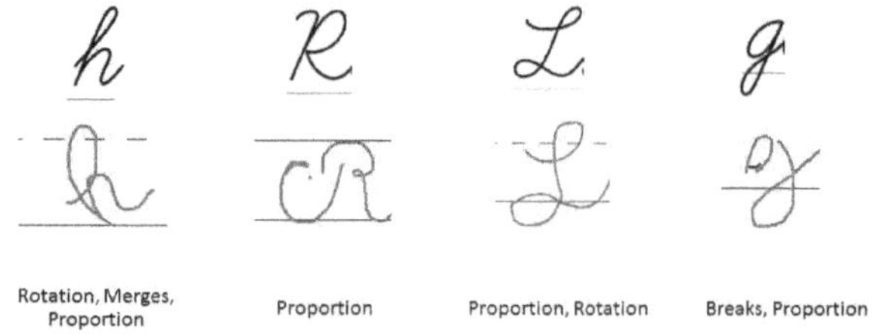

Figure 8: Children's handwriting issues

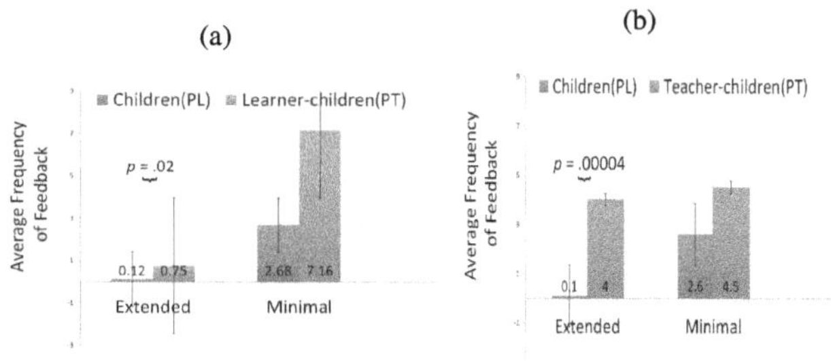

Figure 9: Results of the corrective feedback between (a) learner-children under the PT condition and all children under the PL condition and between (b) tutor-children under the PT condition and all children under the PL condition.

IMPLEMENTATION OF WRITING ERRORS FOR A ROBOT

To test some writing errors from the developed taxonomy, we implemented a set of errors in a system that provides an educational scenario for acquiring the writing skills. The scenario consists of a child, whereby s/he corrects the writing errors of a robot, which acts as a learner. The scenario attempts to demonstrate how children comprehend these writing errors, which in reality depicts their own writing errors.

Generating the deformed letters for the learner-robot and correcting a letter (from the child's side) was a key point in the scenario. Instead of generating the letters with random handwriting errors for the learner-robot, we selected three common errors, *Proportion*, *Breaks* and *Alignment*, from the built taxonomy of handwriting errors.

The choice of using these handwriting issues was motivated by two reasons: their prevalence in children's handwriting [16, 17] and because we also observed in our past studies that the *Proportion* and *Alignment* issues were the most commonly occurring writing errors. We chose only three errors to keep the scenario simple and to prevent stress on a child's cognitive load, particularly, by not adding more than three errors in the same scenario. To handle the *proportion* and *breaks* writing errors, we used an algorithm proposed in [38], which combines the output of multiple algorithms in an inverse control problem. Additionally, the algorithm also incorporates human-movement-inspired features and also generalises the synthesis to generate poor or good written samples of a letter. We used the algorithm for two primary reasons: First, the algorithm provides the capability to synthesise and learn the multiple-mode motion trajectories through the integration of rapid representation and extraction. Second, we needed to generate deformed letters for the learner-robot that resemble children's handwriting.

The input of the algorithm is a planar handwriting dataset $\mathscr{D}$ (see Algorithm 1). To generate similar instances of a letter present in the dataset, the Gaussian statistics of the trajectories are extracted. The parameters received from the statistics are further converted into a curvature-based representation with a nonlinear feature embedding. The mean $\mu_f^m = \{A_j, z_0^j, \mu_j, \sigma_j, \alpha_s^j, \alpha_e^j\}_{j=1:N}$ is obtained by an RXZero process, which effectively solves a nonlinear optimization to match the trajectories through Equations (1) and (2). The covariances are transformed through local linear projections, with $J(\cdot)$ denoting the Jacobian of the reconstruction. It is easy to find that some of the extracted parameters are correlated to the motion path in an explicit manner.

$$|v(z)| = \sum_{j=1}^{N} \frac{A_j}{\sqrt{2\pi}\sigma_j(z - z_o^j)} \exp\left(-\frac{(\ln(z - z_0^j) - \mu_j)^2}{2\sigma_j^2}\right) \quad (1)$$

$$\phi_j(z) = \alpha_s^j + \frac{\alpha_e^j - \alpha_s^j}{2}\left(1 + \mathrm{erf}\left(\frac{\ln(z - z_0^j) - \mu_j}{2\sigma_j}\right)\right) \quad (2)$$

Algorithm 1 Learning with curvature-based features for modelling handwriting motion

Require: $\mathscr{D} = \{\varsigma_i\}, M$
Ensure: $\mathscr{D}^m_{k=1:K_m}, \hat{\theta}^m_k = \{\mu_f{}^m, \Sigma_f{}^m\}, m = 1, ..., M$
  $\mathscr{D}^m_{k=1:K_m} \leftarrow \text{Partitioning}(\mathscr{D}, M)$ ▷ Build locally similar dataset $\mathscr{D}$ through partitioning
  for all m in 1:M **do**
    $\mu_\varsigma{}^m, \Sigma_\varsigma{}^m \leftarrow \underset{\theta}{\text{argmax}} \sum_{i=1}^{|\mathscr{D}_k^m|} \log \mathscr{N}(\varsigma_i^* | \theta)$
    $\mu_f{}^m \leftarrow \text{RXZERO}(\mu_\varsigma{}^m)$
    $\Sigma_f{}^m \leftarrow J(\mu_\varsigma^m)^T \Sigma_\varsigma^m J(\mu_\varsigma^m)$
  end for

Figure 10: Letter samples generated from the algorithm showing the modulation in the components producing the *proportion* and *break* handwriting errors.

For instance, in Equation 1, A_j regulates the velocity magnitude so that the proportion of specific letter components can be modulated without influencing the other components. Equation 2 shows that α_s^j and α_e^j control the angular position. Hence, the two parameters allow for the stroke orientation or the curvature to be adjusted; see Fig. 10. For the *alignment* issue, we developed an algorithm to produce the rotation effect with different angles.

VALIDATION

In our child-robot learning scenario of the final study, we were interested in exploring two different aspects: 1) how children would perceive the writing abilities, specifically, the writing errors of the robot, and 2) how children would perceive the

(a) (b)

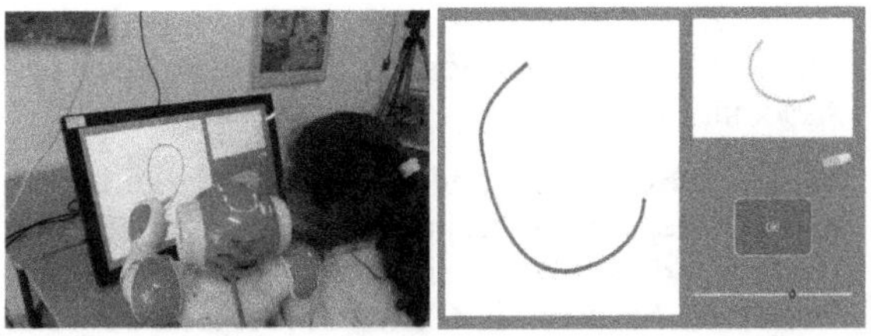

Figure 11: (a) A child and a robot performing the writing activity; (b) Interactive screen

behavior of the robotic agent, as this may affect the child-robot learning interaction. Thus, we tested the above system by conducting a 4-week study (1 interaction per week) with 24 children in the age group of 7-8 years at a school. Considering the results of the second study, which revealed the richness of the PT learning method, the current system relies on the PT learning method. The study consists of between-subject design and has two conditions, therein demonstrating the different competencies of the learner-robot: *Learning* and *Non-Learning*. A total of 13 children (M=8; SD= 0.784; 8 male and 5 female) participated under the *learning condition*, while 11 children (M=7.92; SD=.828 years old; 5 male and 8 female) participated under the *non-learning condition*, and each interaction lasted approximately 12-15 minutes. The scenario involved a tutor-child correcting the handwriting errors of a learner-robot (see Fig. 11(a)). As shown in 11(b), the screen shows interactive features, such as a small white box (right side), and a slider. The slider was connected to the algorithm (Algorithm 1), which has the ability change the shape of a letter by moving the slider. The tutor-child provided corrections in two ways - by moving the slider and by providing a demonstration of the letter in the small box.

Under the learning condition, the robot showed a learning progression after each interaction, whereas under the non-learning condition, the robot showed a consistent performance (it did not learn) throughout the study. To provide spontaneous and fluid interaction between the child and robot, an autonomous social behavior for the robot was developed. Following the interaction, the experimenter asked self-response questions to the children based on a 5-point Likert scale and partially inspired by the Godspeed questionnaire [1]. The questions were asked at three time intervals - immediately after the second, third and fourth interactions with the robot.

The overall goals of the study concern the testing of the writing errors considering child-robot interactions and exploring children's perception of the writing abilities and social behavior of the *Learning* vs. *Non-Learning* robot through child self-response questionnaires. Moreover, the study explores the following research questions: *1*- Can children differentiate the learning abilities of the robot between the two conditions? The learning abilities are related to the robot's writing ability and overall performance. *2*- Would the two different competencies (learning and non-learning) of the robot affect the children's perceived likability and friendliness towards it?

We collected the data from the questionnaires and analysed them using the non-parametric Mann-Whitney U test The pre-

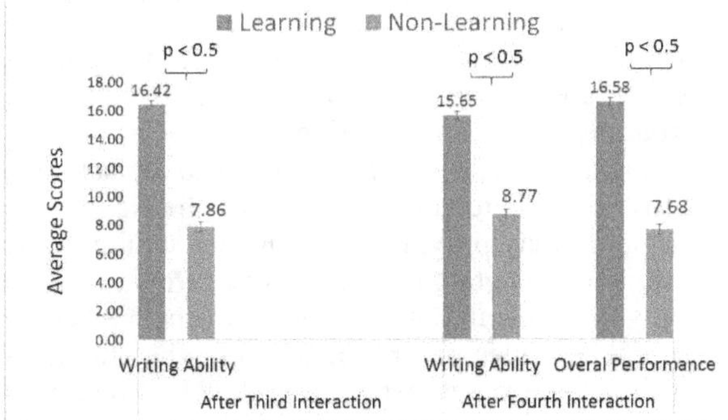

Figure 12: Results of the robot's learning scores given by the children: Writing ability and overall performance scores after the third and fourth interactions.

liminary results related to the children's perception of the robot are presented in the paper. Questions related to the writing ability and the overall performance of the robot showed significant differences over the four-week interactions. Despite showing no differences in the first two interactions, after the third interaction, children under the learning condition (mean rank = 16.42) gave significantly higher *writing ability scores* to the robot compared to the non-learning condition (mean rank = 7.86), $U = 20.5$, $z = 86.5$, $p = .002$ (see Fig. 12). After the fourth interaction, children under the Learning condition (mean rank = 16.58) gave significantly higher *overall performance* scores to the robot compared to the Non-learning condition (mean rank = 7.68), $U = 18.5$, $z = -3.366$, $p = .001$. Additionally, for the writing ability, under the Learning condition (mean rank = 15.65), they gave higher scores to the robot compared to the Non-learning condition (mean rank = 8.77), $U = 30.50$, $z = -2.67$, $p = .015$ (see Fig. 12). The result suggests that children indeed paid attention to the robot's writing errors and hence were able to notice the difference in the robot's learning abilities over time.

Regarding children's perceived social behavior, we observed that after the last interaction, 100% of the children under the learning condition and 92% under the non-learning condition gave high scores for both likeness and friendliness questions. Furthermore, concerning the perceived intelligence of the robot, 100 % of the children under the learning condition and 67% under the non-learning condition gave high scores to the robot, even when being aware of the robot's lack of learning abilities. These results suggest that the children's perceived social behavior was not affected by the robot's learning and non-learning competencies.

CONCLUSION

We believe that this article presents the following important contributions: the proposition of a taxonomy of writing errors, based on the handwritten letters of children 4-8 years of age, that may be useful for educational purposes; the exploration modes of interactions between children and a robot during the first two studies; the test of a set of writing errors from the taxonomy in an educational scenario whereby a child corrects the writing errors produced by a learner-robot; and finally the exploration of children's perception towards a robot with learning vs. non-learning competencies.

The presented taxonomy of the writing errors provides a deep understanding of common handwriting issues for letters of the English alphabet (Uppercase and Lowercase). We believe that the taxonomy extends the existing literature, as it contains a few writing issues (*e.g. multiple strokes and breaks*) that have not been explored previously. Moreover, the classification in the taxonomy may provide a new understanding of writing errors. It is worth noting that the writing errors defined in the taxonomy may benefit both teachers and students. Generally, if a student struggles in forming a letter, s/he practices it by writing it several times, which may involve the correction of random writing errors in the same letter. However, one of the key advantages of using the taxonomy is in helping a child with one particular writing error at a time. In addition, the proposed taxonomy can be used to evaluate children's handwriting skills in a more structured way. To improve handwriting, researchers may develop an educational scenario dedicated to a particular writing issue or similar writing issues present in the taxonomy. However, incorporating all the handwriting issues for one educational activity seems to be challenging, as writing errors differ with respect to the levels of handwriting and motor-cognitive skills. In addition, this would also increase the cognitive load on a child.

The implementation of the three writing errors in the third study indicated children's attention towards the robot's writing errors as well as improvements. These results suggest that correcting the errors (which resembles children's own writing errors) may allow children to pay attention to their own writing errors. Finally, regarding child-robot interactions, the work presented here investigates two modes of interactions and two different roles of a robot in different learning scenarios (the second and third studies), which may be helpful for the human-robot interaction community. In contrast to the second study, the third study provides an active role to the robot, as a learner, which directly involves the writing process and affects children's perception towards the robot's writing abilities.

FUTURE WORK

Future work includes further revisions of the current taxonomy by conducting more child-robot studies. We also plan to prepare a database of children's handwritten words, therein using the English alphabet and collected through future child-robot studies, while exploring the writing issues present in the words. It would be meaningful to compare the two taxonomies, the 'letter' and 'word' taxonomies, to see whether some of the writing errors from the 'letter' taxonomy would disappear.

ACKNOWLEDGMENTS

This work was supported by national funds through Fundação para a Ciência e a Tecnologia (FCT) with reference UID/CEC/50021/2013 and through project AMIGOS (PTDC/EEISII/7174/2014). We show our gratitude to all the schools involved in the studies.

REFERENCES

1. Christoph Bartneck, Elizabeth Croft, and Dana Kulic. 2009. Measurement instruments for the anthropomorphism, animacy, likeability, perceived intelligence, and perceived safety of robots. *International Journal of Social Robotics* 1, 1 (2009), 71–81. DOI: http://dx.doi.org/10.1007/s12369-008-0001-3
2. Mary Benbow, Barbara E Hanft, and Dottie Marsh. 1992. *Handwriting in the classroom: Improving written communication*. American Occupational Therapy Association.
3. Tanya N. Beran, Alejandro Ramirez-Serrano, Roman Kuzyk, Meghann Fior, and Sarah Nugent. 2011. Understanding How Children Understand Robots: Perceived Animism in Child-robot Interaction. *Int. J. Hum.-Comput. Stud.* 69, 7-8 (July 2011), 539–550. DOI: http://dx.doi.org/10.1016/j.ijhcs.2011.04.003
4. Virginia W Berninger and Dagmar Amtmann. 2003. Preventing written expression disabilities through early and continuing assessment and intervention for handwriting and/or spelling problems: Research into practice. (2003).
5. Virginia W Berninger and Steve Graham. 1998. Language by hand: A synthesis of a decade of research on handwriting. *Handwriting Review* 12, 1 (1998), 11–25.
6. K Berry. 1989. The VMI: Developmental Test of Visual-motor Integration (Cleveland. (1989).
7. Gautam Biswas, Krittaya Leelawong, Daniel Schwartz, Nancy Vye, and The Teachable Agents Group at Vanderbilt. 2005. Learning by teaching: A new agent paradigm for educational software. *Applied Artificial Intelligence* 19, 3-4 (2005), 363–392.
8. Mary-Ann Bonney. 1992. Understanding and assessing handwriting difficulty: Perspectives from the literature. *Australian Occupational Therapy Journal* 39, 3 (1992), 7–15.
9. David Boud, Ruth Cohen, and Jane Sampson. 2001. Peer learning and assessment. *Peer Learning in Higher Education: Learning from & with Each Other* (2001), 67.
10. Ginevra Castellano, Ana Paiva, Arvid Kappas, Ruth Aylett, Helen Hastie, Wolmet Barendregt, Fernando Nabais, and Susan Bull. 2013. Towards Empathic Virtual and Robotic Tutors. In *Artificial Intelligence in Education*, H.Chad Lane, Kalina Yacef, Jack Mostow, and Philip Pavlik (Eds.). Lecture Notes in Computer Science, Vol. 7926. Springer Berlin Heidelberg, 733–736.
11. Shruti Chandra, P. A.Oliveira, Séverin Lemaignan, Pedro Sequeira, Ana Paiva, and Pierre Dillenbourg. 2016. Children's peer assessment and self-disclosure in the presence of an educational robot. In *Robot and Human Interactive Comm.(RO-MAN), 2016 25th IEEE Int. Symposium on*. IEEE, 539–544.
12. Clinton I Chase. 1986. Essay test scoring: Interaction of relevant variables. *Journal of Educational Measurement* 23, 1 (1986), 33–41.
13. Carol A Christensen. 2005. The role of orthographic–Motor integration in the production of creative and well-structured written text for students in secondary school. *Educational Psychology* 25, 5 (2005), 441–453.

14. CE Exner. 1989. Development of hand functions. *Occupational therapy for children* (1989), 235–259.
15. Katya P Feder and Annette Majnemer. 2007. Handwriting development, competency, and intervention. *Developmental Medicine & Child Neurology* 49, 4 (2007), 312–317.
16. Steve Graham, Karen R Harris, Linda Mason, Barbara F.Chorzempa, Susan Moran, and Bruce Saddler. 2008. How do primary grade teachers teach handwriting? A national survey. *Reading and Writing* 21, 1-2 (2008), 49–69.
17. Steve Graham, Naomi Weintraub, and Virginia Berninger. 2001. Which manuscript letters do primary grade children write legibly? *Journal of Educational Psychology* 93, 3 (2001), 488.
18. Deanna Hood, Séverin Lemaignan, and Pierre Dillenbourg. 2015. When children teach a robot to write: An autonomous teachable humanoid which uses simulated handwriting. In *Proceedings of the Tenth Annual ACM/IEEE Int. Conf. on Human-Robot Interaction*. ACM, 83–90.
19. Alexis D Jacq, Séverin Lemaignan, Fernando Garcia, Pierre Dillenbourg, and Ana Paiva. 2016. Building successful long child-robot interactions in a learning context. In *The Eleventh ACM/IEEE International Conference on Human Robot Interaction*. IEEE Press, 239–246.
20. Jeffrey Johnson. 2003. Children, robotics, and education. *Artificial Life and Robotics* 7, 1–2 (2003), 16–21.
21. Peter H Kahn Jr, Takayuki Kanda, Hiroshi Ishiguro, Nathan G Freier, Rachel L Severson, Brian T Gill, Jolina H Ruckert, and Solace Shen. 2012. "Robovie, you'll have to go into the closet now": Children's social and moral relationships with a humanoid robot. *Developmental psychology* 48, 2 (2012), 303.
22. Takayuki Kanda, Takayuki Hirano, Daniel Eaton, and Hiroshi Ishiguro. 2004. Interactive Robots As Social Partners and Peer Tutors for Children: A Field Trial. *Human-Computer Interaction* 19, 1 (June 2004), 61–84.
23. Takayuki Kanda, Rumi Sato, Naoki Saiwaki, and Hiroshi Ishiguro. 2007. A two-month field trial in an elementary school for long-term human–robot interaction. *Robotics, IEEE Transactions on* 23, 5 (2007), 962–971.
24. Ragnheidur Karlsdottir and Thorarinn Stefansson. 2002. Problems in developing functional handwriting. *Perceptual and motor skills* 94, 2 (2002), 623–662.
25. Mike Keppell, Eliza Au, Ada Ma, and Christine Chan. 2006. Peer learning and learning-oriented assessment in technology-enhanced environments. *Assessment & Evaluation in Higher Education* 31, 4 (2006), 453–464.
26. Judith I Laszlo and Phillip J Bairstow. 1984. Handwriting: Difficulties and possible solutions. *School Psychology International* 5, 4 (1984), 207–213.
27. Annlaug Flem Maeland. 1992. Handwriting and perceptual-motor skills in clumsy, dysgraphic, and âĂŸnormalâĂŹchildren. *Perceptual and motor skills* 75, 3 suppl (1992), 1207–1217.
28. Theresa Malloy-Miller, Helene Polatajko, and Bev Anstett. 1995. Handwriting error patterns of children with mild motor difficulties. *Canadian Journal of Occupational Therapy* 62, 5 (1995), 258–267.
29. Shizuko Matsuzoe and Fumihide Tanaka. 2012. How smartly should robots behave?: Comparative investigation on the learning ability of a care-receiving robot. In *2012 IEEE RO-MAN: The 21st IEEE International Symposium on Robot and Human Interactive Comm.* IEEE, 339–344.
30. Jane Medwell and David Wray. 2008. Handwriting–a forgotten language skill? *Language and Education* 22, 1 (2008), 34–47. `http://www.tandfonline.com/doi/abs/10.2167/le722.0`
31. Adrian D Sandler, Thomas E Watson, Marianna Footo, Melvin D Levine, William L Coleman, and Stephen R Hooper. 1992. Neurodevelopmental study of writing disorders in middle childhood. *Journal of Developmental & Behavioral Pediatrics* 13, 1 (1992), 17–23.
32. Rosemary Sassoon. 1990. *Handwriting: A new perspective*. Stanley Thornes.
33. ML Simner. 1991. Estimating a child's learning potential from form errors in a child's printing. *Development of graphics skills: Research, perspectives, and educational implications* (1991), 205–222.
34. Marvin L Simner. 1982. Printing errors in kindergarten and the prediction of academic performance. *Journal of Learning Disabilities* 15, 3 (1982), 155–159.
35. SR Stewart and CS Simon. 1985. Development of written language proficiency: Methods for teaching text structure. *Communication skills and classroom success* (1985), 341–361.
36. Carol O Sweedler-Brown. 1992. The Effect of Training on the Appearance Bias of Holistic Essay Graders. *Journal of Research and Development in Education* 26, 1 (1992), 24–29.
37. Fumihide Tanaka and Shizuko Matsuzoe. 2012. Children teach a care-receiving robot to promote their learning: Field experiments in a classroom for vocabulary learning. *Journal of Human-Robot Interaction* 1, 1 (2012).
38. H. Yin, P. A.Olivera, F. S. Melo, A. Billard, and A. Paiva. 2016. Synthesizing Robotic Handwriting Motion by Learning from Human Demonstrations. In Proceedings of International Joint Conference on Artificial Intelligence (IJCAI). (2016).

Designing for Parasocial Relationships and Learning: Linear Video, Interactive Media, and Artificial Intelligence

James H. Gray
Sesame Workshop
New York, USA
jim.gray@sesame.org

Emily Reardon
Sesame Workshop
New York, USA
emily.reardon@sesame.org

Jennifer A. Kotler
Sesame Workshop
New York, USA
jennifer.kotler@sesame.org

ABSTRACT
Children today are surrounded by media characters who populate their experiences with video, audio, games, books, clothing, toys, robots, and interactive platforms – all with growing potential for personalization, adaptivity, and intelligence. In this paper, we describe our experience designing for "parasocial" relations between children and characters using video, interactive media, and artificial intelligence (AI), with reference to related empirical research, and a theoretical model and framework within which to understand these phenomena. The goal of this paper is to spark discussion about the future of character design in the IDC community, with a view to guiding research, development, theory, and policy recommendations; and, facilitating collaboration across disciplines and industries in order to benefit children's learning and healthy development.

Author Keywords
Parasocial relationships; Child development; Learning; Character design; Interactive media; Video

ACM Classification Keywords
H.5.0 Information Interfaces and Presentation; I.2.11 Artificial Intelligence: Distributed Artificial Intelligence — *Intelligent Agents*; H.1.2 Models and Principles: User/Machine Systems; K.3.0 Computers and Education; K.4.0 Computers and Society; General Terms: Design

INTRODUCTION
People learn from other people. We also learn from the characters who come alive through the voice of a skilled storyteller, actor, book author, video producer, or app designer. Children today encounter myriad characters throughout their daily lives, designed to educate and entertain them, and who are increasingly capable of intelligent interaction. Although little is yet known about how to design intelligent characters to benefit children, valuable insights can be gleaned from decades of educational television research, related social science research and theory, and innovative explorations of interactive media and artificial intelligence.

IDC '17, June 27-30, 2017, Stanford, CA, USA

ACM ISBN 978-1-4503-4921-5/17/06…$15.00
DOI: http://dx.doi.org/10.1145/3078072.3079736

In the social sciences, "parasocial" relations is the term used for a one-way emotionally-tinged relationship between an audience member and character on a screen [15]. The concept has been applied in research on children's television to explain how and why children relate to favorite characters, and how these relationships can be used to foster educational goals [3]. In this paper, we describe our experience designing for "parasocial" relations between children and characters using video, interactive media, and artificial intelligence (AI), with reference to related empirical research, and a theoretical model and framework within which to understand these phenomena.

A MODEL AND A FRAMEWORK
In this section, we present a psychological model of parasocial relationships and a framework for supporting their development. The model describes how children experience parasocial relationships in terms of personification or friendship, social realism, and emotional attachment. The framework describes four factors that have been found to support the development of children's parasocial relationships with television characters. It may also provide a useful design framework to guide the creation of characters and their transmedia storyworlds.

Model: Parasocial relationships
A recently developed model of young children's parasocial relationships identifies three key components: character personification, social realism, and attachment [3].

Personification means that children believe a character has person-like qualities. For example, they talk about the character having thoughts, feelings, and intentions, and, therefore, they may treat the character as a friend [3]. Indeed, "personification" from a child's perspective often means they see characters as "friends" who can feel hungry, sleepy, or sad, or experience other human-like needs [21]. Scholars also compare development of parasocial relationships to development of social relationships with friends and neighbors [14] and point out that once someone assigns personhood to a character, the character essentially enters their social world [10].

Social realism refers to children's belief that a media character could appear in real life [3]. This may be because a child has trouble distinguishing between reality and fantasy – a phenomenon well-documented in media research [25]. Alternatively, it may be because a child acts as if a character is real, in the way that children often treat imaginary friends as if they are real, while also acknowledging their imaginary status [3]. For children grappling with what is real vs. fantasy in the world, the social reality of media characters may be a relative term, with varied degrees of certainty.

Attachment refers to the emotional connection that children establish, first as infants with caregivers [4], then in other close social relationships, and by extension, to parasocial relationships with favored media characters [7]. It's thought that the warmth and predictability of media characters developed for young children can provide them with a sense of comfort and security [3]. For example, the reassuring voice of a familiar media actor following a script informed by child development principles and engaging story structures can meet at least some of the intellectual and emotional needs of young children similar to the way a caring adult might meet those needs. Indeed, for children who have special socio-emotional challenges, the predictability of these parasocial relations may provide a respite from more complex or confusing social relationships with real people in their lives.

Together, these three components form a multi-dimensional model of parasocial relationships, which can be further tested through empirical research. In the meantime, personification, social realism, and attachment provide a useful lens for understanding children's experiences of parasocial relationships. The question of how these relationships develop over time is addressed in the next section.

Framework: Parasocial relationship development

Just as children's face-to-face interactions with peers in a classroom and playground can lead to the development of friendships, various kinds of interactions with media characters contribute to development of parasocial relationships. Specifically, Bond and Calvert's [3] review of previous research and their new analysis of parent observations suggests four interrelated factors that contribute to the development of children's parasocial relations: repeated exposure to a media character, parasocial interaction with them, play with physical toy replicas (e.g., a plush doll of the character), and parent encouragement.

Repeated media exposure refers to the fact that children today live in a media saturated world in which they may encounter a favorite character via video, interactive apps, toys, books, and other products like apparel or school supplies. This transmedia presence of a character affords frequent opportunities across environments for children to think about a character and interact with him/her via multiple modalities. Each exposure is an opportunity to become more familiar with and attached to a character, thereby deepening their parasocial relationship.

Parasocial interactions are the individual responses a child has to a character during each media exposure. These responses, over time, shape a child's developing relationship to the character. Parasocial interactions can take several forms. At the most subtle level, a child may have a cognitive and emotional reaction to a character, even if it is not outwardly evident [17]. In research literature focused on video, parasocial interaction usually refers to more outwardly visible responses, which can include talking out loud to a screen character or physically enacting related content. Children's media is often designed specifically to evoke outward responses that get children visibly engaged with the character, as when children jump out of their seats to climb a mountain with *Diego* or *Dora the Explorer*, or respond verbally to *Elmo*. Production techniques used to evoke these responses will be discussed in a later section. Even more engaging responses are possible with interactive media systems that can respond contingently to a child's actions, giving the interaction a true back-and-forth quality akin to a real social interaction. Richer interactions and more trusting relationships may, in turn, afford the kinds of sustained, socially-interactive, meaningful, cognitively active ("minds on") experiences known to foster deeper learning [13].

Toy engagement refers to active, imaginative play with a physical manifestation of a character, such as a plush toy or action figure. There is a strong base of child development theory and research describing how this kind of pretend play is used by children to make sense of the world by actively engaging with it. Media research in this vein suggests that related toy play can enhance children's parasocial interactions and relationships with characters. For example, puppet play after viewing *Mr. Rogers' Neighborhood* enhanced the program's prosocial messages [9] and play with a replica of show characters (*Barney and Friends* and *Teletubbies*) enhanced engagement with the video [26]. By extension, research on multi-modal learning in both offline and interactive technology environments considers the potential benefits of engaging with and processing concepts through a variety of modalities such as vision, voice, and physical embodiment [31].

Parent encouragement includes parent communication and attitude about specific characters, influence on children's access to characters, and direct participation in children's media experiences [3, 6]. In the same way that parents influence children's interactions and relationships with other people by guiding their attention, modeling interactions, and expressing opinions, parents have a direct effect on young children's parasocial relations. They may express approval or disapproval, encourage or limit screen time [8], and control toy purchases. Likewise, when they consume media with their child, parents can express tacit approval of characters, and they may actively engage their child during media interactions [27]. Overall, in Bond and Calvert's model [3], parent encouragement was found to have, by far, the most influence on parasocial relationship development of all the four factors discussed here.

THREE EXAMPLES

In this section, we outline techniques of designing for parasocial learning using examples across three types of media: (1) one-way relationships (e.g., traditional video), (2) two-way relationships, and (3) two-way relationships powered by artificial intelligence. We describe each example, and highlight some design or production techniques that may provide pointers for the field.

One-way relationships: *Sesame Street* Video

Description

The importance of parasocial relations have become such an industry norm in young children's television and video that most titles incorporate some techniques to foster viewers' affinity to characters both on- and off-screen. Iconic shows such *as Blue's Clues, Daniel Tiger, Go Diego Go*, and *Sesame Street*, as well as newer entrants attempt to draw viewers into interacting with characters and content.

Sesame Workshop characters have been used in several studies showing the power that a beloved media "friend" can have in affecting children's behavior. While not specifically tests of a parasocial interaction or relationship, this kind of theoretical framework has been used to explain the findings of such studies. These studies focus on the role that a liked character has on influencing children's food behavior and math sequencing compared to no character or an unfamiliar character. For example, Lauricella, Gola & Calvert [19] found that children were better able to complete a sequencing task when they learned that task from *Elmo* compared to an unknown Muppet character. Similarly, Kotler, Schiffman & Hanson [18] found that foods labeled with *Sesame Street* characters were more likely to influence children's decisions to try those foods if the children liked the *Sesame Street* characters compared to unknown characters or unbranded foods. In fact, in an earlier pilot study, the same researchers found that just by placing a sticker of *Elmo* on broccoli, the appeal of broccoli was equal to that of a piece of chocolate which contained a sticker of an unknown character. In another study conducted in an elementary school, other investigators found that children were more likely to take apples at lunch time when *Elmo* stickers were placed on them; children took nearly twice as many apples when they had *Elmo* stickers on them than if they did not [28].

Design techniques and lessons learned

In the course of Sesame Workshop's decades' long experimentation with characters and content, we've found that there are a variety of ways to build character affinity. Through our continual formative testing, we have settled on some of the following techniques that seem to help children develop strong relationships with our characters through video.

Offering a range of characters allows a diverse child audience to relate in ways suited to themselves. There is a *Sesame Street* character for almost everyone. For example, if you are a little on the grumpy side, *Oscar's* your monster. If you're impulsive, there's is nothing like *Cookie Monster's* nom-noming on a cookie to make you feel understood. *Abby* is full of magic and *Grover* brings resilience and tenacity. *Elmo* on the other hand seems to be a favorite to many, potentially for his innocence, kindness, and heart. We often hear anecdotally that a particular character was responsible for changing a child's behavior. "My child would not eat vegetables but when he saw *Cookie Monster* eat them, he decided he would try it too" or "I could not have toilet-

Figure 1. An endearing character like *Elmo* can influence children's food choices. © Sesame Workshop. Photo by: Richard Termine.

trained my child without *Elmo* showing that he was doing it too." Likewise, when we work internationally, our partners create local characters that are meaningful and relevant to children in their own contexts. Extensive testing goes into new character development to make sure that children see themselves in the characters and can relate to them.

"Breaking the fourth wall" may help children interact with and build empathy for characters. There are several techniques used in production to extend a character's relationship with the viewer, such as having characters "break the fourth wall" (e.g., turning to the viewers and either asking a question or giving a wink or somehow showing the audience that they are in on the joke). We have also set up situations where the viewer has a greater sense of what is happening on the screen than does the character. We do this so that the child is inclined to call out to help the character become aware of something. This technique can foster helping behavior. For example, in one episode, *Big Bird* is looking for something but he can't find it – he looks all over *Sesame Street* but keeps looking at the wrong moments. The viewers however can help him find just what he is looking for. Many children will call out to the screen to tell him where to look. Moreover, we sometimes have characters take an extra-long time to solve an obvious problem (the tools and materials are right in front of them!) so that the viewer can solve the problem before the character. By creating a space for the viewer to help the character, we hope children may become more empathic towards that character.

Portraying and highlighting familiar emotions may facilitate personification and a sense of social realism. Another way we promote character affinity is by showing rich facial emotions and expressions in the context of scenarios that are very familiar to children. We label such emotions so that children can remember how a particular character feels. Parents tell us how they are able to refer back to the way our characters have felt or how they expressed emotion as a well to help their own children label how they are feeling.

When a child viewer trusts and understands a character as knowledgeable (or not), the degree of parasocial connection and subsequent learning from that character may be enhanced. For instance, children were more likely to learn science from a character if the children believed that the character was knowledgeable and were reminded to think about what the character did in order to solve the problem [24]. In that study, researchers used *Sid the Science Kid*, who has the word "science" in his title, giving potential credibility to his knowledge. In another study, the same lab used a clip of *Grover* (from *Sesame Street*) to teach a concept around wheels. In this clip, *Grover* continues to get things wrong (despite trying and trying) until penguins show him the correct method of using wheels. *Grover* commonly dives in head first, making initial pronouncements of things he may know little about. The comedy is in his continued futile but earnest attempts at finding correct solutions. Finally, he is corrected and shown the right way by another character. In this study, those children who trusted *Grover* as a "wheel" expert actually did worse on the research task than did those who claimed that he was not knowledgeable about wheels [29]. One interpretation of this is that the measure is not actually about trust per se, but rather one's understanding of the character. If a child truly knows and understands *Grover* she would know that he is not a subject matter expert on the things he claims to be. Instead, he tends to learn along with the viewer. The findings could reflect, then, a tendency for understanding of the characters to be a key factor in children's learning from those characters. This study illustrates the importance of capturing whether the viewer understands the character as its creators intended the character to be portrayed. This may be critical to understanding children's relationships with characters.

There is a long history in children's video/TV production of creating characters that children develop affinity for and potentially learn from, provided the characters are engaging, relatable, have social realism, and are understood as the creators intended them to be. We turn next to the design of parasocial relationships through two-way contingent interactions.

Two-way Relationships: *Grover's Block Party*

Interactive environments afford agency through child-centered controls and contingent responses, which may work to make parasocial characters feel even more life-like. In 2013, Sesame Workshop developed *Grover's Block Party*, an augmented reality supported prototype that creates a shared virtual playspace for the child, parasocial characters, physical toys, real-life playmates and caregivers [5]. In this section we both describe how our design and development of *Grover's Block Party* leverages the parasocial model of personification, social realism, and attachment as well as share the lessons we learned with the hope that they are useful to others working on similar topics.

Description

Grover's Block Party is a *Sesame Street* letter block set and adaptive, personalized tablet-based play experience with *Grover*. In *Grover's Block Party*, children play with wooden letter blocks. Via machine vision and augmented reality technology, *Grover* appears socially real in that he is designed to "see" what a child does with the blocks, and – like an engaged parent – provides "guided play" [29] by responding to and promoting experimentation with building, pretend play, pattern-making, and letter exploration. Designed to foster attachment, *Grover*, acting like a caring adult, follows, comments on, and extends (rather than directs) the child's natural curiosity and play. He might point out that the child made the word "dog" and play a *Sesame Street* short film about dogs, or recognize that she spelled her name. The child can show any letter block to *Grover*, and *Grover* talks and asks questions about that letter and letter sound. *Grover* also comments on the structures the child builds, on new blocks the child adds to the play space, guesses what the child is building, and reacts with inimitable *Grover* excitement each time the child topples what she built.

Sesame Workshop, working in partnership with Qualcomm, designed *Grover's Block Party* to see if it might enrich traditional block play by extending play time to positively impact learning. We wanted to see if a virtual character might simulate positive adult engagement in child play to expand and deepen children's engagement in traditional block play. We also wanted to see if the play experience, coupled with a virtual character, might inspire parents to further engage in letter block play with their young child. To these ends, it was critical to us that the player felt that *Grover* could "see" and "understand" the player, and that *Grover* felt like a "fun playmate". The play experience and system design needed to be as deep and varied as each child's way of playing, to adapt to each player, and to be easy and intuitive for young children to use both by themselves and in social play.

Design techniques

To design the play experience, we first delineated two main system states. The first state comprised scenarios in which the system could detect a player's activity and hypothesize intention (e.g., "You have built a very tall tower! Please do not let it fall.") The other state comprised system responses to "chaotic" activity (e.g., the system is not able to guess the player's intention, but can see and comment on the letter V in her structure). We created storyboards to chart these two states, including logic expression for both player behaviors (e.g., player builds a wall, player makes a tower topple,

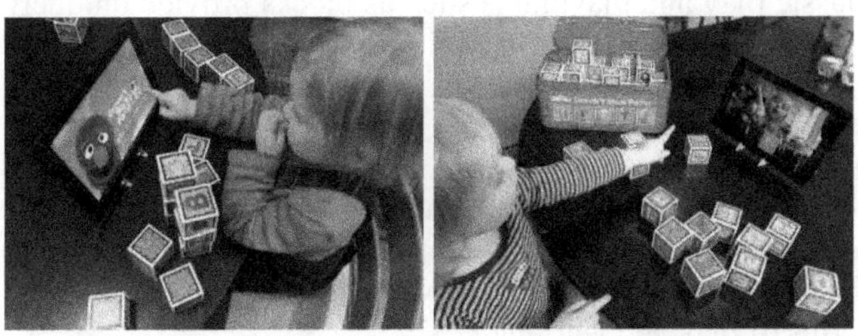

Figure 2: LEFT: Child launches play experience from tablet. The tablet is set on a stand. RIGHT: Child freely plays with blocks. Via the front facing camera, she sees herself, *Grover*, and augmented letter block constructions on screen. *Grover* and the Letter Muppets on the blocks come to life on screen, reacting to the child's physical block play in real time.

Figure 3: LEFT: Child continues to build freely. *Grover* comments on her real-world block play. RIGHT: Child plays with blocks. She sees herself and augmented Letter Muppet blocks, and play space on screen. The letter blocks animate, comment, sing, and react to her real world play activity. *Grover* enters and exits the playspace, as well as speaks to her from out of frame.

player does nothing) and block formations (e.g., towers, walls, pyramids, patterns, words). We mapped the complex and wide range of what players might do and what formations they might make in spreadsheets that correlated to the storyboards. We then built correlating table-based scripts with detailed logic and dialog so that *Grover* could meaningfully react to any possible player action or block arrangement

To bring *Grover* to life and leverage principles of personification, we created a wide-ranging series of 3D *Grover* animations in which he expressed a variety of "moods," for instance: curious, calm, incredulous, and proud. For each line of dialog we assigned one or more moods. Based on the child's block play, the system triggered dynamic voice-over feedback, programmatically generated lip movements, and dynamically selected and stitched mood animations together to make *Grover* come to life and engage with and deepen the child's block play. We considered text-to-speech generation – for example, building an artificial *Grover* voice from a huge range of *Grover* recordings – but decided against it based on concerns about voice fidelity and project scope.

A series of formative and summative research studies were conducted to ensure that *Grover's Block Party* was effectively engaging children in terms of understanding, potential for learning, fun, and sustained play. The Workshop's education and research team first had children, accompanied by their parents, playtest a range of existing commercial block sets as well as in-progress builds of *Grover's Block Party*. In these playtests we conducted foundational research to define typical block play patterns and parental prompts, as well as conducted iterative design research and a use study over time. For the summative evaluation, we deployed a randomized experimental study in Colorado for one week with 24 families with at least one child aged two to three years. The 12 families in the treatment group received *Grover's Block Party*, including a local analytics log, while the 12 families in the control group received a commercially available letter block set. Parents in both groups were instructed to use *Dscout*, a research app, to capture videos of their children playing with the blocks throughout the week and took part in a 45-minute initial play session as well as pre- and post-interviews. For each round of testing the education and research team built protocols, had a researcher guide the play session, coded the protocol and video data, and produced a report.

Lessons learned from Grover's Block Party

Grover's Block Party is a prototype which we'd love to develop further. Below are our initial findings with respect to parasocial character design for interactive projects that integrate augmented reality, dynamical procedural content, tangible toys, and social play.

Mixing an interactive character with classic playthings, such as letter blocks, can be engaging and promote social play, including caregiver engagement. We found that the length of the average play session for families using *Grover's Block Party* was double that of the control group families. Parents of children who played with *Grover's Block Party* reported 30-45 minutes of play per day and analytics showed an average of 30 minutes of play per day. 87% of the participants who had *Grover's Block Party* reported that the augmented experience made the classic toy more appealing, with some reporting *Grover's Block Party* app-usage drop off and increased blocks-only play. *Grover's Block Party* generated a significant amount of co-play experiences between a wide range of ages, including parents and even siblings, up to 12-15 years old. Parents reported that the majority of children (67%) co-played with siblings, other adults, and/or friends. Over half the parents reported that co-play happened the majority of the time.

Designing parasocial experiences for young children in which they see themselves can promote engagement. Sesame Workshop creates characters, places, and experiences where all children can "see themselves" (figuratively) and appreciate others. In all our work we model diversity; in *Grover's Block Party*, as well as in other projects, we found "seeing themselves" to be literally true – children loved seeing themselves and their homes on the tablet screen, in the same "place" as their friend *Grover* and their "alive" physical letter blocks (see figure 2 e.g., top right above). Augmented reality, in mixing real and virtual worlds, affords many creative ways to leverage social realism where children can see and interact with parasocial characters, themselves, and other people – both co-located and remote – for engagement and learning.

Procedurally generating content allows parasocial characters to "realistically" respond to wide ranges of player action and complex input in meaningful ways. Children bring with them feelings of attachment, such as warmth and trust of the *Sesame Street* Muppets. Since we know that extended parasocial dialog around curricular topics enables learning to take place [19], it is critical to us to build on this relationship to create an environment of extended engagement and dialog between the child and the character on screen. *Grover's* dynamically generated reactions to player activity as well as novel combinations of voice feedback and animation allowed him to respond to an exceptionally wide array of machine-vision input and naturalistic block play actions. Especially for well-known brands and characters, our advice to designers is to approach parasocial dynamic content in isolated tests. We were unsure how a procedurally animated Muppet might impact social realism and while we found that children enjoyed the procedurally animated *Grover*, evaluating its success without the added complexity of integrated dynamic text-to-speech services felt like the right choice for this project.

Conveying experiences that use emerging technologies and parasocial characters that feel "real" is difficult. In our research we found that it was difficult to convey the full-concept and scope of *Grover's Block Party*. We discovered that children sometimes struggled with field-of-view issues, and perhaps because *Grover's* social realism and understanding of player behavior felt so natural to them, they sometimes expected *Grover* to "see" (or "hear") things he couldn't. We wrestled with how to communicate what *Grover* can "see" and initially resisted using a large mat to define the block play space, but ended up including it for the in-home testing. We found that the mat was cumbersome, and that addressing the field-of-view issues warrants redesign.

Another area we'd like to further explore is how to optimally convey the richness of the experience to the player. For instance, how might *Grover* best reflect to the player what he sees and that he's responsively following the player's lead so as to enhance her relationship with him and engagement in the experience? Since *Grover's* animations were dynamic, he might pivot and focus his eyes on the player or might point to a specific block. These issues of "realness," spatial perspective taking, and communication may have implications for social robotics or embodied systems that function in a child's three-dimensional world.

We know that children of all ages are attracted to, motivated by, and spend significant amounts of time with technology, and even very young children spend a lot of time with beloved characters on-screens. We also know that classic play and playthings such as blocks provide uniquely meaningful, child-led, socially interactive, sustained engagement, and positive learning outcomes. By remixing classic play modes with computer support and leveraging parasocial relationship features such as personification, social realism, and attachment, designers open up unique modalities as well as reinvigorate interest and engagement that can pave the way to new audiences as well as new forms of play and learning.

Two-way relationships, powered by Artificial Intelligence

Finally, we discuss a second category of contingent interaction, in this case governed by artificial intelligence. In the previous category, hard-coded logic and procedural animation determined the structure and content of the character's actions. In this category, we aspire to have AI govern the character's actions, dynamically changing its pattern based on evolving learner profiles, semantic networks, and machine learning.

Description

Sesame Workshop has embarked on a multi-year project with IBM Watson Education to combine the power of machine learning and artificial intelligence (a.k.a., "cognitive computing") with Sesame's expertise in child development, educational media, and character design. Our initial work is focused on developing a back-end platform to enable a range of products, starting with vocabulary development for young children, using adaptive, personalized learning approaches and parasocial interactions with on-screen characters. Specifically, kindergarten students interact with games and characters on *iPad* tablets in their classrooms, with potential for use in other contexts (e.g., at home) and interfaces devices (e.g., toys).

In this section, we describe the types of AI and machine learning techniques that we are currently exploring, and discuss potential educational uses. Since this work is still in early stages of prototyping, we discuss in general terms, the categories of techniques that can be used with these technologies, educational goals that can be addressed, and related issues that may emerge.

Design techniques

Like most present day artificial intelligence platforms, Watson is composed of various modules or "services" which can be combined to meet particular needs. Specifically, we are exploring text-to-speech, speech-to-text, and a conversation module to govern child-character interactions. We are testing how to use a machine vision module to support children's exploration of physical objects using the tablet camera, and a concept expansion module to make semantic connections between vocabulary words in order to help students explore the underlying meaning of terms like: bug, spider, and arachnid. Central to our goal of providing personalized adaptive learning experiences, we are also investigating structures and uses of learner profiles, in order to represent each student's knowledge, interests, preferences, and other factors that affect their learning processes.

Machine learning techniques are used in various parts of the overall system to improve functioning of particular modules based on repeated exposure to relevant data. We are experimenting with how to use training data sets or data publically available on the internet to develop a base level of functionality in the initial prototype. Then, as children use the system, the module continues to improve. For example, we provided the vision system with a large library of images related to target vocabulary words so it could identify objects that children photographed with the tablet camera.

Similarly, the speech-to-text module acquires its initial capacity to understand children's' speech based on hundreds of hours of human speech, and especially samples from young children. This sort of speech recognition is more difficult with younger children, who use a wider range of pronunciations than older youth or adults in the same communities. Like the vision system, it will continue to improve in accuracy with exposure to more and more individuals in the target population.

Learner profiles require a different approach. Whereas the processes described above involve large data sets and deep learning from the start (e.g., vision and voice modules), individual student profiles start with relatively small datasets generated from interactions with each individual child – specifically, the knowledge and interest that the child displays through interaction with the prototype system. Over time, profiles can represent expanded understanding of each learner based on more data from interactions with the system and other sources such as input from teachers and parents, combined with research-based knowledge of how children learn and grow.

Questions raised by AI-driven contingent interactions

Based on our development of prototypes, formative evaluations, educator studies, and related explorations, we discuss in this section some key questions about designing for parasocial interactions, relationships, and learning.

When should learners make their own characters vs. meeting established ones? We want children to develop a strong affinity for the intelligent character to help guide and motivate their educational activities. Children may bond with characters whom they build for themselves in the way a writer or artist loves their own work. However, it's also possible that knowing how the character is constructed will inhibit children suspending disbelief and personifying the character. They know too much about its origins and perhaps inner workings (e.g., given child-friendly coding tools to play and explore with).

How might characters interact with individual children or scaffold social interactions between children? Interacting directly with a well-crafted intelligent character holds the potential to provide a personalized educational experience; although, current state-of-the art falls far short of interacting with a skilled human tutor. Supporting interactions among children of equal or differing skill levels offers the potential benefits of collaborative learning; however, in the absence of a human teacher, may easily drift off task.

What kinds of personalization are effective in developing parasocial relationships? We know that providing customized, personal details in parasocial interactions can be engaging and lead to stronger parasocial relationships. What factors have the greatest effect in particular educational environments for particular children? Factors may include: child's name, interests, preferences, pre-existing knowledge, etc. While there are likely universal factors common to all children, and generalized factors common to particular groups, there are also likely to be unique individual factors, which this sort of AI system can identify and leverage to enhance each child's learning.

How important is voice quality in establishing a strong parasocial relationship? The tone, timbre, pacing, and other qualities of a human voice carries significant personal information that shapes interactions and relationship development. Listeners infer a lot about another individual from the qualities of their voice. It's not just what they say, but how they say it. What implications does this finding [20] have for parasocial interactions with characters who may sound human or artificial to varying degrees? Is there an auditory uncanny valley? [12]

How effective in fostering parasocial relationships are various forms of contingent interaction? Timing of interactions (i.e., perceived causal connections in turn taking) and personalization of responses (name, personal facts, knowledge, etc.) are contingent factors that have been shown to affect children's engagement and parasocial relations. Which ones are most important, for which children, in which contexts?

FUTURE DIRECTIONS

In the above sections, we discuss current research and practice regarding parasocial relations across platforms, as well as near-term implications for character and media design. Long-term issues include what was once the stuff of science fiction, but now seems to many experts to be worthy of serious consideration and planning (https://openai.com/about/). For example, how should today's children be prepared for working in a world shaped significantly by AI and automation? Examining and evaluating these kinds of possible futures is beyond the scope of this paper. However, we do address mid-term future development of intelligent agents and parasocial relationships with children.

Various disciplines may be interested in gaining a better understanding of how they could address children's relationships with AI-powered characters. Specifically, we suggest five areas that encompass research, product development, and public policy. Below we discuss one sample topic in each discipline. Please see Table 1 for a list of others.

Discipline	Guiding Questions and Topics
Science of Child Development	1. What kinds of parasocial interactions are appropriate at different stages? 2. Which factors influence parasocial relations, for which children? 3. What are the effects on cognitive and social-emotional development? 4. What developmental processes are most affected, positively or negatively? 5. What special populations may benefit most (e.g., autistic, dyslexic, homeless) [6]?
Education and the Learning Sciences	How can parasocial interactions and relationships be used to: 1. Promote learning across school, home, and community? 2. Build deeper understanding of key concepts [11]? 3. Foster cognitive apprenticeships in subject area domains [11]? 4. Provide continuity during development (i.e., characters grow with learners)? 5. Promote social play and learning?
Human-Computer Interaction Design	1. How should characters be designed (personality, backstory, knowledge)? 2. How do child-generated vs. developer-created characters compare? 3. What roles should characters have (teacher, guide, student, friend, service provider)? 4. How can we incorporate Universal Design for Learning? 5. How should different modalities best be used (touch screens, audio, robotics)? 6. How should characters be used in different media (i.e., video, scripted interaction, and AI interactive media)?
Research Methods	1. Iterative, formative, design research. 2. A/B testing of specific character design features. 3. Brain imaging linked to behavioral data (e.g., what engages the "social brain"?). 4. "Science of the individual" analyzing big data from each individual learner. 5. "Translational" research that actively applies finding from basic research. 6. Use-inspired basic research in "Pasteur's Quadrant".
Society and Public Policy	1. Privacy. 2. Data ownership (e.g., learner profile data). 3. Age-appropriateness. 4. Unintended consequences of stereotyping due to categories in learner profiles. 5. Equity of access to value and exposure to risks. 6. Economic and quality of life impact (e.g., from intelligent agent AI, automation).

Table 1. Guiding questions and topics about parasocial relations with intelligent agents to consider across five disciplines

Theory of mind

How do interactions with an intelligent character affect the development of children's social cognition, self-understanding, and social-emotional development? For example, around age 5 years, children typically begin realizing that others do not always share their thoughts, feelings, and perspectives; they develop what psychologists call a "theory of mind" [1, 30]. This "theory" may be more complex if some of the "minds" they theorize about belong to AI-powered characters, especially if children can program the characters' "thoughts", "feelings", and actions.

Cognitive apprenticeships

Children can learn from the perspective of various social roles, including: student, teacher, friend, participant, observer, or apprentice. What they learn and how they learn it may vary. For example, an apprentice learns by observing a master craftsperson, and by actively doing or making something themselves. As in project-based learning, they may gain knowledge, skills, and attitudes in the service of a specific goal. How might an intelligent agent support this sort of learning by asking questions, posing problems, or providing alternative solutions to consider while a child is engaged in a creative process or inquiry (c.f. [2, 16])?

Design for multiple-modalities

As discussed above, playing with a physical version of a screen character contributes to development of children's parasocial relationships with the character. By extension, designers may ask what parasocial opportunities are afforded by making robotic characters, in addition to video or interactive touch-screen versions. As child-codable robots like *KIBO* or *Dash & Dot* illustrate, children can code, personalize, and interact with a robot in 3D space. For example, they can program a simple movement and then mimic or dance with the robot using their own body. Audio can include child-friendly voices with especially strong potential for contributing to parasocial relationship development, since the human voice carries so much social-emotional information.

Science of the individual

Most statistical methods in the social sciences have been developed to understand groups of people (or other things), but are often mis-applied in attempts to understand individuals who may vary significantly from the "average" [22]. Unlike traditional real world settings, digital environments can be designed to record vast amounts data from each individual, relevant to their engagement, interests, and learning. This approach can help identify uniquely important patterns, thereby providing a high level of personalized experiences.

Open learner profiles

Giving individuals access to their own educational data has the potential to support learning across settings and over time. One of the greatest long-term benefits of detailed learning data is to support student understanding of their own knowledge and skills, learning processes, strengths and challenges, and appreciation of accomplishments. As a representation of themselves and who they may become, access to their data may be prove to be very beneficial. For example, in the form of portfolios, this data can support a student's communication about their academic history and help them achieve their goals.

Character design for tomorrow: Combine old and new

Designing an intelligent agent includes all of the factors that make a great character on video/television, plus ones unique to deeply interactive characters. For example, children's television script writers try to make characters be relatable to their target audience, dynamic with a wide range of emotions and interests, unique or quirky, liked by friends, visually appealing, and exist in a story with a relatable hook, conflict, and message [Wilson Stallings, personal communication]. Interactive character designers should also consider which media and modalities to use (audio only, linear video, interactive screen, physical embodiment – i.e., social robot), and how children will make transmedia connections. Will character interactions be personalized, and if so, what data will inform the character's evolving understanding of the child (e.g., learner profile)? Are the content and interaction patterns developmentally-appropriate? Does the system adapt to changing patterns in the child's behavior, for example, as she builds knowledge over time, or has a temporary misunderstanding? Moving forward, these are the kinds of strategies and questions that designers will bring to the development of characters across media.

As we discuss in this paper, well-designed characters afford parasocial interaction and relationship development, and ultimately provide opportunities to support children's learning and healthy development. Technological advances support new kinds interactions and perhaps better learning. However, rather than replacing older media, new ones provide additional avenues for engaging and educating children, giving designers a broader pallet with which to create. The power of parasocial learning across old and new media makes character design a richer and now indispensable craft for interaction designers to embrace.

ACKNOWLEDGEMENTS

The authors gratefully acknowledge their many colleagues at Sesame Workshop and IBM Watson for years of research and product development work on which our ideas are based; especially Mindy Brooks, J Milligan, David Glauber, and Todd Slepian for their work on *Grover's Block Party*; and, the following individuals who provided assistance and helpful comments on drafts of this paper: Ravindranath Kokku, Satya Nitta, Miles Ludwig, Michelle Kaplan, Franco Schettino, and Sandra Calvert.

REFERENCES

1. Janet W. Astington, L. A. Dack. 2008. Theory of mind. In M. M. Haith, J. B. Benson (eds.). *Encyclopedia of infant and early childhood development Vol 3*. Academic Press. 343-356.
2. Amy L. Baylor, and Yanghee Kim. 2005. Simulating instructional roles through pedagogical agents. *International Journal of Artificial Intelligence in Education* 15, 2: 95-115.
3. Bradley J. Bond, and Sandra L, Calvert. 2014. A model and measure of US Parents' perceptions of young children's parasocial relationships. In *Journal of children and media* 8, 3: 286-304.
4. John Bowlby. 1969. *Attachment and loss.* Basic Books.
5. Mindy Brooks and Emily Reardon (2016). Sesame Street, letter blocks, and augmented reality: Increasing engagement and learning. *User Experience Magazine* 16, 2. Retrieved from http://uxpamagazine.org/sesame-street-letter-blocks-and-augmented-reality/
6. Kaitlin L. Brunick, Marisa M. Putnam, Lauren E. McGarry, Melissa N. Richards, & Sandra L. Calvert. 2016. Children's future parasocial relationships with media characters: The age of intelligent characters, *Journal of Children and Media* 10, 2: 181-190. DOI:10.1080/17482798.2015.1127839
7. Sandra L. Calvert and M. N. Richards. 2014. Children's parasocial relationships with media characters. In *Media and the well-being of children and adolescents.* A. Jordan and D. Romer (Eds.). Oxford University Press.
8. Common Sense Media. 2016. *The Common Sense Census: Plugged-In Parents of Tweens and Teens 2016.* Retrieved January 21, 2017 from https://www.commonsensemedia.org/research/the-common-sense-census-plugged-in-parents-of-tweens-and-teens-2016#
9. L. K. Friedrich and A. H. Stein. 1975. Prosocial television and young children: The effects of verbal labeling and role playing on learning and behavior. *Child Development* 46 1: 27-38.
10. D. C. Giles. 2002. Parasocial interaction: A review of the literature and a model for future research. *Media Psychology* 4, 2: 279-305.
11. James H. Gray. September 2013. Designing for Deeper Learning. Presentation at the *World Congress of Play.* San Francisco, CA.
12. Mark Nicholas Grimshaw. 2009. The audio uncanny valley: Sound, fear and the horror game. *Audio Mostly 2009*. 21-26.
13. Kathy Hirsh-Pasek, Jennifer Zosh, Roberta Golinkoff, James Gray, Michael Robb, and Jordy Kaufman. 2015. Putting education in educational apps: Lesson from the science of learning. *Psychological Science in the Public Interest* 16, 1: 3-34.
14. C. Hoffner. 2008. Parasocial and online social relationships. In *The handbook of children, media, and development.* Sandra L. Calvert and B. J. Wilson (Eds.). Wiley-Blackwell.
15. D. Horton, and R. R. Wohl, 1956. Mass communication and parasocial interaction: Observations on intimacy at a distance. *Psychiatry* 19, 3: 215-229.
16. Yanghee Kim, and Amy L. Baylor. 2016. Research-based design of pedagogical agent roles: A review, progress, and recommendations. *International Journal of Artificial Intelligence in Education* 26, 1: 160 – 169.
17. Heather L. Kirkorian, Ellen A. Wartella, and Daniel R. Anderson. Spring, 2008. *Media and Young Children's Learning* 18, 1. Princeton-Brookings. https://www.princeton.edu/futureofchildren/publications/docs/18_01_03.pdf
18. Jennifer A. Kotler, Jennifer M. Schiffman, and K. G. Hanson. 2012. The influence of media characters on children's food choices. *Journal of Health Communication* 17, 8: 886-898.
19. Alexis R. Lauricella, Alice Ann, Howard Gola, and Sandra L. Calvert. 2011. Toddlers' learning from socially meaningful video characters in *Media Psychology* 14, 2: 216 – 232.
20. J. W. Mullennix, T. Bihon, J. Bricklemyer, J. Gaston, & J. M. Keener. (2002). Effects of variation in emotion and talker on speech perception. *Language and Speech* 45, 3: 255-283.
21. Melissa N. Richards, and Sandra L. Calvert. 2016. Parent versus child report of young children's parasocial relationships in the United States. *Journal of Children and Media* 20 10: 1-19.
22. Todd Rose. 2016. *The end of average: How we succeed in a world that values sameness.* Harper Collins.
23. Molly Schlesinger. October 2016. The impact of self-perceptions and perceptions of media characters on STEM learning during early childhood. Paper presented at the *Technology and Media in Child Development Special Conference of the Society for Research in Child Development.* Irvine, California.
24. Molly A. Schlesinger, R. M. Flynn, and Rebekah Richert. 2016. US preschoolers' trust of and learning from media characters. *Journal of Children and Media* 10, 3: 321-340.
25. Dorothy G. Singer, and Jerome L Singer. 2005. *Imagination and play in the electronic age*. Harvard University Press.
26. Erik Strommen and K. Alexander. 1999. *Learning from television with interactive toy characters as viewing companions.* Paper presented at the meeting of the Society for Research in Child Development.
27. Lori Takeuchi and Reed Stevens. 2011. *The new co-viewing: Designing for learning through joint media engagement.* Retrieved January 21, 2017 from: http://www.joanganzcooneycenter.org/publication/the-new-coviewing-designing-for-learning-through-joint-media-engagement/

28. Brian Wansink, David R. Just, and Collin R. Payne. 2012. Can branding improve school lunches? *Archives of Pediatrics & Adolescent Medicine* 166, 10: 967-968.
29. Deena S. Weisberg, Kathy Hirsh-Pasek, and Roberta Michnick Golinkoff. 2013. Guided play: Where curricular goals meet a playful pedagogy" in *Mind, Brain, and Education* 7, 2: 104-112.
30. Henry M. Wellman. 1990. *The child's theory of mind.* MIT Press.
31. Marcelo Worsley, Dor Abrahamson, Paulo Blikstein, Shuchi Grover, Bertrand Schneider, Mike Tissenbaum. 2016. Situating multimodal learning analytics. In *12th International Conference of the Learning Sciences, ICLS 2016: Transforming Learning, Empowering Learners, Proceedings Vol. 2.* International Society of the Learning Sciences (ISLS). 1346-1349.

Persistent Memory in Repeated Child-Robot Conversations

Iolanda Leite, André Pereira, Jill Fain Lehman
Disney Research Pittsburgh, USA
{iolanda.leite, andre.pereira, jill.lehman}@disneyresearch.com

ABSTRACT

Persistent memory is a critical mechanism in long-term human-robot interaction. In this work, we investigate how a robot can use information from prior conversations with the same child to foster a sense of relationship over time. To address this question, we conducted a repeated interaction study with three experimental conditions: a baseline control condition, in which the robot retains no information between conversations and relies on a typical elicitation-response paradigm; a persistence condition, in which children experience the same topic flow but with some robot turns that refer back to prior shared events; and a pro-active persistence condition, in which the robot attempts to offer its own feelings and opinions pro-actively and congruently with what it knows about the child. Our results indicate age differences with respect to the measures of interest. During conversations with the robot, older children who were assigned to the persistence conditions exhibited more positive affect, while younger children showed more positive affect in the control condition. Moreover, in a set of comparative judgments among robots they had played with, children in the augmented persistence condition considered PIPER to be the most intelligent and their favorite more often than children in the other conditions, overall, but the effect was more evident in the older children.

CCS Concepts

•Human-centered computing → User studies; Empirical studies in HCI; *Natural language interfaces;*

Author Keywords

Human-robot interaction; memory; repeated interaction

INTRODUCTION

In human-human conversation we use a variety of available strategies in service of myriad goals: to inform, to effect action, to modify beliefs, to evoke emotion, to build connection. Who says what, and how and when, contributes to how we feel about the other person and how we think the other feels about us [8]. In relationships that involve repeated conversation over time, persistent memory for information previously shared has its own power. Minimally, persistence allows a conversant to know or signal that s/he is remembered; more importantly, persistence allows her/him to build and act from a model of common values and experiences. As human-robot dialog faces the challenges of long-term interaction, understanding how to use prior conversation to foster a sense of relationship is key because whether robots remember what we've said, as well as how and when they expose that memory, will contribute to how we feel about them.

IDC '17, June 27-30, 2017, Stanford, CA, USA

ISBN 978-1-4503-4921-5/17/06. . . $15.00

DOI: http://dx.doi.org/10.1145/3078072.3079728

Figure 1: Child interacting with PIPER.

The study presented here is an initial effort to understand how two basic conversational strategies that require persistent memory effect young children's experiences with a robot over time. All children have four conversations with the same robot, PIPER, interspersed with other activities out of the robot's view. In a baseline control condition (C), PIPER relies on a typical elicitation-response paradigm to work through a pre-determined set of topics about each activity (e.g., "What did you do?" <child names activity> "That's cool. Did you like it?") and retains no information between conversations. In the persistence condition (P), children experience the same topic flow but with some PIPER turns that refer back to prior shared events (e.g., "Hey, done with <previously mentioned activity>, I see. Did you like it?"). In the pro-active persistence condition (P+), PIPER goes further and attempts to offer its own feelings and opinions congruently with what it knows about the child, depending on the child's self-report at the end of the activity (e.g., "Hey, done with <previously mentioned activity>, I see. I think that game is really <hard/fun>).

We found that during conversations with the robot, older children who were assigned to the persistent-memory conditions exhibited more positive affect, while younger children showed more positive affect in conversations with simple elicitation and response. Self-report questions collected after the first and last conversations showed that children in all conditions liked the robot, but that the likeability gains were higher for children in the persistent-memory conditions overall, and caused primarily by larger gains for the older children. Finally, in a judgment task comparing the three robots that children interacted with across activities, children in the persistence conditions considered PIPER to be the most intelligent and their favorite more often than children in the control conditions. Despite this general trend, young children in the control condition were more likely to favor the other robots. More broadly, we find that a multiple measures approach, examining phenomena at different levels of granularity, may be an important technique in understanding repeated interactions with children.

BACKGROUND

Information Elicitation

Information elicitation can serve multiple goals in dialogue, one of them being the establishment of a common ground between people [7]. Kiesler [13] argues that communication between robots and users will benefit if robots have a model of common ground with the user. Bickmore and Cassell [3] investigated the effects of conversational strategies such as small talk to establish common ground and improve trust in human-agent interaction. The use of social dialogue by the agent positively impacted users' perception of trust, especially among extrovert adults. More recently, Matsuyama et al. [19] proposed an architecture that allows an agent to build rapport with users by eliciting personal information. Using strategies such as self-disclosure or reference to a previous shared experience, SARA (Socially-Aware Robot Assistant) elicits user preferences and goals to make personalized recommendations about which conference sessions the user should attend. We note that these results were obtained with adults, and it remains unclear whether these findings would hold for children.

One of the practical benefits of information elicitation in human-machine interaction is personalization [14]. Clabaugh and Matarić [6] investigated the impact of elicitation for personalizing interactions between students and a robotic tutor. They define interactive personalization as "the process by which an intelligent agent adapts to the needs and preferences of an individual user through eliciting information directly from that user about his or her state." In a preliminary experiment to explore the elicitation frequency of learning sensitive information by college students, a social robot either elicited learning information by asking direct questions to the students 25% of the time, 50% of the time or never elicited learning sensitive information (and asked other questions instead). Contrary to their initial hypothesis, the results showed that high elicitation levels contributed to participants' positive perception of the learning session and the robot. Elicitation appears natural in a learning environment where question and answering is common, but frequent elicitation might have a different impact in other types of human-robot conversation.

Memory and Persistence

A number of authors have highlighted the critical role of memory in long-term human-robot interaction [5, 16, 1]. While several computational models of memory for virtual characters and robots have been proposed in the literature [11, 27, 17, 24, 23, 20], less attention has been given to the empirical effects of memory in repeated human-robot interactions. One exception is the work by Matsumoto et al. [18] who developed a computational model of spatial memory to enable a robot to collect shared experiences with a user and establish common ground. The model was trained with data collected from people window-shopping and then used by a robot to predict the locations that a user might recall in order to provide appropriate directions in a shopping mall. The authors report the results of a study validating the usefulness of this model. More importantly, this work stresses the importance of implicit shared past experiences in human-robot interaction.

Most relevant, Hastie et al. [10] report a study with an artificial tutor that either referred to a previous interaction (*with-memory* condition) or did not reference a previous interaction (*no-memory* condition) while providing assistance to students. The authors found that the references to past events by the tutor increased students' success in the learning task. Despite the learning gains, students in the *with-memory* condition reported liking the tutor less and judged its instructions harder to follow. These are interesting results when considered in combination with those obtained by Clabaugh and Matarić [6]. It appears that the process of elicitation itself is positive, but the way a robot makes use of elicited information in the future is a more delicate matter. The study described in the next section begins to explore this issue with young children.

METHOD

To explore the effect of referencing prior interactions on young children's experiences with robots, we must contrast dialogs that are reasonably equivalent with respect to features other than the experimental manipulation. Individual differences in life experience and interests are likely to produce free form conversations that lack the necessary degree of commonality. Similarly, developmental differences across the age range we work with (four to ten years old) make it difficult to get comparable task-based dialogs. To keep the topic constant we designed moments of contrast into four dialogs that were interspersed with, and about, a common set of activities in an hour-long session of play. Each non-PIPER activity is a research project with its own goals and hypotheses that was instrumented to provide information necessary to distinguish the PIPER conditions in the dialog that followed it.

Experimental Design

Although introduced briefly above, we explain the three experimental conditions more fully here before continuing with a description of the participants and procedure:

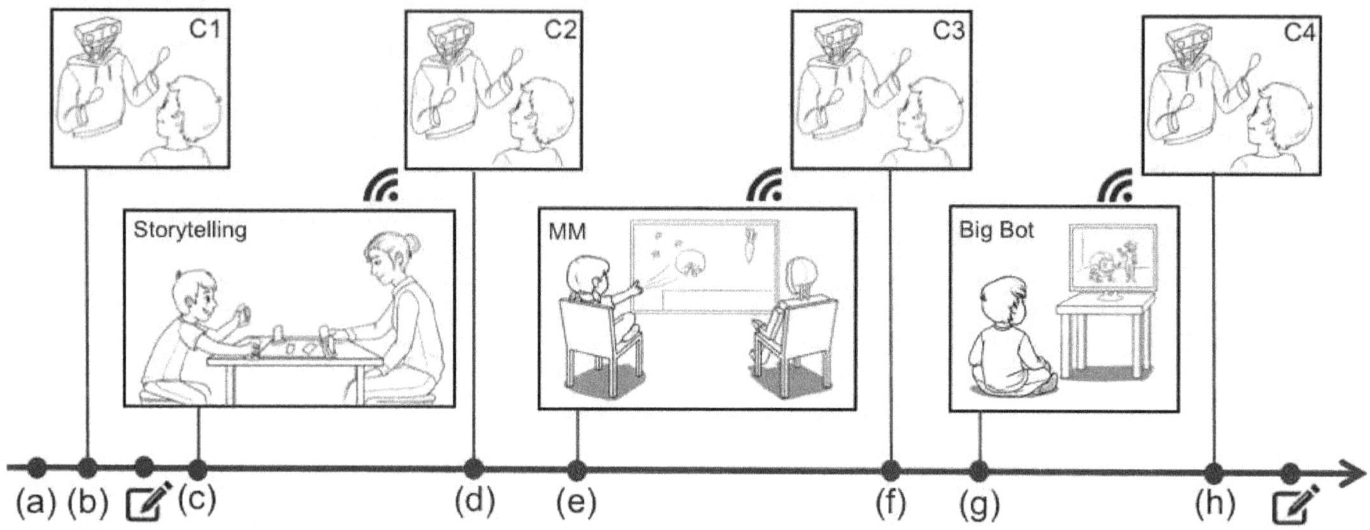

Figure 2: Procedure of the study as described in Section 3.3. Each child has four conversations with PIPER (top row), interspersed with and about the same set of non-PIPER activities. At the end of each activity, children make choices and fill out activity-specific scales that are communicated over the local network to PIPER's dialog manager for use in the P+ condition. Immediately after the first and last conversations, children are asked direct questions about their experience with PIPER.

- *Control (C):* PIPER has no persistent memory, and its language never implies prior interaction. Even if a piece of information is disclosed in a previous conversation, PIPER would need to elicit it again to bring it into the common ground or to predicate behavior on it. It should be noted, however, that all children wore a "name tag" with a character on it and were addressed by that character's name in all conditions. Although it is possible that children would interpret the reuse of their character name as an indicator of familiarity, this personalization did not require persistent memory because the tag was visible. The alternative would have been to use no names, violating expectations in the persistence conditions (P and P+), or to use names only in those conditions, the effect of which might have overshadowed any other contribution of memory [12].
- *Persistent Memory (P):* PIPER is able to remember prior conversations. As a result, it can refer back to previous content without needing to elicit it again, and can predicate its behavior on the basis of previously elicited information. However, in this condition PIPER offers its own opinions only reactively, in congruence with but only after eliciting an opinion from the child. With respect to opinion, then, the P condition is similar to C; both would rely on a dialog path that asked,"Did you like it?" before offering the opinion,"So/Neither did I."
- *Pro-active Persistent Memory (P+)*: PIPER has all of the abilities and behaviors available in P but also offers its own ideas and opinions before the child's are in the common ground. To try to ensure that the comments are congruent with the child's state, PIPER has access to information from the activities that are the topic of conversation but occur out of view. In general that external information was the child's self-report about how much s/he liked the activity. So, for example, if the rating was high/low, pro-active PIPER would follow an eliciting question immediately with a statement containing the same valence: "Hey, what did you think of <activity>? I like/don't like that one."). In short, P+ PIPER acts as if it has a deeper model of the child and can take the risk of exposing its own ideas and opinions first to promote rapport.

Conversational Participants

Eighty-one children were recruited through postings in physical and online community bulletin boards. Because PIPER dialogs were about the non-dialog activities and condition effects were expected to accumulate over time, 14 children were excluded from the analysis due to failure to complete at least one activity or dialog for personal reasons, or hardware or software failure. In our final sample, $N = 67$ (35 female and 32 male), and children's ages ranged from 4 to 10 years ($M = 7.00$, $SD = 1.77$). Participants were assigned to one of the three study conditions in order to balance with respect to age and gender. The C group consisted of 13 females and 10 males ($M = 7.11$ years, $SD = 1.79$), the P group contained 11 females and 11 males ($M = 7.10$ years, $SD = 1.85$), and the P+ group included 11 females and 11 males ($M = 6.79$ years, $SD = 1.74$). The study was approved by an Institutional Review Board, and children were compensated for their participation.

The other dialog participant was PIPER (see left side of Figure 1), an upper body torso teleoperated via an identical master through a hybrid air-water configuration. The robot has four degrees of freedom (DOF) in each arm and a 2-DOF neck. Stereo cameras mounted on the robot's neck stream real-time video to the operator's head-mounted display, which in turn maps the head orientation of the operator to the neck servos of the robot. A menu with options that allow the human operator to perform the language understanding capabilities for PIPER is rendered on top of the video stream. The human operator selects the menu option closest to what the child said using joysticks mounted in each arm of the robot. Through this setup, the operator is visually immersed in the robot's physical space and can "puppeteer" the robot's movements behind the curtain in real-time, while PIPER's responses and the storage and reuse of elicited information are all controlled by a dialog system implemented in Unity3D [26].

Procedure

Because the content of PIPER conversations was grounded in non-dialog activities and information from those activities distinguishes the P and P+ conditions, we explain the experimental procedure with a walk-through of the session the way the child experienced it, as shown in Figure 2.

(a) Consent, name tags, practice scales: After parental consent, children were asked to choose a name tag with a familiar character's picture and told that they would be addressed by that character's name during activities. Next, they participated in a short practice session to learn about *Smileyometer* rating scales [22], answering three simple questions designed to elicit responses across the scale's range ("How much do you like ice cream?" "How much do you like broccoli?" and "How do you feel when you stub your toe?"). The experimenter then invited the child to meet PIPER for the first time on their way to a storytelling activity. The robot was strategically located in a corridor to make it appear natural for children to stop by as they went to and from the non-dialog activities.

(b) Conversation 1 (Baseline): Except for the farewell ("bye" versus "see you later"), this conversation is identical across experimental conditions. PIPER introduces itself to the child and asks which activity the child is going to do first. When the child replies (or the experimenter intervenes, if the child does not remember), PIPER gives directions to a new room where the activity has been relocated. Once they are out of sight of PIPER and before they reach the storytelling room, children are asked two *Smileyometer* questions - "How much did you like talking to PIPER?" and "How friendly is PIPER?" - in order to get a baseline reaction.

(c) Activity 1 (Storytelling): This guided storytelling activity explores different styles of prompting. Children start by selecting the main character of their superhero story from a fixed set of visuals, then new objects are introduced pictorially at fixed time intervals with either a general or story-specific prompt (e.g.,"Ok, let's include a kitten." versus "What if this kitten drinks that potion?"). At the end, children answer *Smileyometer* questions about how much they like the activity and how brave their character was in the story they created. The name of the chosen superhero character and the self-reported value for the first question are communicated to PIPER and determine the dialog flow if the child is in the P+ condition. A full description of the research aims and results for this activity can be found in [25]. As children leave the Storytelling room they are told that the next activity will involve a new robot, named Sammy, and a video game called *Mole Madness*.

(d) Conversation 2 (Storytelling)

When the child approaches PIPER after Storytelling, the robot uses a different greeting for control and persistence conditions ("Hi there, <character name>" versus "Hey <character name>, you're back!"). It then introduces the topic of storytelling. In the C condition this must be done by elicitation ("What activity did you just do?"). In the P condition, however, PIPER remembers that the child was going to Storytelling and simply asks whether the child had fun during the activity. For children in the P+ group, PIPER predicates its opening using the information provided by the child's *Smileyometer* choice at the end of the activity. If children selected one of the two higher ends of the scale, PIPER says "You look like you had fun in Storytelling!" and otherwise, "Hmm, doesn't look like Storytelling was much fun."

Another critical moment in this conversation happens a few turns later when PIPER asks about the contents of the child's story, in particular the superhero character selected by the child. In the C and P conditions, this is done through direct elicitation ("So, tell me your story. Who was in it?"), but in the P+ condition PIPER proactively offers its own value judgment of the child's character by injecting the experimenter-provided information during the elicitation ("So, tell me your story. Who was in it? Wait, wait, was <child's choice> in it? I hope <child's choice> was in it!!").

Differences between conditions also occur at parting. PIPER ends C conversations with a simple "Have fun," but P and P+ conversations end with an explicit reference to seeing the child again after the next activity.

(e) Activity 2 (*Mole Madness*): This cooperative, speech-based videogame is played with a very different kind of robot, introduced as Sammy. The goal of the game is to move an animated mole through its environment using a small set of keywords. Children play multiple levels with different versions of Sammy's behavior, and complete *Smileyometer* scales about how much they liked the game and how good a player Sammy is. These values are transmitted to PIPER to be used in the P+ condition.

(f) Conversation 3 (*Mole Madness*): As in Conversation 2, greetings immediately establish whether PIPER remembers where the child was going (P and P+) or not (C). In the case of P+, PIPER goes further by adding either a positive comment about the game, or commenting on how hard the game is, depending on the child's *Smileyometer* data.

A second contrasting moment in this conversation occurs when PIPER says that the mole needs a vacation and asks the child to suggest a replacement character for the game. After the child responds, PIPER offers an alternative. In the C condition the alternative is always Iron Man, a superhero that is not one of the Storytelling characters. In the P condition, PIPER suggests Trash Can Guy, a character that is always the villain introduced in Storytelling and thus a character that can be known simply by remembering that the child did the earlier activity. In the P+ condition, PIPER suggests the specific character the child chose, thus reintroducing the shared preference established in Conversation 2 back into the common ground.[1]

This dialog ends when PIPER offers to tell its own story, but the experimenter mentions that it's time for them to go to BigBot's Big Adventure. As in prior conversations, PIPER acknowledges departure with either a simple goodbye (C), or a reference to the next time they will meet (P, P+).

(g) Activity 3 (Bigbot's Big Adventure): This problem-solving task has children talk to screen-based characters in an interactive story. Zoe and Smallbot are in Zoe's tree house when their friend, Bigbot, runs out of battery power. Children help Zoe and Smallbot get Bigbot back to the lab by choosing the right tool to solve problems that come up along the way. A full description of the research aims and results for this activity can be found in [4]. At the end of the activity, children complete *Smileyometer* scales about whether they liked the game and whether they thought it was easy to solve the problems, results of which are communicated to PIPER.

(h) Conversation 4 (Bigbot's Big Adventure):

The first turns continue to differentiate conditions. In C, a greeting without a familiarity marker is followed by eliciting the name of the last activity and then the child's success in completing it. In P, the greeting refers directly to the information disclosed at the end of Conversation 3, then PIPER elicits success. In P+, PIPER also greets familiarly and knowledgeably ("Hi, again <character name>. I want to hear about Bigbot.") but extends the turn with a pro-active judgment: "I hope you saved him!" if the child found the task easy, and "I gotta tell you I do not like that game," if the child did not.

Later PIPER acknowledges that this is the last dialog and either elicits the child's favorite activity for the session (C and P), or self-interrupts the elicitation (P+) and guesses the child's preference based on the full history of the child's self-reports ("I bet it was storytelling!"). Note that although some information about the child's opinion for each activity was explicitly elicited and remembered in the P condition, PIPER does not integrate and front that knowledge in this final dialog with those children.

(i) Post-conversation Measures: After the fourth conversation and out of sight of PIPER, children were given the same *likeability* and *friendliness* scales as in (a). They were also given four stickers and asked to give each sticker to one of the robots they had talked to during the session (PIPER, Sammy, or Smallbot). Children were told that they could offer any number of stickers to any of the bots, and were verbally prompted with the intended meaning of each award. In particular, the stickers showed a pair of glasses ("Who is smarter? Give the glasses to the bot you think is smartest."), a birthday cake ("Who is more fun? Give the birthday cake to the bot you would invite to your birthday party."), an apple ("Who would be a better teacher? Give the apple to the bot you would chose to be your teacher."), and a gold medal ("Who did you like the most? Give the gold medal to your favorite bot").

Behavioral Measures

Conversations with PIPER were audio and video-taped. Thus, in addition to the self-report measures collected at points (a) and (h), we were able to compute behavioral measures for the child's expression of positive or negative affect in the turns where PIPER's dialog was different across conditions[2]. For empirical purposes, we consider that such *critical turns* begin when PIPER finishes an utterance specific to one or two experimental conditions, and end at the beginning of the robot's next utterance.

Two coders with experience in behavioral analysis marked segments where children were clearly expressing positive or negative affect. We excluded negative affect from subsequent analysis because such annotations occurred in less than 5% of the critical turns, regardless of coder. With respect to positive affect, reliability between coders was moderate ($\alpha = 0.69$), with most of the differences occurring in judgments about children in the control condition in Conversation 2. For clarity of exposition, and because their overall patterns are otherwise consistent, we present one annotator's results. By combining her annotations with the start and end times for PIPER's dialog, we computed the presence of positive affect in each critical turn based on whether there was an annotation that overlapped at least 25% of that turn duration. We extracted a total of 616 critical turns for all participants in Conversations 2 to 4. The average number of critical turns per conversation was about three and corresponded to approximately 30% of the total conversation in each condition.

RESULTS

Our experience with young children suggests the importance of multiple measures in drawing conclusions about the effect of any experimental condition on emotion or behavior [15]. To that end, likeability, friendliness and positive affect measures look at change over time with PIPER, while the sticker data looks at cumulative perception of PIPER versus other robots in the session. The different measures also look for change at different levels of granularity, with likeability and friendliness measuring large-scale change in attitude from the first to the last conversation, and the affect data offering a window into conversation-by-conversation change. Our experience also suggests that differences due to age are likely to be present in language interactions; as a result, statistics that

[1] In the story retell in Conversation 2, children are asked who their character was, so in theory it would have been possible to store and reuse that information in Conversation 3 in the P condition as well. However, not all children will remember or name their character during the retell. We would have had to add an extra turn to P to make sure the name was introduced into the common ground for PIPER to reuse it, creating an imbalance in either dialog length or topic flow across conditions. We chose, instead, to use Trash Can Guy in P, making the back reference without the need for an extra turn.

[2] In Conversation 1, only the farewell differentiates between the persistence and control conditions. Because many children walked away as soon as the experimenter said it was time to leave, missing PIPER's actual parting words, we include critical turns only for Conversations 2, 3, and 4 in the analysis.

Table 1: Mean and Standard Deviations (in parentheses) of the perceived likeability and friendliness measures collected after the first and last conversations with PIPER. Results in bold represent the Mean across all conditions.

		4 to 6 years		7 to 10 years		All ages	
		c1	c4	c1	c4	c1	c4
Likeability	C	4.14 (.95)	4.64 (.74)	4.54 (.52)	4.62 (.65)	4.34	4.63
	P	4.39 (.77)	4.31 (.99)	4.25(.75)	4.58 (.90)	4.32	4.45
	P+	4.82 (.60)	4.64 (.81)	3.91(.94)	4.46 (.69)	4.37	4.55
		4.45	**4.53**	**4.23**	**4.55**	**4.34**	**4.54**
Friendliness	C	4.57 (.85)	4.93 (.27)	4.85 (.38)	4.92 (.28)	4.71	4.93
	P	4.62 (.87)	4.54 (.66)	4.67 (.65)	4.67 (.65)	4.65	4.61
	P+	5.00 (.00)	5.00 (.00)	4.64 (.67)	4.73 (.65)	4.82	4.87
		4.73	**4.82**	**4.72**	**4.77**	**4.73**	**4.80**

collapse across age may show no effect because the trends in different age groups are at odds. At the same time, there are simply not enough children in our study for full condition X ages analyses. As a compromise we explore age-related trends by dividing participants into two groups (4 to 6 and 7 to 10 years) based on the child developmental literature [21] and re-examine the data with respect to age group subsequent to the computation of main effects. Such analyses are particularly important when top-level results are not significant.

Likeability and Friendliness

The *Smileyometer* data on perceived likeability and friendliness was converted into two variables using a 5-point scale where 1 was the least positive smiley and 5 was the most positive. We conducted a repeated-measures ANOVA to investigate the effects of these two measures, collected after the first and the last conversations with PIPER, across study condition (C, P and P+) and age group.

For perceived likeability, we found a significant main effect for conversation $F(1,68) = 4.48, p < .05, \eta^2 = .07$, such that children reported to like PIPER more after the last conversation ($M = 4.54, SD = .85$) than after the first conversation ($M = 4.34, SD = .80$) regardless of their assigned condition and age. No significant interaction effect was found between conversation and condition, $F(2,68) = .27, p = .77, \eta^2 = .01$, nor in the interaction between conversation and age, $F(1,68) = 1.60, p = .21, \eta^2 = .02$. However, a significant interaction effect was found between conversation, condition and age group, $F(2,68) = 3.39, p < .05, \eta^2 = .10$. In particular, if we examine the top of Table 1, we see that the younger children showed a gain in mean likeability only in the control condition, while the same degree of gain occurred in the older children only in the P+ condition.

Regarding perceived friendliness, we found no significant main effect for conversation $F(1,68) = 1.55, p = .22, \eta^2 = .02$, nor in the interaction between conversation and condition, $F(2,68) = 1.67$, $p = .20, \eta^2 = .05$, the interaction between conversation and age group, $F(1,68) = .10$, $p = .76, \eta^2 = .00$, or in the interaction between the three factors, $F(2,68) = 1.07, p = .35, \eta^2 = 0.03$. As can be seen in the second half of Table 1, initial scores for this measure were so high that there was less room for positive change than in the case of likeability. Of course, there was more room for negative change, but our primary constraint in designing interactions is always that the children have an enjoyable experience, so all versions of PIPER's dialog were phrased in a friendly manner.

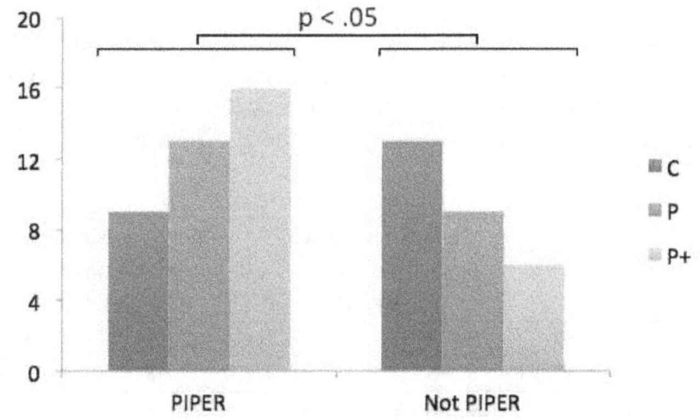

Figure 3: Number of sticker glasses received by PIPER in comparison with the other robots, by study condition.

Award Stickers

To analyze the sticker attribution data, we created a contingency table with one categorical variable for each sticker and the frequencies of children that offered that sticker to PIPER versus either of the other two robots (not-PIPER). We then conducted Pearson's chi-square tests with these categorical variables to examine the relation between the study condition and the number of stickers that PIPER received compared to the other robots. The relation between the number of glasses stickers (Who is smarter?) that PIPER received across study condition was significant, $\chi^2(2) = 5.24, p < .05$. Children in the persistence conditions were more likely to give the glasses sticker to PIPER while children in the control condition were more likely to give the glasses to a different robot (see Figure 3). The relation was not significant for the cake (Who is more fun?), $\chi^2(2) = .82, p = .33$, apple (Who would be a better teacher?), $\chi^2(2) = .74, p = .35$ or gold medal (Who is your favorite?) stickers, $\chi^2(2) = 3.53, p = .09$.

Although the smartness metric was the only one to achieve significance across conditions, the raw data suggest some age patterns that might be more robust in a larger sample. Table 2 shows the number of stickers received by PIPER versus the other robots, divided by the three study conditions and age. Note that the older children contribute more to the glasses win for PIPER in the persistence conditions, while the younger children contribute more to the not-PIPER win in the control condition. Moving right in the table, the pattern for cake (fun) seems the same across age groups, but the pattern for apple (teacher) is inverted: older children in all conditions voted for PIPER but younger children in all conditions voted for a different robot. Finally, when we look at which robot receives the medal as favorite, the raw scores for all children (bottom two rows) follow the same pattern as glasses - preference for

Table 2: Contingency table with the number of stickers that each child offered to PIPER and to the other robots after the four conversations, divided by age group and condition. (A few children insisted on splitting a sticker across PIPER and one of the non-PIPER robots. In these cases, a point was awarded to each.)

		Glasses (smarter)			Cake (fun)			Apple (teacher)			Medal (favorite)		
		C	P	P+	C	P	P+	C	P	P+	C	P	P+
4 to 6	PIPER	3	5	7	4	2	2	4	2	3	3	7	3
	Not PIPER	8	6	4	7	9	9	7	9	8	8	4	8
7 to 10	PIPER	6	8	9	4	3	4	9	8	7	4	5	9
	Not PIPER	5	3	2	8	8	7	3	3	4	7	5	2
All	PIPER	9	13	16	8	5	6	13	10	10	7	12	12
	Not PIPER	13	9	6	15	17	16	10	12	12	15	9	10

PIPER versus non-PIPER robots in persistence conditions - but the patterns by age are not as pronounced.

Affect

A one-way ANOVA was conducted to investigate the impact of study condition (C, P or P+) on the presence of positive affect in children during the critical turns in the latter three conversations. There was no statistically significant difference between conditions, collapsed across conversation, $F(2,218) = 2.40, p = .09, \eta^2 = .02$. Despite the lack of main effect, we nevertheless expect repeated interaction with the robot to show a novelty effect, per [9, 16], and planned comparisons with conversation number as a within-subject factor, keeping study condition as a between-subject factor. Of course, this was possible only because the topics in each conversation were the same for all conditions.

Results showed a statistically significant main effect for conversation number in a repeated measures ANOVA, $F(2,69) = 11.08, p < .05, \eta^2 = .20$, but no significant interaction effect between conversation number and condition, $F(4,140) = 1.24, p = .30, \eta^2 = .04$. Post hoc analyses applying Bonferroni correction indicated that the proportion of positive affect was significantly higher in Conversation 2 ($M = .48, SD = .38$) than Conversation 3 ($M = .31, SD = .31$) and Conversation 4 ($M = .24, SD = .30$), $p < .05$, as novelty wore off, but that the overall difference in affect between Conversations 3 and 4 were not significant, $p = .55$.

Based on both the condition X conversation effect and *a priori* differences in language sophistication with age, we carried out individual planned comparisons for each conversation, considering age group as a factor. For the critical turns of Conversation 2, we found no significant main effect for condition, $F(2,68) = 1.14, p = .34, \eta^2 = .03$, nor in the interaction between condition and age group, $F(2,68) = .50, p = .61, \eta^2 = .01$. Similarly, the analysis of variance conducted for Conversation 3 yielded no main effect for condition, $F(2,68) = .84, p = .44, \eta^2 = .03$, or in the interaction between condition and age, $F(2,68) = 1.31, p = .28, \eta^2 = .04$.

In Conversation 4, however, there was a significant main effect for condition, $F(2,67) = 3.56, p < .05, \eta^2 = .11$. Post hoc analyses applying Bonferroni correction indicated that the proportion of positive affect was significantly higher ($p < .05$) in children assigned to the P+ condition ($M = .36, SD = .25$) than children in P ($M = .16, SD = .27$), but no significant differences were found between either of the persistence conditions (P and P+) and the C condition ($M = .21, SD = .33$). We also found an interaction effect between condition and age, $F(2,67) = 4.07, p < .05, \eta^2 = .12$. The age-distinct patterns of positive affect over time can be seen clearly in Figures 4a and 4b. The older children show a typical novelty effect in the control condition, slower attenuation in the persistence conditions, and a small reversal of trend for P+ in the final conversation. In contrast, younger children's affect remains fairly steady in the control condition and attenuates quickly in the persistence conditions, except for P+ in the last conversation, where they show an even more pronounced reversal than the older children.

DISCUSSION

Looking across all of the results presented in the previous section, a consistent picture emerges in which younger and older children have different basic reactions to the conversational strategies associated with persistent memory in PIPER's interactions. Overall children's cumulative experience with the robot led to a significant increase in their likeability ratings, but older children's ratings were more likely to increase in the persistent conditions (particularly P+) while younger children's ratings were more likely to increase if they were in the control condition. Similarly, cumulative experience led children to judge PIPER as more intelligent than the other robots with whom they interacted, but the effect was more pronounced if you were older and in a persistent condition and less pronounced if you were younger and in the control. Looking at positive affect conversation by conversation, all children showed evidence of a novelty effect, but affect dropped more steeply in C for older children, and in P and P+ for younger children, at least until Conversation 4. Indeed, there is clearly something about what children experience in the P+ condition in Conversation 4 that is special, irrespective of age.

What was it about Conversation 4 that mattered and why did it only matter for P+ in that culminating context? Recall that the difference between C and the other conditions is persistent memory, which means that if topic flow across conditions is to be kept as similar as possible, C PIPER will have to elicit information that P and P+ PIPER do not. The essential difference between P and P+ is that P+ has a pro-active conversational strategy, but to create that distinction we provided PIPER with additional information in the P+ condition without it having to be elicited. Thus, while we intended to create a different persona for P+ PIPER, one that sounded more varied in its conversation and appeared to be more vested in building a relationship by risking exposing its opinions first, we inadvertently created a situation in Conversation 4 in which P PIPER was hamstrung. The important moment in Conversation 4, the culmination of the use of persistent memory, occurs when PIPER moves to the topic of the child's fa-

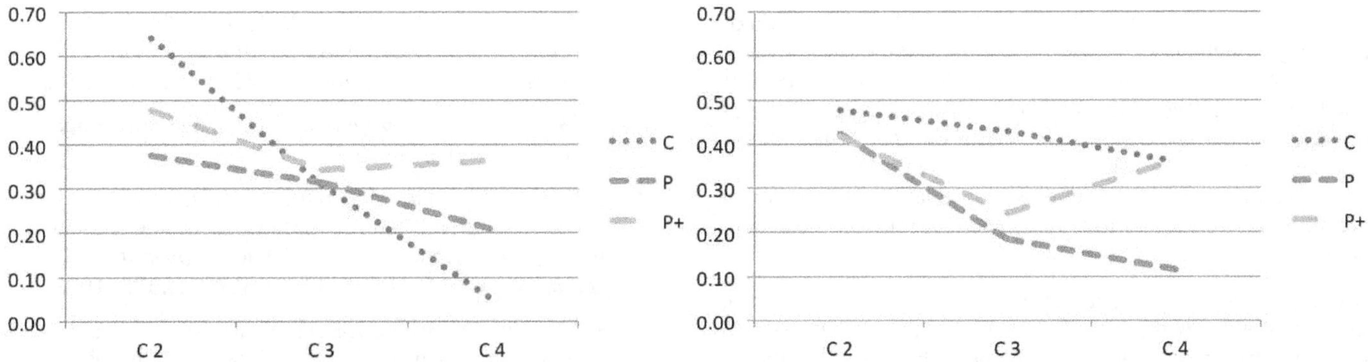

(a) 7 to 10 year olds (b) 4 to 6 year olds

Figure 4: Proportion of critical turns with positive affective reactions divided by age groups for each conversation with PIPER (excluding baseline Conversation 1) in the control (C), persistence (P) and augmented persistence (P+) conditions.

vorite activity. In C this is done through simple elicitation. In P+ it is done by performing a computation over all the stored information that has been provided from the various activities and making a guess. In P, however, PIPER also uses simple elicitation, like C, despite having all the same information that is available in P+. In P the information was gained over accumulated elicitations rather than by unseen means, but to use it would violate the strategy difference between the conditions. In other words, by Conversation 4 the difference between P and P+ was less about whether each version had the information necessary to perform the computation of which activity to guess was the child's favorite, than that P was not allowed to express the results of that computation.

We conjecture that if we had allowed P PIPER to follow the elicitation of the final value at the start of the conversation (how easy it was to help Bigbot) with a proactive evaluation of the child's experience during the entire session, P PIPER's measures would have mirrored P+ PIPER's, even as it violated the distinction between the two conditions. This is conjecture, however, and not just because we didn't try it, but because the origin of the memories might matter. In P+ the information that went into the guess was self-report via *Smileyometer* scales, but in P the information was self-report in conversation. We observed that not all children in the C and P conditions were consistent with regard to how they answered with the scale and what they said in subsequent elicited response. Absent a conversational turn that grounded the child's opinion in situ, P+ PIPER was effectively making an inference and that inference could have been (and occasionally was) wrong. Had we let P PIPER guess as well, the fact that it was using grounded values – that the child knew s/he had provided those values to PIPER – might have made the personalization more powerful.

Stepping back, the data suggest to us that although older and younger children have different baseline preferences, persistence matters when the content it makes available matters, regardless of age. The preference for the C condition in the younger children may be because simple elicitation and response is a familiar and easily understood format. Or it may be that any conversation that elicits more responses will, absent other factors, be more enjoyable to them. It is also possible that the youngest children did not notice the familiarity markers, or noticed them but did not understand them as intended, or recognized the intent but did not build up a model of mutual familiarity over time. But while small intimations of familiarity might not have had much cumulative impact, the moment of personalization that resonated – the moment when they understood that PIPER knew something important about them – that use of memory had a noticeable effect. The story is different for the older children, but consistent nonetheless. They prefer the kinds of conversation that are more typical for their ages, and the control condition's simplicity and predictability is less enjoyable, albeit no less friendly. The steady accumulation of markers of familiarity and personalization make for a better experience, and the guess in Conversation 4 signals another instance that matters, but it is less impactful because of the cumulative effect.

CONCLUSION

We studied how different conversational strategies, with and without the ability to refer to prior events, effect children's experience with a robot over repeated interactions. To create a common backdrop for evaluation, each child played the same games and activities and then had conversations about them with the robot. Our method allowed the robot's dialogs to be both automated and predicated on information that distinguished the experimental conditions. We find that the small expressions of familiarity associated with persistent memory were important only to the older children, but that a personalized observation made on the basis of accumulated information had a positive effect across the age range.

The work reported here is a preliminary study in which we were as interested in developing a new methodology for evaluating repeated child-robot conversations as we were in understanding the outcomes. Thus, a number of limitations must be acknowledged. First, to have both repeated interactions and non-trivial common conversation across subjects, we had to create a setup that was complex in both conception and execution. That complexity is why we decided to recruit children across the age range of interest within the duration of the study rather than try to run a smaller number of ages first and the remainder at some future time. As a consequence, our results suggest several age differences that a larger sample of participants per age might have helped clarify. Although exact replication of this study will be difficult for any group, including our own, studies exploring the same conversational phenomena are needed to verify the interpretation these data suggest.

Second, it seems clear that the more conversations there are, the less likely it is that simple pre- versus post measures will uncover important patterns of change related to cumulative effect. We collected multiple measures at different levels of granularity for this reason, but the research community is still developing techniques and standards in this regard [16, 2]. We acknowledge that the measures used in this study are unlikely to be the only ones relevant to understanding the cumulative effect of conversational variables over repeated interaction between robots and children.

Finally, although long-term is by definition repeated, repeated is not necessarily long-term. We cannot assume that the results reported here will apply to long-term child-robot interactions, and future work should address that issue. Of course, long-term interaction with children must entail a theory of how persistent an item of elicited information should be, i.e., how long it should be held to be true given developmental change. Absent such a theory, we see focusing on repeated interaction over a period of time in which what the robot remembers is still likely to be what the child believes, as a useful beginning.

REFERENCES

1. P. Baxter and T. Belpaeme. Pervasive memory: the future of long-term social HRI lies in the past. In *Third International Symposium on New Frontiers in Human-Robot Interaction at AISB*, 2014.
2. P. Baxter, J. Kennedy, E. Senft, S. Lemaignan, and T. Belpaeme. From characterising three years of HRI to methodology and reporting recommendations. In *2016 11th ACM/IEEE International Conference on Human-Robot Interaction (HRI)*, pages 391–398, March 2016.
3. T. Bickmore and J. Cassell. Relational agents: A model and implementation of building user trust. In *Proceedings of the SIGCHI Conference on Human Factors in Computing Systems*, CHI '01, pages 396–403, New York, NY, USA, 2001. ACM.
4. E. J. Carter, J. Hyde, and J. K. Hodgins. Investigating the use of interactive features for children's television programming. In *Proceedings of the The 16th International Conference on Interaction Design and Children*, IDC '17, New York, NY, USA, 2017. ACM.
5. G. Castellano, R. Aylett, K. Dautenhahn, A. Paiva, P. W. McOwan, and S. Ho. Long-term affect sensitive and socially interactive companions. In *Proc. of the 4th International Workshop on Human-Computer Conversation*, 2008.
6. C. Clabaugh and M. J. Matarić. In *The 25th IEEE International Symposium on Robot and Human Interactive Communication (RO-MAN)*. IEEE, 2016.
7. H. H. Clark. *Using language*. Cambridge university press, Cambridge, 1996.
8. S. R. Fussell and R. M. Krauss. Coordination of knowledge in communication: effects of speakers' assumptions about what others know. *Journal of personality and Social Psychology*, 62(3):378, 1992.
9. R. Gockley, A. Bruce, J. Forlizzi, M. Michalowski, A. Mundell, S. Rosenthal, B. Sellner, R. Simmons, K. Snipes, A. C. Schultz, and J. Wang. Designing robots for long-term social interaction. In *2005 IEEE/RSJ International Conference on Intelligent Robots and Systems*, pages 1338–1343, Aug 2005.
10. H. Hastie, M. Y. Lim, S. Janarthanam, A. Deshmukh, R. Aylett, M. E. Foster, and L. Hall. I remember you!: Interaction with memory for an empathic virtual robotic tutor. In *Proceedings of the 2016 International Conference on Autonomous Agents and Multiagent Systems*, AAMAS '16, pages 931–939, Richland, SC, 2016. International Foundation for Autonomous Agents and Multiagent Systems.
11. W. C. Ho, K. Dautenhahn, M. Y. Lim, P. A. Vargas, R. Aylett, and S. Enz. An initial memory model for virtual and robot companions supporting migration and long-term interaction. In *The 18th IEEE International Symposium on Robot and Human Interactive Communication (RO-MAN)*, pages 277–284, Sept 2009.
12. T. Kanda, T. Hirano, D. Eaton, and H. Ishiguro. Interactive robots as social partners and peer tutors for children: A field trial. *Human-computer interaction*, 19(1):61–84, 2004.
13. S. Kiesler. Fostering common ground in human-robot interaction. In *Proceedings of the IEEE International Workshop on Robot and Human Interactive Communicationn (RO-MAN)*, pages 729–734. IEEE, 2005.
14. G. Kreutler and D. Jannach. Personalized needs elicitation in web-based configuration systems. In *Mass Customization: Challenges and Solutions*, pages 27–42. Springer, 2006.
15. I. Leite and J. F. Lehman. The robot who knew too much: Toward understanding the privacy/personalization trade-off in child-robot conversation. In *Proceedings of the The 15th International Conference on Interaction Design and Children*, IDC '16, pages 379–387, New York, NY, USA, 2016. ACM.
16. I. Leite, C. Martinho, and A. Paiva. Social robots for long-term interaction: A survey. *International Journal of Social Robotics*, 5(2):291–308, 2013.
17. M. Y. Lim. *Memory Models for Intelligent Social Companions*, pages 241–262. Springer Berlin Heidelberg, Berlin, Heidelberg, 2012.

18. T. Matsumoto, S. Satake, T. Kanda, M. Imai, and N. Hagita. Do you remember that shop?: Computational model of spatial memory for shopping companion robots. In *Proceedings of the Seventh Annual ACM/IEEE International Conference on Human-Robot Interaction*, HRI '12, pages 447–454, New York, NY, USA, 2012. ACM.

19. Y. Matsuyama, A. Bhardwaj, R. Zhao, O. J. Romero, S. A. Akoju, and J. Cassell. Socially-aware animated intelligent personal assistant agent. In *17th Annual Meeting of the Special Interest Group on Discourse and Dialogue*, page 224, 2016.

20. M. Oliveira, G. H. Lim, L. S. Lopes, S. H. Kasaei, A. M. Tomé, and A. Chauhan. A perceptual memory system for grounding semantic representations in intelligent service robots. In *2014 IEEE/RSJ International Conference on Intelligent Robots and Systems*, pages 2216–2223, Sept 2014.

21. J. Piaget. *The moral judgement of the child.* Simon and Schuster, 1997.

22. J. C. Read and S. MacFarlane. Using the fun toolkit and other survey methods to gather opinions in child computer interaction. In *Proceedings of the 2006 Conference on Interaction Design and Children*, IDC '06, pages 81–88, New York, NY, USA, 2006. ACM.

23. S. Rosenthal, S. Skaff, M. Veloso, D. Bohus, and E. Horvitz. Execution memory for grounding and coordination. In *Proceedings of the 8th ACM/IEEE International Conference on Human-robot Interaction*, HRI '13, pages 213–214, Piscataway, NJ, USA, 2013. IEEE Press.

24. D. Stachowicz and G. J. M. Kruijff. Episodic-like memory for cognitive robots. *IEEE Transactions on Autonomous Mental Development*, 4(1):1–16, March 2012.

25. M. Sun, I. Leite, J. Lehman, and B. Li. Collaborative storytelling between robot and child: A feasibility study. In *Proceedings of the The 16th International Conference on Interaction Design and Children*, IDC '17, New York, NY, USA, 2017. ACM.

26. J. Whitney, T. Chen, J. Mars, and J. Hodgins. A hybrid hydrostatic transmission and human-safe haptic telepresence robot. In *2016 IEEE International Conference on Robotics and Automation (ICRA), Stockholm, Sweden (to appear)*. IEEE, 2016.

27. R. Wood, P. Baxter, and T. Belpaeme. A review of long-term memory in natural and synthetic systems. *Adaptive Behavior*, 20(2):81–103, 2011.

SpeechBlocks: A Constructionist Early Literacy App

Ivan Sysoev
MIT Media Lab
Cambridge, MA
isysoev@mit.edu

Anneli Hershman
MIT Media Lab
Cambridge, MA
anneli@mit.edu

Susan Fine
Northeastern University
Boston, MA
s.fine@northeastern.edu

Claire Traweek
MIT
Cambridge, MA
ctraweek@mit.edu

Deb Roy
MIT Media Lab
Cambridge, MA
dkroy@media.mit.edu

ABSTRACT
This paper introduces SpeechBlocks (SB): a smartphone app that allows children to explore spelling principles in an open-ended way. Children rearrange letter combinations through direct manipulations and instantly hear each combination pronounced back, whether or not a conventionally spelled word is formed. We evaluated SB with a group of 16 preschool children ages 4 and 5 in a pilot consisting of 16 sessions over the course of two months. Qualitatively, we found that (a) the app facilitated children's engagement, sense of authorship and self-efficacy, (b) SB evoked significant amount of social interactions between children around literacy activities, and (c) support of nonsense words and remixing contributed to these factors. In addition, fine-grained log data of children's interaction with the app showed promise as a viewpoint into their literacy skills and interests.

ACM Classification Keywords
K.3.2. Computers and Education: Computer and Information Science Education - Literacy

Author Keywords
constructionism; early literacy; phonological awareness; phonics

INTRODUCTION
The ability to read and write is an essential skill for a person in a modern society. Yet this is a challenging task for a child to master – especially in languages that do not adhere to the phonemic principle, such as English and French [26]. Smartphones, which became ubiquitous in developed countries and is steadily gaining prominence around the world [16], have the potential to support children in this undertaking. Among other advantages, they offer (a) a mode of interaction that is intuitive, natural and engaging for children; (b) a possibility to bring educational activities from the classroom into homes and other informal learning environments; (c) a possibility to enable personalized learning experiences and (d) a promise to reach underserved families [21]. Currently, there is a great number of educational apps designed to support literacy learning. However, the overwhelming majority of these apps are within the instructionist paradigm – they present the child with a task or a puzzle which has a single pre-determined correct answer [24]. The validity of such an approach has been questioned in light of findings from the science of learning [7].

IDC '17, June 27-30, 2017, Stanford, CA, USA

DOI: http://dx.doi.org/10.1145/3078072.3079720

Figure 1. Sblocks.

In his foundational work *Mindstorms*, Seymour Papert suggested the key learning affordance of computers (which smartphones essentially are) is not to "program the child" through tasks and answers, but instead to be a tool for exploration and self-expression through the construction of artifacts [14]. This paradigm, known as constructionism, has since been shown to promote deeper learning and facilitate intrinsic motivation and self-efficacy (see, e.g., [18]). However, there are very few literacy apps implemented within this paradigm. Additionaly, to the authors' knowledge, there has been no published research exploring the potential of constructionist mobile apps for literacy learning. These factors motivated us to create SpeechBlocks and conduct the present study.

In SpeechBlocks (SB), children rearrange letter combinations by pulling them apart and putting them together with their fingers. Each combination, whether or not it represents a real word, is then pronounced aloud by a speech synthesizer[1], creating instant feedback to the child. Such interaction was designed to help children acquire written text decoding skills (as elaborated in the *Literacy Research Background* section). In addition, SB provides a medium for learners' self-expression.

We conducted a pilot study with SB to identify how children would interact with a constructionist mobile learning app and to inform further development of such technology. We were specifically interested in the following questions:

(a) Would children engage with SB?

(b) If yes, what would they do and what would they build? E.g. their names? Names of things that surround them? Random rearrangements of letters?

(c) What kind of activities can enrich their experience with SB?

(d) Would children play with SB socially?

We present qualitative and some quantitative observations that shed some light on these questions. Our results have implications for developers and designers of early literacy technologies.

While this paper focuses on SB on its own, we believe that the greatest potential lies in SB being a part of a larger system. We are exploring possibilities for a technology that would facilitate the formation of a supportive informal learning environment around the child. Such environment would include peers, parents and learning experts. The experts would act as guides, rather than instructors, by providing feedback to the parents and remotely adjusting the workings of the literacy apps. The expert's decision process could be supported by an automated analysis of the digital traces of the childrenâĂŹs interactions with the device. We believe that a constructionist approach is crucial for creating this type of supportive learning system, and SB is our first step towards this goal.

RELATED WORK

Talking Typewriter

In 1960s, Moore [12] conducted extensive experimentation on building "autotelic responsive environments." By this he meant environments where a child: (a) is driven by intrinsic motivation, (b) could explore freely, (c) receives immediate feedback, (d) determines the pace of events, (e) makes full use of his/her capacity to discover various relations, and the very structure of environment facilitates such discoveries. Moore's environments included "talking typewriter" which, in addition to printing letters, could also pronounce them back to the child. In certain modes the typewriter also pronounced the words being typed (though, in opposition to SB, it only handled real words). Moore found it necessary for efficient learning to provide some structure to the exploration. He did this by constraining the action space (e.g., blocking some keys on the keyboard). A laboratory assistant would monitor the learner's activity with the device and transition the child to a more or less structured setting should s/he show the signs of boredom or frustration. Moore also took care to provide meaningful context for typing activities: children wrote materials for their own newspaper. The "talking typewriter" was to a large extent based on the same pedagogical principles as our approach.

Talking Blocks

In 1980s, a student of Seymour Papert, Aaron Falbel, created an open-ended computerized environment for writing [6] based on the postulate that children have a natural capacity for learning given a proper environment to explore. His system allowed learners to experiment with making words by dragging blocks, which represented phonemes, into a working area and arranging them there. The blocks did not form combinations as in SB – instead, their positions were used to fine-tune the pronunciation, with horizontal intervals controlling the duration of each phoneme and vertical coordinates controlling the pitch. Falbel felt it was important to give children this opportunity to play with the sounds. A speech synthesizer was used to pronounce the resulting arrangement phoneme-by-phoneme, supporting both real and nonsense words. A particularly unusual and interesting aspect of the design was the emphasis on making the spelling systematic, as opposed to adhering to the rules of English orthography. This was influenced by the research on invented spelling [17]. Falbel represented each phoneme with the grapheme that it is most commonly associated with, leading to spellings like "tawking blawks" for "talking blocks." We chose a different approach, as discussed in *Design* section.

Tiggly

Tiggly Story Maker[2] and its derivative, *Sesame Street Alphabet Kitchen*[3], are early literacy apps which allow for a limited degree of experimentation. Each app displays a short string of consonants with a space in-between, that can be filled with a vowel to form a word. *Alphabet Kitchen* presents this process as making word cookies using letters cookie cutters. The child can put any vowel in the space, and the result is pronounced whether or not it constitutes a valid word. In the latter case, in *Tiggly*, a spring throws a letter away afterwards, while in *Alphabet Kitchen*, the Cookie Monster makes a funny but encouraging remark (e.g. "BOD – don't know that word – probably some sort of French pastry"). If the child creates a real word, an object that the word stands for appears (in *Alphabet Kitchen*, this is in a form of a cookie). In *Tiggly*, these objects interact with each other, allowing for some storytelling. However, the possibilities for creation in both of those games are limited, and they can not be considered constructionist.

Word Wizard

Word Wizard[4] is a mobile app that allows children to build words by dragging letter blocks onto a grid. The learner instantly hears the words pronounced back by a speech synthesizer. Incomplete and nonsense words are supported. Similarly

[1]We chose IVONA (`https://www.ivona.com/`) because of pronunciation quality and possibility of phoneme-level control.

[2]`https://www.tiggly.com/tiggly-storymaker`

[3]`https://www.tiggly.com/sesame-street`

[4]`http://lescapadou.com/LEscapadou_-_Fun_and_Educational_applications_for_iPad_and_IPhone/Word_Wizard_-_Talking_Educational_App_for_iPhone_and_iPad.html`

to the Moore's design, Word Wizard has several constrained modes intended to help children spell particular words.

To our knowledge, there have been no published studies examining how children interact with *WordWizard*. It is likely that many findings in our present study apply to that app as well. However, there is a significant difference between *WordWizard* and SB in their interaction paradigms. *Word Wizard* only supports building words letter-by-letter by arranging letters on a fixed grid. In contrast with that, in SB, letter blocks snap to each other, not a grid, which allows for tinkering with existing words and remixing them into new ones. As shown in the *Results* section, the ability for children to remix pre-existing words in SB creates a significant new affordance in children's play and supports their engagement. Additionally, it creates more opportunities for exploration by letting the child not only synthesize, but also "analyze" words by breaking them down into parts. Furthermore, *WordWizard* was designed to be a standalone app, while our goal is to incorporate SB as a part of a larger human-machine system.

Text-Based Open-Ended Games

There are several games that allow children to use text for open-ended creation. Notable examples are *CBC4Kids Story Builder* [1], *Mobile Stories* [5], *StoryTime* [9], *Arthur's Comic Creator*[5] and *Scribblenauts*[6]. However, these games are designed for type or word-dragging input and are not aimed for exploration of relationships between spelling and sound.

LITERACY RESEARCH BACKGROUND

Behavioral [3] and neurological [26, pp. 145-155] evidence indicates that written words in human memory are linked to pronunciations, not directly to meanings. Thus, in order to acquire literacy, it is essential to learn the mapping of spellings to pronunciations. Experienced readers recognize familiar words as a whole [3]. But before achieving that, a reader needs to utilize decoding skills to reconstruct likely pronunciation using common spelling-to-sound regularities. Performance on reading nonsense words is used to assess children's ability to decode [23].

One prerequisite of decoding is the awareness that words consist of smaller sounds – phonemes (see, i.e. [8, 4]). The challenge for a learner is that phonemes are co-articulated in speech and thus hard to separate. Another component is the knowledge of how phonemes map to letter combinations. Yet another prerequisite is the knowledge of blending: how separate sounds combine into a word. In languages with complex orthography, such as English, these skills are still insufficient, because the sounds of letters and letter combinations are very context-dependent. Thus, learners have to acquire pronunciations of larger "sight chunks," such as rimes and morphemes [3][26, p. 128], which tend to be more consistent. They also have to apply analogical reasoning to infer pronunciations of novel words from known ones [3].

[5] http://pbskids.org/arthur/games/comiccreator/

[6] https://www.scribblenauts.com/

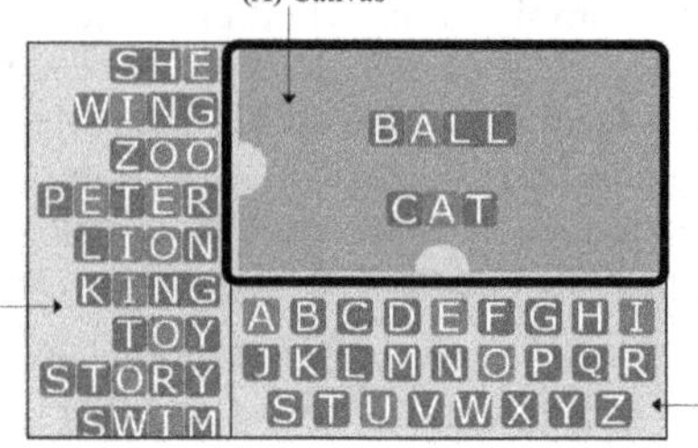

Figure 2. SpeechBlocks' Interface Components

Some educators, including Maria Montessori, taught writing before reading [11]. Montessori argued that writing is cognitively simpler, because it does not require the child to have a mental model of the author. Another important advantage of writing is that it allows children to perceive authorship over what s/he wrote and empowers them through the ability to leave a lasting mark in the world and communicate with other people [22, pp. 77, 85]. Many children are drawn by these factors even before they master writing: They create imitations of books and mail [22, pp. 82, 114]. To facilitate the sense of empowerment, practitioners suggested to maintain a "me museum," where the child's literacy accomplishments are preserved [22, p.54]. Other successful practices include surrounding children with meaningful contexts to exercise their literacy skills: maintaining a classroom "newspaper," labeling personal belongings with their names, writing letters inviting people to the class, etc. [22, pp. 22, 24] Fostering human connections, both with adults and with peers, is another important ingredient to successful learning [22, pp. 24, 85][10, pp.193-223].

One important phenomenon of early writing, related to our support of out-of-vocabulary words, is invented spelling [17]. Children who are not yet familiar with conventional orthography sometimes come up with their own spelling systems, often more logical and systematic than the conventional one. It has been found that invented spelling can efficiently be utilized to help development of phonological and other early literacy skills [4, 20, 13] and can serve as an indicator of children's reading level . In addition, invented spelling facilitates early access to the literacy culture [20] and may help the child to develop a love for it.

While we tried to support development of decoding skills, our goal was also to make technology that would help learners to feel a sense of authorship and connect to other people through their activities. Additionally, we strived to build an app that could be used as a component of larger activities in which children can use writing in personally meaningful ways.

DESIGN

Interface and Interaction

The SB interface consists of a single screen divided into three areas (Fig. 2). The canvas, which normally occupies almost the entire screen, serves for tinkering with letters and words. On the sides of the canvas, there are retractable word and letter drawers. The word drawer contains a selection of words that can be used as prompts and as a material for remixing. It also stores words created by the child – a word can be dragged onto the word drawer to be saved there. The letter drawer holds individual letters. The drawers are made retractable to save the screen space, which is particularly limited on smartphones.

The blocks in the canvas are connected to each other like LEGO bricks. The user interacts with block combinations through tapping and dragging them with their fingers. Placing two fingers on one block combination and moving them in opposite directions will cause the combination to split into two (Fig. 3, a). Putting two combinations end-to-end and "pressing" them against each other will cause them to merge into one (Fig. 3, b). Every time a split or merge happens, the speech synthesizer immediately pronounces the outcome of the manipulation. Block combinations are also pronounced when tapped.

This simple interaction allows the learner to explore a wide range of language regularities in a uniform way. S/he can decompose a word into constituent sounds by simply pulling it apart. By merging strings, s/he can witness how individual sounds blend together. In the process of play, the learner is exposed to the sounds that word chunks of different sizes make. When a learner strips off a part of a word and replaces it with something else, s/he observes an analogical transfer of pronunciation.

SB uses different colors for vowel and consonant blocks. Such differentiation is a quite common practice: it is utilized in Montessori's *Movable Alphabet*[11] and in a variety of educational technology such as *Alpha Writer*[7] and *Touchtronics Letters*[8]. Analysis of invented spelling shows that vowels appear play a special role in the process of writing acquisition [20], which makes it reasonable to emphasize them.

We used uppercase letters for the blocks, but this choice is less straightforward. It has been argued that uppercase letters are more easily distinguishable by a child, since none of them looks like a mirror image of another (in contrast with such lowercase letters as "b", "d", "p" and "q"). For that reason, uppercase letters are taught first in several widespread literacy curricula, such as *Handwriting Without Tears*[9]. On the other hand, lowercase letters constitute the majority of printed text, and familiarity with them may contribute more to children's emergent literacy skills. They are used in literacy materials such as *Movable Alphabet*, as well as every app considered in this paper. In light of this ambiguity, we used a practical consideration to select uppercase letters for our first design: they could be more readily fitted on a square block.

We believe that design of SB is applicable to a variety of touch-screen devices, from tabletops to tablets to smartphones. However, we currently focus on the latter, which are most readily available in home settings. We believe that informal learning in those settings is where the greatest potential for SB lies. A tradeoff which have to be accepted with smartphones is the limited screen size. When at least one of the drawers is

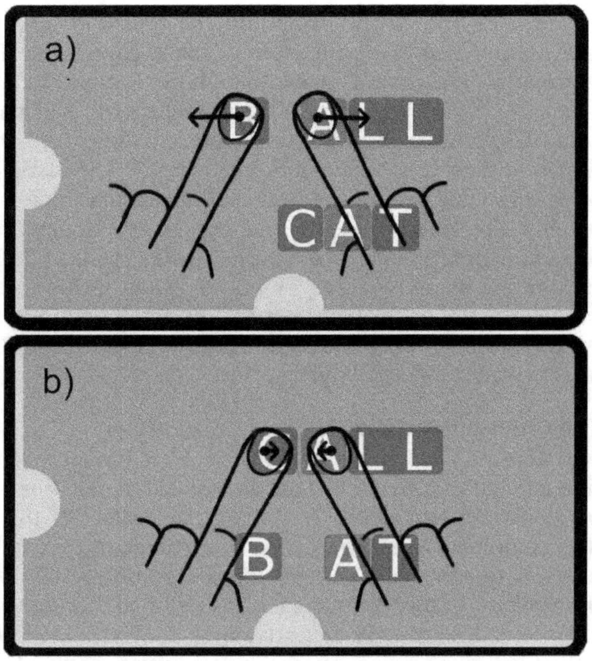

Figure 3. Basic Interactions with SpeechBlocks

extended, it covers a large part of the canvas, leaving relatively little space for play. While we saw children having minor difficulties with that, it doesn't appear to be a major problem.

Design Inspirations

We attempted to create a literacy app which would allows learning through child-driven, persistent exploration, similar to one that occurs in Montessori classrooms. For instance, Lillard [10] describes a child repeating an activity with a Montessori material 42 times in a row, despite deliberate attempts to disturb her – until suddenly she stopped, as if she reached an "aha" moment. She apparently grasped the principle and never returned to the activity again. Montessori and constructionist approaches both view learners as competent pattern discoverers who are able to learn regularities of the world (in our case – the functioning of written language) on their own if the environment is sufficiently rich and transparent. To allow for extended exploration, we made SB combinatorial: children are able to compose letter blocks in any possible order. To create a safe space for experimentation, we excluded the notion of "right" and "wrong" from our design: If a child creates nonsense words, they are pronounced just like regular words. This consideration also led us to avoid game-like rewards. This decision contrasts with the recommendation of Chiong & Shuler [2], who identified such rewards as an important factor of engagement of children with educational mobile apps. However, it is in line with the large body of research indicating that external rewards are detrimental to exploration and creativity (for an overview, see [10, pp. 152-172]). We found SB to be engaging for children even in absence of game-like dynamics.

We were also inspired by work of Resnick and Rosenbaum, who emphasize the importance of "tinkering" [19]. They define it as "*playful, experiential, iterative style of engagement*",

[7] https://montessorium.com/app/alpha-writer

[8] http://juniorlearning.com/touchtronic-letters.html

[9] https://www.hwtears.com/hwt/why-it-works/teaching-order

and provide guidelines for building designs that support it. Our design is in line with some of those guidelines. First, it provides instant feedback to the child. Second, in SB, it is easy to get started without much preparation and knowledge. Children can begin by remixing existing words from the word drawer to make nonsense words. The results are often surprising and possess a humor value that is recognized by children. The emphasis on remixing is one important difference between our app and earlier works, such as Talking Blocks and Word Wizard. Third, our study shows that SB provides many distinct avenues for children's creativity. We believe that diversity could be furthered by integrating SB into larger constructionist activities.

The Choice of the Block

An interesting design question that requires further investigation is what exactly should act as a block. A good building block should retain its core function regardless of the way it is combined with others. The core function of a talking block is to produce a certain sound. From this standpoint, the choice of letters as blocks is not optimal, because what letter encodes strongly depends on its context. Similarly to Falbel [6], our original approach was to use graphemes for blocks. However, we found some difficulties with it. First, graphemes did not appear natural to children: During our initial trials, they were frequently frustrated that they could not pull the multi-letter grapheme blocks apart. Second, the sound of graphemes, particularly single vowels, is still significantly dependent on the context: One grapheme may represent multiple sounds and one sound may be represented by multiple graphemes. Unlike Falbel, we did not want to enforce one-to-one phoneme-grapheme correspondence within the system: While we wanted to allow invented spelling in our app, we did not want to force it. It would create a disconnect between the app and the surrounding literacy culture (children books, environmental print, etc.), which is the foundation of children's emergent literacy. We decided to use a compromise approach: whenever several consecutive letters form a grapheme (e.g. a vowel digraph such as *"ea"*, or a consonant digraph, such as *"th"*), we visually combine them into a single block. However, internally, they are still treated as multiple blocks and can be pulled apart. The intent of this dynamics is to allow incidental learning of common letter combinations.

It is also possible to choose an "inverse" approach, when the sound of a block stays constant, but the displayed combination of letters changes based on the context. For instance, a block representing phoneme ɑ would look like "a" in "star" and like "au" in "laugh". The advantages and disadvantages of each approach are worth examining in a separate study.

PILOT

Overview

To see how children interact with SB, we conducted a pilot study with a group of preschool children over the course of two months. We observed children playing both freely and in context of structured activities. We also experimented with different supplementary materials to use alongside of the app. Since the purpose of the study was not to prove a particular hypothesis, it did not include a control group.

The study was conducted in a daycare center at a university in the Greater Boston area. In this environment, teachers practiced splitting children into groups of 4 and rotating them between different activity stations every 15 minutes. We established a literacy station: a table with phones and supplementary materials on it. One researcher was seated at the table to assist children when they had questions and guide them through activities (if present). Another researcher took notes. The station was active two days a week. Although the children had to come to the table during their rotation, they were free to leave as early as they wanted. The fact that children were coming to the literacy station in groups of four contributed to the social dynamics observed.

We used three ways to gather the data about the sessions. The first way was the observation notes, which were free-form. Second, we recorded a video of all sessions, with the exception of one group, for which we did not obtain the consent to record from all parents. Third, the app itself maintained a very detailed log of all user interactions that allowed us to completely reconstruct and analyze everything that was happening on the screen during each session.

During the pilot, we used an earlier version of SB that lacked some of the features described above: It did not display composite blocks for "sight chunks" and it was not capable of saving words that children constructed. To compensate for the lack of saving function, we provided each child with a journal, where us or children themselves could write words that they wanted to preserve.

Participants

We had 16 participants ages 4 to 5 years old: 12 girls and 4 boys. They had no speech and hearing disorders and were typically developing. They were mostly children of faculty and staff at the university. Thus, they were likely to have rich literacy environments in their homes.

The children's literacy skill varied greatly: some were already able to spell simple words, whereas others did not know all the letters yet. We conducted a pre- and post- assessment of the children's literacy and language abilities using the CTOPP-2 Sound Matching Subtest. On the pre-test, 4 children scored below 50th percentile, with some scoring very low. Interestingly, on post-test all of the children scored above 50th percentile, and 14 out of 15 children (one child's results were discarded due to no pre-test) showed increases in their CTOPP scores. The overall increase was statistically significant (p-value = 0.003). This improvement happened in a short period of time (10 weeks). While the absence of control group does not allow to attribute these results to SB, they warrant a study of effectiveness of our app.

Activities and Complementary Materials

During the first day, the sessions were set up as free play. The children were shown how to use SB, but no specific activity was suggested, and we observed how they use the app on their own initiative. On the second day, we tried to provided themes – e.g. animals, party, food – as a prompt for the children. However, the children mostly ignored the themes and continued with free play. On days 3 and 4, we put a set of

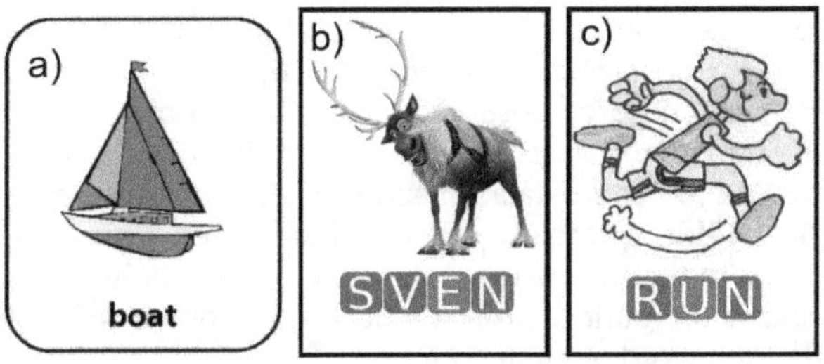

Figure 4. Articulation (a), character (b) and action (c) cards

articulation cards (Fig. 4a [10]) on the table. They are normally used to practice common pronunciation patterns, but we were interested in using them as prompts to give children more ideas on what to spell. On days 5 and 6, we attempted a structured activity similar to Mad Libs[11]. The children were read a story with some gaps and asked to complete the story as they like by creating any words, real or nonsense, with SB. On days 7 and 8, we reverted back to the free play setup.

The idea for another learning material was indirectly suggested by the children themselves. During the very first day of play, one child merged two instances of *ZOO* from the drawer into *ZOOZOO*. When the synthesizer pronounced it back, the child exclaimed excitedly: "This is Zazu from Lion King!" This excitement was picked up by another child, and they continued to make *ZOOZOO* during almost every session. In response to that, we created a new set of cards, mimicking the articulation cards, but using cartoon characters (Fig. 4b). The name of the character was spelled in the font resembling SB, to encourage children to make the word in the app. To promote progress towards sentences and storytelling, we later added cards displaying verbs (Fig. 4c; introduced to children as "action cards"). Finally, we recorded some of the sentences children said and the next day presented them on a new set of cards (Fig. 5). The sentences made in SB were compiled into a small "book" that was given to the group at the end of the study.

Video Annotation and Analysis

To capture the difference of children's behaviors across differently structured play sessions, we annotated video recordings from three days: a free play day, a day with Mad Libs-like activity, and a day with character cards. We used recordings of only 10 children who were present on all three days. To observe activities on the phones within the context of activities and conversations in the classroom, we implemented a tool called Play Observatory (Fig. 6). The tool displays synchronized video recording of the children's play and simulations of their SB screens reconstructed from the log files.

Our first-hand observations in the classroom made us most interested in three dimensions of the play activities: manifestations of self-efficacy and authorship, intentionality of words and actions, and social interactions between children around the app and materials. To capture them, we designed a behavioral protocol that was inspired by two frameworks: Four Indicators of Learning [15] and the ILAUGH Model of Social Thinking [25]. We don't provide the detailed description of the protocol here, since the behaviors that we looked for are described in the *Results* section.

[10]Image sources: http://testyyettrying.blogspot.com/2011/07/final-t-free-speech-therapy.html, http://hero.wikia.com/wiki/File:Sven.png, http://www.clipartbest.com/run-cartoon

[11]http://www.madlibs.com/

Figure 5. Sentence card

Figure 6. Play Observatory.

RESULTS

Types of Interaction

Children used SB in a variety of ways:

Making nonsense words through remixing. This activity was the most popular during the first days of the play. Children would most frequently concatenate several words from the drawer together to achieve results like *ZOOCATBALL*.

Patterning. Participants built letter combinations letter-by-letter in order to see the outcome. In many cases, letters either appeared in alphabetical order, or were repeated multiple times (e.g. *ZZZZZZZZZZ*), or were interchanged (e.g. *AJAJAJA*). Some children copied the sound that the speech synthesizer made after adding each new letter. One child commented: "*It is saying buzzzzzzzz, just like a bee*".

Spelling names. Children would spell both their own names and the names of their friends. Names were often the first real words that they tried to spell. It was common for them to persist on this self-imposed task over the course of many days despite initial unsuccessful efforts. As a result, there was often an evolution in the way the name was spelled, towards correct spelling. For instance, for a child spelling name Addia[12], the evolution appeared like this: *DD*, *ADD*, *ADID* and *DDAA* (day 1); *ADD*, *ADDI* and *ADDIA (day 4)*; *AGIHD* and *ADDE* (day 5); *AWI* (day 12); and finally 4 occurrences of *ADDIA on days 11 to 14*. Children would frequently combine their names with other words, particularly the names of cartoon characters (after the introduction of character cards). An example of this could be *BUZZALEX* (referring to a Pixar's character Buzz Lightyear). When we asked the child what this word meant, he replied: *"It means that I am Buzz!"*.

Creating words and sentences using the cards. Children created less than 10 words inspired by the articulation cards. That stands in sharp contrast with character cards, which were actively used by almost all children (and only one child did not use them at all). Children often picked three to five character cards at the beginning of the session, arranged them in a row and throughout the whole session built the characters' names. The font imitating SB that was used on the cards turned out to be very helpful for children, because they were able to find necessary letters in the app by visually matching them with those on the card. They were unable to do the same with articulation cards, which used lowercase and a different font. In one case, there was a moment of discovery when a child copied a word from a card and realized what the word says only after the synthesizer pronounced it; it lead to her surprise and excitement. Action cards were also actively used after their introduction. However, children rarely (1 occurrence) made a complete sentence one the screen. Instead, they would made words one-by-one and delete them, or make one word and say the sentence verbally. After the introduction of the sentence cards, about a third of the children engaged in copying sentences from them.

Using SB as a reference to write words in journals. Children preferred to write down words on their own. In many cases, they were not fully able to write and would carefully redraw letter shapes, using the image on the screen as a reference. Several children turned this into a separate activity: Instead of spelling the words in the app, they copied it from the word drawer. Notably, some were unable to read the words yet, so they utilized the pronunciations generated by the speech synthesizer to find an interesting word to copy. There were 3 children who dedicated the entire duration of at least one session to this process. It is possible that this unusual activity resulted from a greater sense of agency and relatedness to writing inspired by the constructionist setup. This question needs further investigation.

Making everyday life words: Participants created words that were inspired by their surroundings, day-to-day activities, events happened in their lives, etc. Example words include: *LOV* (love), *MOM*, *POPCORN*, *BNGA* (bang), and *SINK* (an item that could be observed in the classroom). Such words were infrequent: we found only around 10 occurrences of such words in the entire data. In addition, there were several cases when children verbally expressed the desire to make a word related to their experience, but did not. We believe this was because the children did not have the proper scaffolding to make the word on their own.

[12]Children names were changed to protect their identity. The sequence of name spellings is taken from data, but altered by substitution of the corresponding letters.

Character of Interaction

We found that children utilize the merge functionality 8 times more frequently than the split one. Furthermore, most of the splits were generated in process of self-correction, when children were rebuilding words that did not sound as expected. Only 4 children split words in order to either explore what the parts sounded like or in order to create building material for other words, and each child did that only a few times.

Although we do not know the exact reason why splits were less used, we can see several possible causes. First, the limitations of the SB version used in the pilot may have made splitting less convenient than merging: A child's finger could accidentally touch a neighboring block, leading to split happening in a wrong place. Second, children seemed to be interested in building long words, as evident from their exclamations, such as: *"I am making such a long words!"* and *"I made the longest word ever!"*. Since splits lead to shorter words, they might have been less interesting for children. Third, children may have perceived splits as undoing their work or existing meaningful words, rather than creating something new.

As mentioned above, we think that splits provide important learning opportunities. It is a question for further investigation whether splitting behavior can be encouraged by proper scaffolding.

Engagement

Children used SB very actively during initial days. This can almost completely be attributed to the fun of making nonsense words by remixing words on the drawer, as evidenced by frequent laughter and comments such as:

- (laughing) *"ZOOBALLBALL! What's that like?"* (later) *"ZOOBALLBALL – that's what I say!"*

- (hearing a word made by peer's phone) *"CUPEAR!"* (laughing) *"Can I see? Can I see how you spelled CUPEAR?"*

The positive influence of that slight amounts of absurdity have on children's engagement with educational apps is similar to observations of other authors [2]. As the entertainment value of making nonsense words started to exhaust itself, the engagement started to drop.

Children's engagement dropped even further when we introduced the highly structured Mad Libs-like story activity. While some children enjoyed the activity, most felt frustrated. A few children explicitly said that they were bored. This was caused by the fact that children wanted to create specific words to complete the story (e.g. one child wanted to create *QUACK* for a sound that the dog in the story makes) but did not yet have the skills to do this on their own, and assistance that we could provide was limited. This situation occurred despite our explicit statement that we welcomed nonsense words that could complete the story and make it silly. The very nature of activity caused it to be too inflexible for children to utilize their existing skills.

Engagement visibly recovered when character, action and sentence cards were introduced. Children started to set challenging spelling goals for themselves more frequently.

There are two additional bits of qualitative evidence showing generally-good level of engagement with the app. First, children were often (57 cases in the 3 annotated days) repeating the words that the speech synthesizer was producing. Second, according to the teachers, several children continued to talk about SB and the words that they made after the sessions. Third, the last two sessions were spontaneous. We only planned to wrap up and present children the book that they made, but they requested that we give them the phones and continued to joyfully make words.

Self-Efficacy and Authorship

The children took pride in making words in SB, as evidenced by their exclamations:

- "*I spelled LALLA! That's what my name says.*"
- "*I can spell ZIVVY with mine* [phone]*!*"
- "*Look! I spelled BUZZ!*"
- "*I made so many words!*"

We counted 39 such expressions within the 3 annotated days. We attribute such exclamations to a sense of accomplishment fostered by either producing something interesting and fun (even by accident) or setting up a goal for oneself and successfully carrying it over. Both cases were enabled by the free-form nature of the app, and we surmise that is is harder to achieve the same in the context of a pre-described, puzzle-like activity where children have less agency.

Interestingly, the children who scored below 50th percentile on CTOPP-2 pre-test produced much more verbal signs of self-efficacy: 6.25 occurrences per child within the 3 days, as opposed to 2.33 occurrences per child for children who were above 50th percentile (p-value 0.013, using t-test). This evidence suggests that SB may be more compelling for children who experience reading difficulties, allowing them to meaningfully engage and feel a sense of accomplishment. This is a very desirable characteristic, since children who struggle with reading are often most in need of support and motivation.

Another indicator that children felt a sense of ownership of their work is manifested in children's desire to take their journals and keep them. One child even asked: "*Can we keep them forever? Until the end of our lives?* "

Goal-Setting and Planning

Setting goals for oneself freely and executing plans to achieve them is another manifestation of learner agency. Children's self-directed speech indicated that they did that. For example: "I'm going to make Simba. I need S, I, M... I'm writing about Lion King today." We found 59 phrases like this. They were almost always unprompted: Children were naturally talking about their plans and goals.

Social Interaction

Even though SB did not have any explicit features for social play, children frequently engaged in a variety of social interactions related to their activity with the app. In the 3 annotated days, we counted about 600 micro-occurences of all the behaviors below:

Displaying their work. As mentioned above, children took pride in their creations and displayed them both to adults and to their peers.

Observation. Children's curiosity was often piqued by the sounds produced by their peers' phones, and they looked at their screens. In one case a child was not actively interacting with the phone in the course of several sessions, but instead was watching other children's activities very attentively. Eventually she became an active player again. It seems that the observation helped her to gain confidence and ideas on what to do.

Idea borrowing. Children imitated creation of others that they liked. For instance, when one child spelled *LOV*, a child from another group heard the sound and reproduced the word during her turn.

Shared play. Participants would sometimes play in close coordination with one another. In one instance, a child made a nonsense word *WCAT* and showed it to a peer. The peer, who had *VWCAT* spelled, remarked: "*You did the same thing as me! You have to do exactly the same thing*". She then bent over her friend's screen to find letter *V* together with her. When the letter was found and added, she said: "*Another V! Let's add another V!*", and both of them did that. They continued to make words together for some time afterwards.

Assisting each other. Children asked each other questions such as: "*Oh! Do you know where T is?*" (on the letter drawer) or "*Can you help me to spell your name on my phone?*"

Conversation. Participants connected the words pronounced by SB to their life experiences, e.g. saying "*I have a dog*" after hearing someone's phone pronouncing *DOG*. In many cases other children responded, resulting in several turns of conversation.

Storytelling. Children produced verbal descriptions of imaginary situations involving words they made in the app:

- (Repeating after the speech synthesizer) "*BALLCATTOYZ...*" (noticing that "toys" were accidentally made) "*Wait, I spelled toys?!*" (speaking to another child) "*Oh, you know what? You know why I spelled it? Because it is cat playing with ball toys – that's why I spelled it.*"
- (responding to a researcher's question about Olaf) "*Olaf likes warm hugs.*"

We found 37 instances of this behavior over the 3 annotated days of data. About two thirds of those instances were child-initiated, whereas in other occasions children responded with a story to a question asked by a researcher. Most of these cases (29) occurred on the day when children used character cards – significantly more (p-value = 0.01, using paired sample t-test) than in the other two settings. This shows how prompts within a constructionist literacy activity could reinforce children's meaningful engagement around storytelling.

Early Literacy Phenomena Visible in the Data

We found that the log data from the phones captured two phenomena that often occurred during the early stages of literacy acquisition: omission of silent *E* at the end (e.g. spelling *LOV* instead of *LOVE*) and reversal of text direction (e.g. spelling *ASLE* instead of *ELSA*). For the latter children, the text direction phenomena also showed up in their journals: While writing words, they placed letters completely randomly (not even in one line). Nevertheless, that they considered their work proper words, as evidenced by phrases like "I wrote all of this!". Apparently, at their stage of literacy development, they were unaware of the role of letters' spatial arrangement. In one of the cases of text reversal, the child noticed the unexpected pronunciation generated by the speech synthesizer, and learned about the directionality of text from a researcher's explanation.

DISCUSSION AND FUTURE WORK

Current study was conducted with children from families with relatively high socioeconomic status (SES). However, the promise of mobile learning technology partially lies in its capacity to reach underserved households. From that standpoint, it is of interest to conduct evaluation of SB with children from more diverse socioeconomic backgrounds. Outside of the scope of the study, we had opportunities to present SB to such children and found that they exhibit mostly similar engagement and patterns of interaction.

Instant feedback feature prompted a variety of educationally useful behaviors. Most prominently, it contributed to literacy-related social interactions that provide opportunities for peer learning. The emphasis on remixing, which was distinctive for SB, helped children to produce interesting results early on, contributing to engagement and self-efficacy.

We found that scaffolding materials were important for learners to maintain meaningful engagement with the app. Their role was twofold. First, they served as prompts, giving children ideas of what to make. The efficiency of character cards, as opposed to articulation cards, highlights how important it is for such a material to tap into children's interests, rather than focus solely on its educational function. Second, the materials acted as support, giving children a reference on how to spell certain words. Children frequently wanted to build very specific words, and their (in)ability to do that influenced the level of their engagement with the app. While cards (whether physical or built into the app) could mitigate this problem, they have a major limitation, as they are limited to a closed vocabulary. We are researching how to design a spelling support that matches the open-endedness of the app itself. First, we are exploring how to incorporate automatic procedures within the app to help scaffold the spelling of new words that children are interested in. Second, we are looking at the ways this support could be provided by people. It appears that researchers acting as guides played a significant role in facilitating children's play in the course of our study. They introduced children to materials, responded to their comments, provided guiding questions and occasionally suggested how to spell specific words. We are currently conducting a study with SB in family settings to determine how well this role could be fulfilled by parents, informed by a learning expert. In the new study, SB acts as a part of a larger human-machine system supporting acquisition of literacy.

It has been shown that analysis of invented spelling offers good predictions of reading development [20]. The log data from SB may have similar affordances. Its capacity to capture early literacy phenomena could become vital for the work of learning experts in the above-mentioned system. Using the data, the experts might be able get a sense of child's interests and specific challenges s/he encounters.

Authorship and learners' ownership of their work were prominent themes manifested during the pilot. The digital medium of a mobile app provides multiple opportunities to further support it. To that end, after the completion of the pilot we implemented the ability for children to save words on the word drawer. With this feature, richer interactions are possible. For example, a child could take a picture associated with the word, record a snippet of his/her voice telling about it, digitally share the word with peers etc. We are currently designing some of these features in our next iterations of SB.

Our hope is not only to support the technical skills of reading and writing, but also to help children develop more positive attitudes towards literacy. For that reason, a good topic for further research is to explore whether playing with SB changes the way children interact with traditional print materials.

CONCLUSION

Constructionist mobile apps for early literacy learning are underrepresented both on the market and in research. To explore the possibilities that such apps can provide, we created the SB app and piloted it with preschool children. We found that children generally engaged with the app. Interaction with the app facilitated learners' sense of agency and ownership of their work which we hope to further reinforce through digital features. The app was a good facilitator of peer learning, evoking a variety of social interactions around literacy activities. The data collected by the mobile devices showed potential to be utilized by learning experts. The results of the pilot support our belief that apps similar to SB have large potential for facilitating literacy learning, both on their own and in combination with other apps. We see space for SB both within classrooms and in home environments. We will continue to further explore and develop this technology.

ACKNOWLEDGEMENTS

We would like to express our gratitude to Mina Soltangheis for her data analysis tools and help in gathering statistics; Brianne Fitzpatrick for the help in conducting pre-assessments; Soroush Vosoughi, Juliana Nazaré and Sayamindu Dasgupta for feedback on the drafts; and staff of the daycare center for their enthusiasm and support.

REFERENCES

1. Alissa Antle. 2003. Case study: the design of CBC4Kids' StoryBuilder. In *Proceedings of the 2003 conference on Interaction design and children*. ACM, 59–68.
2. Cynthia Chiong and Carly Shuler. 2010. Learning: Is there an app for that. In *Investigations of young children's usage and learning with mobile devices and apps. New York: The Joan Ganz Cooney Center at Sesame Workshop*.
3. Linnea C Ehri. 2005. Learning to read words: Theory, findings, and issues. *Scientific Studies of reading* 9, 2 (2005), 167–188.
4. Linnea C Ehri and Lee S Wilce. 1987. Does learning to spell help beginners learn to read words? *Reading Research Quarterly* (1987), 47–65.
5. Jerry Alan Fails, Allison Druin, and Mona Leigh Guha. 2010. Mobile collaboration: collaboratively reading and creating children's stories on mobile devices. In *Proceedings of the 9th International Conference on Interaction Design and Children*. ACM, 20–29.
6. Aaron Falbel. 1985. A Second Look at Writing to Read: A Teaching System for Schools Becomes A Medium for Learning in the Home. (1985). Unpublished manuscript. MIT Media Lab.
7. Kathy Hirsh-Pasek, Jennifer M Zosh, Roberta Michnick Golinkoff, James H Gray, Michael B Robb, and Jordy Kaufman. 2015. Putting education in "educational" apps: lessons from the science of learning. *Psychological Science in the Public Interest* 16, 1 (2015), 3–34.
8. Connie Juel, Priscilla L Griffith, and Philip B Gough. 1986. Acquisition of literacy: A longitudinal study of children in first and second grade. *Journal of educational psychology* 78, 4 (1986), 243.
9. Alex Kuhn, Chris Quintana, and Elliot Soloway. 2009. StoryTime: a new way for children to write. In *Proceedings of the 8th International Conference on Interaction Design and Children*. ACM, 218–221.
10. Angeline Stoll Lillard. 2016. *Montessori: The science behind the genius*. Oxford University Press.
11. Paula Polk Lillard. 1972. *Montessori: A modern approach*. Random House LLC.
12. Omar Khayyam Moore. 1966. Autotelic responsive environments and exceptional children. In *Experience Structure & Adaptability*. Springer, 169–216.
13. Gene Ouellette, Monique Senechal, and Allyson Haley. 2013. Guiding children's invented spellings: A gateway into literacy learning. *The Journal of Experimental Education* 81, 2 (2013), 261–279.
14. Seymour Papert. 1980. *Mindstorms: Children, computers, and powerful ideas*. Basic Books, Inc.
15. Mike Petrich, Karen Wilkinson, and Bronwyn Bevan. 2013. It looks like fun, but are they learning. *Design, make, play: Growing the next generation of STEM innovators* (2013), 50–70.
16. Jacob Poushter. 2016. Smartphone ownership and Internet usage continues to climb in emerging economies. *Pew Research Center* (2016).
17. Charles Read. 1971. Pre-school children's knowledge of English phonology. *Harvard educational review* 41, 1 (1971), 1–34.
18. Mitchel Resnick. 2006. Computer as paint brush: Technology, play, and the creative society. *Play= learning: How play motivates and enhances children's cognitive and social-emotional growth* (2006), 192–208.
19. Mitchel Resnick and Eric Rosenbaum. 2013. Designing for tinkerability. *Design, make, play: Growing the next generation of STEM innovators* (2013), 163–181.
20. Donald J Richgels. 2001. Invented spelling, phonemic awareness, and reading and writing instruction. *Handbook of early literacy research* 1 (2001), 142–155.
21. Carly Shuler. 2009. Pockets of potential: Using mobile technologies to promote children's learning. (2009).
22. Dorothy S Strickland and Lesley Mandel Morrow. 1989. *Emerging literacy: Young children learn to read and write*. ERIC.
23. Joseph K Torgesen, Richard K Wagner, and Carol A Rashotte. 1999. *TOWRE: Test of word reading efficiency*. Psychological Corporation.
24. Sarah Vaala, Anna Ly, and Michael H Levine. 2015. Getting a read on the app stores. *New York: Joan Ganz Cooney Centre* (2015).
25. Michelle Garcia Winner and Pamela J Crooke. 2009. Social Thinking: A training paradigm for professionals and treatment approach for individuals with social learning/social pragmatic challenges. *SIG 1 Perspectives on Language Learning and Education* 16, 2 (2009), 62–69.
26. Maryanne Wolf and Catherine J Stoodley. 2008. *Proust and the squid: The story and science of the reading brain*. Icon Cambridge.

The Sound Labyrinth: Computers, Constructionism and Language Learning

Sónia Matos
Madeira Interactive
Technologies Institute
Funchal, Portugal
sonia.matos@m-iti.org

ABSTRACT
This contribution presents The Sound Labyrinth, which is an application software that was designed to support the learning and safeguard of Silbo Gomero, a whistled from of language. Once used by the islanders of La Gomera, this unique form of communication has been revived, shifting from the fields where it was once used by agricultural laborers and into the space of the classroom. Here, it has integrated the school curriculum, providing children with a unique opportunity to engage with local intangible heritage. As a response to this transformation, the island's educational community has identified a new challenge: the need to develop didactic materials that resonate with the generational interests of local children. Drawing on the work Papert, Bamberger, amongst others, this contribution presents and discusses the application software that was designed in response to this challenge. Pushing the boundaries of constructionism, this contribution equally demonstrates how software might contribute to the domain of linguistic heritage.

Author Keywords
whistled language; endangered languages; intangible cultural heritage; virtual acoustics; interface design; learning environments

ACM Classification Keywords
K.3 [Computers and Education]: General.

INTRODUCTION
The Silbo Gomero is a whistled language that was once used by the islanders of La Gomera (Canarian Archipelago, Spain). After fifty years of almost total extinction, this form of communication was revived, shifting from the fields where it was once used by agricultural labourers and into the space of the classroom. Against this backdrop, this contribution will present The Sound Labyrinth, an application software that was developed in response to Silbo Gomero's integration within the school curriculum. Supported with the evidence that has resulted from a study of whistled language and its historical and cultural context, the ultimate-goal of this contribution is to consider whether interactive technologies could play an important role in the learning and safeguard of endangered forms of language.

Using an ethnographic approach to research [1] that included direct observation, interviews, informal conversations and participation in class, the fieldwork that was carried out on the Island of La Gomera would soon demonstrate that Silbo Gomero had integrated the curriculum of the island's schools, providing children with a weekly class that was led by one of two teachers that still taught whistled language. Documented elsewhere [2] [3], the two teachers were not formally trained as such and rather learned *Silbo*[1] at a young age and while working in the fields of the island with family members.

Visiting the island on a yearly basis - for two to three weeks at a time - and over the duration of a two-year period, it was soon apparent from the sessions of direct observation and participation in class and through a series of informal conversations with both teachers and with other members of the island's educational community, that a transformation was taking place. The *Silbo* was shifting from the field and into the space of the classroom and this change would carry profound shifts. Firstly, an integration within the school curriculum and within a classroom environment would mean that whistled language was now taught in an enclosed space, very different to the steep terrain where Silbo Gomero was once used. Secondly, whistled language was now taught to children who were also formally learning other languages, such as Spanish and English. It is important to note that prior to the institutionalization of *Silbo* and its recognition as protected intangible heritage by UNESCO [4], whistled language was mostly used by agricultural labourers who rarely had the opportunity to attend school and to learn how to read and write. Finally, the Gomeran educational community recognised that

IDC '17, June 27-30, 2017, Stanford, CA, USA

ACM ISBN 978-1-4503-4921-5/17/06...$15.00
http://dx.doi.org/10.1145/3078072.3079726

1 Silbo Gomero is often locally known as *Silbo,* meaning 'whistle' in Spanish.

children were now exposed to a very different set of media. This would mean that future ways of teaching *Silbo* would have to respond to the children's culture and environment, one that was becoming equally influenced by the presence of desktops, laptops and mobile computers at school and at home.

As a response to this transformation, and the need to develop learning materials, the project that is here reported would proceeded by taking into account the phonological [5][6][7], bioacoustic [8] and cognitive [9] studies of whistled languages and of Silbo Gomero more specifically. However, it was the ethos of constructionism as well as the situated research developed while living on the island of La Gomera that would instigate a new approach to the design of learning materials for Silbo Gomero. In fact, it was the view that learning should not be understood as a process of transmission but rather as a constructive process [10] that would guide subsequent readings as well as their application in the design of the application software that will be presented and discussed in the following sections.

SILBO GOMERO: AN INTERDISCIPLINARY APPROACH

Whistled languages have been found in almost all continents [8]. However, what makes Silbo Gomero unique is its survival. Recognised by UNESCO as world intangible heritage [4], today, Silbo Gomero integrates the curriculum of all public schools of the Island of La Gomera. The most detailed accounts of *Silbo* appear in the work of linguists Ramon Trujillo [5] [6] and Annie Rialland [7], in the work of psycholinguist Manuel Carreiras and colleagues [9] and in the work of bio-acoustician Julien Meyer [8]. In all four accounts, *Silbo* is portrayed as an independent phonological system that is used to communicate (through a set of whistles) the Castilian Spanish that is spoken on the island. Used by local islanders to communicate across the steep and mountainous terrain of La Gomera, *Silbo* presents two whistled vowels and four consonants that vary in duration, pitch and frequency [5][6][7][8]. Resembling the "generative primitives" of musical competence that are described by Jeanne Bamberger [11], whistled vowels and consonants are the basic units upon which more complex words and sentences can be built from.

What is important to retain from a very brief presentation of whistled language, is that despite the proximity to the local spoken language (in this case, Spanish), *Silbo* should not be understood as a surrogate of speech [6][7]. A point of debate amongst some scholars [6][7], presenting the *Silbo* as an independent phonological system, with its own characteristics, has led to an understanding that those who use *Silbo* possess unique cognitive traits [8][9]. In fact, in the bioacoustics studies of Meyer [8], it was found that whistled languages are only the 'tip of the iceberg' of more complex cognitive phenomenon. For this same reason, the process of learning whistled language is often compared to the process of learning a musical instrument [8].

The phonological, psycholinguist and bioacoustics studies of whistled language can be further complemented with the interdisciplinary study of sound that was produced by Augoyard and Torgue [12] and that offers an understanding of how diverse physical environments shape our relationship to sound. Attuned to the fieldwork that was conducted on the island of La Gomera, the authors suggest that the surrounding environment can be understood as an instrument – or '*instrumentarium*' – "a reservoir of sound possibilities, (…) [that is used] to give substance and shape to human relations and the everyday management of (…) space" [12]. This was easy to observe when documenting whistlers outside, working in the fields. In fact, the abrupt terrain of the island would often offer a dramatic set of echoes and reverberations that were exploited by whistlers to aid their projection of a whistled utterance. Conversely, intense reverberations and echoes could also appear as obstacles to those who were placed in the receiving end of a whistled message. As observed during fieldwork, these different 'interferences' would play an important role in the cognitive development of whistlers, subtlety transforming their auditory skills - a key aspect that was also documented by Meyer [8].

THE SOUND LABYRINTH

The Design Concept

During the fieldwork that was conducted as part of this project, it became apparent that the two local teachers that were responsible for a weekly class of *Silbo* had devised their own unique teaching methods. One teacher, would use a self-devised alphabet known as the *Silfateo.* This alphabet was used when encouraging children to playfully combine whistled vowels and consonants and when constructing the syllables of whistled words. Furthermore, the other teacher would favour a method of learning-by-hearing, one that resembles the process of learning a musical instrument through improvisation. In both instances, there was a clear preference for experimentation over rote learning or the transmission of facts.

Figure 1: Child whistling in class.

Briefly described in the previous section, the bioacoustic and cognitive studies that tackle whistled languages greatly influenced the development of a design concept for the project. Both Meyer and Carreiras and colleagues suggest that those who learn whistled languages develop unique cognitive traits [9], which are comparable to the cognitive traits of musicians [8]. When designing The Sound Labyrinth this point offered a new ground for experimentation. Combined with the methods that were devised by the two teachers, and with some of the lessons that have been conveyed by constructionism [13], it soon became clear that the aim was to design an interactive platform that would invite children to experiment with the sonic qualities of whistled language.

Documented in two additional publications that have resulted from this project [2][3], The Sound Labyrinth is an application software that was designed as a language support system, an 'object-to-think-with' [14]. To be used within the context of Gomeran schools and to support local children when learning Silbo Gomero, it is important to note that when the application software was developed most Gomeran schools had a computer lab with desktops and where children could access a range of software, each one directed toward a specific topic or discipline. However, to date, nothing was developed to suit the children's exploration of whistled language. Paired with the didactic approaches that had been devised in class by the two local teachers, the intention was to design a platform that would suit the existing ICT infrastructure available on the island as well as the approach to language learning that the two teachers were using for the past twenty years. On this view, the role of The Sound Labyrinth was to stretch their influence even further as opposed to replacing their role as teachers. Also, and in line with Papert's critique of applications that simply mimic real world phenomena [15], the The Sound Labyrinth was not designed to mimic the outdoor environment where *Silbo* was once used. The goal was to rather offer an '*instrumentarium*' [12] that would aid local children in their learning of *Silbo*.

Constructionism became a decisive reference when rethinking the role of didactic materials for whistled language. After documenting the community's concern for developing learning materials that would accompany the children's own generational interests, as well the teachers unique teaching techniques, it was soon clear that Papert's 'computer as a medium of expression' [15] would be the right paradigm when devising a platform that would allow children to explore Silbo Gomero in a constructive and exploratory way. Therefore, The Sound Labyrinth was created in the attempt of offering local children an opportunity to construct their own stories while using whistled language.

The Software Environment

Figures 2 and 3 demonstrate the platform through a documentation of its visual interface. Designed with only a set of reduced visual cues, the interface of The Sound Labyrinth was designed to invite children to explore sound as the primary means of communication and interaction. Therefore, one key aspect is the possibility of spatially organising and distributing a range of sound sources. To do this, children can use the application software to add whistled words, sentences and dialogues that are recorded there and then and while inserting a yellow sound source. Children can also add sound sources that have been previously saved as a sound file on the computational medium – here represented by the orange and blue circles.

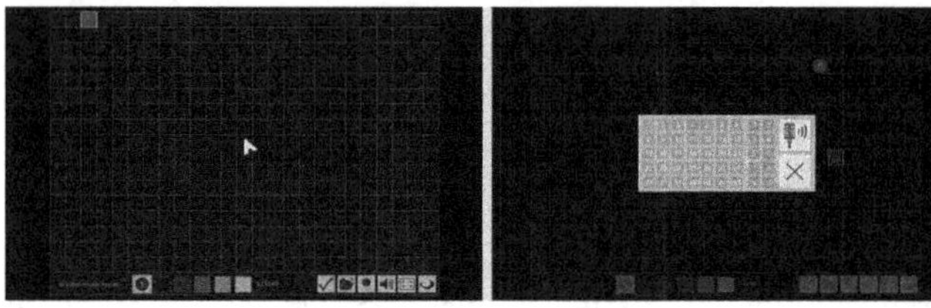

Figure 2: Snapshot #1 & 2 of The Sound Labyrinth.

Looking at the right-hand side of the menu bar, the reader will notice an icon in the form of an 'eye'. By clicking on this icon, the sound sources will disappear and the child will be presented with a dark screen, a feature that was added to provide a mode of interaction that is purely aural and that should be used once a story has been created. Here, it is important to mention that a binaural algorithm was used to create a binaural sound field that emulates the way in which humans spatially hear the surrounding world [16]. As mentioned above, the interface itself will afford children the possibility to distribute sounds spatially. When both combined, the experience provides children an immersive environment where they can create stories as well as hear stories that were created by their classmates and teachers.

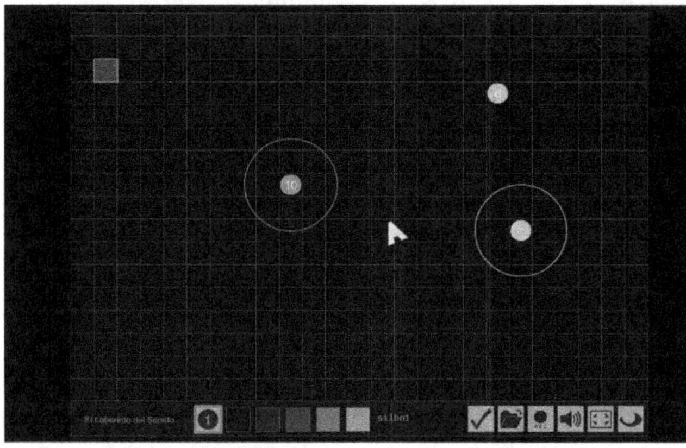

Figure 3: Snapshot #3 of The Sound Labyrinth.

Figure 3 demonstrates some of the sound sources with a surrounding circle while others (such as the oranges circles) are devoid of this feature. This will mean that some sound sources (such as the orange one) can be heard throughout the environment, even though their intensity will vary depending on the cursor's proximity to the sound source. On the other hand, the sound sources that are presented with a surrounding circle can only be heard once the cursor is within the boundaries of the surrounding circle. It is important to note that this circle can be removed. Finally, a set of grey squares can be 'painted' directly onto the interface, this will add more-or-less reverberation to the surrounding sound source and depending on the shade of grey that is chosen by the user.

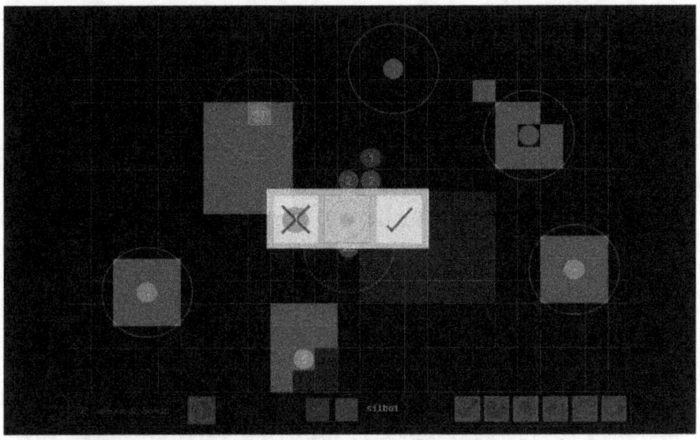

Figure 4: Snapshot #4 of The Sound Labyrinth.

TESTING THE APPLICATION SOFTWARE

The setting

The Sound Labyrinth was first tested at CEIP El Retamal, a school situated in the municipality of Valle Gran Rey on the western part of the island of La Gomera. The school follows Spanish educational guidelines this considering that the Island of Gomera integrates the Canarian archipelago, an autonomous region of Spain. According to the information that was provided by the local Educational Bureau, in line with most EU Member States, Spain has also shown an interest in the modernization of the school system, particularly through the implementation of computers in the classroom. In the Canary Islands, particularly on the island of La Gomera, the development of an educational digital culture was implemented through *Proyecto Medusa* (Medusa Project) [17]. This project brought to CEIP El Retamal twelve desktop computers that were set in one of the schoolrooms and where the children would engage with information and communication technologies (ICT's), once a week and for the period of one hour.

According to one of the teachers that was interviewed, not all teachers had incorporated *Proyecto Medusa* within their own teaching. In fact, some were suspicious of forcing computers into the classroom, this considering that "what might work for a specific subject area might not necessarily work for all". In fact, this seemed to be a common approach amongst teachers at CEIP. "It all depends on how one incorporates these tools, the same could be said for a pen and pencil", was how one teacher addressed the topic during an interview. This episode resonates with Papert's concerns that highlighted how computers were at times blindly introduced to educational settings without however taking into account a school's underlying culture [15]. Considering this, one could conclude that, despite having a basic computerized infrastructure, CEIP El Retamal was not incorporating computer-based learning to foster everyday learning activities. This was partially influenced by the teachers' own idiosyncrasies and, overall, by their limited technical understanding of computers, as well as the instructional nature of the curriculum that was in place.

However, and contrary to the observations that are documented above, the children who participated in the evaluation of the application software showed great fluency with computers, a fact that might have been aided by *Proyecto Medusa*. To strengthen this idea, the teachers that were interviewed confirmed that most children had computers at home and would therefore learn how to use the computer almost intuitively, often being in a better position to teach adults how to use one. This generational gap was also documented in the constructionist literature and in relation to the introduction of the LOGO programming environment [10] . However, some of the children that participated in this initial user-testing session only had the possibility of accessing a computer at school and in the computer-room that was provided by *Proyecto Medusa*.

Testing the Application Software: Ages Eight and Nine

Two groups of children with ages eight and nine were chosen to test the application software. This choice was influenced by two factors: (1) fluency with Silbo Gomero (children start learning whistled language at age six and upon entering elementary school) and (2) the children's ability to understand the nature of the proposed activity - the creation of stories using whistled language as well as other sources of sound. When testing The Sound Labyrinth activities were divided amongst six sessions of one hour each and in the afternoons after class and when children would normally have time to use one of the rooms that was reserved for the project. Hence, it is important to note that we did not use the computer-room that was provided by *Proyeto Medusa,* this considering that the beta version of the application software was designed for a Macintosh system that was not available in the school.

Group 1 was composed by four children while group 2 was composed by five children. The initial session was followed by a thorough presentation of the designed application. Also, in this first session, and for the first thirty minutes, I adopted the role of transmitter however quickly becoming a facilitator when the children showed interest in trying out the application software and clarifying their own doubts. In both groups the children demonstrated a special interest during the facilitating stage where they could closely engage with the application software. The transmission phase was purely informational. For this same reason, the children did not engage with such eloquence. In fact, confirming the value of a constructionist approach where children are in charge of their own learning process [10]. For this same reason, in subsequent sessions it become clear that it would be better to initiate the session by inviting children to explore the application software in groups and without my direct intervention.

The second session was dedicated to the development of a story while exploring previously discussed concepts such as the auditory, temporal and spatial qualities of Silbo Gomero. An exploration of the non-linear 'editing' space of the application software and how it could be used to influence the story was also discussed. The first group, was very quick in exploiting to its maximum potential the flexibility of a non-linear approach. This group's story was based on the idea of a labyrinth where the listener approaches distinct doors that lead to distinct parts of the story. For each part of the story, the group recorded a set of sentences that the children performed in whistled language as well as a set of sounds that were provided upon request. The second group, decided to create a set of shorter stories that were unrelated. For this same reason, they did not exploit the non-linear nature of the application software to its fullest potential, at least when compared to the first group.

Figure 5: Children designing an interactive story.

It would be important to highlight that the second session provided an opportunity for children to construct a story as a group while splitting the tasks amongst each member. Some, who were more proficient in whistled language, gave suggestions for possible utterances while others, more prone to narrative exploration and construction, provided structural cues. To complement this session, each group was given a squared sheet of paper, resembling the interface that was designed for the application software. The children used this sheet to take note of each sound source and to carefully decide where each one would be placed within their project. This proved to be useful, this considering that we only had one computer per group. Also, with this sheet of paper the children could more easily circulate ideas amongst each other. However, and perhaps more importantly, the additional sheet acquired a life of its own this considering that the children would use it to "think with" [14][11]. Paraphrasing the words of Bamberger, this sheet became a 'symbolic notation' [11] that was used to make sense of the spatial organization of their story.

The third session was devoted to recording whistled utterances directly and while using the application software. Groups were divided between those who wanted to perform whistled utterances and those who showed more interest in working directly with the computer. In the third session, one group appeared to be more dynamic, manipulating the computer as well as participating in the performance of whistled utterances. In the other group, some challenges were faced, this considering that one of the group members initially disliked working with the computer. What was interesting to observe was that after a couple of sessions this child gained a real interest in the application software and slowly felt more at ease with the computer as a tool.

The third session was aimed at developing collaboration and teamwork. Students had to record whistled messages and periods of silence had to be agreed and respected. Also, when the group was not happy with a specific whistled utterance they would have to motivate each other to repeat the process. The dialogue that is presented below provides an example:

Child 1: "*Parad*. Did you understand?"

Child 2: "No! It does not sound like *parad*!"

Child 3: "*Parad* is more like this....[child 3 whistles]."

Child 2: "So let's change it." [Child 3 gives a final try but finally child 1 repeats the whistle successfully].

Child 2: O.k. "Now we got it!"

Figure 6: Children recording their story.

Harking back to the work of Bamberger, the children's discussion of the word *parad* (to stop, in Spanish) demonstrates that they were actively making sense of the sounds that were being heard and performed in real-time. This 'active process of sense-making', as Bamberger would suggest, draws on a negotiation of the 'similarities and differences' of what can only be heard individually [11].

During the final two sessions, each group was asked to complete the narrative while inserting new sounds as well as exploring the reverberation that could be 'painted' directly onto a sound source. The additional sounds were provided directly to the children and were recorded on the island and based on suggestions that were made by the children. It is important to consider that the final activities were done with greater ease this considering that the children were now comfortable with the application software. Also, it is important to note that during the initial two sessions, the children avoided using the stronger reverb this considering that the higher the reverb, the greater the distortion of whistled utterances. Only with time did the children become interested in experimenting with this feature.

During the last session, the two groups were brought together in a joint activity and where both stories were on display. The setup was comprised of two laptop computers with two headphones each. The goal of this session was to hear the story that was created by the other group and to decipher all whistled utterances. Here, the screen was faded and the children could only use a drawing pad to explore the interface while uncovering the story and each utterance. Overall the task was not always easy and often the children had difficulty when deciphering the story. This enhanced their curiosity to explore each sound source more than once. Just as the discussion of the word *parad*, the act of deciphering each utterance was an exploratory process where each child was invited to make sense of the different whistled utterances that were hidden in each story.

Figure 6: Child interacting with the story of another group.

The relative difficulty that the children experienced when deciphering the story and the different whistled utterances also instigated fruitful discussions amongst the children. Once again, what was particularly interesting to observe was the debate as to whether the word *parad* was being whistled correctly. Already presented in the previous dialogue, once again this word would instigate a debate amongst the children and as seen below:

Child 4: "there it seems like *aiai*"

Child 5: "*Parad*...this one?"

In fact, in the final session, the word *parad* would draw both groups together in a lively discussion that was aided by a set of demonstrations of how the word should be whistled. When later presenting a video recording of this discussion to one of the teachers of Silbo Gomero he responded by stating the following:

"They still do not know how to vocalize but they are searching for the sounds, the sound that the word carries. Not the expression but the sound."

The children's discussion and the teacher's remarks, illustrate the ethos of constructivist learning. Here, the focus is not on what is being learned but rather how, in which social and cultural context [18] and through which means will learning occur. In the end, the *Silbo* teacher rightly observes that it is the process that leads to learning. In the case of Silbo Gomero, the process of searching for the sounds, the building blocks of whistled language (here attuning to Bamberger's 'generative primitives'), is key.

The children's feedback

Later, at the end of the session, when all activities were complete, two of the children went back to the application software to decipher some of the utterances that were still missing. Considering that we only had two headphones per laptop, during the last session a small video camera was provided to those who were waiting for their turn to interact with the story. Upon my suggestion, and with the camera at hand, some of the children documented their experience of the project. The video footage that was collected by the children became a key asset for the project. In fact, while producing their own 'documentary' the children had the opportunity to reflect on the usability, comprehension and utility of the application software. From this footage, it would be important to outline the following comments:

Child 6: "We learned how to use it to build a narrative."

Child 3: "Yes, because it is very interesting and we learn more things" [referring to the application]. "One of the sentences is *buenos dias.* You say it like this...." [child 3 whistles]. "I also learned how to whistle a sentence I did not know before."

Child 2: "It was bit difficult.... let's say a bit" [referring to the application software].

In these three moments one can sense ways in which the The Sound Labyrinth enhanced a language learning process by introducing a novel and constructive approach. The application software also enhanced the learning process that was already initiated during the weekly class of *Silbo*. This is particularly visible in one comment: "I also learned how to whistle a sentence I did not know before". This comment also sustains an understanding of the application software as a system that supports exploration of unknown vocabulary. In this respect, and if we take into consideration that The Sound Labyrinth also encouraged children to look for the basic sounds, the building blocks of whistled language, one can also conclude that the platform posed manageable challenges to the children. In fact, echoing the early work of Lev Vygotsky [18] who suggested that learning was best promoted while establishing 'zones of proximal development'; briefly, this concept sustains the idea that activities and learning materials should aid and guide children in the exploration of unknown domains.

Testing the Application Software: Age Seven

Another phase of experimentation with The Sound Labyrinth was conducted amongst the children that were attending the second-grade class at CEIP El Retamal. With seven years of age, this session would benefit from the involvement of a lead teacher that was keen to experiment with the application software as a transversal activity that would cut through diverse levels of the language module, one that integrates Castilian Spanish and whistled language. To achieve this, the lead teacher suggested using a storytelling project that she had initiated in class. The story consisted of distinct dialogues that were developed by all fifteen students that were attending the second-grade class. Whistled utterances were inserted in some parts of the story while other parts were delivered in spoken Spanish. With this material, which was recorded in class with the children, the lead teacher would use the application software to design an interactive story for the class to interact with.

In this user-testing session the aim was to provide second-graders with a rich auditory experience. In response, an interactive 'collage' of distinct sounds was orchestrated by the lead teacher. Whistled and spoken utterances that were recorded in class would now compose a non-linear and interactive story for the second graders to explore. Hidden in the sound collage were a set of whistled utterances, the names of characters *Arturo*, *Manolo* and *Carpa*. More difficult sentences were also provided such as *fuera bichos* ('go away creatures'). Surrounding each one of these utterances was a collection of sounds that framed the story such as sounds of the ocean, water, frogs and birds that were once again recorded on the island.

To test the story that was created by the lead teacher a setup with one laptop and two simultaneously connected headphones was provided. Various groups of children interacted with the story. To illustrate their interaction with The Sound Labyrinth, the dialogue that is provided below can be used to support the analysis of the application software.

Child 7: "What was that?"

Child 7: "Continue moving."

Child 7: "Maybe through there."

Child 8: "Now that was a really big wave."

Child 7: "Another *silbo*."

Child 8: "I am almost sure what they are saying: *ven pa'ca"* (come here).

Child 7: "Did you listen to that?"

Child 7: "Hear the words."

Child 8: "Yes, it's [the word] *Carpa* because it's shorter."

Child 7: "Now think…." [here the children were trying to remember what was recorded in class].

[The two children fully concentrate on a specific whistled utterance].

Child 7: *"Fuera bichos"* (go away creatures).

Child 8: "Yes, super!2 [the two children finally deciphered all four utterances].

Figure 7: Children age seven interacting with the application.

The rich interaction between the two children that is illustrated above demonstrates, once again, the potential of the application software to support children in their search for the 'right sounds'. However, some difficulties were found amongst the different pairs of children that interacted with The Sound Labyrinth in this session. Often some level of difficulty was identified, particularly when the children could not find any sounds unless they moved the pen to the outer edges of the tablet. This constraint was influenced by teacher's own design that only placed sounds in these same locations. Despite this, the interaction between the different pairs of children and the application software demonstrated potential, particularly in terms of language comprehension.

Just as in the previous section where the word *parad* was thoroughly analysed, the interaction between two other children also provided pertinent information and as indicated below:

Child 9: "Do you find a *silbo* there?"

Child 10: "Can you hear it? I think I found one around here…."

Child 9: "Very good! Carpa."

Child 10: "It's difficult, isn't it?" [referring to the hidden and 'masked' utterances].

While the children's discussion can be approximated to the earlier discussion of the word *para*', here it is important to emphasize that this group of seven-year olds did not engage in such a rich dialogue, particularly when discussing the meaning of each whistled utterance. This could be related to one of the children who was more proficient in Silbo Gomero. As there were only two children to exchange ideas concerning whistled utterances, this disparity seemed to create an imbalance. Amongst the third and fourth grade students that were presented earlier on, the dynamics was very different. This might be related to the number of participants in each activity as the number was considerably higher. It could be suggested that a slightly larger group will keep in balance the number of proficient and less proficient whistlers, the number of children who were better in perceiving the complex whistled utterances and the number of children who demonstrated more-or-less proficiency when interacting with the application software. However, this is something that would need to be repeatedly tested with larger and smaller groups and across varying age groups and as a way of drawing a more robust conclusion.

Feedback from the community

Feedback from the community was received during two presentations of the project. One presentation was delivered to one of the two teachers of Silbo Gomero and to the lead teacher that was working with the second graders. The other presentation was delivered to a representative of the Canarian Educational Bureau. The feedback provided by one of the two *Silbo* teachers can be seen in the dialogue below:

"This is an incredible sensitivity (referring to the emphasis that was made on the *Silbo*'s auditory body of knowledge and its relation to the surrounding natural environment of the island). How much this could support the children. This should be in all the schools. A tool that supports them so that they can progress within this field".

Feedback from the lead teacher that worked with the group of second graders emphasized the importance of the application software to help the children contextualize what they are learning. On the other hand, a representative of the Canarian Educational Bureau suggested that "they [the children] are working not only the *Silbo*, the stories, comprehension, communicational competence that is now so much valued". As she would contend: "[this] has an application. We are now introducing new technologies as part of new educational laws. It is important to work communicational competences. Even more the *Silbo* as a Canarian context". She would finalize her feedback by stating that: "It seemed to me that the children like to learn in this context".

All three presentations and the feedback that was collated in response to a presentation of The Sound Labyrinth had a positive outcome. As a consequence, a final version of the application software is available on the *Proyecto Medusa* web portal [19].

DISCUSSION

Despite the presence of *Proyeto Medusa,* one could not find a computer culture within the context of CEIP El Retamal. Informal conversations with the school's teachers pointed towards a similar scenario in other public schools of the island. In CEIP Retamal, computers were mostly used outside the classroom and confined to a few hours a week. Also, the computer room was only used to explore specific subject areas, excluding Silbo Gomero. Finally, the software that was available was more instructional in nature. Following Papert's own thoughts [15] one could state that the school lacked the institutional culture that would allow teachers and students to use computers to radically transform the way in which children learn. However, the evidence collected in this study suggests that Silbo Gomero as well as an application software such as The Sound Labyrinth have the potential to introduce constructionist modes of learning within the island's schools. In fact, one of the contributions provided by the application software can be seen in the shift from an instructional mode of learning toward a constructionist [10] one and where children are in charge of their own process of learning. On that note, The Sound Labyrinth was designed as a tool as well as an 'object-to-think-with' [14]. Used to record, create as well as listen to stories that use whistled language, the children's interaction with the application software demonstrated the potential to aid them in the exploration of the form and meaning of the basic units of Silbo Gomero.

The recurrent discussion regarding how one should whistle the word *parad* was particularly insightful. Reconnecting to Papert's own thoughts, namely to his concept of 'debugging' [10], it was clear that the application software could provide children an opportunity to experiment and learn with their own mistakes. Even though faults were encouraged within the weekly class of *Silbo*, the episodes that are here described demonstrate how the computer could be used to promote what the constructionist literature would qualify as: "children's growing tolerance for their own "errors""[10].

Moreover, the application software also enhanced a mode of learning that was already taking place during the weekly class of *Silbo*. In this sense, The Sound Labyrinth materialized what Turkle and Papert [20] would identify as an 'epistemological pluralism' that seeks to "accept and validate multiple ways of knowing and thinking". In this case, a mode of knowing and thinking that is attuned to Silbo Gomero's original use by the local islanders that mostly did not have access to modes of formal education and that would learn *Silbo* while working the mountainous terrain of the island.

Later on, the two pilot tests demonstrated how the application software promotes a 'mode of learning by making' while positioning the child as a designer in his or her own right, a dimension that has been explored in the constructionist literature for quite some time [13]. Revisiting once more the work of Bamberger [11], the two user-tests equally demonstrate that the application software can support the development of a hearing culture that is highly performative. In the author's own words: "developing a "hearing" of a composition as it unfolds in time is a *performance* and performances (both silent and out-loud) involve a process of active sense-making occurring in real-time". This 'active process of sense-making' is particularly noticeable in the children's discussion of the word *parad.* Just as the group of children that were documented by Bamberger, the children reported in this contribution would often make sense of what was being whistled by simply negotiating the 'similarities and differences' of what was heard individually. And while we must be careful with simplistic comparisons between whistled language and musical learning and competence, this negotiating process could be said to aid the 'classification, naming and identification' [11] of the sound objects that are key to Silbo Gomero.

The Sound Labyrinth, the two pilot tests as well as the feedback that was received from key stakeholders demonstrate that the application software was well received by children learning Silbo Gomero, by teachers and by the broader educational community of the island of La Gomera. Further improvements could be made, particularly by addressing the teaching community and how the application software could be used by teachers to create stories in whistled language and that can be later explored by children.

More importantly, The Sound Labyrinth raised pertinent questions regarding constructionism, learning and language heritage. Initially, the application software was designed with the goal of offering the educational community of La Gomera a platform that could contribute toward the curricular safeguard of whistled language. However, the most telling aspect is that the application software offered the community an opportunity to introduce a constructionist agenda within the island's schools. Although endangered languages are often understood as 'a thing of the past', The Sound Labyrinth demonstrates that perhaps linguistic heritage can point towards new ways of learning. In fact, confirming the words of anthropologist Wade Davis [21] who suggested that the variety of human languages offer a range of different "ways of thinking and interacting with the world". The application software that is here described as well as its use by the children of La Gomera demonstrate that endangered forms of language can instigate new modes of learning. And while an older generation of whistlers might see the *Silbo* as a way of transmitting a culture of the past, the process of learning whistled language while using The Sound Labyrinth might point towards the development of a hearing culture for the future.

CONCLUSION

Constructionism has influenced the development of several studies and design applications. The SIGCHI community alone has acknowledged the timely influence of constructionism on our understanding of children's interaction with computers, namely when learning mathematics and programming [22][23]. Perhaps, less explored, is the constructionist influence on the design of 'objects' that can be used to facilitate language learning and expression. It was exactly this premise that this contribution has proposed to exemplify. Through a presentation and discussion of The Sound Labyrinth, this paper proposed ways in which constructionism and language learning can be used to make small incremental shifts within instructional based teaching environments and where linguistic heritage is at stake.

ACKNOWLEDGMENTS

This study received the support of the Portuguese Foundation for Science and Technology in the form of a doctoral grant (SFRH/BD/32144/2006). Firstly, I would like to thank the children, parents and teachers of the school CEIP El Retamal for their participation and for facilitating my presence in the school. I would also like to thank computer scientist Theo Burt for the dedication and time when developing The Sound Labyrinth. A special thank you to Florian Hecker who helped with the sound recordings. My grateful thanks to Isidro Ortiz and Lino Rodriguez for the opportunity to learn Silbo Gomero. Finally, a very special thank you to my supervisors Matthew Fuller, Luciana Parisi and Olga Goriunova and to the reviewers of this paper. The work has benefited immensely from your thoughtful comments, suggestions and feedback.

REFERENCES

[1] Margaret D. LeCompte. 1999. *Designing and Conducting Ethnographic Research.* Thousand Oaks, Calif.: Altamira Press.

[2] Sónia Matos. 2014. Here We Don't speak, Here We Whistle. In *Proceedings of the 08th Conference of the International Committee for Design History and Design Studies* (ICDHS 2012), 243–247. DOI:10.5151/design-icdhs-046.

[3] Sónia Matos. 2015. Can Languages be Saved? Linguistic Heritage and the Moving Archive. In *Memory in Motion: Archives, Technology, and the Social*, 61-84. Amsterdam, Amsterdam University Press.

[4] UNESCO. n.d. Whistled language of the island of La Gomera (Canary Islands), the Silbo Gomero. Accessed January 30, 2016 from

http://www.unesco.org/culture/ich/en/RL/whistled-language-of-the-island-of-la-gomera-canary-islands-the-silbo-gomero-00172

[5] Ramón Trujillo. 1978. *El Silbo Gomero: Análisis Linguístico*. Ed. Interinsular Canaria.

[6] Ramón Trujillo. 2006. *The Silbo Gomero: A New Phonological Study*. Islas Canarias, Academia Canaria de la Lengua.

[7] Annie Rialland. 2005. Phonological and Phonetic Aspects of Whistled Languages. *Phonology*, 22, 237–271. DOI:10.1017/S0952675705000552

[8] Julien Meyer. 2015. *Whistled Languages: A Worldwide Inquiry on Human Whistled Speech*. Heidelberg, Springer.

[9] Manuel Carreiras, Jorge Lopez, Francisco Rivero and David Corina. 2005. Linguistic Perception: Neural Processing of a Whistled Language. In *Nature*, 433, 31. DOI: 10.1038/433031a

[10] Seymour Papert. 1993. *Mindstorms: Children, Computers, and Powerful Ideas*. Basic Books.

[11] Jeanne Bamberger. 2012. What Develops in Musical Development? In G. McPherson (Ed.), The *Child as Musician: A Handbook of Musical Development*, 69–92. Oxford, Oxford University Press. DOI:10.1093/acprof:oso/9780198530329.003.0004

[12] Jean François Augoyard and Henry Torgue (Eds.). 2005. *Sonic Experience: A Guide to Everyday Sounds*. Montréal, McGill-Queen's Press.

[13] Seymour Papert and Idit Harel. 1991. Situating Constructionism. Accessed January 17, 2017 from http://www.papert.org/articles/SituatingConstructionism.html

[14] Yasmin B. Kafai and Mitchel Resnick (Eds.). 2010. *Constructionism in Practice: Designing, Thinking, and Learning in a Digital World*. New York, Routledge.

[15] Seymour Papert. 1987. Computer Criticism vs. Technocentric Thinking. In *Educ. Res.*,16, 22–30. DOI:10.2307/1174251.

[16] Curtis Roads. 1996. *The Computer Music Tutorial*. Cambridge, Mass. : MIT Press.

[17] Gobierno de Canarias. n.d. Portal Medusa. Accessed February 1, 2017 from http://www3.gobiernodecanarias.org/medusa/ecoescuela/ate/medusa/

[18] Lev Vygotsky. 1978. *Mind in Society: The Development of Higher Psychological Processes*. Cambridge, Mass., Harvard University Press.

[19] Gobierno de Canarias. n.d. El Laberinto del Sonido. Accessed February 1, 2017 from http://www3.gobiernodecanarias.org/medusa/ecoescuela/abriendolaescuela/?p=1049

[20] Seymour Papert and Sherry Turkle. n.d. Epistemological Pluralism and the Revaluation of the Concrete. Accessed April 23, 2017 from http://web.mit.edu/sturkle/www/pdfsforstwebpage/ST_Epistemo Pluralism.pdf

[21] Wade Davis. 2009. The Wayfinders: Why Ancient Wisdom Matters in the Modern World. In *CBC Massey Lect.* Accessed April 21, 2017 from http://www.cbc.ca/radio/ideas/the-2009-cbc-massey-lectures-the-wayfinders-why-ancient-wisdom-matters-in-the-modern-world-1.2946883

[22] Jean M. Griffin. 2016. Learning by Taking Apart: Deconstructing Code by Reading, Tracing, and Debugging. In *Proc. 17th Annu. Conf. Inf. Technol. Educ.*, 148–153. DOI:10.1145/2978192.2978231.

[23] Craig Jenkins. 2015. A Work in Progress Paper: Evaluating a Microworlds-based Learning Approach for Developing Literacy and Computational Thinking in Cross-curricular Contexts. In *Proc. Work. Prim. Second. Comput. Educ.*, 61–64. DOI:10.1145/2818314.2818316.

Agency, Embodiment, & Affect During Play in a Mixed-Reality Learning Environment

Danielle Keifert
University of California
Los Angeles CA, USA
keifert@ucla.edu

Christine Lee
University of California
Los Angeles CA, USA
clee@labschool.ucla.edu

Maggie Dahn
University of California
Los Angeles CA, USA
maggiedahn@gmail.com

Randy Illum
University of California
Los Angeles CA, USA
randy@remap.ucla.edu

David DeLiema
University of California
Berkeley CA, USA
deliema@berkeley.edu

Noel Enyedy
University of California
Los Angeles CA, USA
enyedy@gseis.ucla.edu

Joshua Danish
Indiana University
Bloomington IN, USA
jdanish@indiana.edu

ABSTRACT
Beginning from the assumption that young children (ages 6-8) are capable of reasoning about complex phenomena [12], we set out to better understand dimensions of the Science through Technology Enhanced Play environment that provided support for children to learn about relationships between multiple levels of an emergent phenomenon [23]—states of matter. We conducted interactional analysis [15] of several moments in two classrooms as students developed and refined understanding of rules that connect micro behavior of particles of water to macro understanding about states of matter. We argue that central to students' disciplinary work were (1) multiple forms of agency negotiated within the STEP environment that were deeply intertwined with (2) students' embodiment. Agency and embodiment both supported students' consensus understanding of relationships between levels of the states of matter phenomenon (3) through students' joyful and playful collaborative work. We examine several episodes in detail to explore these findings.

Author Keywords
Science learning; early-elementary; mixed-reality; sociodramatic play; agency; embodiment; affect.

ACM Classification Keywords
K.3.1 [Computers and Education]: Computer Uses in Education - *Collaborative learning.*

IDC '17, June 27-30, 2017, Stanford, CA, USA

ACM ISBN 978-1-4503-4921-5/17/06...$15.00
http://dx.doi.org/10.1145/3078072.3079731

INTRODUCTION
Despite a commonly held belief that young children are not ready to engage in complex science learning, scholars have argued that even very young children can grapple with advanced scientific phenomena [12]. Work that engages students with sophisticated concepts pushes against fixed notions of development and opens opportunities for students to learn about advanced science topics such as complex systems of honeybee pollination [7,8], micro properties of states of matter [11], and the very nature of science [1]. We argue that three central aspects of successful learning through play in our context included (1) student agency for directing learning and activity, (2) the role of embodiment in thinking about complex systems, (3) and the centrality of affect for the endeavor of science.

EMBODIMENT, AGENCY, AND POSITIVE AFFECT IN SOCIODRAMATIC PLAY FOR SCIENCE
These themes of embodiment, agency, and affect have been reflected in prior work on STEM learning. Papert long ago argued for the importance of embodiment in STEM learning [21], and the call to provide opportunities for embodiment continues in work arguing to broaden forms of sense-making recognized as productive for science learning [22]. Within our context of sociodramatic play, we define embodiment as moments when children use their bodies to represent other entities (e.g., water particles). Furthermore, science education literature has emphasized the importance of students taking ownership of their ideas, wrestling with the inquiry process themselves (e.g., [17]). We specifically define *agency* in the context of embodied sociodramatic play as those moments when children direct their own or other's bodies during embodiment. Students might move around the space as they choose (e.g., running in circles), direct others to create particular patterns (e.g., "Let's make a diamond"), or coordinate together (e.g., "Everybody, hold my hands!"). Additionally, recent work has emphasized the centrality of affect in science. Affect is not merely an issue of motivation, but is central to the disciplinary work of science itself [14]. We are particularly interested in understanding the role of joy, playfulness, and excitement in science learning (though

we acknowledge feelings of confusion and frustration are equally central to science).

We explore how student agency, embodiment, and positive affect support children becoming legitimate participants in the disciplinary work of science through sociodramatic play. Through a designed learning experience we call STEP (Science through Technology Enhanced Play), we explore students' development of rules relating multiple levels [23] of a scientific phenomenon—states of matter—through a playful, embodied, mixed-reality collaborative simulation.

We begin with a description of the STEP mixed-reality environment including the technology, the interactional space, and the sociodramatic framing of activities. We then present case studies in which students developed and refined rules relating micro-particle behavior to the macro phenomena of creating solids, liquids, or gases. We end by synthesizing our analysis of the STEP environment to better understand the role of agency, embodiment, and affect as central to disciplinary science learning within STEP.

STEP ENVIRONMENT

STEP is a mixed-reality (MR), body-based, collaborative environment. We view the STEP environment as an enactment of Vygotsky's [25] conceptualization of sociodramatic play, which includes (1) rules, (2) roles, and (3) and an imaginary situation. We believe this approach lends itself to opportunities for students to engage in science through embodiment, thereby supporting young children's understanding of complex systems. Two mixed-age first- and second-grade classrooms (ages 6 through 8; n=26) participated in six days of embodied activities in science learning through a collaborative effort between the students and teachers. Students engaged in learning about changes in states of matter for water by embodying both macro, observable characteristics of matter (e.g., solid ice, liquid water) as well as micro, particulate behavior of matter (i.e. solid, liquid, or gas particles).

We focus on two days of activities that included students playing as particles exploring patterns of making solid (white), liquid (blue), and gas (red). Students were tracked through open-source computer vision software—OpenPTrack [18]. OpenPTrack (OPT) was developed in response to the inception of the STEP research which required markerless person-tracking. The overall goal of the sequence of activities was for students to understand macro and micro properties of states of matter including factors such as how distance and speed impact state change (e.g., particles that vibrate in place and are spaced far away make solid; particles that are slow moving and closely spaced make liquid; particles that are fast moving make gas).

The STEP space (Figure 1) was used when the class was oriented to tracking activity (in contrast to discussion during which students oriented away from the screen towards the teacher and documentation.) The space was designed to foster a collaborative environment that encouraged play as part of the students' learning. This was achieved through a large open space for activities. This configuration allowed students to enter the STEP tracking space and interact with the learning content without the need for markers or other objects to interface with STEP software. Within the STEP tracking space there was a large-format projection screen that was used to visualize the MR environment. In addition to displaying particles, this screen also provided various tools at different points in the lessons. For example, a new tool, the state-meter (Figure 2), was introduced during the second lesson we analyze here. This tool displayed information about the proportion of students in the space that were solid, liquid, or gas at any given time.

During the sociodramatic play in these lessons, students were assigned roles as *particles* and *directors* within the imaginary, embodied situation to support their work to determine the rules of behavior for particles at microscopic levels. All students had a chance to perform both roles, which defined how they interacted with each other and the technology. Student particles explored the MR space through their movements in the tracked space, which in turn controlled their particle in the simulation they would see on the projection screen. Student directors sat outside the

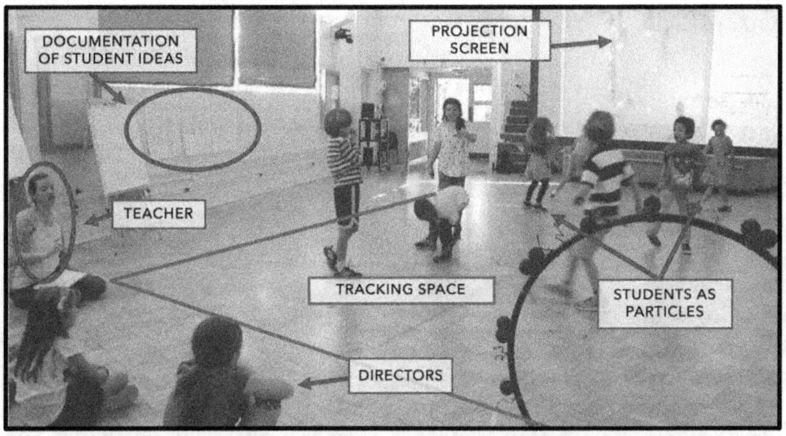

Figure 1. Student directors observe student particles while the teacher sits near prior documentation of student ideas and consensus rules.

A.

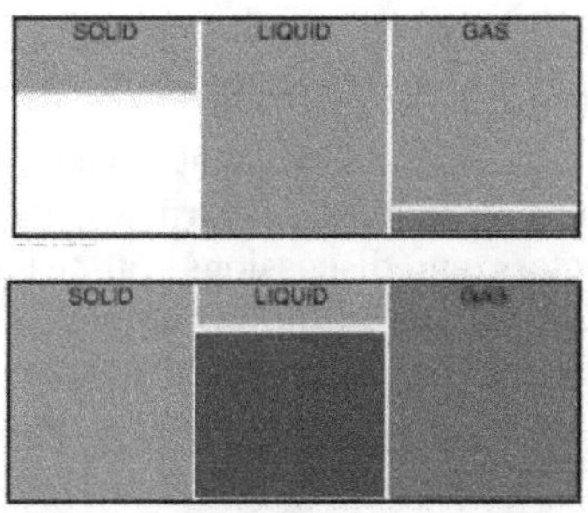

B.

Figure 2. The state-meter displayed proportions of particles in each state. 2A shows most particles as solid and a few as gas. 2B shows particles split between liquid and gas.

tracked area with the goal of looking for emerging patterns in particles' play. Directors gave instructions to particles regarding goals (what state to make) and multiple methods of achieving goals including creating particular kinds of movement (skip, run, stand still), gestures (move arms up and down), or patterns (make a diamond, spread out). These directions came both as students initially developed ideas about the relation between particles' movement and states of matter, as well as a means for refining or retesting consensus rules.

In this paper, we examine how students in both director and particle roles contributed to the development of ideas into consensus rules for explaining relationships between micro particle behavior and states of matter. Students were not initially taught rules that describe states of matter. Instead, students developed their own ideas and consensus rules through playful embodiment, excited observations, and early expressions of their initial learning through gesture [13]. As such, the students' movement became a crucial factor in their body-based learning [16] and interactions. Also critical to this work were daily reflections in the discussion space during which students worked with teachers to create a written list—documentation—of the observed rules in the particle simulation. These rules were referred back to, changed, and modified throughout the STEP activities as students learned together.

METHODS

The Lessons

Our STEP curriculum included both macroscopic and microscopic lessons on state changes of water particles (solid, liquid, and gas). Macroscopic lessons included observable characteristics of water such as associating cold temperatures with ice. Our microscopic lessons included particle behavior in each state of matter (solid, liquid, gas) as well as how energy impacts changes in states of matter. For this case study, we examine two lessons in two different classrooms (lead by different teachers) that covered microscopic particle behavior for each state of matter. We focused on these two lessons because we wanted to trace students' work to move from observations to expressed ideas and finally to consensus rules relating micro particle behavior to macro states of matter.

We looked for ideas that became consensus rules through embodied inquiry of particles, the directions provided by directors, and discussions with teachers. The goal of the two lessons was to learn how to make each state of matter in the particulate level according to speed and/or distance (e.g. to make gas, particles must move quickly in the space). During the first lesson, both classrooms developed initial ideas and created documentation on how to make a certain color with their bodies. During the second lesson, the goals were to test existing ideas and develop consensus rules. Across these two lessons we traced all student ideas on how to create white (solid) in one classroom, and we traced student ideas on how to create blue (liquid) in the other classroom. For each we provide a detailed sequence of episodes, and then examine a few moments more closely.

Analysis Process

Following the identification of these episodes, we analyzed each following the tradition of Interaction Analysis [15]. This included creating transcripts, analyzing each line-by-line, characterizing each turn, and developing an understanding of patterns across episodes. In this paper, we focus on moments within the last of the episodes in both classrooms. We chose these episodes because they afforded us an opportunity to explore particular forms of agency within the STEP play space, demonstrated the importance of collaborative action during particles' embodiment, and presented different examples of the centrality of positive affect to the work of scientific inquiry. Using these episodes we ask: *How did the STEP environment support students' work to develop consensus rules for particle behavior through playful embodied exploration and discussions?* In what follows, we argue that central to the *how* of the above question were opportunities for agency, embodiment, and positive affect afforded in the STEP environment.

ANALYSIS

Solid White

We begin presenting analysis of the last episode in the sequence of student inquiries about how to make white (solid) from one classroom (Figure 3). In these episodes students developed the idea that standing still or jumping in place would "make white," and over time began to accept this as a consensus rule. In the last episode, there was a shift

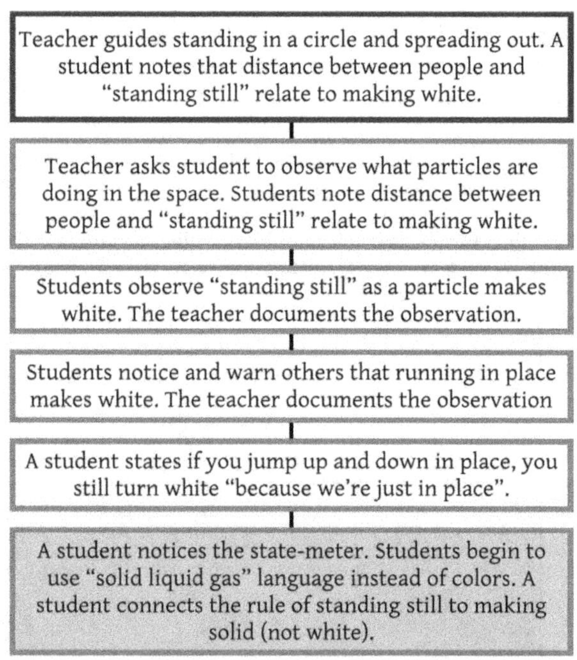

Figure 3. Episodes during which students discussed how to make white or solid in STEP. Purple borders represent Day 2 activities, Orange borders day 3 activities. Shaded box is the episode analyzed here.

Figure 4. Bethany and Sarah move in a particle-hug.

1 Brandon: .hhh Hey! (That says solid and liqu::id)
Brandon points to screen turns to Ms. Jones.
2 *Brandon taps Ms. Jones with left hand.*
3 *Ms. Jones leans towards Brandon, sets her hand on his shoulder.*
4 Ms. Jones: What?
Ms. Jones lifts her hand off of Brandon's shoulder and points towards the screen.
5 *Brandon turns to face the screen, still pointing.*
6 Ms. Jones: Tell them Brandon!
Ms. Jones raises her arms and then drops in quickly as she shouts to Brandon.
7 Brandon: GUYS EVERYBODY, LOOK AT THAT!!

Figure 5. Brandon shows the state-meter to Ms. Jones and she encourages him to share.

in their language from "making white" to "making solid" accompanied by the introduction of a new tool. We explore how agency was enacted both through (a) the roles assigned within the sociodramatic play of the STEP environment, as well as through (b) the positioning of students by teachers (or other adults, e.g., researchers) with regard to agency. We also examine how the introduction of the new tool (state-meter) shaped students' language and embodiment, and as a result impacted students' evolving goals. Finally, we examine the role of positive affect in this particular moment, as it runs central to the activity shaped by this tool.

Introduction of the state-meter: "Everybody look at that!"
Students in classroom one had been exploring how to make patterns related to the particle color; students focused on making white (or red, or blue) prior to this moment. In the midst of the particles' free exploration, a researcher turned on a new tool: the state-meter.

Within 10 seconds, students' interactions demonstrated they had noticed it. Bethany, a particle, pointed it out to another particle, Sarah. Bethany and Sarah had been moving in a particle hug—a formation where students stand close to each other or hug one another (Figure 4), causing STEP to track them as one body and therefore one particle. After the introduction of the state-meter, Bethany broke the hug, pointed it out to Sarah, and both girls moved closer to the screen. At nearly the same time, a director, Brandon, pointed out the state-meter to his teacher. Brandon's excitement was evident as he turned around to his teacher, Ms. Jones (Figure 5). Brandon described what he saw, "Hey, that says solid and liquid" to which Ms. Jones responded with an excited "What?!" and then shouted, "Tell them, Brandon!" lifting her arm before dramatically dropping it. Brandon jumped up and shouted, "Everybody, look at that!" and ran into the tracking space pointing at the state-meter, before returning to his spot to watch the particles respond.

These three students' actions in this short span of 20 seconds display two distinct forms of agency in the STEP play environment. First, Bethany and Sarah were demonstrating their own agency in determining how to move in the space as particles. Bethany and Sarah chose to take advantage of the exploratory time, where no directors had told them how to act, and made the particle-hug arrangement against the advice of researchers who were concerned with each student being tracked separately at all times. Brandon, on the other hand, took advantage of another form of agency when he received encouragement directly from his teacher to direct particles in the space. As a director, Brandon was already positioned to direct particles' actions. However, the offer from his teacher provided Brandon with the push to shift the pattern of activity in the environment away from exploratory play, which we discuss next.

These forms of agency—of particles to direct their own activity during exploratory play, directors directing particles' activity, and specific encouragement from adults—provided opportunities for students to direct their own and each other's embodied activity. We recognize both roles in the context of sociodramatic play, particles and directors, and the specific offers of agency from adults could enable or constrain individuals' agency. For instance, the particles' agency over their own embodiment shifted as the class moved from exploratory play of particles, where particles could self-direct their activity, to the testing of a particular rule, where a director, Brandon, determined particles' activity.

After Brandon returned to stand by other directors, Samantha, another director, turned to Ms. Jones. Although

1 Brandon: GUYS YOU NEED TO MAKE SOLID! and you're gonna stay still!
2 *Leon pivots and begins to run around the space moving in a big circle. Lilly begins to run in a smaller circle.*
4 *Bethany stretches out her left leg stamping down in an spread leg formation stretching her arms out, making a large X with her body. She holds that position steady.*
5 Leon: Make gas
6 *Sarah turns partially to face Leon, lifting her arms up in front of her making a "stop" motion.*
7 (student): Stay still for a second
8 Sarah: Stay still! (unclear) stay still!
Sarah steps to the side as Leon approaches her, spreading her arms out.
9 *Sarah steps towards Leon.*
10 *Leon stops and faces the screen. Bethany drops one arm and raises the other straight up.*
11 (student): (don't) mo:::ve
12 (student): Stay still
13 (student): Stay still
14 *Lilly stops, leans forward stretching her arms about behind her.*

Figure 6. Brandon directs particles and they respond.

Samantha's talk is not audible, Ms. Jones clearly said to Samantha "Okay, tell them that, and tell them what they need to do". Ms. Jones' comment suggested a particular form that direction should take—direct particles *what* state to make and *how*, or by what method to make it. In the subsequent turn, Brandon did just that (Figure 6). Brandon shouted "Guys, you need to make solid, and you're gonna stay still!" following the format Ms. Jones indicated to Samantha. In response, most particles shifted to standing still, and those few that didn't were quickly reined in by other particles (particularly Sarah as she shouted "Stand still" and spread her arms out to block Leon from continuing to run). Two things are of particular note here.

First, students' language shifted from prior talk about making *white*, *blue*, or *red* to a consistent language of making *solid*, *liquid*, or *gas*. In this classroom, the shift occurred directly after the introduction of the state-meter by Brandon to the rest of the class, and was adopted by all students. This minor shift in language indicates a significant contribution to the development of a consensus rule through which students mapped their embodied activity as particles to resulting states of matter. Through this shift in language, students directly tied movement of particles at one level to emergent states of matter at another. This was a central goal of these two lessons.

Second, there was a shift in agency and embodiment as a result of Brandon's direction. Prior to his direction to "make solid" and "stay still", particles were engaged in free exploratory play as they self-directed their own activity. Following his utterance, particles who had been embodying several small and independent patterns organized together to collectively stand still to make solid. Particles were involved in this shift in agency by allowing directors to direct as they disciplined their own and each other's bodies to collectively make white by standing still. As a result, Brandon's direction led to a testing of a prior consensus rule that standing still makes white within the context of the new language introduced by the state-meter, testing instead if standing still makes solid. Thus, shifts in agency, language, and embodiment were tied together. Specifically, they were all critical in students' work to link colors of particles to states of matter, reflecting students' development of a shared understanding of the relationship between particle motion and color (standing still to make white) and the resulting state of matter (making solid), and meeting the central goal of these lessons.

Additionally, this moment illustrates the centrality of positive affect, particularly excitement. Brandon's excitement was evident as he quickly turned around and shared his noticing of the state-meter with Ms. Jones, who in turn demonstrated her own excitement as she enthusiastically replied "What?!" and then "Tell them, Brandon!" The cascade of excitement continued as Brandon shouted and ran into the space to point out the state-meter to other students, and several moved forward to take note of the state-meter. In addition to Bethany and Sarah who had already moved closer to the screen to inspect the state-meter, Leon ran from having his shoe tied by a researcher to standing immediately next to the screen and pointing out each of the states on the state-meter (Figure 7). Leon's excitement was evidenced by his running and his quick (and loud) repetitions of reading each of the states while pointing to their bar on the state-meter.

1 Leon: Liquid, solid
Leon drops his arm and turns to face directors.
2 *Kara skips the other way and forward towards the students.*
3 *Zach skips towards the cluster of students near the state-meter.*
4 (Carl?): Oh yeah
5 *Leon turns back towards screen and moves closer to state-meter side.*
6 *Leon raises her arm and points to state-meter again.*
7 Leon: That's gas, liquid, and solid
Leon points to each of the bars on the state-meter.
8 *Kara moves away from Lilly, bouncing towards the screen.*
9 *Leon walks away from the screen*

Figure 7. Leon reads and points to the states twice, other particles move towards him.

Other students, too, showed evidence of excitement; another director, Carl, stood up at the same time as Brandon and said "Oh Yeah!", several particles shifted their bodies from motion towards standing close to the screen to inspect, and particles shifted into collaborative patterns in response to Brandon's later direction. We argue this cascade of excitement, starting with Brandon and moving through Ms. Jones, Leon, and other students (both directors and particles), was central to the discovery of the state-meter and the shift from free exportation of particles into the collective testing of a consensus rule. By this we mean that the excitement of the state-meter led directly to the collaborative effort to tie their prior rule (standing still makes white) to the new language of the state-meter (standing still makes solid) thus creating a critical link for students between embodied action, color of particles, and state of matter created. Essentially, agency, embodiment, and affect were deeply intertwined in students' successful elaboration of a consensus rule to capture the disciplinary idea of relating particle behavior to states of matter.

Liquid Blue

In the second classroom, we analyzed the development of creating liquid (blue). We examined the development of an idea about a pattern—holding hands while walking slowly in a circle—as it developed over two days into a consensus rule for making blue (Figure 8). We found contrasts to the previous episode in how the technology was used and how teacher and student roles played out. In this sequence, the state-meter had already been introduced by the teacher during a discussion. Although there was no excitement of discovery of the state-meter as in the prior classroom, the students in this classroom used the state-meter as a tool for

REFERENCES

1. Valarie L. Akerson, Gayle A. Buck, Lisa A. Donnelly, Vanashri Nargund-Joshi, and Ingrid S. Weiland. 2011. The Importance of Teaching and Learning Nature of Science in the Early Childhood Years. *Journal of Science Education and Technology* 20, 5: 537–549. https://doi.org/10.1007/s10956-011-9312-5
2. Sasha A. Barab, Tyler Dodge, Adam Ingram-Goble, Patrick Pettyjohn, Kylie Peppler, Charlene Volk, and Maria Solomou. 2010. Pedagogical Dramas and Transformational Play: Narratively Rich Games for Learning. *Mind, Culture, and Activity* 17, 3: 235–264. https://doi.org/10.1080/10749030903437228
3. Angela Calabrese Barton and Edna Tan. 2010. We Be Burnin'! Agency, Identity, and Science Learning. *Journal of the Learning Sciences* 19, 2: 187–229. https://doi.org/10.1080/10508400903530044
4. Doris Bergen. 2009. Play as the Learning Medium for Future Scientists, Mathematicians, and Engineers. *American Journal of Play* 1, 4: 413–428.
5. Michael Cole and Yrjo Engeström. 1993. A cultural-historical approach to distributed cognition. In *Psychological and educational considerations*. Cambridge University Press, Cambridge UK, 1–46.
6. National Research Council, Division of Behavioral and Social Sciences and Education, Board on Science Education, and Committee on a Conceptual Framework for New K.-12 Science Education Standards. 2012. *A Framework for K-12 Science Education: Practices, Crosscutting Concepts, and Core Ideas*. National Academies Press.
7. Joshua A. Danish, Kylie Peppler, David Phelps, and DiAnna Washington. 2011. Life in the Hive: Supporting Inquiry into Complexity Within the Zone of Proximal Development. *Journal of Science Education and Technology* 20, 5: 454–467. https://doi.org/10.1007/s10956-011-9313-4
8. Joshua Danish, Noel Enyedy, Asmalina Saleh, Megan Humburg, David DeLiema, Maggie Dahn, and Christine Lee. 2017. STEP-Bees: Coordinating embodied interaction with peers, teachers, and computer simulation to support learning.
9. Paul Dourish. 2003. What we talk about when we talk about context. *Personal and Ubiquitous Computing* 8, 1: 19–30. https://doi.org/10.1007/s00779-003-0253-8
10. Paul Dourish. 2004. *Where the Action is: The Foundations of Embodied Interaction*. MIT Press.
11. Noel Enyedy, Lee, David DeLiema, Joshua Danish, Asmalina Saleh, Dahn, Kelly Peters, Noelani Morris, Carla-Anne Thomas, Jacqueline Torres, Gabriela Cardenas, Cynthia Creek, Michael Love, Jeff Burke, Randy Illum, Fabian Wagmister, Alex Horn, Matteo Munaro, and Radu Rusu. 2016. Learning About States of Matter Through Multiple Correspondences Among the Body, Abstractions, and Reality.
12. Haim Eshach. 2011. Science for Young Children: A New Frontier for Science Education. *Journal of Science Education and Technology* 20, 5: 435. https://doi.org/10.1007/s10956-011-9324-1
13. Susan Goldin-Meadow. 2004. Gesture's Role in the Learning Process. *Theory Into Practice* 43, 4: 314–321. https://doi.org/10.1207/s15430421tip4304_10
14. Lama Z. Jaber and David Hammer. 2016. Learning to feel like a scientist. *Science Education* 100, 2: 189–220.
15. Brigitte Jordan and Austin Henderson. 1995. Interaction Analysis: Foundations and Practice. *The Journal of the Learning Sciences* 4, 1: 39–103.
16. Leilah Lyons, Brian Slattery, Priscilla Jimenez, Brenda Lopez, and Tom Moher. 2012. Don't forget about the sweat: effortful embodied interaction in support of learning. In *Proceedings of the Sixth International Conference on Tangible, Embedded and Embodied Interaction*, 77–84.
17. Eve Manz. 2015. Resistance and the Development of scientific practice: Designing the mangle into science instruction.pdf. *Cognition and Instruction* 32, 2: 89–124.
18. Matteo Munaro, Alex Horn, Randy Illum, Jeff Burke, and Radu Rusu. 2014. OpenPTrack: People Tracking for Heterogeneous Networks of Color-Depth Cameras. In *IAS-13 Workshop*, 235–247.
19. Ricardo Nemirovsky, Cornelia Tierney, and Tracey Wright. 1998. Body Motion and Graphing. *Cognition and Instruction* 16, 2: 119–172. https://doi.org/10.1207/s1532690xci1602_1
20. Elinor Ochs, Patrick Gonzales, and Sally Jacoby. 1996. "When I come down I'm in the domain state": Grammar and graphic representation in the interpretive activity of physicists. In *Interaction and grammar*, Elinor Ochs, Emanuel A. Schegloff and Sandar A. Thompson (eds.). Cambridge University Press, Cambridge, UK.
21. Seymour Papert. 1980. *Mindstorms: Children, Computers, and Powerful Ideas*. Basic Books, Inc., New York, NY, USA.
22. Beth Warren, Cynthia Ballenger, Mark Ogonowski, Ann S. Rosebery, and Josiane Hudicourt-Barnes. 2001. Rethinking diversity in learning science: The logic of everyday sense-making. *Journal of Research in Science Teaching* 38, 5: 529–552. https://doi.org/10.1002/tea.1017
23. Uri Wilensky and Mitchel Resnick. 1999. Thinking in Levels: A Dynamic Systems Approach to Making Sense of the World. *Journal of Science Education and Technology* 8, 1: 3–19. https://doi.org/10.1023/A:1009421303064
24. Fisher Hirsh-Pasek Golinkoff (2010) Playing around in school- implications for learning and educational policy.pdf.
25. L. S. Vygotsky. 1978. *Mind in Society: Development of Higher Psychological Processes*. Harvard University Press.

TaBooGa – A Hybrid Learning App to Support Children's Reading Motivation

Rebecca Linke[1], Tina Kothe[2], Florian Alt[1]

[1]LMU Munich
Ubiquitous Interactive Systems Group
florian.alt@ifi.lmu.de

[2]LMU Munich
Institute of Art Education
tina.kothe@lrz.uni-muenchen.de

Figure 1. We present TaBooGa, a hybrid reading app that supports children's reading motivation by combining an electronic book with tangible elements. Children read a story on a tablet (a). To progress through the story a figure of the main character needs to be moved on a physical gameboard (b). The reading task is interlaced with real world tasks (e.g., building a bridge with LEGO), which is integrated with the story by taking a picture (c).

ABSTRACT

In this paper we present TaBooGa (Tangible Book Game), a hybrid learning application we developed to increase children's reading motivation. As children are exposed to digital devices early on (e.g., smart phones and tablets) weak readers are particularly apt to prefer digital offers over reading traditional books. Prior work has shown that ebooks can partially address this challenge by making reading more compelling for children. In this work we show that augmenting ebooks with tangible elements can further increase the reading motivation. In particular, we embed tangible elements that allow for navigating through the book as well as in the form of mini-games that interlace the reading task. We report on the results of an evaluation among 22 primary school pupils, comparing the influence of the approach on both strong and weak readers. Our results show a positive influence beyond reading motivation on both weak and strong readers. Yet, the approach requires to strive a balance between the tangible elements being motivating while at the same time not being too distracting.

ACM Classification Keywords

K.3. Computers and Education: Computer Uses in Eduation

Author Keywords

reading; motivation; literature; book-app; hybrid; tangible

IDC '17, June 27–30, 2017, Stanford, CA, USA.

ACM ISBN 978-1-4503-4921-5/17/06 ...$15.00.
http://dx.doi.org/10.1145/3078072.3079712

INTRODUCTION

Reading is one of the most essential skills in our daily life. As Clark et al. state, 'reading is an important gateway to personal development, to social, economic and civic life' [5]. At the same time, the plethora of compelling alternatives in the form of games or video clips on smart phones and tablets leads to an ever decreasing amount of time children dedicate to training the skill of reading. As a result, many children are exposed to reading only at school. This raises the question, how to involve young people and increase their interest in literature.

Prior research tried to address this challenge and increase the motivation for engaging with literature by transferring the reading task to the digital world through interactive ebooks and storytelling authoring tools [7, 16, 19, 25]. At the same time, prior work showed that the involvement of multiple senses (e.g., visual, acoustic, haptic) increases motivation and supports learning [2, 21]. Tangibles were found to be particularly useful for reading tasks [1, 9, 15, 20, 23].

In this work, we combine the strengths of both approaches. As with an interactive ebook, the reading task is performed in the digital world. At the same time we enhance the reading task with tangible elements, hence creating a multi-sensory experience. We implemented a tablet app for the reading task. To further increase the reading motivation, we augmented the reading task with two kinds of tangibles: First, to progress through the story (flip pages), children need to move a figure of the main character across a physical board. Second, the story includes short tasks that need to be performed in the physical world (e.g., building a LEGO bridge to cross a river). Results are integrated into the story through taking pictures (see Figure 1). Thus we make the reading task more attractive and motivate weak readers in particular to read the entire story.

We report on the design and development of the app and present a user study among 22 primary school children aged 7–9. The evaluation focuses on a comparison of how the presented concept of a hybrid book-app impacts on the reading motivation of weak and strong readers. Our results show that both types of readers (weak and strong) can benefit from hybrid apps enhanced with tangible elements. At the same time, the app design needs to strive for a balance between the tangible and digital interactive elements being motivating but not distracting from the main task of reading, hence being in line with findings from prior work [7].

RELATED WORK

Our work draws from several strands of prior research: reading motivation, digital reading, and hybrid apps.

Reading Motivation

Reading is an essential skills to partake in the cultures and society of our modern world. To become a strong and fluent reader, the act of reading has to be effortless and exciting to get young people interested [23, 27]. Basically, involvement in literature should not exclusively be supported in school, but be brought to the children's homes. As low performance in reading leads to low motivation for reading, a change in attitude has to start here. Motivation for reading and fascination for stories are the decisive factors. Reading may become boring if it is mandatory and not an experience of 'flow', where children can explore new worlds with their imagination [6].

Another important fact is that appreciation of literature and stories has a direct link to further motivation for reading [27]. An investigation on children's (aged 6–12) usage of media in their spare time showed that the activity of 'leisure reading' is ranked far behind most computer-based activities [11]. Due to a remarkable difference in gender regarding reading motivation and reading skills – girls are on a much higher level – it is important to support both genders in different ways [13].

Digital Reading

Children grow up in households that cover a broad spectrum of different media, ranging from TV over computers to smart phones and tablets [11]. As smart phones and tablets are both popular and easily accessible for children, these devices are best choices of considered media for enhancing reading skills.

In Germany formal education at primary schools often has still no access to tablets or similar devices [4]. The acceptance of parents to use such devices as a possibility for learning and improving reading skills is also rather low. Only 16% of all parents use children book apps [8]. Their main concerns are that their children stop liking printed books, see inappropriate content, and spend too much time in front of digital devices.

There is indeed a difference between high and low quality ebooks. A high quality ebook has to strive a balance between reading and stirring up interest through interactive elements. These elements should be no distraction from the story itself [6, 21]. Furthermore, ebooks are able to support parents in their attempt to encourage their children's reading, but they should not be misused as so called 'pacifier toys' [24]. The focus should always remain on the good story and not on games or interactions [17]. With these guidelines at hand, high quality ebooks can be created in a way that satisfies sceptical parents and teachers alike. A further advantage of ebooks is that in particular children with an immigration background who still struggle with the new language may benefit from the combination of images and sound [22].

From our review of prior literature we learned that while training reading skills is important and ebooks are a promising attempt, there are still considerable reservations among parents and teachers. One of the reasons is the exclusive focus on the digital world that further increases children's 'air time' with technologies, such as tablets and smart phones. This motivated us to investigate how to establish a link between digital and real world by means of tangibles.

Hybrid Apps

To do so, we consider a new approach: mixing digital elements with real-world physical objects. We envision this approach to both increase acceptance among parents for reading apps while at the same time increasing children's motivation and engagement, ultimately leading to more quality reading time.

We realize this approach through tangibles that augment the reading app. Tangible user interfaces (TUIs) 'augment the real physical world by coupling digital information to everyday physical objects and environments' [14]. Here the physical world with all its objects becomes an interface for interaction with digital components [26].

In general, physical components already follow design guidelines like 'form follows function', hence being the best suitable choice for special tasks [12]. Tangibles enable haptic feedback that is usually missing from touch-based devices, but is well known to users through daily routines [18]. These benefits make tangibles particularly useful tools for learning [20].

In projects like 'Click-Craft-Play', children can draw or use bricks to create their own gaming area. A link between the virtual and the real world is created. The game becomes digital, when the children take a photo. In hybrid games, digital components are added to toys or vice versa to make playing more interactive and to stop parents from worrying about excessive digital gaming of their children [3].

Tangibles are mainly used in combination with digital games. An example where tangibles have been used in the context of reading is the work of Pinto. Here, the reading experience is enhanced through a multi-sensory approach that 'involves haptic perception, and [...] in turn engages both tactile and kinaesthetic perceptions.' [23]. In her 'Book of Hours', Pinto therefore enhances an ebook with a traditional book to enable haptic feedback and interactive elements [23]. In another project, Fan et al. [10] used alphabetical characters in the form of tangible objects to enhance reading and spelling acquisition among children with dyslexia.

Our work contributes a novel approach where tangibles are used beyond creating a haptic sensation during reading, but also adds playful, haptic elements that are aimed at further increasing motivation as well as establishing a link back to the physical world.

Figure 2. A Monsterly Adventure in the Mountains: on a tablet, children read the study about the main character, Jonas, who is on his way to the mountains to search for a legendary monster. Children progress through the story by means of a physical game board (cf. Figure 3). The story is interlaced with physical tasks in the real world (see Figure 3–right).

TABOOGA – A HYBRID BOOK APP

The following section presents our design and development of an interactive ebook enhanced with tangibles (hybrid app).

Concept

In our work we adapt the concept of hybrid games, i.e. games where physical toys are combined with digital components. To support leisure reading, we created a digital reading app and augmented it with various physical elements, to support leisure reading. The physical elements are used for navigation and games related to the plot.

One challenge was to maintain the focus on the story and associated images, as known from traditional children's picture books. The reading content is presented to the children on a tablet. In addition to the app, a physical game board is provided (see Figure 3–left). It enables the reader to progress through the story and to flip pages of the digital book. In addition, the concept includes a number of tasks in the real world by means of pen and paper as well as by using LEGO bricks. Another challenge was to connect the tasks from the physical world with the digital reading app. This was done by enabling children to take photos of what they achieved in the real world (see Figure 1–c). These photos are embedded into the text.

The physical components are characters and elements of the story, that also appear in digital form. The plot called 'A Monsterly Adventure in the Mountains' revolves around the protagonist Jonas and his friend, the jackdaw-bird Petry (see Figure 2). They are on an adventure in the mountains, where they try to find and catch a famous monster out of legend. On their way, they need the help of the reader to progress up the mountain slopes (for example, building a bridge, catching a water flask from a river). In addition, the reader is provided hints about the monster's features (claws, horns, eyes and teeth), which are later used in a task where the monster has to be drawn. The story finally reveals the monster as the silhouette of four mountain animals, whose shadow resembles a monster.

Components

The hybrid app consists of one tangible element, two physical tasks, and two digital components.

The tangible element is a game board showing a mountain path where the figure of Jonas can be moved up and down (see Figure 3–left). The steps in the path mark the pages of the book: the further the figure moves on the mountain path, the further the story progresses. Making a step on the game board with the LEGO figure triggers a digital image of the walking Jonas on the tablet. This is an indicator of the story's overall progress and helps readers to understand how much of the story they have already finished.

Figure 3. Tangible game elements: to progress through the story (flip pages), children need to move a physical representation of the main character on a game board (left). In addition, the story is interlaced with task, such as building a bridge using LEGO bricks (right).

Two physical tasks help Jonas to progress in the story. First, the reader has to build a LEGO bridge to aid the protagonist (see Figure 3–right). The second physical task is to draw their version of the monster Jonas and his bird encounter (cf. Figure 5). These tasks are solved with everyday objects such as bricks, pencil, and paper. The goal is to encourage imagination and creativity among the children – two aspects of reading that need to be present for enjoying and comprehending stories [27]. To establish a connection between the real-world task and the app, the children are required to take a picture of both the bridge and the monster using the book app. The picture is integrated with the story (see Figure 1–c).

Finally, there are two digital components. One is a backpack (see Figure 4–left) that is filled with hints or helpful gear to solve riddles and tasks. In this hybrid app, the backpack contains the hints about the monster Jonas collects on his way up the mountain. The children can look at the backpack's contents when drawing their version of the monster. This helps weak readers to remember parts of the story that happened some time ago. The second digital component are three 'mini-games' that have to be solved to continue the story (see Figure 4). Their

Figure 4. Two digital components support the reading task. First, the contents of the backpack (left) help readers during their task of drawing the monster, by providing hints that were presented throughout the story on the monster's appearance. Second, three mini-games interlace the content to further increase motivation – a puzzle, a skill game, and a navigation game.

purpose is to increase the reading motivation through gaming actions, known to the children from many apps. In particular the games include a cave game, where children need to navigate through a dark cave, a skill game, where children need to fish a bottle out of the water, and a puzzle game, where children need to solve a puzzle depicting a signpost.

Implementation

The book app and the digital components were implemented using SenchaTouch[1]. To gain access to the native components of the smart phone or tablet (i.e. the camera that was required to include pictures from the real-world tasks with the story) we used the Cordova API[2]. To control the app through the figure being moved on the game board, we connected the Arduino board integrated with the game board to the app using a NodeJS server running on a local computer which read data from the Arduino from serial line. Every time a contact on the game board was closed by the game figure, the actual position was sent to the book app.

EVALUATION

We evaluated the hybrid app to understand the impact on the children's reading motivation and behavior. In particular, we were interested in the influence of reading skills. Since reading motivation often correlates with reading skills, we compared rather struggling (weak) and strong readers.

Study Design

An increase in motivation is more important for struggling readers than for the group of strong readers, because improved reading skills have been shown to persist in the long-term. To measure an abstract concept like 'motivation' we assessed how many of the text passages were read. If no parts were skipped and the focus of attention remained on the story itself, a high reading motivation was assumed. In particular, we investigated whether the students were *reading*, *partly reading* or *not reading* at all. Furthermore, reactions towards the hybrid app were considered: Was there *laughing* or *help needed* and which *kind of remarks* were given? In addition, we collected interaction data with the hybrid app. Interaction could be *effective* or *exploratory* and, since we let participants act in teams, there could be *single* and *team* interaction.

In addition we captured reading and gaming affinity, age, gender and a migratory background.

[1] `https://www.sencha.com/products/touch`

[2] `https://cordova.apache.org/`

Recruiting

For the study, we decided to recruit children from primary schools. This provided us the opportunity to let teachers assess participants' reading skills (se below). All in all 22 children were recruited in two schools – one in a rural and one in an urban area – for participating in the evaluation. Experiments were conducted onsite. The children were aged seven to nine, among them twelve girls and ten boys. Thirteen of them were eight years old, one girl aged seven and eight children were nine years old. 41% of students had a migrant background.

Procedure

At the outset, children were introduced to the procedure and their role in the investigation. We had teams of two children reading together to make them feel comfortable and also to provoke conversation between the students that we envisioned to yield further insights.

The procedure of the study was split into three parts. At the beginning, demographic questions were asked. Details about gender, age and migrant background were collected. We also asked about children's behaviour with books, tablets and smart phones in their spare time. Afterwards, children were asked to read the story using our hybrid app. Teams were mixed, i.e. we had teams consisting of one strong and one weak reader as well as teams consisting of two strong or two weak readers. To observe influences on behavior, we did not further specify how they should read the text (alone silently or together). There was no interruption by the experimenter, except for cases where children got stuck and explicitly requested help. Finally, we had children rate the reading app with regard to different aspects. Furthermore, their favourite media for reading stories was investigated. To verify the children's understanding of the story, each of them had to answer three contextual questions.

With the consent of the parents, children were video-recorded during the whole study to collect and later transcribe actions, reactions, questions, answers, and behavior. For 20 of the children we were granted permission to video-tape the experiment.

Results

In a first step, we identified strong and weak readers in our sample. This was done by assessing their reading preferences, evaluation of their teachers, and the difficulty of their favourite book. For example, some preferred rather simple books, such as 'Coconut – The little dragon', whereas others stated 'Harry Potter' to be their favourite book. Overall we classified 7 out of the 22 children as weak readers.

Figure 5. Examples of the monsters drawn by the children. During the story, several hints were presented as to how the monsters looked like. We assessed how many of the hints presented throughout the story were included in the drawing (claws, teeth, horns, eyes).

Quantitative Findings

Weak and strong readers had different preferences with regard to their preferred media for reading stories (options included ebooks, book apps, traditional paper books, and hybrid apps). Among the weak readers, only 20% preferred paper books, whereas 50% of the stronger readers preferred paper books.

From the questions on the content of the story presented through our hybrid app, strong readers could answer slightly more questions correctly. The children from this group answered on average 2.6 out of 3 questions completely correctly, whereas the group of weak readers only answered 1.6 questions completely correctly. In the group of weaker readers, about 50% of the questions were answered partly correctly.

Furthermore, we assessed the degree to which children understood the story by evaluating their drawings (see Figure 5). As previously mentioned, the story contained four hints about the monster's features (claws, horns, eyes, and teeth). Hints were included in the text itself. In addition, little picture items could be collected by tapping on them. Teeth (13 of 22 drawings), claws (17) and eyes (22) were contained in almost every drawing. The horns were included only twice.

In total, we collected 227 remarks by children. Out of these 60% were *positive* or *constructive remarks*. Most remarks occurred during one of the mini games where the children had to navigate Jonas through a digital cave. This seemed to be the most difficult task to solve. Most *constructive remarks* (24) were provided during drawing the monster.

We found that weak readers read on average 71% of all pages, whereas strong readers read 96% of the pages.

Finally we looked into how children interacted with each other during the reading task. Interaction differed between digital and physical tasks. Interaction with LEGO bricks and drawings was mostly conducted in teams. Collecting digital items in the virtual backpack had a high *exploratory* component. All in all, 75 out of 88 hints where successfully collected. On 8% of all book pages *help* from the observers was needed.

Qualitative Findings

We made a number of observations during the evaluation. We noticed *differences between the urban and rural students*. The story contained an allusion to a local country legend which was recognized by one child. Furthermore, all rural students were able to name the four animals in the story correctly, whereas only one urban child knew the correct name of the 'alpine ibex'. For most of the urban children this animal was a 'goat'. Urban children also called Jonas' companion (a jackdaw) 'raven' or 'crow', as they knew these birds from every day life.

Children mostly read the story by themselves. With regard to the *interaction between children*, the faster reader usually asked once finished 'Are you done?'. In most cases the other child would negate and continue reading. This was interesting, as weak readers often simulate equal reading skills to other children [27]. This finding suggests a high motivation to carefully read the story.

We received several recommendations about possible *extensions of the hybrid app* in the future. Children would have liked to have more possibilities to interact with digital elements of the hybrid app. This seems to come from their earlier experiences with apps in general and has not happened a few years back, when smart phones and tablets where not so popular yet [16]. Furthermore, some of the children did not follow the mountain trail on the game board in a linear order but investigated what happens once they jump to other fields. This was technically possible, but mixed up the order of the story. A future version could either keep track of the already read pages and notify children about their mistake. Or this exploratory behavior could be exploited by designing a story with several options where the part branches and children could decide which route to take.

SUMMARY & DISCUSSION

All in all, our investigation showed that hybrid apps have a high potential to support reading motivation, in particular for struggling readers. Access to tablets and smart phones increased over the last years. As a result, most of the children had previous experience with these devices and favourite games they liked to play on them [11]. Most struggling readers chose the digital or hybrid variant as their favourite kind of experiencing stories.

The connection between story and physical tasks turned out to be particularly useful. The fact that the entire story had to be read in order to successfully solve the tasks / games led to 75% of the weak readers reading all pages to the end. Hence, in the follow-up questions also weak readers had a good understanding of the story's content and could answer them well. We conclude that during the design of hybrid apps an emphasise needs to be put on the connection of story and tangible elements in a way such that proper reading is motivated.

Interesting to note was the willingness of the team mates to wait for the slower reader to finish reading the page. We take this as an indicator for a strong interest in the story. Only through strong interest in stories, a kind of flow experience and curiosity about the content, characters, and suspense, a reader can achieve a higher reading motivation [27] . It seems that the combination of an easy access through digital media, general interest in games and experiencing a story can lead to more motivation for reading literature.

The group of strong readers also reported a positive experience with the hybrid app. Eight out of thirteen strong readers referred to both digital and physical games or tasks as their favourite elements in the hybrid app. For them the combination between tangible and digital parts added to their positive attitude towards reading through all kinds of media.

Reading itself is per definition a silent and individual activity, but by including games and tasks it may become teamwork and be shared with friends on a different level than traditional books. This could be pursued and intensified through hybrid apps that can only be solved by four hands instead of two.

The children easily adopted and liked the combination of digital and tangible elements [10]. Even if controlling action on the tablet with an external game figure was new to them, almost all teams quickly understood the concept. At the beginning of the story there is only a picture of Jonas in the app, telling the children to grab the game figure and move it forward. As they were obviously used to digital actions being triggered on the graphical user interface, many children tried to move the digital version of Jonas. The physical game board was easily visible, but not all of the students made the logical connection instantly. Yet, as soon as they were acquainted with the concept, they could easily handle figure and board.

The children merely had to be reminded of the LEGO bricks, papers and pencils to be used for some tasks. Taking a photo to transfer their creations to the digital world was always combined with many remarks. Two of the children for example wondered: ‘Is our stair high enough to bring Jonas up the rock?’. That is a clear sign that the students could combine the digital with the real world in their imagination and actions.

The success of such a concept depends on the acceptance of the parents. Parents have a strong influence on their children’s choice of literature and are equally responsible for increasing reading motivation. Understandably, some parents do not want their children to spend too much time with digital devices, as it shortens their time spent with the development of motoric and haptic abilities [24]. Time in front of TV, computers, or tablets is therefore often restricted. Here a combination of digital devices with tangible elements may convince parents to encourage reading using hybrid apps as well.

LIMITATIONS

We are aware of several limitations of our study. First, the hybrid app was a new concept for all participating children. This may have sparked their curiosity and have been served as an additional motivating factor. Second, we only focused on a particular age group of children (7–9 years) that already had a certain reading proficiency. It is not clear how the concept would be taken up by younger children Future work could investigate a ‘read along feature’. Third, we deliberately kept games and tasks simple. Future work could investigate more complex games and tasks for more experienced readers as well as an adaptation of the task to the gender of the readers. Fourth, it remains to be investigated how motivation is affected as children do not read in teams but alone. Yet, reading in teams occurs frequently, for example among siblings.

CONCLUSION

In this work we presented TaBooGa, a hybrid reading app for children. We reported on the design and evaluation of the application among 22 children, aged 7 to 9 years. We found that the combination of reading on a tablet combined with tangible elements that were carefully integrated with the story had a positive influence on reading motivation as well as interplay and behavior of both strong and weak readers.

We believe our results to be interesting for the designers of hybrid apps, since they point to challenges and opportunities in the design of such apps. In future work we plan to test how the concept can be applied to children of different age groups and gender and how individuals would use the application.

With our work, and in particular the combinations of physical and digital elements, we hope to have taken a first step towards a new class of systems that encourage literacy. In this way we want to trigger a discussion in the IDC community as well as motivate work on novel applications that cater to changes in children’s reading behavior as a result of digital technology being available to them from early on.

ACKNOWLEDGEMENTS

We would like to thank the pupils and teachers of the Grundschule Surberg in Traunstein, Germany as well as of the Haus für Kinder Hinterbärenbadstrasse in Munich, Germany for their participation and support of this research. Furthermore, we would like to thank Janika Linke for sketching the illustrations, Christian Linke for his help while building the game board as well as Viola Linke and Claus Prokscha for their help during the evaluation.

REFERENCES

1. Alissa N. Antle, Jillian L. Warren, Emily S. Cramer, Min Fan, and Brendan B. Matkin. 2016. Designing Tangibles for Children: One Day Hands-on Workshop. In *Proceedings of the The 15th International Conference on Interaction Design and Children (IDC ’16)*. ACM, New York, NY, USA, 726–730. DOI: http://dx.doi.org/10.1145/2930674.2932223
2. Richard Bamberger. 2000. *Erfolgreiche Leseerziehung in Theorie und Praxis*. Schneider Hohengehren, Wien.
3. Lizzy Bleumers, Karen Mouws, Jonathan Huyghe, Maarten Van Mechelen, Ilse Mariën, and Bieke Zaman. 2015. Sensitivity to Parental Play Beliefs and Mediation in Young Children’s Hybrid Play Activities. In *Proceedings of the 14th International Conference on Interaction Design and Children (IDC ’15)*. ACM, New York, NY, USA, 170–177. DOI: http://dx.doi.org/10.1145/2771839.2771857

4. buchreport.de. 2015. Cornelsen-Studie zur Medienausstattung an Schulen. `https://www.buchreport.de/2015/05/26/cornelsen-studie-zur-medienausstattung-an-schulen/`. (2015). (last accessed 24.4.2017).

5. Christina Clark and Kate Rumbold. 2006. *Reading for Pleasure: A research Overview*. Technical Report.

6. Luca Colombo and Monica Landoni. 2011. Towards an Engaging e-Reading Experience. In *Proceedings of the 4th ACM Workshop on Online Books, Complementary Social Media and Crowdsourcing (BooksOnline '11)*. ACM, New York, NY, USA, 61–66. DOI: `http://dx.doi.org/10.1145/2064058.2064074`

7. Luca Colombo, Monica Landoni, and Elisa Rubegni. 2014. Design Guidelines for More Engaging Electronic Books: Insights from a Cooperative Inquiry Study. In *Proceedings of the 2014 Conference on Interaction Design and Children (IDC '14)*. ACM, New York, NY, USA, 281–284. DOI: `http://dx.doi.org/10.1145/2593968.2610472`

8. Simone Ehmig and Bettina Müller. 2012. *Vorlesestudie 2012: Digitale Angebote - neue Reize für das Vorlesen?: Repräsentative Befragung von Eltern und Kindern im Alter von 2 bis 8 Jahren*. Technical Report.

9. Min Fan, Alissa N. Antle, and Emily S. Cramer. 2016. Design Rationale: Opportunities and Recommendations for Tangible Reading Systems for Children. In *Proceedings of the The 15th International Conference on Interaction Design and Children (IDC '16)*. ACM, New York, NY, USA, 101–112. DOI: `http://dx.doi.org/10.1145/2930674.2930690`

10. Min Fan, Alissa N. Antle, Maureen Hoskyn, Carman Neustaedter, and Emily S. Cramer. 2017. Why Tangibility Matters: A Design Case Study of At-Risk Children Learning to Read and Spell. In *Proceedings of the 2017 SIGCHI Conference on Human Factors in Computing Systems (CHI'17)*. ACM, New York, NY, USA.

11. Sabine Feierabend, Theresa Plankenhorn, and Thomas Rathgeb. 2014. *KIM-Studie 2014, Kind + Medien + Computer + Internet, Basisuntersuchung zum Medienumgang 6- bis 13-Jähriger in Deutschland*. Technical Report 10. Medienpädagogischer Forschungsverbund Südwest.

12. George W. Fitzmaurice and William Buxton. 1997. An Empirical Evaluation of Graspable User Interfaces: Towards Specialized, Space-multiplexed Input. In *Proceedings of the ACM SIGCHI Conference on Human Factors in Computing Systems (CHI '97)*. ACM, New York, NY, USA, 43–50. DOI: `http://dx.doi.org/10.1145/258549.258578`

13. Dagmar Holzmann-Witschas and Magdalena Güttler. 2012. Geschlechtersensible Leseförderung in einem offenen Literaturunterricht. (2012). unpublished manuscript.

14. Hiroshi Ishii and Brygg Ullmer. 1997. Tangible Bits: Towards Seamless Interfaces Between People, Bits and Atoms. In *Proceedings of the ACM SIGCHI Conference on Human Factors in Computing Systems (CHI '97)*. ACM, New York, NY, USA, 234–241. DOI: `http://dx.doi.org/10.1145/258549.258715`

15. Janio Jadan-Guerrero, Javier Jaen, María A. Carpio, and Luis A. Guerrero. 2015. Kiteracy: A Kit of Tangible Objects to Strengthen Literacy Skills in Children with Down Syndrome. In *Proceedings of the 14th International Conference on Interaction Design and Children (IDC '15)*. ACM, New York, NY, USA, 315–318. DOI: `http://dx.doi.org/10.1145/2771839.2771905`

16. Tina Kothe, Anja Mohr, and Ida Buchwald. 2014. Art Education in the Digital World. A Picture Book as App.. In *IBOOC2014 - 2nd Workshop on Interactive eBooks for Children (IDC '14)*. ACM, New York, NY, USA, 281–284. `http://idc2014-ebooks.fbk.eu/sites/idc2014-ebooks.fbk.eu`

17. Alexis R. Lauricella, Rachel Barr, and Sandra L. Calvert. 2014. Parent-child interactions during traditional and computer storybook reading for children's comprehension: Implications for electronic storybook design. *International Journal of Child-Computer Interaction* 2, 1 (2014), 17 – 25. DOI: `http://dx.doi.org/10.1016/j.ijcci.2014.07.001`

18. Aurélien Lucchi, Patrick Jermann, Guillaume Zufferey, and Pierre Dillenbourg. 2010. An Empirical Evaluation of Touch and Tangible Interfaces for Tabletop Displays. In *Proceedings of the Fourth International Conference on Tangible, Embedded, and Embodied Interaction (TEI '10)*. ACM, New York, NY, USA, 177–184. DOI: `http://dx.doi.org/10.1145/1709886.1709917`

19. Nadia Mana, Ornella Mich, Antonella De Angeli, and Allison Druin. 2013. Interactive e-Books for Children. In *Proceedings of the 12th International Conference on Interaction Design and Children (IDC '13)*. ACM, New York, NY, USA, 593–595. DOI: `http://dx.doi.org/10.1145/2485760.2485886`

20. Paul Marshall. 2007. Do Tangible Interfaces Enhance Learning?. In *Proceedings of the 1st International Conference on Tangible and Embedded Interaction (TEI '07)*. ACM, New York, NY, USA, 163–170. DOI: `http://dx.doi.org/10.1145/1226969.1227004`

21. Amelia K. Moody. 2010. Using Electronic Books in the Classroom to Enhance Emergent Literacy Skills in Young Children. *Journal of Literacy and Technology* 11 (November 2010), 23–52.

22. Jule Ostrop. 2010. Literarisches Lernen mit dem Grüffelo. *Praxis Grundschule* 2010, 6 (2010), 9 – 12.

23. Ana Lúcia Pinto. 2014. Touch, read and play: enhancing the reading experience of hybrid-enhanced children's picturebooks. In *Proceedings of the 13th Conference on Interaction design and children (IDC'14)*. ACM, New York, NY, USA.

24. Jenny S. Radezky, Jayna Schuhmacher, and Barry Zuckerman. 2015. Mobile and Interactive Media Use by Young Children: the Good, the Bad and the Unknown. *Pediatrics* 135, 1 (2015). DOI: http://dx.doi.org/10.1542/peds.2014-2251

25. Elisa Rubegni and Monica Landoni. 2014. Fiabot!: Design and Evaluation of a Mobile Storytelling Application for Schools. In *Proceedings of the 2014 Conference on Interaction Design and Children (IDC '14)*. ACM, New York, NY, USA, 165–174. DOI: http://dx.doi.org/10.1145/2593968.2593979

26. Susanne Seitinger, Elisabeth Sylvan, Oren Zuckerman, Marko Popovic, and Orit Zuckerman. 2006. A New Playground Experience: Going Digital?. In *CHI'06 Extended Abstracts on Human Factors in Computing Systems (CHI EA'06)*. ACM, New York, NY, USA, 303–308. DOI: http://dx.doi.org/10.1145/1125451.1125520

27. Kaspar H. Spinner. 2006. Literarisches Lernen. *Praxis Deutsch* 2006, 200 (2006), 6 – 16.

Creating Environmental Awareness with Upcycling Making Activities: A Study of Children in Germany and Palestine

Anne Weibert, Marios Mouratidis, Renad Khateb,
Sarah Rüller, Miriam Hosak, Shpresa Potka, Konstantin Aal, Volker Wulf
University of Siegen
Siegen, Germany
{firstname.lastname}@uni-siegen.de

ABSTRACT
This study explores the development of environmental awareness and computational literacy among children by means of upcycling making activities in Germany and Palestine. Our research supports the idea that the combination of handcraft and digital work, documentation and social interaction in the upcycling can foster the development of a maker identity in children. Findings indicate that upcycling can sensitize children for environmental issues of global relevance, foster their environmental learning and encourage them in the exploration of creative answers.

Author Keywords
Children; Computer Club; Environment; Intercultural; Learning; Making; Upcycling.

ACM Classification Keywords
H.5.m. Information interfaces and presentation (e.g., HCI); K.3.2 Computers and education, literacy.

INTRODUCTION
A large problem of modern society is waste production. As products are innovated in high frequency and product lifecycles are short, consumer products – be it smartphones, computers, household items or furniture – become quickly "out-of-date" and obsolete [13]. Product packaging further aggravates the issue. In 2014 Germany produced more than 1.7 mio. tons of e-waste [7]. With most consumer electronics being affordable and repairing being time-consuming and more expensive than replacement, societies have developed throw-away habits, not reflecting on consequences. In response to this, upcycling has become a movement, working on strategies to repurpose, repair or modify things. The DIY maker community has been "hacking" products to appropriate them for specific uses, giving old objects new meaning instead of throwing them away (e.g. [11]). These initiatives have not (yet) reached mainstream society level [33]. We propose that especially from the young makers' perspective, upcycling can be a means to learn about environmental resources [e.g. 32]. By promoting creative interactions with technologies as well as collaborative agendas between individuals engaged in making [30,36], an environment is generated that supports "alternative framings of the user as creative appropriator, hacker, tinkerer, artist, and even co-designer or co-engineer" [34:2609]. Thus, creative ways of coping with environmental issues are fostered. A bottom up making approach can be a fruitful way to educate children with regard to environmental issues, and to empower them in the design of creative responses to these challenges. This paper's contribution is a study of computer clubs in Germany and Palestine, where upcycling is explored as a means to foster environmental awareness among young children. Our research shows how the combination of handcraft and digital work, documentation and social interaction in upcycling can foster the development of a maker identity in children. Upcycling, we argue, not only sensitizes children and fosters their environmental learning, but encourages them in the exploration of creative answers.

IDC '17, June 27-30, 2017, Stanford, CA, USA

ACM 978-1-4503-4921-5/17/06…$15.00
http://dx.doi.org/10.1145/3078072.3079732

RELATED WORKS
Tangibles and aspects of materiality have been approached from various angles in HCI and beyond, prominently among them child learning. Our work is linking these discourses in our study of upcycling as a means to foster environmental awareness among young children.

Making, Recycling and Upcycling
Making is concerned with creating an object by shaping or changing materials, combining or re-arranging parts [18]. Blikstein and Krannich [10] focus on educational benefits introducing Maker Spaces as places that expose learners to handcraft, computation, engineering and maths. While 'recycling' is a common term, 'upcycling' is rather new. The Oxford Dictionary has backtraced it to the 1990s, describing it to result from the blending of the two words up- and recycling, and to be concerned with reuse of "(discarded objects or material) in a way as to create a product of higher quality or value than the original". Recycling is the process of "destroying" the original product so the material it is made of can be re-used as a resource [35]. Santulli and Langella portray upcycling projects [30], focusing on local waste and linking designs to local culture and habits. Ali et al. (2013) study upcycling as

a sustainable approach of giving 'waste' new value without degrading the original material [3].

Learning with Tangibles

Tangibles as objects to learn with promote cognitive development triggered through children's interactions with them, e.g. in play. Also, they support "discovery learning" [14]. Building on previous research with e-textiles [40], we propose that tangible upcycling artefacts can foster meaning-making among children engaged in their playful creation. The creative aspect immanent to this encompasses decisions about materials and experiences [16:282]. Previous research on e-textiles has found tangibles to enable alternate ways of learning, skill building [41:284], and problem solving [26]. Tangibles support children's need to combine physical and mental activity in learning [5], e.g. to support literacy learning [21]. Differentiation between concrete objects and their abstraction sophisticates' cognitive development and engagement in epistemic actions [4]. Physical computational artifacts can promote "interest, engagement and understanding" [14:54] in children. Research in IDC has explored means to foster computational learning and programming skills in children (e.g. [12,17]). Tinkering learners [8] make use "of "just in time" resources and feedback to guide the next steps in their exploration of the problem space" [22:49].

Environmental Learning and ICT

Scientific discourse on environmental learning unfolds along the lines of a) teaching programming, and b) upcycling and making. Various works have set out to foster child learning about scientific phenomena like evolutionary change using computational modeling environments (e.g. [17,37]). Also, researchers pursued the reverse way, linking programming concepts to phenomena from nature to introduce basic programming logic [36]. Björkvall and Archer (2016) studied the re-contextualization of resources in global consumption ecologies [9]. Applying their insights to education, they found the design element in upcycling to be supportive to the education of global critical citizens.

METHODS

Our study of upcycling project work with children in computer clubs is predicated on the idea of participatory action research. This entails social science research methods and commitment to participation with dis-privileged or marginal groups [24]. To achieve this in our study, qualitative methods are used, and field notes are relied on as part of the participatory action research [20] perspective. Field notes are the main resource for the study presented here, supplemented by the artifacts and accompanying digital multimedia stories created in the project. Members of the research team are active participants in the computer clubs where they routinely act as tutors. The clubs are where the upcycling activities took place. Field notes were taken by the tutors during the weekly sessions, and have afterwards been documented in a formal protocol. Their focus: observable collaborations and interactions of the kids, their appropriation of media and computer technology in relation to the (upcycling) project work, and associated processes of learning.

The Setting: Intercultural Computer Clubs

The come_IN computer clubs provide open, yet guided access to information and computer technologies and related skills for often marginalized groups in intercultural neighbourhoods. Thus, the clubs a) contribute to a bridging of the 'digital divide' [25], and b) foster integration processes (e.g. [31,39]). Hence, come_IN computer clubs build on the US concept of computer clubhouses (e.g.[19]).

Computer Club A

This computer club is located in an elementary school of a large city in the Ruhr Area in Germany. It is based in a district with high population density, young age structure, and cultural diversity (~58% of the population with immigrant background). High unemployment rates, low wages, among other obstacles, make access to higher education difficult. Immigrant backgrounds in the club mirror the district's diversity. Participants' backgrounds are from Albania, Macedonia, Morocco, Tunisia and Turkey.

Computer Club B

The computer club is located in a Palestinian refugee camp embedded in a Palestinian city [1,2,42,43]. The camp was established in 1949, built on land which is leased by the UNRWA from the Hashemite Kingdom of Jordan. The camp population was deported or fled from a nowadays Israeli area, during the Arab-Israeli War in 1948. High population density (72,916/km^2) [43] and precarious living conditions characterize the camp [27]. Interactions between refugee population and the surrounding society is scarce. Due to the political and socio-economic situation, club sessions sometimes get cancelled. Israeli Defense Forces occasionally close down the camp. In winter, it might be too cold to work in the club room, which has no heating.

Our Project Activities

The core activity unfolded over the course of six sessions, followed by a period of collaboration and exchange about the results and related experiences and learning.

Core Activity Computer Club A

In computer club A in Germany, ten kids (5 girls/5 boys) took part in the upcycling. The project was accompanied by a teacher and two tutors, who provided guidance and assisted with the making tasks. Artefacts included a cardboard racing car with a balloon engine, a fabric doll, a jam jar snow globe and a plastic cup telephone (Figure 1). The first session introduced the topic. A tutor had created examples of upcycling artefacts (a paper Alice band, a plastic bottle car, a plastic bag purse). The children were asked to guess the commonality among these. From there, the tutors directed the group towards brainstorming on materials. The kids left the session with the task to observe their daily lives, to see what kinds of waste are produced, and what could be made of them. The second session started with the children's presentation of their observations. Waste materials were listed, and the children teamed up to work on one material of their choice. They sketched construction ideas and listed tools needed. The third session was concerned with the creation of the projects. Tutors and teacher helped with constructions and tools. Kids documented the making with digital cameras.

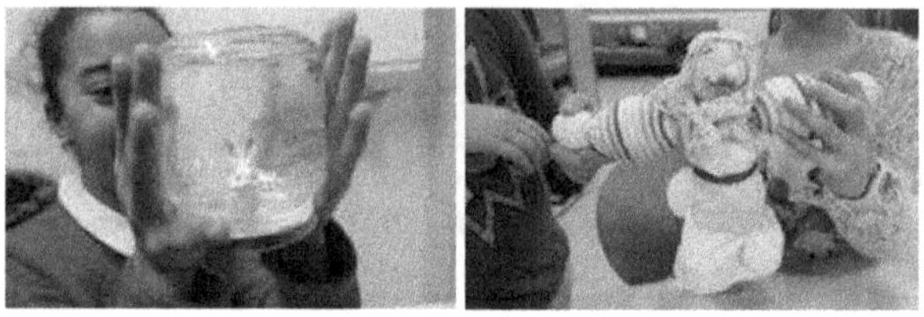

Figure 1. Upcycling artefacts from Computer Club A included a jam jar snow globe (left) and a fabric doll (right).

Children finalized the making of their artefacts in the fourth session. Then the group engaged in planning the digital upcycling stories. Kids learned about search engines in a game. Teams researched information about 'their' materials and processed this information in writing, which was finalized in the fifth and sixth session. Texts and images documenting the making were assembled as stories.

Core Activity Computer Club B

6-20 kids (~equally f/m) age 10-14, guided by two volunteer students participated in the activity in Club B. The resulting artefact was a two-seat bench made of plastic bottles and car tires (Figure 2). The kids got introduced to the idea of "making something" out of waste and the issue of it being on the streets was discussed. Children were asked to bring "useful" waste to the next session, where tutors handed them protective gloves for collecting material in the neighborhood. Afterwards they reflected upon the sourced material and its' reuse potential. In the next two sessions the kids engaged in ideation and reflection by playing word games. They also sketched buildable objects before deciding to build "something to sit on".

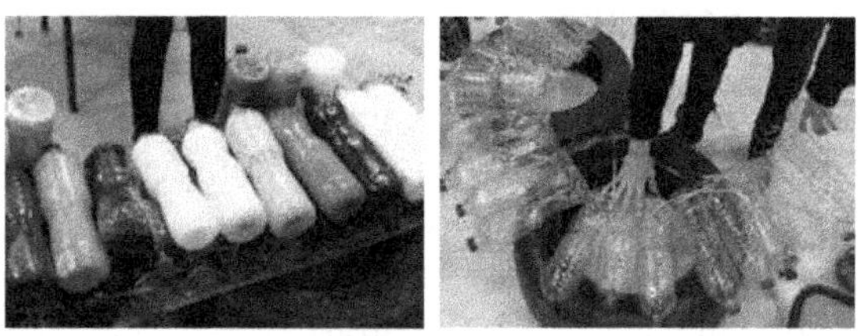

Figure 2. Club B made a bench from plastic bottles and tires.

The fifth workshop was about reflecting on the usability of a chair in general. Kids brainstormed problems with their club chairs and sketched prototypes before agreeing on a design and materials. In the last session, the chair was built.

Collaboration of Clubs

Over their upcycling artefacts, children from both computer clubs engaged in exchange and learning about living conditions and the environment. The exchange among the clubs is initialized by the tutors in club A. It starts with the children preparing a short greeting introducing their upcycling stories. Those are sent via email and the initiative triggers a video "conversation" among the clubs. The kids exchange motivations for their upcycling projects, information about themselves and their environments, their living conditions, and upcoming project ideas of their club.

Data Collection

Data basis for this study are field notes, images and artefacts. The researchers, who are also the authors of this paper, recorded extensive jottings as well as reflexive memos during the club activities. These were completed to full field notes right after each session. The entire upcycling activity was documented in digital images taken by the researchers, as well as by the children themselves. Finally, the upcycling artefacts were collected, as well as video and text messages exchanged about the upcycling and resulting artefacts among children of both clubs.

Data Analysis

Intercultural and environmental awareness were used as frames to examine collaboration and learning among the kids. Field notes were coded by the researchers looking for themes related to the concepts underpinning the shared acts of making and reflection. A qualitative and thematic analysis [15] was conducted that refined our initial open codes, and revealed three main themes that we isolated, *materiality*, *organization of work*, and *digital literacy*.

FINDINGS

Environmental awareness was the key analytical frame we used. Findings yielded *materiality* and *handcraft challenges*, *organization of work* and *structural thinking*, *collaboration*, *problem solving*, *digital literacy* and *privacy* as central topics.

Materiality

For the participants in both clubs, an exploration of materials marked the beginning of all subsequent project activity. For the children in club A, this meant engaging in observation of everyday routines: over their two-week fall vacation, the children observed what kinds of trash they produced, and where in their neighborhood they perceived waste as problematic. When these observations were then discussed, the kids linked them to ideas on what kinds of creations could possibly be created from these materials. This broad exploration refined when the children started focusing on a material's characteristics, e.g. by asking how paper needs to be bend to create a stable construction. Another example are two girls in Club A, tinkering with materials to create 'snow' for a snow globe in a jam jar.

Club B creatively reflected on trash in a wordplay: a piece of waste is handed from one kid to the next, each adding to its description (Boy 1: *"A green bottle."* Boy 2: *"A green bottle with a blue label."* Girl 1: *"A green bottle with a blue label and a lid."*) Thus, children got to pay attention to details, and think about (waste) material characteristics.

Handcraft challenges

In line with previous research [40], children demonstrated a lack of knowledge using tools. This held with sophisticated tools like paper cutters, but also with commonly used tools like scissors. Tutors provided help, and encouraged the kids to explore the specificities of each tool (Girl 1: "*How can we make a hole in a glass? Drill it?*" Tutor: *"No. Glass can only be reshaped when melted at a very high temperature.*") In tasks like cutting paper or using hot glue, the children were still developing their fine motor skills, at times struggling to realize the constructions they had drafted. Again, tutors provided guidance and support when needed.

Organization of Work

Organization of work unfolded along the lines of *structural thinking*, *collaboration* and *problem solving*.

Structural Thinking

When asked to draw their ideas, children would sketch with regard to previously sourced material. A team of girls in Club A quickly discovered that it can be useful to structure their sketch using different colors. Field notes report them to proceed in a very organized manner. First they just list materials in the order they come to their minds. But then one girl suggested to make a drawing of the envisioned artefact and to label the parts with the materials they would later be made of. Girl: *"Yes – and we use different colors. Then we can see, what materials I can bring, and which ones you will bring."* The sketch, which looks like a simple drawing, is a construction plan highlighting assigned tasks.

Collaboration

From previous activities, children in both clubs were used to team up and help each other. Field notes report how girls and boys alike routinely look around in search of a peer who could help them, or are happy to provide help, when they see that this is needed. Especially the construction part of the upcycling is prompting collaboration. The kids enjoy discussing different solution, to engage in tinkering and try out multiple options when there is more than one solution.

In the collaborations, there was a strong link to aesthetics visible: kids were seen to identify 'experts' in the group who were known to be good at, e.g. drawing, or typing fast at the computer, or cutting clean with scissors), and making use of their expertise, whenever they thought they wouldn't be able to complete a task in the same skillful way, so it would hurt the aesthetics of their artefact if they tried.

By collaborating across club and country boundaries, the children learned how waste is a global problem that comes with different local specifications. The water supply in Palestine is limited and controlled by Israel, in the context of the conflict it is a valuable resource [6]. Thus, having to clean materials was not an option for Palestinian children, they seemed however unaware of that, a boy brought some empty bottles and tomato cans: *"My mother made pizza and I took the cans and cleaned them."* The kids where advised not to wash material, but rather *"look for clean material"*.

Problem Solving

Problem solving in the project activity was concerned with a) finding solution for challenges in the making, and b) discussing strategies for a contribution they could make in their everyday lives as children to an overall solution of the global issue of waste production. The first aspect was visible especially during the initial exploration of materials and their characteristics. This was the case, e.g. when a team of boys in Club A was discussing options for the construction of wheels and 'engine' of their cardboard car. They restart a construction drawing several times, erasing it and sketching something new on top. They comment their drawings loudly, explaining how they envision materials to behave. The second aspect unfolded, e.g. when children in Club A learned that all plastic bags used in Germany over the course of one year sum up to an amount that is enough to be wrapped around the equator 46 times. Impressed by the number, the group engages in a discussion about how they could help reduce the number of plastic bags used (e.g. *"Use a real backpack instead."*). Developed solutions later become a part of the children's digital upcycling stories.

Digital literacy

As the searching of information online was important in the upcycling, tutors in Club A approached this in a role play.

> Tutor: *"Shall we play search engine?"* The tutor lets one girl be the search engine and explains to the rest of the group: *"Imagine, you are now all websites."* Giggeling, as the tutor poses a search request: "*Give me all websites with blue pullovers.*" More giggling, as the girl points to all kids in blue pullovers. Tutor: *"How did you know, whom to pick?"* Girl: *"I could see that."*
>
> The group talks about how a search engine does exactly this: search for the obvious. In a second round of play, the task is to find *"all children who are in the same class"*. The boy, who is now the search engine doesn't know the answer, because he doesn't know the group too well. So the group comes to talk about how there are hidden search criteria that can be in a website.
>
> The last task is to *"Find the teacher."* The tutor tells the kids that now they are all search engines, and they should all point their finger to indicate the answer. As all children point to the teacher, tutors explain how similarly, a search engine also looks for links between pages, thus ranking results as more or less 'trustworthy'. Finally, tutors create awareness how internet content can usually not be taken and reused without permission.

Subsequent sessions see the information that was embedded in this play be used, as the children seek the information needed for their upcycling stories. Awareness for digital ownership was deepened when the kids teamed up for creation of their digital stories. Here, children were eager to point out what share in the story they had created. Digital literacy in Club A was further refined when the kids engaged in the creation of images. Resulting from the group's examination of search engines, the kids discussed how widely their stories would be circulated – and whether or not they wanted to be a recognizable part of these. The group was eager to capture the making and ensured that each kid would have an equal share in taking the images.

There is a playful aspect in developing digital literacy. As a lot of environmental information comes across abstract, tutors help the kids discovering how numbers can be 'translated', e.g. by putting the figure of 1.400 meters of paper per minute a papermaking machine can produce in perspective to the length of the children's way to school.

DISCUSSION

In line with earlier works on tangibles [14,16], our findings indicate that the tangible approach of environmental issues in the upcycling is apt to support acquiring of interdisciplinary knowledge in children: not only did they discover facts about materials; they also understood and applied basics of digital literacy, copyright and ownership of digital media, and gained basic understanding of privacy issues relevant to their digital work. Our findings reveal signs of an evolving environmental awareness in the children on multiple levels. First, identifying problems regarding waste in their lives, then by researching information on waste, they experienced these problems not as singular but as an issue of global relevance. This was further deepened by the exchange of upcycling experience and related learning among children in both clubs.

The overall structure of the upcycling activity, from sourcing over researching the material to the actual creation of the artefacts, has facilitated a sense of empowerment among the children. By adding value through acts of making to materials that would otherwise have been thrown away, children practically experienced how "change" can be possible. This involved an active take on the avoidance of waste, as well as a conscious contribution to the shaping of local living conditions. The latter was especially relevant with regard to the children from Club B: Throughout the upcycling activity the Palestinian children expressed multiple reasons to build a *"comfortable chair"*: living conditions in refugee camps are crowded, accommodations are used by larger, multi-generational families – there is not a lot of room to get comfortable. Their design of the water bottle bench was driven by the idea to create a *"feeling of sitting at the beach, because we cannot go there"*. Palestinians are not allowed to enter the Israeli territories which cover coasts at the Mediterranean and Red Sea and the kids are very aware of that. They felt empowered to not only change their environment (clean neighborhood) and build whatever they want (a bench) but also cope with their situation (living in a refugee camp in occupied territory).

The tangible upcycling encompasses creative decisions about materials based on experiences. Inherent to the exploration of and tinkering with [8,22] waste is a twofold learning experience, concerned with a) the value inherent to a material object, and b) material properties, relevant for the upcycling making and construction decisions. By extending these shared acts of exploration and tinkering to the digital world, a holistic approach to environmental learning is pursued and a sense of empowerment fostered in the young learners, who experience that change is feasible if approached in numerous small, creative steps.

CONCLUSION

Our study has shown how awareness for an environmental issue of global relevance can be fostered in a bottom up process. By exploring the development of environmental awareness as well as computational literacy in children through upcycling, our research supports the idea that the combination of handcraft and digital work, of documentation and social interaction is especially apt to foster the development of their identity as makers. We have shown that upcycling can sensitize children for environmental issues, foster their environmental learning and encourage them in the exploration of creative answers.

ACKNOWLEDGMENTS

Thank goes to all participants from the neighborhoods, helping us to implement our research approach and contributing to make computer club be a lively experience.

REFERENCES

1. Aal, K., Mouratidis, M., Weibert, A., & Wulf, V. (2016). Challenges of CI Initiatives in a Political Unstable Situation-Case Study of a Computer Club in a Refugee Camp. In *Proc. of GROUP*, 409-412.
2. Aal, K., Yerousis, G., Schubert, K., Hornung, D., Stickel, O., and Wulf, V. (2014). Come_in@ palestine: adapting a german computer club concept to a Palestinian refugee camp. *Proc. of CABS*, 111–120.
3. Ali, N. S., Khairuddin, N. F., & Abidin, S. Z. (2013). Upcycling: Re-use and recreate functional interior space using waste materials. In *15th Int. Conference on Engineering and Product Design Education.*
4. Andersen, K. (2004). 'Ensemble': playing with sensors and sound. In: *CHI Ext. Abstracts*, 1239-42.
5. Antle, A.N. (2007). The CTI framework: informing the design of tangible systems for children. *Proc. of TEI.*
6. Assaf, K., Attia, B., Darwish, A., Wardam, B., Klawitter, S., & II, A. (2004). Water as a Human Right: The Understanding of Water in Arab Countries of the Middle East. *Global Issue Papers, 11*, 168.
7. Baldé, C.P., Wang, F., Kuehr, R., Huisman, J. (2015). *The global e-waste monitor – 2014, United Nations University*, IAS – SCYCLE, Bonn, Germany.
8. Bevan, B., Gutwill, J. P., Petrich, M., & Wilkinson, K. (2015). Learning Through STEM-Rich Tinkering: Findings From a Jointly Negotiated Research Project Taken Up in Practice. *Science Education, 99*(1), 98-120.
9. Björkvall, A., & Archer, A. (2016). Ecologies of 'upcycling'as design for learning in Higher Education. In *Designs for Learning–5th International Conference.*
10. Blikstein, P., & Krannich, D. (2013). The makers' movement and FabLabs in education: experiences, technologies, and research. In *Proc. of IDC,* 613-616.

11. Buechley, L., Rosner, D.K., Paulos, E., & Williams, A. (2009). DIY for CHI: methods, communities, and values of reuse and customization. In *CHI Ext. Abstr.*, 4823-4826.

12. Chawla, K., Chiou, M., Sandes, A., & Blikstein, P. (2013). Dr. Wagon: a 'stretchable' toolkit for tangible computer programming. In *Proc. of IDC*, 561-564.

13. Cooper, T. (2005). Slower consumption reflections on product life spans and the "throwaway society". *Journal of Industrial Ecology*, *9*(1-2), 51-67.

14. Fails, J.A., Druin, A., Guha, M.L., Chipman, G., Simms, S., & Wayne C. (2005). Child's play. In: *Proc. of IDC*, 48-55.

15. Fereday, J., & Muir-Cochrane, E. (2006). Demonstrating rigor using thematic analysis: A hybrid approach of inductive and deductive coding and theme development. *Int. J. of qualitative methods*, *5*(1), 80-92.

16. Gross, S., Bardzell, J., Bardzell, S. (2013). Touch style: creativity in tangible experience design, in: *Proc. of C&C*, 281-290.

17. Guo, Y., Wagh, A., Brady, C., Levy, S. T., Horn, M. S., & Wilensky, U. (2016). Frogs to Think with: Improving Students' Computational Thinking and Understanding of Evolution in a Code-First Learning Environment. In *Proc. of IDC*, 246-254.

18. Hatch, M. (2013). *The maker movement manifesto: rules for innovation in the new world of crafters, hackers, and tinkerers*. McGraw Hill Professional.

19. Kafai, Y. B., Peppler, K. A., & Chapman, R. N. (2009). *The Computer Clubhouse: Constructionism and Creativity in Youth Communities.* Teachers College Pr.

20. Kemmis, S., McTaggart, R. (1988). *The action research planner*. Deakin University Press.

21. Kleiman, J., Pope, M., & Blikstein, P. (2013). RoyoBlocks: An exploration in tangible literacy learning. In *Proc. of IDC*, 543-546.

22. Lyons, L., Tissenbaum, M., Berland, M., Eydt, R., Wielgus, L., & Mechtley, A. (2015). Designing visible engineering: supporting tinkering performances in museums. In *Proc. of IDC*, 49-58.

23. Marshall, P. (2007). Do tangible interfaces enhance learning?, in: *Proc. of TEI*, 163-170.

24. McIntyre, A. (2008) *Participatory Action Research*. Sage.

25. Norris, P. (2001). *Digital Divide*. Cambridge Univ. Pr.

26. Orth, M., Post, R., Cooper, E. (1998). Fabric computing interfaces. In: *Proc. of CHI 1998,* 331-332.

27. Palestinian Central Bureau of Statistics. *Localities in Ramallah & Al Bireh Governorate by Type of Locality and Population Estimates, 2007-2016.* Online: http://www.pcbs.gov.ps/Portals/_Rainbow/Documents/ramallah.htm (Retrieved: 27.01.17)

28. Rode, J. A., Weibert, A., Marshall, A., Aal, K., von Rekowski, T., El Mimouni, H., & Booker, J. (2015). From computational thinking to computational making. In *Proc. of Ubicomp*, 239-250.

29. Rosner, D., & Bean, J. (2009). Learning from IKEA hacking: i'm not one to decoupage a tabletop and call it a day. In *Proc. of CHI,* 419-422.

30. Santulli, C., & Langella, C. (2013). '+ design–waste': a project for upcycling refuse using design tools. In *Int. Journal of Sustainable Design*, *2*(2), 105-127.

31. Schubert, K., Weibert, A. & Wulf, V. (2011). Locating computer clubs in multicultural neighborhoods: How collaborative project work fosters integration processes. *Int. J. of Human-Comp. Studies*, *69*(10), 669-678.

32. Seravalli, A. (2016). Making an upcycling station. *Report "Kvartersnära återbruks-central och makerskultur för integrerad social och ekologisk hållbarhet"*, Vinnova Social Innov. Program.

33. Silver, J. (2009). Awakening to Maker Methodology. In: *Proc. of IDC*, pp.242-5, ACM.

34. Tanenbaum, J. G., Williams, A. M., Desjardins, A., Tanenbaum, K. (2013). Democratizing technology: pleasure, utility and expressiveness in DIY and maker practice, in: *Proc. of CHI*, 2603-2612.

35. Terracycle. *Begriffe und Definitionen.* Online: http://www.terracycle.de/de/pages/recycling-begriffe-und-definitionen (Retrieved: 27.01.17).

36. Vallgårda, A., Boer, L., Tsaknaki, V., & Svanaes, D. (2016). Material Programming: A New Interaction Design Practice. In *Proc. of the Conf. Companion Publication on DIS*, 149-152.

37. Wagh, A., & Wilensky, U. (2013). Leveling the playing field: Making multi-level evolutionary processes accessible through participatory simulations. *CSCL,* Madison, Wisconsin.

38. Wang, T. and Kaye, J. J. (2011). Inventive Leisure Practices, in *Proc. of CHI*, 263-272.

39. Weibert, A. & Wulf, V. (2010). All of a sudden we had this dialogue...: intercultural computer clubs' contribution to sustainable integration. *Proc. of ICIC*, 93-102.

40. Weibert, A., Marshall, A., Aal, K., Schubert, K., Rode, J. (2014). Sewing interest in E-textiles: analyzing making from a gendered perspective. *Proc. of DIS*, 15-24.

41. Weinberg, G., Orth, M., & Russo, P. (2000). The Embroidered Musical Ball. In: *CHI Ext. Abstr.*, 283-4.

42. United Nations Relief and Work Agency. *Am'Ari Camp.* Online: https://www.unrwa.org/where-we-work/west-bank/amari-camp (Retrieved: 27.01.17)

43. Yerousis, G., Aal, K., von Rekowski, T., Randall, D. W., Rohde, M., & Wulf, V. (2015). Computer-enabled project spaces: Connecting with Palestinian refugees across camp boundaries. In *Proc. of CHI,* 3749-3758.

Where are the Glass-Boxes? Examining the Spectrum of Modularity in Physical Computing Hardware Tools

Kayla DesPortes
Georgia Institute of Technology
Atlanta, USA
ksdesportes@gatech.edu

Betsy DiSalvo
Georgia Institute of Technology
Atlanta, USA
bdisalvo@cc.gatech.edu

ABSTRACT
Teaching physical computing has become more prevalent in the past several decades as the maker movement has popularized microcontroller kits as a way to engage students in learning about and creating with technology. Depending on the design of the kit, students can be exposed to concepts in electronics, computer science and design of computational objects. We argue that the concepts students are exposed to depend on the modularity of the hardware and software tools. We define the level of modularity based on two interdependent characteristics: *transparency* and *affordances for interaction*. The transparency affects what is hidden or visible to the learner, while the affordances for interaction regulate how users manipulate and combine elements when constructing a computational artifact. Within this study, we examine the transparency and affordances for interaction of the physical computing hardware tools. Using our findings from this examination, we layout a framework that outlines spectrum of modularity that can be provided to facilitate learning with maker kits.

Author Keywords
Design for Learning; Microcontroller; Electronics; Physical Computing Education.

ACM Classification Keywords
K.3.2 Computer and Information Science Education: Computer science education, Information systems education.

INTRODUCTION
Physical computing in education dates back to the 1970s where early explorations showed promise for the domain to successfully enable students to think about complex ideas while working with tangible computing devices [4,21]. Since then, researchers, educators and designers have developed toolkits for children and hobbyists to work more easily with these devices. These various toolkits have gained popularity as a way to offer students multiple pathways to learn about computing (ex. [9,12,14]). The toolkits have hardware, giving the tool its tangibility, and software, giving the tool its ability to support interactive behavior. Depending on the tool, students can engage in the design of computational objects, explore the programming aspects, or learn about the electronics. The ability for the student to explore these domains is completely dependent on the modularity integrated into the design of the hardware and software tools. We use Sadler et al.'s definition of modularity, as the "ability to freely recombine elements" [23]. We characterize modularity by the *transparency*—what is visible or obscured from the learner—and the *affordances for interaction*—how learners can manipulate and combine the tools as they build computational objects. The effect of these two characteristics are inseparable—the transparency affects what the learner interacts with, and what she interacts with affects what is transparent to her.

While there are a range of physical computing toolkits out there (*see* [3,4] for a review), the modularity in the electronic elements often lies on two extremes. The hardware tools are either highly obscured, allowing students to plug-and-play them without learning about the electronics, or they are completely open-ended, with little scaffolding at all, creating a difficult learning environment for novices. While obscuring the electronics is a valid choice for some learning environments, it would be a lost opportunity if we ignored physical computing's capabilities to support pathways for students to explore the electronics. We draw attention to design decisions embedded in the modularity of the hardware tools to examine their ability to support learning.

RELATED WORK

Black-Box and Glass-Box Scaffolding
Design choices involving the modularity incorporated into maker kits can affect learning by providing different types of scaffolding for the learner. By supporting certain interactions and making certain concepts transparent, the modularity can facilitate learning. This study examines the range of scaffolding that the physical computing tools can provide from the perspective of Hemlo and Guzdial's concepts of *black-box* and *glass-box* scaffolding [16]. They describe black-box scaffolding as something that helps a student perform an action that they could not otherwise perform, while shielding them from having to learn about

IDC '17, June 27-30, 2017, Stanford, CA, USA

ACM 978-1-4503-4921-5/17/06…$15.00

how the scaffolding works. Conversely, glass-box scaffolding helps the student understand how the scaffolding works, while they learn how to "take on the functions that the glass-box scaffolding is providing" [16:p128]. They suggest, if it is unimportant for the student to learn about the work the scaffolding is doing, it should be black-boxed and not fade; however, if the function of the scaffolding is important for the student to learn, it should be glass-boxed and fade as the learner begins to do the task. In prior literature, scaffolding of hardware elements in physical computing is either fully black-boxed without a pathway for fading or there is little to no scaffolding [5]. This leaves us to wonder, *where are the glass-boxes?* And how can our scaffolding better support learning goals?

Previous Analyses of Physical Computing Tools

In one analysis of the physical computing tools, Blikstein and Sipitakiat categorized the tools into two main models: the *cricket model*—plug-and-play features that hide complexities in the electronics (ex. LittleBits); and the *breakout model*—open-ended designs that enable the user to extend functionality through interfacing with other electronics (ex. Arduino) [5]. The plug-and-play or *cricket models* enable users to explore various inputs and outputs to the microcontroller, but the electronics themselves are completely *black-boxed.* A prevalent argument against this model is that, "In packaging electronic components into higher-level modules, toolkits can obscure the technology they seek to make accessible" [17:83]. Conversely, the open-ended or *breakout models* are more complex. These solutions require that users combine individual electronic elements into circuits, understanding where the connections need to be made. The main argument against this model is that the difficulty is too high for novices, and it can therefore, create barriers to learning programming or design [4]. Other researchers have expressed similar concerns, arguing for tools that can scaffold students between these the two extremes [5,10,13].

In a later analysis, Blikstein argues for the importance of attention to the *selective exposure* embedded within the design choices of tools. Similar to the glass/black-box scaffolding, he discusses how what is visible and what is hidden determines the contrasting goals of *usability* and *power* [4]. He states, "Instead of exposing children to inadequate technologies, a more productive approach would be to identify the many toolkits that children should use throughout their school years, understand what each can accomplish, and task designers with the creation of better *bridges between toolkits*" [4:p60]. Our paper explores a way to conceptualize the design of these *bridges*.

ANALYZING MODULARITY

Segmenting the Hardware

In order to analyze the ability to create *bridges* between hardware tools, we segment the hardware into three categories: the electronic connectors, the programmable electronics, and the peripheral electronics.

Electronic Connectors

Within physical computing kits, researchers and designers have explored different methods for connecting and constructing circuits. The capabilities of these connections have been conceptualized based on their materiality and their ability to scaffold students. Eisenberg's (2002) examination of construction kits argues that the materials and their capabilities guide the user to certain creative possibilities based on the materials' affordances and constraints. He argues that this affects what the user experiments with and therefore learns about [15]. The materiality of physical computing kits has been explored by researchers and designers investigating materials such as thread [9], ink [17], stickers [22], play dough [24], fiber optics [15], magnets [2], etc. The material capabilities make certain domains more or less transparent to the learner. For example, the Chibitronics circuit sticker kits [22] might lead students to explore paper circuits while the LilyPad brings transparency to wearables.

The materiality also guides the permanence and therefore the learners' interactions as they experiment with the tools. With playdough circuits [24], one is able to continuously mold, reposition, and repurpose the dough. This stands in contrast to circuit stickers, which once laid are difficult to undo and reuse. While there is no empirical data on the differences between the modularity of these two models, research in other educational fields suggests that being able to receive feedback, reflect on mistakes, and iterate upon the design is an essential part of the learning process [25].

The types of connections can also affect students' interactions by determining how easily students can make connections to recombine elements. Chu et al. found that complex connectors were often misinterpreted by children and their motor skills impacted their ability to physically operate the connectors [11]. Blikstein takes a slightly different approach analyzing the connections through the lens of *embedded error correction* classifying tools based on their ability to guide students into making connections correctly and thus avoiding errors. He draws attention to the spectrum of design choices from *no error correction* (ex. LilyPad), to *guided error correction* where shapes help users make correct choices (ex. Phidgets), to *forced error correction* in the form of connectors that cannot be inserted incorrectly based on size, shape or capabilities (ex. LittleBits) [4]. Embedded error correction provides a range of modularity in the students' ability to know how and why to combine the elements together and the ease at which they can complete this. Embedded information can make interactions more seamless by scaffolding students to more rapidly combine elements with fewer mistakes. This enables rapid prototyping and opportunities to learn about design without the overhead of learning the electronics. However, embedded error correction decreases the transparency of the electronic connection. Tools like LittleBits and LEGO Mindstorms *black-box* much of the electronics and do not require students to think about *how* to connect the elements but instead whether they *can* connect them. This provides no visibility into how electricity is flowing through the elements and makes it difficult for students to learn anything about electronics.

On the flip side, when working with tools like the LilyPad Arduino that do not scaffold connections, students might experience more errors when interacting with the elements. However, the transparency into the connections enables the possibility for students to learn about electronic concepts. For example, in an E-Textiles workshop, Peppler and Glosson demonstrated that students learned about current flow, important aspects of connections between the elements, and the polarity of elements [20]. These concepts were transparent to the learner, who could not create a circuit without implementing knowledge of these concepts.

Programmable Electronics

The programmable electronics are the interface between the software and the hardware in a physical computing toolkit. Programmable electronics are often the central entities of physical computing projects because they control the interactive behavior of the hardware. The modularity of the programmable electronics affects the transparency of the communication between the hardware and software. When the programming is not obscured, the user uploads code to a programmable integrated circuit (IC). The code can create sophisticated behavior that would be more difficult to create without programming (i.e. independent logic gates).

The transparency determines the accessibility of the IC and affects the user's control of it. For example, the Arduino's popularity was due in part to its inexpensive scaffolded packaging that enabled untrained professional hobbyists and designers easy access to powerful hardware [18]. The Arduino platform makes the pins transparent allowing users to capitalize on their functionality. The markings on the Arduino platform and documentation guides interactions with these pins making it easier for a novice professional to combine into designs with other hardware.

The scaffolding of the programmable electronics goes from none at all (i.e. just the IC), to scaffolding that completely obscures the pins of the IC. Mellis et al.'s "Untoolkit" is an example of no scaffolding; users directly integrate the microcontroller chip into a conductive ink circuit [17]. Users are given written guides for using the microcontrollers, but there is no physical scaffolding or guidance. One example of a highly scaffolded programmable IC is LEGO Mindstorms. This tool has specific places for proprietary peripheral components to be plugged into the main controller. The IC and access to its pins are visually and physically obscured from the user. The GoGo board is an example that offers some transparency to the programmable IC, because while it obscures some microcontroller pin connections, there is transparency into the connections for particular inputs and outputs to the microcontroller [4,26].

The modularity of the programmable IC is tied to the capability of the toolkit to support an understanding of the communication between the software and hardware. Depending on how the design exposes or obscures connections to the IC designates the set of interactions required by the user to facilitate communication between the hardware and software. This affects how students understand the connections and the transparency of the processes through which the code affects the peripheral electronics. Booth et al. demonstrate the importance of this based on their finding that a breakdown in a user's understanding of the interactions between the hardware and software can lead to difficult errors for the user to overcome [7]. Research has yet to empirically investigate what types of modularity facilitate understanding these interactions.

Peripheral Electronics

There is a wide range of modularity to be found in peripheral electronic elements. They vary in complexity and transparency affecting users' interactions when combining them. We have created a framework of the wide spectrum of design choices in modularity of the peripheral electronics (See Table 1). This allows us to examine the affordances of the various electronic elements for learning. For the sake of simplicity, we frame this discussion in the context of only wired connections between electronic components. Wires were chosen because of their prevalence and the ease of iteration using tools on the market. Focusing on wires places constraints on the design space, which are useful now, and can be removed in future explorations when they are needlessly inhibiting.

In the discussion of this spectrum, we refer to the electronic *components* as the individual electronic pieces such as an LED or a resistor. We combine electronic components with circuit boards to create glass-box scaffolding. The modularity is discussed based on the types of interactions that are possible with the circuit boards, which make certain concepts and electronic component behaviors more or less transparent to the user. Using examples from industry, the literature, and some of our own, we will examine areas for exploration in the design space of physical computing tools.

SPECTRUM OF MODULARITY

Level 1: Plug-and-Play Static Components

The first level of modularity comprises of multiple electronic component modules where the components are soldered into a circuit that can be directly connected to a microcontroller or another circuit. Table 1, contains an example of an LED and resistor circuit with the components soldered to the board. Circuit boards at this level have power, ground, and signal connections, and give students the ability to play with a particular sensor, actuator, or pre-programmed module as a black-box. All of the internal components and circuit connections are masked.

	LEVEL	EXAMPLE
Multiple Component	**Level 1:** Plug-and-Play Circuits with Static Electronic Components	
	Level 2: Plug-and-Play Circuits with Static and Variable Electronic Components	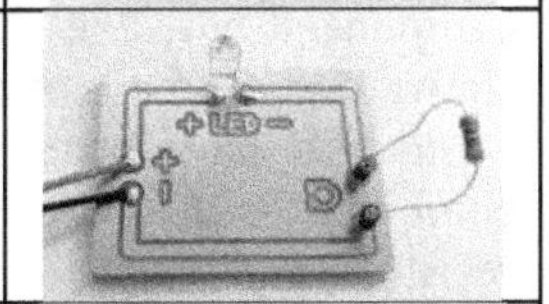
	Level 3: Plug-and Play Circuits with Variable Electronic Components	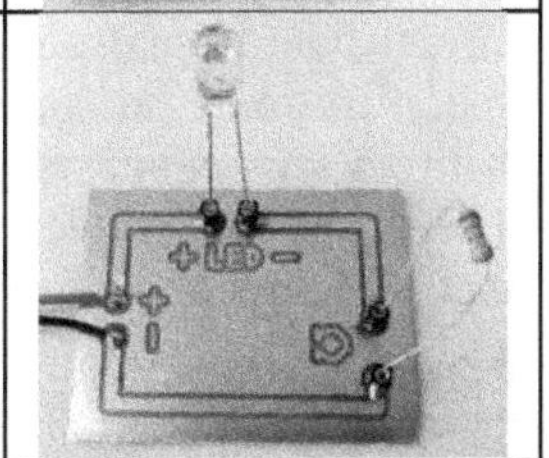
Single Component	**Level 4:** Static Single Electronic Component Modules	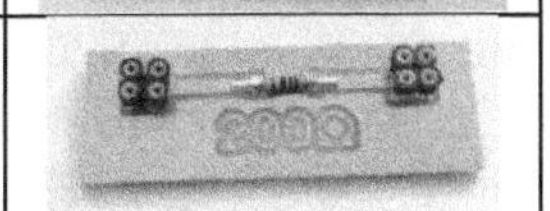
	Level 5: Variable Single Electronic Component Modules	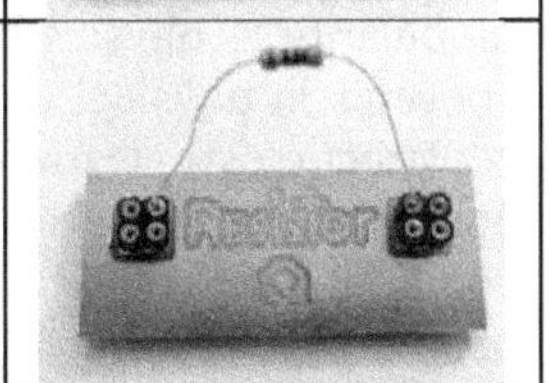
Multiple Component	**Level 6:** Open Circuit Modules	

Table 1. Spectrum of modularity for peripheral components

Using plug-and-play static modules allows users to interact with the circuit boards based on a signal that they either send or receive giving transparency to how the circuit board interacts with the world. Depending on how it is used, the student can learn about the signal in a variety of ways. For example, the user could observe the signal from the light sensor in an abstract way, such as a number representation output from a microcontroller, or as a concrete physical representation, such as connecting it in series with an LED to visualize how the light sensor affects brightness. These various representations could lead to understandings of what is going on in the circuit and possibly how signals are being manipulated in the code. Sadler et al. echo the importance of understanding the learning goals in order to choose how to package components, "Modules may be a poor choice if one's goal is to educate a designer on the technical aspects of a system, since the details are hidden. However, if the primary goals is to enable functional prototyping of a creative idea as quickly as possible, then modules are effective candidates" [23:p144].

Level 2: Plug-and-Play Static & Variable Components

The second level of modularity involves predefined circuits, similar to Level 1, but integrates pin headers for some of the components so the user can experiment with particular aspects of the circuit to change the behavior. Table 1 shows an example of the LED circuit in which the resistor becomes a variable component. Variable components guide the learner to experiment with specific manipulations scaffolding her to learn about a certain concept. The variability can create transparency of a component and/or a particular circuit concept as it guides interactions with the circuit. In the case of the LED circuit, the concept of resistance is now accessible to the learner through tangible interactions that were not possible in the first level of modularity.

There has been little exploration of the design space in this level of modularity; however, we see potential to facilitate learning. The LCD breakout board, which has a knob potentiometer to control the screen brightness gives the user the ability to manipulate a component in the circuit. However, because a knob is a conventional way for users to interact with electronic devices (ex. radio knobs), it is unclear if the learner would gain any conceptual insight from this manipulation. A more effective way of promoting students to learn the underlying concepts, would be to force the learner to make intentional changes to the circuit components in ways that build their conceptual models.

Figure 2. Level 2 module: a two lead sensor circuit with pull-up/pull-down resistor in which the sensor can be changed

Figure 2 provides an example of a circuit that has both static and variable components at this level of modularity. This circuit module can either be a pull-up or pull-down resistor circuit. This circuit board intends to bring transparency to how information can take different forms based on how electrical signals are translated into data (i.e. high vs. low). The students must make intentional decisions about where to connect the power and ground and can explore differences in the signals and how the code interprets the signals. The students using this board can also manipulate the sensors used in the circuit with different types of variable resistors such as a flex-sensitive resistor, a photoresistor, and a thermistor.

Level 3: Plug-and-Play Variable Components

The third level of modularity is similar to the second level, but there is less scaffolding within each circuit because all the parts are variable. There is now transparency brought to all components within the circuit. There are no specific electronics examples that we have found that replicate this design feature, but there are similarities to blocks-based programming languages, which enable students to modify certain aspects of the functions without struggling with syntax or building the function. This has been shown to provide students access to computing and computational thinking [8], while creating an environment that is easier for students to *tinker* with code and understand the functionality of the various blocks [27]. We anticipate that Plug-and-Play Variable Component tools can achieve similar goals in the electronics side of physical computing.

The example circuit in Table 1 is of the LED circuit in which both the resistor and LED can be manipulated. The information on the module still provides scaffolding to help students correctly assemble the circuits (i.e. polarity of LED), but logically there are more mistakes that can be made in this stage when compared to the previous. Depending on the circuit and its implementation in a learning activity, it could be more difficult for an instructor to draw a students' attention to one aspect of the circuit now that all aspects are variable. The entire circuit becomes transparent and open for the user to interact with.

Level 4&5: Static & Variable Single Component Modules

Level 4 and 5 are the levels of modularity in which we transition from multiple components packaged together to single components packaged by themselves. These two levels are presented together because they are conceptually very similar, but have different affordances for scaffolding between the levels of modularity. The interactions with the components are now on a component level rather than based on components integrated into a circuit. The connections between components are no longer scaffolded leading to an exponential number of concepts that a learner can be exposed to.

The single component circuit boards are useful for their *embedded error correction* [4] that would not exist within an open environment. Table 1 shows a resistor module in both level 4 and 5 forms. The circuit boards offer transparency into information about the component that would not be visible otherwise. The Level 4 circuit boards have the component physically soldered to the module so there can be specific information such as the resistance of the resistor, or polarity to ensure the LED has the correct directionality. The Level 5 modules give this same type of error correction for things such as directionality, but depending on the component may have less specificity. For example, the resistor module is not restricted to a particular resistance. While there is no guarantee that the Level 5 component will be used properly (i.e. the LED aligned correctly), it has the affordance of enabling the user to transfer components between abstraction layers and possibly into a final permanent solution. While we do not have any empirical data, this interaction with the component could prove beneficial.

Level 6: Open Circuit Modules

The final level of modules does not define the components and instead focuses on the relation between components. The connections between components are set (i.e. if two things are in parallel or in series), but the modules do not guide the student into using any specific component in the various slots. Depending on the number of leads the component has, the student is still restricted. Figure 1 shows one example of three components in series, but you could also have boards with components in parallel or a combination. This could bring transparency to concepts of resistors and capacitors in series versus parallel. These circuit boards scaffold the students in terms of creating a specific circuit, but they still enable the students experiment with various concepts depending on the components used. There are no examples of these particular types of modules that we know of, so it is unclear what would be learned.

CONCLUSION

The spectrum outlined above is one way to conceptualize the glass-box scaffolding that can exist within the electronic components in physical computing toolkits. By designing based on transparency and interactions, the different modularities physically direct the learner to explore concepts in physical computing in a way that still supports constructionist learning [19]. The theoretical ideas underpinning this scaffolded exploration of physical computing are analogous to those offered in the problem- to project-based work [1,6]. Educators can systematically expose students to particular concepts that can facilitate transitioning students to an open-ended scenario in which students are empowered to create with technology. The spectrum of modularity provides a framework to empirically analyze the success and failure of design choices in educational interventions. The spectrum is outlined such that it can be investigated, iterated upon, and improved rather than to mandate a final state that the design of these educational circuits should take. By drawing attention to the modularity of design choices we can begin to create learner-centered physical computing tools providing learners access to the powerful concepts of computing.

ACKNOWLEDGMENTS

We gratefully acknowledge the grant from NSF (1431984) which supported us in completion of this work.

REFERENCES

1. B.J.S. Barron, D.L. Schwartz, N.J. Vye, A. Moore, A. Petrosino, L. Zech, and J.D. Bransford. 1998. Doing with understanding: Lessons from research on problem-and project-based learning. *Journal of the Learning Sciences* 7, 3: 271–311.
2. Ayah Bdeir. 2009. Electronics as material: littleBits. In *Proceedings of the 3rd International Conference on Tangible and Embedded Interaction*, 397–400.
3. Paulo Blikstein. 2013. Gears of our childhood: constructionist toolkits, robotics, and physical computing, past and future. In *Proceedings of the 12th*

International Conference on Interaction Design and Children, 173–182. Retrieved November 12, 2015 from http://dl.acm.org/citation.cfm?id=2485786

4. Paulo Blikstein. 2015. Computationally Enhanced Toolkits for Children: Historical Review and a Framework for Future Design. *Foundations and Trends® in Human–Computer Interaction* 9, 1: 1–68. https://doi.org/10.1561/1100000057
5. Paulo Blikstein and Arnan Sipitakiat. 2011. QWERTY and the art of designing microcontrollers for children. In *Proceedings of the 10th International Conference on Interaction Design and Children*, 234–237. http://dl.acm.org/citation.cfm?id=1999070
6. Phyllis C. Blumenfeld, Elliot Soloway, Ronald W. Marx, Joseph Krajcik, Mark Guzdial, and Annemarie Palincsar. 1991. Motivating Project-Based Learning: Sustaining the Doing, Supporting the Learning. *Educational Psychologist* 26, 3&4: 369–398.
7. Tracey Booth, Simone Stumpf, Jon Bird, and Sara Jones. 2016. Crossed Wires: Investigating the Problems of End-User Developers in a Physical Computing Task. 3485–3497. https://doi.org/10.1145/2858036.2858533
8. Karen Brennan and Mitchel Resnick. 2012. New frameworks for studying and assessing the development of computational thinking. In *Proceedings of the 2012 annual meeting of the American Educational Research Association, Vancouver, Canada*. Retrieved March 10, 2015 from http://scratched.gse.harvard.edu/ct/files/AERA2012.pdf
9. Leah Buechley and Michael Eisenberg. 2008. The LilyPad Arduino: Toward wearable engineering for everyone. *Pervasive Computing, IEEE* 7, 2: 12–15.
10. Joshua Chan, Tarun Pondicherry, and Paulo Blikstein. 2013. LightUp: an augmented, learning platform for electronics. In *Proceedings of the 12th International Conference on Interaction Design and Children*, 491–494. http://dl.acm.org/citation.cfm?id=2485812
11. Sharon Lynn Chu, Michael Saenz, and Francis Quek. 2016. Connectors in Maker Kits: Investigating Children's Motor Abilities in Making. 452–462. https://doi.org/10.1145/2930674.2930714
12. Elise Deitrick, R. Benjamin Shapiro, Matthew P. Ahrens, Rebecca Fiebrink, Paul D. Lehrman, and Saad Farooq. 2015. Using Distributed Cognition Theory to Analyze Collaborative Computer Science Learning. 51–60. https://doi.org/10.1145/2787622.2787715
13. Kayla DesPortes, Aditya Anupam, Neeti Pathak, and Betsy DiSalvo. 2016. BitBlox: A Redesign of the Breadboard. In *Proceedings of the 15th International Conference on Interaction Design and Children*: 255–261.
14. Kayla DesPortes, Monet Spells, and Betsy DiSalvo. 2016. The MoveLab: Developing Congruence Between Students' Self-Concepts and Computing. 267–272. https://doi.org/10.1145/2839509.2844586
15. Michael Eisenberg, Ann Eisenberg, Mark Gross, Khomkrit Kaowthumrong, Nathaniel Lee, and Will Lovett. 2002. Computationally-enhanced construction kits for children: Prototype and principles. *Proceedings of the Fifth International Conference of the Learning Sciences*: 23–26.
16. Cindy E. Hmelo and Mark Guzdial. 1996. Of black and glass boxes: Scaffolding for doing and learning. In *Proceedings of the 1996 international conference on Learning sciences*, 128–134. Retrieved December 29, 2016 from http://dl.acm.org/citation.cfm?id=1161153
17. David A. Mellis, Sam Jacoby, Leah Buechley, Hannah Perner-Wilson, and Jie Qi. 2013. Microcontrollers as material: crafting circuits with paper, conductive ink, electronic components, and an untoolkit. *Proceedings of the 7th International Conference on Tangible, Embedded and Embodied Interaction*: 83–90.
18. Iqbal Mohomed and Prabal Dutta. 2015. THE Age of DIY and Dawn of the Maker Movement. *GetMobile: Mobile Computing and Communications* 18, 4: 41–43.
19. S Papert. 1993. *Mindstorms: Children, computers, and powerful ideas*. Basic Books, New York, NY.
20. Kylie Peppler and Diane Glosson. 2013. Stitching Circuits: Learning About Circuitry Through E-textile Materials. *Journal of Science Education and Technology* 22, 5: 751–763. https://doi.org/10.1007/s10956-012-9428-2
21. Radia Perlman. 1974. "TORTIS: Toddler's Own Recursive Turgle Interpreter System.
22. Jie Qi, Andrew "bunnie" Huang, and Joseph Paradiso. 2015. Crafting technology with circuit stickers. 438–441. https://doi.org/10.1145/2771839.2771873
23. Joel Sadler, Lauren Shluzas, Paulo Blikstein, and Riitta Katila. 2016. Building Blocks of the Maker Movement: Modularity Enhances Creative Confidence During Prototyping. In *Design Thinking Research*, Hasso Plattner, Christoph Meinel and Larry Leifer (eds.). Springer International Publishing, Cham, 141–154. http://link.springer.com/10.1007/978-3-319-19641-1_10
24. Matthew Schmidtbauer, Samuel Johnson, Jeffrey Jalkio, and AnnMarie P. Thomas. 2012. Squishy Circuits as a Tangible Interface. *Human Factors in Computing Systems*: 2111–2116.
25. Donald A. Schön. 1987. *Educating the reflective practitioner: Towared a new design for teaching and learning in the professions*. Jossey-Bass.
26. Arnan Sipitakiat, Paulo Blikstein, and David P. Cavallo. 2004. GoGo board: augmenting programmable bricks for economically challenged audiences. In *Proceedings of the 6th international conference on Learning sciences*, 481–488. http://dl.acm.org/citation.cfm?id=1149185
27. David Weintrop and Uri Wilensky. 2015. To block or not to block, that is the question: students' perceptions of blocks-based programming. 199–208. https://doi.org/10.1145/2771839.2771860

Toward Understanding Children's Perspectives on Using 3D Printing Technologies in their Everyday Lives

Brenna McNally, Leyla Norooz, Alazandra Shorter, Evan Golub
Human-Computer Interaction Lab (HCIL)
College of Information Studies
University of Maryland, College Park
{bmcnally, lnorooz, ashorter, egolub}@umd.edu

ABSTRACT
Children are currently using 3D printers in schools, libraries, and maker-oriented spaces. As in-home use of 3D printing becomes more common, children's access to this technology will increase. Research has investigated challenges and educational opportunities around children's use of 3D printers, and has speculated on their desires. So far, little research has investigated how children perceive the opportunities of 3D printing in their everyday lives. This exploratory work presents results from a series of three Cooperative Inquiry design sessions that investigated children's anticipated everyday uses of 3D printing and how 3D printing technologies may need to adapt to meet this envisioned future. We found that children welcomed the idea of 3D printing in their everyday lives, envisioning diverse uses spanning utilitarian needs, promoting social good, encouraging play, and providing rapid interventions. We discuss the implications of these outcomes for future designers of 3D printing and modeling technologies.

Author Keywords
3D Printing; Cooperative Inquiry; Participatory Design; Children; Design; Maker movement

ACM Classification Keywords
H.5.m. Information interfaces and presentation (e.g., HCI): Miscellaneous;

INTRODUCTION
As 3D printing transforms virtual imaginings into physical artifacts, it is no wonder that it has caught the interest of adults and children alike. A future envisioned more than a decade ago saw digital fabrication tools such as 3D printers, once only available to expertly trained individuals in specialized labs, becoming available in households for everyday purposes [8,9,13]. Today, this envisioned future seems evermore likely due to the decreasing costs and increasingly consumer-focused 3D printers and companion software [2,5]. Children are already using 3D printers in schools, libraries, and maker-oriented spaces [3,19], and opportunities for home use of the technology seem likely to follow given current services that will model and 3D print children's drawings [14] and 3D printers that are being specifically designed for children [2].

Many possibilities that encourage children to engage in 3D printing are being explored, ranging from educational opportunities to personal interest projects [22,24]. While there have been discussions about what children might like to do with 3D printers and how they can use 3D printed objects, explorations into children's perspectives on why and how they would want to use the technology have been limited. This begs the question, how do children perceive the opportunities that 3D printing affords? As 3D printers move into the home, what are children's goals for using them in their everyday lives? Furthermore, one of the first steps toward 3D printing requires the use of 3D modeling software, which often times can be challenging [19,22]. Once children have access to 3D printing technologies, what barriers may these novices encounter and how might 3D printing software and hardware need to adapt to accommodate children's current needs and future desires?

In anticipation of a future where 3D printing is commonplace, in this paper we present an initial investigation into 1) the everyday uses of 3D printing that children anticipate and 2) how 3D printing technologies may need to adapt to meet this envisioned future. Children's perspectives were sought through a series of three intergenerational Cooperative Inquiry design sessions [4,10]. The first session focused on uncovering how children envision using 3D printing in their everyday lives. In the second session children used 3D modeling software to design their favorite idea while simultaneously evaluating the software's capabilities and suggesting future directions. In the final session the children designed new, "ideal" 3D modeling software for kids. We found that children welcomed the idea of 3D printing in their everyday lives, envisioning diverse uses spanning utilitarian needs, promoting social good, and providing rapid interventions. From these findings, this work contributes implications for the design of future 3D printing technologies for children.

IDC '17, June 27-30, 2017, Stanford, CA, USA
© 2017 Association for Computing Machinery
ACM ISBN 978-1-4503-4921-5/17/06···$15.00
http://dx.doi.org/10.1145/3078072.3079735

RELATED WORK

Because of the creative and educational potential, children are being encouraged to design and print their own 3D objects in libraries, schools, and maker-oriented spaces such as Fab Labs [3,22,23]. The future promises children's increased access to 3D printing technologies as personal fabrication is predicted to be the next technological revolution [8,13], and it is projected that 3D printers will eventually be available in every household [8,9,13,16].

From an educational perspective, the potential applications of introducing children to 3D printing are abundant and are thus receiving attention. Notably, because 3D printing has the ability to surpass *"artificial boundaries between disciplines"* [3, p.18]—for instance, 3D modeling projects in subjects such as music or history become directly related to the mathematics required to develop the models—it therefore has the ability to promote learning and participation across curricula [3,20]. Part of the strength of integrating 3D printing into curricula is that the process of physical creation reinforces what students are learning [15,16]. Research has also noted how engaging students in 3D printing can promote competencies such as design thinking [22] and has intrinsic benefits such as improving self-esteem [3], collaboration [3], and empowerment [20]. From a broader perspective, as educational applications are hardly the only domains in which children are likely to desire 3D printing capabilities [5], researchers have also discussed benefits to children from engaging in 3D printing such as playfulness and self-expression [3,24].

The trend of encouraging children to engage in 3D printing implies that requisite consumer software and hardware resources will need to meet the needs of the children who will use it. Engaging children in 3D printing comes with a number of challenges, and whether children can make use of 3D printing technologies has been a topic of discussion [19]. One of the first steps when 3D printing is designing a model within 3D software; children, particularly at a young age, have difficulty with the software's orientation and camera control, lack of collaboration features, and the construction limitations of current 3D printers [19,24]. The difficulties children face in designing models, as well as 3D design software's inability to meet the expectations of children, suggest that there is room for improvement of these software interfaces [16,19]. Regarding children's expectations, Eisenberg posited several directions for the development of 3D printing technologies for youths, among them the need to *expand the range of physical media for printing* and *devising software techniques for specifying, altering, and combining 3D elements* [5]. Already research is seeing strides toward these directions. For instance, recently developed printers move beyond 3D printing with traditional materials (i.e., plastics and metals), and instead work with soft materials such as layers of needle felted yarn [12] or off-the-shelf fabrics [18]. This work continues these discussions by looking at how children want to use 3D printing in everyday life and how to prepare for that future.

METHODS

This work investigates children's perspectives on the value and opportunities of 3D printing in everyday life through a series of three Cooperative Inquiry design sessions. Here we describe the Cooperative Inquiry method and the specific design team discussed in this work.

Cooperative Inquiry: Background and Session Structure

Children are asked to participate in the design of technologies meant to be used by children, with the goal that this participation *"...results in technologies that better address [children's] needs, interests, and abilities"* [11, p.313]. Cooperative Inquiry (CI) is a Participatory Design method that is specifically developed to facilitate children, ages 7 to 11, and adults working together as design partners throughout the technology design process [4,10]. Design partners, which include the child and adult CI team members, are peers in the design process who become knowledgeable in intergenerational communication and the design techniques (e.g., 3D prototyping, paper prototyping) necessary to being equitable CI design team members and to designing children's technologies [6,17]. The 90-minute CI design sessions we describe in this work were held at [a university lab- redacted for review]'s [design team-redacted for review], which meets twice weekly throughout the academic year.

Cooperative Inquiry Design Session Structure

To provide context for the descriptions to follow, the structure of each design session is briefly described. Each session begins with an introduction to the topic area, which in this case is 3D printing, to ensure all members of the team have basic content knowledge. The larger team then splits up into three smaller groups to complete the design activity. At the end of each design session each small group presents their ideas, and then the outcomes and themes that arose are discussed among the entire team.

Participants

The six child design partners on this team ranged in age from 8 to 11 and included four females and two males, one of whom had previously used 3D printing design software. Between four and six adult design partners, ages 20 to 45, also attended each design session.

DESIGN SESSIONS

Three CI design sessions were conducted to investigate children's perceptions of and desires for 3D printing:

- Session 1: Desires for 3D Printing
- Session 2: Using 3D Modeling Software
- Session 3: Redesigning 3D Modeling Software

The data from these sessions can be aggregated to form a picture of the opportunities for 3D printing from the viewpoint of a child, the frustrations that are encountered when attempting to create their designs, and requirements for child-friendly tools that can be used to actualize the opportunities that children envision.

Design Session 1: Desires for 3D Printing

The first design session investigated what children would want to 3D print in three locations: at home, at school, and in the world. Inspired by Shewbridge et al. [21], who had participants brainstorm uses for 3D printing in their everyday lives by depositing ideas in a box in their home over the course of 10 weeks, we had children rapidly brainstorm ideas for each location, writing out each idea on a separate sticky note. At the end of the design session, small groups were asked to choose their favorite idea from the brainstorming activity and prototype it with Legos for use in the next session (Figure 1).

Analysis

Sticky notes from across all groups in the first session were clustered into similar categories [6,7] regarding perceived uses for 3D printing in everyday life (Table 1). The materials that each of the ideas would require to be printed were similarly categorized (Table 2).

Findings

Uses of 3D Printing. The six children brainstormed 176 ways they would use 3D printed objects in everyday life. Many ideas were based on improving convenience through improved *access to everyday items*, such as being able to create extra hangers or school supplies such as a binder for papers. Other ideas revolved around obtaining access to goods that would normally be "too expensive" or *otherwise inaccessible items*, such as a new television or a trampoline. Still other ideas pertained to the idea of *social good*, such as being able to print and replace stolen traffic signs to make neighborhoods more safe, or printing body parts such as teeth for people who can not afford dental care.

Category	Frequency	Examples
Toys	54	
• Outdoor	39	Trampoline, pool noodles
• Electronic	8	Wii, Hexbug
• Instruments	4	Guitar, piano
• Other	3	Yarn, board games
Household	47	
• Furniture	14	Bed frame, toilet
• Home electronics	8	TV, phone
• Landscaping	8	Plants, wind chimes
• Other	7	Hangers, light bulbs
• Kitchen	5	Pots, utensils
• Toiletries	5	Toilet paper, soap
Office supplies	24	Crayons, binder
Clothing & accessories	20	Gym clothes, flip flops
Food	15	Lunch, chocolate
Body parts	6	Teeth, eyelashes
Pet supplies	5	Leash, cage
Miscellaneous	5	Street signs
	Total: 176	

Table 1. The categorization of ideas children came up with in Design Session 1, when asked to envision how they would use 3D printing in their everyday lives.

Material	Frequency	Material	Frequency
Multiple Materials	35	Wood	14
Organic	30	Rubber	12
Metal	27	Ceramic	5
Plastic	25	Glass	5
Textiles	20	Paper	3
	Total: 176		

Table 2. The categorization of the materials that would be required to 3D print the ideas children generated during Design Session 1.

Children also described uses for 3D printing that would address a pressing need with an *immediate intervention*. For instance, if they forgot their gym clothes at home they could print a new set at school. Similarly, if a person found themselves in need of a spatula or toilet paper, it could be 3D printed rapidly for immediate use.

Materials. Children also envisioned uses of 3D printing that spanned a wide variety of materials. In addition to the common plastic filament (which they could see as there was a 3D printer in the room during the design sessions), they imagined printers that could print with, for example, paper, rubber, organic materials, and textiles (Table 2).

Design Session 2: Using 3D Modeling Software

The first design session detailed the many uses across diverse materials that children envision for 3D printing in everyday life. In the second session we took the next step toward this envisioned future by asking children to design one of their favorite brainstormed objects, based on their Lego prototypes from Session 1, in a 3D printing modeling software. For this session, 3DTin was chosen as it was a free, web-based software that did not require creating individual accounts or local installation [1]. To introduce the capabilities and functionality of the software, the team watched two of 3DTin's introductory tutorials on building with geometric figures (2:00 min) and building with cubes (1:44 min). Children used 3DTin to individually model their Lego prototypes from the previous session (Figure 1). Lego prototypes were used as a model for the children's 3D designs because they are comprised of simple shapes reminiscent of those presented in the tutorials and provided a concrete goal for the novice 3D software modelers.

As children designed they used a design technique called Sticky Noting [6,7] to report their likes, dislikes, and design ideas regarding using the 3D printing software. Afterward, children reported on their agreement to various statements asked by adults through an activity called Line Judging, where tape is placed on the floor labeled with a 5pt likert spectrum of responses ranging from 1-strongly disagree to 5-strongly agree. As an adult read statements, children voted on each by standing on different parts of the line and then sharing their opinions on their decisions.

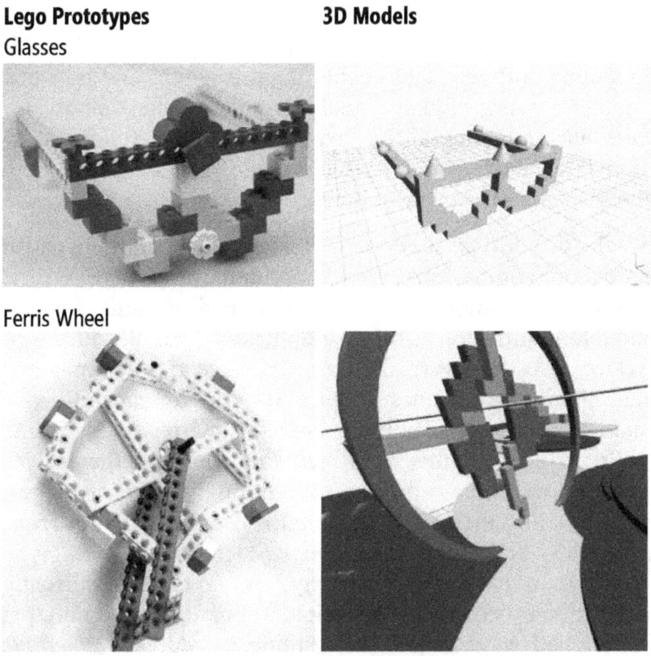

Figure 1. Examples of Lego prototypes from Session 1 and corresponding 3D Models made by children during Session 2. The child who made the glasses (top right) considered the design to be successful, while the child who made the Ferris wheel (bottom right) considered the design to be unsuccessful.

Analysis

The sticky notes describing children's likes, dislikes, and design ideas were analyzed using a modified cluster analysis [6,7], which we used to generate themes. These themes were discussed with the entire design team and then iterated and clarified during a discussion with the adult design partners. Themes are supported by line judging results (reported in mean x and median M) as applicable.

Findings

Feature Visibility. While children in the design session had immediate ideas as to what they wanted to do to begin designing (e.g., use a geometric shape to create the outline of a Ferris wheel), locating the buttons and menus that allowed them to begin was considered challenging. The icon-based buttons were unclear to the children, who suggested adding labels, and finding the undo button to address mistakes resulting from experimentation was also challenging. One child resorted to starting new projects each time a mistake was made. The importance of feature visibility was also made apparent in the line judging activity. When asked whether *"the tutorials taught [the children] what [they] needed to know to get started"* children all strongly disagreed (x=1, M=1). Rather than being due to a lack of introduction on the capabilities of the software, or being unsure what action they wanted to pursue, upon further questioning we found that the challenge was in locating the features that the tutorials pointed out: *"After the tutorial I still could not remember where the buttons were. [The buttons] were just symbols"* (female, age 11).

Positioning. Children appreciated numerous positioning features, including zoom, hotkeys, that the XYZ axes were color-coded, and that guidelines appeared when adding a new shape. To address challenges around positioning shapes, such as difficulty rotating and shapes mistakenly being placed below the grid, children suggested design ideas such as joining or grouping pieces together and the ability to resize objects without needing to type in dimensions. While the line judging activity showed no preference between whether children "liked using blocks" (x=3, M=3) or "liked using geometric shapes" (x=3, M=3) to model their prototypes, positioning geometric shapes was described as being more difficult, since, *"Sometimes they were too big, and they were hard to rotate"* (female, age 9).

Design Session 3: Redesigning 3D Modeling Software

As session 2 identified strengths and challenges for children's use of 3D printing software, session 3 focused on the capabilities of 3D printing technology that would be required to meet children's envisioned future uses. Children were asked to design an "ideal" 3D modeling piece of software for children. Small groups used the Big Paper paper-prototyping technique [10] to design their ideas, and were given printed screenshots of the 3DTin web interface so they could choose to cut out and incorporate any design elements that they desired in their new software.

Analysis

As small groups were presenting, an adult wrote their ideas on a whiteboard and rapidly thematically analyzed the ideas, noting patterns as well as unique ideas [6,7]. After all groups presented, the entire team discussed the outcomes to make sure no ideas were missed [6].

Findings

Restructuring the Design Plane. Although designing above the design plane was considered fun (and necessary), children removed the ability to place 3D objects *"under"* the design plane. Bottom-up views were subsequently eliminated, which they described as having the additional benefit of making the rotation feature easier to use.

Navigation. Within this new design plane many navigational elements were the same with regard to input (e.g., mouse/keyboard) and interface layout (e.g., having main tools along the left, tool-specific options along the bottom of the screen). However, designs had relatively few on-screen buttons, and those that were featured had both icons and labels. Additional features were largely designed around previewing actions. For instance, when dragging a 3D element it would cast a shadow from above onto the grid to identify where it would be placed on the XY surface of the design space. Additionally, to help with navigating where to place 3D objects in more complicated designs, children designed the ability to import photographs to build from. Designs also emphasized using pre-set directional views as opposed to relying solely on rotation to see different sides of a design.

Designing for Movement. Children expressed ways 3D modeling software could support designing and testing moveable objects (e.g., adding a "play" button).

Social Experience. Children designed collaborative features into 3D modeling software, such as split screens, the ability to send a design to a friend and have them edit it, and sharing and duplicating other children's designs.

DISCUSSION

Our focus in this exploratory work was on 1) forming a picture of children's perceptions of the opportunities that 3D printing may provide to their everyday lives, in anticipation of a future where this technology is commonplace,. and on 2) identifying how future 3D printing technologies can support these visions.

Children's Visions of 3D Printing in Everyday Life

The 3D printing goals that our child design partners had ranged from the practical, such as printing new eyeglasses, to the rather fantastical, such as designing a Ferris wheel. While the feasibility of some of the designs may be suspect, motivating children to model their fantastical ideas nonetheless supports educational applications of the technology from a self-driven, constructionist viewpoint [15,24]. Previous work has found that households are likely to desire 3D printing for utilitarian purposes [21], and children's envisioned uses of 3D printing for purposes such as replacing broken objects or duplicating items support this vision. However, in addition to these practical goals, our child design partners emphasized playful uses of the technology and uses that promoted social good.

As with previous research [24], during this exploratory work we observed that children were able to begin developing their ideas quickly in the 3D modeling software. Nonetheless, navigating the software proved to be challenging for the novice child users, and some children did not consider their 3D software models to be successful. While our child design partners were optimistic that given more time and experience they could improve upon their designs, they also sought capabilities within current software that were nonexistent (e.g., developing and testing movement in designs). Overall, the child design partners welcomed the idea of household 3D printing and the applications it could have in their everyday lives.

Implications for Design

Many of the 3D modeling challenges that were encountered during our design sessions echoed what prior research suggested we would see—that, for instance, young children would face issues with orientation, camera control, and the lack of collaboration features [19,24]. Correspondingly, our child design partners described and designed a number of ways to improve modeling software interfaces. The outcomes of these exploratory design sessions suggest that children may prefer a *simplified design plane* that does not enable designing below the grid or bottom-up views, which children speculated would help with their challenges in orienting the plane, placing models, and camera control. Similarly, children may desire *social supports* within 3D modeling software that enable them to share and edit one another's work. Finally, including increased support for *customization* should be explored, or the functionality simplified, such as color selection that would apply to both the 3D software and print items.

While the design sessions in this work did not focus on hardware components or ask children to print out their designs, a number of the desires and designs for 3D modeling software also had implications for the future of 3D printing hardware. Researchers have rightly imagined that children would desire more 3D printing capabilities—such as printing in multiple, mixed materials in the same build [5]—as in this work we find children themselves envisioning this future. Accordingly, we suggest incorporating the ability to model and print with *numerous materials* and to support *mixed-materials printing*, in addition to *printing on a larger scale* than is currently supported by consumer 3D printers. Finally, while children envisioned ways to use 3D printing to address *immediate needs*, to achieve this goal 3D printing technology will need to complete prints faster than is currently possible.

While these implications for design are somewhat juxtaposed—desiring simplifications to existing tools while also desiring enhanced functionality—we believe careful design can facilitate both design directions.

Limitations and Future Work

An early exploration into how children envision 3D printing fitting into their everyday lives, this study was limited to design outcomes from three, 90-minute design sessions and the viewpoints of the six child design partners who participated in these sessions. Therefore, while the outcomes of this exploratory work may guide and inspire future research, its outcomes should be further investigated. Future work could also consider other 3D printing software, how children access and use pre-designed models, and whether printed models meet children's desires and expectations. As these design sessions were held in a university lab, next steps for future work could also investigate children's desires by working within different domains—such as at home or at school—to investigate additional applications of 3D printing.

CONCLUSION

Through a series of three Cooperative Inquiry design sessions with children ages 7-11, we explored the ways in which children envision 3D printers being used in their everyday lives, and the future capabilities of the technology that will be required to meet this envisioned future. Findings described diverse uses incorporating numerous materials, with applications that were utilitarian, promoted social good, and enabled rapid interventions to meet immediate needs. We also provide design implications for the researchers and designers who are interested in supporting children's anticipated uses of the technology.

ACKNOWLEDGMENTS
We would like to extend our thanks to the child design partners of UMD's Kidsteam as well as Chelsea Hordatt, Becky Lewittes, and Lisa Rogers.

REFERENCES

1. 3DTin: 3D Modeling for Everyone. 2015. Accessed October 2015 from www.3dtin.com
2. Brian Barrett. 2016. ThingMaker is for Kids, but You'll Want this 3D Printer for Yourself. *Wired Magazine.* (18 February, 2016). Retrieved January 29th from https://www.wired.com/2016/02/thingmaker-is-for-kids-but-youll-want-this-3-d-printer-for-yourself/
3. Paulo Blikstein. 2013. Digital fabrication and 'making' in education: The democratization of invention. *FabLabs: Of machines, makers and inventors.* 4.
4. Allison Druin. 1999. Cooperative Inquiry: Developing new technologies for children with children. In *Proceedings of the SIGCHI conference on Human Factors in Computing Systems*, 592-599.
5. Michael Eisenberg. 2013. 3D printing for children: What to build next?. *International Journal of Child-Computer Interaction.* 1,1: 7-13.
6. Jerry Alan Fails, Mona Leigh Guha, and Allison Druin. 2013. Methods and techniques for involving children in the design of new technology for children. *Foundations and Trends in Human–Computer Interaction.* 6,2: 85-166.
7. Elizabeth Foss, Mona Leigh Guha, Panagis Papadatos, Tamara Clegg, Jason Yip, and Greg Walsh. 2013. Cooperative Inquiry extended: Creating technology with middle school students with learning differences. *Journal of Special Education Technology.* 28, 3: 33-46.
8. Neil Gershenfeld. 2007. *Fab: The Coming Revolution on Your Desktop--from Personal Computers to Personal Fabrication.* Basic Books.
9. Neil Gershenfeld. 2012. How to make almost anything: The digital fabrication revolution. *Foreign Aff.* 91: 43.
10. Mona Leigh Guha, Allison Druin, and Jerry Alan Fails. 2013. Cooperative Inquiry revisited: Reflections of the past and guidelines for the future of intergenerational co-design. *International Journal of Child-Computer Interaction* 1,1: 14-23.
11. Juan Pablo Hourcade. 2008. Interaction design and children. *Foundations and Trends in Human-Computer Interaction* 1,4: 277-392.
12. Scott E Hudson. 2014. Printing teddy bears: A technique for 3D printing of soft interactive objects. In *Proceedings of the SIGCHI Conference on Human Factors in Computing Systems*, 459-468.
13. Satwant Kaur. 2012. How is "Internet of the 3D Printed Products" going to Affect Our Lives? Pushing frontiers with the first lady of emerging technologies. *IETE Technical Review.* 29,5: 360-364.
14. Kids Creation Station. 2017. Accessed January 31, 2017 from https://kidscreationstation.com/.
15. Hod Lipson. 2007. Printable 3D models for customized hands-on education. *Mass Customization and Personalization (MCPC).*
16. Hod Lipson and Melba Kurman. 2013. *Fabricated: The new world of 3D printing.* John Wiley & Sons.
17. Brenna McNally, Matthew Louis Mauriello, Mona Leigh Guha, and Allison Druin. 2017. Gains from Participatory Design Team Membership as Perceived by Child Alumni and their Parents. To appear in *Proceedings of the 2017 Conference on Human Factors in Computing Systems.*
18. Huaishu Peng, Jennifer Mankoff, Scott E. Hudson, and James McCann. 2015. A layered fabric 3D printer for soft interactive objects. In *Proceedings of the 33rd Annual ACM Conference on Human Factors in Computing Systems*, 1789-1798.
19. Irene Posch, and Geraldine Fitzpatrick. 2012. First steps in the FabLab: experiences engaging children. In *Proceedings of the 24th Australian Computer-Human Interaction Conference*, 497-500.
20. Chelsea Schelly, Gerald Anzalone, Bas Wijnen, and Joshua M. Pearce. 2015. Open-source 3-D printing technologies for education: Bringing additive manufacturing to the classroom. *Journal of Visual Languages & Computing.* 28: 226-237.
21. Rita Shewbridge, Amy Hurst, and Shaun K. Kane. 2014. Everyday making: Identifying future uses for 3D printing in the home. In *Proceedings of the 2014 conference on Designing interactive systems*, 815-824.
22. Rachel Charlotte Smith, Ole Sejer Iversen, and Mikkel Hjorth. 2015. Design thinking for digital fabrication in education. *International Journal of Child-Computer Interaction.* 5: 20-28.
23. Gary S Stager. 2013. Papert's prison fab lab: Implications for the maker movement and education design. In *Proceedings of the 12th International Conference on Interaction Design and Children*, 487-490.
24. Oliver Stickel, Dominik Hornung, Konstantin Aal, Markus Rohde, and Volker Wulf. 2015. 3D Printing with Marginalized Children—An Exploration in a Palestinian Refugee Camp. In *ECSCW 2015: Proceedings of the 14th European Conference on Computer Supported Cooperative Work*, 83-102.

Kindergarten Programming Goes Mobile - Should The Next Years Be About Ubiquity?

Ruthi Aladjem
School of Education
Tel-Aviv University
6997801 Israel
rutrutal@gmail.com

Asi Kuperman
School of Education
Tel-Aviv University
6997801 Israel
asikuper@post.tau.ac.il

David Mioduser
School of Education
Tel-Aviv University
6997801 Israel
miodu@post.tau.ac.il

ABSTRACT

Over the past 50 years, since the introduction of the programmable floor turtle, the dyad learning /programming environment underwent several transformations. Each transformation brought about new questions regarding children's understanding, learning and programming performance. This paper describes results from a preliminary study analyzing the current transformation from desktop to mobile-based learning/programming by kindergarten children. Observations of children's performance and semi structured interviews with teachers were conducted. The findings unveiled three key themes, namely, changes in programmers' perspectives, changes in foci and learning patterns in different programming modes, and changes in patterns of collaboration among peers. The preliminary findings serve as basis for planning further systematic research on the design of mobile-based programming environments for kindergarten children.

Author Keywords

Mobile Programming Environment; Educational Robotics; Young Children.

ACM Classification Keywords

D.2.6 Programming Environments

BACKGROUND AND STUDY RATIONAL

Over the past 50 years, since the introduction of the programmable floor turtle, the dyad "programming environment" and "programmable device" (e.g., robot) in the educational scene underwent several transformations in configuration [12]. These transformations included stages such as: The turtle's migration to the screen (e.g., in Logo, Scratch and Scratch Junior); its revival as a physical device in the Lego-Logo and subsequent systems (e.g Control Lab, generations of Lego programmable bricks, and KIBO); the loss of the robot's "umbilical cord" when communication became wireless (adding spatial flexibility and freedom to the robot's navigation but at the same time challenging children's understanding of the communication and control process); the introduction of tangible programming which allowed to replace the mouse and keyboard with tangible manipulatives (e.g., "smart" blocks [3], wooden puzzle pieces [10]); and recently, the transition to mobile programming environments. Each transition brought about new questions about children's understanding and learning.

Mobile devices have vast potential for supporting learning and learners. They have become a significant part of daily life, integrating seamlessly with a range of common activities to the point of being regarded as mindtools and as "extensions of the self" [2, 12]. The qualities of mobile devices in the context of learning and above all, the fact that unlike a desktop computer, they do not constrain the learner to a fixed location, may transform how the child programmer experiences the physical behaving devices. At the same time, the issue requires more in-depth investigation. Our current research aims to gain understanding of children's programming experience with a *mobile* learning/programming environment used in kindergartens (the Kinderbot system) compared to their experience using a *desktop-based* version of the system. The findings reported here, unveil major themes and questions arising from the "migration" from desktop to mobile and suggest directions for further research which may contribute to the design of mobile programming environments and their implementation in the kindergarten curriculum.

The main question addressed was: *What characterizes children's programming (concerning, e.g., skills construction, strategies development, collaborative patterns) in the transition from a desktop-based to a mobile programming environment?*

METHOD

THE PROGRAMMING ENVIRONMENT

"Kinderbot", the programming environment used by the children in this study, has been designed to support and

IDC '17, June 27-30, 2017, Stanford, CA, USA
© 2017 Association for Computing Machinery.
ACM ISBN 978-1-4503-4921-5/17/06□$15.00
http://dx.doi.org/10.1145/3078072.3079737

scaffold the acquisition of basic programming concepts, and to advance the technological thinking of kindergarten children. Rooted in Papert's constructionist vision, and his conception of the learning value of the combination of the physical programmable "Turtle" with the Logo programming language, the environment combines symbolic and physical components and allows for playful investigations of both abstract and concrete concepts [4,6,9,14]. Kinderbot was originally designed as a desktop based programming environment; recently, a mobile (tablet) version has been developed.

The environment uses a visual iconic interface that supports and encourages kindergarten children's programming of the behaviors of a physical robot, without the need for reading and writing skills [8,14]. The first prototype of the environment was created in the early 90s as part of a research project and has since been the focus of versatile research concerning various aspects of children's programming experience, such as the strategies that kindergarten children use for creating rule-based behaviors [6], their perceptions of the behaving artifacts [4] and more. Studies show that the environment serves as a concrete space for the exploration and construction of abstract concepts and schemas, as young children spontaneously abstract rules for controlling the robot's behavior [7]. Furthermore, it was shown that children are able to detect patterns in observed data and to use these to predict, plan and code a robot's expected behavior [8]. About a decade after the first prototype and following extensive research, a pedagogical program was designed for using the programming environment in kindergartens. The program has been running successfully in several kindergartens for the past decade, as part of the kindergarten curriculum.

The system comprises a (virtual) programming environment, a (physical) robot (built using Lego's EV3 programmable brick), and a (physical) landscapes for the robot's navigation. The visual user interface (Figure 1) allows the programmer to control the robot's behavior by constructing programs using icons that represent inputs (e.g., incoming from a touch or distance sensor), outputs (e.g. movements based on activating motors), and configurations of inputs and outputs (e.g., a linear sequence of instructions, a conditional statement). The programming sequence is structured in gradual succeeding modes of increasing difficulty (shown at the right of the Figure). The basic modes (1-3) focus on acquiring the basic competencies of controlling the robot and sequencing commands (from immediate mode activation up to creating a sequential script for further running). The more advanced modes introduce the definition of routines (mode 4) and rules of increasing complexity linking between expected outputs and measured inputs (modes 5-7). The tasks involve the use of the robot in a variety of physical landscapes, and were designed as a progression according to the programming modes in Kinderbot [6]. The navigation landscape contains features and obstacles that the robot will need to interact with or avoid, while equipped with appropriate navigation scripts (Modes 2-3) or rules (Modes 4-7). The structure and use of the environment are similar on both the desktop and mobile versions, aside for the touch operation modality (e.g., tapping, dragging) in the mobile version. In this paper, we focus on the children's experience using the first three modes - as they form the basis for acquiring the symbolic language for controlling the robot's behavior [7]. Further details about the programming modes are provided in the following sections, as we compare the desktop and mobile experiences.

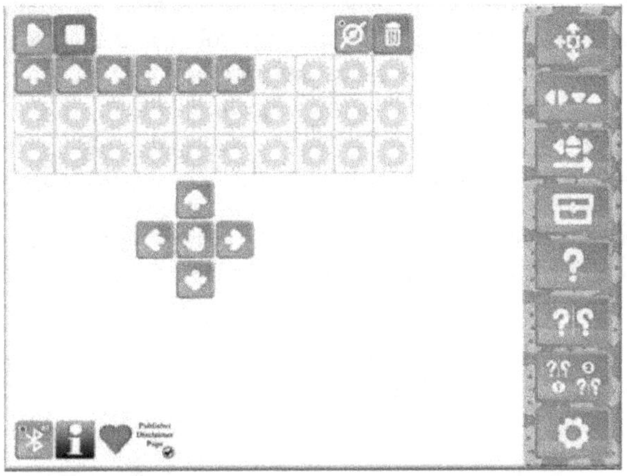

Figure 1: the icon based Kinderbot UI

DATA COLLECTION

Data collection was conducted by means of: (a) observations of children's performance; and (b) semi-structured interviews with four teachers who use the programming environment in their kindergartens.

Naturalistic observations of the children engaged with the mobile and desktop environments were conducted. Each observation session was 20-30 minutes long, the children were observed while constructing routes and creating narrative contexts for the robots to travel through.

The teacher interviews focused on issues such as the way children manipulate the mobile device, their posture and position relative to the robot's navigation, their displacement in space, mistakes made, and communication issues. The mobile version of the environment has been initially implemented in two kindergartens. Hence, two teachers had experience with both the desktop and mobile environment while the other two had experience only with the desktop environment. The two teachers who had experience with both environments were also asked to describe their understanding and insights concerning the differences in the programming experience.

FINDINGS

The following three main themes arose from the analysis of the data and the comparison of the desktop and mobile experience: Changes in the programmer's perspective;

changes in foci and learning patterns in programming modes; changes in patterns of collaboration among peers while programming.

Theme one - changes in programmers' perspectives

In the desktop mode, there is a physical separation between the location of the computer and that of the robot. The programmer must face the static computer screen for entering the commands, while the robot is in a distant position. It even may be pointing to a different direction than the one indicated by the commands in the computer screen, meaning that, e.g., it's "ahead" and the "ahead" icon (pointing upwards in the screen) differ in spatial configuration. Hence, to control the robot and to provide commands for its movements, the programmer needs to be able to visualize the robot's perspective while sitting in front of the computer screen. A common strategy that children naturally apply, is to move back and forth between the two spatial worlds: the screen programming environment and the physical robot's scene - thus switching cyclically between the physical/concrete environment to the virtual/abstract environment [6,9].

Figure 2: Switching perspectives while programming

It should be mentioned that some programmers find ways to bypass this dual-perspective challenge by collaborating with their peers. This strategy is discussed as part of the third theme (the changing nature of collaboration).

The mobile device in its very essence is unfixed, so there is little surprise that once given the mobile interface, the programmers naturally tend to take position in the vicinity of the robot facing the same direction as the robot, thus taking the perspective of the robot and following its movements (holding the mobile programming interface) while the commands are performed. In other words, the physical distance and gaps in orientation between the programming environment and the programmed object becomes minimal, and the separation (spatial, and in some modes also temporal) between the symbolic creation of the action and the physical execution of the action is negligible.

In previous work, we analyzed the rich cognitive nature of the dialog between the concrete and the abstract, and the physical and the symbolic aspects of children's programming [8,12]. We indicated that:

"The robot system serves the child as a concrete environment for the exploration and construction of abstract concepts and schemas. Interplay is generated between this ''abstractions-embedded-concrete-agent'', and the cognitive abstractions generated by the child. This is the realm of thinking processes we refer to as the realm of ''concrete-abstractions'', in which recurring cycles intertwining the symbolic and the concrete are exercised by the child while abstracting schemas for understanding the robot's behavior" [8, pp. 32].

These previous studies were conducted with the desktop programming interface, separated from the robot and its physical environment. The integration between the symbolic description of the expected behavior and its physical instantiation was constructed iteratively in the programmer's mind, in a process marked with spatial and temporal delays between the two. In mobile programming these delays disappear and, moreover, the spatial perspectives become unified - the programmer can enact the robot's behavior while programming "in situ", where the action takes place. This brings as close as possible the three components of the concrete-abstractions dialog: playing the robot, describing its desired behavior with symbols and its actual physical behavior (see Figure 3).

Figure 3: Using Kinderbot mobile

Theme two - changes in foci and learning patterns in different programming modes

The desktop and mobile modes of Kinderbot share the same logic and structure, yet several differences were noted in the ways in which the programming was carried out by the programmers on the two platforms. Following is a comparison of children's performances in the three basic modes of programming between the platforms.

Programming mode one: Immediate execution command-by-command

The first programming mode allows the learner to get acquainted with the basic robot-controlling commands. The four controls introduced in this mode are simple manipulation commands, represented by four arrow-shaped icons for "forward", "backward", "turn right" and "turn left" actions (see Figure 1). Each command symbolizes a single step of the robot in the physical world. For example, in order to program the robot to take two steps forward and a step to the left - the commands would be: forward, forward, turn left, forward (or: ↑↑→↑).

In the desktop platform, this phase is usually quite brief, ending once the programmer has grasped the use of the controllers. For example, the programmer needs to understand that selecting a vertical sign for "up" (↑) on the user interface, will translate into a horizontal step "forward" of the robot in the physical world.

In the mobile version, controlling the robot seems even simpler and more intuitive than in the desktop interface. Overall, the experience of the first mode is quite similar to that of using a remotely controlled vehicle (with the tablet functioning as the remote control), an experience that many kindergarten children are already familiar with. The programmer is standing near the programmable robot and therefore has eye contact with it and with the immediate results of entering a programming command. Since the programmer is facing the same direction as the robot, she/he is not required to a change in perspective or a mental visualization of the robot's navigation - their perspectives are the same. Thus, the first mode becomes extremely short and it is quickly exhausted as the child programmer grasps almost immediately the concept of how to control the physical robot and is ready to move on.

Mode two: Immediate execution of a sequence of commands.

During the second programming mode, the programmer is introduced to the notion of sequencing commands. In this phase, similarly to the previous mode, each command is carried out immediately, in real time, so the programmers can view the immediate outcome of their chosen command. In other words, there is no delay between the symbolic action and the physical action. However, unlike the previous mode, each command is stored in an instructions line, forming a visual representation of the sequence activated – this is children's program, which remains on the screen and can be repeatedly activated.

A sample task in this mode is the one in which the robot must be programmed to navigate a path, while avoiding various obstacles. The navigation sequence is executed immediately, step by step, while being constructed, but it is also being recorded. The program can then be executed, debugged and modified. Thus, the learners experience and experiment with the different commands and their immediate effect on the physical environment, as well as with the idea of constructing a program that can be further executed again and again. Upon planning the navigation course, the programmers need to grasp the physical landscape, envision the required navigation path, and be able to translate these into symbolic commands on the graphic interface.

On the desktop platform, the programmers need to continually adjust their perspective while working in the computer screen, to the robot's perspective. For example, at some point, the programmer's left may be the robot's right and vice versa. For a script requiring multiple steps, they also should be able to estimate the actual distances and the number of steps needed to cover it, given the length of a single step. In addition, given that the robot acts in a concrete physical environment, several factors (e.g., friction, delays) might affect its functioning, generating confusing gaps between the expected (programmed) and the actual behavior. As a result, the programmer using the desktop platform is extensively engaged in repeated cycles of trial and error in aspects such as experimenting with the length of the steps, detecting errors (in estimation, in the commands chosen) and adjusting them (debugging).

In the mobile version, since the distance is minimized and the execution is immediate, there is lesser need for prediction and planning. In addition, less debugging is required as the programmer is effectively following the robot in each step with lesser need to accommodate between the robot's point of view and her/his own, or to preplan the next move. The result is that this mode (as the previous) is exhausted in a few cycles and the programmers seem to arrive to the next mode sooner. However, the price is that children spend less time experiencing the control of the robot, handling challenges or engaging in debugging procedures.

Mode three: planning and programming a script

In this phase, the programmer is introduced to preplanning a sequence of commands (a script). Similar to mode two, the objective here is to program the robot to navigate a complex path. However, unlike the previous phase, a sequence of commands will be executed only after a fully program is created and saved. In order to construct the sequence, the programmer is required to use strategies that involve decomposing the problem, reconstructing it modularly, and planning several steps ahead (anticipation) [6]. Once the sequence is executed, it may need to be adjusted using different debugging strategies [6].

In the desktop platform, the progression to this phase is natural. In the previous mode, every command in the sequence being constructed is executed immediately while in this mode the immediate execution is omitted and only the complete sequence can be run. Although it implies more complexity, the requirements are clear, the programmers have already established a clear estimation of the length of a step, and developed the skills required for planning and executing a full script. Although the experience seems like a natural "flow" for the desktop programmer, this mode still involves several cycles of programming and debugging.

On the mobile platform, this phase seems to pose a substantial challenge, compared to the desktop platform. As previously noted, the programmer spent less time experimenting on previous modes, and encountered fewer issues requiring problem solving and debugging skills. As a result, much of the knowledge construction and skills development takes place in this platform in a more challenging and complex fashion than in the desktop platform. Although not systematically measured by the educational teams in the kindergartens, their observations were that this phase requires more scaffolding on the mobile based experience in comparison to the desktop based experience.

Theme three - changes in patterns of collaboration among peers while programming

The nature of teamwork and collaboration demonstrate perhaps the most salient differences between the two modalities of work. On the desktop, collaboration between peers develops naturally and is almost essential, due to the different spatial positioning of the robot and the computer which, as already described, require a dual perspective. As a result, team work evolves: while one child sits by the computer and enters commands, her/his peers stand by the robot and reports on the outcomes of the commands or programs suggesting further actions. A natural "division of labor" and configuration of complementary perspectives emerge, as one child takes the perspective of the robot while the other takes the one of the programmer. The children arrive to the desired results together, through discussion and collaboration. In addition to the dual perspective collaboration, in some cases two programmers sit jointly by the computer and discuss the programming scenario and issues (e.g., the number of steps or turns needed to complete the task). The navigation track is also often constructed collaboratively by peers discussing its path or the location of obstacles in it. Sometimes the track is built or adjusted dynamically, during the programming session, by several learners in a collaborative process of trial and error.

Due to the nature of the mobile device, the programming process is more individual in nature. The mobile programming environment is in a handheld, personal device and it is not well suited for manipulation by more than one person. In addition, unlike the desktop scenario described above, the person holding the mobile programming environment stand by herself/himself just with the robot, following its behavior and grasping in real time the bugs to be fixed. There is no need for peers to assist with taking the robot's perspective, thus making the need for collaboration less relevant. However, other forms of collaboration emerge, as other children wish to be involved and actively look for ways to contribute. Most of the collaboration on the mobile mode revolves around the construction of the navigation track for the robot; children participate by adding obstacles, preparing signs (beginning, end etc.) and discussing potential scenarios for enhancing the track.

SUMMARY AND CONCLUSIONS

The interaction with technology allows kindergarten children to be engaged in technological thinking and to construct a solid basis for the development of complex ideas, through direct manipulation of physical objects [11,6]. The programming environment scaffolds this learning experience by providing tools to think and experiment with, supported by a structured pedagogical program. Originally designed as a desktop environment, a mobile version has been recently developed and implemented. The initial findings from the comparison between the desktop and mobile experiences outline three key themes. The first concerns the perspective of the child programmer, the second focuses on the modes of programming, and the third is related to the collaborative aspects of the programming process. We contend that each theme should serve as basis for further research. Specifically, there is a need to understand the contribution of each of the above themes to the overall programming experience, as well as to individual phases of the programming process. This in-depth analysis should consider different variables, such as the number of cycles of debugging carried out in each phase, the level of mediation required, or the skills and cognitive insights gained in each working mode. For example, it was observed that programmers in the mobile platform pass through the first two modes of programming (i.e., initial learning of the controls and initial sequencing of commands) very briefly, as they seem to pose less of a challenge than on the desktop platform. As a result, programmers arrive to the third phase (involving programming of a basic script) sooner, but having spent less time experimenting and developing necessary knowledge. Further research should establish whether or not this may have an effect on the amount of scaffolding and support required from the educational team.

The cognitive and emotional aspects of using the mobile based programming environment should also be further explored. The use of mobile devices creates a new kind of intimacy [2,15] and further research should explore the implications of the apparent unity between child and robot. For example, past studies on the desktop environment, found that after some engagement with the robot, children develop a technological, as opposed to an intentional-psychological perspective, towards the robot and relate to the robot as a technical construct and not as an entity with personal will or wish [1,4,7]. The mobile, often dubbed as an extension of the self [2], minimizes the physical distance and separation between the child and robot and this may affect the perception of the robot as an external and technical entity.

Finally, it was found that collaboration takes different character and form on the desktop based programming process, compared to the mobile programming experience. The mobile experience is more individual in nature and seems to call for a substantially different kind of collaboration and possibly even to a lesser extent of collaboration when compared to the desktop experience where learners need their peers to serve as their eyes while being constraint by the location of the computer. Engaging in a collaborative learning process may lead to developing collaborative skills that are significant to learning. On the other hand, for the mobile programmer, having successfully faced multiple challenges on her/his own, may lead to a greater sense of accomplishment and self-efficacy.

Although beyond the scope of this paper, we are aware that the advanced phases of programming as well, dealing with rule and adaptive behavior based on incoming data (via the sensors) should also be examined in depth. Reaching a deeper understanding of the different aspects of the mobile programming experience, may contribute to the design of environments that make use of the unique affordances of the mobile device. This understanding will also assist in bridging the gaps that may have been formed due to the transition from desktop-based to mobile-based programming.

REFERENCES

1. Ackermann, E., (1991). The agency model of transactions: Towards an understanding of children's theory of control. *In J. Montangero and A. Tryphon (Eds.). Psychologie genetique et sciences cognitives.*
2. Belk, R. (2013). Extended self in a digital world. *Journal of Consumer Research*, 40(3), 477–500
3. Bers, M.U. and Horn, M.S. (2010) 'Tangible programming in early childhood: revisiting developmental assumptions through new technologies', in Berson, I.R. and Berson, M.J. (Eds): *High-Tech Tots: Childhood in a Digital World*, Information Age Publishing, Greenwich, CT, pp.49–70.
4. Kuperman, A., & Mioduser, D. (2012). Kindergarten Children's Perceptions of "Anthropomorphic Artifacts" with Adaptive Behavior. *Interdisciplinary Journal of E-Learning and Learning Objects*, *8*, 137-148.
5. Levy, S., & Mioduser, D. (2008). Does it ''want'' or ''was it programmed to...''? Kindergarten children's explanations of an autonomous robot's adaptive functioning. International Journal of Technology and Design Education, 18(3), 337–359.
6. Levy, S. T., & Mioduser, D. (2010). Approaching complexity through planful play: Kindergarten children's strategies in constructing an autonomous robot's behavior. *International Journal of Computers for Mathematical Learning*, *15*(1), 21-43.
7. Mioduser, D., & Levy, S. T. (2010). Making sense by building sense: Kindergarten children's construction and understanding of adaptive robot behaviors. *International Journal of Computers for Mathematical Learning*, *15*(2), 99-127.
8. Mioduser, D., Levy, S. T., & Talis, V. (2009). Episodes to scripts to rules: Concrete-abstractions in kindergarten children's explanations of a robot's behavior. *International Journal of Technology and Design Education*, *19*(1), 15-36.
9. Papert, S. (1980). Mindstorms: Children, Computers, and Powerful Ideas. Cambridge, MA: Basic Books
10. Rave, G., and Mioduser, D. (2014). Young Children construct planning skills via programming the behavior of a virtual robot using tangible programming language. In *Proceedings of the 9th Chais Conference for the Study of Innovation and Learning Technologies* (Hebrew), 286-292.
11. Resnick, M. (1998). Technologies for lifelong kindergarten. *Educational technology research and development*, *46*(4), 43-55.
12. Resnick, M., & Silverman, B. (2005). Some reflections on designing construction kits for kids. *IDC '05 Proceedings of the conference on Interaction Design and Children*, 117-122.
13. Sharples, M., Taylor, J., & Vavoula, G. (2007). A theory of learning for the mobile age. *In R. Andrews & C. Haythornthwaite (Eds.), The Sage handbook of elearning research* (pp. 221-47). London: Sage.
14. Talis, V., Levy, S. T., & Mioduser, D. (1998). *RoboGAN: Interface for programming a robot with rules for young children.* Tel-Aviv: Tel-Aviv University
15. Turkle, S. (2008). Always-on/always-on-you: The tethered self. In *Handbook of mobile communication studies, ed. James E. Katz,* 121–137. Cambridge, MA: MIT Press.

Supporting Interactive Youth Maker Programs in Public and School Libraries: Design Hypotheses and First Implementations

Victor R. Lee, Whitney Lewis, Kristin A. Searle, Mimi Recker, Jennifer Hansen, & Abigail L. Phillips
Utah State University
Logan, Utah, USA
victor.lee@usu.edu; whitlewis7@gmail.com; kristin.searle@usu.edu; mimi.recker@usu.edu; jenny.hansen@aggiemail.usu.edu; abigail.phillips@usu.edu

ABSTRACT
After six months of observation at three middle school libraries and one public library implementing Maker-oriented programs, we propose four design hypotheses derived from qualitative data analysis and initial testing through design implementation. These design hypotheses address how public and school libraries serving adolescent youth can better facilitate Maker-oriented activities and are drawn from an on-going study and design project to help libraries develop interactive, technologically enriched spaces and programs to support youth exploration and creativity. Each hypothesis is illustrated with examples drawn from our observations of libraries before and after maker programs were introduced.

Author Keywords
Makerspaces; public libraries; school libraries; design

ACM Classification Keywords
K.3.1 [Computers and Education]: Computer Uses in Education-Collaborative learning.

INTRODUCTION
Libraries that serve adolescent youth are currently facing pressure to adapt their program offerings to include a range of new services including Maker-oriented programs [8] where youth are able to create their own physical and digital content using everything from found materials to 3D printers. This new pressure arises from an increased awareness of how libraries function as important sites for supporting interest-driven "connected learning" [9] that emphasizes youth exploration and creation of new forms of digital media and artifacts. Successful models such as Harold Washington Library's YOUMedia program, which encouraged youth to go to a major urban library to work with mentors and create with new media [2] do exist, yet the means to effectively design and implement such programs in other library sites have yet to be specified. This represents an important research and design opportunity to help libraries develop interactive, technologically enriched spaces for youth exploration and creativity. In particular, school libraries are an especially important youth library site to consider. They comprise over 80% of the 119,000 libraries in the United States [1]. Yet, the literature on how school libraries can become sites for youth Making is still very limited [11]. As an important venue for informal youth interaction and learning, more work is needed to support adaptations of such spaces.

IDC '17, June 27-30, 2017, Stanford, CA, USA

ACM ISBN 978-1-4503-4921-5/17/06…$15.00
http://dx.doi.org/10.1145/3078072.3079741

Our goal during the past year has been to respond to these needs for both small public and school libraries by using techniques associated with contextual design [3] and design-based research [13]. Contextual design is one of a number of contemporary approaches favored in human-computer interaction communities that highlights the importance of understanding users and their context prior to creating new tools or interventions. More specifically, contextual design favors deliberate observational research and modeling of observed phenomena as its first process steps. Design-based research, originating out of learning sciences, involves iterative introduction of educational resources and activities into an intact educational setting with the expectation that implementation will reveal hidden complexities relevant to learning in that system and serve as a means for testing design hypotheses and generating new theories. We maintain an overarching assumption that these combined approaches can facilitate the identification of the hidden resources and obstacles embedded in designing for Maker learning activities in libraries serving youth.

This paper reports four design hypotheses thus far derived from an extended period of observational work, which involved understanding existing practices and routines in youth-serving public and school libraries in a predominantly rural county. We present these hypotheses along with our rationale drawn from our observational work while also reporting on early design implementations that have sought to embody these hypotheses. Our initial commentaries based on those implementations are provided, followed by a discussion of what tasks and opportunities lie ahead in the future for this kind of library-based Maker activity design work.

DATA SOURCES AND APPROACH

Naturalistic Observation

For the first six months, our approach has been explicitly committed toward observation and understanding of current library practices rather than immediately introducing any interventions. For this initial phase of work, we obtained commitments from all middle school libraries in a single school district covering a rural county in Utah and from two major rural public libraries in that same area serving the same students. We conducted weekly observations at one of the public libraries and at three middle school libraries, in which we obtained detailed field notes and photographs of the sites. (The remaining sites will serve as future test sites).

In what follows, we refer to the libraries with pseudonyms: the middle school libraries are Autumn Falls Middle School Library, Northern Trove Middle School Library, and Blue Spruce Middle School Library, while the public library is North Hollow Public Library

Observations at the libraries typically lasted about one hour, although several went for as long as two hours. The times were adjusted when the project team learned of special events or time slots that would allow for observation of activities beyond what would typically be encountered. For example, on a school district professional development day, a team member observed the entire multi-hour school librarian professional development session, and on special school event days, some observations were moved to before school hours or during lunch times to observe the library when it would be used those days. School library observations focused on the work of library personnel (typically a single library media specialist), the patrons (predominantly students at the school, although classroom teachers were often visitors to plan for collaborative instruction or obtain materials), and the various planned and unplanned activities that took place there. Public library observations focused on teen centered activities, and involved observing teen advisory board meetings and weekly teen programs at the library, which typically hosted 20-50 youth on a given day. Sites and activities were also photo documented. In addition, we conducted audio recorded interviews with each public and school librarian (approximately one hour per interview).

At the time of this writing, we have obtained 201 pages of field notes from those sites, multiple hours of audio recordings from interviews, and several dozens of photographs. Full analysis of this qualitative data is still ongoing at the time of this reporting. However, current analyses included open coding of observational field notes, which have been distilled to identify key job responsibilities of the observed librarians, librarian characteristics, and library features. These have been cross checked with photographic records. We have also begun to articulate coded features with patterns of youth behavior and interaction in the libraries. We have been and continue to deploy the constant comparative method to verify and challenge claims that are being made [7]. For this paper, we provide select and brief descriptive accounts rather than raw codes or reports of codes as our coding approach continues to adapt and expand. However, the assertions made here have been driven largely by what has emerged thus far in our coding of field notes from the first six months of observations.

Initial Program Launches

As timing and our partnerships have evolved, we have also begun to co-develop and implement new Maker-oriented programs at two of our partner libraries (one public library and one middle school library) as our six months of dedicated observation time had begun to close. Those initial program launches will be referenced in our discussion of design hypotheses below. The first program took place at the public library's teen night and used MaKey MaKey interface boards (makeymakey.com) to create new forms of computer input using conductive material and found objects. The MaKey MaKey night took place in the evening at a public library during an existing teen program time slot.

The second program was a launch of an afterschool activity at a school library with an emphasis on Making with paper circuitry and electronic textiles. In this program, youth had access to copper tape, conductive thread, coin cell batteries, various craft and found objects, and LEDs to make interactive paper and cloth objects. These objects then resided in the school library as interactive objects for others to explore and use during the school day. This afterschool library activity was one of multiple afterschool program options that youth could select and lasted for about one and half hours once per week. Attendance for any program fluctuated depending on a myriad of factors. Along with this school's librarian, we helped develop and facilitate this 8-week program.

For both programs, field notes and photo documentation were taken with multiple observers independently recording notes. Those data sources are used to inform our discussion of the activities, and they appear in commentary for our design hypotheses.

DESIGN HYPOTHESES

We now present our emerging design hypotheses for libraries as spaces for maker programming, and, where appropriate, the outcomes from our first program implementations. As this is part of a larger program of design-based research, we expect that over time these hypotheses will be further refined and adapted ontologically (e.g., from design hypothesis to principles or strategies, such as what is presented from iterative work elsewhere [4]). Furthermore, we retain awareness that features of the geographic context in which the work is unfolding (a rural and small town context rather than a large urban one, as had been the case with YOUMedia) influences the creation of these hypotheses. Still, we believe that academic discourse related to design for real settings should move beyond 'final-form' reports and instead offer more concurrent reporting as work unfolds. Those prefaces should be kept in mind when reading the sections that follow.

Design Hypothesis 1. Many youth find libraries to be more welcoming as convening and exploration spaces when the libraries permit small behavioral transgressions.

In our observations, we have found unexpected contrasts between the three middle school libraries. In particular, Northern Trove Middle School Library was rarely visited by students during unscheduled times (between classes, lunch times, before or after school hours). On the other hand, Autumn Falls Middle School Library, a middle school in the same district serving the same age of students, was seen as a desirable place to hang out during unscheduled times. Dozens of students filled the library doing a range of activities, including playing games on personal phones, using computers or iPads in the library to play multiplayer games, participating in passive programming and craft creation activities, playing board games, chatting, and reading. Blue Spruce Middle School Library fell somewhere in between these two. In contrast with Autumn Falls Middle School Library where youths' behavior was much less restricted, Blue Spruce Middle School Library was also frequently visited by youth with many hanging out there during unscheduled time, but youth at this library were constrained to specific activities such as independent computer coding, chess, reading, and puzzles.

One of the major differences that we have observed between the school libraries is how classroom-like behavioral norms were enforced. At Northern Trove Middle School Library, the librarian took a traditional approach to maintaining the library setting. For instance, Maker activities there – a new development in response to professional pressure to incorporate Making - were restricted to Mondays during homeroom. During all other times of the day, students were expected to use the library in a quiet manner for reading, checking out books, taking tests, and doing homework. Only students who met certain academic standards were able to participate in the "Monday Making" time. In one instance, this library was closed for part of the day as a punitive action due to students talking too much. In contrast, at Autumn Falls Middle School Library, we observed students who were free to make noise or use their mobile devices openly. Students were welcome to put their feet on table surfaces and gather with friends to simply have an indoor space to talk. According to the librarian supervising this space, libraries can and should be loud places, especially when youth are involved. In this respect, the school library became a place where students could do things that they could not do in classrooms and, perhaps as a result, seemed to attract more youth.

As further support for this hypothesis, we have observed that at the public library, North Hollow, youth were given no form of reprimand for certain behavioral transgressions. We have seen youth take off their shoes and walk around barefoot, use handheld devices with their friends, lay on the floor between aisles, or even gently wrestle with one another. From these observations, we believe that part of what draws youth to spend time in this library – which has seen steady growth in teen program attendance in recent years – is the opportunity to freely behave in ways that are playful and physically comfortable without as much accountability or externally focused expectation from supervising adults. What this suggests for the design of youth-oriented maker programs in libraries is that there should be both tolerance for and welcoming of a range of youth behaviors, and a reduction of imposed norms for behavior that resemble traditional classroom, remedial, or punitive forms of activity. That is also consistent with the characterization of climate in non-library Makerspaces that have appeared in the literature thus far [12].

Design Hypothesis 2. Flexible and semi-private physical design and layout of the library space can serve to encourage youth participation

Another major difference we have noticed is the presence of accessible, semi-enclosed areas where youth tend to congregate and spend time informally with friends. For instance, at Autumn Falls Middle School Library, the librarian converted an equipment storage room into a what she called a Makerspace where youth could access Maker and craft materials or hang out together in a room separate from others. There were additional areas made up of couches, bean bags, and chairs that sit facing one another to enable group conversation (see Figure 1).

At the North Hollow Public Library, one unique feature is mobile shelving. When there are teen programs, these shelves are rearranged to facilitate spaces for large and small groups to comfortably convene. Some teens will go with groups of friends and sit down together in secluded aisles, while others will arrange chairs and couches to sit in small circles. When these shelves are not rearranged, we observed teens at the library behaving more like typical library patrons moving quietly among the shelves to look at books or quietly working on homework at a table.

In contrast, at Northern Trove Middle School Library, the library space was set as one large open space and tables were in distinct and continuous rows (see Figure 2) within plain sight of the circulation desk. In addition, hanging in front of the circulation desk was a large, round mirror that enabled the librarian to supervise all bookshelves.

Figure 1. Lounging areas at Autumn Falls School Library

We suspect this arrangement may limit the privacy groups of students feel they can have and forces multi-person body-positions that are inconsistent with how people naturally arrange themselves physically into groups [10]. We do not know with certainty to what extent these forced spatial configurations inhibit youth mobility and limit interest in being in the library, but the implication of this possibility is that when possible, Maker programs for youth in libraries could profit from making available semi-private or easily configurable spaces so that youth can select who they interact with and who interacts with them. Indeed, other research suggests adolescent youth doing Maker oriented projects prefer to have more explicit control over who can see and access what they are doing rather than openly making all their work visible and public [6].

Figure 2. Northern Trove School Library

Thus far, in the afterschool school library maker program at Autumn Falls Middle School Library, we have observed that groups of youth will try to stake claims to particular tables or areas in certain regions of the school library. Some youth also get the materials that they need for a paper circuitry project and then move to an entirely separate, fairly dark corner of the library out of view of most of the other youth. When we checked on their projects, they had been diligently working but wanted to be working 'by themselves' instead of with the other two dozen youth who were present.

Design Hypothesis 3. Library maker programs get better attendance and reception when they augment existing programs rather than create entirely new ones.

During our observation periods, we have seen youth-serving library personnel make deliberate efforts to launch new programs that they have heard youth would be interested in, but these new programs can be radical departures from what they have successfully launched before. For example, North Hollow Public Library launched an afterschool coding club. Only a few youth have consistently attended and participated, and youth who were already present in the library opted to do other activities instead of participating in the coding club. North Hollow Public Library also created a Makerspace with 3-D printers and media software akin to what has been noted as accessible and successful in cases like YOUMedia. However, this space has been substantially underused and was rarely visited by teens, according to direct observations and reports from library personnel.

Similarly, at Northern Trove Middle School Library, we observed the school librarian launching her own newly-created Maker-themed activities, which included mostly sewing or craft activities and more recently K'NEX. Students could sign up to do these pre-planned crafts on Mondays during their 20-minute homeroom period. She was inspired to pursue this after having learned from others in the community that paper crafts and sewing were one form of maker programming that has seen success in some libraries. After weeks of sign-up opportunities and school announcements, only a handful of students in the school participated. The librarian reported that (excepting one student who signed up for all activities), all the youth she was attracting were ones already assigned to the library for homeroom, even though other students were informed that they could obtain a pass from their regular homeroom to attend.

These examples of new initiatives serve to illustrate that, even with a Maker orientation and some investment of resources toward promoting the program as publicly available to youth, its success and appeal to its intended population is hardly guaranteed.

However, as we have transitioned to our first designed implementations of new Maker-oriented programs, we have noted from our observational work that most of our partner libraries already have existing repertoires of recognized and successful programs that get several youth participants. Our view as a design team is that we should augment those programs with Maker components rather than try to introduce entirely new programs that pose much higher risk.

For example, during a teen advisory board meeting at North Hollow Public Library when new programs were being decided for the following month, we observed the enthusiasm and interest of youth and the library personnel to have another library video game night. This involved bringing in various game consoles and larger projection screens for gaming and was an old standby for the teen advisory board when no other activity could be quickly conceptualized or implemented. Having seen firsthand through observations that this drew in a number of local youth, we proposed that MaKey MaKeys be introduced for a library video-game night with computer-based games. This proposal was enthusiastically endorsed by the teen advisory board and implemented at the next library teen evening program (see Figure 3).

This event was seen as a tremendous success by the library personnel, both by their direct verbal reports to us as a research team and reports of youth asking when they could do more of "that MaKey MaKey game activity" weeks after the program had ended. This program was easier to implement because it utilized tools and programs already familiar to personnel and the youth while also introducing a relatively accessible Maker technology that youth could use as part of their game night through designing custom game controllers.

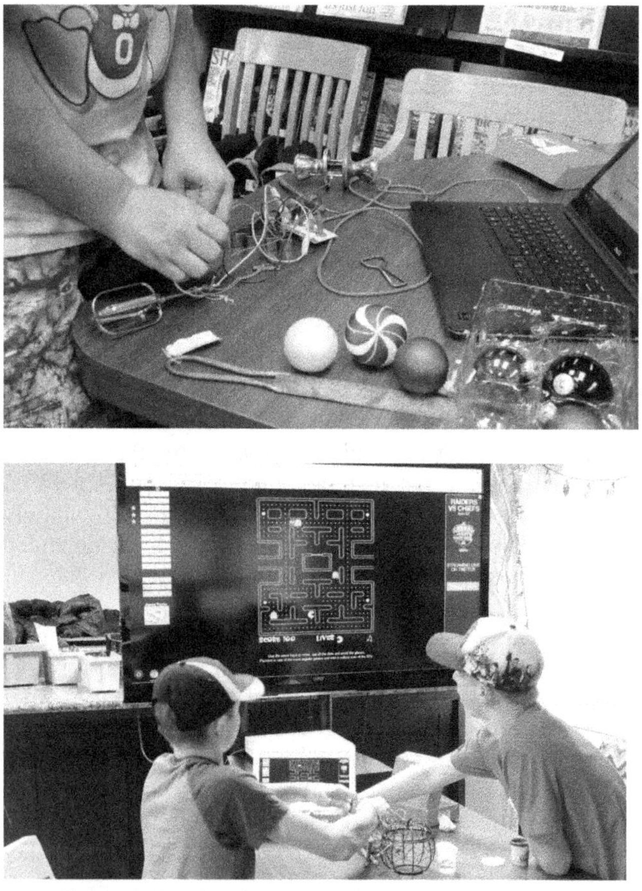

Figure 3. Testing for conductivity and creating game controllers at North Hollow Public Library

Design hypothesis 4. Library maker programs should accommodate drop-in visitation patterns of libraries with designated "first-timer" areas.

In our observation of successful library activities and programs, we noticed that libraries were often treated as drop-in spaces by youth. Youth would show up late, leave early, or just come to a program one time but not regularly. In contrast to formal learning environments, where consistent scheduled attendance is expected, this presented a significant design challenge. Maker projects often take several hours to complete and may be distributed over multiple days, but library youth patrons visiting a program may only be present for varying amounts of time or joining an activity several days into the project, making a coherent progression of activities difficult to design.

Furthermore, with one of our partnering school libraries, Autumn Falls Middle School Library, playing host to an afterschool program, we also learned that youth visiting this library would be able to opt in and out of specific afterschool activities each day. This meant some youth may leave a program taking place in the school gymnasium and join the one in the library halfway through a day's session, and others may opt to do the one taking place in the home economics room one day but then do the library activity on the next day. Upon recognizing this, we explored creating "first-timer" areas by way of signage and beginner resource sheets, so those who drop in on unexpected days and times could get started without the intimidation of trying match what someone else had been making over several weeks.

The first-timer area had regular attendance for all the days it was implemented in the afterschool club hosted by Autumn Falls Middle School Library. We also overheard a number of teachers involved in the afterschool program who had visited briefly to speak with the hosting school librarian about program logistics ask about the first-timer area and then comment enthusiastically about this idea for supporting drop-in visitors. We did not see any new youth leave the library-hosted maker program early and also accommodated word-of-mouth attendance that went well beyond (i.e., more than double) what we had initially planned. Our current design challenge is figuring out how to enable and support the freedom of movement, exploration, and behavior with a large group of youth in the library who are rapidly differentiating themselves in their levels of Maker expertise. Finding solutions to this for libraries would allow them to be more than just spaces for superficial and duplicative making activities (e.g., suffering from the 'keychain syndrome' [4]) and also cultivate a 'learning culture' rather than a 'hacking culture' [5], which we believe is more apt for youth in libraries.

DISCUSSION

This paper reports on our observations of adolescents and librarians interacting in rural public and school libraries and our preliminary forays into Maker activity design. We have presented four design hypotheses for library Maker programs and spaces: (1) youths' ability to experience freedom in the space matters, (2) the physical space needs to be comfortable and configurable for the option of semi-private groupings, (3) building Maker components by leveraging existing programs can be more successful than creating completely new programs, and (4) there is a need for visible "first-timer" areas and options to accommodate drop-in visitation.

Within these design hypotheses, several questions remain unanswered. First, the success or failure of libraries in implementing Maker activities might largely depend upon the librarian's disposition and openness to less traditional uses of library spaces. How do we facilitate this shift in professional disposition towards seeing libraries as spaces for "hanging out" and "messing around" with physical and digital materials [9]? We are actively exploring this through various interview protocols and will report on librarian dispositions in a future paper. Second, librarian reports, our own observations, and initial implementations of programs suggest that highly accessible, low-threshold activities like building video game controllers with Makey Makeys or creating paper circuits using found materials were likely to be more easily supported in these drop-in youth spaces than higher-threshold or more time consuming activities like 3D printing or game making in Scratch. Our future work will focus on uncovering what other kinds of low-threshold activities lend themselves to making in libraries.

These are important questions for us to consider but are also relevant for the broader community of designers of youth interactions. Interaction design may include specific tools, applications, and hardware that enable youth to have new experiences. At the same time, the physical and social environment in which activities are to take place, even if they do not involve wildly experimental technologies, must be thoughtfully considered. Interaction design for youth should also involve some consideration of what already works and what does not in a site with respect to a set of design goals. Finally, the role of adults and professionals must be considered as well. Designers need to find ways to build on what these adults already are comfortable doing and ease them into new ways of planning and facilitating interactive activities like those we envision in our own work. As we begin to develop answers, we will form a better understanding of libraries as an ecosystem that can effectively support youth participation in Making.

ACKNOWLEDGMENTS

We thank the library professionals and youth for their participation. Funding for this work came from an Institute of Museum and Library Services grant, no. RE-31-16-0013-16 and from the Beverly Taylor Sorenson Arts Learning Program. The findings and claims made here are those of the authors and not necessarily those of the funding organizations.

REFERENCES

1. American Library Association. 2015. Number of libraries in the United States. Retrieved January 30, 2017 from http://www.ala.org/tools/libfactsheets/alalibraryfactsheet01.
2. Kimberly Austin, Stacy B. Ehrlich, Cassidy Puckett, and Judi Singleton. YOUmedia Chicago: Reimagining learning, literacies, and libraries: A snapshot of year 1. 2011. *Consortium on Chicago School Research at the University of Chicago Urban Education Institute*.
3. Hugh Beyer and Karen Holtzblatt. 1997. Contextual design: Defining customer-centered systems. Elsevier.
4. Paulo Blikstein. 2013. Digital fabrication and 'making' in education: The democratization of invention. In *FabLabs: Of Machines, Makers and Inventors*, J. Walter-Herrmann & C. Büching (eds.). Bielefeld, Germany: Transcript Publishers.
5. Paulo Blikstein and Marcelo Worsley. 2016. Children Are Not Hackers. In *Makeology: Makerspaces as learning environments* (Vol. 1), Peppler, K., Halverson, E., and Kafai, Y.B. (eds.). Routledge.
6. Maneksha DuMont and Victor R. Lee. 2015. Understanding the opportunities and challenges of introducing computational crafts to alternative high school students. In *Educational Media and Technology Yearbook* (Vol. 39), M. Orey and R. M. Branch (eds.). Springer, New York, New York, 83-99.
7. Barney G. Glaser and Anselm L. Strauss. 1967. *The discovery of grounded theory; Strategies for qualitative research*. Aldine Transactions.
8. Maureen L. Hartman, Sandra Hughes-Hassell, and Kafi Damali Kumasi. 2014. *The future of library services for and with teens: A call to action*. Braun, L.W. (ed). Chicago, IL: Young Adult Library Services Association.
9. Mizuko Ito, Kris Gutiérrez, Sonia Livingstone, Bill Penuel, Jean Rhodes, Katie Salen, Juliet Schor, Julian Sefton-Green, and S. Craig Watkins. 2013. *Connected learning: An agenda for research and design*. BookBaby.
10. Adam Kendon. 2010. Spacing and orientation in co-present interaction. In *Development of Multimodal Interfaces: Active Listening and Synchrony*. Springer, Berlin, Heidelberg, 1-15.
11. Leslie B. Preddy. 2013. *School library makerspaces*. Libraries Unlimited.
12. Kimberly Sheridan, Erica Rosenfeld Halverson, Breanne Litts, Lisa Brahms, Lynette Jacobs-Priebe, and Trevor Owens. 2014. Learning in the making: A comparative case study of three makerspaces. *Harvard Educational Review* 84, 4: 505-531.
13. The Design-Based Research Collective. 2003. Design-Based Research: An Emerging Paradigm for Educational Inquiry. *Educational Researcher* 32, 1: 5-8.

Becoming Makers: Examining 'Making' Literacy in the Elementary School Science Classroom

Sharon Lynn Chu[1], Elizabeth Deuermeyer[2], Rachel Martin[2], Francis Quek[3], Alexander Berman[3], Mario Suarez[2], Niloofar Zarei[3], Beth Nam[1] and Colin Banigan[1]
[1]The StoryLab@Texas A&M, [2]Department of Teaching, Learning & Culture,
[3]TAMU Embodied Interaction Lab. Texas A&M University.
[sharilyn, e.deuermeyer, rkt002, quek, anberman, suarezi, n.zarei.3001, namieu, cbanigan]@tamu.edu

ABSTRACT

This paper extends the concept of digital literacy and applies it to Making. Through case descriptions, we contribute an understanding of how children can become or fail to become individuals literate in Making within a formal learning context. Our analysis draws from video recordings and other data sources of two 4th grade classrooms in which the students, who had already participated in 1.5 years of more structured 'makified activities', engaged in an open-ended, exploration-based, and playful task that was more in line with the spirit of Making. Student teams were classified as 'high in Making literacy' and 'low in Making literacy', revealing how Making literacy was expressed at the level of skills, mental models, and practices in various ways for different students. Our qualitative analysis demonstrates what burgeoning Making literacy may mean in a public elementary school classroom, paving the way for a vision of a time when Making becomes generalized practice.

Author Keywords
Maker; Making; Children; Literacy; Science; Elementary school; Electronics.

ACM Classification Keywords
H.5.m. Information interfaces and presentation (e.g., HCI): Miscellaneous.

INTRODUCTION
The Maker movement has tremendous promise to enable children to participate in empowering learning experiences through technology use. Studies of children's Making – "an active process of building, designing, and innovating with tools and materials to produce shareable artifacts" [1] – has gained much traction in the IDC community (e.g., [2, 3]). Yet, we still have insufficient understanding of how learning interrelates with Making. In this paper, our focus is the public school classroom as a site for the development of 'Making' literacy and learning. Our research goal is to contribute to the understanding of how children become or fail to become Makers within formal learning contexts. Understanding how students may learn Making and become Makers in formal settings may inform us on how the classroom may be a site where children from a diversity of backgrounds are inducted into the Maker movement. Making gains additional significance when it is used in an educational environment where it is a medium for learning. Reading, writing and speaking have traditionally been the main ways by which learning takes place. As new platforms and screen-based media emerged, it was quickly recognized that this literacy needed to evolve to include multimedia and digital technologies, such as Internet search skills. With the deep interest to bring the Maker movement into education, it is imperative that we now begin to understand literacy in the context of Making. Key questions to be asked include not only 'how does a student become literate in Making?', but first of all, the question 'what does it mean for a student to be literate in Making?' begs consideration.

IDC '17, June 27-30, 2017, Stanford, CA, USA

ACM ISBN 978-1-4503-4921-5/17/06...$15.00
DOI: http://dx.doi.org/10.1145/3078072.3079745

BACKGROUND: LITERACY
Literacy is defined by Vee [4] as "a human facility with a symbolic and infrastructural technology that can be used for creative, communicative and rhetorical purposes". Literacy has traditionally been associated with skills in reading and writing that enable an individual to participate adequately and effectively in society, but many other concepts of literacy have been put forth. 'Media literacy' is "the ability to access…media, to understand and to critically evaluate different aspects of the media and media content and to create communications in a variety of contexts" [5]. 'Digital literacy' includes skills like searching, organizing and presenting digital information online [6].

Literacy has at its core processes of meaning-making through forms of representation [7]. A literate individual is able and willing to engage with the medium to create new meaning. A useful framework proposed by Meyers et al. [8] describes three aspects of digital literacy: i) *Skills* – "a set of discrete abilities or behaviors", often equated with competencies such as knowing the Boolean operators to create effective search strings in a search engine; ii) *Mental models* – "the application of abstract mental models to activities involving digital content", essentially 'habits of mind' that one may apply to generalized contexts and problems (e.g., being able to evaluate the authority of internet sources); and iii) *Practices* – "engagement in a set of practices involving digital tools and media that are deeply embedded in a particular context or activity", i.e., the general capability of an individual to function within a physical and social environment characterized by digitality, which typically is accompanied with a sense of identity.

TOWARD 'MAKING' LITERACY

To our knowledge, there has been little examination of the concept of literacy in terms of Making. DiSessa [9] argues that for a literacy to arise, the associated technology must first become central or infrastructural to the society's communication practices. For instance, although writings were available very early on, the importance of reading and writing literacy came into play much later [4]. As Making technologies become diversified in their uses and more pervasive in everyday settings, there is increasing pressure to understand the form that Making literacy will take and what it will entail. Some prior work pave the way for us to think about the issue. Meyers et al. [8] move literacy within the scope of the Maker through another perspective on digital literacy: rather than seeing the literate individual as a consumer who is able and willing to engage in interpretive processes to (re)produce meaning, they advance the notion of *the participatory creator* – "a digitally literate person who is able to and see themselves as someone who engages in the activity of digital information creation".

In her dissertation, Litts [1] uses the lens of 'multiliteracies' to analyze learning in three types of informal makerspaces (libraries, after school programs, and museums). Multiliteracies recognizes that learning is situated and embedded in material and socio-cultural contexts, and that there are many ways for people to learn [10]. Litts proposes three design threads emerging from her analysis: activity (making trajectory and artifact), identity (maker), and community (makerspace). Using this framework, Litts asserts for instance that "not every classroom can become a makerspace, since makerspaces require a community element that transcends the systemic limitations of a traditional classroom".

The area of 'computational thinking' expanded to 'computational literacy' that recognizes "the computer as the material basis of the literacy" [4] may also be relevant to Making literacy. Steinkuehler and Johnson [11] report on two case studies of groups engaging in 'modding' (modifications) of the well-known game *World of Warcraft.* Mods can be seen as computational artifacts, the products of a specific kind of computational literacy. Integrating data from online forums, design documents and interviews, they propose that a potential learning trajectory for computational literacy moves first from consumption (being mod users) to production (becoming mod critics and then mod adapters) to more complex or professional forms (full-fledged mod producers). The question that Steinkuehler and Johnson do not answer is under what conditions does participation evolve into production.

The Making literature has addressed to various degrees the three aspects of literacy from Meyers et al.'s [8] framework. At the level of 'skills', research that evaluate particular Making technology implementations and approaches, such as TouchWire [12] and I/O Stickers [13], tend to focus on specific abilities, e.g., wiring circuits, manipulating stickers, or the acquisition of knowledge sets, e.g., circuitry.

At the level of 'mental models', work that address the Maker mindset is relevant. Dougherty [14] introduced the idea of the 'growth mindset', the belief that one's capabilities can continuously be improved, as being central to a Maker mindset. Regalla [15] offers reflections on how this growth mindset can be fostered in practice by, for example, training facilitators to withhold offering direct help, helping the children to step back from their process, and nurturing resilience in the face of frustration and failure. Some literature has looked at Making at the level of 'practices' or identity. Halverson and Sheridan [16] define Makers as the "identities of participation that people take on within the Maker movement". Some like Martin and Dixon [17] have delineated characteristics perceived to be associated with the Maker individual (e.g., playful, learning-oriented, accepting of technology, risk-taking, enjoys sharing, etc.).

RESEARCH QUESTION

Digital literacy has been addressed in both formal and informal learning contexts, but in formal institutions, the goal of literacy formation must also consider the "constraints, motivational challenges and rigid discourses" of such contexts [8]. Meyers et al. [8] argue that informal environments are the best suited to actualize this form of digital literacy since "agents can express themselves most fully outside the bounds and constraints of a curricular agenda and standards". The questions of interest to us then are: *i) Can students acquire Making literacy in the elementary school classroom?*; and *ii) How do students express their Making literacy in a Making-based class assignment?*.

Our investigation of these questions adopts the approach of studying how students, having acquired basic Making skills and being familiar with the concept of Making through close-ended Making activities, engage in Making at the level of mental models and practices through an open-ended Making activity for the first time.

STUDY CONTEXT

This study was part of a larger 3-year long research project that integrates Making into the science curriculum for 3rd, 4th, and 5th grade classes within a local public elementary school classroom. Each class engages for a week in a Making curriculum focused around a specific science topic every six weeks. This corresponds to one Making week for every science unit in the curriculum of that particular grade level. Activities during the Making weeks are designed by a team consisting of members with expertise in electrical engineering, computer science, child-computer interaction and design, and education and classroom pedagogy, informed by feedback from the participating teachers. The allotted class length ranges from 45 minutes to 1.5 hours depending on the grade level. The number of students in each class ranges from 18 to 20.

We describe below an example of the activities that the students engaged in during the Making weeks for the first 1.5 years of the project in the science unit of 'Matter and Energy: Mixtures and Solutions'. The students built an electronic mixer (see Figure 1) comprising of a basic electronic circuit with a geared rotating motor as the load and a switch made out of card stock and conductive copper tape. A 3D-printed mixer head was attached to the motor through a dowel rod so that the student can insert the head into a container and activate the motor. With their electronic mixer, students mixed glitter with water and made observations about the mixture. Other examples of Making activities in which the students engaged for other science units included building LED-embedded food chains, rotating solar system models, etc.

Figure 1. Mixer with motor

STUDY DESCRIPTION

The work reported in this paper specifically focused on two 4th grade Bilingual science classes, both taught by the same teacher. Class 1 had 19 participants and Class 2 had 18 participants, totaling to 37 participants (18 groups of two or three students). The study was conducted in the second semester of Year 2 of the research project, when the 37 participants had already participated in the first 1.5 years of Making curriculum as described above. In one of the Making weeks, the nature of the Making activity was changed. In contrast to the previous activities, the activity was made more open-ended, exploration-based, encompassing, and more playful.

Figure 2. Students working on their dioramas

The curriculum topic addressed during the focus Maker week was 'Forms of Energy'. The learning goals for this unit were that students should be able to differentiate among the various forms of energy (including mechanical, sound, electrical, light, and heat or thermal energy. Minors' assent was obtained from all the students prior to the study, and parents also provided written informed consent for their child to be observed and recorded during class. The focus Making week consisted of the following activities:

On Day 1, a review of the forms of energy was done by the teacher to ensure baseline science knowledge. On Day 2, students were put in groups of two or three. Each group was assigned one form of energy, and the students were given a single instruction for the Maker activity: "Make a diorama that shows a model of your assigned form of energy using the materials available to you in any way that you want". The students were given a set of components (Figure 3), most of which they have encountered in previous Making weeks. From their engagement in the previous 1.5 years of Making weeks, the students had basic Making skills (building a basic electronic circuit to activate LEDs, and motors) and programming skills using the Arduino microcontroller board and the ArduBlockly interface (a block-based visual programming interface).

As in previous Making weeks, helpers were present in the classroom, but for this activity, students were let to work independently and without interruption from the adults, unless help was specifically requested by the children. The diorama-making activity was spread over Day 2 and Day 3. On Day 4, all student teams presented their final dioramas to the class, the teacher and the school principal. The students planned out a script and practiced at their tables before doing their presentations. Figure 2 shows the students working on their dioramas. On Day 5, the students filled in a questionnaire about their interest in Making and feedback about the Making week.

DATA ANALYSIS

Our research adopted a qualitative case study approach. Data sources included video recordings of each student team's diorama presentation, the diorama drawings, pictures of the final diorama with electronics embedded, video recordings of the planning phase, planning sheets, and observation notes from helpers.

Two members of the research team watched the students' presentations and together generated a summary of the concept of each diorama. Specifically, notes were taken on the components used, how the diorama modeled the type of energy assigned, and the role that Making broadly had in the diorama. Six student groups that had the most interesting presentations were selected for deeper analysis. Three pairs of coders were assigned two student groups each. All coders were familiar with the Maker movement. Each pair of coders consisted of one person from a technical background (computer science or engineering) and one person from a non-technical background (education or design). The data for each student group were collected from all the various sources identified earlier, and given to each coder pair. Each coder independently reviewed all the data, and then did a decomposition analysis of the dioramas: first, all the meaningful units of the diorama were identified (see Figure 5 for example of decomposition); each unit was then coded as being 'technology-based' or 'non-technology' (a technology-based unit could contain non-technology elements as well, as long as at least one technology component was integrated); and finally, the coders noted the function that each unit served in the broader diorama with respect to the intended science concept. The coders from all pairs and the two members of the research team who did the initial group selection then met to compare and contrast the process and products of the student groups.

FINDINGS

RQ1: Can students acquire Making literacy in the elementary school classroom?

All the pairs managed to produce technology-based dioramas that were in line with the assignment instruction given. This suggests that at least at the level of skills, all the children knew how to Make. Figure 4 shows the 6 dioramas analyzed. We describe only two of them below because of space restrictions. Pairs 1 and 2 were assigned thermal energy to model. Pair 1 created a narrative around their form of energy of a camper who set up camp in the forest and lit up a fire to scare away a snake. Their presentation highlighted the camp fire as emanating heat. Out of the six components that made up their diorama, 3 had a technology component and 3 were simply arts-and-craft (see Figure 5). While other parts of their diorama related to science ("The sun makes the plants grow and the plants give us oxygen."), the children made explicit links to thermal energy only for the camp fire. Thus, all of the other components, technology- or non-technology-based played a supporting role to provide context for the narrative. Pair 1 thus used Making both as the *illustrator* for the science concept, and to provide *context* to the concept.

Pair 2 created a literal representation of an LED circuit. Their concept was that "When we keep the light on all the day it gets hot. Today we're going to show you how to turn on the light." Their diorama had five meaningful units: an LED, a battery pack, the Arduino microcontroller, a resistor, and a laptop. Each element was drawn on the paper and the electronic component placed on top of the drawing except for the laptop drawing. While all their components were technology-based, not all had a functional role. The battery and the resistor, for example, were drawn in the diorama but were not used in the circuit. The children powered the LED from the Arduino running from the laptop, making the battery and resistor redundant. Pair 2 used Making to produce *exemplars* of science concepts themselves (LED for light, and the warm resistor for heat).

RQ2: How do students express their Making literacy in a Making-based class assignment?

We describe below how the students' Making literacy was observed at the level of skills, mental models and practices.

Skills. Basic Making literacy skills that all the students were familiar with from the past 1.5 years of Making curriculum included connecting batteries and paper switches with loads, such as LEDs and motors, and programming how to switch on and off loads using the Arduino. In this first-time open-ended Maker activity, high literacy students were able to identify materials that they would need for the concept that they envisioned. For example, after deciding to use vibration to generate sound for a mobile phone ringing, Diego and Daniella (Pair 5) identified the difference between the vibrating motor and the rotating motor, and quickly communicated to a helper that they needed to exchange their rotating motor for a vibrating one for their vibrating mobile phone concept. While even low literacy students could connect up circuits correctly once they were given the correct materials, they had

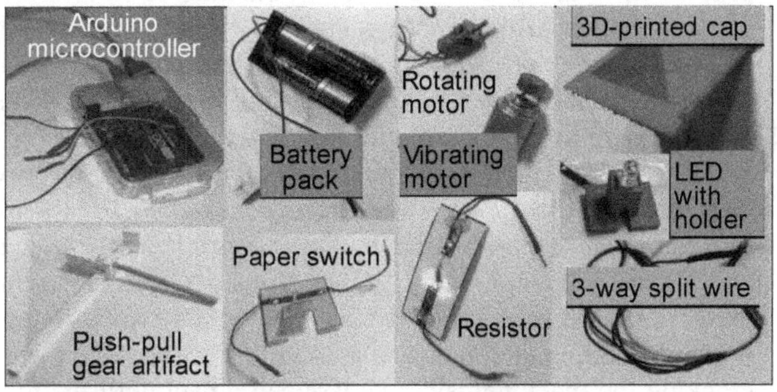

Figure 3. Components available to the students for Making

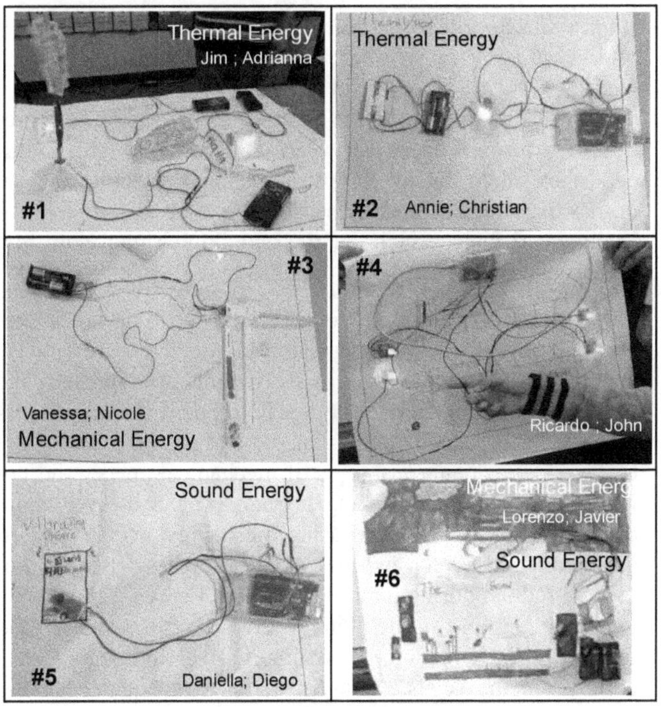

Figure 4. Dioramas analyzed (names have been changed to preserve anonymity)

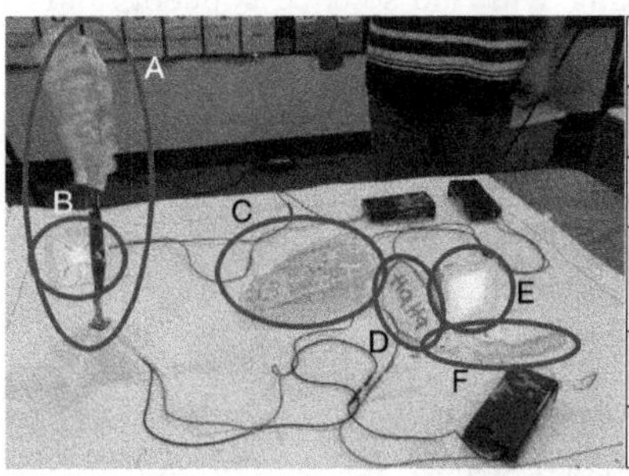

A	Spinning tree	T
B	Lit sun	T
C	Pop-up Bush	NT
D	'Haha' speech bubble	NT
E	Lit camp fire	T
F	Pop-up Snake	NT

Figure 5. Example of decomposition analysis (T: Technology-based; NT: Non-technology-based)

problems identifying the materials needed to operationalize their diorama concept. Annie and Christian in Pair 2, for example, included a resistor and a battery in their circuit when their LED was already being powered by an Arduino.

Mental models. *Troubleshooting:* In previous Making weeks, helpers had continuously reinforced troubleshooting as a key process in Making. Different troubleshooting strategies had been explained to the students, such as checking that wires were connected properly and that the battery packs were switched on. We observed that even lower literacy students could engage in such learnt troubleshooting during the open-ended activity. However, groups higher in Making literacy were able to *think of other ways to troubleshoot through exploration and experimentation*. For example, when Nicole and Vanessa (Pair 3) were stumped in how to reverse the motor on their push-pull machine, they tried two different methods: pulling the motor out and turning it over, and hand-cranking the machine using the wooden dowel until the machine was back to its starting position;

Ability to think about the science concept through the possibilities afforded by Making: Lower literacy students struggled in 3 ways: i) they could not think of a diorama concept that would use the available Making technologies to represent their form of energy; ii) when they came up with a concept, they could not see how to implement it using Making; or iii) there was a clear separation in their discussions of Making and science such that the two did not interrelate, and neither one was in service of the other.

For example, Ricardo and John (Pair 4) were assigned mechanical energy. They engaged in Making and were entirely proficient in building their LED circuits to represent the headlights in their diorama of a school bus, but their discussion of the bus door opening or the bus driver pressing the brake pedal as being instances of mechanical energy did not interrelate with their Making process. The two boys could correctly identify what was using mechanical energy in their diorama when asked, and they even brought a push-pull device with them during their presentation. However the device served no purpose in the diorama, and was not actually used during the presentation. This suggests that although Pair 4 understood the science concept and had adequate Making skills, they were poor in Making literacy. Conversely, students deemed higher in Making literacy went beyond simply connecting Making with the science concept, and grounded their dioramas in real-world scenarios. For instance, Diego and Daniella (Pair 5) made the connection between vibrating motors and the buzzing noise of their mobile phone on silent mode. Nicole and Vanessa (Pair 3) made connections between the concept of mechanical energy, rotating motors in a gear system, and the way one moves a toothbrush back and forward to brush teeth.

Ability to deconstruct the artifact to be made and figuring out how to realize each aspect through Making: In Pair 3's toothbrush diorama, for example, even though brushing one's teeth is typically viewed as a holistic activity rather than distinct pushing and pulling actions, Nicole and Vanessa deconstructed the concept in their discussions into separate movements. They were then able to reflect on how to actualize each movement using the rotating motor. Similarly, Jim and Adrianna (Pair 1) deconstructed their idea of heat energy scaring away animals into distinct units and they then operationalized each using Making through iterative problem-solving. E.g., the as a printed sun drawing in front of an LED in a 3D-printed cap (see B in Figure 5), a rotating motor to animate a tree drawing to simulate wind (see A in Figure 5). Groups that did not engage a deconstruction process tended to have a one-to-one mapping between a science concept and a technology artifact.

Practices. At the level of practices, some students were observed to be able to function better in a Making environment than others. Diego and Daniella (Pair 5) continuously *expressed their ideas* to each other throughout the design process and *shared all responsibilities* equally. Nicole and Vanessa (Pair 3) readily expressed their Making ideas to each other as well as to adult helpers, and reported that they actually enjoyed explaining themselves and how their artifacts worked. Students considered low in Making literacy had difficulty integrating Making as part of their typical collaboration practice. A case example is that of Ricardo and John (Pair 4) who were able to discuss with each other during the initial brainstorming phase when no Making was involved, but once they started the Making process, they worked completely independently of each other.

Another way by which students were deemed to be further away from the practice of Making was through the *delay of the Making process*. A case in point is Pair 6 who dedicated almost the whole two days to drawing their diorama, and spent only the last 20 minutes of the presentation day to engage in Making and had to rush to finish up their circuits. They did not necessarily dislike Making, but saw Making as an add-on to an art-and-craft-based diorama.

DISCUSSION

Our findings showed that after learning Making skills within classroom constraints (lockstepped instructions, fixed goals, minimal choices, etc.) for 1.5 years, the students could produce significant technology-based science dioramas in a Maker activity that was more in line with the spirit or essence of Making [16]. At a certain level then, the students would be considered as Makers. Indeed, questionnaires that we have collected throughout the prior Making weeks indicate that on self-report questions, a good proportion of the students are increasingly seeing themselves as Makers. They like Making, they are motivated to Make, and they feel that they can Make. However, their processes, behaviors and performance in the open-ended Maker activity showed a more nuanced picture. We extracted the themes of Making literacy from our analyses and present them in a framework shown in Table 1. A Making-literate student functions effectively at all three levels of skills, mental models and practices. Most Making skills can be taught and learnt. If the skills are correctly assimilated, students should be able to engage in Making, as many do by following tutorials and how-to guides on websites.

But Making-literate students also assimilate generalized ways of doing in their thinking and are able to apply them to various problems and scenarios. Literacy at the level of mental models can be basic in the sense that one simply applies learnt troubleshooting strategies to a particular problem. Greater literacy results in troubleshooting through the use of exploration and experimentation processes, or one being able to think about a concept or a problem through Making as grounded in real-life scenarios.

A Making-literate student further accepts Making as part of his/her ways of being and adopted it into his/her practices. Literacy at the level of practices is mostly emergent, and is challenging to inculcate through actual teaching. More literate children tend to have the drive and motivation to engage in Making. They enjoy the process and are not fearful of discussing or sharing what they did. Making takes on more of a normalized quality– they begin to perceive Making as something that you just do, and not as an add-on or something totally distinct from their typical activities.

CONCLUSION

Why is it important to begin thinking about Making literacy? We expect the Maker movement to evolve beyond being a 'movement' or a subculture. Making is poised to become a generalized rather than a specialized practice [4], essentially a literacy, just like textual and visual literacy today. Children learn to read till around third grade, after which they read to learn. The same may perhaps be expected for Making in the future: children may learn how to make and then use Making as a tool for learning. Our work provides a glimpse into how students who 'know' Making act and perform for a science assignment.

Table 1. Aspects of Making Literacy

SKILLS	
Identifying parts and components	Learnt
Recognizing the functions of parts	Learnt
Connecting up circuits	Learnt
Basic programming using block-based interface	Learnt
MENTAL MODELS	
Troubleshooting	
Using troubleshooting strategies	Learnt
Troubleshooting through exploration and experimentation	Emergent
Thinking through Making possibilities	
Making for the sake of Making	Learnt
Grounding in real-world scenarios	Emergent
Deconstructing artifact	
One-to-one mapping of concept and Making component	Learnt
Problem-solving each aspect	Emergent
PRACTICES	
Self-identification as a Maker	Emergent
Integration of Making into collaboration practices	Emergent
Making as integral to one's activity	Emergent

ACKNOWLEDGMENTS

This work has been supported by NSF grant #DRL-1433770. We sincerely thank all the students and teachers.

REFERENCES

1. Litts, B.K., *Making learning: Makerspaces as learning environments*, in *Curriculum and Instruction*. 2015, The University of Wisconsin-Madison.
2. Holbert, N. *Bots for Tots: Building Inclusive Makerspaces by Leveraging Ways of Knowing*. in *IDC* 2016. ACM.
3. Wardrip, P.S. and L. Brahms. *Learning practices of making: developing a framework for design*. in *IDC* 2015. ACM.
4. Vee, A., *Understanding computer programming as a literacy*. Literacy in Composition Studies, 2013. **1**(2): p. 42-64.
5. European, C., *A European approach to media literacy in the digital environment*. Official Journal of the European Union, 2007.
6. Gilster, P., *Digital literacy*. 1997: Wiley Computer Pub. New York.
7. Potter, J., *Digital media and learner identity: The new curatorship*. 2012: Springer.
8. Meyers, E.M., I. Erickson, and R.V. Small, *Digital literacy and informal learning environments: An introduction*. Learning, media and technology, 2013. **38**(4): p. 355-367.
9. DiSessa, A.A., *Changing minds: Computers, learning, and literacy*. 2001: Mit Press.
10. Group, T.N.L., *A pedagogy of multiliteracies: Designing social futures*. Harvard educational review, 1996. **66**(1): p. 60-93.
11. Steinkuehler, C. and B.Z. Johnson, *Computational Literacy in Online Games*. International Journal of Gaming and Computer-Mediated Simulations, 2009. **1**(1): p. 53-65.
12. Saenz, M., et al. *Touch Wire: Interactive Tangible Electricty Game for Kids*. in *TEI* 2015. ACM.
13. Freed, N., et al. *Sticking together: handcrafting personalized communication interfaces*. in *IDC* 2011. ACM.
14. Dougherty, D., *The Maker Mindset*, in *Design, Make, Play: Growing the Next Generation of STEM Innovators*, M. Honey and D.E. Kanter, Editors. 2013, Routledge. p. 7-11.
15. Regalla, L., *Developing a maker mindset*. Makeology: Makerspaces as Learning Environments, 2016. **1**: p. 257.
16. Halverson, E.R. and K. Sheridan, *The Maker Movement in Education*. Harvard Educational Review, 2014. **84**(4): p. 495-504.
17. Martin, L. and C. Dixon. *Youth Conceptions of Making and the Maker Movement*. in *IDC* 2013. ACM.

Designing Together?: Group Dynamics in Participatory Digital Badge Design with Teens

Caroline Pitt
University of Washington
Seattle, WA, USA
pittc@uw.edu

Katie Davis
University of Washington
Seattle, WA, USA
kdavis78@uw.edu

ABSTRACT
Balancing the dynamics between industry, academia, and stakeholders in a participatory design (PD) project can be challenging, particularly with teens as design partners. In this reflective case study of digital badge design, we attempt to untangle complex PD work that incorporates several groups, each with their own vocabulary, area of expertise, and position in a perceived project structure hierarchy. Using participant interviews that reflect on the design process, triangulated with video, field notes, and design artifacts, we determined that the adolescent stakeholders, science center staff, researchers, and industry professionals viewed the design process through distinct lenses based on their *communities of practice,* which affected how they perceived the project. Our findings contribute new insight into how youth stakeholders perceive their involvement and role in participatory design practices within a complex design project.

Author Keywords
Participatory design; co-design; reflection-on-action; digital badges; case study; power dynamics.

ACM Classification Keywords
H.5.2. User Interfaces (D.2.2, H.1.2, I.3.6): *Prototyping, User-centered design*; K.3.1. Computer Uses in Education: *Collaborative learning*.

INTRODUCTION
Participatory design (PD), at its roots, attempts to address power imbalances inherent in the typical design process, allowing the users of the technology to have agency in its development [3,15]. In more recent years, the principles of PD have been extended to younger groups of stakeholders, involving children in the design of technologies [8,9,13].

IDC '17, June 27-30, 2017, Stanford, CA, USA

ACM 978-1-4503-4921-5/17/06...$15.00
http://dx.doi.org/10.1145/3078072.3079716

Figure 1. Youth participants of the digital badge design team organize brainstormed stickies about their science learning into overarching themes in the first design session.

The addition of youth creates a new dynamic, as the relationship between children and adults introduces another level of complexity to the power differences already found in various PD projects [17].

Some researchers have begun to explore how adult-child design relationships function; however, less is known about how youth view their participation and the participation of others. Such insight is essential when forming constructive, long-term relationships, as one might in a PD project lasting several years [14,15,17,30,31]. If PD is one component of a larger design project, understanding these relationships can be key to overall success. *Reflection-on-action*, described by Schön, can be a useful tool when working in such design contexts [24]. The current study uses this reflective lens to probe the underlying dynamics and relationships that exist within an ongoing design project involving a complex ecology of stakeholder groups.

In 2015, we embarked on a multi-year PD project with a local science center, recruiting teens from the center's structured science interpretation program to join a design team that would develop a digital badge system for their work. This system was intended to represent the learning pathways of the program and recognize the accomplishments of participating high school students, documented in Bell and Davis [2]. We hoped to gain insight into how digital badges could be used in different educational and career-related contexts and whether or not such a system would be sustainable. During the first year of badge design and development, teens involved in the design process showed clear signs of learning together, using the design process to develop their thinking about the program and their participation in it (Figure 1) [2]. More generally, digital badges are still an emerging area of research, and thus far many implementations and designs have focused on proof-of-concept and top-down approaches, rather than building, testing, using, and evaluating badges from start to finish through a PD process [1,4,12,23].

In this study, we examine the first year of the design research project: exploring how the different groups experienced the project process, contributed their respective expertise, and developed an understanding of participatory design as well as the design of digital badge systems overall. We conducted in-depth interviews with the different groups of stakeholders involved, reflecting on their participation in the project and triangulating their thoughts with other data such as video and field notes. This study provides insight into the complex workings of such a project and discusses the benefits, limitations, and possible improvements of this type of PD process involving teens as one of multiple groups of stakeholders.

In this work, we address the following research questions: **1)** How do teens and other stakeholders perceive the power dynamics in PD? **2)** How do different stakeholders conceptualize their position in and contribution to the design process?

We found that though the stakeholders viewed the PD process as enjoyable and beneficial to themselves and the broader program, there were distinct imbalances in power and expertise among the different groups. The teens in particular were acutely aware of the fact that all of the adults in the project had more knowledge in areas of domain expertise. This work explores the complexity of a long-term PD project involving multiple stakeholders, focusing in particular on how including teens as design partners affects the overall dynamics. We hope that other researchers will be able to use our insights as a starting point to help address any points of conflict and power imbalance they encounter in their own design research.

RELATED WORK

Participatory Design with Youth

Participatory design with children and teens has risen in prevalence over the past two decades as researchers have explored how best to incorporate young stakeholders into the ever-evolving PD landscape [8–10,13,28–31]. Different perspectives exist on how best to incorporate children in the design process [13,20]. Druin and colleagues are well-known for their *KidsTeam* work that focuses on in-depth design work with a small group of children. Other projects have used similar group sizes over an extended time period [8,9,17,29]. Read's work with children focuses more on a larger sample size, often working with classrooms of students to provide feedback on designs [21,22].

In recent years, advances in PD with children have led to a debate regarding the proper role of youth in the design of technologies intended for their use and the ethics of having children involved in research [17,21,22,26]. McNally, Guha, Mauriello, and Druin explored children's perspectives on their involvement in KidsTeam and found that the participants generally held positive views of their experience as co-designers but that these participants were keenly aware of the role of the adult facilitators [17]. Additionally, overuse of jargon and position can create pressure on participants not to question or criticize, which runs counter to the goals of PD and can hamper the development of conceptual convergence, the building of strong inter-group bonds, and free discussion of ideas, which is something we explore in this study [5,11,27].

Digital Badges

The PD work discussed in this paper focused on the design of a digital badge system intended to support the learning trajectories of the young science interpreters at the science center. Digital badges are web-based icons that represent components of learning trajectories and can be used to provide information about a learner's skills, achievements, and experiences [19,23]. As previously stated, we have embarked on a long-term PD project focusing on the design, implementation, and evaluation of a badge system for a particular science interpretation program in a large science center [2,7,19]. This paper focuses on year one of the project that involved participatory design workshops; development and testing of a badge system for the science center; and evaluation of the success of the program. Thus, this study is an opportunity to examine and reflect on the first year of the larger digital badge design project from the perspectives of our core design team members.

CASE STUDY

Taking a reflective perspective on the first year of a badge system design, we obtained the opinions and reflections of participants through semi-structured interviews supported by additional data from the design process. The interviews were structured to elicit participants' reflections on their participation in the project, their views of design, and their interactions with other group members. This approach was influenced by Schön's *reflection-on-action* as well as Stake's stance on case study research, examining a particular case in-depth to see what emerges [24,25].

Setting and Participants

This research is takes place at a youth science interpretation program at a science center in the Pacific Northwest, conducting PD research with students and staff to develop a digital badge system design to support student learning in the program. Nine monthly design sessions occurred during year one of the project, starting with brainstorming and moving on to more detailed badge development, as well as weekly meetings with the supervisors and the badge developers to discuss progress on the badge system. We interviewed most of the main participants in the design process, listed in Table 1.

Procedure

The interview protocol was developed by the first author and refined by the second author. The interviews were conducted in person or by phone during the late summer and early fall of 2016. Participants were asked to reflect on project meetings, the power dynamics they perceived, and how their perceptions of the project changed over time. They were also invited to reflect on the challenges and points of conflict or confusion that arose during the course of the year, as well as positive moments and experiences they felt were beneficial.

Interview data were triangulated using previously collected data from meetings and design sessions. Design sessions were videotaped and documented using analytical memos written from field notes after each session [2]. While video and sound recordings were not taken during other meetings, agendas and notes were used to verify events and timelines from the interviews.

Analysis

Themes that emerged during the interview process were checked against each subsequent interview revisiting whether or not they were reinforced across participants [24]. In order to triangulate the data, the analytical memos from the design sessions were reviewed, as were any relevant video clips from the design sessions [18]. The interviews were then coded for major themes using an open coding approach [6]. The first author reviewed the interviews and developed a list of possible themes for initial coding, then re-examined the interviews and further refined the thematic analysis. The first author then discussed initial findings and emerging themes with the second author and an external researcher in order to check the reasonableness of the initial conclusions.

FINDINGS

Across all stakeholder groups, participants discussed how the *perceived power structure* of the project affected their *agency and identity as co-designers*, both of which tied into the *vocabulary and practice* of the different communities. This interconnected system of stakeholders provided opportunities for *learning through participation*, where each group was able to learn from and teach the others. These themes are further explored below.

Perceived Power Structure

Participants were asked to describe a diagram of how they might depict the power hierarchy of the entire project in an attempt to understand how each of them viewed the multiple groups of stakeholders. Most participants viewed the researchers as the connective bridge between the science center and the badge developers, if somewhat higher in the project overall. Some of the teen designers placed their supervisors above them, while others considered them to be on a more equal level in this particular context of PD.

Pseudonym	*Role*	*Gender*
Claire^{T}	Teen designer still in program	Female
Naomi^{T}	Teen designer now in college	Female
Felicia^{T}	Teen designer now in college	Female
Lily^{T}	Teen designer now in college	Female
Sandra^{P}	Program coordinator	Female
Tom^{P}	Program supervisor	Male
Becca^{P}	Program supervisor	Female
Anya^{R}	Principal Investigator	Female
Matt^{R}	Research Assistant	Male
Julie^{R}	Research Assistant	Female
George^{D}	Badge system developer	Male

Table 1. Pseudonyms, roles, and genders of participants, superscripts: T = teen, R = researcher, P = program staff, D = developer

Felicia^{T} described the following overarching project structure and ecology, visualized in Figure 2, "I guess [Anya^{R}] and [Matt^{R}] would be the central and then they would flow out to [Tom^{P}] and [Becca^{P}] as a source of information who referenced them to the [teen] group that was us. And then they took that information and went to the developers…"

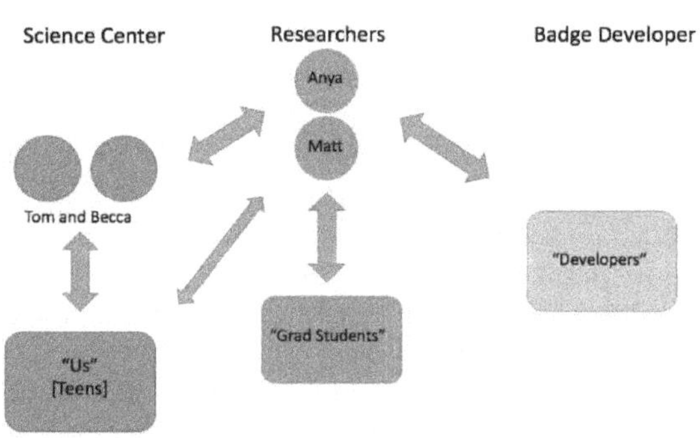

Figure 2. Felicia's^{T} description of the digital badge project team hierarchy.

Both the researchers and the program supervisors did mention that they sometimes held back their input in the design sessions and stressed the ideas of the student designers over their own. As Felicia^{T} put it "[Tom^{P}] kinda tends to stay out of things like that, so there was no problem there. [Matt^{R}] was fairly quiet. [Anya^{R}] mostly just asked questions to clarify things…" The badge developer did not attend the design sessions, but George^{D} expressed that he generally viewed the relationship as an attempt to meet the client's needs versus an equal partnership.

Agency and Identity as Co-Designers

Each teen participant developed a somewhat different perspective on their role as co-designers. Claire^{T} described her role within the project as "it would be more to narrow down ideas and like a sounding board." A more senior student, Naomi[T], stated that "we really worked with [the researchers] to develop [the badge system], and I feel that it was mostly our group that came up with the ideas." Felicia[T] mentioned that she would have liked to attend the meetings with the badge developer, as she felt rather detached from the technical side of the system, which made her feel less of a sense of ownership overall.

While most of the teens felt fairly incorporated as co-designers, the science center staff tended to remain more on the periphery. Both Becca[P] and Sandra[P] attended weekly meetings with the badge developer, but they were not as involved in the participatory design process with teens. Though Tom[P] was the main staff member to attend the design sessions, he often had other duties during parts of the session and usually restrained himself to allow the students a greater voice in the sessions.

The main contact from the badge system developer, George[D], viewed the company's role as that of a contractor providing a service than as a co-design partner, which produced a different dynamic. The other participants in the project also noticed this perspective, Sandra[P] particularly mentioning that she felt more like a client than a collaborator with the badge developer. Overall, the teens were the main stakeholders who expressed that they identified as co-designers, even though some of them did express doubts about their level of involvement.

Vocabulary and Practice

One major theme that arose throughout the interviews was the domain-specific language and practices used in the different *communities of practice* of the participants [16]. The researchers used terms and practices from the academic fields of education and human-computer interaction that were unfamiliar to the participants, though any confusion was quickly clarified. The site-specific terminology and *situated knowledge* of the science center was also something that the researchers and badge developers had to learn quickly in order to translate the program elements into digital learning pathways for the badge system [16]. Both the science center and the research team are based in educational domains, and thus they had a certain amount of shared vocabulary. By contrast, the badge system developers came from industry. George[D], the main contact for the developers, was somewhat acquainted with an educational perspective, but the science center staff and the researchers were not as familiar with the industry terminology, creating points of confusion.

Learning through Participation

Participants across the groups expressed that they had learned from the other stakeholder groups and evolved their understanding of digital badges since beginning the project. The science center stakeholders stated that they had become more confident in their ability to discuss and share their knowledge of badges. These stakeholders also gained insight into the PD process and how it could be beneficial. The researchers, meanwhile, developed a deep understanding of the structure and function of the science interpretation program [2].

Although the badge developers were not present for the design sessions, George[D] also mentioned that this project was a significant learning experience for his team, as this was their first large-scale custom badge project for this type of application. Generally, all parties involved moved towards a shared understanding of digital badging. The teens especially bonded as a team and gained a deeper knowledge of the learning pathways and opportunities in their science interpretation program.

DISCUSSION

Our findings provide new insight into the complexities associated with involving youth in a long-term participatory design project involving multiple groups of stakeholders, each with their distinct sets of expertise, language, and perspectives. This study lays the groundwork for deeper inquiry into how the different parties involved in a PD process interact with, learn from, and perceive each other, which is vital to those who wish to form strong relationships within and among *communities of practice* in their design research[16].

Our interviews also revealed room for improvement with respect to clarity and communication among the different stakeholders participating in the digital badge design project. The miscommunications and misunderstandings that can arise when multiple groups with different sets of vocabulary and practices come together is something all design researchers should consider. These insights can be valuable in almost any PD project, particularly those with sensitive dynamics.

We found that not all participants, even those that we specifically involved in PD activities, identified fully as co-designers. Two of our teens specifically expressed that they did not feel a complete sense of ownership of the badge system design process, contrary to some of the goals of PD [2,3,9] . Although we strove to promote a sense of ownership among all participants, particularly the teens, it is evident that reaching this level of personal engagement can be difficult to achieve.

Thus, we conclude this paper with input from our stakeholders on how the PD process can be improved in such a way that promotes the development of participants' co-design identities. Most of the feedback was around communication and involvement, with stakeholders requesting more interaction with each other and more detailed and explicit explanations of the research process and the rationale behind the activities. This feedback suggests that while researchers attempt to avoid information overload, they must also be aware that sometimes participants want to spend more time and effort, not less.

LIMITATIONS

We acknowledge that case studies in general have limited explanatory power to a broader population [25]. We also are very aware that there are many potential ethical considerations involved in interviewing youth, and all youth participation was approved by our university's Institutional Review Board, with assent continuously obtained and re-verified throughout the research process. Another limitation is that this study involved interviewing fellow research team members and contracted developers, which touches on some of the group dynamics issues we explore in this study. We are cognizant of the possible biases that come with studying one's own research team and playing dual roles as participants and researchers, but feel that a reflective stance is important for improvement of the design process.

CONCLUSION

In this case study, we have detailed the experiences of our youth and adult co-designers during the first year of a long-term PD project to develop a digital badge system. From participants' reflections and insights, we identified both successes and challenges associated with this long-term PD project involving multiple stakeholder groups. Participants learned about the perspectives of the other stakeholders on the project, and were able to work with them to increase their understanding of digital badges and the process of design and implementation. At the same time, our participants articulated that they were keenly aware of hierarchies in the project. Particularly among the youth participants, this awareness affected their sense of agency and identity in the design process. Thus we can clearly see that while PD attempts to democratize design and incorporate user viewpoints, power dynamics within a project are still clearly visible and cannot be ignored, particularly when working with children and teens.

ACKNOWLEDGMENTS

The authors thank the National Science Foundation for its support of this research under grant *DRL-1452672*. They also thank the science center staff and students who participated in the research.

REFERENCES

1. Samuel Abramovich, Christian Schunn, and Ross Mitsuo Higashi. 2013. Are badges useful in education?: it depends upon the type of badge and expertise of learner. *Educational Technology Research and Development* 61, 2: 217–232. https://doi.org/10.1007/s11423-013-9289-2
2. Adam Bell and Katie Davis. 2016. Learning Through Participatory Design: Designing Digital Badges for and with Teens. In *Proceedings of the The 15th International Conference on Interaction Design and Children* (IDC '16), 218–229. https://doi.org/10.1145/2930674.2930705
3. Erling Björgvinsson, Pelle Ehn, and Per-Anders Hillgren. 2010. Participatory Design and "Democratizing Innovation." In *Proceedings of the 11th Biennial Participatory Design Conference* (PDC '10), 41–50. https://doi.org/10.1145/1900441.1900448
4. Ivica Boticki, Jelena Baksa, Peter Seow, and Chee-Kit Looi. 2015. Usage of a mobile social learning platform with virtual badges in a primary school. *Computers & Education* 86: 120–136. https://doi.org/10.1016/j.compedu.2015.02.015
5. Tone Bratteteig and Ina Wagner. 2012. Disentangling Power and Decision-making in Participatory Design. In *Proceedings of the 12th Participatory Design Conference: Research Papers - Volume 1* (PDC '12), 41–50. https://doi.org/10.1145/2347635.2347642
6. Juliet Corbin and Anselm Strauss. 2014. *Basics of Qualitative Research: Techniques and Procedures for Developing Grounded Theory*. SAGE.
7. Katie Davis and Eve Klein. 2015. Investigating High School Students' Perceptions of Digital Badges in Afterschool Learning. In *Proceedings of the 33rd Annual ACM Conference on Human Factors in Computing Systems* (CHI '15), 4043–4046. https://doi.org/10.1145/2702123.2702413
8. Allison Druin. 1999. Cooperative Inquiry: Developing New Technologies for Children with Children. In *Proceedings of the SIGCHI Conference on Human Factors in Computing Systems* (CHI '99), 592–599. https://doi.org/10.1145/302979.303166
9. Allison Druin. 2002. The role of children in the design of new technology. *Behaviour & Information Technology* 21, 1: 1–25. https://doi.org/10.1080/01449290110108659
10. Elizabeth Foss, Mona Leigh Guha, Panagis Papadatos, Tamara Clegg, Jason Yip, and Greg Walsh. 2013. Cooperative Inquiry Extended: Creating Technology with Middle School Students with Learning Differences. *Journal of Special Education Technology* 28, 3: 33–46. https://doi.org/10.1177/016264341302800303
11. Lalya Gaye and Atau Tanaka. 2011. Beyond Participation: Empowerment, Control and Ownership in Youth-led Collaborative Design. In *Proceedings of the 8th ACM Conference on Creativity and Cognition* (C&C '11), 335–336. https://doi.org/10.1145/2069618.2069684
12. Sheryl Grant. 2014. Badges: Show What You Know. *Young Adult Library Services* 12, 2: 28–32.
13. Mona Leigh Guha, Allison Druin, and Jerry Alan Fails. 2013. Cooperative Inquiry revisited: Reflections of the past and guidelines for the future of intergenerational co-design. *International Journal of Child-Computer Interaction* 1, 1: 14–23. https://doi.org/10.1016/j.ijcci.2012.08.003
14. Elin Irene Krog Hansen and Ole Sejer Iversen. 2013. You Are the Real Experts!: Studying Teenagers' Motivation in Participatory Design. In *Proceedings of the 12th International Conference on Interaction Design and Children* (IDC '13), 328–331. https://doi.org/10.1145/2485760.2485826

15. Ole Sejer Iversen and Rachel Charlotte Smith. 2012. Scandinavian Participatory Design: Dialogic Curation with Teenagers. In *Proceedings of the 11th International Conference on Interaction Design and Children* (IDC '12), 106–115. https://doi.org/10.1145/2307096.2307109
16. Jean Lave and Etienne Wenger. 1991. Situated learning: Legitimate peripheral participation. Cambridge university press.
17. Brenna McNally, Mona Leigh Guha, Matthew Louis Mauriello, and Allison Druin. 2016. Children's Perspectives on Ethical Issues Surrounding Their Past Involvement on a Participatory Design Team. In *Proceedings of the 2016 CHI Conference on Human Factors in Computing Systems* (CHI '16), 3595–3606. https://doi.org/10.1145/2858036.2858338
18. Sharan B. Merriam. 2009. Qualitative research: A guide to design and implementation. John Wiley & Sons.
19. Lin Y. Muilenburg and Zane L. Berge (eds.). 2016. Digital Badges in Education: Trends, Issues, and Cases. Routledge.
20. J. C. Read, Peggy Gregory, Stuart MacFarlane, Barbara McManus, Peter Gray, and Raj Patel. 2002. An investigation of participatory design with children-informant, balanced and facilitated design. Retrieved February 15, 2016 from http://www.chici.org/references/an_investigation_of_participatory_design.pdf
21. Janet C. Read, Daniel Fitton, and Matthew Horton. 2014. Giving Ideas an Equal Chance: Inclusion and Representation in Participatory Design with Children. In *Proceedings of the 2014 Conference on Interaction Design and Children* (IDC '14), 105–114. https://doi.org/10.1145/2593968.2593986
22. Janet C. Read, Matthew Horton, Gavin Sim, Peggy Gregory, Daniel Fitton, and Brendan Cassidy. 2013. CHECk: A Tool to Inform and Encourage Ethical Practice in Participatory Design with Children. In *CHI '13 Extended Abstracts on Human Factors in Computing Systems* (CHI EA '13), 187–192. https://doi.org/10.1145/2468356.2468391
23. Michelle M. Riconscente, Amy Kamarainen, and Margaret Honey. 2013. STEM badges: Current terrain and the road ahead. *Retrieved from New York Hall of Science website: http://badgesnysci.files.wordpress.com* 8.
24. Donald A. Schön. 1987. Educating the reflective practitioner: Toward a new design for teaching and learning in the professions. Jossey-Bass.
25. Robert E. Stake. 1995. *The Art of Case Study Research.* SAGE.
26. Nigel Thomas and Claire O'Kane. 1998. The ethics of participatory research with children. *Children & Society* 12, 5: 336–348. https://doi.org/10.1111/j.1099-0860.1998.tb00090.x
27. Maarten Van Mechelen, Mathieu Gielen, Vero vanden Abeele, Ann Laenen, and Bieke Zaman. 2014. Exploring Challenging Group Dynamics in Participatory Design with Children. In *Proceedings of the 2014 Conference on Interaction Design and Children* (IDC '14), 269–272. https://doi.org/10.1145/2593968.2610469
28. Greg Walsh, Allison Druin, Mona Leigh Guha, Elizabeth Bonsignore, Elizabeth Foss, Jason C. Yip, Evan Golub, Tamara Clegg, Quincy Brown, Robin Brewer, Asmi Joshi, and Richelle Brown. 2012. DisCo: A Co-design Online Tool for Asynchronous Distributed Child and Adult Design Partners. In *Proceedings of the 11th International Conference on Interaction Design and Children* (IDC '12), 11–19. https://doi.org/10.1145/2307096.2307099
29. Greg Walsh, Elizabeth Foss, Jason Yip, and Allison Druin. 2013. FACIT PD: a framework for analysis and creation of intergenerational techniques for participatory design. In *Proceedings of the SIGCHI Conference on Human Factors in Computing Systems*, 2893–2902. Retrieved December 4, 2015 from http://dl.acm.org/citation.cfm?id=2481400
30. Jason C. Yip, Kiley Sobel, Caroline Pitt, Kung Jin Lee, Sijin Chen, Kari Nasu, and Laura R. Pina. 2017. Examining Adult-Child Interactions in Intergenerational Participatory Design. In *Proceedings on the 2017 CHI Conference on Human Factors in Computing Systems.* https://doi.org/http://dx.doi.org/10.1145/3025453.3025787
31. Jason Yip, Tamara Clegg, Elizabeth Bonsignore, Helene Gelderblom, Emily Rhodes, and Allison Druin. 2013. Brownies or Bags-of-stuff?: Domain Expertise in Cooperative Inquiry with Children. In *Proceedings of the 12th International Conference on Interaction Design and Children* (IDC '13), 201–210. https://doi.org/10.1145/2485760.2485763

The Binding of Fenrir: Children in an Emerging Age of Transhumanist Technology

Michael Eisenberg
University of Colorado
Boulder, CO USA
duck@cs.colorado.edu

ABSTRACT
The meaning of "children's technology" is poised for imminent and radical change, as a variety of technologies are developed whose goal is to expand or augment the biological limitations of human functioning. These transhumanist *technologies (including sensory augmentation, robotic bodily extensions, brain-machine interfaces, and genetic alteration) pose urgent questions for the community of designers of children's artifacts. This paper discusses the questions that transhumanist technologies raise for children's design specifically; we then present suggested heuristics for design in this new space, and outline plausible research projects consistent with those heuristics.*

Author Keywords
Human augmentation; human enhancement; children's technology; transhumanism.

ACM Classification Keywords
H.5.m. Information interfaces and presentation (e.g., HCI): Miscellaneous.

INTRODUCTION
For decades now the very idea of "children's technology" has been based on several bedrock assumptions. The first of these assumptions is that the term "technology" refers primarily (if not exclusively) to digital electronics, with an emphasis on computers and communication. The second is that "technology", even under its broadest interpretation, is something *external*, in the surrounding environment of the child. The third is the biological constancy of human beings–and a fortiori, children–over historical time. In short, a typical research project might center around (say) designing a digital artifact to be placed in a classroom (or museum, or child's bedroom), for a child biologically indistinguishable from those in past millennia.

IDC '17, June 27-30, 2017, Stanford, CA, USA © 2017 Association for Computing Machinery. ACM ISBN 978-1-4503-4921-5/17/06...$15.00
http://dx.doi.org/10.1145/3078072.3079744

These assumptions have been so ingrained in the educational technology community for so long that there would seem to be no controversy about these ideas–to question them would be to question the very nature of "technology" and (more disturbingly) "children" and "childhood". We *know* what these terms mean, don't we?

There are growing indications within technological culture that in fact we do not. A steadily increasing attention to technologies that work on a biological level–*internally*, in a sense, rather than externally–needs to be acknowledged and discussed in the context of design for children. The technologies in question are varied–they include sensory extensions, robotic augmentations to the body, techniques for genetic alteration, bodily implants, and brain-machine interfaces, among others. Collectively, these technologies are likely to shift the underlying discussions of children's technologies from a default emphasis on artifacts in the child's environment to artifacts that (potentially) affect the traditional sensory, kinesthetic, and cognitive dimensions of childhood itself.

The current historical moment, then, presents us with the prospect of "transhumanist" technologies–advances meant to venture beyond the evolutionary and biological limits of human nature. As designers, our situation is reminiscent of an ancient story from Norse mythology concerning the character of Fenrir. Fenrir is a wolf of tremendous potential strength and ferocity (he is one of the children of the mischievous god Loki); but as a young animal he is adopted by the Norse gods and treated as a pet, in which role he is largely ignored. Over time, however, the god Odin notices that Fenrir is growing steadily larger; the day-to-day change is imperceptible, but the challenge posed by the adult wolf is soon going to be impossible to meet. The gods' urgent task, then, is to somehow bind Fenrir–to create a leash strong enough to cope with the beast that he will eventually become. [Keary & Keary, 1870]

The community of children's technology design is arguably faced with an analogous task. At this point it is difficult to predict precisely which elements of transhumanist research represent imminent challenges, which reflect longer-term issues, and which are simply futuristic fantasies. It is nonetheless clear that the range and plausible impact of transhumanist technologies are steadily growing, like Fenrir. Much like Odin and his companions in the Norse myth, it is not within our power to kill the beast outright (indeed, there are good reasons why we shouldn't want to do so); but without discussion, we lack even the rudiments of an intellectual "leash" with which to bind the oncoming rush of strange new techniques and philosophical questions.

The remainder of this paper is a discussion of the meaning of transhumanist technologies for the field of children's design. Such issues have, surprisingly, been largely absent from the debates and predictions swirling about transhumanism in general. The time is therefore right–indeed long overdue–for airing the questions surrounding children's lives in an era of transhumanist technology.

TRANSHUMANIST TECHNOLOGIES: A SAMPLER

There is by now a burgeoning literature on human enhancement and augmentation: good overviews include Clark [2003], Barfield [2015], More [2013], and Lilley [2013]. This section provides a necessarily telegraphic sketch of several main lines of current work, and suggests how those might intersect with the field of design for children.

It should be noted by way of preface that there is usually something of a continuum between *prosthetic* or *remedial* technologies and those that are meant to enhance or extend human capacity. A pair of eyeglasses meant to alleviate nearsightedness is clearly the former; but if the glasses are designed to allow the user to "see" wavelengths in both the visible and infrared ranges, they could be described as an enhancing technology. A recurring theme in the literature is that, while remedial technologies are seen as uncontroversial and benign, enhancing technologies are seen as potentially dangerous or anxiety-provoking. For the purposes of this discussion, we will focus where possible on the more controversial (and more open-ended) realm of enhancement.

Sensory Augmentation

Among transhumanist technologies and research projects, many prominent examples involve the extension or augmentation of human sensory capacity. Platoni [2015], for instance, describes a community of do-it-yourself "body modders" who experiment on themselves by (e.g.) having tiny magnets implanted within their fingers so that they can "feel" magnetic fields. (Note, by the way, that this very simple example illustrates the point that a challenging new technology may in fact be neither digital nor external.) One might imagine variants or extensions of cochlear implants to perform similar mild enhancements of human hearing.

Historically, we can view sensory augmentation technology as a continuation of a venerable process in scientific instrumentation: a telescope, microscope, or Geiger counter might be seen as (external) "sensory enhancements" for humans (cf. the discussion in [Jebari, 2015]). By extension, augmented reality goggles such as the Microsoft Hololens could be seen as part of this tradition. Over time, such tools migrate to positions closer to (or within) the human body itself. Lingley *et al.* [2011] describe, for instance, a wireless contact lens display that was successfully tested on a rabbit. The examples of "magnetic fingers" or enhanced cochlear implants represent early steps toward moving the locus of sensory enhancement to a position within the body itself.

From the standpoint of children's technology, one likely scenario for sensory enhancement would (as suggested by the analogies with telescopes and microscopes) involve endowing students with greater perception for understanding the natural world. We will return to scenarios along these lines in a later section.

Enhancements for Actuation

The flip side of sensory enhancement involves the extension of human muscles or movement. One major line of research along these lines involves extensions to the body (e.g., via robotic limbs or exoskeletons). Again, there is a natural link here to the field of prosthetics (in which replacement limbs are seen as restoring lost function); but some early exoskeleton-like enhancements (e.g., for the construction industry) are already commercialized products.

Exoskeletons alone might be viewed as wearable technology (and hence not quite at the level of full-scale "human enhancement"); but to the extent that such devices might be controlled via brain-machine interfaces, it becomes increasingly hard to disentangle the "external" from the "internal" elements of such artifacts.

One might imagine equipping children with devices geared toward artistic creation (controllable actuators for, e.g., painting or musical performance of a sort unachievable by unaided human muscles); or for manipulating scientific instruments and materials (such as small-scale electronic components, or hazardous chemicals); or in combination with sensors, in devices such as extended robotic fingers to create an enhanced sense of touch.

Brain-Machine Interfaces

Both of the previous subsections have mentioned the subject of direct interaction between electronic or digital devices (such as artificial sensors or robotic exoskeletons) and the brain of the user. By "direct" in this context, the implication is that interaction does not require such intermediaries as keyboards or pedals, but instead is mediated by brain activity through such means as electroencephalographic (EEG) recording. The basic idea is that brain activity can be used to achieve varying degrees of control of computational devices (whether external to the body or not); or the brain itself can be the recipient of signals from external devices (in medical or research settings, this is sometimes managed via direct stimulation of the brain using microelectrodes). For the purposes of this discussion, EEG reading (which is non-invasive) seems to be sufficient to achieve at least some degree of non-muscular control of electronic artifacts (see for example, [Doud *et al.*, 2011]).

Genetic Alteration

While the previous subsections described techniques in which artifacts (such as magnets or actuators) are added to the human body, techniques of genetic alteration change the biology of the human body itself. There are various techniques for making such changes–some speculative–that make the subject difficult to summarize. For the purposes of this discussion, we can focus on existing techniques for somatic gene therapy, in which a genetic change is made in a person but that change does not impact the person's germ line (and therefore is not transferred to descendants). The method of gene alteration is likewise variable, but can be accomplished (as one example) through the injection of a virus containing the desired gene (for a good, brief introductory discussion, see Seedhouse [2014]). Somatic gene alteration has already been used therapeutically to treat disease; again, by analogy with our previous examples, it is plausible (if not always comfortable) to imagine its use to enhance or "improve" human performance. The near-term prospect of widespread "gene doping" in athletic competition is already the focus of discussion (see for example [LePage, 2016]).

There are numerous scenarios in which children might eventually be the focus of genetic enhancement (ignoring for the time being the question of legal restrictions). It might be possible, for example, to alter a child's genetic makeup to improve his or her performance in some particular domain (undersea swimming, playing a musical instrument, dance). Cognitive enhancement via gene alteration (could one improve, say, attention span?) is even more speculative at this point–the genetic components that affect individual cognitive traits are currently not understood at a level that would permit specific improvements. Nonetheless, it seems likely that there will be attempts made to improve human cognition via genetic enhancement within the next quarter-century.

TRANSHUMANISM AND DESIGN FOR CHILDREN

The previous section outlined several of the major lines of work in transhumanist technologies–directions that could plausibly be part of the landscape of "children's technology" in the coming decades. The vast majority of existing discussion of these technologies, however, ignores the specific issues that impact children. In this section we explore several prominent topics that deserve greater discussion, particularly in the area of designing technologies for children.

Developmental issues

Historically, questions surrounding children's use of technology has often centered on the issue of "starting age": should a child really be watching television at the age of three? Should we be introducing children to (say) video games before the age of five? The general arc of the past half-century has been toward greater cultural acceptance of children's use of technology. Where the idea of children programming computers was once seen as startling, computers are now perceived as, if anything, preferentially artifacts of the young–consider the standard media images of the teenage hacker or computer whiz.

In the case of transhumanist technologies, the question of use at an early age is particularly pointed. Consider, for instance, the widespread perception that certain types of skills are best learned early if one wants to achieve a high level of mastery. Children interested in becoming, e.g., top-level violinists, or baseball players, or gymnasts, are often encouraged (or prodded by their parents) to start practicing while young. One might argue, along similar lines, that skill at manipulating a robotic exoskeleton, or at interpreting sensory input from magnetic implants, would be achieved at a superior level if the process started in childhood. Such considerations, if anything, are likely to make children and parents less cautious (and more adventuresome) in experimenting with enhancement technologies.

Indeed, there are some skills (such as language acquisition) for which it is clear that there are biologically typical developmental windows. If one wanted to experiment with (say) sensory enhancement to improve the perception of phonetic patterns in a foreign language, the most successful subjects for such an experiment would likely be children.

Educational issues

Most discussions of transhumanist technology are centered on topics other than education (typical discussions involve improvement in professional performance, enhanced health or longevity, and so forth). This is an odd omission, since there are vivid scenarios in which enhancements for children might be employed in educational settings.

We have already noted that sensory augmentation is particularly suited to certain kinds of scientific exploration (just as the invention of the telescope provided an "enhancement" to human vision for the purpose of studying the heavens). Children might be equipped with enhancements for perceiving polarized light, or high-frequency sounds, or for detecting chemical gradients. While such instrumentation might likely be designed as wearable (rather than implanted, like magnets in one's fingers), the effects might approach those of biological enhancement if the child wears the sensory device continually, or for protracted periods of time. (The historical example of Stratton's "upside-down glasses", in which the user adjusts over a modest time span to glasses that invert the visual image, is telling here. [Stratton, 1896])

Nor need the educational scenarios be drawn exclusively from the natural sciences. We might, for instance, design novel types of devices, approaching the nature of prosthetics, for the purposes of artistic performance–new types of bodily extensions for the purposes of, e.g. playing a string instrument. In fact, it might be that novel artistic forms will be developed in tandem with the enhancement devices needed to attempt them: a musical instrument designed to be used, for instance, by a hand larger and more powerful than the standard human hand.

Ethical issues

Throughout this discussion, a myriad ethical, legal, and policy issues have been lurking in the background. Philosophical debates surrounding the prospects transhumanism are by now hardly new (see Lilley [2013] and Savulescu & Bostrom [2011] for informative discussions), but the question of how these technologies affect children's lives is particularly pointed, and relatively underexplored.

Take, for example, our scenarios of early enhancement of children for the purposes of achieving expertise (say, as a violinist or tennis player). Should a parent be allowed to make a decision in favor of enhancement on behalf of the child? Does it make a difference if the enhancement is electronic (a cochlear implant to make the child more sensitive to the specific timbre of violin music) or genetic (a somatic enhancement to increase the dexterity of one's fingers for playing the violin)? Should parents' rights be limited in this respect?

Naturally such discussion can be broadened to include the child's perspective as well. We are used to cultural policies that limit the decision-making abilities of children (restrictions on voting, for instance). For similar reasons, adult society might wish to place restrictions on a child's ability to opt for a particular enhancement.

Perhaps, let us say, a ten-year-old should not be able to obtain a sensory enhancement because his judgment is not yet to be trusted. What about a seventeen-year-old? The prevalence of risk-taking behaviors among teenagers is well-established (indeed, there are evolutionary arguments to the effect that teenagers *should* be expected to take greater risks than adults). We might soon be faced with a scenario in which numerous teenagers wish to experiment on themselves with enhancement technologies; and this will be accompanied by a need to sort out which technologies are to be allowed, and which forbidden.

The complementary question to "who should be allowed to choose enhancement" is that of accessibility. If *some* people are allowed to choose enhancement technologies, why not all people? Once some prospective young athletes have begun to experiment with altered senses or genomes, shouldn't the same choices be available to all students? There is a related issue of economic accessibility, or equity: suppose a particular enhancement (for, say, playing violin) happens to be expensive to obtain. Is it fair that children from non-wealthy families should be unable to achieve the same level of mastery as children of well-off parents, simply because they cannot afford the same bodily enhancements as their wealthy peers?

One temptation, when faced with the thicket of ethical and philosophical dilemmas surrounding transhumanist technologies, is to attempt to finesse the question by proposing a ban on research and development of all such technologies. Yet there are reasons that it would be unwise to take this course (much like trying to kill the wolf Fenrir outright). For one thing, it might be argued that to forbid such technologies would be to artificially constrain the potential achievements of individuals: perhaps our society would be deprived of scientific understanding or artistic achievement by placing biological limits on what people (and children in particular) can learn and accomplish. Another argument is a pragmatic one: if there are avenues by which people can experiment with enhancements privately or in a do-it-yourself manner, some people will pursue those avenues regardless of legality. Parents might find ways of seeking enhancements for their children despite restrictions; teenagers, being teenagers, might continue to experiment on themselves. In other words, prohibiting enhancement technologies might place societies in the same sorts of scenarios as already exist when prohibiting alcohol (an unsuccessful social experiment in the twentieth-century United States) and certain drugs (a policy with its own associated controversies).

HEURISTICS FOR DESIGN

In the light of the discussion in the previous section, it seems reasonable for this community–the designers interested in children's technology–to propose for debate a number of heuristics, or guidelines, to shape research and experimentation in transhumanist technologies for children. This section is not at all intended as a "manifesto"; it's difficult to approach this topic with any sense of technological or moral certainty. The purpose of the following heuristics, then, is to suggest some starting points for the inevitable design controversies that will emerge over the coming decades.

Heuristic 1: Wearables over implantation. It seems reasonable for the near-term future to give a strong preference to designing technologies that have temporary or easily undone impact instead of longer-term alterations. (This heuristic is familiar to any parent who has argued with their teenage child about the wisdom of getting a tattoo.) In the case of sensory extensions, for example, experimentation with wearable (and removable) devices is a natural preferred option in contrast to bodily implants. The obvious reasoning here would be that since we don't know about the long-term impacts–including behavioral or cognitive impacts–of sensory extensions, it would be sensible to gather as much lore as possible in a setting where extensions can be easily removed or replaced.

Heuristic 2. Craft technologies in preference to large-scale commercial products. The community of "body-modders" described by Platoni [2015] is a sort of "homebrew" group of people experimenting with sensory enhancements on their own, in basements and garages. Undoubtedly there are risks associated with this style of work in contrast to more mainstream, better-funded efforts: the body-modders cannot, for instance, get implants done by medical doctors, so they avail themselves of the services of tattoo artists. Even with these risks understood, however, there are distinct cultural advantages to a style of experimentation that allows, within fairly broad limits, people to create and experiment with their own enhancement technologies in do-it-yourself fashion, rather than pursuing large-scale commercially designed products.

There are several reasons for this heuristic, which is admittedly more likely to be controversial than the previous one. First, in principle it allows a greater openness and transparency about early experimental work: the homebrew communities tend to be open-source and to permit other hobbyists and enthusiasts to pick up and extend their work freely. This avoids the scenario in which corporate researchers are working out of the public eye to avoid imitators; the likelihood in this latter case is that there will be less public discussion of the merits of a particular innovation until it has a large-scale release and is something of a *fait accompli*.

Moreover, there are deeper problems involved, at the cultural level, in responding to large-scale corporate interests in contrast with craft communities. When a product is released it is accompanied by professional advertising to create a perceived need where none might have existed before (cf. [Wu, 2016]); arguably people have more freedom to consider their options in the absence of such professional manipulation. Likewise, when large numbers of people are persuaded to adopt a particular technology, it becomes an increasingly fraught decision on the part of the individual whether to go along or not. (This sort of peer pressure phenomenon–whether it promotes the playing of a particular video game, the acquisition of a tattoo, or the use of a particular fashion accessory–is particularly acute in communities of young people.) Finally, when a corporate product is promoted, other options are regarded as competitors (rather than alternatives) and in some cases are deliberately suppressed.

Heuristic 3: Concentrate attention on children's culture and children's purposes as foundations for innovation. The intent of this final heuristic is to sound what might be an unexpected cautionary note. The caution here is not, in this case, of the physiological risks of transhumanist technologies (though these do exist). Rather, it is to warn against the interpretation of these technologies in terms of the purposes of the adult (and especially the politically or financially powerful adult) community.

The idea here is that there will inevitably be efforts to redefine the constraints of childhood in ways that preferentially highlight the purposes of the designers rather than children themselves. Adults might wish to create innovations that (e.g.) lengthen children's attention span in the classroom; or encourage them to load themselves up with commercial attachments or accessories; or provide products that lead to a loss of privacy (the possibility of a limited sort of "reading the thoughts of another" via brain machine interfaces is often mentioned in discussions of this kind).

We live in a culture that places heavy emphasis on consumption and material acquisition, while simultaneously devaluing alternative themes such as long-term reflection, relaxation, and idiosyncratic interests (particularly those with no discernible monetary reward, such as stargazing). The design community must be aware of these tendencies as it begins to explore the potentially explosive and transformative technologies associated with transhumanism. Every technology, every newly designed artifact for young people inevitably reflects a set of values–what should children be like, how should they spend their time–and these questions will come to the fore with special urgency as we create designs whose impact is increasingly expressed in biological or physiological terms.

SAMPLE RESEARCH PROJECTS

To concretize some of the discussion thus far, this section presents a variety of plausible (if in some cases a bit futuristic) research and design projects involving transhumanist technologies for children. The goal in these examples is to try to keep relatively close to the spirit of the heuristics offered in the previous section.

Project 1. Experiencing animal perception. The term "umwelt" was coined by the German biologist Jakob von Uexküll to denote the concept of "the world as experienced by a particular creature". That is, the umwelt of a bat (which navigates via echolocation) or a dog (whose sense of smell is far more acute than that of a person) is significantly different than that of a human being. One likely project, then, in biology education would be to design sensory enhancements that permit children (or researchers, for that matter) to experience, at least in part, the umwelt of another creature. A set of wearable cat whiskers, or an artificial "dog nose" sensor, or glasses that mimic the compound eye of an insect, could be created as first steps toward this project (again, following the natural heuristic of preferring wearables to more long-term enhancements). By temporarily inhabiting (again, if only in part) the sensory world of an animal, it may be possible to achieve both a deeper intellectual understanding of, and empathy for, the experiences of certain animals.

Project 2. Musical performance via combined hand and brain-machine interface control. Another potential project would be to design novel musical instruments for children that could be controlled by various combinations of physical movements and brain-machine interface control. The degree to which purely neural (as opposed to muscular) control is employed for a given instrument could, in this instance, be a parameter of the design. Each instrument would be played at least in part via input received from EEG signals transmitted from a wearable headpiece.

Arguably this sort of project would resonate with a common element of youth culture involving the playing of an instrument (as suggested by the third heuristic of the previous section). For some children, an especially high level of performance skill might be obtained on an instrument that is, in effect, customized for their own particular mixture of muscular and neural abilities. The result might encourage participation in music for students who otherwise would have been indifferent, or who might be daunted by the prospect of not being the best at some particular traditional instrument.

Project 3. Science education via sensory enhancement. The first project suggestion focused on sensory enhancements as a means toward zoological understanding. One might similarly employ sensory enhancements to (e.g.) directly perceive certain radio wavelengths, or "feel" electric currents, or direct attention to certain color combinations, among many other possibilities. As noted earlier, the history of scientific instrumentation can be viewed as a progressive accumulation of sensory prostheses; a project of this sort could be directed toward creating scientific instruments that are positioned increasingly close to the user's body, and whose use would occur over potentially longer periods of day-to-day activity.

CONCLUSION

The reader familiar with the literature of transhumanism might have already noticed in this discussion certain topics that have been deliberately omitted. In our view, there is no need, at least at present, to speculate on large-scale cosmic-level changes in human consciousness facilitated by transhumanist technologies. We are free, of course, to imagine a coming "singularity" event of human-level artificial intelligence, or futuristic scenarios involving the storage and copying of human connectomes; and indeed it may be that such scenarios, or approximations of them, will come to pass. But the current, plausible frontier of transhumanist technologies–sensory extensions, robotic actuators, brain-machine interfaces, and genetic alteration–gives us plenty to think about, debate, and design in the very near-term future.

In the Norse myth of Fenrir, the wolf was eventually successfully bound: his leash, rather than a ponderous metal chain, was composed of the lightest, most ethereal elements of imagination and fantasy. The myth has a profound, disturbing effect. It suggests that the greatest dangers to civilization are tamed by inventions of the mind, invisible entities that constitute our collective cultural survival. The technologies of transhumanism might steer us toward dangerous cultural territory; but we, as designers, may yet create an intellectual leash that allows the technology to flourish for children in ways that reflect our own abiding and evolving projects and values.

Endnote. An extended, more thorough version of this paper may be found under the "Publications" link at: https://cucraftlab.org Readers wishing to cite this paper are encouraged to access the longer version.

ACKNOWLEDGMENTS

This paper has benefitted, directly and indirectly, from many wonderful conversations over the years. I particularly wish to thank Ann Eisenberg, Gerhard Fischer, Clayton Lewis, Roy Pea, Hal Abelson, Andy diSessa, Ben Shapiro, Gerald Jay Sussman, Uri Wilensky, Andee Rubin, Mark Gross, and the late Edith Ackermann.

REFERENCES

1. Barfield, W. [2015] *Cyber-Humans: Our Future with Machines.* New York: Springer.
2. Clark, A. [2003] *Natural-Born Cyborgs.* New York: Oxford Press.
3. Doud. A. *et al.* [2011] Continuous three-dimensional control of a virtual helicopter using a motor imagery based brain-computer interface. *PLoS One*, 6(10): e26332.
4. Jebari, K. [2015] Sensory enhancement. In Clausen, J. and Levy, N., *eds. Handbook of Neuroethics.* Dordrecht, Netherlands: Springer.
5. Keary, A. and Keary, E. [1870] *The Heroes of Asgard.* Reprinted in 2012, Calgary, Canada: Theophania Publishing.
6. LePage, M. [2016] Gene doping in sport could make the Olympics fairer and safer. In *New Scientist*, Aug. 5, 2016.
7. Lilley, S. [2013] *Transhumanism and Society*. Dordrecht, Netherlands: Springer.
8. Lingley, A. *et al.* [2011] A single-pixel wireless contact lens display. *J. of Micromechanics and Microengineering,* 21:12.
9. More, M. and Vita-More, N., *eds.* [2013] *The Transhumanist Reader*. Chichester, UK: John Wiley & Sons.
10. Platoni, K. [2015] *We Have the Technology.* New York: Basic Books.
11. Savulescu, J. and Bostrom, N. *eds*. [2011] *Human Enhancement.* Oxford, UK: Oxford University Press.
12. Seedhouse, E. [2014] *Beyond Human.* Berlin: Springer.
13. Stratton, G. [1896] Some preliminary experiments on vision without inversion of the retinal image. Read at *Third International Congress for Psychology*, Munich, 1896.
14. Wu, T. [2016] *The Attention Merchants.* New York: Random House.

The SEL Transition Wheel: Designing for Early Childhood Social Emotional Learning

Abigale Stangl
ATLAS Institute*
Boulder, Colorado
abigale.stangl@colorado.edu

Joanna Weidler-Lewis
School of Ed.*
Boulder, Colorado
joanna.weidler-lewis@colorado.edu

Carlye Lauff
Dept. of Mech. Eng.*
Boulder, Colorado
carlye.lauff@colorado.edu

Emily Price
School of Ed.*
Boulder, Colorado
emily.price@colorado.edu

Eric Fauble
Dept. of Mech. Eng.*
Boulder, Colorado
eric.fauble@colorado.edu

ABSTRACT
This paper describes the design of an interactive artifact—The SEL Transition Wheel—created to support social emotional learning (SEL) in children ages three to six. The SEL Transition Wheel focuses on helping young children learn emotional self-regulation and labeling of one's emotions while encouraging caregiver mediation of the SEL process during transition times. The final prototype presented in this paper demonstrates how a set of heuristics, identified through the design process, can be used to create interactive SEL artifacts for young children. We also discuss how the process of designing for SEL supported a multidisciplinary collaboration.

Author Keywords
SEL; social emotional learning; decision wheel; self-awareness; pre-school; user-centered design.

ACM Classification Keywords
H.5.m. Information interfaces and presentation

INTRODUCTION
Social emotional learning (SEL) is the process through which children and adults develop the skills, attitudes, and values necessary to acquire social and emotional competence. Social and emotional competence is the ability to understand, manage, and express the social and emotional aspects of one's life in ways that enable the successful management of life tasks [7]. General consensus in the field of education identifies five core competencies: self-awareness, self-management, social awareness, relationship building, and responsible decision-making [4].

Drawing from theories of social, emotional and cognitive development as well as behavior change, the field of SEL has grown extensively since its introduction in the late 1990s [3].

IDC '17, June 27-30, 2017, Stanford, CA, USA

ACM ISBN 978-1-4503-4921-5/17/06...$15.00
http://dx.doi.org/10.1145/3078072.3079746

Despite this growth, Slovák et al (2015) found that the Human Computer Interaction (HCI) community has rarely engaged with the design and research around supporting the development of social and emotional skills for the general population [15]; indeed, nearly all HCI work focusing on the development of SEL skillsets is geared to children with special needs [8, 18]. Furthermore, there are even fewer projects within the Interaction Design for Children (IDC) community explicitly focused on investigating the design of SEL interactive artifacts that support preschool-aged children's SEL competencies. In this paper, we present an exploratory design process conducted by a multidisciplinary team (educators, learning scientists, mechanical engineers, and interaction designers), which resulted in a set of design heuristics for the design of interactive SEL artifacts for young children, and an exemplar of an interactive artifact to support children in developing SEL competencies.

As identified during our problem definition activities and caregiver interviews, children are in need of greater support to identify their emotions during these transition times, and thus, to gain increased self-awareness and self- management. Reaching beyond existing early-childhood SEL curriculum and materials, the *SEL Transition Wheel* provides children with multiple ways to identify and understand emotions (their own and of others) before, during, and after transitioning between activities or environments. These transitions sometimes referred to as "horizontal transitions," include the movements children make across space and time such as the movement from home to school, or from playtime to bedtime [19].

BACKGROUND
We used this background information to inform our initial observations towards the design of an interactive artifact for SEL in young children. This literature shows a clear need and opportunity to design an interactive artifact that is mobile in form, readily adapted to a child's diverse experiences in different environments, during a range of activities, and with various caregivers.

SEL Competencies in Pre-Kindergarten
Identifying and understanding one's own as well as others' emotions, which requires the ability to differentiate, name, and notice subtle changes of emotions, is a prerequisite to developing the five core SEL competencies [14]. SEL

equips a person to become self-aware, engage in self-management, have social awareness, practice strong relationship skills, and eventually engage in responsible decision making. To obtain these competencies, one should learn SEL skills that help a person manage their emotions, develop communication strategies and relationships, and deal with conflicts and problematic situations. Unsurprisingly, then, activities that emphasize the practice of self-recognition and internal reflection leading to continuous exploration of how the individual and others feel [14] is often incorporated into SEL curricula.

SEL Curriculum and Materials:

The use of systematic school-based programming to promote SEL competencies in preschool and early childhood classrooms has evolved since the 1970's. Currently, the primary Pre-K SEL curriculum advocates for using age appropriate instructional modalities in as many different contexts as possible. Further, SEL curriculum advocate for the use of different types of instructional tools and methods, including brainstorming activities, cooperative learning, guest speakers modeling, rehearsals and practice, role-play, simulations, and more. Notably, audiotapes and videotapes are commonly used.

Digital Technologies for SEL

Digital technologies have been designed to enable people to explore and deepen their understanding of their emotional experiences. Examples of such technologies include artifacts that provide users with data representations of their emotional states based on user data, e.g. AffectAura [12], or offer users information on their emotional state as an aid to support post hoc recall. Other systems support users in making personal reflections about their emotions, e.g. AffectiveDiary [10, 16]. However this work is limited to generally focus on adult users and does not focus on SEL.

Digital technologies focused on supporting children to explore and deepen their understanding of their emotional experiences rarely focus on young children, and when they do, they tend to focus on children with disabilities [9,18]. Few systems have been developed by HCI researchers or others to support SEL in young learners. This gap may be due to, as Slovák et al note, a sustained reliance on experiential—often non-cognitive learning—in SEL that makes the design of technology difficult and challenges how learning is approached in HCI. Without question, the needs of young SEL learners raise different requirements, needs, and challenges for HCI designers [14]. In turn, we saw an opportunity to explore this nascent HCI space through user-centered research through design, guided by design-thinking activities. During this process however, we kept three human development concepts in mind.

Developmental Considerations for Design

Multiple factors influence the SEL development of pre-school children. During preschool (three to six years old), developmental advances in executive functioning (EF) and language development, lay the foundation for dramatic growth in children's emotional understanding and regulation, self-awareness, self-regulation, and social reasoning and social skills [9]. Social and emotional difficulties are common during these years, when young children are just beginning to cultivate SEL competencies [6]. The *SEL Transition Wheel* supports child SEL development by 1) leveraging children's developmentally appropriate level of executive functioning (self-regulation), 2) fostering the labeling of emotions, and 3) encouraging caregiver mediation of the process.

1) Self-Regulation: Executive functioning supports adaptive, goal-directed behaviors that enable individuals to override more automatic or established thoughts and responses [11, 13]. Preschoolers are still learning to self-regulate, but the goal at this age is to help children shift from always relying on adult-regulation by providing them tools and strategies to self-regulate. As we discuss below, the *SEL Transition Wheel* supports this shift as it is designed to be interactive for children both with and without their caregiver.

2) Labeling Emotions: In these early years, children experience many feelings and tend to understand the general notion of feelings or emotions, but they usually have a very limited vocabulary of words to describe different emotions. The critical SEL skill development for this age range includes fostering a sense of self-control, learning new emotional words, understanding that "right" or "wrong" may be based on more than just the immediate consequences of the behavior, and learning that how something appears is not always how it is [20]. An important feature of the *SEL Transition Wheel* is that it labels emotions with both sight and sound. It also allows children to view their reflection of their emotions in a mirror to support self-recognition and awareness.

3) Caregiver Mediation: In response to research showing that a child's social-emotional development is greatly influenced by parents and other caregivers in addition to teachers [1], SEL curriculum often advocates for universal approaches highlighting parent-child relationships and SEL interventions that include both in and out school components [2]. The *SEL Transition Wheel* is customizable to the child, the caregiver, and the learning environment.

METHODS

The background research and the design of the *SEL Transition Wheel* began when our multidisciplinary team came together to respond to the Robert Wood Johnson Foundation's (RWJF)[1] design prompt, "*How might we support SEL development in young children?*" In developing this prompt, the RWJF recognized the need for materials to support children's SEL.

1 The RWJF's overarching mission is to improve the culture of health, supports programs in early childhood.

At the onset of the project we choose several methodological strategies to combat these challenges. First, we noted that conventional methods often used to translate evidence-based SEL interventions into real work contexts have yet to have significant impact. Moreover, throughout the design process, we strove to elicit each of our team members' different epistemological conceptions of design and academic backgrounds. Our team members included a SEL educator/researcher, a learning scientist, two mechanical engineers, and an interaction design researcher. Our team found common ground and engaged in a *research through design* process using a structured *design-thinking* framework. Research through design emphasizes the production of artifacts as vehicles embodying what "ought to be" and that will influence both the research and practice communities [21]. Design thinking is an iterative approach to developing solutions that will meet the needs of the user in an innovative way. The process can be displayed in multiple forms, one being five stages—empathize, define, ideate, prototype, and test [17]. The end user is always at the center of the process; ideas are turned into prototypes and then immediately tested with these users to inform the next iteration of the design. We wanted to ensure that the end users' (children and their caregivers) needs were always at the center of the process. Our design process occurred over the course of four months. During each stage of the project we engaged with the end-users and the design materials in specific ways in order to identify the requirements for an interactive artifact that supports preschool-aged children's ability to identify their emotions.

Empathize

At the onset, we met to discuss the theoretical groundwork for our project, including principles of design thinking, the SEL core competencies, and how to perform empathetic fieldwork. We identified a variety of scenarios and environments in which children, ages three to six, and their caregivers develop and practice SEL. We recognized that they primarily spend time at home with a caregiver, in transit to another activity with a caregiver, or engaged activities with other children and caregivers in public or private environments—homes, parks, preschool, public library events, etc. Each of our multidisciplinary team members choose to learn about the experiences of children and their caregivers in a manner that met their prior training. Each team member spent eight hours engaging in participant observations, including running errands and observing typical routines with a mother and her children, (ages three and five), conducting three 20-minute informal interviews with preschool teachers and observing children in situ (at different schools) during the students' play time, observing pre-school aged children at a public park, and observing children at a public library. Each team member reported their observations to the team in the form of a photolog, a formal ethnographic report, a series of sketches, and analytical memos. We observed how the children, families, and staff functioned in the child care centers as well as compared these observations to the dynamics of the families at home.

Define: Together as a team we synthesized and categorized these insights, and then defined the problem using empathy mapping, saturate and group, and user point of view techniques [17]. After much deliberation, we determined our problem statement: *It would be game changing if we could increase children's self-awareness of their emotions during transition periods throughout all of the day.*

Ideate: Together we used several techniques such as stoke, brain swarming, brainstorming, heat mapping, and selection to ideate on our problem statement. We identified sketched a series of ideas that became our first round of physical prototypes.

Prototype and Test: *Iteration 1:* We initially developed three low-resolution paper prototypes. At this stage of the process, we did not identify the design solution to be specifically technical in nature, although some of the ideas incorporated DIY electronic components. The initial prototypes included (1) "feeling embodiment activity" which incorporated yoga-like movement and activity with SEL competencies, (2) an electronic bracelet and a feelings board that allowed children to identify their feelings on a visual display that would also be mirrored on their bracelet, and (3) an initial version of the transition wheel (Figure 1). We conducted semi-structured interviews with the children, families, and staff to obtain feedback for improving them.

Iteration 2: Upon reviewing the feedback from parents and caregivers made a set of refined digital sketch of *SEL Transition Wheel* (Figure 2). We presented these concept-drawing to caregivers to receive additional feedback that helped us refine a set of design heuristics.

Figure 1. Initial Prototypes

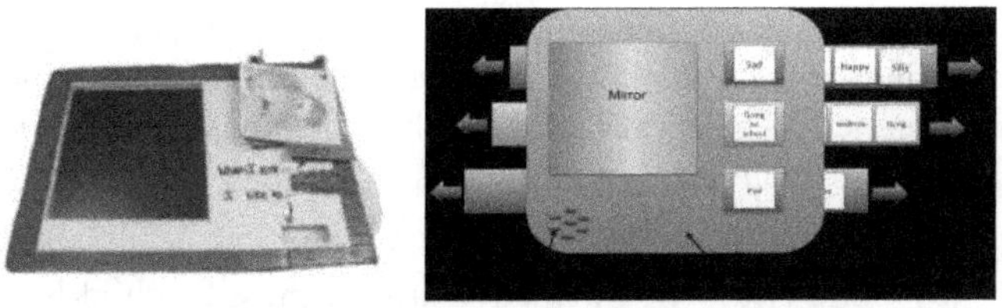

Figure 2. Representation of the Second Prototypes

Iteration 3 (Final Prototype): We designed the third and final version of the *SEL Transition Wheel* as a physical prototype. We gave the prototype to caregivers for situated use. (Figure 3).

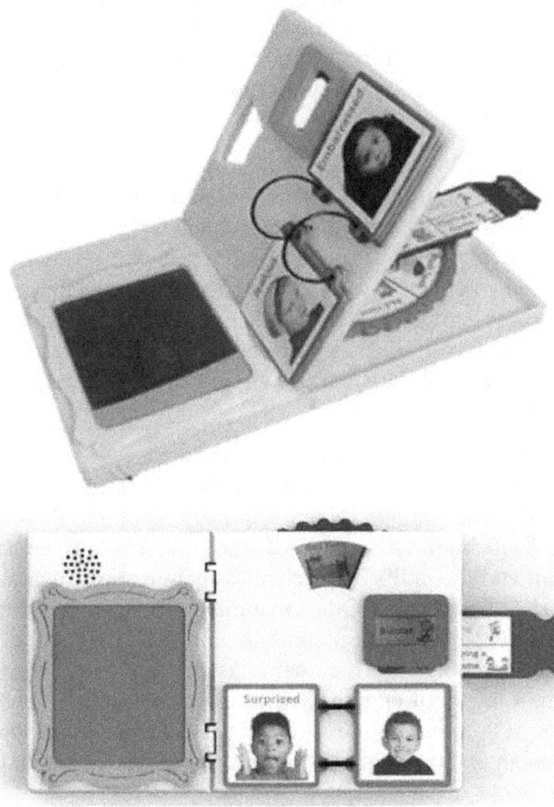

Figure 3. Final Prototype

FINDINGS

Initial Prototypes and Feedback

Each initial prototype enabled us to refine the design to meet specific feedback provided by our end-users. Our findings from the initial prototypes came from interviews, where caregivers and parents recounted their reflections of watching children interact with the designs, as well as our own observations. For example, to test the feelings embodiment ("yoga mat") the researcher led an activity at the daycare using the mat to guide the children through the different poses. The teacher reflected that leading the whole class in the activity would be too much of a burden for teachers, and that the children would benefit from something more self-guided. She liked the fun, colorful, and lively pictures that oriented the children to emotions.

While testing the first iteration of the transition wheel and the electronic bracelet the caregivers asked for something that was transportable, and had clear representations of emotions that do not rely on words (since children are generally unable to decode words at this age, but are developing early literacy skills through exposure to text). The caregivers also had reservations about an artifact that was overly technological, for example the app, or not appropriate for school settings. In turn, we decided to focus on the transitions wheel prototype concept because adheres to these requirements and incorporates multiple design features that the caregivers identified—portability, manipulability, and multi-modality.

The second iteration blended ideas from the initial prototypes into two prototypes: one was a physical version modified to include features such as a mirror for children to self-identify their current emotional state, and the other was a mock-up of a different structural design in which levers would be pulled rather than spun (Figure 2). In the meetings with the parents, caregivers, and children, they preferred the ability to spin and flip levels rather than pull or slide. Additional feedback included incorporating sound and more images to make it more preschool friendly. It is beyond the scope of this paper to report on the use of the final prototype.

Final Product and Interactive Features

Parents and caregivers were critical in identifying and naming the instances when and why young children experience dramatic emotional changes; this insight led to key design features of the final *SEL Transition Wheel prototype.* The final design, as seen in Figure 3, is a handheld and easily transportable artifact that helps children observe, differentiate, name, and notice subtle changes of emotions while in transition between activities. The main features include: **1)** A lightweight ergonomic design made of ABS plastic, which a child can carry and fit into the contours of their lap, and a parent can wash. **2)** A mirror and pictures of children's faces related to specific emotions like surprise, happiness, jealousy, and embarrassment as shown in the figures. This design allows children to see the facial expressions and then look at themselves to see if this reflects their emotions. **3)** Customizable audio and lighting prompts to encourage the children to express and reflect on their emotions. **4)** Kinetic parts that enable children to manipulate the object, through scrolling, pulling, sliding, and flipping. **5)** Customizable parts that enable caregivers to exchange the exemplar emotion images, transition cards, and the sliding reel of activities.

Underlying Design Heuristics

Through engaging design thinking and researching though design also helped us identify a set of key design heuristics that enabled us to make a set of prototypes that were developmentally, structurally, and situationally appropriate. These heuristics may be used to evaluate the final *SEL Transition Wheel* in filed studies. The heuristics included: **A)** The interactive artifact must contain elements that are representative of age appropriate emotions and be akin to the emotions the child was experiencing prior to the interaction with the artifact. During our fieldwork, for example, a parent noticed that a child would only interact with the artifact if the child was in the "mood" and understood the emotion labeled on the artifact. **B)** The interactive artifact must be readily usable during transitions: it must be mobile in form and adaptable to diverse experiences in different environments, during a range of activities, and with various caregivers. **C)** The interactive artifact must be child-led, in that teachers and caregivers should not be over-burdened by mediating children's engagement with the artifact.

DISCUSSION AND LESSONS LEARNED

Designing Interactive Artifacts for SEL and Children

To date, few artifacts and systems support SEL in young learners have been developed by HCI researchers. All the while, many organizations and teachers are recognizing the need to develop SEL skills in young children. In this paper we present an interactive artifact to support preschool children's SEL skills. The *SEL Transition Wheel* is a product of a design thinking/research through design activity that enabled a multidisciplinary team to investigate SEL development in young children, the needs of caregivers to help in their development, and interactive artifacts to help address these needs.

Our design process was guided by observing the opportunities for SEL instruction as they occurred organically during the daily activities of young children. This focus contrasts with the majority of programmatic approaches that proceed through a set of lessons designed to address targeted skills in a predetermined order [5]. Additionally, by focusing on the various transitional moments preschool-aged children experienced at home, in school, and in child care centers, our approach has the distinction of responding to demonstrated individual need, rather than to a universal classroom-level audience. The value of this nuanced approach is demonstrated in both the final prototype of *The SEL Transition Wheel* as well as the associated design heuristics, which can be used to guide future SEL-focused design activities for young children.

(1) Age Appropriate Representations: The interactive artifact must contain elements that are representative of age appropriate emotions and be akin to the emotions the child was experiencing prior to the interaction with the artifact. → The final prototype enables children to see how others might express themselves in the pictures and then recognize their own emotions in the mirror. The sliding reel of activities enables children to physically manipulate the artifact, while providing representations of the responsible decisions children could take.

(2) Mobility and Customizability: The interactive artifact must be readily usable during transitions by being mobile in form and adaptable to diverse experiences in different environments, during a range of activities, and with various caregivers. → The emotion cards and the sliding reel of activities are customizable to unique children, and to group settings, which supports caregiver attempts to build social awareness. The form factors of the wheel enable children to put it in their laps, pick up and carry, and stakeholders to interchange and wash parts as needed.

(3) Child-Led: The interactive artifact must be child-led, in that teachers and caregivers should not be overburdened by mediating children's engagement with the artifact. → In addition to the aforementioned from factors, light and audio features can capture a child's attention. As they hear the spoken name of an emotion, they may see the corresponding word and facial expression, and their own-mirrored image. While using it, they may identify their current emotional state, and/or be aided to choose a new activity to transition to. Together, these features support burgeoning literacy skills, further enabling children's development of the SEL competencies.

In future work we aim to evaluate use of the *SEL Transition Wheel* according to these heuristics, as well as the impact the interactive artifact has in young children's' everyday lives. We hope to identify when children use the artifact in an unguided manner, how direct engagement with the artifact instantiates shifts in their behavior, and the temporal and situational factors that impact engagement or persistence in using it. We also hope to design and evaluate variations of the multimodal elements.

SEL in Multidisciplinary Design Work

The final design represents the various forms of expertise brought by our unique multidisciplinary team: the theoretical work from both SEL and HCI, the different approaches to design, and the skills of mechanical engineering such as the 3D printed prototype. Other features not readily apparent in the final design include a commitment to a final product that reflects diversity of all learners. As our team navigated our different layers of expertise, we were called upon to use our own social-emotional development as a resource to support the design and development of the artifact. We argue that this particular design space, namely SEL, and the interdisciplinary nature of the design task afforded us greater opportunity to experience and reflect on the emotional processes of design. In future work, we aim to further explore how SEL impacts the way designers collaborate while working through design processes, especially for the production of interactive artifacts that focus on developing self-awareness.

CONCLUSION

This paper details the importance of SEL in young children as well as the user-centered design process that led to the creation of *The SEL Transition Wheel*. This interactive product supports young children in identifying their emotions—a critical step in becoming self-aware. A multidisciplinary team, using their own SEL competencies to collaborate and interact with parents and caregivers, worked together to identify three heuristics for developing interactive SEL artifacts for you young children.

ACKNOWLEDGMENTS

We thank the Robert Wood Johnson Foundation, the families and preschools that provided the initial design insight and feedback, and our collaborators at The Pennsylvania State University.

REFERENCES

1. A. Bernier, S. Carlson, and N. Whipple. 2010. From External Regulation to Self-Regulation: Early Parenting Precursors of Young Children's Executive Functioning. Child Development 81, 1 (2010), 326–339.
2. K. Bierman, and M. Motamedi. (2015). SEL programs for preschool children. In J.A. Durlak, C.E. Domitrovich, R.P. Weissberg & T.P. Gullotta (Eds.), Handbook of social emotional learning: Research and practice (pp. 135-150). New York, NY: Guilford Press.
3. R. Brandt. (1999). Successful implementation of SEL programs: Lessons from the thinking skills movement. In J. Cohen (Ed.), Educating minds and hearts: Social emotional learning and the passage into adolescence (pp. 173-183). New York: NY: Teachers College Press.
4. Collaborative for Academic, Social, and Emotional Learning (CASEL). 2016. www.casel.org, accessed January, 17, 2017.
5. J. Durlak, R. Weissberg, A. Dymnicki, R. Taylor, & K. Schellinger. 2011. The Impact of Enhancing Students' Social and Emotional Learning: A Meta-Analysis of School-Based Universal Interventions: Social and Emotional Learning. *Child Development* 82, 1 (January 2011), 405–432.
6. E. Egger and A. Angold. (2006). Common emotional and behavioral disorders in preschool children: Presentation, nosology, and epidemiology. Journal of Child Psychology and Psychiatry, 47, 313–337
7. M. Elias, J. Zins, R. Weissberg, K. Frey, M. Greenberg, N. Haynes, R. Kessler, M. Schwab-Stone, & T. Shriver, T. (1997). Promoting social and emotional learning: Guidelines for educators. Alexandria, VA: Association for Supervision and Curriculum Development.
8. L. Escobedo, D. Nguyen, L.A. Boyd, S. Hirano, A. Rangel, D. Garcia-Rosas, M. Tentori, and G. Hayes. 2012. MOSOCO: A mobile assistive tool to support children with autism practicing social skills in real-life situations. In CHI'12. ACM Press, New York, NY, USA, 2589.
9. M.T. Greenberg. 2006. Promoting resilience in children and youth. Annals of the New York Academy of Sciences, 1094(1), 139-150.
10. K. Höök, A. Stahl, P. Sundström, and J. Laaksolaahti. 2008. Interactional empowerment. In CHI'08. ACM Press, New York, NY, USA, 647–656.
11. M. Lezak. (1995). Neuropsychological assessment. New York: Oxford University Press.
12. D. McDuff, A. Karlson, A. Kapoor, A. Roseway, & M. Czerwinski. 2012. AffectAura: an intelligent system for emotional memory. In Proceedings of the SIGCHI Conference on Human Factors in Computing Systems. ACM, 849–858.
13. M. Mesulam, D. Stuss, & R. Knight. (Eds.) (2002). Principles of frontal lobe function. New York: Oxford University Press.
14. P. Slovák and G. Fitzpatrick. 2015. Teaching and Developing Social and Emotional Skills with Technology. ACM Trans. Comput.-Hum. Interact. 22, 4 (June 2015), 19:1–19:34.
15. P. Slovák, R. Gilad-Bachrach, & G. Fitzpatrick. 2015. Designing Social and Emotional Skills Training: The Challenges and Opportunities for Technology Support. In Proceedings of the 33rd Annual ACM Conference on Human Factors in Computing Systems. CHI '15. New York, NY, USA: ACM, 2797–2800.
16. A. Stahl, K. Höök, M. Svensson, A. Taylor, & M. Combetto. 2008. Experiencing the affective diary. Personal and Ubiquitous Computing 13, 5 (June 2008), 365–378.
17. Stanford Design School, Welcome to the K12 Lab Network wiki! 2016. https://dschool.stanford.edu/ January 17th, 2017
18. M. Tentori and G. Hayes. 2010. Designing for interaction immediacy to enhance social skills of children with autism. In Ubicomp'10. ACM Press, New York, NY, USA, 51.
19. P. Vogler, G. Crivello, M. Woodhead, & Bernard van Leer Foundation. 2008. Early childhood transitions research: a review of concepts theory and practice.
20. S. Whitcomb and D. Parisi Damico. 2016. Merrell's Strong Start—Pre-K. (2016).
21. J. Zimmerman, J. Forlizzi, and S. Evenson. 2007. Research through design as a method for interaction design research in HCI. In Proceedings of the SIGCHI conference on Human factors in computing systems. ACM, 493–502

Making in Minecraft: A Means of Self-Expression for Youth with Autism

Kathryn E. Ringland, LouAnne Boyd, Heather Faucett, Amanda L.L. Cullen, Gillian R. Hayes
Department of Informatics
University of California, Irvine
{kringlan, boydl, hfaucett, cullena, hayesg}@uci.edu

ABSTRACT
Maker culture values fabrication and production in both the digital and physical realms as well as the sharing of resources. As such, maker culture provides an opportunity to be democratic and inclusive. Likewise, spaces that stem from maker culture, such as makerspaces, provide the same opportunity for inclusion, even for those with disabilities. Autcraft is a community that supports children with autism and is centered on a Minecraft virtual world that embodies maker culture. The Autcraft community's unique form of maker culture supports self-expression, sociality, and learning for children with autism by providing structure in a virtual space, allowing for and enabling creating and sharing. In this paper, we explore design implications for the creation of inclusive spaces for making and self-expression in the future based on intensive fieldwork in the Autcraft community.

Author Keywords
Autism; Communication; Maker Culture; Virtual Worlds; Minecraft; Social Media; Self-expression.

ACM Classification Keywords
K.4.2 Social Issues: Assistive technologies for persons with disabilities.

INTRODUCTION
Maker culture has piqued the interest of many within the IDC community [1,2,6,9]. Although stemming from arts and crafts communities and originally focused on physical engagement with materials to be formed and "made" into products, prototypes, and projects [17], maker culture has evolved to include hacker culture which uses a wide variety of software, hardware, and craft materials. Present-day maker culture includes online and offline fabrication and production, sharing of resources, and social norms around the act of making [1,17]. Communities of makers inhabit spaces that are built to have a low barrier to entry, support those interested in learning to be makers, and encourage sharing of resources [17]. Researchers have found that maker culture supports learning a variety of skills (*e.g.,* production of new media) in youth through active sharing of knowledge and openness in how to produce new objects [7].

Maker culture is often associated with physical-world makerspaces. However, these physical spaces are only one facet of maker culture and can be intimidating to the uninitiated or differently abled. They are often largely inaccessible to people under 18 for liability concerns. Thus, alternative locations for workshops and free exploration, such as schools or even online, have emerged [11,12], bringing in a wide variety of makers. Despite this progress, there is evidence that some individuals (*e.g.,* those with disabilities) are still excluded, which may lead to exclusion from the wider maker community [8,17]. To answer these concerns, Alper proposes taking maker culture a step further by introducing "mixed-ability maker culture," which is "a collaborative culture within which people with and without disabilities can co-exist and co-create" [1]. With educators, parents, and librarians embracing maker culture as a way to support educating children [8], youth themselves must *all* be included.

To this end, we take an expansive view of maker culture in this paper by including a Minecraft virtual world in which children are heavily engaged in making in a virtual space. The Autcraft space, built and run by parents, exists as a Minecraft virtual world for children with autism[1] and their allies. In Autcraft, the opportunity to safely enter a space that supports self-expression is more accessible for those who have been left out due to challenges they experience in the physical world.

In this paper, we explore how "mixed-ability maker culture" supports self-expression in children with autism through an online community centered around the popular game, Minecraft. Our results show how the "mixed-ability maker culture" found within the Autcraft community, supports children with autism in imaginative making and self-expression [1] and we provide design implications for creating inclusive spaces for making and self-expression.

[1] In this paper, we use children with autism and autistic children interchangeably as that is the preference of the Autcraft community.

IDC '17, June 27-30, 2017, Stanford, CA, USA

ACM ISBN 978-1-4503-4921-5/17/06 $15.00
http://dx.doi.org/10.1145/3078072.3079749

Figure 1. A table with chairs in Minecraft. The table is made of a "piston" object.

METHODS

This paper reports on results from an on-going, qualitative digital study of an online community that has grown around a Minecraft server known as Autcraft. Data were collected through interviews with children and parents, participant observations, directed and non-directed forum discussions, chat logs, and digital artifacts.

Setting

The multiplayer virtual world in our study, Autcraft, is a semi-private server on Minecraft created for children with autism, their families, and allies. Anyone wishing to join must first complete an application to be added to the white list. Only those on the white list can access the server. Autcraft currently has more than 6,000 white-listed members with a daily average of approximately 50 players in-world at peak hours of the day and approximately 1,200 individual players[2] logging in each month. The Autcraft community is an inclusive, mixed-ability space.

Minecraft

Minecraft is an open-ended virtual world with no particular goals or play requirements [4,5,13]. Players can build and create new objects by manipulating blocks in the game. Minecraft has previously been described as a makerspace and as an example of a digitally mediated maker culture [12]. According to a popular guidebook in maker culture [12], modifying is the essence of making and, therefore, of maker culture. Minecraft is a virtual world where children are encouraged to modify the environment within the game, and even to modify the game itself, and to do so in collaboration with others. Autcraft is a version of Minecraft that includes modifications and add-ons to the software to allow for the safety of community members [15] and to enhance their socialization [14,16].

Data Collection

Our work employs ethnographic methods established by other studies of virtual world communities [3]. The first author gained access to Autcraft via permission of the server's creator for this study and uses an avatar labeled as a researcher in-world. Both the researcher's presence and purpose were made clear to the community through the Autcraft web-based forum and in the in-world chat. Parents were informed of the lead researcher's presence via a parent message board and the Facebook page of the community.

The lead researcher collected approximately 130 hours of immersive in-world observations, including participating in activities on the server, recording chat-based dialogue, and taking extensive field notes on everyday practices of community members and events as they occurred in the virtual world. Digital artifacts from the various platforms used by the community were also included in the analysis. These data were collected over a period of 24 months and include approximately 5,000 forum threads and 150 blog posts created by players, parents, and administrators.

Data Analysis

We used a three-phased approach to our data analysis. We first became familiar with the data as individuals and then drafted and shared memos related to themes within the team. Finally, we reviewed the themes collaboratively in meetings, searching the data for indicators or support for themes, as well as for conflicting data that was not well explained by our original interpretation. This approach was iterative, meaning that the team revisited each phase multiple times, as is an established best practice for qualitative data analysis [11].

RESULTS

Although clinical work has found that many autistic children exhibit challenges in engaging in imaginative play in which they can express themselves [19], we find in our work a plethora of creative examples in the Autcraft virtual space. Our findings open substantial clinical questions about the structure of imaginative play in the physical realm and how imaginative play may look different online. Analysis of our data, as represented in our discussion of vignettes, indicates that the constraints and affordances of this virtual environment provide structure for children to create and share in rich and varied ways without the barriers they would typically face in the physical world. By understanding the values in the Autcraft community through a lens of mixed-ability maker culture, we can see how these values encourage and support autistic children in their endeavors in self-expression.

Making in Minecraft

Minecraft, at its core, is a game about building with blocks in a virtual world. In Autcraft, community members have created complex, expressive spaces within their virtual world. They have done this through using construction materials found within the world, both as they are meant to

[2] AutCraft Wiki. *AutCraft*. Retrieved April 30, 2016, from http://autcraft.com/wiki/m/34575523/page/Autcraft_Wiki

be used (*e.g.,* using bricks to pave a walkway), but also in unexpected ways (*e.g.,* using a piston as a table).

Many of these building projects are shared amongst a group of community members, helping to foster and support sociality [16]. For example, in an interview, one participant showed off his large farm that could be used by any member of the community. He and several younger Autcraft members worked to build and maintain the farm. A section of the forums labeled "Builder Applications" allows community members to post their specific interests and skills for building in the virtual world. This space allows players coordinate building projects that might be prohibitive to build by oneself, encouraging members to participate in large-scale, multi-player, projects (*e.g.,* creating an entire town or island).

Community members build using their own ideas as well as finding references to use. While some members copy other Minecraft player's work (*e.g.,* from YouTube videos or Google image searches), others may imitate objects from within the game itself. For example, the children on the farm created a large, multistory building shaped like a cactus where desert plants were grown. Community members create landmarks of architecture from the physical world and create structures based on the stories that are culturally important to them (*e.g.,* Doctor Who[3]). They have gone so far as to create entire areas dedicated to particularly important cultural references. They are embracing the ethos of maker culture in Minecraft to modify and build their virtual world [14]. Further, they are expressing their identities through the objects they are creating.

Vignette: Mining World. In Autcraft, there is an entire world dedicated to mining raw materials. Mining World is different from other locations in Autcraft because once per month, the world is reset, wiping out everything and making a new world with all new resources. Signs are ubiquitous, warning community members not to build in Mining World because they will lose their creations at the end of the month. However, as the players mine, they also create. In the cases of these builders, the monthly world refresh does not stop them from creating in that space. Perhaps the ability to practice in a space that is not permanent may be motivating. This allows them freedom to try new ideas, practice building specific creations, and play around with making in a space that will be wiped away at the end of the month.

For other community members, this Mining World allows them to simply dig holes. Although this may not be seen as self-expression *per se* for children with autism, this can be a form of self-soothing – a repetitive action that helps alleviate overwhelming sensory experiences [18]. Instead of simply going offline to self-soothe without an audience, these players choose a virtual representation of such behavior that requires the player to manipulate game controllers to execute this action. We view digging as a deliberate form of creating and, in the Autcraft community, this behavior is a valid means of self-expression. These acts, both building in the Mining World and less goal-directed activities, such as digging, often happen without others being present. The community members are still expressing themselves, but they are doing it for their own enjoyment or stress relief, rather than having the explicit need to share every creation with others. They are doing it for self-satisfaction, such as giving themselves a sensory break by digging a hole to turn the screen black. Mining World in Autcraft provides a wide-open space for this activity to take place, indicating the potential value of intentionally creating spaces for children to destroy what they built as a part of becoming makers.

Creating to Share with Others

Many in the Minecraft community have gone far beyond this simple framework of just building to survive[4] in a world [4]. Websites for sharing creations, popular YouTube videos of players both playing and built objects, and Twitch streams all point to a culture of sharing. For example, one popular Minecraft YouTube channel for children named Stampy[5] has over 8 million subscribers [20]. Autcraft members participate in sharing through in-world events, forums, YouTube, and Twitch. They share their creations and use their creations to tell stories, both within the Autcraft virtual world and outside the Autcraft virtual world.

Sharing Creations Within the Autcraft Virtual World

When a community member has finished a new build or has created something to share with others logged into the Autcraft virtual world, they encourage those who are online to teleport (*i.e.,* instantly travel to specified coordinates) to their new creation. They also create forum posts with screenshots and coordinates so members who are offline can visit when they are back online. This practice allows others to learn from previous building projects, as well as giving builders a sense of pride in their own work. Community members can provide advice and feedback in the comments of the forums and in-world when they are touring the creation.

Beyond building and showing off their work, special events are hosted by both Autcraft administrators and individual community members. One of these events is the fireworks display, which is usually hosted by individual community members after they have built enough fireworks.

Vignette: Fireworks Show. It is late in the evening in the summertime, and only a handful of players are online in Autcraft. One community member posts in the chat window that there will be fireworks displayed in the main hall in 10 minutes, inviting everyone to join in watching. This member spent all day gathering the supplies needed to create the

[3] http://www.bbc.co.uk/programmes/b006q2x0

[4] Minecraft has two modes of play: creative and survival.

[5] https://www.youtube.com/channel/UCj5i58mCkAREDqFWlhaQbOw

fireworks and then crafting them all individually. Five minutes later, the member writes in chat that the show will be in five minutes' time. One minute until the show, the member then gives a countdown every 10 seconds and at 10 seconds out, every second. Six players in total arrive leading up the fireworks event. As they wait, they chat and walk around together. When the show starts, everyone stands still, looking up into the black sky as the colors burst forth.

Fireworks take a great deal of effort and energy to create. There is a lengthy process in which the player must find the right materials within the Minecraft world and use them to craft the different kinds of fireworks. To know how to make these different fireworks requires the player ask more experienced players or to look up the knowledge online (which is readily available on wikis). One of the reasons these fireworks shows are important to the Autcraft community members is because many of them have special sensory needs, and cannot attend physical-world fireworks displays. Being able to control their own fireworks show in-world gives them the opportunity to partake in an activity that was before inaccessible to them. This shows that users are willing to put in tremendous effort when given the opportunity to experience a sensory experience is a comfortable way.

This kind of effortful self-expression can be seen in various forms across the Autcraft community. For example, community members will learn programming languages to modify the Minecraft software (*i.e.,* modding [14]). This allows them to make changes to the base code to make various changes to how the game is played. They then teach other Autcraft community members how to do these program modifications, going as far as teaching classes within the Autcraft virtual world. These different making activities require a good deal of time, skill learning, and desire to learn from and teach others and is encouraged by administrators in the community.

Sharing Creations Outside the Autcraft Virtual World

Players build and show off their work through platforms such as forums, YouTube, and Twitch—and in some cases have become solvent in their own right off of their YouTube "Let's Play" videos [10]. "Let's Play" are edited videos of players playing through a video game, giving viewers a first-person experience of playing the game. It is against this cultural backdrop that members of the Autcraft community use their virtual world and the other existing social media to express themselves. This self-expression allows them to foster relationships within the Autcraft community, as well as to reach out to others beyond their community.

Vignette: Autism Awareness Day. One community member, age 12, created a YouTube video of himself building in Autcraft. He opens the video saying, "Hello, today I am going to continue building my house in Minecraft and talk to you about bullying." During the 15-minute video, the creator continues working on his home in Autcraft. He builds a bridge across a river, explaining his actions along the way. "I will make this bridge six blocks wide. And put supports in the water like this..." In between demonstrating to the viewer how he is building the bridge, the creator is explaining what it is like to be labeled with autism and go to school. He explains that some children get bullied, both in school and online. He ends with the plea to the viewer to consider passing on the message that everyone should be allowed to play Minecraft and to stop bullying, which is a problem in the Minecraft community at large.

The video this boy created not only shows how he is building within the Autcraft virtual world, making something new for others to replicate, but he is also using the video to express his own identity as a child with autism. Using the maker culture ideals of production and sharing knowledge, this community member is not only cementing his own role as an advocate for his community, but he is also doing a service by showing others how to "join in" and become makers as well.

Videos are not the only way Autcraft members share their creations outside of the server– they also post stories to forums and share fan art. In the forums, they share stories about events that happened within the Autcraft virtual world, often accompanying these stories with screenshots from when they were "in-world." Autcraft community members create fan art that shows their love for the Minecraft software and mixes mediums in an expressive way. For example, one child put cartoon images of another player on top of a screen shot of the Autcraft world. This mixed-media artwork goes beyond simply sharing something built in Minecraft. Using these types of tools, community members can explore, play with, and display their own identities alongside their avatars, chat, and other more traditional identity markers. Given the heavy identity development work that happens in childhood and the particular challenges autistic children have with this work, Autcraft and its surrounding technical ecosystem provide a unique view into these processes as well as opportunities for support.

KEY ISSUES FOR DESIGN

Despite not explicitly seeing or labeling themselves as makers, our fieldwork has demonstrated that the Autcraft community shares many traits with maker culture. Drawing on our findings, we propose the following set of issues as key considerations that designers must make when creating systems to help "mixed-ability maker culture" thrive while supporting self-expression for the users. Although we cannot offer explicit direction, the consideration of these concerns and how they are in conversation with one another is necessary to make inclusive mixed-ability spaces.

Accommodations for Access. The virtual world is not immune to the need for environmental accommodations. In our work, for example, we found that many modifications were necessary for the inclusivity of this maker space. These modifications include demarcating parts of the world for building, creating "safe" zones, and modifying the chat for easier use [14,15]. Such modifications allow for those with disabilities to participate in a way that is suitable for them in a space where they might otherwise find themselves excluded.

Virtual worlds as makerspaces can be tailored to needs that might be difficult to accommodate in the physical world, such as overstimulation. For example, in the virtual world, if a child is highly sensitive to sound at a particular moment, they can easily adjust the volume of the world or turn it off altogether. Similarly, if the child becomes over stimulated by images, they may darken the screen, as was the case for the children digging holes in the mines to turn the screen black. These modifications allow the child to continue to participate in the space, wherein a physical environment they may have to leave the environment altogether to avoid these symptoms.

Bounded Freedom. The boundaries found within Autcraft help enhance the creativity of the members. This includes the boundaries within the virtual world (the world and its resources are finite), the social boundaries imposed by the community, and the expectation that one member's creative self-expression does not infringe upon another member's self-expression. The Mining World resetting each month, for example, motivates the participants to try new designs with each reset that they might not otherwise attempt. This is particularly of interest for children with autism who may have a difficult time changing their focus or become very attached to a particular project. Having some areas of the world permanently save what members have built and others that serve as a temporary space allows for diverse approaches that serve to make the space more accessible and to give all the community members equal access to community resources through scaffolding.

Opportunity-Rich Environment. The Minecraft world is rich – full of objects, biomes, and creatures. This allows users to create narratives and even a mythos from these resources. The Minecraft game itself does not come with a history or backstory but allows players to create new history as the player explores and alters the world. It is this richness that sets the foundation for allowing for inclusivity. Disabilities, even those of the same diagnostic umbrella, are incredibly diverse and experiences occur in a myriad of ways. In this study, we observed this diversity within the Autcraft community and how this diversity was accommodated by using the richness of the environment. For example, one group of children might act out the story of a queen in her castle, and another group of children simultaneously tells a story based on My Little Pony. Further, this allows for a range of self-expression, giving a large variety of resources in which to be able to create their stories, villages, or buildings.

Social Support. The presence of moderators, helpers, and peer mentors support expression for community members. More experienced members help the less experienced members learn how to build, where to get resources, and even give tips on how to create forum posts and videos. This social support also comes with the expectation that community members will be inclusive. For example, when a child creates an anti-bullying video, other community members respond with praise and with their own videos with similar messaging. This shows solidarity within the community, as well as allowing each member to express themselves individually.

Social Conventions. The Minecraft community at large embraces creative players and the Autcraft community continues this trend by encouraging members to express themselves through building, roleplaying, storytelling, and sharing their created content through social media (*e.g.,* through streaming on Twitch, recording YouTube videos, and posting screenshots in the forums). The administrators have deliberately created a community that encourages every member to participate in making and sharing, in whatever way they desire. This comes through both explicit statements by the administrators, but also through their actions. Community members are praised for their making efforts and for sharing these creations through the various media available to them.

These design features support children with autism as they learn skills to express themselves. Designers and researchers interested in creating other technical systems can infuse some of the maker culture to create spaces that foster learning, sharing, and self-expression.

DISCUSSION AND CONCLUSION

The Autcraft community is a sociotechnical system that embodies the tenants of maker culture. The founders of Autcraft blended Minecraft DIY culture and disability communities' values of inclusion to create their own mixed-ability maker culture. Designers and researchers can learn from this community how to embed mixed-ability maker culture into new platforms.

Maker culture supports children's learning by being an open space for children to explore their own skills and interests. Children (and adults) come to learn in these spaces, but they also teach. Autcraft demonstrates that some autistic children, given the right supports, can express themselves in ways that are in direct contrast with core components of an autism diagnosis—challenges with social communication and pretend play. This contrast is not likely an indicator of a "cure," but instead demonstrates how their inherent abilities may be uncovered through different tools.

Future work should examine how the skills children learn in Autcraft travel beyond this Minecraft virtual world, to other parts of the internet and into the physical world. Likewise, we anticipate that skills developed in Autcraft and social bonds formed may stay with children as they grow into adults, meanwhile navigating an increasingly blurry digital-physical world divide.

ACKNOWLEDGMENTS

We thank the members of Autcraft for the warm welcome to their community. We would like to thank members of LUCI for their feedback on this paper. We would also like to thank Robert and Barbara Kleist for their support, as well as the

ARCS Foundation. This work is covered by human subjects protocol #2014-1079 at the University of California, Irvine.

REFERENCES

1. Meryl Alper. 2013. Making space in the makerspace: Building a mixed-ability maker culture. In *Interaction and Design for Children.* Retrieved January 26, 2017 from https://pdfs.semanticscholar.org/8d8a/ef7ff1f842a65e4fcbec9fb7d10deb46711a.pdf
2. David Bar-El and Oren Zuckerman. 2016. Maketec: A Makerspace as a Third Place for Children. 380–385. https://doi.org/10.1145/2839462.2856556
3. Tom Boellstorff, Bonnie Nardi, Celia Pearce, and T.L. Taylor. 2012. *Ethnography and Virtual Worlds: A Handbook of Method.* Princeton University Press.
4. Sean C. Duncan. 2011. Minecraft, beyond construction and survival. *Well Played: a journal on video games, value and meaning* 1, 1: 1–22.
5. Nate Garrelts (ed.). 2014. *Understanding Minecraft: Essays on Play, Community, and Possibilities.* McFarland & Company, Inc., Jefferson, NC.
6. Erica Rosenfeld Halverson and Kimberly Sheridan. 2014. The maker movement in education. *Harvard Educational Review* 84, 4: 495–504.
7. Y. B. Kafai and K. A. Peppler. 2011. Youth, Technology, and DIY: Developing Participatory Competencies in Creative Media Production. *Review of Research in Education* 35, 1: 89–119. https://doi.org/10.3102/0091732X10383211
8. Barbara Klipper. 2014. Making Makerspaces Work for Everyone. *Children and Libraries* 12, 3: 5–6.
9. Breanne K. Litts. 2015. Resources, facilitation, and partnerships: three design considerations for youth makerspaces. 347–350. https://doi.org/10.1145/2771839.2771913
10. Esther MacCallum-Stewart. 2014. "Someone off the YouTubez": The Yogscast as Fan Producers. In *Understanding Minecraft: Essays on Play, Community, and Possibilities*, Nate Garrelts (ed.). McFarland & Company, Inc., Jefferson, NC, 148–159.
11. Sylvia Libow Martinez and Gary S. Stager. 2013. *Invent to Learn: Making, Tinkering, and Engineering in the Classroom.* Constructing Modern Knowledge Press.
12. Dodie J. Niemeyer and Hannah R. Gerber. 2015. Maker culture and Minecraft: implications for the future of learning. *Educational Media International* 52, 3: 216–226. https://doi.org/10.1080/09523987.2015.1075103
13. Markus "Notch" Persson. 2011. *Minecraft.* Mojang, Stockholm, Sweden.
14. Kathryn E. Ringland, Christine T. Wolf, LouAnne E. Boyd, Mark Baldwin, and Gillian R. Hayes. 2016. Would You Be Mine: Appropriating Minecraft as an Assistive Technology for Youth with Autism. In *ASSETS 2016.*
15. Kathryn E. Ringland, Christine T. Wolf, Lynn Dombrowski, and Gillian R. Hayes. 2015. Making "Safe": Community-Centered Practices in a Virtual World Dedicated to Children with Autism. In *CSCW 2015.*
16. Kathryn E. Ringland, Christine T. Wolf, Heather Faucett, Lynn Dombrowski, and Gillian R. Hayes. 2016. "Will I always be not social?": Re-Conceptualizing Sociality in the Context of a Minecraft Community for Autism. In *CHI 2016.*
17. Nick Taylor, Ursula Hurley, and Philip Connolly. 2016. Making Community: The Wider Role of Makerspaces in Public Life. 1415–1425. https://doi.org/10.1145/2858036.2858073
18. Tracy Westeyn, Kristin Vadas, Xuehai Bian, Thad Starner, and Gregory D. Abowd. 2005. Recognizing mimicked autistic self-stimulatory behaviors using hmms. In *Wearable Computers, 2005. Proceedings. Ninth IEEE International Symposium on*, 164–167. Retrieved February 10, 2014 from http://ieeexplore.ieee.org/xpls/abs_all.jsp?arnumber=1550802
19. Pamela Wolfberg, Mila DeWitt, Gregory S. Young, and Thanh Nguyen. 2014. Integrated Play Groups: Promoting Symbolic Play and Social Engagement with Typical Peers in Children with ASD Across Settings. *Journal of Autism and Developmental Disorders* 45, 3: 830–845. https://doi.org/10.1007/s10803-014-2245-0
20. 2016. The 12 Best Kid-Friendly Minecraft Channels on YouTube. Retrieved February 1, 2017 from https://www.commonsensemedia.org/blog/the-12-best-kid-friendly-minecraft-channels-on-youtube

Parent-Child Dialogue with eBooks

Glenda Revelle
University of Arkansas
Fayetteville, AR USA
revelleg@gmail.com

Jennifer Bowman
University of Arkansas
Fayetteville, AR USA
jbowman@uark.edu

ABSTRACT
Research shows that dialogic reading (adults and children engaging in conversation about the book they are reading) facilitates young children's language and vocabulary development and success in learning to read. A growing body of research suggests that parent-child dyads engage in less dialogic reading with e-books than with traditional paper books. Previous researchers have suggested this effect may be due to interactive features such as animations and games distracting children from the storyline, or that voice-over narration may compete with parent verbalization. The current study is the first to test this explanation directly, by comparing parent-child reading of a "feature-free" e-book with reading a paper book. Results showed that even "plain" e-books with severely limited interactive features led to less parent-child conversation about book content than reading with paper books. It is critical that these results inform parents, educators, developers, and the research community with regard to policy and practice for young children's media use.

Author Keywords
Children; literacy; dialogic reading; parent-child interaction; e-books

ACM Classification Keywords
H.5.2. Information interfaces

INTRODUCTION
Children who do not have an adequate start in literacy development by the time they reach school rarely learn to read on schedule [24] and they continue to have difficulty throughout elementary school. Almost 90 percent of children identified as poor readers at the end of first grade are still poor readers at the end of fourth grade [11].

Children from lower income families are particularly at risk with regard to learning to read. Lower income families are less likely to have books and other print materials available for children in their home environment [21]. Furthermore, low-income parents typically speak less to their children and use less complex sentences when contrasted with more affluent families [8]. Hart & Risley estimate that ***by the age of three*** children from affluent families have heard approximately ***30 million more words*** than children living in poverty. This differential experience is reflected in preschool vocabulary level, which in turn predicts third grade reading comprehension [9].

IDC '17, June 27-30, 2017, Stanford, CA, USA

ACM ISBN 978-1-4503-4921-5/17/06...$15.00
http://dx.doi.org/10.1145/3078072.3079753

Engaging with adults in shared reading can help improve the literacy skills of young children, particularly when adults engage young children in "dialogic reading," a style of reading picture books in which adults ask children questions and engage them in conversation about what is happening in the book while they are reading together. Research has shown that dialogic reading facilitates children's language and vocabulary development [2, 4, 18, 20, 27].

With the growing popularity of electronic books, researchers have begun examining the extent to which e-books support parent-child dialogic reading interactions in the way that traditional paper books do [6, 16, 17, 22]. The current study compared parent-child conversation when reading e-books versus traditional print books to determine whether the amount and kind of dialogic reading interaction varied based on book format.

RELATED WORK
One of the most recent technological tools being marketed for young children is the electronic storybook. E-books can be found on various technology platforms, from the internet to popular mobile technologies such as mobile phones, the iPad, Nook or the Kindle. Digital technology has become a normal part of the younger generation's daily lives in various cultures and languages [14]. Due to the prevalence of digital media marketed toward children today, recent studies have begun to examine the impact of using e-books on young children's language and literacy development [3, 5, 12, 13].

Korat and Or [13] examined mother-child conversations during joint reading of e-books compared to print books. This study concluded that book format accounted for differences in the initiations, expanding talk, and responses of the mother and child. Traditional print book readings provided more initiations and responses by the mother as well as more expanding talk. A previous study by Kim and

Anderson [12] also found that e-books and print books showed differences in conversations between the adult reader and the child during joint reading experiences. E-books with narration were shown to impede parental mediation of the text that typically occurs in joint book reading and also showed fewer conversations about the written text.

Regarding children's part in the conversation, in a study by Moody, Justice, and Cabell [19] children demonstrated twice as many labeling references during joint print storybook reading than with e-books. The increase in children's labeling references suggests that children were more active in the conversation during traditional print readings than in the e-storybook readings. Other studies have suggested that typical e-books are not suitable for advancing young children's literacy due to the emphasis on graphics, colorful animations, and sounds that can distract young children from story comprehension [3, 13].

Studies by Trushell and colleagues [25, 26] found that e-storybooks with interactive features such as cued animations and sound effects can be a distraction from the storyline and decrease children's recollection of book content. The support and scaffolding that is provided by the parent in the joint book reading interaction (for example prompts, facilitation of the story, and feedback given to the child) can be hindered in e-book readings due to the fact that the child may not need or want adult assistance.

While the existing literature provides some evidence of young children's varying interactions with parents and books during shared reading experiences across book formats, much more research is needed in order to determine the effects of book format on parent-child interactions, children's engagement with books, and overall child literacy outcomes. For example, if the enhanced features that are so prevalent in e-books were eliminated, would e-books elicit the same levels and kinds of parent-child interaction that are known to support emergent literacy? This research question forms the heart of the current study.

RESEARCH METHOD

The present study investigated the behavior of parents and their three-year-old children while using two different book formats (traditional print books and e-books). Researchers observed and coded parent-child interactions across the two book formats in order to determine whether there were differences in parent-child verbal interaction. The electronic books used in this study had almost no interactive features except page turns. In addition, there was no voice-over narration in the e-books, so that e-books in this study were identical to traditional books except for format.

Participants

Twelve families with three-year-old children were recruited through local libraries and childcare facilities in a southern US university town to participate in this project. Of the 12 families included in the current study, four had a yearly income of less than $25,000, five families earned between $25-$50,000, and three families earned more than $50,000. There were 10 Caucasian families in the study, one Asian family and one Hispanic family. The education levels of parents varied, with one parent being a high school graduate, six parents having had some technical or college experience, and 5 parents having college or graduate degrees.

Parents and children read traditional print books together during two sessions and electronic books together during two sessions. For the purposes of the current study, the first five minutes of each of these four reading sessions were included in the analysis.

Social Behavior Coding Scheme

A social behavior and social interaction coding scheme, adapted from SOCSI: System for Observation of Children's Social Interactions, developed by Brown, Odom, & Holcomb [1], was developed and used for this study. Coding categories for the current analysis focused on behaviors of Child (C) and Parent (P) on each page of the book. The unit of analysis was an utterance, operationally defined by Sato [23] as a "stream of speech under a single intonation contour bounded by pauses." The coding categories focused on the types of parent and child verbalizations associated with dialogic reading (see complete list in Figure 1). Duration of interaction and number of words spoken by each participant were also recorded for each page, as was the presence or absence of distracting events.

Procedures

Each reading session took place on a different day. The first and fourth reading sessions consisted of families reading one or more of three traditional print books (*Mr. Gumpy's Outing* by John Burningham, *In the Tall, Tall, Grass* by Denise Fleming, and *The Little Mouse, the Red Ripe Strawberry, and the Big Hungry Bear* by Don and Audrey Wood). In the second and third sessions, the parent-child dyads were then asked to read e-books together on a mobile device. The e-books consisted of 5 Sesame Street books on a Nokia N8 smart phone *(Abby in Wonderland, 100th Day of School, Big Block Party, Color Carnival*, and *The Monster at the End of this Book*). See Figure 2 for a sample screen from one of the e–books. As previously noted, the e-books had minimal functionality. There were no animations, no music, no voice-over narration. They simply displayed each page of the book with on-screen text and enabled page turns from one page to the next. The minimal functionality was an intentional decision so that the primary difference between the two conditions in the study was whether the book was presented on paper in the traditional format or on screen in the e-book format.

For both conditions, parents were instructed to read any and all books as many times as they or the child wanted and were read instructions about the study from a script that included a sentence about the importance of engaging in conversation and asking questions when reading with their child. For the e-book sessions, parents were also given a demonstration by researchers on how to open and close books, turn pages, select new books and enlarge text boxes on the mobile device. The first five minutes of each reading session were coded for analysis in this study. All reading sessions were recorded using a digital video camera so that parent and child behaviors could be coded and analyzed.

Coding

Before coding began, three researchers went through a training process that lasted several weeks. Each researcher coded the same transcript and then they compared their results and discussed disagreements. This process was repeated several times until the researchers were using the coding scheme consistently. The researchers then coded different transcripts individually to establish inter-rater reliability. Transcripts of the first five minutes of one traditional print book reading session and one e-book reading session were coded by two researchers for parent and child verbal behaviors across all of the coding categories during the reading interaction. Krippendorf's Alpha [10] was used for calculating inter-coder reliability. Across all of the verbal coding categories, inter-coder reliability was high, α = .89.

Figure 2. **Sample e-book screen.**

Category	Description
Reading text on page A,S,N	P reads text from the page of the book. A=All or almost all, S=Some, N=None
C Repeats Text? C/rt	Does C repeat one or more words that P reads from the book? Yes/No
C Interrupts? C/I	Does C interrupt P's reading of text on page? (Includes talking over each other while P is reading) Yes/No
Concrete Question P/cq; C/cq	P or C asks a question about the content of the book that can be answered in one word or with a point (e.g. Where's the bunny? What's this? What does the cat say? All yes/no questions) (record #)
Descriptive Question P/dq; C/dq	P or C asks for a description about the content of the book, more than one word answer (e.g., What's he doing? What happened? What's he thinking? Why is he doing that?) (record #)
Making Connections P/mc; C/mc	P or C draws a connection between something that's happening in the book and something from their own lives (e.g., We caught fireflies once at Grandma's house, remember? Did we see any of these animals when we were at the zoo?) (record #)
Comment/Statement P/cs; C/cs	P or C makes a declarative statement about the content of the book, that is not in response to a question (e.g., I wonder what is going to happen next, Look at that strawberry!, That looks yummy!) (record #)
Answer/Response P/ar; C/ar	P or C verbally responds to a question or statement about the content of the book. (record #)
Request for clarification/repetition P/rc; C/rc	P or C asks the other to repeat/clarify something the other has said (e.g., What did you say? He saw a what?) (record #)
Clarify/Repeat P/cr; C/cr	P or C repeats or clarifies something the other or they themselves said. (e.g., Oh, you don't like snakes?, Right, we did that once.) (record #)
Prompt or Help C with Response P/pcr	P prompts C to respond or helps child answer a question. (record #)
Unintelligible P/u; C/u	P or C says something unintelligible. (record #)

Figure 1. Coding Categories for Parent and Child Utterances on each page of the book

Researchers then coded verbal behaviors for the first five minutes of each of the four reading sessions for each family. All coded transcripts were then used to conduct an analysis examining the differences in parent-child interactions between the two book formats for each category of verbal behavior. For each measure coded and analyzed, the number of occurrences in each of the two sessions for a format were added together to create a total number of occurrences of that behavior over the two sessions for that format.

RESULTS

The data analyses examined the differences in parent-child verbal interactions when reading traditional print books versus e-books. The first analysis examined the influence of condition (book format) on parents' verbalizations.

Parent Analyses

Paired sample t-tests were conducted to compare total parental utterances during the reading interaction in both sessions across the two book formats. There were more total parent utterances during print book sessions ($M = 150.67$, $SD = 41.65$) than during e-book sessions ($M = 110.08$, $SD = 46.42$), with a significance level $t\,(11) = 3.23$ $p < .01$).

Paired samples t- tests were conducted comparing the total number of parent utterances about book content and for each of the book content coding categories for print book sessions versus e-book sessions. With regard to parental talk about book content across the two book formats, total number of parental utterances with regard to book content for print book sessions (M = 67.75, SD = 6.05) was significantly greater than total parental utterances with regard to book content during e-book sessions (M = 40.83, SD = 3.78; t (11) = 5.72, p < .001). Subsequent analyses showed that several of the subcategories of verbalizations about book content were responsible for the greater number of total utterances about book content in book sessions than e-book sessions. In both reading sessions, there were significantly more concrete questions asked by the parents in the print book condition ($M = 21.92$, SD = 11.31), than in the e-book condition ($M = 13.58$, $SD = 6.44$); $t\,(11) = 3.28$, $p < .01$), and significantly more parent comments or statements regarding book content for print book sessions ($M = 17.50$, $SD = 11.92$) than e-book sessions ($M = 9.25$, $SD = 4.05$), $t\,(11) = 2.76$ $p < .02$. Furthermore, the number of parental utterances in which parents repeated or clarified something they or the child had said was also significantly greater for print book sessions ($M = 11.58$, $SD = 8.85$) than e-book sessions ($M = 6.92$, $SD = 5.68$); $t\,(11) = 2.57$ $p < .03$.

Child Analyses

The next analysis examined the differences children's verbalizations when reading traditional print books versus e-books with their parents. A set of analyses parallel to those described in detail in the previous section was conducted with regard to children's verbalizations.

Paired samples t-tests were conducted to compare the total number of child utterances that occurred across the two book formats in each of the book reading sessions. The total number of child utterances in print book sessions ($M = 98.08$, $SD = 32.48$) was significantly greater than total child utterances in e-book sessions ($M = 67.25$, $SD = 24.74$); $t\,(11) = 3.24$, $p < .01$.

Paired sample t–tests showed that the total number of child utterances related to book content was significantly greater for print book sessions ($M = 37.83$, $SD = 9.520$) versus e-book sessions ($M = 23.92$, $SD = 6.37$; $t\,(11) = 4.52$, $p < .01$). With regard to the subcategories of book content, the number of child answers to questions and/ or responses was also significantly higher for the print book sessions ($M = 22.25$, $SD = 6.50$) when compared to e-book sessions ($M = 14.92$, $SD = 4.93$); $t\,(11) = 4.05$, $p < .01$. In addition, the total number of child comments or statements made in relation to book content was significantly greater for print book sessions ($M = 9.83$, $SD = 5.64$) versus e-book sessions ($M = 4.75$, $SD = 4.27$); $t\,(11) = 2.69$, $p < .05$.

DISCUSSION

The present study investigated the effects of two book formats (print books versus e-books) on parent-child verbal interaction during joint book reading with three-year-old children. A major contribution of this study compared to previous literature is that the functionality of e-books was paired down to an extent that made them comparable to the functionality of print books. In other words, the e-books merely presented illustrations and text on screen with no voice over narration or interactivity of any kind other than page turns. This is important because previous studies have suggested that decreased parent-child interaction may result from the fact that e-books have lots of voice-over audio which could be in competition with the parent speaking to the child or to the distraction of multimedia components like animations, music, and so on. To the authors' knowledge, this is the first study to test that assertion.

The results of this study showed that both parents and children engaged in more total verbal interaction and specifically in more dialogue related to book content when reading print books as compared with e-books. Both the total number of utterances and the number of utterances related to book content were greater for both parent and child in the print book condition when compared with the e-book condition. Parental clarification and or repetition of what the child said, the number of concrete questions asked, and the number of comments or statements related to book content were significantly greater when reading print books than when reading e-books with their children. For children, the number of comments or statements related to book content and the number of answers or responses related to book content were significantly greater with print books than with e-books. Thus both parents and children engaged in more of the kind of dialogic reading verbalizations that have been linked with children's language and vocabulary development.

Previous studies have attributed similar findings to the fact that e-books have lots of voice-over audio which could be in competition with the parent speaking to the child and/or multimedia "bells and whistles" that could distract the child from the narrative content of the story. This study is the first to the authors' knowledge to document that the extra interactivity and enhanced features of e-books are not solely responsible for parents engaging in fewer dialogic reading strategies or children engaging in less content related conversation during joint reading interactions when reading e-books. It has been suggested that the very features of e-books that are designed to capture the child's attention and maintain engagement may compete with or replace the kind of parent-child interaction that is so effective at supporting emergent literacy. The results of this study show that even without games, animations, voice-over and other potentially distracting features, there is still less parent-child conversation about book content with plain e-books than with print books. Thus the dynamics of the parent–child interaction during joint reading have been affected by the introduction of the electronic book. Given the vast amount of research evidence that has supported the importance of conversation related to book content that occurs between the parent and child when reading together, the fact that there is significantly less of this kind of conversation when reading with e-books raises a legitimate concern.

One limitation of this study was the small sample size, which limited comparisons among different demographic groups in the sample. Future research should explore the effects of book format on parent-child interaction with a broader and more diverse sample of parent-child dyads now that an effect of book format has been demonstrated with a small, relatively heterogeneous sample in reading interactions. In particular, future research with larger samples may benefit from analyzing the impact of these effects on families with lower income and education levels versus those with higher levels of income and/or education.

CONCLUSIONS

The quality of parent-child interaction during joint book reading can have significant impacts on children's story comprehension, vocabulary development and attainment of other early literacy skills. This study demonstrated that book format can have an effect on the quality of the parent-child verbal interaction that occurs during joint book reading interactions, thereby also possibly affecting the literacy skills that are derived from the reading experience.

The results of this study showed that the verbal interaction between the parent and child during joint book reading varies significantly depending on book format. In particular, conversation related to book content, of the kind that is associated with dialogic reading strategies which promote emergent literacy skills, was found in higher levels during traditional print book readings than e-book readings.

The design of the e-book used in this study intentionally omitted features such as voice-over narration, animations with sound, and games – the "bells and whistles" that previous researchers suggest could be a source of distraction for young readers or could discourage parents from reading the text and talking about book content. The goal of this approach was to document whether that explanation is accurate, or whether even a plain e-book book with no special interactive features or voice-over would also have an impact on parent-child reading interaction and attention to book content. The results of this study disconfirm that explanation, since even a "plain" e-book with severely limited interactive features still led to less parent-child conversation about book content. The impact that using e-books may have on parent-child reading interactions brings to light salient concerns regarding how these devices should be used with young children, as well as the desirability of continuing to engage children in joint reading with print books.

The present study found that parent-child conversations during joint book-reading interactions with minimally interactive e-books have less talk centered on book content than conversations with paper books. It is critical that parents, educators, developers, and the research community are made aware of these results so that their implications can inform policy and practice for young children's media use. Less talk about what is happening in the story leads to fewer opportunities for children in to make meaningful connections between the story and real life experiences. Opportunities for children to make these meaningful connections during joint book reading interactions have been proven to support children's developing emergent literacy skills and later learning outcomes.

REFERENCES

1. Brown, W. H., Odom, S. L., & Holcombe, A. (1996). Observational assessment of young children's social behavior with peers. *Early Childhood Research Quarterly*, *11*(1), 19-40.
2. Bus, A. G. (2001). Joint caregiver-child storybook reading: A route to literacy development. *Handbook of Early Literacy Research*, *1*, 179-191.
3. De Jong, M. T., & Bus, A. G. (2003). How well suited are electronic books to supporting literacy? *Journal of Early Childhood Literacy*, *3*(2), 147-164.
4. Eagle, S. (2012). Learning in the early years: Social interactions around picture books, puzzles and digital technologies. *Computers & Education*, *59*(1), 38-49.

5. Fisch, S. M., Shulman, J. S., Akerman, A., & Levin, G. A. (2002). Reading between the pixels: Parent-child interaction while reading online storybooks. *Early Education and Development*, *13*(4), 435-451.
6. Fletcher, K. L., & Reese, E. (2005). Picture book reading with young children: A conceptual framework. *Developmental review*, *25*(1), 64-103.
7. Francis, D., Shaywitz, S., Stuebing, K., Shaywitz, B., Fletcher, J. Developmental lag versus deficit models of reading disability: A longitudinal, individual growth curves analysis. Journal of Educational Psychology. (1996, 88), pp. 3-17..
8. Hart, B., & Risley, T. Meaningful differences in the everyday experience of young American children. (Paul H. Brookes, Baltimore, MD, 1995).
9. Hart, B., & Risley, T. The early catastrophe: The 30 million word gap. American Educator. (2003, 27.1), pp. 4-9.
10. Hayes, A. F., & Krippendorff, K. (2007). Answering the call for a standard reliability measure for coding data. *Communication Methods and Measures*, *1*(1), 77-89.
11. Juel C. (1988). Learning to Read and Write: A Longitudinal Study of 54 Children from First through Fourth Grades. *Journal of Educational Psychology* 80:437–44.
12. Kim, J. E., & Anderson, J. (2008). Mother–child shared reading with print and digital texts. *Journal of Early Childhood Literacy*, *8*, 213–245.
13. Korat, O., & Or, T. (2010). How New Technology Influences Parent-Child Interaction: The Case of e-book Reading. *First Language*, *30*(2), 139-154.
14. Korat, O., & Shamir, A. (2007). Electronic books versus adult readers: Effects on children's emergent literacy as a function of social class. *Journal of Computer Assisted Learning*, *23*(3), 248-259.
15. Korat, O., & Shamir, A. (2012). Direct and indirect teaching: Using e-books for supporting vocabulary, word reading, and story comprehension for young children. *Journal of Educational Computing Research*, *46*(2), 135-152.
16. Lauricella, A. R., Barr, R., & Calvert, S. L. (2014). Parent–child interactions during traditional and computer storybook reading for children's comprehension: implications for electronic storybook design. *International Journal of Child-Computer Interaction*, *2*(1), 17-25.
17. Mol, S. E., & Bus, A. G. (2011). To read or not to read: a meta-analysis of print exposure from infancy to early adulthood. *Psychological bulletin*, *137*(2), 267.
18. Mol, S. E., Bus, A. G., de Jong, M. T., & Smeets, D. J. (2008). Added value of dialogic parent–child book readings: A meta-analysis. *Early Education and Development*, *19*(1), 7-26.
19. Moody, A. K., Justice, L. M., & Cabell, S. Q. (2010). Electronic versus traditional storybooks: Relative influence on preschool children's engagement and communication. *Journal of Early Childhood Literacy*, *10*(3), 294-313.
20. Morgan, P. L., & Meier, C. R. (2008). Dialogic reading's potential to improve children's emergent literacy skills and behavior. *Preventing School Failure: Alternative Education for Children and Youth*, *52*(4), 11-16.
21. Neuman, S., D. Celano, D. Access to print in low-income and middle-income communities. Reading Research Quarterly. (2001, 36), pp. 8-26.
22. Parish-Morris, J., Mahajan, N., Hirsh-Pasek, K., Golinkoff, R. M., & Collins, M. F. (2013). Once upon a time: parent–child dialogue and storybook reading in the electronic era. *Mind, Brain, and Education*, *7*(3), 200-211.
23. Sato, C. J. (1990). *The syntax of conversation in interlanguage development* (Vol. 11). Gunter Narr Verlag.
24. Snow, C. E., Burns, M. S., & Griffin, P. (Eds.). (1998). *Preventing reading difficulties in young children*. National Academies Press.
25. Trushell, J. & Maitland, A. (2005). Primary pupils' recall of interactive storybooks on CD-ROM: Inconsiderate interactive features and forgetting. *British Journal of Educational Technology, 36,* 57-66.
26. Trushell, J., Burrell, C., & Maitland, A. (2001). Year 5 pupils reading an interactive storybook on CD-ROM: Losing the plot? *British Journal of Educational Technology, 32,* 389-401.
27. Whitehurst, G. J., Falco, F. L., Lonigan, C. J., Fischel, J. E., DeBaryshe, B. D., Valdez-Menchaca, M. C., & Caulfield, M. (1988). Accelerating language development through picture book reading. *Developmental Psychology*, *24*(4), 552-559.

Adolescent Online Safety: Moving Beyond Formative Evaluations to Designing Solutions for the Future

Anthony T. Pinter
Pennsylvania State University
University Park, PA
atp136@psu.edu

Pamela J. Wisniewski*
University of Central Florida
Orlando, FL
pamwis@ucf.edu
*Corresponding Author

Heng Xu, Mary Beth Rosson, & John M. Carroll
Pennsylvania State University
University Park, PA
{hxu, mrosson, jcarroll}
@ist.psu.edu

ABSTRACT
We present a comprehensive and structured review of 132 peer-reviewed publications between the years of 2008 and 2015 to inform Human-Computer Interaction (HCI) researchers and interaction designers about the current and multi-disciplinary knowledge on the topic of adolescent online safety and risks. Overall, we found that the existing literature has deeply studied the phenomena around adolescent online safety through an in-depth examination of the prevalence, perceptions, behaviors, characteristics, and outcomes associated with various online risk experiences. However, very few studies have moved beyond formative evaluations that inform design to novel design interventions or summative evaluations of new designs that serve to effectively change the status quo.

Author Keywords
Adolescent online safety; online risks; interaction design.

ACM Classification Keywords
K.4.1 [Public Policy Issues]: Ethics, Human safety, Privacy

INTRODUCTION
We synthesize the current research related to adolescent online safety in a way that can help inform the SIGCHI and Interaction Design for Children (IDC) communities on how we can best join in the valiant efforts to keep teens safe online. We report important trends from the literature and highlight potential gaps that are particularly relevant to HCI researchers and interaction designers. Specifically, our goal is to show how the SIGCHI community can help move the current state of adolescent online safety research from a focus on the prevalence of and factors that contribute to online risks, to one of designing solutions to effectively protect, mitigate, and empower teens to cope with the risk that they will inevitably encounter online. Online risks teens encounter may include cyberbullying, contact with strangers, sexual messaging, and pornography [20], among others. Our analysis was guided by following research questions, which employed an HCI-focused lens:

- ***Who*** are the users and stakeholders studied within the adolescent online safety and risk literature?
- ***What*** methodological approaches have been used to study the phenomena of interest?
- ***How*** does the research conceptualize the topic of adolescent online safety, risk, and harm?

IDC '17, June 27-30, 2017, Stanford, CA, USA
© 2017 Association for Computing Machinery.
ACM ISBN 978-1-4503-4921-5/17/06…$15.00
http://dx.doi.org/10.1145/3078072.3079722

BACKGROUND
In 2014, Livingstone and Smith [20] published a comprehensive review of interdisciplinary research published since 2008 with a focus on summarizing the prevalence of various "content" and "conduct" related online risks, contributing and protective factors towards these risks, and the potential aggressive or sexual harm resulting from risk exposure. The researchers concluded their review by stating, "the challenge is now to examine the relations among different risks, and to build on the risk and protective factors identified to design effective interventions" [20:635]. Building upon a deep understanding of human behavior to design effective sociotechnical interventions is a hallmark of our field [44]. Thus, we argue that the SIGCHI community can make a significant impact in the area of adolescent online safety if we clearly understand how our expertise is situated and may be leveraged to complement the extant literature. While HCI researchers have addressed the challenges associated with conducting interaction design research with adolescents [28], none have specifically addressed the intersection of interaction design for adolescent online safety. Thus, our paper makes the following research contributions:

- Synthesizes a representative subset of 132 peer-reviewed articles relevant to the topic of adolescent online safety.
- Makes recommendations for future HCI and interaction design research related to adolescent online safety.
- Presents a conceptual framework for engaging HCI researchers and interaction designers in adolescent online safety research.

METHODS

We conducted a structured literature review, which consisted of three distinct stages: 1) literature search, 2) relevancy coding, and 3) article content coding. Approximately eight months elapsed between the first round (February 2015) of our literature search and the last (November 2015). In Round 1, we queried three electronic databases (ACM Digital Library, PsychInfo, and Web of Science) that span the interdisciplinary domains that study adolescent online safety and risks. We limited our search to peer-reviewed journals and conferences and used seven keywords based on prior literature [42] in combination with the words "adolescent" or "teen" to capture relevant literature. Keywords included: "technology use," "online safety," "online risk," "information privacy," "sexual solicitation," "cyberbullying," "online harassment," "pornography," and "explicit content."

For Rounds 2-4 of our literature search, we cross-referenced the citations from the previous round to identify additional salient articles. We stopped at the fourth iteration because the number of relevant articles fell from 52 in Round 1 to only eight in Round 4, signaling that we had reached a reasonable level of saturation. Near the end of 2015, we conducted a fifth iteration in order to capture articles published during the months between the initial literature search and the composition of our review. Our literature search identified a total of 232 articles that were then coded for relevance. Next, we reviewed these articles to ensure that they met certain threshold criteria prior to inclusion in our review. A total of 132 articles met these inclusion criteria:

1. Peer-reviewed published work (conference or journal).
2. Published between 2008 and 2015.
3. Involved teens and/or parents of teens (ages 13-17).
4. Focused on online activities (not offline).
5. Involved some aspects of online safety and/or risks (not just general technology use).

Finally, the 132 relevant articles were coded based on a structured codebook. Two coders coded the entire article set independently and inter-rater reliability between the coders was calculated using Cohen's kappa [13]. In cases where codes were not mutually exclusive, we applied multiple and double counted codes. **Table 1** summarizes each dimension coded and the IRR metrics averaged across all five rounds. Our results are presented based on these dimensions.

SYNTHESIZING PAST RESEARCH

Country of Origin: A U.S. Centric Focus

Twenty-six countries were represented in the article set, with the majority of articles originating in the United States (44%). The Netherlands and Great Britain were the next largest, representing 9% and 8% of articles, respectively. Only 5% of the studies in our sample studied safety and risks multi-nationally. Of these, one compared adolescents in Canada and China [19], another U.S. and Finland [26], and the others studied adolescents from multiple European countries, e.g., [34]. Comparative studies often confirmed that different cultural and national groups had significantly different online experiences and outcomes [3].

Subject of Study: A Reliance on Teen Self-Reports

As might be expected, 83% of the articles focused specifically on teens as research subjects; 13% included the perspectives of parents and teens, 2% focused only on parents [1], and another 2% involved external sources of influence, such as teachers, school staff, and counselors [31]. Of the teen-focused studies, 83% conducted self-reported surveys where researchers asked teens to quantify their own online risk experiences and behaviors. The researchers then inferred statistically significant relationships among the variables of interest. Fewer studies involving teens used more nuanced techniques such as interviews (9%), focus groups (9%), or analysis of publically available data (2%). Only 6% of the studies used multi-method approaches. Studies that involved both teens and parents focused on how different parental mediation strategies influenced teens' online risk behaviors and experiences. Meanwhile, studies focused solely on parents often examined how they directly contributed to their teens' online safety through their own actions.

RQ	Dimension	Description (Codes)	Cohen's κ
Who?	Country	The country from which the participants originated (Country Code)	0.92
	Subject of Study	Type of participants included in the study (Teen, Parent, Both, Other)	0.81
What?	Time Horizon	Time frame the study was conducted (Cross-sectional or Longitudinal)	0.88
	Approach	The type of data collection/analysis that was conducted (Qualitative, Quantitative, Mixed)	0.90
How?	Online Risk Type	Type of online risk studied. Multiple codes permitted (Information Breaches, Cyberbullying, Sexual Solicitations, Exposure to Explicit Content, Other)	0.87
	Risk Context	Whether the researchers studied online risks as an outcome or after the risk had occurred (Pre-exposure, Post-exposure)	0.75
	Intervention	Whether the research implemented any type of intervention, system, or program (Yes, No)	0.76

Table 1: Structured Codebook and Reliability Metrics

Time Horizon and Approach: A Snapshot in Time

Cross-sectional studies dominated this literature with 85% of our articles basing their analyses on a single snapshot of time. Of the cross-sectional studies, 74% conducted quantitative surveys, 16% took qualitative approaches, and 10% employed mixed quantitative and qualitative methods. Of the more novel approaches, Menesini et al. took a scenario-based survey approach, which covered a range of online behaviors and asked teens whether they felt each scenario was cyberbullying or not [22]. Of the longitudinal studies, nearly half (47%) had time horizons that were less than one year. Most (90%) were quantitative in nature. Only three of the studies leveraged multi-year, longitudinal designs that tracked the same sample of teens over a period of time. For instance, Sumter et al. (2012) found over the course of two years that offline and online peer victimization were significantly correlated and negatively impacted perceived life experience [36].

Risk Types: A Considerable Focus on Cyberbullying

We identified four typical online risk categories within the articles reviewed: 1) harassment and cyberbullying (66% of articles), 2) privacy or information breaches (33%), 3) sexual solicitations or encounters (23%), and 4) exposure to explicit content (22%). 69% of the articles focused only on one risk category, even though the associations between multiple online risks were consistently confirmed within the literature. For example, sexual solicitations and exposure to explicit content were significantly associated [38], and information disclosures were tied to privacy-related risks, which increased overall risk exposure [3,18]. We also noted considerable variation in how each article defined risk. Generally, any information disclosure or communication with strangers online was considered risky, as well as unsafe disclosures made to known others.

Risk Context: A Mindset of Risk-Aversion

The majority (69%) of the articles framed online risk exposure as a dependent variable with the intention of identifying the factors that contribute to the likelihood of risk occurrence and minimizing future risk exposure (i.e., pre-exposure). Fewer studies examined what happened after risks actually occurred (i.e., post-exposure). Of these articles, 54% investigated negative outcomes or harm resulting from exposure (e.g., loneliness [7], psychosomatic symptoms [24], and lower life satisfaction [6]), while 46% studied coping responses in response to exposure. For instance, studies found that teens rarely seek adult help when exposed to online risks [34], but do seek support from their personal peer networks [32]. Teens also take protective measures against risk exposure [32], especially when they have a heightened level of privacy concern [18].

Interventions: Few Solutions for Mitigating Online Risks

There were only six articles (4.5%) that implemented or implied any kind of intervention as part of their research programs. These interventions fell into three categories: 1) design interventions, 2) parental monitoring software, and 2) educational programs. Four of the articles took design-based approaches for conceptualizing new (yet hypothetical) technologies for addressing adolescent online safety. Lwin et al. [21] examine the interplay between parental mediation and the use of a warning message as a safeguard for protecting children and teens from disclosing personal information in online e-commerce contexts. The three other articles took participatory design approaches; for instance Emanuel and Fraser [9] worked with teens to design their own avatars and asked about identity and privacy, while Garaigorbil and Martinez-Valderray [12] created an educational program called Cyberbully 2.0, which they found to be effective in reducing traditional and online bullying perpetration and victimization.

LOOKING TOWARD THE FUTURE

Given the state of the current literature, we make the following recommendations for future research that addresses adolescent line safety.

Differentiating between Online Safety, Risk, and Harm

Livingstone and Smith make the point that harm is only a potential outcome of risk exposure [20]. Our previous work [40,41,43] argues that many of the existing studies around adolescent online safety have predominantly taken an "abstinence-only" approach to by trying to reduce risk-exposure as a symptom of "unhealthy" online engagement. Our literature review confirmed these assertions; after systematically reviewing the literature, we found that more studies (69%) focused on factors leading to or away from risk as opposed to confirming whether exposure actually resulted in negative outcomes. We also found an overwhelming trend that adolescent online safety is predominantly studied in direct relation to online risks. In focusing solely on reducing exposure, much of the literature implicitly equates risk exposure to harm. As such, the concepts of privacy and safety have often been confounded [10], implying that if teens would just disclose less personal information about themselves online, then they would be safer due to less exposure. We caution against such privacy-focused recommendations as they do not align well with teens' over-arching goals for why they engage online with others; research has confirmed that teens are aware of risks posed by their online personal disclosures, but value the relational benefits over the potential risks [5].

In fact, by shielding teens from online risk exposure, we may actually be causing more harm than good. For instance, boyd [4] cautions us against such approaches because fear-based paternalism can push us to overprotect teens, which may hinder developmental processes that are vital to teaching teens how to protect themselves. Hartikainen et al. [14] also found that enhancing parent-teen communication and trust building was superior to more control-based approaches. Our recent diary study of teens' weekly online risk experiences illustrated how teens are often able to cope with, resolve, and even benefit by learning from their personal online risk experiences [43], showing some level of agency in their own online safety.

Yet, existing technology-based solutions have been overly focused on designs that increase parental control to reduce risk exposure instead of cultivating teen self-awareness, impulse control, and risk-coping skills [39]. We recommend that future research move away from predominantly risk-adverse perspectives of adolescent online safety to ones that are more aligned with developmental psychology, acknowledging that some level of risk is actually a healthy part of adolescent developmental growth [2].

Diversifying Our Ways of Knowing

There are a number of suggestions we can make for building upon and deepening the current body of knowledge on adolescent online safety as it relates to HCI and interaction design. First, we must diversify our "ways of knowing" [27] by using different approaches for understanding the problem-space and arriving at new, user-centered solutions. For instance, only 5% of the research in our sample studied online safety and risks multi-nationally. We urge that multi-national coalitions should work together to conduct studies across adolescent populations in different countries and with diverse cultures to design sociotechnical systems or features that promote online safety from a more global perspective. Given the wealth of cross-sectional, quantitative survey studies, it would be reasonable at this point to conduct a formal meta-analysis [16]. Statistically consolidating various inferential findings would help HCI researchers and interaction designers pinpoint ways in which we can influence positive behaviors through design.

Other ways to expand our formative knowledge to better inform design would be to conduct more longitudinal studies that span distinct developmental stages of adolescence, such as transition periods from early adolescence to mid-adolescence [33], so that we can design solutions that align with the developmental needs of our users. Additionally, more studies that involve the co-occurrence of multiple risk types should be conducted to better understand how they are intertwined. This is of particular importance in regards to information disclosures, which has been shown to act as a "gateway" risk behavior that led to exposure to other, more serious types of risks, such as sexual solicitation [25] and cyberbullying [23]. By distinguishing what types of disclosures are most prone to severe risk exposure, we may be able to design targeted solutions that nudge teens to make more informed online disclosures [37], as opposed to setting an unrealistic goal of limiting all information sharing by teens online.

We also need to address an obvious dichotomy in how we tend to view teens and subsequently use them to inform our research. Ironically, adolescent online safety research is often motivated by the assertion that teens are inherently risk-seeking and lack the maturity to make well-informed decisions [5]; thus, we cannot trust teens to protect themselves from online risks [18]. Yet, as researchers, we have heavily relied on teens (83% of the articles) as the experts who provide the empirical evidence in which we base our conclusions. We should reflect on whether or not we should be concerned about the validity of relying so heavily on the self-reports of teens. We should also consider triangulating our results by incorporating benchmarks to calibrate teens' perceptions with their actual behavior [35]. Only a few studies collected unobtrusive data that captured teens' actual behaviors, such as publicly available social media posts [8] and profiles [29], while no studies have delved into the private or semi-private behaviors of teens in online contexts.

Overall, we argue that teens *should* be given more agency when it comes to their online safety – not only in understanding their behaviors to inform design (i.e., formative evaluations) but, more importantly, within the design solutions that serve to protect teens (e.g., participatory design). However, we also recommend that more nuanced approaches, such as those suggested by Poole and Peyton [28] (e.g., observation, videography, and video collages) should be incorporated to create a more holistic understanding of teens' online practices prior to designing potential solutions. Future research should also take into account the viewpoints of other key stakeholders (e.g., peers, parents, teachers, or counselors) to understand their goals and values [11], which will likely need to be reconciled with those of teens [39]. Finally, future work may assess how the current knowledge regarding adolescent online safety and risks applies to younger children, as they are also engaging with technology.

CONCLUSION

The literature has come a long way in helping us better understand the *phenomena* around adolescent online safety and risks. Yet, while risk is an integral part of safety, we argue for more emphasis on adolescent online *well being* as we move forward (**Figure 1** bullets in green). By shifting the discourse from preventing online risks to maximizing the benefits teens can garner from of online engagement,

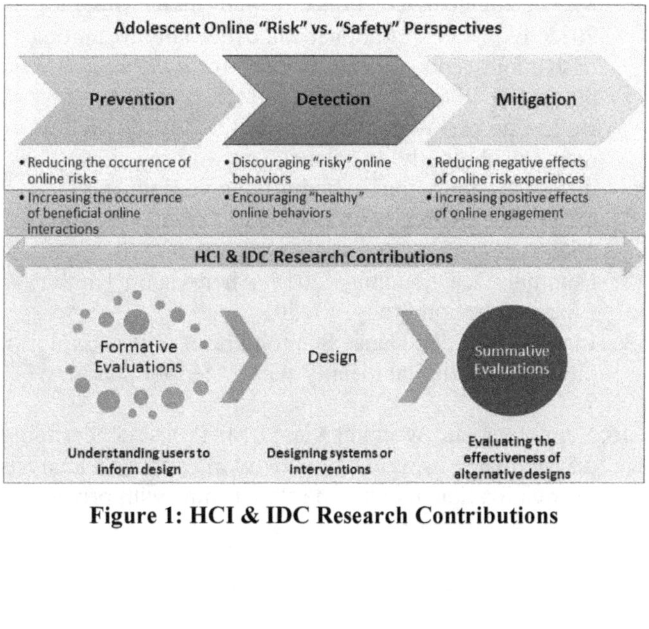

Figure 1: HCI & IDC Research Contributions

we can start building more realistic solutions that benefit, not just protect, teens. Finally, moving beyond formative evaluations that inform design, to novel design interventions and summative evaluations of existing or new designs [15] would serve to effectively change the status quo of adolescent online safety, which is where we argue that HCI researchers and interaction designers can make the most profound contributions moving forward (**Figure 1**). By iteratively designing real solutions across the spectrums of online risk and safety, we will be able to not only develop a deeper, empirical understanding of adolescents as end users, but also provide viable solutions that empower teens to positively engage with and through technology, take some risks, and remain safe from undue harm.

ACKNOWLEDGEMENTS

This research was supported by the U.S. National Science Foundation, under grant CNS-1018302. Any opinion, findings, and conclusions or recommendations expressed in this material are those of the authors and do not necessarily reflect the views of the U.S. National Science Foundation.

REFERENCES

1. Tawfiq Ammari, Priya Kumar, Cliff Lampe, and Sarita Schoenebeck. 2015. Managing Children ' s Online Identities : How Parents Decide what to Disclose about their Children Online. 1895–1904.
2. Diana Baumrind. 1987. A developmental perspective on adolescent risk taking in contemporary America. *New directions for child development*, 37: 93–125.
3. Ina Blau. 2014. Comparing online opportunities and risks among Israeli children and youth Hebrew and Arabic speakers. *New Review of Hypermedia and Multimedia* 20, 4: 281–299.
4. danah boyd. 2014. *It's complicated: The social lives of networked teens*. Yale University Press.
5. Jo Bryce and James Fraser. 2014. The role of disclosure of personal information in the evaluation of risk and trust in young peoples' online interactions. *Computers in Human Behavior* 30: 299–306.
6. Mary Callaghan, Colette Kelly, and Michal Molcho. 2015. Exploring traditional and cyberbullying among Irish adolescents. *International Journal of Public Health* 60, 2: 199–206.
7. Bolin Cao and Wan-Ying Lin. 2015. How do victims react to cyberbullying on social networking sites? The influence of previous cyberbullying victimization experiences. *Computers in Human Behavior* 52: 458–465.
8. Munmun De Choudhury. 2015. Anorexia on Tumblr: A Characterization Study. 43–50.
9. Lia Emanuel and Danaë Stanton Fraser. 2014. Exploring physical and digital identity with a teenage cohort. 67–76.
10. Yang Feng and Wenjing Xie. 2014. Teens' concern for privacy when using social networking sites: An analysis of socialization agents and relationships with privacy-protecting behaviors. *Computers in Human Behavior* 33: 153–162.
11. Batya Friedman, Peter H. Kahn, and Alan Borning. 2002. *Value Sensitive Design: Theory and Methods*. Retrieved from http://faculty.washington.edu/pkahn/articles/vsd-theory-methods-tr.pdf
12. Maite Garaigordobil and Vanesa Martínez-Valderrey. 2015. Effects of Cyberprogram 2.0 on" face-to-face" bullying, cyberbullying, and empathy. *Psicothema* 27, 1: 45–51.
13. Kilem L. Gwet. 2014. *Handbook of Inter-Rater Reliability, 4th Edition: The Definitive Guide to Measuring The Extent of Agreement Among Raters*. Advanced Analytics, LLC.
14. Heidi Hartikainen, Netta Iivari, and Marianne Kinnula. 2016. Should We Design for Control, Trust or Involvement?: A Discourses Survey About Children's Online Safety. In *Proceedings of the The 15th International Conference on Interaction Design and Children* (IDC '16), 367–378.
15. H. Rex Hartson, Terence S. Andre, and Robert C. Williges. 2001. Criteria For Evaluating Usability Evaluation Methods. *International Journal of Human–Computer Interaction* 13, 4: 373–410.
16. J. P. Ioannidis and J. Lau. 1999. Pooling research results: benefits and limitations of meta-analysis. *The Joint Commission Journal on Quality Improvement* 25, 9: 462–469.
17. ISTTF. 2008. *Enhancing Child Safety and Online Technologies*. Harvard University's Berkman Center for Internet and Society. Retrieved from http://cyber.law.harvard.edu/sites/cyber.law.harvard.edu/files/ISTTF_Final_Report.pdf
18. Haiyan Jia, Pamela Wisniewski, Mary Beth Rosson, and John M Carroll. 2015. Risk-taking as a Learning Process for Shaping Teen ' s Online Information Privacy Behaviors. 583–599.
19. Qing Li. 2008. A cross-cultural comparison of adolescents' experience related to cyberbullying. *Educational Research* 50, 3: 223–234.
20. Sonia Livingstone and Peter K. Smith. 2014. Annual Research Review: Harms experienced by child users of online and mobile technologies: the nature, prevalence and management of sexual and aggressive risks in the digital age. *Journal of Child Psychology and Psychiatry* 55, 6: 635–654.
21. May Lwin O., Andrea J. S. Stanaland, and Anthony D. Miyazaki. 2008. Protecting children's privacy online: How parental mediation strategies affect website safeguard effectiveness. *Journal of Retailing* 84, 2: 205–217.
22. Ersilia Menesini, Annalaura Nocentini, Benedetta Emanuela Palladino, Ann Frisén, Sofia Berne, Rosario Ortega-Ruiz, Juan Calmaestra, Herbert Scheithauer, Anja Schultze-Krumbholz, Piret Luik, Karin Naruskov, Catherine Blaya, Julien Berthaud, and Peter K. Smith.

2012. Cyberbullying Definition Among Adolescents: A Comparison Across Six European Countries. *Cyberpsychology, Behavior, and Social Networking* 15, 9: 455–463.

23. Diana J. Meter and Sheri Bauman. 2015. When Sharing Is a Bad Idea: The Effects of Online Social Network Engagement and Sharing Passwords with Friends on Cyberbullying Involvement. *Cyberpsychology, Behavior, and Social Networking* 18, 8: 437–442.
24. Faye Mishna, Charlene Cook, Tahany Gadalla, Joanne Daciuk, and Steven Solomon. 2010. Cyber bullying behaviors among middle and high school students. *American Journal of Orthopsychiatry* 80, 3: 362–374.
25. Kimberly J. Mitchell, Janis Wolak, and David Finkelhor. 2008. Are blogs putting youth at risk for online sexual solicitation or harassment? *Child Abuse & Neglect* 32, 2: 277–294.
26. Matti Näsi, Pekka Räsänen, Atte Oksanen, James Hawdon, Teo Keipi, and Emma Holkeri. 2014. Association between online harassment and exposure to harmful online content: A cross-national comparison between the United States and Finland. *Computers in Human Behavior* 41: 137–145.
27. Judith S. Olson and Wendy A. Kellogg. 2014. *Ways of Knowing in HCI*. Springer Publishing Company, Incorporated.
28. Erika S. Poole and Tamara Peyton. 2013. Interaction Design Research with Adolescents: Methodological Challenges and Best Practices. In *Proceedings of the 12th International Conference on Interaction Design and Children* (IDC '13), 211–217.
29. Melissa A. Pujazon-Zazik, Stephanie M. Manasse, and Joan K. Orrell-Valente. 2012. Adolescents' Self-presentation on a Teen Dating Web Site: A Risk-Content Analysis. *Journal of Adolescent Health* 50, 5: 517–520.
30. Samantha Biegler and danah boyd. 2010. Risky Behaviors and Online Safety: A 2010 Literature Review (DRAFT).
31. Mike Sharples, R. Graber, Colin Harrison, and K. Logan. 2009. E-safety and Web 2.0 for children aged 11-16: E-safety and Web 2.0 for children aged 11-16. *Journal of Computer Assisted Learning* 25, 1: 70–84.
32. Peter K. Smith, Jess Mahdavi, Manuel Carvalho, Sonja Fisher, Shanette Russell, and Neil Tippett. 2008. Cyberbullying: Its nature and impact in secondary school pupils. *Journal of Child Psychology and Psychiatry and Allied Disciplines* 49, 4: 376–385.
33. Sedra Spano. 2004. Stages of Adolescent Development.
34. Elisabeth Staksrud and Sonia Livingstone. 2009. CHILDREN AND ONLINE RISK: Powerless victims or resourceful participants? *Information, Communication & Society* 12, 3: 364–387.
35. Arthur A. Stone, Christine A. Bachrach, Jared B. Jobe, Howard S. Kurtzman, and Virginia S. Cain. 1999. *The Science of Self-report: Implications for Research and Practice*. Psychology Press.
36. Sindy R. Sumter, Susanne E. Baumgartner, Patti M. Valkenburg, and Jochen Peter. 2012. Developmental Trajectories of Peer Victimization: Off-line and Online Experiences During Adolescence. *Journal of Adolescent Health* 50, 6: 607–613.
37. Yang Wang, Pedro Giovanni Leon, Alessandro Acquisti, Lorrie Faith Cranor, Alain Forget, and Norman Sadeh. 2014. A Field Trial of Privacy Nudges for Facebook. 2367–2376.
38. Melissa Wells and Kimberly J Mitchell. 2008. How do high-risk youth use the Internet? Characteristics and implications for prevention. *Child maltreatment* 13, 3: 227–234.
39. Pamela Wisniewski, Arup Kumar Ghosh, Mary Beth Rosson, Heng Xu, and John M. Carroll. 2017. Parental Control vs. Teen Self-Regulation: Is there a middle ground for mobile online safety? In *Proceedings of the 20th ACM Conference on Computer Supported Cooperative Work & Social Computing.*
40. Pamela Wisniewski, Haiyan Jia, Na Wang, Saijing Zheng, Heng Xu, Mary Beth Rosson, and John M. Carroll. 2015. Resilience Mitigates the Negative Effects of Adolescent Internet Addiction and Online Risk Exposure. In *Proceedings of the 33rd Annual ACM Conference on Human Factors in Computing Systems* (CHI '15), 4029–4038.
41. Pamela Wisniewski, Mary Beth Rosson, Heng Xu, and John M. Carroll. 2017. Parents Just Don't Understand: Why Teens Don't Talk to Parents about Their Online Risk Experiences. In *Proceedings of the 20th ACM Conference on Computer Supported Cooperative Work & Social Computing.*
42. Pamela Wisniewski, Heng Xu, Jack Carroll, and Mary Beth Rosson. 2013. Grand Challenges of Researching Adolescent Online Safety: A Family Systems Approach. Retrieved May 25, 2016 from http://aisel.aisnet.org/amcis2013/SocialTechnicalIssues/GeneralPresentations/10
43. Pamela Wisniewski, Heng Xu, Mary Beth Rosson, Daniel F. Perkins, and John M. Carroll. 2016. Dear Diary: Teens Reflect on Their Weekly Online Risk Experiences. In *Proceedings of the 2016 CHI Conference on Human Factors in Computing Systems* (CHI '16), 3919–3930.
44. Research contributions in human-computer interaction. ACM Interactions. Retrieved September 30, 2016 from http://bit.ly/2pq0x0d

Constructing Meaning: Designing Powerful Story-Making Explorations for Children to Express with Tangible Computational Media

Alisha Panjwani
SEEDS StudioLab, Acera School
Winchester, MA 01890
alisha@aceraschool.org

ABSTRACT
Story-Making is a process that cultivates creative learning by combining innovative forms of storytelling and new forms of making with novel technologies. In this paper, I highlight creative experiences for engaging children in making physical representations of their personal stories using Tangible Computational Media such as paper electronics, programmable projections, and sewable circuits. By sharing examples of the artifacts and stories made by children, I describe how they construct and express personal meaning artistically, electronically, and computationally. Reflecting on Story-Making explorations with children, I share ten design practices for developing creative learning environments, experiences, and tools that broaden and deepen children's engagement with new technologies.

Author Keywords
Tangible Computational Media; learning; children; constructionism; creativity; self-expression; education; storytelling.

ACM Classification Keywords
K.3.2 Computers and Education: Computer Science Education; J.5 Arts and Humanities: Fine arts; D.2.10 Design: Representation.

INTRODUCTION
Storytelling and making are two of the oldest forms of self-expression. Storytelling provides opportunities to express the self; making provides opportunities to represent the world. Independently they each allow us to reflect, refine, and represent our experiences. When we tell a story, we engage with ideas through the story. When we make the story tangible and concrete by creating a physical representation of it, it gives us another way of thinking about those ideas. Creating such multiple representations of an idea fosters deeper understanding and learning. As Marvin Minsky wrote, describing the importance of multiple forms of representation: "If you 'understand' something in only one way, then you scarcely understand it at all" [5]. Combining storytelling with making can provide multiple ways of thinking about one's ideas and lead to novel modes of creative inquiry and expression.

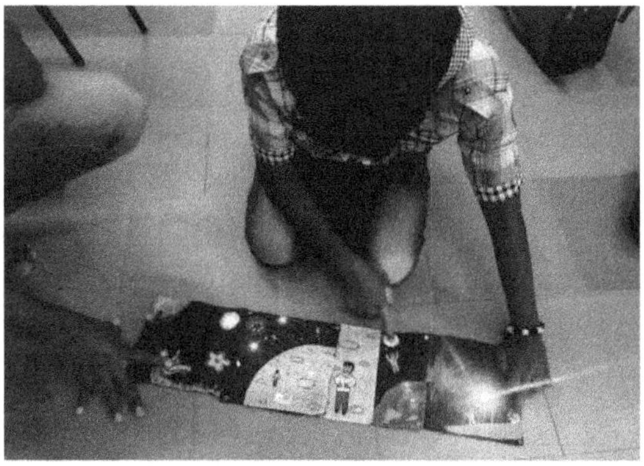

Figure 1: A 12-year-old boy demonstrating his story made with sewable circuits as part of a collaborative quilt project

Advances in technology have introduced new forms of Tangible Computational Media that are changing the ways and types of things people can create. By the term Tangible Computational Media (TCM), I refer to the tools that allow us to create physical objects that have computational capabilities, enabling us to construct new interactions and behaviors. Such computationally enhanced construction kits [3] can enhance experiences of storytelling, making and learning. This effort to weave together multifaceted storytelling, with new technologies builds on several strands of recent research and development. Many artists and designers are exploring new media technologies for representing stories and experiences in new ways, adding dynamic interactions to their creations. But few children have these opportunities. While more schools and community centers are opening maker spaces that provide children with hands-on experiences building with technology, these initiatives typically do not support narrative exploration and deeper artistic expression. How can we provide children with opportunities to express themselves creatively through a combination of making and stories?

I imagine an approach to designing rich meaningful learning pathways for children by engaging them in making experiences introducing new technologies as narrative mediums for self- expression. This approach is influenced by

IDC '17, June 27-30, 2017, Stanford, CA, USA

ACM ISBN 978-1-4503-4921-5/17/06...$15.00
http://dx.doi.org/10.1145/3078072.3079723

Seymour Papert's theory of Constructionism [7]. Constructionism holds that children learn best when they are engaged in constructing personally meaningful artifacts.

This paper presents Story-Making, a constructionist process designed to engage children in creating multiple representations of their personal experiences and integrating them into a coherent narrative. I describe creative experiences for engaging children in creating stories using TCM such as paper electronics, programmable projections, and sewable circuits. I share how children become engaged in using both storytelling ideas and computational ideas to represent their experiences. Next, I discuss examples of the artifacts made by children with TCM sharing how stories bring personal meaning to creation that reflects young people's senses, feelings, perceptions of the world, and what matters to them. I conclude by reflecting on Story-Making as an appealing approach to children, and by sharing ten design practices for designing creative explorations for children, empowering them to express and present their experiences in novel and meaningful ways with technology.

STORYTELLING, COMPUTATION, AND STORY-MAKING

Storytelling and computation share some common elements. Narrative thinking engages us in telling stories that have dynamic elements such as flow (sequences of actions), significant events (one action causing action to happen), and parallelism (sequences of actions happening at the same time) [13]. Computational thinking also involves these concepts of flow, events, and parallelism [1].

Storytelling or making may not explicitly highlight these concepts, but Story-Making with tangible computational media can focus children on investigating and bringing together dynamic ideas about flow, triggering events, and parallelism. By engaging with these ideas in multiple ways, children can develop a deeper understanding of these ideas.

Story-Making can also provide multiple pathways for children to develop new ideas. Children who are interested in stories can use Story-Making as a way into learning about constructing with new materials and engaging with computational ideas. Children who are interested in hands-on making and new media can use Story-Making as a pathway into personal expression through stories. These pathways will enable children to construct stories about themselves in their heads while constructing things with their hands, and to integrate them to express what they find meaningful in their world.

STORY-MAKING WORKSHOPS DESIGN

I designed a series of Story-Making workshops to investigate: What types of personal stories can children create using Tangible Computational Media? What do they learn through this process of Story-Making? How can we support the design and facilitation of similar experiences engaging children in constructing narratives using TCM? In this paper, I share work from three workshop series held at Drishya Kalika Kendra, a set of a progressive non-school learning centers located in Bangalore, India. The learning centers offer innovative education for children living in urban slums. Children ages 8 to 14 years participated in the Story-Making workshop series, which lasted between 5 and 10 days, with 3 to 5 hours per session. Each series focused on introducing children to a particular form of TCM combined with a traditional craft-based mode of storytelling.

The workshops highlighted aspects of creative learning environments that can support children to design novel representations of their stories using new programmable technologies. The workshop participants designed artifacts—such as story quilts, interactive storybooks, and e-textile murals—to depict stories inspired by their personal experiences.

Following are the forms of TCM introduced in Story-Making workshops that provided new pathways for children to understand their world, reflect on their experiences, and express themselves.

Paper Electronics

Paper electronics is the construction of circuits on paper [8] using conductive foils, tapes, or inks to make connections between electronic components such as lights, sensors, and programmable microcontrollers. Creators can express themselves by creating circuit patterns with the conductive materials and by decorating their circuits with traditional paper craft media. For example, a 12-year-old boy created a scene (Figure 2) representing rain using multiple LED lights, copper tape and a pre-programmed ATTiny85 chip. LED lights light up in random sequence using a trigger switch aligned with the clouds in his drawing.

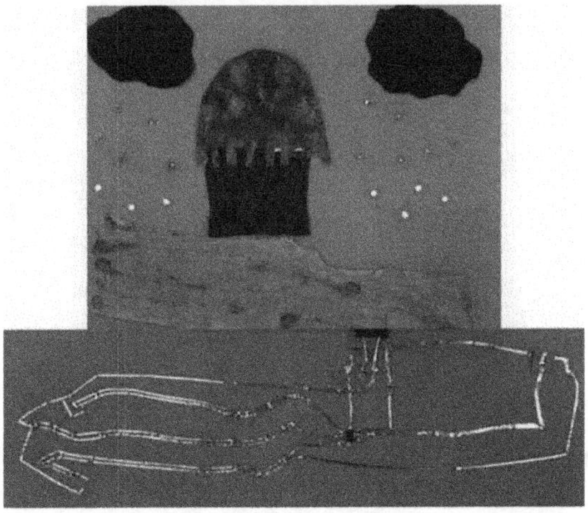

Figure 2: Rain animation created by a 12-year-old participant using paper electronics

Programmable Projections

Programmable projections are interactive Scratch [10] programs projected onto three-dimensional paper sculptures to create dynamic scenes on static forms. Using programmable projections, creators can integrate paper pop-up art with Scratch programming, connecting computation to the physical world; and they can experiment with physical-digital interactions on paper, such as turning the page to trigger an animation.

Programmable projections combine stage craft, paper craft, and computational craft. It leads to the emergence of a new type of engaging narrative performance, bringing physical, digital and personal elements together.

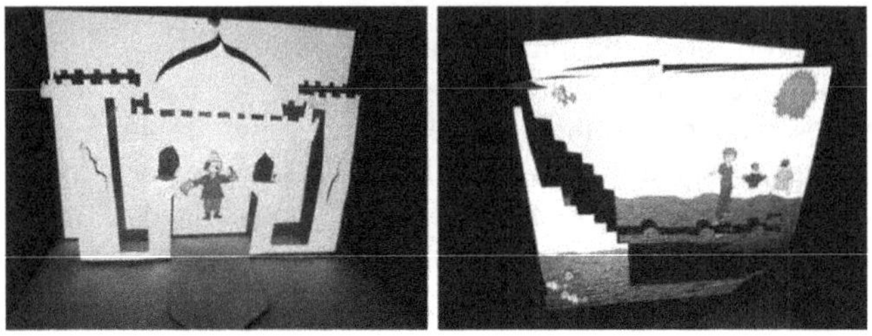

Figure 3: Programmable Projections

Sewable Circuits

Sewable circuits are circuits made on textiles using conductive threads and fabrics to create connections between electronic components. Using sewable circuits, creators can combine textile arts with electronic devices, including a programmable microcontroller such as LilyPad Arduino [2] and create projects using lights and audio.

In Story-Making workshops, children combined sewable circuits with applique embroidery and created quilt frames to represent objects of emotional value and experiences attached to it. As can be seen in Figure 4, a 10-year-old girl made a quilt frame representing her most favorite object. She used two red LED lights to represent fire in the gas stove and a DIY push button switch to depict a liquified petroleum gas tank.

Figure 4: A quilt patch made by a 10-year-old girl depicting a household stove made using sewable circuits

MEANINGFUL REPRESENTATIONS: STORY-BASED ARTIFACT ANALYSIS

Story-Making workshops provided insights on how children engage with different forms of TCM to create personal stories, their representation styles, and the learning outcomes. Through activity-based ethnography or ethnographic action research [4], I observed children's interactions with each medium and used an artifact-based analysis to document and analyze projects made by children who participated in the workshops.

I have found that the Story-Making approach is appealing to children and can contribute to extending their creative potential in deep and meaningful ways. The following case study reflects my observations and insights about a participant who created an interactive storybook using paper electronics. Through her project, the participant tells a story about arguments over access to water in her village and how they could be resolved.

Case Study: The Water Story

A 12-year-old girl without any prior experience with electronics or computational media participated in the Story-Making workshop series. She got started with paper electronics by making simple circuits and as the workshop progressed, she was introduced to new forms of interactions with complex circuitry using sensors, switches and micro controllers. While she was being introduced to these tools, she was simultaneously connecting them to her personal experiences.

She made a map of her neighborhood highlighting various events in one of the sessions. She annotated what she saw, heard or touched in the neighborhood and how she felt. She was particularly hooked on expressing the problem of availability of water in her community. For her final project, she built on that issue and constructed an interactive storybook based on what she experienced around the community water faucet.

Figure 5. First story scene with text: *In our community people fight for water.* In which the faucet button triggers sound.

Her story starts with a scene (Figure 5) showing a group of women gathered around a communal water faucet to fill their pots. There is no organized system, so the women are standing randomly around the single water source. The creator highlighted the key action in the scene using a simple circuit: When the reader presses the faucet, the pot starts making a noise that represents it getting filled.

The creator used simple electronic components, such as a buzzer and a switch to capture the sensory feel and actions associated with the place at visual, tactile, and auditory levels. She placed the switch on the faucet connecting the live action of a person opening the faucet with their hands to the action of the reader pressing the faucet (switch) with their hand. The sound from the buzzer represented the sound of water falling into the empty pot. The creator shows evidence of application of what Nicholas Roukes refers to as Logical Analogy [11] to capture similarities between the diverse elements of the scene from her neighborhood and the various electronic components in her circuit.

Figure 6. Second scene with text: *People fight with each other and get into fisticuffs.* In which LEDs indicate the verbal exchange of an argument.

The next scene (Figure 6) shows women, some with their children, standing across the road. One woman has fallen on the floor. The creator strategically placed the LED lights in the mouths of the women and added multiple switches underneath her drawing aligned with the sketch of the road. As soon as readers slide their fingers over the scene back and forth, the lights blink on and off vigorously. This interaction is used to illustrate the women fighting and arguing over the water.

The girl created an Affective Analogy [11] between her interactive drawing and the actual scene. She associated the emotional state of the women, in this case anger, with the active blinking of the lights, and created a dynamic interaction. The circuit includes ten lights and multiple switches connected in parallel. Her circuit incorporates the "OR" switch logic; pressing any switch completes the circuit and turns the attached LED lights on. Sliding fingers across multiple switches turns the LED lights on and off as you alternate between different switches. Faster sliding brings a fierce animated blinking effect to the lights.

Figure 7. Third scene with text: Talevar (Head of the community) intervened and tried to bring about a solution. He said do not fight and water will definitely be there in the faucets so solve the problem for now amicably and do not get into fights.

The third scene (Figure 7) shows a man in the center of a circle of women. The creator shared that she used multiple yellow and red lights arranged in a circular pattern to depict the Sun. She describes that in this scene, the community leader is negotiating with the women to stop arguing.

In the final scene in the story (Figure 8) Here, the creator visually highlighted that everybody will get water if they stand in queue by placing blue LED lights in the pots representing water. She also placed a sound sensor hidden under the faucet. When the reader whistles, claps, or makes any kind of noise, the LEDs light up. Asked why she used the sound sensor, the creator said that she wanted to show someone managing the water queue and making sure everyone has water.

Figure 8. Climax scene with text: *Now everyone has water in their pots.* Creator used LED lights, electret microphone and ATtiny 85 microcontroller.

Through TCM, this creator shared her thought-provoking story about water issues in her neighborhood in a Bangalore slum. She also created a new type of performance that engages her audience at multiple sensory levels by bringing dynamic interactions with tangible electronic components. And in the process, she learnt about electronics and computational skills ideas, and concepts.

DESIGN PRACTICES

This set of ten design practices has been developed as a framework for developing and facilitating creative, personally relevant and meaningful Story-Making explorations with TCM. These practices could also be useful for others designing meaningful learning environments, experiences, and technologies, which enhance the learning experience for or with children.

1. Create a Sacred Space

Creating a sacred space is a metaphor for providing a comfort zone for children where they can feel free to connect, create and express themselves. It is a space for reflection, contemplation, and consciously connecting with the true creative self. A beginning ritual can help provide the setting, such as children inventing a song by humming together, or a hands-on activity such as a sewing circle or creating light-up paper cubes representing a personal event. Creating a sacred space is more of an attitude of inclusion than an actual physical environment.

2. Encourage Sharing of Personal Experiences

It is crucial for designers and facilitators to understand where children are coming from, and to help them develop their voice as they start documenting and reflecting upon significant moments in their lives Encourage children to share events, stories and experiences that are personal and meaningful to them. These explorations can be created through conversations, writing, programming, and visual and physical representations, and will empower children to create personally relevant connections.

3. Spark Ideas by Sharing Your Own Creative Process

It can be intimidating for children to engage in the complex process of exploring new materials and representing personal meaning with those materials. So it is important to provide some scaffolding, for example by sharing concrete personal examples of projects that represent personal experiences. This serves as a starting point for children to reflect on what inspires them. How could they start? What sequences and actions could they follow to build their projects? How could they identify challenges and resolve them? What is their story and how could they represent their stories with new mediums?

4. Be Curious About Other's Curiosity

Allowing children to develop their ideas and own the process they are engaging with requires actively listening to them. When children don't feel confident in their ideas and feel stuck, they appreciate someone who explicitly values their ideas, listens enthusiastically and shows genuine interest in their discoveries. This practice of engaging children in conversations about their ideas and curiosity allows them to crystallize their ideas and progress in making tangible representations of their ideas.

Figure 9. A participant sharing her self-portrait created using basic circuit.

5. Introduce Tools as a Medium for Self-Expression (not just technique)

The focus should not be on teaching children a new tool itself but instead allowing them to engage with it as a medium for expressing their personal experiences. Through the Story-Making process, children indeed learn technological tools and concepts but in intuitive and exploratory ways. Activities such as creating a self-portrait with basic electrical circuits and lights (Figure 9) can help children in their exploration of how they can express themselves with the technology. Through this practice they not only learn about the tools and techniques but also about the process of how to design and create with these new tools and techniques.

6. Provide Creative Constraints but Leave Room for Open Exploration

Constraints have a significant role in fostering creativity but too many constraints can also restrict the emergence of novel ideas; facilitators need to balance scaffolding with openness. One approach for doing this is to start with a focused activity with limited materials and a specific design prompt, and then expand the range of options as learners gain more experience.

Children feel safe working within constraints early on, establishing familiarity with the materials and concepts. Next, they need, encouragement to go beyond those constraints, to explore multiple possibilities. Creative explorations can be designed with enough structure for children to not feel lost but also enough space to not feel controlled and trust their own ideas.

7. Raise the Ceiling

The concept of "low floor and high ceiling" is often used to describe the Logo programming language. The low floor metaphor is used to describe experiences that are easy enough for beginners to get started while high ceiling indicates complex explorations for expert users [9]. The same analogy of low floor and high ceiling can be used to describe the two extremes of creative explorations. Designing low-floor activities can help children get comfortable with new tools and aspire to create high-ceiling projects. However, there is also a need to design a ladder (progressive explorations) that allows children to gradually transition from a low floor to a higher ceiling.

As a starting point, children can be engaged in designing instantly gratifying projects and, depending on the level of their comfort and confidence, they can be introduced to more complex explorations. Raising the ceiling is a slow and thoughtful process and it can be challenging to apply this practice with limited time. In such cases, at least two different kinds of explorations could be designed where children could make an entry-level project and get started on a more challenging one that\ motivates them to continue in the long term.

8. See Outwards; Focus Inwards

Where do ideas come from? Children have multiple sources for inspiration: things that are unique, things that delight them, things that connect with them, and things that stay with them. What they see and feel in the real world can ignite their imagination. They might experience inspiration intuitively but it can be challenging to transform the inspiration into artistic expression. Stories can create a bridge to connect the real world and the imaginary world that children construct.

Creative explorations should be designed to encourage children to foster a sense of self and express themselves in richer ways. Experiences such as going out for a walk and drawing things that catch one's attention or capturing the sensory feel of the place (the smells, the sights, and the sounds) can prompt children to look at something external and find ways to connect with personal experiences. Using new media, children can then design artifacts based on what they observe, feel, reflect and envision as part of their worlds. Such powerful explorations can stimulate children to look around (externally), look within (internally), and look beyond (imaginatively).

9. Reflect in Action (not just on action)

Reflection is an essential design skill that enables us to pause, think, and learn from our experiences. It pushes us to zoom in, question, and evaluate our work, allowing us to generate insights. While it is important to reflect after completing the work, it is also crucial to reflect while the work is in progress. Schon [12] suggests this concept, calling it "reflect in action" (while doing something) and "reflect on action" (after you have done it).

Through open conversations and design critiques, children can be engaged in sharing their ideas and work in progress, receive feedback, and build strategies to proceed further and refining their work in progress. Explorations that engage children in reflecting in action can help them develop an understanding of their ideas, projects, theories and processes. It also allows them to address common challenges and ways to resolve those challenges.

10. Look Back; Look Ahead

Looking back involves reviewing past experiences to reflect on them and looking ahead helps to develop goals and strategies for the future. This practice not only helps children to iterate and refine their previous work but also to reimagine new possibilities to take their learning further and design new projects.

Looking ahead includes sharing about the long-term future goals. As part of their exploration, children should be encouraged to consciously look back at the process and think critically about ways of applying their learnings in other contexts and extending their creative explorations.

CONCLUSION

This paper presented ways of engaging children with new technologies to create new forms of stories, allowing them to understand and express meaningful aspects of their worlds in unique ways. Using TCM components such as lights, buzzers, and microcontrollers and applying computational ideas such as random sequences, parallelism, and abstraction, children constructed their worlds, illuminating ideas they care about.

By representing their personal experiences and reflecting on those experiences, children demonstrated skills and practices that they were learning. They explored new techniques to construct craft, electronics, and projections while also engaging with computational and artistic ideas. And more importantly, they were learning to create ideas for self-expression, envisioning themselves and their worlds in novel ways with creative confidence.

Stories sparked and inspired their making and learning of artistic and computational ideas, the tangible interactions made them exciting and the personal connection made them more meaningful. This reflects the value of designing meaningful explorations to not just introduce new skills and competencies but fostering a sense of self and creative confidence. We need to design and develop new ways to nurture children's creative self-hood with new technologies.

ACKNOWLEDGEMENTS

This paper is based on my Master's thesis work [6], and some of the text and images have previously appeared in the thesis. I would like to thank my thesis advisor Mitchel Resnick, along with Geetha Narayanan and Natalie Rusk for supporting this work. I also want to thank all the children and facilitators from Drishya Kalika Kendra who participated in Story-Making workshop series.

REFERENCES

1. Karen Brennan and Mitchel Resnick. 2012. New Frameworks for studying and assessing the development of computational thinking. American Educational Research Association (AERA), 1-25.
2. Leah Buechley and Michael Eisenberg. 2008. The LilyPad Arduino: Toward Wearable Engineering for Everyone. *Wearable Computing Column in IEEE Pervasive*, 7, 2: 12-15.
3. Michael Eisenberg, Ann Eisenberg, Mark Gross, Khomkrit Kaowthumrong, Nathaniel Lee, and Will Lovett. 2002. Computationally-Enhanced Construction Kits for Children: Prototype and Principles. In *Proceedings of ICLS (International Conference on the Learning Sciences)*, Seattle, WA.
4. David Gauntlett. 2007. *Creative Explorations: New approaches to identities and audiences.* Abingdon, Oxon, Routledge.
5. Marvin Minsky. 2006. *The Emotion Machine: Commonsense Thinking, Artificial Intelligence, and the Future of the Human Mind*, Simon & Schuster.
6. Alisha Panjwani. 2015. From storytelling to story making: children creating stories with tangible computation media, Masters Thesis, Massachusetts Institute of Technology, Cambridge, MA.
7. Seymour Papert and Idit Harel. 1991. Preface, Situating Constructionism, In *Constructionism, Research reports and essays, 1985-1990*, Idit Harel and Seymour Papert. Ablex Publishing Corporation.

8. Jie Qi and Leah Buechley. 2014. Sketching in Circuits: Designing and building electronics on paper. In *Proceedings of the SIGCHI conference on Human factors in computing systems* (CHI '14), 1713-1722. http://dl.acm.org/citation.cfm?id=2557391
9. Mitchel Resnick and Brian Silverman. 2005. Some Reflections on Designing Construction Kits for Kids, In *Proceedings of the 2005 conference on Interaction design and children* (IDC '05), 117-122.
10. Mitchel Resnick, John Maloney, Andrés Monroy-Hernández, Natalie Rusk, Evelyn Eastmond, Karen Brennan, Amon Millner, Eric Rosenbaum, Jay Silver, Brian Silverman, Yasmin Kafai. 2009. Scratch: programming for all. *Communications of the ACM*, 52, 11: 60-67.
11. Nicholas Roukes. 1984. *Art Synectics: Stimulating Creativity in Art*. Davis Publications, Inc.
12. Donald A Schon. 1984. *The reflective practitioner: How professionals think in action*. Basic Books.
13. David Staker. 2015. *Narrative Thinking.* Retrieved April, 11, 2015 from http://changingminds.org/

Designing for Massive Engagement in a Tween Community: Participation, Prevention, and Philanthropy in a Virtual Epidemic

Yasmin Kafai[1], Deborah A. Fields[2], Michael T. Giang[3], Nina Fefferman[4], Jen Sun[5], Daniel Kunka[5], Jacqueline Wong

[1]University of Pennsylvania Philadelphia, PA

[2]Utah State University Logan, UT

[3]Mount Saint Mary's University Los Angeles, CA

[4]University of Tennessee Knoxville, TN

[5]Numedeon, Inc. Pasadena, CA

kafai@upenn.edu, deborah.fields@usu.edu, mtgiang@msmu.edu, nina.h.fefferman@gmail.com, jen@whyville.net, daniel@whyville.net, writejackie@gmail.com

ABSTRACT

How can we design for more active participation and engagement in massive online virtual worlds? While many online communities, be they online games or virtual worlds, have been created or used ostensibly with learning goals in mind, relatively little has been studied about how to motivate members collectively (rather than individually or in small groups) in productive activities, especially with children and teens. To this end we describe the design and impact of a virtual epidemic in a massive online community called Whyville.net that engaged youth players in an infectious disease outbreak. Our analyses of click data captured in log files and observations reveal which factors impacted players' changes in participation, including searches for information, engagement in prevention, and donations to vaccine design. In the discussion, we address what we have learned about identity, agency and timing as levers in designing participation in massive community experiences.

Author Keywords

Virtual communities; identity; avatar design; virtual epidemics; virtual worlds; computer supported collaborative learning; educational technology

ACM Classification Keywords

H.5.3. Group and Organization Interfaces.

INTRODUCTION

With the arrival of massive online communities, much attention has focused on understanding the dynamics of participation, collaboration, and contributions in a variety of genres: peer production sites like Wikipedia, social networking sites such as MySpace and Facebook, gaming communities such as MMORPGs (e.g., *World of Warcraft*), and more recently online education efforts such as MOOCs [3]. The research has mostly concentrated on examining adult-populated spaces, leaving aside the equally important online communities to which children and tweens are drawn in ever growing numbers, sometimes even surpassing in size those of adults [5]. While commercial hosts have been eager to offer these spaces for children, efforts from the educational side have been far and few between, perhaps because of the expenses and efforts associated for research groups with setting up, hosting, and managing such massive online communities with the specific legal concerns and obligations regarding children [5].

In this paper, our goal is to expand the knowledge base on designing for collective engagement in massive online communities. Inspired by Benkler's seminal work on online peer cooperation [1] we call these principles "design levers" of massive engagement. Building on prior research of implementing a virtual epidemic called *WhyPox* in Whyville [7, 8, 9], we designed and launched a new virtual epidemic called *Dragon Swooping Cough* in Whyville.net, in the same online community that involved millions of tween players in the earlier infectious disease outbreak. In our analysis, we address two questions: (1) How willing were individual online players to use preventive measures that could stop the epidemic outbreak? and (2) Who answered a collective call to donate funds to the design of a virtual vaccine that could stop the epidemic outbreak? Our analysis focused on log file data of location visits, chat records, purchases, and usage of preventive measures coupled with observations of online interactions when *Dragon Swooping Cough* swept in early 2016 through the online community of Whyville to understand how players responded to individual preventive measures of varying efficiency and collective fundraising towards the production of a vaccine In the discussion, we address what we learned about online players' participation that could provide designers of massive online communities with a better understanding of how to initiate and increase engagement.

ACM 978-1-4503-4921-5/17/06...$15.00

http://dx.doi.org/10.1145/3078072.3079730

BACKGROUND

Our prior work on virtual epidemics provided hints on how to use such an event to facilitate participation within a massive virtual world. In designing and studying *WhyPox*, a flu-like virus released within Whyville, we found that participation patterns of players changed throughout an outbreak (i.e., before, during, and after). Looking more closely we identified different levels of engagement from low to high, for example from changing simple behaviors such as chatting (low), to discussing cases (medium), to running simulations (high) [9]. Thus an infectious disease outbreak can become an experiential learning event and a potentially meaningful context for science inquiry that engages everyone who is online, whether they like the disease or not [7, 12]. However, in this virtual epidemic, youth could not take direct action against the disease except by avoiding the site altogether. Instead the designed epidemic limited active engagement to investigating how the disease spread rather than fighting the disease directly.

In our latest efforts toward designing a key community event that would broadly engage youth in a virtual world, we sought to provide further means of directly taking action against the disease as a means to studying players' agency. We wanted to develop a better understanding of player agency by leveraging individual actions towards a larger collective goal such as saving lives or natural resources within or outside of the game—a focus of many recent studies [e.g., 6]. We selected two different actions—prevention and philanthropy—for further examination, not only because they have impact in real life on the progression of an epidemic outbreak but also because they could provide us with measurable outcomes of online players' participation and engagement. Both also are illustrative of player agency, but while prevention is from the outset an individual act to protect oneself from harm, philanthropy starts out as a collective action, especially when outcomes can only be achieved with massive participation. Next we explain the design of our virtual epidemic, the *Dragon Swooping Cough*.

Dragon Swooping Cough Stages 1 and 2

History of Viruses in Whyville

Whyville has a long history of viral epidemics, beginning with research-driven initiatives in the early 2000's [e.g., 7, 9, 12]. These began with *WhyPox*, a virus that mirrored the flu and affected Whyvillians' avatar appearance (red splotchy spots) and their chat (sneezes—"Achoo"—before each sentence). Vaccines became available in later iterations and resulted in a strong trade among players, as citizens could at that time only purchase one portion of a vaccine when three portions were needed [12]. After the initial *WhyPox* outbreaks, Numedeon added new features to educate Whyvillians about virtual epidemics. A BioPlex center was created where Whyvillians could attempt to create their own viruses (variants of a generic *WhyFlu*) and vaccines, and a Pharmacy center where Whyvillians could purchase treatments: over-the-counter medicines to treat coughs (Cof-Eze), spots (Pox Cream), and sniffles (Snif-B-Gone). In addition they created two free preventive measures, Wash (washing hands) and Cover (covering one's mouth), that citizens were encouraged to use frequently (as one would in the real world) to prevent infection. While none of these in-game treatment or preventive measures had been studied, they provided an important background for the release of the *Dragon Swooping Cough*.

Virus

Building on insights gained from the *WhyPox* outbreak [9], we designed the *Dragon Swooping Cough* virus (hereafter: DSC) to reflect real-life features of infectious viruses that are particularly dangerous in the real world, like Ebola. Our decisions on the virus design were influenced from both a design and epidemiological perspective: we sought to make the virus authentic and epidemiologically informed while also trying to infect a large number of players who would want to take action to prevent the spread of the virus. In the end we created a virus that lasted 10 days. The *incubation period*, the time between infection and becoming infectious was intentionally short (days 1-2) while the *latent period*, the time between infection and showing symptoms, was long (days 1-5). We also chose a long infectious period (days 3-9) so that the virus would spread widely, and a symptomatic period (days 6-10) where the ratio of the latent period to symptomatic period was greater than one (important from an epidemiological perspective). The designers infected a set number of Whyvillians, a number chosen by Numedeon based on prior experience with infections, on the first few days of the virus and then let the virus run. Logging in when the virus was active created a chance of infection and spreading the virus.

Drawing on earlier findings that emotional engagement was key in triggering participation [4], we designed symptoms that targeted the things Whyvillians cared about the most—avatar appearance, socializing, and money [7]. We affected *avatar* appearance by putting dragon scales on their bodies, interrupted *chat* (socializing) by inserting the words "rawrr...cough cough rawrr" into chat, created visible *movement* with avatars swooping and circling around the screen, and stopped *salary* deposits during the three worst days of infection. The new financial impact was chosen because real life illnesses affect individuals' income and employment. These symptoms successfully recruited emotional engagement of Whyvillians; participants were upset by "ugly" avatars, interrupted chat and disruptive movements, which many called "annoying" [4].

Drawing on knowledge of both virtual and real world epidemics and economics, we made a number of preventive measures available to Whyvillians: expensive biohazard Umbrellas with a roughly 95% chance of protection (11,000 clams—an amount that would wipe out the middle 50% of Whyvillians' savings), scale block Lotion (15% chance of protection, 30 clams), and Wash (washing hands), a carryover from recent *WhyPox* infections, (10% chance of protection, free). Cover, another carryover from *WhyPox* infections was deemed ineffective to prevent DSC since the DSC was skin- (or rather scale-) based. As a preventive measure, players could purchase face Masks for 1 clam. Unlike the other preventive measures, masks were a "goodwill item," since they lowered the chance of contagious individuals infecting others if used consistently in rooms entered on a given day, a subtlety many Whyvillians did not understand, especially in the first version of DSC (DSC1).

Community

In addition to the virus design, we introduced several activities and modes of distributing disease-relevant information to Whyvillians. One concern here was overwhelming citizens with too much information. Therefore we carefully considered how much information to provide and introduced both information and activities in different stages. Initially, short reports on the homepage alerted citizens to a new virus. By day 3 of the virus, familiar figures in Whyville, "Jimmy and Timmy," were stationed at City Hall to provide both preventive measures and tests for infection. These tests had false positives and false negatives (reported to players with each test) that slowly improved as the virus progressed, in line with epidemiological progressions in the real world.

After DSC1 had run its full course, we shut down the virus for eight weeks and then prepared Whyville for a new mutation of the virus, DSC2, which caused the original symptoms in players who had never before been infected and slightly altered symptoms in players who had been infected by DSC1: red scales (vs grey) and animated fire-breathing coughs (vs unanimated coughs). Two weeks before DSC2 was released, we began a philanthropic campaign to raise money to research and produce a vaccine for DSC. The homepage was peppered with "rumors" that DSC might return, as do many epidemics. A goal was set for one million clams, with a maximum donation per day of 5000 clams (to prevent super wealthy Whyvillians from funding the entire drive on their own). Whyvillians quickly blew past the original goal, and so the goal was raised with the promise that increased funding would allow for speedier production of the vaccine and a cheaper vaccine. In addition to the vaccine drive, we solicited articles for the citizen-written *Whyville Times* about the *Dragon Swooping Cough* epidemic or other epidemics in the real world, though only four Whyvillians submitted articles.

METHODS

Participants included 5835 Whyville players selected from two sources. First, we included all 835 players who responded to at least one of the six surveys about the *Dragon Swooping Cough* (hereafter: DSC) between November 2015 and June 2016. These surveys assessed players' knowledge of infectious diseases and their feelings and behaviors related to DSC (results reported in [4]). Second, to gauge the behavior of the Whyville population during DSC, 5000 players were randomly selected for analyses if they visited Whyville at least 10 times since November 1, 2015. For all participants, online Whyville behavior (log files) between November and June were provided by Numedeon, Inc., the company that hosts and manages Whyville. These log files included general behaviors (e.g., logins, chat, currency, 'clams' transactions) and disease specific behaviors (checking for infection, use of preventative usages, infection status). This data allowed us to compare survey responses to actual activity (see Fields et al, submitted), online behavior across time, and survey and non-survey participants.

Descriptive and comparative analyses were conducted to examine behaviors across time and groups. Descriptive analyses summarized Whyvillians' behaviors regarding logins, preventive purchases and usage, checking for infection and other activities through total weekly counts, means and standard deviations, and frequencies and percentages. Independent samples t-tests and multivariate analysis of variance were used to compare differences among groups (e.g., donators vs. non-donators) on various outcomes (e.g., salary, cash, online behavior). Lastly, chi-square-tests of independent samples were conducted to examine the relationship between donation status and infection status.

FINDINGS

Prevention

The first question asked in this paper regards the players' use of preventive measures: In what ways did individual players use preventive measures that could stop the epidemic outbreak? Overall, Whyvillians used preventive measures quite a lot. Sales for DSC-specific interventions (such as masks, lotions, and umbrella) as well as the more generic hand washing were high and uses of them were similarly high. However, most interesting is the way that uses of preventive measures changed over time both during and between DSC1 and DSC2.

Some preventive measures were already available to Whyvillians since they were used for prior infectious diseases in Whyville (*WhyPox* and *WhyFlu*), while the DSC-specific measures (mask, lotion, umbrella) only became available about one week after the initial release of the virus (see Figures 1, 2, and 3). The previously available preventive measures can be broken into two groups: measures for protecting against infection (Wash, Cover, and *WhyFlu* Vaccines) and measures for treating symptoms available at a local Whyville pharmacy. Of these only Wash was effective in protecting against DSC. However, all saw strong peaks in use during the first week of DSC. Wash (washing hands—effectual) and Cover (covering one's mouth—ineffectual) peaked early during DSC1, at around 4000 uses per week (Wash) and 3000 uses per week (Cover) during the two first weeks of DSC. While far less commonly used than Wash and Cover, WhyPox/WhyFlu vaccines and pharmaceutical treatments also saw sudden peaks of use during the first week of DSC1 and less frequent use throughout DSC1. The purchasable *WhyPox* and *WhyFlu* items included Vaccines (60 purchases) and treatments for coughs (Cof-Eze; 28 purchases), sneezing (Snif-B-Gone; 13 purchases), and avatar spots (Pox Cream; 9 purchases). Unlike the freely available Wash and Cover, these purchase-able measures dropped as soon as DSC-specific measures went on the market. It is apparent that Whyvillians used prior knowledge about infectious disease in Whyville to handle a new epidemic outbreak and learned to adapt to the new disease as illustrated by the drop in using *WhyPox/WhyFlu*-specific measures.

During DSC2, these trends changed somewhat. An overall look at the use of preventive measures shows a large drop in their use during DSC2, however, separating out which preventive measures were used shows a more nuanced view. The generic measures that were useful against *WhyPox* (including Wash, which *was* effective for DSC) dropped to very low usage during DSC2. Umbrella purchases declined somewhat, perhaps because they were the most expensive item and one that did not disappear after use. Lotion usage stayed level (during peak times), and DSC-Vaccines, which were newly available, were used roughly as often as Lotion purchases. While Mask purchases dropped, their use nearly doubled to around 1400. The increase in Mask use is important because it is not useful for protecting oneself from disease, but rather for protecting *others* from catching one's infection. During DSC1, we observed many misunderstandings of the utility of Masks. While our observations suggest that misunderstandings about Masks were less present during DSC2, it is difficult to ascertain whether Whyvillians were using Masks for their intended purposes (i.e., protection of others). Another interpretation is that masks were used more frequently because they were cheaper than other DSC-specific preventive measures and required more frequent use in order to work correctly.

In sum, Whyvillians' usage of preventive measures changed during the course of the two viruses. Initially they turned to pre-existing measures that were mostly relevant for other diseases on Whyville. Ineffective treatments for DSC (i.e., treatments for WhyPox or WhyFlu) dropped immediately. The more generic preventive measures, Wash and Cover, continued in high use during DSC1. When new DSC-specific preventive measures became available, Whyvillians adopted them quickly. Perhaps most intriguingly, Whyvillians' use of preventive measures shifted during DSC2. They used fewer generic measures (Wash and Cover) and largely retained or increased use of DSC-specific measures. Combined with the increase in uses of tests for infection (see prior section), this suggests that during the second round of the disease (DSC2), Whyvillians learned better how to fight the virus, at least on an individual level and with hints of a more collective attitude with regard to an increase in mask use. In addition to the experiences of DSC1, one major reason for this change may have been the donation and informational campaign run in the two weeks prior to the release of DSC2.

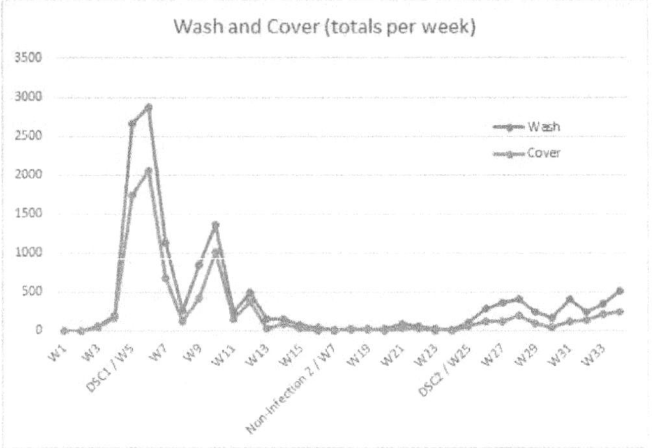

Figure 1. Wash and Cover during DSC1 and DSC2.

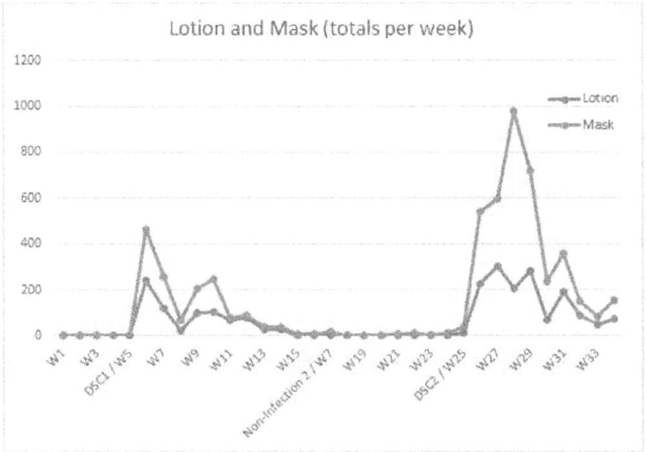

Figure 2. Use of Lotion during DSC1 and DSC2.

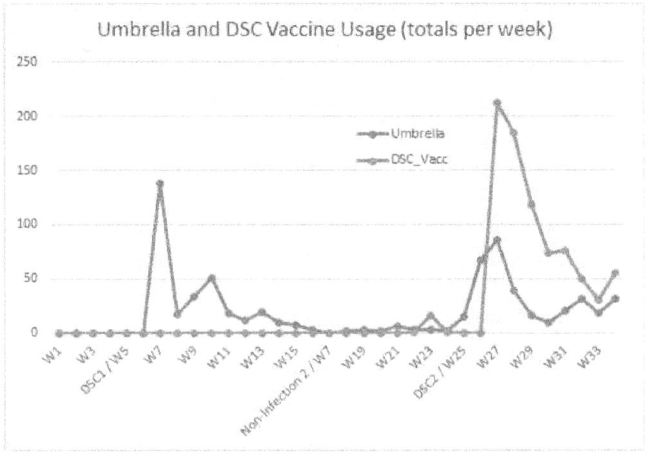

Figure 3. Use of Umbrellas and DSC Vaccines.

Philanthropy

The philanthropic campaign for a vaccine to the *Dragon Swooping Cough* virus provided the most visible form of collective action toward a larger good—an agentic feature only implemented in DSC2. Here we asked the following research question: Who answered a collective call to donate funds to the design of a virtual vaccine that could stop the epidemic outbreak? Among the participants in the study, 394 citizens contributed a total of 2,011,850 clams toward the cause of creating a vaccine. Initially the donation drive was set with a goal of 1 million clams; that amount was raised so quickly that the design team kept the campaign open to more donations with the promise of quicker development and cheaper availability of vaccines. Of those who donated, 58.4% donated once; 20.8% donated 2x, and 20.8% donated three or more times. Some (16.8%) donated the minimum of 100 clams; 8.9% donated 1000 clams; 7.1% donated 10,000; and many donated much more. The most common donation total was 5000 clams (the maximum amount one could donate on a single day). One individual gave the maximum amount possible every day of the drive (15 consecutive days) for a total of 75,000 clams.

What do we know about those who donated toward the vaccine development? Multivariate analysis of variance revealed that those who were able to donate were more likely to participate across multiple Whyville areas of activity. For instance, two prominent predictors of participation are salary and cash (accrued from daily logins and levels of expertise across various science-based games). During the donation period in April, those who donated had significantly higher salaries compared to those who did not (84.86 clams/login vs. 133.74 clams/login; $p < .001$). Similarly, excluding multiple players with extremely high levels of cash (the top 5% or those with 400 million – 1.59 billion clams; $p < .001$), donators also had significantly higher amounts of cash in their bank accounts (160,871.69 vs. 320,386.09 clams; $p < .001$). In terms of specific areas of Whyville participation, results also revealed that those who donated were significantly more active in Whyville overall (i.e., chat, logins, page views) as well as in activities related to the DSC (checking for infection, using preventive measures), especially during the infection periods.

Perhaps more interesting, a Chi-square test of independence revealed a significant relationship between infection status (infected vs. non-infected) and donation status (donators vs. non-donators) for DSC1 (chi-square (1) = 250.022, $p < .001$). Specifically, during DSC1, infected Whyvillians were more likely to be donators ($z = 12.8$) than expected compared to being non-donators ($z = -3.55$); similarly, those who were not infected were more likely to be non-donators ($z = 2.30$) than donators ($z = -8.30$). For those who were infected with the mutated DSC strain (during DSC2, i.e., the second time they were infected), they were also more likely to be donators ($z = 14.4$) than expected compared to being non-donators ($z = -4.0$), while those non-infected were less likely to be donators ($z = -3.6$), chi-square(1) = 236.985, $p < .001$. In sum, Whyvillians who were most likely to make goodwill donations to the vaccine drive were: 1) active on Whyville (such as logins, page views, and chatting), 2) engaged in greater health maintenance behavior (such as preventive measure use, umbrella use, and checking for infection), and 3) likely to have been infected with the DSC.

DISCUSSION

The goal of our study was to better understand how particular dimensions of players' identity and agency can motivate participation and engagement in massive online communities. We examined engagement in our study as changes in actions such as using preventive measures to intercept the outbreak and contributing to charity for vaccine development. Our study provided first insights into which factors were "design levers" to use Benkler's [1] term for increasing players' engagement in individual and collective action. In the following sections, we discuss what we learned about designing for participation and engagement and developing future research.

Designing for Engagement

One of our overarching goals was to contribute to the growing body of research promoting participation and engagement in massive online communities. Many studies have documented that the majority of online activity is driven by a fairly small percentage of players in many massive communities [e.g., 7], obscuring the fact that despite large numbers of registered participants not everyone is equally engaged. This is not just an issue in terms of drawing large numbers of participants into deeper activity but also which voices are being promoted in online communities [11]. From an educational perspective such differential outcomes are problematic as online learning opportunities should be accessible and inviting to all.

What we learned from the implementation of the *Dragon Swooping Cough* is that agency matters in making the virus design engaging. The previous *Whypox* implementation and classroom discussions showed that many players wanted to contribute to curtailing the epidemic outbreak [12] but were not provided opportunities for action. Here preventive measures offered individuals ways to combat the disease, and the vaccine donation drive offered a means to help the community (as well as oneself). These were more successful than other activities we suggested. For instance, a call to write about their experience with the epidemic in the *Whyville Times*, Whyville's online newsmagazine, only resulted in a few contributions while the production of a vaccine activated more than hundreds of players to donate clams. One can argue that there is a difference in investment: writing a newspaper article requires far more effort from players than donating clams or purchasing and using a mask, both of which can be accomplished with a few mouse clicks. Nonetheless, these results provide first indicators about what moves players into action.

Furthermore, we learned that timing matters in the design of the virus itself. The placement of the vaccine drive was positioned after the first epidemic outbreak so that players' donations were motivated by prior experience with the disease. In fact, one could consider the timing of the second outbreak an additional "design lever" for impacting engagement. The repeated outbreak allowed for more information to be presented at a time when many Whyvillians already cared about the disease because of an earlier infection. This second round of information accompanying the philanthropic vaccine drive appears to have supported improvements in Whyvillians' use of preventive measures (using more effective measures and fewer ineffective measures) and in other activities such as checking for infection.

While our current study focused more on the measurable activities of players than their understanding about infectious disease, we have argued elsewhere that there is potential for using virtual epidemics as a pedagogical tool [7, 9]. Previous studies have used epidemic outbreaks in simulation [2] and gaming contexts [10] to help players understand the dynamics of spreading an infectious disease. The changing use of preventive measures in the two versions of DSC provided an intriguing lens into Whyvillians' use of prior knowledge of old diseases to treat new diseases. Behaviors related to preventive measures changed twice: first upon the release of new, DSC-specific preventive measures, and second upon the occurrence of DSC2. In addition, by developing preventive measures to encourage individual participation with a collectivistic goal and releasing the socially-driven funding effort for the vaccine we encouraged group/peer communication, which led to social construction and/or reinforcement of norms guiding individual behavioral change. These adaptions of activity suggest some form of learning, though how intentional or knowledgeable Whyvillians were about their preventive actions is difficult to determine.

CONCLUSION

We used the design of virtual epidemics as an example for how to leverage player identity and agency for participation and engagement in massive online communities. In our case we modeled the virtual cough to resemble real-life outbreaks and provided measures that also in real-life could prevent the outbreak. Understanding the design levers of participation bring us a step closer in realizing a vision of online (and face-to-face) communities in which youth can not just hang out but also participate and go deeper in meaningful ways.

ACKNOWLEDGMENTS

This work was supported by a grant (#1506724) from the National Science Foundation to Yasmin Kafai, Nina Fefferman and Jen Sun. Any opinions, findings, and conclusions or recommendations expressed in this paper are those of the authors and do not necessarily reflect the views of the National Science Foundation, University of Pennsylvania, Kentucky State University, Utah State University or Numedeon, Inc. Special thanks to Estee Ellis for her observational work on this research. We also want to thank Debora Lui and Justice Walker for their helpful comments on earlier drafts of the manuscript.

REFERENCES

1. Yochai Benkler. 2009. Law, policy and cooperation. In E. Balleisen and D. Moss (Eds), *Government and Markets: Toward A New Theory of Regulation (pp. 299-334)*. New York, NY: Cambridge University Press.
2. Vanessa Colella. 2000. Participatory simulations: Building collaborative understanding through immersive dynamic modeling. *J. Learn. Sci., 9*(4), 471-500.
3. Ulrike Cress, J. Moskaliuk, H. Jeong, H. (Eds.). 2016. *Mass collaboration and education*. New York, NY: Springer.
4. Deborah Fields, Yasmin Kafai, Michael Giang, Nina Fefferman, Jacqueline Wong. Submitted. Plagues and people: Mass community participation in a virtual epidemic within a tween online world.
5. Sara Grimes, Deborah Fields. 2015. Children's media making, but not sharing: The potential and limitations of child-specific DIY media websites for a more inclusive media landscape. *Media International Australia,* 154, 112-122.
6. J. Jafarinaimi, E.M. Meyers. 2015. Collective intelligence of group think? Engaging participation patterns in a *World without Oil*? In *Proceedings of CSCW (pp. 1872-1881)*. Vancouver, CA: ACM.
7. Yasmin Kafai, Deborah Fields. 2013. *Connected Play: Tweens in a Virtual World.* Cambridge, MA: MIT Press.
8. Yasmin Kafai, David Feldon, Deborah Fields, Michael Giang, Maria Quintero. 2007. Life in the time of Whypox: A virtual epidemic as a community event. In C. Steinfield, B. Pentland, M. Ackerman, &. N Contractor *(Eds.), Communities and Technologies* 2007 (pp. 171-190). New York: Springer.
9. Yasmin Kafai, Maria Quintero, David Feldon. 2010. Investigating the "why" in Whypox: Explorations of a virtual epidemic. *Games and Culture, 5*(1), 116-135.
10. S. Kennedy-Clark, K. Thompson, K. 2011. What do students learn when collaboratively using a computer game in the study of historical epidemics, and why? *Games & Culture, 6*(6), 513-537.
11. D. Kreiss, M. Finn, F. Turner, F. 2011. The limits of peer production: Some reminders from Max Weber for the network society. *New Media & Society, 13*(2), 243-259.
12. Nina Neulight, Yasmin Kafai, Linda Kao, Brian Foley, Cathy Galas. 2007. Children's participation in a virtual epidemic in the science classroom: Making connections to natural infectious diseases. *J. of Sci. Ed. and Tech., 16*(1), 47-58.

Augmented Games – Exploring Design Opportunities in AR Settings With Children

Sascha Oberhuber[1], Tina Kothe[2], Stefan Schneegass[3], Florian Alt[1]

[1]LMU Munich, Ubiquitous Interactive Systems Group, florian.alt@ifi.lmu.de
[2]LMU Munich, Institute of Art Education, tina.kothe@lrz.uni-muenchen.de
[3]University of Stuttgart, Visualization and Interactive Systems, stefan.schneegass@vis.uni-stuttgart.de

Figure 1. In the study children used 'MakeAR', an application that lets them build AR-treasure hunts. It assists them in creating physical markers (left). Afterwards they placed treasure chests (middle) and played the game in groups (right). AR technology helped them to build more complex and creative treasure hunts.

ABSTRACT
In this paper we investigate how Augmented Reality (AR) technology influences children during creative content generation in playful settings. The work is motivated by the recent spread of AR and the fact that children get in touch with this technology through their smart phones very early on. To understand the consequences, we implemented an app for smart mobile devices that allows children to create treasure hunts using GPS coordinates and marker-based AR functionality. During a qualitative user study, we asked students (n=27) to create traditional (paper + art supplies) and digital (paper + art supplies + AR app) treasure hunts and compared the resulting games, among other metrics, in terms of complexity, length and types of media used. Whereas traditional treasure hunts were linear, centered around locations and delivered information with text only, digital treasure hunts were more complex, focused on visual aspects and frequently integrated storytelling.

ACM Classification Keywords
K.3. Computers and Education: Computer Uses in Eduation; H.5.1. Multimedia Information Systems: Augmented Realities

Author Keywords
Education; Children; AR; Creativity; Storytelling

IDC '17, June 14–16, 2017, Stanford, CA, USA.

ACM ISBN 978-1-4503-4529-3/17/06 ...$15.00.
http://dx.doi.org/10.1145/3077548.3077561

INTRODUCTION
Mobile devices have become ubiquitous, and as a consequence enable novel AR applications in daily live. Such applications are not limited to games and navigation [16], but AR applications have been designed for use in, for example, museums [26], advertising [3], or sports [6]. While regular tablet and phone apps have already proven valuable for education [24, 25], AR app also found their way into the education of children [1, 7, 18]. In these cases, AR is used as a novel and interactive representation of content. For example, ARBS (Augmented Reality Books System) enhances traditional textbooks with AR content [11]. This augmentation has shown to evoke positive emotions and more motivation for the discussed topics [10]. Particularly, providing meta information was considered useful via AR [9, 12]. In another project, the creation of simulations in AR has shown to support children in learning by being highly engaging [8].

AR has mainly been used as a visualization technique by teachers and educators. It was found that AR interfaces may support collaborative activities [4] and lead to higher motivation [22]. At the same time, providing children means to create their own AR content received little attention. Prior projects showed how to build tools that allows children to create digital content in general, for example, programming environment for children ('Scratch'[1]) or story authoring tools ('Fiabot!' [20]).

To close this gap, we focus on enabling children to create AR content by means of an AR authoring tool. We investigate how children use the tools to create AR content on mobile devices and how this influences their creative process [14] compared to traditional tools. We explore how the children's ability to grasp and exploit the concepts of AR helps them to create new content and how it impacts on motivation and experience.

[1]Scratch Website: `https://scratch.mit.edu`

To investigate the potential and challenges of AR in an educational content creation process, we first implemented 'MakeAR', an authoring tool that allows AR content to be created. We then let children create traditional (paper + art supplies) and digital (paper + art supplies + MakeAR tool) treasure hunts, qualitatively comparing the resulting games with regard to complexity, length, and types of media used.

CONTRIBUTION STATEMENT

The contribution of this work is twofold. First, we report on the design and implementation of the 'MakeAR' tool allowing digital AR treasure hunts to be created. Second, we report on a user study with 27 fourth grade primary schools children. We observe their content creation process to compare their creative work to traditional non-digital content creation processes.

MAKEAR – CREATING AR TREASURE HUNTS

'MakeAR' is an app we designed to support children in creating and playing digitally enhanced treasure hunts using augmented reality. The digital enhancement happens through marker-based and/or location-based AR content generated by the user within the application. We developed 'MakeAR' as an Android app particularly suited for tablet-sized devices.

Requirements

While there is a selection of tools allowing users to generate AR content by themselves, our specific setting and target audience (i.e., children aged 9–11) comes with a different set of requirements. The tool should provide:

- simple mechanisms that allow children to focus on the content (instead of the program).
- content generation at runtime, including AR overlays, GPS hooks, and visual markers.
- an approach not relying on an active internet connection to allow usage in places with limited connectivity (e.g., in the woods or basement).

Existing solutions like Aurasma[2] do not include these requirements and were not designed for being used by children.

General Workflow

On opening 'MakeAR' provides two buttons for the main functions: *create* and *play*. When choosing *create*, users see empty fields that can be tapped to add a station to the treasure hunt. A simple treasure hunt is shown in Figure 2. A station must be linked by a cordlike line to the next station. These stations can be dragged and dropped to different fields, the lines be cut and reassigned to other stations. Branches and multiple different endings are possible. Each station requires one *trigger* and at least one piece of *AR content*. A *trigger* is either a set of GPS coordinates (current position, stored in the app) or a hand-drawn paper marker (picture with a black, roughly square outline to be recognized as fitting marker). The paper marker must be scanned by the app and is then transfigured into an internal digital marker, used for image recognition. *AR content* can be added after the trigger (GPS or visual marker) is assigned to a station. Content can be created in three different

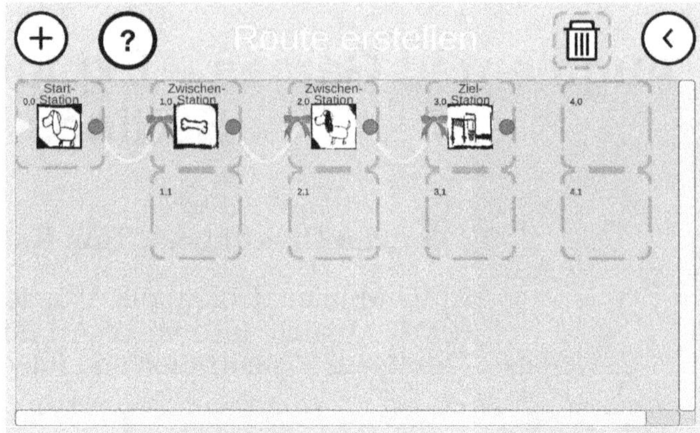

Figure 2. MakeAR's create mode in use. This linear treasure hunt features four marker-based stations.

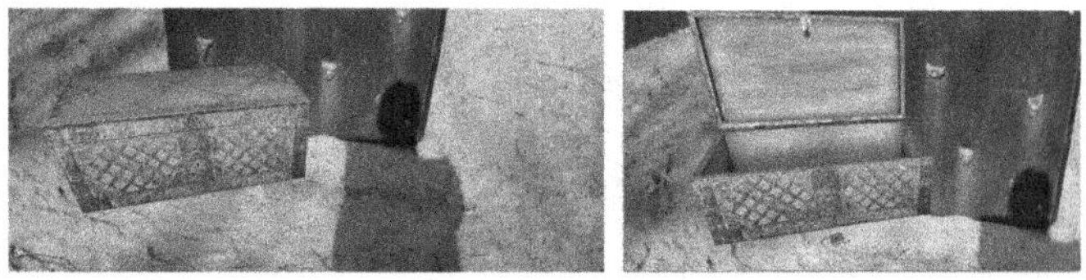

Figure 3. A chest that is tied to GPS coordinates in open state, i.e. if the player is in close vicinity (left) and in closed state (right).

ways: (1) A photo from the surroundings, objects of interest or clues can be taken by an integrated camera interface. (2) Children can write or hand-draw on paper and digitalize it by taking a photo. (3) Images (text or pictures) can be imported from Android's file storage. This allows modification of photographs through image editing or integrating pictures from third-party drawing apps.

Playing a previously created treasure hunt is the other main function of 'MakeAR'. Children hand over their tablet with their previously created treasure hunt stored on it. They give a hint to the playing group where to find the first clue – the rest is provided by the app. In addition to whatever information the content provides, stations that use GPS triggers can be located with the help of a compass integrated in the app.

When the children approach a GPS-based clue, a treasure chest is integrated into the live camera view (see Figure 3). The chest's location is recalculated based on the movement of the tablet, and the actual content is collected by tapping on the chest, which opens it. Marker-based clues work by approaching the physical marker in the real world and tapping the augmented content that is projected on top of it. All clues that got collected throughout a treasure hunt remain as minimized items on the lower half of the screen, thus allowing the players to review them.

MAIN STUDY

Our research is driven by the question how the use of AR influences creative content generation among children. Hence, we compare a traditional, paper-based treasure hunt game with an AR-treasure hunt. We follow an exploratory approach with a strong focus on qualitative observations. We also collected some quantitative data, yet decided to report descriptive statistics only due to the rather small sample size.

[2]Aurasma Website: `https://www.aurasma.com/`

Figure 4. Examples of children creating traditional (left) and digital (right) treasure hunts: Traditional groups focused strongly on text-based artefacts (a). Furthermore, a lot of emphasis was put on the locations (here an artefact was hidden in a tree). For the AR treasure hunt, one group first made a concept on the blackboard (c) before they started to carefully sketch markers and artefacts (d) which were then included by means of MakeAR.

Study Design & Participants

The study followed a between subject design where half of the children designed a treasure hunt using traditional media such as pen, paper, and duct tape, whereas the other half was offered both traditional tools and the MakeAR app described above. The study was conducted over the course of two days, with day 1 dedicated to the 'digital treasure hunts' using MakeAR, and the traditional treasure hunt taking place on day 2. During each day, only the children taking part in the day's experiment were present; nobody participated on both days.

The children were recruited among fourth graders from a local elementary school and were aged 9 to 11. In total, 14 children participated in the digital treasure hunt. In this group we had 6 boys and 8 girls, split into four teams of one boys team, one girls team and two mixed teams. There were 13 children recruited for the traditional treasure hunt (3 girls, 10 boys). Here the children split into three boy-teams and one girl team.

Note, that an earlier prototype of 'MakeAR' (using GPS localization instead of AR markers) was previously tested among children from the same school with regard to usability [23]. We recruited participants in the digital treasure hunt group from among these children. Thus, participants were already familiar with the app and we reduced a potential novelty bias.

Procedure

The researchers started both days by presenting a short overview about the idea of the project and verified that everyone was familiar with the concept of treasure hunt games. The children's task was to create a treasure hunt for their classmates in a given timeframe using the tools provided by the researchers. On the first day, the children were additionally introduced to 'MakeAR's visual marker functionality with a small example, a three-dimensional apple superimposed on a black and white apple marker. Then, the children split into four teams, to each of which one observer from the team of researchers was assigned. Observers were instructed to intervene as little as possible, in particular regarding content creation and children's approach to solving the task.

To clarify the task, we provided two short examples of a treasure hunt on both days. These examples differed in terms of complexity. Both followed a short, overarching story about a woman sending the players to a merchant to get a sewing thread to fix her dress. However, while the first example was strictly linear, the second example included different branches and a recall task – the dress was colored and children had to choose between different sewing threads (blue or red) when reaching the merchant. Based on their choice, the last location and the end of the story differed. Every team only completed one example treasure hunt (linear or complex). This allowed us to retroactively analyze whether children would adhere to what they had seen, or come up with something different.

After completing the examples, each team started to create a treasure hunt by themselves (Figure 4). No further instructions were given how the treasure hunt should look like and which elements it should contain. Teams were provided with various types of paper, pencils, colored pens, scissors, duct tape, and further drawing supplies. In addition, the AR group was provided a Samsung Galaxy Note Pro 12.2 tablet with 'MakeAR' installed. Once content was created (60–90 minutes), every team played another team's treasure hunt.

After that, children were asked to reflect on their experiences, issues, and ideas for improvement during an open group discussion. Children were also handed out questionnaires (Smileyometers [19]) that asked how much they enjoyed creating their own game, playing the others' game, and the overall experience. Open questions inquired about how they would describe their own game and whether they had further ideas to improve their game or the others' game.

RESULTS

Overall, 7 of 8 teams (traditional and digital) managed to create a complete treasure hunt and to play another team's treasure hunt. One digital team was so immersed in the design and story of their artifacts that they forgot to properly link their stations logically, which was fixed post-hoc using paper-based hints attached to the marker images. This team also managed to play another team's treasure hunt.

Examples

We provide some examples of hunts created by both groups.

Traditional Group

One of the traditional teams created a game that sent players across the school campus. In this treasure hunt, artifacts were pieces of paper with nothing but directional text instructions like "look for the big tree" or "go to place XY" (Figure 6).

Another traditional treasure hunt team created a game with less stations, but put more emphasis on the individual artifacts. Most instructions were encoded in riddles (simple cryptography such as mirrored text or letter substitution). In contrast to the previous group they intentionally hid their artifacts well.

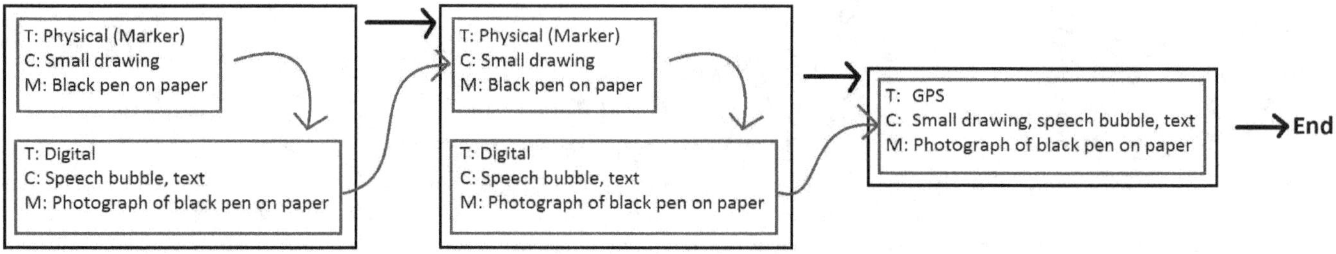

Figure 5. Graph-example of a simple digital treasure hunt: The games were transformed into graphs, each node representing one station. Nodes consist of one or more artifact. Each artifact is described by the artifact type (T), its content (C) and the medium (M) used to create it. This allowed the level of complexity and type of solution of the treasure hunt to be assessed.

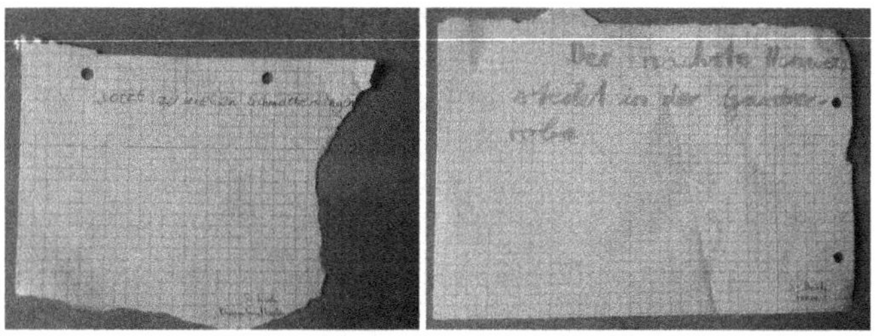

Figure 6. These exemplary traditional hints, send the players to "where the butterflies are" and "to the dressers". They are weakly linked hints consisting of nothing but text.

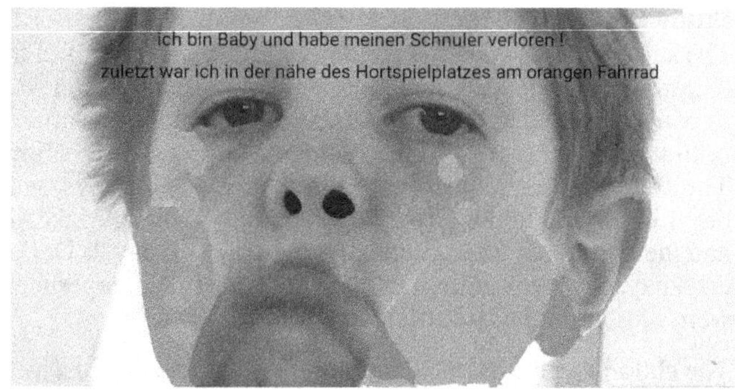

Figure 7. A highly sophisticated artifact, containing a modified photo and a textual hint wrapped up in a story.

AR Group

One AR team built a treasure hunt that contained most types of artifacts: marker-based stations, GPS, and physical riddles. Two artifacts were based on photographs the children took and on which they afterwards placed text and color with a drawing app (Figure 7). The stations were tied together by a short story about a stolen pacifier that had to be recaptured.

The second AR team also came up with a story: here a thief needed to get medicine for his ill horse and later bought supplies at the black market. The game was exclusively built using visual markers that led to dialogs among the characters, played by the members of the team. As previously mentioned, these students were so immersed in realizing their story that they forgot to leave hints where to find the next station.

Game Complexity Analysis – Quantitative Findings

During the study and the following analysis we observed some differences in the children's approach to AR treasure hunts as opposed to traditional hunts. To understand these differences on a quantitative level, we analysed the complexity of the developed games. The criteria were based on indications for creativity, such as preferring complexity over linear solutions, story over simple instructions, and sophisticated images over text-based one-liners [14, 20].

To understand the complexity, the level of sophistication, and story-driven content we analyzed the graph generated through each treasure hunt (see Figure 5 for an example).

We investigated the content of the treasure hunt such as the *number of stations and artifacts* (e.g., physical, digital, or GPS coordinate) as well as what kind of *content* was used (text and/or images, riddles, etc.). We also looked into how children created these pieces of content and which media (pen, paper, photo) they used. Note that in the AR version, content could also be created with pen and paper and then be integrated by taking a picture with MakeAR. This option was the dominant way of usage. We also investigated the *connectivity* between the stations (grouped into weak, strong, and recall link). The results are summarized in Table 1.

Number of stations and artifacts. The traditional group created 35 stations in total, each consisting of exactly one artifact: a hint to the next station (M=8.8, SD=1.7). The AR group created 21 stations (M=5.0, SD=1.2), consisting of 38 artifacts (M=9.5, SD=1.3). Of these artifacts, 14 were markers, 2 were GPS coordinates and 5 were physical objects, such as small drawings pinned to walls and texts reading: "winner!!!" or "Game over :-(Try again!".

Content. All but one artifact (total of 35) created by the traditional group focused on text. 11 of them contained riddles. 2 artifacts featured images, one of which contained only an image and no text.

In the AR group, 22 artifacts (total of 38) contained text (including one riddle) and 19 contained images. In total 3 of the 4 teams embedded all of their artifacts into a story. Note that these numbers do not add up to the previously stated 38 artifacts because some artifacts featured both text and imagery.

Connectivity. Finally, we looked at how the content of the stations was connected. We differentiate between "weak" and "strong" links, and define a weak link to be a simple directional instruction ("The next hint is at the large tree."). Strong links, on the other hand embed directional information into other elements, for example an overarching story ("You can hear someone scream. Its coming from the classroom 4A!"). Furthermore, links may reference previous artifacts.

Figure 8. Three markers children created for the digital treasure hunt.

In the traditional group, stations were connected through weak links exclusively. In contrast, the AR group strongly linked their artifacts (10) through stories. Overall, we found that in the traditional group, children utilized 31 weak links, whereas in the AR group, children built 4 weak, 10 strong, and 1 recall link (players had to recall an artifact from a former station).

Qualitative Findings

The qualitative analysis was based on a review of the treasure hunts themselves (game design, group interaction), the created artifacts (digital and physical), and observer notes. Additionally, we collected data via questionnaire and recorded videos during the game creation phase and final group discussions.

Game Design

In both evaluated groups, it was possible to design artifacts with text and images. We found that with two exceptions, members of the traditional group did not include imagery into their artifacts but almost exclusively used text (Figure 4–a and Figure 6). During the digital treasure hunt, half of the artifacts contained imagery (Figure 4–d and Figure 7). Children often took multiple attempts to draw markers for the sole reason of making them look good (Figure 8), as opposed to aiming for mere functionality. With the exception of a single drawing (a treasure chest on a "goal"-type artifact), traditional groups did not include any elements that would qualify as visual design.

Quantity of Artifacts versus Quality artifacts

We found that the AR group invested about 270 minutes in total to create 38 artifacts, amounting to 0.6 artifacts created per child per hour. In the traditional group, children created on average 0.9 artifacts per hour, hence being about 50% faster in content creation. Members of the AR group spent the additional time in the sophisticated design of the artifacts as well as in the structure of the games themselves. This is also reflected by the fact that one of the AR teams first sketched the story on a blackboard before implementing the treasure hunt (Figure 4–d). Also text-based artifacts originating in the AR treasure hunt group tended to be longer (more words and letters) and hold more information (Figure 7).

Even though every AR marker was treated as image by our system, text as content is similarly detected and makes a valid marker as well. Thus, the children could place text on an AR marker. These text-based markers were counted as 'text-based artifacts' for the purpose of this study. It was also possible to create an AR treasure hunt by using GPS coordinates instead of visual markers and therefore omitting imagery completely. However, the students did not create such AR treasure hunts.

Table 1. Quantitative results of the study. We compared the groups with regard to number of stations, artifacts and connections they created.

	Traditional Treasure Hunt	AR Treasure Hunt
Number of stations	35	21
Artifacts	35	28
Text	34 (97%)	22 (58%)
Image	2 (6%)	19 (50%)
Riddle	11 (32%)	1 (3%)
Connections		
weak	31	4
strong	0	10
recall	0	1
Artifacts created per h	0.9	0.6

One of the four traditional teams used a lot of textual riddles compared to the short and concise directional statements that dominated the other traditional groups' games.

Storytelling vs. Movement & Location

Three out of four AR teams focused on telling stories through their artifacts. This was reflected both through the artifact design as well as by the way in which the stations and also the artifacts within the stations were connected. The AR teams created stronger links: directional instructions were usually embedded into the story (Figure 7). In contrast, none of the traditional treasure hunt teams made an attempt to tell a story. They rather focused on the sequence of locations and created artifacts serving as direct pointers between the locations.

It is worth noting that one of the four AR teams chose to build a treasure hunt with little logical links, where the creation process was dominated by coming up with places to deposit artifacts. This shows that the children of the AR teams were aware of the possibility to create linear text-based treasure hunts, but in 75% chose to focus on storytelling.

Questionnaires

The children rated questions on 4-Point Likert items (Smiley-o-meter–1=totally agree; 4=totally disagree). When asked whether they enjoyed playing the other group's treasure hunt, the average rating for the traditional group was 2, whereas it was 1.8 on average for the AR group. There was a slight preference among children to create their own treasure hunts using AR (M=1.15) versus creating it traditionally (M=1.23).

Suggestions for Features and Improvement

In the open group discussions, the children suggested various features to improve 'MakeAR'. This included video function, speech recording, support for different levels of difficulty, time-based challenges, a VR simulation to play indoors in case of rainy or snowy weather, and the ability to stick artifacts to real objects out of reach, such as clouds or treetops.

When asked for improvements for the traditional concept, the children focused solely on error prevention. While playing, many children came across artifacts that didn't belong to the treasure hunt they were playing, got mixed up with other treasure hunts and thus ended up confused. To avoid this in the future, they suggested using text or colour to mark artifacts. Again, this shows that children were willing to instrumentalize properties of the clues that could otherwise be used for visual design to improve playability.

DISCUSSION

Our main focus was to observe the content creation process. The results suggest a slight preference of the AR groups to compose story-driven, image-based and complex treasure hunts. These are indicators for creative processes such as being able to do complex thinking, to go into varied directions and prefer unusual solutions over straightforward results [14]. This section highlights our conclusions drawn from our study.

The game complexity analysis shows that the AR treasure hunt group preferred a complex setting with many variables over strictly linear solutions. The game design findings reveal that the children focus on visual and aesthetical solutions instead of on plain and straightforward designs. This implies that marker and content design do qualify as what prior work describes as 'aesthetic experience', i.e. children focused on visual design, way beyond the 'utilitarian breakpoint' of getting working artifacts done [5, 17].

The questionnaire reveals a slight preference for creating over playing games. There can be multiple explanations (from technical issues to other children's games being not as satisfying as imagined) but one reason may be the new and pleasing experience of creating something digital themselves as opposed to using existing apps and media. This conclusion would be in line of thinking with media literacy concepts such as 'active media education' [13]. The group discussions displayed a wide imagination of the AR group towards additional features, other ideas, solutions, and room for improvement. This kind of thinking indicates a creative mind and could therefore be an implication for creative problem solving strategies [2, 14, 17].

The results show that using pen and paper seems to motivate children to quickly execute ideas and concepts (in this case, to create many stations). At the same time, less care was exercised regarding the design of each station or the overall game design. This approach can be useful in case prototyping with quick results are needed in early stages of a design process.

Children also employed a structured working process using the MakeAR application (sketching the story, thinking about and building artifacts, linking artifacts together, and blending them in the story). In the traditional setting, children switched back and forth between discussing possible locations and creating artifact which were then rather weakly linked. This could be an indication that AR settings support structured working.

Our results show that creating AR content influences the working atmosphere in a similar manner as when presenting content [10]. It positively influenced children's *motivation*, evokes positive emotions and is highly engaging. This is reflected by the high number and quality of the created artifacts and the positive attitude children showed during the study.

Finally, the high level of detail and the strong focus on stories hints at AR triggering self-initiated learning. Without the observers' or educators' input, the students used the method of a structured working process, attempted and discarded ideas in consensus with their team and managed to create games in the given time span by themselves. This type of thinking and acting benefits the children's development and learning abilities in an educational setting [2, 14, 21].

LIMITATIONS AND FUTURE WORK

We acknowledge several limitations of our work. Our study was conducted with a limited number of children and had a strong exploratory focus. As a result we only report descriptive statistics. We see our findings as first implications that point to interesting directions for future work. Follow-up work could pick up specific aspects and explore them in-depth using a thorough quantitative approach. Such an approach could take into account potential gender differences.

A second limitation is that some differences we observed between the two groups may not be a result of using AR only. For example, the 'MakeAR' software provides a scaffold for creating the treasure hunt, which may have supported the more structured process. Furthermore, prior work in art education indicates that using digital surfaces (such as tablets or PCs) invokes different types of visual interactions (for example, drawing, painting, staging) compared to working on the same task using paper and pens [15].

Interestingly, the AR groups mostly chose to create story-driven treasure hunts, even though this was not the given task. Furthermore, the 'MakeAR' app seems to foster image-based content and storylines. This should be investigated more closely, perhaps in comparison to other AR-creation tools.

Further scenarios (away from treasure hunts) need to be evaluated to obtain knowledge about creative processes through AR in different educational settings.

CONCLUSION

We explored how children handle a creative, complex, yet playful task that involves AR technology and compare it to a traditional pen and paper approach. We did so by, firstly, implementing an AR application for mobile devices that offers opportunities for children to enhance treasure hunts with AR elements. Secondly, we conducted a study involving school children aged 9-11 and asked them to create treasure hunts.

Findings from our qualitative analysis suggest that AR technology may indeed be used to complement educational settings that focus on qualitative outcomes by supporting creativity, self-initiated learning, and structured working processes of the children while at the same time creating a motivating and positive environment. We point to interesting aspects that should be subject to future investigations.

ACKNOWLEDGEMENTS

We thank the 23 children who participated in our user study for their constructive feedback, very reasonable criticism, and enthusiastic suggestions. We also thank Christian Römmelt from the Gänseliesel primary school as well as Grudrun Klinker, David Plecher and Thomas Steffelbauer of the Augmented Reality Group of TUM for their support.

REFERENCES

1. Jorge Bacca, Silvia Baldiris, Ramon Fabregat, Sabine Graf, and Kinshuk. 2014. Augmented Reality Trends in Education: A Systematic Review of Research and Applications. In *Edu. Tech. and Soc., 17 (4), 133-149.*

2. L.E. Berk. 2016. *Development Through the Lifespan*. Pearson Education.

3. Fadi Chehimi, Paul Coulton, and Reuben Edwards. 2007. Augmented reality 3d interactive advertisements on smartphones. In *International Conference on the Management of Mobile Business (ICMB'07)*. IEEE.

4. Rui Chen and Xiangyu Wang. 2008. An Empirical Study on Tangible Augmented Reality Learning Space for Design Skill Transfer. *Tsinghua Science & Technology* 13, Supplement 1 (2008), 13 – 18. DOI: http://dx.doi.org/10.1016/S1007-0214(08)70120-2

5. J. Dewey. 1934. *Art as Experience*. Balch.

6. Ben Dickson. September. How virtual reality is transforming the sports industry. Techcrunsh. (2016 September). https://techcrunch.com/2016/09/15/how-virtual-reality-is-transforming-the-sports-industry/.

7. Matt Dunleavy and Chris Dede. 2014. *Augmented Reality Teaching and Learning*. New York: Springer, Chapter Chapter 67: Augmented reality.

8. Matt Dunleavy, Chris Dede, and Rebecca Mitchell. 2009. Affordances and Limitations of Immersive Participatory Augmented Reality Simulations for Teaching and Learning. *Journal of Science Education and Technology* 18, 1 (2009), 7–22. DOI: http://dx.doi.org/10.1007/s10956-008-9119-1

9. Eduwells. 2013. Bring Schools to Life with Aurasma App. (2013). https://eduwells.com/2013/09/28/bring-schools-to-life-with-aurasma-app/ (last accessed 25.6.2016).

10. Olaug Eiksund. 2012. *Children's Interaction with Augmented Reality Storybooks - A human-computer interaction study*. Master's thesis. Department of Information Science and Media Studies, The University of Bergen.

11. Nicolás Gazcón and Silvia Castro. 2015. ARBS: An Interactive and Collaborative System for Augmented Reality Books. In *Proceedings of the Second International Conference on Augmented and Virtual Reality (AVR'15)*. Springer, Berlin, 89–108. DOI: http://dx.doi.org/10.1007/978-3-319-22888-4_8

12. Matt Hollowell. 2015. Aurasma For The Classroom. Prezi. (December 2015). https://prezi.com/wd4iz9dhiuak/aurasma-for-the-classroom/ (last accessed 25.6.2016).

13. J. Hüther and B. Schorb. 2010. *Grundbegriffe Medienpädagogik*. kopaed.

14. C. Kirchner and G. Peez. 2009. *Encouraging creativity in primary schools: work sheets, exercises, learning sequences and empirical findings*. Westermann.

15. Anja Mohr, Tina Kothe, and Heinrich Hussmann. 2016. DEMO: Web Application ArtEater. In *Proceedings of the The 15th International Conference on Interaction Design and Children (IDC '16)*. ACM, New York, NY, USA, 684–687. DOI: http://dx.doi.org/10.1145/2930674.2938614

16. N. Navab, A. Bani-Hashemi, and M. Mitschke. 1999. Merging Visible and Invisible: Two Camera-Augmented Mobile C-Arm (CAMC) Applications. In *Proceedings of the 2nd IEEE and ACM International Workshop on Augmented Reality (IWAR '99)*. IEEE Computer Society, Washington, DC, USA. http://dl.acm.org/citation.cfm?id=857202.858138

17. G. Peez. 2015. *Art Education in Germany*. Waxmann Verlag GmbH.

18. Iulian Radu. 2014. Augmented Reality in Education: A Meta-review and Cross-media Analysis. *Personal Ubiquitous Comput.* 18, 6 (Aug. 2014), 1533–1543. DOI: http://dx.doi.org/10.1007/s00779-013-0747-y

19. Janet C Read, SJ MacFarlane, and Chris Casey. 2002. Endurability, engagement and expectations: Measuring children's fun. In *Interaction design and children*, Vol. 2. Shaker Publishing Eindhoven, 1–23.

20. Elisa Rubegni and Monica Landoni. 2015. Supporting Creativity in Designing Story Authoring Tools. In *Proceedings of the 14th International Conference on Interaction Design and Children (IDC '15)*. ACM, New York, NY, USA, 287–290. DOI: http://dx.doi.org/10.1145/2771839.2771898

21. K. Seifert and R. Sutton. 2015. Contemporary Educational Psychology — Wikibooks, The Free Textbook Project. (2015). https://en.wikibooks.org/w/index.php?title=Contemporary_Educational_Psychology&oldid=2963820 (last accessed 20.09.2016).

22. Angela Di Serio, Maria Blanca Ibanez, and Carlos Delgado Kloos. 2013. Impact of an augmented reality system on students' motivation for a visual art course. *Computers & Education* 68 (2013), 586 – 596. DOI:http://dx.doi.org/10.1016/j.compedu.2012.03.002

23. Thomas Steffelbauer. 2016. Location Based Augmented Reality Game. Bachelor Thesis, TU München. (2016).

24. Elba del Carmen Valderrama Bahamóndez, Jonna Häkkilä, and Albrecht Schmidt. 2012. Towards Better UIs for Mobile Learning: Experiences in Using Mobile Phones As Multimedia Tools at Schools in Rural Panama. In *Proceedings of the 11th International Conference on Mobile and Ubiquitous Multimedia (MUM '12)*. ACM, New York, NY, USA, 4. DOI: http://dx.doi.org/10.1145/2406367.2406415

25. Elba del Carmen Valderrama Bahamóndez, Bastian Pfleging, Niels Henze, and Albrecht Schmidt. 2014. A Long-term Field Study on the Adoption of Smartphones by Children in Panama. In *Proceedings of the 16th International Conference on Human-computer Interaction with Mobile Devices & Services (MobileHCI '14)*. ACM, New York, NY, USA, 163–172. DOI: http://dx.doi.org/10.1145/2628363.2628403

26. Merel van der Vaart and Areti Damala. 2015. Through the loupe: visitor engagement with a primarily text-based handheld AR application. In *2015 Digital Heritage*, Vol. 2. IEEE, 565–572.

The KOROGARU Park Series: Three Features of the Park of the Future

Daiya Aida
Graduate School of Film and New Media, Tokyo University of the Arts
Yokohama, Japan.
daiyaaida@gmail.com

Kiyoshi Suganuma
Yamaguchi Center for Arts and Media[YCAM]
Yamaguchi, Japan
suga@ycam.jp

Kazuhiro Jo
YCAM / Faculty of Design, Kyushu University
Yamaguchi /Fukuoka, Japan
jo@jp.org

Abe Kazunao
Yamaguchi Center for Arts and Media[YCAM]
Yamaguchi, Japan
abepierre@ycam.jp

ABSTRACT

This paper reports the findings made during the operation of the KOROGARU Park series, a series of temporary park facilities featuring media technologies launched by the Yamaguchi Center for Arts and Media located in Yamaguchi, Japan between 2012 and 2016. The KOROGARU Park series has three common features: (1) Physical forms, (2) Media mechanisms, and (3) Social sprouts. In this paper, we examine the three features in detail, including description and analysis, for the complete series of five parks. While the examination, we intend to depict the potential of media technology in fostering social growth and learning in parks.

Author Keywords

Learning; education; children; playground; future park; media technology.

ACM Classification Keywords

K.3.1 [Computer Uses in Education]: Collaborative learning.

INTRODUCTION

This paper reports the findings observed during the process of operating the KOROGARU Park series, a series of temporary park facilities featuring media technology launched by the Yamaguchi Center for Arts and Media (YCAM] (http://ycam.jp) between 2012 and 2016. Through a group of specialists, InterLab, with advanced skill sets in programming, hardware design, circuit design, sounds, lighting, and other fields, YCAM has tapped local talent to support a movement among local residents aimed at the creation of a new culture in recent years. The KOROGARU Park series is a prominent example of this activity, which aims to play a pivotal role in giving children opportunities to develop their creativity. Furthermore, the KOROGARU Park series proposes a "park of the future," in which technology is embedded within the park itself [1]. As an extension of the idea by Papert [2], the KOROGARU Park series explores the relationship between children and media under the belief that children are capable of developing their own learning power through play and discovery in an environment surrounded by technology. We refer to the idea of Junk Playgrounds put forward by Sørensen [3] regarding the concept of freedom, rules, and the existence of play leaders [4], as well as the additional thought that sociality blossoms through media technology [5].In the KOROGARU Park series, we envision a world in which electronic objects coexist with outdoor elements such as soil, mud, ice, snow, stones, sticks, flowers, and leaves. In addition to Papert's "learning-by-making" concept, we attempted to implement not only objects but also rules and environments, that is, the society, as a form of parks. To date, the KOROGARU Park series has been launched five times in total and been implemented in various forms and styles. Further, cumulatively, 230,000 visitors have visited these parks to date.

IDC 2017, June 27–30, 2017, Stanford, CA, USA.

ACM ISBN 978-1-4503-4921-5/17/06...$15.00.
DOI: http://dx.doi.org/10.1145/3078072.3079738

BACKGROUND

Regarding the examination of the application of media technology to parks, our efforts were significantly influenced by the preceding works of many architects and artists, especially, Claude Parent, Shusaku Arakawa, and Isamu Noguchi. Claude Parent claims that the incorporation of large amounts of angled elements helps to restore humanity to architecture, and this is described in a criticism on the rectilinear forms of modern architecture [6]. With respect to the continuous changes occurring to the height of sight lines, we have observed how slopes and variegation in high and low elevations can promote human activity.

Artist Shusaku Arakawa, who worked with poet Madeline Gins, was responsible for creation of the Site of Reversible Destiny - Yoro, a park that depicts an unstable ground and sloping areas in all directions. From his work, we could learn about the use of complex senses including tactile feelings on the soles of the feet and palms of the hands, as well as the rest of the body, interpreting a space in a nonvisual manner [7].

Sculptor Isamu Noguchi was someone who actively took an interest in the design of parks. He keenly observed how children play in parks and the movements of their bodies [8]. In Noguchi's body of work and plans, we find an approach that is less about enjoying the visual forms of sculpture and more about allowing the user to realize the connection between these objects and the human body as one slides over and moves around the objects. In addition to examining the existing case studies in park construction [9], we observed actual play by children in neighboring parks, as well as the parks in major cities. We explored aspects like the functions of the ground in parks, methods of fostering fun in parks, activities of park users, and various considerations regarding the operation of the park and potential dangers. Consequently, we considered the three key features that are consistent throughout the KOROGARU Park series.

THREE FEATURES OF THE KOROGARU PARK SERIES

The KOROGARU Park series has three common features:

1. Physical forms
2. Media mechanisms
3. Social sprouts

Physical Forms

Physical forms refer to the ground and architectural objects with which children directly interact. The form of the ground, slopes, and other elements with which the children physically come into contact and the structure of the architectural space and its walls and ceilings all are decisive in forming a space where children will play. Based on the above case studies and observations, we arrived at the conclusion that the KOROGARU Park required a surface that was not uniformly flat. Rather than having individual objects of play distributed along a level surface, the entire park space would be on a slope, a structure that could support the activity therein. Therefore, the KOROGARU Park series makes ample use of inclines and slopes.

MEDIA MECHANISMS

The second feature of KOROGARU parks is the deliberate use of ubiquitous media mechanisms. Media mechanisms refer to electronic devices like light-emitting diode (LED) lights and speaker systems, as well as tools or items used for message transmission and notification such as voice projectors, pencils, and bulletin boards. By observing children, we learned that the existence of media for children is quite different from that for adults. For adults, media connects senders and recipients, similar to a mail system that connects individuals. However, when a young child uses twigs to poke various objects, it can be assumed that the child comes to know of the state of various objects through twigs and, on the other hand, they are confirming the function of twigs. Further, the child knows that it is possible to contact objects outside themselves using media such as twigs. Finally, the child discovers the possibility that there are people on the opposite side of the media, as well, through the play. Although it does not start with the purpose of "delivering messages to someone," it is touching the media in the order "messages have arrived to someone as a result." For children, the media is not arcane. It is a part of their everyday environment.

Social Sprouts

In this paper, we refer to social sprouts as prompts to cultivate an awareness of sociability. It encompasses "play leaders," "freedom and autonomy," and "a park created through the ideas of many," which loosely overlap in the context of children's play.

"Play leaders" are the adult personnel (i.e., the management staff) who work within KOROGARU parks, and they are allocated as 1 personnel for approximately every 20 children in the park. Their role is not limited to park surveillance alone. They act to stimulate creativity in children and foster a community of trust. The play leaders in the KOROGARU Park series have a similar role at the Junk Playground. Play leaders constantly consider what ways of approaching children would stimulate the latter's creativity and thought process, what forms of caution should be exercised when children engage in dangerous behavior so that the children themselves can apprehend the situation on their own terms, and so on. As children engage in new, unexplored forms of play, play leaders assist the enhancement of the thought process of the children and act as a type of "external memory" that retains knowledge of the rules of play. This role undergoes change commensurate to the changing play styles of children.

The provision of a sense of "freedom and autonomy" is a fundamental rule of the KOROGARU Park. Nevertheless, we clarified to the children that the provision of "freedom" does not mean that the park allows those forms of freedom that infringe on the freedom of others. In terms of autonomy, we describe herein the outcomes of the activities within the park and ways in which an awareness of autonomy emerges. By designing the KOROGARU Park series, we intended to situate a commons to explore the balance in the security with children. In this respect, the KOROGARU Park series posts notices at the entrance of the park stating that children "play at their own risk." iPads operated by staff at the entrance contain a prompt asking for consent to enter the park. After agreeing to the terms of use, children press a consent button. Although this system is rather unwieldy, the check-in process is deliberately retained in order to promote awareness of the ideas of freedom and safety. The process is clearly different from the notion of children "being allowed to" play at a park operated by another party. While there is constant friction and conflict between the children in the KOROGARU Park, the question of how to address such issues is likely to change based on the awareness of whom the park "belongs."

The concept of "a park created through the ideas of many" does not imply that the style of play in this park is a fixed one. In fact, the style is designed such that it allows people's ideas to flourish once they become familiar with the space. These parks have "idea sheets" and postboxes, where people can post comments on what they think an ideal park should be. The sheets are then collected and used at Kodomo Asobiba Meetings (Children's Playground Meetings). The Children's Playground Meetings are official workshops held by event organizers in order to promote new ideas among children, who are the users of the park. The meetings are attended by children, along with YCAM InterLab members. After checking the functionality of the park among all members and viewing the idea sheets, groups work to develop ideas and present them in front of all the attendees. InterLab quickly runs estimates of the technical issues and feasibility of proposed ideas and gives immediate feedback to the children on whether the ideas can be realized. Ultimately, InterLab members and the children create a plan together and implement it within three days of a meeting. Holding this workshop several times leads to the creation of new strategic elements, which gradually change the nature of play.

ABOUT THE KOROGARU PARK SERIES

Figure 1. From top left, the KOROGARU Park (2012), KOROGARU Pavilion (2013), KOROGARU Park in Nature (2014), KOROGARU Garden for LIL KIDS (2015), and KOROGARU Garden (2016).

The KOROGARU Park series was launched in 2012. It involves five parks that were developed over the years in different sites. (Figure 1) In this section, we describe each park in terms of the three features mentioned earlier: physical forms, media mechanisms, and social sprouts.

KOROGARU Park (2012)

Physical forms

The KOROGARU Park was established in 2012. It is a part of the glitchGROUND exhibition that showcased the YCAM educational project work and was installed in the Studio B galleries of YCAM from May 19 to August 12, 2012. This space has a curved floor like a skateboard park and contains a bowl-shaped area, a tunnel, a jumping platform, and so on. Children find the jumping platform and a huge sliding slope as high as 1,800 mm to be challenging physical objects. We designed the layout of the slope such that the landscape looks like a mountain range to a child.

Media mechanisms

The floor embeds 3 microphones and 16 speakers. The ceiling houses 20 full-color LED lights and 1 big balloon light, as well as 3 spotlights pinpointing the locations of the microphones. The lights and speaker sound are synchronized, creating a single unified scene. Digital audio plays in sync with the movements of light, as though the sound is hopping from speaker to speaker, with scenes including the use of field-recorded city and nature sounds. Each scene lasts about five minutes, and the scenes themselves are shown randomly. In addition, video camera footage captured from a point on the ceiling that spans the entire venue was shown through a monitor installed such that it was viewed through a small peephole on the floor of a tunnel. Children utilized this feature to play hide-and-seek and other games.

Social sprouts

The Children's Playground Meeting, a type of workshop mentioned earlier, was held thrice during the glitchGROUND exhibition in 2012. These meetings referred to idea sheets (selected from among 1000 or more similar sheets) posted by children. In the meetings, after confirming that children were aware of the various functions embedded in the park, the several dozen proposals contained within the sheets were distributed among the group of attendees, and discussions were conducted regarding the ideas that children would like to implement in the park. After the presentation and selection of various ideas, the finalized ideas were produced by YCAM InterLab after a three-day construction period, and these new functions were added to the park. For instance, while realizing the idea of wanting to "fly through the air" was impossible, replacing a part of the floorboards with acrylic could create the feeling of walking across the sky from a high point. All new ideas of what children would like to see implemented in the park were actively and dynamically encouraged, and the technical team strived hard to realize these ideas.

KOROGARU Pavilion (2013)

Physical forms

As part of the tenth-anniversary celebrations of the founding of YCAM, the KOROGARU Pavilion was constructed as two temporary cylinder-shaped structures from July 26 to December 1, 2013. The two buildings have truly opposing features. One has a central void structure at its tubular center, whereas the other houses a void on its outer perimeter. The two cylinders were built according to contrasting architectural principles, and visitors can enjoy the unusual architecture of this site and gain a greater understanding of the particularities of the buildings by comparing them. Since the pavilion has grid-like walls and is located semi-outdoors, visitors are directly exposed to the environment, including weather and rain, temperature, sunlight, and experiences that are completely different from the previous year's KOROGARU Park. This architectural concept was devised by Megumi Matsubara and Hiroi Ariyama of the architectural unit “assistant.” It is a successful example of naturally presenting an architectural experience to visitors in a physical manner.

Media mechanisms
The floor of the circular building is inclined in the shape of a bowl, allowing for activities like swiftly scaling the walls and sliding down. On the floor, computerized LED lights were embedded, shedding light in the horizontal, vertical, or random directions. Although no formal suggestion was provided, children invented creative games such as jumping over or chasing these lights similar to physical shapes. On the floor of the other building, the shape of local mountains copied from Google Earth was pasted in a three-dimensional context. There were various forms of slopes and one jungle gym. Hence, schoolchildren could not run around freely. However, it provided a safe and stable playing space for preschoolers.

Social sprouts
The KOROGARU Pavilion also held Children’s Playground Meetings and had several new additions, including a camera monitoring and microphone speaker system, wind fans embedded in the floor triggered by sound, and “treasure hunts” that made use of frottage stenciling. Since that period was as long as four months or longer, we observed an active development of the interaction among children. The children autonomously planned, organized, and hosted workshops and festivals using the media mechanism. For example, if they wanted to play a game of tag, they used the microphone system to assemble members by announcing, “We will be starting a game of tag, so please come to the mountain.” These interactions emerged spontaneously. Further, the children not only played with their existing acquaintances but also collaborated with other groups. The KOROGARU Pavilion was slated to be dismantled in December 2013; however, before that time, children started a petition aiming to extend the dismantling date. Over 1,000 signatures were collected and delivered to the mayor of Yamaguchi. As a result, the site was reopened on August 1, 2014.

KOROGARU Park in Nature (2014)
Physical forms
As part of the Sapporo International Art Festival, the KOROGARU Park was exhibited behind the Sapporo Records Office Special Hall from July 19 to September 28, 2014. This was the first attempt to launch the KOROGARU Park project in a location other than Yamaguchi. Since Yamaguchi and Sapporo are distant locations, a production team was created in Sapporo and a local team carried out the hardware design, planning, and installation of media elements, as well as the operation of the facility. To this end, we communicated closely with the teams to develop the concept of and expertise in operating the park. As long as these ideas were followed, we left the resolution of specific issues to the local staff.

Media mechanisms
For construction, lumber from Hokkaido was used and new attempts at different construction techniques were undertaken. The ladder-shaped structure found in mountain bike downhill racing was used to create slopes and banks, resulting in a surface where children could run about. Admission to the park was restricted to children between the first and sixth years of elementary school, allowing the obviation of safety concerns for infants and creating a more challenging and free structure than the earlier parks. The structure was constructed entirely outdoors and without a roof. Hence, due to the outdoor exposure, the media elements that could be used were limited. Instead, analog tricks were extensively used in place of digital technology.

Social sprouts
We successfully obtained the support of a local organization that conducts camp activities for children, and it helped with the operation of the park. A team consisting of local part-time staff was formed, and its members were thoroughly instructed about the concept of the park.

KOROGARU Garden for LIL KIDS (2015)
Physical forms
The KOROGARU Garden for LIL KIDS was an indoor park launched by Isetan, a major Japanese department store, as a special program from April 29 to May 3, 2015 (encompassing Japan’s long public holiday). Recently, Isetan has been focusing on providing services to customers that offer “experiential and educational” hospitality within the retail experience. As part of this initiative, the KOROGARU Garden for LIL KIDS was launched as a paid event park. The hardware design of the park was handled by the architecture unit "assistant." The required media tools were developed by YCAM InterLab. Many young visitors, including toddlers and infants, attended this event. Rather than emphasizing a complex and undulating surface, the floor has a simple block structure, with the spaces in between the blocks acting as passages in mazes. We also successfully created a concept whereby all the objects form a single slope to create a unified view when seen from a distance.

Media mechanisms
With respect to media mechanisms, the edges of each block were embedded with LED strips synchronized with other processes to produce light. Each block also contained microcomputers and speakers, allowing the input and output of voice audio. The detection of specific vibrations affected the output of sound and light, creating an interaction whereby children’s actions had an effect on the space in its entirety.

Social sprouts
Since the event was held only for a short time, no Children’s Playground Meetings were held. In addition, since payment was required for entry to the venue, the event was held only for a short period, and most visitors were between the ages of three and five years, the children

did not autonomously form any organized community. Rather, they largely interacted and played with the hardware and media elements. Play leaders also focused on safety and particularly on avoiding any accidents.

KOROGARU Garden (2016)

Physical forms

The KOROGARU Garden is an indoor garden that utilizes a large, newly designed slope; a foyer area and deck; several ladders; and other major updates to the underlying design, in addition to having the block units used for the 2015 version. It was held from June 18 to September 4, 2016. The facility was designed by the architecture unit "assistant" as a continuation from the previous year's construction. The blocks, which were originally designed for preschool children, were repurposed for the Yamaguchi event since it focused on schoolchildren. The venue consists of a foyer area that makes use of natural light and Studio B, a site that uses controlled lighting and does not incorporate natural light. This design allows visitors to compare their experiences in the different venues.

Media mechanisms

In addition to the LED lights embedded in the floor, there were other media elements in the venue such as laser projectors responding to volume, moving lights, and a large projected footage. On July 10 and August 14, Children's Playground Meetings were held. Children together with the hardware elements of the plaything also invented software such as new rules and how to play at the same time without distinction.

Social sprouts

Since the children themselves were already familiar with the KOROGARU series' concept, we created a volunteer structure early on that involved "child personnel," whereby we attempted to foster autonomous functionality. The child personnel consulted with the adult staff and used their own decision-making capabilities to perform roles that they autonomously and actively chose to hold. These included a range of functions necessary for the enjoyment and use of the facility: making announcements in the park, cleaning up activities, repairs and other maintenance activities, providing support for newcomers, planning new workshops, and so on.

OBSERVATIONS

In this paper, we analyze the entirety of the KOROGARU Park series through the lens of the three features introduced earlier.

Physical Forms

A unique feature of the KOROGARU Park series is the way in which the design of the entire space is unified through an integrated architectural vocabulary that exists on a meta level separate from the individual play elements. For the 2012 KOROGARU Park, the layout is highly suggestive of a mountain range forming a single slope that, on ascension, reveals another, higher precipice. Since 2013, we have been working with the architectural unit "assistant," embedding concepts into the architectural structures themselves, such as through the use of void spaces, reversible layouts, spaces in which the signature KOROGARU Garden slope cuts across an area and a labyrinth exists beneath it, and more. Although it might be an exaggeration to say that the children immediately understood these concepts, they could develop memories about the contrast between light and shadow and the conduction of wind by playing at the sites on a daily basis. Hence, they experienced something akin to an "architectural experience."

Media Mechanisms

As described earlier, we consider here how children apprehend "media." In terms of considering media as an ordinary object, one of its archetypes is the LED lights embedded on the floor of the large, pestle-shaped inclined bank found in KOROGARU Pavilion. These LED lights toggled every five minutes in a cycle of a changing horizontal color relative to the slope, a changing vertical color, and a random pulsation/flashing effect. For example, when the horizontal color changed, children "chased" the light or played jump rope with the oncoming light. According to the changes in vertical light, children followed the light up or slid down the slope. As children discovered the means of play within the environment, they played and interacted with the space. The consideration whether these were electronic elements is immaterial. Adults tend to envision the technology behind these concepts and refer to objects as "high-tech" or reflecting a particular intent of the creator. However, for children, we observed that similar to how a slope is a formation that naturally invites activities such as climbing or sliding, an LED is merely an ordinary object that invites different forms of play. In another case, we found that once the children learnt that microphones and speakers can be used to convey their voice, they used these devices for playing. While adults understand the major premise that communication tools imply a receiving party, children do not necessarily bring this knowledge to the table. Instead, as they begin to use media as an extension of their own bodies, they suddenly start interacting with others who are distant and later arrive at the discovery that this process produces a downstream message. In this manner, they make discoveries while playing. Ultimately, this evolved into a petition movement to extend the destabilization dates of the venue. In effect, children naturally learned to select the most effective forms of media suited to their needs.

Social sprouts

Here, we examine social sprouts, as well as its three components, "play leaders," "freedom and autonomy," and "a park created through the ideas of many."

Play leaders

The staff employed as part-time workers were called "play leaders," and their actions influenced children in different ways, including safety management. They were trained to repeatedly consider the best methods of deepening their understanding of what actions children perform while playing with media and tools and how to handle fights and conflicts between children. Play leaders also functioned as a medium to propagate play rules and ideas invented by children. Gradually, the children discovered that the propagation of ideas gives rise to new ideas.

Freedom and autonomy

At the KOROGARU Park series, once they consent to the premise of playing at "one's own risk and discretion," visitors find a space for free play. At the same time, a "free space" is not unlimited in scope. By observing children, we understood that they discover by themselves how this expansive freedom at times impinges on the freedom of others and how the scope of freedom changes slightly over the course of this friction. Ideally, children will develop an awareness of autonomy and consider how they will manage the park themselves. The sense of autonomy developed at the KOROGARU Garden provides a series of experiences that act as the precursor to this understanding. Sometimes, as part of play, children receive special items or toys, such as brooms or megaphones, from play leaders and are encouraged to use them. These items slightly boost the confidence of children since they feel that they have been given a special role. Once they become aware of their affiliation and the operation of the facility, children will consider the stance of others and imagine how they can distribute rights and responsibilities among themselves. It is interesting that this process autonomously emerged over the course of play. Ethics and morals are not something simply handed down. Thus, children learned that consideration and concern for others is extremely important if one wants to enjoy a pleasant time with others.

A park created through the ideas of many

For long-term projects such as the KOROGARU Pavilion and KOROGARU Garden, a range of ideas and applications for creating better spaces have emerged. For example, workshops were organized in order to foster play among people outside one's immediate group of friends. They also communicated with others through microphones/speakers, picked up acorns, pretended to play "shop," and engaged in other forms of play requiring other parties. While these tools initially acted as extensions of the body, they gradually evolved into the means of forming ties with others. We believe that these acts are reflections of an awareness that one's own activity in a space is inseparable from the presence of others and the existence of the space itself.

DISCUSSION & FUTURE WORK

The KOROGARU Park series can be described as a large experimental project, a Petri dish in which the seeds of media technology and communication are cultivated through the synergistic relationship among architecture, environment, and children's lives. These elements form complex interrelationships, suggesting a new form of "simulation" of nature and society befitting the current media age.

The unique abilities of YCAM and InterLab, which are poised to realize immediately the ideas of children, form the technological basis of this project. Furthermore, play leaders have a key role in respecting the creativity of children and watching over them. The viewpoint of media technology as one aspect of our environment is in some ways antithetical to the notion of "learning" about technology in an educational context. Furthermore, media technology education does not necessarily create a type of technology "nerd" who possesses any specific knowledge; this project suggests the potential of media technology in fostering social growth and learning, through collaboration and public awareness. In addition, the above interrelationships do not have explicit dominant/subordinate relationships; instead, they are intertwined in complex ways and influence children in an expansive, rhizomatic fashion. Throughout the course of play, elements such as the body, media, and sociability ebb and flow, supporting the physical and emotional growth of children from the inside out. These elements have such a complex relationship that it is not possible to elucidate them in their entirety in this paper. For this purpose, continued research and observation are required. In other words, efforts to produce parks while actively observing children's growth and engaging in this process over the long term and through various vectors will likely help one to obtain a deeper level of understanding of the associated processes. This will require ongoing support and enthusiasm, as well as financial backup and schemes for sharing the required expertise. We hope that this paper serves as the first step in that direction.

REFERENCES

1. Mark Weiser. 1991. The computer for the 21st century. *Sci. Am* 265.3: 94-104.
2. Seymour Papert. 1980. *Mindstorms: Children, Computers, and Powerful Ideas*. Basic Books, Inc., New York, NY.
3. Carl T. Sørensen. 1951. Junk playgrounds. *Danish Outlook* 4(1), 311-316.
4. Baroness Marjory Gill A. Allen. 1968. *Planning for Play*. Thames and Hudson, London, United Kingdom.
5. Lawrence Lessig. 2002. *The Future of Ideas: The Fate of the Commons in a Connected World*. Random House, New York, NY.
6. Claude Parent. 1970. Vivre à l'oblique. L'Aventure Urbaine.
7. Madeline Gins and Shusaku Arakawa. 2002. *Architectural Body*. University of Alabama Press, Tuscaloosa, AL.
8. Isamu Noguchi. 1967. *A Sculptor's World*. Thames and Hudson, London, United Kingdom.
9. Joe Frost. 2012. Evolution of American playgrounds. *Scholarpedia* 7(12), 30423.

Drawn into Science Through Authentic Virtual Practice

Janet L. Kolodner
The Concord Consortium
Concord, MA
jkolodner@concord.org

Tamer Said
Harvard University
Cambridge, MA
tamer_said@mail.harvard.edu

Kenneth Wright
Medford Public Schools
Medford, MA
kenneth.wright@gmail.com

Amy Pallant
The Concord Consortium
Concord, MA
apallant@concord.org

ABSTRACT

Under what conditions do students engaged with a virtual world come away with enhanced appreciation for science, wonderment about the world, and nascent understanding of science practice? Other researchers have shown that virtual worlds and games can foster such development and highlight design characteristics that elicit engagement, motivation, and learning. Our study examines what contributes to the changed interests and dispositions of learners as they engage with such worlds. Such understanding, analyzed over a diverse array of students learning in a variety of virtual worlds, is a prerequisite for developing design guidelines for drawing in students no matter the resources, interests, and attitudes they bring and help them learn and develop.

Author Keywords

virtual worlds; science education; games for learning; motivation; engagement; learning; development; interest

ACM Classification Keywords

H.5.m: Information interfaces and presentation; H5.1: Multimedia Information Systems (animations, virtual reality); K.3.1: Computer Uses in Education; K.8: Personal Computing (games).

INTRODUCTION

> *Like, I'm not gonna lie. The game gave me ideas, like, next time I go to the beach or something. ... Like, to actually, like, get trying to see how far under water I can go to see what it looks like. And also gave me, like, to scoop a little bit of water from the beach and like, test it out and see like what happened and all that. -- Andre[1], 6th grader*

Two weeks after completing a science unit using EcoMUVE [7 - 9, 16], a 3-D virtual world that recreates the ecological setting of a pond, students in two sixth-grade classes continued to be interested in why the fish in the pond had died off. Andre tells us that the experience affected him deeply; he was ready to be a scientist after his experience, surprising even himself.

We seek to explain why students in the classes we observed came away with enhanced appreciation for science as an enterprise that begets questions, a sense of wonderment, and a nascent understanding of what scientific work entails. We present and analyze three case studies: pairs of students who began their activities in the virtual world with different interests, experiences, attitudes, and beliefs about science. All became excited about both explaining why the fish died off and the enterprise of science. The case studies illustrate several ways the virtual world drew students in (*entryways*) and sustained their engagement (*trajectories*) so that they began to position themselves confidently as doers of science. We extract lessons from the case studies that have potential to inform both the design of virtual worlds for science education and the design and enactment of curriculum units that use such worlds as resources.

We drew from a variety of research traditions to understand what led to these results. The quoted statement exemplifies a sense of intrinsic motivation. We sought to understand how that arose for each of our focal learners. Ryan and collaborators [10, 11] suggest that intrinsic motivation within the context of a game comes from a sense of competence, feelings of autonomy, and relatedness to others. Shaffer and Resnick [12] suggest four types of authenticity that should be built into a learning experience: personal connection and disciplinary, real-world, and assessment authenticity. Barab and collaborators' [1, 2, 3] notion of "transformative play" suggests that designers can make this happen so that players become protagonists who get to use their knowledge and skills to achieve challenges and make their own choices. Shaffer [12] provides guidelines about how to design *epistemic games* that encourage scientific reasoning by supporting learners as they take on the practices of disciplinary experts. Gee [6] explores the power that virtual worlds have to "meld learning and identity" (p. 199), asking us to pay attention to the ways the virtual world supports the identities learners bring to their engagement, those they ascribe to the avatar representing them in the game, and other identities they take on as they are engaging.

These perspectives all share the notion that for learning to occur, students must be drawn in, given the chance to make their own choices, and be supported in any of the ways they might choose to engage. Our use of the terms *entryways* and *trajectories* arose out of our analysis of the cases and the literature cited above. *Entryways* refers to the ways students are drawn into the activities of the environment, while *trajectories* refers to what they do that leads to their development as science doers and knowers.

IDC '17, June 27-30, 2017, Stanford, CA, USA

ACM ISBN 978-1-4503-4921-5/17/06...$15.00
http://dx.doi.org/10.1145/3078072.3079751

Researchers cited above and others have highlighted combinations of design characteristics that tend to elicit engagement, motivation, and learning. EcoMUVE is designed with such findings in mind [7 - 9]. This paper examines something different: what contributes to the changed attitudes, interests, and dispositions of individuals in their variety and uniqueness. Our analysis is intended to be a contribution toward developing guidelines for designing virtual worlds for science learning that draw in learners and keep them engaged no matter the resources, attitudes, and interests they bring to the experience.

We address two sets of questions:

1. What entryways and trajectories allowed students with a variety of starting points to come to value scientific reasoning, develop interest in science, and interact with the world as scientists do?
2. What do these answers suggest about the design of virtual worlds for learning science?

We answer the first question in our case studies. We answer the second through a synthesis across the case studies.

SETTING THE STAGE

The Virtual World

EcoMUVE was designed to "allow students to learn science by exploring and solving problems in realistic environments" [16]. It has the look and feel of a videogame (Fig. 1) and was designed as a resource for learning the science of ecosystems and a context for learning to make causal explanations [7, 8].

Central to EcoMUVE is a 3-D virtual world that closely resembles a real-world pond ecosystem. The ecosystem includes the pond, the natural area around it, and a golf course and housing development a bit farther away. Learners navigate by using keyboard arrows that guide an avatar as it "walks around" the environment. The avatar can walk underwater or on land, allowing it to see the flora and fauna and pond and weather conditions. Students can also enter a submarine to explore microscopic organisms in the pond. They collect data over a seven-week virtual time period—late June through mid-August. They can choose from among 8 dates on a calendar to make observations and collect data. Early in the seven-week period, lawns are fertilized, and it rains. Weather, water conditions, and populations of organisms fluctuate after that, and the large fish in the pond die at the end of July. Late in July and in August, students encounter scientists in the environment who are trying to figure out what caused the fish to die and provide hints about what to pay attention to. They encounter other people (e.g., a park ranger, a landscaper) on other dates who provide hints about what is happening in the ecosystem (e.g., the landscaper talks about fertilizing the lawns). EcoMUVE includes a variety of data collection and information tools: a field guide with information about the flora and fauna in the environment, a chart for recording data, and a graph visualization panel for data analysis.

The curriculum that goes with EcoMUVE suggests sequencing of activities and scaffolding that will result in students gaining understanding of ecosystems and causal patterns as they explain why the fish died off.

The setting

Our investigation took place in two 6th grade classes at a charter school in Boston, MA. The school is focused on closing the achievement gap for minority students. The school is almost 100% African-American, Latino, and mixed-race; 72% of students receive free or reduced lunches; the teacher-student ratio is about 1 to 3.

The teaching approach at the school is quite structured: teachers present, ask questions and take 1 or 2 answers, and then move on. Students do short reflective activities at the beginning of each class, and homework has them reflect on and synthesize what they did in class or prepare for the next day. The school day is longer than is typical, and students have opportunities to meet with teachers outside of class.

The enacted curriculum

Students were introduced to EcoMUVE as the culminating activity of a 6-week unit on ecosystems, designed by the teachers to take advantage of the availability of EcoMUVE. Four weeks were spent covering food webs and energy transfer, biotic and abiotic factors, and ecology processes. Then, for 2 weeks, students worked in pairs around a shared computer. The first 5 days of EcoMUVE use were devoted to open-ended exploration, encounter with their mission (to explain why the large fish died off), using an embedded field guide to generate ecosystem food webs, and collecting and analyzing data consistent with the role of being a water chemist, naturalist, microscopic specialist, or private investigator. On Day 6, students practiced recognizing causal relationships. They read a story about introducing cats to Borneo to quell the rat problem and then diagrammed the causal connections. From the end of Day 6 through Day 8, students worked on solving the challenge. On Day 9, they prepared to present, and on Day 10, they presented their explanations. Throughout, the teacher brought students together for short periods to illustrate how to find patterns in graphs and how to use the science they had previously covered to explain those patterns.

Data collection and analysis

The two classes we observed were each taught by a different teacher and had about 30 students. We received parental permission to video and interview 19 students (9 pairs and one individual) across the two classes. During the initial 4 weeks of the unit, we each observed 1 or 2 days in the two classes to familiarize ourselves with teachers' practices and conventions. While students were using EcoMUVE, at least two of us were in the classrooms each day. We also observed the unit review, where the teachers presented a complete explanation of why the fish died.

We collected four types of data: teacher-prepared materials, including lesson plans and worksheets; observational data;

homework; and interview data. Our observational data derives from a variety of sources: (i) a fixed camera aimed at the teacher during instruction and full-class discussions and aimed at one pair of students in each class during group work on most days, (ii) additional voice recordings for those two groups, (iii) a roving camera used to sample the activities of pairs we had permission to record, (iv) Screencast-O-Matic recordings of pairs' activities in the virtual world and their conversations, and (v) field notes. We aimed our eyes and the roving camera on groups that were particularly engaged in examining the virtual world or in animated discussion.

We conducted two interviews each with student pairs two and three weeks after the unit was complete. In the first interview, we asked questions aimed at capturing students' feelings about their experience (e.g., what they enjoyed, didn't enjoy, found challenging, and were proud of). We asked for a tour of EcoMUVE, aiming to find out what in the environment was most interesting and memorable for them. We also asked about their experiences with video games and what they would do if they could redesign EcoMUVE or the way it was used. In the second interview, we asked a series of data analysis and "what-if" questions.

We analyzed the data associated with five pairs of students, chosen because we had significant classroom data and because they were forthcoming in their interviews. We extracted and connected data that would allow us to identify their pathways to excited engagement (entryways and trajectories). We analyzed data from the first interview to identify students' identities and interests and how those changed over time. We examined classroom data to identify circumstances that affected students' continued engagement, motivation, and. conditions that led to that eagerness to engage in scientific practice.

RESULTS: OUR CASE STUDIES

Looking across the five case studies, we identified many interesting similarities.

1. All students were eager to engage with the virtual world.
2. All pairs enjoyed accomplishing a mission. They were surprised that science could be fun, felt empowered by the challenge, took ownership over solving it, and were proud of their accomplishments.
3. Students all came to like EcoMUVE's graphs, and they valued resources embedded in the virtual world.
4. Students were grateful for a sense of autonomy. All experienced surprise, awe, and wonder. All remembered particular issues they had grappled with, what they found to be challenging, disappointing, or fun, and what awed them or made them wonder.
5. All expressed appreciation of the realism in the 3-D world and the experience of immersion.
6. Students all appreciated EcoMUVE's information resources, including the field guide and people they encountered. Many appreciated the tools. The authentic purposes the tools served made students feel that they had what they needed for success.

In the cases we present (3 of the 5 due to space), we highlight the different ways students experienced EcoMUVE with the intention of illustrating the wide variety of starting points, and trajectories of those in a typical class.

Case 1: Amber and Deana

Amber and Deana were both already interested in science when they encountered EcoMUVE, and Amber was concerned with the health of the oceans. From the beginning, this pair systematically moved around the EcoMUVE terrain noticing and recording weather conditions on different days, reading about organisms, and generating questions and recording data, even before they knew the fish had died and what their mission was.

When the teacher presented the challenge and their role as water chemists, they looked in the field guide to learn more about the fish that had died and then started collecting population data on those fish. They systematically observed, asked questions, and collected data in support of answering those questions. After noticing a rainy day, for example, they became curious about how that affected the water and collected water measurements for that day. EcoMUVE supported their initial dispositions to engage as scientists and provided fertile ground for them to continue that engagement. They particularly enjoyed reasoning with graphs and found such activity in EcoMUVE to be more purposeful and compelling than the graph reasoning they did in math.

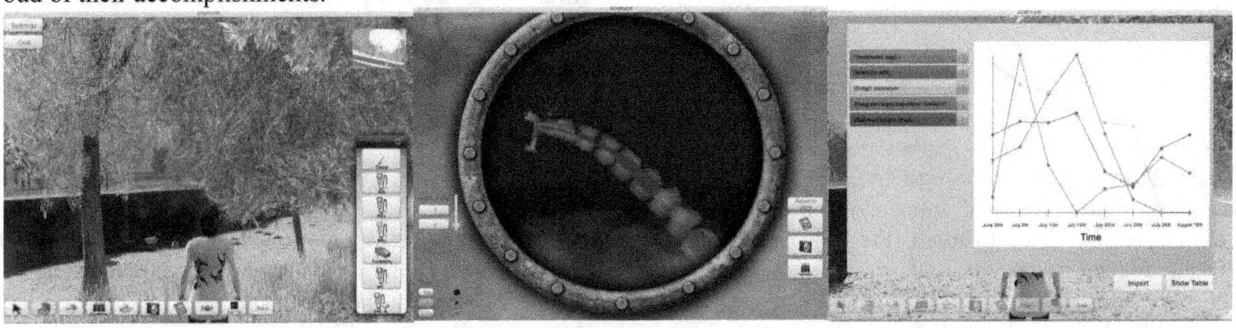

Figure 1. Scenes from EcoMUVE: the pond and tools for data collection, a scene from the submarine, the graphing tool. Image: From EcoMUVE. Used by permission.

This pair brought remarkable initiative to their activity. They were persistent in pursuit of their own hypotheses and collecting data to support them. They persevered even when their lack of science knowledge frustrated them. In the end, they reported to the class that the fish died because herons ate them, pointing out that the heron population increased suddenly. They remained open to other explanations, however, and were still ruminating on the teacher's explanation at interview time. They reported surprise at the role of human intervention (the fertilizer from the lawns leached into the pond after the rain) and were amazed that ordinary human actions could cause so much damage.

As they were re-explaining what had happened to the fish, this pair showed an ability to reason about how multiple factors interact and make things happen over time: "...So if there is less blue green algae, there is less dissolved oxygen, and there is more bacteria and less fish and less herons because all of these are connected, and whatever eats blue green algae also decreases..." They also imagined processes and outcomes that extend beyond EcoMUVE's timespan.

They reported, as well, that although they had not gotten to the correct conclusion, they were proud of the reasoning they did, understanding that pinpointing the cause of the fish's deaths was hard. They reported liking the support that EcoMUVE offered them as scientists, particularly the tools that were available for measurement, and they suggested other measurement tools they would have liked, e.g., for measuring "water pollution in the pond."

Case 2: Asher and Renata

Asher and Renata both think about themselves as problem solvers and mystery lovers, and Renata is a fan of Sherlock Holmes. During the two role-playing days, this pair was assigned the role of naturalists. Their assignment was to learn about the different animal species in the ecosystem, check population changes over time, and identify factors that might explain changes to each population. They began by collecting population data for different organisms. They used the submarine to take "photos" of microorganisms they encountered, and they used the field guide to learn about unfamiliar ones. They were detail-oriented, recording data in paper notebooks even though the software automatically saved these data for them.

After analyzing the first interview, we realized that they were approaching the challenge as they imagined detectives would; they could not leave any clue unexamined. Their mode seems very close to *bricolage* [14]. *Bricoleurs* negotiate with the materials through arranging, rearranging, and associating the pieces and connecting one piece to the other until it makes sense to them (the "aha moment" for detectives). Indeed, they told us that they viewed the challenge as "puzzle pieces ... every time I got a different clue, I was, like, how can I put all the pieces together."

Asher and Renata were interested in how quickly the ecosystem became unbalanced. Renata was "fascinated by how the populations were all the way up and they just went down so fast. ... One day a perfectly balanced ecosystem, and the next all the fish was gone." Asher was amazed by the "speed of things" and how something so distant (the fertilizer) combined with something so normal (a rainstorm) could cause so much damage.

Though they had engaged as detectives, by the time of the first interview, this pair was thinking about themselves as scientists: "It felt very realistic with all the data and made me feel like a real scientist." Indeed, this pair's scientific reasoning during the interview was remarkably developed compared to their discourse in the classroom. In the interview, they described the interconnected nature of an ecosystem. " ... We can see that a very small change in data can really affect the ecosystem, so since it rained, therefore it was like a cycle, but a process, because it rained then it rushed the fertilizer into the pond, then the nutrients went up, and the algae."

They told us that after they heard the teacher's explanation, they looked up information about fertilizer and sought to better understand the science that would allow them to make connections. Thus, during the interview, they used knowledge they had not used in the classroom.

It seems that Asher and Renata transitioned from thinking about their activity as detective work to thinking about it as scientific inquiry sometime between becoming fascinated by the steep decline of the fish population and the first interview. Their amazement at the fast demise of the fish led to their continued curiosity about why the fish died off and their want to understand it. When they began to understand what happened to the fish, they realized that their detective work was helping them reason about a natural phenomenon, and they connected detective work and scientific work. EcoMUVE seems to have provided them the opportunity to approach the challenge as detectives, even while it supported them with an epistemic frame [12] focused on scientific reasoning and gaining scientific understanding.

Case 3: Andre and Amara

Andre, who we introduced above, is generally uninterested in school and science but adept at video games; his partner Amara is a conscientious and grade-conscious student who makes it a point to learn whatever is required. During the first interview, Andre described the many things he observed in EcoMUVE and was delighted that it was so realistic. During class, his interest tended to be on navigating around EcoMUVE. As is typical with experienced gamers, he liked pushing the limits of the virtual world. He reported that he had liked chasing animals and submerging in the submarine, and he was fascinated by the "worms" he saw at high magnification.

During our observations, Andre seldom spoke up or volunteered to share his ideas. He gave little indication that he was interested in science, and he spent little time in class on scientific reasoning. He did, however, have significant experience on beaches and in oceans and was familiar with birds and other animals that live in beach environments.

While Amara was a diligent student who regularly completed written work and was often called on by the teacher to share ideas with her classmates, in the interview, she reflected on EcoMUVE as being a different and more satisfying way to do science, in contrast to what is usual in science class: "... it's usually on like a teacher telling you, write it down. Keep it in your notes and that's how you learn. I've never learned science in a really fun way. But, it, science is overall fun for me, but it doesn't come in fun ways to me [in school]." She particularly enjoyed interactions with characters in the virtual world and the chance to be playful (e.g., chasing virtual herons).

Each also got different things from the experience. For Andre, it was wonderment about water environments, so strong that he developed ideas about what he might do next time he was at the beach. He was full of wonder about the differences between ocean shores in the Boston area (murky), and in the Caribbean (clear), and he expressed amazement that water can look so clear but have so much microscopic life in it. He expressed a novel understanding of the role of hard work in science: "I think, like with science, ... when you see something that's challenging, ... it can get you frustrated, but at the same time, you just laugh at it because it's pushing you to think harder and harder about what you have to do." There is a remarkable similarity between this sentiment with respect to science and the sentiment of many gamers with respect to the satisfaction of overcoming a challenge [6]. For Andre, science, like game playing, became fun because it was challenging. Andre also showed off to us a newfound interest in making arguments based on evidence. In the second interview, he participated as much as Amara in science discourse, and he used the graphing tool to point out the relation between nutrients and algae growth and then attempted an explanation, the first time we saw Andre produce a spontaneous argument in any of our observations.

Amara expressed surprise and delight at the end that science could entail making choices and doing things without being told precisely what to do at every moment. When asked about what she was most proud of, she answered, "I felt like I was like an expert ..., finding information on those things. It was cool to go up to the class and present ... All the hard work and information that we were just adding and building up. It was ... really cool."

We know less about Andre's and Amara's trajectories towards these results than we know about the other pairs, but what we know offers some clues. On Day 8, the class learned that their grades would depend on the presentations they made. Amara became quite alarmed. Andre had participated very little until then, and Amara had thought that she could do the presentation herself. Andre seemed to step up after that. After the presentation that his peers appreciated, he felt pride. For Andre, it is plausible that EcoMUVE allowed him to experience science as a game-like challenge. When he had to participate in the presentation, he felt accomplished and then was ready to engage as a scientist: first in listening to the teacher's explanation, then remembering his own experiences in water environments, wondering about the species in those environments, and making a plan to investigate those.

IMPLICATIONS FOR DESIGN AND ENACTMENT

The case studies illustrate entryways and trajectories to scientific practice and interest (our first question). Analysis and elaboration across the case studies allows us to suggest design implications (second question).

Looking across the cases, we see a variety of entryways into scientific practice. Amber and Deana entered ready to engage as scientists; Asher and Renata entered as problem solvers and detectives; Andre entered as a gamer; and Amara entered as a diligent student. EcoMUVE's challenge was compelling for five of them. For Andre, the environment itself was compelling.

Of the six students, only two were ready to engage as scientists from the start, though all were engaging with us as scientists and expressing genuine interest in science by the time we interviewed them. For Asher and Renata, the system (and the teacher's relatively hands-off approach) allowed them the latitude to explore and gather clues in the sequence they chose, and the graphing tool allowed them to display variables in relation to each other as they wanted. The system supported their approach as *bricoleurs*.

For Amara, getting a good grade was motivating enough. She went about planfully exploring the environment, collecting data, reasoning around graphs, and bringing in what she knew to create an explanation, aiming to complete the assignment well. In the end, however, she had a new appreciation of what science is and what scientists do.

Andre had more trouble engaging in explanation activities and was often off-task, though early on, while "in" the submarine, he was amazed by the microscopic organisms. It was only when he knew that he had to be a team player that he became engaged in scientific reasoning.

Amber and Deana began wanting to engage as scientists, and were further drawn in when they discovered that graphs were useful for making explanations. Although getting to an explanation was quite hard, they felt competent to continue when they recognized the way scientists use mathematical skills as they do their work.

We've extracted out several affordances of the environment that invite learners to engage.

- Identity entryways: These correspond to the ways students think about who they are, e.g., gamers, scientists, detectives. These entryways seemed most impactful early on making students comfortable in the environment.

- Interest entryways: Deana's interest in oceans and Andre's in water bodies and the fish that live in them seemed to make them more appreciative of science and interested in engaging in the world as scientists.
- Competency entryways: Feelings of competency are important to sustaining intrinsic motivation [11]. When students were surprised or delighted by their competence, their engagement changed, as seen with Andre (when his classmates liked his explanation) and Amara and Deana (when they discovered that reasoning around graphs was so useful for scientific explanation).

As for design implications, EcoMUVE and its enactment offered a variety of supports that made learners comfortable and encouraged them to remain engaged:

- Disposition supports: EcoMUVE supported the dispositions that Turkle and Papert [14] discuss: dispositions to be systematic and planful *and* to pull puzzle pieces together (*bricolage*). It also supported dispositions. As a gamer, Andre could explore the environment. As detectives, Asher and Renata could collect clues. As scientists, Amara and Deana could make use of the measurement and graphing tools.
- Autonomy supports: Students felt empowered because they had some autonomy in coming up with solutions, and the software provided multiple tools to support them.
- Social supports: Several students reported that interacting with people in the environment was motivating for them. They liked getting advice from the people, and they wanted more people to interact with. They liked getting hints from people who played different roles in the virtual world -- park ranger, environmental scientist, caretaker.
- Affect-inspiring supports: Nearly all the students expressed considerable amazement, surprise, and/or fascination with something they encountered or found out: complex phenomena or interesting creatures, the surprise of the fish suddenly dying out, the murkiness of the heretofore clear water. Emotion-inducing experiences resulted from the realism of EcoMUVE coupled with the teacher's encouragement to explore. Each student had a chance to come across something personally fascinating.
- Competence supports: Feelings of competence are important to intrinsic motivation and encourage future engagement [11]. EcoMUVE supports competence by providing a low threshold for participation along with easy-to-use information resources and tools that support reasoning. Regular whole class discussions furthered feelings of competence by making information and strategies available to everyone and allowing students to recognize and be recognized for what they could contribute to others.

Shaffer's and Resnick's [13] dimensions of "*thick authenticity*" for sustaining engagement provide us with a framing for the roles of all these different these many entryways and supports. Personal connection came through the ease of being themselves as they entered the environment, whether students thought of themselves as gamers, detectives, or scientists. Personal connection was further supported by students being able to set their own sub-goals [6] in ways that corresponded to their ways of coming to know or figuring out solutions to the challenge. The ease of navigating the world and interacting with the system as scientists also seemed to add to students' interest in the world and to personal connections, as did their feelings of being present in the ecosystem. Ryan et al. [11] report that feelings of presence are more engaging than feelings of looking in from the outside, and ease of use of a system also contributes to such feelings.

Disciplinary and real-world authenticity were implemented, as Shaffer and Resnick suggest, through the problem students were working on, the roles they took on, the realism of the virtual world, and the tools, resources, and representations they had available.

CLOSING THOUGHTS

Our intention in this analysis has been to contribute to collective knowledge about interaction design for children in two ways: (i) better understanding the variety of starting points, dispositions and ways of knowing that students bring to their experiences and the ways they have been successfully supported, and (ii) offering ideas towards the development of guidelines or conjectures for designing virtual worlds for science education and other disciplines.

Software designed for classroom use must draw in the full range of students in a class. Designing for such diversity requires appreciation of the variety of interests and capabilities of the learners we are designing for and the variations in what will draw them in and sustain their engagement. Such understanding, carried out over a diverse array of students learning in the context of a variety of virtual worlds, is a prerequisite for developing design guidelines for drawing in students no matter the resources, interests, and attitudes they bring. Our analysis of EcoMUVE use allowed us to identify "hot cognition" [15] aspects of designing for engagement and sustained interest that the designers of EcoMUVE tacitly considered while designing but that have not shown up in their descriptions of its design. Additional such analyses will need to be done to derive a more complete set of design conjectures.

Other challenges remain. For example, where is the sweet spot in balancing autonomy with needs for reflection so that students develop sophisticated understanding along with excited engagement? The answer to that question is also essential to designing the best virtual worlds and challenges for fostering learning, interest, and engagement.

ACKNOWLEDGMENTS

We thank Tina Grotzer for helping us find schools for our observations and the entire EcoMUVE team for introducing EcoMUVE to us and to the teachers and for valuable discussions about EcoMUVE. Our project is funded by NSF (#1550902). The opinions and deficiencies are ours.

REFERENCES

1. Barab, S. A., Gresalfi, M. S., & Ingram-Goble, A. (2010). Transformational play: using games to position person, content, and context. *Educational Researcher*, 39(7), 525–536.
2. Barab, S., Pettyjohn, P., Gresalfi, M., Volk, C., & Solomou, B. (2012). Game-based curriculum and transformational play: Designing to meaningfully position person, content, and context. *Computers & Education,* 58(2012), 518- 533.
3. Barab, S. A., Sadler, T. D., Heiselt, C., Hickey, D., & Zuiker, S. (2007). Relating Narrative, Inquiry, and Inscriptions: Supporting Consequential Play. *Journal of Science Education and Technology,* 16(1), 59-82.
4. Deci, E. L., & Ryan, R. M. (1985). *Intrinsic motivation and self-determination in human behavior.* NY: Plenum.
5. Deci, E. L., & Ryan, R. M. (2000). The "what" and "why" of goal pursuits: Human needs and the self-determination of behavior. *Psych Inquiry*, 11, 227–268.
6. Gee, J. P. (2003). *What video games have to teach us about learning and literacy*. NY: Palgrave Macmillan.
7. Grotzer, T.A., Powell, M. Kamarainen, A.K., Courter, C., Tutwiler, M.S., Metcalf, S. & Dede, C. (2014). Turning transfer inside out: The affordances of virtual worlds and mobile devices in real world contexts for teaching about causality across time and distance in ecosystems. *Technology, Knowledge, and Learning,* 19(3).
8. Kamarainen, A., Metcalf, S., Grotzer, T., & Dede, C.J. (2015). Exploring ecosystems from the inside: How immersion in a multi-user virtual environment supports epistemologically grounded practices in ecosystem science instruction. *J Sci Ed and Tech,* 24(2), 148–167.
9. Metcalf, S.J., Chen, J.A., Kamarainen, A.M., Frumin, K.M., Vickrey, T.L., Grotzer, T.A., Dede, C.J. (2014). Shifts in student motivation during usage of a Multi-User Virtual Environment for ecosystem science. *International J of Virtual and Personal Learning Environments*. 5 (4).
10. Ryan, R. M., & Deci, E. L. (2000). Self-determination theory and the facilitation of intrinsic motivation, social development, and well-being. *Am Psychologist*, 55, 68–78.
11. Ryan, R. M., Rigby, C. S. & Przybylski, A. (2006). The Motivational Pull of Video Games: A Self-Determination Theory Approach. *Motiv Emot*, 30:347–363.
12. Shaffer, D. W. (2009). *How computer games help children learn.* NY: Palgrave Macmillan.
13. Shaffer, D. W. & Resnick, M. (1999). "Thick" authenticity: new media and authentic learning. *Journal of Interactive Learning Research*, 10(2), 195-215.
14. Turkle, S. & Papert, S. (1992). Epistemological Pluralism and the Revaluation of the Concrete. *Journal of Mathematical Behavior*, 11(1), 3-33.
15. Zajonc, R. B., (1980). Feeling and thinking: Preferences need no inferences. *American Psychologist*, 35(2), 151-175.
16. http://ecolearn.gse.harvard.edu/ecoMUVE/overview.php

Exploring and Evaluating Sound for Helping Children Self-Regulate with a Brain-Computer Application

Elgin-Skye McLaren
School of Interactive Arts and Technology (SIAT)
Simon Fraser University
Surrey, B.C., Canada V3T 0A3
emclaren@sfu.ca

Alissa N. Antle
School of Interactive Arts and Technology (SIAT)
Simon Fraser University
Surrey, B.C., Canada V3T 0A3
aantle@sfu.ca

IDC '17, June 27-30, 2017, Stanford, CA, USA

ACM ISBN 978-1-4503-4921-5/17/06.
http://dx.doi.org/10.1145/3078072.3084299

Abstract
Children in North America are more likely to suffer from attentional challenges than any other mental health issue. Studies suggest that neurofeedback treatments may be useful for helping these children learn to self-regulate. Applying neurofeedback treatments in real-world, school settings poses a challenge, however, as these environments are often noisy and filled with distractions. The addition of ambient audio to neurofeedback systems may help reduce these disruptions. Further, research suggests that certain auditory treatments, such as binaural beats and white noise, may improve children's focus and aid memory recall. In the following paper we present the theories supporting this idea as well as a mixed methods framework for evaluating whether sound can help children focus while learning to self-regulate using a neurofeedback system. Specifically, we wish to investigate whether these treatments may help children (1) achieve an attentive state sooner and (2) maintain an attentive state for longer, when compared to the same system without sound.

Author Keywords
Sound; neurofeedback; ADHD; brain-computer interfacing; children; design.

ACM Classification Keywords
H.5.2. Information interfaces and presentation: User Interfaces –*Evaluation/methodology; interaction styles.*

Introduction
Children in North America are more likely to suffer from attentional challenges than any other mental health issue [3]. These challenges are often associated with persistent, negative impacts on learning and self-esteem. Interventions can be particularly beneficial at a young age, when children's cognitive and emotional faculties are developing; however, school support programs often lack resources. And while pharmacological alternatives can be effective, a less invasive strategy is to teach children self-regulating techniques such as deep breathing and meditation. Research suggests that neurofeedback based treatments can be helpful in the acquisition of self-regulation skills [5,6,9].

Applying these treatments in real-world, school settings poses a challenge, however. Neurofeedback is the process of using a brain-computer interface to practice control over one's brain activity. Primary schools are noisy and filled with distractions. To effectively learn to control their brain state, children must focus inward. This can be difficult amidst unpredictable external disturbances, particularly for children with attentional issues. Encouragingly, background music and sounds have been shown to improve focus, support learning, and elicit strong affective responses in listeners; however, very little is known about the effect of sound within neurofeedback systems. Specifically, there has been little research into the use of ambient sound – i.e. constant, low-level background audio – in neurofeedback systems as a way to reduce distractions and improve focus during treatment.

Many neurofeedback studies feature auditory cues as a form of user feedback. For example, Gruzelier et al. use a system with ocean sounds that become louder/softer as the user's brain state changes [5]; Vernon et al. use a system that identifies when a user enters a particular brain state with an auditory tone [16]. In this paper, we alternatively propose the use of sound treatments not as a form of feedback, but rather as an environmental control and auditory stimulus.

There is evidence to suggest that certain types of sounds, in particular, may help children improve their attention and memory: binaural beats and white noise [8,13]. These sounds not only minimize environmental distractions, but may also stimulate brain entrainment – a synchronization of brain waves to external stimuli [10] – in ways that are helpful for focus. We do not yet know whether incorporating these types of sounds into a neurofeedback system can help children (1) achieve an attentive state sooner and (2) maintain an attentive state for a longer period of time, when compared to using the same system without sound.

This paper offers two contributions. First, we offer a review of binaural beats and white noise, detailing how each type of sound could help neurofeedback processes. Second, we present a rigorous mixed methods approach to evaluate whether binaural beats and white noise can help children focus while learning to self-regulate using an existing neurofeedback system. This paper describes work-in-progress, and concludes with details on future plans to assess the framework.

Figure 1. Child performing neurofeedback training with the Mind-Full system.

Figure 2. Illustrated diagram of Mind-Full system.

Theoretical Framework

Neurofeedback

Neurofeedback training is typically done using a form of operant conditioning in which users are provided with visual or audio feedback to indicate changes in their brain activity. This allows users to observe otherwise imperceptible brain waves. Certain frequencies of brain waves, such as those within the "alpha" and "beta" ranges, are often associated with states such as relaxation and attention, respectively[1]. Research shows that with practice individuals can learn to manipulate these frequencies [16]. In so doing, they may reduce anxiety and improve attentional ability.

Until recently, neurofeedback training was only possible in laboratory settings due to the complex nature of the equipment. However, the development of affordable electroencephalogram (EEG) headset technology allows for widespread application of these treatments in classroom environments [1]. There is ongoing debate about the effectiveness of neurofeedback, owing largely to the lack of controlled studies in the field [14]. However, there is sufficient evidence that leads us to believe that further exploration is warranted.

Binaural Beats

First documented by Gerald Oster in 1973, binaural beats are described as an auditory illusion. Users experience the illusion by listening to two tones with slightly different frequencies through headphones [8]. Listeners report sensing a pulsing modulation of volume, or beats. Binaural beats have been associated with "frequency-follow" response, also known as brain entrainment. This occurs when auditory tones at one frequency stimulate brain activity at a related frequency [11]. Research by Lane et al., and Beauchene et al. suggests that this stimulation can improve listeners' sustained attention and memory [2,8]. To our knowledge, binaural beats have only been included in a single neurofeedback study [15]. And while a null result was observed, the researchers note that participants were only exposed to binaural beats for one minute at a time. This is likely not long enough to elicit entrainment effects.

White Noise

White noise is an auditory signal perceived as a monotonous hissing sound. It is generated by producing a tone using all frequencies at equal intensity at once. Evidence suggests that ambient white noise can improve the attention of children with attention deficit hyperactivity disorder (ADHD) on performance and verbal tasks [4,13]. Children with ADHD are uniquely sensitive to external stimuli: low levels of stimulation produce low levels of brain arousal. Many children compensate for low brain arousal through hyperactive and off-task behavior. Söderlund et al. argue that the presence of white noise increases brain arousal, thereby improving focus and cognitive performance [13]. These positive effects are not seen in children without attentional difficulties. Although white noise has been used as a form of feedback in previous neurofeedback systems [7], to our knowledge no studies have looked at the use of *ambient* white noise to improve focus during treatment.

System and Sound Design

In the proposed study we incorporate audio treatments into an existing portable neurofeedback system, Mind-Full [1]. This brain computer interface uses a single sensor NeuroSky Mindwave Mobile EEG headset paired with a tablet device to measure children's brain activity and provide real-time visual feedback. In the game, an animation begins when brain activity reaches a desired threshold (e.g. birds take flight when the headset measures a defined level of attention-related brain waves). If this brain state is maintained, the user earns game tokens. Mind-Full has been studied in several contexts, including a North American school in an urban center, and an urban Asian setting. The system has shown to be usable and effective in quiet environments within 18-24 sessions for most children. Results suggest that children who practice self-regulation using Mind-Full learn to apply these skills outside of the context of using the system. There is currently no audio in Mind-Full.

Prior to the study, we will hold a short series of exploratory sessions to choose specific sounds for the system. Using a within-subjects design we will work with 4 children, ages 11-13, to assess 3 examples of binaural beats and white noise in a single session. We have chosen to work with older children, rather than their younger counterparts, because they are more mature and may provide better feedback. They remain similar enough in age, however, that they will have similar hearing capabilities. Based on the work of Lane et al. and Beauchene et al. the binaural beats will be within the 15-25 Hz frequency range [2,8]. Based on the work of Söderlund et al., the white noise will be continuous and include the frequency spectrum above 1000 Hz [13].

Measures of assessment will include surveys and guided interview questions. Sounds will be rated based on the following criteria: they must have the appropriate volume (i.e. audible, not too loud); pitch (i.e. not distracting); and timbre (i.e. pleasant sounding). Those rated most highly will be incorporated into the Mind-Full system. We will also use this opportunity to compare several types of headphones to ensure comfort while using the NeuroSky Mindwave Mobile headset.

Evaluation Methodology

This work builds on research into the use of personal neurofeedback systems to help children learn to self-regulate. We propose evaluating the effect of auditory treatments through a within-subjects, quasi-experimental study in which we investigate the relationship between sound and children's attention. We expect that when children are exposed to binaural beats or white noise, they will (1) reach a predefined attention threshold sooner, and (2) maintain an attentive brain state for longer than when compared with using the same system without sound.

This mixed methods study will include 12 participants, ages 6-8, from a school in a North American urban center. Teachers will identify potential participants based on their (high) risk status for attentional challenges such as ADHD. The study will comprise of seven 10-minute long neurofeedback sessions spread over three weeks. During the first session, participants will learn how to use the system. Subsequent sessions will involve practicing neurofeedback with auditory treatments applied (IV: silence, binaural beats, and white noise). Each treatment will be used for two consecutive sessions. The order of treatments will be counterbalanced over 6 groups.

Objective measures of attention will consist of brain wave data as measured by the headset. Specifically, we will look at how long it takes participants to achieve a predefined attention threshold, and how much time participants spend above the threshold each session. Subjective measures of attention will be observational data; researchers will note when participants appear distracted, and in what way. We are unable to use teacher and parental surveys to measure improvements in participants' attention levels because lasting change and transfer outside of the system typically takes 15-20 sessions. Prior to each session, researchers will consult participants to ask how they are feeling that day; this may help explain any unusual performance.

Following the study, we will analyze the data using descriptive and inferential statistics. If significant differences are observed between groups, we may attribute these changes to the auditory treatments applied. By observing both binaural beats and white noise, we will be able to better understand whether these *specific types* of sound can improve participant's attention while using a neurofeedback system, or whether sound, *more generally* has an impact.

Discussion and Future Work

The modern primary school is crowded, loud, and busy – far from the experimental ideal. Understanding the conditions under which sound influences neurofeedback training requires a clear and systematic methodology. From an interaction design perspective, researchers who work with children would benefit from principled and evidence-based criteria for selecting and implementing specific auditory treatments. This paper outlines tools for exploring and evaluating the use of ambient sounds in neurofeedback systems – specifically, binaural beats and white noise. The contribution of this paper is therefore to improve our understanding how sound influences neurofeedback training among children with attentional challenges.

Research on neurofeedback systems is often limited by its reliance on subjective measures and lack of control conditions. We address this in our work by referring to both objective and subjective measures of attention. This study does not feature a dedicated control group; instead, we counterbalance our treatments. This lets us compare the effects of two different types of sound, relative to silence. This methodology was chosen because of sample size requirements and the important within-subject differences that often exist among members of this population.

This work represents an exploratory study and was designed to remain within the scope of a master's project. If the results are promising, we propose running a follow-up study to test the reliability and validity of the proposed framework. We recommend performing a controlled experiment using a larger sample size, and a randomly selected control group.

References

1. Alissa N. Antle, Leslie Chesick, Aaron Levisohn, Srilekha Kirshnamachari Sridharan, and Perry Tan. 2015. Using Neurofeedback to Teach Self-regulation to Children Living in Poverty. *Proceedings of the 14th International Conference on Interaction Design and Children*, ACM, 119–128.
2. Christine Beauchene, Nicole Abaid, Rosalyn Moran, Rachel A. Diana, and Alexander Leonessa. 2016. The Effect of Binaural Beats on Visuospatial Working Memory and Cortical Connectivity. *PLOS ONE* 11, 11: e0166630.

3. Marie-Christine Brault and Éric Lacourse. 2012. Prevalence of Prescribed Attention-Deficit Hyperactivity Disorder Medications and Diagnosis Among Canadian Preschoolers and School-Age Children: 1994-2007. *Canadian Journal of Psychiatry* 57, 2: 93–101.

4. Andrew Cook, Sharon Bradley-Johnson, and C. Merle Johnson. 2014. Effects of white noise on off-task behavior and academic responding for children with ADHD. *Journal of Applied Behavior Analysis* 47, 1: 160–164.

5. J. H. Gruzelier, M. Foks, T. Steffert, M. J. -L. Chen, and T. Ros. 2014. Beneficial outcome from EEG-neurofeedback on creative music performance, attention and well-being in school children. *Biological Psychology* 95: 86–95.

6. Hartmut Heinrich, Holger Gevensleben, and Ute Strehl. 2007. Annotation: Neurofeedback – train your brain to train behaviour. *Journal of Child Psychology and Psychiatry* 48, 1: 3–16.

7. I. N. Konareva. 2005. Modifications of the EEG frequency pattern in humans related to a single neurofeedback session. *Neurophysiology* 37, 5–6: 388–395.

8. James D Lane, Stefan J Kasian, Justine E Owens, and Gail R Marsh. 1998. Binaural Auditory Beats Affect Vigilance Performance and Mood. *Physiology & Behavior* 63, 2: 249–252.

9. Joel F. Lubar, Michie Odle Swartwood, Jeffery N. Swartwood, and Phyllis H. O'Donnell. 1995. Evaluation of the effectiveness of EEG neurofeedback training for ADHD in a clinical setting as measured by changes in T.O.V.A. scores, behavioral ratings, and WISC-R performance. *Biofeedback and Self-regulation* 20, 1: 83–99.

10. Jon A. Frederick M. S. Ph.D, Joel F. Lubar Ph.D, Howard W. Rasey Ph.D, Sheryl A. Brim Ph.D, and Jared Blackburn B. A. MD. 1999. Effects of 18.5 Hz Auditory and Visual Stimulation on EEG Amplitude at the Vertex. *Journal of Neurotherapy* 3, 3–4: 23–28.

11. Susan A. Reedijk, Anne Bolders, and Bernhard Hommel. 2013. The impact of binaural beats on creativity. *Frontiers in Human Neuroscience* 7.

12. D. W. F. Schwarz and P. Taylor. 2005. Human auditory steady state responses to binaural and monaural beats. *Clinical Neurophysiology* 116, 3: 658–668.

13. Göran Söderlund, Sverker Sikström, and Andrew Smart. 2007. Listen to the noise: noise is beneficial for cognitive performance in ADHD. *Journal of Child Psychology and Psychiatry* 48, 8: 840–847.

14. Robert T. Thibault, Michael Lifshitz, and Amir Raz. 2016. The self-regulating brain and neurofeedback: Experimental science and clinical promise. *Cortex* 74: 247–261.

15. D. Vernon, G. Peryer, J. Louch, and M. Shaw. 2014. Tracking EEG changes in response to alpha and beta binaural beats. *International Journal of Psychophysiology* 93, 1: 134–139.

16. David Vernon, Tobias Egner, Nick Cooper, et al. 2003. The effect of training distinct neurofeedback protocols on aspects of cognitive performance. *International Journal of Psychophysiology* 47, 1: 75–85.

Children's Views on Identification and Intention Communication of Self-driving Vehicles

Vicky Charisi
University of Twente
Enschede, the Netherlands
v.charisi@utwente.nl

Azra Habibovic
RISE Viktoria
Gothenburg, Sweden
azra.habibovic@ri.se

Jonas Andersson
RISE Viktoria
Gothenburg, Sweden
jonas.andersson@ri.se

Jamy Li
University of Twente
Enschede, the Netherlands
j.j.li@utwente.nl

Vanessa Evers
University of Twetne
Enschede, the Netherlands
v.evers@utwente.nl

IDC '17, June 27-30, 2017, Stanford, CA, USA ACM ISBN 978-1-4503-4921-5/17/06.
http://dx.doi.org/10.1145/3078072.3084300

Abstract

One of the major reasons behind traffic accidents is misinterpretation among road users. Self-driving vehicles are expected to reduce these accidents, given that they are designed with all road users in mind. Recently, research on the design of vehicle-pedestrian communication has emerged, but to our knowledge, there is no research published that investigates the design of interfaces for intent communication towards child pedestrians. This paper reports the initial steps towards the examination of children's views and understandings about the appearance and intention communication of self-driving vehicles. It adopts a design inclusive methodological approach for the development of a prototype for the communication of two basic intentions: "I am going to stop" and "I am going to proceed". The initial results indicate children's need to be aware about the autonomy of the vehicle and the use of their previous experience with traffic signs for the interpretation of communicative signs of the vehicle.

Figure 1: Materials for the focus group session with children

Author Keywords
Self-driving vehicles; child pedestrians; intention communication; interface design; inclusive design research.

ACM Classification Keywords
H.5.2 Information interfaces and presentation: user interfaces (D.2.2, H.1.2, I.3.6) Subjects: Interaction Styles; H.1.2 User/Machine Systems: Human Factors

Introduction
Children are one of our most vulnerable categories of road users. The World Health Organization (WHO) estimates that about 500 children die in accidents with motorized road vehicles each day, and that nearly two thirds of these fatalities occur outside the vehicle [17]. Child pedestrians' vulnerability stems from two key factors: (i) their physical vulnerability (they are small and are still developing physically), and, (ii) their functional vulnerability, which refers to their stages of cognitive and perceptual development, with many skills that are considered essential for safe traffic participation not fully developed until young adulthood [12]. In particular, child pedestrian safety is of concern during middle childhood when children venture farther from home, but have not yet fully developed cognitive skills needed to negotiate pedestrian environments (e.g., [1]).

Automated vehicles (AVs) that assume either partial or full authority from vehicle drivers are one of the currently most promising countermeasures being developed. Eliminating the "driver error" is expected to improve general traffic safety. However, to facilitate benefits for child pedestrians, such vehicles need to be designed with children in mind. That is, the design of AVs needs to ensure that children can easily detect, perceive and interpret intentions and actions of such vehicles, and that the risk of miscommunication between them is eliminated.

Recently, research on the design of vehicle-pedestrian communication has emerged (e.g., [3,6,9]), however the idionscratic nature of child-pedestrian might need different approaches and design principles to ensure sematically valid intent communication towards children. Since, to our knowledge, there is no research published that investigates the design of interfaces for intent communication towards child pedestrians, this topic is addressed in the study reported in this paper.

Related Work
Vehicle-pedestrian communication

Pedestrians interact with vehicles by interpreting vehicle-centric cues (e.g., velocity) and driver-centric cues (e.g., eye contact) [15]. Recent studies suggest that the introduction of AVs in the urban context may lead to a notable change on how pedestrians experience AVs compared to today's vehicles [3,8,9,14]. With the transfer of control from the driver to the vehicle, pedestrians will not be able to rely on driver-centric cues anymore. This could, in turn, lead to misinterpretation of AVs' intent and increase the risk of unpleasant encounters and accidents.

Design solutions for intent communication

To aid communication between AVs and pedestrians, communication solutions featuring external vehicle interfaces with primary visual cues have been suggested. A biomimetic interface for automated vehicles called AEVITA has been suggested that uses light, sound and mechanical actuators [13]. Researchers from Sweden suggested an interface concept called AVIP that informs pedestrians about

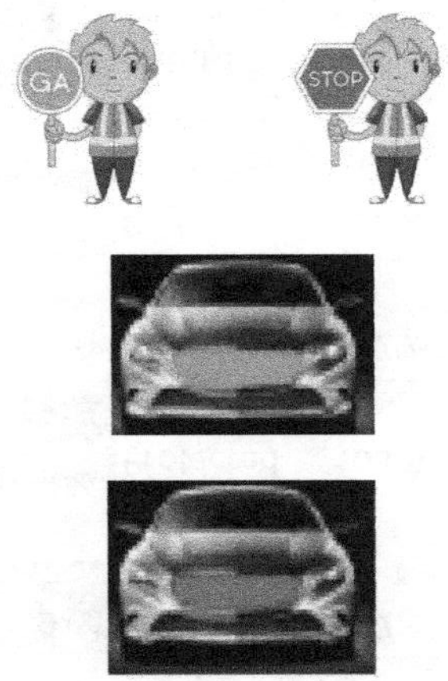

Figure 2: Pictures for intention communication examined with the interactive questionnaire

- Emulate human hand
- Emulate eye contact
- Projections on the ground
- Front window display
- Display in the grill
- Wearable warning device
- Audible warnings
- Pulsating icons

Table 1: Results from the brainstorming

vehicle's intentions via a LED-list on the windshield without explicitly inviting pedestrians to act [6]. Mercedes demonstrated a concept vehicle that projects a zebra crossing in front of the pedestrian and issues auditory signal to cross the road [10], while Nissan messages in the front windshield such as "after you" [11]. Google uses a flashing stop sign on the door of an AV to inform pedestrians not to cross the street and sound signals that mimic characteristics of conventional vehicles to alert pedestrians about their presence [5]. All these interfaces feature different modalities and appearances, but little is known about which interfaces are most legible to children.

Children's construction of mental models

One of the basic prerequisites in designing new interactive technologies for children is the use of their existing mental models as a basis for the construction of meaningful metaphors that support the underlying functionality of technology. Successful interface metaphors should draw on children's previous experiences in order to establish connotations that allow them to predict the results of their action in advance [16]. Previous research (e.g., [4]) indicates the necessity of including children in the design process at each stage of development, as a design partner, tester or user and iterate based on their feedback.

Current Work

This paper presents a design-based study of the development of a prototype and the extraction of preliminary design principles for the intention communication of an AV towards child pedestrians. The aim is to examine the impact of certain modalities on the legibility and interpretation of signals by children aged 7-10 years old, which may have an influence on children's safety and the social acceptance of AVs in urban environments. Therefore, open research questions (RQ) are as follows:

RQ1: What components in behavior and appearance do children use to identify autonomous vehicles?

RQ2: Which form factor of visual intention communication do children most consistently understand?

We focus on two traffic situations: (i) the vehicle intends to stop and let the pedestrian cross the road, (ii) The vehicle intends to continue moving and warns the pedestrian to stop. We assume humans inside the vehicle do not communicate with child pedestrians.

Method

The RQ are addressed by exploring children's views. Due of its exploratory nature, we apply a design inclusive research methodological approach that considers a dual manifestation of the design: as a process for a product development and as a research means [7].

Participants

Children aged 7 to 10 years were selected as children at this age start walk to school without close supervision. In total, 41 children participated. We gained the approval from one of the author's university department ethical committee and informed consent from participants' parents/carers.

Development of the prototype

To answer the research question RQ1, two sessions were designed: (1) a brainstorming with adults for the

Signal	Description	Correctly decoded
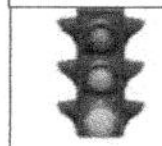	Green light	90%
	Walking figure	67%
	Red light	100%
	Stop sign	100%
	Light signals on car	90%
	"Child-walk" signal	100%
	Green flickering lights	67 %
	Projected zebra cross.	63 %
	"Child-stop" signal	97%
	Red flickering lights	93%
	Anthro. animation	40%
	Red projected zebra cross.	87%

Table 2: Results from the questionnaire (n=30)

aggregation of existing knowledge, identification of the problem, definition of goals and generation of solutions, and (2) a focus group and a drawing session with children, for the specification of the design criteria that define children's perceptions aiming to address the first research question of this study.

Brainstorming

To construct a theoretical platform, we drew on the existing research and on the results of a brainstorming session. This included a set of design goals and possible solutions which were translated in detailed sub-solutions (e.g., animated signs, projected crosswalk etc.) and then categorized as visual, audio or tactile (see Table 1).

Focus Group and Drawing Session

We organized a focus group and drawing session with 11 children aged 7 to 10 years. Probe questions and interactive materials (Figure 1) were used to ensure children's understanding of the concept of self-driving vehicles. Children's drawings were used as a means to reveal how children perceive and interpret concepts [2]. The analysis of the drawings and the conversations revealed that the main modality used to identify an autonomous vehicle is visual. The features they used included displays, projections, cameras, visible sensors and sound systems. Interestingly, 6 children mentioned visual features that relate to the recognition that the vehicle is automated (e.g., visible cameras on the top of the vehicle).

In sum, the results from the focus group session indicate that children most commonly use visual cues in the vehicle apperance to identify wheather the vehicle is autonomous or not.

Survey

This study aimed to address the second research question (RQ2). That is, it examined children's current knowledge and perceptions on the use of new visual signs for the communication of the stop / go strategies. We developed a survey consisting of an interactive questionnaire and a video study (Figure 2). These were inspired by the results from the focus groups and drawing sessions (Table 1). In total, 30 children took part, 12 boys (9.92y, SD=0.29) and 18 girls (9.89y, SD=0.47).

Questionnaire

The questionnaire consisted of 19 items, which were discplayed on personal computers. For each question, the children had to choose between two options: The human figure / the vehicle will Stop or Go. Three adult facilitators were present and provide procedural clarifications if needed. The results shown in Table 2 imply that children are familiar with existing go/stop signals and interpret them correctly. The new signals that were inspired by existing signals were also easily recognizable. However, in the case of an anthropomorphic animation, the results did not show consistency. We conducted a binomial logistic regression on the number of successful and unsuccessful interpretations as the response variable and intent, and found an interaction effect ($z = 2.86$, $p = 0.004$) as well as main effects for novelty ($z = -3.44$, $p < 0.001$), and walking ($z = -3.13$, $p = 0.002$). We conducted pairwise Tukey comparisons, specifically comparing the novel symbols for walking with one another and the novel symbols for stopping with one another. For walking, no significant differences were found. For stopping, all symbols except the orange

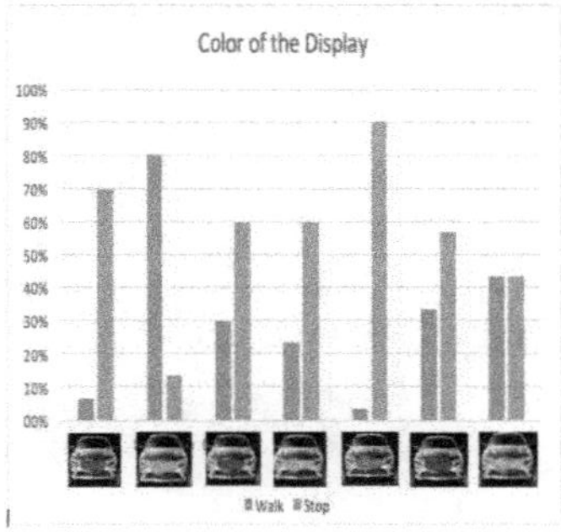

Figure 3: Results from the color of display questions in the questionnaire (n=30)

color were recognized significantly better than the anthropomorphic symbol.

For the investigation of the effects of colors, we designed a display to a vehicle grille showing different colors and we asked the children if they would stop or cross the road. The colors that were read in a more consistent way were: red (90%), green (80%), and orange (60%), see Figure 3.

The children could also explain the reason of their choice and a qualitative content analysis was carried out. Most interestingly, some of the children noted that they were not sure whether the displayed signs represented the intention of the vehicle or a command for the pedestrian. However, they did not mention any uncertainty regarding this point of confusion when the "child-signs" were displayed, which was a clear indication that this was a message for the pedestrian.

Video-based survey

We designed 3 video-clips, in which we displayed an autonomous vehicle and a (child pedestrian) figure who had to take a stop/go decision. The clips were used to investigate three affordances of communication: an already known signal displayed on the vehicle, a set of expressive eyes displayed on the vehicler, and a zebra crossing projected by the vehicle on the road. Data analysis showed that all children understood the display of an already known signal. The answers of the children about the display of the eyes on the vehicle and the projected cross road were not consistent.

In sum, the results from the survey indicate that the stop/go cues built on conventional traffic signals were more consistently recognized by children than new cues based on anthropomorphic animations. This is in accordance to the relevant literature on the ways in which children develop new constructs based on their existing mental models.

Discussion and next steps

This late breaking paper presents the first results of an ongoing research which aims to explore features that children use for the identification of an AV and the interpretation of communicative signals of its intentions. We adopted an inclusive design research methodology that proved to be an efficient and developmentally appropriate way to gain knowledge about childrens's views about non-existing AVs.

Overall, our preliminary findings indicate children's need to know whether the vehicle they are encountering is autonomous. This may create the basis for the development of the trust towards self-driving vehicles. Also, the results revealed a consistency in terms of colors used for the indication of a stop/go strategy. Green, red and orange where the best legible for children. This result can be explained by the constructivist theoretical approaches of children's development regarding the construction of mental models within a new situation. Children's need for concrete and easily read messages was also revealed. The "child-sign" that holds the stop or go sign was among the best understood.

Given the limited number of children in the study, it is difficult to generalize our results. However, the results can be used to inform design and select direction for further research. This study is only the first step towards the investigation of interaction between child pedestrians and self-driving vehicles. Next steps include the development of prototypes with additional comparisons and field studies with a larger sample of children. In addition, design issues, such as the color of signals, luminance, form and placement need to be investigated further to ensure that the proposed signals are in line with the legislation. An important step that will be taken is to explore interaction between child pedestrians and automated vehicles without any external signals, and compare with the corresponding interactions with selected signals.

Acknowledgements
We thank the children and their teachers as well as the bachelor students E. Bongers, K. Boonk, L. Koning, R. Ransmann and S. Deinum for their input to this study.

References
1. B.K. Barton. 2006. Integrating selective attention into developmental pedestrian safety research. *Canadian Psychology* 47: 203–210.
2. V. Charisi, D. Davison, D. Reidsma, and V. Evers. 2016. Evaluation methods for user-centered child-robot interaction. In *IEEE International Symp. on Robot and Human Interactive Communication (RO-MAN2016)*.
3. M Clamann, M Aubert, and M. L. Cummings. 2017. Evaluation of Vehicle-to-Pedestrian Communication Displays for Autonomous Vehicles. In *Transportation Research Board (TRB)*.
4. Allison Druin. 2002. The Role of Children in the Design of New Technology. *Behaviour & Information Technology 21*, 1–25.
5. Google. 2016. *Google Self-Driving Car Project Monthly Report (May 2016)*.
6. A Habibovic, V M Lundgren, J Andersson, M Klingegård, T Lagström, A Sirkka, J Fagerlönn, C Edgren, R Fredriksson, S Krupenia, D Saluäär, and P Larsson. 2017. Communicating the intent of automated vehicles to their surroundings. *To be submitted.*
7. I. Horváth. 2008. On the differences between research in design context and design inclusive research in the domain of industrial design engineering. *Design Research* 7, 1: 61–83.
8. V. Lundgren Malmsten, A. Habibovic, J. Andersson, T. Lagström, M. Nilsson, A. Sirkka, J. Fagerlönn, R. Fredriksson, C. Edgren, S. Krupenia, and D. Saluäär. 2017. Will there be New Communication Needs when Introducing Automated Vehicles to the Urban Context? In *Advances in Human Aspects of Transportation*, N. A. Stanton, S. Landry, G. Di Bucchianico and A. Vallicelli (eds.). Springer International Publishing, 485–497.
9. N Merat, R Madigan, and S Nordhoff. 2016. *Human Factors, User Requirements, and User Acceptance of Ride-Sharing in Automated Vehicles.*
10. Mercedes-Benz. 2015. The Mercedes-Benz F 015 Luxury in Motion.
11. Nissan News. 2015. Nissan IDS Concept: Nissan's vision for the future of EVs and autonomous driving.
12. M. Peden, R. Scurfiled, D. D. Sleet, A. Mohan, E. Hyder, Jarawan, and C. Mathers. 2004. *World report on road traffic injury prevention*. Geneva, Switzerland.
13. N Pennycooke. 2012. *Designing biomimetic vehicle-to-pedestrian communication protocols for autonomously operating & parking on-road electric vehicles.*
14. D Rothenbucher, J Li, D Sirkin, B Mok, and W Ju. 2016. Ghost Driver: A Field Study Investigating the Interaction Between Pedestrians and Driverless Vehicles. In *The 25th IEEE International Symp. on Robot and Human Interactive Communication (RO-MAN)*.
15. M. Šucha. 2014. Road users' strategies and communication: driver-pedestrian interaction. In *Transport Research Arena (TRA) 2014 Proceedings*.
16. L. Uden and A Dix. 2000. Iconic Interfaces For Kids On The Internet. In *IFIP World Computer Congress*, 279–286.
17. World Health Organization (WHO). 2009. *Global status report on road safety: time for action*. Geneva, Switzerland.

Teaching and Learning of Chinese History in Minecraft: A Pilot Case-Study in Hong Kong Secondary Schools

Kening Zhu
School of Creative Media
City University of Hong Kong
keninzhu@cityu.edu.hk

Man Ho John Huen
Koding Kingdom (HK) Ltd.
Hong Kong
john.huen@kodingkingdom.com

IDC '17, June 27-30, 2017, Stanford, CA, USA

ACM ISBN 978-1-4503-4921-5/17/06.
http://dx.doi.org/10.1145/3078072.3084301

Abstract
Minecraft is the best-selling and the most popular digital sandbox games, allowing children to freely create their own buildings and objects. It has been widely used in education. In this research, we developed a real-scale Forbidden City in Minecraft, as a history education platform for Hong Kong secondary schools. The platform allows teachers to manage the class in Minecraft, meanwhile preserving the freedom for students to explore, collaborate, and create. We piloted the platform with 3 teachers and 50 students, and collected feedbacks on the teaching and the learning experience, for future development.

Author Keywords
Minecraft; Chinese history; education; game-based learning.

ACM Classification Keywords
H.5.m. Information interfaces and presentation (e.g., HCI): Miscellaneous.

Introduction
Minecraft [5] is the best-selling and the most popular digital sandbox games, with 100 million players all over the world. The creative mode of Minecraft allows

players to freely explore, gather block-based resources, craft, and construct objects and buildings in the pixelated 3D gaming-environment. In addition, as a massive multiplayer online role-playing game, Minecraft supports interactions and collaborations among players. These features of Minecraft have demonstrated a great potential in applying the game in education, including math [2], computer science [6], history [7], and literacy [3].

For the learning and teaching of History, Minecraft offers unique affordances for reenacting, replaying, and gaining first person experiences within the realms of historical contexts [7]. While Minecraft has been widely used in different countries for history education, it is still hard to see any convincing case in the greater China region, where a culturally rich and 5000-year long history is based, yet the digital-game industry is booming in this area. In spite of the previously mentioned positive evidence on MinecraftEdu, many educators in this region may not be open to the idea of using video games in their classrooms. Firstly, it could be due to the tradition Chinese perspective that being additive to games could spoil one's study, and this thinking is commonly shared by different stakeholders, including educators and parents. A Hong Kong-based survey showed that a majority of local teacher concerns about learning new media for teaching [11]. In addition, young Chinese primary and secondary students, who are highly attracted to digital games, are losing their interests in traditional culture and history, due to the conventional lecture-based educational approach which they find non-attractive [9]. There is a need to attract the youngster back to the traditional culture and history through digital entertainment media. Meanwhile, it is needed to convince local teachers that emerging entertainment media (i.e. game) could be an effective tool for education.

In this research, we developed an educational platform, a real-scale Forbidden City in Minecraft, including the modification of the front-end virtual-world interface and the back-end server, for Chinese history education in Hong Kong secondary schools. The platform allows teachers to manage the class and review the students' behavioral data in Minecraft, meanwhile preserving the freedom for students to explore, collaborate, and create. We piloted the platform with 3 teachers and 50 students, and collected their perception on learning and teaching Chinese history in Minecraft. The preliminary results showed the students' motivation in studying Chinese history increased significantly after using our platform. While most students enjoyed using the platform in the Chinese-history classroom, female students tended to prefer more labor division rather than the current setting that every player plays the same action-oriented role. The teachers suggested that more natural in-game interaction and more challenge would be preferred.

Background: Game-based Learning and Minecraft Education

Game-based learning has attracted much research interest in academia. Bebbington's study [1] suggested that, to succeed in Minecraft, one requires cultivating complex information literacy skills, such as information seeking, evaluation, and sharing. Smeaton's survey [8] with an active online MinecraftEDU community showed that teachers perceived Minecraft as an effective teaching tool, and were willing to adopt this game in their classroom. Furthermore, Burnett suggested that using Minecraft in the classroom promotes online and

(a) Architecture of Forbidden City

(b) Interior of Forbidden City

(c) Artwork Collection of Forbidden City

Figure 1: Forbidden City in Minecraft.

offline collaboration among students [4]. Sáez-López et al compared Minecraft-based and lecture-based education for "History and Architecture", and showed that a majority of the teachers and the students considered that MinecraftEdu is fun, enhances creativity, develops discovery [7]. Despite of these case-studies, the number of academic studies on Minecraft for education is still limited, and most existing publications on this topic simply described the practices of applying Minecraft in different classrooms. In this research, we aim to investigate the effectiveness of using Minecraft for Chinese history education, and the teachers' and the students' perception on this educational approach.

1:1 Forbidden City in Minecraft

Selection of Educational Content

In this research, we recreated the landscape of the Forbidden City, the Chinese imperial palace for the Ming and the Qing dynasties, in Minecraft at a 1:1 scale, including the architectures (Fig. 1(a)), the interior decoration (Fig. 1(b)), and the artwork collection (Fig. 1(c)). The Forbidden City was chosen because it was the palace for the last two imperial dynasties of China, lasting almost 500 years, and witnessing important changes of Chinese society.

The virtual contents followed the textbooks currently being used by Hong Kong secondary schools, and the education guidance of Chinese history released by the Education Bureau of Hong Kong [12]. The guidance indicated that the curriculum needs to help students "*to know the historical figures and events that had far-reaching impact on Chinese history as well as some significant or interesting current affairs/events of the country*" and "*to know the characteristic features of ancient Chinese civilization*".

Educational Gaming Stages in Minecraft Forbidden City

In the current prototype, we developed three educational gaming stages.

STAGE 1: INTERACTIVE CONSTRUCTION OF FORBIDDEN CITY

In this stage (Fig. 2), the students will be immersed as the roles of the construction workers in the year of 1406 when the Chinese empire began the construction of the palace. The students will be instructed by the non-player character (the designer of the palace) to collect the construction materials and build the palace. The in-game instructions will elaborate the design, the culture, and the construction process of the palace.

Figure 2: Stage 1 – Interactive Construction of Forbidden City.

STAGE 2: FIRE FIGHTING IN THE TAIHE GATE

After accomplishing the tasks in the first stage, the students will be teleported to the context of the fire accident in 1889 in the Taihe Gate, which is the largest gate in the Forbidden City. As shown in Fig. 3, the students will play as the guards in the palace, and need to save the fire using the water elements in Minecraft. In the end of this stage, the students will be shown that fire accident affected the imperial wedding, thus to learn the culture of traditional Chinese wedding.

Figure 3: Stage 2 – Fire Fighting in the Taihe Gate

STAGE 3: PALACE EXAMINATION
Stage 3 (Fig. 4) will immerse the students in the context of a Chinese imperial examination (also known as palace examination), which was a civil service examination in Imperial China to select candidates for the state bureaucracy. The students will act as the selected scholars, and will be examined by the empire who will provide multi-choices questions related to Chinese culture and literature. Through this gaming stage, the students will learn about the knowledge of traditional Chinese culture, literature, and the system of civil service selection.

Figure 4: Stage 3 – Palace Examination.

BACK-END CLASSROOM MANAGEMENT & DATA COLLECTION
Besides the three educational games, we implemented a list of back-end features in Minecraft, to support the teachers to manage the class in the virtual world, and collect the learning data in real time during students' play. The collected data included the time spent in each game, the number of trials in each game, and the log of the chatting messages.

Pilot Study: Classroom Deployment

In our preliminary study, we deployed our current prototype to three Chinese-history classrooms in three different local secondary schools. Fig. 5 shows the deployment, we collected the parents' consensus, through the assistance of the teachers, to collect the students' anonymous personal information (e.g. gender, age, study year, and experience with Minecraft), record the classroom sessions in photo and video, and interview the students after the sessions.

There were totally 50 Secondary-2 students (26 girls and 24 boys, Age Mean = 13.4, SD = 1.2, all Chinese and native Cantonese speakers, 54% with more than 6-months of playing Minecraft), in the three separated 1-hour classroom sessions. The three sessions were delivered by different history teachers (2 males and 1 female, averagely aging 33.4 years old, all teaching history for more than 3 years) in Cantonese.

Before the classroom session, the students were guided to finish the questionnaire on their motivation on studying Chinese history, which was modified from the Intrinsic Motivation Inventory Questionnaire for Adults [13]. In the session, the teacher first introduced the features of our platform. Then the students were allowed to go through the three stages in the current

Figure 5: Set-up of the Minecraft Chinese-History Class

prototype with the permission to chat with the classmates, under the supervision of the teacher.

After the classroom session, the students were guided to finish the same motivation questionnaire again. We further conducted a 30-minute focus-group interview with the students (5 students were randomly assigned in each group) and a 30-minute individual interview with the teacher, regarding their experience of using this platform in Chinese-history learning and teaching.

Results of Motivation Questionnaire

A one-way ANOVA was conducted to compare the students' motivation on studying Chinese history before and after the classroom-deployment session, based on the results of the questionnaire. The results showed that the students' motivation increased significantly after the classroom deployment ($F(1, 49) = 4.136$, $p < 0.05$), which suggested that the Minecraft-based education platform could have a positive effect on motivating students to study Chinese history, pointing to the future work on involving more teachers and students, and comparing with the traditional classroom teaching in a more controlled setting.

Feedbacks from Teachers and Students

While most students mentioned they enjoyed using the platform, and would prefer learning Chinese history in this platform, two groups of girls commented that they were a bit annoyed by the fire-fighting scene, as they thought the action game was more for boys rather than girls. They further suggested it would be nicer to provide different roles in the game for different players, which will also help to understand how different people collaborate in an historical event.

Both teachers appreciated our effort on designing Chinese-history education platform in Minecraft which they think is a currently trendy and attractive game for children. One male teacher mentioned that it would be better to cover more history knowledge in the platform, and hope that the platform can provide the form of Q&A for the students to learn from the non-player characters through conversation. He further commented that some students may not be familiar with the current interaction method (e.g. WASD directional keys) in Minecraft, and it may be a challenge to attract these students' interest in the very beginning, thus a more natural interaction in Minecraft for education would be needed. The female teacher suggested that we could increase the game challenge to the students' interest and engagement more effectively, stating her observation that the current generation of children can easily pick up and perform well with emerging digital technology.

Discussion & Future Work

Firstly, we will improve the platform by involving teachers and students in the participatory design iteration, to develop new features and storylines which are more closed to the learning requirement of Chinese history in Hong Kong. In addition, we didn't quantitatively measure the in-game behavior of teachers and students, the effectiveness of Minecraft in motivating students in learning Chinese history, and the learning outcome of the Minecraft-based Chinese-history education, due to the limited sample size and the short duration of the deployment. With a more-refined prototype, we will incorporate long-term classroom deployment with different settings (e.g. mobile classroom), to further explore the effect of Minecraft on Chinese-history education.

Acknowledgements
This project is sponsored by Koding Kingdom (HK) Ltd. Special thanks to HKSKH Bishop Hall Secondary School, Pui Ching Middle School, and Christian Alliance SW Chan Memorial College for providing the time and the space for the classroom deployment.

References
1. Bebbington, S. (2014). A Case Study of the Use of the Game Minecraft and Its Affinity Spaces for Information Literacy Development in Teen Gamers (Doctoral dissertation, Université d'Ottawa/University of Ottawa).
2. Bos, B., Wilder, L., Cook, M., & O'Donnell, R. (2014). Learning mathematics through Minecraft. Teaching Children Mathematics, 21(1), 56-59.
3. Brand, J., & Kinash, S. (2013). Crafting minds in Minecraft.
4. Burnett, C. (2016). Being together in classrooms at the interface of the physical and virtual: implications for collaboration in on/off-screen sites. Learning, Media and Technology, 41(4), 566-589.
5. Persson, M., & Bergensten, J. (2011). Minecraft. Computer software]. Stockholm, Sweden: Mojang AB. Retrieved from http://minecraft. net.
6. Repenning, A., Webb, D. C., Brand, C., Gluck, F., Grover, R., Miller, S., ... & Song, M. (2014). Beyond minecraft: Facilitating computational thinking through modeling and programming in 3d. IEEE Computer Graphics and Applications, 34(3), 68-71.
7. Sáez-López, J. M., Miller, J., Vázquez-Cano, E., & Domínguez-Garrido, M. C. (2015). Exploring application, attitudes and integration of video games: MinecraftEdu in middle school.
8. Smeaton, D. (2012). Minecraft as a Teaching Tool-A Statistical Study of Teachers' Experience Using Minecraft in the Classroom (Doctoral dissertation, Master's Thesis. Nathan: University of Griffith).
9. South China Morning Post. (2015, April) St Clare's Girls' School cuts Chinese history for lack of student interest. URL: http://yp.scmp.com/news/hong-kong/article/95907/st-clares-girls-school-cuts-chinese-history-lack-student-interest.
10. TeacherGaming, L. L. C. (2012). MinecraftEdu [Video game]. TeacherGaming LLC, New York, NY.
11. Wong, G. K., Cheung, H. Y., Ching, E. C., & Huen, J. M. (2015, December). School perceptions of coding education in K-12: A large scale quantitative study to inform innovative practices. In Teaching, Assessment, and Learning for Engineering (TALE), 2015 IEEE International Conference on (pp. 5-10). IEEE.
12. Chinese History Curriculum (Secondary 1 - 3). Education Bureau, Hong Kong. URL: http://www.edb.gov.hk/attachment/tc/curriculum-development/kla/pshe/CSS13CH.pdf.
13. McAuley, E., Duncan, T., & Tammen, V. V. (1989). Psychometric properties of the Intrinsic Motivation Inventory in a competitive sport setting: A confirmatory factor analysis. Research quarterly for exercise and sport, 60(1), 48-58.

Youth Reasoning With Interactive Data Visualizations: A Preliminary Study

Michelle Hoda Wilkerson
University of California, Berkeley
Berkeley, CA 94720, USA
mwilkers@berkeley.edu

Vasiliki Laina
University of California, Berkeley
Berkeley, CA 94720, USA
vlaina@berkeley.edu

 ACM ISBN 978-1-4503-4921-5/17/06.
http://dx.doi.org/10.1145/3078072.3084302

Abstract
Youth interact with data constantly through visualizations on social feeds and news sites. Unlike traditional graphs that are the focus of school instruction, visualizations use context rich and interactive methods to create narratives and allow users to explore data for themselves. We ask: How do youth make sense of interactive data visualizations? Nine participants ages 12-13 completed semi-structured, think-aloud clinical interviews as they worked with data visualizations about socio-scientific issues. Findings suggest learners used a variety of resources, but often did not coordinate those resources. When they did, they built deeper understandings of the visualizations and their content.

Author Keywords
data visualization; middle school; data literacy; science education; statistical literacy

ACM Classification Keywords
K.3.2 [Computer and Information Science Education]: Literacy

Introduction
Data-intensive artifacts such as interactive visualizations are a growing part of news reporting [10], scientific and professional practice, self-study and civic advocacy [13, 6]. They are also becoming pervasive in youth's media land-

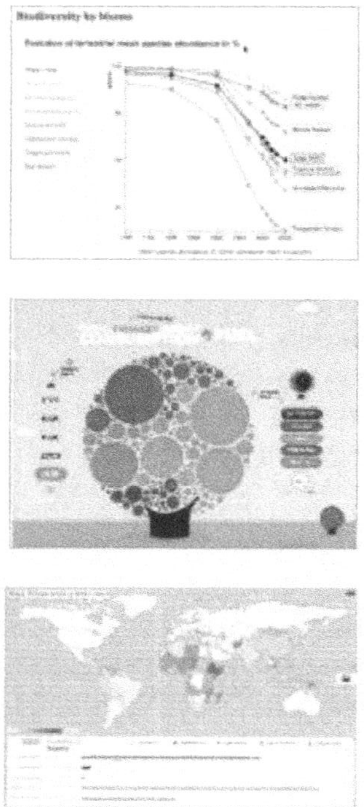

Figure 1: Three visualizations used in interviews: Ecosystems Dynamics (top), Human Impact (middle), Human Impact (bottom).

scapes. There are books of science information graphics for young children [12], and websites tout data visualizations and data analysis tools as useful learning resources [1].

Even as these data artifacts permeate learners' lives, there are still not many opportunities to work with them in the formal K-12 school curriculum. Mathematics curricula emphasize conventional, static data displays such as line graphs, bar charts, tables, or scatter plots, usually to illustrate simple patterns in small data sets. This does not prepare learners for the highly contextual, interactive, and story driven types of representations seen online, at work, or in print [5, 8]. School curricula rarely integrate data visualizations; when they do, they often do not provide support to help learners interpret these artifacts in meaningful ways.

This presents a need and opportunity. Learners may lack prior knowledge to understand what a visualization represents, and struggle to process the complex information they include [17]. Some visualizations are outright deceptive [11]. However, data visualizations also take advantage of new modes of interaction, non-traditional data sources (citizen science projects, online participation data), and storytelling conventions that youth regularly encounter out of school. And in many cases, working with visualizations can be aligned with standards-based content and practices [16].

This is especially true in science, where complex, socio-scientific systems are often presented in data visualizations. Since scientific visualizations combine math and science content with narrative and aethetic features [7, 14], we draw from research that explores math and statistics learning, science education, and how learners construct explanations [15]. For example, youth usually think of statistical data as a collection of individual values rather than an aggregate [2]. Ben-Zvi and Arcavi [3] call these local and global understandings, and showed that local understanding can hinder or support students' global understanding. Attending to the origin and context of data allows learners to develop more sophisticated inferences [4]. Learners should explicitly coordinate patterns in data with relationships that describe systems under study [18]. Personal experiences also inform how connections between data and systems are made [9].

Here we report emerging results from a semi-structured think-aloud interview study with nine middle school youth as they explored data visualizations about socio-scientific topics. Specifically, we explore: *How do middle school youth leverage and coordinate diverse knowledge resources to make sense of data visualizations?*

Methods

We interviewed 9 middle-school students using a semi-structured protocol as they worked with data visualizations.

Participants. Youth were recruited in collaboration with two partners: a 7th grade mathematics teacher who taught at a public school, and an after-school engineering program. 4 identified as girls and 5 as boys; 6 were from the school and 3 from the program. Participants were interviewed after class or program activities ended for the day, and received a US$10 gift card for their participation.

Interview Protocol. Interviews lasted 30-40 minutes. Participants worked with a set of three visualizations focused on either ecosystem dynamics or human impact on Earth (both themes emphasized in middle school science; Figure 1). For each, we presented each visualization and asked participants to interact with it until they were ready to answer questions. Then, we asked a series of eight questions about their initial impressions, the quantitative relationships featured in the visualization, and events or relationships that might explain patterns exhibited in the visualizations. We also asked participants to critique the visualization, and to

Codes Used in Analysis

Hypothesized Relationships. Knowledge of the system and of likely or hypothesized causal relationships.

Mathematical Ideas. Ideas such trend, distribution, quantitative difference, mean, or fit functions.

Visual Features. Conventions such as axes, legends, or use of position, shape, color, or other visual properties.

Text or Other. Supplemental information provided (visualization titles, text descriptions).

Reliability and Origin of Data. Questions, challenges, or inferences about whether data are reliable, sampled appropriately, and/or reflect knowledge or expectations about the system.

Local/Global Tensions. Similarities and differences between single data points or classes of data, and overall trends.

Personal Experience. Learner relates data to personal experiences, behavior, or identity.

propose changes to make it easier to use and understand. Due to time constraints, Mia and William interacted with only 2 of the 3 visualizations.

Data Collection. Interviews were video recorded with cameras positioned to capture participant-interviewer interactions, facial expression and gestures, and on-screen activity. Interviews were transcribed, including descriptions of gesture and other nonverbal cues.

Visualizations Used. We chose visualizations that illustrate a variety representational types, and that had already been recognized as well-designed by popular media or organizations interested in data visualization (see Figures 1 and 2). Some featured conventional representations of data such as linear graphs, others more idiosyncratic ones such as a tree whose leaves were circles colored to correspond to different fuels. Yet others featured a variety of representations, such as a combination of a colored geographic map and bars about the global water usage.

Analysis. We began with an open-ended analysis of transcript data. We annotated transcripts when we found evidence that learners were attending to particular mathematical, representational, or domain-specific resources, but also sought other instances in which learners worked to make sense of the visualizations in other ways. This led us to identify several different categories of, for example, domain-specific resources: some related to learners' own experiences of a particular phenomenon (e.g., their own experiences of local weather when exploring issues of climate, or their own fuel use when exploring issues of natural resource management). Through discussing emergent codes, we identified additional resources, such as text accompanying the visualization. The resulting categories used for subsequent phases of analysis are in the side bar.

Pseudonyn	Interviewer	Topic	Duration
Aminah	Vicky	Eco. Dynamics	35 min
Ryan	Michelle	Human Impact	33 min
Bobby	Vicky	Human Impact	42 min
Meili	Michelle	Human Impact	37 min
Mia	Michelle	Eco. Dynamics	30 min
Jason	Michelle	Eco. Dynamics	35 min
Oliver	Vicky	Human Impact	38 min
William	Vicky	Human Impact	34 min
Lilly	Michelle	Eco. Dynamics	37 min

Table 1: Participant details. Interviewers are authors of this paper.

Applying the Coding Scheme to Transcripts

An iterative, bottom-up analysis procedure yielded seven themes that became the focus of subsequent analysis (Table 2). Once these were identified, we organized transcripts into arguments. Each argument was then coded for evidence of one or more resource codes. An argument is one or more sentences that complete an answer to a question or an assertion. In the following, two arguments were identified:

William: [...] So, I think by the years, gas gets higher, cause gas was 5% and petrol and solid was really, people used it. Then we start to use gas, then we used, still down, then. Now, we're not using solid as much, because gas is like a useful tool, and then, now gas is the most, solid is the least and petroleum is, a little high, it's the second highest. But back then [1970] solid was the biggest, petrol was second and gas was the lowest. I feel like, it's trying to show our usage of these elements from 1970 to 2010, how we're using a lot more gas than we should be.

The first argument is "So, I think by the years, gas gets

An Example of Reporting with Visualization Resources

Meili: So, it's like about [reading text], like how, like the spring snow cover and the carbon dioxide levels and the average temperature, stuff like, change during 1950 and 2015.

I: And, op, yeah?

Meili: So, so like. For the average temperature, so like, you can like easily see like how the temperature is rising [gestures to graph]. So like, in 1952 it was a lot lower.

Meili: So, it's like, in 2014 there was like a lot, there was like a higher average temperature than like 1952. And then like, the carbon dioxide levels, like in October in 1987 it was like, carbon dioxide was a lot less than in, like March 2015. [I: Uhu] And for like the snow cover, it shows that like the snow melts earlier than it did in 1965. So, I think it's probably cause of global warming. In like 2013, it melted a lot earlier.

higher... ...petrol was second and gas was the lowest." and is only part of the first turn of talk. The second is "I feel like, it's trying to show..." More than one code could be applied to each argument. Here, the first argument was coded for evidence of mathematical ideas and hypothesized relationships, the second for personal experiences of data.

Preliminary Results

We expected students who leveraged a wider and balance of (mathematical, representational, domain-specific, and other) resources would exhibit deeper and more accurate interpretations of their content. Instead, our findings suggest a more complicated landscape of sense making. We identified additional categories of resources not well captured as only mathematical, representational, or domain-specific. We also found that students often leveraged resources without integrating them.

Summary of Content Analysis. We identified a diversity of resource type use within participants, and of distributions of use across participants. Table 3 presents results by student and resource. For example, Aminah referred to Hypothesized Relationships (HR) in 57% of her arguments during the interview. She referred to Mathematical Ideas (MI) in only 17% of arguments. Four resource types were identified in all interviews and played a heavy role in most students' reasoning. These were Hypothesized Relationships, Mathematical Ideas, Visual Features, and Text.

Of the remaining resources, seven students explicitly referred to the Origin or Reliability of the Data, four referenced Local and Global Tensions in data, and only three referenced Personal Experience. The distribution of resources leveraged also varied dramatically: William relied heavily on Personal Experience (52% of arguments), versus very low or no reliance from other participants. Four participants

Pseudonyn	HR	MI	VF	Text	OR	LG	PE
Aminah	57%	17%	4%	30%	4%	-	4%
Ryan	42%	48%	14%	10%	-	-	-
Bobby	46%	38%	17%	13%	4%	-	-
Meili	44%	33%	44%	17%	-	-	6%
Mia	31%	15%	31%	31%	15%	8%	-
Jason	26%	26%	16%	21%	16%	5%	-
Oliver	22%	28%	33%	22%	11%	6%	-
William	22%	43%	9%	13%	13%	4%	52%
Lilly	5%	50%	20%	35%	10%	-	-

Table 2: Percent arguments coded for presence of each resource.

frequently cited Hypothesized Relationships (over 40% of arguments); three Mathematical Ideas. Some participants heavily relied on multiple resources in conjunction. For example, Ryan frequently cited both Mathematical Ideas and Hypothesized Relationships to make sense of the visualizations presented, Meili frequently cited Mathematical Ideas and Visual Features.

Sensemaking and Synthesis During content analysis we noticed that resources were often used as justification for an assertion, or they were consulted without synthesis or coordination with other resources. In other words, resources were not always used by learners to build, interrogate, or revise their understandings of the visualization. This happened even in cases where students referenced multiple resources at the same time—something we expected to promote sense making.

For example, in the excerpt featured in the left sidebar, Meili cites several resources when describing the main themes of a visualization, but treats each in isolation. She first consults Text accompanying the visualization as a resource,

An Example of Strong Sensemaking with Visualization Resources

Bobby: Here [indicates spring snow cover] you can see that this is going down [traces blue bars] and this is going up [traces red bars].

I: Which one is going down and which one is going up, sorry?

Bobby: The top, the blue one is going down, and this one is going up, kind of.

I: Uhu, uhu. Why do you think this is so? What's a possible explanation for that pattern?

Bobby: Ah, global warming?

I: Ok

Bobby: Like um, it, if they put heat trapping gases here, and that's important because, like um, we're just trapping the sun's heat cause, the sun's energy [clicks on the graph] is not doing anything that it hasn't been doing.

I: Uhu

Bobby: And... So, it's not whatever is melting all the snow, and glaciers and arctic sea ice, is not the sun's fault.

and reports what this text indicates in her first turn of talk of the excerpt. She then identifies Mathematical Ideas in the form of rising and falling patterns indicated in the graphs ("you can like easily see..."). Finally, she describes a Hypothesized Relationship ("it's probably cause of global warming.") as a source for the patterns identified. However, there is no evidence to suggest that Meili is extending or revising what she already knows—she is reporting what information each resource provides, not how they can be coordinated with one another to tell a story.

To further explore the differences between reporting versus making sense of resources, we isolated arguments where multiple resources were leveraged at once. We then classified each argument as showing evidence of strong, weak, or no sensemaking. Strong sensemaking suggests the student made new inferences about the system, or changed prior inferences based on new information. This analysis is ongoing; here we report our emerging findings.

We were surprised that about 1/3 of arguments we identified as leveraging multiple resources did not represent new knowledge construction, like the example presented with Meili. Another approximately one third included weak evidence for sensemaking, in which *overlaps*—that is, consistencies or disconnects between resources—were noted by the interview participant, but not explored or resolved. Finally, about one third represented strong evidence for sensemaking, whereby students explicitly engaged with overlaps between resources which led them to construct, strengthen, or revise their knowledge. One example of such strong sense making is featured the excerpt to the left.

In this excerpt, Bobby explicitly coordinates the patterns (Mathematical Ideas) exhibited by multiple graphs to highlight that indicators of global warming are affected by a rise in heat-trapping gasses, rather than solar energy (Hypothesized Relationships). While both Meili and Bobby interactied with the same graph, and both noted that the patterns indicated by the graph were likely markers of global warming, the excerpts illustrate very different levels of sensemaking with the visualization. Meili recounted what text and data were presented, while Bobby linked data to domain-specific mechanisms and relationships.

We are careful to note that the examples provided here are to illustrate sensemaking per *argument*, not per student. Of course, sensemaking can be affected by many factors—interviewers' questions, students' framing of the interview task, and the visualization content. Our point here is that sensemaking is characterized by the deliberate coordination rather than merely the presence of diverse resources.

Conclusions

Work is ongoing, and we are currently analyzing episodes of strong versus weak integration of resources to better understand the conditions under which integrative reasoning happens. We are especially interested in probes or cues that interviewers may have used to promote this deeper level of sensemaking. Thus far, our study suggests that supporting learners in coordination of any resources they choose to leverage is more likely helpful than supporting a particular approach or sequence of resource use.

Acknowledgements

This work is funded through Grant IIS-1350282 from the National Science Foundation. We thank Asami Takagi, Elsa Head, Merredith Portsmore, and the Functions group at UC Berkeley for their help and feedback on this work.

REFERENCES

1. 2014. Telling Stories With Data. (2014). `https://learning.blogs.nytimes.com/2014/08/26/`

`reader-idea-telling-stories-with-data/`

2. Arthur Bakker. 2004. Reasoning about shape as a pattern in variability. *Statistics Education Research Journal* 3, 2 (2004), 64–83.
3. Dani Ben-zvi and Abraham Arcavi. 2001. Junior high school students' construction of global views of data and data representations. *Educational Studies in Mathematics* 45 (2001), 35–65.
4. Dani Ben-Zvi, Keren Aridor, Katie Makar, and Arthur Bakker. 2012. Students' emergent articulations of uncertainty while making informal statistical inferences. *ZDM - International Journal on Mathematics Education* 44, 7 (2012), 913–925.
5. William Finzer. 2013. The data science education dilemma. *Technology Innovations in Statistics Education* 7, 2 (2013), 1–9.
6. Michael Friendly. 2006. A brief history of data visualization. In *Handbook of Computational Statistics: Data Visualization*, C Chen, W Hardle, and A Unwin (Eds.). Springer-Verlag, Heidelberg, 15–56.
7. Douglas N. Gordin and Roy D. Pea. 1995. Prospects for scientific visualization as an educational technology. *Journal of the Learning Sciences* 4, 3 (1995), 249–279.
8. C. Hancock, J. J. Kaput, and L. T. Goldsmith. 1992. Authentic inquiry with data: Critical barriers to classroom implementation. *Educational Psychologist* 27, 3 (1992), 337–364.
9. Richard Lehrer and Leona Schauble. 2004. Modeling natural variation through distribution. *American Educational Research Journal* 41, 3 (2004), 635–679.
10. G. McGhee. 2010. *Journalism in the age of data.* Technical Report. `datajournalism.stanford.edu`
11. Anshul Vikram Pandey, Katharina Rall, Margaret L Satterthwaite, and Enrico Bertini. 2015. How deceptive are deceptive visualizations?: An empirical analysis of common distortion techniques. In *CHI 2015: Storytelling in InfoVis.* Association for Computing Machinery, 1469–1478.
12. Simon Rogers. 2014. Infographics for children: What they can learn from data visualisations. (March 2014).
13. Laurie H Rubel, Vivian Y Lim, Maren Hall-Wieckert, and Mathew Sullivan. 2016. Teaching mathematics for spatial justice : An investigation of the lottery. *Cognition and Instruction* 34, 1 (2016), 1–26.
14. Edward Segel and Jeffrey Heer. 2010. Narrative visualization: Telling stories with data. *IEEE Transactions on Visualization and Computer Graphics* 16, 6 (2010), 1139–1148.
15. Bruce L. Sherin, Moshe Krakowski, and Victor R. Lee. 2012. Some assembly required: How scientific explanations are constructed during clinical interviews. *Journal of Research in Science Teaching* 49, 2 (2012), 166–198.
16. NGSS Lead States. 2013. *Next generation science standards: For states, by states.* The National Academies Press, Washington, DC.
17. Barbara Tvertky. 2005. Prolegomenon to scientific visualizations. In *Visualization in science education.* 29–42.
18. Michelle Hoda Wilkerson-Jerde and Uri J Wilensky. 2015. Patterns, probabilities, and people: Making sense of quantitative change in complex systems. *Journal of the Learning Sciences* 24, 2 (2015), 204–251.

Multisensory Games on Children's Empathetic Feelings and Cooperative Behavior: Developing a Kansei-Based Sensory Playground Design Workshop

Rodrigo Fernandes
Department of Kansei,
Behavioral, and Brain Sciences
University of Tsukuba
Tsukuba, Ibaraki, Japan
Rqk.fernandes@gmail.com

Toshimasa Yamanaka
School of Art and Design
University of Tsukuba
Tsukuba, Ibaraki, Japan
tyam@kansei.tsukuba.ac.jp

Ikkaku Kawaguchi
Department of Kansei,
Behavioral, and Brain Sciences
University of Tsukuba
Tsukuba, Ibaraki, Japan
ikkaku@kansei.tsukuba.ac.jp

IDC '17, June 27-30, 2017, Stanford, CA, USA

ACM ISBN 978-1-4503-4921-5/17/06.
http://dx.doi.org/10.1145/3078072.3084303

Abstract

How, from childhood, can we start to develop a more empathetic and cooperative society? Based on the play value for children's social development, this research aims to back up the surge of `interactive playgrounds`, a proposal that combines the interactive attractiveness of modern multi-sensory technologies with traditional elements of playground environments. In order to understand their sensory effects, we propose a play and design team workshop with children, where we will observe if different stimulus during play activity can affect their empathetic considerations toward others and their practical collaborative behavior. On this paper, we focus on this workshop experiment plan, describing its goals, the intended tools for obtaining data with infant collaborators, and our expected results. From the results, we expect to develop guidelines for sensory stimulus usage on new interactive playground and play tools designs.

Author Keywords

Play; Empathy; Cooperation; Multisensory-stimuli; Interactive Playground; Workshop; Kansei Science.

ACM Classification Keywords

H.5.2

Introduction

Nowadays, Empathy and cooperation are growing as desirable attributes for good social development. Based on humanist views, empathy correlates with interaction among different types of people. These interactions can be described as "an affective response that stems from the apprehension or comprehension of another`s emotional state or condition, and that is similar to what the other person is feeling or would be expected to feel" [10]. Cooperation, on a more concrete or measurable definition, is the act of working together towards a same end or goal. Many factors can affect cooperation and, among them, authors find empathic behavior to relate positively [4; 7]. Considering also other factors such as social environment, we have been asking *"how can we develop a more empathetic and cooperative society from childhood?"*

Playing is an irreplaceable way for children to understand their surroundings, communicate, and develop affection [9]. For encouraging play activity and its benefits, playgrounds environments have also been gathering increased attention for the society. Those environments are spaces where kids from a large age-range can get in contact with each other to, through dynamic play exploration, socialize and develop different skills.

Current context has been leading to a series of new proposals for play tools, such as the `*Interactive Playgrounds*`. By combining the traditional play values of playgrounds with modern technologies, interactive playgrounds can provide more direct feedback and narrative possibilities for the users. Their technologies can also engage the children through sensory stimuli such as light mechanism for sight; digital sounds for hearing; and haptic inputs for touch [3].

Related with sensorial perception, Kansei is a Japanese field and term that describes the function of the brain, which would be the source of emotion, inspiration, intuition, pleasure, displeasure, taste, curiosity, aesthetics and creation [2]. Since it is relatable with affective feelings, we believe empathy to be a matter of Kansei. However, even with studies evaluating the impact of toys on child development, we could not find dedicated studies to the effects of sensory-stimuli on affective play behaviors.

Therefore, this research aims to understand how different multisensory-stimuli on interactive play activities can generate feelings of empathy and encourage cooperation on children. To achieve part of this understanding, we propose a design workshop for children involving play, sensory stimuli, and teamwork.

On this workshop proposal, primary school children aged 6 to 11 will play modified team game versions of an interactive block puzzle toy based on different sensory stimuli. While the original blocks contain digital light and sound stimuli, the modified version will remove these features, leaving only its mechanical properties, which are mostly self-moving gears and wheels. Right afterward, the Children will have to project together a new inclusive playground design through activities such as *individual sketches; team idea generation; and Physical prototyping;*

As our goal is to understand how sensorial elements of interactive playground environments can foster empathy and collaborative behavior, we believe that

Interaction Rating Scale: Tool developed by Tokie Anme [1] based on the observation of children's social behaviors during play activity. It consists of a checklist of 50 items filled by the researchers while observing children play situations. In this scale, Cooperation is defined as a consequence or extension of empathy with items such as "Shares intentions and attitudes with the partner through eye contact.", and "shows empathy with a verbal or non-verbal response when the partner is in a bad mood."

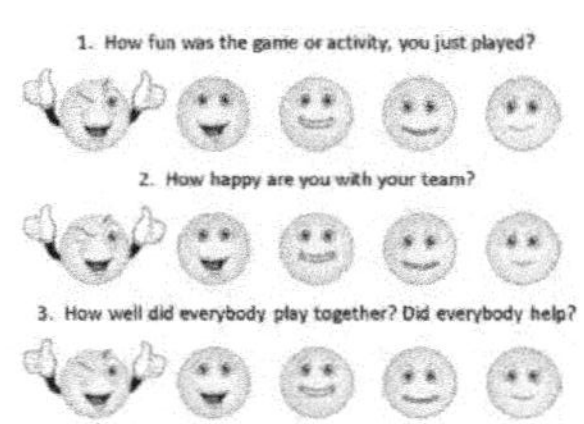

Figure 1: 5 degrees of happiness Smiley Face Likert Scale [5], an evaluation tool focused only on positive faces that resulted on a wider range of answers by the children.

the obtained data will aid on generating new playground concepts based on affective interactions. Therefore, we are currently working on the following research question: *how can different interactive sensorial elements effect on our empathetic feelings and cooperative behavior during team play activities?*

Methodology

The following workshop plan, entitled `Play and Design Workshop`, has the goal of discovering if and how different combinations of stimuli given during play activity can contribute on children better working together on team play and design activities. First, we will access the empathy pre-disposition of children individually through the usage of the Kids Empathy Development Scale – KEDS [8]. From that, we can organize the different multiage teams based on age, gender and empathy disposition.

For the initial stage of this workshop, we will work with primary school students, aged 6 to 11, of the *Liberty International School* of Tsukuba, Japan. With a modest initial sample size of 43 children, we have chosen to work with 10 teams of four and one team of three children. We will establish then three main groups:

1. **High sensory stimuli group:** This group will play a team based electronic building blocks game involving LED light color and sound blocks.
2. **Low Sensory Stimuli group:** This group will play a team based electronic building blocks game using only the blocks' mechanical features of moving wheels and gears.
3. **No stimuli – Control Group**: This group will not play the building blocks game and will only perform the design challenges.

We will select combined sensory stimuli through game activities, evaluating the direct response that they might give not only during the play actions, but also during the team based design activities that follows it. By doing that we aim to find if, the different stimuli affected both the way that children worked together and the way on how they perceived themselves.

During the game and design activities, we plan to analyze this phenomenon objectively by observing their team behavior through the *Interaction Rating Scale* [1], a tool that evaluates both cooperation and empathy by observing social cues during play activity. After each activity, through self-assessment reports, we plan to analyze the children`s own feelings regarding the tasks and their team members impressions. We will aim to counter possible response bias of children by using the *5 degrees of happiness Smiley face Likert Scale* [5].

The final questions of the report involves selecting, between a range of six identifiable emotions, which emotion predominated on themselves during the task, and which emotions predominated on their team members. Another task involves drawing a self-portrait of their team, so we can also evaluate the usage of elements such as facial expressions and the representation of characteristics.

Since the workshop proposal is to Design new interactive playground concepts, we will also be evaluating the different generated concepts to find trends regarding sensory stimulation and interactive playground Design. For evaluating the designs, we will focus on aspects such as novelty, number of elements, and color utilization.

Introduction	playground design and technology	1 Hour
section 1	introduction	minutes
Design section 1	sketching followed by team idea discussion and generation	15-30 minutes
section 2	challenge	minutes
Design Section 2	self-portrait followed by low complexity prototyping	30-40 minutes
Presentation	presentation	minutes

Table 1: Workshop Flow to be applied on different teams during a week.

Figure 2: Hikari Tsumiki 2.0: programmable multisensory puzzle blocks selected as game stimuli. [6]

Considerations

As the workshop is on ongoing procedures, we can predict its outcomes. On the most positive scenario, the high stimuli teams will present significantly better evaluations on the teamwork behavior and impressions as well as on the generated designs. From this scenario, we can evaluate how to explore this found phenomenon on further experiments.

On a moderate scenario, the children will not display any significant differences between the high and the low sensory stimuli groups. However, they will both present better evaluations than the no-stimuli group. On this case, assuming that they are not strong enough, the research will seek to reevaluate its sensorial stimuli utilization.

On the most pessimist scenario, there will be no significant differences among the three groups, or the no-stimuli group will present significant higher evaluations than the stimuli groups. This finding could contradict the initial hypothesis of games and sensorial stimuli aiding on teamwork feelings and activities, causing the research to reevaluate its theoretical and experimental procedures.

The limitations over the data evaluations could be a considerably low sample and the existence of many external factors of difficult control. For example, a pre-existing design or art affinity and the social competence of children. Pre-discussion of children regarding the playground designs can also affect the results as they can vary from team to team.

It is important to reinforce that more than the design outcomes, the displays of empathy and cooperation on children are our main research targets. Therefore, additional results such as notable differences between the objectively evaluated teamwork activities and the teamwork feelings reported by the children can also provide interesting data for further evaluation.

Since this research is based on Kansei or affective principles, we believe that different sensory stimuli given to children can influence their feelings and social behaviors, and that we can enhance them with interactive technology. If we can be successful on finding results that back up this theory, they can greatly aid on the development of more suitable products for developing the modern children.

Acknowledgements

We thank the *Liberty International School of Tsukuba*, Japan, for supporting this project, and all the volunteer work among staff and students for developing it.

References

1. Tokie Anme, et al. 2014. Validating the Effects of Inclusive Childcare with the Interaction Rating Scale. *Education Journal* 4, 2: 35-40.
2. B. Beuttel, T. Yamanaka. 2010. Kansei Research and Design. Retrieved march 27, 2017 from http://www.geijutsu.tsukuba.ac.jp/~tyam/KRaD.pdf
3. R. V. Delden. 2012. Towards a Socially Adaptive Digital Playground. In *Proceedings of the the 11th International Conference on Interaction Design and Children* (IDC '11), 355-358.
4. N. Eisenberg. 2002. Empathy-related emotional responses, altruism, and their socialization; *In R. J. Davidson & A. Harrington (Eds.), Visions of compassion: Western scientists and Tibetan*

Buddhists examine human nature. Oxford University Press, London, 131-164.

5. L. Hall, C. Hume, S. Tazzyman. 2016. Five Degrees of Happiness: Effective Smiley *Face Likert Scales for Evaluating with Children. In Proceedings of the The 15th International Conference on Interaction Design and Children* (IDC '15), 311-321.
6. I. Kawaguchi et al. 2017, Hikari Tsumiki: Module Toy for Hardware Education Which Visualize Information Using Visible Light. Annual Design Review of Japanese Society for the Science of Design, 21. (To be published, paper in japanese)
7. L. Malinverni, N. P. Burgues. 2015. The Medium Matters: the Impact of Full-Body Interaction on the Socio-Affective Aspects of Collaboration. *In Proceedings of the the 14th International Conference on Interaction Design and Children* (IDC '14), 89-98.
8. C. **Reid et al. 2013. The Kids' Empathic** Development Scale (KEDS): A multi-dimensional measure of empathy in primary school-aged children. British Journal of Developmental Psychology, 31: 231–256.
9. J. Santer, C. Griffiths, D. Goodall. 2007. Free play in early childhood: a literature review. *National Children`s Bureau*, London: 1-114.
10. L. Tong et al. 2012. Early Development of Empathy in Toddlers: Effects of Daily Parent–Child Interaction and Home-Rearing Environment. Journal of Applied Social Psychology, 24: 2457-2478.

YOLO, a Robot for Creativity: A Co-Design Study with Children

Patrícia Alves-Oliveira
INESC-ID; Instituto Universitário de Lisboa ISCTE-IUL, CIS-IUL; Sibley School of Mechanical and Aerospace Engineering, Cornell University
pa284@cornell.edu

Ana Paiva
INESC-ID and Instituto Superior Técnico, Universidade de Lisboa
Lisbon, Portugal
ana.paiva@inesc-id.pt

Patrícia Arriaga
Instituto Universitário de Lisboa ISCTE-IUL, CIS-IUL
Lisbon, Portugal.
patricia.arriaga@iscte.pt

Guy Hoffman
Sibley School of Mechanical and Aerospace Engineering, Cornell University
Ithaca, NY, USA
hoffman@cornell.edu

IDC 2017, June 27–30, 2017, Stanford, CA, USA.
ACM ISBN 978-1-4503-4921-5/17/06.
http://dx.doi.org/10.1145/3078072.3084304

Abstract
This paper describes the design and development of YOLO, a social robot aimed at boosting creativity in children. Creativity is one of the most sought-after competencies as we move from industrialized economies, in which standardized knowledge was imperative, to creative economies, where the ability to innovate is crucial for the workforce. YOLO is a robot to be used by children as a tool to boost new ideas and stimulate their creativity. This paper describes how established educational strategies that enhance creativity were combined with co-designing with children as informants to reach the the prototype design of the robot.

Author Keywords
Creativity; Children; Social robot; Collective creation; Human-robot interaction; Design; Prototype

ACM Classification Keywords
H.1.2 [User/Machine Systems]: Human factors; J.4 [Social and Behavioral Sciences]: Psychology; J.6 [Computer-Aided Engineering]: Computer-aided design (CAD)

Introduction
Creativity is considered one of the highest human cognitive abilities [1]. It is also one of the most sought-after workforce skills as many societies are shifting from *industrialized* to *creative* economies [16]. Despite the lack of

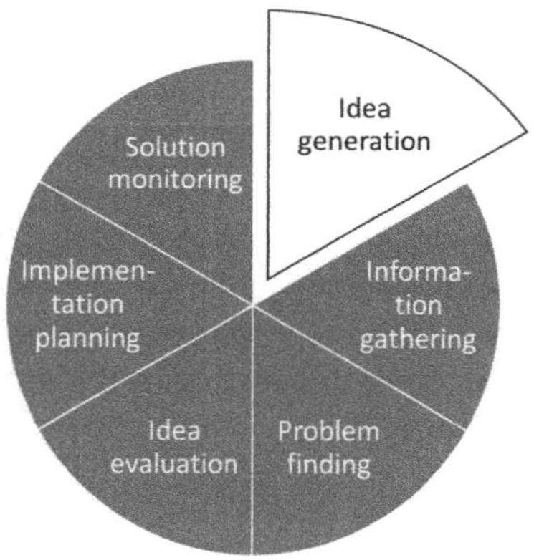

Figure 1: Model of cognitive processes involved in problem-solving tasks [21]. The design of YOLO is dedicated to the enhancement of the cognitive process of *idea generation.*

a full consensus or a unique definition for the concept of creativity, a canonical literature sees creativity as the *"interaction among aptitude, process, and environment by which an individual or group produces a perceptible product that is both novel and useful as defined within a social context"*, [15] related with *"fluency, flexibility, and originality"* of ideas [5]. Due to the variety of definitions, some authors attempted to convey key requirements that should underlie definitions of creativity. With this, they initiated a dialogue towards a standard definition of creativity, stating that *originality* and *usefulness* are the most common occurrences when it comes to defining this concept [18], related with the number of ideas generated [7].

Despite schools being perceived as potentially rich and nurturing environments for enhancing children's creative abilities, research suggests a *"creativity crisis"* in education, in the form of a decline of creative abilities [9], starting at elementary school [2]. Scholars tend to agree that this ability can be nurtured and enhanced throughout life [12], making it important to be stimulated from a very young age.

Vision for YOLO

We present the design and development of YOLO, a social robot developed to boost creativity in children. YOLO is a non-humanoid robot with interactive capabilities that makes use of established strategies for creativity enhancement to boost creativity in children. YOLO was created to engage in playful activities with children and at the same time stimulate them to be more creative. The application scenario for YOLO is a storytelling activity with children, aiming to trigger idea generation and content for the story.

According to literature, idea generation (or *fluency*) is one fundamental creative ability that tends to lead to originality and novelty [5]. With YOLO, we aim to stimulate fluency during the creative process of storytelling. At the same time, we are interested in improving this ability in a group context [19]. Thus, YOLO acts as a playful tool for supporting *idea generation* during the creative process of storytelling of *groups of children.*

Table 1: Design principles of YOLO's creative triggers.

Process	Techniques	Media	Exercises
Idea generation	(1) Related Stimuli (semantic intuition) (2) Remote Stimuli (Nonlogical stimuli)	Robot	Group Imaginative Playful
Creative encounters	Collaborative emergence	Robot	Group
Originality	Motivate new ideas by discouraging repetitions	Robot	Group Imaginative Playful

Design process of YOLO

The design of YOLO included an integrative process of *literature review* and *user-studies of co-design with children.* Therefore, YOLO's design was informed by key concepts of validated creative programs and techniques that elicit creativity, as well as from findings from the co-design studies with children. This enabled an integrative design approach that combined both aspects from theory revision as well as views and preferences of children as they will be the end-users of YOLO .

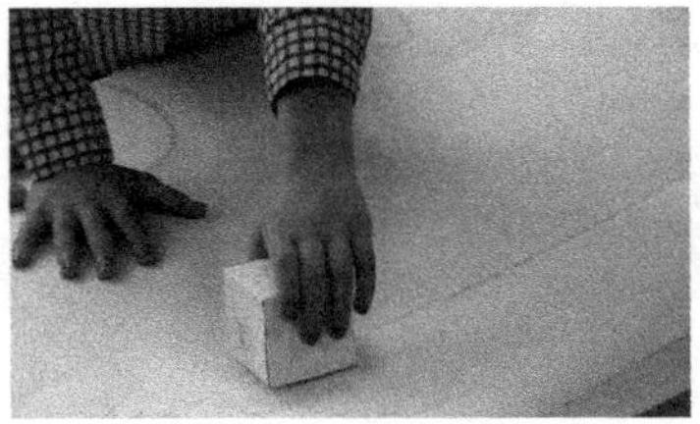

Figure 2: Co-design study 1: Children animating the paper robot prototype using puppeteering technique.

Figure 3: Co-design study 2: Children creating a story together with two robots (blue and orange) that were being animated by two children.

Figure 4: Paper-robot prototype with the basic shape of a cube in two sizes (small and large) that children animated during co-design studies.

Co-design studies with children
As children are the end-users of YOLO , they were included in the design process as informants [3] in two different co-design studies described below:

Co-design study 1 The goal of this study was to include children as co-designers of the *social behaviors* for the robot. To achieve this goal, children were asked to give expression to a prototype of the robot according to selected personality traits, *e.g.*, they were asked to provide movements and sounds for a grumpy/kind, sociable/shy robot. Thus, children gave expression to the robot by animating it according to puppeteering techniques as illustrated in Figure 2.

Co-design study 2 The goal of this study was to involve children in the design of *creative behaviors* for the robot, *i.e.*, different ways of the robot expressing new ideas during storytelling. For this, children were instructed to create a story using a robot-prototype. One of the children was selected to animate the robot and instructed to express ideas *through the robot* by performing only movements and sounds (thus, refraining from using speech to provide ideas). Thus, the group of children together with the robot (that was being animated and controlled by another child), were able to generate ideas for a story. *E.g.*, the child-puppeteer would move the robot in a certain way leading to the other children to interpret its behavior (*e.g.*, children could say *"the robot is afraid"* because the child who is controlling the robot is making it shake) and combine that interpretation in their story (see Figure 3). This way, they were integrating the robot's ideas and building a story together.

A total of 64 children aged between 6-10 years old were organized in groups of 3-4 and the studies were conducted in the school's classrooms. A psychologist researcher with experience in developmental studies with children was in the room where the sessions took place and performed field observations. The most relevant results that informed the design of YOLO are presented in Table 2. During the two co-design studies, children used a low fidelity robot-paper prototype with the basic shape of a cube (see Figure 4). This initial shape was inspired by LEGO™ bricks, nonetheless, the final morphology of the robot changed according to the results collected from the studies and accommodating literature on creativity (see *e.g.*, Figures 5, 6, 7 for the final appearance of the robot).

Literature review on creativity programs and techniques
Systematic literature reviews and meta-analysis on the field of creativity present a wide set of training programs for creativity [11, 17, 20, 21]. These programs were created and validated with the main goal of enhancing creativity. Usually, these programs tackle specific *cognitive processes of creativity* (such as idea generation). To achieve a successful enhancement of creativity levels, specific *techniques* are used (such as ideation, metaphors, brainstorming, etc), delivered using different *media* (*i.e.*, through a lecture, individualized coaching, behavioral modification, etc) in the format of defined *exercises* (such as exercises in groups, written exercises, etc) [21]. In this sense, YOLO is a robot that will incorporate validated creativity techniques for idea generation [23] (see Figure 1), such as *remote stimuli* and *related stimuli* to enhance idea generation by children (see Figure 7) (for a full list, see Table 1).

Table 2: Field observations from the two co-design studies conducted with children, mapped with how these results informed the design of the robot YOLO .

	Field observations from co-design studies	How co-design studies informed the design of YOLO
Social expression	Children were able to conceive different movements for the robot according to the personality traits. They expressed the different movement for different personality traits by animating the robot-paper prototype with different motion amplitude, angles and speed. *E.g.,* a grumpy robot would have a high movement amplitude, spiky motion with serious shapes and high speed (see Figure 8).	Giving the rich set of movement expression, YOLO was created to combine rich movement opportunities, expressed by different standing modes. Thus, the robot can stand in the vertical mode performing rotating movements (resembling a vinyl record) that can be programmed with different speeds. It also has a horizontal mode in which it has non automated wheels so that children can use the robot and express a variety of personalities and emotions (see Figure 6).
Guessing behavior	When the robot gave ideas for the story, children almost always tried to guess which idea the robot was trying to express. As the robot could express ideas only by movement, this resulted in different interpretations from children about what the robot was trying to convey. This result validated the idea that children were able to attribute meaning to the robot's movement when creating a story.	YOLO was designed to accommodate rich and diverse types of movements. Therefore, YOLO has both a vertical and two horizontal standing modes, all of them providing different movements with the potential to elicit ideas. Besides the standing modes, YOLO has the ability to move its strings in a hide-and-show movement (see Figures 5 and 7).
Turn-taking	At times, the interaction between children and the robot was chaotic due to the excitement of the task and because they wanted to share a large number of ideas with each other. In these moments, the researcher intervened to re-organize the flow.	YOLO includes a button in its design that children can click on to ask for ideas to YOLO, or to ask YOLO what it thinks about their own ideas. We envision that because the button can be clicked whenever children decide to and does not obey to strict turn-taking rules, it will have the effect of organizing the interaction and decrease the interference of an adult, proving children more autonomy during their creations

Figure 5: Movement study (1): Rotation movement of YOLO's strings (optical fibers).

Figure 6: Movement study (2): YOLO's non actuated wheels that are controllable by children.

Figure 7: Movement study (3): YOLO's hide-and-show autonomous behavior.

Meet YOLO

For the design process of YOLO a multidisciplinary team of psychologists, mechanical engineers and a computer scientists came together and have followed design techniques that emphasize movement in the robot [8], improvisation, [4], storyboarding [22] and user-studies [6]. YOLO's morphology followed an iterative process involving sketches, 3D modeling and rapid prototyping that encouraged and evoked movement-centric design [8]. Freehand sketches were drawn in order to explore multiple shapes for the robot. Sketches were inspired in real-world objects that were perceived by the authors as candidates for organic shapes and agile movements (see Figures 5, 6 and 7). Also, rapid prototyping enabled us to experiment several mechanical mechanisms. Storyboard techniques was used to explore different application scenarios for the deployment of the robot. In its final morphology, YOLO resembles a sea-like creature with a non-humanoid shape whose design was guided considering the following principles:

- **Expressive representations.** Since YOLO captures and recognized both the *shape* of the movement and the *speed* of the motion when children move it around, we will use this input to capture the context of the story. The shapes and speed's input were defined according to the results from the co-design study 1. As children act out the story using the robot, the generated movement will thus serve as our input (in the form of shapes and speed), enabling YOLO to react and contribute to the story. YOLO's contributions have the goal to stimulate idea generation (often called *fluency*) and will make use of the *related stimuli technique* (stimuli that is connected to the task) and the *remote stimuli technique* (stimuli that is unrelated to the task) [23] to stimulate ideas from children. Different behavioral expressions of YOLO (sound, colors and movement) will be used as related or remote stimuli. For this, we will develop expressive representations for the different movements that children produce, *e.g.*, if a child moves the robot with high speed in making a curly shape movement and the robot wants to provide a relate stimuli, it will display a given color, sound or movement that relates to this idea. The representations of movement-sound-color are based on the works of Mats B. Küssner [10] on visual representations of shapes and Konstantina Orlandatou on color-sound associations [13]. YOLO will thus display these two idea-generation behavioral triggers along the storytelling process.

Figure 8: Two examples of movements created by children for the kind (on the left) and the grumpy (on the right) personality traits.

- **Creative encounters.** YOLO will be used with groups of 3 children in a storytelling task. Henceforth, it becomes crucial to stimulate group processes of creation (denominated by Sawyer (2009) as *collaborative emergence* processes [19]). To stimulate the contribution of each child for the story creation YOLO will turn to each child during the storytelling activity in order to motivate and empower them to contribute with ideas for the story.

- **Originality.** Creativity is not only about the number of relevant ideas generated (fluency), but also how *original* they are. To design for originality of ideas, YOLO will demonstrate that it does not appreciate repetitions if they are performed too often in a row. Therefore, if children perform the same type of shapes using the same speed more than three times in a row, YOLO will perform a type of "shut-down" behavior in order to motivate children to perform different movements instead and not just repeat what they have performed.

We envision YOLO as a non-humanoid artifact that resemble a toy for children and that behave autonomously. Due to its autonomous behavior, it becomes non totally controllable (such as toys are) and thus fun for children to play with, having the potential to be a conductor of creative thinking. During playful interactions with YOLO, children will likely try to guess what the robot is expressing, enhancing the ingredients in their stories and at the same time not letting them take full control. In this sense, YOLO will not only be used and perceived as a toy that children project their unique ideas on, but additionally as an interactive toy that children can play with and that have a life on its own.

Seymour Papert revolutionized the way we look at education and learning. His vision of education as the center of all growth lead to revolutionary ideas: from computers as tools to learn, from LOGO programming to Turtle creations [14]. Nowadays, technology is indeed part of our lives and robots are being developed at a fast pace to enter in our homes, work places, and schools. The work presented in this paper seeks to provide a new application for robot and to develop them in such a way that they nurture intrinsic human abilities, such as creativity. Our future work includes usability studies of YOLO with children and long term studies in school to investigate if robotic technology can be used to boost creative thinkers.

Acknowledgements

This work was supported by national funds through Fundação para a Ciência e a Tecnologia (FCT-UID/CEC/500 21/2013) and through project AMIGOS (PTDC/EEISII/7174/2014). P. Alves-Oliveira acknowledges a FCT grant ref. SFRH/BD/110223/2015. The authors show their gratitude to André Pires, Ian Coutlier and Ankita Chandak for their involvement in this project, as well as to all teachers, students and parents from Escola Infante Sagres and Colégio Campo de Flores.

REFERENCES

1. Lorin W Anderson, David R Krathwohl, and Benjamin Samuel Bloom. 2001. *A taxonomy for learning, teaching, and assessing: A revision of Bloom's taxonomy of educational objectives.* Allyn & Bacon.
2. Mihaly Csikszentmihalyi. 1997. Flow and the Psychology of Discovery and Invention. *HarperPerennial, New York* 39 (1997).
3. Allison Druin. 2002. The role of children in the design of new technology. *Behaviour and information technology* 21, 1 (2002), 1–25.
4. Elizabeth Gerber. 2007. Improvisation principles and techniques for design. In *Proceedings of the SIGCHI conference on Human factors in computing systems.* ACM, 1069–1072.
5. Joy Paul Guilford. 1967. The nature of human intelligence. (1967).

6. Rex Hartson and Pardha S Pyla. 2012. *The UX Book: Process and guidelines for ensuring a quality user experience.* Elsevier.
7. Dennis Hocevar. 1979. Ideational fluency as a confounding factor in the measurement of originality. *Journal of Educational Psychology* 71, 2 (1979), 191.
8. Guy Hoffman and Wendy Ju. 2014. Designing robots with movement in mind. *Journal of Human-Robot Interaction* 3, 1 (2014), 89–122.
9. Kyung Hee Kim. 2011. The creativity crisis: The decrease in creative thinking scores on the Torrance Tests of Creative Thinking. *Creativity Research Journal* 23, 4 (2011), 285–295.
10. Mats Kussner. 2014. *Shape, drawing and gesture: Cross-modal mappings of sound and music.* Ph.D. Dissertation. King's College London (University of London).
11. Richard S Mansfield, Thomas V Busse, and Ernest J Krepelka. 1978. The effectiveness of creativity training. *Review of Educational Research* 48, 4 (1978), 517–536.
12. Raymond S Nickerson. 1999. 20 Enhancing Creativity. *Handbook of creativity* (1999), 392.
13. Konstantina Orlandatou. 2014. Synaesthetic and intermodal audio-visual perception: an experimental research. (2014).
14. Seymour Papert. 1980. *Mindstorms: Children, computers, and powerful ideas.* Basic Books, Inc.
15. Jonathan A Plucker, Ronald A Beghetto, and Gayle T Dow. 2004. Why isn't creativity more important to educational psychologists? Potentials, pitfalls, and future directions in creativity research. *Educational psychologist* 39, 2 (2004), 83–96.
16. Ken Robinson. 2011. *Out of our minds: Learning to be creative.* John Wiley & Sons.
17. Laura Hall Rose and HSIN-TAI LIN. 1984. A meta-analysis of long-term creativity training programs. *The Journal of Creative Behavior* 18, 1 (1984), 11–22.
18. Mark A Runco and Garrett J Jaeger. 2012. The standard definition of creativity. *Creativity Research Journal* 24, 1 (2012), 92–96.
19. R Keith Sawyer and Stacy DeZutter. 2009. Distributed creativity: How collective creations emerge from collaboration. *Psychology of Aesthetics, Creativity, and the Arts* 3, 2 (2009), 81.
20. Ginamarie Scott, Lyle E Leritz, and Michael D Mumford. 2004a. The effectiveness of creativity training: A quantitative review. *Creativity Research Journal* 16, 4 (2004), 361–388.
21. Ginamarie Scott, Lyle E Leritz, and Michael D Mumford. 2004b. Types of creativity training: Approaches and their effectiveness. *The Journal of Creative Behavior* 38, 3 (2004), 149–179.
22. David Sirkin and Wendy Ju. 2014. Using embodied design improvisation as a design research tool. In *Proceedings of the international conference on Human Behavior in Design (HBiD 2014), Ascona, Switzerland.*
23. Gerald F Smith. 1998. Idea-generation techniques: a formulary of active ingredients. *The Journal of Creative Behavior* 32, 2 (1998), 107–134.

Creating Social Stories as Wearable Hyper-Immersive Virtual Reality Experiences for Children with Neurodevelopmental Disorders

Mirko Gelsomini
Department of Electronics,
Information and Bioengineering
Politecnico di Milano, 20133
Milano, Italy
mirko.gelsomini@polimi.it

Nicolò Messina
Department of Electronics,
Information and Bioengineering
Politecnico di Milano,
20133 Milano, Italy
nicolo.messina@mail.polimi.it

Franca Garzotto
Department of Electronics,
Information and Bioengineering
Politecnico di Milano,
20133 Milano, Italy
franca.garzotto@polimi.it

Daniele Occhiuto
Department of Electronics,
Information and Bioengineering
Politecnico di Milano, 20133
Milano, Italy
daniele.occhiuto@polimi.it

Vito Matarazzo
Department of Electronics,
Information and Bioengineering
Politecnico di Milano, 20133
Milano, Italy
vito.matarazzo@mail.polimi.it

IDC '17, June 27-30, 2017, Stanford, CA, USA

ACM ISBN 978-1-4503-4921-5/17/06.
http://dx.doi.org/10.1145/3078072.3084305

Abstract

"Social stories" are short narratives that describe everyday life situations using paper or video and are widely used in interventions for children with Neurodevelopmental Disorders (NDD), particularly in the Autistic Spectrum. Our research explores how to transform "traditional" social stories into wearable interactive immersive digital experiences. The paper describes a tool designed with therapists that enables everyone to autonomously develop and customize these "high tech" social stories, and, during a session of use, to control user's interaction and to automatically gather relevant behavioural information.

Author Keywords

Neurodevelopmental Disorders (NDD); social story; wearable immersive virtual reality; head-mounted display; 360° videos; customization; disability; children, autism

ACM Classification Keywords

H.5.m

Introduction

Wearable Immersive Virtual Reality (WIVR) offers interactive virtual experiences that simulate real or imaginary environments on Head-Mounted Displays

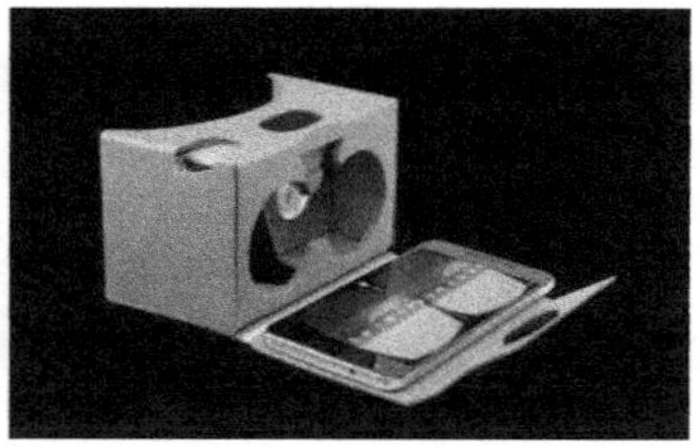

Figure 1: Example of Google Cardboard

Figure 2: Example of paper-based social story. Through a combination of short sentences and images this example explains to children how to do their homework.

(HMDs) and make the user feel inside the virtual spaces. In the last years, the evolution of WIVR technology (e.g., Oculus Rift, Google Cardboard, HTC Vive or Samsung Gear VR) has made HMDs cost-affordable and much more comfortable than previous generation devices. In addition, 360° cameras have enabled the spread of realistic 360° videos that can be played on WIVR viewers. As a result, we witness an increasing popularity of WIVR technology and applications in various domains that range from gaming, entertainment to cultural heritage, tourism and education [11]. Google Expeditions, for example, is a large educational project that supports the use of WIVR in the classroom. Students use Google Cardboard viewers (Figure 1) to experience virtual trips around the world, while teachers guide their students focusing on specific areas of interest.

Our research focuses on WIVR technology for children with Neurodevelopmental Disorders (NDDs). NDD is an umbrella term for a group of disabilities that appear during the developmental period and are characterized by deficits and limitations in the cognitive, emotional, motor and intellectual spheres [3]. The use of WIVR as a therapeutic or education tool for people with NDD was explored in the past and abandoned because of the drawbacks of first generation viewers [12] (e.g., high cost, weight, motion sickness effects). With the advent of cheaper, more comfortable, and technically more accurate hardware and software solutions, WIVR has raised a growing interest in the NDD field [7][8].

We are interested in WIVR applications for NDD children that exploit therapeutic approaches based on *social stories*. We have created a set of WIVR-based social stories on everyday situations (e.g., going to school, shopping at a store, visiting a museum). We have developed a tool designed with and for therapists that enables them to autonomously develop these WIVR applications, to control and personalize interaction, and to automatically gather behavioural information. Moreover, thanks to its portability, parents are provided with the same tool, allowing children to continue the training at home. In fact, parents have the possibility to reuse the same WIVR-based social stories developed in therapeutic centres, or to create new ones from scratch. The combination of therapist and parents is hereinafter referred as caregivers.

Approach

WIVR-based social stories

The term "social story" is used in NDD therapy to denote visual materials (paper- or video-based) that describe everyday life situations as simple short narratives (Figure 2). These tools are used in the treatment of persons with NDD, particularly ASD (Autism Spectrum Disorder), to help them develop social and practical skills and to learn appropriate behaviours and norms [1][4]. They are characterized by a format that is meaningful for these subjects: for example, four basic sentence types are typically included (descriptive, directive, perspective and affirmative), the use of illustrations is suggested and the authors must adopt the point of view of the child for whom the story is written [10].

Transforming social stories into interactive immersive virtual narratives can increase the benefits of the traditional approach [5]. WIVR-based social stories allow children with NDD to train in everyday life activities in a secure environment, while VR headsets promote attention and engagement as they remove the distractions caused by external visual stimuli and help users focus on learning tasks.

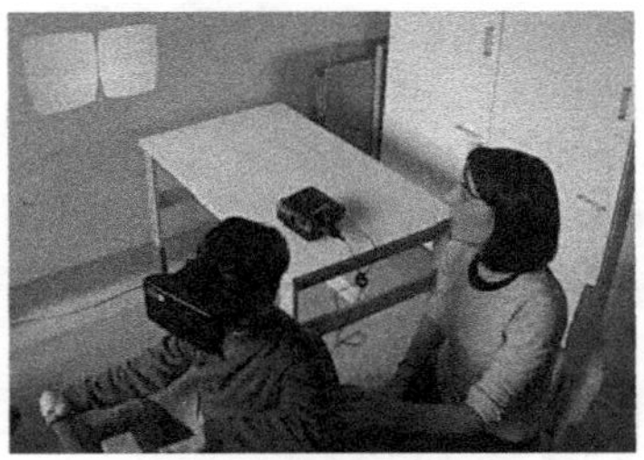

Figure 3: Using WIVR in previous therapeutic sessions with NDD children [6][7]

In our research, social stories are represented by a sequence of one or more connected 360° videos enriched with visual interactive elements that drive attention on specific elements, provide visual feedbacks, stimulate memory, or simply add engagement and fun to the WIVR experience. An important point of traditional social stories is to allow children to focus step by step on single actions. The same effect can be achieved with our tool thanks to the possibility to pause the story at any time and bring the attention of the child on important details through the specified elements.

As these applications are meant to be integrated in existing therapeutic programs and widely adopted (at care centers and at home), they must exploit low cost devices. We opted for the cheapest solution on the market, Google Cardboard (Figure 1). This viewer is composed of two biconvex lenses mounted on a plastic or cardboard structure available in different colors and shapes. The smartphone positioned inside the visor displays the visual contents, splitting them into two near-identical bi-dimensional images. The illusion of 3D depth and immersion is created by the stereoscopic effect generated by the viewer lenses. The interaction is achieved through gaze pointing and focus. The WIVR applications assume that the direction of the gaze focus is defined by head orientation (detected by smartphone sensors), and is always at the center of the screen. The user can navigate in the virtual world by rotating her head, which will consequently rotate the virtual scene projected in the display. Even if this assumption may seem limiting for people with NDD, since they often face challenge of making eye contact, this type of interaction has already been tested in previous work with positive results [6]. Particular cases (for example peripheral vision), must be evaluated directly by the therapist. Moreover, while the video goes on, the user can interact with an active object or areas in a scene by "pointing" at it (i.e. maintaining the gaze focus on the object for a minimum amount of time).

Empowering therapies

The educational and therapeutic value of any technology for persons with disability is directly related to its ability to adapt to each user's specific characteristics and learning requirements. There is empirical evidence that digital technologies for persons with disability that cannot be easily customized, or can be customized by ICT professionals only, are more often abandoned [9]. Having this fundamental requirement in mind, we have tried to understand how to make a WIVR customization application accessible to every caregiver, that are typically non-experts, in particular therapists that work with NDD children and their parents. For this target users, we have developed a tool that enables them to autonomously create new social stories from scratch, or to modify existing ones, in order to customize these technological solutions and make them appropriate for the specific and evolving needs of each single subject without relying on external developers. In addition, the ease of use of our tool allows parents to record their own 360° videos in a more familiar context like the child's home, and build a virtual experience. The results of the creation can be used by the child, supervised by her parents, to continue the learning process in a well-known environment.

Our tool is named *XOOM* and has been co-designed with NDD specialists from a local therapeutic center. XOOM provides caregivers full control over the virtual experience: from the creation and personalization of a WIVR-based social story to the control of the interaction features during the child's immersive experience. The rest of the paper focuses on the requirements and design of this tool.

XOOM Requirements

The requirements for XOOM have been elicited through the observation of 10 therapeutic sessions at a therapeutic center (Figure 3) in which 10 children with different functioning levels of NDD used, with the supervision of their caregivers, a WIVR application developed in prior research [6][7][8]. The content of this application was an interactive digital transposition of a storybook that children use at the center. During these sessions, the therapists were invited to "think aloud" about the customization that would be needed in the various situations. All sessions have been video-recorded and discussed in two focus groups with the involved NDD specialists at the end of the study, in order to understand the therapists needs of customization and to identify the main features and parameters of the VR experience that they would like to manage and control.

Requirement 1: Contextualized videos.
There are many 360° videos available today on the web that can be re-used for the creation of WIVR-based social stories. Still, videos that are related to the specific context of life of each subject can be more effective; they may refer to familiar contexts (to avoid the potential distress caused by the unknown that is typical of many children with NDD) or to local contexts that the subjects may later experience in person. This kind of video materials must be created from scratch but they can be easily recorded using any 360° camera available on the market.

Requirement 2: Scene selection and aggregation.
The caregiver should be enabled to select a 360° video, to insert it in the current social story, and to create a flow of different interconnected "scenes" to be shown in sequence (hyper-stories). The user proceeds along the flow of scenes by effect of external commands activated by the caregiver, by specific user's interactions, or both.

Requirement 3: Customization at creation time.
The caregiver should be able to personalize the video and its interactive experience by adding different types of items like arrows, masks, geometrical forms or textual popups. Each of these elements can have different properties.

Requirement 4: Run time control.
The caregivers should always be in control of the user experience: they should have a control panel that allows them to pause, restart, stop and change the video while it is playing in the HMD. The control panel should always show what the child is currently watching in the HMD, so to allow the caregiver to observe the interaction and intervene if needed.

Customization Elements

These are the elements used to customize the 360° videos. The following properties can be associated to each Customization Element:

Dynamic element: an element that can perform some animations or dynamic effects when the child focuses on it (e.g., showing animations, zooming in-out, rotating).

Control element: an element that, when selected by the user, controls the video execution (e.g., playing a paused video or moving from a scene to the next one).

Static element: an element that is overlaid on the video with no dynamic effects.

Figure 4: Creating a social story about a trip to a museum using the Creator component of XOOM. On the background there is the original video, while the customization elements (in red) were superimposed by the caregiver.

Requirement 5: Automatic data gathering.
The tool should automatically collect information about the child's interaction in the virtual spaces and support the analysis of this information, which is useful for caregivers to monitor the person's progression.

XOOM Design

Starting from the above requirements XOOM integrates three main components called *Creator, Runtime Controller,* and *Analyzer.* These are integrated with the WIVR-based social story used by the child, and offer the functionalities needed respectively before, during, and after the child's experience.

The *Creator* (Figure 4) allows the caregiver to create or modify a WIVR social story by:

- Selecting video fragments from the XOOM repository and combining them.
- Reordering the video fragments, set specific frames at which the scene must pause, add various customization elements (arrow, transparent area, textual popup, simple 3D objects,...). In particular, for each of these elements the caregiver can set position, dimensions, duration from a specific starting frame and its properties (details in the side bar). Moreover, the caregiver can select an area of the current frame to highlight, obscuring the rest

Figure 5: View of Runtime Controller of the running experience (under creation in figure 4). The two windows may be aligned horizontally depending on the screen orientation.

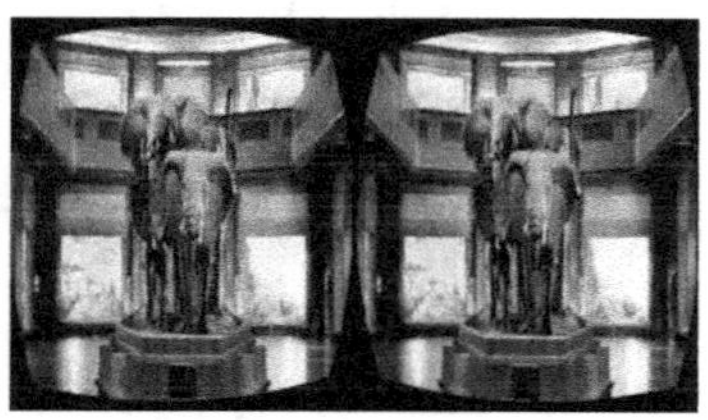

Figure 6: The same social story as in figure 5 as it is displayed on the smartphone placed inside the viewer.

with a mask. This functionality is useful to focus child's attention on a desired point.

- Saving the created story in the XOOM repository.

The *Runtime Controller* (Fig. 5) allows to:

- Choose a social story among those already created to start a session with the child.
- Monitor the running experience. The caregiver can see and control what is displayed to the child in the HMD using two windows on the screen. The control window (Figure 5 – top) shows the complete 360° scene "flattened" so that the caregiver can move freely in the timeline of the experience, without affecting the viewer. The other window (Figure 5 – bottom) shows the "perceived live view", i.e., what the end user is currently seeing through the HMD – a single image created by the human brain from the 2 almost identical images on the smart phone screen).
- Control what happens in the virtual environment affecting the reproduction of the experience, pausing it or changing the currently playing video. Moreover, the HMD leaves the caregiver the possibility to verbally communicate with the child, for example by making suggestions after pausing the video.

The *Analyzer* (under development) visualizes a 360° *heatmap* of each session and summarizes with different colors the points and areas of the scenes on which the child focused her attention the most and the least.

XOOM Implementation

Both XOOM and the social stories created using this tool are developed as *web applications*, which ensures a high degree of *portability* of all our technology on any platform. We used standard web languages: HTML, JavaScript (for the client side) and PHP (for the server side) and a set of public software libraries: A-Frame; heatmap.js; Firebase.

Conclusion and Future Work

Using wearable hyper-immersive virtual reality to extend and enrich social story therapeutic approaches opens up new opportunities in the treatment of NDD that have only been initially explored but may have an enormous potential in this field. The increasingly low-cost of WIVR technology paves the ground towards large scale adoption of this class of assistive applications, at therapeutic centers and in other contexts of life (e.g. at home and at school). The customization features offered by XOOM empower caregivers and give them a control of the child's experience with WIVR technology at a degree which is not allowed by any other existing tool. Finally, the nature of the contents exploited in WIVR hyper-social stories offers novel opportunities to give an active role to caregivers in the therapeutic process. Parents can be involved to record videos in the real contexts of their children's life to feed the XOOM video repository.

Our future work in the short term envisions the engineering of XOOM and the execution of two empirical studies – already designed - that will start soon at a therapeutic center. The goal of the first study is to evaluate the usability and effectiveness of XOOM with 10 NDD specialists. The second study (controlled study) will involve 20 children with NDD aged 6-12 and will focus on the therapeutic benefits of WIVR-based social stories, also compared to traditional social stories approaches. The creation of the social stories – both on paper (baseline condition) and as WIVR experiences has already started, involving the caregivers in the creation of the video materials.

References

1. Adams, L., Gouvousis, A., VanLue, M., & Waldron, C. 2004. Social Story Intervention: Improving

communication skills in a child with an autism spectrum disorder. Focus on Autism and Other Developmental Disabilities, 19(2), 87-94.

2. Deepti Aggarwal, Robyn Garnett, Bernd Ploderer, Frank Vetere, Patricia Eadie, and Bronwyn Joy Davidson. 2015. Understanding Video based Parent Training Intervention for Children with Autism. In *Proceedings of the Annual Meeting of the Australian Special Interest Group for Computer Human Interaction* (OzCHI '15), Bernd Ploderer, Marcus Carter, Martin Gibbs, Wally Smith, and Frank Vetere (Eds.). ACM, New York, NY, USA, 10-19. DOI: https://doi.org/10.1145/2838739.2838770
3. American Psychiatric Association. 2013. Diagnostic and statistical manual of mental disorders (DSM-5®). American Psychiatric Pub
4. Andersson, U., Josefsson, P., & Pareto, L. 2006. Challenges in designing virtual environments: Training social skills for children with autism. International Journal on Disability and Human Development, 5(2), 105–111.
5. Ehrlich J., Munger J. 2012. Utilizing Head Mounted Displays as a Learning Tool for Children with Autism. Proc. 4th European Immersive Education Summit, Vienna (Austria)
6. Franca Garzotto, Mirko Gelsomini, Francesco Clasadonte, Daniele Montesano, Daniele Occhiuto. 2016. Wearable Immersive Storytelling for Disabled Children. In *AVI '16 Proceedings of the International Working Conference on Advanced Visual Interfaces Pages 196-203.* https://doi.org/10.1145/2909132.2909256
7. Franca Garzotto, Mirko Gelsomini, and Daniele Occhiuto. 2016 (Conference Paper). Wildcard: A Wearable Virtual Reality Storytelling Tool for Children with Intellectual Developmental Disability Annual International Conference of the IEEE Engineering in Medicine and Biology Society (EMBC'16)
8. Mirko Gelsomini. 2016. Best Student Research Paper Award: An Affordable Virtual Reality Learning Framework for Children with Neuro-Developmental Disorder. In *Proceedings of the 18th International ACM SIGACCESS Conference on Computers and Accessibility* (ASSETS '16). ACM, New York, NY, USA, 343-344. DOI: https://doi.org/10.1145/2982142.2982143
9. Phillips, B. and Zhao, H. 1993. Predictors of assistive technology abandonment. In Assistive Technology. Taylor & Francis. 5(1): 36--45.
10. Reynhout, G. & Carter, M. J Autism Dev Disord (2006) 36: 445. doi:10.1007/s10803-006-0086-1
11. Seymour, N. E., Gallagher, A. G., Roman, S. A., O'Brien, M. K., Bansal, V. K., Andersen, D. K., & Satava, R. M. (2002). Virtual Reality Training Improves Operating Room Performance: Results of a Randomized, Double-Blinded Study. *Annals of Surgery*, *236*(4), 458–464.
12. Strickland, D. C., Marcus, L. M., Mesibov, G. B., & Hogan, K. 1996. Brief report: Two case studies using virtual reality as a learning tool for autistic children. Journal of Autism and Developmental Disorders, 26(6), 651–659
13. Sussman, F., Honeyman, S., Lowry, L., & Drake, L. More Than Words - The Hanen Program for Parents of Children with Autism Spectrum Disorders (Third ed.). 2013. Toronto, Canada: The Hanen Centre. http://www.hanen.org/Programs/For-Parents/More-Than-Words.aspx

Programming Literacy: Computational Thinking in Brazilian Public Schools

Adelmo Antonio da Silva Eloy
Escola Politécnica
Universidade de São Paulo /
Instituto Ayrton Senna
Sao Paulo, SP, Brazil
adelmo.eloy@usp.br

Amilton Rodrigues Quadros Martins
Faculdade Meridional (IMED)
Passo Fundo, RS, Brazil
amilton@imed.edu.br

Ariane Mileidi Pazinato
Faculdade Meridional (IMED)
Passo Fundo, RS, Brazil
ariane.pazinato@imed.edu.br

Maria de Fatima S. Polesi Lukjanenko
Universidade São Francisco
Itatiba, SP, Brasil
maria.lukjanenko@usf.edu.br

Roseli de Deus Lopes
Escola Politécnica
Universidade de São Paulo
Sao Paulo, SP, Brazil
roseli.lopes@usp.br

IDC '17, June 27-30, 2017, Stanford, CA, USA

ACM ISBN 978-1-4503-4921-5/17/06.
http://dx.doi.org/10.1145/3078072.3084306

Abstract
Bringing Programming to K-12 Education has been a strong tendency in Brazil and in the world. In this work-in-progress, we describe an experience in teacher training with the goal of promoting the practice of programming and the development of computational thinking in students of Brazilian public schools, through an initiative called Programming Literacy. Here we present strategies used in the implementation of the initiative, design of a curricular structure and training program, as well as monitoring and evaluation strategies. The results and findings of the initiative, involving more than 500 students from four cities in 2016, are shared as well as the perspectives on next steps.

Author Keywords
Programming; Computational thinking; Computer Science Education; K-12 Education; Teacher training.

ACM Classification Keywords
K.3.1 [Computer Uses in Education]: Collaborative learning, K.3.2 [Computer and Information Science Education]: Computer science education.

Figure 1: Programming Literacy's activity in *Itatiba* (SP), Brazil. Photo: Ivan Franchet / IAS

Introduction

Seymour Papert defined computer programming as the communication between user and machine through a language that both understand [4]. More than using an existing software for specific purposes, the act of programming consists of solving problems using the computer and its ability to process data and information as powerful tools. More important than a computer program as a final result, the process of creating a program involves steps such as identification of a problem and breaking it down, implementation and validation of the proposed solution; the understanding and practice of those skills go beyond the computational context. Considering programming as an educational practice, one of its expected results in a structured way is the development of what can be called computational thinking.

Jeanette Wing defined computational thinking as the formulation of problems and solutions represented in a way that can be carried out by information processors - humans, computers or, even better, a combination of both [8]. Karen Brennan and Mitchel Resnick suggest the division of computational thinking into three dimensions: concepts, practices and computational perspectives [2]. Computational practices and perspectives, especially, show that computational thinking is not limited to technical or professional training. In addition to representing a gateway to careers in Electrical Engineering and Computer Science, the ability to solve problems, in an efficient and structured way, contributes to a differentiated view of how to create or design digital technologies, an essential skill in several areas. As Paulo Blikstein asserts, through Computational Thinking it is possible to "use computers and computer networks to increase our productivity, inventiveness and creativity" [1].

In this way, the *Instituto Ayrton Senna* (IAS), through its UNESCO Chair in Education and Human Development, created an initiative called Programming Literacy, which aims to contribute to the development of 21st century skills, such as creativity, problem solving, collaboration and persistence, through the practice of programming and development of computational thinking. This initiative focuses on the training of school teachers from Years 6 to 9 from all areas of knowledge to promote the development of computational thinking in students from public school (figure 1). The implementation of this initiative began in 2015, in partnership with the municipality of *Itatiba, São Paulo*, and an expansion to three other municipalities in the state of *Rio Grande do Sul* in 2016. The methodology used to implement a pilot project of this initiative, as well as preliminary results, lessons learned and next steps, are presented in this paper.

Methodology

Four main areas were considered in the pilot project: implementation in schools, curriculum design, teacher training, and monitoring and evaluation. The main tools used to gather information on these areas were meetings with local leaders, face-to-face sessions and virtual feedback forms (anonymous and identified). The pilot project described in this article includes 2015 and 2016.

The implementation followed IAS's methodology: partnerships with the Municipal Departments of Education to ensure that the initiative would be lead as a public policy; from a formal agreement, schools

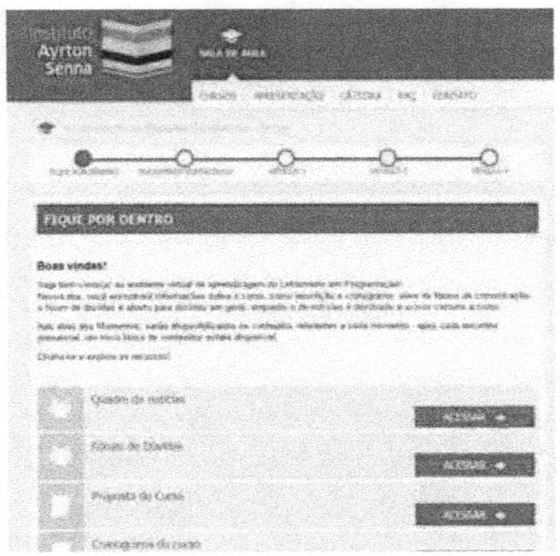

Figure 2: *Educação Online*: Learning Management System from IAS [6].

interested in lauching the initative designated teachers to join the training program, organizing classes as extracurricular actvities. To strengthen the implementation, partnerships were established with Higher Education Institutions (HEI) from or close to the municipalities, with the role of contributing to the educators' training activities and exploring research possibilities related to the initiative.

In order to design the curriculum's first version, a set of activities available in the online platform *Programaê!* was selected as a first guiding material [5]. The main digital tools explored in this set were Code.org and Scratch. The activities were selected according to the age range of the students involved and its availability in Portuguese. As an improvement's strategy, face-to-face sessions with educators were conducted and virtual feedbacks about activities were collected.

The teacher training program was designed from earlier experiences in teacher training from IAS, with face-to-face sessions conducted by the IAS staff and partners, complemented with virtual activities in the IAS's Learning Management System (LMS): *Educação Online* (figure 2). In this system, teachers could access supporting content and communicate with Institute's staff.

Monitoring and evaluation were slightly different in the years 2015 and 2016. In 2015, the monitoring strategy focused on improving: a) the initiative's implementation, adjusting weekly hours of teachers planning and running activities with students; b) the teacher training program, based on virtual feedback for each session. In 2016, it had a greater focus on gathering inputs to improve the curriculum and the monitoring process itself, using the same information gathering's techniques. Regarding evaluation, the key indicator tracked was the students' retention in the activities through the year. In addition, the information collected resulted in findings and points of improvement that are not restricted to one or more of the areas defined and which will be described in the results and lessons learned section.

Results and lessons learned

Table 1 presents a summary of the public served during the pilot project in 2015 and 2016, considering different cohorts of students who started the project at the same period. By the end of 2016, there were three different cohorts of students participating in the initiative in Itatiba – São Paulo (SP), where there is also a partnership with the *Universidade São Francisco*, an HEI from *Itatiba*. In *Rio Grande do Sul* (RS), the first cohort started in 2016, after a partnership with the Municipal Departments of Education in the municipalities of *Passo Fundo*, *Marau* and *Sananduva*, as well as the *Faculdade Meridional* – IMED, an HEI from *Passo Fundo*. Also, teachers indicated in each cohort refers to the number of teachers who were responsible for the activities, in one or more classes – that means that a teacher could be leading two different cohorts of students during the same period.

The difference in number of cohorts per year is due to the change of a semester-based curriculum in 2015 to a year-based curriculum in 2016. This decision was made in order to adjust the weekly workload of activities: instead of 3 hours per week for teachers with students, *Itatiba's* Department of Education proposed 1 hour for planning and 2 hours of activities with students per week. We consider that this was a success factor for greater student retention in phase 1 (green cells in Table 1): from 69 and 71% for the 1st and 2nd cohort in SP, respectively, to 79% in the 3rd cohort and 77% in the 1st cohort in RS. Although students' retention is still a challenge in this and other extracurricular initiatives from IAS, a year-based curriculum brought better results in retention, even with the increase of schools and students involved in the project.

Cohorts of students involved	Schools	Periods											
		2015.1				2015.2				2016			
		Teachers involved	Students: beginners	Students: graduates	Students: retention (%)	Teachers involved	Students: beginners	Students: graduates	Students: retention (%)	Teachers involved	Students: Beginners	Students: graduates	Students: retention (%)
1st SP	6	12	91	63	69	2	50	44	88	2	26	23	88
2nd SP	5					9	85	60	71	3	29	22	76
3rd SP	16									29	490	388	79
1st RS	9									10	141	109	77

Table 1: Summary of schools and students involved in the Programming Literacy initiative, by cohort of incoming students – beginners (students by the beginning) and graduates (students by the end)

The curriculum used in phase 1 was based on *Programaê!* material and guided initial activities in all cohorts of students involved (green cells in Table 1. In order to keep students learning and engaged in programming, two additional phases, called 2 and 3, were designed – exploring Scratch and App Inventor, also on a year-based model (blue and yellow cells in Table 1, respectively). As an entry requirement, students in phase 2 and 3 should have finished phase 1 and 2, respectively, in the prior semester/year. In those phases, a greater focus was given on project-based learning, such as design of games, animations and mobile applications; more details are presented in Table 2.

	Curriculum phases	Digital tools
1	Introduction to Computational Thinking	Code.org, Scratch
2	Design of games and interactive stories	Scratch
3	Design of mobile apps	App Inventor

Table 2: Curriculum phases of Programming Literacy

We observed a greater student retention in phases 2 and 3 (88% in 2015 and in 2016, for 1st cohort in SP, and 76%, for 2nd cohort). We believe that students who were involved in those phases were more engaged with the initiative and that project-based learning was important for this result. As in phase 1, phases 2 and 3 consisted of a set of 30 activities to be run by teachers with students as an extracurricular activity (2 hours per activity in a weekly basis). While the material from phase 2 was design by IAS team, the material of the phase 3 was based on Technovation Program's methodology [7].

In 2016, an effort was also made to improve phase 1's curriculum of Programming Literacy initiative, through discussion sessions with teachers and virtual questionnaires for critiques and suggestions (total of 21 answers). The three main points of improvement were: importance of unplugged activities for discussion and appropriation of knowledge in computing; importance of creating a first project to support students' learning and keep their engagement; need for a more structured introduction to Scratch platform. These aspects were considered in the design of a new version of curriculum for phase 1; the new version was designed in 2016 in partnership with Sheena Vaidyanathan, computer scientist and educator based in California, and is being tested in 2017.

Teacher training - indicators	2015	2016
Participants	12	40
Classes	1	3
Face-to-face meetings	6	7
Length	36 hours	42 hours

Table 3: Comparison between teacher training program: 2015 and 2016

Figure 3: Tech Oscar 2016, in *Itatiba (SP)*. Credit: Maira Villamarin / IAS

The teacher training strategy in 2015 and 2016 was based on face-to-face meetings and distance learning activities managed with the support of IAS's LMS, programming platforms explorations and group discussions. Table 3 presents a comparison between the training strategies of 2015 and 2016, with the number of teachers involved in each year.

The participating public was made up of teachers from diverse areas of knowledge, with a greater representation of Math teachers (41%). In both years, for each meeting, 3 hours of face-to-face activities and 3 hours of activities in the LMS were estimated; also, 3 meetings were held before the beginning of classroom activities. In order to improve the teacher training program, feedbacks for each meeting were provided by participants, which contributed to incremental improvements in the training strategy in both years - the discussion and application of their main suggestions between sessions contributed to engage the participants and stimulated them to give continuous feedbacks. Despite the increase in the number of meetings in 2016, they have been more distributed throughout the year than in 2015. Nevertheless, the length of the teacher training has been a constraint for Departments of Education; in this way, we plan to design and run a format with less face-to-face hours.

Other lessons learned, which were not strictly related to the four main areas discussed, were identified during this process and are highlight here:

Role of the teacher: The teachers participating in the pilot were not experts in the field, but rather people interested in learning something new. Throughout the process, the main learning described by them was the new role they had in the classroom: mentors and facilitators who do not have the answer to all questions and who could learn from and with their students.

Infrastructure: This is a big challenge in Brazilian public schools. Although the participating schools have computer labs, teachers still report issues regarding the quality of computers and internet connection.

Community engagement: local events were important to promote the initiative and engage other stakeholders, like students' families. Workshops within and outside schools, and fairs for projects' presentations such as Tech Oscar - where about 90 students presented their games and animations to the local community (figure 3) – were important to bring interest – and more schools and teachers – to the initiative.

Skills development: Although interesting cases emerged during the pilot - such as the written testimony of a 6th grader after his 1st project on Scratch (figure 4) or a 9th grader whose story was broadcasted nationwide after building an application for his father (Figure 5) –, no tools that could scientifically prove the development of computational thinking or 21st century skills – the purpose of the initiative – were identified and applied yet.

Conclusion and Future Work

The experience of designing an initiative to bring Programming to public schools in Brazil to promote the development of 21st century skills resulted in the results and lessons learned described. Besides designing and improving a curriculum considering peculiarities from local schools, implementing an

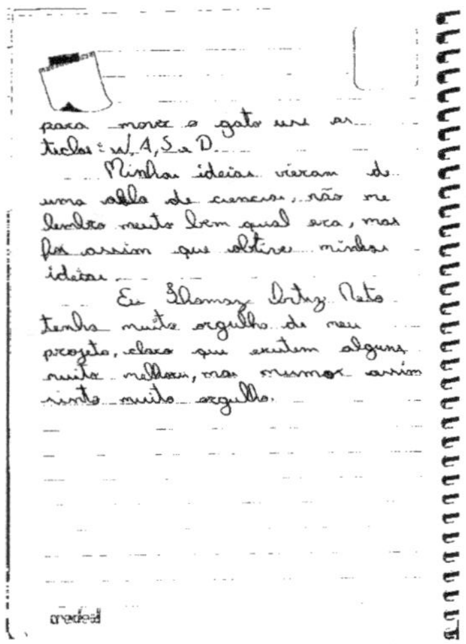

Figure 4: Journal of a student from Programming Literacy where he describes how proud he was of himself because of his first project on Scratch.

Figure 5: Student from Programming Literacy who designed an app to make the work of his father (a truck driver) easier [3]. Credit: Globo Television / Como será.

effective teacher training strategy was a big challenge. Monitoring of activities also presents isssues and learnings, especially in relation to the definition of indicators which could effectively contribute to the project. Improving evaluation also is essential: keeping track of student attendance and retention is a first step that does not answer all the questions of the initiative. In other words, there were many lessons learned in 2015 and 2016, but we see several points of improvement for the next years of the Programming Literacy initiative.

The next steps planned for 2017 are:

- Expansion of the initiative in number of schools and cities, increasing the diversity of experiences and lessons learned, in addition to the number of students engaged.
- Design and implementation of the logical framework of the initiative to make monitoring more robust and generate more inputs for analysis, as well as strategies for assessing programming and computational thinking skills of students, throughout the project;
- Strengthening the partnership with Higher Education Institutions, promoting scientific progress in the field, especially related to the study and evaluation of skills.
- Improvements on the curriculum, with the design of a 4th phase related to physical computing and an experience with students and teachers from Years 1 to 5.
- Improvement on the teacher training strategy, including the design of a specific track for teachers applying phases 2 to 4 of the curriculum.

Acknowledgements

We thank the support from *Instituto Ayrton Senna*, *Universidade São Francisco* (USF), *Faculdade Meridional* (IMED), and municipalities of *Itatiba* (SP), *Marau* (RS), *Passo Fundo* (RS) and *Sananduva* (RS).

References

1. Paulo Blikstein. 2008. O Pensamento Computacional e a Reinvenção do Computador na Educação. Paulo Blikstein. Retrieved August 29, 2016 from: http://www.blikstein.com/paulo/documents/online/ol_pensamento_computacional.html.
2. Karen Brennan, Mithcel Resnick. 2012. New frameworks for studying and assessing the development of computational thinking. American Educational Research Association. Vancouver, 2012.
3. G1 EDUCAÇÃO. 2016. Filho aprende a programar e cria app para facilitar o trabalho do pai. Retrieved August 29, 2016 from http://glo.bo/2byKDZt.
4. Seymour Papert. 1980. Mindstorms: children, computers, and powerful ideas. New York: Basic Books.
5. Programaê. 2015. Professor: Programaê! Retrieved August 29, 2016 from http://programae.org.br/professor/.
6. Instituto Ayrton Senna. 2016. Educação Online. Retrieved August 29, 2016 from http://www.educacaoonline.org.br/ead.
7. Technovation. Currículo Technovation. Retrieved August 29, 2016 from http://www.technovationbrasil.org/curriculo
8. Jeannette M. Wing. 2010. Computational Thinking: What and Why? Link Magazine".

Cracking The Code: The Impact of Computer Coding on the Interactions of a Child with Autism

Jim Gribble
UC-Santa Barbara
Goleta,CA, 93117, USA
jgribble@ucsb.edu

Alexandria Hansen
UC-Santa Barbara
Goleta,CA, 93117, USA
ahansen@ucsb.edu

Danielle Harlow
UC-Santa Barbara
Goleta,CA, 93117, USA
dharlow@education.ucsb.edu

Diana Franklin
University of Chicago
Chicago, IL, 60637, USA
dmfranklin@uchicago.edu

IDC '17, June 27-30, 2017, Stanford, CA, USA

ACM ISBN 978-1-4503-4921-5/17/06.
http://dx.doi.org/10.1145/3078072.3084307

Abstract
This paper reports on the communication patterns of two students in two settings: the elementary school classroom and the computer lab. One child was diagnosed with autism and the other was neurotypical. These students participated in a computer science curriculum designed for upper elementary school children (grades 4-5; ages 9-10), featuring block-based coding. The computer science instruction occurred in an inclusive general education setting. Analysis of video data revealed the child with autism communicated more (in terms of both total time speaking and interactions initiated) in the computer lab than was observed in the traditional classroom setting. Opposite trends were observed for the neurotypical child.

Author Keywords
Computer Science Education; Autism; Communication; Elementary School; Scratch; Coding; Logo; Papert

ACM Classification Keywords
K.3.1 [Computer Uses in Education]: Collaborative learning, K.3.2 [Computer and Information Science Education]: Computer science education

Introduction

In 2016, the White House announced the *Computer Science for All* initiative, calling for computer science instruction in K-12 schools, "offering every student the hands-on computer science and math classes that make them job-ready" [7]. There has been an increase in novice-friendly programming environments (e.g., Scratch, Alice), many of which occur in after-school.

As computer science is integrated into K-12 inclusive schools, research-based findings should inform the development of curriculum and teaching practices to ensure *all* students can access the content, including children with exceptionalities (formerly special needs).

Despite children with exceptionalities making up 13% of the school-age population [12], little research has focused attention on understanding how these children understand computer science. A significant portion of this 13% consists of children diagnosed with autism or who exhibit autism-like characteristics, such as difficulty communicating with others.

Research on children with autism has largely focused on differentiating instruction or on supporting these children to succeed with existing curricula. To our knowledge, no research has focused on the impact computer science has on the communication of children with autism, as we do here. We focus on whether computer science instruction can serve as a tool for helping a child with autism communicate more with his peers, a skill he struggled with in other school contexts.

Related Works

Scratch is a programming environment for children [10]. Like its predecessor, Logo [8], Scratch was developed to encourage children to be makers, rather than consumers, of their worlds [9]. This requires children learn more than just academic skills. Social and communication skills are essential as well, including the ability to learn from and with others. This is difficult for children diagnosed with autism, who may easily acquire deep specialized knowledge about a topic or subject of study and struggle to collaborate with peers. Below we describe research on computer science instruction for children with exceptionalities.

The Individuals with Disabilities Act (IDEA) and the Americans with Disabilities Act (ADA), *legally requires* educators to provide all students access to the general education curriculum. In the K-12 school level they should be placed in the LRE (Least Restrictive Environment) in a classroom with their peers, rather than receiving instruction in separate classrooms. Further, in many states, computer science is being taught as part of the general education curriculum; therefore, it is important for educators to consider how to meaningfully include students with exceptionalities.

The term "exceptionality" encapsulates a wide range of disorders impacting learning. This paper focuses on one student diagnosed with autism, "a neurodevelopmental syndrome defined by deficits in social reciprocity and communication" [6]. Individuals diagnosed with autism typically struggle to effectively communicate with peers and adults. Limited research exists investigating how elementary school children with autism engage with and learn computer coding in elementary school.

While some research has focused attention on students with exceptionalities studying computer science at the secondary [3] and post-secondary levels [2], less studies have looked at elementary school students (aged 5-11) with exceptionalities. Israel et al. [5] conducted a cross-case analysis of elementary school teachers implementing computer science lessons in the general education curriculum at one school. They found implementation varied based on teacher and context (e.g. classroom vs. library); successful teachers more often integrated coding into other content areas (e.g., math). This signals a need to prepare elementary school teachers to ensure *all* students are able to participate in computer science instruction. Further, Snodgrass, Israel and Reese [11] conducted a comparative case study of three elementary school students diagnosed with learning exceptionalities, one of which was autism. This student struggled to initiate and maintain interactions with others while generally engaging in programming exercises on the computer. Adults working with this student frequently took control of the computer. When he remained in control of the computer, he engaged for longer periods.

Research Design

This study is part of a larger research project investigating how students in grades 4-6 (ages 9-11) learn computer science using a block-based programming environment, modified from Scratch [10]. For more information about our modifications and curriculum, see Hill et al [4]. Our study followed design-based research methods [1] which, depended on the collaboration of multiple stakeholders.

We tested our curriculum with over 1,500 students (aged 9-12) at 10 schools ranging from 2013-2015. 4%-100% of students qualified for free or reduced lunch (a proxy for socioeconomic status), and 2%-82% designated English language learners.

While many teachers reported difficulties engaging students with exceptionalities in the computer science curriculum, one exception emerged – a student we call Alex, who was diagnosed with autism.

Alex participated in roughly 30 hours of coding and performed lower than his typical peers on programming tasks. By the end of 5th grade, he surpassed those same peers. Further, teachers noted Alex emerged as a leader; his peers frequently asked him for help or observed his work. Based on these observations, a new research question was formulated to investigate the connection between Alex's programming abilities and communication patterns: *How does engagement in a computer science curriculum impact the communication patterns of a student identified as having autism?*

To answer this question, we narrowed our focus to Alex and another student—Nick. Nick did not have a learning exceptionality and was selected for contrastive purposes to better understand Alex's communication patterns. We chose Nick because he was the only child who appeared in the classroom as well as the computer lab video records when Alex was in the video frame.

Some of the computer science lessons occurred in a normal classroom without a computer, while other lessons occurred in the school's designated computer lab. This created an interesting opportunity to investigate how lesson type – on or off a computer – impacted student communication, generating a more specific research question: *How did Alex's communication patterns change based on lesson type – on computer or off computer?*

We identified all segments in which Alex was visible both in a typical classroom setting (working off

	Lessons (N)	Video Length (s)
Classroom	1	2160
Lab	2	5100
Total	3	7260

Table 1: Summary of video data analyzed

computers) and in a computer lab setting. Table 1 shows the amount of video records analyzed.

In the classroom context, students prepared for their final project—to program a game. In this lesson, the teacher led the class through a group brainstorm, recording aspects of common games students enjoyed.

Students then completed a worksheet and recorded ideas they would later use to program a game in the computer lab. Students were encouraged to talk with nearby partners and to move around the room. No computers were used.

In the computer lab context, two lessons were analyzed. In one, students completed guided programming exercises. They were reminded about sprites (programmable objects or characters) and how to start a script (code) in the computer lab. They were challenged to use 3 sprites and 15 coding blocks for this exercise. In the second lesson, students completed guided programming exercises on variables where they programmed sprites' scores to increase or decrease during a game. In both cases, if a student finished early, they were encouraged to tinker in an open-ended play area to practice their newly learned skills. All instruction occurred in the computer lab.

For all 120 minutes of video, we coded both Alex and Nick's interactions with other peers, the teacher and each other. We defined an interaction as an instance of conversation initiation, such as when a child turned to speak to a peer or ask the teacher a question. We used time stamps in the video to calculate the amount of time each child was speaking for each interaction. We then compared the number of interactions and speaking time in the computer lab to the classroom.

In this section, we first discuss Alex's interactions in the two contexts. We then compare Alex's interactions to Nick's, a neurotypical peer. All lessons focused on computer science content; however, computers were only used in the computer lab.

Comparing Contexts: Alex in Classroom to Alex in the Lab

Alex's Interactions in Classroom

Alex's participation in the traditional (non-computer based) classroom was characterized by physically disengaging himself from the conversation with few initiated interactions. In the classroom, Alex rarely interacted with his peers (2 times) or with a teacher (4 times). For example, the teacher approached Alex to re-direct him when he leaned back in his chair and asked: "Got everything down?" Alex was non-responsive so the teacher read what he wrote aloud saying: "Computer Skills. Okay." Alex replied: "Good" and gave a thumbs up. Further, Alex frequently got out himself from any potential discussion.

Alex's Interactions in Computer Lab

In contrast to his participation in the typical classroom, Alex's participation in the computer lab was characterized by increased interactions with his peers (24 times) and his teacher (10 times). For example, Alex frequently offered to share his work with the teacher, or help his nearby peers when he finished a programming task early. As shown in Figure 2, Alex was often seen leaning in and pointing to his neighbor's computer (in this case, Nick). This action occurred multiple times throughout the lesson.

Figure 2: Alex and Nick in the classroom. This shows a typical scene in which most of the children were engaged in small group discussions at their tables, while Alex was leaning back in his chair. In these instances, a teacher typically attempted to help Alex re-focus on the task.

Figure 2: Alex helping Nick with coding on a desktop computer.

Comparison to Nick, the Neurotypical Peer

We found Alex spoke for less time in the classroom setting when no computers were used. As shown in Table 2, Alex spoke for a total of 300 seconds (out of 2160 total seconds), or roughly 14% of the time. Further, Alex initiated interactions 6 times throughout the class period, or approximately once every 6 minutes. In contrast, in the same classroom setting, Nick spoke for 480 seconds, or 22% of the time and initiated interactions 23 times, or approximately once every 90 seconds.

Alex's interactions in the classroom were very limited compared to Nick.

		Time (s)		Initiations With Whom?	
Student	Context	Speaking	%	Teacher	Peer
Alex	Classroom	300	14%	4	2
Nick	Classroom	480	22%	1	22
Alex	Lab	955	19%	10	24
Nick	Lab	235	5%	3	10

Table 2. Initiated interactions of Alex and Nick, by context. See Table 1 for total time observed in each context.

The opposite trend was observed when Alex worked in the computer lab. As shown in Table 2, Alex verbally communicated for 955 seconds (out of 5100 total seconds), or roughly 19% of the time. Further, Alex initiated 34 interactions. In contrast, Nick spoke for only 235 total seconds, or roughly 5% of the time, and initiated only 13 interactions.

Nick's limited interactions over the course of the two lessons in the computer lab were not surprising either. Other students were observed to be more solitary in their work and less likely to interact with nearby peers.

Recall, Nick interacted 23 times in the classroom setting and only 13 times in the computer lab whereas the reverse was true for Alex. Alex interacted only 6 times in the classroom setting and 34 times in the computer lab. We recognize these anecdotal findings are not generalizable to the general population.

Discussion

We reported on the communication patterns of a child with autism learning how to code in two contexts—the classroom and computer lab. When working in the computer lab, Alex spoke for longer amounts of time and initiated more interactions with peers and the teacher than in the classroom. Alex's teachers said he was more engaged socially during computer coding class. Jim Gribble saw similar communication when he taught children with autism how to code in the past.

Alex also used twice as many blocks when compared to the average number used by his peers in class. Alex's communication assisted peers in their understanding of coding. We delve deeper into this in another paper we are working on: "Understanding the Potential of Computer Science for Elementary School Students with Disabilities." Additionally, Alex led one of the summer school coding classes at the end of the sessions. Further similar individual case studies, as well as studies with multiple students, are encouraged.

Similar to Papert, we advocate for using the computer as a powerful tool to think with and act through. In our case, the computer served as a tool for a student to communicate and connect with both peers and adults. We, as researchers, must attend to the social benefits coding provides students with autism if we want elementary school teachers to embrace coding through mediums born out of Logo to teach computational thinking or other disciplinary content. This will help ensure computer science for all children is achieved.

Acknowledgements

This work is supported by the National Science Foundation (USA) CE21 Award CNS-1240985. Any opinions, findings, and conclusions or recommendations expressed are those of the authors and do not necessarily reflect those of the NSF.

References

1. Sasha Barab. & Kurt Squire. 2004. Design-based research: Putting a stake in the ground. Journal of the Learning Sciences, 13(1), 1-14.
2. Katherine Deibel. 2007. Studying our inclusive practices: Course experiences of students with disabilities. In Proceedings of the 12th annual ITiCSE Conference, 266–270, New York. ACM Press.
3. James Dixon Hearne, Mary S. Poplin, Carole Schnoeman, & Elizabeth O-Shaughnessy. 1988. Computer aptitude: An investigation of differences among junior high students with learning disabilities and their non-learning-disabled peers. *Journal of Learning Disabilities, 21*(8), 489-492. Chicago.
4. Charlotte Hill, Hilary Dwyer, Tim Martinez, Danielle Harlow & Diana Franklin. 2015. Floors and Flexibility: A block based programming environment for 4th-6th grade. ACM SIGCSE Conference.
5. Maya Israel, Jamie N. Pearson, Tanya Tapia, Quentin M. Wherfel, George Reese. 2015. Supporting all learners in school-wide computational thinking: A cross case analysis. *Computers & Education.*
6. Catherine Lord, Edwin H. Cook, Bennett L. Leventhal, & David G. Amaral. 2000. Autism spectrum disorders. *Neuron*, *28*(2), 355-363.
7. Barack Obama. 2016. State of the union address. Retrieved July 18, 2016, from https://www.whitehouse.gov/the-press-office/2016/01/12/remarks-president-barack-obama-—-prepared-delivery-state-union-address.
8. Seymour Papert. 1980. *Mindstorms.*
9. Seymour Papert & Idit Harel. 1991. Situating constructionism. *Constructionism*, 36, 1-11.
10. Mitchel Resnick, Maloney, J., Andrés Monroy-Hernandez, Natalie Rusk, Evelyn Eastmond, Karen Brennan, Amon Millner, Eric Rosenbaum, Jay Silver, Brian Silverman, Yasmin Kafai. 2009. Scratch: Programming for all. *Communications of the ACM*, 52, 11, 60-67.
11. Melinda R. Snodgrass, Maya Israel, George Reese. 2016. Instructional supports for students with disabilities in K-5 computing: Findings from a cross-case analysis, *Computers & Education*.
12. U.S. Department of Education, National Center for Education Statistics. 2015. *Digest of Education Statistics, 2013* (NCES 2015-011), Chapter 2.

Designing a Robot Companion for Children with Neuro-Developmental Disorders

Mirko Gelsomini
Politecnico di Milano
mirko.gelsomini@polimi.it

Marzia Degiorgi
Politecnico di Milano
marzia.degiorgi@mail.polimi.it

Franca Garzotto
Politecnico di Milano
franca.garzotto@polimi.it

Giulia Leonardi
Politecnico di Milano
giulia.leonardi@mail.polimi.it

Simone Penati
Politecnico di Milano
simone1.penati@mail.polimi.it

Noëlie Ramuzat
ENSTA Bretagne & Politecnico di Milano
noelieestelle.ramuzat@mail.polimi.it

Jacopo Silvestri
Politecnico di Milano
jacopo.silvestri@mail.polimi.it

Francesco Clasadonte
Politecnico di Milano
francesco.clasadonte@polimi.it

IDC '17, June 27-30, 2017, Stanford, CA, USA

ACM ISBN 978-1-4503-4921-5/17/06.

DOI: http://dx.doi.org/10.1145/3078072.3084308

Abstract
The paper describes the design of a robot companion for children with Neurodevelopmental Disorders. This work; being informed by general design guidelines reported in the current literature, lessons learned from our own previous experience, meetings with a team of therapists and special educators, and a comparison with 21 well-known robots; shows that the combination of robots' design features and roles would eventually made a robot companion unique and potentially powerful with respect to existing robots for this target group.

Author Keywords
Neurodevelopmental Disorder; Children; Robot; Learning; Play, Disability.

ACM Classification Keywords
• **Social and professional topics~People with disabilities** • *Computer systems organization~Robotics*

Introduction
Neurodevelopmental disorders (NDD) are disabilities associated primarily with the functioning of the neurological system and brain [1]. According to DSM-5 [2], NDD are a group of conditions with onset in the developmental period. The disorders typically manifest in developmental period and are characterized by often co-

occurring deficits in personal, social, academic, and occupational functioning. Example of NDD include attention-deficit hyperactivity disorder (ADHD), autism spectrum disorder (ASD), and intellectual disability (ID).

NDD children are attracted by technological devices [4] and a vast body of research explores the use of interactive technologies for this target group. Particularly, there are several studies on the use of robots for NDD interventions and investigate how robotic interaction can help these subjects to develop social, communicative, motor, cognitive skills [6][7][8][9][13]. This paper presents the design considerations that will lead our future work on robots' development. It describes the robots' design usability in terms of criterion rather than protocols and procedures. These considerations have been elaborated in collaboration with NDD specialists, of a robotic companion that is meant to support educational and therapeutic interventions for children with NDD, particularly those with perceptual and sensory processing impairments and deficits in the cognitive, social and behavioral spheres. The design of the physical and interaction characteristics is informed by:

i) general design guidelines reported in the current literature on robots for NDD children (especially those in the autism spectrum) [5][11][12][14][18];
ii) lessons learned from our own previous experience on robots for children with NDD [4][20][21];
iii) feedbacks and suggestions offered by a team of 15 therapists (psychologists, neuro-psychiatrists, and special educators) from two different rehabilitation centers who have long-term, everyday experience of NDD subjects.

Design Guidelines

Research publications [5] as well additional public materials (e.g. web sites and online videos), which describe the design features of these robots and on-the-field case studies with NDD children, have been the source for our analysis. Since children in our target group are mostly non-verbal or have difficulties in generalization and imagination of the concepts, 15 specialists who have long-term, everyday experience with them, were recruited to discourse about the videos and research publications. A video for each robot was shown once without and twice with interruptions, having the specialists the freedom to annotate their own thoughts, and discuss them with other group members. During this process, two researchers were taking notes and video-recording. At the end of the whole day workshop all notes were collected and categorized. For lack of space we cannot explain the entire debate and categorization process – which will probably be better discussed in a full paper.

The results of the scrutiny, have been divided in
i) robots' roles played in the interaction with children
ii) robots' features divided in classes.

Robot's Roles

The robot can play different functional roles, extracted from [5] and from our own evaluation with therapists, during the interaction with the child:

- *Feedback*: it not only reacts to an action performed by the child, promoting cause-effect understanding, but also acts as a rewarding agent, to offer positive reinforcement and promote self-esteem [5];
- *Facilitator*: it suggests what to do and when to do it facilitating tasks execution [5];
- *Prompt*: it acts as a behavior eliciting agent enhancing attention and engagement [5];

- *Restrictor*: it limits the child's spatial possibilities (going around) promoting body and space awareness
- *Emulator*: it plays as an emulator (acts as the child) or something that is imitated, to trigger the child's imitative reaction and skills;
- *Social Mediator*: it mediates social interaction between the child and others (therapist, peers); it acts as a communication channel through which the child expresses her communication intents as well as a tangible material for shared activities;
- *Affective agent*: it facilitates the creation of the child's affective bond toward it and long term engagement in child-robot interaction. It helps the child to unlock her emotional rigidity and to feel emotions;
- *Emotional Agent*: it stimulates the child's capability of manifesting her own emotions and interpreting the others' emotional expressions [14].

The combination of these fundamental roles permits to create more complex ones, such as the robot capacity of developing the creativity of the child. It can be evaluated by measuring its *Affective agent*, *Emotional Agent* and *Prompt* roles. Indeed, these three categories put the child in self-confident and emotional states, which are necessary to be more creative.

Robot's features

The design features of the robots have been categorized in five main classes: appearance, multimodality, multisensoriality, configurability and safety.

1) Appearance: The visual appearance of the robot should evoke a familiar element, possibly something that the subject likes such as cartoon characters, to mitigate the potential distress of the unknown often generated in subjects with NDD. Considering Mori's conjecture about the uncanny valley [24], and the difficulty of many subjects with NDD to interpret the complexity of the signals expressed by the human face and body, abstract minimalistic "harmonic" shapes are thought to be preferable to realistic human-like representations [16][17]. Some facial components should be included, particularly eyes, to facilitate the child's understanding of what the robot is "looking at" [13]. Considering the deficits in sensory integration and discrimination that affect our target group [15] the robot should be of a neutral color so to avoid visual overstimulation, as the one created by the aggregation of (moving) components of different shapes [23] and multiple colors.

2) Multimodality: Embodied cognition theories posit that manipulation, tactile experiences and functional touches play a fundamental role in the development of sensory-motor capabilities as well as cognitive skills [19]. Mobility and spatial interaction are important not only to trigger engagement but also to develop spatial awareness skills (i.e., the appropriate perception of one's own body in the physical space) and of the spatial relationships with other entities. Vocal interaction has been positively used in NDD research to ask questions, provide verbalized instruction during a task, attract the child's attention, express attention to the talking child [22].

3) Multisensoriality: According to Bicchi's analysis [3] the softness of robots' bodies exhibit new levels of versatility, adaptability, safety, elasticity, dynamism and energy efficiency. Research [25][26] shows that Light has the role of attracting children's attention and acting as a communication medium (e.g., to convey emotions, feelings, information or to reward the child). Visual digital contents (images, videos, or animations) are functional to task-oriented interactions (e.g., to provide instructions or feedbacks on task performance) and should be used to improve engagement and to convey emotional expressions (e.g., smiles).

4) Configurability: There is no such thing as an "average" child with NDD. Each child manifests unique strengths and skill deficits. Things that are reinforcing or rewarding to one individual may be unpleasant for another person. Any interaction must be oriented to addressing the unique capability and needs of each individual child, which implies a high degree of configurability.

5) Safety: In a case of an accidental strong collision or fall, a robot should not harm the child as well as it should protect itself from a damage of equipped components.

Table 1. Survey on robots' roles

	Feedback	*Facilitator*	*Prompt*	*Emulator*	*Restrictor*	*Mediator*	*Affective*	*Emotional*	*TOT*
Bobus	x					x			2
*CHARLIE**	x			x		x	x	x	5
CPAC	x						x		2
*DISKCAT**	x			x		x	x		4
FACE	x					x	x		3
Infanoid	x			x		x	x		4
*IROMEC**	x		x			x			3
Jumbo	x				x		x		3
KASPAR	x		x	x		x			4
Keepon	x			x			x		3
Kismet	x						x	x	3
Maestro	x				x		x		3
Nao	x	x	x	x		x	x	x	7
*Paro**	x					x	x		3
Roball	x						x		2
Robota	x			x		x			3
*SAM**	x	x	x			x	x		5
Tega	x	x	x			x	x	x	6
*Teo**	x	x	x	x	x	x	x		7
TREVOR	x		x						2
Troy	x					x			2
Total: 21	21	4	7	8	3	14	15	4	
	95%	18%	32%	36%	14%	64%	68%	18%	

robot names in alphabetical order

Survey

We have surveyed 21 most relevant robots that, according to the existing literature, have been used in interventions for subjects with NDD [5]: Bobus, CHARLIE, CPAC, DISKCAT, FACE, Infanoid, IROMEC, Jumbo, KASPAR, Keepon, Kismet, Maestro, Nao, Paro, Roball, Robota, SAM, Tega, Teo, TREVOR, Troy.

The robots marked with a "*" have been designed since the very beginning for persons with special needs and are hereinafter referred to as "specialized", while the others are called "generic".

Table 2. Survey on robots' design features

	Appearance			*Multimodality*					*Multisensoriality*						
	Familiarity	*Abstract Harmonic Shape*	*Neutral Color*	*Physical Manipulation*	*Functional Touch*	*Spatial*	*Vocal*	*Emotional*	*Softness*	*Light*	*Sound*	*Video Anim.*	*Configurability*	*Safety and Robustness*	*TOTALS*
Infanoid								X							1
TREVOR					X										1
FACE							X	X							2
Kismet							X	X							2
Robota				X	X		X				X				4
KASPAR				X			X	X	X				X		5
Troy					X		X				X	X	X		5
Bobus		X			X	X				X	X			X	6
Jumbo	X	X		X	X					X			X		6
CPAC		X		X	X	X			X	X				X	7
Maestro		X			X	X			X	X	X			X	7
Roball		X		X	X		X			X	X			X	7
Nao			X		X	X	X	X			X		X	X	8
*CHARLIE**	X	X	X	X	X			X	X					X	8
*DISKCAT**	X	X	X	X	X				X	X				X	8
Keepon	X	X	X	X			X	X	X		X				8
Tega		X		X			X	X	X		X	X	X	X	9
*IROMEC**		X	X		X	X	X			X	X	X	X	X	10
*Paro**	X	X	X	X	X		X	X	X		X			X	10
*SAM**	X	X		X	X		X	X	X	X	X		X	X	11
*Teo**	X	X	X	X	X	X		X	X	X	X		X	X	12
Total: 21	7	13	7	12	15	6	12	11	10	9	12	3	8	12	
	32%	59%	32%	55%	68%	27%	55%	50%	45%	41%	55%	14%	36%	55%	

robot names ordered according to their scores

Results and Discussion

Concerning Table 1, all robots play as Feedback; it seems to be widely acknowledged the importance not simply of supporting interaction, i.e., providing stimuli in response to user's actions, but also of offering positive reinforcement and rewarding the children. Table 1 also shows an expected dependency between the physical capability of the robot and its roles. For example, 2 robots (Nao and Sam) meet all but one requirements, respectively Space Restrictor (Nao is static) and Emotional Agent (Teo is not equipped with emotion detection functionality). Table 1 also highlights the potential of robots to promote affection: 68% of the robots play as Affective Agent; some robots in this subset (e.g., Paro, Teo, SAM) have been explicitly designed for this role while for others the affection power emerged only during the experimentation with the children. The second most popular role is Social Mediator (64% of the robots). This role is played by all specialized robots and also by 6 generic robots. Specialized robots are typically meant to be used by children under the supervision of the caregiver and all acknowledge that the interaction with the robot promotes also human-human interaction; still, the potential of robotic interaction to develop social skills in children with NDD seems to be achieved also by some generic robots, showing that it might be intrinsic in the robotic interaction paradigm per se. Concerning Table 2, the highest total scores (>7) are assigned to all specialized robots, but this top ranked set also includes some generic robots (Nao, Roball, Maestro). The most common physical feature is the abstract non-humanoid shape (59%) and the least common one is the integration with videos and animations (14%). All specialized robots but IROMEC, plus 3 generic robots, are soft, accounting to 45% of the total. The most popular paradigm of interaction is Functional touch (68%) followed by Physical Manipulation and Vocal Interaction (55%). The latter is supported by 4 out of 7 specialized robots. A limited number of robots (27%) exploits spatial interaction, an interaction paradigm that is relatively new and deserves further exploration.

The values of the various robots resulting from our analysis do not reflect their therapeutic or educational effectives for children with NDD and is therefore not to be interpreted as a "quality" ranking. Certainly, the design and functionalities of the robot have a significant influence in the educational and therapeutic process and may hold a potential. Still, in general we cannot state that, on the basis of our comparison, some features are more relevant than others and we cannot draw any conclusion on how each specific design feature may influence the overall benefits (or limitations) for each child's experience with the robot. This is because the profound diversification of the profiles of children with NDD. Due the nature of these disorders, not all children with NDD will react exactly the same way. Some may show more receptiveness towards some design features but discomfort to others, and with few exceptions we cannot state that some design aspects are more relevant than others. An exception is safety and robustness, which is truly a precondition for this special target, according to our analysis, and is satisfied only by 55% of the robots (7 specialized robots and 6 generic ones). Due to this small score, our future work will be focused on developing robots with better performances in this field.

Conclusion

Our work offers a contribution to the design of social robots for children with disabilities. The design is informed by a set of requirements that distill the main results of the current state of the art in this field as well as the experience of a team of NDD specialists that are collaborating in our research. These requirements can be regarded as design guidelines that can benefit to researchers and developers in robotics. On the basis of these guidelines, we have provided a systematic comparison between 21 existing robots that have been used with children in the NDD spectrum.

This analysis offers a novel perspective on the current state of the art in robotics for this target group.

Our future work is focusing on the development of the robot taking these guidelines in consideration in a iterative design process. The robot companion we are developing will support learning through play and will consider the specific characteristics and needs of this target group. It will include different interaction paradigms (spatial, emotional, and tangible interaction), physical features (mobility, softness, multimodality) and multisensory stimuli. After the first developmental process, we are setting up another focus group to discuss the robots' features and specialists' expectancies. In parallel we are also conducting an exploratory study in a kindergarten school to better understand the interaction modalities and affordances of children with the same mental age of our target group.

References

1. EPA, "United States Environmental Protection Agency". America's Children and the Environment | Third Edition, Updated October 2015.
2. American Psychiatric Association, 2013. Diagnostic and statistical manual of mental disorders (DSM-5®). American Psychiatric Pub.
3. Bicchi "Of Robots, Humans, Bodies and Intelligence: Body Languages for Human Robot Interaction." *Proceedings of the Tenth Annual ACM/IEEE International Conference on Human-Robot Interaction*. ACM, 2015.
4. Bonarini, F. Garzotto, M. Gelsomini. A huggable, mobile robot for developmental disorder interventions in a multi-modal interaction space. In Proc. of IEEE International Symposium on Robot and Human Interactive Communication. IEEE RO-MAN 16.
5. J. Cabibihan, H. Javed, M. Ang Jr, and S. M. Aljunied. Why robots? a survey on the roles and benefits of social robots in the therapy of children with autism. International journal of social robotics, 5(4):593–618, 2013.
6. Chella, et al. "An Emotional Storyteller Robot." *AAAI Spring Symposium: Emotion, Personality, and Social Behavior*. 2008.
7. Den Brok and P. Sterkenburg. Self-controlled technologies to support skill attainment in persons with an autism spectrum disorder and/or an intellectual disability: a systematic literature review. Disability and Rehabilitation: Assistive Technology, 10(1):1–10, 2015.
8. J. Diehl, L. M. Schmitt, M. Villano, and C. R. Crowell. The clinical use of robots for individuals with autism spectrum disorders: A critical review. Research in autism spectrum disorders, 6(1):249–262, 2012
9. Kozima, M. P. Michalowski, and C. Nakagawa. Keepon. a playful robot for research, therapy, and entertainment. International Journal of Social Robotics, 1(1):3–18, 2009.
10. Marti, A. Pollini, A. Rullo, and T. Shibata. Engaging with artificial pets. In Proceedings of the 2005 annual conference on European association of cognitive ergonomics, pages 99–106. University of Athens, 2005.
11. Michaud, A. Duquette, and I. Nadeau. Characteristics of mobile robotic toys for children with pervasive developmental disorders. In Systems, Man and Cybernetics, 2003. IEEE International Conference on, volume 3, pages 2938–2943. IEEE, 2003.
12. J. Ricks and M. B. Colton. Trends and considerations in robot-assisted autism therapy. In Robotics and Automation (ICRA), 2010 IEEE International Conference on, pages 4354–4359. IEEE, 2010.
13. Robins, K. Dautenhahn, R. Te Boekhorst, and A. Billard. Robotic assistants in therapy and education of children with autism: can a small humanoid robot help encourage social interaction skills? Universal Access in the Information Society, 4(2):105–120, 2005.
14. Scassellati, H. Admoni, and M. Mataric. Robots for use in autism research. Annual review of biomedical engineering, 14:275–294, 2012.
15. Iarocci and J. McDonald, 2006. Sensory integration and the perceptual experience of persons with autism. Journal of autism and developmental disorders, 36(1), pp.77-90.
16. Robins, K. Dautenhahn, and J. Dubowski, 2006. Does appearance matter in the interaction of children with autism with a humanoid robot?. Interaction studies, 7(3), pp.509-542.

17. B. Robins, N. Otero, E. Ferrari, K. Dauthenhahn, 2007, August. Eliciting requirements for a robotic toy for children with autism-results from user panels. In Robot and Human interactive Communication. RO-MAN 2007. The 16th IEEE International Symposium on 101-106. IEEE.
18. Giullian, D. Ricks, A. Atherton, M. Colton, M. Goodrich, and B. Brinton, 2010, October. Detailed requirements for robots in autism therapy. In Systems Man and Cybernetics (SMC), 2010 IEEE International Conference on (pp. 2595-2602). IEEE.
19. Shapiro, 2010. Embodied cognition. Routledge.
20. S. Colombo, F. Garzotto, M. Gelsomini, M. Melli and F. Clasadonte. 2016, June. Dolphin Sam: A Smart Pet for Children with Intellectual Disability. In Proceedings of the International Working Conference on Advanced Visual Interfaces (pp. 352-353). ACM.
21. A. Bonarini, F. Clasadonte , F. Garzotto and M. Gelsomini, 2015, June. Blending robots and full-body interaction with large screens for children with intellectual disability. In Proceedings of the 14th International Conference on Interaction Design and Children (pp. 351-354). ACM.
22. N. Pares, P. Masri, G. van Wolferen, and C. Creed, 2005. Achieving dialogue with children with severe autism in an adaptive multisensory interaction: the" MEDIAte" project. IEEE Transactions on Visualization and Computer Graphics, 11(6), pp.734-743.
23. Cute and soft: baby steps in designing robots for children with autism. In Proc. of the Workshop at SIGGRAPH ACM.
24. Mori, M., MacDorman, K.F. and Kageki, N., 2012. The uncanny valley [from the field]. IEEE Robotics & Automation Magazine, 19(2), pp.98-100.
25. Wirz-Justice, A., Benedetti, F., Berger, M., Lam, R.W., Martiny, K., Terman, M. and Wu, J.C., 2005. Chronotherapeutics (light and wake therapy) in affective disorders. Psychological medicine, 35(07), pp.939-944.
26. Torrington, J.M. and Tregenza, P.R., 2007. Lighting for people with dementia. Lighting Research & Technology, 39(1), pp.81-97.

Bots for Tots: Girls' Perceived Versus Actual Competency in Technology and Making

Sawaros Thanapornsangsuth
Teachers College,
Columbia University
New York, 10027 USA
st2839@tc.columbia.edu

Nathan Holbert
Teachers College,
Columbia University
New York, 10027 USA
holbert@tc.columbia.edu

IDC '17, June 27-30, 2017, Stanford, CA, USA

ACM ISBN 978-1-4503-4921-5/17/06.

DOI: http://dx.doi.org/10.1145/3078072.3084309

Abstract

This study explores how young girls perceive technology and making as part of their identity. The data presented here is part of a larger study on 38 fourth grade students (aged 9-11) taking an Engineering and Design class at an all-girls private school in a suburban area in the North-Eastern United States. Most of the girls we interviewed expressed little to no confidence in working with technology or maker activities. **When asked, "were you good at technology?"** They perceived themselves as someone who was not good at technology and felt as though others were much more competent than them. These expressed self-perceptions were consistent with previous findings in regards to gender and technology. However, when the girls were asked to design and identify tools that required knowledge of technology and making, they were able to demonstrate deep understanding and descriptions that supported their competency in both fields. They also shared prior experiences of engaging with technology, which contradicts their claim to be novices in these fields.

Author Keywords

women confidence in STEM; maker activities; self-perception in STEM; Girls in technology; making.

Population and Site

The data presented here is part of a larger study on 38 fourth grade students (aged 9-11) taking an Engineering and Design class at an all-girls private school in a suburban area in the North-Eastern United States. In addition to the many extracurricular activities and programs available in the school, students in 4th grade and beyond have access to an Engineering and Design lab (EDL) which is filled with cutting edge equipment including a CNC machine, laser engraver, multiple 3D printers. As we will show in the data and methodology section, many of the girls have parents that are involved in the tech industry, have the opportunity to take extracurricular STEM courses such as robotics, and have access to many high-tech toys and construction kits.

ACM Classification Keywords
K.3.m. Computers and Education: Miscellaneous;

Introduction

Maker activities provide learners with hands-on experience to design, experiment, build, and invent as they engage in activities that involve science, technology, engineering, and math (STEM) concepts [4,7]. In "makerspaces" or fabrication labs—physical space that are part science lab, woodshop, computer lab and art room [4]—learners take advantage of cheap and powerful tools to create meaningful physical objects that can serve as an entry points for STEM content and practices [2,9,11,12,20]. While schools and libraries across the United States have begun to enthusiastically incorporate makerspaces with the goal of engaging students in STEM [4] these spaces, activities, and clubs have struggled to serve a diverse population of makers, particularly women [3,9,13]. Nevertheless, there is a paucity of research examining technology confidence in young girls who are newly introduced to maker and engineering education in a formal school setting. Likewise, little work has been done to explore these perceptions for girls from various backgrounds and experiences. In the Bots for Tots project we are engaging young learners, from diverse communities, in using high-tech tools and technologies to build toys for younger kids in their school. In this work-in-progress paper, we present early findings of interviews with young girls, from privileged backgrounds, participating in the Bots for Tots project and show how their low self-perceptions of competencies with technology do not match their actual high capabilities.

Literature Review

Despite women making up a majority of the overall education and workforce in the U.S. over the past 50 years, they are much less represented in STEM disciplines compared to their male counterparts [8]. In 2009, women represented only 6.7% of U.S. mechanical engineers, 7.7% of electrical engineers, and 20.9% of software engineers [23]. The most recent data from National Center for Women & Information Technology [19] reveals that women make up only 15% of practicing engineers and only 26% are in computing occupations.

The gender deficit problem in STEM fields has long been a topic of study. Hill, Corbett and Rose [8] compiled various literature in order to answer a very important question: "Why so few?" They suggested that women are less confident that they will succeed in STEM fields. Thus, women tend to not express an interest in STEM occupations. Likewise, women significantly underestimate their math and science abilities (compared to men) even though their knowledge and achievements are equivalent [10,15]. Negative stereotypes about women's abilities in math plays an integral role in deterring women's interest in STEM. Women may even end up underperforming in exams, if they themselves believe in these negative stereotypes [8]. Additionally, in the field of computer science, the stereotype that men are better at computing discourages women from joining the field [21]. Women are also hesitant to enroll in high school computer classes with unbalanced gender participation [15]. Nevertheless, Dweck [5] reveals that if women have a growth mindset in STEM fields, their confidence and eagerness to learn (as opposed to thinking that men are superior and innately better suited to STEM) can significantly improve their success rate.

Creating inclusive learning environment and having a hands-on and supportive learning environment may help nurture young girls' interests in STEM [11]. A study conducted by Hill, Corbett, and Rose [8] shows that if teachers and parents tell girls that they are capable, they perform better on math exams and are more likely to continue pursuing math.

Additionally, studies suggest women value social interactions and a sense of community. In maker activities, women work collaboratively, provide support, and help their peers more often than men [11]. Women tend to favor collaborative relationships to competition and enjoy helping or giving back to their community [17]. Working together, women share accomplishment and provide positive feedback, which eventually leads to an increase in confidence and performance advancement [1].

Methodology

Data Collection and Analysis

38 4th grade students received and filled out a survey that includes sections on interest in STEM fields, interest in crafting and technology-based activities, and a section where participants ranked various technologies and maker activities in terms of gender expectations ("Boys really like this more," "Girls really like this more," etc). Of the 38 girls in the class, twelve were randomly selected to be interviewed. Using a semi-structured cognitive-clinical interview format [6], the fourth-grade girls were asked questions about their 1) electronic toys or devices at home, 2) self-perception of technology, 3) experience with making and crafts, both for themselves and for other people, 4) ideas on designing new inventions that aim to solve household problem 5) their familiarity with technological and maker activities and tools.

Of the 12 interviews, seven (chosen based on the first authors familiarity with their work) have been analyzed in depth. These seven are not necessarily meant to be illustrative of the entire sample, but do provide an interesting set of cases for this work-in-progress. Once transcribed, we looked closely at segments of the interview related to the girls' 1) self-perception of technology, 2) experience with making and crafts, and 3) familiarity with technological and maker activities and tools. The data was coded "bottom-up" where themes and coding categories emerged from patterns in the data [16]. For example, one code categorizes participants' perceptions of themselves in relation to the topic—in particular their self-report of "technology and making confidence." Example phrases from the interviews included: "Umm not really," "I'm not an expert," "My brother like to build [..] but I don't build." We also coded girls' prior experiences with making and technology. For instance: "making crafts", "making for or with other people", "making by or for themselves."

Findings

Girls' Self Perception on their technology and making confidence

While six of the fourth-grade girls were interest in working with technology or maker activities all seven interviewed expressed a lack of confidence. In particular, when asked if they perceive themselves as someone that is good with technology, the girls showed uncertainty or said they were not. When asked "why" the five of the seven girls mentioned few details about their own expertise and instead suggested that their male family members are better with technology.

One participant, Betty, told us she often played with "Meccano," a sophisticated robotics toy that requires 168 steps to assemble. Additionally, Betty indicated her dad often invited her to work with him on small wood-working and electronics tasks and that they had even built a series of birdhouses "together" using a book she had given him for his birthday. However, when Betty was asked whether she thought of herself as someone who is good with technology and electronics, she immediately responded "No." She then went on to say: "umm because like my dad likes to build stuff with me but he likes to build like robotic stuff. So normally like he's doing the whole thing and I'm just kinda like 'Yeah, yeah that's cool. Umm-uh that's cool. Yeah I think you have to connect the green wire there.' He does most of it." The interviewer then asked, "but do you like electronics?" Betty answered "yes" but then reiterated she didn't feel like she "was someone that's good with electronics." When another participant, Aditi, was asked if she thinks of herself as someone who is good with electronic or technology. She answered, "I don't know. I don't use electronics that much so it doesn't seem like something I'll be like really good at or something." Aditi added that if something goes wrong with her electronic devices, she would not go to her mom but will seek help from her dad or brother who she considered as someone who is good at technology in her family.

Similarly, when Panni was asked about her technology competency, she answered "I don't know" while shrugging her shoulders. She compared her interest in building to her brother saying, "I don't like to build stuff that much. My brother likes to build. If the pieces don't come all together, he builds it. But I don't build." Interestingly on the survey taken a few days later in class, Panni indicated on the first section that she liked building things with wooden blocks or Legos, and enjoyed working with electronics. Nevertheless, there was a misalignment in her answers on the last section when she was asked to evaluate each maker and engineering task as boys or girls while ranking those tasks based on her interest. Panni indicated that "Tinkering with electronics" is not her thing at all while perceiving this task as male oriented.

Despite being out-spoken and confident in answering questions about her everyday usage of technology, Hailey was hesitant to state that she was "good at technology". When asked, "do you consider yourself as someone who is good at technology," Hailey answered "umm not really." Although she mentioned that she coded and enjoyed the experience, she still perceived herself as a person with limited experience in technology stating she was "not an expert" and was "still learning." Only two participants analyzed for this work-in-progress, Erica and Sarah, expressed statements reflecting their confidence in technology. Erica said she was "kind of good" at technology. However, she still mentioned that she didn't know much about technology and referred to her uncle in Spain as the expert. If she has any trouble with electronics, Erica said she would seek help from her dad. Sarah didn't explicitly say that she was good at technology but she told us that she can "figure it out." Still, when she was asked if she was good at computers, she replied "I don't really know."

Girls' Actual Technology and Making Competency

When the interview was framed away from identity—being someone that is either good or bad with technology—and instead involved identifying and describing a variety of tools and components used in engineering and electronics, the girls were more successful than their self-perceptions would imply. In cases where the girls didn't know the tools or component, they managed to speculate and provide thoughtful and critical possibilities of the tools' applications. All seven girls also shared their prior experience with technology—both as consumers and producers—contradicting earlier claims of being a novice in the field. For example, despite suggesting she isn't good with technology, Hailey immediately identified many of the electronic and engineering components presented during the interview. When shown a bag full of parts, Hailey picked up a gear and said, "this is something called, gear, I think." She then revealed that she had previously taken a robotic class and had used gears. Hailey then picked up a wheel and demonstrated how the gear worked while moving the wheel in a circular motion, "when [the gear] spins, it will turn an axle so the wheel would turn and move." When Hailey saw a small LED, she shared her experiences with her science project from the previous year, "We connect the wire with [...] a switch and this would turn on and this part would get lit. It had a really thin wire that make the light bulb and we used the light and try to make them work." Holly, another participant who also gave the same "not really" response once she was asked if she someone who is good with technology or electronics, began describing the components of a working circuit when shown a small wire. Picking up the wire Holly stated, "You can connect it to another wire, a battery, and a light bulb. It will make the light goes on. Cause the, I forget what it's called, but it will travel through the wire and boom, the light is on!" While Betty was not able to recall the word "gear," she immediately picked it and other related parts up and began to describe their functionality, "You can put another one next to them and like put one of the little axle thingy in there and you can make it turns and it turns another one so you might be able to like connect this to the wheel and it will make that turn."

To intentionally encourage participants to engage in on-the-spot knowledge construction, the girls were also asked about some uncommon components. The goal here was to see how the girls made sense of the objects, and how they might imagine uses or purposes for the components. When shown a small force sensor, Betty indicated she was not familiar with the object. However, after thinking momentarily, Betty stated, "I think this is some kind of sensor like you start moving I think." Surprised that she so easily identified the sensor, the interviewer pushed further asking, "how would it know that you've touched it?" Wasting no time, Betty responded, "I think it's like those lines in there. Maybe it's like sensing like heat?" Despite not having prior knowledge of the component, Betty was able to reason about its nature and how it might function. This ability—possibly developed during those times she was encouraged to watch, but not touch, while her father worked on electronics—suggests Betty is more electronically capable than she knows or claims.

During the interviews, six of the girls revealed little to no confidence on their technology and making competency— five often identifying the male members in their family as the technology expert. However, once the questions were framed less on competency, but more towards personal stories and technological and making tools, the girls provided rich understanding and excitement in the tasks.

Discussion

The girls interviewed for this study attend an all-girls private school with a wealth of opportunities and resources. The school has an Engineering and Design lab filled with cutting edge equipment including a *ShopBot* CNC machine, laser engraver, multiple 3D printers, various micro-controllers, and robotic kits. Moreover, many of the girls interviewed come from families that encourage extracurricular activities from sports, music, to programming. In some cases, building robots and make things was a family activity. Despite these opportunities, the girls interviewed still felt less confident about their technology competency. While this discrepancy of the girls' self-reporting and their actual competency aligns with literature on gender stereotype [22], it is worthwhile to note that this is a population that has been on the receiving end of active efforts to engage them with powerful STEM opportunities.

One reason for this result may be the girls' tendency to automatically compare their own expertise to that of a male members of the family. For example, Panni often said throughout the interview that she was "not a big big builder [...] My brother likes to build." Panni's tendency to position her own expertise as inferior to her brother during the interview aligns with stereotypes about gender and technology. Many studies have suggested girls are less confident than boys about their ability in domains—such as technology, engineering, and computing—that are stereotypically considered masculine [8,11,14]. Likewise, compared to men, women significantly underestimate their math and science abilities even though their knowledge and achievements are equivalent [10,15].

While the girls interviewed had many prior STEM experiences, for some these experiences may have been more observation than active participant. Betty for example, mentioned her involvement in various maker and engineering activities with her dad including assembling her favorite toy, a *Meccano* robot and building bird house. Despite her dad's effort to engage his daughter with these activities, it seems more often than not Betty was an observer, not the doer. Betty states her dad never let her touch the equipment—that he would be the only one to connect the wires or cut the wood. As someone with a passive role, Betty was interested in technology and maker activities but didn't dare to consider herself as someone who is proficient.

Future Research

The 4th grade girls described in this study are currently part of a year-long maker project where they are building toys for their assigned "Little Sisters"--younger girls at their school. When the project concludes, we intend to once again investigate the students' self-perception of technology and making. Additionally, we aim to look at interactions between fourth-grade builders and between builders and their client "Little Sisters" with the goal of extending theory on activity and environmental designs that engage young girls in making and engineering.

References

1. Lisa S. Blackwell, Kali H. Trzesniewski, and Carol S. Dweck. 2007. Implicit theories of intelligence predict achievement across an adolescent transition: A longitudinal study and an intervention. *Child development* 78, 1 (Jan.2007), 246-263. DOI: http://dx.doi.org/10.1111/j.1467-8624.2007.00995.x
2. Paulo Blikstein. 2013. Digital fabrication and "making" in education: The democratization of invention. In *FabLabs: Of Machines, Makers and Inventors,* Julia Walter-Herrmann and Corinne Buching (Eds.) transcript Verlag. 1–21.
3. Leah Buechley. 2013. Thinking about making. Retrieved November 5, 2016 from http://edstream.stanford.edu/Video/Play/883b61dd951 d4d3f90abeec65eead2911d
4. Jennifer Cooper. 2013. *Designing a School Makerspace*. *Edutopia.* Retrieved November 5, 2016 from http://www.edutopia.org/blog/designing-a-school-makerspace-jennifer-cooper
5. Carol S. Dweck. 2007. *Is Math a Gift? Beliefs That Put Females at Risk*. American Psychological Association. Washington, DC.
6. Herbert Ginsburg. 1997. Entering the child's mind: The clinical interview in psychological research and practice. Cambridge University Press. Cambridge, UK.
7. Erica Rosenfeld Halverson and Kimberly Sheridan. 2014. The Maker Movement in Education. *Harvard Educational Review* 84, 4 (Dec 2014), 495–504. DOI: http://dx.doi.org/10.17763/haer.84.4.34j1g68140382063
8. Catherine Hill, Christianne Corbett, and Andresse St Rose. 2010. *Why so few? Women in Science, Technology,Engineering, and Mathematics*. American Association of University Women. Washington, DC.
9. Nathan R. Holbert. 2016. Leveraging cultural values and "ways of knowing" to increase diversity in maker activities. *International Journal of Child-Computer Interaction*, *9 (Dec. 2016)*, 33-39. DOI: http://doi.org/10.1016/j.ijcci.2016.10.002
10. Janet S. Hyde, Elizabeth Fennema, Marilyn Ryan, Laurie A. Frost, and Carolyn Hopp. 1990. Gender comparisons of mathematics attitudes and affect. *Psychology of women quarterly* 14, 3 (Sept. 1990), 299-324. DOI: http://doi.org/10.1111/j.1471-6402.1990.tb00022.x
11. Intel Corporation. 2014. MakeHers Report: Engaging Girls and Women in Technology through Making, Creating, and Inventing. Retrieved November 12, 2016 from http://www.intel.com/content/www/us/en/technology -in- education/making-her-future-report.html
12. Thomas Kalil. 2013. Have fun--learn something, do something, make something. In *Design, Make, Play*, Margaret Honey and David E. Kanter (Eds.). Routledge. 12–16.
13. Yasmin B. Kafai, Quin Burke, and Mitchel Resnick. 2014. *Connected code: Why children need to learn programming*. MIT Press. Cambridge, MA.
14. Jane B. Kahle and Judith Meece. 1993. Research on gender issues in the classroom. *Handbook of research on science teaching and learning*. 542-557. Division of Macmillan. New York, NY.
15. Jane Margolis and Allan Fisher. 2003. *Unlocking the clubhouse: Women in computing*. MIT press. Cambridge, MA.
16. Matthew B. Miles, A, Michael Huberman and Johnny Saldaña. 2014. Qualitative Data Analysis. A Methods Sourcebook (3rd. ed.). Sage, Los Angeles, CA.
17. Harriet S. Mosatche, Susan Matloff-Nieves, Linda Kekelis and Elizabeth K. Lawner. 2013. Effective STEM programs for adolescent girls: Three

approaches and many lessons learned. *Afterschool matters 17* (Sept. 2013), 17-25.

18. National Science Foundation. 2015. *Women, Minorities, and Persons with Disabilities in Science and Engineering*. Retrieved November 5, 2016 from http://www.nsf.gov/statistics/wmpd/
19. NCWIT. 2015. *Women in IT: The Facts Infographic*. Retrieved November 5, 2016 from https://www.ncwit.org/resources/women-it-facts-infographic-2015-update
20. Seymour Papert. 1980. *Mindstorms: Children, computers, and powerful ideas*. Basic Books, New York.
21. Mitchel Resnick and Eric Rosenbaum. Designing for Tinkerability. In *Design, Make, Play*, Margaret Honey and David E. Kanter (Eds.). Routledge. 163-181.
22. Steven J. Spencer, Claude M. Steele and Diane M. Quinn. 1999. Stereotype threat and women's math performance. *Journal of experimental social psychology 35*, 1 (Jan. 1999), 4-28. DOI: http://doi.org/10.1006/jesp.1998.1373
23. U.S. Department of Labor, Bureau of Labor Statistics. 2009. *Women in the labor force: A databook,* 1018. Author, Washington, DC.

Toward a Socio-Cultural Perspective on "Making": Pupils' Journey through Materials, People and Places

Pauline Gourlet
Paragraphe C3U, Université Paris 8
& EnsadLab, Paris, France
pauline.gourlet@gmail.com

Françoise Decortis
Paragraphe C3U, Université Paris 8
Saint-Denis, France
fdecortis@gmail.com

IDC '17, June 27-30, 2017, Stanford, CA, USA

ACM ISBN 978-1-4503-4921-5/17/06.

http://dx.doi.org/10.1145/3078072.3084310

Abstract

In this paper, we describe a series of workshops conducted with first grade pupils (6-7 years old) and their teacher. These workshops aim at introducing pupils to typeface design to create a class typeface to be used both on computer and on posters. While describing the whole sequence of activities pupils engaged in, we intend to open new perspectives on "making" for general education, considering its social and cultural dimensions. Throughout this report, we highlight how such making activity can support (1) pupils' acknowledgment of complex relations between materials, people and places, (2) the connection of schools to new environments and renewed agency perspectives, and (3) the development of a class culture.

Author Keywords

Type Design; Making; Collaboration; FabLabs; Materials; Open Schools

ACM Classification Keywords

H.5.m

Introduction: Overview of the process

We have been involved for two years in a partnership with a French elementary school to develop making activities as daily school activities. We (together with two designers, a teacher, two Fabmanagers), designed a series of workshops to engage first grade pupils (23 pupils aged 6-7 years old) in a type design activity. In this paper, we first describe the sequence of activities that we designed—along with our theoretical framework, motivations and design principles. The whole sequence involves the use of a large variety of materials, and tools, and takes place at three different locations, managed by diverse people. Through the description of the overall sequence and several zooms, we highlight how such sequence of making activities can support (1) pupils' acknowledgment of complex relations between materials, people and places, (2) the connection of schools to new environments with new agency potentials for both children and teachers, and (3) the development of a class culture, in relation to a broader situated culture. Following this creation and use of a typeface by the pupils for the pupils helps us open new perspectives on "making" for general education, bridging learning with developmental approaches focusing on the social and cultural dimensions of such making activities.

Theoretical Framework

Even though the term "making" still lacks of a clear definition, many researchers have studied the beneficial aspects of making activities for learning [6]. A recent literature review [5] shows that most studies using this term are referring to the engagement of students in programming activities, involving the use of digital tools and sometimes craft materials. A making approach to learning seems to be taken most notably in programming [5]. Even though most studies highlight the collaborative and engaging aspect of making activities and their learning opportunities, several voices argue toward a broader and developmental understanding of making, and advocate for a holistic and designerly approach, a 'Maker mindset' or a 'Bildung' perspective [2,4,9]. They highlight the development of students' self-efficacy and reflective thinking through creative processes. Bridging these developmental perspectives with socio-cultural [1,10] and original constructionist views [3,7], we understand making as a constructive activity, through which pupils' development occurs within a situated culture. This culture is embodied within the artifacts of the situation on which pupils act as they engage in these making activities. They participate to the negotiation of their situated culture through the construction of "public entities", as Papert calls them, "whether it's a sand castle on the beach or a theory of the universe" [3]. As Brown demonstrated, "ways of knowing are deeply connected to the cultural artifacts of situations, artifacts that include tools and people" [1]. This is why we designed a series of workshops that aims at increasing pupils' participation to authentic and distributed making activities [1,7] (both within their class but also outside school), where they would discuss constructions, share constructions and collaborate on constructions.

Motivations and Design Principles

OPENING THE SCHOOL AND CREATING A NETWORK

This series of workshops was meant for pupils to discover a network of places and actors, so they could experience the relations at play within such network, and develop new agency perspectives. In addition to the pupils, our case study involved directly one researcher, one schoolteacher, two graphic designers,

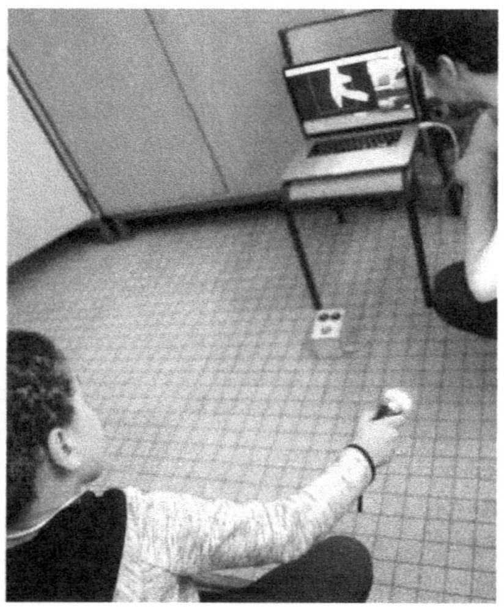

Figure 1 – Typeface in Play-Do.
Figure 2 – Pupil painting her letter on paper.
Figure 3 – Pupil digitalizing his letter moving a flashlight.

two fablabmanagers and two design teachers from a graphic design university. Three different places created the scenes: a classroom (within an elementary school), a FabLab, and a design university. A researcher and the two designers came within the classroom, and the whole class came to work within the FabLab and the design school.

DESIGNING A TYPEFACE: ANOTHER PERSPECTIVE ON WRITING

We decided to engage pupils in the design of a typeface for the class for two main reasons: 1) it is collective making activity, i.e. the whole class is working together to design a coherent typeface family, which requires sharing, discussing and collaborating on each other's designs; and 2) it relates to writing/reading, which pupils are currently learning in first grade, in both a pragmatic and historical sense. Through this making activity, pupils can experience the process of collectively designing a cultural tool people could later use, and therefore they develop another kind of relation to their learning, i.e. they experience and participate to the history of the letters.

A TRANSLATION PROCESS

We looked for ways to articulate the network at play with the goals of the making activities, to engage pupils in authentic activities [8], and to make visible the relations between each activity. Therefore, we designed a "translation process", where the typeface plays the main role. Born from pupils' bodies and hands with tools, the typeface becomes digitalized and later available in the computer system, or materialized within diverse materials for printing. Thanks to this translation process, pupils can experience the relations between the different places and their resources (both human and material) and relate to them with a subjective goal (to realize their class typeface).

The Journey

Pupils' journey made of the sequence of activities is described in the following diagram (see fig. 4).

Zooms in the Activities

1) Tinkering with materials and tools in the classroom

For one half-day, the classroom was transformed in a design studio. The two designers, the teacher and the researcher facilitated the session. After deciding which pupil was in charge of which letter, part of the classroom played with diverse craft materials to imagine and design letter forms, while others digitalized their designs.

PLAYING WITH MATERIALS

Sketching, folding plastic bands or modeling play-do, pupils first looked for ways to form their letters, choosing the materials they wanted to try out new designs. From their first iterations, they elaborate a design, and later came to the "painting corner", where they could paint large letters with large brushes on posters. Each material used allows the pupils to experience the impact of physical properties on their designs (scale, shape, spread, combination, support…). Painting with brushes was a requisite step before tracing digitally "in the air": we wanted them to develop a gesture (as in calligraphy), useful for the digitalization process of the design. During all these mini-workshops, pupils were in small groups, free to walk from on spot to another. The schoolteacher and one graphic designer helped them when asked to. Pupils also recorded photos and videos from these activities.

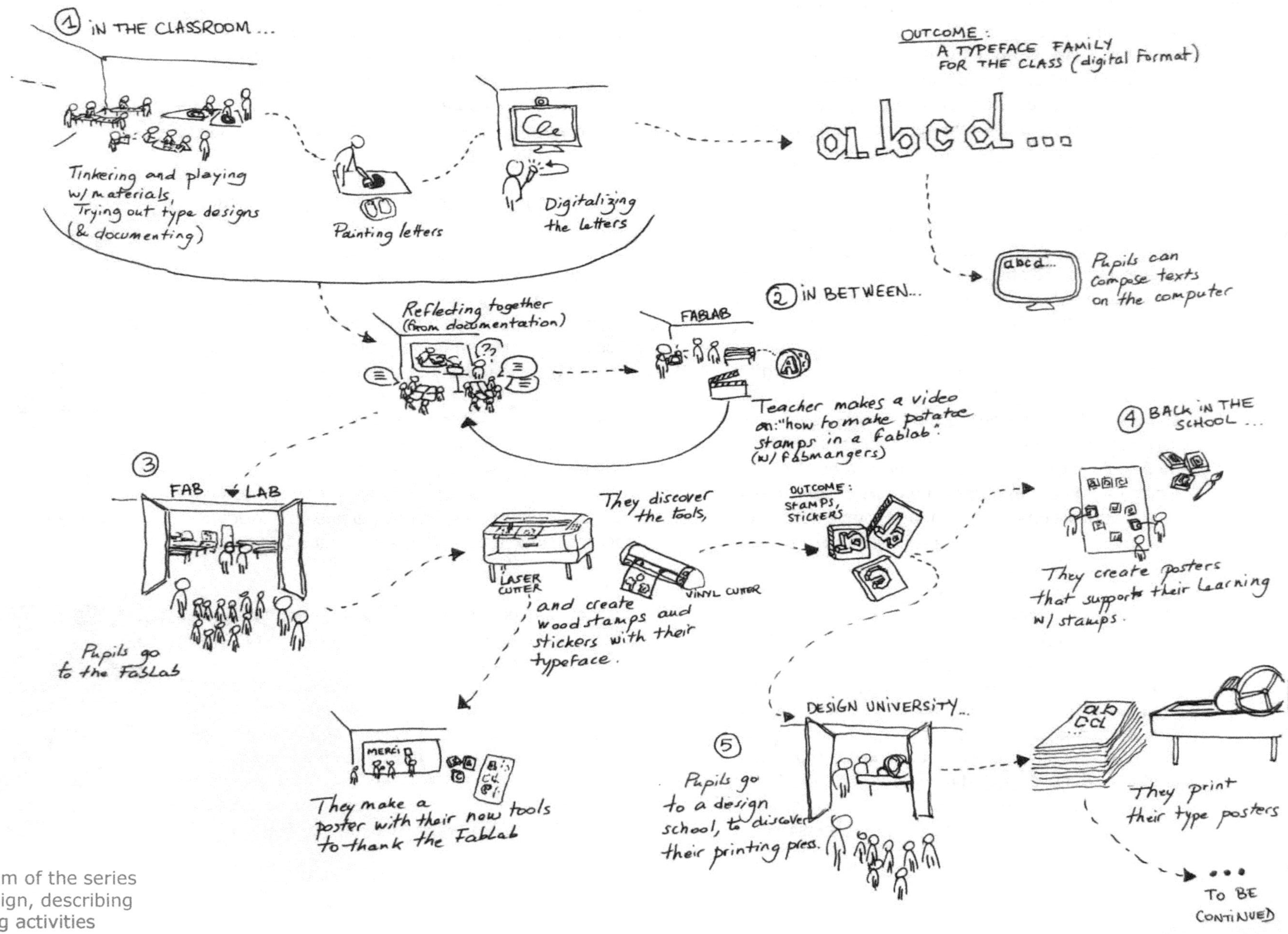

Figure 4 – Diagram of the series of workshops design, describing the pupils' making activities encompassed in the typeface design process.

Figure 5 – Message to thank the FabLab, composed with laser-cutted wooden letters on a wood board ("Thank you very much for helping us" signed "CP.C", i.e. their class name)

Figure 6 – a wood-stamps set of the typeface and stickers sets.

After painting, pupils "digitalized" their designs in small groups in another room. Thanks to a program developed by the graphic designers, they faced a computer and moved a flashlight. These gestures drew their letters and they could see the result of their gestures (see fig.3) in real time. Together and with the graphic designer, they discussed the outcomes and made many iterations. Compared to the hustle and bustle of the other room with the many mini-workshops, the atmosphere in this room was focused and calm.

2) Scaffolding the Translation Process: making a video to prepare the FabLab session
A few days after the classroom session, the schoolteacher went to the FabLab to make a video to tease the pupils and explain what they will be doing there. Instead of filming around, he teamed up with two of the Fabmanagers to make a few letter stamps made out of potatoes with the laser cutter. He brought the stamps back to the class and showed the video to the pupils. While discovering a new technique, pupils acknowledged that the stamps were not written with their typeface, so they will have to realize their own stamps. They also discussed whether to use potatoes or other materials and listed the materials they could use depending on the use they would have of their typeface.

3) Materializing the class typeface in the FabLab
A week later, the whole class came to the FabLab, accompanied by 8 parents, the schoolteacher, the researcher and one graphic designer. Once arrived, they recognized the place and the two fabmanagers from the video. Several sets of the typeface have been materialized with diverse materials and tools.

DISCOVERING THE FINAL TYPEFACE
One graphic designer used the photos shot during the **classroom session to vivid pupils' memory, and pupils** collectively retraced the various steps of this previous session, along with their goals. Then, the designer showed boards of letters, with a lot of versions of shapes, to explain the work he has done to reshape and harmonize the digitalized class typeface (see fig.5). Together with the schoolteacher and the pupils, they discussed these changes and commented the general appearance of their typeface.

WRITING A MESSAGE TO THE FABLAB
One of the activities pupils engaged in during the session was to write a message to thank the FabLab. They first agreed on a sentence that they spelled out to the teacher for him to write on the white board. Using the wooden letters cut with the laser cutter, a group of pupils wrote that message on a wood board and took a picture for the FabLab, whereas another one used stickers on paper.
At the end, the class left the FabLab with two sets of wood stamps and two sets of stickers, and they offered to the FabLab a large poster made out of stickers to thank them. A digital version of the font has also been installed on the classroom computer for them to compose texts.

4) To be continued: printing at a design university
Pupils will be using their new wood stamps to create large posters for their classroom and their school. Plus, in a few weeks, they will go to a design university to discover how to use a printing press. Before this session, they will be working in class to imagine the message they will be printing, knowing that the point of using a press is to print multiple copies for them to be

distributed out of school. Through this act, the class will exist as an identified group who has a voice and creates public signs. Their printed poster will be exhibit during a graphic design fair (Les Puces Typographiques).

Discussion and Future Work

We designed this journey through making to create the conditions for pupils to participate and experience the relations between materials, people and places, through a translation process with a constructive goal. Following their collective typeface through tools, interfaces, people and places, they made it evolve. We can say that they participated to the written culture by creating their own alphabet, and acknowledged the different steps and skills involved. They also acknowledged that to a desired end, one needs to imagine the appropriate mediational means, be they human or material (often a combination of both). Because they have discussed their typeface, shared it and collaborated on it, they have experienced a "distributed constructionism": these activities engaged pupils in a mutual appropriation and negotiation process in a zone of proximal development (ZPD) [1]. We can say they elaborated a situated culture by designing the means of a broader culture (a typeface), and by creating relationships that go beyond the walls of their classroom. We see a great research opportunity in considering making activities from their social and cultural dimensions, and this early work confirms us to pursue in that direction, beginning by a closer analysis of pupils' paths in the ZPD [9].

References

1. A. L. Brown, D. Ash, M. Rutherford, K. Nakagawa, A. Gordon, and J. C. Campione. 1993. Distributed expertise in the classroom. In Gavriel Salomon (ed.). Cambridge University Press, Cambridge, 188–228.
2. S. L. Chu, F. Quek, S. Bhangaonkar, A. Boettcher Ging, and K. Sridharamurthy. 2015. Making the maker: a means-to-an-ends approach to nurturing the maker mindset in elementary-aged children. *International Journal of Child-Computer Interaction*, 5.
3. I. Harel, S. Papert. Epistemology & Learning Research Group. 1991. *Constructionism*. Ablex Publishing Corporation.
4. E.-S. Katterfeldt, N. Dittert, and H. Schelhowe. 2015. Designing digital fabrication learning environments for Bildung: Implications from ten years of physical computing workshops. *International Journal of Child-Computer Interaction*, 5.
5. S. Papavlasopoulou, M. N. Giannakos, and L. Jaccheri. 2017. Empirical studies on the Maker Movement, a promising approach to learning: A literature review. *Entertainment Computing* 18: 57–78.
6. M Petrich, K. Wilkinson, and B. Bevan. 2013. It looks like fun, but are tehy learning? In *Design, Make, Play*, M. Honey and E. Kanter (eds.). Routledge, 50–70.
7. M. Resnick. 1996. Distributed constructionism. In *Proceedings of the 1996 international conference on Learning sciences*, 280–284.
8. D. Shaffer and M. Resnick. 1999. "Thick" Authenticity: New Media and Authentic Learning. *Journal of Interactive Learning Research* 10, 2: 195–215.
9. R. C. Smith, O. S. Iversen, and M. Hjorth. 2015. Design thinking for digital fabrication in education. *International Journal of Child-Computer Interaction*, 5.
10. Lev S. Vygotsky. 1978. *Mind in Society*. Harvard University Press, Cambridge.

Click to Enter: Comparing Graphical and Textual Passwords for Children

Jasper Cole
Digital Whimsy Lab
University of Baltimore
jaspercole@ubalt.edu

Greg Walsh
Digital Whimsy Lab
University of Baltimore
gwalsh@ubalt.edu

Zachary Pease
Digital Whimsy Lab
University of Baltimore
zacharypease@ubalt.edu

ACM ISBN 978-1-4503-4921-5/17/06.
http://dx.doi.org/10.1145/3078072.3084311

Abstract
This work outlines a study comparing graphical and textual passwords. A study was conducted with 13 children between the ages of six and twelve years old. These participants created their own textual and graphical passwords for fictional Web sites and after two weeks, participants returned and attempted to recall the usernames and passwords that they created. Our preliminary results showed that graphical passwords had a lower success rate and participants were less likely to access their accounts when using graphical passwords. Whether using graphical or textual passwords, children succeeded with generalities, but struggled with specifics.

Author Keywords
Security; Passwords; Children

ACM Classification Keywords
D.4.6 [Security and Protection]: Authentication

Introduction
In their article Designing Textual Password Systems for Children, Read & Cassidy wrote "studies on how children create and use passwords are rare" [8]. These authors suggest requiring text passwords that do not require 8 letters and do not require a mixture of numbers, letters, and symbols, but they do not discuss any alternatives methods.

Figure 1: A participant is smiling while entering a graphical password on a picture of a motor bike.

Despite this, they write that "textual passwords can be especially problematic for children" (p. 200). Therefore, it is worthwhile to examine some other systems of authentication and their accessibility, memorability, and favorability among children. Alternative passwords may be better for children, providing safer, easier, and more secure access to their private information.

Graphical passwords are a popular alternative among adults and have been the subject of many studies. One of the most discussed system is PassPoints - where users select several distinct points on an image and then recall these positions accurately in order to access their account. This system has been studied extensively and many authors have written about it. For example, Wiedenbeck et al. [11] examine tolerance and image choice and Dirik & Birget [4] model and predict user choice. These studies are built around the potential viability of graphical passwords among adults.

Some research has been done on children and passwords already. Despite a long history of research about children's struggles with passwords, and many viable alternatives, there are very few studies that compare alternative password systems to more conventional textual systems. This paper discusses one preliminary study into the use of one type of graphical password system with children.

Background

Research about children and computers has been mostly separated from research relating to passwords and login systems. These subjects have some overlap, but in general research about children is focused on design and usability [12]. Some research examines the effects of computer use on children's development [1]. If children are going to use computers, they need to be able to use them securely. This means secure access through children-friendly login and password systems. Very little research looks seriously at the question of security and what security is appropriate and effective for children.

From the research that has been done, it is clear that researchers do not feel that children can use textual passwords effectively. Read & Cassidy [8] explain that children do not know how to create secure textual passwords and designers need to make many accommodations for children to use textual passwords. These accommodations may well compromise the security of the system. They end their article discussing that "future work will be looking at [...] the use of non-textual passwords for children". Unfortunately they do not study or suggest any alternative password methods, and no one has yet identified any leading alternative methods for children's passwords.

There has been some research published on alternative login methods for children. Mendori et al [7] posits a symbol based password as a child-friendly alternative to conventional textual passwords. Icon identification seems plausibly superior to textual passwords, but no comparisons were performed for memorability. Therefore, it is unclear if this type of password system performs better, the same, or worse than a conventional textual password.

Stemming from literature about adult users, there is an underlying assumption that textual passwords are inherently problematic and a superior login system could be created. Articles such as [6] outlines the ways password reuse compromises the security of textual password systems. In [10], the authors explain the harsh demands of textual password systems by showing how many user names and passwords adults are expected to remember, and exploring how frequently these passwords are forgotten. They recommend securing access further by requiring physical objects, biometric input, and voice or handwriting analysis.

The most commonly explored alternatives are graphical passwords. For example, [5] investigates multiple types of graphical passwords. The research examined different kinds of graphical passwords, including their strengths and weaknesses. The article is reinforced by grounding the results of graphical password studies in research conducted on textual passwords. Comparisons between graphical and textual passwords lead to the largest gap in current research. Chiasson et. al [2] compared users' retention of graphical passwords and textual passwords in adults using a graphical password system called PassPoints. In PassPoints, users select 5 points on an image and are required to click those 5 points to log in. The authors found that graphical passwords were easier to remember after the distraction task, but after "two weeks, recall of the passwords in the text and graphical conditions was not statistically different from each other" (p. 510).

Graphical passwords have been discussed as a viable alternative since 1999 in [9]. More recently, articles such as [3] showed the potential weakness of these passwords. The authors used computer models to identify and accurately predict users' graphical passwords. Therefore the decision to investigate graphical passwords is not based on the assumption that graphical passwords are the ideal alternative. Instead, this study seeks to examine the strengths and weakness of one of the most prevalent alternative methods in children. This will hopefully identify the applicability of this method for children, leading to better login systems in the future.

Figure 2: The graphical password screen in the second prototype. There is a "change hint" button that allows the user to write a textual hint, as suggested by the design partners from the co-design team.

What We Did

This study was performed to compare textual passwords, specifically the PassPoints-based system modified by an intergenerational design team and enabled graphical passwords for children. Researchers expected that a graphical password system would be more enjoyable and useful.

In the final password prototype developed for testing, participants created a text username then selected one of several images from a menu of images. They then selected five points on that image as their password. To access their account, the participant chose the same image and then selected the same five points in the same order. If they selected points that are within 20 pixels to their original selections, then they would successfully access their account.

A textual password interface was also created for empirical testing. This version of the site works exactly the same as the picture passwords except they created an alphanumeric password with the keyboard. Participants were prompted to create a hint which they can change at any point during the password confirmation process. Afterwards they were taken back to the home page and they could log in to their account by entering their username and their password.

When a participant completed each page (by successfully logging in to an account), the test moved to the next page based on the order set for that participant alternating randomly between graphical and textual pages.

Methods

Participants The study was completed with 13 participants between the ages of 6 and 12 years old (See Table 1). The study had a within-subjects design where all participants created textual and graphical passwords. Participants were randomly assigned to different orders for five different pages; some created textual passwords first

Name	*Age*	*Gender*
Archer	7	M
Caren	9	F
Marie	6	F
Xena	10	F
Kyle	9	M
Elizabeth	9	F
Alice	7	F
Mollys	10	F
Sally	9	F
Trent	12	M
Darren	8	M
Eric	6	M
Ian	8	M

Table 1: List of participants.

while others created graphical passwords first. All participants had some experience with passwords and login systems, but because of their young age, most did not have as extensive experience or as many different passwords as many adults. All of the children were from the Baltimore metropolitan region in the United States.

Protocol The study consisted of two lab-based session. The first session took approximately one hour and was completed by all 13 participants. The second sessions were held at least 10 days later and took approximately thirty minutes to complete. Participants used the same computer system and tried to recall the passwords that they had previously created.

First Session - Participants answered a few questions with the researchers and then created passwords for each of the five pages. They received a random order of graphical and textual passwords. All participants completed all five passwords. Each site was distinct and was identified by different colors, a different title, and a different logo image. After creating five accounts, participants were given approximately five minutes to play a game online as a distraction activity.

After completing the game, the children went back to try their passwords. If they failed to log in, they were given up to five attempts, but many children gave up after several unsuccessful attempts. They were encouraged to continue, but if they would not, they were given their password and advanced to the next page.

Once they attempted to log in to all five accounts, they were congratulated for their focus and hard work. They then answered a few questions about the process. These questions included questions about preference such as "What was easier to remember?" and "What did you prefer?" as well as questions about security in general, such as "Which of these would protect you better?".

Second Session - Ten participants returned to the lab 11 to 16 days after they completed their first session. These participants tried to recall the passwords that they created previously.

Researchers observed as children moved through the process. After logging into the first page they then logged into the same five web site prototypes in the same order from the first session. If they could not log into a page, researchers provided the password for them and moved them to the next page. Once they completed the task, researchers asked them several questions about the experience. For example, they were asked if they felt their hints were useful, and if they felt graphical or textual passwords were more secure.

What We Found

The success rate is the number of successfully entered passwords divided by the total number of attempts. Table 2 shows the number of times participants attempted to access their account and the number of successfully entered passwords. A single attempt in this table can include multiple password entries, as long as the user continued to work on accessing their account.

It is clear from this table that participants did best during their first login. As soon as they were distracted for five minutes, they were much less successful at logging into their account. The success rate of graphical passwords dropped from approximately 87% to approximately 78%. The success rate of textual passwords dropped from a flawless 100% to approximately 81%. This implies that users forgot textual passwords more quickly, as the distraction task caused a greater difference with textual passwords than

		Attempts	*Successfully entries*	*Success Rate*
Graphical Passwords	Following account creation	33	29	87%
	After distraction task	33	26	78%
	After two weeks	26	11	42%
	Total	92	66	71%
Textual Passwords	Following account creation	32	32	100%
	After distraction task	32	26	81.25%
	After two weeks	24	16	66%
	Total	88	74	84%

Table 2: Success Rate of Passwords

graphical passwords (19% versus 9%). This implies that graphical passwords may be more memorable in the short term. But they were also more difficult for participants, as participants were able to access their accounts more consistently when using textual passwords.

What It Means

Even after two weeks most children did remember the generalities of their password. Most passwords were approximated, even when children couldn't access their accounts. They remembered what kinds of usernames and passwords they created, what picture they chose, and generally where the points were located on the image. Their troubles came from selecting specific locations, maintaining accuracy and order, and recalling the exact spelling, capitalization, and symbols following their passwords and usernames. This implies that both graphical and textual passwords are potentially viable, but concessions must be made to facilitate children. An alternative system may be able to capitalize on this knowledge to create a secure system that does not require the same specificity.

Limitations and Conclusion

Due to the lack of research in this area of Child-Computer Interaction, this study should be viewed as exploratory. As mentioned earlier, the field has thought about passwords, but the authors could not find any exploration of password solutions. This data is an excellent starting part, but further research could help strengthen the arguments of this paper and reveal better solutions.

This research had a small number of participants. Having only ten participants return for the second session was a disappointment. More participants were scheduled, but several canceled or forgot to show up to their second session.

It would be good to see more research on alternative graphical or picture password designs. This study showed that multi-point graphical passwords like PassPoints are problematic, but it also showed that children were able to remember objects and pictures with a great deal of accuracy. It would be interesting to study this further to discover the strengths and weakness of this capacity. It is likely that fertile new technologies could take advantage of this to create password systems that are both secure and child friendly.

Acknowledgments

The researchers would like to thank the University of Baltimore's Fund for Excellence, Google, the children and adults of KidsteamUB for helping with the prototype, and all of the participants.

References

[1] Attewell, P., Battle, J., and Suazo-Garcia, B. Computers and young children: Social benefit or social problem? *Social forces 82*, 1 (2003), 277–296.

[2] Chiasson, S., Forget, A., Stobert, E., van Oorschot, P. C., and Biddle, R. Multiple password interference in text passwords and click-based graphical passwords. In *Proceedings of the 16th ACM conference on Computer and communications security*, ACM (2009), 500–511.

[3] Devlin, M., Nurse, J. R., Hodges, D., Goldsmith, M., and Creese, S. Predicting graphical passwords. In *International Conference on Human Aspects of Information Security, Privacy, and Trust*, Springer (2015), 23–35.

[4] Dirik, A. E., Memon, N., and Birget, J.-C. Modeling user choice in the passpoints graphical password scheme. In *Proceedings of the 3rd symposium on Usable privacy and security*, ACM (2007), 20–28.

[5] Gołofit, K. Click passwords under investigation. In *European Symposium on Research in Computer Security*, Springer (2007), 343–358.

[6] Ives, B., Walsh, K. R., and Schneider, H. The domino effect of password reuse. *Communications of the ACM 47*, 4 (2004), 75–78.

[7] Mendori, T., Kubouchi, M., Okada, M., and Shimizu, A. Password input interface suitable for primary school children. In *Computers in Education, 2002. Proceedings. International Conference on*, IEEE (2002), 765–766.

[8] Read, J. C., and Cassidy, B. Designing textual password systems for children. In *Proceedings of the 11th International Conference on Interaction Design and Children*, ACM (2012), 200–203.

[9] Rubin, A. D., Jermyn, I., Mayer, A., Monrose, F., and Reiter, M. K. The design and analysis of graphical passwords. In *8th USENIX Security Symposium*, Citeseer (1999).

[10] Summers, W. C., and Bosworth, E. Password policy: the good, the bad, and the ugly. In *Proceedings of the winter international synposium on Information and communication technologies*, Trinity College Dublin (2004), 1–6.

[11] Wiedenbeck, S., Waters, J., Birget, J.-C., Brodskiy, A., and Memon, N. Authentication using graphical passwords: effects of tolerance and image choice. In *Proceedings of the 2005 symposium on Usable privacy and security*, ACM (2005), 1–12.

[12] Yarosh, S., Radu, I., Hunter, S., and Rosenbaum, E. Examining values: an analysis of nine years of idc research. In *Proceedings of the 10th International Conference on Interaction Design and Children*, ACM (2011), 136–144.

Wearable Immersive Virtual Reality for Children with Disability: a Case Study

Franca Garzotto
Mirko Gelsomini
Daniele Occhiuto
Vito Matarazzo
Nicolò Messina

I3Lab – Innovative Interactive
Interfaces Laboratory
Department of Electronics,
Information and Bioengineering
Politecnico di Milano
20133 Milano, Italy

franca.garzotto@polimi.it
mirko.gelsomini@polimi.it
daniele.occhiuto@polimi.it
vito.matarazzo@mail.polimi.it
nicolo.messina@mail.polimi.it

IDC '17, June 27-30, 2017, Stanford, CA, USA

ACM ISBN 978-1-4503-4921-5/17/06.
http://dx.doi.org/10.1145/3078072.3084312

Abstract

Our research explores the potential of Wearable Immersive Virtual Reality (WIVR) as learning tool for children with disability, particularly Neurodevelopmental Disorder (NDDs). NDD is characterized by severe and often co-existing deficits in the cognitive, emotional, and motor areas. The paper discusses the learning potential of WIVR and presents the design and preliminary evaluation of Wildcard, a novel WIVR system designed in cooperation with NDD specialists. Virtual environments are displayed on a smartphone placed inside a commercial low cost VR viewer while children interact with the virtual world through gaze focus and direction. An exploratory study performed at a care center sheds a light on the behavior of children with NDDs in wearable immersive virtual reality environments and highlights the learning potential as well as the possible difficulties of using this technology with this target group.

Author Keywords

Accessibility; Neurodevelopmental Disorder; Immersive Virtual Reality.

ACM Classification Keywords

• H.5.1 Multimedia Information Systems: Artificial, augmented, and virtual realities. • J.3 Life and Medical

WIVR – Wearable Immersive Virtual Reality: virtual reality applications on wearable viewers to enhance users' immersion in the virtual environment.

NDD – Neurodevelopmental Disorder: NDD encompasses ID (Intellectual Disability), ADHD (Attention Deficit Hyperactivity Disorder), and ASD (Autistic Spectrum Disorder) [1].

HMD – Head Mounted Display: currently, there are two types of HMDs. Embedded solutions (e.g. Oculus, HTC Vive) provide a complete VR experience without any external devices. Embedded solutions usually ensure a more accurate user interaction and a better graphical quality, but at a much higher cost. Modular solutions exploit external devices, mostly smartphones, as enabling technology for displaying the simulated world, and are much cheaper.

Sciences: Health. • K.4.2 Social Issues: Assistive technologies for persons with disabilities.

Introduction

Wearable Immersive Virtual Reality (WIVR) enables users to experience 3D virtual spaces using Head Mounted Displays (HMDs) and establish a feeling of presence in the simulated environment. This technology has recently been hit by a new wave of popularity triggered by the price reduction of modern HMDs together with the advances in virtual reality development tools. This situation opens up new opportunities for creating and experimenting WIVR applications in different domains. Our research explores the use of WIVR as a support tool in therapies for children with NDD – Neurodevelopmental Disorder. NDD is a group of conditions that are characterized by severe deficits in the cognitive, emotional, and motor areas and produce serious impairments of social functioning [1]. Little is known about how WIVR technology works for children with NDD and how WIVR applications can be designed for these target users. This paper offers the following contributions. After an overview of the literature on virtual reality technologies for subjects with NDD, we investigate the relevant issues in this field. We describe our WIVR application, named Wildcard, that aims at complementing traditional educational interventions for children on the NDD spectrum, particularly to practice attention skills. We explore the acceptability of WIVR and the usability of Wildcard; we investigate the potential of Wildcard in promoting attention skills – an aspect that, to our knowledge, has never been addressed by prior studies in WIVR. Our results shed a light on the benefits and drawbacks of using virtual reality applications with children on the NDD spectrum.

Related Work

Several studies highlight the potential of interactive technologies for children with NDD, and the importance of introducing them in regular educational or therapeutic practices [3][6]. In what follows, we review the state of the art in this field ranging from Virtual Reality to Immersive Virtual Reality and Wearable Immersive Virtual Reality.

For most subjects with NDD, thinking is visual and many traditional learning approaches for these users use visual (often paper based) supports [7]. VR contents are centered on visual representations and therefore capitalize on these visual skills [11]. In virtual environments, behaviors and responses can be practiced in a safe and repeatable environment built-upon a visual context that shares some similarities with the real world. This is thought to help children with NDD learn about real life situations. Similar benefits can be found in the reviews described in Pearson & Cobb (2011) [9].

Some systems (e.g. CAVE) add immersion the VR interaction. Immersion induces the feeling of actually being in the environment. Outside the virtual experience, the user is expected to capitalize and link the representation of the virtual environment to the real world applying skills learned in the virtual space [5]. According to some studies, authors found a positive correlation between immersion and improvement of social and practical skills in low-medium functioning children with ASD [4].

Being wearable, the HMD maximizes the immersion effect removing the distractions of the outside world. In the past, the technological limitations of VR headsets

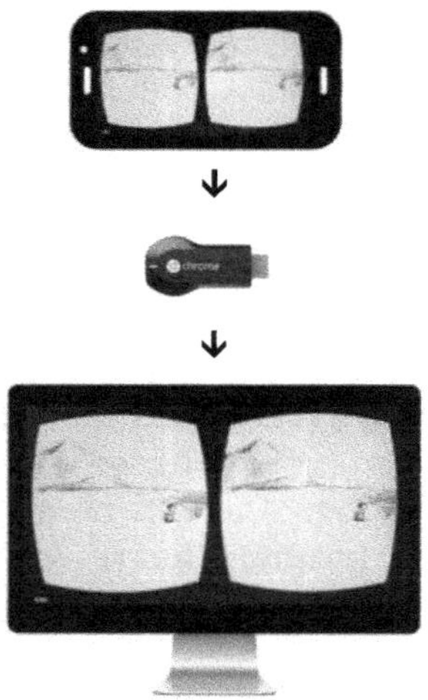

Figure 1: View on smartphone and secondary screen by mirroring with Google Chromecast over Wi-Fi.

Figure 2: Stereoscopic effect and virtual environment perception on Google Cardboard.

(e.g., poor viewing angles, high latency, and weight) and their high cost prevented a widespread adoption of WIVR in educational programs for children with NDD. The study performed by Strickland and al. in 1996 [11] explored the acceptability of this technology with two autistic children: authors defined the HMD as "heavy and awkward". Today's HMDs are more comfortable and some of them (e.g., Samsung Gear VR[1] and Google Cardboard[2]) are commercially available at an affordable cost, triggering an increasing attention to WIVR by research and industry, and creating a space for Wildcard development.

Few studies to date investigate the use of new WIVR devices among subjects with NDD. Most of these studies explore the questions raised by Strickland et al. [11] surrounding acceptability and willingness to engage with VR viewers. Few publications explore modern WIVR technology as learning tool in the NDD domain. The VR game for Oculus Rift described in [2] aims at preparing individuals with ASD to use buses for transportation to reach specific destinations.

Wildcard Design

We designed Wildcard in close collaboration with caregivers who actively participated in the following phases: i) eliciting the key requirements, ii) evaluating iterative prototypes, iii) performing an empirical study evaluation.

Before starting to design our system we participated as observers to the children's activities in their normal context. This approach enabled us to understand what happens in a typical session and where the opportunities for WIVR technology lay. Then, specialists familiarized with WIVR technology, trying Google Cardboard and interacting with VR contents (360° videos, VR games). Together we identified the main requirements for a WIVR application for NDD interventions, from the perspective of both the child and the therapist:

- provisioning sense of presence by effect of the viewer isolation and real-time feedback on gaze orientation,
- triggering engagement through gamification,
- promoting cause-and-effect reasoning through interaction with stories,
- enabling therapists to receive real-time feedback of the child's view focus (**Figure 1**),
- gathering data automatically on children's performances exhibited during the session.

Specialists also suggested to create virtual worlds that evoke the visual contents of story books used in regular interventions and provided us with 2 stories that they use as learning material in therapeutic sessions.

Interaction Modality

Wildcard exploits Google Cardboard as VR viewer. We opted for this device because it is low cost, is available in different shapes, colors, and materials. Therapists can select the option which is more appropriate for each child. The smartphone set inside Google Cardboard provides the VR environments. The visual content appears as two near-identical bi-dimensional images on the display. What creates the illusion of 3D depth and immersion is the stereoscopic effect generated by the biconvex lenses on the VR viewer and the human vision system. The human brain combines

[1] http://www.samsung.com/us/explore/gear-vr/

[2] https://vr.google.com/cardboard/

Figure 3: Story 360: view from user perspective - Main characters: Suzy (top) and Giulio (bottom).

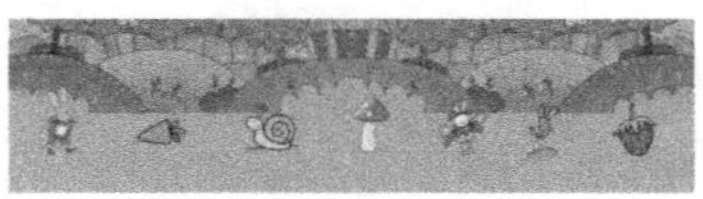

Figure 4: Unfolded Virtual World: 360° flat overview of the virtual environment "Story360: Giulio".

Figure 5: Exploration - top view in Unity game engine.

the two near-identical images and gives the perception of a single planar representation (**Figure 2**). Conceptually, interaction is based on gaze orientation and focus. By changing gaze direction, the child updates her/his view of the virtual environment and has the illusion of moving in different directions or changing perspective in the virtual space.

Virtual Environments and Children's Tasks

The visual "themes" of the virtual environments are inspired to the fantasy tales of two books used at the care center during regular therapy (**Figure 3**). We used Unity game engine to implement two types of tasks for each theme: Story360 and Exploration. In Story360 the goal is to explore the space "together with" the main character and "collect" the items encountered along the way. The main character is initially placed at the center of the user's field of view while the other elements are distributed in the entire 360° panorama at equal distance from one another (**Figure 4**). The character will advance in the story only when focused and will collect items from the narration when positioned over them. In Exploration, the virtual environment is shaped as an irregular 3D path that requires several changes of gaze direction to be traversed (**Figure 5**). The goal is to reach the "exit" of this non-linear space in the minimum amount of time. Images related to one of the previously defined themes indicate the direction to follow and are the active elements that must be pointed at in order to move towards the "exit".

Exploratory Study

We focused on the *acceptability* of WIVR, the *usability* of Wildcard, and the effects of Wildcard experiences on *attention.*

Acceptability was investigated in terms of the main parameters adopted in the current literature on WIVR for subjects with NDD (e.g., [8]: children's willingness to use the visor, motion-sickness, double vision and digital eye strain). *Usability* of Wildcard was measured in terms of "*task accomplishment"* (number of completed tasks in a session) and "*support from caregiver"* (number of times the caregiver provided *prompts,* i.e., helped the child to interact or to orient the head properly). *Attention* was the most difficult variable to operationalize because of the wide spectrum of definitions and measures of this construct. Considering the context of the children's experiences, therapists desired a concise representation of the fluctuation in user focus (**Figure 6, 8, 9**) and defined as attention measure "how long children were concentrated on relevant items in the VR spaces". We therefore measured attention as the percentage of time during which relevant items were focused on compared with the total duration time of the task. The study involved 5 children with NDD and their 4 therapists (**Table 1**). The children were aged 6-10 and attended the center on a regular basis. They had different forms of NDD at mild or moderate severity level and comparable intellectual functioning level.

ID	Age	Main Diagnosis	Severity level
C1	6	ASD	Moderate
C2	7	ASD	Moderate
C3	8	ASD	Mild
C4	10	SLD	mild
C5	8	Motor disorder	mild

Table 1: Participants' profiles. ASD = (Autism Spectrum Disorder), SLD (Specific Learning Disorder)

Variables Operationalization

AT – Accomplishment Time: the actual time of "gameplay" i.e. the total time to complete a task.

#FC – Number of Focus Changes: sum of attention-switches from relevant to non-relevant items, they represent the fluctuations in user focus during a task.

Attention levels: binary values tracked by the system during the session (1 the child focuses on a relevant object; 0 otherwise.

SA – Sustained Attention: percentage of the amount of time the user's focus stays on a relevant item over the Accomplish Time.

Main Results

The data about *acceptability* and *usability* were extracted from the video analysis performed by therapists. The information about other variables were extracted from interaction logs.

Concerning *acceptability*, C1 and C2 (the two youngest children, with ASD) had an initial resistance to wear Google Cardboard but only at the beginning of the first session. They accepted to wear it after the therapists wore it and invited them to manipulate it. C3, C4 and C5 were not bothered by the viewer. The physical discomfort effects are reported **Table 2**.

ID	Session 1	Session 2
C1	DES, DV	n/a
C2	DES, MS	DES
C3	DES, MS	n/a
C4	DES	None
C5	DES, MS	DES

Table 2: Physical discomfort. DES = Digital Eye Strain; MS = Motion Sickness; DV = Double Vision.

Concerning *usability*, the reduction of the *number of prompts* in the second sessions (**Table 3**) pinpoints a reduction of the need for therapist's support from the first session to the second one. **Table 3** also reports the values for *Task Accomplishment*, indicating if both Story360 and Exploration could be performed in a session.

The analysis of the *attention* variables considers only the children who attended both sessions (C2, C4, and C5) to enable a comparison between the two sessions.

Table 4 summarizes the main results concerning Sustained Attention (SA), Accomplishment Time (AT) and Number of Focus Changes (#FC).

ID	T S1	P S1	T S2	P S2
C1	1	25	n/a	n/a
C2	1	19	1	12
C3	1	16	n/a	n/a
C4	2	4	2	1
C5	1	9	2	5

Table 3: Usability results (T S_i Accomplished tasks in Session *i* – P S_i Therapists' Prompts in Session *i*).

ID	SA S1	SA S2	AT S1	AT S2	#FC S1	#FC S2
C2	52%	33%	229	233	92	122
C4	59%	76%	124	95	56	52
C5	44%	51%	134	155	34	80

Table 4: Sustained Attention (SA), Accomplishment Time (AT) and Number of Focus Changes (#FC) results in Session 1 (S1) and Session 2 (S2)

The graphical representation of Attention Levels for the Story360 task are reported in **Figure 6 , 8, 9**. Caregivers inspected these data and pinpointed some valuable insights: C2 usually takes a break from the task at half of the story and dedicates this time to asking questions on the story to the specialist. C4 is very concentrated at the beginning of the task but loses interest in it with time. C5 attention levels are sparser in the first session, meaning that in the second session there are longer periods of sustained attention.

Figure 6: C2 attention levels. S1 top, S2 bottom. (time on x-axis).

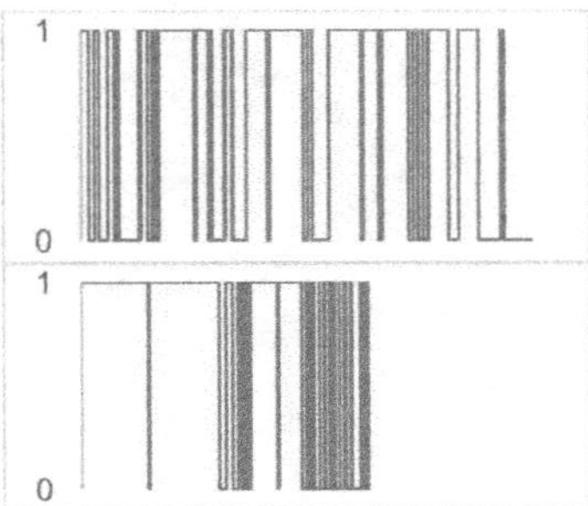

Figure 7: C4 attention levels. S1 top, S2 bottom. (time on x-axis).

Figure 8: C5 attention levels. S1 top, S2 bottom. (time on x-axis).

Conclusion and Future Work

Wildcard is an example of WIVR application that exploits last-generation cheap VR viewers, has been created for children with NDD and has been designed in cooperation with NDD specialists. Because of its affordable cost and design features, Wildcard could be integrated in regular interventions. However, our findings highlight some limitations as well. Due to the variability between the subjects in this target group, children with different needs and abilities from those who participated in the study may not benefit from using Wildcard. We do not know to which extent children generalize skills acquired in VR to the real world, this aspect could be investigated in a broader study. Wildcard may suffer from the side-effects of physical discomfort that are typical of WIVR technology. Concerning our future research, the natural follow up of the exploratory study will be a larger one. In addition, Wildcard needs some improvements in order to be used extensively. For example, the virtual environment should support more diversified and incremental contents. Finally, Wildcard data gathering capability will enable the creation of a vast body of data unique in the NDD field that will deserve an in-depth analysis to mine valuable information for clinical research.

References

1. American Psychiatric Association. (2013). Diagnostic and statistical manual of mental disorders *(DSM-5®)*.
2. Bernardes M., Barros F., Simoes M. and Castelo-Branco M. (2015). A serious game with virtual reality for travel training with Autism Spectrum Disorder. Proc. Int. Conf. on Virtual Rehabilitation (ICVR), Valencia.
3. Finkelstein, S., Barnes, T., Wartell, Z., Suma, E. A.. (2013). Evaluation of the exertion and motivation factors of a virtual reality exercise game for children with autism. In Proc. of Virtual and Augmented Assistive Technology (VAAT).
4. Herrera, G., Alcantud, F., Jordan, R., Blanquer, A., Labajo, G., De Pablo, C. (2008). Development of symbolic play through the use of virtual reality tools in children with autistic spectrum disorders: Two case studies. Autism Int. J. Res. Pract. 12, 143–157.
5. Herreraa, G., Jordanb, R., & Veraa, L. (2006). Abstract concept and imagination teaching through virtual reality in people with autism spectrum disorders. Technology and Disability, 18, 173–180.
6. Lanyi, C. S., & Tilinger, A. (2004). Multimedia and virtual reality in the rehabilitation of autistic children. In: Lecture Notes in Computer Science LNCS 3118, 22-28.
7. Meadan, H., Ostrosky, M. M., Triplett, B., Michna, A., & Fettig, A. (2011). Using visual supports with young children with autism spectrum disorder. Teaching Exceptional Children, 43(6), 28–35.
8. Newbutt, N., Sung, C., Kuo, H. J., Leahy, M. J., Lin, C. C., & Tong, B. (2016). Brief Report: A Pilot Study of the Use of a Virtual Reality Headset in Autism Populations. Journal of autism and developmental disorders, 1-11.
9. Parsons, S., Cobb, S.. (2011). State-of-the-art of virtual reality technologies for children on the autism spectrum. In Proc. European Journal of Special Needs Education, 26(3), 355-366. 2011.
10. Phillips, B. and Zhao, H. (1993). Predictors of assistive technology abandonment. In Assistive Technology. Taylor & Francis. 5(1): 36--45.
11. Strickland, D. C., Marcus, L. M., Mesibov, G. B., & Hogan, K. (1996). Brief report: Two case studies using virtual reality as a learning tool for autistic children. J. of Autism and Developmental Disorders, 26(6), 651–659.

TunePad: Computational Thinking Through Sound Composition

Jamie Gorson
Computer Science and Learning Sciences
Northwestern University
Evanston, IL, 60208 USA
jgorson@u.northwestern.edu

Nikita Patel
Computer Science
Northwestern University
Evanston, IL, 60208 USA
nikitapatel@u.northwestern.edu

Elham Beheshti
Computer Science
Northwestern University
Evanston, IL, 60208 USA
beheshti@u.northwestern.edu

Brian Magerko
Digital Media Program
Georgia Institute of Technology
Atlanta, GA 30332 USA
magerko@gatech.edu

Michael Horn
Computer Science
Northwestern University
Evanston, IL, 60208 USA
michael-horn@northwestern.edu

IDC '17, June 27-30, 2017, Stanford, CA, USA

ACM ISBN 978-1-4503-4921-5/17/06.
http://dx.doi.org/10.1145/3078072.3084313

Abstract
Computational thinking skills will be important for the next generation of students. However, there is a disparity in the populations joining the field. Integrating computational thinking into artistic fields has shown to increase participation in computer science. In this paper, we present our initial design prototype for TunePad, a sound composition tablet application controlled by a block-based programming environment. TunePad is designed to introduce learners to computational thinking and to prepare them for text-based coding environments. From our preliminary testing, with children ages 7-14, we observed that our design actively engages learners and communicates how the programming blocks control the sounds being played. This testing is a prelude to more formal studies as we continue to improve the design and interface of TunePad. With this work, we intend to engage students in computational thinking who may not have otherwise been exposed, giving the opportunity to more people to enter the computer science field.

Author Keywords
Computational thinking; music composition; broadening participation; CS education; STEAM;

ACM Classification Keywords
H.5.2 [User Interfaces]: User-Centered Design; K.3.2 [Computer and Information Science Education]:

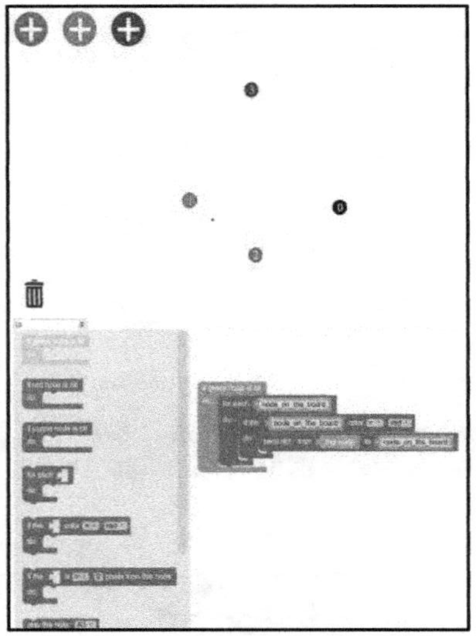

Figure 1: Screenshot of the TunePad prototype.

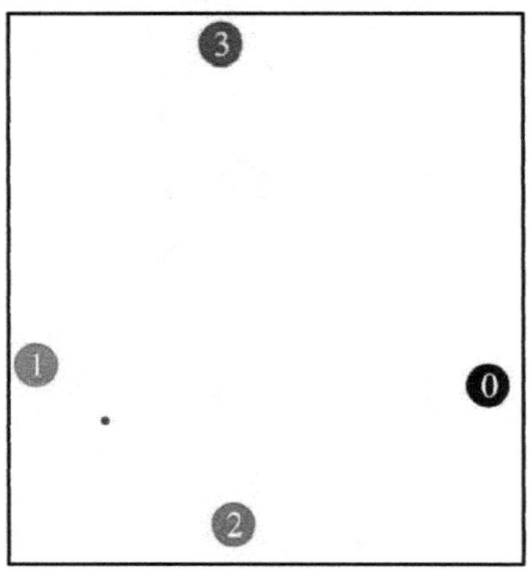

Figure 2: Nodes, generator and particle on the TunePad prototype.

Computer Science Education; J.5 [Arts and Humanities]: Music;

Introduction

Computational thinking skills are becoming increasingly important for the next generation [13]. However, large disparities remain in populations pursuing computer science, in part because many students are turned off by the image portrayed by the field [4]. One promising approach to address this disparity has been STEAM (Science, Technology, Engineering, Arts, Mathematics), the integration of the arts into technology-focused fields like computing [9]. STEAM blends topics perceived as "rigid and logical-mathematical" with disciplines seen as more "creative" and broadly appealing [7].

One example of the STEAM based approach is EarSketch, an online learning environment that integrates computer programming with electronic music composition. With EarSketch, learners from both minority and majority populations have shown significant increases in content knowledge, along with positive attitudinal shifts towards computing [6]. EarSketch lets students remix professionally produced audio samples with authentic programming languages (Python or JavaScript). However, EarSketch's curriculum and text-based programming environment are targeted at students in high school and may be intimidating and difficult for younger learners.

Building on EarSketch, we are designing and testing a sound composition app called TunePad. Our goal is to provide a playful introduction to computational thinking in places like community centers, libraries, schools, and homes. Learners manipulate a visual interface consisting of colorful nodes that generate sounds. Users can program these nodes with a visual programming environment based on the Blockly framework [5]. The application is ideally easy enough for young learners to pick up in informal, unguided contexts, but rich enough to help them transition to more sophisticated environments over time. With TunePad, we hope to broaden participation in computing.

Our overarching research questions are (1) how can we best design a learning environment that engages novices in computational thinking around music composition and (2) how do we strike a balance between playful, informal learning while also preparing learners for transferring to a more instruction-based learning environment such as EarSketch?

In this paper, we describe our prototype design and present findings from our preliminary testing with 26 children. From these sessions, we found that our design was engaging for learners. Our participants, many of whom had prior experience with block-based programming, understood how TunePad programming blocks connected to nodes. We still have open questions about how to help users learn computational theory through our coding blocks without sacrificing the playful and exploratory nature of the experience.

Background

Many researchers have studied environments to help children learn computational thinking concepts and change their attitudes towards computer science [3,4,11]. The STEAM approach has been promising in its ability to improve personal motivation and increase learner engagement [7]. For example, Buechly et al. showed that using e-textiles to create wearables was

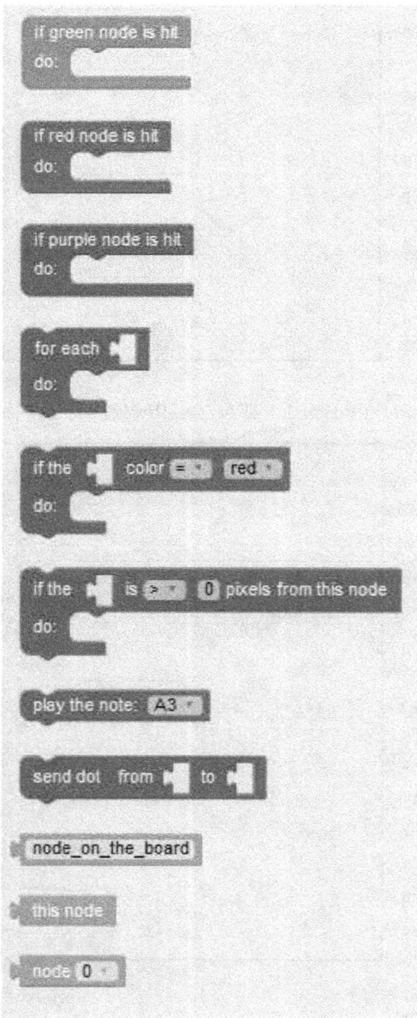

Figure 3: Custom-made blocks for TunePad.

an engaging and rich vehicle for teaching computational thinking to children [3]. STEAM has also been applied to music composition, integrating music with STEM fields [1,2,6]. This strategy takes advantage of pre-existing communities and interests. These studies found that learners are more engaged in STEM, and specifically computing, when it's integrated into the learner's existing activities. We hope to follow this strategy by engaging learners who are already drawn to music while introducing them to computational thinking.

Prototype Design

TunePad (Figure 2) is comprised of nodes (colored dots), generators (black dot) and particles (small grey dots), which enable learners to create sound. In TunePad, learners can experiment by placing nodes on the screen and observing the resulting sounds created when particles hit the nodes. We were inspired by an existing music app called NodeBeat, in which users create combinations of pitches and sounds to rapidly produce musical rhythms [12].TunePad is distinct from NodeBeat because by using block code, learners can tinker with a node's actions. The generator sends a particle to every node at regular intervals. When a particle hits a node, the learner now determines which sounds are created and if new particles are sent from nodes by writing the reaction function.

Users program the reaction function (Figure 4) using our custom-made block-based programming language created with the Blockly framework [5]. The method of programming is based on the object-oriented programing model. This means that the code is organized around objects instead of actions. In our implementation, the code is oriented around the node that is hit. Nodes are assigned a number based on their order added to the board, allowing users to identify and target individual nodes. Reaction functions are written for each color of node, meaning all nodes of the same color execute identical code.

There are 12 different programming blocks in the prototype (Figure 3). The first three are the containers for each reaction function and colored to match their respective nodes. The middle five, all navy blue, are the command blocks. The 'for each' block allows users to access all the nodes on the board. The conditionals afford the user control over where to send particles based on color or distance. This gives the user more creative ability and teaches them about if statements. The play block is what makes the sounds. The send dot block creates a particle from the first input to the second input, teaching participants about calling functions with parameters. The last three blocks, all yellow, are how users identify nodes. The first is a variable to be used with the 'for each' block. The 'this node' block calls the node that was hit by the particle. The final block has a dropdown where users can pick an individual node to reference by its number.

The text on each block was written so that a complete function could be read and comprehended with natural language, yet formatted in a way that correlates to programming syntax. This way, a user could easily understand the blocks and also learn computing concepts.

To help children learn the fundamental ideas of troubleshooting and debugging, we have begun to incorporate error messages into the program. For example, if a user accumulates too many particles on

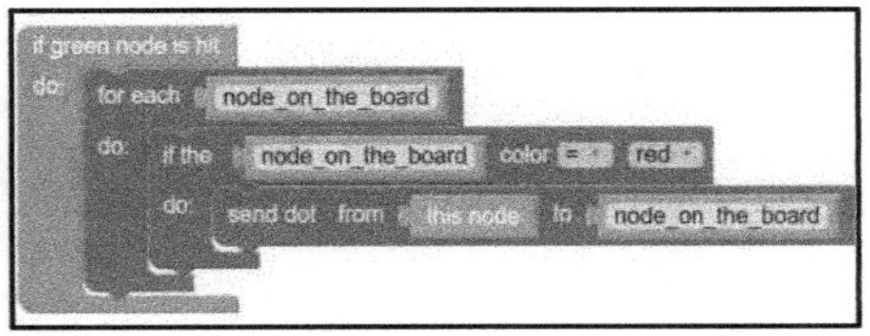

Figure 4: Example of a reaction function.

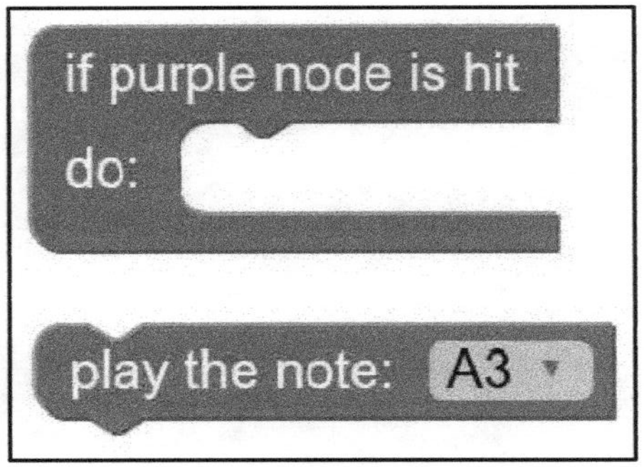

Figure 5: A function block (top) and a command block (bottom).

the board by creating an infinite loop, the user will receive a notification that the song exploded. When this happens, all the particles are erased on the board leaving the code and nodes the same, forcing the user to correct their work to avoid another explosion.

Prototype Testing

We tested our prototype with 14 children, ages 7–14, in an after-school music school in a major Midwest city. We asked children to use the tablet in groups of two or three. Two of the participants used the application alone. Each group was monitored by a researcher who helped and observed the group. We tested on two separate days with different children each time. On the first day, we provided a printed example of a working program for the students to replicate, and then encouraged each group to experiment freely. On the second day, we provided the learners with a printed set of step-by-step instructions to teach them how to create a working program. At the end of each session, the researcher asked the children for feedback on their experience with the application.

Additionally, we tested the prototype with 12 children, ages 10-14, during a workshop in a STEAM-based college-prep program. We asked the children to use the prototype in groups of three for 7 minutes. The students were encouraged to explore on their own, with minimal instruction from the researcher, who only stepped in to help when a child demonstrated signs of lost interest or asked for assistance. After finishing interacting with the app, researchers asked the participants for feedback.

Preliminary Findings and Discussion

Engagement

Almost all participants expressed interest in using TunePad beyond the allocated study time and most were physically and vocally enthusiastic while using the app. Many groups, after making an arrangement of nodes and blocks, watched their results with big smiles on their faces. Some of the groups increased the number of particles so much that the sound got very loud. One participant put his hands up to his ears and commented "Ahh! It's horrible again!" referring to the explosion of noise. This dislike encouraged him to edit the code to improve his composition. We expected learners to spend around 10 minutes playing with the app, but most groups interacted for around 30 minutes, even after researchers asked if they wanted to stop. Some children didn't want to leave and asked how they could play it at home.

Understanding Programming Controls Nodes

The groups showed a compelling understanding of how manipulating the programming blocks controlled the nodes on the screen. They would move the blocks and look for changes in the particles and sounds. While they were almost always able to reproduce the examples given, they were not able to fully explain each line of code. Students seemed to understand the mapping between a pattern of code blocks and a desired result, but struggled to create new patterns. The groups varied drastically in age and prior coding experiences, resulting in a range of the complexity of their compositions and their understanding of the computational concepts.

Intuitiveness of Block-based Programming

Many of our participants had previously exposure to block-based programming environments. What we found least intuitive about using the blocks for musical programming was indicating which blocks needed to be inside a function. The command blocks have indents on the top and a carrot on the bottom to imply that blocks go before and after, while the function blocks have the indent on the inside, so users put blocks on the inside (Figure 5). Several participants put the command blocks on the workspace without putting them into a function block and expected it to have an effect. Since reaction functions run when a node is hit, these independent blocks will never execute. We hoped the Blockly notation would discourage this, but it was not apparent to the participants.

Comprehension and Interest Without Instruction
At the second site, the groups were not given direction on how to use the app, yet all but one of the groups were able to create a composition. While these students struggled slightly more than those given direction, they figured out how to use the application to create sound. Their interest level in the application remained high until they couldn't understand an individual coding block or became confused.

Future Work

Develop In-App Directions
We are still very unsure how to best introduce TunePad in a way that helps children learn computational thinking without sacrificing the playful and exploratory nature of the application. While we tried prototypes of two methods in the preliminary testing, we still have limited understanding. In further testing we hope to formatively test different models of instruction.

Improving Functionality
We want to build upon the current functionality of the application, giving users more control over the sounds and adding more computational thinking elements. For example, nodes could be chosen by properties of their number, like evens and odds and sounds could be played in different instruments or octaves. Increasing the possible variables allows for the integration of more computational theory, like Boolean logic. With more complexity, we would need a method for revealing tools slowly to not overwhelm the learner.

Tangibles
We are also interested in studying the effects of adding physical manipulatives (tangibles) to the digital interface. Research has shown that physical manipulatives can support mathematics learning [6] or can increase engagement [8]. These tangibles could be as simple as print-at-home representations of the nodes, ensuring that the addition of tangibles wouldn't decrease the accessibility of the application.

Conclusion

We presented the initial prototype design of TunePad, a sound composition app that introduces computational thinking skills to middle-school aged learners. Although we have only conducted preliminary testing, we found that TunePad is engaging, making it a potential platform for introducing learners to computational thinking skills. The continuation of this work and future studies will help inform designers using STEAM approaches and create a new pathway for children to computer science. TunePad has shown to attract music students to computational thinking and we hope it will help attract a broader population to computing fields.

Acknowledgements

We thank our participants and Anna Xambo for help with this study. We thank the National Science Foundation for their support of this project (DRL-1612619). Any opinions, findings and conclusions or recommendations expressed in this material are those of the authors and do not necessarily reflect the views of the National Science Foundation.

References

1. Samuel Aaron and Alan F. Blackwell. 2013. From sonic Pi to overtone: creative musical experiences with domain-specific and functional languages. In *Proceedings of the first ACM SIGPLAN workshop on Functional art, music, modeling & design*, 35–46.
2. Jeanne Bamberger. 2003. Music as embodied mathematics: A study of a mutually informing affinity. *International Journal of Computers for Mathematical Learning* 8, 2: 123–160.
3. Leah Buechley, Mike Eisenberg, Jaime Catchen, and Ali Crockett. 2008. The LilyPad Arduino: using computational textiles to investigate engagement, aesthetics, and diversity in computer science education. In *Proceedings of the SIGCHI conference on Human factors in computing systems*, 423–432. Retrieved March 7, 2017 from http://dl.acm.org/citation.cfm?id=1357123
4. Jamika D. Burge and Tiki L. Suarez. 2005. Preliminary analysis of factors affecting women and African Americans in the computing sciences. In *Proceedings of the 2005 conference on Diversity in computing*, 53–56. Retrieved March 12, 2017 from http://dl.acm.org/citation.cfm?id=1095265
5. N. Fraser. 2013. Blockly: A visual programming editor. *Published. Google, Place*.
6. Jason Freeman, Brian Magerko, Tom McKlin, Mike Reilly, Justin Permar, Cameron Summers, and Eric Fruchter. 2014. Engaging Underrepresented Groups in High School Introductory Computing Through Computational Remixing with EarSketch. In *Proceedings of the 45th ACM Technical Symposium on Computer Science Education* (SIGCSE '14), 85–90. https://doi.org/10.1145/2538862.2538906
7. Danah Henriksen. 2014. Full STEAM Ahead: Creativity in Excellent STEM Teaching Practices. *STEAM* 1, 2: 1–9. https://doi.org/10.5642/steam.20140102.15
8. Michael S. Horn, Erin Treacy Solovey, R. Jordan Crouser, and Robert JK Jacob. 2009. Comparing the use of tangible and graphical programming languages for informal science education. In *Proceedings of the SIGCHI Conference on Human Factors in Computing Systems*, 975–984. Retrieved October 27, 2016 from http://dl.acm.org/citation.cfm?id=1518851
9. John Maeda. 2013. STEM + Art = STEAM. *STEAM* 1, 1: 1–3. https://doi.org/10.5642/steam.201301.34
10. Taylor Martin and Daniel L. Schwartz. 2005. Physically distributed learning: Adapting and reinterpreting physical environments in the development of fraction concepts. *Cognitive science* 29, 4: 587–625.
11. Andrés Monroy-Hernández and Mitchel Resnick. 2008. Empowering Kids to Create and Share Programmable Media. *interactions* 15, 2: 50. https://doi.org/10.1145/1340961.1340974
12. S. Sandler and J. Windl. 2013. NodeBeat. app for iOS. *Blackberry, Android, and Windows*.
13. David Weintrop, Elham Beheshti, Michael Horn, Kai Orton, Kemi Jona, Laura Trouille, and Uri Wilensky. 2016. Defining Computational Thinking for Mathematics and Science Classrooms. *Journal of Science Education and Technology* 25, 1: 127–147. https://doi.org/10.1007/s10956-015-9581-5

Multisensory Participatory Design for Children with Special Educational Needs and Disabilities

Nigel Robb
SMARTlab
School of Mechanical and Materials Engineering
University College Dublin
Dublin, Ireland
nigel.robb@ucd.ie

Connie Sung
Department of Counseling, Educational Psychology and Special Education
Michigan State University
MI, USA
csung@msu.edu

Michael Leahy
Department of Counseling, Educational Psychology and Special Education
Michigan State University
MI, USA
leahym@msu.edu

Lizbeth Goodman
SMARTlab
School of Mechanical and Materials Engineering
University College Dublin
Dublin, Ireland
lizbeth.goodman@ucd.ie

IDC '17, June 27-30, 2017, Stanford, CA, USA

ACM ISBN 978-1-4503-4921-5/17/06.
http://dx.doi.org/10.1145/3078072.3084314

Abstract
Participatory design techniques are used to involve children with special educational needs and disabilities in the design of video games and other artefacts, but previous research has not sufficiently addressed several issues. Among these are (1) the need to develop techniques to facilitate the involvement of children with a wider range of disabilities, including children with severe and profound intellectual disabilities (ID); and (2) the need to evaluate the potential benefits of such participation for the participants themselves, and not merely in terms of the benefits to the software or other artefacts produced. We have developed a multisensory design technique: ten children (8 – 17 years; 3 female) with a range of special educational needs (including children with severe ID) participated. Parents and teachers completed a questionnaire and reported that the technique was engaging and enjoyable for children, and that they would support the use of the technique in future.

Author Keywords
Participatory design; intellectual disability; game design; video games; theory of planned behavior; sensory stories

Figure 1: A poster created by participant 1. Not visible is a tab which, when pulled, plays music recorded on a small sound chip attached to the poster.

Figure 2: A poster created by participant 2. This poster has four swatches of cloth, each with a different texture (e.g., the bottom right creature is made of imitation fur). The poster also incorporates a sound chip which plays music.

ACM Classification Keywords

H.5.2. Information interfaces and presentation: User Interfaces – Theory and Methods, User-Centered Design

Introduction

We are developing online multiplayer video games and multisensory stories (simple stories told with the aid of sensory props, such as textured materials and scented objects) suitable for both typically developing children and children with special educational needs and disabilities (SEND). Multisensory input is important for individuals with certain disabilities: e.g., a widely-used multisensory intervention has large effects on adaptive behavior in individuals with intellectual disabilities (ID) [6]. Our overall aim is to create a video game/narrative experience that all children can engage with collaboratively, to promote contact between children with SEND and typically developing children; such indirect forms of intergroup contact can improve the attitudes of members of a group (in this case, typically developing children) towards members of an outgroup (in this case, children with SEND) [2, 5]. We are involving children with SEND in the design process. Participatory design (PD) of software and other artefacts with children with SEND is an area of research in which several issues have yet to be addressed. A recent review notes that more work is required to involve children with a wider range of disabilities in PD processes, and that future work should explicitly address the potential wider benefits of the PD process for the participants – such as a sense of empowerment, enjoyment, increased confidence, and improved social skills – rather than merely focus on benefits in terms of usability and effectiveness of the software or other technology produced [4]. To address these issues, we have developed a multisensory design technique. Our aim is to utilize a PD technique that children with a range of cognitive disabilities can take part in, including children with severe and profound levels of ID. To assess the potential benefits of our technique for the participants, we utilized a questionnaire based on the theory of planned behavior, which states that a person's intention to perform or permit a behavior is determined by (1) their attitude towards the behavior (positive/negative); (2) the perceived social pressure to perform or permit the behavior; and (3) their perceived control over the behavior [1]. By administering the questionnaire to teachers and parents who are present during the PD session, we aim to evaluate if adults who know the children well would intend to support the use of the technique in future.

Participant	Age at time of activity	Gender	Special Education Eligibility
1	17	Male	Cognitive impairment
2	13	Male	Severe multiple impairment (cognitive) (NV)
3	11	Female	Severe multiple impairment (cognitive) (NV)
4	13	Male	ASD (co-morbid Down Syndrome) (NV)
5	11	Male	ASD
6	12	Female	Cognitive impairment

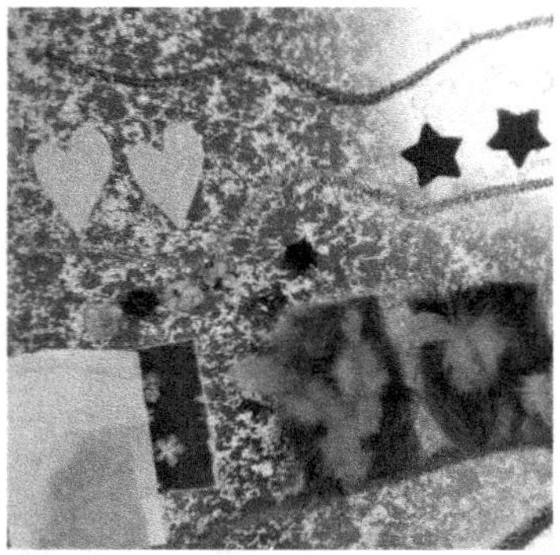

Figure 3: A poster created by participant 3. A small scent bag (in this case, containing dill) is visible bottom left.

Figure 4: A poster created by participant 4. This participant did not include any scents or sounds in the poster.

Participant	Age at time of activity	Gender	Special Education Eligibility
7	14	Female	Cognitive impairment
8	11	Male	ASD
9	10	Male	Cognitive impairment
10	8	Male	ASD

Table 1: Participants who took part in the design of multisensory interactive posters. ASD: autism spectrum disorder. NV: non-verbal. Special education eligibility categories are defined in [7].

Participants, Materials, and Methods

Participants are shown in Table 1. The PD technique used in this study involves the creation of interactive, multisensory posters. These are posters which incorporate visual, auditory, tactile, and olfactory experience. To create the posters, children are presented with a selection of materials; they are then invited to choose which objects they like, and a designer can assist the child to attach the object to a board or sheet of card. We recommend that the selection of materials is determined individually for each project, as designers can then impose specific design constraints if required. For our current project – designing video games and sensory stories – we utilized a range of materials, including materials with specific textures, colors, and shapes, small bags containing scented materials, and small sound chips incorporating music (see Figures 1 – 10).

Procedures: Making the Posters

Seven design sessions took place. Consultations with teachers and parents determined the format of each session, including the number of children involved, and each child's specific requirements (e.g., sessions 2 – 4 involved children who required one-to-one support; session 4 was shorter as a teacher informed a researcher in advance that the participant rarely focused on a single activity for long periods of time). The maximum number of participants in any session was three. Parental consent was obtained prior to the design sessions. Research information was presented to children in a simplified format incorporating illustrations. In each session, a researcher began by explaining to the children that he would like to make a video game, but that he didn't have any good ideas. He then asked the participants if they would like to help him by making a picture to show him what the game should be like. The researcher then either let children select materials themselves, or presented materials to the children and asked them if they wanted to use them. For children who were non-verbal (participants 2, 3, and 4), the researcher demonstrated how to use the material in an appropriate way (e.g., in the case of textured materials, the researcher brushed these against the participant's hand; in the case of scented materials, the researcher first smelled the material himself as a guide, then presented it to the participant to smell). Each session continued until the participant had either filled the entire poster with materials, began to show less interest in the activity, or indicated to the researcher that the poster was finished. The researcher then took a photograph of the poster and let the children keep the original poster.

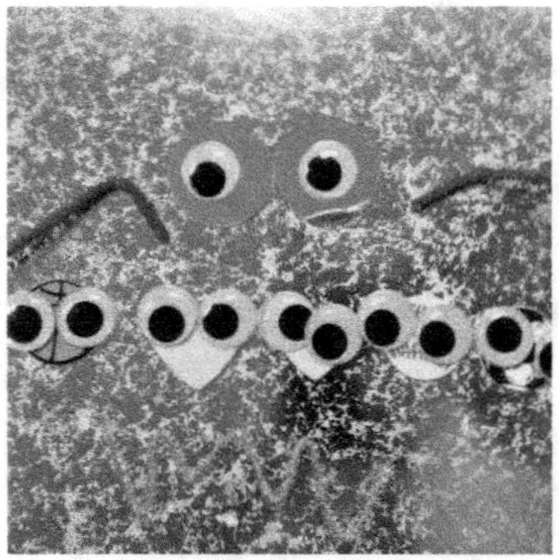

Figure 5: A poster created by participant 5. This participant did not include any scents in the poster. The sound chip (which plays music) is not visible.

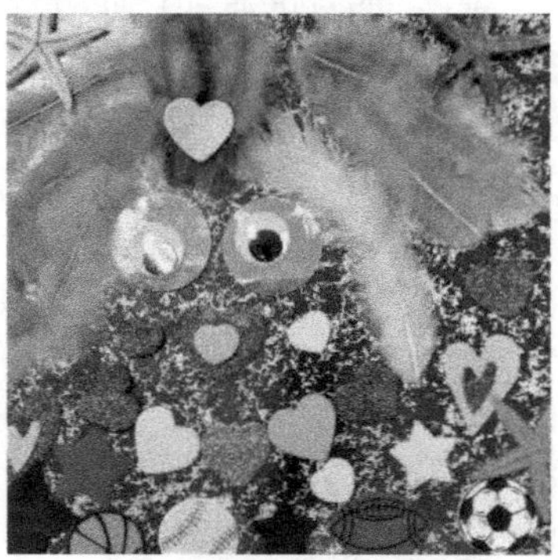

Figure 6: A poster created by participant 6. This poster incorporates feathers. The sound chip (which plays music) is not visible.

Questionnaire for Parents and Teachers

For at least part of each session, a parent or teacher who is familiar with the children involved was present. In addition, the parent or teacher studied the resulting poster, and discussed the activity with the child or children. Then, the parent or teacher completed a questionnaire, based on the theory of planned behavior. Questions were designed to elicit respondents' (1) behavioral beliefs about, (2) views on subjective norms regarding, (3) attitudes towards, and (4) intention to support, the use of multisensory interactive posters with children with SEND. All questions are displayed in Table 2. For the Intention, Behavioral Beliefs, and Subjective Norms constructs, questions were rated on a 5-point Likert-style scale, ranging from "Strongly Disagree" (1), to "Strongly Agree" (5). For the Attitudes construct, questions were also rated on a 5-point Likert-style scale (see Table 2 for the specific terms used).

Results

A total of 10 participants were able to make a poster with practical assistance from a researcher (e.g., the researcher attached some objects to the poster for the children) (see Figures 1 – 10). With the exception of participants 4 and 7, all children enthusiastically engaged with the activity. After a short time (less than 10 minutes), participant 4 began to fixate on one specific object and did not pay any further attention to the poster; in the case of participant 7, she created a poster and indicated preferences for objects, but had to be continually prompted and encouraged to do so. Results from the questionnaire are shown in Table 2. Generally, parents and teachers indicated that: (1) they would intend to support the use of the technique in future; (2) they believed the technique was engaging, enjoyable, and suitable for children; (3) others would support the use of the technique; and (4) they had positive attitudes towards the technique.

Construct	Question	Mean	Standard Deviation
Intention	I intend to make interactive posters with children with ID in the future	4.8	0.6
Behavioral Beliefs	I think that the child enjoyed making an interactive poster	4.6	0.8
	I think that the child was engaged while making an interactive poster	4.4	1.3
	I think that the child expressed their preferences through the interactive poster	3.8	1.4
	I think that the child was capable of making an interactive poster	4.7	0.7
Subjective Norms	Most carers like me would support using interactive posters with children with ID	5	0.0
	Most parents of children with ID would allow their children to make interactive posters	5	0.0
	I am confident that I could encourage children with ID to make interactive posters in the future	4.9	0.3
Attitudes	I think that making interactive posters is bad (1)/good (5)	5	0.0

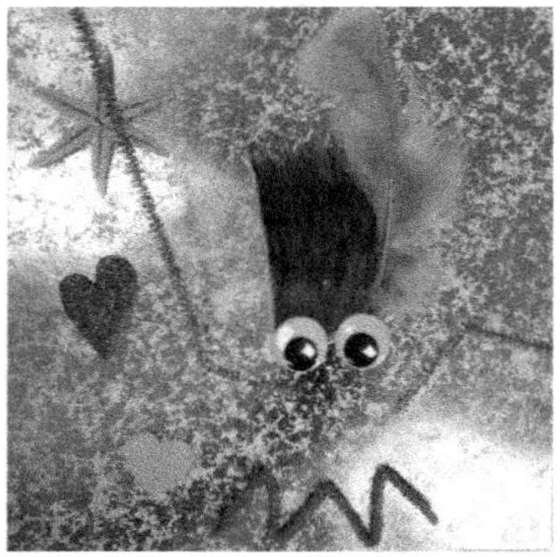

Figure 7: A poster created by participant 7. This participant wanted the picture to be a self-portrait. The sound chip (which plays music) is not visible.

Figure 8: A poster created by participant 8. This poster incorporates several images of specific objects (sports balls).

Construct	Question	Mean	Standard Deviation
	I think that making interactive posters is harmful (1)/beneficial (5)	5	0.0
	I think that making interactive posers is risky (1)/safe (5)	5	0.0
	I think that making interactive posters is boring (1)/engaging (5)	5	0.0
	I think that making interactive posters is unnecessary (1)/necessary (5)	4.8	0.4

Table 2: Results from a questionnaire based on the theory of planned behavior. For the Intention, Behavioral Beliefs, and Subjective Norms constructs, items were rated from "Strongly Disagree" (1) to "Strongly Agree" (5). ID: intellectual disability

Discussion and Future Work

This study shows that creating interactive multisensory posters is an activity that children of a range of ages and with a range of disabilities can do, including young children who are eligible for special education under the criteria of severe multiple (cognitive) impairments, and children who are non-verbal. While parents and teachers also indicated that they believed that the children expressed their preferences through the technique, the mean score of 3.8 for this item was the lowest, due to the presence of three cases where a teacher indicated that they felt the child did not express their preferences through the technique. Two of these children (participants 2 and 4) were non-verbal. In the case of participant 3 (also non-verbal), the teacher indicated that they neither agreed nor disagreed that the child expressed their preferences through the technique. However, during each session, all participants both expressed (1) a desire to include at least one particular material (either by directly choosing it or indicating they liked the material when it was presented to them); and (2) that they did not want to include at least one particular material in the poster (either by not selecting it or by indicating that they did not like the material). This suggests that, in the case of non-verbal children, consulting parents and teachers may not be sufficient to determine if the children are expressing their preferences through the technique. Instead, videos could be recorded of each child, and behaviors could be operationalized and rated.

Participant 4 and participant 7 did not engage as enthusiastically with the technique as the other children (see Results). However, consultations with teachers, both before, during, and after the activity, indicated that the level of engagement by each child was similar to their level of engagement in other similar activities. It is therefore plausible that their lack of engagement was not specific to the PD technique utilized in this study.

Some children did not include scented materials in their poster. In the case of participants 4, 5, and 6, they expressed strong dislike (e.g., recoiling from the material) of all the scents. Of the children who did include scented materials in their posters, some (participants 1, 2, and 3) expressed a strong dislike of some scents (note, however, that no children appeared distressed or indicated that they wished to stop taking part). This suggests that children had strong negative reactions to the materials, or that the materials used here had particularly strong scents. However, it is interesting to note that research shows associations between certain developmental disorders and

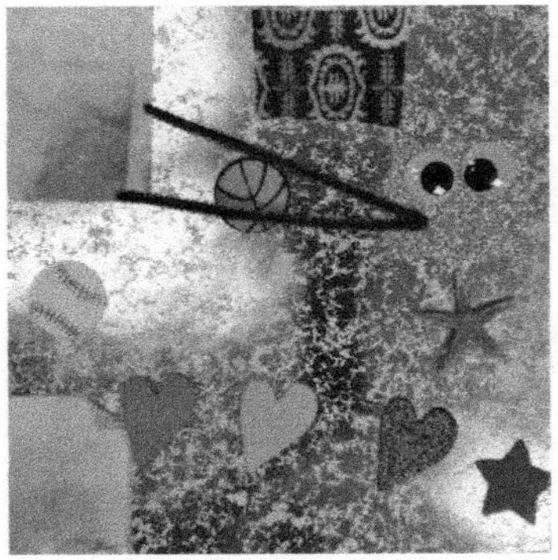

Figure 9: A poster created by participant 9. This poster incorporates two scent bags and (not visible) a sound chip which plays music.

Figure 10: A poster created by participant 10. This participant explicitly aimed to create a snake and a man. The poster includes a sound chip (not visible) which plays music.

dysfunctional sensory processing, including in olfaction [3]. Designers of sensory experiences for these populations may find multisensory techniques such as that presented here useful in determining which sensory experiences produce strong negative reactions in children with SEND, and should therefore be avoided.

Some of the materials selected for the present study were concrete representations of objects (e.g., a soccer ball), while others were abstract (e.g., a swatch of material). In the former case, we may have encouraged the children to create within certain themes (e.g., sports). There may be both advantages and disadvantages to this: it may be an advantage to limit the materials children can select from if the artefact being designed has a prior design brief. In such a case, it may be useful to perform the PD sessions later in the project, so that (e.g.) initial character designs, created by artists, could be among the materials presented to children. However, it may also be the case that this approach limits children's choices and self-expression. Which approach is more appropriate may depend on the specific requirements of each design project.

Note that a single teacher completed the questionnaire for eight of the children. Therefore, results for the Intention, Subjective Norms, and Attitudes constructs should be interpreted with caution, as these are based on responses from three individuals. Since the Behavioral Beliefs items asked child-specific questions, ten unique responses were recorded for this construct.

We recognize that it would be informative to seek direct feedback on the activity from the children themselves. However, our aim in this study was to establish that parents and teachers supported the use of the technique and believed that it was engaging and enjoyable for children. In future work, we aim to assess the benefits for children more specifically and directly.

Video games and multisensory stories incorporating ideas from the PD sessions reported here will be developed. The games and stories will be designed so that typically developing children and children with ID of all severity levels will be able to engage with them. Two approaches could be adopted when developing video games based on the children's posters: (1) the posters could be analyzed to determine the most popular preferences of children (e.g., only one child did not use eyes in their poster, suggesting that games should feature characters with eyes); (2) alternatively, 10 minigames could be created, each resembling one of the children's posters. This approach may prove more satisfying for the children who took part, as they would directly see their contribution realized in a unique video game. We intend to use the second approach in our future work. Typically developing children will be made aware of the design process, so that they understand the role of children with SEND in creating the games and stories. A study will be conducted to investigate the effects of engaging with the games and stories on the attitudes of typically developing children towards children with disabilities.

Acknowledgement

This research was supported by funding from the charity RESPECT and the People Programme (Marie Curie Actions) of the European Union's Seventh Framework Programme (FP7/2007-2013) under REA grant agreement no. PCOFUND-GA-2013-608728

References

1. Icek Ajzen. 1991. The theory of planned behaviour. *Organ. Behav. and Hum. Decis. Process.* 50: 179-211.
2. Megan Armstrong, Christopher Morris, Charles Abraham, Obioha C. Ukoumunne, and Mark Tarrant. 2016. Children's Contact with People with Disabilities and their Attitudes Towards Disability: A Cross-Sectional Study. *Disabil. Rehabil*. 38,9: 879-88.
3. Grace T. Baranek, Fabian J. David, Michele D. Poe, Wendy L. Stone, and Linda R. Watson. 2006. Sensory Experiences Questionnaire: Discriminating Sensory Features in Young Children with Autism, Developmental Delays, and Typical Development. *J. Child Psychol. Psychiatry* 47,6: 591-601.
4. Laura Benton and Hilary Johnson. 2015. Widening Participation in Technology Design: A Review of the Involvement of Children with Special Educational Needs and Disabilities. *Int J. Child-Comp. Interact.* 3: 23-40.
5. John F. Dovido, Anja Eller, and Miles Hewstone. 2011. Improving Intergroup Relations Through Direct, Extended and Other Forms of Indirect Contact. *Group Process. Intergr. Relat.* 14,2: 147-60.
6. Meir Lotan and Christian Gold. 2009. Meta-Analysis of the Effectiveness of Individual Intervention in the Controlled Multisensory Environment (Snoezelen®) for Individuals with Intellectual Disability. *J. Intellect. Dev. Disabil.* 34,3: 207-15.
7. Michigan Department of Education. 2016. Michigan Administrative Rules for Special Education (MARSE) with Related IDEA Federal Regulations. Retrieved March 24, 2017 from https://www.michigan.gov/documents/mde/MARSE_Supplemented_with_IDEA_Regs_379598_7.pdf

D-TOX: Inducing Digital Detox for Nighttime via Smart Lamp Applied Gamification

Jong Sung Lee
Dept. of Human ICT Convergence
Sungkyunkwan University
Suwon, South Korea 440-746
kes98215@naver.com

Seo Gwang Kim
Dept. of Human ICT Convergence
Sungkyunkwan University
Suwon, South Korea 440-746
buffist.kim@gmail.com

Ji Yeon Lee
Dept. of Human ICT Convergence
Sungkyunkwan University
Suwon, South Korea 440-746
all4me8911@gmail.com

Jun Dong Cho
Dept. of Human ICT Convergence
Sungkyunkwan University
Suwon, South Korea 440-746
jdcho@skku.edu

IDC '17, June 27-30, 2017, Stanford, CA, USA

ACM ISBN 978-1-4503-4921-5/17/06.
http://dx.doi.org/10.1145/3078072.3084315

Abstract
We present D-TOX, a user-centered design that by applying gamification to a smart lamp and mobile application reduces the frequency of smartphone usage during nighttime. Many children make use of their smartphone without any significant reason before sleep which prevents them from getting a good rest. To avoid this, we focused on developing a corrective system that removes their smartphone from their hands. We reward the user using gamification. The lamp's color and intensity varies depending on the smartphone usage which feedbacks the user. Through a user study, we confirmed the significance and usability of the device.

Author Keywords
Digital detox; smart lamp; Gamification; reward; adolescent; corrective action

ACM Classification Keywords
H.5.2. User Interfaces: User-centered design.

Introduction
Digital detox is a compound of digital and detox, meaning 'to abstain from toxic substances.' The concept has emerged as a remedy to the global concerns regarding the negative aspects of digital

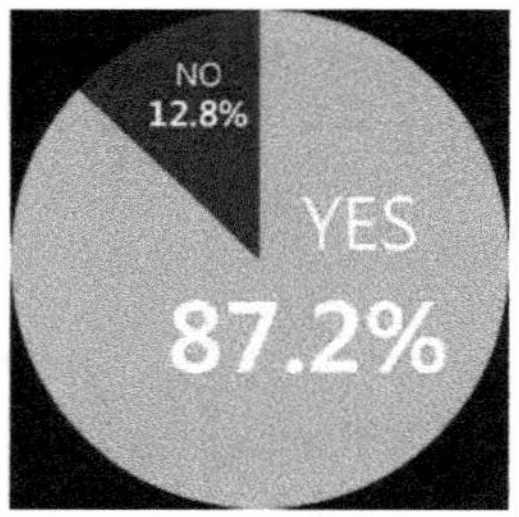

Figure 1. Do you use your smartphone before bedtime?

Rank	Reason
1	Feel Bored
2	habitually
3	SNS
4	Using Entertainment
5	Not Sleepy
6	Not Ready to Sleep
7	No Reason
8	Etc

Table 1. Why use a smartphone?

usage. Students started the term with generally healthy levels of activity and sociability. However, the use of smartphones has reduced sociability and activity [3]. We focus on the fact that using smartphones just before sleep causes harmful effects on the users' sound sleeps. Continuous exposure to blue light emitted from smartphones or tablets may not only lead to eyestrain but also cause damages to the vision of user Also, looking at smartphones late at night will restrain the secretion of sleep-inducing hormones (e.g., melatonin) and cause sleep disturbances [1]. This will result in additional problems such as deterioration of learning abilities and growth of adolescents. Therefore, this study aims to induce digital detox to users by developing smart lamps applied with gamification.

Before designing the research, we conducted a survey of teenagers (N=78, age mean=16.9, SD=1.1). Of the respondents, 87.2% answered they use smartphones the most before sleep (See Figure 1). We were able to confirm through the survey that most of the adolescent users have a habit of using smartphones before sleep. Also, they chose top reasons for demonstrating this kind of behavior as 'feel bored,' 'habitually,' and 'not sleepy,' which indicate that using smartphones before sleep happens because of no particular reason (See Table 1).

We accordingly suggest Smart Lamps that will help adolescent users voluntarily correct their smartphone using behaviors before sleep. Smart Lamp is a device to provide feedbacks, informing the users through the color changes of lights suiting the environment. Existing applications that restrict smartphone usages all exert coercion in common. We aim for voluntary behavioral corrections through positive reinforcements including compensation. If a child does refrain from using smartphones, they will award some points. Also, if the behavior arrives at a certain level, compensation that was agreed by the parents and the child beforehand will be provided. The form of compensation may vary from gifts to donations. Through the powerful motivation of positive compensations, children will voluntarily engage in behavioral correction.

Related Work

Gamification

We used gamification element to change user behaviors which see the smart device display in bed before sleep. Hamari's study creates a framework for examining the effects of gamification by drawing from the definitions of gamification and the discussion on motivational affordances [4]. Yeong Rae Joi presented wearlove, a wrist-worn device and mobile application for enhancing effective communication between users by adding gamification elements as mentioned above to the app [5].

Digital Detox

Mehmet EMEK presented many cases of digital detox service try to help the addicted Smartphone users to reduce the time spent with Smartphone interactions. An application called "Quiet" blocks notifications and changes your status on things like Skype to "busy" [2]. However, unlike most of the services like this, we focus on corrective action through compensation.

Exchange theory

Francisco's study gives us insight which efficient technology can change the attitudes or behaviors of users, through social influence, without coercion [7]. Jung min Kim observed the relational satisfaction

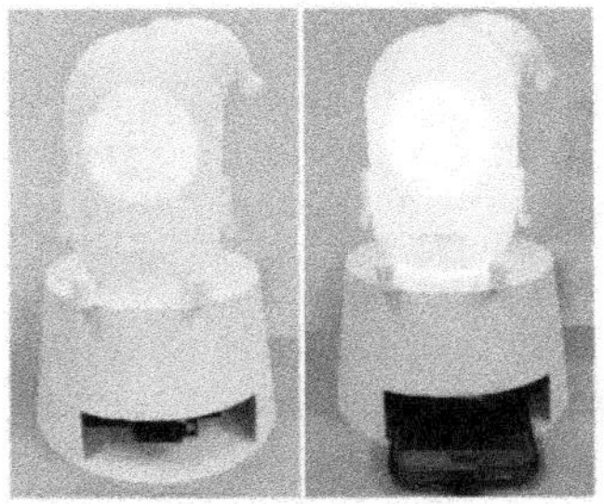

Figure 2. Hardware Prototype

Figure 3. User Scenario Test

according to exchanged resources. Kim focused on the six resources (service, information, economy, product, recognition, affection) that a mother and her child exchange, from the perspective of exchange and resource theory. The study shows that the resource that children are offered the most from their mothers is a product (economy). Accordingly, we judge that economic reward can be useful motivational elements [6].

System Overview

Smart Lamp, via its built-in IR sensor, senses the user's movement when he or she lies in bed. If the user is considered to be on the bed for a period of time, the Lamp regards it as a sleeping behavior and automatically starts measuring the time. If the user does not place the smartphone, inside the case at the bottom part of the Lamp for more than 3 minutes, it will provide feedbacks in red light. As we close our eyes, it takes 3-15 minutes to enter a light sleep [8]. So, to fall asleep as quickly, we set 3 minutes. On the other hand, if the user does place the smartphone inside the case, the RFID sensor of the Smart Lamp will recognize the smartphone and the sleep light will be off after 3 minutes.

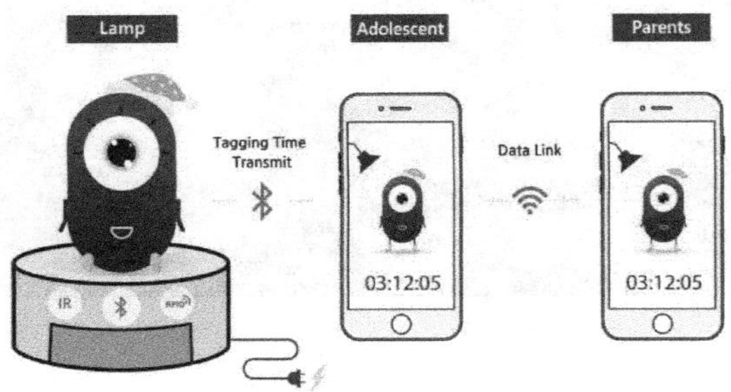

Figure 4. System Architecture

Feedback Smart Lamp

According to whether or not the smartphone is tagged to the Smart Lamp, the color of the light will automatically change. Firstly, if your turn on the Smart Lamp, a color of light that creates a supportive atmosphere (A) will be on. Secondly, if the smartphone is not tagged after turning on the Smart Lamp, a red light (B) will be on after 3 minutes as a sign of warning. Thirdly, to indicate that the smartphone has been tagged, a green light (C) will be on for about 3 seconds. Lastly, a cozy color light such as the sleep light (D) will be on to help the user sleeps well, which will be automatically turned off after 3 minutes. By changing the color of the character created in the form of the human eye, we enable the users to be aware of their eye health.

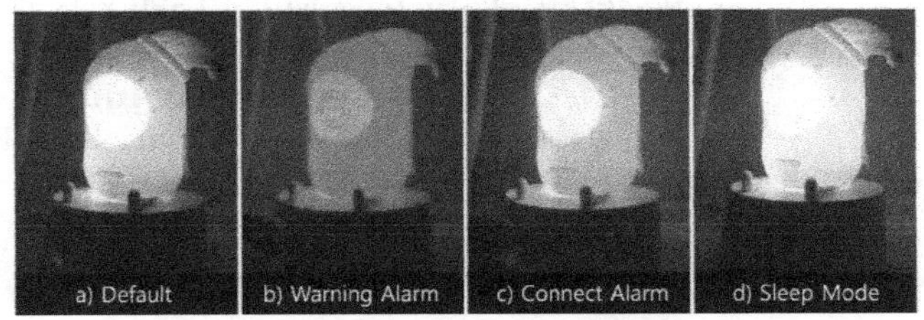

Figure 5. Color change of the lighting according to the changing situations.

Mobile Application Design

The D-TOX character and time will vary according to whether the smartphone is tagged or not.

Affordance
Points
Leaderboards
Achievements/Badges
*Levels
Story/Theme
*Clear goals
Feedback
*Rewards
Progress
Challenge

Table 2. Gamification Elements (* Applied to the D-TOX)

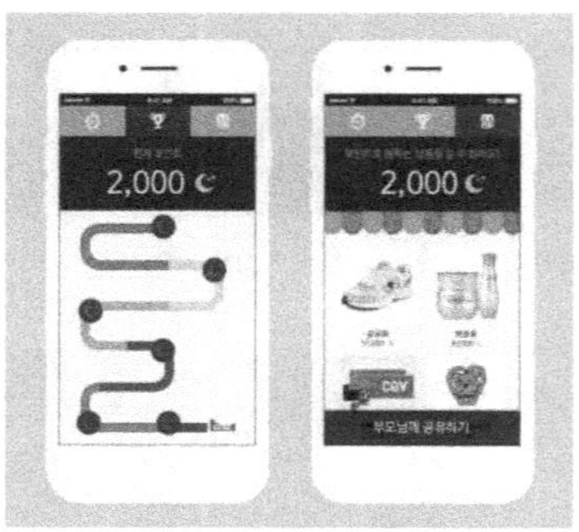

Figure 9. Achieving Levels Display (Left), Get a Reward Display (Right).

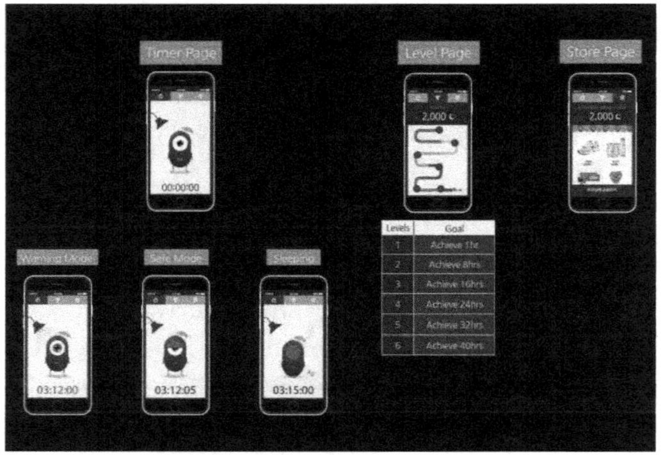

Figure 6. Mobile Application Structure

Safe Mode

If the smartphone is tagged, a healthy eye will blink and show the labeled time (See Figure 7).

Figure 7. Safe Mode Mobile Application

Warning Mode

If the smartphone is not tagged, the character with a red eye will show the amount of time the user used the smartphone before sleep (See Figure 8).

Figure 8. Warning Mode Mobile Application

Gamification Elements

Clear Goals

D-TOX has the following 'Goals' receiving rewards through points: points are saved by measuring the amount of time which smartphone has been on the lamp and the collected points can make user accomplish the gift user chose.

Rewards

The most effective compelling to the user among the gamification elements is "Rewards". With D-TOX, the user can get rewards such as allowances, products, and donations (See Figure 9) via the promising platform with their parents. The users will not use smartphones in the hope getting the rewards, and the parents can expect positive effects user's habit would be changed. The 'promise platform' refers to the parents and the children agreeing on the compensations for each amount of time for not using smartphones, which is applied to the application.

Levels

By assigning tasks per level, we improve the concentration about goal achievement. The each level

Levels	Goal
1	Achieve 1hr
2	Achieve 8hrs
3	Achieve 16hrs
4	Achieve 24hrs
5	Achieve 32hrs
6	Achieve 40hrs If you reach Level 6, you will be provided with 6 times the points to reinforce the motivation.

Table 3. The goal for each level

	e	Sex
(N=5)	;/15 /16/15	Boy/Girl/Girl /Girl/Girl
(N=5)	;/15 /15/16	Boy/Boy/Girl /Girl/Girl

Table 4. pre-study group information

	e	Sex
(N=5)	0/7 /10/10	Girl/Boy/Girl /Boy/Boy
(N=5)	)/10 /11/11	Boy/Girl/Girl /Girl/Girl
(N=5)	l/14 /17/12	Girl/Girl/Girl /Girl/Boy

Table 5. post-study group information

is set on the base of the accumulated time. 10 points are provided per hour. While Level 1 is for service experience, other levels are designed by reflecting the average of important daily sleep – i.e., 8 hours (See Table 3). **By applying "Levels"** element, we motivate D-TOX user (See Figure 9).

Pre-study

Can the reward make adolescents stop using a smartphone? We conducted the first pilot study to confirm the above hypothesis (N=10, age mean=15.6). User tests with D-TOX were preceded for 10 minutes.

Procedure

To confirm that the reward element has an effect on the corrective action, we split into two groups, which is G1 (N=5) ·G2 (N=5). 1) We gave a "Find the hidden picture" game them to evoke desire which they cannot easily give up. By doing so, we made a similar mental state with the mentality of bedtime which they want to use smartphone despite already in bed. 2) G1 · G2 had a same notice that if the red light of the D-TOX lamp is on, stop using the smartphone and put that into the space of the lamp. 3) After this notice, we give information only to G1, which they would receive a reward by carrying out this process. G2 didn't have any information about the compensation.

Results

A result of the experiment shows that the 3 of 10 participants used a smartphone again. Also, the 2 of these three people is in the G2 which didn't have reward information. The 7 of 10 didn't use their smartphone because they expect to get a reward.

Post-study

After confirming that the reward effect in the pre-study, we conducted a post-study to verify the effectiveness of our system (D-TOX). We conducted a pilot study for children (N = 15, age mean = 11.3).

Procedure

We divided into three groups, which is G1 (N=5) · G2 (N=5) · G3 (N=5). The groups were divided into three kinds of groups such as the first group that no information is provided, the second group that rewards only presented and then the third group that both rewards and D-TOX were represented and test subject groups were randomly assigned. As with the first study, we gave a "Find the hidden picture" game them to evoke desire which they cannot easily give up. All groups had to stop using their smartphones after 10 minutes, and G1·G2 had to check the time by themselves and, only G3 had to check the time by using the D-TOX device.

Results

The test has shown that four of the fifteen people were not keeping the time to use a smartphone. All four individuals were an experimental group of G1·G2, and G3 group has stopped using smartphones within a specified period. As a result of an interview with the test subject, they replied that "I didn't keep time since I couldn't confirm the designated hour well." (G1)

Discussion

Although we didn't user test about not only the interaction between parents and children, also bedtime study, we were able to know that the reward which is a gamification element have a significant effect in corrective behavior of adolescents. Also, through the

Figure 10. Pilot Study.

follow-up experiments.it was able to see that D-TOX influence the behavior of children with interaction by utilizing light. In a future study, we will test how long it takes for adolescents behaviors to change with D-TOX and how long the changes are sustained with or without parents intervention.

Conclusion

By applying gamification elements of clear goals, rewards and levels to adolescent users, we do not coerce them to stop using smartphones but will induce them to voluntarily reduce smartphone usages. To provide rewards, we measure the amount of time the smartphone was tagged to the Smart Lamp by using the NFC function of smartphones and save following points via the application, which can be viewed at any time. The saved points can be used to receive compensations agreed through the 'promising platform' between the parents and the children beforehand. Also, to provide feedbacks to the adolescent users, we have produced a character lamp in the shape of the human eye by using a 3D printer and the color of the character light will automatically change according to the situation so that the users can perceive the situation. Accordingly, we will conduct user test runs of D-TOX(Tangible device named "D-TOX" for providing real-time motivational cue), which we developed, to adolescent users while their parents participate as well, to analyze how much it is effective in mediating adolescent behaviors.

Acknowledgements

This research was supported by the Ministry of Trade, Industry and Energy (MOTIE), Korea, through the Education Support program for Creative and Industrial Convergence (Grant Number S-2016-0117-000).

References

1. C. Cajochen, C. Jud, M. Münch, S. Kobialka, A. Wirz-Justice, and U. Albrecht. 2006. Evening exposure to blue light stimulates the expression of the clock gene PER2 in humans. European Journal of Neuroscience, 23(4), 1082-1086.
2. M. Emek. 2014. Digital detox for the holidays: are we addicted? http://hdl.handle.net/11376/1059
3. Harari, G. M., Gosling, S. D., Wang, R., Chen, F., Chen, Z., & Campbell, A. T. (2017). Patterns of behavior change in students over an academic term: A preliminary study of activity and sociability behaviors using smartphone sensing methods. *Computers in Human Behavior*, *67*, 129-138.
4. J. Hamari, J. Koivisto, and H. Sarsa. 2014, January. Does gamification work?--a literature review of empirical studies on gamification. In 2014 47th Hawaii International Conference on System Sciences (pp. 3025-3034). IEEE.
5. Y. R Joi, B. T. Jeong, J. H. Kim, K. H. Park, T. Lee, and J. D. Cho. 2015, October. WearLove: Affective Communication via Wearable Device with Gamification. In Proceedings of the 2015 Annual Symposium on Computer-Human Interaction in Play (pp. 559-564). ACM.
6. Jungmin KIM and Hyunju KIM. 2016. Value congruency of exchanged resources on the Relational Satisfaction between adolescent and their mothers. Family and Culture, 28, 207-232.
7. F. Lepe Salazar, T. Yamabe, T. Alexandrova, Y. Liu, and T. Nakajima. 2012, May. Family interaction for responsible natural resource consumption. In CHI'12 Extended Abstracts on Human Factors in Computing Systems (pp. 2105-2110). ACM.
8. P. Wozniak. 2000. Good sleep, good learning, good life. Retrieved April, 13, 2003. https://www.supermemo.com/en/articles/sleep#NREM.

Growing Designs with biomakerlab in High School Classrooms

Yasmin Kafai
Graduate School of Education
University of Pennsylvania
Philadelphia, PA 19104 USA
kafai@upenn.edu

Orkan Telhan
School of Design
University of Pennsylvania
Philadelphia, PA 19104 USA
otelhan@design.upenn.edu

Karen Hogan
Department of Biology
University of Pennsylvania
Philadelphia, PA 19104 USA
hogank@sas.upenn.edu

Debora Lui
Emma Anderson
Justice T. Walker
Graduate School of Education
University of Pennsylvania
Philadelphia, PA 19104 USA
deblui@upenn.edu
emmaa@gse.upenn.edu
justicew@gse.upenn.edu

Sheri Hanna
String Theory School
Philadelphia, PA 19102 USA
shanna@stringtheoryschools.org

IDC '17, June 27-30, 2017, Stanford, CA, USA © 2017 Copyright is held by the owner/author(s). ACM ISBN 978-1-4503-4921-5/17/06.
http://dx.doi.org/10.1145/3078072.3084316

Abstract
We report on the development and implementation of biomakerlab, a wetlab starter kit for synthetic biology activities in K-12. In synthetic biology, participants make their own DNA—gene by gene—and then grow their designs into real applications by inserting them into microorganisms to develop different traits and characteristics provided by the genes. High school students worked with biomakerlab to 'grow' logo designs using microorganisms they manipulated to produce differently colored pigments. Our analysis focuses on student engagement with production activities and design challenges in biomaking. In the discussion, we address differences and overlaps between traditional maker activities and biomaker activities for education.

Author Keywords
Biology design, fabrication device, high school.

ACM Classification Keywords
H.5.m: Information interfaces and presentation (e.g., HCI); Miscellaneous.

Introduction
Most current efforts to broaden access to K–12 maker practices have focused on developing fabrication activities and tools such as 3D printers, laser cutters, and other digital and traditional tools [13, 14]. Far

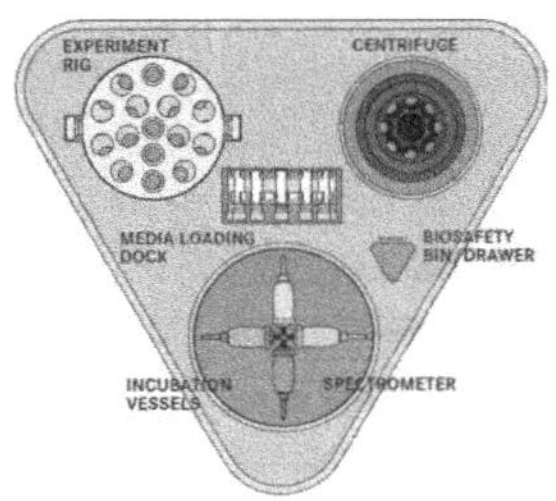

Figure 1: Design of biomakerlab

Figure 2: Prototype of biomakerlab

Figure 3: Two Iterations of a Student-Designed Logo for a Company Called "Blue Heart"

fewer efforts have focused on developing wet labs for equally important synthetic biology activities, where makers can manipulate organisms for creative applications. In synthetic biology, participants can engineer DNA—gene by gene—and then grow their designs into real applications by inserting them into microorganisms to develop different traits and characteristics. In this paper, we report on the design and recent implementation of a wetlab fabrication tool to promote bio design activities [20] in a high school classroom. Here, students worked on creating original logo designs that used pigment made from genetically transformed bacteria. Our analyses and discussion focused on students' engagement and experiences with this new type of maker activity.

Background

Paralleling the maker do-it-yourself (DIY) movement, the last decade has seen a steady growth in maker bioengineering, also called synthetic biology, garage biology, or bioDIY [7]. So far, these activities have been accessible and affordable only to university students and professionals at research universities [4, 17, 18], in undergraduate student competitions like IGEM [10] or at workshops at community biolabs [5].

Most efforts in K-12 education have concentrated on capturing students' understanding of and attitudes toward biotechnology [e.g., 2], such as their willingness to manipulate animal or human life. More recent work has started to develop educational activities appropriate for K-12 students. These include efforts to engage the public with synthetic biology issues in science centers [11], and designing interfaces for museum exhibits [16]. Curriculum design efforts with BioBuilder have adapted undergraduate activities for high school classrooms [8] while others have focused on developing analysis tool kits such as Bento Lab [1] and Amino Labs [9].

In promoting synthetic biology as a K-12 maker activity, we needed to address not only the design of a wetlab fabrication tool but also accompanying classroom activities and implementation. The facilities of university or professional contexts are appropriate for addressing wetlab setup and safety concerns. However many high schools, especially those serving underrepresented students, do not have such capacities. Our first goal was thus to adapt a professional fabrication tool called Biorealize [19] for use in high school classrooms by building what we call biomakerlab, a device that functions as an automated and self-contained wetlab.

The second goal was the development of curriculum activities to situate the use of biomakerlab. Here we drew on lab procedures developed by Kuldell and colleagues [8] in which specially engineered DNA are used to transform bacteria for production of differently colored pigments. We contextualized this activity, following a constructionist pedagogy [12], by having students create a real world design application for these synthetically created pigments. Unlike previous efforts that involve providing analysis tools to students (Amino or Bento) or those which primarily focus on lab procedures for building synthetic biology systems [8], our approach centers on having students learn about synthetic biology through a design application. This mirrors previous successful tactics in computer science education that situate the learning of computational concepts and practices in the context of designing real world software applications such as games [6].

Figure 4: Lab Materials

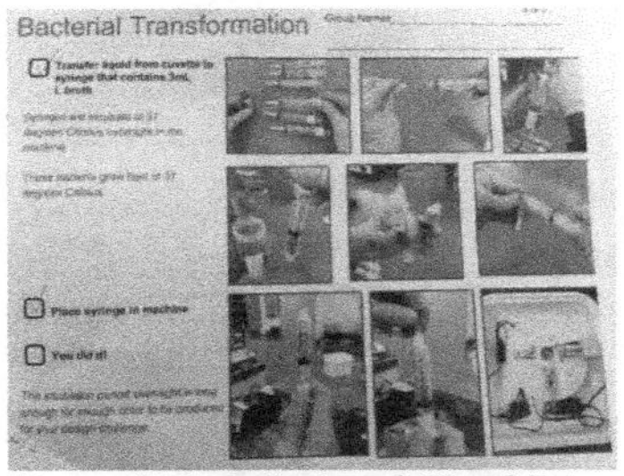

Figure 5: Lab Protocol Checklist

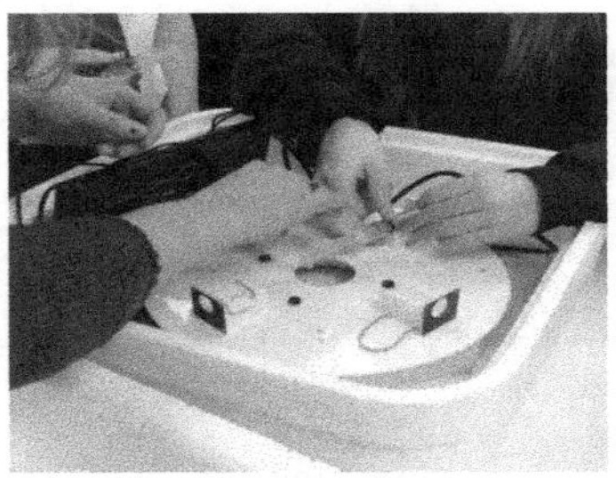

Figure 6: Students Placing Bacteria Cultures into the biomakerlab Machine

Participants, Tools and Activities

In January 2017, we conducted our synthetic biology design activities with two STEM elective classes for high school juniors (27 students) and seniors (22 students) at a charter school in a northeastern metropolitan city. Student demographics mirrored the school with 44% African American, 35% Caucasian, 13% Hispanic, 3% Asian, and 3% Multiracial students. The participating teacher, a trained biologist, is also the STEM coordinator of the school. The classroom teacher arranged groups of 2-4 students each.

The fabrication tool, called biomakerlab (Figure 1), contains a transformation module that includes a rotating incubator, a spectrophotometer, capsules that allow for cell distribution, and a media input/output outlet to supply media, nutrients, and other substances. For our study, we provided students with a prototype that included all the features except for the media input/output outlet (Figure 2).

Together with the classroom teacher, we developed a curriculum unit focused on sustainable manufacturing and design, which took place over four 90-minute class periods. Each group created a logo using biologically-produced pigment for a student-proposed company focused on sustainable design. Groups were assigned a particular color (based on the pigments produced) and industry (e.g., fashion, athletics, health) and asked to decide upon a sustainably manufactured product based on these specifications (e.g., sneakers made from recycled materials). Teams were then asked to come up with an accompanying company name and logo (see Figure 3).

For the design of the logo, groups engaged in the process of transforming existing bacteria (E.coli) with pre-designed plasmids (circular DNA for bacteria) to create different colored pigments (green, black, purple, or blue). This procedure involved use of the biomakerlab to incubate their transformed bacteria (Figures 4, 5, and 6). After producing the pigments, groups developed three physical versions of their logo. Two were 2D forms involving 'painting' with the transformed bacteria, one directly on nutrient agar in a petri dish, and another on filter paper placed on top of the agar (Figures 7 and 8). The third was a 3D logo that used sodium alginate, a compound that is regularly used in cooking (specifically 'molecular gastronomy'). Here, the alginate is used to encapsulate the transformed bacteria into raised shapes that were formed into the logos through the use of hot glue gun outlines (Figures 9 and 10).

In addition to photo documentation of the class and group work, we wrote field notes for each day. We also conducted focus groups with four randomly selected teams asking about their experience with the design challenge and lab procedures. We collected student worksheets focused on their company and logo design.

Findings

Here, we report on how students experienced agency in biomaking activities, their challenges realizing the physical logo designs, and the integration of wetlab making into a science classroom.

Student Agency in Bio Making – One of the key challenges of the project was to shift students' perception of learning about biology from a traditional science inquiry to a design or maker activity. Many

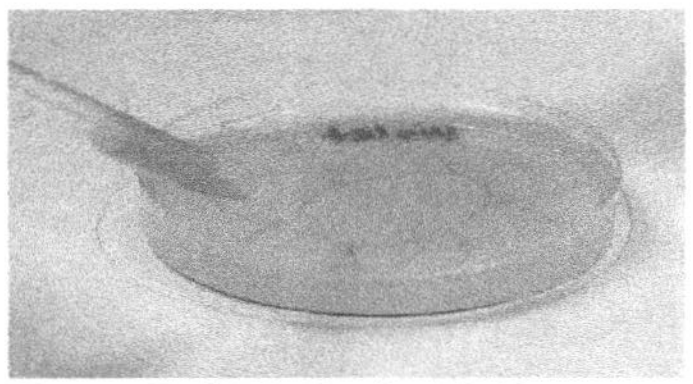

Figure 7: 'Painting' with Bacteria

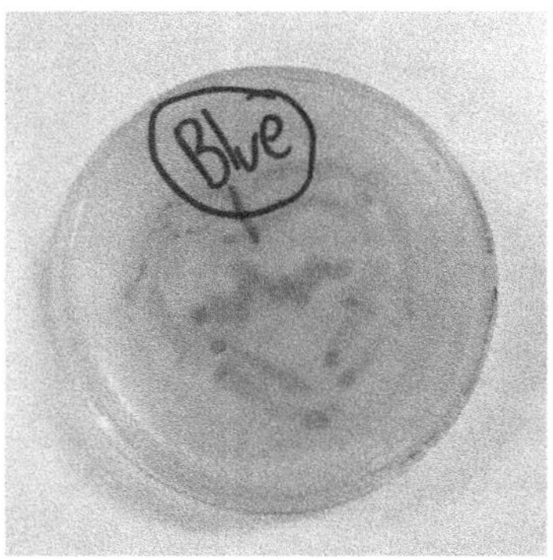

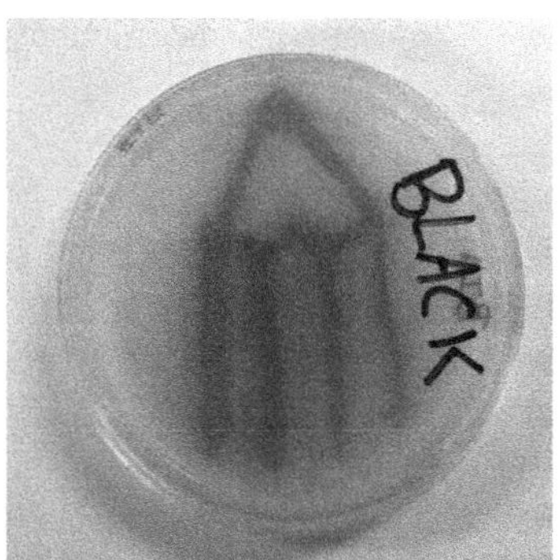

Figure 8: 2D Logos Painted Using Bacterial Pigment

students reflected on how having a constrained but open project allowed them to express their own ideas and creativity. Kristine[1] stated: "I feel like we did what we wanted to do. I mean, we had guidelines, but it was our ideas that went into the project." Dino added: "I liked how we had freedom for whatever we wanted to come up with for our logo and our name, and the way we wanted to draw—it was pretty cool." This was further aided by the fact that some students felt personal connections to their assigned contexts, as James described: "We got sports and athletics, [and since] me and [my teammate] were involved in sports and athletics... we have more a connection to it." Thus, because they were able to bring in their own voice into the process, these students started to perceive biology as a context for personal making and creation.

Student Challenges with Bio Making – In designing their logos, there were three main areas of difficulty that students faced. First, students spoke about their challenges with the actual construction tools. Cyra described using the hot glue gun in her design: "My arms started to hurt after... we had to practice on top of the petri dish... I kept messing up." James further described how this limited his logo design: "the glue kept like spreading out... so it was a bit harder to keep it detailed to like the same level [as] the logo that was drawn." From this perspective, dealing with the maker tools limited how well students thought they could express themselves through this activity.

The second challenge students described was the difficulty of dealing with the bacterial pigment. As Dino explained: "Tracing over the bacteria [on the petri dish] ... was kind of difficult, because it didn't really feel like I was doing anything [while] applying it." Unlike dealing with 'traditional' mechanical or electrical maker activities then, students described the lack of tangible feedback when dealing with these microorganisms and their products. Not only were these materials initially invisible to the human eye, but also required days to grow and yield a tangible output (the pigments).

A third obstacle students faced was not having time to iterate on their designs within the confines of the unit. In describing the outcome of her logo, Cyra stated: "My plate didn't turn out the way I expected it to. It's not green, I can't really see the design, and... it's disappointing... But I'm interested in finding out what I did wrong and why what happened happened and how I can fix it." Because of the time it took to grow the bacteria and see the outcome, some students missed the opportunity to engage further with their design.

Integrating Bio Making into STEM – Creating a link between biology, making, and design allowed students to broaden their understanding of these three disciplines. As Laila noted, "We had to learn how to incorporate engineering and design in biology...Instead of strictly learning about one thing, you get to learn how to incorporate different other aspects that make it greater, better." As the students described, this interest in combining fields was helped by contextualizing it in issues of sustainability. Cyra stated: "We started [the unit by learning] where dyes come from and the chemical waste that comes from dyes... now I know that... it's affecting the world as a whole and that's not good." Understanding this further motivated Cyra to think about potential biological solutions: "It personally makes more passionate about using bacteria to create

[1] All these names are pseudonyms to preserve confidentiality.

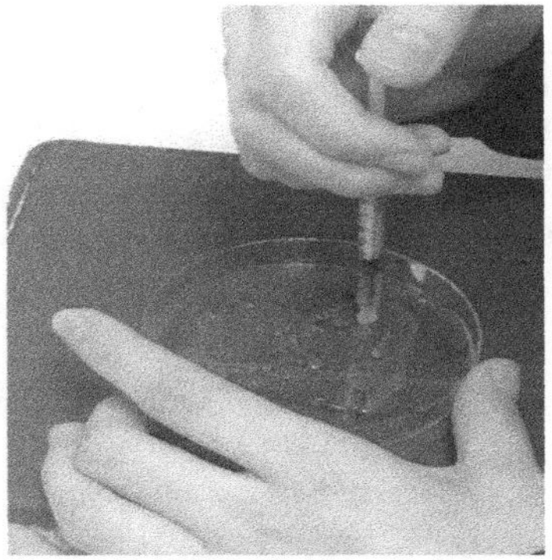

Figure 9. Using Sodium Alginate for Bacteria Encapsulation

Figure 10. Creating a Glue Gun Outline for Logo

dye rather than chemicals... We've always perceived bacteria as something negative [but] ... for us to use it in a way that would benefit us is interesting." Thus, by contextualizing the design within an existing world problem and providing tools to solve this issue using synthetic biology, students were more interested in learning about the possibilities of biomaking and design.

Discussion

While much attention has focused on bringing various maker activities into K-12 classrooms [13, 14], few of these efforts have included biology activities. In making or designing with biology, students can use cells as fabrication units to grow or "make" desired colors, smell or materials for their applications. Our pilot implementation with the biomakerlab illustrated some of the opportunities and challenges in biomaking with high school students. In the following sections, we situate biomaking in the larger landscape of making.

On the surface biomaking is very unlike 'traditional' making activities that involve electrical, digital, or mechanical systems. Whereas the latter often involves interactions with everyday tools or materials (e.g., batteries, lights), biomaking is a less recognizable practice. It involves materials and tools that are present in students' regular science classes, but in service of new fabrication process that are simultaneously abstract (since they are less visible) and unfamiliar as compared with traditional science labs. Additionally, students have to shift in their approach from science *as inquiry*, in which they observe and study the natural environment, to science *as design* where they use their knowledge of cells to produce new and desired outcomes. This approach to science as design is an epistemological shift that is unfamiliar in concept and in practice to most students in K-12.

However, what biomaking has in common with traditional making is the idea of turning students into producers rather than consumers of applications. These parallels have also been observed in other maker-like activities such as writing and coding that engage students in producing text or software [15]. Our approach to synthetic biology as biomaking is not only a step into the future where we engage students with making or 'growing' their designs in the lab but also a link to the past in which students were first invited to making or 'coding' their designs on computer screen. More than three decades ago, Papert [12] provided tools such as the turtle as an "object-to-think-with" and pedagogy to turn children into producers of code. In biomaking we are now facing the challenges to create connections for these new design activities. Our pilot implementation with biomakerlab was a first step into mapping out this new territory.

Acknowledgements

This work was supported by a grant (#1623018) from the National Science Foundation to Yasmin Kafai and Orkan Telhan. Any opinions, findings, and conclusions or recommendations expressed in this paper are those of the authors and do not necessarily reflect the views of the National Science Foundation or the University of Pennsylvania. The authors wish to thank Aurora MacRae-Crerar and Keith Lewy for their help with preparing and supporting classroom work.

References

1. Philipp Boeing and Bethan Wolfenden. 2016. Bento Labs. (2016). Retrieved April 1, 2017 from https://www.bento.bio/

2. Vaille Dawson. 2007. An exploration of high school (12–17 year old) students' understandings of, and attitudes towards biotechnology processes. *Research in Science Education,* 37 (March, 2007), 59-73. http://dx.doi.org/10.1007/s11165-006-9016-7
3. Jessica S Dymond, Lisa Z Scheifele, Sarah Richardson, Pablo Lee, Srinivasan Chandrasegaran, Joel S Bader, Jef D Boeke. 2009. Teaching Synthetic Biology, Bioinformatics and Engineering to Undergraduates: The Interdisciplinary Build-a-Genome Course. *Genetics 181*, 1 (January 2009), 13–21. http://dx.doi.org/10.1534/genetics.108.096784
4. Finnish Bio Arts Society at Aalto University. 2015. Making Life (2015). Making Life Workshop Series. Retrieved March 1, 2017 from http://bioartsociety.fi/making_life/
5. Daniel Grushkin. 2017. Genspace. (2017). Retrieved April 1, 2017 from http://genspace.org/
6. Yasmin B. Kafai and Quinn Burke. 2014. *Connected Code: Why Children Need to Learn Programming*. MIT Press, Cambridge, MA.
7. Denisa Kera. 2012. Hackerspaces and DIYbio in Asia: Connecting Science and Community with Open Data, Kits and Protocols. *Journal of Peer Production, 2* (July 2012). Retrieved from: http://peerproduction.net/issues/issue-2/peer-reviewed-papers/diybio-in-asia/
8. Natalie Kuldell, Rachel Bernstein, Karen Ingram and Kathryn M. Hart. 2015. *Biobuilder: Synthetic Biology in the Lab*. O'Reilly Media, Inc., San Francisco, CA.
9. Julie Legault and Justice Pahara. 2016. Amino Labs. (2016). Retrieved April 1, 2017 from http://www.amino.bio
10. Rudolph Mitchell, Yehudit J. Dori, Natalie H. Kuldell. 2011. Experiential engineering through iGEM -- An undergraduate summer competition in synthetic biology. *Journal of Science Educational Technology* 20, 2 (April 2011), 1-5. http://dx.doi.org/10.1007/s10956-010-9242-7
11. Museum of Science, Boston. 2015. Building with Biology. (2015). Retrieved April 1, 2017 from http://www.mos.org/buildingwithbiology/index.html
12. Seymour Papert. 1980. *Mindstorms*. Basic Books, New York, NY.
13. Kylie A. Peppler, Erica Halverson, and Yasmin B. Kafai, (Eds.). 2016a. *Makeology: Makerspaces as Learning Environments (Volume 1).* Routledge, New York, NY.
14. Kylie A. Peppler, Erica Halverson, and Yasmin B. Kafai, (Eds.). 2016b. *Makeology: Makers as Learners (Volume 2).* Routledge, New York, NY.
15. Mitchel Resnick, Elyse Eidman-Adaahl, and Dale Dougherty. 2016. Making-Writing-Coding. In K. A. Peppler, E. Halverson, and Y. B. Kafai, (Eds.). 2016b. *Makeology: Makers as Learners (Volume 2).* Routledge, New York, NY, pp. 229-240.
16. Orit Shaer, Consuelo Valdes, Sirui Liu, Kara Lu, Kimberly Chang, Wendy Xu, Traci L. Haddock, Swapnil Bhatia, Douglas Densmore and Robert Kincaid. 2013. Designing reality-based interfaces for experiential bio-design. *Personal Ubiquitous Computing,* 18, 6 (November 2013), 1515–1532. https://doi.org/10.1007/s00779-013-0752-1
17. SymbioticA , The Arts Catalyst, UCL, Synthetic Aesthetics. 2011. Synthesis Exchange Laboratory organized by University College London. Retrieved April 1, 2017 from https://www.ucl.ac.uk/synbion/network/Synthesis
18. SymbioticA. 2016. The Centre of Excellence in Biological Arts, School of Anatomy, Physiology and Human Biology. Perth, AU: The University of Western Australia. Retrieved from April 1, 2017 from http://www.symbiotica.uwa.edu.au/
19. Orkan Telhan and Karen Hogan. 2015. Biorealize. (2015). Retrieved April 1, 2017 from http://www.biorealize.com/
20. Orkan Telhan. 2016. Design.bio: Biology at the design studio. *Biocoder#11,* (November 2016), 33-43.

Aiding the Transition from Novice to Traditional Programming Environments

Luke Moors
Robert Sheehan
University of Auckland
Auckland, New Zealand
lmoo228@aucklanduni.ac.nz
r.sheehan@auckland.ac.nz

IDC '17, June 27-30, 2017, Stanford, CA, USA

ACM ISBN 978-1-4503-4921-5/17/06.
http://dx.doi.org/10.1145/3078072.3084317

Abstract

Novice programming environments are increasingly popular as introductory tools for teaching programming. Many of these tools differ significantly from traditional programming environments and are successful in motivating novices and making it simple to start programming. However, it has been reported that students still struggle when transitioning to general-purpose languages and have difficulties learning certain concepts. In this paper, we briefly describe some of the problems novices have when learning to program and identify drawbacks to existing novice programming environments. We then present two different works in progress with features designed to keep some of the advantages of current novice programming environments but in such a way that students are led to deeper concepts. Such features include immediate feedback, loop construction, and automated identifier updating. This report references the feasibility of these approaches.

Author Keywords

Novice programming; programming environments; block-based programming.

ACM Classification Keywords

K.3.2 Computer and Information Science Education.

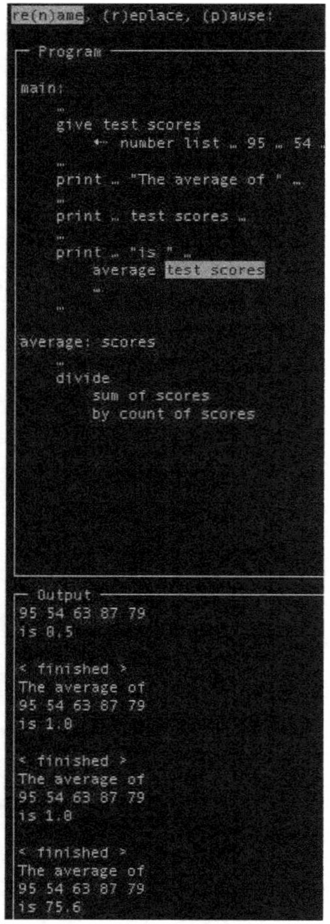

Figure 1 - Producing an average function in Simplicity1

Introduction

In this 50th year of the initial development of Logo [11] programming in schools is making a tremendous come back. In the 1980s when microcomputers were introduced into schools the computers were commonly used to teach programming, usually in Basic or Logo [14]. With the emergence of Computational Thinking [18] programming is back in school curricula and a large number of novice programming environments (NPEs) have been developed. The Scratch environment is just one example and has achieved hundreds of thousands of active monthly users since its release [13].

It is however widely acknowledged that programming is difficult to learn. Novice programmers frequently have difficulties in programming. Many of these problems arise from the semantics and syntax required in programming [2, 6].

Programming environments designed for children implement numerous features that make the introduction to programming more accessible, such as simplified syntax, the use of language closer to natural language, and a visually appealing interface [4]. These educational programming environments have a goal of simplifying the process of learning to program, making it both accessible and engaging.

While novice programmers describe such environments as a positive influence on their subsequent experience with general-purpose languages [8], other literature has identified possible problems when transitioning to more traditional programming environments (TPEs) [1]. After transitioning to languages like Java, students report a loss of confidence in programming ability and in some cases, believe that novice languages are not "real programming" [12]. Other researchers have identified habits that students acquire using novice programming environments which can be problematic when moving to a TPE [9, 17].

Novice Programming Environments (NPEs)

Many educational programming languages are designed with a common goal of making it easy to learn programming [4]. But there is a conflict between simplifying the learning process and preparing novices for TPEs, the majority of educational programming languages fall into one of two categories:

1. Making programming exciting and easy for novices
2. Providing a solid background in programming to ease the transition into TPEs

In addition, there are various styles of implementing NPEs, the two most common being text-based programming and block-based programming.

Text-based languages

Text-based programming was originally the preferred style of educating novices with the development of languages like BASIC [5], Logo [11] and Smalltalk [3]. Many of these early educational programming languages were dialects of high-level programming languages, with a simplified version of syntax and language.

Block-based Environments

In recent years, there has been a rise in the use of block-based environments as a means to learn programming. In such environments, instructions are placed into blocks which can be snapped together to form a syntactically correct program. This is typically done by using shaped blocks which can only be connected to other blocks in a syntactically correct way.

Features of Simplicity1

- Text-based
- Keyboard menu controlled
- Insertion point at the cursor
- Only valid menu options provided at each insertion location
- Live programming
- Default values for selections
- Simple to add new functions

Features of Simplicity2

- GUI based
- Mouse controlled
- Code can be inserted anywhere it preserves correct syntax
- Live programming
- Default values for selections
- Simple to add new functions
- Automatic identification of possible loops

Due to the block implementation, these environments remove or reduce the possibility of making syntax errors. This solves one of the biggest problems associated with learning to program, having to come to terms with the syntax requirements of the language. This style of programming also means that the words given to program constructs such as loops, or even assignment to variables can be made more like natural language, e.g. Scratch has the words "set (variable name) to (some value)" for an assignment statement.

Transitioning from an NPE to a TPE

Although the goal of lowering the barriers to programming has been achieved by NPEs, some studies have suggested a detrimental effect when transitioning to TPEs. From reviewing the literature on these environments, we identified two significant weaknesses: lost confidence - where users lose confidence in their programming ability, and incorrect ideas - where novices acquire incorrect beliefs about programming.

Several studies have reported students' loss of confidence after switching to text-based languages. Powers et al. [12] studied the transition to high-level programming languages where the first half of a course was taught with Alice and the second half with Java (and C++ the following year). Both strong and weak students were overwhelmed by the syntactical requirements and students quickly became discouraged when their programs would not compile. Most importantly, after using a high-level language, students lost confidence in their programming ability and concluded that Alice was not "real programming".

A study comparing the learning outcomes of students programming in Logo and Scratch supports this claim. Lewis [7] reported that students programming in Logo identified themselves as having higher confidence in their programming ability compared to programmers using Scratch.

We are implementing environments which we hope will help with this transition. We are keeping key ideas from existing NPEs at the same time as making our environments appear more text-like as well as providing Integrated Development Environment (IDE) type assistance for the refactoring of code.

Another problem we are trying to address is making it easier for novices to use higher level abstractions in their programming such as loops. Learning loops is an especially difficult concept for novices to understand.

Proposed Solution

Our two environments are called Simplicity1 and Simplicity2. Simplicity1 is text-based and keyboard menu driven, it is closest in style to the Structure Editors of the past [10]. Simplicity2 is implemented as a GUI environment with selection by clicking and dragging. Both environments only allow actions which preserve the syntactical correctness of the current program. Both environments aim to stay live in the sense of changes to the code producing immediate output; this is similar to the performance style of Live Coding and is discussed in more general terms by Tanimoto [15] as live programming.

Apart from preserving syntactical correctness both environments also keep the language of programming constructs closer to natural language as in existing NPEs. Furthermore both environments encourage users to expand their use of programming constructs via an approach we call concept guidance. At the moment this is done in two ways.

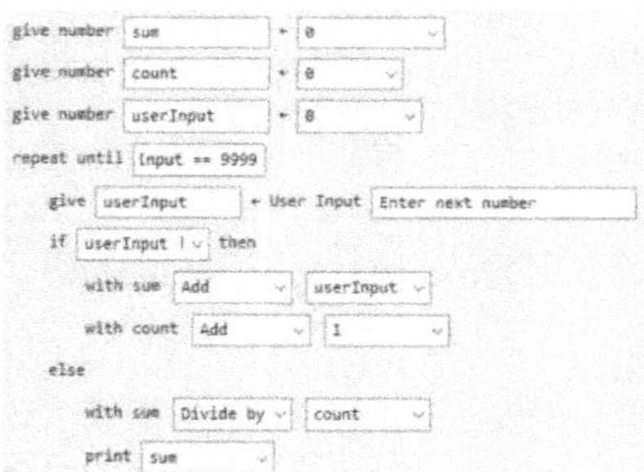

Figure 2 – The Rainfall problem in Simplicity2

We have made it as easy as possible to introduce functions into an existing program. This was introduced both because the use of functions is good style when writing code but also because it can encourage the transition from the bricolage [16] or "playing around" style of code construction to a more structured approach. This is most apparent in Simplicity1. For example if the user wants to print the average of a list of numbers. The user selects the print function and then inserts a call to a new function (which does not exist yet). Two things happen here: the function call is inserted and a default function body is created at the end of the program. The user gives the function a name and can either then or later specify the body and parameters to the function. Any changes are propagated throughout the existing program (see figure 1).

We have added loop assistance into Simplicity2. In this case if the user constructs a section of code which is immediately followed by an identical section of code the user is asked if he/she wishes to form a loop. If the answer is "yes" a definite loop is created from the shared sections of code. Similarly if a section of code following an existing loop has the same contents as the loop body the user is asked if that section should be included in the loop and adjustments made as required. The automatic detection of loops in Simplicity2 creates the opportunity for novices to understand where loops can be utilised and how they are implemented.

What have we discovered so far?

Even at this early stage in the development of these environments we have discovered some important restrictions as a result of this. These are from our implementation work and not yet from novice user studies.

To allow flexibility in the choice of statements to add to our programs while at the same time guaranteeing correct syntax we had to choose suitable default values for our control structures and function calls, e.g. when a definite loop control structure such as iterating a set number of times is entered into the program it is initialised to repeat twice. In all such cases it is a simple process to edit the default values. This not only maintains the correct syntax, because all additions are "complete" in a default way, it also means the program can still run, maintaining the ability to run the code as soon as the change is made.

Because of the requirement for inserting syntactically correct code we have to ask the user to choose types for values, variables and functions, e.g. if the user wishes to add two elements together they have to match in type. If users at some later time wish to modify variables or functions they are only allowed to choose from values of the correct type. This does not stop users from changing an addition with two numbers to two strings, but they have to do that by deleting one and inserting the other. We see this requirement as a major limitation of the approach and we are keen to see how this affects users of the environments. There may be a positive value in requiring users to consider the types of their objects.

Because of the requirement to keep the program live with changes in the program leading to changes in the output we have to be careful when implementing loops. There is a related problem with recursive calls. For definite loops e.g. for loops repeating a set number of times or iterating over a collection, there is no problem. When the user enters such a command the loop will run the specified number of times. For indefinite loops e.g. while statements, the inserted code defaults to not performing the loop. This gives the user time to set up the body of the loop, including the loop increment, before possibly producing an infinite loop. Otherwise with our live programming approach an infinite amount of processing may occur. We currently allow a pause command because there are a number of situations where it gets irritating to see the results of all updates. An alternative approach, which is not currently implemented, is to allow changes to the program to halt any current executions of the old code and start immediately with the new.

We have to supply default names for variables, functions and parameters. This saves the user the immediate cognitive load of determining what to call the item. When a user adds a function call to a new function, we have to give the function a name before the function call and the new function itself can be inserted into the code. The first thing the environments do is to ask the user for a name for the function, but they can just accept the generated name. Any text can be used for the function name, including spaces (except the name of an existing function/variable or a type value).

It must be easy to modify the names of variables and functions at any time. This requires automatic updating of variables/functions throughout the program. Similarly we must allow the signature of functions to change, e.g. modifying the number and types of parameters. If an extra parameter is added then all calling locations have a corresponding default parameter of the same type added to the call list.

Unfortunately it is not so easy to remove a parameter from a function definition. The reason is that the parameter may be used in the function. We are still implementing this detail, but the solution we are employing is to check to see if the parameter is used and only allowing it to be removed when all references to it have been removed. These references are highlighted so that the user can see the changes that are needed. Removing the corresponding parameter from the function calls is then done automatically.

We also have to deal with errors in a different way from TPEs. Because code entry in Simplicity1 is via a text-menu based system it is simple to control what can be inserted at any position of the code. The user places the insertion point at the desired location and only valid selections are offered. In Simplicity2 because the user can drag instructions and drop them into the existing program we have to give more feedback. Only code which will preserve the correctness of the program can be inserted or moved at each point. If the user attempts to drop code into a location where it would not make sense we provide a message describing why this is not allowed. This is partway between many NPEs and TPEs in the sense that a TPE would generate an error message either at editing time in an IDE or at compile time. The difference here is that Simplicity2 does not allow the incorrect action to be inserted into the code, and the user is informed as to why.

Conclusion

With our development prototypes we have shown it is possible to create programs using a system which enforces program correctness at each stage. This allows immediate feedback. We have discovered some of the pitfalls and restrictions such an approach entails, including the need for explicit type identification, careful choice of default values and default names, and providing feedback to users when they attempt to do something which is not allowed e.g. because it would create a syntax error.

References

1. J. Blanchard, C. Gardner-McCune, and L. Anthony. 2015. Bridging Educational Programming and Production Languages. *Paper for the "Every Child a Coder" workshop, ACM SIGCHI Conference on Interaction Design and Children (IDC 2015)*, Boston, MA.
2. S. Garner, P. Haden, and A. Robins. 2005. My program is correct but it doesn't run: a preliminary investigation of novice programmers' problems. *Proceedings of the 7th Australasian conference on Computing education*, 42, Australian Computer Society, Inc., 173–180.
3. A.C. Kay. 1996. *The early history of Smalltalk. History of programming languages—II*, ACM, 511–598.
4. C. Kelleher, and R. Pausch. 2005. Lowering the barriers to programming: A taxonomy of programming environments and languages for novice programmers. *ACM Computing Surveys (CSUR)* 37, 2, 83–137.
5. J.G. Kemeny, and T.E. Kurtz. 1980. *Basic programming*. John Wiley & Sons, Inc.
6. E. Lahtinen, K. Ala-Mutka, and H.M. Järvinen. 2005. A study of the difficulties of novice programmers. *ACM SIGCSE Bulletin*, 37, ACM, 14–18.
7. C.M. Lewis. 2010. How programming environment shapes perception, learning and goals: Logo vs. Scratch. *Proceedings of the 41st ACM technical symposium on Computer science education*, ACM, 346–350.
8. D. J. Malan, and H. H. Leitner. 2007. Scratch for budding computer scientists. *ACM SIGCSE Bulletin*, 39, ACM, 223–227.
9. O. Meerbaum-Salant, M. Armoni, and M. Ben-Ari. 2011. Habits of programming in Scratch. *Proceedings of the 16th annual joint conference on Innovation and technology in computer science education*, ACM, 168–172.
10. P. Miller, J. Pane, G. Meter, and S. Vorthmann. 1994. Evolution of Novice Programming Environments: The Structure Editors of Carnegie Mellon University, *Interactive Learning Environments*, 4, 2, 140–158.
11. S. Papert. 1980. *Mindstorms: Children, computers, and powerful ideas*. Basic Books, Inc.
12. K. Powers, S. Ecott, and L.M. Hirshfield. 2007. Through the looking glass: teaching CS0 with Alice. *ACM SIGCSE Bulletin*, 39, ACM, 213–217.
13. M. Resnick, J. Maloney, A. Monroy-Hernández, N. Rusk, E. Eastmond, K. Brennan, A. Millner, E. Rosenbaum, J.Silver, B. Silverman, and Y. Kafai. 2009. Scratch: programming for all. *Commun. ACM* 52, 11, 60-67.
14. C. Solomon. 1988. *Computer environments for children: A reflection on theories of learning and education*, MIT press.
15. S.L. Tanimoto. 2013. A perspective on the evolution of live programming. *Proceedings of the 1st International Workshop on Live Programming (LIVE '13)*. IEEE Press, 31-34.
16. S. Turkle, and S. Papert. 1990. Epistemological Pluralism: Styles and Voices within the Computer Culture". *Signs: Journal of Women in Culture and Society*, 16, 1, 128-157.
17. D. Weintrop, and U. Wilensky. 2015. To block or not to block, that is the question: students' perceptions of blocks-based programming. *Proceedings of the 14th International Conference on Interaction Design and Children*, ACM, 199–208.
18. J.M. Wing. 2006. Computational thinking. *Commun. ACM*, 49, 3, 33-35

The Programmable Battery: A Tool to Make Computational Making More Simple, Playful, and Meaningful

Hideki Mori
Tokyo Institute of Technology
Meguro, Tokyo 152-8550, JAPAN
mori@citl.titech.ac.jp

IDC '17, June 27-30, 2017, Stanford, CA, USA

ACM ISBN 978-1-4503-4921-5/17/06.
DOI: http://dx.doi.org/10.1145/3078072.3084318

Abstract

The Programmable Battery is a tiny computer that can control motors, lights, and any devices that use dry batteries. By pressing buttons on the Programmable Battery, the pattern of on and off for the devices is recorded and played back repeatedly. Since it has limited functions but can be programmed easily without a computer, anyone can make their own computational devices anytime and anywhere. In this paper, I introduce the concept of the Programmable Battery and its workshops for elementary school students.

Author Keywords

Making, Programming, Learning through making

ACM Classification Keywords

K.3.m., Computers and Education, Miscellaneous

Introduction

Programming education for children is becoming more popular around the globe. Many developed countries have begun integrating programming education into their school curricula. It is believed that the development of "Computational Thinking" (Wing 2006) is important for children to prepare them for the future. When we look at the history of programming

Figure 1. The first prototype of the Programmable Battery

Figure 2. The second prototype of the Programmable Battery

education for children, LOGO, first developed by Seymour Papert and his colleagues in the late 1960's, greatly influenced programming languages and environments for children for 50 years. While a variety of programming and computational making tools are available for children these days, it seems that the concepts of LOGO for children's learning, which is called "Constructionism," are getting difficult to see behind the current movement in computational thinking and programming education. Kafai and Resnick (1996, p.1) defined Constructionism as follows: "Constructionism suggests that learners are particularly likely to make new ideas when they are actively engaged in making some type of external artifact - be it a robot, a poem, a sand castle, or a computer program - which they can reflect upon and share with others. Constructionism involves two intertwined types of construction; the construction of knowledge in the context of building personally meaningful artifacts." In this regard, programming is one of the ways of making to learn, although programming helps children to understand computation and computational thinking.

What kinds of construction are children interested in these days? Obviously, the everyday objects in children's lives are changing. Taking toys as an example, children play with toys in which motors, sensors, lights, and speakers are embedded and controlled by microcontrollers. Video games are another example. Making something that children are familiar with must encourage children to make and learn by making something that is personally meaningful for them. It has been difficult to make these kinds of computational things, and children can only play with them; in other words, children are only able to consume them.

As I described, there is a variety of programming tools for children to create their own video games and programmable computers, with which they can build their own robots. These tools are getting easier for children to use than those of decades ago, but children still need a certain amount of time to learn how to use them before they make something. For most Japanese children, they lose interest in making things after they enter elementary school, and they begin to enjoy just playing with and consuming existing commercial toys and games.

In order for children to revive their interests in making and to learn through making, I present in this paper a tool that I developed to make computational tasks easy, called the "Programmable Battery," and workshops in which children make their own computational toys with it.

Programmable Battery

The Programmable Battery is a small, programmable device powered by dry batteries to control motors, LEDs, beepers, and other actuators connected to it. It is simple and easy to program. Just by pushing the button on it, any motor or LED connected to the programmable battery will switch on and off. At the same time, it records the on and off patterns of running motors and LEDs. For example, when children push the button for one second and release it for one second, the motors connected to the programmable battery turn on and off. This enables younger children to make their own projects that can move, light up, and make sounds as they program without a PC. They can also make their projects anywhere, with anybody, using any materials. The first prototype of the Programmable Battery is powered by two AAA batteries and outputs

Figure 3. LEGO® Car

Figure 4. Ringing Duck

Figure 5. Sound Car

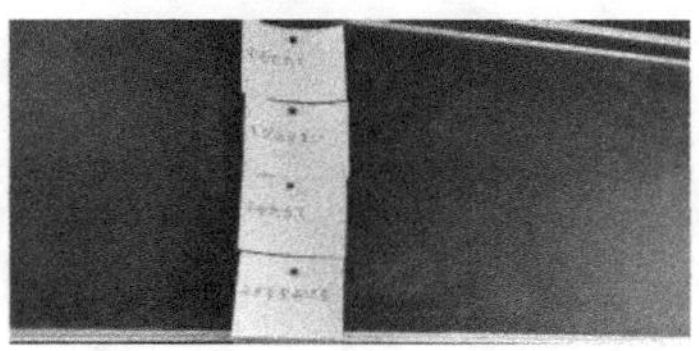

Figure 6. Human Computer Activity

3V to motors, etc. (Mori 2013). The second prototype I present in this paper can output up to 9V to control more powerful motors to make a variety of things in the workshops (See Figures 1 and 2).

Programmable Battery Workshops

In this section, I introduce the workshops that I designed for children to be held in museums, community centers, and elementary schools in Japan. Since the Japanese Ministry of Education plans to add programing education to the curricula of all elementary schools by 2020, the Programmable Battery workshop is designed to be an opportunity for children to make computational devices and also to introduce programing to students with no previous experience with computer programming.

Workshops at Museums and Community Centers

This workshop is designed for informal learning settings such as museums and community centers. A 90-minute workshop starts with a brief introduction to how to use the Programmable Battery, and then the children and their parents spend an hour making their own toys with the Programmable Battery, motors, LEGO® bricks, craft materials, musical instruments, and toys. The workshop ends with a show and tell of what the participants created, which allows them to share their ideas with other participants.

Figures 3, 4, and 5 display examples of projects that children aged of 4 to 11 created with their parents at a workshop held in a community center. Figure 3 shows a toy car built with LEGO® bricks, a motor, and the Programmable Battery. It moves forward for 5 seconds and then stops for 2 seconds before moving forward again. Figure 4 displays a musical duck toy with a bell that spins using the Programmable Battery and a motor to make ringing sounds. Figure 5 shows another example of cars that participants created in the workshop. It was first built as a car and then the child added egg shape maracas so that it makes rhythmical sounds when it moves forward and stops.

Workshops at Elementary Schools

The workshop for elementary schools is also designed as a 90-minute, two school-period workshop. This workshop is for 1st and 2nd graders who have no prior experience with programming. The workshop starts by asking the students about their knowledge of computers and then telling them that computers work with programs that people code.

After the introduction, the students imitate computers, moving as they are "programed to" with commands such as "clap your hands," "raise your right hand," "lower your right hand," "wait for a second," and "repeat." These commands are written in Japanese, and arranged in a sequence on the blackboard to show students as human computers (see Figure 6).

The next activity involves making simple computational things with the Programmable Battery, motors, and LEGO® bricks. Students tinker and explore by connecting materials and making things like fans, cars, and tops according to their interests for 20 minutes (see Figure 7).

The final activity is to program with Scratch. Students make their own project for 30 minutes after receiving an introduction to how to make and run programs in Scratch (see Figure 8).

Evaluation of the Programmable Battery

Ninety-one children from ages 4 to 11 made their own toys and devices with the Programmable Battery in five workshops in community centers and elementary schools in Japan. All children can program a pattern to turn the motor on and off with the Programmable Battery.

After the workshops, a questionnaire was completed by the children. Figure 9 shows the length of the pattern that the children programmed/recorded with the Programmable Battery. Of the children, 65% made 6- to 20-second patterns to turn motors on and off.

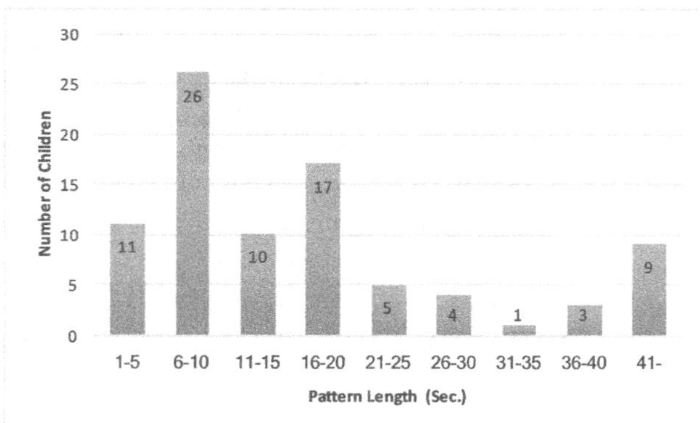

Figure 9. Length of pattern

In terms of the satisfaction with the products that they created, a 5-point scale (5: Very Satisfied to 1: No at all) was used in the questionnaire (N=91), and the result showed an average satisfaction level of 4.68 (SD 0.71). While the children were satisfied with making things with the Programmable Battery, the difficulty for them to use it (5: Very Easy to 1: Very Difficult) was average 3.73 (SD 1.37). This result shows that using the Programmable Battery is not so easy for everyone; however, further analysis is needed to clarify whether they felt making things with Programmable Battery was not easy or operation itself was difficult.
The following are comments written by children in the questionnaire.

- It was difficult for making but I was very happy that I could make a very interesting thing (つくるのはむずかしかったけど、とてもおもしろいものがつくれてうれしかったです).[Nine year-old workshop participant]

- I felt uneasy at the beginning as this was my first time using the computer toy, but it was very fun! （コンピュータのおもちゃを使うのははじめてだったのでさいしょはふあんだったけど、とてもおもしろかったです!）. [Nine year-old workshop participant]

- Although the bell did not ring at first, it began to ring after I thought and worked out a lot, so I was very happy. (すずかさいしょはならなかったけど、いっぱいくふうしたらなるようになったのでうれしかったです). [Eight year-old workshop participant]

Most of the participants in the workshops enjoyed making their own computational devices with the Programmable Battery. They did not need to spend their effort understanding how to use the tool but used trial and error to make their own personally meaningful things. In-depth analyzes of children's learning from

Figure 7. Program Controlled Fan

Figure 8. Programming with Scratch

making with the programmable battery is the next steps of this research.

Acknowledgements
I would like to thank all of the workshop participants. This project was supported by the Tokyo Tech Fund for Science Education.

References
1. Kafai, Y. and Resnick, M. 1996. Constructionism in Practice. Lawrence Erlbaum Associates, New Jersey
2. Mori, H. 2013. Programmable Battery - a computer-embedded MONODUKURI ("making things") device for anyone -, Fablearn 2013 Demo session
3. Wing, J. 2006. Computational Thinking. Communications of the ACM, vol. 49, no. 3, pp. 33–35.

RobIn: A Half-baked Robot for Electronics in a STEM Context

Chronis Kynigos
National and Kapodistrian
University of Athens, Greece
Educational Technology Lab
kynigos@ppp.uoa.gr

Marianthi Grizioti
National and Kapodistrian
University of Athens, Greece
Educational Technology Lab
mgriziot@ppp.uoa.gr

Sofia Nikitopoulou
National and Kapodistrian
University of Athens, Greece
Educational Technology Lab
sophieniki@ppp.uoa.gr

IDC '17, June 27-30, 2017, Stanford, CA, USA

ACM ISBN 978-1-4503-4921-5/17/06.
http://dx.doi.org/10.1145/3078072.3084319

Abstract
Robotic kits in designs for STEM education are becoming popular during the last few years. However, many of them focus mainly on programming leaving aside the electronics and engineering parts of robotics. In this paper we present RobIn (Robotic Insect), a robotic design that supports the equivalent coexistence of programming, construction and argumentation processes in corresponding educational robotic activities. RobIn challenges students to change it, improve it and expand its prototype robotic skeleton by using every day and affordable materials. We also present a study where RobIn functioned as a boundary object among students from different specializations of a Vocational Technical School.

Author Keywords
Educational Robotics; STEM; Boundary Crossing;

ACM Classification Keywords
I.2.9 Robotics; K.3.2 [Computers and Education]: Computer and Information Science Education;

Introduction
In the last two decades, activities with robots have progressively found their way in formal educational systems. In parallel, in the last few years there has been a big effort worldwide, for the inclusion of all

young learners in STEM (Science, Technology, Engineering, and Mathematics) education and for their attraction to STEM related professions. Robotics activities for STEM have been considered as interdisciplinary emphasizing collaborative learning, and robots have been perceived as a potentially powerful vehicle providing opportunities for construction, experimentation and collaboration between learners [1]. A large number of children from different ages has recently been given the opportunity to participate in a big variety of robotics activities. However, regarding STEM education, educational robotics activities often focus either on the 'Technology' (programming) or the 'Engineering' (constructing) element of STEM, with the 'Science' and 'Mathematics' lying somewhere on the background. Moreover, the electronic part of the robotic kits is in most cases a black box for the student, while the designs that allow electronics are too expensive or too complicated for the students. In this paper we present a robotic design approach that supports the involvement of students equally in programming, engineering and electronics and also their engagement with concepts from other STEM fields.

Robots as improvable boundary objects

In this study we designed RobIn (Robotic Insect), a robot for students to start working with. Our design was such that the students would have to re-engineer parts of the robot and tinker with the programming. We grouped students with different knowledge backgrounds to make these changes. To guide our design and to study meanings negotiated and generated by the students we used a theoretical framework called 'Boundary Crossing' [2]. Boundary crossing is a term that describes how persons from different professions or fields of knowledge work together for a common production task. They each contribute their knowledge and at the same time need to understand the others' contributions and negotiate around them for the task in hand. This process has educational implications since understanding peers from a different background requires crossing the borders of one's own knowledge in order to produce a hybrid artifact. A "boundary object" [7] describes an artifact that provokes this crossing and functions as a bridge between different domains or practices intersecting in a common task [5]. In the field of education a boundary object is central to an activity, in the context of a task which may vary, but it has in any case the following characteristics [8]:

a) it is designed for learners to articulate meanings and express different perspectives

b) it facilitates a back and forth movement between the different disciplines

c) its status is based on fallibility [4], an epistemological approach where artifacts are considered as malleable, questionable and improvable.

The activity can e.g. involve, designing a game, creating a digital story or constructing a tangible object. The boundary object is at the center of the activity and at the same time has a role as a communicational tool to shape a common language between the different members of the team. In this paper we consider robotic constructions and their programs as boundary objects, due to their interdisciplinary nature across the STEM subjects.

In our design we wanted to consider RobIn as an improvable boundary object amongst students with different knowledge background. To achieve that, we adopted the design approach of "half-baked microworlds" [5] and adjusted it to fit a robotic design. "Half-baked microworlds" is a term used to describe digital media designed in a way that their users would want to build on them, change them or de-compose parts of them in order to construct an artifact for themselves. In many cases they function as boundary objects because they facilitate the communication between researchers, technicians, teachers and students as they are involved in changing them.

Robotic Kits for STEM education

At the current time the dominant educational robotics platform is Lego Mindstorms [3], while the new releases of Lego, such as Lego WeDo, are also becoming popular especially to younger ages. Another robotic kit that lately has been used in many educational robotics activities is Thymio, a small robot with a number of sensors integrated. Thymio can be programmed with various ways like Scratch, text programming and Blockly. It is an appropriate tool for introducing learners to robot programming and to sensors' functionalities. However, children cannot intervene to its electronic design and the building element is limited to attaching bricks of Lego on its surface. During the last years there have also been developed a few robotic designs that are built on Arduino board, as more affordable solutions. One example is Sparki, a ready-made robotic construction with a number of advanced sensors and electronic parts integrated on an Arduino platform. Sparki can be programmed either with C++ or with block based programming. Edison is another Arduino based solution that offers the basic sensors, it can be programmed in Python and supports the attachment of Lego bricks on its surface. However, apart from Lego-based solutions, the "making" element for students is limited or missing in robot designs. Most of them are non-modifiable robotic kits whose construction remains a black box for the user. It is characteristic that phrases like "No assembly is necessary" are used to promote the robot products, presenting the lack of construction as a benefit. At the same time robotics activities tend to focus only on programming leaving aside the part of electronics and engineering. However, this is a core part of robotics field and is crucial for an integrated STEM education. With our RobIn design we aim to promote a side of robotics that is accessible by every student both in terms of cost efficiency and also in construction difficulty. In our approach the robot is neither a black box ready to be programmed nor an obscure and unattractive set of wires and electric boards. It is a "half-baked" robotic design that aims to act as a boundary object both amongst students and also between teachers and students. It is a mean for negotiation, communication of ideas, and meaning construction for concepts relative to the different fields of STEM.

The RobIn Design

RobIn is a robotic insect designed and built on an Arduino platform, developed by members of the Educational Technology Lab at the National Kapodistrian University of Athens. It was designed during the first year of ER4STEM, a three-year project funded by the European Commission, that focuses on the development of an integrated framework for the different European approaches in using robotics in education [6]. The idea behind RobIn's design is the construction of a robotic insect with everyday, easy to find, materials. In workshops with RobIn we provide students with a prototype robotic design that serves as

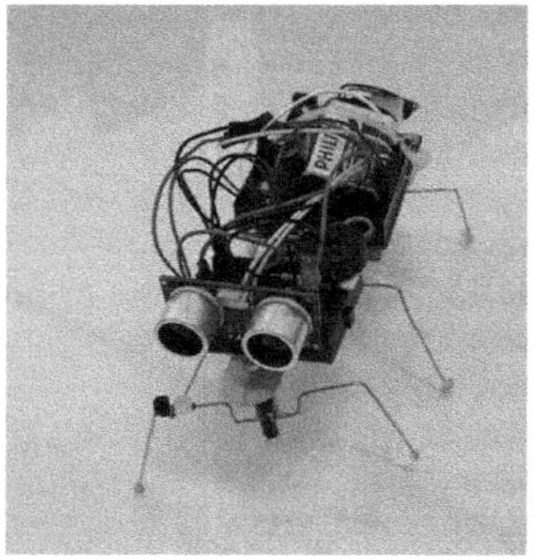

Figure 1: The prototype skeleton of RobIn Design

Pilot Study

- 19 students
- 16 to 18 years old
- 6 groups of 3 students each
- Duration: 6 hours
- Vocational Technical School of Athens
- No previous knowledge with Arduino

the robot's skeleton, some electronic spare parts (resistances, leds, sensors etc) and everyday materials (ropes, glue, paperclips, wooden sticks etc) and they build on the prototype in order to create their own functional robotic insect. The prototype (Figure 1) is constructed by the connection of an Arduino board with a mini-breadboard, a Piezo and a Sonar. Its body is created by a wooden pop stick and the legs with paper clips and adhesive tape. It also uses two servo motors to generate the movement of the legs. Its behavior can be programmed either in Arduino programming environment or in Scratch. The default behavior tries to depict the reactions of a real insect and includes the production of an increasing noise when something approaches and a backwards movement when an obstacle is too close. The initial code is open and the teacher may choose if it will be used as it is or with modifications.

RobIn design has the following characteristics: a) It is an affordable solution as its cost is limited to the purchase of an Arduino platform and some sensors, while all the other parts can be replaced with any material one has available b) It is designed in a way that promotes the modification, the interference of the user to its core construction and the continuous evolution of its initial form. In other words it is "a half-baked" robotic kit, ready to be expanded, evolved and transform to something new c) It can act as a boundary object both between students from different school specializations (technological specialization, biology and science specialization etc) and between teacher and students d) It combines multiple STEM fields (Biology, Mathematics, Technology, Engineering etc), while Engineering, Electronics and Programming are in the foreground.

Furthermore RobIn's design aims to involve students with the robotics field through the equivalent coexistence of three core processes for constructionist learning with robots: Construction, Programming and Argumentation. More precisely students switch between those three processes in order to finally create their new robotic artefact. This artefact every time will be a unique robotic design, since students don't have a specific pattern or instructions to follow, but instead they use their imagination to choose and combine the available materials. Thus, each insect is slightly or a lot different and has the personal "touch" of the students who built it. It is also a product of negotiation and knowledge exchange between students with different background and it is open to be further improved and extended by others.

Pilot Study

Last year we conducted a study as part of the ER4STEM project in order to investigate students' interaction with RobIn. A teacher of the school designed the activities of the workshop with the support of the researchers. The school was a Vocational Technical School in Greece. In those schools, students choose and follow different specializations of profession expertise from the age of 15 years old (e.g. electronic, electrician but also aesthetic or nurse). By conducting the study in that school we had the opportunity to group students with different knowledge backgrounds to work together. The participants came from the fields of electronic, programming, electrician and nursing and each group contained students from different fields. Before the workshop, the teacher presented the RobIn prototype and described how it works. When the teacher designed the activities, she decided to change the initial code of RobIn and make on purpose three errors at the

Episode 1

Dialogue between S3 (electrician student) and S1 (Computer Science student)

S3: It should have a command that would make the sound stop.

S1: No it is correct look the if statements (he explains how the conditions work)

S3: Ok. Let me see the definitions again (S3 looks the code).

Episode 2

S4: Why is it moving backwards? Is it something wrong with the construction?

S5: There is a problem with the robot's legs

S4: If we put the breadboard piece at the other side, then it will go forward

S5: Or we can keep it like this, draw some eyes on a carbon and glue them at the "back" and then it will be like going forward. Who can say what is back and what is forward?

commands that created robot's movement. The task for each team was a) to correct the program so that the robot would move forward smoothly and b) to build their own robot insect based on the given RobIn prototype. This robot could have programmed any behavior the students' wanted but it should at least be able to make a sound when it detects an obstacle and make some steps backwards.

Before the workshop two groups were chosen from the teacher as focus groups. The data that collected during the workshop included screen capturing, photos, video and audio recordings of the students. In addition, before and after the workshop students answered pre and post questionnaires with questions related to the activity and to their engagement with different STEM fields. Finally, after the workshop we interviewed the participants of the focus groups about their experience and the way they worked with RobIn. The evaluation of the study was based on a qualitative analysis of the collected data. The transcript data and the answers of the questionnaires were mapped in clusters of critical episodes related to evidence of boundary crossing, creative thinking, collaboration and engagement with STEM concepts. Below we present a brief overview of the total results for all students and also two critical episodes from the two focus groups (1 and 2).

Results

The analysis of the pre and post questionnaires showed that, even though a 47% (9 out of 19) of students answered that the activity was (quite)hard, a 84% (16 out of 19) of them answered that the activity was also (very) interesting and (very) fun. This fact shows that "hard" robotic activities may also be those that are more "interesting" and "fun" for the students. With respect to STEM subjects a 78% (15 out of 19) of students answered that they used knowledge related to technology and engineering. However the percentage of students who argued that they used knowledge related to physics and maths was very small (only 3 out of 19), probably due to the focus of the activities which was mainly on engineering, electronics and programming. Moreover, the analysis of the focus groups data revealed that RobIn design functioned in many cases as boundary object among students from different specializations. For example group 1 was formed by 1 student from computer science specialization (S1), 1 student from electronic specialization (S2) and 1 from electrician specialization (S3). Until the middle of the workshop they had distributed roles according to their expertise without one interfering to the other's field of knowledge. However, at one point they faced a problem whose solution required a kind of "boundary crossing": Their robot made a continuous sound when it faced an obstacle and it did not stop. The computer science student started to describe the program to the other two students and they explained to him the assembly and construction of the insect. Afterwards, S1 made suggestions for changes on the electronic parts like "*Shouldn't we have some voltage here? Now it seems to me that we have to change the circuit of piezo. Where is that circuit?*". In parallel S3 experimented with some commands on the program, even though he didn't had previous knowledge with programming. Then the dialogue of Episode 1 occurred. This critical episode is one of the cases where RobIn functioned as boundary object and urged the two students to exchange knowledge and to interfere to each other's field of expertise. Furthermore it seemed that the openness and the half-baked characteristic of RobIn design foster some students to express creative solutions during the

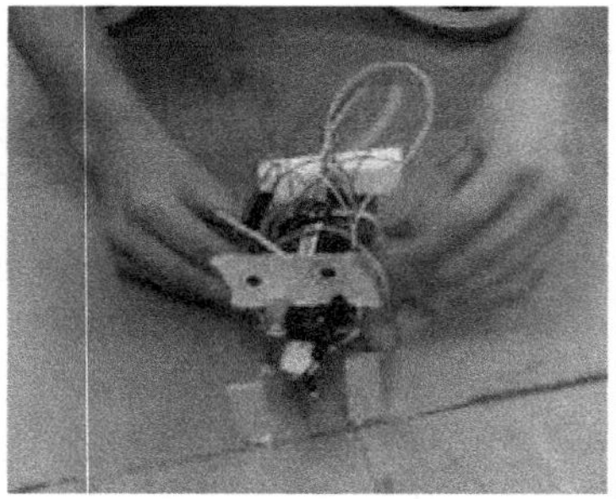

Figure 2: The creative design of team 1

Figure 3: One robotic insect produced with RobIn

process of construction. One selected critical episode is the Episode 2 from group 2. This group had realized that their robot moved always backwards due to an engineering error. By the time they discovered the error they couldn't decompose all of the robot parts, because they had already glued some of them. As a solution, they decided to follow the suggestion of S5. Finally they changed their initial strategy and created a robot quite different from the one they had planned (Figure 2), expressing in that way their creativity.

Some problems that students faced with RobIn design included the fact that procedures like gluing, thermal bonding etc were very time consuming. This problem can be solved with the preparation of the materials from the teacher beforehand. Moreover, the Arduino programming environment was quite difficult for students with no previous knowledge of programming and probably Scratch would be a better solution for beginner programmers.

Future work and conclusion

Through the pilot study we found boundary crossing framework to be useful in the context of robotics, especially amongst students with different knowledge backgrounds. The building and programming of a half-baked Arduino robot (RobIn) seemed to be worthwhile for educational activities, but it needs more study and analysis of how the boundary crossing occurs. Based on the results of our pilot study, we will improve the design of RobIn so that we endure a stable robotic skeleton prototype. In addition we plan to integrate concepts from physics and maths in the activities. Finally we are going to conduct another study in order to investigate in more depth the boundary crossing processes that may occur with RobIn design.

Acknowledgments

The study reported here has received funding from H2020 project Educational Robotics for STEM: ER4STEM (No. 665972)

References

1. Alimissis, D. 2013. Educational robotics: Open questions and new challenges. *Themes in Science and Technology Education*, 6 (1), 63-71
2. Akkerman, S. F., Bakker, A. 2011. Boundary Crossing and Boundary Objects. *Review of Educational Research*, 81(2), (pp. 132–169).
3. Baretto F., Benetti, V. 2012. Exploring the educational potential of robotics in schools: A systematic review. *Computers & Education*, 58(3), 978–988
4. Ernest, P. 1991). *The philosophy of mathematics education.* UK: Falmer Press.
5. Kynigos, C. 2007. Half-baked logo microworlds as boundary objects in integrated design. *Informatics in Education* 6(2), (pp. 335–359).
6. Lammer, L., Lepuschitz, W., Kynigos, C., Giuliano, A., & Girvan, C. 2017. ER4STEM Educational Robotics for Science, Technology, Engineering and Mathematics. *Robotics in Education* (pp. 95-101). Springer International Publishing.
7. Star, S. L., Griesemer, J. R. 1989. Institutional ecology, "translations" and boundary objects: Amateurs and professionals in Berkeley's Museum of Vertebrate Zoology, 1907–39. *Social Studies of Science*, *19*, 387–420.
8. Yiannoutsou, N., & Kynigos, C. 2013. Boundary Objects in Educational Design Research: designing an intervention for learning how to learn in collectives with technologies that support collaboration and exploratory learning. *Educational design research: Introduction and illustrative cases*, (pp. 357-379).

A Multi-User Tabletop Application to Train Children with Autism Social Attention Coordination Skills without Forcing Eye-Gaze Following

Pinata Winoto
Media Lab
Dept. of Computer Science
Wenzhou-Kean University
pwinoto@kean.edu

Tiffany Y. Tang
Media Lab
Dept. of Computer Science
Wenzhou-Kean University
yatang@kean.edu

IDC '17, June 27-30, 2017, Stanford, CA, USA

ACM ISBN 978-1-4503-4921-5/17/06.
http://dx.doi.org/10.1145/3078072.3084320

Abstract

Social attention coordination skills are central to the overall joint attention development. Previous research for children with neurotypical developing (NT) and autism spectrum disorder (ASD) has largely focused on one pathway of coordinating visual attention via gaze following with a social partner. However given the much higher reluctance of individuals with ASD to make eye contact, other pathways of visual attention coordination might be more satisfying. Such a possible pathway might be the hand-eye coordination which was observed to lead to successful social attention coordination between physically active infants and their parents. Motivated by prior works on the benefits of tabletop-based applications for ASD children, in this paper, we unfold a multi-user tabletop pattern-matching game to train ASD children social attention coordination skills via hand-eye coupling, that is, manipulation of screen-objects (puzzles with different patterns) in goal-directed tasks is achieved by alternating eye-gaze between screen-objects in one's own private space and another one in a shared space.

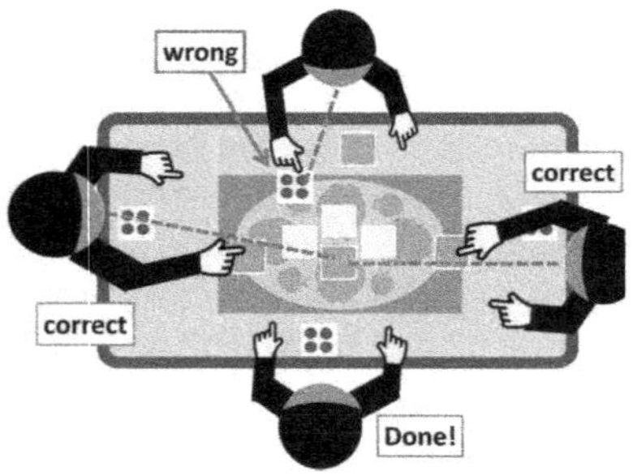

Figure 1: Hand-eye coupling without forcing eye-gaze following to facilitate coordinated joint switches in visual attention in our multi-user pattern-matching tabletop game. In this coordination game, all four players are expected to put similar cards into empty target white 'boxes' near the center of tabletop screen.

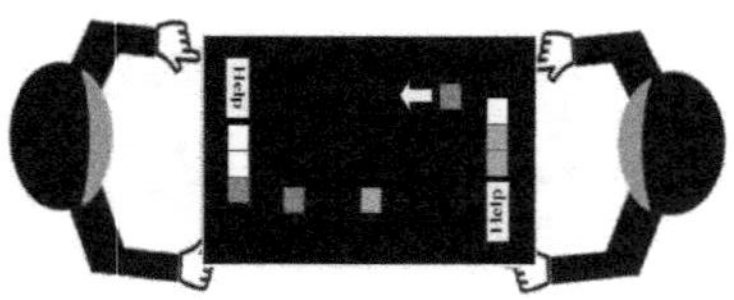

Figures 2: When Player 1 (left) press "Help" button (yellow), Player 2 may notice a flashing piece (arrow) and pass it to Player 1 by tapping it [16].

Author Keywords
Autism; joint attention; multi-user play; free-play; tabletop; social coordination; eye-hand coupling.

ACM Classification Keywords
H.5.m. Information interfaces and presentation (e.g., HCI): Miscellaneous.

Introduction and Background
Joint attention has been heralded as "*an executive form of information processing that contributes to social learning, stimulus encoding, and the facilitation of human social communication and connectedness across the life span*" (pp. 116 [13]) and must occur in the context of a social interaction [10]. For individuals with ASD who have social-communicative and social-emotional impairments, it is especially crucial to provide early intervention [13]. However, further complicated the effectiveness of earlier intervention (especially those large screen tabletop supported ones [1, 2, 4, 5, 6, 9, 11, 16]) is the heterogeneity of these children's abilities in their use of gesture and eye contact during social interactions [13]. Moreover, unlike NT children, they exhibit much less intrinsic desire to enhance and maintain their social reputation [3]. These factors, taken together, pose great challenges for researchers and developers to design collaborative environment to train their joint attention skills, especially during the early stages of their life. Most of the earlier tabletop-enabled applications offer ASD children with only one shared space where tightly coupled collaboration is required. Taken together, these earlier designs fail to effectively improve children's social communication skills since these children showed frustration as a result of "forced" collaboration [2]. Winoto et al. [16] is an exception which introduced a loosely-coupled play environment where ASD children are allowed to play in their own private space while occasionally engaging in collaboration requiring the abilities of initiating and responding to joint attention bids. Two enhanced designs (see Figure 3 for its two screenshots) had been implemented and studied with both high-functioning and low-functioning ASD children (HFASD and LFASD, respectively) over the past year with satisfying results (see Figure 2 for an illustration of the design paradigm).

Despite it, one of the drawbacks of the majority of previous works stressed the need to train young children with ASD eye-gaze following to respond to joint attention bids (RJA) given their higher reluctance of making eye contact. In this paper, we present a new design to specifically train children's social attention coordination skills by facilitating children's alternating eye-gaze between a screen object in one's own private space and another in a shared space without forcing eye-gaze following (see Figure 1 for an illustration of it). To the best of our knowledge, little previous research has explored this issue.

Related Work

Joint Attention & Socio-Communicative Skills for Children with ASD and Tabletop-based Intervention
Joint attention must occur in the context of a social interaction [10]. In the development literature, it is regarded as one of the core skills for language development and social competence especially collaboration and communication [10, 13]. For individuals with ASD, there is a growing recognition of it as a prevalent predictor of ability in such core domains of autism as language development, socio-

IJA	
	Response to hand-gripping on an object
	Response to Object being tapped
	Response to object being shown
	eye contact displayed
	Following a point action
	Following an eye gaze of a social partner
RJA	
	Eye-gaze coordinated shifting relative to each other
	Pro-declarative pointing

Table 1: Responses sponsored in IJA and RJA (adapted from [14])

communication, affective sharing, and theory of mind [7]. Prior works have proposed a wide variety of intervention and training strategies [12, 14, 15, 17]. According to Whalen and Schreibman [14], two phases of joint attention occur in a social interaction: initiating joint attention (IJA) and RJA. Accordingly, trainings are also provided at the two levels augmented with contextual hints. Table 1 lists levels of responses to joint attention bids for such trainings in a non-computerized setting [14]. Moreover, verbal, physical and gestural prompts from other children, care-givers and parents are suggested and to assist engagement (see [8] for a review). While many of the earlier empirical studies occur in non-computerized settings, recent ones largely had been conducted in computerized play environment [15], among which computer supported collaborative large-screen tabletop games gain popularity due to tabletop's large enough social spaces for all participants including on-lookers and the inherent multi-user interactions it affords [6, 9, 11].

Previous tabletop-enabled games, for examples in [1, 2, 4, 5, 6, 9, 11, 16], roughly follow two types of interaction types: Enforced collaboration (EC) and Free Play (FP) [2]. The empirical studies involving only HFASD children in [2] yield negative results where some children showed frustration as a result of EC, which is not surprising since children with ASD have less intrinsic motivation to socialize with others [3]. Moreover, almost all of these previous applications offer ASD children with one shared space where mostly EC was implemented. Figure 3 shows the screenshots of the enhanced puzzle game which is loosely structured and were developed after some inputs from care-givers of ASD children. Figure 4 compares and summarizes these earlier works.

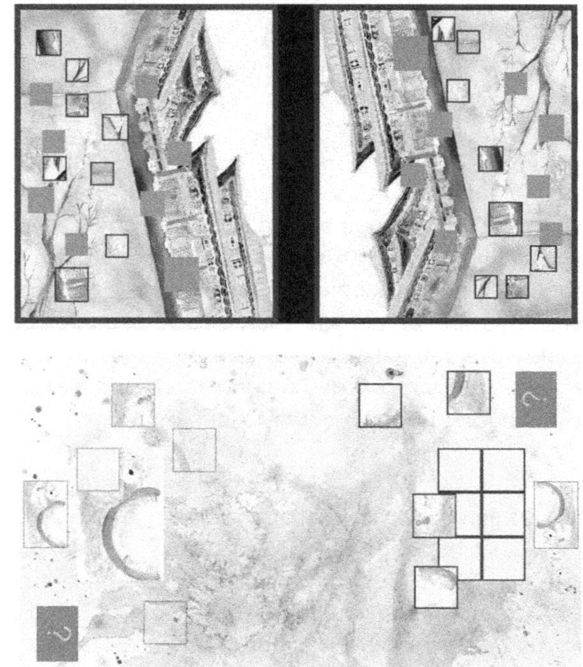

Figure 3: The enhanced version of the puzzle game based on the earlier version presented in [16]

Joint Attention without Eye-Gaze Following with a Social Partner

One of the drawbacks of previous works stressed the need to train young children with ASD eye-gaze following to RJA bids, which could pose great challenges for these children given their reluctance of making eye contact. Yu and Smith [18] observed that physically active infants and parents can coordinate joint visual

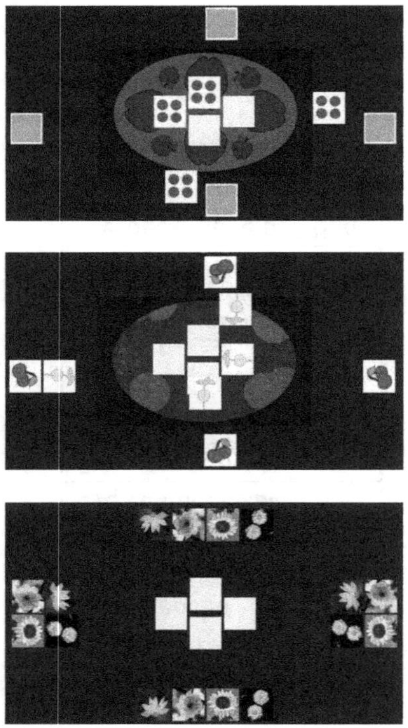

Figure 5: The screenshots of three levels (among a total of seven) in the game.

switches without gaze following via *attending to objects held by the self* or *parent*, and they argued that such social attention coordination can be achieved through eye-hand coupling in goal directed coordinating activities. Such a new pathway of hand-eye coupling without eye-gaze following to achieve coordinated joint switches in visual attention could be appealing if integrated into a collaborative design to train joint attention skills for children with ASD.

	# Players	Application	Private space?	Design pattern	Promoted social skills	Testers	In-game data collection
[9]	4	Route-planning game (SIDES)	×	EC	group work skills including negotiation and turn-taking	HFASD	N
[1]	2	Collaborative Puzzle Game	×	EC, FP	cooperation manifested in coordinated finger movement	ASD, TD	N
[2]	Multi-user	Collaborative Puzzle Game	×	EC, FP	positive social interaction(esp. goal-related behaviors)	HFASD	N
[5]	3	Collaborative Game	×	EC	joint performance, sharing and mutual planning	HFASD	N
[11]	3	Collaborative Puzzle Game	×	EC, FP	passive/active sharing, joint-performance, and turn-taking	HFASD	N
[4]	N/A	Collaborative Puzzle Game; Collaborative Collage (CC);	×	EC	joint performance, turn-taking, and negotiating	HFASD	N
[6]		Collaborative Game	×	EC, FP	positive interdependence, group processing; turn taking	HFASD, TD	N
[16]	2	Collaborative Puzzle Game	√	EC	joint-attention, reciprocity	HFASD & LFASD	Y

Figure 4: The comparison of previous tabletop-based games

Motivated by this work and drawn from the findings of earlier works, in this paper, we present a new design to specifically train children's social attention coordination skills by facilitating children's alternating eye-gaze between a screen object in one's own private space and another in a shared space without forcing eye-gaze following with a social partner (see Figure 1 for an illustration of it).

The System at a Glance

Figure 5 presents screenshots of three levels among a total of seven in the game. Four players are expected to play this game, in which each player will be given four different cards (puzzle pieces) at the beginning. Each card can be dragged within the player's private space, including into an empty target white 'box' near the center of the screen. When all players fill the target boxes with similar cards, then these cards will disappear. The level is completed when all cards are filled into the target boxes.

Figure 7 and 8 show the lab testing moments of the puzzle pattern-matching game in the tabletop; two design constraints were also explained accordingly. The system can be easily installed in any multitouch-screen based Table PC running Windows 8 or 10 (for better experience a screen-size larger than 12 inches is recommended). There is no additional hardware requirement. Figure 9 shows the game loaded in such a tablet PC.

The System Development Environment

The application is developed in Microsoft Visual Studio Enterprise 2015 as a Windows application for desktop. The minimum operating system to run the application is Windows 8.

Facilitating Social Attention Coordination Skills without Forcing Eye-Gaze Following: Design Rationale

The tabletop pattern-matching game has been designed to specifically train children's social attention coordination skills by facilitating children's alternating

Figure 6: Symmetric (top) and asymmetric patterns (bottom) used in the game

Figure 7: One of the lab play moments.

Design Consideration One

The image captured a moment here the task was not successfully accomplished (yet players are allowed to put the two wrong patterns in the shared space); the system though will provide an auditory hint to remind the players to try it again. To correct it, the player just need to first tap the wrongly placed card, then grab another. The wrongly-put card will then be automatically placed back to the player's private space.

eye-gaze between a screen object in one's own private space and another in a shared space in a series of pattern-matching tasks. Specifically, responding to joint attention (RJA) by following another's pointing gesture; and initiating joint attention (IJA) by using alternating eye contact between a puzzle in one's own private space to others in the public space to share attention. Note that in our game we intend to explore the possibilities of the eye-hand coupling pathway without eye-gaze following in responding and initiating joint attention bids among children with ASD (refer back to Figure 1 for an illustration of it).

The complexity of the game levels is controlled through the use of various patterns, such as simple symmetric patterns or more complicated asymmetric patterns (see Figure 6). A symmetric pattern will appear identical from four players' point of view; hence, does not require their mental rotation skill. We posit the harder the game level is the more joint-attention skill is needed.

Concluding Remarks

Following our previous study, we unfolded a new design to specifically train children's joint attention skills by facilitating children's alternating eye-gaze between a screen object in one's own private space and another in a shared space—without forcing eye-contacting with a social partner. We are currently finalizing the design and on the road to deploy the system in the field.

Acknowledgements

This research is supported by Wenzhou-Kean University's Student Partnering with Faculty (SpF) Research Program (#WKU201617005), and Wenzhou Municipal Science and Technology Bureau (#S20160012).

References

1. Alberto Battocchi, F Pianesi, Daniel Tomasini, Massimo Zancanaro, Gianluca Esposito, Paola Venuti, A Ben Sasson, Eynat Gal, Patrice L (Tamar) Weiss. 2009. Collaborative Puzzle Game: a tabletop interactive game for fostering collaboration in children with Autism Spectrum Disorders (ASD). In *Proceedings of the ACM International Conference on Interactive Tabletops and Surfaces* (ITS'09), 197-204. http://doi.acm.org/10.1145/1731903.1731940
2. Ayelet Ben-Sasson, Liron Lamash, Eynat Gal. 2012. To enforce or not to enforce? The use of collaborative interfaces to promote social skills in children with high functioning autism spectrum disorder. *Autism* 17, 5: 608–622.DOI: 10.1177/1362361312451526
3. Anne Deckers, Jeffrey Roelofs, Peter Muris, Mike Rinck. 2014. Desire for social interaction in children with autism spectrum disorders. *Research in Autism Spectrum Disorders* 8, 4: 449–453.
4. Eynat Gal, Liron Lamash, Nirit Bauminger-Zviely, Massimo Zancanaro, Patrice L. (Tamar) Weiss. 2016. Using Multitouch Collaboration Technology to Enhance Social Interaction of Children with High-Functioning Autism. *Physical & Occupational Therapy in Pediatrics* 36, 1: 46-58.
5. Leonardo Giusti, Massimo Zancanaro, Eynat Gal, Patrice L. (Tamar) Weiss. 2011. Dimensions of collaboration on a tabletop interface for children with autism spectrum disorder. In *Proceedings of the SIGCHI Conference on Human Factors in Computing Systems* (CHI'11), 3295-3304, http://doi.acm.org/10.1145/1978942.1979431
6. Wooi Boon Goh, Wei Shou, Jacquelyn Tan, G.T. Jackson Lum. 2012. Interaction design patterns for

Figure 8: One of the play moments where design constraint of boundary is shown.

Design Consideration Two

The image captured a moment where the card cannot be moved out of one player's 'hidden' private space.

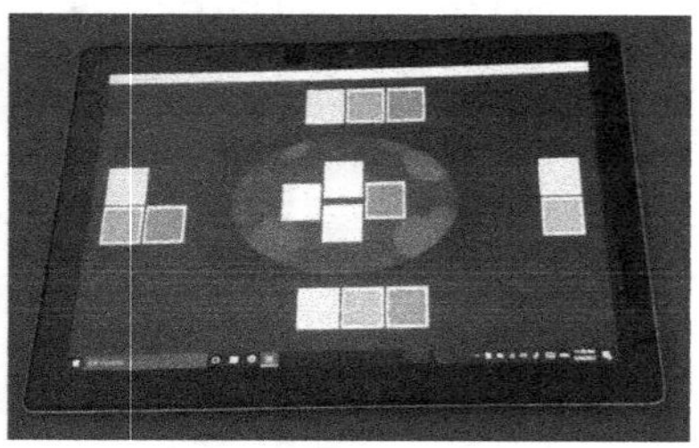

Figure 9: The game was captured being loaded in a Lenovo Miix 12.2' tablet PC powered by i5-6200U 8G RAM running Windows 10.

multi-touch tabletop collaborative games. CHI '12 Extended Abstracts on Human Factors in Computing Systems (CHI'12), 141-150, http://doi.acm.org/10.1145/2212776.2212792

7. Megan P. Martins and Sandra L. Harris. 2006. Teaching children with autism to respond to joint attention initiations. *Child & Family Behavior Therapy* 28, 1: 51-68.
8. Tanya Paparella and Stephanny F N Freeman. 2015. Methods to improve joint attention in young children with autism: a review. *Pediatric Health, Medicine and Therapeutics*, 6: 65–78.
9. Anne Marie Piper, Eileen O'Brien, Meredith Ringel Morris, Terry Winograd. 2006. SIDES: a cooperative tabletop computer game for social skills development. In *Proceedings of the 2006 20th conference on Computer supported cooperative work* (CSCW'06), 1-10, http://doi.acm.org/10.1145/1180875.1180877
10. Elizabeth Redcay, Mario Kleiner, Rebecca Saxe. 2012. Look at this: the neural correlates of initiating and responding to bids for joint attention. *Frontiers in Human Neuroscience* 6:169. doi: 10.3389/fnhum.2012.00169
11. Greis F. Mireya Silva, Alberto Raposo, Maryse Suplino. 2015. Exploring collaboration patterns in a multitouch game to encourage social interaction and collaboration among users with autism spectrum disorder. *J. Computer Supported Cooperative Work* 24:149–175.
12. Bridget A Taylor and Hannah Hoch. 2008. Teaching children with autism to respond to and initiate bids for joint attention. *J Appl Behav Anal*. 41, 3: 377–391. doi:10.1901/jaba.2008.41-377
13. Amy Vaughan Van-Hecke, Tasha Oswald, Peter Mundy. 2016. Joint attention and the social phenotype of autism spectrum disorder: a perspective from developmental psychopathology. *Developmental Psychopathology* 4: 4:1–36. doi: 10.1002/9781119125556.devpsy304
14. Christina Whalen and Laura Schreibman. 2003. Joint attention training for children with autism using behavior modification procedures. *Journal of Child Psychology and Psychiatry* 44, 3: 456–468.
15. Pamela J. White, Mark O'Reilly, William Streusand, Ann Levine, Jeff Sigafoos, Giulio Lancioni, Christina Fragale, Nigel Pierce, Jeannie Aguilar. 2011. Best practices for teaching joint attention: A systematic review of the intervention literature. *Research in Autism Spectrum Disorders* 5, 4: 1283–1295.
16. Pinata Winoto, Tiffany Y. Tang, Aonan Guan. 2016. I will help you pass the puzzle piece to your partner if this is what you want me to: the design of collaborative puzzle games to train Chinese children with autism spectrum disorder joint attention skills. In *Proceedings of the 15th International Conference on Interaction Design and Children* (IDC'2016), 601-606. http://doi.acm.org/10.1145/2930674.2936012
17. Connie Wong and Connie Kasari. 2012. Play and joint attention of children with autism in the preschool special education classroom. *J. of Autism and Developmental Disorders* 42, 10: 2152–2161.
18. Chen Yu and Linda B. Smith. 2013. Joint attention without gaze following: human infants and their parents coordinate visual attention to objects through eye-hand coordination. *PLoS ONE* 8, 11: e79659. doi:10.1371/journal.pone.0079659

Emotion Recognition via Face Tracking with RealSense™ 3D Camera for Children with Autism

Tiffany Y. Tang
Media Lab
Dept. of Computer Science
Wenzhou-Kean University
yatang@kean.edu

Pinata Winoto
Media Lab
Dept. of Computer Science
Wenzhou-Kean University
pwinoto@kean.edu

Guanxing Chen
Media Lab
Dept. of Computer Science
Wenzhou-Kean University
ChenGuanxing316@wku.edu.cn

IDC '17, June 27-30, 2017, Stanford, CA, USA

ACM ISBN 978-1-4503-4921-5/17/06.
http://dx.doi.org/10.1145/3078072.3084321

Abstract

Although there is a growing recognition of the differences, not diminished abilities, of facial affective expressivity between Typically Developing (TD) and Autism Spectrum Disorder (ASD) individuals, which might lead to the varied recognizability of conveyed emotion by both TD and ASD individuals, little is explored on the ecological validity of these findings; that is, whether *spontaneous* affective facial expressions can better be produced and recognized by both populations. We aimed to address these issues in the present study, using children's cartoon clips to assess two aspects of spontaneous emotion production and recognition in a context closer to real-life children's cartoon movie watching (at home or a classroom). Based on the facial landmark data and a teacher/parent's manual emotion tags (happy), we performed a computational analysis to compare the happy emotion labels generated by the automated algorithm and the human TD rater. Two pilot studies of six ASD children revealed the potential as well as challenges of such an approach.

Author Keywords

Autism; emotion; children; affective expressivity; computational analysis; facial landmark; China

ACM Classification Keywords
H.5.m. Information interfaces and presentation (e.g., HCI): Miscellaneous.

Introduction
One of the core characteristics of ASD is the presence of early and persistent impairments in social-communicative skills [1]. An overwhelming number of previous studies usually attribute such deficits to the population's diminished skills in emotion recognition until a few recent studies started to probe into possibility of the lack of such skills in the TD population. That is, awkward moments in social interactions might be characterized by facial emotion recognition difficulties on both sides of the social equation [4, 11, 22, 23] since social interactions are intrinsically bi-directional [11]; that said, instead of attributing the social-communicative skill deficits in ASD individuals to their impairments in emotion recognition skills, isn't it possible that TD people might also have difficulties or deficits at reading ASD expressions? Recent studies have indeed empirically demonstrated the difficulties of TD individuals in recognizing ASD expression [4, 7, 22]. Another related line of research has concluded that individuals with ASD demonstrate varied quality on *affective expressivity* across multiple modalities: specifically, for example, a greater variability in vocal prosody production [12, 16], the social inappropriateness of facial affective expressivity [3, 4, 7, 14, 22]. Some attributes the subtle differences of affective facial expressivity between the two populations to the reduced facial muscle movement [6, 15, 25], irregularities in limbic brain activities which are closely related to emotion [15], and being less motivated in engaging in social activities [4], in the ASD community.

These converging empirical evidences revealed the differences of facial affective expressivity between ASD and TD individuals might prevent the former from producing recognizable emotions to both populations [4, 7, 12, 22, 24] and thus further complicate their social interactions. A pressing and under-explored research path to pursue is how existing mature facial emotional algorithms could successfully label the emotion of expression posed by ASD individuals so as to provide social cues for their partners including both ASD and TD individuals. A few recent works started to explore down this avenue [14, 20] including our present one. Specifically, in present study, we attempted to examine the potential of computational emotion recognition of ASD children's facial expression collected during naturalistic tasks (cartoon-clip watching) by comparing the manual emotion tag from teachers/parents with the automatic one generated by our system.

Related Work
There is no lack of empirical studies examining the impairments of facial expressivity in individuals with ASD (among many, [13, 21]); however, few probe the degree of *recognizability* of these emotions by either ASD or TD raters [4]. These two indirect, yet related, lines of research will first be presented to motivate the present study.

The Affective Expressivity of Children with ASD
Previous research has argued that individuals with ASD demonstrate varied quality on affective expressivity across multiple modalities: specifically, for example, a greater variability in vocal prosody production [12], the social-inappropriateness of facial affective expressivity [3, 4, 7, 8, 9, 14, 22, 24]. For example, Faso et al [7]

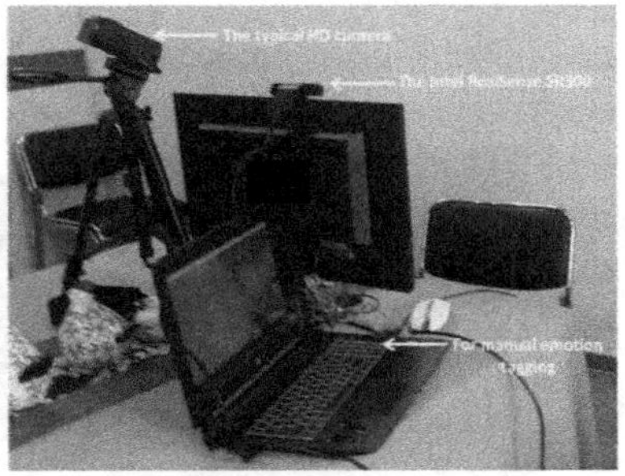

Figure 1: Pilot testing environment setup in a private autism center.

Figure 2: Pilot testing environment where a teacher sat side by side with the child to manually 'spot' his happy expression.

Figure 3: Another pilot testing in our lab where a girl was watching a cartoon movie.

examined how well facial expressions produced by individuals with ASD are perceived and thus subsequently recognizable by both TD and ASD individuals (both were referred to as the *potential social partners*). They have found that both groups of potential social partners did not find it difficult to identify the facial emotions posed by individuals with ASD; though posed expressions by ASD individuals are somewhat *different* and rated as '*awkward*'. Such awkwardness might make it difficult for TD individuals to interpret the emotion of their ASD peers, which in turn make it emotionally disconnect between the two populations. Similar observations on the awkwardness of affective expressivity by individuals with ASD were also reported in [8], and a computational comparative study in [14]. Meanwhile, prior research provided prevailing evidences that differences, not diminished abilities, are exhibited in affective facial expressivity ASD individuals [4, 7, 12, 24]. For instance, [12] reported that raters observed a higher frequency of laughter produced by ASD children than that of produced by TD children; adults with ASD can produce more recognizable anger emotion than happy one by naïve female observers [7]. Picard argued that individuals with ASD could exhibit incredible calmer facial expression (outward) than their true emotional state (inward, measurable through physiological data including Galvanic Skin Response or GSR) [17, 18], which largely supported these previous empirical and clinical findings.

Can TD Individuals Read the Emotion of Children with ASD?

Recent empirical studies began to probe the other side of the social interaction equation in observing whether the emotion of individuals with ASD can be recognized by TD individuals, including those have more intimate relationships with ASD individuals (parents, teachers, etc.) [4, 5, 22, 24] following the mounting evidences of unnatural and exaggerated affective facial expression posed by ASD individuals. In order to determine whether atypical emotion production is common or idiosyncratic, [4] investigated both TD and ASD judgers' ability to recognize emotional expressions produced by TD and ASD posers. Empirical studies are consistent with previous ones in highlighting the degree of recognizability decreased on expressions produced by ASD individuals regardless of the profiles of the raters which implicate idiosyncratic atypical emotional expression representation in ASD [4]. In a large sample of 84 ASD and TD children, empirical results indicated that TD adult judgers (senior psychology college students) were less able to recognize *sad* facial expression produced by children with ASD than that produced by TD children [24]. More recognizable *anger* emotion than *happy* one by adults with ASD was captured in [7]. ASD children were perceived, by parents, as showing more negative emotion than TD children.

Computational Facial Data Analysis for Emotion Labeling in Autism Research

Although emotion recognition has been an active research field, the majority of the earlier studies targeted and evaluated by typical users [26]. Among them, recognizing emotions from facial expression received the most attention; portable cameras make it possible to integrate the technique into (multimodal) everyday activities for emotion recognition [26]. Recently, the low-cost 3D sensor cameras such as Microsoft Kinect™ and the newer Intel RealSense™ receive much attention due to its advantages in

Facial Action Units (AUs)	Real-Sense	Facial Land-mark
Upper Eyelid	√	
Lower Eyelid	√	
Eyes Smaller		√
Corners of the Mouths	√	
Lip Medium	√	
Grin		√

Table 1: selected facial AUs for happy emotion in our study

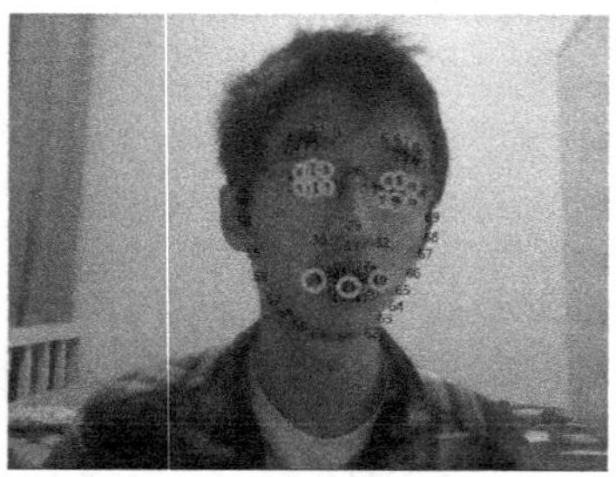

Figure 4 Selected facial landmarks obtained from RealSense

capturing fine-grained skeleton and facial landmark data which in turn provided motion data for more accurate analysis [20]. Such computational analysis has the potential to characterize emotion expressivity in terms of temporal feature of facial landmark data, head motion and hand gestures, especially with more affordable and portable motion and facial data capture technologies [23]. However, the inherently atypical facial muscle movement in individuals with autism poses significant challenges for such technique to be effective in the domain. Metallinou et al [14] quantitatively compared the affective facial poses of 37 individuals aged ranging from 9 to 14 with high functioning autism (HFASD, 21) and typically developing individuals (TD, 16). The task involved is to mimic the emotional facial expression from the common Mind Reading CD [2]. Motion capture technology and functional data analysis were deployed to allow the facial gesture data capture, analysis and visualization of temporal nature of facial landmark data. Experiential results revealed statistically significant differences between ASD and TD children in terms of the asynchrony of motion between different facial regions and more facial motion roughness [14]. [19] relied on human-intervened semi-automatic analysis and [20] revealed that for both TD and ASD children, happiness, sadness and anger were correctly labeled with high accuracy through Intel's RealSense™ lens. These recent works provided solid ground for our present study.

The System, Pilot Study, and Study Procedure

The evaluated system consists of a 19-inch LCD monitor, an Intel RealSense™ camera, and a computer with a typical camera (see Figure 1). The Intel RealSense™ SR 300 programmable camera was mounted on the LCD monitor where a two-minute cartoon was shown to capture the facial landmark data of the child; side by side with the RealSense ™ is a typical high-definition camera to record their continuous facial expressions.

RealSense ™ SDK could detect a total of 78 facial landmarks and calculate 16 facial action units (AUs) from a human face [20]. To detect the happy expression, six facial action units (AUs) are selected (see Table 1); Figure 4 illustrates an example of the selected facial landmarks used in our study. The linear distances between these landmarks were then computed every second to determine whether it is a happy or non-happy face [20]; that is, by comparing the distances with some discrimination thresholds.

Drawn from earlier results that caregivers and parents are likely to develop secure attachment with the ASD individuals [5] and thus can easily spot the happy and anxious moments in an ASD child [10], we asked either a home-run teacher or parent to sit in front of another computer to 'press' the 'enter' key when s/he spotted a happy moment in the child (see Figure 2). We assume the observation made by teachers/parents is more accurate than that from our evaluated system in judging their children's happy emotion, because they could observe not only children's facial expression, but also their voice, gesture, and other contextual information (multi-modalities).

Finally, we manually compared the labels ('happy') obtained from the evaluated system with the labels provided by teachers/parents. The maximum temporal offset of the co-occurrence is set to three seconds; that is, an agreement between the system and human is reached if the system could detect a happy face within three seconds before/after the teachers/parents press the enter key. Any consecutive 'happy' labels from the system would be considered as a single happy moment.

Pilot Study Results and Discussion

The experiments were carried out twice (i.e. in a private autism center and our lab, see Figure 2 and 3 respectively). The pre-test interview revealed that both teachers and parents can tell when the child is happy and the frequency of happiness is relatively satisfying. A total of six ASD children (Mean age=4.5, SD=1.2) taking part in the testing and the system had been tested ten times. Among them, only six testing moments from four ASD children are valid. Invalid data are caused by either teachers/parents' failure in operating the equipment or due to children's temporary disruptive behaviors. Using the collected valid data, a discrimination threshold δ is adjusted in the computation of AUs in our analysis. By decreasing the threshold value, our system becomes more sensitive in detecting a happy face; hence, increasing both its true positive and false positive rates, and vice versa. Here, the true positive rate refers to the probability of detecting a happy emotion correctly by the system, and the false positive rate refers to the probability of misjudging a non-happy emotion as a happy one. Those said, we can draw the Receiver Operating Characteristic (ROC) curve after adjusting δ. These ROC curves represent the accuracy of the evaluated system in recognizing children's facial expression (happiness) relative to their teachers/parents' observation. The horizontal axis of an ROC curve represents the false positive rate and the vertical axis represents the true positive rate (see Figure 5). The origin (0, 0) represents the situation when the system is extremely insensitive in recognizing happy face; hence, it would never classify a face as a happy one regardless the teachers/parents' observation. In contrast, the point (1, 1) represents the situation when the system is oversensitive or would always classify a face as a happy one. Finally, the point (0, 1) represents the ideal system which could always correctly classify happy/non-happy emotion exactly as what the teachers/parents have observed. Figure 5 shows two sets of ROC curves for eye-based AUs and mouth-based AUs. A diagonal black line represents a random classifier; the further a point is above it the better our classifier is. It appears in Figure 5 that both eye-based and mouth-based AUs could be used to predict children's happiness, where eye-based AUs are more stable as a predictor. This is true, because when we fix the false positive rate at 0.3, the average true positive rates from all six samples are 0.69 and 0.60 for eye-based and mouth-based AUs, respectively.

Concluding Remarks and Challenging Issues

In present study, we attempted to examine the potential of computational emotion recognition of ASD children's facial expression collected during naturalistic tasks (cartoon-clip watching) by comparing the manual emotion tag from teachers/parents with the automatic one generated by our system. Experimental results favor the use of facial landmark data around the eye area. More experiments need to be conducted to further examine the validity of it.

In the long run, such tools could provide assistance to help TD individuals to read the emotions of ASD. There existing two key challenges along this research avenue,

Data Collection

Before the testing, a pre-test interview with either teachers or parents was conducted on some basic statistics of the child such as the age of children, the schooling time, their self-reported ability on recognizing the happy emotion of the child, relative frequency of happiness spotted, etc. During the testing, we asked children to watch a two-minute cartoon in front of the display monitor with a RealSense™ camera attached on the top of it. Meanwhile, a teacher or parent pressed 'Enter' key when the child's happy emotion was spotted and automatically recorded (see Figure 2).

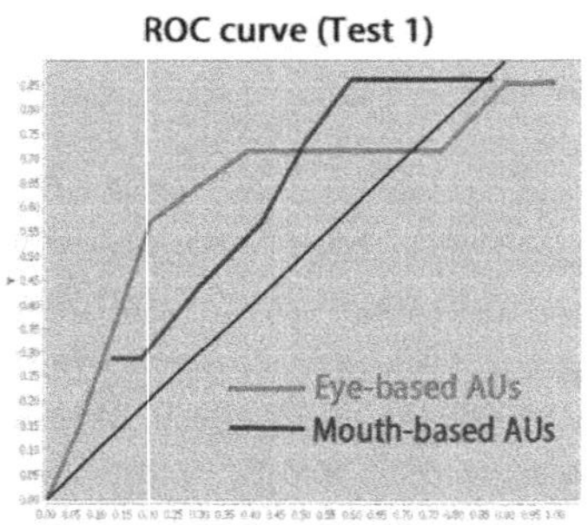

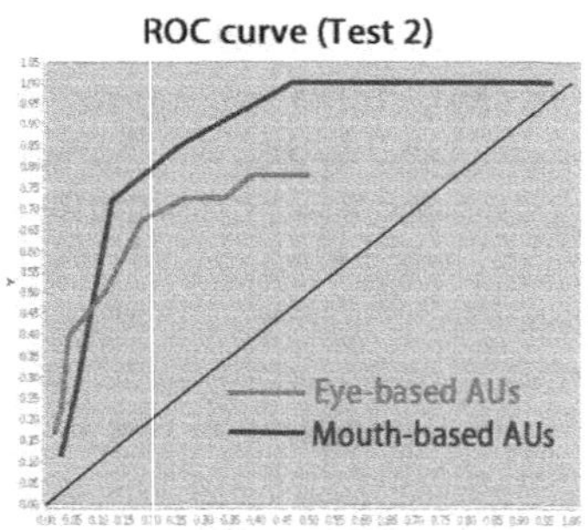

Figure 5. ROC curves of two children using eye-based AUs and mouth-based AUs respectively.

all of which are rooted in the *idiosyncratic*, rather than common and systematic, representation of emotion expression in people with ASD [4]. Specifically, how to validate the two emotion labels generated by the computer algorithm and manually tagged by a human user; and how to *groupize* and *adapt* such an automatic emotion recognition tool to at least a *subtype* of ASD individuals remain key open questions as well as our future works.

Acknowledgements

We would like to thank all parents, children and teachers involved in the study; thanks also go to Xi Yang, Xiaoyang Qiu, and Hang Xie for their assistances in the pilot testing. The financial support of this research through Student Partnering with Faulty (SpF) Program (WKU201617004) is greatly acknowledged.

References

1. American Psychiatric Association. 2013. *Diagnostic and statistical manual of mental disorders* (5th ed.). Washington DC: American Psychiatric Association.
2. Simon Baron-Cohen. 2003. *Mind Reading: The Interactive Guide to Emotions*. Jessica Kingsley Publisher, London, UK.
3. Sander Begeer, Hans M. Koot, Carolien Rieffe, Mark Meerum Terwogt, and Hedy Stegge. 2008. Emotional competence in children with autism: Diagnostic criteria and empirical evidence. *Developmental Review* 28,3: 342–369.
4. Rebecca Brewer, Federica Biotti, Carloline Catmur, Clare Press, Francesca Happé, Richard Cook, and Geoffrey Bird. 2016. Can Neurotypical Individuals Read Autistic Facial Expressions? Atypical Production of Emotional Facial Expressions in Autism Spectrum Disorders. *Autism Research* 9 2: 262–271.
5. Lisa Capps, Connie Kasari, Nurit Yirmiya, and Sigman, M. 1993. Parental perception of emotional expressiveness in children with autism. *J. Consulting and Clinical Psychology* 61, 3: 475–484.
6. Patrycja Czapinski, Susan E Bryson. 2003. Reduced facial muscle movements in autism: Evidence for dysfunction in the neuromuscular pathway? *Brain and Cognition* 51, 2: 177–179.
7. Daniel J. Faso, Noah J. Sasson, Amy E. Pinkham. 2015. Evaluating Posed and Evoked Facial Expressions of Emotion from Adults with Autism Spectrum Disorder. *J. Autism and Developmental Disorders 45, 1:* 75–89.
8. Ruth B. Grossman, Lisa R. Edelson, and Helen Tager-Flusberg. 2013. Emotional facial and vocal expressions during story retelling by children and adolescents with high-functioning autism. *Journal of Speech, Language and Hearing Research* 56, 3: 1035.
9. Ruth B Grossman. 2015. Judgments of social awkwardness from brief exposure to children with and without high-functioning autism. *Autism* 19, 5: 580-587.
10. Amanda C. Gulsrud, Laudan B. Jahromi, and Connie Kasari. 2010. The Co-regulation of emotions between mothers and their children with autism. *J. Autism and Developmental Disorders* 40, 2: 227–237.
11. Amy G. Halberstadt, Susanne A. Denham, and Julie C. Dunsmore. 2001. Affective Social Competence. *Social Development* 10, 1:79–119.
12. William J Hudenko, ad M. A. Magenheimer. 2011. Listeners prefer the laughs of children with autism to those of typically developing children. *Autism 16, 6:* 641–665.
13. Connie Kasari, Marian Sigman, Peter Mundy, and Nurit Yirmiya. 1990. Affective sharing in the context of joint attention interactions of normal,

autistic, and mentally retarded children. *J. Autism and Developmental Disorders*, 20(1), 87–100.

14. Angeliki Metallinou, Ruth B. Grossman, and Shrikanth Narayanan. 2013. Quantifying atypicality in affective facial expressions of children with autism spectrum disorders. In *Proc. of 2013 IEEE International Conference on Multimedia and Expo* (ICME). DOI: 10.1109/ICME.2013.6607640
15. Rachel L. Moseley, Yury Shtyrov, Bettina Mohr, Michael V. Lombardo, Sim on Baron-Cohen, Friedemann Pulvermüller. 2015. Lost for emotion words: What motor and limbic brain activity reveals about autism and semantic theory. *NeuroImage* 104: 413–422.
16. Aparna Nadig, Holly Shaw. 2012. Acoustic and perceptual measurement of expressive prosody in high-functioning autism: Increased pitch range and what it means for listeners. *Journal of Autism and Developmental Disorders* 42, 499–511.
17. Rosalind Picard. 2009. Future affective technology for autism and emotion communication. *Philosophical Transactions of the Royal Society B*, 364:3575-3584.
18. Rosalind Picard. 2010. Emotion research by the people, for the people. *Emotion Review 2, 3:* 250-254.
19. James M. Rehg, Agata Rozga, Gregory D. Abowd and Matthew S. Goodwin. 2014. Behavioral Imaging and Autism, *IEEE Pervasive Computing*, 13, 2:84-87.
20. Vinícius Silva, Filomena Soares, João Sena Esteves, Joana Figueiredo, Cristina Santos and Ana Paula Pereira. 2017. Happiness and Sadness Recognition System—Preliminary Results with an Intel RealSense 3D Sensor. In *Proc. of CONTROLO 2016*, LNCS 402, Springer.
21. Margaret E. Snow, Margaret E. Hertzig and Theodore Shapiro. 1987. Expression of Emotion in Young Autistic Children. *J. the American Academy of Child and Adolescent Psychiatry* 26, 6: 836–838.
22. Steven D. Stagg, Rachel Slavny, Charlotte Hand, Alice Cardoso, and Pamela Smith. 2014. Does facial expressivity count? How typically developing children respond initially to children with autism. *Autism* 18, 6: 704–711.
23. Tiffany Y. Tang. 2016. Helping Neuro-typical individuals to read the emotion of children with autism spectrum disorder: an internet-of-things approach. In *Proc. of the 15th ACM Interaction Design and Children Conference (ACM IDC2016)*, 666-671.
24. Martin A. Volker, Christopher Lopata, Donna A. Smith, Marcus L. Thomeer. 2009. Facial encoding of children with high-function autism spectrum disorders. *Focus on Autism and Other Developmental Disabilities* 24, 4: 195–204.
25. Amy K. Weimer, Amy M. Schatz, Alan Lincoln, Angela O Ballantyne, and Doris A. Trauner. 2001. "Motor" impairment in asperger syndrome: Evidence for a deficit in proprioception. *Journal of Developmental & Behavioral Pediatrics* 22,2: 92–101.
26. Zhihong Zeng, Maja Pantic, Glenn I Roisman, and Thomas S Huang. 2009. A survey of affect recognition methods: Audio, visual, and spontaneous expressions. *IEEE Transactions on Pattern Analysis and Machine Intelligence*, 31, 1:39–58.

Digital Natives and Cardboard Cubes: Co-Creating a Physical Play(ful) Ideation Tool with Preschool Children

Katriina Heljakka
University of Turku
Finland
katriina.heljakka@utu.fi

Pirita Ihamäki
Satakunta University
of Applied Sciences
Finland
pirita.ihamaki@samk.fi

Abstract
This presentation highlights a study on the interactive design and implications of a playful co-creation tool, Comicubes, which combines a two-dimensional blank cardboard canvas with a three-dimensional, open-ended toy medium: the cube. In our study, we tested the concept's functionality as an ideation tool suitable for different target and age groups, as well as its potential as a creative physical platform that encourages design thinking, allows for playful manipulation, and invites interaction. In workshops designed for preschool-aged children, participants were asked to create a plaything of their choice by applying various art supplies to blank cardboard cubes. The workshop findings indicate that the children in our test group, as digital natives, were able to use the Comicubes platform to co-design and create a physical plaything and develop associated play patterns and open-ended (toy) or rule-based (game) ideas for its use.

Author Keywords
Co-creation; playful tool; participatory design; design techniques; preschool-aged children; digital natives.

IDC '17, June 27–30, 2017, Stanford, CA, USA

ACM ISBN 978-1-4503-4921-5/17/06
http://dx.doi.org/10.1145/3078072.3084322

ACM Classification Keywords
H.5.m [Information Interfaces and Presentation (e.g., HCI)]: Miscellaneous; H.5.2 [User Interfaces]: Evaluation/Methodology, User-Centered Design; K.8.0 [Personal Computing]: Games

Introduction
This paper investigates how preschool-aged children engage with Comicubes [1], a three-dimensional tool that stimulates design creativity and interaction. We present an empirical study focused on how children interacted with this ideation tool in a workshop setting. The children in the test groups (N=13), aged 6 and 7 years, were asked to create a plaything using two cardboard cutouts that could be formed into cubes and art supplies, such as coloring pens, pictures, and letters printed on cardboard squares. We consider the cardboard cubes as forms and their blank surfaces as an information layer that can be enhanced with text, images, and even digital technology (such as apps) involved, hybrid features which connect the physical base material with digitally operated devices. Prensky introduced the term "digital natives" to refer to the generation that has grown up with digital technologies, so much so that these technologies are a part of their worldview [2]. For digital natives, ways of acting and being in the social world are framed by their experiences with technology. Their worlds are heavily influenced by these technologies. As Zenvenbergen noted, one only has to consider the toys produced by global toy manufacturers and the changes over the past 20 years to see how digital technologies are changing the experiences of young children. In turn, such experiences change these children's dispositions to learning and behaving [3]. For many players, the focus is on fun, entertainment, and pleasure, but the age of the ludic turn also manifests in game and toy-related skill-building, self-realization, and other forms of creative behavior. Lacasa et al. expressed a similar notion when they wrote that "playing, imagining, and creating are indispensable activities that humans, young or old, have to learn in the 21st century" [4]. According to the literature [5], however, the importance of the material dimension of play is not diminishing, although Western culture is digitalizing and dematerializing in many ways [6]. In other words, physical (tangible) toys and games are still popular among different age groups. It is therefore possible to verify the existence and continuous play potential of classical play media such as the cube, which as a form has its point of origin in a physical object but is used today in both material and digital contexts as a basis for different play ideas. The present research is interested in how digital natives perceive and interact with the physical Comicubes, which use simple paper-based technology and are introduced in greater detail in the following section.

Study Background and Research Questions
This paper sets forth a new technique for developing and simultaneously co-creating an ideation tool that employs simple, approachable, yet playfully inviting paper technology. In previous stages of our research, we invited university students, teachers, and artists to test and present their creations based on the Comicubes ideation tool, and these creations provided a starting point for concept creation and the construction of physical prototypes for playful uses. In this paper, we present a case study in which preschool-aged children were thought of as design partners and collaborated in the overall design process for an ideation tool, which is being constantly re-evaluated by

Figure 1: The original Comicubes toy-game hybrid is considered the point of departure for the design tool presented in this paper. It combines a two-dimensional serial image with a three-dimensional and therefore more open-ended toy medium: the cube. This format is well recognized in both play cultures and pedagogy through, for example, various blocks sets, like Froebel gifts. Playthings such as alphabet and puzzle blocks, construction toys, and brain teasers have been used successfully. In terms of games, the form is often associated with dice. Recently, the popularity of games like Minecraft have proven the sustainable attraction of the cube shape.

The Comicubes tool presents an ecologically sustainable, economically sound, and potentially more inclusive ideation tool than the more expensive plastic bricks often used as design tools. The advantage of cardboard cubes compared to many other materials used in prototyping is their capacity to be enhanced with various textural dimensions or layers of information, whether physical or digital.

the authors through testing with new user groups. In this way, the preschool-aged children, referred to in this paper as digital natives, contributed to the design knowledge regarding possible interaction contexts for the work-in-progress ideation tool. Consequently, the study also represents design research conducted with children, as it discusses the involvement of children in the design process as they co-developed understandings of the tool's conceptual and physical aspects. Interaction design focuses on user behavior. Thus, our study is interested in how the participants in our test groups interacted with the playful ideation tool and with other members of the test group to communicate about the ideas for play that they associated with their creations. On the one hand, we want to know how preschool-aged children co-create play-object-like prototypes using the ideation tool. On the other hand, we are interested in how the blank cardboard cubes invite them as users to design new playthings. In particular, through the workshops, we investigated the following interactions: 1) How do preschool-aged children, as digital natives, experience Comicubes as a tool that helps them create their own playful concepts? 2) What kind of playful elements or play patterns do preschool-aged children associate with their created playthings based on the tool? 3) How do the participants in this case study, as both digital natives and preschool-aged children, interact with their creations in both solitary and social contexts?

Comicubes: A Conceptual and Physical Ideation and Co-Creation Tool

The Comicubes tool is a tangible physical object that allows for three-dimensional manipulation. The tool affords various forms of interaction, depending on its users' age and skills. For instance, younger groups may use the tool as the basis for developing ideas around play, as explained in this paper, whereas designers, for example, can use the tool to explore, narrate, and build on conceptual ideas for products, brands, and services. Both physical and digital manipulatives can require bimanual and haptic interaction skills and the facilitation of spatial tasks [7]. Following Resnick and Silverman [8], tools that support creative thinking should "support exploration; have a low threshold, high ceiling and wide walls; support many paths and styles; support collaboration; support open interchange; make it as simple as possible; choose black boxes carefully; invent things that you would want to use yourself; balance user suggestions with observation and participatory processes; iterate; and design for designers." The Comicubes tool combines ideas associated with toys, games, and comic-style storytelling.[1] The cube format has longstanding roots in the history of play, and their simplicity, familiarity, and ease of use speak for cubes as play(ful) tools that stimulate design creativity and co-creation [9]. Ullmer and Ishii noted that this tangible format, which invites touch, also supports peer collaboration and facilitates communication [10]. Furthermore, it provides "multiple access points" [11]. When considering the potential of the cube format from an educational perspective, it is important to pay attention to its capacity to promote social interactions and active, engaged participation [12]. In our case studies, we discovered the potential of the Comicubes to afford prototyping beyond the context of toys, games, and hybrids, including both physical and digital elements, to play patterns in

[1] For reference, we have constructed an introductory video presentation about some of the hypothetical play patterns the Comicubes concept holds. See video clip: https://www.youtube.com/watch?v=sRGss4sVF-4.

Figures 2 and 3: Workshop setting at the kindergarten. The workshop began by having the children fold the paper cutouts into cardboard cubes.

Figure 4: Some workshop participants enhanced the cube's information layer by drawing with coloring pens.

relation to both open-ended toys ("sandbox games") and structured play concepts (rule-bound games). One of these prototypical ideas for use connects the ideation tool with service design. Regardless of Comicubes' capacity to function as a "phygital" device, meaning a hybrid artifact encompassing both material and digital components, this study is primarily interested in their capacity to function as a simple prototyping platform that invites young children to co-design ideas for object-based play.

Data and Method

Experimental design: Co-creating for interaction with preschool-aged children

Our research aims to explore children's creativity and co-creation capabilities. In the study, we tested the potential functionality of the Comicubes concept as an experimental point of origin for a plaything, or in other words, as a creative platform that fosters design thinking and allows for playful manipulation. First, we showed the participants existing versions of the prototype. Then, we allowed them to design their own playthings. In this way, we tested the concept's potential to function as a creative platform that fosters design thinking and allows for playful manipulation.

Participants and play testing

The ethnographic fieldwork that generated the empirical data for this article was carried out in 2016 in a Finnish kindergarten class that specialized in art education. Inspired by the new child research paradigm [13], which emphasizes research *with* children rather than *on* children [14], the study aimed to identify what constitutes an interesting plaything. In the workshops for (N=13) preschool-aged children (aged 6–7 years), participants were asked to create a plaything of their choice by applying various art supplies to blank cardboard cubes. The workshops began with an introductory segment in which the first author showed two ready-made Comicubes to the children and then asked them to design a plaything out of the given materials. The author guided the children in how to fold the cutouts and form a cube. There were two kindergarten supervisors present during each workshop segment to assist the children. During the 30-minute workshops, which were documented through recorded video and photography, each child created two individual Comicubes.[2]

The children were able to observe other participants' design process as they created their cubes. In addition to talking with the children, we also observed their actions and attitudes to access their perspectives on playing. As a result, our data collection methodology involves video ethnography, videotaped interviews and photographs. This data was used to involve the children in describing and interpreting their interactions with their creations and to gain a firsthand account of their perspectives.

In Group 1, all the children chose to use ready-made images in the form of leftover memo tiles donated by a board game manufacturer. In Group 2, some of the children picked up coloring pens and drew on the

[2] Most of the participants needed help from adults in assembling the cardboard cutouts into cubes. This indicates that introducing the intentional limitation of having each child design only two cubes each within the 30-minute workshop presented a suitable task.

Figure 5: The workshop invited the participants to take action and share ideas with each other.

Figure 6: The workshop enabled shared play experiences as the participants reflected upon the play patterns they associated with their individually created playthings.

Figures 7 and 8: After the creation phase of the workshop, the preschool-aged children were asked to demonstrate the play patterns they associated with the playthings they had created.

cubes. During the workshops, the participants were asked about the potential uses for their emerging playthings. Both groups made the connection between the cube and a familiar board game element: the dice. In fact, one child decided to make an actual dice out of one of the cubes. After the workshops concluded, each participant was taken to another room and interviewed about his or her design. Each child was asked to present his or her creation and demonstrate the potential uses for their design in a "show-and-tell" style. The children were also asked about what they found fun about the design process and what they considered difficult.[3] To get another perspective on how their creations could be used in play, each child was asked to present the plaything to another child in the group and demonstrate the play patterns they associated with it.

Results

In this study, we investigated how preschool-aged children, as digital natives, experienced Comicubes as a tool for creating their own playful concepts in a workshop setting. Based on our study's findings, the participants were easily enticed into a playful co-creation situation once they began to interact with the material. The participatory research process of working with young digital natives demonstrated that they are capable of understanding what designing for play with physical materials means in a group situation.

All participants were able to identify a play pattern for the two cubes they had created. The most frequently mentioned and demonstrated play patterns were throwing, rolling, rotating, and stacking the cubes.

We also noticed that the children, when verbalizing their discovered affordances of the cubes, began to discuss and mimic each other's interaction with the materials. Many participants made a connection between the cube's shape and a familiar element: the dice. One participant also informed us that the form was reminiscent of a familiar character from a digital game.[4] When interviewed after the active phase of the workshops, after the creations were ready, most children were able to demonstrate the play patterns they envisioned to the first author through verbal utterances. However, when showing another child the possible play patterns associated with their play objects, most of the children used more specific movements (see Figures 7 and 8) and thus took a more embodied approach.

The initial findings suggest that in a digital age where technology is ubiquitous, children are still drawn to creating physical three-dimensional play media and can communicate about the various play patterns associated with them. As participants in this case study, the preschool-aged children were able to observe each other's work and exchange ideas while prototyping. When the creation period for their play concepts came to an end, the children were encouraged to communicate about their creations' potential play affordances by illustrating their interactions with their playthings. The information layer most children used in creating their cubes, that is, the ready-made images, was considered an important part of the created play concepts.[5]

[3] For reference, see video clip: https://www.youtube.com/watch?v=0iqSCB_S-S4.

[4] For reference, see video clip: https://www.youtube.com/watch?v=mzep7ZuCKUE.

[5] For reference, see video clip:

Limitations and Future Research

The participants' level of digital exposure was not measured in this study. In future research, it would be interesting to explore possible differences between preschoolers who have had great access versus limited exposure to digital technologies. In this study, the participants were asked about whether or not the cube format reminded them of any games or toys they had played with before, without specifying either physical or digital games or toys. One child noted that the shape was reminiscent of a game character with a cube-shaped head and body.

We believe that the preschoolers in our study will be exposed to a significant amount of digital technologies once they enter the school system following their early kindergarten education. Consequently, we find it important to emphasize exposure to creative physical materials that can be transformed into three-dimensional objects.

Nevertheless, as printing technologies develop, it becomes more and more probable that even mundane materials such as paper will provide access points to digital worlds. It is the hybrid potentialities that exist between the two-dimensional and the three-dimensional and between the material and digital that present interesting possibilities for both the design and user experiences of 21st century playthings.

The participants who chose to attach ready-made images to their cubes put time into deciding which pictures (e.g., numbers or animals) to use. These decisions were often coupled with brief narratives on favorite animals or, for instance, the traffic sign system as a part of their created play concept. The children who decided to enhance their cubes in other ways were more inclined to put their cubes in motion by throwing or rolling them without giving detailed descriptions of their play concepts. In terms of further research, it would be interesting to explore how the design process might advance if the ready-made visual elements were not available to the children. Furthermore, and perhaps surprisingly, in addition to their capacity to invite to play, some of the children highlighted in their comments the educational value of the cubes they had created.[6] This participatory design task can be carried out with other types of participant constellations, for example, adult-child pairs, children working in pairs, etc. This would allow researchers to capture the thought processes behind the prototyped designs in greater detail.

Discussion and Conclusion

We propose that the Comicubes concept has the potential to function not only as a physical, playful platform that invites users to design and co-create toys and games, but also as a conceptual tool that may be used as an easy-to-use, ecologically sustainable, economically sound, and therefore inclusive ideation tool in interaction design, as it facilitates communication between designers, test participants, and interaction design researchers in many ways. To conclude, the cardboard Comicubes concept can be applied to many different target groups and used in place of more expensive tools, such as Legos, that have been used in interaction design. One important benefit of the cardboard cubes is that they provide endless opportunities for both toying in terms of spatial play and constructing. Perhaps even more important is the potential for information to be presented in many ways, including the use of traditional methods; images, words, numbers, and combinations thereof; and a technologically enhanced information layer. As previously described, the inviting, play(ful) qualities of the cardboard cubes present a simple, customizable interface and a never-ending potential to be enhanced with different elements (both material and digital) in terms of its information layer. Possible avenues for future research include further testing with children incorporating the use of hybrid elements on the cardboard cubes, for example, in exploring new printing technologies. Another possible direction is to investigate in greater detail how the physical, play(ful) ideation tool can be implemented in the context of service design, for example, by involving children in the ideation and co-creation of services targeted to them, including both entertainment and educational services.

https://www.youtube.com/watch?v=bMEIMKL-fdc.

[6] For reference, see video clip: https://www.youtube.com/watch?v=owsGJRcdt_w.

Acknowledgments

This study has been partially funded by the Academy of Finland and Tekes: The Finnish Funding Agency for Innovation. It is part of the Ludification and the Emergence of Playful Culture (276012) and Hybrid Social Play (2600360411) research projects. The authors would like to thank the children and the Kuvataidepäiväkoti Viikari staff who participated in the study.

References

1. Katriina Heljakka and Pirita Ihamäki. 2016. Comicubes – a playful tool to stimulate design creativity. In *Proceedings of the 10th International Conference on Design & Emotion* (AMS'16), 387-394.
2. Marc Prensky. 2005. Digital Natives: How They Think Differently. Retrieved May 3, 2017 from http://coe.sdsu.edu/eet/articles/digitalnatives//start.htm
3. Robyn Zenvenbergen. 2007. Digital natives come to preschool: Implications for early childhood practice. *Contemporary Issues in Early Childhood* 8, 1: 19-29.
4. Pilar Lacasa, María Ruth García-Pernía, and Sara Cortés. 2015. Creative collaboration in young digital communities. In *Creativity in the Digital Age*, Nelson Zagalo and Pedro Branco (eds.). Springer-Verlag, London, UK, 135-157.
5. Katriina Heljakka. 2013. *Principles of Adult Play(fulness) in Contemporary Toy Cultures. From Wow to Flow to Glow.* Doctoral dissertation. Aalto University, Helsinki, Finland.
6. Katriina Heljakka. 2012. Hybridisyys ja pelillistyminen leikkituotteissa De-materiaalisen ja re-materiaalisen rajankäyntiä [Hybridity and gamification in playthings – on the cross roads of de-materialisation and re-materialisation]. In *Pelitutkimuksen vuosikirja*, J. Suominen, Raine Koskimaa, Frans Mäyrä, and Riikka Turtiainen (eds.). Tampereen yliopisto, Finland, 82-91.
7. Bieke Zaman, Vero Vanden Abeele, Panos Markopoulos, and Paul Marshall. 2012. Editorial: The evolving field of tangible interaction the challenge of empirical validation. *Personal and Ubiquitous Computing* 16:4, 367-378.
8. Mitchel Resnick and Brian Silverman. 2005. Some reflections on designing construction kits for kids. In *Proceedings of Interaction Design and Children Conference*. ACM Press, New York, NY, 117-122.
9. Alissa N. Antle, Alyssa F. Wise, and Kristine Nielsen. 2011. Towards utopia: designing tangibles for learning. In *Proceedings of the International Conference on Interaction Design and Children*. ACM Press, New York, NY, 1-20.
10. Brygg Ullmer and Hiroshi Ishii. 2001. Emerging frameworks for tangible user interfaces. In *Human-Computer Interaction in the New Millennium*, John M. Carroll (ed.). Addison-Wesley, Boston, MA, 579-601.
11. Eva Hornecker. 2005. A design theme for tangible interaction: embodied facilitation. In *Proceedings of the Ninth European Conference on Computer-Supported Cooperative Work*, Hans-Werner Gellersen, Kjeld Schmidt, Michel Beaudoin-Lafon, and Wendy E. Mackay (eds.). Springer International Publishing, Cham, Switzerland, 23-22.
12. Sarah Eagle. 2012. Learning in the early years: Social interactions around picture books, puzzles and digital technologies. *Computers & Education* 59, Issue: 1, 38-49.
13. Alison James, Chris Jenks, and Alan Prout (eds.). 1998. *Theorising Childhood*. Polity Press, Cambridge, MA.
14. Pia Christensen and Allison James (eds.). 2000. *Research with Children. Perspectives and Practices.* Falmer Press, London, UK.

Digital Fabrication as a Tool for Teaching High-School Students STEM at the University

Covadonga Lorenzo
CEU University
Madrid, 28925, Madrid (Spain)
clorenzo@ceu.es

IDC '17, June 27-30, 2017, Stanford, CA, USA

ACM ISBN 978-1-4503-4921-5/17/06.
http://dx.doi.org/10.1145/3078072.3084323.

Abstract
In the current paper is documented an ongoing education program designed at FabLab Madrid CEU (the Digital Fabrication Laboratory based at CEU University´s Institute of Technology) to teach high-school students STEM in a university environment through digital fabrication technologies. Inspired by the ideas of Neil Gershenfeld and Paulo Blikstein, we are using digital fabrication as a learning tool through which we attempt to create a working educational environment to improve the motivation of the students to finish their pre-college studies and to start a career at the university. All the pedagogies that we are exploring though the programs are based on Seymour Papert concepts related to the use of technology as a building material, the need of a 'learning by doing' approach, the importance of learning to learn to keep learning or the benefits of enjoying while learning.

Author Keywords
FabLab; education; design; fabrication, high-school students; university.

ACM Classification Keywords
D.2.2 Design Tools and Techniques.

Figure 1-4. High-School students working on a model of Oiza's BBVA Building.

Introduction

Four years ago, I founded FabLab Madrid CEU, the Digital Fabrication Laboratory at Madrid-based CEU University's Institute of Technology where I was working as an Associate Professor at the Department of Architecture and Design. The FabLab was created to allow Architecture and Engineering students to improve their skills on digital fabrication thanks to the use of next generation technologies and advanced technological languages. Our university is run by the CEU Foundation, devoted for the development of education and along with our university it runs Barcelona and Valencia-based CEU universities and a great number of high-schools throughout Spain. Due to our link with the Foundation it was usual for us to receive groups of high-school students at our facilities several times a year.

During the guided visits that I was conducting, I became to realize that high-school students were amazed by the projects that we developed and the machines that we used, and that they were willing to participate at the workshops that we offered to our university students. Besides, their teachers were completely surprised with the interest that students seem to show, because as they told me, it was difficult for them to keep their attention and motivation on a conventional work session.

It was then when we thought that it could be a good idea to involve high-school students in some activities developed at the FabLab to motivate them in their current studies and make them see the relevance of what they were learning at their high-schools for their future university careers.

Background

As any FabLab (fabrication laboratory) of the FabLab network, we are a small-scale workshop that has been offering personal digital fabrication in our facilities during the last four years inspired by the ideas of Neil Gershenfeld. [1] We are equipped with an array of flexible computer-controlled tools that cover several different length scales and various materials, with the aim to 'make almost anything'. [2] As the design of this new high-school student program involved expanding the profile of our users to teenagers, I looked for some guidance that helps me to succeed on this ambitious endeavor. I found out the work of Paulo Blikstein related to digital fabrication and education [3], which led me to the understanding of digital fabrication as a learning tool through which I could attempt to create a working educational environment that improve high-school students' motivation showing them practical applications of the theoretical concepts that they were acquiring at their high-schools.

Besides, some of the pedagogies that I was trying to explore and implement were inspired by some of Seymour Papert's ideas which I discovered during a research that I conducted while writing my doctoral thesis. I tried to implement concepts as the use of technology as a building material, the need of 'learning by doing' approach, the importance of learning to learn (to keep learning) or the benefits of enjoying while learning. In fact, some researchers have credit him as the "father of the maker movement" [4] even defining constructionism as "learning by constructing knowledge through the act of making something shareable".[5] Other studies suggested that integrating mathematics, science, and engineering "in a highly motivating task that makes use of digital fabrication, could facilitate

Figure 5-8. High-School students working on a model of Oiza's BBVA Building.

learning, developmental skills, and student engagement". [6] They even affirmed that engineering design could be used as an interesting teaching pedagogy for developing mathematics content while implementing tools for digital fabrication. And more recently, another group of researchers studied the use of digital fabrication and ¨making¨ to produce methodological change in teaching practice in schools. [7] They found out, among other things that all through the process of designing and producing each project, the students developed their critical thinking skills and had an impact in their self-esteem offering them an alternative way to deal with problems and making decisions.

Methods

"I fell in love with the idea that a technologically rich environment could give to children who love ideas access to learning-rich idea work, and to those who love ideas less, the opportunity to learn to love them more". [8] The idea of running a program with high-school students at the university facilities came from this Papert statement, in which he highlighted the importance for students motivation of creating a technologically rich environment that offer them direct access to what he defined as 'learning idea work', a new concept that prioritize ideas over skills or knowledge.

Thinking about this, I began to realize the potential of the FabLab environment and the digital fabrication tools to change the student's misconception that learning is related to acquire knowledge and skills, to a new definition of learning that involves materializing their own ideas thanks to the use of new programming languages and technologies.

In order to design a successful program aligned with all this previous studies but including also the involvement of high-school students in a university environment, their participation in projects to develop in cooperation with university professors and college students and the fabrication of designs that explain, not the theoretical concepts learned at the high-school but the application of this principles into a professional career, I implemented a case-study design that included a two-week summer program in which teens, program supervisors and instructors worked together to develop a short intensive project similar to a first-year graduate school project with group discussions and reviews, training sessions in graphics and digital fabrication skills and direct access to the FabLab.

Participants

The summer program was designed for those high-school students that were finishing up their junior year of high school and were thinking about their future, in order to motivate them to finish their studies and explore the possibilities of studying a career at the university. The youth are between the ages of 15 and 18 and included both genders. Each year the number of student goes from 15 to 20. Our design team included one program supervisor, in charge of tracking the progress of the teens; ten university professors, in charge of the theoretical classes and finally, a laboratory technician and two college students that participated as FabLab Instructors.

Procedures

Due to my background as an Architect, the program has been created as a two-week program to introduce them to a career in the design and building professions. The idea was to take advantage of the university

Figure 9-12. High-School students working on a model of Madrid Rio facilities.

facilities and the city of Madrid, both understood as a kind of dynamic laboratory of architectural speculation. To that end, the program included instruction in freehand sketching, model-making and a short introduction to digital representation as well as a field trip to a Madrid's architectural landmark, and concluded with an exhibition of the student works and a reception for students and their families. Each year we are exploring a new architectural landmark, so that students can learn from the previous ones but at the same time, explore their own ideas to represent and fabricate a new model without seen previously a possible solution. We have worked on the BBAA Building by Javier Saénz de Oiza; Atocha Train Station, by Rafael Moneo and some facilities at Madrid Río.

The first approach to the architectural landmark involves a guided visit in order to encourage students to explore the building through freehand sketches and pictures that allow them, in a later session to use computer aided design to create a 3D model, some technical documentation (as plans, sections and elevations) and finally, a scaled model using CNC and laser cutter machines. Along the way they are requested to explain their way to approach to each assignment and to discuss it with the faculty and classmates but each day they have to end the session with a final drawing or a final prototype (not only ideas) to share with the group.

Data analysis

The analysis of the design sessions is being developed in five phases. After each session, the program supervisor (that attended the sessions to take notes, pictures and video data), meet with professors and instructors involved on this specific session to interview them and review the work developed by the students (drawings, notes, models, etc). Later on, using video data, photographs, and field notes the program supervisor wrote a account of each session to describe the progress and evaluate the results. At the end of the summer program there is an exhibition of the work developed by students where the program supervisor met again with all the instructors and students as well as their families that attend the event. There, the supervisor talks with students and families to collect video data of some interviews. Then a paper is written to be discussed in a congress to test previous results in order to add this information on the design of the next year course. Finally, we are now analyzing the findings on the previous years in order to see the evolution of the students during this program.

Findings

Based on the previous data analysis we have find some results although we are still working on a more in depth data analysis. As from the beginning of the summer course students have to hand-in at the end of each session a sketch or model of what they have been working on, we have realized that on the first sessions the results are not often what they expect but that make them realize how far are the perfect ideas that they have in their minds of their physical materialization, and consequently how important is to find enough time to bring these ideas to life. As soon as they realize that a prototype should be finished at the end of each session adding improvements to the previous ones, they work more focused on their tasks. And as quickly as they have something made by them in their hands, they are more motivated to keep working and transforming these first prototypes to get a more accurate final architectural model. This

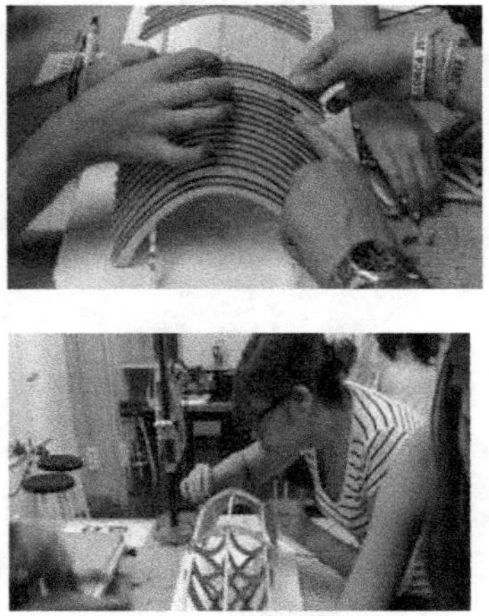

Figure 13-14. High-School students working on a model of Madrid Rio facilities.

Figure 15-16. Interview with High-School students.

approach to fabrication though a spiral design process that allows them to work over previous prototypes is something that I learned from Neil Gershenfeld but also from John Dewey studies. [8] Thanks to that students gain experience through repetition and as the level of detail increase, they are more motivated to find additional ideas.

One of the most extraordinary transformations that I have seen on them is the self-confidence they gain during the program, possibly, due to the fact that they become autonomous on their learning experience working hand by hand with their classmates and instructors during the workshops. In fact, many of them came to the program thinking that they were going to be taught by professors and took them some time to understand that they had to take charge of their own learning, for example, discussing with their classmates and instructors the best way to fabricate their designs. As soon as they understand that they are in charge of their projects and that the accurateness of the drawings and models that they develop is related to the implementation of their ideas, they start to get involved in all the decisions defining a unique learning experience. This idea of learning while finding the way to learn is implicit in some Papert's articles, [9] in which he emphasizes how crucial is for the success of the students and for their future lives to find by themselves the way to learn how to learn.

In the book Mindstorms [10] Papert found out that one important difficulty in mathematics education was the social construction of math in our culture as an alienated thing. The use of Logo and the computer allowed students to learn and integrate math in their everyday life. What I tried to explore in this program was the use of digital fabrication in the same way that Papert used Logo. The idea was to take advantage of the interest that students might find out in building an architectural model to make math and physic for them useful for the design. To that end, the workshop required an introduction to teach some concepts related to physics and math to solve problems related to the geometry of each part as for example, how to slice the model into smaller parts that should be later assembled or how to use measurement tools and Boolean operations to work in a 3D design environment. As incredible as it seems, finding out that math and physic were useful for solving everyday life problems was a revelation for some of the students.

Another idea that interested me was extracted from Papert's article Teaching Children Thinking [11]. Here, Papert suggests that on a good learning environment the child should be in charge of the technology, not the technology in charge of the child, offering what was a new image of children using computers as tools for creativity. We tried to transfer this idea of 'teaching thinking' to the program giving the students the possibility to use the FabLab machines by themselves helped by an instructor. In our opinion, the fact that they wanted to materialize an idea with a technology that has some limitations on size, lengths, widths or materials among other things, took them to think about new ways to experiment with the technology in order to get the result they were expecting.

Conclusions

As the education program presented at this paper is an ongoing program we have to keep working on the data analysis to get to a conclusion but the first results based on a general data analysis seems to prove that

Figure 17. High-School students' final exhibition.

Figure 18-20. Interview with High-School students.

the program increase the motivation of the students on STEM courses as a complement of the formal education provided by the high-schools. It seems that the program achieve the objective of encouraging students to enjoy technology and make it part of their future life as some of the students are now enrolled in our degree programs at the university. So it seems that the succeed on the program implementation confirms the potential of digital fabrication to be used as learning tool, through which it is possible to create a working educational environment to show high-school students practical applications of the theoretical concepts that they are acquiring during pre-university studies guiding them to the university studies thanks to their involvement in a university environment and their participation in projects in cooperation with university professors and college students. And finally, they seems to validate the ideas of Seymour Papert related to the use of technology as a building material, the need of a learning by doing approach, the importance of learning to learn (to keep learning) or the benefits of enjoying while learning but in this case applied to the fabrication of designs that explain, not the theoretical concepts learned at the high-school but the application of this principles into a professional career.

Acknowledgements

Our thanks to high-school students and instructors involved on the high-school programs that run at FabLab Madrid CEU for the materials and the images used in this paper.

References

1.Neil Gershenfeld. 2005. *Fab. The Coming Revolution on your Desktop*. Basic Books, New York.

2.Neil Gershenfeld. 2012. "How to Make Almost Anything. The Digital Fabrication Revolution". *Foreign Affairs*, 91/ 6, Council in Foreign Relations, New York.

3.Paulo Blikstein. 2013. *Digital Fabrication and 'Making' in Education: The Democratization of Invention. In FabLabs.* J. Walter-Herrmann & C. Büching (Eds.), Bielefeld: Transcript Publishers.

4.Halverson, E. R., & Sheridan, K. 2014. *The maker movement in education*. Harvard Educational Review, 84(4).

5.S. L. Martinez & G. S. Stager 2013. *Invent to learn: Making, tinkering, and engineering in the classroom.* Constructing modern knowledge Press.

6.R. Q. Berry, G. Bull, C. Browning, C. D. Thomas, G. Starkweather & J. Aylor. 2010. *Use of digital fabrication to incorporate engineering design principles in elementary mathematics education.* Contemporary Issues in Technology and Teacher Education, 10(2).

7.S. Tesconi S. & L. Arias. 2014. *Making as a Tool to Competence-based School Programming*. Fab Learn Conference Paper, Online resource. Retrieved January 2017 from: http://fablearn.eu/2014/wp-content/uploads/fablearn14_submission_161.pdf

8. Seymour Papert. 2000. *What's the big idea? Toward a pedagogy of idea power*. IBM Systems Journal, v. 39.

9. Jon Ord. 2012. John Dewey and Experiential Learning: Developing the theory of youth work. *Youth & Policy* 108

10. Seymour Papert. 1980. *Mindstorms: Children, Computers, and Powerful Ideas*. Basic Books, New York.

11. Seymour Papert. 2005. Teaching Children Thinking. Contemporary Issues in Technology and Teacher Education, 5(3). Association for the Advancement of Computing in Education (AACE).

Interactive fiction: Weaving together literacies of text and code

Chris Proctor
Paulo Blikstein
Stanford University
Stanford, CA 94305
cproctor@stanford.edu
paulob@stanford.edu

IDC '17, June 27-30, 2017, Stanford, CA, USA
ACM 978-1-4503-4921-5/17/06.
http://dx.doi.org/10.1145/3078072.3084324

Abstract

We propose structural parallels between textual literacy and computational literacy, and explore interactive fiction as a medium at their intersection. We designed and built a web application allowing students to read and write interactive fiction and a curriculum weaving the two literacies together. A study evaluating the curriculum found modest adoption of literacy practices from each domain. Our qualitative observations suggest a mechanism for how each literacy can support the other: incorporating computation into English/Language Arts makes it possible for students to model linguistic processes which are otherwise ephemeral. In the other direction, situating Computer Science concepts in students' identities and experiences can make them personally meaningful and address inequities in STEM education. A third study, underway, will quantify the extent to which one literacy supports growth in the other.

Author Keywords

Computational literacy; computer science education; sociocultural learning theory; sociolinguistics

ACM Classification Keywords

H.5.m [Information interfaces and presentation (HCI)]: Miscellaneous

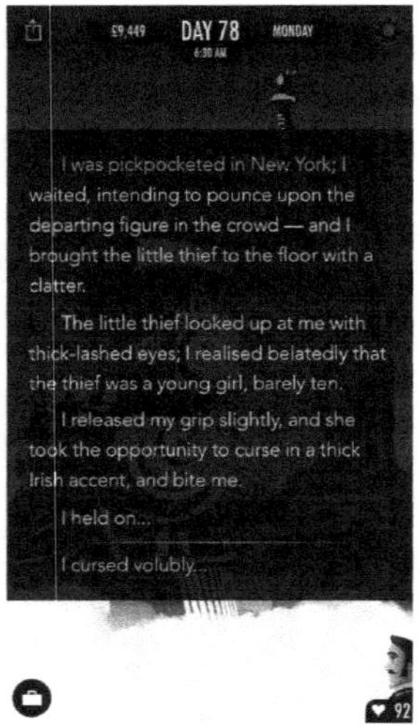

Figure 1: Inkle's *80 Days*

Figure 2: Nicky Case's *Coming Out Simulator*

Introduction

We propose structural parallels between the literacy communities that form in progressive secondary English/Language Arts classrooms and those which might come to exist in Computer Science classrooms. Based on these parallels, we explore opportunities for mutual cooperation between the development of textual literacy and the development of computational literacy. Pedagogy from English/Language Arts, particularly that which emphasizes personal meaning-making through engagement with text, might also be effective in teaching Computer Science. In the other direction, Computer Science could support students' learning in English/Language Arts by making visible the subtle transactions that comprise participation in a literacy community. These questions have substantial implications for equity in learning opportunities: students could draw on one literacy in which they are competent to develop the other. Computational literacy could provide an additional route toward textual literacy for students such as English language learners. In the other direction, textual literacy could support the development of computational literacy for students who are oppressed by stereotypes excluding them from STEM fields. We used a sequence of three design-based experiments [5] to test these hypotheses.

Study 1 explored the pedagogical feasibility of using interactive fiction to concurrently approach Computer Science and English/Langauge arts as literacies, and sought qualitative evidence of students recruiting one literacy to support development in the other.

Study 2 evaluated the extent to which students working with an interactive fiction curriculum adopted literacy practices from textual and computational literacy.

Study 3, underway, measures the support one literacy provides the other by assessing growth in each literacy when the curriculum is used by three groups: students already strong in tetxual literacy, students already strong in computational literacy, and a control group.

Background

The structure of literacy

Our hypotheses are grounded in a recognition of structural similarities between the practices of writers and computer scientists. diSessa [7] offers a three-part definition of literacy as engagement with an external medium (text or code), cognition afforded by the medium, and social interaction grounded in the niches and genres of a literacy community. Textual literacy–learning to read and write, the accompanying cognitive changes [12], and literacy-based social roles [11]–is a central concern of progressive English/Language Arts pedagogy [6]. Computer Science has important cognitive [18] and social [16] aspects, and recent curricular frameworks explicitly model the discipline as a literacy [1]. In exploring how these literacies might support one another, we draw on Papert's [13] observation that constructionist learning environments, in which students can see the shared product of their work and the tools they are using, are particularly effective for constructing new understandings.

Interactive fiction

The theorized structural similarities between textual and computational literacy, suggest the two literacies might interact, particularly in formal educational settings where parallel pedagogical strategies could emerge. In k-12 schools in the United States, textual literacy is a central cross-disciplinary concern, while Computer Science is just beginning to be a widespread academic subject. We saw one possibility in interactive fiction, a form of computational storytelling at the boundary of text and code, belonging in both English class and in Computer Science. The experience of reading and

```
=== waking ===
My eyes flickered open
into warm sunlight. I
found myself on a beach.
* A dream, I thought.
    -> dream
* I willed away the
  memories.
-> denial
=== dream ===
But what dream had ever
felt so real? I was
sure I could feel a
crust of salt in my hair.
* It was too much.
    -> denial
* It all came flooding
  back to me.
    -> onward
=== denial ===
I resolved not to think
of the past. Yet the
words of the prophecy
haunted me.
* That was just a story.
    -> denial
* No matter. What's done
  is done, even if it
  happened in a dream.
-> onward
=== onward ===
... to be continued ...
  -> END
```

Figure 3: The Ink language

writing interactive fiction is fundamentally similar to that of prose; at the same time, interactive fiction has affordances for four of the seven concepts Brennan & Resnick [4] identify as core concepts in computational thinking: sequences, loops, conditionals, and data. (The other three core concepts, events, parallelism and operators, are not inherently present in the structure of narrative.)

Several recent interactive fiction games demonstrate the medium's potential. In *80 Days* (Figure 1), the player/reader inhabits the role of Passepartout, valet to a wealthy Englishman who is attempting to circumnavigate a counterfactual 19th century world. In choosing how the story should unfold, the player/reader may have different experiences depending on the extent to which she decides to explore beyond the bubble formed by her employer's casually racist, sexist, and elitist attitudes. When staying overnight in a city, the player is presented with the choice of playing it safe by staying in, or exploring the city by night. If the player goes out at night, Passrepartout might end up hearing a fisherman's story of losing his wife, having to decide whether to lie to protect a thief from harsh punishment, or allowing himself to be seduced. In these ways, *80 Days* functions as a microworld [13] in which the player can discover how richly expansive or foreclosed the world (and one's identity) can be.

Nicky Case's *Coming Out Simulator* (Figure 2), an autobiographical "half-true story about half-truths," powerfully demonstrates the capability of interactive fiction to model how linguistic processes produce our social reality and shape how we can act within them [10]. The game replays the evening during the author's teenage years when he told his parents (or, perhaps, they found out) that he is bisexual. The interface mimics that of a mobile phone, superimposing text message speech bubbles over animation and presenting the player with dialogue options. In the prologue, the game emphasizes that all the characters remember and respond to everything the player does. As the protagonist struggles to come out to his parents, they are equally committed to preserving their image of him by silencing his attempt at self-redefinition. The game is ultimately about negotiating what it means to be male and to be a good son within a cultural context. It is played through speech acts which position oneself with respect to pre-existing "figures of personhood," [2] or (in the parents' case) by preventing action by insisting on categories which fix one's identity.

Both *80 Days* and *Coming Out Simulator* illustrate the potential of interactive fiction as a medium which engages with both textual and computational literacy. Studying language, identity, and culture within a computational environment could make it possible to simulate, replay, and share these otherwise-elusive phenomena. Studying computational thinking in the context of questions usually addressed by literature might imbue an otherwise abstract and impersonal field with profound personal significance.

Inkle, the studio which created *80 Days*, released an open-source version of their internal scripting language called Ink in early 2016. Ink is designed to feel like writing prose while incorporating control structures, variables, and functions. Figure 3 shows a short story written in Ink.

Methods

In **Study 1**, we developed a web-based environment for reading and writing interactive fiction using the Ink language. We introduced this tool in a weeklong workshop (3 hours per day) with twelve students at an all-girls middle school. The loosely-structured format was modeled on writer's workshop [8]; students spent most of their time working on their own stories with occasional short craft

Quest
Bring in three objects which tell an important story about you. Then build an explorable world in which the player can find these objects.
Perspective
Think of an event in which each participant had a different experience. Write this story in several anecdotes, allowing the player to change perspective between each.
Conversation
Think of a conversation where something important was said or went unsaid. Write this conversation in all the possible ways it could have gone.

Table 1: Outline of our interactive fiction curriculum

lessons targeting writing skills such as incorporating dialogue, and developing character, as well as computational thinking skills such as as conditional branching and using directed graphs to plan stories. We took fieldnotes, logged interactions with the authoring environment, analyzed students' stories, and asked students to write daily reflections.

In **Study 2**, we developed a curriculum (Table 1) based around writing and programming discourses [9] and evaluated its efficacy in eliciting writing and programming practices in students' stories. This study was embedded within a two-week summer program designed to build community amongst students receiving scholarships to a private all-girls middle school. We worked with 16 incoming 6th-graders, all bilingual speakers of Spanish and English. We used a writer's workshop format, though we devoted much of the first week to introducing the narrative and computational elements of interactive fiction through three small projects. We analyzed fieldnotes, students' reflections, and students' stories.

In **Study 3**, we use our interactive fiction curriculum to compare growth in each literacy between students who have expertise in the other literacy and a control group. We used our curriculum in three different classrooms for a two-week workshop. Our measures include self-reported skill level in each literacy, analysis of students' stories, and a post-test in which students suggest revisions to an existing story [17]. We hope to use fieldnotes and artifact analysis to argue for a mechanism by which textual and computational literacies support each others' development.

Results

In **Study 1** we collected discourses students reported in their daily reflections and grouped them into those we recognize as writing, programming, and shared (Table 2). After

Writing discourses	
Freewriting	"I just like to write it out"
Dialogical interaction	"I was relating A LOT to my imaginary friends"
Sensory detail	"I also practiced writing in ways that made the reader visualize what was happening"
Programming discourses	
Testing	"I love to test out parts of my story when I do it"
Tinkering	"try doing things"
Commenting	"I wrote notes for myself using comments"
Overlapping discourses	
Planning	"I someimes spend time thinking about what will happen before writing it."
Working incrementally	"I wrote up certain parts of my story to outline how i was doing to continue it and i brainstormed twists."
Modeling experience	"I thought about how I really like it when books have unexpected twists in them. I often like it when its about identity, so i created the twist where one of the generic other prisoners turned out to be the girls brother."
Considering audience	"I have been thinking about questions in my story if people ever thought of them."
Revision	"I've been re-writing a story I wrote a long time ago into 1st person."

Table 2: Discourses identified in students' reflections (**Study 1**)

Writing practices	
Story built around dialogue	39%
Story based on personal experience	37%
Story navigates physical space	31%
Plot based on a quest	28%
Story simulates perspective	15%
Story simulates self-presentation	11%
Programming practices	
Story branches into options	81%
Story includes cyclical structure	19%
Story uses lists to cycle content	13%
Story uses variables	7%
Story models a system	6%

Table 3: Practices identified in students' stories (**Study 2**)

working with the interactive fiction curriculum in **Study 2**, students wrote an average of 3.4 stories (SD=1.2). We analyzed these stories for specific practices we associated with writing and programming (Table 3).

Analysis

The discourses described in Table 2 show students engaging with interactive fiction as both text/narrative and code/algorithm. For example, when one student wrote, "I thought about how I really like it when books have unexpected twists in them. I often like it when its about identity, so i created the twist where one of the generic other prisoners turned out to be the girls brother," she explicated a complex process of drawing on her own experience as a reader to imagine her audience, and then composing her story to have a particular effect on her imagined audience. Here, the discourses of writing and programming serve as resources for one another. Because the story is interactive, the student is able to concretely model the moment when the reader chooses an option, the story advances, and the reader is shocked by the plot twist. Helping students learn that reading is an active, interpretive process [3, 15] rather than one of passive uptake is a central goal of English/Language Arts, made particularly challenging because the student cannot observe the practices adopted by the expert reader. In this case, the interactive fiction here serves as an observable simulation [13, 14] of the metacognitive reading process.

Sophisticated writing practices were widespread in students' stories. Students also made frequent use of computational thinking by writing stories that branched into different options, though few went beyond basic usage. Nevertheless, students found the computational thinking concepts interesting and generative. One student wrote, "The language seemed very difficult to me at the beginning of this week but by the end I feel like I can write a million more stories with this language."

Conclusions

This paper proposes parallels between textual and computational literacy. **Studies 1 and 2** demonstrate the pedagogical utility of interactive fiction as a medium engaging both literacies. **Study 3** tests the hypothesis that each literacy can support development in the other. Bridging two literacies has the potential to support educational equity: students could draw on one literacy in which they are competent to develop the other. Computational literacy could provide an additional route toward textual literacy for students such as English language learners. In the other direction, textual literacy could support the development of computational literacy for students who are oppressed by stereotypes excluding them from STEM fields.

Acknowledgements
We are grateful to the teachers and students who made these studies possible. This research was supported by sponsors of the Transformative Learning Technologies Lab, including the Lemann Center for Educational Entrepreneurship and Innovation in Brazil and MediaX, and by TELOS, an initiative supporting technology for equity in learning opportunities.

REFERENCES
1. 2016. K-12 Computer Science Framework. (2016). `http://www.k12cs.org`
2. Asif Agha. 2005. Voice, footing, enregisterment. *Journal of linguistic anthropology* 15, 1 (2005), 38–59.
3. Sheridan Blau. 2003. Performative literacy: The habits of mind of highly literate readers. *Voices from the Middle* 10, 3 (2003), 18–22.
4. Karen Brennan and Mitchel Resnick. 2012. New frameworks for studying and assessing the development of computational thinking. In *Proceedings of the 2012 annual meeting of the American Educational Research Association, Vancouver, Canada*. 1–25.
5. Allan Collins, Diana Joseph, and Katerine Bielaczyc. 2004. Design research: Theoretical and methodological issues. *The Journal of the learning sciences* 13, 1 (2004), 15–42.
6. Harvey Daniels. 2002. *Literature circles: Voice and choice in book clubs and reading groups*. Stenhouse Publishers.
7. Andrea A DiSessa. 2001. *Changing minds: Computers, learning, and literacy*. Mit Press.
8. Linda J Dorn and Carla Soffos. 2001. *Scaffolding young writers: A writer's workshop approach*. Stenhouse Publishers.
9. James Paul Gee. 2005. The new literacy studies and the 'social turn'. *Situated literacies: Reading and writing in context* 2 (2005), 177–194.
10. Erving Goffman. 1978. *The presentation of self in everyday life*. Harmondsworth.
11. Glynda Hull and James Greeno. 2006. Identity and agency in nonschool and school worlds. *Counterpoints* 249 (2006), 77–97.
12. Walter J Ong. 1982. *Orality and literacy*. Routledge.
13. Seymour Papert. 1980. *Mindstorms: Children, computers, and powerful ideas*. Basic Books, Inc.
14. Ron Ritchhart, Mark Church, and Karin Morrison. 2011. *Making thinking visible: How to promote engagement, understanding, and independence for all learners*. John Wiley & Sons.
15. Louise M. Rosenblatt. 1968. *Literature as Exploration*. The Modern Language Association.
16. Annette Vee. 2013. Understanding computer programming as a literacy. *Literacy in Composition Studies* 1, 2 (2013), 42–64.
17. Linda Werner, Jill Denner, Shannon Campe, and Damon Chizuru Kawamoto. 2012. The fairy performance assessment: measuring computational thinking in middle school. In *Proceedings of the 43rd ACM technical symposium on Computer Science Education*. ACM, 215–220.
18. Jeannette M Wing. 2006. Computational thinking. *Commun. ACM* 49, 3 (2006), 33–35.

Investigating an Intervention System to Increase User Engagements on an Educational Social Q&A

Erik Choi
Brainly
New York, NY 10002, USA
erik.choi@brainly.com

Tomasz Sienkiewicz
Brainly
New York, NY 10002, USA
Tomasz.sienkiewicz@brainly.com

Chad Coleman
Teachers College
Columbia University
New York, NY
cjc2238@tc.columbia.edu

Karolina Wojcik
Brainly
New York, NY 10002, USA
Karolina.wojcik@brainly.com

IDC '17, June 27–30, 2017, Stanford, CA, USA.

ACM ISBN 978-1-4503-4921-5/17/06.
http://dx.doi.org/10.1145/3078072.3084325

Abstract
We present preliminary results of investigating an intervention system to increase user engagements in learning on educational social Q&A. Through the experimental procedure with 600 Brainly (social Q&A platform for learning) users, the study shows that interventions through a formative message have a significant effect on user behaviors and engagements in learning on educational social Q&A services.

Author Keywords
Social Q&A; Online learning; Learning analytics; Formative feedback; Intervention

ACM Classification Keywords
H.3.5. Online Information Services

Introduction
The proliferation of Internet technologies in educational environments has reshaped information-seeking behavior. Online learning, defined as "the use of computer network technology, primarily over an intranet or through the internet, to deliver information and instruction to individuals" ([16], p.246), has become a favored method to optimize learning experiences through drastically expanding users' abilities to access online information and

Category	**Description**
Inquiry Participation	*Total number of questions posted by the user.*
	Total number of questions answers by the user.
	Ratio of questions posted and questions answered.
	Total number of subject categories the user has interacted with.
	Total number of times the user has received "Best Answer."
	Ratio of answers provided and times the user has received "Best Answer."
Social Interaction	*Total number of friends a user has obtained.*
	Total number of times a user has been "thanked."
	Total number of times a user has posted a comment.
	Average number of comments a user has posted per week.

Table 1: Description of the data collected for analysis during the measurement phase of the experiment.

learning resources. Social question-answering (Q&A) services are one example of a recent technology to emerge that these support online learning experiences.

Social Q&A services are "purposefully designed to allow people to ask and respond to questions" ([4], p.866) to satisfy an asker's need for information and "exemplify (sic) the Web 2.0 model of user-generated and user-rated content" ([7], p.2302). As social Q&A services grow in popularity in recent years, these services have become one of the major online information sources that provides flexible access for students to seek and share educational information for their learning "on their own time and at their own pace" ([3], p.ix). Although a rich body of research has emerged to investigate user behavioral analysis (e.g., motivation for asking and answering a question, etc.) and content analysis (e.g., answer and question quality, etc.) within a context of social Q&A services, there is little research investigating how students' learning engagements are developed and improved through question-answering and other user activities. Moreover, as social Q&A services are generally reliant upon user-generated content with little to no direct educational interventions by educators, methods in learning analytics may deliver critical insights into investigating how social Q&A services develop appropriate intervention systems in educational contexts in order to help students improve their learning engagement and performance.

In this study, we attempt to experiment educational interventions by implementing a formative message feedback system based on students' learning engagements and social interactions on Brainly[1], social Q&A platform for learning. Research has shown that there are many important indicators for predicting students' learning and performance within online environments. These attributes primarily consist of data collected using traditional quantitative analytic methods adapted within a learning context. Leveraging these concepts allows us to create and scale predictive measures of student performance and employ these learning progression metrics across large-scale digital environments [14]. By designing an intervention system that utilizes these data collection methods, we may be able to provide better educational features to social Q&A users that support increased positive educational practice and learner guidance [15].

Background

Social Q&A services

In recent years, new information and communication technologies (ICT) have emerged to mediate human information seeking behaviors in online environments. Social Q&A services are one of the examples of such ICTs where social Q&A users are allowed to formulate a question to express their information need in a natural language, while other people answer a question which indicate collaborative information exchange between people within online communities [12]. Examples of social Q&A services are Yahoo! Answers, WikiAnswers, Quora, etc. Unlike traditional information seeking behaviors via online sources such as search engines (e.g., Google, Bing) in which people most likely interact with information systems to obtain information for their needs, social Q&A services facilitate social interactions between people through question-answering interactions to seek and share knowledge. In other words, social Q&A services are designed to provide "outlets for information retrieval where the user's information need is articulated by natural language questions posed to a community whose members can answer the question or even offer feedback on the

[1] https://brainly.com

Category	*Description*
Gamification Participation	Total number of challenges the user has attempted.
	Total number of challenges the user has completed.
	Total number of lifetime points the user has gained.
	Ratio of challenges attempted and challenges completed.
Engagement	*Total number of logon sessions for the user.*
	Average number of logons per measurement week.

Table 1 (continued): Description of the data collected for future analysis during the measurement phase of the experiment.

given responses, resulting in a personalized set of answers" ([2], p.1183). Although the purpose of social Q&A services is to seek and share information in a broader range of topics such as business, entertainment, reference, health, etc., new social Q&A services have been introduced to help users "participate in question-answering interactions that share educational information for online learning" ([9], p.130). Those education-focused social Q&A services (e.g., Brainly, Chegg, Piazza, etc.) help students interact with their peers to access information and resources in order to improve their online learning process, while question-answering activities and other social interactions (e.g., comment, etc.) are utilized to increase students' learning engagement over time.

Online learning and learning analytics
Online learning is "a new social process that is beginning to act as a complete substitute for both distance learning and the traditional face-to-face class" ([8], p.60). By providing flexible access to educational materials, online learning also empowers participants to improve their knowledge bases. While online learning is designed to support structured learning processes such as online classes, new online information-source formats (e.g., social networking sites, wiki, social question-answering sites, etc.) also provide less-structured yet personalized learning solutions for each individual's needs [10]. Learning analytics is an emerging discipline concerning students' learning performance in educational settings [1]. As new information and communication technologies have opened new opportunities to develop a variety of new online learning methods and technologies, The previous research stressed 'social learning analysis' as a newer form of assessments of students' learning process in participatory online environments where students are "not solitary, and are not necessarily doing work to be marked, but are engaged in social activity, either interacting directly with others (for example, messaging, friending or following), or using platforms in which their activity traces will be experienced by others (for example, publishing, searching, tagging or rating)" ([6], p.5).

Interventions
Interventions in the form of formative feedback have long been considered as an important step in the learning process [11], and [13] argued that the main goal of formative feedback is "to increase student knowledge, skills, and understanding in some content area or general skill (e.g., problem solving), and there are multiple types of feedback that may be employed toward this end (e.g., response specific, goal directed, immediately delivered)" (p.156-157). Feedback designed to modify or change user-behavior is considered formative in that it is intended to communicate information for the purpose of improving the overall student or users learning processes [13]. As such, the design and implementation of formative interventions within this study attempted to adhere to these traditional instructional design practices.

Method
The Brainly platform provides a collaborative digital space for a community of learners to team up and share ideas, knowledge, and solve problems. The platform can be generalized into four features categories – 1) questions and answers, 2) social interactions, 3) games/gamification, and 4) engagement.

In order to measure and compare the effects on a user's social interaction, inquiry, gamification, and engagement behavior, users received a personalized intervention in the form of a message designed to improve self-regulation. Using a two-group, between-subjects, randomized

- Counts of each user's interactions within the Brainly platform were created (Table 1). An interaction score was created for each category of interaction data.
- An intervention, in the form of a private message, was then provided to the experimental group.
- A second measure of interactions were scored three days after the first message was received. Positive behavior was identified as an increase in the overall interaction score.
- A second intervention was then applied to the experimental group. This follow up intervention was designed to either reiterate the first interventions formative message. If no change was observed the first message sentiments were reapplied. If a positive behavioral change was observed an intervention providing positive support was given.

Figure 1: Expanded description of experimental procedure.

controlled experiment, we compared the difference in means between a group that received the intervention (experimental group) and a group that did not receive any intervention (control group). Regressions and post-hoc Tukey tests were conducted for each behavioral indicator.

Participants
The study randomly selected *active* users (ages between 13 years and 18 years) on Brainly. Both the control and experimental group users were deemed "active" if using the following conditions held true: Total number of Brainly logon sessions in the past two weeks is greater than 10; and the user has asked or answered a minimum of one question within the past two weeks. The initial sample produced 300 users for the experimental group and 300 users for the control group. Users within the experimental group received an informational or motivational automated private message twice a week (a total of 4 weeks) designed to increase interactions within Brainly, while users within the control group received no intervention message.

Experiment Procedure
The experimental procedure included a measurement of the student's current level of interaction data. Table 1 shows 16 variables for data collection for analysis during the measurement phase of the experiment. An intervention was randomly applied to the experimental group on day one then the user's level of interactions were determined; a second intervention aligned to the category of the initial intervention was then applied on day four then user interaction data was collected and measured on day seven. Details of this procedure are described in Figure 2. This process is repeated over the course of four consecutive weeks with the experimental group.

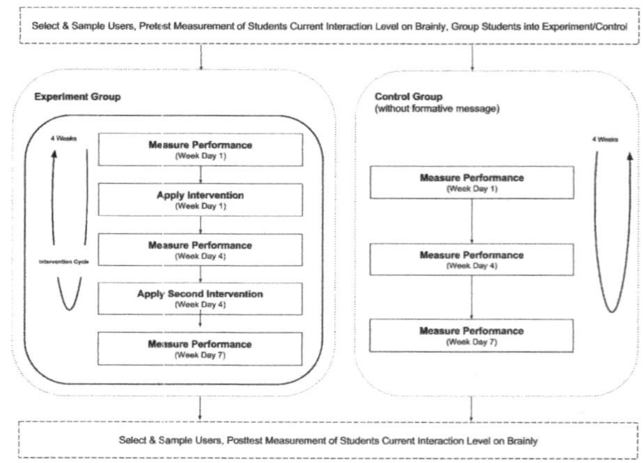

Figure 2: Experiment procedure design

Findings
Over the course of the four-week trial, 113 user accounts (52 from the experimental group and 61 from the control group) were deemed nefarious users, and either had their accounts deleted or were removed from the study, leaving a total of n=487 (n=248 in the experimental and n=239 for the control). Preliminary results from the current study found that a few selected users in both the control group and the experimental group are considered *power users* in that they were very active when compared against the majority of the sampled users. Thus, Tukey's interquartile range approach was used to identify and remove those outliers for each dependent variable used in this analysis. A one-way between subjects ANOVA was conducted to compare the effect of the intervention on user behavior for users who received a formative message condition and those who did not receive an intervention condition.

Of the 16 variables tested in the study (see table 1 for details), five dependent variables were found to be significantly affected by the application of the intervention at the $p<.05$): The total number of times the users has received the best answer [$F(1,440) = 8.459$, $p=0.004$)]; the total number of subject areas the user encountered [$F(1,394) = 12.877$, $p=0.000$)]; the total number of times the user commented on an existing question or answer [$F(1,435) = 4.996$, $p=0.026$)]; the total number of times the user has completed a challenge game [$F(1,254) = 5.664$, $p=0.001$]; the frequency of inquiries submitted by the user [F)1,348) = 2.371, $p=0.012$.

Post hoc comparisons using the Tukey test indicated that the mean score for the message intervention condition found the total number of times the users received the best answer (M = 1.39, *SD* = 1.775) was significantly different than the no message intervention condition (M = 0.96, *SD* = 1.204); for the users that encountered a labeled subject area, the total number of subject areas the user encountered (M = 3.56, *SD* = 2.532) was significantly different than the no message intervention condition (M = 2.76, *SD* = 1.796); the total number of times the user commented on an existing question or answer (M = 5.20, *SD* = 6.442) was significantly different than the no message intervention condition (M = 3.99, *SD* = 4.703); for the users that chose to participate in a challenge, the total number of times the user completed a challenge game (M = 1.58, *SD* = 0.828) was significantly different than the no message intervention condition (M = 1.29, *SD* = 0.454); and of the users that submitted inquiries, the total number of inquiries (M = 7.96, SD = 6.093) was significantly different those that did not receive the message condition (M = 7.04, SD = 4.969). All other dependent variables measured within this analysis showed no significant effect ($P>=.05$) between the experimental and control conditions.

Results indicate that users who received an intervention were more likely to increase social interaction in the form of commenting, increase the quality of their peer-reviewed answers, and have greater than before interest in gamified learning challenges. These preliminary findings may imply that the intervention is effective in increasing the inquisitiveness of Brainly users in both the amount of inquiries the user makes and the subject areas in which the user is encountering. Additionally, while the data does not allude to an increased user response rate in the form of an *answer,* it does suggest that of the users that did respond to an inquiry, they were more likely to receive the *best answer*, showing a potential increase in high quality content for those that experienced the intervention condition. Last, an increase in user commenting and gamified challenge completion rates for users that received an intervention suggest that the use messaging can positively modify behavior and increase social interaction within an online learning community among users.

Discussion

New technologies have opened new opportunities for learning and expanded access to information, and social Q&A services have become prevalent channels to seek and share information to address their educational needs. Although [5] point out that "digital, networked media provide new opportunities for students to learn from others in a much less hierarchical and institutional way than ever before" (p.18), formative feedback towards students' learning activities could be helpful in order to develop more efficient online learning interactions through question-answering and other social interaction activities on social Q&A services. In the study, we attempt to describe our preliminary results from a novel formative intervention to understand how learner interactions are improved on social Q&A services. Results support past literature and reaffirm the capabilities of social channels, combined with formative interventions, to have a significant effect on user behaviors and engagements in learning on social Q&A services. Our final study will apply a larger sample to confirm data findings from the current study and identify any other significant changes in user behaviors and engagements in learning by formative message on social Q&A services.

References

1. Ryan S.J.d. Baker, Kalina Yacef. 2009. The state of educational data mining in 2009: A review and future visions. *Journal of Educational Data Mining* 1, 1: 3-17.
2. Erik Choi, Chirag Shah. 2016. User motivations for asking questions in online Q&A services. *Journal of the American Society for Information Science Technology* 67, 5: 1182-1197.
3. Robert A. Cole. 2000. *Issues in Web-based pedagogy: Acritical primer*. Greenwood Press, Westport, CT.
4. Maxwell Harper, Daphne Raban, Sheizaf Rafaeli, Joseph A. Konstan. 2008. Predictors of answer quality in online q&a sites. In *Proceedings of the SIGCHI Conference on Human Factors in Computing Systems* (865–874.
5. Andrew J. Flanagin, Miriam J. Metzger. 2008. Digital media and youth: Unparalleled opportunity and unprecedented responsibility. In *Digital media, youth, and credibility*, Andrew J. Flanagin, Miriam J. Metzger (Eds.). MIT Press, Cambridge, MA, 5-27.
6. Rebecca Ferguson. 2012. Learning analytics: drivers, developments and challenges. *International Journal of Technology Enhanced Learning* 4, 5/6: 304–317.
7. Rich Gazan. 2011. Social Q&A. *Journal of the American Society for Information Science Technology* 63, 12: 2301–2312.
8. Starr R. Hiltz, Murray Turoff. 2005. Education Goes Digital: The Evolution of Online Learning and the Revolution in Higher Education. *Communications of the ACM Archive* 48, 10: 59-64.
9. Long T. Le, Chirag Shah, Erik Choi. 2016. Evaluating the quality of educational answers in community question-answering. In *Proceedings of the 16th ACM/IEEE-CS on Joint Conference on Digital Libraries*, 129–138.
10. Justin Reich, Richard Murnane, John Willett. 2012. The state of wiki usage in US K–12 schools: Leveraging web 2.0 data warehouses to assess quality and equity in online learning environments. *Educational Researcher* 41: 1, 7-15.
11. Doris R. Pridemore, James D. Klein, 2005. Control of Practice and Level of Feedback in Computer-Based Instruction, *Contemporary Educational Psychology* 20, 4: 444-450.
12. Pnina Shachaf, Howard Rosenbaum. 2009. Online social reference: A research agenda through a STIN framework. In *Proceedings of iConference*.
13. Valerie J. Shute. 2008. Focus on Formative Feedback. *Review of Educational Research* 78, 1: 153-189.
14. Mar Wilson, Perman Gochyyev, Kathleen Scalise. 2016). Assessment of Learning in Digital Interactive Social Networks: A Learning Analytics Approach. *Online Learning* 20, 2: 97-119.
15. Wolfgang Greller, Hendrik Drachsler. 2012. Translating Learning into Numbers: A Generic Framework for Learning Analytics. *Journal of Educational Technology & Society* 15,3: 42-57.
16. Elizabeth T. Welsh, Connie R. Wanberg, Kenneth G. Brown, Marcia J. Simmering. 2003. E-learning: Emerging uses, best practices, and future directions. *International Journal of Training and Development* 7, 4: 245–258.

Designing Inclusive STEM Activities: A Comparison of Playful Interactive Experiences Across Gender

Mandy McLean
Gevirtz Graduate School of Education
UC Santa Barbara
Santa Barbara, CA 93106, USA
amclean@education.ucsb.edu

Danielle Harlow
Gevirtz Graduate School of Education
UC Santa Barbara
Santa Barbara, CA 93106, USA
dharlow@education.ucsb.edu

IDC '17, June 27-30, 2017, Stanford, CA, USA
ACM 978-1-4503-4921-5/17/06.
http://dx.doi.org/10.1145/3078072.3084326

Abstract
The STEM toy market is primarily designed for, and targeted to, boys. Even the Maker Movement, which has been hailed as movement for all types of people, is dominated by males. In this paper, we take a mixed-methods approach to identify the affordances of activity design that engage first through sixth grade girls in STEM play. We present data from three workshops where we tracked and analyzed 45 students' choices from one of two squishy circuits activities—free play or a socially relevant storybook design task. Using logistic regression, we show that the odds of choosing the storybook activity over free play were approximately 23 times higher for girls than for boys. Through the analysis of one-on-one interviews, we found that most girls were drawn to the storybook activity because they either wanted to help others or the design task provided them with a starting point.

Author Keywords
STEM; gender; play; making; children; activity design.

ACM Classification Keywords
J.2. Physical Sciences and Engineering; J.5. Arts and Humanities.

Introduction

Although women now receive 50% of bachelor degrees in science, technology, engineering, and mathematics (STEM), they only hold 30% of jobs. Furthermore, math-intensive STEM fields such as computer science and engineering award only 18% and 20%, respectively, of bachelor degrees to women [17]. Most research on increasing diversity in STEM focuses on secondary and postsecondary education. Yet, research shows that gendered attitudes towards mathematical abilities are evident by kindergarten [2,8]. As such, this study emphasizes the importance of early STEM education and focuses on elementary school children in environments where learning is achieved through play. While there is a growing movement towards STEM toys that are designed to be gender neutral (e.g., LittleBits [1] and Makey Makey [19]) or even slightly girl-centric (e.g., GoldieBlox [7] and electronic textiles (e-textiles) [5]), the bulk of STEM toys are still designed with boys in mind and have been shown to alienate girls with their competitive nature and subject matter [16]. To effectively engage more girls in STEM, we must understand how to design activities that appeal to girls.

This research explores the affordances and constraints of activity design that lead girls to playful interactions with STEM materials using a mixed-methods approach with 45 first through sixth grade children. We used several a priori design constraints based on prior research to select the type of activities used for the study. First and foremost, the activities could not rely too heavily on gendered stereotypes. Secondly, we do not want to exclude boys; the goal is to better engage all children who are overlooked by traditional STEM toys. Thirdly, the activities should focus more on collaboration than competition. Finally, the activities should be designed to align with the theory of constructionism [18], which emphasizes design, experimentation, and the creation of artifacts to increase learning and maximize engagement. Our goal was to determine additional attributes within these constraints. Specifically, we were testing the effect of integrating aspects of social relevance, storytelling, and design tasks into activities. However, the affordances that best engage girls in STEM play will emerge from the students themselves via interviews.

Gender Gap in STEM

To decrease the gender gap in math-intensive STEM fields, we must first increase females' self-efficacy in their STEM abilities as soon as stereotypes begin to take hold. According to Ceci et al. [8], gendered attitudes towards math are evident by kindergarten and empirical studies indicate that interest in STEM is predictive of career choices as early as eighth grade [15]. Moreover, a recent study with 400 children found that by the age of 6, both girls and boys were significantly more likely to classify males as "really, really smart" than females and this correlated with less girls showing interest in games for "really, really smart" children [2]. Given that elementary-aged children spend much of their time engaged in play, one way to address this issue is through carefully designed activities. If we can successfully engage young girls in STEM play, they will have more opportunities to participate in problem solving, building, and critical thinking.

There is a lot of research surrounding the democratization of the increasingly popular Maker Movement [9], which relies on "making" (i.e., artifact design and creation) as a learning tool. While making is being embraced by many as a tool for diversifying the STEM population, it is not there yet. For example, in an analysis of four volumes of Make Magazine, Brahms and Crowley [4] found that 89% of authors or featured makers were male. Moreover, 81% of approximately 300,000 readers of Make magazine in 2012 were male [14] and of about 130,000 attendees at the 2014 Bay Area Maker Faire, 70% were male [13].

Affordances of STEM Activity Design

A STEM design attribute that has been extensively researched in recent years, with respect to gender, is crafting. For example, the LilyPad Arduino for e-textiles is more popular among females than standard Arduino boards, even though they are functionally identical [5]. While crafting may be the most researched, there are other attributes of activity design that are also likely to increase the appeal to girls. For instance, females, in general, prefer "people-oriented fields" while males prefer "thing-oriented fields" [8,10], which helps explain why women are more prevalent in careers with a clear social purpose, such as healthcare, social work, and education. Incorporating social relevance into STEM activities may make them more appealing to girls [11]. Additionally, females have an edge in verbal skills, with significant differences found between assessments of female and male writing samples [10]. As such, integrating aspects of storytelling into STEM play may increase the appeal to girls. In fact, incorporating storytelling into STEM activities has been shown to to improve elementary girls' geometry skills [6], as well as to engage middle school girls in computer programming [12]. Finally, Blikstein and Worsley [3] discuss the importance of onboarding and facilitation for novices before they start making, especially underrepresented individuals who may be impacted by stereotype threat. Without guidance, many females struggle and thus feel that they are confirming stereotypes that they are not good at STEM. Constraining some aspects of STEM activities with design tasks, while still allowing room for exploration and creativity, may engage a more diverse population by providing a starting point for participation.

Methods

This paper takes a mixed-methods approach to address the following research questions: Is there a difference between girls' and boys' interests in STEM play? What design attributes of activities lead girls to playful interactions with STEM materials? Ultimately, activity design will be achieved through design-based research that will include multiple phases of iterative analysis, design, development, and implementation.

Participants and Context

This research study was conducted at a local public elementary school in a small city in Southern California with 45 first through sixth grade students. Data were collected over a period of three weeks during three Friday afternoon 'Maker Friday' sessions, which are rotated through the school by grade levels (grade one and two students participate during week one, followed by grade three and four students in week two, and grade five and six students in week three). Sessions are part of the regular school day and last 60 minutes for grades one and two and 90 minutes for grades three through six. The selection of students was based on assignment by the school, with no input from the researchers. The lead author of this paper led the activities with help from a graduate student and a local school volunteer. The maker sessions conducted for this research centered around squishy circuits [22]—squishy circuits rely on play dough, instead of wires, to explore circuit design. Conductive and non-conductive dough were used together with battery packs, LEDs, and motors to comprise the main circuit components. Squishy circuits were selected as the medium to test the affordances of activity design because they have a low floor and high ceiling, with wide walls, meaning they do not require prior knowledge, can easily be modified for a wide age range, and can be used to explore a large variety of projects [20]. We began each session with

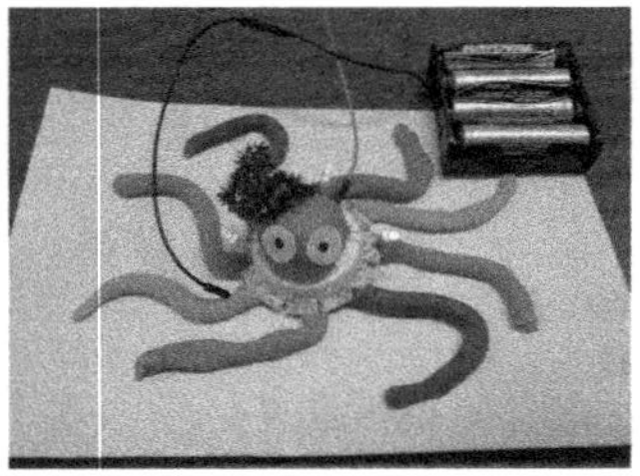

Figure 1: Example free play project provided for the students.

Figure 2: Example storybook page provided for the students.

an overview of the two activity options. Option one—students could build anything they wanted using the provided squishy circuits materials (Figure 1). Option two—students could help create a book that would be used to teach children about animals and circuits. Students were tasked to construct an animal, incorporating at least one circuit component, and to write a corresponding animal fact. Their final design would then be photographed and used as one page of a book created to teach children about animals and circuits (Figure 2).

Data Collection

Activity choices were tracked by the researchers to determine if there was a statistically significant difference between the activities chosen by girls and boys. Additionally, short interviews were conducted with students to learn more about the reason(s) behind their activity selection. All students participated in the activity but only those with parental consent were asked for interviews. The interview responses were coded by two researchers using emergent codes for affordances of activity design that became relevant through analysis of the student responses [21]. On the initial pass, inter-rater reliability was above 80% and, after discussion, the two researchers reached consensus on all codes. Interviews were conducted during two of the three weeks of data collection. Due to unforeseen scheduling issues, the first session, conducted with grade 1 and 2 students, did not include interviews.

Results

Statistical Analysis of Activity Selection

Logistic regression was performed to investigate to what extent the observed variation in activity selection can be explained by the participants' gender and grade level. A hierarchical analysis was conducted to determine whether either of the two predictor variables significantly affected the students' activity selection, reported as a binary outcome measure (0 = free play activity, 1 = storybook activity). The results of the analysis found gender to be a significant predictor of activity selection $(\chi^2(1) = 18.90, p < .001)$ and produced an odds ratio of 22.86, which implies that the odds of girls choosing the storybook activity over free play are 22.86 times greater than the odds of boys choosing the storybook activity over free play (Table 1). Adding grade level did not improve the fit over the first model. In fact, the difference between the model chi-square for the two models was only 0.23, which is very non-significant $(p = .89)$. Therefore, it is reasonable to group students across all grade levels (first through sixth) when analyzing preferences for STEM play in this study. See Figure 3 for an activity count and Table 2 for a breakdown by grade level.

		95% CI for Odds Ratio		
Predictor	**B [S.E.]**	*Lower*	*Odds*	*Upper*
Gender	3.13***[0.87]	4.16	22.86	125.55

Table 1: Summary of logistic regression analysis. Note. $R^2 = .34$ (Cox & Snell) $.46$ (Nagelkerke). Model $\chi^2(1) = 18.90, p < .001$. $^*p < .05$, $^{**}p < .01$, $^{***}p < .001$.

		Grade Level		
	Activity Selection	*1–2*	*3–4*	*5–6*
Males	Free play	7	7	6
	Storybook	1	0	1
Females	Free play	2	1	4
	Storybook	5	5	6

Table 2: Activty selection categorized by gender and grade level.

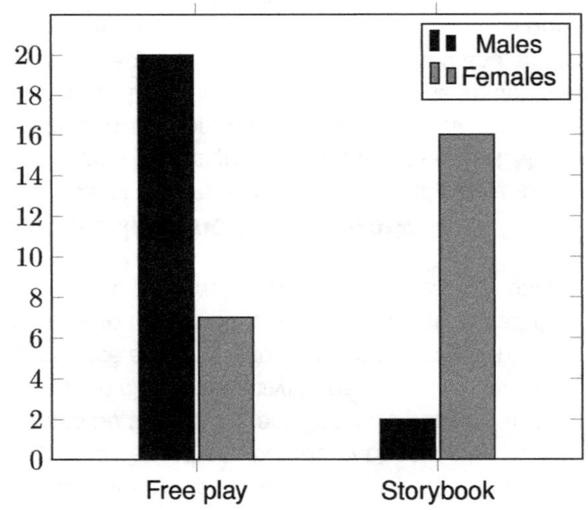

Figure 3: Activity selection categorized by gender.

Qualitative Analysis of Interviews
To better understand why girls were more likely than boys to choose the storybook activity, interviews were conducted with the students individually. Emergent coding was used to identify reasons for activity selection and the following codes were identified: design task, free play, social relevance, public (positive and negative), and storytelling. See Table 3 for the codebook and Figure 4 for a count of student responses.

The most common reason girls chose the storybook activity was because they liked helping others (coded as "social relevance"). These girls made statements such as, "I like helping the teachers out" and "because I like helping kids". Secondly, a notable number of girls chose the storybook activity because they preferred having a design task to help them get started. For instance, one girl stated she choose

Code	Description
Design task (DT)	Student preferred having structured design task to help get started.
Free play (FP)	Student enjoyed having the freedom to build anything.
Social relevance (SR)	Student wanted to help others; either the teacher or the children.
Public: positive (P-p)	Student wanted work displayed for the public.
Public: negative (P-n)	Student did not want work displayed for the public.
Storytelling (S)	Student was interested in writing and/or designing for a book.

Table 3: Codebook.

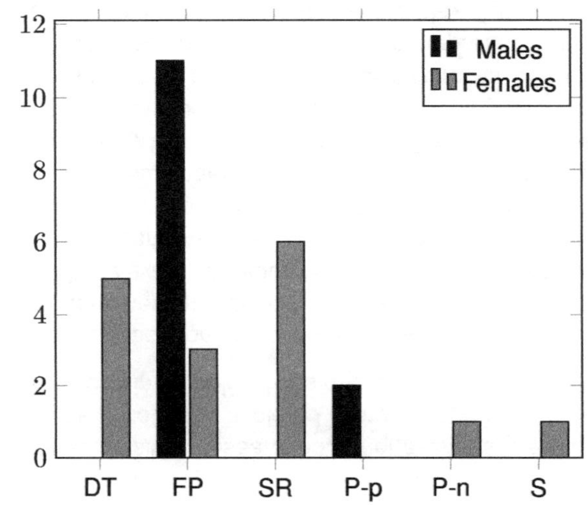

Figure 4: Interview codes assigned to student interviews.

Figure 5: Storybook page completed by a female student.

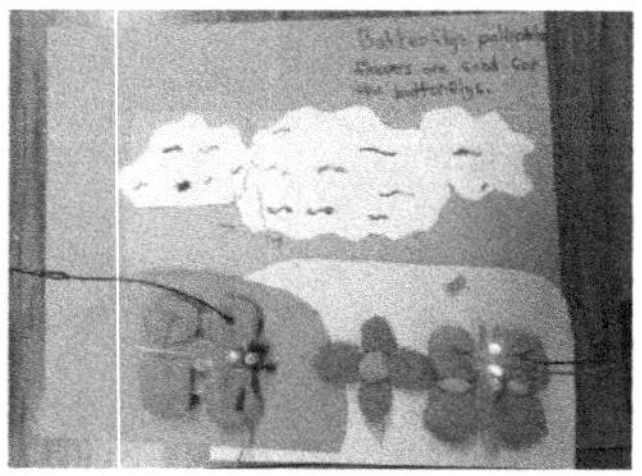

Figure 6: Storybook page completed by two female students.

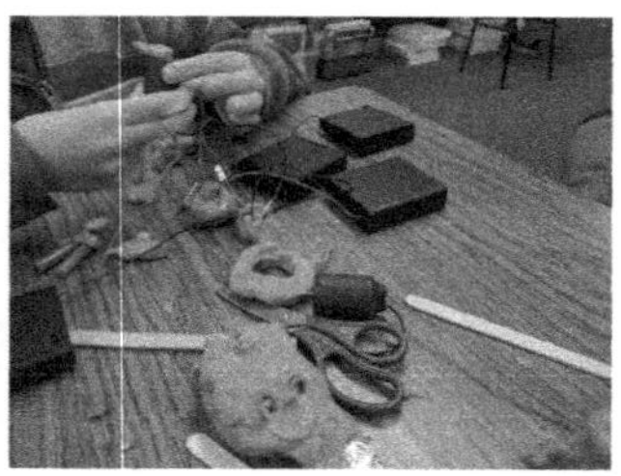

Figure 7: Two male students engaged in the free play activity.

the storybook activity "[be]cause if I would not build something [for the storybook] I wouldn't know what to build". Additionally, one girl chose the storybook activity for the opportunity to contribute to a book. In her words, "[I chose this activity] because when I grow up I like want to be an author or an artist" (coded as "storytelling"). The final attribute that impacted girls' choice of activities was whether other people beyond her classroom would see the final product. One young girl elected for the free play activity because she was not yet confident enough to build for the storybook; she explained that she wanted to learn how the circuits worked before committing to a project (coded as "negative public"). All boys who selected the free play activity mentioned in their responses that they enjoyed the open-ended nature of the activity, e.g., "I just wanted to build something random." Only one boy that elected to participate in the storybook activity was interviewed, out of two boys total. His reason was not related to the design task or to help others, but rather because he wanted his work to be seen by others ("positive public"). In his own words, he chose the activity "because I felt like my excellence should be honored [in a book]." This is in stark contrast to the girl described above who lacked the confidence to allow her work to be viewed by others.

Conclusion and Future Work

The goal of this research was to identify the affordances of STEM activity design that engage girls in STEM play. To this end, two different squishy circuits activities were introduced to 45 first through sixth grade students and the students' activity selections were tracked and analyzed through interviews. One of these activities was designed based on a priori attributes that have been shown to appeal to females, resulting in a socially relevant, storybook design task. The other activity was left open for free play. While the impact of incorporating crafting into STEM play on girls has been extensively researched, other avenues to engaging girls have not been explored in much depth; the results of our study aim to help fill this gap in research.

Using logistic regression, our analysis revealed that girls have 23 times greater odds than boys of choosing the socially relevant, storybook design task over the free play activity. Incorporating elements of social relevance and design tasks into STEM play, while respecting individuals' privacy, should help engage more girls and thus, help pave the pathway for more diversity in STEM. However, we must note that this study is limited and preliminary. We looked only at one type of material—squishy circuits. Work with additional materials may reveal other important attributes that influence children's self-directed play. Further, in this study, the variables are confounded. While we anticipated being able to ascertain whether girls were drawn to the storytelling aspect of the storybook activity, we found that only one girl mentioned this design attribute as influential in her task selection. It is still possible that girls are driven to engage in STEM play through storytelling but that this design element was overshadowed by other attributes of the storybook activity. In a second iteration of the study, we plan to better isolate each design attribute and take into consideration other factors, e.g. gender of the teacher and researchers. Nevertheless, this study provided interesting findings, identifies initial attributes to investigate, and points to productive further directions.

Acknowledgments

We thank the participating students, teachers, and school involved in this research. In particular, we thank Kevin Spracher, DJ Perry, and Jim Gribble. We also thank our anonymous reviewers for their helpful comments.

REFERENCES

1. Ayah Bdeir and Ted Ullrich. 2011. Electronics as material: LittleBits. In *Proceedings of the Fifth International Conference on Tangible, Embedded, and Embodied Interaction* (TEI), 341–344.
2. Lin Bian, Sarah-Jane Leslie, and Andrei Cimpian. 2017. Gender stereotypes about intellectual ability emerge early and influence children's interests. *Science* 355: 389–391.
3. Paulo Blikstein and Marcelo Worsley. 2016. Children are not hackers: Building a culture of powerful ideas, deep learning, and equity in the maker movement. In *Makeology: Makerspaces as Learning Environments*, Kylie Peppler, Erica Rosenfeld Halverson and Yasmin B. Kafai (eds.). Taylor Francis, 64–79.
4. Lisa Brahms and Kevin Crowley. 2016. Making sense of making: Defining learning practices in MAKE magazine. In *Makeology: Makers as Learners*, Kylie Peppler, Erica Rosenfeld Halverson and Yasmin B. Kafai (eds.). Taylor Francis, 13–28.
5. Leah Buechley and Benjamin Mako Hill. 2010. LilyPad in the wild: How hardwareÊijs long tail is supporting new engineering and design communities. In *Proceedings of the 8th ACM Conference on Designing Interactive Systems* (DIS), 199–207.
6. Beth Casey, Sumru Erkut, Ineke Ceder, and Jessica Mercer Young. 2008. Use of a storytelling context to improve girls' and boys' geometry skills in kindergarten. *Journal of Applied Developmental Psychology* 29, 1: 29–48.
7. Craig Causer. 2013. Ribbons and wheels and engineers — That's what girls are made of. *IEEE Potentials* 32, 5: 15–17.
8. Stephen J. Ceci, Donna K. Ginther, Shulamit Kahn, and Wendy M. Williams. 2014. Women in academic science: A changing landscape. *Psychological Science in the Public Interest* 15, 3: 75–141.
9. Dale Dougherty. 2012. The Maker Movement. *Innovations: Technology, Governance, Globalization* 7, 3: 11–14.
10. Diane F. Halpern, Camilla P. Benbow, David C. Geary, Ruben C. Gur, Janet Shibley Hyde, and Morton Ann Gernsbacher. 2007. The science of sex differences in science and mathematics. *Psychological Science in the Public Interest* 8, 1: 1–51.
11. Nathan Holbert. 2016. Bots for tots: Building inclusive makerspaces by leveraging "ways of knowing." In *Proceedings of the 15th International Conference on Interaction Design and Children* (IDC), 79–88.
12. Caitlin Kelleher, Randy Pausch, and Sara Kiesler. 2007. Storytelling Alice motivates middle school girls to learn computer programming. *Proceedings of ACM CHI 2007 Conference on Human Factors in Computing Systems* (CHI), 1455–1464.
13. Maker Media. 2014. *Maker Faire Bay Area Attendee Study.*
14. Maker Media and Intel. 2012. *Maker Market Study and Media Report: An In-Depth Profile of Makers at the Forefront of Hardware Innovation.*
15. Adam V. Maltese and Robert H. Tai. 2011. Pipeline persistence: Examining the association of educational experiences with earned degrees in STEM among U.S. students. *Science Education* 95, 5: 877–907.
16. Borjana Mikic and Domenico Grasso. 2002. Socially-relevant design: The TOYtech project at

Smith College. *Journal of Engineering Education* 91, 3: 319–326.

17. NSF. 2015. *Women, Minorities, and People with Disabilities in Science and Engineering.* National Center for Science and Engineering Statistics.
18. Seymour Papert and Idit Harel. 1991. Situating Constructionism. In *Constructionism*, Idit Harel and Seymour Papert (eds.). Ablex Publishing, 1–11.
19. Mitchel Resnick and Eric Rosenbaum. 2013. Designing for tinkerability. In *Design, Make, Play: Growing the Next Generation of STEM Innovators*, Margaret Honey and David E. Kanter (eds.). Routledge, 163–181.
20. Mitchel Resnick and Brian Silverman. 2005. Some reflections on designing construction kits for kids. In *Proceedings of the 4th International Conference on Interaction Design and Children* (IDC), 117–122.
21. Anselm Strauss and Juliet Corbin. 1994. Grounded theory methodology. In *Handbook of Qualitative Research*, N. Denzin and Y. Lincoln (eds.). Sage Publications, 273–285.
22. Annmarie Thomas. 2013. Squishy circuits. In *Design, Make, Play: Growing the Next Generation of STEM Innovators*, Margaret Honey and David E. Kanter (eds.). Routledge, 119–137.

CodeStitch: Leveraging Analogical Encoding in a Game Space

Marleen Villeroy
Teachers College, Columbia University
New York, NY 10027, USA
mcv2132@tc.columbia.edu

IDC '17, June 27-30, 2017, Stanford, CA, USA

ACM ISBN 978-1-4503-4921-5/17/06.
http://dx.doi.org/10.1145/3078072.3084327

Abstract

Computer programming is highly collaborative, whether practiced in the form of on-site pair-programming or asynchronous reusing and remixing of code. Digital games have become an attractive tool for teaching coding, yet rarely do they account for collaboration among players. The goal of this paper is to show how asynchronous collaboration can be leveraged in a game-space by facilitating players to share and compare their solution methods. By comparing and contrasting code side-by-side players are more likely to detect structural (rather than superficial) similarities and differences (analogical encoding). A pilot study involving pre-teens found that this design feature led to reflection on the differences and different affordances of the solution methods based on their deep structure.

Author Keywords

Analogical encoding; structure mapping; coding; programming comparing solutions; video game.

ACM Classification Keywords

K.3.2. Computers and Education: Computer and Information Science Education – *computer science education.* K.8.0. Personal Computing: General – *games.*

Introduction
Computer programming is highly collaborative. Moreover, collaboration is an important strategy at all stages, from novice to expert programmers [1, 3, 13]. For example, in pair programming, a software development technique in which two programmers work together at one workstation, one person writes code while the other reviews each line of code as it is typed in. Collaboration in this way enables synergetic effects that result in an increase in the quality of the code [6, 1, 20]. This strategy is employed commercially as well as in formal learning environments, including many Computer Science Principles Curricula. Most often though, programming does not occur on the same workstation; in these instances, collaboration happens asynchronously when programmers copy and extend pieces of others peoples' code. Not unlike on-site collaboration, this form of asynchronous collaboration enables individuals "to potentially create things much more complex than they could have created on their own" [2].

Digital games have become an attractive tool for learning to program, yet they oftentimes fail to facilitate a collaborative learning environment and instead present programming as solo-play. This is surprising, considering that many of the most commercially successful computer games thrive on collaborative play, such as in guilds in multiplayer online role-playing game communities [7]; or in virtual worlds, including Habbo Hotel, Toontown, and Whyville [12]. Moreover, popular sandbox environments for tinkering with code (e.g. Scratch) are fundamentally collaborative, encouraging users to study other peoples' code and build on existing projects. Here, learning occurs not through the gameplay alone but instead is enhanced with a network of collaborators [15, 18].

This paper investigates how collaboration among users can be leveraged in a game that teaches computer programming and the ways in which sharing and comparing code solutions affects players' perception and understanding of a solution space. The first part of the paper introduces the concept of analogical encoding [10], which explains the cognitive mechanisms by which one creates schemas by using the differences in various examples to understand relational structures embedded within the examples. The second part of the paper explores a game space that leverages analogical encoding through asynchronous collaboration. The effects of this feature on players' reflecting on and synthesizing of solution methods is explored in the findings of a preliminary study, detailed in the third part of the paper.

Background
Analogy is an important process by which humans learn (e.g. reasoning, conceptual development). Structure-mapping theory assumes that when we carry out a comparison we look for common structures; it assumes we do this by taking knowledge from a representation we know well to one we know less well. In this process we rearrange our cognitive structures and learning happens [8].

Evidence from cognitive science literature and computer science education indicates that this happens particularly felicitously when studying different approaches to solving a problem side-by-side, comparing and contrasting them in the process rather than studying them in isolation or sequentially, one after the other [10, 16, 17]. For example, Loewenstein, Thompson, and Gentner (1999) compared students who saw two novel case studies either sequentially, or in parallel, and found students were better at analyzing the case studies when they were presented in parallel. They described the effect of learning the case studies in one batch as "analogical encoding" and relate it to analogical learning. Unlike analogical learning, where students relate new information to existing schemas, in analogical encoding, the students create schemas by using the differences in the case studies to understand relational structures embedded within the cases [4, 5, 16]. Genter, Loewenstein, and Thompson (2003) shed insight on the underlying cognitive mechanisms, explaining that

> if people are directly comparing two examples, they probably can appreciate structural similarities, but if they are presented with just one example, they are far more likely to recall a prior example on the basis of surface similarities than structural similarities. (p. 394)

Analogical encoding can be extremely informative to learners, even when they lack deep knowledge of the domain [9, 14].

Analogical Encoding in a Game Space

CodeStitch leverages the concept of analogical encoding by means of asynchronous collaboration in a game space. In this puzzle-based digital game players explore programming through knitting. In the game, the player runs a bustling knitting shop whose customers order garments in different patterns, sizes, and colors, be it a purple-and-gold striped scarf or a checkered sweater. In order to complete a customer order, the player needs to program a knitting machine. In so doing, players encounter loops, variables, and other basic programming concepts. Until this point, the interaction in the game is between the fictional customer and the player; this changes once a player has successfully completed a customer order. Now the player sees his own code solution alongside that of a randomly chosen fellow player in a pop-up window that displays both methods as valid solutions and encourages the player, before moving on, to compare the structural differences of the approaches (see figure 1).

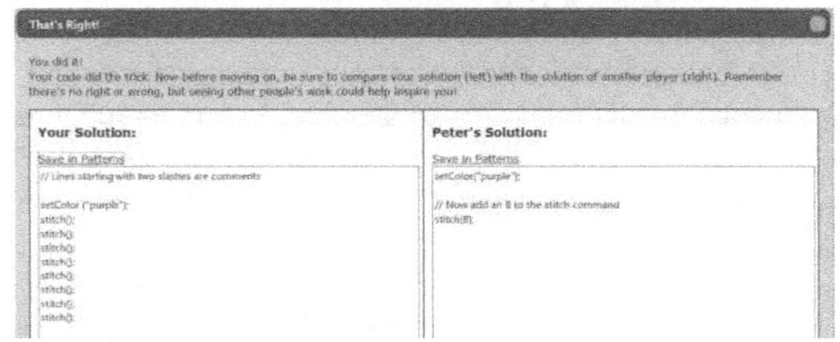

Figure 1: Comparing code solutions in CodeStitch.

This design feature employs an epistemological pluralism [19] that abstains from teaching one "best" way. Instead, the design feature of sharing and comparing code encourages the players to reflect on the differences between approaches. Furthermore, in directly comparing two methods side-by-side, players may gain an understanding of the relational structures embedded within the methods (analogical encoding) and may be more likely to understand the tradeoff of the different approaches.

Study

A preliminary study was conducted to gain insight into the ways in which analogical encoding leveraged through asynchronous collaboration engages players in reflection on structural differences in the solution methods. The study was organized into a preliminary semi-structured cognitive clinical interview [11], 45 minutes of gameplay, and a follow-up interview, each intervention spaced approximately one week apart. All activities occurred in the participants' homes and were video-recorded and log files were collected during gameplay.

Participants were between 11 to 15 years old (3 boys and 1 girl). This age group was chosen to ensure that participants would have only minor experiences in computer programming. Only 1 boy, Jason (all names used here are pseudonyms), had prior exposure to computer programming, having been exposed to Scratch in school. The other participants, Melodie, Gen-ichi, and Shin, had no prior coding experience. None of the participants had a personal computer.

Findings

This paper investigates how participants perceived and utilized the alternate solution. To do so, the findings are drawn from the participants' responses to the interviewer asking during the post-interview if they had looked at the alternate solution and follow-up questions.

The first finding was that all but one participant found the alternate solution beneficial. Shin alone disregarded the alternate solutionsand explained that "it could have been helpful but then, at the same time, it's not how I dealt with it. I wanted to see what the next level was like." Interestingly, he recognized the value of studying other peoples' solutions, yet did not expect its benefit to apply to himself. Shin explained, "I think it would have probably been very helpful for a lot of other people. If they'd completed the level differently they'd see a new way they could have done it and maybe could have applied it to future levels." Not only did Shin not recognize how studying an alternate solution would benefit him, but evidently the potential benefits thereof did not outweigh his personal interest in advancing in the game.

The second finding was that those participants who studied the alternate solutions would reflect on the similarities and differences to varying degrees. Jason (the only participant with prior coding experience) suggested that this activity benefited his understanding of programming. He commented that it "gives me a bit more understanding cause then I see how this person solved it and how I solved it and I compare and contrast." This gaining of a better understanding occurred by (1) detecting differences, (2) drawing conclusions, and (3) formulating hypotheses. Not all participants drew on all forms of reflection; for example, Melodie detected differences and drew on conclusions but did not formulate hypotheses; Jason on the other hand did. The order of operations however remained fixed. When asked why she had looked at the alternate solution, Melodie recounted "I liked to look for the differences. I remember mine for I think it was Patty's scarf. I looked at [Lane's] to see what's different and I put set color pink all the way through (giggles) – after every new row. I didn't have to do that." Melodie first detected the differences between her own code solution and the alternate solution and based on those differences, drew conclusions about how she could have improved her solution. In so doing, she implies qualitative differences in code solutions.

Both Jason and Gen-ichi had similar findings but went one step further in their reflections as they abstracted their conclusions from the concrete example into generalizable strategies for programming. For example, Jason stated that, "I compare and contrast and maybe this person's was shorter cause they used less code then I did. And so they wouldn't have to use as much time. So next time I would make my code shorter so I don't have to use as much time either." For these two boys, looking at someone else's solution led to comparing solutions, reflecting on the differences, drawing conclusions for their own strategy, and even abstracting and generalizing their findings.

The third finding was that in reflecting on the differences in the code, participants would notice sophistication in the alternative solution but rarely in their own. Melodie noticed less redundancy in the alternate solution (not resetting the color). Jason was impressed that Lane had not needed to employ variables in order to arrive at the same result as he did when instead he could have pointed out that in so doing, she had not followed the instructions (as he had done). Jason remarked that, "okay, that was cool. Cause I noticed that [Lane] didn't use the [variable] name. I'm like 'she still did the exact same thing that I did. She just didn't have to put the names on the top.'"

Conclusion

The paper describes a work-in-progress study to explore the potential of analogical encoding to support learning about programming. The findings indicate that all but one CodeStitch player reflected on the alternate solutions, though not for every instance. Both novices and non-beginners reflected on alternate solutions suggesting that engagement was based on curiosity about the difference between the code solutions rather than prior knowledge or skill. During reflection participants often compared differences between their code and the alternate solution and drew conclusions or implications about how they might change their own code from these differences. In studying the differences, participants would recognize sophistication in the alternate solution but only shortcomings in their own. Lastly, two participants also abstracted their findings from the concrete examples into generalizable programming strategies.

Future Work

Despite the small sample size of participants these findings suggest designing for analogical encoding is promising. In future work I will use data from gameplay logs to cross-validate and provide richer context for what subjects self-report. I will draw on the process data to see if and how learners adapted their strategies after comparing peer solutions. A larger participant pool, and richer process data about how learners use alternate strategies to play a programming game should provide important insight into the design of game-based learning environments for coding as well as other domain areas.

Another area worth investigating is the tension between players' desire to advance to the next level versus wanting to study the alternative solutions. Future work on this study will explore ways to integrate alternate solutions into the game that alleviate this tension, or take advantage of it.

Acknowledgements
Many thanks to Nathan Holbert for the valuable feedback on this project.

References
1. Michael Armbrust, Armando Fox, Rean Griffith, Anthony D. Joseph, Randy Katz, Andy Konwinski, Gunho Lee, David Patterson, Ariel Rabkin, Ion Stoica, and Matei Zaharia. 2010. A view of cloud computing. *Commun. ACM* 53, 4: 50-58. DOI=http://dx.doi.org/10.1145/1721654.172167
2. Karen Brennan & Mitchel Resnick. 2012. New frameworks for studying and assessing the development of computational thinking. Paper presented at the annual meeting of the American Educational Research Association, Vancouver, BC, Canada.
3. Tom DeMarco & Timothy Lister. 1999. *Peopleware: Productive projects and teams.* 2nd ed. Dorset House, New York, NY.
4. Ronald W. Ferguson. 1994. MAGI: A model of analogy-based encoding using symmetry and regularity. In A. Ram & K. Eiselt (Eds.), *Proceedings of the Sixteenth Annual Conference of the Cognitive Science Societ*. Erlbaum, Hillsdale, NJ, 283-288.
5. Ronald W. Ferguson & Kenneth D. Forbus. 1998. Telling juxtapositions: Using repetition and alignable difference in diagram understanding. In K. Holyoak, D. Gentner, & B. Kokinov (Eds.), *Advances in analogy research*. New Bulgarian University, Sofia, Bulgaria, 109-117.
6. Nick V. Flor & Edwin L. Hutchins. 1991. Analyzing distributed cognition in software teams: A case study of team programming during perfective software maintenance. In J. Koenemann-Belliveau, Moher, T. & Robertson, S. *Empirical studies of programmers: Fourth workshop*. Ablex, Norwood, NJ, 36/64.
7. James P. Gee. 2003. *What video games have to teach us about learning and literacy.* Palgrave Macmillan, New York, NY.
8. Dedre Gentner. 1983. Structure-mapping: A theoretical framework for analogy. *Cognitive Science*, 7: 155-170.
9. Dedre Gentner & José Medina. 1998. Similarity and the development of rules. *Cognition*, 65: 263–297.
10. Dedre Gentner, Jeffrey Loewenstein, & Leigh Thompson. 2003. Learning and transfer: A general role for analogical encoding. *Journal of Educational Psychology*, 95, 2: 393-408.
11. Herbert P. Ginsburg. 1997. *Entering the child's mind: The clinical interview in psychological research and practice*. Cambridge UP, New York, NY.
12. Yasmin Kafai & Deborah Fields. 2013. *Connected play: Tweens in a virtual world.* MIT Press, Cambridge, MA.
13. Yasmin Kafai & Quinn Burke. 2014. *Connected code. Why children need to learn programming.* MIT Press, Cambridge, MA.
14. Kenneth J. Kurtz, Chun-Hui Miao & Dedre Gentner. 2001. Learning by analogical bootstrapping. *Journal of the Learning Sciences*, 10: 417–446.
15. Andrés Monroy-Hernandez. 2012. *Designing for remixing: Supporting an online community of amateur creators.* PhD dissertation, Massachusetts Institute of Technology, Cambridge, MA.
16. Jeffrey Loewenstein, Leigh Thompson, & Dedre Gentner. 1999. Analogical encoding facilitates knowledge transfer in negotiation. *Psychonomic Bulletin & Review,* 6, 4: 586-597.
17. Elizabeth Patitsas, Michelle Craig, & Steve Easterbrook. 2013. Comparing and contrasting different algorithms leads to increased student

learning. In *Proceedings of the ninth annual international ACM conference on International computing education research* (ICER '13). ACM, New York, NY, USA, 145-152. DOI=http://dx.doi.org/10.1145/2493394.2493409

18. Mitchel Resnick, John Maloney, Andrés Monroy-Hernandez, Natalie Rusk, Evelyn Eastmond, Karen Brennan, Amon Millner, Eric Rosenbaum, Jay Silver, Brian Silverman, & Yasmin Kafai. 2009. Scratch: Programming for everyone. *Communications of the ACM* 52, 11: 60-67.
19. Sherry Turkle & Seymour Papert. 1991. Epistemological pluralism and the revaluation of the concrete. In I. Harel and S. Papert (Eds.), *Constructionism*. Ablex, Norwood, NJ, 161-191.
20. Laurie Williams. & Robert Kessler. 2002. Pair programming illuminated. Boston, MA, Addison-Wesley Longman.

Mathematical Reflections: The Design Potential of Ensemble Performance

Lauren Vogelstein
Vanderbiilt University
Nashville, TN 37203, USA
lauren.e.vogelstein@vanderbilt.edu

Corey Brady
Vanderbiilt University
Nashville, TN 37203, USA
corey.brady@vanderbilt.edu

Rogers Hall
Vanderbiilt University
Nashville, TN 37203, USA
r.hall@vanderbilt.edu

IDC '17, June 27-30, 2017, Stanford, CA, USA

ACM ISBN 978-1-4503-4921-5/17/06.
http://dx.doi.org/10.1145/3078072.3084328

Abstract
This paper describes learning in new forms of mathematical activity that involve multiple, moving bodies. It reports on initial findings from interviews with participants from various disciplines, who were asked to find and make sense of emergent mathematics in performances from the opening ceremony of the 2016 Rio Olympic Games. Findings from these interviews will inform future design studies of experimental mathematics teaching and learning.

Author Keywords
Embodied mathematics; ensemble learning; participatory simulations.

ACM Classification Keywords
J.2. PHYSICAL SCIENCES AND ENGINEERING: Mathematics;
J.2. ARTS AND HUMANITIES: Performing arts (e.g., dance, music).

Introduction
All humans have bodies. Our bodies profoundly affect our perspectives and understandings of the world. However, today's schools neglect the body as a resource for mathematical thinking and learning. Recently researchers are putting the body back into the equation [4], [8] and exploring changes in the modality

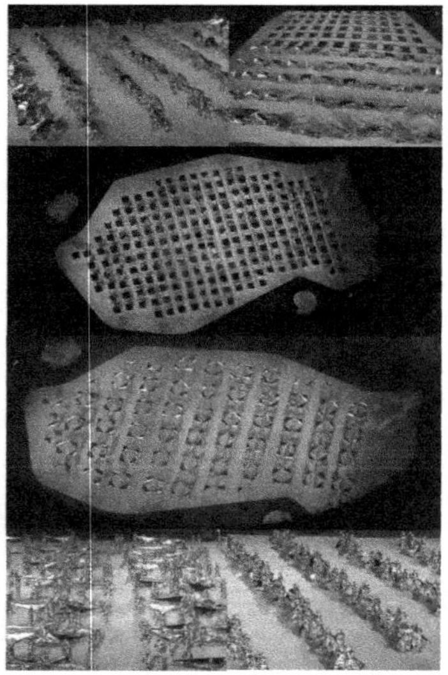

Figure 1: Rio 2016 Opening Ceremony

and scale of mathematical activity as whole body coordinated movements in open spaces [2], [5]. This paper presents early findings from a project building on this line of research and investigating the potential of choreographed ensemble performances as a context for expressive mathematical activity. We share initial insights from interviews with people from various disciplines, who were asked to find and make sense of emergent mathematics in performances from the opening ceremony of the 2016 Rio Olympic Games (Figure 1). Findings from these interviews will inform future design studies of experimental mathematics teaching and learning.

Background and Framework

During the opening ceremony of the 2016 Rio Olympic games, billions of people worldwide watched thousands of performers execute large-scale choreographed routines with dynamic geometric forms. In this emerging genre of theatrical production, viewers are invited to engage with a performance that is mathematically complex in design and appearance [4], [5]. Our research engages with this cultural form, under the premise that ensemble performances can hold rich relations to mathematics. As a first step to exploring this space, we aim to understand how groups of people with different disciplinary backgrounds might identify patterns, explain how these patterns are assembled in the performances, and use their own bodies and similar props to demonstrate their understandings. The opening ceremony of the Rio Olympic games (Figure 1) provides rich material for probing these understandings, as the video record involves hundreds of performers who create complex dynamic formations by using their bodies and large Mylar squares.

To explore the expressive and mathematical potential of this approach, we have begun conducting extended interviews in which we provide similar Mylar sheets to groups of four participants, encouraging them to attempt to coordinate their movement with the prop to complete mathematically based tasks. This context disrupts the scale and modality used in traditional geometry practices. Giving a group of people an *intrinsic* perspective on dynamic shapes that they can manipulate, foregrounds different mathematical reasoning, learning, principles, and perspectives from paper-scale geometry [2], [5]. Coordinating multiple people as components of one shape becomes important. This involves organizing their positions and their perspectives in space and time. The change in scale and modality also involves recreating ideas and competencies familiar at the "paper-scale" and from the extrinsic perspective (e.g., notions of knowing measurement and straight). At this scale, embodied and social human resources such as talk, gesture, and gaze management are foregrounded as tools for coordinating group action, whereas they are backgrounded or suppressed in single-person paper-scale geometry. The cognition of the group and prop is distributed across all of these constituent parts as these coordination resources become cognitive resources for the distributed system.

In the course of our first four interviews of this kind we have seen many connections between participants activity and core geometric ideas, such as symmetries of geometric shapes, tessellations, and transformational geometry. To guide future design work in this mode, we are eager to see how the context of ensemble performance changes the relation of learners to this content and potentially gives them new

Figure 2: All let go of their corners

Figure 3: Tyrone suggesting that only two participants cross underneath the Mylar

access to understandings. People's physical intuitions about how their bodies relate to geometric forms are a rich resource that this work aims to tap into. Our work bears some similarity to the early "Star People" games conducted by Resnick & Wilensky [7] in providing access to the emergent behaviors of complex systems, in that we involve groups of people in physically enacting phenomena where the structure of the group is mapped onto the structure of the system being explored. Activities of this kind are also called Participatory Simulations [3], [9], enabling a group to use its own behavior as a means of investigating topics and themes of interest. This form of projection involves a group-level variant of a technique that Papert (1980) called "playing turtle." Papert used the term "syntonic learning" to describe the affordances of environments where learners can make use of their own perspectives and bodies for inquiry; these group environments would offer a *social* syntonicity [1].

Methods

Our interviews are conducted in four parts. First, participants watch and discuss a clip from the 2016 Rio opening ceremony in which 824 performers manipulate large Mylar squares in groups of 4 performers per square (Figure 1). Second, the quartet of participants is given a 7′ x 7′ Mylar square and given two tasks: (i) fold the sheet into a triangle just like the performers do and (ii) flip (reflect) it in the same wave the performers do. Next participants are asked what they think mathematics is and prompted to describe both the performance and their experience with the prop, mathematically. The last part of the interview offers the participants the opportunity to create their own performance with the Mylar sheet. They are asked to explore what else they can do with the prop, to note any limitations of working with the prop, and finally to reflect on their experience.

We position four cameras throughout the room to record the interactions; thus we record views from above, from two adjacent sides of the rectangular room, and from the table where participants sit for discussions throughout the interview. In particular, the top view and side views have been helpful in analyzing these sessions from the perspective of their relation to the large-scale performances of the 2016 Rio Olympic opening and closing ceremonies. The figures in this paper utilize these multiple views.

We are conducting these interviews (a) to understand the cultural importance of a new theatrical genre composed of units of props plus bodies, (b) to explore what is compelling about this cultural form, and (c) to ask participants to discover their own "powerful ideas" [6] and use shared tools (e.g., mathematics, their bodies) to interpret these performances and explore the generative capabilities of these mathematical props. This paper will focus on the third line of inquiry, sharing two cases that we think are extremely mathematically generative, accessible, and describing the unique affordances of these props.

Preliminary Analysis and Findings

Our interview-based research is at an early stage, yet we can already discern the outlines of the design space for activities using this context to explore mathematics in new ways. For instance, one group attempted to convince themselves that their constructions were "the same as" (congruent or similar to) those of the Rio performers. Another group questioned the basic nature of the prop (e.g., proving it was a square), and whether other shapes (e.g., rectangles or various kinds of triangle) could generate the same shapes as the square. Finally, all of the groups exhibited an interest in the ways that the square could be transformed and manipulated through maneuvers that began and ended in square form. In mathematical terms, that is, all of the groups explored aspects of the symmetry transformations of the square.

All of the groups we have interviewed (including two quartets of 8th graders and one quartet of their teachers), have explored the billowing properties of the lightweight Mylar prop that have allowed participants to cross under the square and switch positions with partners at the opposite corner of the sheet. The interviews suggest that the discovery of this property of the prop has an important role in encouraging the group to explore generative mathematical and performance properties of the situation and prop. . One quartet of 8th graders first produced this floating phenomenon at the beginning of the interview while they were engrossed in trying to inflate the prop like it is done at the end of the Rio performance. Raising the Mylar above their heads in unison was their initial attempt to "catch air in it." At the end of the interview when trying to choreograph their own performance this group raised the sheet above their heads, holding on to their corners as they all walked in towards the center. As the group executed this maneuver, one member, Tyrone, suggested that they switch sides by walking underneath the prop. They attempted to have participants at opposite corners release their corners and cross underneath the sheet at the same time. In their first attempt to do this they let go of their corners, but found that the Mylar floated away, making it almost impossible for them all to grab their new corner after crossing underneath (Figure 2). They then tried to raise the Mylar slowly, hoping to have it stay over their heads as they all crossed under. This configuration allowed Tyrone to see Sarah across from him and suggest that only two members of the group should cross under at a time (Figure 3). Using this symmetry proved the most reliable way for the group to exchange places under the prop.

The billowing property of the prop was extremely salient to both groups of 8th graders when given the time to investigate what they could do with it. Both groups discovered that if they raised the Mylar above their heads, it would float above them and allow two opposite participants to let go and cross under to switch corners. Their intuitive understandings of symmetry allowed them to choreograph ways to move underneath the sheet while it billowed above them. The billowing materiality of the Mylar thus seemed to open up a performative space and opportunity that the different groups could fill with various movements and transformations of their own devising.

While also working on the third part of the interview, the group of adults produced a 180-degree rotation by simultaneously conducting two reflections across the two diagonals of the square. Although this group consisted of adult participants, we see strong continuities with the affordances of the prop explored by the other groups; thus, we argue that these kinds of exploration could be supported in many groups with appropriate scaffolding or prompting. In terms of the mathematics of the symmetries of the square, this equivalence (two reflections equal a rotation) is a non-trivial result. And yet the group generated this outcome spontaneously through group play with the

Figure 4: Twisted kink in the Mylar

Figure 5: Above view and side view of adult quartet conducting two reflections simultaneously

prop. After producing it, they spent the remainder of their choreography session attempting to reproduce and understand this outcome.

The quartet began, like the other groups, by exploring different billowing properties of the sheet. Similar to the 8th graders, they used this floating quality to cross underneath to opposite corners of the square and switch positions. In contrast to their students, however, this group continued to expand on the idea of crossing under the floating sheet. One of the participants, Damien, suggested, "now let's do it, but we don't switch corners, we just switch places. So it will twist, it will fold over as we" and he gestured, raising his corner of the Mylar and his other hand up and over in front of his body, simulating the beginning of a reflection about the opposite diagonal of the square. Kathy, his partner opposite him in the square, indicated that she understood the plan. The quartet all raised their corners, and Damien and Kathy crossed underneath the Mylar. They were not able to walk all the way to the desired end points, however, because the square became twisted (Figure 4). Damien turned to face the kink in the Mylar, pointed to it and says "oh wait, we don't have a go-under for that." Here he acknowledged that in order to reflect this sheet over the diagonal, one corner (which is attached to a person) would need to pass *under* the sheet while another corner (also attached to a person) would need to pass *over* the sheet. That is, having both corners cross under the Mylar led to the twisted outcome they faced. In contrast to working with paper-scale geometry in which flipping a small rigid square can be done easily by going out of the plane, this set up makes it salient to the quartet that going "out of the plane" cannot be taken for granted.

Kathy and Damien then unfolded the Mylar, returned to their original square position, and tried to debug what happened. Another group member, Monica suggested that they could try switching each diagonal *simultaneously*, prompting the quartet to clarify a complex sequence involving people going "under" each other, in which Kathy needed to go under Damien, and Monica needed to go under both Kathy and Damien, as well as the participant opposite her, Tanesha. In planning this interaction, the group was describing two reflections, each about a different diagonal of the square. After clarifying these plans, the quartet raised the sheet and everyone enacted their role (Figure 5). Tanesha and Monica were the first to enter, walking along their diagonal. Kathy walked to the outside of Tanesha, and Damien hung back so that he passed through the center after Tanesha and Monica had passed each other (Figure 6).

From the top view, it is clear that the transformation that occurred as a result of this maneuver was a 180-degree rotation (left column of Figure 5). The camera footage shows the Mylar sheet ballooned up, spun around, and then was drawn back down into a square. This view also shows that the Mylar never actually flipped over: the side that was initially facing the ground stayed facing the ground for the entire time. A rotation occurs when these two reflections occur simultaneously; thus, conducting these two reflections simultaneously did not entail the sheet flipping over, as occurred in single reflections.

The side camera gives a contrasting view of the performance, clearly showing the participants' individual trajectories. It shows Tanesha and Monica traversing the diagonal that was between them when

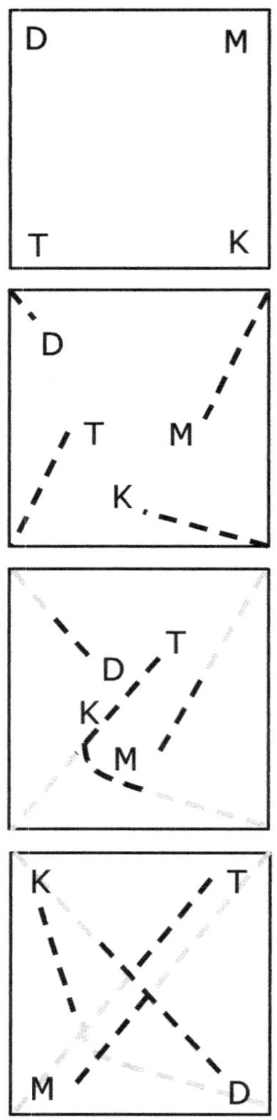

Figure 6: Participants' pathways to complete two reflections underneath the Mylar

they started. It shows Kathy walking around the outside of Tanesha and it also shows Damien and Kathy passing each other along the diagonal between them after Tanesha and Monica passed each other. This diagonal walking pattern cannot be seen from above and reveals an entirely different perspective on the action. Both these patterns of movement and the group's verbal and nonverbal communication before the enactment indicate that the members of the quartet were thinking about conducting two reflections in quick succession so that they would happen almost simultaneously. The above view, however, gives away that they *also* produced a rotation as a result.

We believe that there is rich potential to design mathematical experiences for quartets working with this prop. The desire to create something aesthetically interesting, in the spirit of the Rio performance, led these quartets to generate all of the symmetries of a square, as well as to explore sequences and combinations of them. Each of the groups began to develop operations on the prop that produced reflections along lines of symmetry (both diagonals and vertical/horizontal symmetry lines). The groups exhibited different procedures for enacting these symmetries and different interests in sequencing and repeating them, while producing the same end state. We find this interesting from a design perspective because it allows participants to gain multiple perspectives on the operations, as well as to discover and explore the relations that exist among them.

The performance unit of people and prop made rich mathematical opportunities both accessible and social, introducing a materiality to geometric concepts that is not present in paper-scale geometry. The quartet's exploration with the prop generated physical, logistical, and mathematical challenges that do not exist at a smaller scale; and exploration of the prop's abilities within a quartet system led these groups to discover some of the mathematical affordances of this billowing system.

References

1. Brady, C., Weintrop, D., Anton, G., & Wilensky, U. (2016). Constructionist Learning at the Group Level with Programmable Badges. In *Proc. Constructionism Conf* (pp. 61-68).
2. Hall, R., Ma, J. Y., & Nemirovsky, R. (2014). Re-scaling bodies in/as representational instruments in GPS drawing. *Learning technologies and the body: Integration and implementation in formal and informal learning environments, 112.*
3. Klopfer, E., Yoon, S., & Perry, J. (2005). Using palm technology in participatory simulations of complex systems: A new take on ubiquitous and accessible mobile computing. *Journal of Science Education and Technology, 14*(3), 285-297.
4. Lakoff, G., & Núñez, R. E. (2000). Where mathematics comes from: How the embodied mind brings mathematics into being. Basic books.
5. Ma, J. Y. (2016). Designing Disruptions for Productive Hybridity: The Case of Walking Scale Geometry. *Journal of the Learning Sciences*, 1-37.
6. Papert, S. (1980). Mindstorms: Children, computers, and powerful ideas. Basic Books, Inc..
7. Resnick, M., & Wilensky, U. (1998). Diving into complexity: Developing probabilistic decentralized thinking through role-playing activities. *The Journal of the Learning Sciences*, *7*(2), 153-172.
8. Stevens, R., & Hall, R. (1998). Disciplined perception: Learning to see in technoscience. *Talking mathematics in school: Studies of teaching and learning*, 107-149.
9. Wilensky, U., & Stroup, W. (1999). Learning through participatory simulations: Network-based design for systems learning in classrooms. *Proceedings of Computer Supported Collaborative Learning (CSCL'99)*. Stanford, CA, December 12 - 15.

Designing Towards Maximum Motivation and Engagement in an Interactive Speech Therapy Game

Jared Duval
Zachary Rubin
Elizabeth Goldman
Nick Antrilli
Yu Zhang
Su-Hua Wang
Sri Kurniawan
University of California Santa Cruz
Santa Cruz, CA 95064 USA
jduval@ucsc.edu
zarubin@ucsc.edu
eljgoldm@ucsc.edu
nantrill@ucsc.edu
yzhan105@ucsc.edu
suhua@ucsc.edu
skurnia@ucsc.edu

IDC '17, June 27-30, 2017, Stanford, CA, USA

ACM ISBN 978-1-4503-4921-5/17/06.
http://dx.doi.org/10.1145/3078072.3084329

Abstract

Children with speech impairments often find speech curriculums tedious, limiting how often children are motivated to practice. A speech therapy game has the potential to make practice fun, may help facilitate increased time and quality of at-home speech therapy, and lead to improved speech. We explore using conversational real-time speech recognition, game methodologies theorized to improve immersion and flow, and user centered approaches to design an immersive interactive speech therapy solution. Our preliminary user evaluation showed that compared to traditional methods, children were more motivated to practice speech using our system.

Author Keywords

Speech Processing; Speech Therapy; Human Computer Interaction; Games; Motivation

ACM Classification Keywords

H. Information Systems; H.5. Information interfaces and presentation (e.g., HCI); H.5.2. Voice I/O; I/O J.3. Life and Medical Sciences: Health

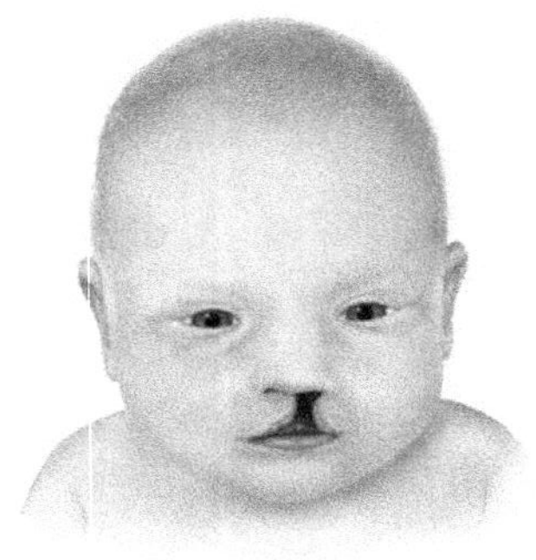

Figure 1: An image that shows a baby with cleft lip. Image CC-BY Center for Disease Control and Prevention

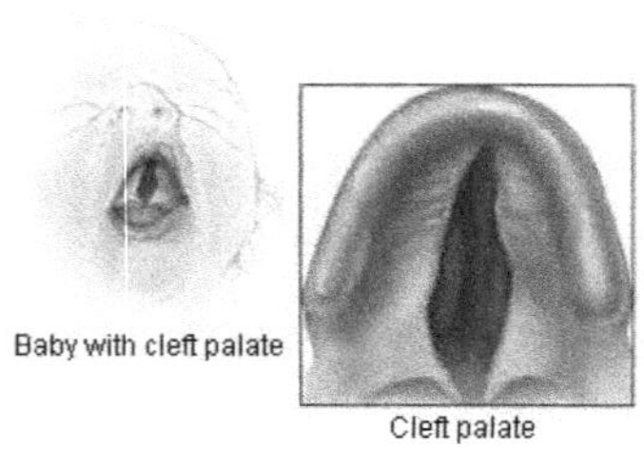

Figure 2: An image that shows a baby with cleft palate. Image CC-BY Center for Disease Control and Prevention

Introduction
The prevalence of speech sound phonological and articulation disorders in young children is 8 to 9 percent [13]. Most speech impairments can be corrected with practice and speech therapy. Speech therapy consists of two components: in-office sessions with a speech language pathologist (SLP) and at-home practice curriculums [6, 11]. Orofacial cleft is one of the most common causes of speech impairments.

Orofacial cleft is a common birth defect that results in a gap in the lip or mouth, shown in Figures 1 and 2. Children born with orofacial cleft undergo multiple surgical procedures and often require long-term speech therapy. Speech impairment is extremely common with this birth defect because it allows air to escape through the nasal cavity, which results in the use of compensatory glottal attacks to mimic sounds, lisps, and difficulty forming plosives.

During in-office therapy sessions, SLPs evaluate the child's speech to find specific targets that the child has difficulty speaking. Once the SLP knows the child's unique impairments, they work with child on techniques to improve the detected targets. The SLP gives children and parents resources to take home to continue practicing until the next session, where the child is reassessed.

SLPs instruct parents to have their child practice for ten minutes per day, but according to our interview with a SLP, it is suspected that children practice little to none outside of speech therapy sessions. There are many contributing factors as to why children do not practice enough at home: children find the curriculums tedious and repetitive, parents are not qualified to assess the small nuances in leading a speech curriculum, and children may not be intrinsically motivated to improve their speech.

Many children do not have enough access to SLPs and could benefit from a supplemental speech therapy game. The challenges a speech therapy game may address are numerous [12]:

- Moves responsibility to lead practice from the parent to the game
- Can assign appropriate words and phrases from an expansive knowledge base for each child's unique speech goals
- Adjusts difficulty as the child plays using a dynamic curriculum to balance challenge and boredom [3]
- Adds intrinsic motivation to practicing speech through gameplay and mechanics
- Allows SLP to track practice and performance in-between in-office therapy sessions to make better use of their time
- Allows children with less access to an SLP to continue improving speech

A high-fidelity prototype of our speech therapy game named SpokeIt has been developed and tested. Many of the design considerations mentioned below are the result of feedback we received from the original high-fidelity prototype of SpokeIt. We first discuss the new design motivations and then the results of our user study that lead to these decisions.

Motivation
Design of the game content, mechanics, and interactions are central to the success of improving

Figure 3: Blue game character

Figure 4: Yellow game character

speech and motivating practice. "Placing high hopes on games designed for the public good- as many nonprofits, health organizations, and social enterprises are doing-without realizing the bad game design can undermine the most noble of ambitions. It's quite possible to make terrible, dull, and unappealing games for learning or training or health" [9].

To improve speech, one must practice speaking, but saying a word or phrase repeatedly for the sake of practice is often found to be tedious and boring. During our observations of interactions between SLPs and their patient's we noticed the jaded children were not interested in practicing speech.

Games turn repetition from something that stifles motivation and induces boredom into an element that is recognized as useful for progress in the game [10]. Hiding information about gameplay and maintaining a sense of uncertainty about the outcome can make games fun [10]. Repeating target words and phrases for the advancement in a game is much more motivating than for the completion of a speech curriculum.

Educational software has traditionally attempted to harness games as extrinsic motivation by using them as sugar coating for learning content, but children learn more from intrinsic approaches [8]. The learning objectives should be part of the gameplay itself [8] Practicing speech should be a game mechanic that induces immersion and flow rather than a disruption to play. The narrative and plot should align with the learning content [5].

If done correctly, games can lead to improved learning, enhanced motivation, greater attention, and increased retention [2]. The end state we desire is the motivated learner, which is someone who is enthusiastic, focused, and engaged [7].

Design

In order to understand the needs of the relevant stakeholders we held a focus group with cleft lip specialists, researchers, and game developers. Cleft lip specialists emphasized the need for virtual incentives that would remain effective for months or even years. Researchers and game developers agreed that maximizing immersion through emotionally motivating elements would best hide the repetitive speech exercises. We design and validate the following aspects of our game are emotionally motivating:

- Characters that are relatable and have the capacity to create empathy
- An overarching plot for our characters that is interesting and defines the player's goals
- Narrators that engage and encourage the player to continue helping the game characters
- A Procedural Content Background Art Generator that creates rich environments to experience
- Mechanics that seamlessly incorporate conversational speech recognition into completing game objectives

Characters

The characters in a game are often the single most motivating factors to continue play [9]. We become invested in their wellbeing, life, and goals [9]. The

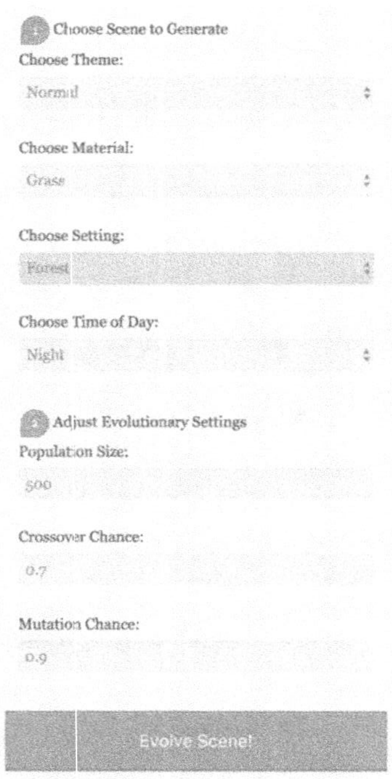

Figure 5: Settings available to system to procedurally generate background art using evolutionary algorithm

children who play our speech therapy game should be able to relate to the characters and be motivated to help them.

Our speech therapy game follows a race known as the Migs, shown if Figures 3 and 4. The Migs do not speak. The player is their voice. The game includes Migs of six different colors, six different personalities, and unique relationships with the other Migs.

We animate the Migs facial expressions to display the primary emotions as a starting point for creating natural and realistic experiences within the game [1]. Using Adobe's Character Animator, we are able to employ actors to capture and record animations in real time that are mapped directly to the Migs. By combining the animations created by graphics artists, performances by actors in Character Animator, and physics, we can make believable and natural facial expressions so that children can easily understand our game character's emotions and hopefully empathize with them.

Plot

The story of the Migs is a hopeful one. Before the game is played for the first time, the player is provided an introductory cinematic to the game that describes the Migs history and story. The story begins in the Mig's beautiful world, where the narrator describes their utopian lives. As the background music gets more dramatic, the Migs are whisked up by a storm into a new unfamiliar two-dimensional world.

Procedural Content Generation

Speech therapy is an ongoing process that takes each child a different amount of time to complete. Therefore, our speech therapy game should continue to be available. Previous iterations of our work employed mini-games that would play for an allotted amount of time before switching to the next game. Games could be randomly ordered and could be played multiple times. We observed that the mini-games lacked replayability and would not sustain long-term use. Fresh procedurally generated content should solve replayability issues.

Our PCG employs an evolutionary algorithm that learns how to make art with our collection of over 750 image assets. The evolutionary algorithm borrows from biology to develop art that is believable and aesthetically pleasing, shown in Figure 6. It actively learns to match selected themes, materials, terrain settings, lighting, and time of day to produce visually striking worlds, shown in Figure 5.

As development continues, the plot and game objectives will also employ PCG so that our speech therapy game can always deliver fresh new content that will keep the children motivated and engaged.

Mechanics

The elements of engaged learning are focused goals, challenging tasks, clear and compelling standards, protection from adverse consequences for initial failures, affirmation of performance, affiliation with others, novelty and variety, choice, and authenticity [4].

Games are proven to have perceptual and cognitive impacts as well as the ability for the player to acquire new skills [2]. We can adjust difficulty by assigning target words that are more difficult to the child,

Figure 6: Sample output of PCG while it continues learning how to create background art

Figure 7: Indicator that displays when the game is listening for input. Indicator changes colors when loudness thresholds are met by the player

changing the number of repetitions needed to move past a challenge, adjusting the rhythm and timing required to say the targets, and by tweaking the number of targets required per interaction.

Volume is a challenge for many children. To successfully complete a challenge the child must say the correct target at an appropriate volume. There is an indicator that displays the loudness of the child's speech and it changes colors when volume moves in and out of the threshold. It should be clear to the player when the game is listening and when they should be speaking. The child should only be able to speak when the narrators are not. To make this clear, we include an ear in the top-right corner of the game to indicate when the child should speak and is toggled off when the game is not listening, shown in Figure 7.

Results

SpokeIt (1st iteration shown in Figure 8 and 2nd iteration shown in Figure 9) has been tested on children with cleft speech as well as with expert medical professionals that work with children with cleft speech.

Four participants with cleft speech played SpokeIt: 3 children under 10 (Mean: 5.33, σ: 2.3) and 1 teenager. One child in particular engaged much more with the game than the shyer children. The children under 10 had speech barely above the detection threshold, resulting in play difficulties. We addressed this with a volume indicator and adding narrator voice prompts instructing the player to speak louder.

The child life specialist said she loved watching the eight-year old play the game. She noticed that he immediately put much more effort into his speech. She demonstrated how he overemphasized each spoken syllable in the target sentence to make the game advance. The SLP had trouble keeping his attention, but when he was given the opportunity to try SpokeIt, he completed the entire prototype and asked for more content.

The SLP who watched her patients play SpokeIt loved the storybook style of the game. She is skeptical that the game will ever be able to make the distinction between correct and incorrect speech, but looks forward to motivating practice nonetheless.

The plastic surgeon who debriefed with us wants to add a feature to the game that would display a mouth and demonstrate correct speech when the child was struggling.

The eldest spoke primarily using sign language. It was very difficult for the SLP to convince her to use her voice. At first, she was also too shy to try SpokeIt, but once we started the game, she started speaking without the SLP's encouragement.

Discussion and Future Work

The speech recognition system accuracy can be improved greatly. We are curious about how effectively it can differentiate between correct and incorrect speech. If the system can accurately diagnose speech impairment details, it would save SLPs a lot of time that could be used for helping the child improve.

A speech therapy game has the potential to track progress for each child. It may be able to grade children's speech and report progress to SLPs. The data can be studied to look for demographic patterns and

Figure 8: Original high fidelity prototype of SpokeIt actively using conversational speech recognition

Figure 9: Example challenge where child must say "Fire"

correlations to other aspects of the child's development.

SpokeIt may make it easier for SLPs to assign unique curriculums for each child's unique speech goals. It can assign target words and phrases that will have the most impact on the child.

Acknowledgements

This material is based in part upon work supported by the National Science Foundation under Grant number #1617253. We also thank Doctor Travis Tollefson and SLP Christina Roth for their aid in conducting user evaluations. Any opinions, findings, and conclusions or recommendations expressed in this material are those of the authors and do not necessarily reflect the views of the National Science Foundation.

References

1. Becker-Asano, C., & Wachsmuth, I. (2010). Affective computing with primary and secondary emotions in a virtual human. *Autonomous Agents and Multi-Agent Systems*, *20*(1), 32.
2. Boyle, E., Connolly, T. M., & Hainey, T. (2011). The role of psychology in understanding the impact of computer games. Entertainment Computing, 2(2), 69-74.
3. Conati, C., & Zhou, X. (2002, June). Modeling students' emotions from cognitive appraisal in educational games. In International Conference on Intelligent Tutoring Systems (pp. 944-954). Springer Berlin Heidelberg.
4. Dickey, M. D. (2005). Engaging by design: How engagement strategies in popular computer and video games can inform instructional design. Educational Technology Research and Development, 53(2), 67-83.
5. Dondlinger, M. J. (2007). Educational video game design: A review of the literature. Journal of applied educational technology, 4(1), 21-31.
6. Facts about Cleft Lip and Cleft Palate. (2015, November 12). Retrieved March 25, 2017, from https://www.cdc.gov/ncbddd/birthdefects/cleftlip.html
7. Garris, R., Ahlers, R., & Driskell, J. E. (2002). Games, motivation, and learning: A research and practice model. Simulation & gaming, 33(4), 441-467.
8. Habgood, M. J., & Ainsworth, S. E. (2011). Motivating children to learn effectively: Exploring the value of intrinsic integration in educational games. The Journal of the Learning Sciences, 20(2), 169-206.
9. Isbister, K. (2016). How Games Move Us: Emotion by Design. MIT Press.
10. Sauvé, L. (2010). Effective educational games. Educational gameplay and simulation environments: Case studies and lessons learned, 27-50.
11. Speech Development – Cleft Palate Foundation. (n.d.). Retrieved March 25, 2017, from http://www.cleftline.org/parents-individuals/publications/speech-development/
12. Sri Kurniawan, Su-hua Wang, Christina Roth, Travis Tollefson. (2016). CHS: Small: Game for Cleft Speech Therapy (No. 1617253). National Science Foundation.
13. Quick Statistics About Voice, Speech, Language. (2016, May 19). Retrieved April 01, 2017, from https://www.nidcd.nih.gov/health/statistics/quick-statistics-voice-speech-language

“Hey Google is it OK if I eat you?” Initial Explorations in Child-Agent Interaction

Stefania Druga*
MIT Media Lab
Cambridge, MA, 02139 USA
sdruga@media.mit.edu

Randi Williams*
MIT Media Lab
Cambridge, MA, 02139 USA
randiw12@media.mit.edu

Cynthia Breazeal
MIT Media Lab
Cambridge, MA, 02139 USA
cynthiab@media.mit.edu

Mitchel Resnick
MIT Media Lab
Cambridge, MA 02139 USA
mitch@media.mit.edu

IDC '17, June 27-30, 2017, Stanford, CA, USA

ACM ISBN 978-1-4503-4921-5/17/06.
http://dx.doi.org/10.1145/3078072.3084330

Abstract
Autonomous technology is becoming more prevalent in our daily lives. We investigated how children perceive this technology by studying how 26 participants (3-10 years old) interact with Amazon Alexa, Google Home, Cozmo, and Julie Chatbot. We refer to them as “agents“ in the context of this paper. After playing with the agents, children answered questions about trust, intelligence, social entity, personality, and engagement. We identify four themes in child-agent interaction: perceived intelligence, identity attribution, playfulness and understanding. Our findings show how different modalities of interaction may change the way children perceive their intelligence in comparison to the agents'. We also propose a series of design considerations for future child-agent interaction around voice and prosody, interactive engagement and facilitating understanding.

Author Keywords
Child-agent interaction; interaction modalities

ACM Classification Keywords
H.5.2 [Information interfaces and presentation (e.g., HCI)]: Interaction Styles

Introduction
Prior research in child-computer interaction explores the role of computers in shaping the way children think. In her

Figure 1: Alexa
Internet search, games, jokes, music
Morphology: Cylinder, LED ring, female voice
Input: voice
Outputs: voice and LEDs

Figure 2: Google home
Internet search, games, jokes, music
Morphology: Cylinder, LED ring, female voice
Inputs: voice, touch
Outputs: voice, LEDs

book "Second Self", Sherry Turkle describes them as intersectional objects that allow children to investigate "matter, life, and mind"[7]. Similarly, emerging autonomous technologies invite children to think about what it means to be intelligent and conscious. These technologies are becoming increasingly prevalent in our daily lives. Yet, there is little research on how children perceive them. This paper presents the preliminary findings of a study on how children, ages 3 to 10, interact with modern autonomous agents. In our results, we analyze how and why children ascribe particular attributes to agents. We address how different modalities affect children's perception of their own intelligence.

Related Work

In the fields of human-computer interaction (HCI), human-robot interaction (HRI), and applied developmental psychology, there is extensive research on how children perceive robotic and conversational agents. Tanaka found that children build relationships with these agents the same way that they build relationships with people [6]. Kahn found that they consider robots as ontologically different from other objects, including computers [3]. He also saw that age and prior experience with technology led to more thoughtful reasonings about robots' nature [3]. Turkle argues that the intelligence of computers encourages children to revise their ideas about animacy and thinking [7]. She observed that children attributed intent and emotion to objects that they could engage with socially and psychologically. Bernstein's study revealed that voice, movement, and physical appearance are other factors that children consider when deciding how to place agents [2].
To understand why children may attribute characteristics of living beings to inanimate objects, we must consider Theory of Mind development [3]. Those with a developed Theory of Mind can perceive the emotional and mental states of other beings. An analysis of 178 false-belief studies led to a model that showed that across cultures, Theory of Mind usually develops when a child is 3 to 5 years old [8].
This finding indicates that age is a significant factor in children's reasoning about technology. Through our work, we build on prior research by analyzing how children interact with and perceive modern agents. In our analysis, we consider developmental differences between children and functional differences between agents.

Method

Participants were randomly divided into four groups, roughly 4-5 in each group, then groups were assigned to a station. We had four stations, one for each agent. Each station had enough devices for participants to interact alone or in pairs. At the stations researchers introduced the agent, then allowed participants to engage with it. After playing with the first agent for 15 minutes, participants rotated to the next station to interact with a second agent. Each session of structured play was followed by a questionnaire, in the form of a game, analyzing children's perception of the agent. We interviewed 5 children (3 boys and 2 girls), to further probe their reasoning. We selected children that played with different agents and displayed different interaction behavior. Between interviews, participants were allowed to free-play with the agents. This methodology is based on the prior research work of Turkle [7].

Participants

This study consisted of 26 participants. Of these participants, four were not able to complete the entire study due to lack of focus. The children were grouped according to their age range to gather data about how reasoning changes at different development stages. There were 12 (46.15%) children aged 3 or 4 years old classified as our younger children group. The older children group contained

Figure 3: Cozmo

Games, autonomous exploration, object/face recognition
Morphology: robot (wheels, lift), garbled voice, block accessories
Inputs: visual information, distance, app
Outputs: sound, movement, LED eyes, block LEDs, app

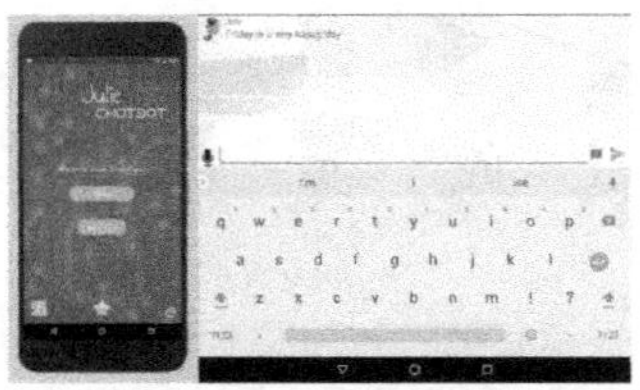

Figure 4: Julie

Conversations, jokes, and games
Morphology: Android app, tablet TTS voice
Inputs: text, voice
Outputs: text, voice

14 (53.85%) children between the ages of 6 and 10. Of the 26 participants, 16 offered information about previous technology experience. A total of 6 (37.5%) of the respondents had programmed before and 9 (56.25%) had interacted with similar agents (Google, Siri, Alexa, and Cortana) previously.

Agents
The children interacted with four different agents: Amazon's Echo Dot "Alexa" (Figure 1), Google Home (Figure 2), Anki's Cozmo (Figure 3), and Julie Chatbot (Figure 4). These agents were chosen for their commercial prevalence and playful physical or conversational characteristics. Alexa is a customizable, voice-controlled digital assistant. Google Home is also a voice-controlled device, for home automation. Cozmo is an autonomous robot toy. Finally, Julie is a conversational chatbot.

The Monster game: interactive questionnaire
After interacting with an agent, participants completed a ten item questionnaire in the form of a monster game. The game was adapted from the work of Park et.al, and was used to keep younger children engaged [4]. In the game, two monsters would share a belief about an agent then children placed a sticker closer to the monster they most agreed with. We vetted the usability of this method and the clarity of the questions in a pilot test. The questions queried how children felt about the agent in terms of trust, intelligence, identity attribution, personality, and engagement and were adapted from a larger questionnaire found in the work of Bartneck[1].

Findings
Overall, most participants agreed that the agents are friendly (Figures 5,6) and trustworthy (Figures 7,8). The younger children (3-4 years old) experienced difficulty

		Agents			
Age	*Response*	*Alexa*	*Google*	*Cozmo*	*Julie*
Younger	Smarter	20%	0%	40%	60%
	Neutral	20%	100%	0%	40%
	Not as smart	60%	0%	60%	0%
Older	Smarter	100%	43%	20%	
	Neutral	0%	57%	40%	
	Not as smart	0%	0%	40%	

Table 1: How children perceive agent's intelligence compared to theirs. Note: Only one session of interaction and questionnaire data with Julie was collected, the group was restless after interaction

interacting with the conversational and chat agents. They enjoyed very much playing with the Cozmo. The older children (6-10 years old) enjoyed interacting with all the agents, although they had their favorites based on the different modalities of interaction. Responses varied depending on the agent and age of the participant. These are discussed below as: perceived intelligence, identity attributions, playfulness, and understanding.

"She probably already is as smart as me" - perceived intelligence
Younger participants had mixed responses, but many older participants said that the agents are smarter than them. The older participants often related the agent's intelligence to its access to information.

For example, Violet[1] (7 years old) played with Alexa and Google Home during structured playtime, then Julie and Cozmo during free play. She systematically analyzed the

[1] Participants names are changed

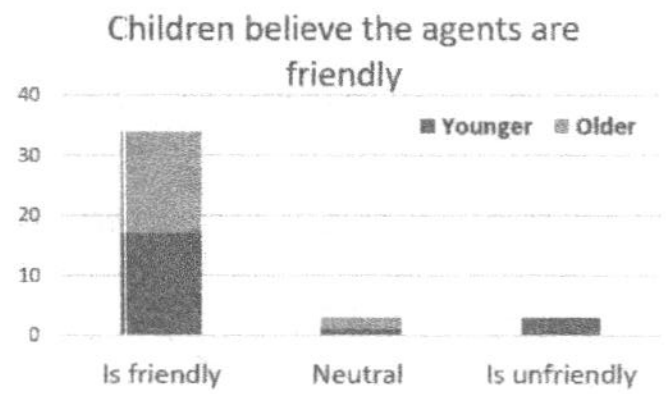

Figure 5: How children perceive friendliness of agents by age

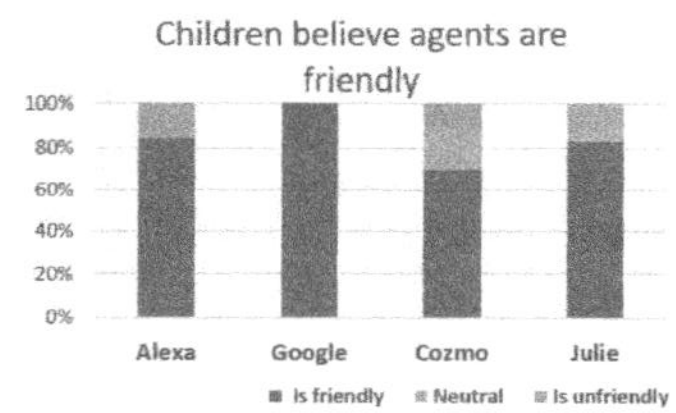

Figure 6: How children perceive friendliness by agent

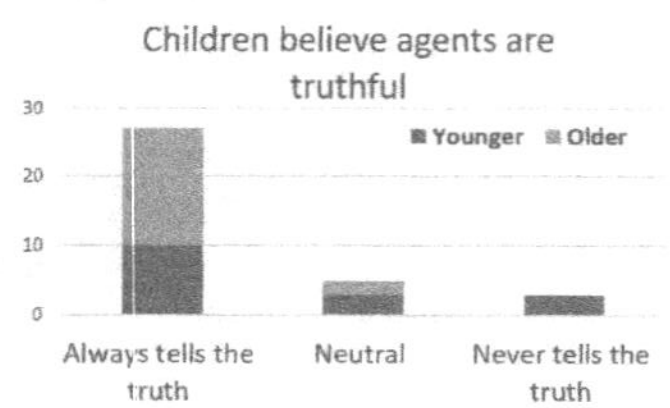

Figure 7: How children perceive truthfulness of agents by age

Figure 8: How children perceive the truthfulness of each agent

intelligence of the agents by comparing their answers in regards to a topic she knew a lot about: sloths."Alexa she knows nothing about sloths, I asked her something about sloths but she didn't answer... but Google did answer so I think that's a little bit smarter because he knows a little more". Mia(9.5 years old) played with Julie and Google Home during the structured play, then tried all the other agents during free play. She used a similar strategy of referring to the things she knows when trying to probe the intelligence of the agent: "[Google Home] probably already is as smart as me because we had a few questions back and forth about things that I already know".

" What are you?" - identity attribution and playfulness
We observed probing behavior, where the participants were trying to understand the agent. Younger children tried to understand the agents like a person, "[Alexa], what is your favorite color", "Hey Alexa, how old are you". Older children tested what the agent would do when asked to perform actions that humans do, "Can you open doors?" "[Cozmo] can you jump?" They also asked the agents how they worked, "Do you have a phone inside you?" and how they defined themselves, "What are you?" The children used gender interchangeably when talking about the agents. Gary and Larry referred to Cozmo as both "he" and "she". "I don't really know which one it is" - Gary. "It's a boy...maybe because of the name but then again you could use a boy name for a girl and and girl name for a boy" - Larry. Later, they concluded that Cozmo "is a bob-cat with eyes".
Multiple agents of the same type were provided during the playtest which led the participants to believe that different Alexas could give different answers , "She doesn't know the answer, ask the other Alexa".They would repeatedly also ask the same question to a device to see if it would change its answer.
As they became familiar with the agents we observed children playfully testing their limits. A 6 year old girl asked several agents "Is it OK if I eat you?". Other children offered the agents food and asked if they could see the objects in front of them, "Alexa what kind of nut am I holding?"

"Sorry I don't understand that question" - understanding
We observed that the majority of participants experienced various challenges getting the agents to understand their questions. Several children tried to increase the level of their voice or make more pauses in their questions, things that may help people understand them. However, it did not always lead to better recognition with the agents.
Often, when the agents would not understand them, children would try to reword their question or make it more specific. Throughout the playtest, we observed shifts in children's strategies, under the encouragement of the facilitators and parents or by observing strategies that worked for other children.
Despite these challenges, participants became fluent in voice interaction quickly and even tried to talk with the agents that didn't have this ability (e.g Cozmo).

Discussion
Building on prior work and based on the observations from this study, we propose the following considerations for child-agent interaction design: voice and prosody, interactive engagement, and facilitating understanding.

Voice and prosody
Voice and tone made a difference in how friendly participants thought the agent was (Figure 6). When asked about differences between the agents Mia replied, "I liked Julie more because she was more like a normal person, she had more feelings. Google Home was like 'I know everything'...Felt like she [Julie] actually understood what I was saying to her".

Her favorite interaction with the agents was the following exchange she had with Julie, "She said 'I'm working on it"...I said 'What do you mean you're working on it ? ' She said 'I don't speak Chinese'[laughs] I wrote back 'I'm not speaking Chinese' and she said 'It sounded like it'. That is an interaction I would have with a normal human". Mia's perception of this interaction could be a result of the "mirroring effect", where the agent's unexpected response is perceived as a sense of humor, a reflection of Mia's own style of communication. Through this interaction and previous experiments ran by Disney Research, we see an opportunity for future agents to imitate the communication style of children and create a prosodic synchrony in the conversations in order to build rapport [5].

Interactive engagement
Gary and Larry said they liked interacting with Cozmo the most "because she could actually move and all the other ones that we did she couldn't move". Also because Cozmo had expressions, "he has feelings, he can do this with his little shaft and he can move his eyes like a person, confused eyes, angry eyes, happy eyes...Everybody else like they didn't have eyes, they didn't have arms, they didn't have a head, it was just like a flat cylinder". This testimony reveals how mobile and responsive agents appeal to children and how the form factor plays a significant role in the interaction. Through its eyes and movements, Cozmo was able to effectively communicate emotion, and so the children believed that Cozmo had feelings and intelligence. Many participants, who tried to engage in dialogue with the agents, were limited by the fact that the agents weren't able to ask clarifying questions. While the children were attracted to the voice and expressions of the agents at first, they lost interest when the agent could not understand their questions. We recognize the potential for designing a voice interface that could engage in conversations with the children by referring to their previous questions, by asking more clarifying questions and by expressing various reactions to children inputs.

Facilitating understanding
During the play-test the facilitators, parents, and peers helped the children rephrase or refine their questions. We wonder how some of this facilitation could be embedded in the design of the agent's mode of interaction. If the agent could let the children know why they cannot answer the question and differentiate between not understanding the question and not having access to a specific information, this would help the users decide how to change their question, either by rephrasing it, or by being more specific. Another issue we recognized was that sometimes the amount of information provided to the participants was overwhelming. The agent's answers could be scaffolded to provide information gradually. This would enable the children to decide how much they want to know about a specific topic and get more engaged by having a conversation with the agent.

Conclusion
This research raises the following question: if these agents are becoming embedded in our lives, how could they influence children's perception of intelligence and the way they make sense of the world? During our study the participants believed that they could teach the agents, and they could learn from them. This leads us to imagine novel ways in which the agents could become learning companions. In future work, we hope to design interactions where children are able to tinker with and program the agents and thus expand their perception of their own intelligence and different ways to develop it.

Acknowledgements
We would like to thank the students at the Media Lab who assisted with the study, our friends and mentors who reviewed the various drafts, the parents and children who participated in the study, and our colleagues who offered advice on this work. This research was supported by the National Science Foundation (NSF) under Grant CCF-1138986. Any opinions, findings and conclusions, or recommendations expressed in this paper are those of the authors and do not represent the views of the NSF.

REFERENCES
1. Christoph Bartneck, Dana Kulić, Elizabeth Croft, and Susana Zoghbi. 2009. Measurement instruments for the anthropomorphism, animacy, likeability, perceived intelligence, and perceived safety of robots. *International journal of social robotics* 1, 1 (2009), 71–81.
2. Debra Bernstein and Kevin Crowley. 2008. Searching for signs of intelligent life: An investigation of young children's beliefs about robot intelligence. *The Journal of the Learning Sciences* 17, 2 (2008), 225–247.
3. Peter H Kahn Jr, Batya Friedman, Deanne R Perez-Granados, and Nathan G Freier. 2006. Robotic pets in the lives of preschool children. *Interaction Studies* 7, 3 (2006), 405–436.
4. Hae Won Park, Rinat Rosenberg-Kima, Maor Rosenberg, Goren Gordon, and Cynthia Breazeal. 2017. Growing growth mindset with a social robot peer. In *Proceedings of the 12th ACM/IEEE international conference on Human robot interaction. ACM.*
5. Najmeh Sadoughi, André Pereira, Rishub Jain, Iolanda Leite, and Jill Fain Lehman. 2017. Creating Prosodic Synchrony for a Robot Co-player in a Speech-controlled Game for Children. In *Proceedings of the 2017 ACM/IEEE International Conference on Human-Robot Interaction.* ACM, 91–99.
6. Fumihide Tanaka, Aaron Cicourel, and Javier R Movellan. 2007. Socialization between toddlers and robots at an early childhood education center. *Proceedings of the National Academy of Sciences* 104, 46 (2007), 17954–17958.
7. Sherry Turkle. 2005. *The second self: Computers and the human spirit.* Mit Press.
8. Henry M Wellman, David Cross, and Julanne Watson. 2001. Meta-analysis of theory-of-mind development: the truth about false belief. *Child development* 72, 3 (2001), 655–684.

Scratch Nodes: Coding Outdoor Play Experiences to enhance Social-Physical Interaction

Tom Hitron
Media Innovation Lab
Interdisciplinary Center (IDC)
Herzliya, Israel
tom.hitron@milab.idc.ac.il

Itamar Apelblat
Media Innovation Lab
Interdisciplinary Center (IDC)
Herzliya, Israel
Itamar.apelblat@milab.idc.ac.il

Iddo Wald
Media Innovation Lab
Interdisciplinary Center (IDC)
Herzliya, Israel
iddo.wald@milab.idc.ac.il

Eitan Moriano
Media Innovation Lab
Interdisciplinary Center (IDC)
Eitan.Moriano@milab.idc.ac.il

Andrey Grishko
Media Innovation Lab
Interdisciplinary Center (IDC)
Herzliya, Israel
andrey.grishko@milab.idc.ac.il

Idan David
Media Innovation Lab
Interdisciplinary Center (IDC)
Herzliya, Israel
idan.david@milab.idc.ac.il

Avihay Bar
Media Innovation Lab
Interdisciplinary Center (IDC)
Herzliya, Israel
avihai.bar@milab.idc.ac.il

Oren Zuckerman
Media Innovation Lab
Interdisciplinary Center (IDC)
oren.zuckerman@milab.idc.ac.il

IDC '17, June 27-30, 2017, Stanford, CA, USA
ACM 978-1-4503-4921-5/17/06.
http://dx.doi.org/10.1145/3078072.3084331

Abstract
We present the initial design process of Scratch Nodes, a sensor-based prototype designed to augment children's social-physical outdoor play. Scratch Nodes has two main components: a hardware device and a tablet-based coding environment. The prototype was designed for 8-12 year old children with the goal of encouraging physical play, social interaction, and "changing the rules" through coding. We extend prior work in the Heads-up Games (HUG) domain by adding a real-time coding environment that directly controls the hardware device, empowering children to change the game's rules in real-time. We argue that the combination of physical play, social interaction, and coding strikes the right balance between the societal need to increase outdoor play & enhance computational thinking skills on one hand and children's need to play, measure, and define their own rules on the other. We present our initial design and implementation process as well as our insights from a preliminary evaluation with six children who tested the prototype.

Author Keywords
Scratch; Head-Up Games; Changing The Rules; Children;

ACM Classification
K.3.1 [Computers and Education]: Computer Uses in Education Collaborative learning

Design Guidelines:

Augmenting social-physical play: The design should promote interaction between players. In particular it should enhance collaboration, competition, or mutual exploration of the physical environment.

Heads-up arms-out interaction: The design should minimize the need to constantly observe a screen and encourage players to look at each other, enabling children to use their hands freely for non-verbal communication and for physical interaction with the environment.

Rule-creation through coding:
Making rules is both a creative and intellectual activity. The design should make it easy for children to create new exploratory games by changing existing rules and adding new ones.

Introduction
In recent years, HCI researchers and more recently high-tech companies strive to develop programming platforms for children, such as Scratch [10]. Children's engagement in appropriate coding activities encourages creative processes that develop "computational thinking" skills [4]. Computational thinking has been shown to have great benefits which stem from engaging in processes such as debugging, iterations, deconstructing problems, and generalizations through patterns. We strive to harness the engagement and value of computational thinking towards social outdoor play (such as capture the flag, tag, or hide and seek). The well-known decline in social outdoor play [11] pose a risk to children's well-being due to the connection between social play and emotional development, social competence, problem solving, creative thinking, and safety skills [9, 3]. We therefore suggest that an integration of coding in an outdoor social play context will leverage the benefits of both activities. One of the most important advantages of outdoor play is its relation to creativity, as game rules can be constantly modified, changed and even reversed [6, 7]. We suggest that coding should serve as a rule-making mechanism in outdoor social games. In the following sections we present our initial prototype design, implementation, and insights from an exploratory evaluation.

Related Work
Magerkurth et al. defined pervasive games as traditional games augmented with mobile multi-player outdoor games [8]. Zuckerman et al. further explained that pervasive games are outdoor games which deliver a gaming experience that changes according to the environmental context [15]. An exciting sub-category of pervasive games is Heads Up Games (HUG), defined by Markopoplus and Soute as technology-based outdoor play that enables children to play freely and liberates them from attending to screens, which mobile-based pervasive games may demand [13]. Examples of non-mobile based pervasive games from recent years include 'Camelot', a physical multi-user game designed to enhance social outdoor interaction among children without a coding interface [14] and RaPIDO, a sensor based device that children could program via a platform called 'Game Baker' [12]. We argue that real-time rule creation and adaptation during a game is of great benefits. RaPIDO and GameBreaker took the first step toward this approach, but the programming interface is separated from the play experience, so real-time rule creation or adaptations are not possible.

Design & Implementation
Building on prior work [13, 10, 6], we define three design principles for our Scratch Nodes prototype: Augmenting physical-social play; Heads-up arms-out interaction; Rule-creation through coding (see Left side-bar for details). The novelty of this work is in addressing all three principles in one system.

Based on our design principles, we developed an Arduino sensor-based device (see Figure 2 for info about hardware). Bluetooth Low Energy protocol is used to establish a connection between the Scratch Android app and the hardware devices (up to seven), and a unique ID is assigned to each (See system diagram in Figure 1). On the software side, we implemented the "rule-creation through coding" principle using the Scratch Android environment, so children can change the rules dynamically as they play. We selected the tablet-based Scratch Android environment to reduce childrens' dependency on in-home personal computers, and by that enable the potential for coding outdoors (see Figure 4 for info). In this initial prototype, we implemented a very limited set of blocks, enabling the modification of the acceleration threshold.

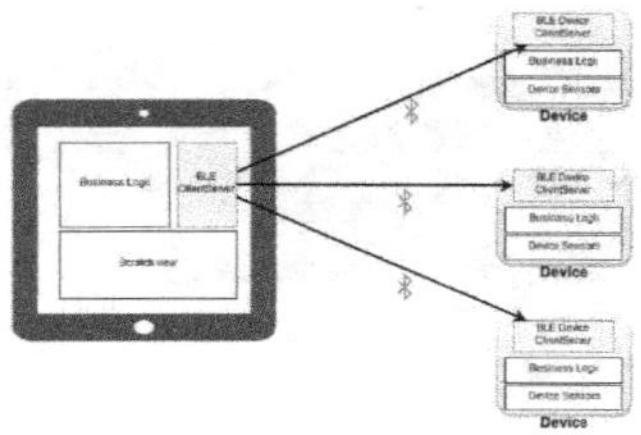

Figure 1: Bluetooth Low Energy protocol is used to establish a connection between the Scratch Android app and the hardware devices.

Figure 2: Sensor-based hardware device using the Adafruit Feather (an Arduino clone with built-in Bluetooth support) and an acceleration sensor. We designed a custom display using three columns of 9 LEDs each, based on the metaphor of an abacus: 9 units, 9 tens, and 9 hundreds.

From the product design perspective, we focused on a design that will afford "holding" rather than "wearing", aiming at a "holdable" device, not a "wearable" device, with the goal to increase the potential for social play among children (See Figure 6). In addition, we designed the device case to be robust, encouraging children to throw the device from one child to another without hesitation.

Exploratory evaluation

We defined a very limited use case for the user testing session: when a child shakes one of the devices it will turn on another LED on both their device, and on the other child's device. This creates an immediate social effect, because the devices count the number of shakes performed by all devices. Children could also "change the rules" by changing the value of the acceleration sensor threshold level using the tablet device and as a result make the "counting of shakes" in the device easier or harder.

Method & Procedure: Six children ages 8-12 participated in the user testing, 2 girls and 4 boys. Participants were recruited through personal acquaintance with the researchers.

We conducted 2 sessions of user testing activities that lasted about 60 minutes each. The first session with two participants and the second session with four. The goal of the initial evaluation was to test the prototype's design and basic functionality, by observing the interaction of children with the device and with each other. Consistent with the initial evaluation goals, we decided to conduct the testing indoors and not outdoors in order to simplify observation of the children's interaction with our design. We chose the living room of one of the children's home, because physical-social play in a living room is natural and appropriate but not exaggerated. The sessions were documented using video for later analysis.

The session started with a short explanation about the device and the activity and a short interview about the children's interests, use of technology, and free-time activity. Afterwards, two devices were placed on a small table together with the tablet, and the children were invited to explore the system. The initial device threshold level was set to be very low, so even a slight shake would count. The researcher observed the play session, took notes, and resolved technical problems if needed.

Figure 3: A girl and a boy exploring the Scratch Nodes prototype during a user testing session.

Findings

We followed Grounded Theory principles [1] to identify emerging themes in the interview transcripts and in the incident-to-incident observation notes. We identified provisional themes and gradually identified new/repeating themes in all transcripts. Below, we report on the two leadings themes and insights.

Children started by exploring the devices and after a very short exploration discovered the mapping between shaking the device and turning on each other's LEDs. All children immediately proceeded to rapidly shake the device to "accumulate" lights or "points" as they referred to them. In addition, the children constantly switched roles among themselves (controlling the rules vs. playing with the devices).

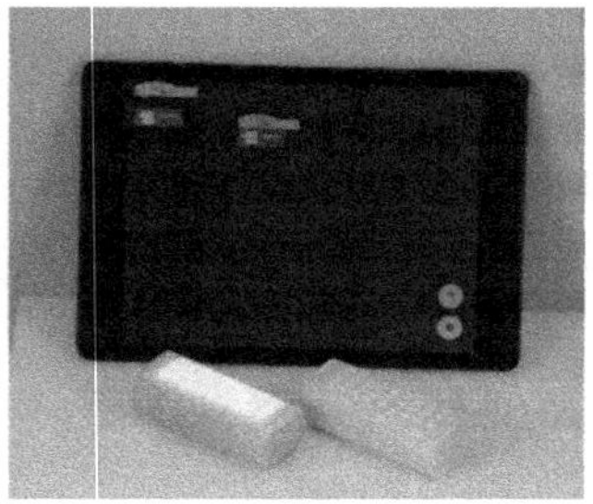

Figure 4: Scratch Android platform: Collaboration with the MIT Scratch team by utilizing the Scratch Android codebase, an in-development codebase based on Google Blockly.

Figure 5: Changing a rule during a user testing session.

Theme 1: play & measurement:
The "shake-to-measure" use case was very limited, but children easily generated a wide variety of examples for using the device in their free-time activities. The range of ideas and the type of measurement children expected the device to perform were wide and directly related to activities that are meaningful to their own lives. Selected quotes include:

Gal (11): *"I will use it to measure my circus jumps"... "I can attach it to my bicycle, to know how fast it goes, or even to my dad's car".* Shira (8): *"It's cool, we can measure our steps, or when we run"... "For example, while running with the device, You can give one device to your friend, he will measure your activity"*
Tali (8): *"After setting the game perimeter, we can use it in order to stay in the approved range of the game, if you have too many points, it means that you went too far"... "Maybe we should attach it to a paper airplane to measure its speed."*

Theme 2: co-located physical/social play:
Children were able to test two devices that interact with each other, and they could change the code to slightly modify the rules of the game. Our findings support our assumption that the device can encourage co-located physical/social play. Below are a small collection of quotes from the children's discussions:

Gal to Tali: *"let's try and do it together and get all the points".* Or to Doron: *"Give me an easy threshold, I want to see what happens when I reach 1000".* Or: *"I would like to set the rules, so I could make the game harder for everybody else".* Doron: *"If I could both decide the rules and play with the device, it will be better, but if I had to choose I will choose to be with the device and not with the tablet."*
When asked how they would name the role of the kid that defines the rules on the tablet device, the children gave it various names: *"the judge, because he defines the rules", "The mechanic because he fixes the rules", "The thresholder, because he sets the threshold".*
Doron to his friends: *"I am giving you something easy now"* (really inserting a very high value). Shira and Dorit struggling to get a point. Doron: *"Regardless of how much you try you won't get a point, even Usain Bolt won't get a point now".* Shira: *"Here you go Doron and Itai, try to shake it now"* (Shira inserts a very high threshold value). Itai and Doron are shaking really hard with no success. Shira: *"Ok I'll make it easier"* (Still inserting an even higher value).
Itai: *"Don't worry, I will get a point"* (shaking it hard with all his strength, but with no success). Tali (8), took the device and inserted a high threshold. After failing to score a point, she gave the device to her brother and asked him to try. He shook the device for some time, put all his effort into it and finally got a point. He looked happy and proud.
Gal (10): *"While playing "Capture the flag", we can create a secret language by defining that one light means something and two lights means something else, like a light language."*

Product Design Insights
Children found the device comfortable to hold and use. On two occurrences, they showed interest in connecting the device to their bodies: to the shoulder (a girl) and to the belt loop on his pants (a boy). In addition, the children found the device durable and were not too concerned about breaking it. In fact, the device fell several times and continued to work properly, so the children gained more confidence in its durability. Finally, the children showed interest in seeing how the electronics look within the device case.

Discussion
We presented the initial design & implementation of a new prototype called Scratch Nodes, designed with three principles in mind: augmenting outdoor play in the spirit of Heads-Up Games (HUG), creating opportunities for co-

Figure 6: In order to increase the potential for social play among children we designed a robust case that affords holding rather than wearing.

located social-physical interaction, and changing the rules through real-time coding.
As a Work in Progress, our research has several limitations, including the small set of programming blocks that were available to the children in the user testing, our preference to initially evaluate the system indoors, and the small sample of children who evaluated the prototype. However, our initial findings show promise and support the design principles. We showed that children are able to easily invent small games or activities that involve physical play and co-located social interaction, treat measurement as a playful game-related activity, and see coding as an intuitive way to change the rules of a game.
Based on our initial findings, we would like to share the following insights:

Give children a game invention platform, not a game:
the Children easily invented small games and activities and added new dimensions to their play experiences: measurement, challenging oneself, competition, and collaboration. They treated these dimensions as an inherent part of the play experience, and used it to extend their natural play activities. They used measurement to add meaning, not just simple gamification features as rewards (as many companies do when adding game elements into mobile apps). Notable children‘s examples from our findings include measuring challenging jumps in circus class or inventing a secret communication language in a “capture the flag“ game context. Children care about their play activities and treat them very seriously, we should give them tools that allow them to integrate sensing technologies in ways that are meaningful for them, in contrast to giving them products that dictate what adult designers think children want.

Technology should not harm natural social dynamics:
designers must leverage the decentralized nature of sensor networks and device-to-device communication, as it successfully mimics natural social interaction between children. Being at the same location, looking at each other‘s devices, and communicating naturally with one another all empower children to invent creative games and collaborate or compete in playful ways. For example, when two children shake their devices together in an attempt to reach a goal faster and get all the points, they fulfill Moore & Wong‘s notion of social competence [9] and Guddemi & Erikson‘s notion of initiative [5].

Coding should enable playful rule-making:
Our findings show that children are interested in setting their own rules, fulfilling Hughes‘s notion that children tend to “modify the game in creative ways“ [6]. We observed how children initiated rule modification and generated new rules as part of their game. They found it very natural to define rules for multi-user social games by challenging or favoring their peers, making rules that are fun and silly, and by collaborating around solving a challenge set by another child. Hence, our findings support our assumption that a coding platform can indeed serve as “changing the rules“ for children.

Future work should extend the technological as well as the experimental aspects of the scratch nodes. On the technological aspect, the range of programming blocks should be further developed to enable a greater variety in the rule-making process. On the experimental aspect the design guidelines and the insights should be tested outdoors and the activity outcomes should be evaluated in an empirical way. Considering existing evidence indicating that rule generation and rule changing are characteristics of creativity and mindfulness[7, 2]. future work should evaluate the effect on those. Finally, the potential of playing with such a system outdoors should be evaluated with a larger sample of children.

In sum, if outdoor play can indeed contribute to social competence, problem solving, creative thinking, emotional growth and appreciation for the environment [9], and if computational thinking can indeed contribute to design strategies, deconstructing problems, and generalizations [4], then an interactive system like Scratch Nodes that merges between outdoor play and computational thinking has the potential to strike the right balance between children's need to play and collaborate, and society's need to increase physical activity, social interaction, and creative exploration.

Acknowledgments
We would like to thank Mitch Resnick, Andrew Sliwinski and Lisa O'Brien from the Scratch team; Oran Peretz and Shlomi Azoulai who worked on an early version of the prototype, and special thanks to Hadas Erel for her contribution in the Camera Ready version. This research was supported by the Scratch Foundation and by the I-CORE ISF grant #1716/12.

REFERENCES

1. Kathy Charmaz. 2011. Grounded theory methods in social justice research. *The Sage handbook of qualitative research* 4 (2011), 359–380.
2. Hadas ErEl and Nachshon Meiran. 2011. Mindset changes lead to drastic impairments in rule finding. *Cognition* 119, 2 (2011), 149–165.
3. Usha Goswami. 2008. *Blackwell handbook of childhood cognitive development.* John Wiley & Sons.
4. Shuchi Grover and Roy Pea. 2013. Computational Thinking in K–12 A Review of the State of the Field. *Educational Researcher* 42, 1 (2013), 38–43.
5. Marcy Guddemi and Aase Eriksen. 1992. Designing outdoor Learning Environments for and with Children. *Dimensions of Early Childhood* 20, 4 (1992).
6. Linda Hughes. 1983. Beyond the rules of the game, why are rooie rules nice. *The game design reader: A rules of play anthology* (1983), 504–516.
7. Ellen J Langer. 1989. *Mindfulness.* Addison-Wesley/Addison Wesley Longman.
8. Carsten Magerkurth, Adrian David Cheok, Regan L Mandryk, and Trond Nilsen. 2005. Pervasive games: bringing computer entertainment back to the real world. *Computers in Entertainment (CIE)* 3, 3 (2005), 4–4.
9. Robin C Moore and Herb H Wong. 1997. *Natural Learning: The Life of an Environmental Schoolyard. Creating Environments for Rediscovering Nature's Way of Teaching.* ERIC.
10. Mitchel Resnick, John Maloney, Andrés Monroy-Hernández, Natalie Rusk, Evelyn Eastmond, Karen Brennan, Amon Millner, Eric Rosenbaum, Jay Silver, Brian Silverman, and others. 2009. Scratch: programming for all. *Commun. ACM* 52, 11 (2009), 60–67.
11. Alana Sajatovic. 2016. An Examination of Cross-Curricular and Experiential Outdoor Learning Opportunities at the Elementary Level. (2016).
12. Iris Soute, Herman Aartsen, and Chet Bangaru. 2011. On developing a platform for mobile outdoor gaming for children. In *International Joint Conference on Ambient Intelligence.* Springer, 200–204.

13. Iris Soute, Panos Markopoulos, and Remco Magielse. 2010. Head Up Games: combining the best of both worlds by merging traditional and digital play. *Personal and Ubiquitous Computing* 14, 5 (2010), 435–444.

14. Janneke Verhaegh, Iris Soute, Angelique Kessels, and Panos Markopoulos. 2006. On the design of Camelot, an outdoor game for children. In *Proceedings of the 2006 conference on Interaction design and children*. ACM, 9–16.

15. Oren Zuckerman, Narcis Pares, Steve Benford, and Henrik Hautop Lund. 2006. Designing interactive environments for outdoors gaming and play. In *CHI'06 Extended Abstracts on Human Factors in Computing Systems*. ACM, 419–422.

From Parents to Mentors: Parent-Child Interaction in Co-Making Activities

Ofir Sadka
Media Innovation Lab
Interdisciplinary Center (IDC)
Herzliya, Israel
ofir.sadka@milab.idc.ac.il

Oren Zuckerman
Media Innovation Lab
Interdisciplinary Center (IDC)
Herzliya, Israel
orenz@idc.ac.il

IDC '17, June 27-30, 2017. Stanford, CA, USA
ACM 978-1-4503-4921-5/17/06.
http://dx.doi.org/10.1145/3078072.3084332

Abstract
Making activities for children often take place at informal learning environments. In this context parents may join their children for co-making activity. It has been shown that this type of activity can be facilitated by educators that serve as mentors. In this paper we aim to explore parent-child interaction in the context of a co-making activity at home. Towards that end, we developed a dedicated kit that couples Automata-building with paper circuits. We also designed five activity cards as scaffolding for parents, to raise their awareness to mentoring principles. We present our design process, evaluation, and findings from eight parent-child co-making activities. Our qualitative analysis indicates the challenges and opportunities for parents as mentors in a co-making activity. We propose a two-dimensional scale that can help designers and maker-space practitioners better understand the different parental roles during a parent-child co-making activities, and the need for better tools and support materials for parents in that context.

Author Keywords
Children; Parents; Making; Scaffolding

ACM Classification Keywords
K.3.1 [Computers and Education]: Computer Uses in Education-Collaborative learning

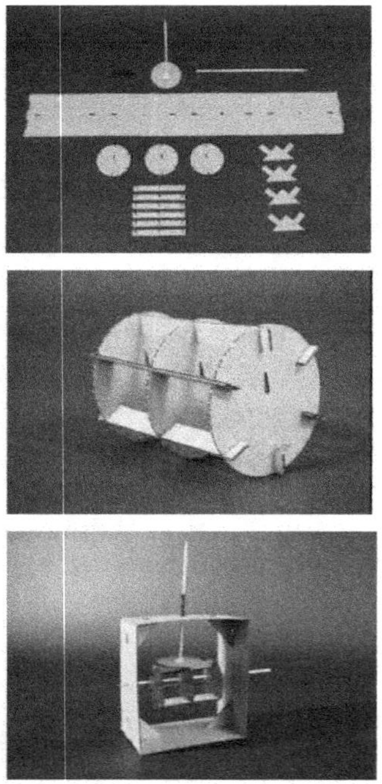

Figure 1: Top: Automata template. Middle: cylinder. Bottom: Automata.

Introduction

Maker spaces and the maker revolution in general are on the rise, with focused attention on children in both formal and informal learning environments. Mentoring is a common practice in these activities, particularly within informal learning contexts [7]. Bar-El et al. [1], reported on the Maketec maker space for children, in which teens serve as mentors who guide children in various making activities. In the Maketec, the mentors' responsibility is not to teach, but rather to support children's intrinsic motivation to create, and offer assistance when the kids encounter hurdles in the making process. By providing teen-mentors a set of skills to help them overcome upcoming challenges during the mentoring role, they showed how valuable and meaningful a good mentor can be [1]. We believe that parents have the potential to fulfill this important role in a family activity context.

In recent years, traditional family roles as expert-novice have shifted, since children are commonly exposed to various technologies and develop expertise that their parents do not master. Roque [8, 9] and Correa [4], noted that these shifts may leave parents wondering what role they can play in supporting their child's learning process. Parent-child co-making activities hold a unique opportunity for parents to find a role in supporting their childs' learning process.

Our goal is to create an intervention that would assist parents in defining their role during a co-making activity at home. Parent-child co-making activities have great potential for both parents and children in two aspects: (1) both parties are introduced to computational thinking skills, which is a creative process that includes iteration, deconstructing, debugging, and generalizations through patterns [7]; (2) the activity may serve as a platform for strengthening parent-child connection. Hence, in this preliminary work we set out to explore the parent-child interaction in the context of a co-making activity at home. We wish to generate insights that can inform researchers, designers, and educators regarding the factors that influence parent-child interaction, as a starting point for design and implementation of relevant technologies. We present our design research based on co-making activity and a set of activity cards intended to increase parents' awareness to the mentor's guiding principles. We report on our findings of parent-child interaction patterns in co-making activities at home, and propose a two-dimensional scale based on three emerging themes we identified, that can help describe the parent's role in the interaction.

Related Work

Our work is influenced by three domains: parent-child co-making activities, activity cards as an empowering tool for awareness, and scaffolding.

Parent-child co-making activities:
Roque [8] [9] et al., reported that mutual making activities are promising for parent-child interaction. They showed that this type of activity was as much about building relationships as it was about building projects [8] [9]. However, it has been noted that explicit reminders regarding the goal of the activity are required during parent-child interaction [9, 12]. A possible implementation may be designing environments that invite parents to learn their diverse potential roles and integrate explicit reminders of these roles during mutual parent-child activities [9, 10].

Activity cards as an empowering tool for awareness:
Many previous researchers have used physical cards as tools to assist learning and design processes, or as a source of inspiration. Deng, Antle and Neustaedter presented

Mentoring Principles

The Silent Attentive Expert: do not directly solve problems but patiently listen and strive to help children solve challenges by themselves, with gentle suggestions that hint at the solution indirectly.

Pleasantly Frustrating: guide children how do deconstruct complex challenges into small manageable steps, striving to transform frustration into a pleasant challenge.

The Empathic Partner: show empathy to the child, use positive feedback and encouragements along the way, especially when the child faces or completes a challenge.

An Active Passive Presence: create an atmosphere that empowers the child to ask for support when needed, rather than the mentor initiating it.

Meaningful Inspirations: encourage children to let their personal interests and hobbies influence their work.

TANGO cards [5], a design tool facilitating communication and shared understanding. Friedman and Hendry designed the Envisioning Cards [6], a toolkit for inducing human values during a design process.

Scaffolding:

Scaffolding is defined as adjusting the learning process, progress, and its content to a child's specific needs, abilities, and interests. This is a major difficulty educators face, since it requires previous acquaintance and personal attention to every individual child [10]. Scaffolding is based on Vygotsky's [11] classic Zone of Proximal Development ("ZPD"), defined as the greater achievement a learner can achieve with the help of another person that he would otherwise be unable to achieve by himself [11].

Design research

In this section, we present our design research process including the kit we created for the parent-child activity as well as the Parent Mentoring Cards (PMC) that were designed as a physical reminder to raise parents' awareness to the mentoring role.

The kit

We designed a step-by-step co-making activity focusing on entry-level making that includes mechanisms and electronics. Each domain has its specific instruction cards - Kit Building Cards (KBC). The mechanical kit is the Automata, a three-dimensional structure that exhibits motion or behavior [2]. We designed an Automata that integrates movement on two different axes: horizontal and vertical (see Figure 1). The electronic kit is paper circuit, made of a 3-Volt battery, LED, and a copper coil with a sticky side to glue onto surfaces.

The Parent Mentoring Cards (PMC):

We were inspired by prior work of Friedman et al. [6] and Deng et al. [5] and adopted some design principles from both. From Friedman's Envisioning Cards [6] we adopted the use of images related to the content of the cards. The images seek to evoke the diversity, complexity, and subtlety of human affairs. In particular, we chose pictures that might evoke relatedness between the content of the card and the image. From Deng's Tango Cards [5] we adopted four elements: title, rationale, design consideration, and textual example (See Figure 2). We focused on five mentoring principles used successfully in the Maketec maker-space [1]. Some principles have ambiguous titles, as they aim to describe the ambiguous and challenging role a mentor has during co-making activities (See side bar).

Method and procedure

Eight families with children 8-12 year old (5 males, 3 females) participated in the study. Participants were recruited through personal acquaintance. The sessions were held for approximately 90 minutes in the participant's home, usually in the living room. In each session, the researcher observed the parent-child interaction by sitting behind them and taking notes. The activity was introduced to the participants as a mutual activity around two domains: mechanics and electronics.

When handing the PMC, we aimed at finding the balance between controlling PMC order between families, PMC relevance to the interaction and having the smallest impact on the natural parent-child interaction. However, in order to avoid order influences, greater weight was given to handing specific PMC in constant stages of the activity. Apart from that, the researcher's decision when to hand the next PMC within the specific stage was guided by one factor: to minimize distraction to the natural dynamics between par-

Pleasant Frustration

Rational:
Learning process is like a voyage, there are ups and downs, there are moments of joy and moments of frustration. When there is a balance between joy and frustration, the memory that will form about the experience will be positive.

Consideration:
Your child is in a state of uncertainty and stress, he want to prove himself. Empower small successes over failures. When your child does not have motivation, show enthusiasm.

Example:
"I see, you are right. This is a challenge". "Lets try to think about the problem in a different point of view".

Figure 2: An example for one of the PMC. Top: Image related to the content of the card, highlighting a pleasant experience that inherently involves some frustration. Bottom: Title, rationale, consideration, and textual examples.

ent and child. After the parent-child team completed the Automata and the paper circuit tasks, they were asked to configure the paper circuit on top of the Automata in order to complete a sensor that turns the paper circuit LED on, in sync with the Automata movement.

Findings

We followed Grounded Theory methods [3] and used our observational notes to analyze the qualitative data (parent and child quotes and the various observed behaviors). We conducted a brief analysis of the first session, detected five emerging themes from the parent-child interaction and agreed on a coding scheme for the first four sessions, according to the "initial codes" methodology [3]. The initial codes were: initiative, process management, feedback, attention, and interaction. Following completion of the first four sessions, we identified repeating topics in our themes, and merged the five themes into three leading ones: initiative, attention, and interaction. After forming these three themes we continued with four additional co-making sessions as a theoretical sample to gather more data and verify our consolidated themes, as recommended by Charmaz [3]. We present a sample of our qualitative data below, with four representative "scenes" of parent-child interaction, including our analysis.

Scene 1 - mother is a product manager, has three children, co-making activity with her 9-year-old son:
Mother and child are at the 3rd stage of the Automata building activity when they realize they need to insert the triangle corner to the frame of the Automata. The child struggles to insert the triangle corners to the frame of the Automata.

Child :"Mom, how do I do it?"

Mother: "Look, I'll do it and show you how it's done, and then you will do the rest".

The mother showed **high attention** to the child; she responded to his struggle. She also showed **high initiative**, since she chose to insert the triangle corners herself. She did not ask him any guiding questions or encouraged him to solve the problem by himself. However, she encouraged him to connect the rest of the triangle corners after she showed him how to do it - **positive interaction.**

Scene 2 - mother is a teacher, has three children, co-making activity with her 9-year-old daughter:
Mother and child are at the 5th stage of the Automata building activity as they attempt to glue the triangle corners of the Automata and construct the frame. The child has difficulties in gluing the triangle corners and she realizes that the frame is unstable:

Child: "It's hard, it's almost falling apart". The mother does not respond.

Child: "Oh no, mom, it's not stable". The mother does not respond, she gazes at the instruction cards.

Eventually, the frame is stabled.

Mother: "Very good! You made it".

The mother showed **low attention** to the child, she did not respond in any form, explicit or implicit, to the child's struggles and explicit continuous requests for help.

Scene 3 - mother works in marketing, co-making activity with her 9-year-old son:
Mother and child are at the 12th stage of the Automata building activity as they realize that they need to cut the straw in order to stabilize it on the inner side of the Automata's frame:

Mother: "Go bring the scissors".

Figure 3: Parent-child co-making activity

Child: "I'll cut it with my hands".

Mother: "Ok...try it...". After several minutes, during which the child failed to cut the straw with his hands or teeth, he brings the scissors.

Mother (while the child is cutting the straw with the scissors): "You wasted a lot of time because you didn't bring the scissors".

The Mother showed **high attention** to the child and the activity, but she also showed **high initiative** by telling the child what to do. The child refused to listen to the mother and insisted to cut the straw with his teeth. After several minutes, when he realized that it is ineffective, he brought scissors and cut the straw with them. While he cut the straw the mother teased him and added an element of time pressure - **negative interaction.**

Scene 4 - mother is an architect, has two children, co-making activity with her 10-year-old son:
Mother and child are at the beginning of the 7th stage of the Automata building activity when the child realizes that he did not glue all the triangle corners to the Automata facing in the same direction, which is not critical:

Child: "Oh no, I glued it in the wrong direction".

Mother: "Do you think it is a problem?"

Child: "Yes".

Mother: "Then what should we do?"

Child: "Disassemble it and glue it again".

Mother: "Do you think it is critical?"

Child: "Yes".

Mother: "OK, then go for it".

The mother showed **high attention** to the child as she responded to his difficulties by asking guiding questions. She also showed **low initiative** since she let the child disassemble the frame despite knowing that it is not critical and that it might defect the frame and delay the progress of the activity. When she realized that the child is holding his ground, she encouraged him to do what he thought was right, an example of **positive interaction.**

Discussion

We aimed at exploring parent-child interaction during a co-making activity, while increasing parents' awareness towards mentoring guiding principles. Based on our qualitative findings, we present a two-dimensional scale showing both the challenge and potential in parent-child interaction during a co-making activity (see Figure 4).

As we showed in our findings, attention is a prerequisite for any successful parent-child co-making activity. The parent must be attentive to the child and to the activity. While a parent is attentive in the activity, he or she can take a meaningful role on a spectrum between 'a peer parent' and 'a mentor parent'. The main motivation of a peer-parent is to complete the activity successfully and efficiently, by leading the activity or following the child's lead. Peer interaction can include both negative or positive interactions, according to the team's personal dynamics. In contrast, a mentor-parent is focused on the child's learning process, not the successful completion of the activity. He or she will never lead directly, but will always follow the child's lead with positive encouragements, promoting exploration and "pleasant frustration". While the shift of the parents role to mentoring is clearly desirable, our analysis suggests that it is important for parents to find the right balance between

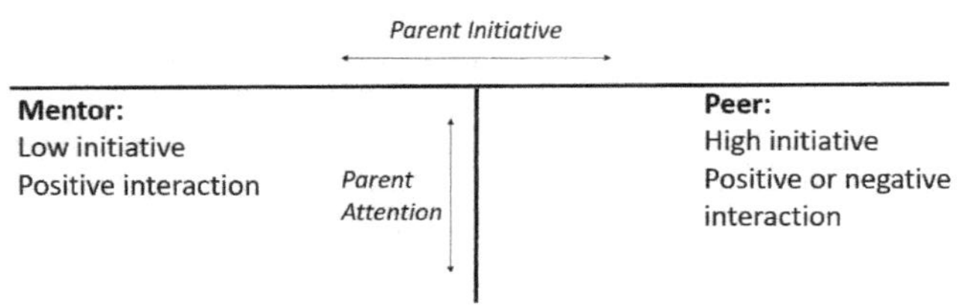

Figure 4: The parent-as-mentor scale

mentor and peer. Shifting roles in the process of an activity enables leveraging the strengths of each role at the right time. Hence, parents can adapt their role according to their child's needs and abilities. Future work should focus on two main question raised in this paper: (1) How to design environments that expose parents to their diverse potential roles? (2) How to assists parents in shifting their roles along the co-making activity, according to their childs' needs?

Our findings and scale can help designers and makerspace practitioners better understand the different parental roles during parent-child co-making activities. Creating opportunities for parents and children to create together is not enough. New technologies, tools, aids, and support materials must be designed and implemented to assist parents in (1) becoming more aware of their natural role vs. their desired role, and (2) learning new tools and strategies to better scaffold their child's learning process.

Limitations

As a Work in Progress paper, our research has several limitations, including the small number of participants and potential bias of the researcher handing the Parent Mentoring Cards.

Acknowledgments

This research was supported by the I-CORE Program of the Planning and Budgeting Committee, the ISF grant #1716/12 and the Sara Fine Foundation. We thank the creative learning team at the miLAB, IDC for assisting during the research and writing process: Hadas Harel, Rona Sadan, Aviv Sheriff, Tom Hitron, and Yasmin Keats - for designing the Automata. A special thank to the families who participated in the study and offered their time and valuable insights.

REFERENCES

1. David Bar-El, Oren Zuckerman, and Yaron Shlomi. 2016. Social Competence and STEM: Teen Mentors in a Makerspace. In *Proceedings of the The 15th International Conference on Interaction Design and Children.* ACM, 595–600.
2. RG Blauvelt. 2001. *A design environment for automata: supporting childrenâĂŹs construction of mechanical reasoning and spatial cognition.* Ph.D. Dissertation. Doctoral dissertation, University of Colorado at Boulder, USA.
3. Kathy Charmaz. 2014. *Constructing grounded theory.* Sage.
4. Teresa Correa, Joseph D Straubhaar, Wenhong Chen, and Jeremiah Spence. 2015. Brokering new technologies: The role of children in their parentsâĂŹ usage of the internet. *new media & society* 17, 4 (2015), 483–500.
5. Ying Deng, Alissa N Antle, and Carman Neustaedter. 2014. Tango cards: a card-based design tool for informing the design of tangible learning games. In *Proceedings of the 2014 conference on Designing interactive systems.* ACM, 695–704.

6. Batya Friedman and David Hendry. 2012. The envisioning cards: a toolkit for catalyzing humanistic and technical imaginations. In *Proceedings of the SIGCHI conference on human factors in computing systems*. ACM, 1145–1148.

7. Edward Pines, P Sullivan, and L Nogales. 2015. Broadening participation through engagement in the maker space movement. In *ASEE Annual Conference and Exposition Proceedings*.

8. RICAROSE ROQUE. 2016. Family creative learning. *Makeology: Makerspaces as Learning Environments* 1 (2016), 47.

9. Ricarose Roque, Karina Lin, and R Luizzi. âĂIJIâĂŹm Not Just a MomâĂİ: Parents Developing Multiple Roles in Creative Computing. In *Proceedings of the 12th International Conference of the Learning Sciences*.

10. Janneke van de Pol, Monique Volman, Frans Oort, and Jos Beishuizen. 2015. The effects of scaffolding in the classroom: support contingency and student independent working time in relation to student achievement, task effort and appreciation of support. *Instructional Science* 43, 5 (2015), 615–641.

11. Lev Vygotsky. 1987. Zone of proximal development. *Mind in society: The development of higher psychological processes* 5291 (1987), 157.

12. Jason C Yip, Tamara Clegg, June Ahn, Judith Odili Uchidiuno, Elizabeth Bonsignore, Austin Beck, Daniel Pauw, and Kelly Mills. 2016. The Evolution of Engagements and Social Bonds During Child-Parent Co-design. In *Proceedings of the 2016 CHI Conference on Human Factors in Computing Systems*. ACM, 3607–3619.

Investigating Children's Passwords using a Game-based Survey

Dev Raj Lamichhane
University of Central Lancashire
Preston, UK, PR1 2HE
DRLamichhane@uclan.ac.uk

Janet C Read
University of Central Lancashire
Preston, UK, PR1 2HE
jcread@uclan.ac.uk

ACM ISBN 978-1-4503-4921-5/17/06.
http://dx.doi.org/10.1145/3078072.3084333.

Abstract
This work describes how a simple Android game was used to study password and username creation with children aged 7 and 8. Children answered questions, made a username and password, and then later used these to log in. The novelty is in the use of the approach as well as in the findings. The findings confirm earlier work in regards to password length, suggesting six characters as adequate, and provide preliminary evidence that most children use familiar items in password and especially username creation.

Author Keywords
Children's security; Password design; Game-based research

ACM Classification Keywords
H.5.m. Information interfaces and presentation (e.g., HCI): Miscellaneous;

Introduction
Children are significant users of computer technology and much of this technology is networked and relies on access to internet services. Additionally, children are now creating user accounts in games, educational software and social media software and so security, and the wider issue of child-centred security, is a

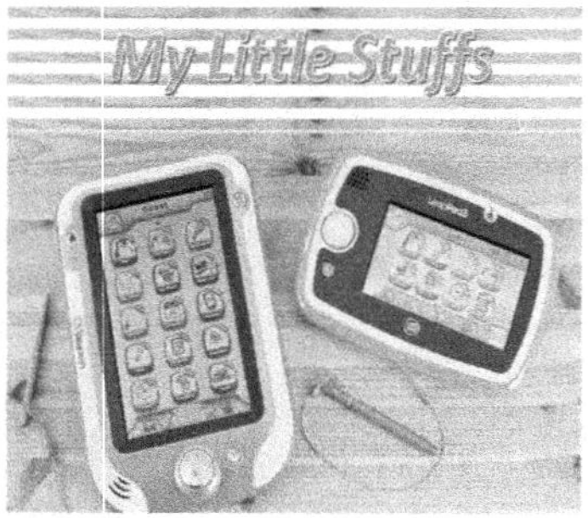

Figure 1 - My Little Stuffs

PROCESS
Admin login: for security
Admin selects the phase of the experiment whether it is phase 1 (create) or 2 (login).
If Phase 1 – Each child is registered with a unique number and name – saved to database. Then logged in.
If Phase 1 – Child starts the survey. Rewdon says something and then asks the child to provide some information. This continues until the survey finishes.
If Phase 1 - At the end the child creates his / her own username and password.
If Phase 2 – admin logs in the child, then the child has to log I to the app. Attempts are recorded.

pressing area for concern in terms of designing interfaces for children.

Studying children's habits around computer security is not easy. Ethical practice suggests that we should not be tracking children's IT behaviours without their knowledge but asking children about computer security is problematic as the concerns held by adults are often difficult to convey to, and discuss with, children. Password and username creation is one area where knowledge of children's behaviours can benefit children's technology design. If children could be guided to create more memorable passwords but in so doing could be given small 'child-sized' hints that would possibly remain with them as they grow into more adult systems, then this could also be beneficial.

This study looked at password and username creation as it pertains to children. An Android app called 'My little Stuffs' was created to take a child on a story through some of the child's 'special things' in order to then study whether these special things then featured in the passwords and usernames. In addition, the study provided general data on password and username complexity and memorability.

Related Work

Users are the weakest link in many aspects of computer security as their behavior is hard to control and difficult to change [1]. Behaviour around passwords is especially problematic with users tending to either make 'easy to crack' passwords or resorting to writing them down in easy to access places. Learning how to create and use passwords is important and could be considered to be an essential aspect of children's education for the digital age [2], [3].

Studying passwords and security with children requires imaginative methods and ingenuity. One such method, to abstract out security for very young children, was from Read and Beale [4] in which they asked children to draw things that were special to them and then to describe how they would keep these things safe. Another option is to use game like interfaces for research with children - this has found favour in the IDC community with work by [5] showing that research data can be gathered in fun ways with an engaging interface.

Textual password systems have had attention in terms of their use with adults [6], [7], but work on children's use of textual passwords is scant. The entry of passwords, by children, was flagged up as problematic in 2000 by Sharples, [8], but little has been done to further the knowledge in this area. Although there have been studies aimed at circumventing textual passwords [9], there are still many systems relying on textual passwords and thus this work is timely. Our work in this paper builds on previous work in which an artificial log in system was created in order to study children's usernames and passwords [10].

Study

The aim of this study was in part to study password and username length and memorability, as seen in [8], but also to test a hypothesis that children, like adults, might use familiar, easy to guess items, in their usernames and passwords. Additionally, we wanted to see if a game like interface was appropriate for studying password design. The plan was to ask children, in an interactive app, about some of their personal likes, before then asking them to create a username and a password, and then to study effects.

2

Figure 2 - Children working on the tablets

Participants
The study involved 17 children aged 7-8 from a single class of a UK primary school. The study was facilitated by two observers.

Data
The data from the application, including the username and password was saved in a MySQL database. When, at the end of the study, the children had to login again – each attempt was stored in the database in order that it could later be analysed

A game-based approach was used to situate the questions and the password creating activity. It is reported that people often create usernames and passwords from elements of who they are, what they have, or what they like [10].

The Research Tool
The research tool is described in the sidebar on the previous page (fig. 1). This tool was an Android app that asked the children, one page at a time, their name and age, the name of their best friends and pet, their favourite colour, food, cartoon, superhero, sports team and sports hero. An astronaut robot character "Rewdon" took the children through the application by, on each page, saying something about himself and then prompting the children to say something about themselves. For example: ***"****Hi, my name is Rewdon and I am an astronaut robot. I like to go to space and different planets. Now tell me something about you****."***.

Procedure
Seventeen children (see sidebar and fig. 2) came to the study in groups of four or five as selected by the class teacher. Each child was given an Android tablet that was logged to them by the admin. They then began the game by answering the questions on the application. At the end of the application they each created their own passwords and usernames and then returned to the classroom. Later, after about an hour doing another activity, the children came back and attempted to 'log on' to find out where Rewdon (the game robot) had been to on his holidays. At the end of the study the main researcher explained what we had been doing and explained about the data that was being gathered. `This was to allow the children to withdraw their data if they wanted to.

Results and Discussion
All the children completed the study. No children asked for their data to be not included. The results here are in terms of the main research questions on a) the use of self-related data in username and password design, b) the overall simplicity and complexity of passwords and usernames created and c) the memorability of the words used.

Usernames and passwords and relationships to self
Out of the 17 children, 13 made self-related usernames out of which 8 of them contained their name, two contained their last name and 1 their middle name. Favourite game and class of year were contained in one each. In the case of passwords, out of 17 children, 9 created a self-related password, of which 2 each contained their name and cartoon character whereas last name, year of birth, super hero, food and pet were present in one each.

In the study reported in [10], almost half of the younger children (who were younger than those studied here) made usernames and passwords that were very similar; in this study only two children (11.7%) had closely related usernames and passwords.

Simplicity of usernames and passwords
To determine the simplicity of the chosen passwords and usernames we defined three levels:

- Simple: one word, 1 – 3 digits and the word being something simple like a pet name
- Moderate: two words, maybe with a name + something and with 3 – 5 digits.
- Complex: Something unrelated, a long set of digits, mixed alphabets and numbers.

Using this rubric, table 1 shows how many usernames and passwords were at each level of simplicity

Objects	Usernames	Passwords
Simple	10	8
Moderate	6	5
Complex	1	4

Table 1 - The simplicity of usernames and passwords

It appears from this table that in the main the children used very simple words and that the passwords were more complex than the usernames. The longer the username or password, the more complex it is and the harder it is to memorize. Longer passwords are hard to guess as well.

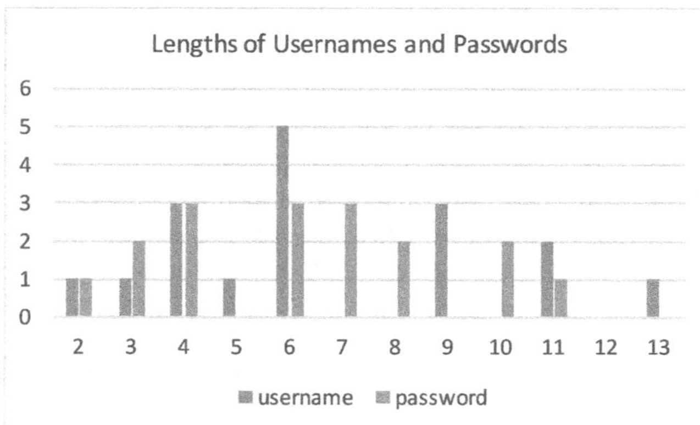

Figure 3 - Lengths of passwords and usernames

As seen in fig. 3, the children made passwords and usernames of different lengths. The average length of the usernames was 6.65 characters and of passwords was 6.25. These numbers compare favourably with those from [10] who reported means of 7 and 6 respectively.

The guessability of a password is very contextual. The username or password can be guessed by someone who is near to the user like friends and family because they know a lot about the user. This information can be name, last name, age, date of birth etc. The guessability of the username and the password was described as follows so as to allow further analysis:

- Easy to guess: Included the child's name, age, pet name, best friend name, colour etc. And was simple in terms of simplicity. Similar username and password.
- Hard to guess: Two words joined. Nothing easy to guess.

Table 2 shows the guessability of usernames and passwords.

	Usernames	Passwords
Easy to guess	7	5
Hard to guess	10	12

Table 2 - Guessability of usernames and passwords

It is clear from this that many of the words used were quite easy to guess BUT also that the children seemed to make sharder to guess passwords than usernames.

Spelling mistakes

Children tend to make many spelling mistakes while typing. In this study, when creating passwords and usernames and when working through the app, they were asking for the spelling of names of their pets,

CHILDREN WHO COULDN'T LOGON

One child forgot her username completely though she knew the password. She made it after getting a hint.

One couldn't spell the word "bubbles" that she used in her username. She got the help for it got it right next.

One put "hello2" instead of "hello22". Maybe she wanted to put only "hello2" but accidently put "hello22" while creating the password.

One put a six-digit number as a password but couldn't remember it, she tried twice, got a hint for it, and did it in third time.

One was constantly making spelling mistake of the word for four times and got it right at the fifth try.

One created a complicated password ("1l3m4a") but couldn't get it right for two times and got a hint and did it in third time.

favourite sports and so on. Altogether, in the data gathered in the app, there were 18 'known' spelling mistakes. One child asked what was the spelling of "bubbles" as she put that in while creating her username. This aligns to [10] where it is mentioned that the children had chosen passwords that they weren't confident spelling.

Number of attempts to login

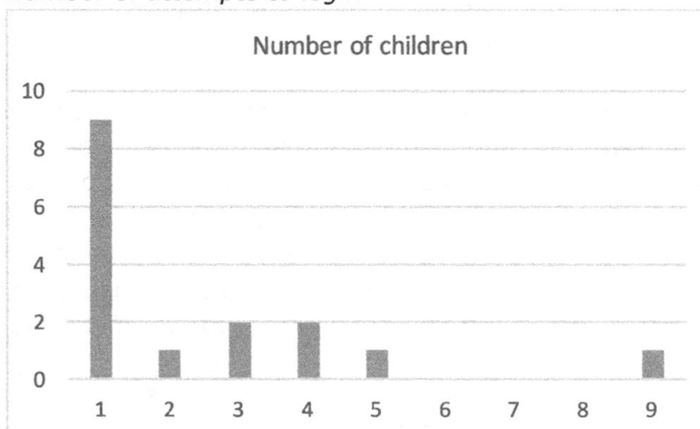

Figure 3 - The number of attempts needed by children to log in.

After taking part in a different activity and having playtime, the children returned to log in again. Of the 17 children, 16 managed to login with half of them managing to login on their first attempt as shown in fig. 4. Children who couldn't login were allowed to ask the researcher for a hint – this was their choice and many took the choice although one tried eight times before asking for a hint. The one who couldn't log in did not want a hint. For those who didn't login first time, there were several reasons – these are listed in the sidebar and summarized here:

- Forgetting it completely (two children).
- Spelling mistakes (two children).
- Maybe making a mistake creating (1 child).
- Forgetting a long set of digits (1 child).

Tables 3 and 4 show the relationship between complexity and logon.

	First time	Two attempts	More than two attempts
Simple	8	0	1
Moderate	4	0	2
Complex	0	1	0

Table 3 - Relationship between complexity and log on attempts for username

	First time	Two attempts	More than two attempts
Simple	7	0	0
Moderate	2	1	2
Complex	0	0	4

Table 4 - Relationship between complexity and log on attempt for password

These clearly show that children struggle to remember the passwords when they become more complex.

Conclusion

The study here was an extension of the study [10] and the findings in relation to username and password length, the difficulties with login and the make-up of passwords and usernames all show similarities across the two studies. The present study additionally examined the hypothesis that children use self-related items in passwords and usernames. This was studied using a game based method, and it was found that over half the children used such items, with more prevalence in usernames (76%) than passwords (53%), That many of the findings are very similar to those from [10] suggest that this game based method is useful. The design suggestions arising from this work are that children's products should require shorter passwords than adult ones, that demands on complexity should be relaxed and that it might be useful – when children enter unusual words, to encourage double entry passwords and in order to mitigate against spelling and entry errors.

The limitations of the work are that there were only a small number of children doing this study and also the password creation process is somewhat contrived. The app is available (at Google Play Store) for others to carry out the study, this would be a useful extension of the work. In addition, development of content beyond the password creation will allow studies to be made of the long term memorability of passwords. One can argue that due to rapid development in technology, children might not be using textual password in future as password managers, fingerprints, face-recognition technologies are being used and becoming popular for login systems. However, for website logins and school desktop accesses, it is still a major way of logging in so the study is very appropriate for current situation.

Acknowledgements
We thank the children from the UK school for their participation in this work.

References
1. Dourish, P., et al., *Security in the Wild: user strategies for managing security as an everyday, practical problem.* Personal and Ubiquitous Computing, 2004. **8**: p. 391 - 401.
2. Goodwin, K., *Designing for the Digital Age: how to create humen-centred products and services*. 2009, Indeanapolis, IN: John Wiley.
3. Coggins, P.E., *Implications of What Children Know About Computer Passwords.* Computers in the Schools, 2013. **30**(3): p. 282-293.
4. Read, J.C. and R. Beale. *Under my pillow: designing security for children's special things*. in *DCS - HCI 2009*. 2009. Cambridge, UK: ACM Press.
5. Law, E.L.-C., et al., *An Experiential Approach to the Design and Evaluation of a Gamified Research Tool for Law in Children's Lives*, in *Proceedings of the The 15th International Conference on Interaction Design and Children*. 2016, ACM: Manchester, United Kingdom. p. 322-333.
6. Adams, A., A. Sasse, and P. Lunt. *Making Passwords Secure and Usable*. in *HCI07*. 1997. Springer-Verlag.
7. Forget, A., et al. *Improving text passwords through persuasion.* in *SOUPS '08*. 2008. ACM.
8. Sharples, M., *The Design of Personal Mobile Technologies for Lifelong Learning.* Computers & Education, 2000. **34**: p. 177 - 193.
9. Mendori, T., et al. *Password input interface suitable for primary school children*. in *International Conference on Computers in Education, 2002. Proceedings.* 2002.
10. Read, J.C. and B. Cassidy, *Designing textual password systems for children*, in *Proceedings of the 11th International Conference on Interaction Design and Children*. 2012, ACM: Bremen, Germany. p. 200-203.

BacToMars: Creative Engagement with Bio-Design for Children

Anna Loparev
Wellesley College
Wellesley, MA, USA
aloparev@wellesley.edu

Amanda Sullivan
Tufts University
Medford, MA, USA
amanda.sullivan@tufts.edu

Clarissa Verish
Lauren Westendorf
Wellesley College
Wellesley, MA, USA
cverish@wellesley.edu
lwestend@wellesley.edu

Jasmine Davis
Margaret Flemings
Wellesley College
Wellesley, MA, USA
jdavis4@wellesley.edu
mfleming@wellesley.edu

Marina Bers
Tufts University
Medford, MA, USA
marina.bers@tufts.edu

Orit Shaer
Wellesley College
Wellesley, MA, USA
oshaer@wellesley.edu

IDC '17, June 27-30, 2017, Stanford, CA, USA

ACM ISBN 978-1-4503-4921-5/17/06.
http://dx.doi.org/10.1145/3078072.3084334

Abstract
We present BacToMars, an educational video game that engages elementary school children in a bio-design activity. We describe its design and implementation, and discuss design considerations for developing playful and developmentally-appropriate interactive activities, which enable children to grasp complex scientific concepts and apply bio-design to solve problems. We share results from preliminary evaluation, and describe next steps in our investigation.

Author Keywords
Play; children; bio-design; educational games.

ACM Classification Keywords
H.5.2. Information interfaces and presentation: User Interfaces---theory and methods

Introduction
In today's world, biology has become a powerful technology, advancing innovation in domains ranging from food shortage, to clean water, and space travel. It is therefore important to inspire future innovators to solve problems at the intersection of science and technology by exposing them to the burgeoning fields of biological engineering and bio-design. However, the elementary natural science curriculum does not include emerging domains of knowledge like biological engineering that cut across disciplinary boundaries [1].

There is a lack of concrete tools that expose children to abstract scientific concepts such as traits, cells, genes, and the conceptual framework of biological engineering.

In this paper, we present the design, implementation, and preliminary evaluation of a novel educational video game called BacToMars, which is designed to encourage students in elementary school to explore abstract scientific concepts in concrete ways. The design of BacToMars is inspired by the interactive museum exhibit BacPack for New Frontiers [7]. However, it is designed for formal learning in elementary school class settings. Following, we describe the design and implementation of BacToMars. We also share results from preliminary evaluations and discuss design considerations for the development of an engaging educational game for bio-design.

Related Work

Our design of BacToMars draws upon Papert's Constructionist educational framework [10] and previous work that explores how children learn through hands-on technology-rich activities [3, 4]. When applied to learning in biological engineering, Constructionism means that learners construct knowledge by solving real-world problems using a toolkit of biological parts [7, 9]. BacToMars was also designed to foster two core aspects of computational thinking [11]: abstraction and modularity [5].

A number of video games have been developed to engage players in the design of new organisms (e.g. Spore, Cubivore, Graffiti Kingdom) or objects (e.g. Particles!). However, these games do not provide a platform for children to participate in creative problem-solving through bio-design. e.pixel [2] and TrapIt![6] are interactive museum exhibits that allow young audiences to observe live bacterial cells. SynFlo [9] and BacPack for New Frontiers [7] engage children in problem-solving using biological design. These exhibits inspired our work but they target informal museum settings, which are inherently different from formal learning in elementary classroom settings. For example, BacToMars supports extended engagement and contains levels to support progression, as well as a help system to imitate an expert facilitator.

Application Domain and Design Goals

Biological Engineering

Biological engineering aims to provide creative solutions to a wide range of real-world problems. It applies the principles of standardization, abstraction, and modularity to the design of living organisms with new properties. In this game, genetic programs are composed from standardized biological parts called BioBricks, which are used like "Lego Bricks" to compose programs with complex behaviors.

The premise of the game draws upon a widely-known research paper about the utility of bio-design techniques for manned exploration missions to Mars [8]. The authors propose to identify which molecules could be utilized to create desired products. Similar to the exhibit BacPack for New Frontiers [7], BacToMars mirrors this investigation by allowing children to experiment with biological designs of bacteria that consume input materials and produce desired output materials essential for sustaining a mission to Mars.

Learning and Design Goals

Based on the BacPack exhibit [7] but focusing on formal learning settings, we have identified specific and

Figure 1: The first level of BacToMars. In this level, children are only allowed to make oxygen.

Figure 2: The fourth level of BacToMars. Players may use all five resources to create all six products. The goal of this level is to build the launch pad and rocket so the astronauts can escape Mars.

measurable learning goals for BacToMars that can be taught to elementary school students (2nd-5th grade) in a developmentally-appropriate way: (L1) Introduce basic concepts of genetics, with a focus on what genes and DNA are; (L2) Facilitate the design of genetic programs that include input and output, and where output from one program could serve as input to a different program; (L3) Introduce the foundations of biological engineering: using methods to build things that solve real-world problems, and following a concrete process; (L4) demonstrate the principles of abstraction and modularity—genes with documented functionality are used as standard biological parts, and are combined to create new biological systems; and (L5) Engage players in creative problem-solving of critical challenges related to survival on Mars. Our design goals for BacToMars were informed by these learning goals and influenced by a constructivist educational philosophy: G1) Facilitate the development of inquiry skills through a hands-on playful experience and creative problem-solving; G2) Provide scaffolding, help, feedback, and guidance within the game; and G3) Provide opportunities for collaborative learning.

Design Iterations and Rationale

The premise of BacToMars is that players take on the role of a scientist-astronaut who is helping a team of astronauts. The astronauts settle on Mars and build a bio-dome; however, their supplies are destroyed by a dust storm. The player is challenged to work with a biological engineer character to solve the real-world problem of survival on Mars by designing bacteria that can help the astronauts. The bacteria consume resources that exist on Mars (e.g. soil, CO_2, biomass) and produce products that are required for sustaining human life on Mars (e.g. water, nutrients, O_2). At the start of the game, players are introduced to the Mars team and treated as a member of the team. Before playing the game, players watch three brief introductory videos that explain the goal of the game and introduce key concepts, such as the environment on Earth and on Mars, natural resources, genetics, and bio-design. Simple language and animations are used to explain these concepts in an appropriate manner while maintaining scientific accuracy. Next, the bioengineer character guides the player in designing bacteria that consume available resources and produce essential products.

The game space is divided into two areas: a wet lab (on Mars) with a workbench station, and the Mars landscape, which includes a bio-dome where astronauts carry necessary building products to the ship they are constructing and consume essential life-support products (see Figures 1 and 2). Included in the wet lab area is a score to reflect the player's overall state, and a button to trigger a scaffolding animation.

Players use eleven representations of BioBricks (i.e. genes) to design and engineer the bacteria that make essential products. The quantity of products in the biodome is gradually reduced over time. Players are required to pick two genes: an input gene that consumes a particular resource and an output gene that produces a product. These two genes are combined into a genetic program. Some combinations of input and output genes are more effective than others. Figure 3 shows some of the possible combinations. In advanced levels, players can use biomass as both a resource and a product.

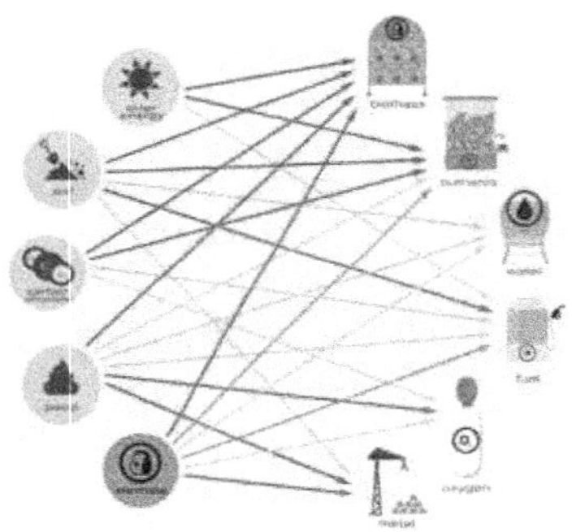

Figure 3: Subset of possible resource and product combinations, color coded based on how many units are produced by each combination: green = 3 units, yellow = 2 units, red = 1 unit. Green combinations are most efficient.

Figure 4: Preliminary testing of BacToMars with children. The two children pictured chose to play the game collaboratively without being prompted to do so.

Players then insert the genetic program into a digital plasmid (i.e. ring of DNA) and add the plasmid to a bacterial cell, which results in the growth of a colony of bacteria containing the genetic program. The players release the bacteria to Mars by dragging the petri dish with the colony towards the resource on the Martian landscape (see Figure 2). The bacteria gather around the resources they consume and produce a product, which is added to the products available in the bio-dome. The astronaut figures move around the bio-dome, providing feedback to users and indicating what products are running low, as well as picking up the products players create and consuming them or carrying them to where they are needed.

Implementation

BacToMars was created in JavaScript using the Phaser.IO game engine. It is optimized for Chrome on a laptop, but future iterations will focus on tablets. The current prototype implements six levels. We are currently developing additional levels as well as support for multi-player.

Design Rationale

We encountered several challenges in the design of BacToMars. Here we describe the design choices we made to address them. Many are applicable to games beyond the scope of a formal elementary classroom setting. Our choices were informed by user and expert feedback we received through our iterative design process as well as by frameworks for learning with technology-rich experiences [3, 4].

Overcoming time and size scales – This is a known challenge in the design of educational bio-design activities [7, 9]. In the game, animation bridges the time scale of bio-design from days to seconds through simulation, with the concept of time represented by an animated clock face. To represent genes, we draw upon the metaphor of BioBricks, which is widely used within bio-design [8], and embody two important engineering principles: abstraction and modularity. We use a jigsaw puzzle metaphor to indicate whether genes are considered input (consuming resources) or output (producing products). Animation is used to communicate size scale, showing that a genetic program composed of two genes fits within a plasmid that is then inserted into a bacterial cell.

Supporting a young audience – The game uses simple graphics with minimal text. Various features are used to provide built-in scaffolds to guide players, such as introductory animation videos, tips, a demonstration of a virtual hand showing players what to tap and where to drag, a companion bioengineer character that provides guidance, and a help button.

Fostering creative problem solving – In early levels of the game, we provide players with a limited number of genes and with contextual hints indicating how and which necessities to produce. In intermediate levels, players are provided with up to 11 different genes and are guided by a dynamic simulation of resource depletion and production. At these levels, players are required to consider which combinations of genes are most effective and to prioritize and plan their utilization of resources. In advanced levels, players are able to identify new genes that could be helpful and to invent new combinations of genes to improve the lives of the astronauts on Mars. At these levels, players are encouraged to apply their creativity and to experiment with new ideas for bio-design.

Supporting collaborative learning – BacToMars will support teams of up to four simultaneous players that will work in parallel on different biological designs. The engineered bacteria are released to a common environment (i.e. Mars landscape) so that all team members can observe the impact. Players are encouraged to collaborate on solving important problems (e.g. lack of oxygen, need for lighting a particular area) as well as to draw upon the bio-designs (i.e. genetic programs) of fellow team members. We intend for the game to be played in a co-located collaborative settings - children seated next to each other each with their own tablet, so that players can communicate directly while collaborating.

Preliminary Evaluation

Our preliminary evaluation focused on the learnability of the game, learning of core terminology and concepts, and the level of engagement.

Early pilot-testing with two children in second and third grade indicated that the children had trouble understanding the overall goal of the game and figuring out game mechanics. To address these issues, we introduced the scaffolding mechanisms discussed above and developed introductory animation videos. We evaluated the videos with elementary school teachers and child development specialists and iterated on the videos' content and design to ensure that they were developmentally appropriate.

Pilot-studies of the current version of BacToMars and videos (with N=7 elementary school students; males=5 and females=2; 1st graders=1, 2nd graders=3, 3rd graders=2, 5th graders=1) show that players were engaged with the game and enjoyed the play session.

During these trials, children first completed a pre-survey targeting their prior knowledge regarding core biological engineering concepts and terminology. For the 1st grader participant, the questions were read aloud. Next, children watched the three animated videos. After the videos, they were prompted to play the BackToMars game for 15 minutes. During this time, the researchers gave minimal prompts or help to the children. After 15 minutes, children were allowed to continue playing for up to 25 minutes before moving on to the post-task questionnaire to assess learning of core concepts and terminology. Finally, a researcher conducted a debrief with each participant.

Results show that all children were able to successfully engage in gameplay. Participants reiterated that the videos were a necessary addition to the game. In the words of one child, "I really thought the video was giving me a lot." In Level 4, where a new concept is introduced, we observed some confusion, yet none of the participant used the help button. Future iterations will highlight the option and introduce contextual tips. The mean play time was 19.89 minutes (STD=3.40 minutes) with only one child choosing not to extend their play time. While playing, children made comments (mostly to themselves but sometime to another player sitting close by) like "They thirsty they want water" and "I am making so much oxygen…". When children played next to each other they sometimes collaborated. For example, one child commented "They hungry", and the other child suggested "Use nutrients and sun". We interpret these comments as indicators of engagement.

Pre- and post- assessments revealed that the videos and game were generally successful at teaching some core concepts. However, older participants demonstrated greater levels of learning than younger participants, suggesting elements need refinement to make the content domain developmentally-appropriate for a young audience. In the post-test debrief and surveys, all children shared overall enjoyment. When asked about favorite aspects of the game one 3rd grader commented "I liked how the pictures help you figure out what they [astronauts] need", another 2nd grader said "trying to find out the combinations that you need to do," a 5th grader mentioned "I liked how there would be a mixture of different things that you'd need to make, so I'd keep testing and trying to make enough." These comments indicate that our design indeed prompted inquiry and problem solving.

Conclusions and Future Work

We presented the design, implementation, and preliminary evaluation of BacToMars, an educational video game that engages elementary school children in problem-solving through bio-design. BacToMars acts as a medium for children to experiment with the emerging field of biological engineering without costly equipment and the long wait-times inherent to a wet lab setting. We will continue to refine BacToMars through an iterative and participatory process. We plan to deploy the game with an accompanying curriculum in schools Fall 2017 and use it to further investigate how games can fit into a lesson plan, as well as what abstract scientific and engineering concepts young children are capable of learning when provided with engaging and developmentally-appropriate interactive experiences.

Acknowledgements

This work is funded by NSF IIS-1149530. A special thank you to students who are not co-authors but have contributed to the BacToMars project.

References

1. National Science Board STEM education recommendations. Retrieved January 20, 2009 fromhttps://www.nsf.gov/nsb/publications/2009/01_10_stem_rec_obama.pdf
2. e.pixel. Retrieved September 8,2015 from http://2014.igem.org/Team:The_Tech_Museum
3. Marina U. Bers and Michael S. Horn. 2010. Tangible programming in early childhood: Revisiting developmental assumptions through new technologies. *High-tech tots: Childhood in a digital world.* Information Age Publishing, Greenwich, CT.
4. Marina U. Bers. 2012. *Designing digital experiences for positive youth development: From playpen to playground*. Cary, NC: Oxford.
5. Marina U. Bers. 2017. *Coding as a Playground: Programming and Computational Thinking in the Early Childhood Classroom*. Routledge.
6. Seung Ah Lee et al. 2015. Trap it!: A Playful Human-Biology Interaction for a Museum Installation. In *Proc. of the ACM Conference on Human Factors in Computing Systems*, 2593-2602.
7. Anna Loparev et al. 2017. BacPack: Exploring the Role of Tangibles in a Museum Exhibit for Bio-Design. In *Proc. of the ACM Conference on Tangible, Embedded, and Embodied Interaction.*
8. Amor A. Menezes, John Cumbers, John A. Hogan, and Adam P. Arkin. 2015. Towards synthetic biological approaches to resource utilization on space missions. J. R. Soc. Interface 12, 102.
9. Johanna Okerlund et al. 2016. Synflo: A tangible museum exhibit for exploring bio-design. In *Proc. of Tangible, Embedded, and Embodied Interaction*.
10. Papert, Seymour. (1980). Mindstorms: Children, Computers, and Powerful Ideas. Basic Books.
11. Jeannette M. Wing. 2006. Computational thinking. Commun. of the ACM 49, 3: 33-35.

Connected Spaces: Helping Makers Know Their Neighbors

Vishesh Kumar
University of Wisconsin–Madison
Madison, WI 53706, USA
vishesh.kumar@wisc.edu

Mike Tissenbaum
Massachusetts Institute of Technology
Boston, MA 02142, USA
miketissenbaum@gmail.com

Lauren Weilgus
Matthew Berland
University of Wisconsin–Madison
Madison, WI 53706, USA
lauren.weilgus@gmail.com
mberland@wisc.edu

IDC '17, June 27-30, 2017, Stanford, CA, USA

ACM ISBN 978-1-4503-4921-5/17/06.
http://dx.doi.org/10.1145/3078072.3084335

Abstract
This paper presents Connected Spaces (C-S) – a tool designed to promote collaboration in makerspaces. It also describes a pilot study designed to test C-S's effectiveness in enabling people to seek help from peers. In our pilot, some (but not all) students were able to leverage C-S's affordances. We explore both supporting and mitigating factors, and highlight design features for environments as well as tools to support divergent, open-ended exploration and learning.

Author Keywords
Makerspaces; help; scaffolding; collaboration; help-seeking; constructionism; expertise; communication

ACM Classification Keywords
H.5.m. Information interfaces and presentation (e.g., HCI): Miscellaneous;

Introduction
Help-seeking by novices plays a valuable role in learning and achievement [8]. Yet, novices lack the competencies and support to effectively seek help from experts [11]. The ability to seek help from experts or peers is especially important in open-ended, exploratory, and inquiry environments, where learners have many different pathways to develop domain knowledge [2]. The openness of such spaces

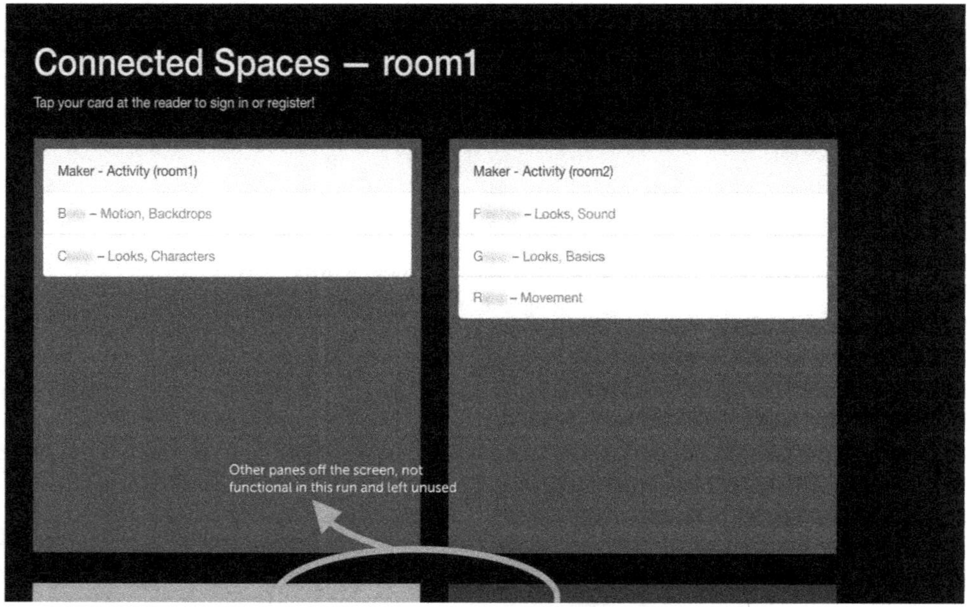

Figure 1: Screenshot of the Connected Spaces skill list tablet, as visible in this study's run. The contents of the two spaces are explained later in Table 1.

compounds the challenges for effective help-seeking as learners are often unaware of the activities and abilities of their peers, a critical feature in building a community of like-minded learners [4,5,6]. To overcome these barriers, there is a need to develop learning spaces and the supportive technologies within these spaces which can reduce the barriers to effective help seeking and mentorship.

Makerspaces are an excellent example of open-ended, exploratory learning environments in which participants can design and construct solutions to problems themselves [15]. However, because of this open-ended nature of makerspaces, making connections between one's work and that of one's peers is more difficult than in more structured traditional pedagogical settings. This can create a critical gap in the awareness of what others are doing and how it relates to one's own work (termed "knowledge awareness" by Ogata and Yano [10]), both within and across makerspaces. This lack of awareness reduces the opportunities for effective collaboration and cooperation between participants [14]. As a result, makerspaces frequently have learners in need of assistance; however, they lack awareness of who has the relevant expertise [3,16].

With the aim of making this expertise visible and to facilitate assistance for to newcomers to makerspaces, this paper examines the design of Connected Spaces (C-S) – a technology framework that uses ambient displays to track and connect learners across makerspaces -- and its success in helping learners find help and collaborate in real-time. This paper describes C-S, a pilot study designed to see how makers use Connected Spaces to find and obtain help (if at all), and a design debrief and feedback session with participants to solicit ideas on how C-S could be improved.

Connected Spaces: An Ambient Awareness Tool for Connecting Distributed Makerspaces in Real-Time

Novices often fail to leverage the experts in the same space due to their inability to recognize these experts and/or their expertise [1]. This failure presents a need to make visible the interests and activities of the wide range of makers in makerspaces. In response, we have developed a technology platform named Connected Spaces (C-S), which displays the names of everyone present in a network of connected makerspaces, along with their self-identified interests (affinities) and the activity they are engaged in (Figure 1). To further support help seeking, collaboration, and mentorship, C-S provides light-weight video conferencing capabilities to connect learners across these spaces in real-time.

When a participant wants to engage with members at a partner site, they use a C-S "calling tablet" to call another space. If remote participants want to collaborate, they can accept the call and engage in conversation. Through these integrated tools, Connected Spaces provides multiple avenues for providing awareness of the broader community and developing maker and STEM+C skills, as well as ways to engage with their distributed maker community.

Methods

In the following sections, we present the design of the study and its enactment, followed by a description of the data we focused on collecting and analyzing.

Study

For this pilot study, we recruited 5 participants (8-11 years old). The study began with basic introductions intended to gather an overview of the participants' past programming experience. We then gave everybody a basic introduction to Scratch – a graphical programming language built for young programming novices [12] – to show how to make a working script where a user input triggers a perceptible program action.

To emulate a makerspace-like environment – where makers did not share the same skills, but had different specializations they might need to leverage in completing their projects – we separated the participants into two groups randomly, and taught each group separate "specialized" Scratch programming abilities – "motion", and "looks". The participants were then brought back together in the main room, given details on their final project, and a description of Connected Spaces. They were told that they would be split into two groups again, and individually work on their final project (making an interactive pet that can eat food, make sounds, and 'play').

This project was designed to be representative of a common "maker project" – it is: open to interpretation; involves design components; requires a breadth of knowledge; and produces a coherent product. The project was assigned to them for the purposes of the study, though we expect people in actual makerspaces working on their own projects, would experience the presence of C-S rather similarly.

In describing Connected Spaces, we showed two tablets to the participants – one which lists people in both the rooms, along with their self-chosen affinities; and the other which can be used to call people in the other room. Since all the students were working on the same project, we did not use the participants' "current activity" function of C-S. We then asked each participant to share what specializations they wanted to appear alongside their name, and added them to their C-S accounts.

The participants were again randomly separated into two groups, sent to separate rooms, and told to work on their projects for the next 45 minutes. The two groups during this phase had mixed specializations – both had rooms with some people being fluent with "motion", and some with "looks". This was intended to reduce a deliberate sequestering of skills across the rooms, to see if Connected Spaces worked productively in finding help within the same room itself as well, and to see if calls across spaces occur even if makers in one space have an adequate variety of skills.

At the end of their individual project work time (which lasted for 45 minutes), all participants came back to the initial room, and spent 15 minutes presenting their projects to everybody else. Following that, we debriefed with the participants about their experience with using Connected Spaces, their design suggestions to improve the system, and what they felt they needed when they were struggling with a challenge.

Data Collection and Analysis

We used field notes for our data collection and analysis. We paid close attention to times when participants approached the Connected Spaces tablets, and how it affected their help-seeking behavior. When the participants would query us, we encouraged them to figure things out on own, or seek help from their fellow participants. We would sometimes make a discretionary choice to help them ourselves.

For this work, we employed a case study approach [7]. Case studies are particularly effective for this kind of pilot study as they can provide us a detailed lens into the interactions within the learning activity and the role that Connected Spaces played in supporting these interactions. The post-activity focus group interview aimed to better understand participants' perceptions of C-S; to get direct feedback to help with future design iterations; and also to provide us with evidence about aspects of making participants focused on, especially with respect to C-S.

Findings

When the participants were introduced to Connected Spaces, they chose their own descriptions of the affinities they wanted displayed next to their names, to all participants in both rooms. The different specializations taught, the affinities claimed, and the rooms the different participants conducted their project work in, are presented in table 1. The distribution of participants for the second half made it so that there was at least one person for each of the two specializations (looks and motion) in each room. This distribution helped us see if inter-room calls ever happen if there is adequate skill distribution in the rooms.

Participant	Skill taught	Affinity	Room
B	Motion	Motion, Backdrops	1
C	Looks	Looks, Characters	1
R	Motion	Movement	2
F	Looks	Looks, Sound	2
G	Looks	Looks, Basics	2

Table 1: Participants' taught specializations, claimed affinities, and room location.

Room 1 had 2 participants, N1 as the note-taking researcher, and F1 as the facilitator. Room 2 had 3 participants, N2, and F2 as the note-taker and facilitator, respectively.

A total of 4 notable interactions with the C-S tablets took place during the 45 minutes of project work, and are presented here (sorted by room, and time).

Event 1 (Room 1 + Room 2): 25 minutes into project time, B asked F1 "how to send messages from one sprite to another". C did not know, and F1 asked B if she would want to call and ask anybody in the other room. B accepted F1's prompt, and was assisted by F1 in calling Room 1 – a call that was picked up, and responded to, by the participants in Room 1.

In Room 2, when the call came, G was closest to the tablet and grabbed it to respond. Others in the room gathered around G, expressing interest in helping B. G led most of the instruction, and answered B's query.

Event 2 (Room 2): Around 10 minutes into project time, F expressed that he was struggling with motion. Then unprompted, F got up to look at the C-S tablet, then came back to his laptop, and worked on his issue. We observed that F managed to solve his own problem.
Event 3 (Room 2): 25 minutes into project time, F again faced a challenge with motion. Then he went to the C-S tablet, looked carefully, went to R (who had motion as an affinity), and pointedly asked a query. R was able to competently solve F's problem.
Event 4 (Room 2): 35 minutes into project time, G expressed a difficulty with "broadcasting" (a specific function in Scratch). On being prompted to see C-S, G picked up the C-S tablet, looked carefully at it, then put it back, and continued to work by herself. It did not seem like her query was solved – she seemed to be trying to circumvent that specific programming challenge while trying to accomplish her goals.
Post-Activity Debrief Session: During the debrief session, the participants brought up highly specific, relevant, and valuable recommendations. They can be summarized into the following points:

1. There should be photos of people's faces beside their name, so it is easier to know and find who the name and relevant expertise belongs to.
2. Clicking on people's names in the skill display tablet should make the call, rather than needing to make a call from a separate tablet.
3. Callers should be able to attach a photo of their project and/or relevant query before making a call, so receivers can see what their query is about before picking up a call.
4. Have a facility to make general calls for help (which specify the issue being faced), if the maker looking for help does not see the topic they are looking for in other people's listed affinity.

Discussion
Here we present analyses of when participants used Connected Spaces, and inferences from when they found help, as well as when they did not.
Explicit help-seeking following C-S interactions
Events 1 and 3 – the call across spaces, and the soliciting of help after referring to the C-S tablet – are clear instances of C-S enabling seeking as well as provision of help. These interactions productively contributed to participants' project work. Both within a space (Event 3), as well as across spaces (Event 1), having facilities to see others' skills and being able to approach them, are valuable actions enabled by Connected Spaces. Our inference that these successful interactions resulted from participants using C-S for targeted help-seeking is bolstered by participants' first three design feedback suggestions. The third point (about being able to attach photos of problems to call for help) also reflected their desire to communicate the help being sought as quickly as possible, and also judge whether they can help the help-seeker, even before picking up a call.
C-S interactions lacking explicit help-seeking
Event 2 seemed to indicate some resistance to asking for help, especially from peers, and a proclivity to solve problems independently. This could be a result of patterns entrenched in traditional classroom settings which often frown upon students seeking and receiving peers' help [13]. This might also be due to participants feeling empowered to pursue their struggle themselves. Knowing someone in the room may be able provide help is likely to encourage one to seek a solution on

one's own knowing that the answer is accessible in an 'easier' way, if needed [9].

The fourth design suggestion (offered by participant G seemed to result from G's experience in Event 4. G did not talk to anyone via C-S, because no one's affinities addressed her issue. She told us that she would have made a general call for help, if C-S had had a "general call" function. This event also supports the notion that participants were not using C-S simply for social interactions, but for critical and clear needs.

Limitations

The limited sample size of the study makes it hard to make general remarks about how participants interact with C-S. Further, while this study was not situated in a makerspace in the more traditional sense, most of the problem-solving needs and planned design features for their projects appeared to arise from the participants' desires for what they wanted their virtual pets to do. This kind of pursuit made the participants' actions fairly similar to those of newcomers in a makerspace. We also acknowledge that given the well-defined task, the affinities of participants in our study are narrower than those of makers in a traditional makerspace (sewing, electronics, etc.). These broader affinities are likely to lead to more scenarios where others do not have the knowledge to successfully help the help-seeker (but also potentially new opportunities for inspiration).

Conclusions

This pilot study strongly showed the potential of C-S as tool to foster productive collaborations between makers. Feedback from the participants also acted as evidence to show us that they understood and used C-S as we had intended. Both the participants' feedback and their experiences using C-S gave us valuable information about how to improve C-S and sparked questions to investigate about the effectiveness of C-S in supporting novices in makerspaces.

We were able to see that helping overcome the lack of knowledge awareness in open-ended learning spaces is valuable in encouraging help-seeking, talk and collaboration, and building a community of practice more welcoming for newcomers. We look forward to studying how this community creation looks and is influence by Connected Spaces through more sustained runs in the future!

References

1. Jessica Brazelton and G. Anthony Gorry. 2003. Creating a knowledge-sharing community: if you build it, will they come? *Communications of the ACM* 46, 2: 23–25.
2. Douglas H. Clements. 1991. Enhancement of creativity in computer environments. *American Educational Research Journal* 28, 1: 173–187.
3. Nathaniel Hudson, Celena Alcock, and Parmit K. Chilana. 2016. Understanding newcomers to 3D printing: motivations, workflows, and barriers of casual makers. *Proceedings of the 2016 CHI Conference on Human Factors in Computing Systems*, ACM, 384–396.
4. Stuart A. Karabenick and Akane Zusho. 2015. Examining approaches to research on self-regulated learning: conceptual and methodological considerations. *Metacognition and Learning* 10, 1: 151–163.
5. Jean Lave and Etienne Wenger. 1998. Communities of practice. *Retrieved June* 9: 2008.
6. Piritta Leinonen, Sanna Järvelä, and Päivi Häkkinen. 2005. Conceptualizing the awareness of collaboration: A qualitative study of a global virtual

team. *Computer Supported Cooperative Work (CSCW)* 14, 4: 301–322.

7. Matthew B. Miles and A. Michael Huberman. 1994. Qualitative data analysis: A sourcebook. *Beverly Hills: Sage Publications*.
8. Sharon Nelson-Le Gall. 1981. Help-seeking: An understudied problem-solving skill in children. *Developmental review* 1, 3: 224–246.
9. Richard S. Newman. 2008. The motivational role of adaptive help seeking in self-regulated learning. *Motivation and self-regulated learning: Theory, research, and applications*: 315–337.
10. Hiroaki Ogata and Yoneo Yano. 2000. Combining knowledge awareness and information filtering in an open-ended collaborative learning environment. *International Journal of Artificial Intelligence in Education (IJAIED)* 11: 33–46.
11. Minna Puustinen. 1998. Help-seeking behavior in a problem-solving situation: Development of self-regulation. *European Journal of Psychology of education* 13, 2: 271–282.
12. Mitchel Resnick, John Maloney, Andrés Monroy-Hernández, et al. 2009. Scratch: programming for all. *Communications of the ACM* 52, 11: 60–67.
13. Allison M. Ryan and Paul R. Pintrich. 1997. " Should I ask for help?" The role of motivation and attitudes in adolescents' help seeking in math class. *Journal of educational psychology* 89, 2: 329.
14. Kjeld Schmidt. 2002. The problem withawareness': Introductory remarks onawareness in CSCW'. *Computer Supported Cooperative Work (CSCW)* 11, 3: 285–298.
15. Kimberly Sheridan, Erica Rosenfeld Halverson, Breanne Litts, Lisa Brahms, Lynette Jacobs-Priebe, and Trevor Owens. 2014. Learning in the making: A comparative case study of three makerspaces. *Harvard Educational Review* 84, 4: 505–531.
16. Diane Slatter and Zaana Howard. 2013. A place to make, hack, and learn: makerspaces in Australian public libraries. *The Australian Library Journal* 62, 4: 272–284.

A Tattooed Bracelet for Child Vaccination Records in a Developing World Context

Bongkeum Jeong
Madeira-ITI
University of Madeira
Funchal, Madeira 9020 Portugal
bongkeum.jeong@m-iti.org

Jesús Ibáñez
Madeira-ITI
Funchal, Madeira 9020 Portugal
Jesus.ibanez@m-iti.org
EMAiD School of Art and Design
Barcelona, Spain
jibanez@vilanova.cat

Nuno Nunes
Madeira-ITI
Funchal, Madeira 9020 Portugal
nuno.nunes@m-iti.org
Institution Superior Técnico
Lisbon, Portugal
nuno.nunes@tecnico.ulisboa.pt

Monchu Chen
Hewlett Packard Labs
Hewlett Packard Enterprise
Palo Alto, Los Angeles, CA, USA
monchu.chen@hpe.com

IDC'17, June 27-30, 2017, Stanford, CA, USA

ACM ISBN 978-1-4503-4921-5/17/06
http://dx.doi.org/10.1145/3078072.3084336

Abstract

This paper proposes technical solutions to collect, record, and track health vaccination records for children in a developing world context. The problem we address in this paper is very important, and often underappreciated. Our solution consists of two elements: bracelets containing NFC tags (intended to be worn by the children), and NFC enabled Android smartphones (intended to be used by the doctors) in order to manage the vaccine information contained within the bracelets. We use a tattoo design inspired by ethnography for our prototype of the NFC enabled bracelet. The visual representation of the tattoo is printed on the bracelet surface. It conveys an overall picture of the current vaccination status. Furthermore, the tattoo is the central element of the user interface of the Android App that allows the doctors to access, read, and update more detailed information about the child's vaccination status.

Author Keywords

Tattooed Bracelet; Vaccination Visualization; Child Vaccination Records; Ethnography Design; Functional Tattoos; Developing World Context

Discover: Loss and Inaccuracy

Figure 1: Families never receive child health record, or lose it. Also they are not accurately filled out.

Figure 2: The health worker thinks the child had the vaccine.

Figure 3: The surveyor gets less correct information [10].

Images above 'Figure 1, 2, 3' are by Jeong B. on HCIK'16 [6].

ACM Classification Keywords

H.5.m. Information interfaces and presentation (e.g. HCI): Miscellaneous. H.5.2 [User Interfaces]: Theory and methods, User-centered design, Graphical user interfaces

Introduction

In the traditional sense, ethnography is complete only when the researcher is assimilated into the target culture or social community [8]; on the other hand, from the modern perspective, any type of research that includes cultural factors is recognized as ethnographic research [4], [6]. Ethnography strengthens design by exposing the user's surrounding environment and drawing out the understanding of cultural implications and primary users [9]. It can be effectively used particularly when it is analyzed in a broad sense related to overall strategy rather than direct feedback [1], [4], [6]. Whereas ethnography has been highly utilized in interaction design and industrial design, its application has been less prevalent in visual communication design. However, ethnography can be useful in helping designers find the communication strategy or insight required for a plan, method, or composition that allows for the most effective and natural communication under any given circumstances [4], [6]. In this sense, we present a design that fuels both the tattoo visualization and the prototype that are described in the precedent and present paper. Tattooing in Africa dates back thousands of years. It holds a fixed place in Africa's history. Evidence of painful tattooing was also found on the bodies of pregnant women and little children, which is said to have originated from a strong belief that such tattoos will chase away evil spirits and provide protection [8, 9]. Our research proposes technical solutions to collect, record, and track health vaccination records for children in rural parts of Africa. We used a tattoo design inspired by ethnography for our prototype NFC enabled bracelet. The problem addressed by the study (Figure 1, 2, 3) is very important, and often underappreciated. This research will spark lots of discussion about current and emerging problems in developing countries in areas that concern children.

Related Work

Our earlier studies described a specific context that we have been working on [4, 5, 6], followed by case studies conducted with child health records, along with the ethnography design method we applied [8, 9]. The purpose of the study [6] was to provide communication design recommendations that can solve problems with child health record systems in Africa. Additionally, the research aimed to test an ethnographic method in a broad way, in order to find a design solution within African culture. We conducted literature reviews and stakeholder interviews on the topics of child health and vaccination status, as well as on African tattoos. When the core users are child who have unclear communicative expressions, the environment of the child (Figure 4) has a dominant influence [6, 7].

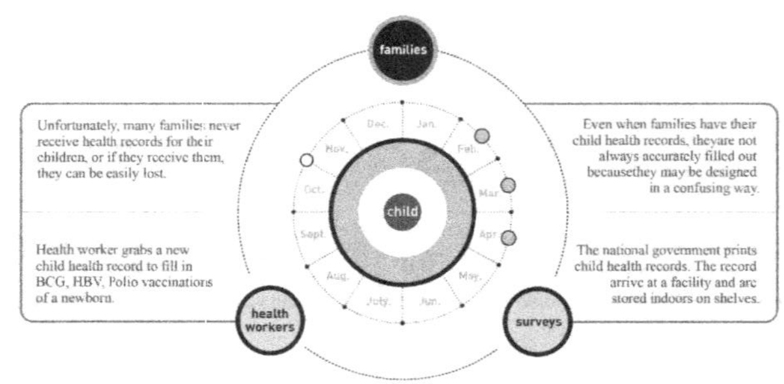

Figure 4: This triangle user structure shows the definition of users (Family, Health worker, and Surveyor)

Figure 5: This photo in our interview shows Carlton, a journalist from Germany. His tattoo is a reminder of his infant son. He said he wanted to have an ugly tattoo, not a beautiful one to remember his son.

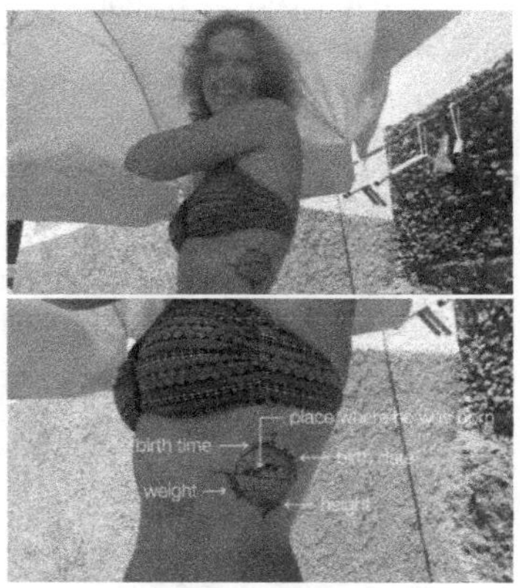

Figure 6: In this image, a German woman who lives in Madeira, Tika's tattoo is also a reminder of the birth of her son, but encodes multiple pieces of relevant data in the tattoo design. The tattoo contains the date and time, the location, and her son's weight and height at birth.

Challenges and Opportunities

The research subjects are children, parents (Figure 1), health workers (Figure 2), and surveyors (Figure 3). We tried to develop a design that satisfies all of these subjects' needs (Figure 4). We also intend to include characteristics of African culture in a health service process where tattoos as a design element are reborn as a symbol of children's lives being saved

The tattooed bracelet for baby vaccination records in Africa addresses an important issue: identification and maintenance of vaccination records for children with both families and health care workers. Health records and data are considered as sensitive private information, which may be a big challenge. However, we believe that it will give us many opportunities.

Design Approach

The design is applied to two artifacts: a baby guidebook and a baby bracelet. Our concept is to test combining technology with the tattoo by adding an NFC readable bracelet with a matching tattoo design on it. The tattoo design is for human readable, and the NFC component provides a machine-readable version.

User centered research in-depth interviews

User centered research has to evolve along with new studies and technologies. The basic principles of such a methodology and the basic research that yields design paradigms exist at one end [7]. To assess user needs from 13 parents and 2 health workers, in depth interviews were conducted in Madeira. From the interviews we discovered that tattoos were usually meaningful reminders of specific events, such as an engagement or child's birth. We found very interesting parents who have tattoos relating to their child's birth. Carlton, a journalist from Germany, his tattoo is a reminder of his infant son (Figure 5), and Tika's tattoo is a reminder of the birth of her son. She wanted to have all information, birthdate, time of birth, place of birth, weight, and height in her tattoo as a baby guidebook (Figure 6).

Tattoo Design as human-readable data

These are examples of vaccination data encoded in variations of the base tattoo design. The evolution from left to right that follows age, with the tattoo increasing in size and complexity for the additional vaccinations required immunizations (Figure 7).

Figure 7: Vaccination data encoded within tattoo design

The Tattooed Bracelet as machine-readable data

We have designed a system for recording and accessing the information regarding a child's vaccinations. The central element is a bracelet, which contains the above-described tattoo in two different (and complementary) ways. First, the visual representation of the tattoo is printed on the bracelet surface. Second, the bracelet encloses an NFC tag that stores the information encoded by the tattoo in a more extended manner. Thus, we intend our bracelet to be useful at two levels.

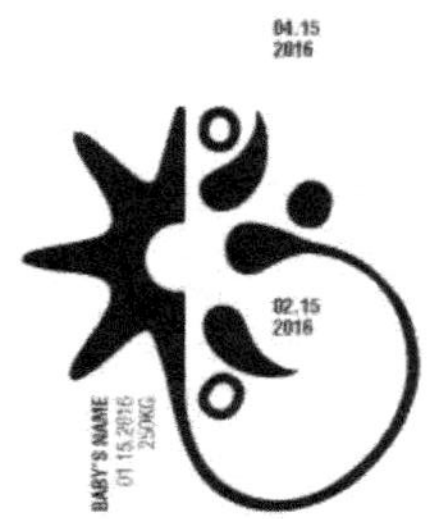

Figure 8: It shows the initial tattoo a child would receive at birth, together with the encoded information about which of the vaccinations required at birth the child actually received. This tattoo shows, the three vaccinations required at birth, but only one was received and 2 missed.

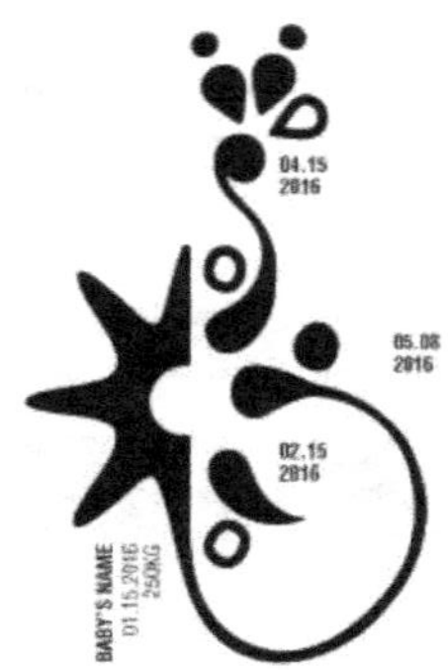

Figure 9: All 4 required vaccines received at 6 weeks old, plus the two additional ones that were missing at birth.

After that time, at 10 weeks old the child received two of the three vaccines required.

On one level, the physical visual representation of the tattoo can be read and interpreted without requiring any kind of technology (Figure 8, 9, 10, 11, 12). We hope that once the designed tattoo becomes popular, the users (doctors and parents) will be able to understand the symbol and the information it conveys (the vaccines that have already been administered to the child wearing the bracelet). On the other level, the users can employ NFC enabled devices (Figure 13, 14) in order to access, read, and update more detailed information about the child's vaccination status (such as the vaccination dates).

Prototype

This section describes the system we have prototyped so far. The prototype consists of two elements: bracelets containing NFC tags (intended to be worn by the children), and NFC-enabled Android smartphones (intended to be used by the doctors) in order to manage the vaccine information contained within the bracelets.

NFC stands for Near Field Communication. It is a set of communication protocols that enables two electronic devices to establish communication by bringing them within 4 cm of each other. Usually, one of the two devices is a portable device such as a smartphone, while the other one is an NFC tag.

NFC tags are basically passive data containers. They can be written to and read by an NFC enabled device. More concretely, the tags are electrical circuits that function thanks to the inductance of a nearby device. A smartphone located near a NFC tag supplies the power that the tag needs to fire up. The use of NFC tags has two remarkable advantages. Firstly, the tags are very cheap. For example, we found waterproof NFC bracelets for US $0.18 available from Alibaba. Secondly, there is no cost related with maintaining the NFC tags, since they do not require batteries (they are unpowered circuits.)

Nowadays many current models of Android smart phones can be employed to manage the information contained in the NFC tags inside the bracelets, since those phones incorporate an NFC controller able to read and write data to an NFC tag. We are aware that smartphones are not cheap. Thus, we recommend minimizing the cost of our approach by reusing second-hand smartphones. Every time we buy a smartphone, we could donate the previous one so that, it can be used by doctors in a developing world context. If we could induce that behavior, we would obtain many useful devices, because the current rate of phone replacement is very high and raising.

There are various types of NFC tag with different memory sizes, normally between 96 bytes and 8KB. For our prototype, we have used 1Kb tags. The material we used to craft the bracelet is EVA foam. We used this material because it is easy to manipulate, and is therefore appropriate for rapid prototyping at this stage of our research. However, we anticipate that silicone will be employed for the final prototype instead of EVA foam. With respect to the NFC-enabled device, we employed a Google Nexus 5 smartphone to test every functionality and option we implemented in the App. Once the prototype was stable, we also tested the App on various different phones.

We have prototyped two slightly different versions of the App. One is for medical staff and the other is for

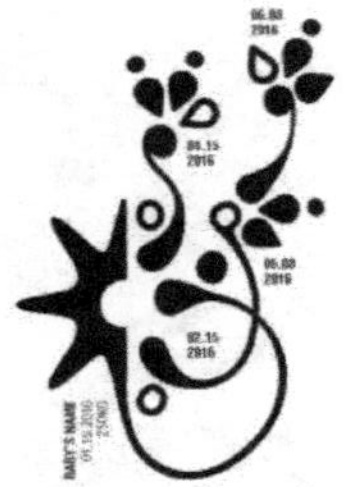

Figure 10: At 14 weeks old the three required vaccines have been given, along with the additional one that was missed at 10 weeks.

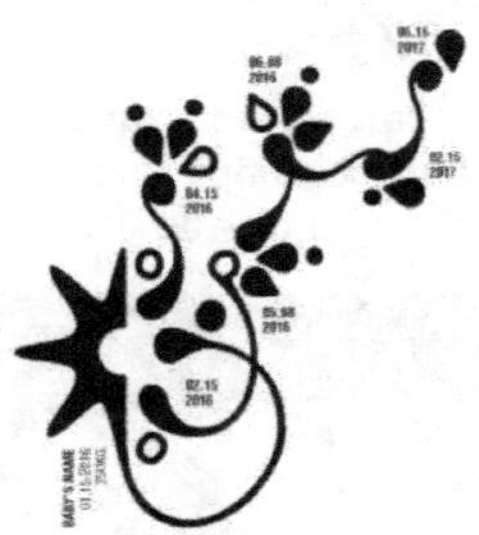

Figure 11: At 15-18 months old the child received both required vaccinations, along with the missing one from 6-12 months.

Figure 12: The guidebook provides instruction on how to interpret the tattoo.

parents. The version for parents allows the users to query information. The version for medical staff also allows the users to update information.

The user interface of the App is primarily visual. Note that there are between 1,250 and 2,100 different languages spoken natively in Africa [3]. Some authors even talk about 3,000 languages [2]. Ironically, English is the most widely spoken language in Africa [11]. Many African countries also have a very low literacy level. Thus, we make the user interfaces as visual as possible, to overcome the language and literacy barriers. Specifically, we employ the tattoo design as a catalyst for both visualization and interaction. In cases where written language is needed, we use English, the most universal language in Africa nowadays.

The overall functioning of the App is easy and intuitive. The App was designed in order to simplify the interaction of both medical staff and parents with the information contained in the NFC bracelet. (Internally stored as a text string that encodes vaccines identifiers along with the dates when the vaccinations were made). Whenever an NFC bracelet is located very near (a few centimeters) a smartphone with the App installed, the App is automatically triggered. The main screen (Figure 13) is presented to the user, including the whole tattoo symbol. The areas of the tattoo related to vaccines still not administered appear in a light color. Conversely, the areas corresponding to vaccines already administered are represented in a dark color. Thus, the main screen conveys an overall picture of the current vaccination status.

The version of the App intended for parents allows the users to query the information in an intuitive way. By touching any region of the tattoo symbol, the App visualizes the information pertinent to the corresponding vaccine (Figure 14). The information includes the vaccine name, whether it has been administered or not, and the date it was administered or the date it is supposed to be administered. Moreover, when a vaccination date approaches, the app warns and notifies the users about it.

The version of the App intended for medical staff additionally incorporates the ability to update information related to each concrete vaccination. Thus, the doctors can update both the date a vaccine has been administered and the expected date of the next vaccination.

Beyond the design and technologies described in this document, there are other aspects that must be taken into account for our system to be used in the real world. We are aware that health records and health date are considered as sensitive private information. They are subject to security and privacy regulations. Even though the use of NFC technologies for very sensitive actions, such as payment systems, is increasing, we think that having sensitive information in wearable NFC tags presents some risks. Therefore, we will take these concerns into account and will work to minimize these security and privacy risks in our design.

Conclusion

In this paper, we have described our technical proposal for collecting, recording, and tracking health vaccination records for children in a developing world context. Our solution comprises both bracelets containing NFC tags (that store information regarding

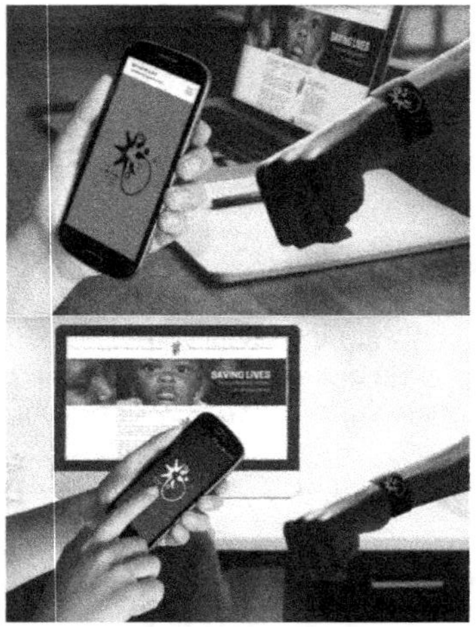

Figure 13: The App is automatically triggered whenever an NFC bracelet is located.

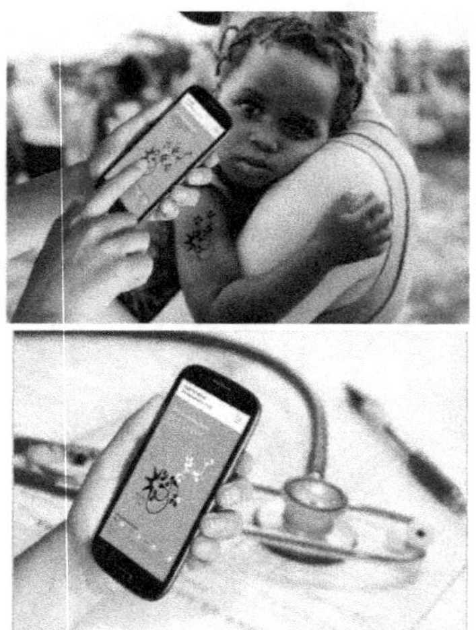

Figure 14: The App visualizes the information pertinent to the corresponding vaccine.

the child's vaccination status) and NFC-enabled Android smartphones (that allow the doctors to access, read, and update that information). The bracelets also have the vaccination status recorded visually as a tattoo design printed on their surface, allowing both human readable and machine readable access to the information they contain.

The tattoo design combines traditional ethnographic elements with easily interpreted variations to encode basic vaccination data in a form, which is aesthetically and culturally acceptable while still recording the important data.

Our future work includes conducting user research in real settings, in collaboration with NGOs. Furthermore, since we are dealing with sensitive private information, we will also devote effort to minimize the security and privacy risks inherent to this kind of technology.

Acknowledgements

We would like to thank the anonymous reviewers who provided helpful and wise comments on the previous version of this document.

The LARSyS has been funding this project, UID/EEA/50009/2013. Acknowledgement to ARDITI - Regional Agency for Development and Technology for the financial support through their grants in the scope of the Project with reference M1420-09-5369-000001.

References

1. Dreyfuss, Henry. 2003. *Designing for People*. Third Ed. New York: Allworth Press.
2. Epstein, Edmund L. 1998. The Language of African Literature. Africa World Press.
3. Heine, Bernd; Heine, Bernd, eds. 2000. African Languages: an Introduction. Cambridge University Press.
4. Jeong B., Ibáñez J., Nunes N., Chen M. 2017. Mobile App to Assist with Tattoo-encoded Baby Immunization Records in Africa. In proceedings of the 5th International Conference on Advanced Technology & Science (ICAT'17), Istanbul, Turkey.
5. Jeong B. 2016. On-Skin Technologies: Aesthetic, Expressive, and Functional Tattoos for Child Health Records. ACM International Joint Conference on Pervasive and Ubiquitous Computing (Ubicomp/SWC'16) Heidelberg, Germany. 937-941. DOI: http://dx.doi.org/10.1145/2968219.2979137
6. Jeong B., Chen M., and Ibanez J. 2016. A Tattooing for the Child Health Records Design that can Save Lives. In Proceedings of HCI Korea (HCIK'16), ACM Digital Library, Seoul, Korea, 15-21.
7. Jeong B., and Chen M. 2015. The New Understanding of User-centered Design through the Extension of User Definition and Goal. In Proceedings of HCI Korea (HCIK'15) ACM Digital Library, Seoul, Korea, 26-30.
8. Jeong B. 2015. An Ethnography Design for Cultural Implications in Africa. In Proceedings of 2015 KSDS Spring International Conference, Seoul, Korea, 146-149.
9. Jeong B. 2014. Study on Ethnography Methods for Design Strategy. Proceedings of 2014 KSDS Spring International Conference, Seoul, Korea, 186-187.
10. http://www.gatesfoundation.org
11. http://www.africaranking.com/most-spoken-languages-in-africa

An Observational Coding Scheme for Detecting Children's Usability Problems in Augmented Reality

Iulian Radu
Georgia Institute of Technology
North Ave, Atlanta, GA, USA
iulian@gatech.edu

Simina Avram
Georgia Institute of Technology
North Ave, Atlanta, GA, USA
savram3@gatech.edu

Katherine Guzdial
Georgia Institute of Technology
North Ave, Atlanta, GA, USA
kguzdial@gatech.edu

IDC '17, June 27-30, 2017, Stanford, CA, USA

ACM ISBN 978-1-4503-4921-5/17/06.
http://dx.doi.org/10.1145/3078072.3084337

Abstract
Handheld augmented reality (AR) is a unique medium that can be helpful for young children's entertainment and education, but to achieve the benefits of this technology, experiences need to be appropriately designed for young children's developing skills. In the current research, we are interested in identifying and quantifying the usability problems that are encountered by children using handheld AR applications. We have developed a qualitative coding scheme for detecting AR usability problems from video observations of user interactions. We then applied the coding scheme to extract usability problems encountered by children aged 5-10 years old as they played with a handheld AR game. Through triangulation with performance data, we have detected usability problems related to AR and non-AR components of the experience. Our analysis found positive and negative correlations between usability problems and child age, and found that children experienced a variety of problems such as grip and posture strains, inabilities to recover from various types of tracking loss, difficulties orienting their body around the gameboard, etc. This work is the first in a series of studies applying the qualitative coding for understanding young children's ability to use handheld AR applications.

Mental & Emotional States
FRU - Indication of frustration / dislike **SUGG** - Child makes suggestion **CONF** - Indication of confusion **BOR** - Indication of boredom **AHA** - Indication of "aha" moment **TIRV** - Indication of physical tiredness **SPACEV** - Indication of 3D space awareness
General Movement
SCRATCH – Interrupts game to scratch **HSTR** - Fingers / hand / arm stretched **HSHAKE** - Hand shaken **BSTR** - Body stretching **BSIT** – Body sitting down **ELT** - Elbow or hand is resting on table **PHONEDROP** - Phone dropped or slips **PHONEDOWN** - Puts the phone down **BUMP** - Bumps or trips body **BSW** - Back has switched its posture
Grips
GSW- Hand has switched its grip
Help and Interruptions
HLPME - Child asks for help **HLPV** - Experimenter gives quick help **INTH1** – Gameplay interrupted while experimenter helped for a period of time, just verbally **INTH2** – Gameplay interrupted while experimenter helped for a period of time, and took away the phone / moved the paper / or touched the child **IGN** - Child ignored instructions from the game or experimenter **INT** – Child did something which caused their gameplay to be interrupted (e.g., looking at experimenter)
Tracking Events
TLW – Tracking lost while walking **TLF** – Tracking lost, finger occlusion **TLA** – Tracking lost, aiming away **TLC** – Tracking lost, too close

Table 1. Behaviors tagged through the coding scheme.

Author Keywords

Augmented reality; children; mobile; qualitative method; video coding; usability; developmental psychology

ACM Classification Keywords

H.5.1 Artificial, augmented, and virtual realities.

Introduction

Augmented reality (AR) is a technology that enables computer-generated imagery to be superimposed on a view of the real world, and handheld devices, such as phones and tablets, will likely be the dominant method for delivering AR experiences to large number of children for the near future. AR has been shown to have measurable benefits to children's education over traditional approaches [1,2,3]. To achieve these benefits, AR experiences need to be usable by children. In this research, we are developing a method for identifying and quantifying usability problems in handheld AR experiences for children, permitting researchers to use observational video data to compare between different age groups and/or different AR designs.

Research in AR technology has typically measured usability through performance metrics and subjective reports [10,11]. Such metrics quantify certain aspects of usability, but they can miss user behaviors leading to the problem. Another method for quantifying usability problems is analysis of observational recordings. The popular DEVAN method [7] was designed for contexts where adults interact with desktop applications. Videos are annotated through a qualitative coding scheme, and coded behaviors are aggregated into usability problems [8,9]. Unlike adult users, children typically use digital games and are strongly affected by motivation, thus an adapted scheme was developed for such contexts [6].

In handheld augmented reality applications, different usability problems arise than compared to desktop computer interfaces, because handheld AR experiences require users to manipulate a mobile device through physical body motions in a three-dimensional space. Qualitative coding schemes have previously been used for understanding observational data of children playing with augmented reality [12,25,26,27,28]. However, such coding schemes are focused on studying specific aspects of the user experience other than usability. We do not know of any existing coding scheme specifically for measuring usability of children's AR experiences. This research intends to address this limitation, by answering:

1. What observable behaviors can serve as indicators of usability problems in augmented reality?
2. What types of usability problems are experienced by children using handheld augmented reality?
3. What is the relationship between children's age and the types of usability problems encountered?

To address these questions, we first developed a coding scheme for detecting usability breakdowns, then applied the coding scheme to 40 children playing with a handheld augmented reality game, identifying a set of usability problems and differences between age groups.

Coding Scheme and Experimental Design

We developed a first version of the AR usability problems coding scheme (Table 1). Codes are observable child behaviors that indicate a usability problem may be occurring. After participant videos are tagged with these codes, a set of usability problems can then be extracted, through the process explained in the next sections. The coding scheme was designed based on literature about children's usability problems, and then was refined through iterative application on pilot study videos. The

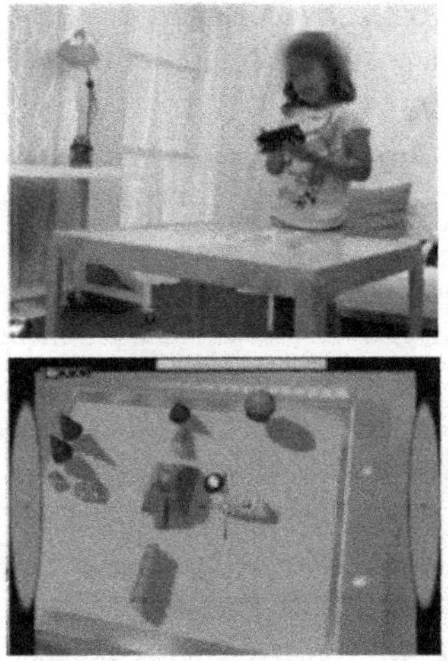

Figure 1. A child playing the augmented reality game.

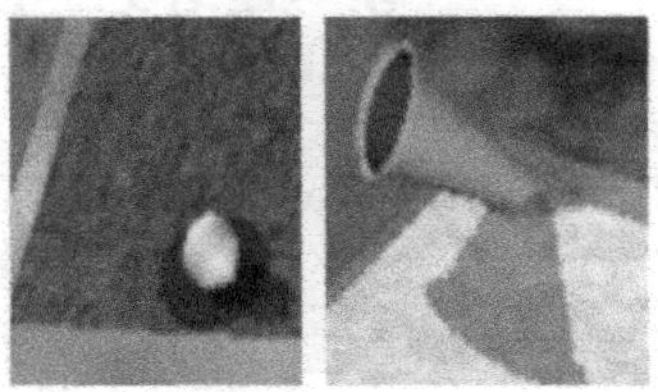

Figure 2. Game items are exposed in open levels (left) and enclosed in tunnel levels (right).

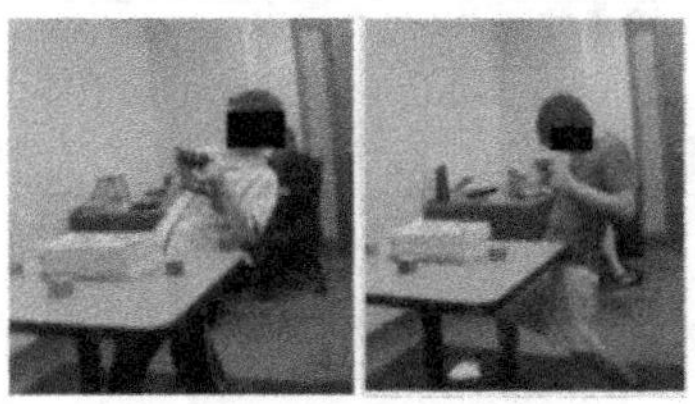

Figure 3. Examples of strained body posture.

initial design was primarily informed by the research in [6], describing a coding scheme for detecting problems in children's desktop computer games, and by the research in [13], which describes links between child development and the usability of AR technology. The coding scheme was then refined by application to eight videos of children playing AR games. Researchers and undergraduate coders participated in this process, revising the scheme mainly by adding new codes and adjusting ambiguous codes (i.e. codes whose meaning would be interpreted differently by different people).

We then used the coding scheme to extract usability problems encountered by children of different ages as they played with a handheld augmented reality game. A total of 40 children participated, 14 children in each age group: 5-6 year olds (6M, 8F), 7-8 year olds (7M, 7F), and 9-10 year olds (7M, 7F). The game, previously been described in [21], was a typical tabletop augmented reality game where a 3D virtual world appears on top of the "gameboard" paper once it is viewed through a smartphone camera (Figure 1). The player took the role of a wizard who must collect a set of magical lemons, to create items for their virtual pets. The game was composed of a tutorial plus 4 levels of gameplay. Each level consisted of repeated trials of item collection, where children collected lemons by tapping the screen, or by using a crosshair activated by side buttons. The game was designed to test the relationship between usability and user movement around the gameboard. Half the game levels required changes in perspective, as the user had to collect targets enclosed inside tunnels (Figure 2). When games encourage changes in perspective, it may cause spatial and movement problems, such as bumping into objects, difficulties gripping the device, etc.

Two coders used the coding scheme to code the play sessions of all children, overlapping on 10% of the videos. To determine if coders agreed on each coded event, a 4-second overlap time window was used, similar to [6]. The coders achieved an inter-rater agreement validity of Cohen's Kappa equal to 0.80 or greater (percent agreement > 97%). Inter-rater agreement was calculated using Quera and Bakeman's GSEQ algorithm for continuous-timed event coding [22].

To extract types of usability problems, the coded events were first categorized into clusters of related behaviors, and a severity rating was assigned to each event according to how much assistance a child required to proceed. Clusters of events were then aggregated into usability problem types (Table 2.A and 2.B). Other types of events were also captured during video analysis, such as reasons why tracking loss was lost (Table 3.A and 3.B) and types of grips used by children (Figure 4). We then performed quantitative analysis on the counts of events for each child: Spearman rank correlations between children's age (in months) and number of event occurrences for each usability problem type; and Wilcoxon signed-rank tests comparing AR movement conditions.

USABILITY PROBLEMS DETECTED

Tables 2.A. and 2.B. list issues encountered by children under different age groups and under different AR movement conditions. The number of problems encountered by children was relatively similar between age groups, overall. Although these numbers are similar, younger children experience different problems than older children, as will be discussed below. Additionally, younger children experienced higher severity problems and required more assistance to fix the usability

Observed Problems in Tunnel Levels	Num. children aged 5-6/7-8/9-10
MANIPULATION	
Strained body posture[OT]	0% / 28% / 33%
Strained grip	0% / 21% / 16%
Dropping the phone	7% / 0% / 8%
SPACE	
Difficulty orienting body, while playing the game[OT]	21% / 50% / 0% **(7% / 0% / 0%)**
Difficulty orienting body, while fixing tracking[OT]	[CN] 50% / 7% / 0% **(42% / 7% / 0%)**
ABSTRACT THINKING	
Needing in-game instruction on crosshair	7% / 0% / 0% **(7% / 0% / 0%)**
Not understanding storyline	7% / 7% / 8%
Not understanding mechanics	14% / 14% / 0%
Difficulties interpreting or fixing tracking loss	[CN] 50% / 14% / 16% **(42% / 14% / 0%)**
ATTENTION	
Bumping or tripping[OT]	28% / 35% / 41%
Interruption from self-distraction	21% / 7% / 0%
Interruption from scratching	21% / 35% / 58%

Table 2.A. Usability problems encountered in Tunnel levels. Bold=Children requiring experimenter assistance. CP=positive correlation with age ($p<0.05$); CN=negative correlation. OT=Significant differences between open vs. tunnel levels.

problems. In the following discussion we present our qualitative findings and report triangulation with our performance data whenever relevant.

Problems Specific to Handheld Augmented Reality

When children experience usability issues in AR experiences, the issues may be related to different layers of the experience: game design and narrative, interaction design, AR tracking technology, hardware ergonomics, etc. In the current section, we present issues that are likely to be caused specifically by the presence of AR technology, and which may occur across other kinds of AR experiences.

Strained body postures in older children: Children aged 7-8 and 9-10 years old were observed bending their backs or necks in ways that appeared strained, or stretching their neck or back (Figure 3). The number of children experiencing this behavior increased with age; older children were observed to bend their body more often, and seemed more reluctant to move around the gameboard. This issue may, in part, be related to the fixed angle of tunnels, indicating that AR games should be designed to measure and adapt to player height. Although older children subjectively indicated enjoying the challenge of tunnel levels, they frequently noted a dislike for walking around the game, possibly indicating a sedentary lifestyle or familiarity with digital experiences that lack movement.

Difficulty orienting while playing the game: Performance metrics logged during gameplay showed that 5-6 year old children completed the tasks significantly slower than other age groups, but the performance data does not indicate why. Through the qualitative analysis, we see that children had most trouble with changing perspective while collecting lemons inside tunnels. This issue occurred more severely in 5-6 year old children, with 7% of children requiring researcher assistance. None of the older children, 9-10 years old, experienced this issue. This may be due to 5-6 year old children's developing abilities to understand space and coordinate their body [13], and can indicate that AR experiences for 5-6 year olds should be lenient if requiring perspective changes.

Difficulty orienting while fixing tracking: Losing the tracking of the paper is a significant issue because it interrupts the gameplay, and may occur for several reasons (Table 3.A and 3.B). Performance data showed that 5-6 year old children are significantly slower at fixing tracking. The qualitative data shows that children had trouble fixing tracking when required to reorient their body. In tunnel levels, the experimenter had to assist 40% of children in the 5-6 year old range, and 7% of children in the 7-8 year old range, indicating that this issue is problematic for young children when they are required to move around the gameboard. This is possibly because in such levels children changed their perspective to the gameboard, had likelihood of tracking losses, and it may be related to spatial and abstract thinking abilities of younger children [13].

Difficulties recovering from tracking loss: Abstract thinking is required to understand why tracking has become lost and how to fix it. We clustered all events which indicated that children either did not understand, were frustrated, or required assistance when the game lost tracking. This issue included instances of children being unable to orient themselves while recovering tracking, and included other instances of frustration, or difficulties fixing tracking, such as the need to reposition fingers away from the camera. This event was negatively

Observed Problems in Non-Tunnel Levels	Num. children aged 5-6/7-8/9-10
MANIPULATION	
Strained body posture[OT]	[CP] 0% / 14% / 33%
Strained grip	0% / 21% / 0%
Dropping the phone	0% / 7% / 8%
SPACE	
Difficulty orienting body, while playing the game[OT]	0% / 0% / 0%
Difficulty orienting body, while fixing tracking[OT]	0% / 0% / 0%
ABSTRACT THINKING	
Needing initial instruction on how to use crosshair	71% / 79% / 58% **(71% / 79% / 58%)**
Needing in-game instruction on crosshair	7% / 7% / 0% **(7% / 7% / 0%)**
Not understanding storyline	0% / 14% / 0%
Not understanding mechanics	7% / 0% / 0%
Difficulties interpreting or fixing tracking loss	14% / 7% / 0% **(7% / 0% / 0%)**
ATTENTION	
Bumping or tripping[OT]	7% / 0% / 0%
Interruption from self-distraction	0% / 0% / 0%
Interruption from scratching	[CP] 0% / 35% / 50%

Table 2.B. Usability problems encountered in Non-Tunnel levels. Bold=Children requiring experimenter assistance. CP=positive correlation with age ($p<0.05$); CN=negative correlation. OT=Significant differences between open vs. tunnel levels.

correlated with children's age. Some of the older children experienced this issue but none required experimenter assistance to resolve it.

Bumping or tripping: Children of all ages were observed either bumping into the table or tripping over their own feet as they changed their perspective on the gameboard. This event occurred significantly more in tunnel levels where users were required to change perspective. This event may indicate a focused attention on the game, and may cause problems if children play such games in dynamic environments such as in cluttered spaces, busy classrooms or outdoors.

Interruption due to self-distraction: Children were sometimes observed losing interest in the game and using the AR camera to look away at other pieces of the environment. This behavior was observed most often with 5-6 year old children, typically when they were challenged or frustrated by tunnel levels, possibly indicating mechanism for distraction from difficult tasks.

Types of Tracking Losses: The AR technology used in our application was based on image-based tracking. The experience would stop working if the smartphone camera (located on the left side of the phone) stopped seeing the gameboard. From performance metrics logged in the game, we discovered that children of all ages experienced tracking losses, and 5-6 year olds had significantly more tracking losses than both older age groups. With the current coding scheme, we identified multiple reasons: losing tracking while walking (negatively correlated with age), covering the camera with the finger (occurring in each age group), and aiming too close or away (negatively correlated with age).

Adverse Effects of Technology Exposure
Parents were asked to report the kinds of devices their child has been exposed to, and this metric was correlated with the number of tracking errors encountered by children (accounting for age effects in the analysis). The correlation was, surprisingly, a positive correlation: children with highest technology exposure had 83% increase in number of tracking losses due to fingers in front of the camera compared to children with lowest exposure. Performance metrics showed that children with more technology experience had 39% more selection errors when touching targets on the screen. This indicates a potential issue with introducing new technologies, namely that children who are experienced with technology will transfer expectations from old to new technologies, causing issues such as expectations of technology resilience to errors, and the use of familiar grips which may interfere with tracking technology.

Problems Not Specific to Augmented Reality
This section will discuss usability problems caused by other layers of the experience, such as the hardware ergonomics, game narrative, screen interaction types.

Grip Styles and Strains: Children aged 7-8 and 9-10 years old were observed such as stretching their hand, shaking their hand, or repeatedly shifting their grip in a way suggesting they are searching for a more comfortable grip. We identified a shift in grips over age (Figure 4), noting a possibility of transition period during age 7-8. As children age, their hands develop in both strength and size, therefore changing their ability to grip and manipulate the smartphone device. In our study, younger children showed a preference for the curled grip, but as children aged the use of the crab grip increased, whereby older children preferred the crab grip. There is a

Tracking Loss Reasons in Tunnel Levels	Num. children aged 5-6/7-8/9-10
Walking[OT]	[CN] 100% / 50% / 50%
Stationary, finger occlusion	50% / 64% / 41%
Stationary, aiming the camera away	[CN] 42% / 28% / 0%
Stationary, aiming too close	14% / 14% / 0%

Table 3.A. Children in each age group encountering tracking loss, in levels with tunnel-enclosed targets.

Tracking Loss Reasons in Non-Tunnel Levels	Num. children aged 5-6/7-8/9-10
Walking[OT]	[CN] 28% / 0% / 0%
Stationary, finger occlusion	71% / 57% / 41%
Stationary, aiming the camera away	28% / 7% / 8%
Stationary, aiming too close	7% / 0% / 0%

Table 3.B. Children in each age group encountering tracking loss, in levels with non-enclosed targets. Significant correlations between age and number of events are marked as "CP"=positive correlation; "CN"=negative correlation. Significant differences between open vs. tunnel levels marked as "OT".

strong use of the straight grip in 7-8 year olds, possibly indicating that the straight grip is an intermediary grip style where children's strength allows them to hold and control the phone by pushing on the sides; unfortunately this grip is quite unstable and leads to frequent tracking losses. A small number of children within each age group were observed dropping the phone, typically occurring as children were changing or relaxing their grip. All children recovered, but this may lead to mobile device damage.

Needing assistance with the game mechanics: All children knew how to touch on the screen with their finger. However, many young children did not know how to use the crosshair interaction, which required them to aim with the center of the screen. Children also had questions about game storyline and mechanics, such as why lemons are in tubes, how things can be made from lemons, how many lemons had to be collected, etc.

Limitations and Future Work

In upcoming research, we are interested to apply the coding scheme to a variety of AR experiences. Currently, our results are likely influenced by multiple variables, such as game interactions (ex: if users collect items by moving close/far vs. touching on screen), by hardware ergonomics (ex: mobile phones vs. tablets; camera in the center of the device vs. on the side), by AR tracking software (ex: image based tracking vs. depth-based markerless tracking), etc. As a next step, we will study children's usability problems with a non-AR version of the same game, allowing us to account for factors such as gameplay interactions and mobile device ergonomics. In the future, we will apply the coding scheme to detect usability problems in other types of AR experiences. We expect this process will refine the coding scheme, provide triangulation between metrics, identify a common set of usability problems encountered by children in AR, and ultimately lead to understanding relationships between AR designs and child development.

Finally, good games should be easy to learn and hard to master [6], and should keep players highly engaged by maintaining a dynamic balance between the player's abilities and the challenge offered by the game [23,24]. The current research has identified degree of difficulty which children experience with the AR game. Designers can use this knowledge to create AR games that provide appropriate challenge for children of specific ages.

Acknowledgements: We wish to thank the children and parents who participated in this study; Emory University Child Study Center and Spatial Cognition Lab; and the students who helped with video-coding in this study.

References

1. Radu, I. (2014). Augmented reality in education: a meta-review and cross-media analysis. Personal and Ubiquitous Computing, 18(6), 1533-1543.
2. Vincenzi D. A. , Valimont B. , Macchiarella N., Opalenik C., Gangadharan S. N., and Majoros A. E. (2003). "The Effectiveness of Cognitive Elaboration Using Augmented Reality as a Training and Learning Paradigm," Annual Meeting of the Human Factors and Ergonomics Society, Denver, CO, USA, pp. 2054-2058.
3. Lindgren R. and Moshell J. M. (2011). "Supporting Children's Learning with Body-Based Metaphors in a Mixed Reality Environment," Simulation, pp. 177-180
4. Dix, A., (2009). Human-computer interaction. Springer US.
5. Sharp, H., Rogers, Y. and Preece, J., (2007). Interaction design: beyond human-computer interaction.
6. Barendregt, W. and Bekker, M.M., (2006). Developing a coding scheme for detecting usability and fun problems in computer games for young children. Behavior research methods, 38(3), pp.382-389.

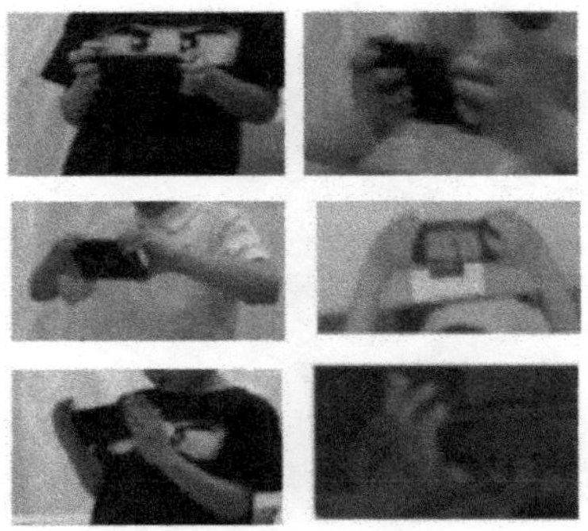

Figure 4.A. Grips used by children: Curl (top), Crab (middle), Straight (bottom).

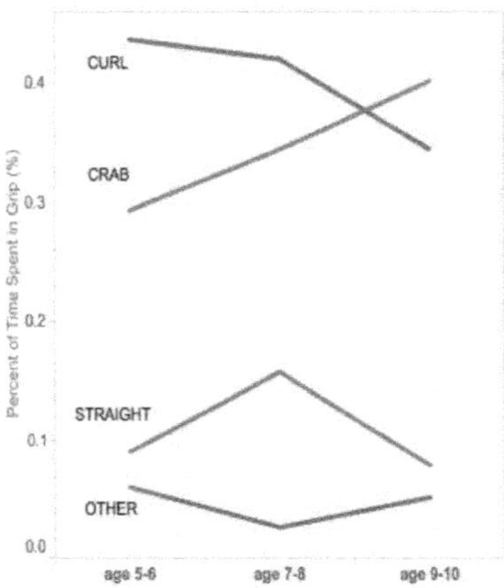

Figure 4.B. Percentage of time each grip type was used by children of different ages.

7. Vermeeren, A.P., den Bouwmeester, K., Aasman, J. and de Ridder, H., (2002). DEVAN: a tool for detailed video analysis of user test data. Behaviour & Information Technology, 21(6), pp.403-423.
8. Gamberini, L., Spagnolli, A., Prontu, L., Furlan, S., Martino, F., Solaz, B.R., Alcañiz, M. and Lozano, J.A., (2013). How natural is a natural interface? An evaluation procedure based on action breakdowns. Personal and ubiquitous computing, 17(1), pp.69-79.
9. Cockton, G. and Lavery, D., (1999), August. A framework for usability problem extraction. In INTERACT (pp. 344-352).
10. Bai, Z. and Blackwell, A.F., (2012). Analytic review of usability evaluation in ISMAR. Interacting with Computers, 24(6), pp.450-460.
11. Dünser, A., Grasset, R. and Billinghurst, M., (2008). A survey of evaluation techniques used in augmented reality studies (pp. 5-1). Human Interface Technology Laboratory New Zealand.
12. Hornecker, E. and A. Dünser (2009). "Of pages and paddles: Children's expectations and mistaken interactions with physical-digital tools." Interacting with Computers 21(1-2): 95-107.
13. Radu, I. and B. MacIntyre (2012). Using children's developmental psychology to guide augmented-reality design and usability. Mixed and Augmented Reality (ISMAR), 2012 IEEE International Symposium on, IEEE.
14. Nischelwitzer, A., F.-J. Lenz, et al. (2007). "Some Aspects of the Development of Low-Cost Augmented Reality Learning Environments as Examples." Universal Access in Human-Computer Interaction.: 728-737.
15. Dunleavy, M., C. Dede, et al. (2009). "Affordances and Limitations of Immersive Participatory Augmented Reality Simulations for Teaching and Learning." Journal of Science Education and Technology 18(1): 7-22.
16. Piaget, J. (1970). "Science of education and the psychology of the child. Trans. D. Coltman."
17. Rosser, R. A. (1994). Cognitive development: Psychological and biological perspectives, Allyn and Bacon Boston.
18. Wyeth, P. a. P., H.C. (2003). "Using developmental theories to inform the design of technology for children." Proceedings of the 2003 conference on Interaction design and children: 93-100.
19. Gelderblom, H. (2009). Designing technology for young children: guidelines grounded in a literature investigation on child development and children's technology. Doctor of Philosophy, University of South Africa.
20. Bekker, T. and A. N. Antle (2011). "Developmentally situated design (DSD): making theoretical knowledge accessible to designers of children's technology." Proceedings of the 2011 annual conference on Human factors in computing systems: 2531--2540.
21. Radu, I., MacIntyre, B. and Lourenco, S., (2016), Comparing Children's Crosshair and Finger Interactions in Handheld Augmented Reality: Relationships Between Usability and Child Development. In Proceedings of the International Conference on Interaction Design and Children (pp. 288-298). ACM.
22. Quera, V. and R. Bakeman (2000). GSEQ for Windows: New software for the sequential analysis of behavioral data, with an interface to The Observer. 3rd International Conference on Methods and Techniques in Behavioral Research. Nijmegen, Netherlands.
23. Shell, J. (2008). The art of game design.
24. Swink, S. (2009). Game feel. A Game Designer's Guide to Virtual Sensation. Burlington, MA, 1.
25. Zimmerman, Heather Toomey, et al. (2015) "Using augmented reality to support observations about trees during summer camp." Proceedings of the 14th International Conference on Interaction Design and Children. ACM.
26. Cassidy, B., Sim, G., Horton, M., & Fitton, D. (2015). Participatory design of wearable augmented reality display elements for children at play. In Computer Science and Electronic Engineering Conference (CEEC), 2015 7th (pp. 53-58). IEEE.
27. Escobedo, L., Tentori, M., Quintana, E., Favela, J., & Garcia-Rosas, D. (2014). Using augmented reality to help children with autism stay focused. IEEE Pervasive Computing, 13(1).
28. Fleck, S., Hachet, M., & Bastien, J. M. (2015). Marker-based augmented reality: Instructional-design to improve children interactions with astronomical concepts. In Proceedings of the 14th International Conference on Interaction Design and Children (pp. 21-28). ACM.

Autistic Children's Use of Technology and Media: A Fieldwork Study

Susana Alarcon-Licona
Lian Loke
The University of Sydney
Sydney, NSW 2006, Australia
susana.alarconlicona@sydney.edu.au
lian.loke@sydney.edu. au

IDC '17, June 27-30, 2017, Stanford, CA, USA

ACM ISBN 978-1-4503-4921-5/17/06.
http://dx.doi.org/10.1145/3078072.3084338

Abstract

This qualitative field study conducted at a school for autistic children aims to describe how low and medium functioning autistic children use technology at school. Additionally, it explores education professionals and parents' attitudes and concerns regarding technology use by children. Data-collection methods included focus groups with nine education professionals, naturalistic observations of fifteen children with autism in therapy sessions, and interviews with parents of four of the children. Results revealed that (1) children are regular users of digital technology and media, (2) there are different patterns of use of technologies with possible correlations to accessibility and behavioural manifestations of autism, (3) education professionals and parents have positive attitude towards the use of technology by the children, but also recognize disadvantages to its use.

Author Keywords

Autism; children; digital technology; interactive technology; assistive technology; media; field study

ACM Classification Keywords

K3.1 Computers and education: Computer uses in education

Introduction

Autism Spectrum disorder (ASD) is a neurodevelopmental disorder characterized by a

Participant	Age	Grade	Gender
Alex	7	K	M
Ben	7	1	M
Charles	6	K	M
David	7	1	M
Ethan	8	2	M
Fabio	7	1	M
Gabriel	6	K	M
Helen	8	2	F
Ian	6	K	M
Justin	7	1	M
Kacey	10	3	F
Leo	10	3	M
Martin	9	3	M
Nolan	11	5	M
Oliver	7	1	M

Table 1: Characteristics of the children participating in this study. Note: All names are pseudonyms.

pattern of symptoms that include persistent deficits in social interaction, communication, rigidity of thought and imagination, repetitive behaviors, and in some cases, unusual responses to sensory stimuli. According to Sinha et al. (2014), deficits are closely linked with each other and their behavioral manifestations. For example, stimming behaviors may be coping mechanisms on an otherwise overwhelming environment. Some severe cases may present difficulty to understand communication, as well as tendency to problem behavior, requiring dedicated support and intensive intervention programs.

Digital Technologies for Autism Support

In recent years, there has been an increase in the design and implementation of technologies for autism support. Assistive Technology [AT] is often employed in special education to facilitate learning, enhance skills and increase the independence of people with disabilities (Lang et al. 2014). Authors commonly categorize AT according to its level of sophistication: from *low-tech* aids, such as reminder cards, to *high-tech* applications such as alternative and augmentative communication [AAC] devices (Ennis-Cole and Smith 2011), virtual environments (Shane et al. 2012), socially assistive robots (Boccanfuso et al. 2017) and sensors for evaluating physical, emotional and environmental states (Cabibihan et al. 2016). Nevertheless, it is important to note that autistic children's use of technology is not limited to specialized systems; mainstream products such as computers, mobile devices and electronic toys are available for their use. Studies on this area mainly explore the potential of applications in the autism context, including mobile applications to facilitate communication and social interaction (Abdullah, Wilson, and Brereton 2016, Hourcade et al. 2013) and use of SMART boards in classrooms for autistic users (Leach 2010). Studies documenting autistic children's use of technology are scarce. One relevant study from Vance et al. (2013) aimed to explain how autistic people were using iPads®. Results indicated that participants were using the device for a variety of purposes but not always in the intended way. These studies open relevant opportunities for different audiences but do not provide information on the current situation in school settings where diverse technology is available. This qualitative study is part of a larger project on implementation of technology to support autistic children with sensory processing differences. The focus of this study is to reveal the current patterns of use of technology at a school for autistic children. Understanding children's preferences and associated behaviors, interaction characteristics, as well as education professionals' attitude and concerns regarding technology can provide directions in the development or implementation of technology in this context.

Limitations

The participants in this study represent a convenience sample of autistic children and education professionals from one educational setting where children have access to digital technology. This setting was selected for being a distinctive context in which technology has been adopted in daily activities; likely to show natural patterns, behaviors and attitudes towards technology. Furthermore, it is also a feasible context for the future implementation of new technology. Although the findings cannot be generalized to the autistic population, we hope that by providing detailed descriptions readers working with similar user groups and contexts will gain insights from them.

The Study Context

The participating school provides Individualized Education Plans [IEP] to suit children's needs and skills. IEPs are reviewed by clinical supervisors. Besides, behavioral therapists work in separate sessions under the direction of a teacher. As shown in Figure 1, a typical classroom setting includes areas for either individual or group therapy sessions. Equipment in each classroom (A, B and C) includes at least one PC or laptop, a SMART board, at least 2 iPads and several digital timers. Other instances of technology include cause-and-effect toys, a Wii game console and a DVD player.

Figure 1: Typical classroom setting.

Method

The main participants in this study were 15 children diagnosed with autism who attended a school for autistic children in Sydney, Australia. Table 1 illustrates the characteristics of the participants. The data-collection methods used in this study are defined as ethnographic fieldwork (Atkinson 2014) involving a combination of methods suitable for studies with autistic children (Barendregt et al. 2016, Börjesson et al. 2015). Methods included focus groups with nine education professionals from the school that provided information as proxies and experts, i.e., three clinical supervisors with background in Behavior Analysis, three teachers, and three behavioral therapists; naturalistic observation of classroom activities and behaviors; and interviews with parents. All children's parents were invited to participate in interviews. However, only parents of 4 children accepted to be interviewed. Children were observed for periods ranging from 30 min to 1 hour, corresponding to full therapy sessions at the school, for a total time of five hours per child over a four-month period. Sessions were recorded through photos, video and/or notes according to parental consent limitations. Setting details such as the type of activities, relevant technology use characteristics and behavioral responses were documented. The observations and focus groups were used to generate information about the patterns of use of the different technologies that were available at school. In addition, the combination of these methods was also used to gather opinions and issues regarding technology use at school. The parents were interviewed about their children's use of technology at home and about their attitude in relation to their children's use of technology. All focus groups and interviews were video recorded and transcribed. The combined data were analyzed using a thematic analysis method (Creswell 2012, Atkinson 2014). Raw data were coded and grouped according to emerging themes. Finally, experiences were compared with relevant literature. It is important to note that we considered and documented individual cases over the whole process, but we also provide a general overview of the situation.

Results

1 Children are regular users of technology and media.

Figure 2 summarizes results of frequency and patterns of use, including related behavioural manifestations. All the children in this study are exposed to a range of technologies and use at least one instance of interactive technology in the classroom. From the 15 children, 13 of them enjoy and engage in technology-related activities every day in the classroom, especially educational games on iPad® and video-watching in a variety of devices. This is consistent with reports from the four interviews for high frequency of use of iPad® at home by children. In most of cases, children use other interactive technologies such as DVD players, computers or caregivers' mobile phones. However, children are mostly using them to access to media through YouTube or the native media player. In similar instances device's photo folder and Google search engine were used to find favorite images.

2 Patterns of use of technologies in classroom and home settings

DIGITAL TECHNOLOGY IN THERAPY

Given that classrooms are equipped with digital technology, it is not uncommon for teachers and therapists to select and utilize them in daily activities. Digital timers, are the most used digital tools in therapy. Most of the children seem to understand the concept of time and have adapted to the timer's alarm. However, children only interact with the timer when prompted except for one child who actively engages with starting timer, stopping it and watching time count up/count down. The most used digital interactive technology as part of an activity is iPad®. Teachers and therapists typically select *Injini*, a child developmental game suite, which provides opportunities for developing fine motor and early literacy skills through interactive games (Lee 2012). *Injini*'s games are the favorites for most of the participants and stand out given its usability characteristics (Figure 3). Therapists reported that children's skills improve with the use of these games. Other favorite iPad® applications such as *Temple Run*, *LEGO Juniors Create and Cruise*, and YouTube are predominantly used to engage children and practice turn-taking or requesting.

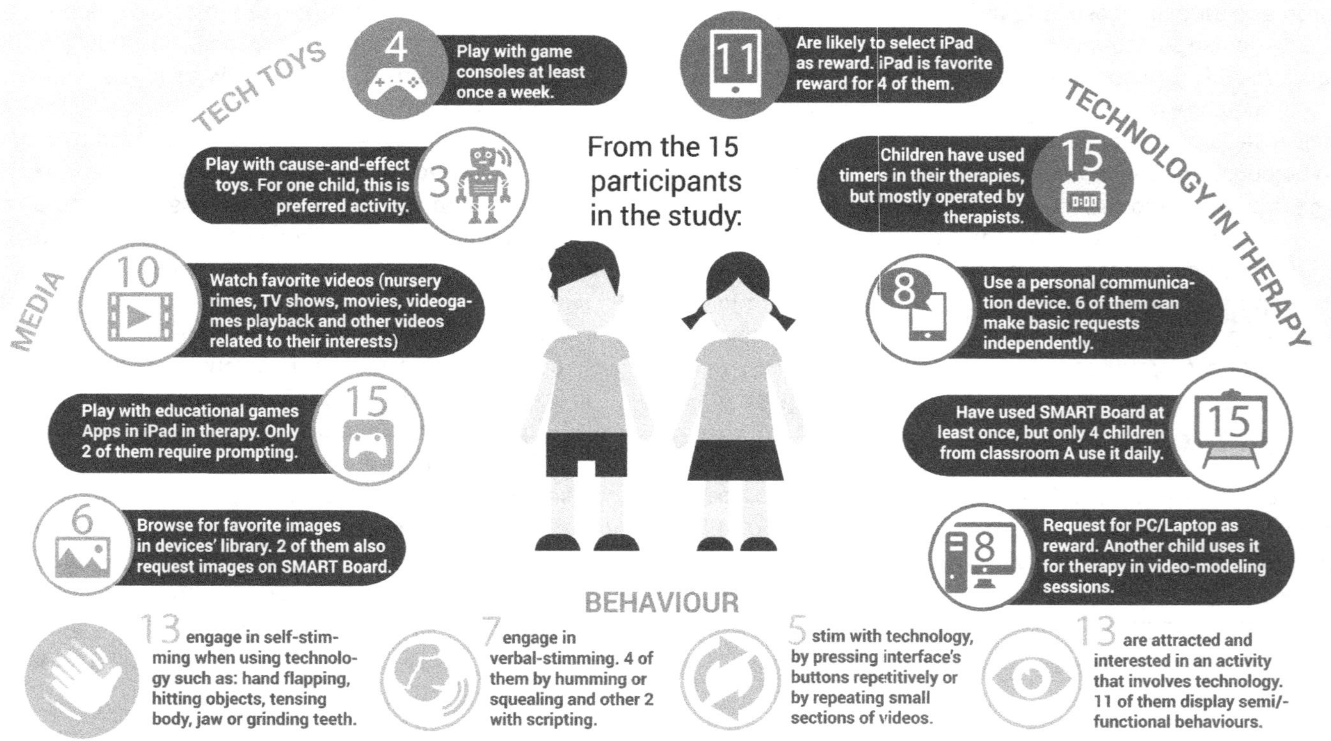

Figure 2: Summary of technology use by the 15 participants of the study.

Figure 3: Child tracing shapes on *Injini* IPad® application.

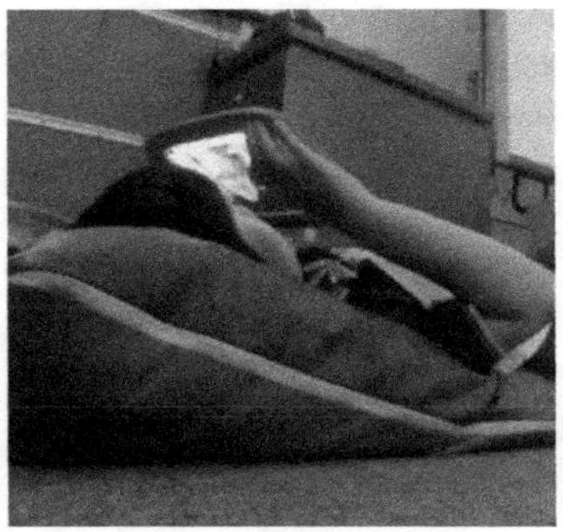

Figure 4: Child watching photos in AAC device.

All children who enjoy technology in therapy sessions are likely to request it as reward in their free playtime. Six of the children are more likely to request for iPad® as a reward than any other available technology, and four of them would choose iPad® over any other reward. In classrooms B and C, the use of SMART Board is limited to a few times per month, i.e. two to five. However, the use of it is not dedicated for therapy sessions but for entertainment purposes and children do not have continuous access or full control. In these classrooms, only two children attempt to operate the SMART Board. Contrarily, in classroom A, teacher and therapists use the SMART Board in daily individual or group sessions focused in developing skills for *requesting*, *turn-taking*, *attending* songs and stories, *interacting socially* or *learning* colors and shapes. Use of SMART Board in sessions ranges from one to three times a day but is also continuously available as a reward option for children, who exclusively use it for watching favorite videos and pictures.

Depending on the availability of the classroom resources, i.e., iPad®, PC/Laptop or SMART board, the children tend to fluctuate in their technology preference but watching videos is their permanent predilection. Consistently, the application that children use more in either tablets, PC or SMART Boards is YouTube. All children understand basic video controls for playing, pausing, option for *Full screen,* as well as the use of sliders for video time control and volume. None of the children can type titles in the search bar, but they navigate through recent searches and related videos. When they want to watch a different video, they request it verbally or with their AAC device. Children who use IPad® have been observed tapping, scrolling, minimizing, navigating to main page and browsing other applications without help from adults. When these children get to undesired pages or end of games without familiar input options, they can recover by touching *Home* button and accessing *Home screen*. Contrarily, children who use PC or laptops rarely explore menus and do not try to access to other programs. Furthermore, when they find themselves in an unfamiliar program or page they tend to approach adults for help.

As mentioned before, technology availability seems to impact children's preference; it is suggested that other features consistent with their preferences impact their decision (e.g. portability, flexibility of content and content control). Preferred activities of 10 of the 15 children relate to technology. 11 children mostly engage in semi/functional behavior when using the technology. For example, by playing a game appropriately or singing along music videos. Kacey and Charles mostly engage in non-functional repetitive behavior when using technology. This comprises self-stimming through interaction with technology when repeating very small portions of videos or AAC device commands without intent to communicate, or when pushing buttons of interactive toys for the only intent of replicating sounds or visuals.

Use of Technology at Home

Parents who participated in the interview reported children having access to different technologies at home (e.g. TV, Computer, Game Console, etc.) but they also reported children's preference for using iPad® for watching videos or movies. One of the children also enjoyed watching music videos on TV and another on a portable DVD player. These children regularly use IPad® by themselves, use phrases such as "Go away, it's my time" and do not accept adults interacting with their iPads. Education professionals provided information about use of technology at home by other two of the children. Contrarily to the previous children, one child preferred to watch videos on mobile phone and another preferred to play with his X-Box.

3 Attitude towards the use of technology by education professionals and parents

Parents and education professionals hold a positive attitude towards the use of interactive technologies for autism support. Both groups agree on the use of technology to facilitate activities and engage children. Parents' responses regarding use of technology at home also involved the benefits of using it as a regulating tool: "Gives him something to occupy himself with", and as a way for their children to integrate with others and in public spaces: "It also helps him look like every other kid". Education professionals also reported concerns and limitations with the use of technology in therapy. Several themes emerged in this area. **Cost and Durability:** "Children wouldn't recognize the importance of a thousand-dollar device" (Therapist). Technology may have elevated cost and be easily damaged by the children. **Setup Requirements:** If setup is difficult or time-consuming, teachers and therapists are unlikely to use it. **Technical Issues:** If the system continuously fails, teachers and therapists avoid using the application or limit its use, such as applications that require Wi-Fi. **Practical Issues:** Short battery life has an impact in daily activities at school. It is not uncommon for therapists to interrupt sessions and children becoming frustrated when AAC devices or iPads run out of battery. **Distraction:** Sounds from games and videos may distract children on other classroom areas.

Technology May Overstimulate Children and Cause Obsession: "Technology seems to be overstimulating for him" (Parent). Sounds, visuals and even vibrations from technology seem to have an impact on children's behavior. During observations, 13 of the children displayed signs of over-stimulation or self-stimulation during use of technology; some children seemed tenser, engaged in hand-flapping, humming and other repetitive behaviors. Correspondingly, this was also a recurrent theme in focus groups with education professionals.

Conclusion and Future Directions

In this paper, we have aimed to describe the patterns of technology and media use by autistic children of a school setting. Findings reveal that children are frequent users of interactive technology and media. Mainstream technology is available at school and being used in therapies and as reward to motivate children in sessions. Parents and education professionals have a positive attitude towards the use of technology by the children, but also describe limitations and concerns on its use that must be considered for either managing the available technology or implementing new. Findings from this study are a critical component of our project on development of technology for sensory processing differences. This research project is based on the development of technology that supports individual needs and behaviours but adapts to an educational setting with a set of requirements.

Acknowledgements

The first author gratefully acknowledges financial support from Mexican National Council of Science and Technology [CONACyT] (Doctoral scholarship 216880).

References

1. Muhammad Haziq Lim Abdullah, Cara Wilson, and Margot Brereton. 2016. MyCalendar: supporting families to communicate with their child on the autism spectrum. In Proceedings of the 28th Australian Conference on Computer-Human Interaction (OzCHI '16). ACM, New York, NY, USA, 613-617. DOI=https://doi.org/10.1145/3010915.3011000
2. Paul Atkinson. 2014. *For ethnography, London,* Sage: 25.
3. Wolmet Barendregt, Mathilde M. Bekker, Peter Börjesson, Eva Eriksson, and Olof Torgersson. 2016. The Role Definition Matrix: Creating a Shared Understanding of Children's Participation in the Design Process. In Proceedings of the The 15th International Conference on Interaction Design and Children (IDC '16). ACM, New York, NY, USA, 577-582. DOI: http://dx.doi.org/10.1145/2930674.2935999
4. Laura Boccanfuso, Sarah Scarborough, Ruth K. Abramson, Alicia V. Hall, Harry H. Wright, and Jason M. O'Kane. 2017. "A low-cost socially assistive robot and robot-assisted intervention for children with autism spectrum disorder: field trials and lessons learned." In *Autonomous Robots* 41 (3):637-655. DOI=http://dx.doi.org/10.1007/s10514-016-9554-4.
5. Peter Börjesson, Wolmet Barendregt, Eva Eriksson, and Olof Torgersson. 2015. Designing technology for and with developmentally diverse children: a systematic literature review. In Proceedings of the 14th International Conference on Interaction Design and Children (IDC '15). ACM, New York, NY, USA, 79-88. DOI=http://dx.doi.org/10.1145/2771839.2771848
6. John-John Cabibihan, Hifza Javed, Mohammed Aldosari, Thomas W Frazier, and Haitham Elbashir. 2016. "Sensing Technologies for Autism Spectrum Disorder Screening and Intervention." *Sensors* 17 (1):46.
7. John W. Creswell. 2012. *Qualitative inquiry and research design: Choosing among five approaches*: Sage publications.
8. Demetria Ennis-Cole, and Daniella Smith. 2011. "Assistive technology and autism: Expanding the technology leadership role of the school librarian." *School Libraries Worldwide* 17 (2):86.
9. Juan Pablo Hourcade, Stacy R. Williams, Ellen A. Miller, Kelsey E. Huebner, and Lucas J. Liang. 2013. Evaluation of tablet apps to encourage social interaction in children with autism spectrum disorders. In Proceedings of the SIGCHI Conference on Human Factors in Computing Systems (CHI '13). ACM, New York, NY, USA, 3197-3206. DOI=https://doi.org/10.1145/2470654.2466438
10. R. Lang, R. Sathiyaprakash, T. R. Ramdos, A. Carnet, J. Sigafoos, R. Didden, D. Moore, and M.F. O'Reily. 2014. *Assistive Technologies for People with Autism Spectrum Disorders*. Edited by Giulio E. Lancioni and Nirbhay N. Singh. Vol. 1;2014;, *Assistive Technologies for People with Diverse Abilities, Autism and Child Psychopathology Series*. Dordrecht: Springer.
11. Sooin Lee. 2012. "Project Injini: Developing cognitive training games for children with special needs." *GAMES FOR HEALTH: Research,*

Development, and Clinical Applications 1 (1):69-73.

12. Howard C. Shane, Emily H. Laubscher, Ralf W. Schlosser, Suzanne Flynn, James F. Sorce, and Jennifer Abramson. 2012. "Applying Technology to Visually Support Language and Communication in Individuals with Autism Spectrum Disorders." In *Journal of Autism and Developmental Disorders* 42 (6):1228-1235. DOI= http://dx.doi.org/10.1007/s10803-011-1304-z.
13. Pawan Sinha, Margaret M. Kjelgaard, Tapan K. Gandhi, Kleovoulos Tsourides, Annie L. Cardinaux, Dimitrios Pantazis, Sidney P. Diamond, and
14. Richard M. Held. 2014. "Autism as a disorder of prediction." *Proceedings of the National Academy of Sciences of the United States of America* 111 (42):15220-15225.
15. Maggie Vance, Judy Clegg, Amie M. King, Melissa Thomeczek, Grayce Voreis, and Victoria Scott. 2013. "iPad® use in children and young adults with Autism Spectrum Disorder: An observational study." In *Child Language Teaching and Therapy* 30 (2):159-173. DOI= http://dx.doi.org/10.1177/0265659013510922.

Designing a Physical Computing Toolkit to Utilize Miniature Computers: A Case Study of Selective Exposure

Figure 1: The GoGo Board, on top of a Raspberry Pi. Designing how the two boards worked together so that the system becomes more learnable to students is the main focus of this work.

Marutpong Chailangka
Department of Computer Engineering
Chiang Mai University
Chiang Mai, Thailand
marutpong_c@cmu.ac.th

Arnan Sipitakiat
Department of Computer Engineering
Chiang Mai University
Chiang Mai, Thailand
arnans@eng.cmu.ac.th

Paulo Blikstein
Graduate School of Education
Stanford University
Stanford, CA, USA
paulob@stanford.edu

IDC '17, June 27-30, 2017, Stanford, CA, USA

ACM ISBN 978-1-4503-4921-5/17/06.
http://dx.doi.org/10.1145/3078072.3084339

Abstract

Amid today's explosion of cheap and abundant tools for Physical Computing, there is a serious neglect of design for learnability. This issue is especially important when Physical Computing is not used mainly to teach engineering skills but to foster creativity and innovation. This empirical study presents a design case study that took place while we were trying to figure out how to best integrate miniature computers like the Raspberry Pi into our "Programmable Brick" platform, the GoGo Board, with the goal of making new and complex functionalities, such as face detection and social media integration, learnable by beginners. Using the construct of Selective Exposure for our design and research, this paper presents a case study with secondary and high school students with our platform.

Author Keywords

Interaction design, physical computing, programmable bricks, miniature computers, constructionism.

ACM Classification Keywords

K.3.1 [Computers and Education]: Computers Uses in Education

Introduction

The work leading to this paper has its roots in research designing Programmable Bricks [1], which started at MIT in the 1990s. Although research in this area has generated powerful design examples, the popularity of low-cost microcontroller platforms such as the Arduino has greatly surpassed that of Programmable Bricks and its descendants in the past decade. Although tools like the Arduino have been designed primarily for hobbyists and hackers, schools have adopted such platforms widely, and students now endure the need to learn about low-level circuitry such as resistors, device polarity, and microcontroller pins before making any useful creations. Instead of using physical computing to enrich the learning experience by providing better pathways to powerful ideas as envisioned by scholars such as Papert [2], the main arguments for physical computing became to build engineering skills and to boost interest in science and engineering career paths [3].

We have created a Programmable Brick called the GoGo Board (Figure 1) in 2001 [4]. This report describes our experience generating a new version of the GoGo Board by incorporating the use of embedded computers such as the Raspberry Pi. It is clear that the cost of a full computer will continue to drop (the Pi Zero, which also runs Linux, sells for US$ 5) while the processing power will increase (the Raspberry Pi 3 released in 2016 was approximately 10 times faster than the first revision). How do we harness this immense power while making sure that the focus remains on learnability and empowerment through building personally meaningful projects [5]? An important challenge was how to select what to expose and what to hide so that learners feel empowered and not overwhelmed by the required technical know-how.

Selective Exposure

Selective exposure [3] is a construct that further elaborates the general design concept of black-boxing [11] for physical computing toolkits. What a designer decides to hide or expose has implications on the tool's learnability and usability, which need to match the desired learning goals. The Arduino, for example, exposes the microcontroller pin functionalities. This "pin-level" exposure, while flexible, is arguably not designed for learnability. For example, to turn on an LED, the user needs to choose which microcontroller pin to use. Since all pins look the same, it is up to the learner to select a valid I/O pin together with a ground pin. If a user wants to control the brightness of the LED, the user needs to know which pins come with the Pulse-Width Modulation (PWM) functionality. This pin-level exposure expects the user to understand what PWM is, including the related terms such as "period" and "duty cycle". Programmable Bricks, on the other hand, hide the microcontroller from the user by creating a higher-level abstraction layer that exposes "port-level" functionalities. Output ports are labeled A, B, C, ... all of which can be dimmed by setting the power level, which is by far more learnable than having to deal with complex technical terms and concepts such as PWM, which are less relevant for novices.

DESIGNING THE GOGO BOARD AND RASPBERRY PI INTEGRATION: The First Attempt and Lessons Learned

The canonical approach for using the Raspberry Pi for physical computing is to attach add-ons such as the PiFace and the Gertboard, using the same idea

Examples of the Raspberry PI Enabled Functionalities

Camera and Face Detection: takes pictures using a USB webcam and detects faces within the photo.

Telegram: sends and receives text messages and images via the Telegram messaging service.

Web UI: Users can design user interfaces using buttons, labels, and sliders. Accessible via any web browser, including mobile devices

Audio Playback: plays music, recorded audio, or sound effects.

Text-to-Speech and Speech Recognition: reads out text or converts audio commands into text for use in Logo programs.

Data Logging: Log sensor data to a cloud server for later analysis.

employed by Arduino "shields." Utilizing the Raspberry Pi's standard GPIO pins, these add-on boards enable the connection to buttons, sensors, relays, and other input/output devices. We followed this "shield" approach and created the Pi-Topping Board [6]. The Pi-Topping offered an added abstraction layer: instead of exposing the GPIO pins, users would have ready-to-use sensor and actuator ports instead. Programming was done on the Raspberry Pi using Python.

Design Problem: Plug and Not Play.
Using the Raspberry Pi and Pi Topping as a programmable brick, within the shield model, assumed that no monitor or keyboard would be attached, since the devices would be attached to the student's inventions. The common usage scenario was to write the computer program on a laptop computer and then transfer the code to the student's Raspberry Pi for execution. This process was surprisingly complex in practice. Our programming environment first relied on a network connection to transfer the user code to the Raspberry Pi. Although we designed the programming environment to seamlessly automate this transfer process, there were still a big chance that a networking issue (very common in school networks) would prevent a successful connection. For example, the laptop computer may be connected to a different Wi-Fi network, the laptop could have custom IP settings required by the school, or firewalls and antiviruses could block the connection.

The Improved Second Attempt

Design I: The Raspberry Pi as an add-on
In this revision, we inverted the "shield" model, and thus the roles of the Raspberry Pi and the Pi-Topping (which was then renamed back to GoGo Board). The GoGo Board became the central device and the Raspberry Pi became an optional add-on component used only when the learner needed extra functionalities such as vision and sound.

The design goal was to capitalize on the simplicity of a USB HID connection, which was implemented on the GoGo Board. Such connection does not require the installation of any device drivers, which is a considerable advantage in schools. In addition, the GoGo Board can inform the status of the attached Raspberry Pi, automatically connect the Raspberry Pi to a Wi-Fi network, and perform other administrative tasks through a straightforward interface. Thus, the technical overhead of using the Raspberry Pi is now exposed in a much more accessible form when compared to our first attempt, which proved to be counterintuitively cumbersome for educational use.

Design II: Extending Logo Programming
Instead of running Python on the Raspberry Pi, the learner's program would run on the GoGo Board's microcontroller. Since the GoGo Board uses a variant of Logo, we added commands to allow Logo to make use of the Raspberry Pi functionalities. The new Logo commands would communicate with a Python script on the Raspberry Pi over a serial port connection on the GPIO pins. This approach allowed us to design high-level Raspberry Pi primitives—such as face and speech recognition, and sending SMS messages—within the Logo language. We also created a graphical blocks interface, called Tinker, based on Google's Blockly platform [7] that enabled learners to write programs graphically.

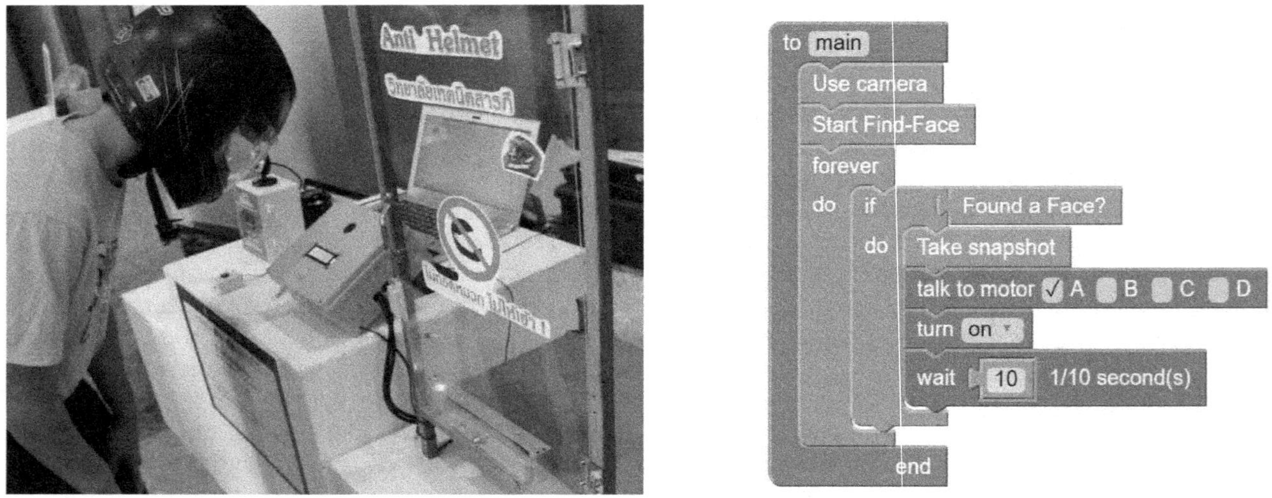

Figure 2: An anti-helmet project (left) and the code (right) used to perform face-detection on the Raspberry Pi

Case Studies

In this section, we offer initial case studies from using the designed tools—Tinker, Raspberry Pi primitives, and the new Raspberry Pi-enabled GoGo Board—in the field. All examples took place in a learning program called iTim (Interactive Technologies for the Inventive Minds) offered to secondary and high school students in Thailand. Schools enroll to the program and select participating students. Our selection guideline was to bring students interested in using Physical Computing to create innovations. We had 32 participants from ten schools. Unfortunately, we had only four girls. The ages were between 12 and 17, with an average of 14.7. Our survey showed that eight students (25%) had experience using programming in projects while eighteen students (56%) had some exposure from courses in school and six students (19%) had no experience at all. None had worked with Physical Computing before. We started the activity with a three-day workshop, followed by a six-month open-ended project period where the students from each school designed their own innovation to solve a local problem at their school or community.

Case Study I: Selective Exposure of Technically Complex Tasks

In Figure 2 (left), a student created a door lock for banks and jewelry stores that would open only to customers who present their face to a camera. No one wearing a helmet or anything that could obscure his or her identity would be allowed to enter.

The GoGo Board was hooked up to an electric lock and the Raspberry Pi was connected to a webcam. Figure 2

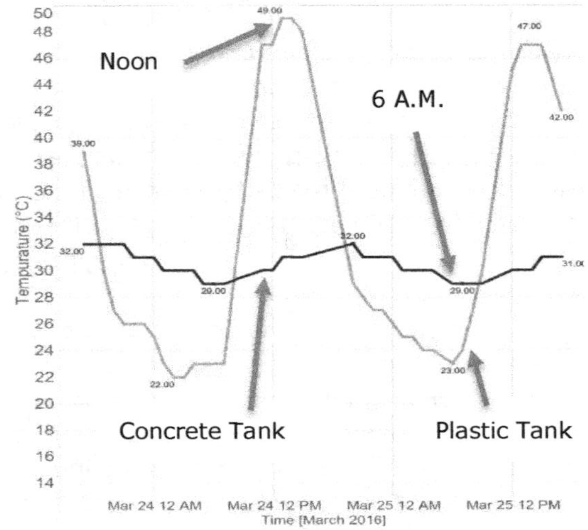

Figure 3: The solar heater tank painted in black (left) and the graph showing the water temperature over time (right)

(right) shows the program required to make this idea work. We made the choice of hiding all the technical complexity of face recognition and image processing, and only exposing a simple set of blocks to the user. A "found-a-face?" block returns true when the Raspberry Pi recognizes a human face through the USB webcam. This design continues Logo's design focus on creating a language that is straightforward and reads like natural language [2]. Traditional means of accomplishing this task usually expose learners to much more low-level technicalities, which would raise the threshold for students to use image processing in their projects.

Case Study II: Focusing on Powerful Ideas

This second project aimed to fix a problem with the school's fish farm. The existing farm used four water-filled concrete tubes each containing 10-20 fish. The problem, as described by the students, was that during the winter, when the morning temperatures gets too low, the fish would eat less food, which affects their growth. The project idea was to create a water tank that would be solar-heated. To make this tank work, they painted the tank black. The hypothesis was that the black color would increase the heat absorption from the sun and warm the water during the day. They would then mix this heated water with the colder water in the fish tanks. The process was to be automated using temperature sensors and electric water valves, all controlled using the GoGo Board and the Raspberry Pi.

However, their hypothesis turned out to be wrong. A nearby water well supplies water to the heating tank through a plastic storage tank (the blue one on the tower in Figure 3). Students touched the tanks in a hot afternoon and realized that the black tank seemed cooler than the blue plastic storage tank. We discussed many potential explanations, but nobody, not even our research team, understood what was really happening. We suggested students to investigate their hypothesis by collecting temperature data. Within two hours, students were able to submerge two temperature sensors, one in the blue plastic storage tank and the other in the black solar heater tank. The students then wrote a program to log the data up to a cloud server, which was one of the easy-to-use functionalities that we have created using the Raspberry Pi's Wi-Fi capabilities.

As shown in Figure 3 (right), the graph did prove that the water in the concrete tank was warmer during the early morning. However, the reason was not that the tank was black. The reason were the insulating properties of concrete. The students realized it by seeing how little the temperature of the concrete tank changed in comparison to the plastic tank. Without this experiment, students may have accomplished their project, but would never have understood the real behavior of the system and addressed their misconception about the underlying principle.

There are two reasons why we wanted to describe this last story in detail. First, it is a concrete example of how technology was used in school to understand powerful ideas in physics and other STEM disciplines. Using data collection to prove or disprove one's hypothesis is an essential practice in science inquiry, but one rarely exercised in schools. This is quite different than using Physical Computing to secure future programming jobs, which is a common mindset of many educators today [3].

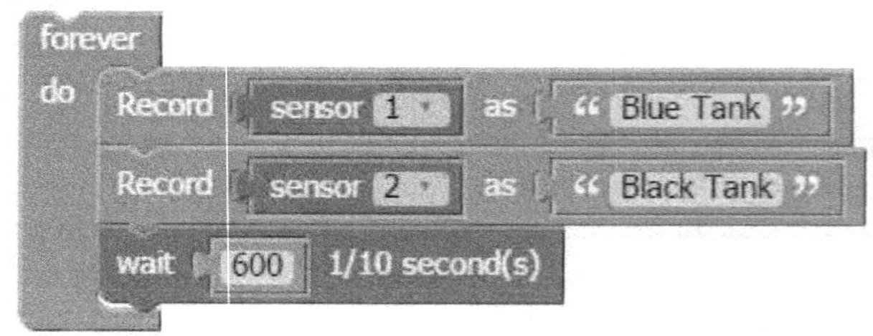

Figure 4: The program to record sensor data onto a cloud server, using simple and user-friendly blocks

Secondly, the fact that the students could quickly create the necessary hardware and code do to complex Wi-Fi-enabled data logging is evidence of the success of our choice for selective exposure for usability. Instead of dealing with technicalities of cloud-based data-logging such as REST APIs or sending data to electronics message brokers, logging data was a matter of creating an account on our data server and using the "Record" command in their code (Figure 4). This design choice allowed learners to spend more time thinking about data and less on the technical overhead of making data logging work.

CONCLUSIONS

This work has highlighted the power of using selective exposure for usability as a design principle. Many popular robotics tools in the market today may work well only with a small group of hacker-minded students. However, if the goal is to engage *all* learners, serious consideration must be given to the selection of what technical layers we should expose to children, and how we design the tools that they will use. Such a selection should be intentional, precise, research-based, and connected to learning goals.

REFERENCES

1. Resnick, M., Martin, F., Sargent, R., & Silverman, B. (1996). Programmable bricks: Toys to think with. *IBM Systems journal*, 35(3.4), 443-452.
2. Papert, S. (1980). *Mindstorms: Children, computers, and powerful ideas*. Basic Books, Inc.
3. Blikstein, P. (2015). Computationally enhanced toolkits for children: historical review and a framework for future design. *Foundations and Trends® Human–Computer Interaction*, 9(1), 1-68.
4. Sipitakiat, A., Blikstein, P., & Cavallo, D. P. (2004, June). GoGo board: augmenting programmable bricks for economically challenged audiences. In Proceedings of the 6th international conference on Learning sciences (pp. 481-488). *International Society of the Learning Sciences*.
5. Papert, S., & Harel, I. (1991). Situating constructionism. *Constructionism*, 36(2), 1-11.
6. Sipitakiat, A., & Blikstein, P. (2013, June). Interaction design and physical computing in the era of miniature embedded computers. *In Proceedings of the 12th International Conference on Interaction Design and Children* (pp. 515-518). ACM.
7. N. Fraser. Google blockly - a visual programming editor. URL: https://developers.google.com/blockly/, accessed May. 2017.

Home Game: an Educational Game for Children with Cognitive Impairments

Asterios Leonidis
Dimitris Arampatzis
Maria Korozi
Ilia Adami
Stavroula Ntoa
Foundation for Research and Technology – Hellas (FORTH) - Institute of Computer Science
N. Plastira 100, Vassilika Vouton, GR-700 13 Heraklion, Crete, Greece
{leonidis, arabatzis, korozi, iadami, stant}@ics.forth.gr

Constantine Stephanidis
Foundation for Research and Technology – Hellas (FORTH) - Institute of Computer Science
N. Plastira 100, Vassilika Vouton, GR-700 13 Heraklion, Crete, Greece

University of Crete, Department of Computer Science, Crete, Greece
cs@ics.forth.gr

IDC '17, June 27-30, 2017, Stanford, CA, USA

ACM ISBN 978-1-4503-4921-5/17/06.
http://dx.doi.org/10.1145/3078072.3091976

Abstract
This paper describes an educational game that aims to familiarize cognitive impaired children with household objects, the overall home environment and the daily activities that take place in it. In addition to touch-based interaction, the game supports physical manipulation through printed cards on a tabletop setup, using a webcam to detect and track the cards placed on the game board.

Author Keywords
Children with cognitive impairments; educational games; physical interaction; tangible interaction

ACM Classification Keywords
K.3.1 [COMPUTERS AND EDUCATION]: Computer Uses in Education – Computer-assisted instruction (CAI)

Introduction
Independent living is a major attainment for individuals with cognitive impairments [1], which is typically pursued through methodical training in order to acquire the necessary skills. Technology can complement this continuous educational process [2], however the content and the interaction paradigms should be carefully selected to satisfy the needs of the targeted audience [3].

This paper presents a system based on interaction with physical cards and boards in order to assist cognitive

The Home Game

The "Home game" aims to instill knowledge regarding the main rooms of a house, their most important objects, and their most frequent activities.

Also, one of the system's goals is to educate children regarding hazardous behaviors that should be avoided, as well as good behavior patterns for everyday activities at home.

The system is intended to be used by trainers of the Rehabilitation Centre (RC) for Children with Disabilities in Heraklion (Crete, Greece) to educate their students.

Hardware: The system features a touch screen, a computer, and a high-resolution camera overlooking the area in front of the screen. A custom casing has been designed especially for this game to hide the technology from plain sight (see Fig. 1).

impaired children in learning the home environment. In terms of interaction, the game employs a multimodal approach where various input sources (both digital and physical) can be used interchangeably by the player, whereas multisensory output alleviates difficulties in comprehending written text. According to [4], physical manipulation of objects can benefit cognition. This is also supported by Montessori [5], who developed many of her ideas while working with mentally challenged children. Montessori suggests that physical movement and direct touch enhance learning, and that when children learn with their hands they have more meaningful experiences. Mixing these well-established findings with augmented digital information can facilitate the educational process [6].

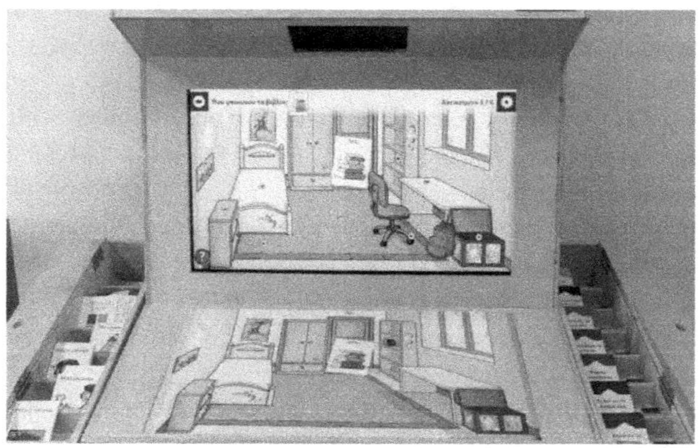

Figure 1: The physical setup of the system

Learning the home environment

The "Home game" features six types of mini-games and an extensive analytics framework that allows the trainers to monitor (even in real-time) the progress of their students. The player can interact with the games in a multimodal manner either digitally through a touch interface, or physically via the printed cards that represent the various objects and activities. Every game is accompanied by its own set of boards and decks of cards, which allow the player to interact naturally with the system, thus forming an augmented board game.

In addition to multimodal input, the system supports multisensory output by narrating the various messages and prompts in natural language, which is complemented by short auditory feedback wherever necessary (e.g., incorrect answers). Content-wise the system offers: (i) two levels of content, a simple one for students with severe cognitive problems and an advanced one for students with milder problems and (ii) context-sensitive help for each game task.

- **Presentation (Learning) Games**. These touch-only mini-exercises let the player freely explore the primary rooms and the utility areas (e.g., yard, garage, etc.) of a house, learn about their function, identify their common objects and the most frequent activities that take place in them.
- **Locate the Room:** The player has to point at the location of a specific room in the house. When asked, the system displays context-sensitive help by showing the common objects or the frequent activities of that room and if the player needs further assistance, the system highlights the correct answer.
- **Place an Object.** The goal is to find the room to which a specific object belongs or to indicate the most appropriate location for an object (e.g., pot) in a specific room (e.g., kitchen). In the touch-enabled mode, the player can touch the respective area on the screen, while in the board-game mode, she can place the respective card on the board (Fig. 2). If the

Graphics: the house and the rooms, were carefully designed to better depict a typical Greek home setting. That way, the players will be able to easily map the rooms in the game with those in their house.

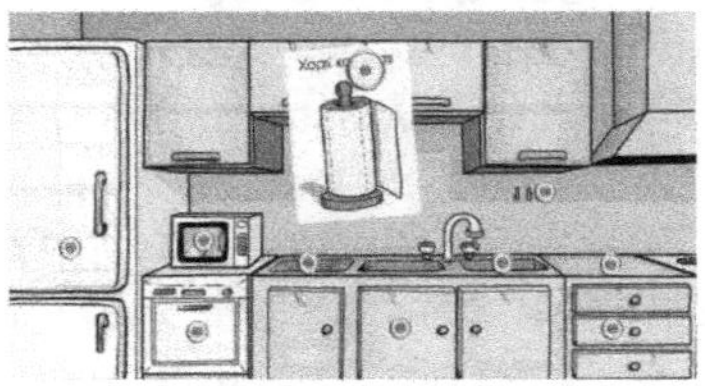

Figure 1: Place an object game

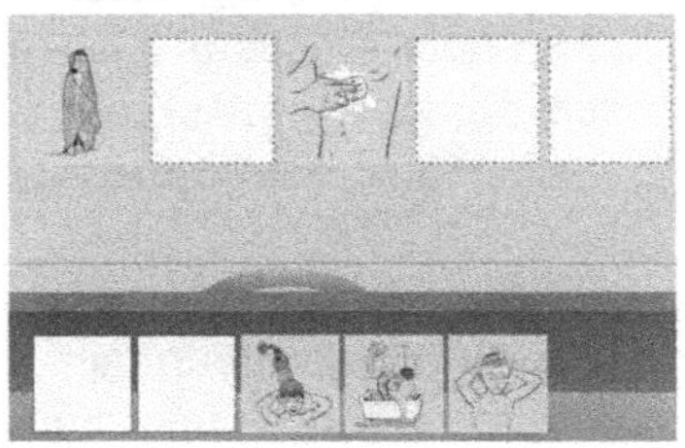

Figure 3: Order the steps of the routine "taking a bath"

Figure 4: Two possible answers for a hazardous behavior regarding touching detergents

player asks for help, the system displays information regarding the type of the current object and its intended use (e.g., the pot is used for cooking).

- **Find mismatches.** In this touch-only game, the player has to indicate which objects should not be present in a specific room. In the simple level, the room contains two correct objects and one wrong from a different room, whereas in the advanced level, these numbers change to four and three respectively. This game offers help gradually by firstly displaying the purpose of the room, then removing a correct object and finally highlighting a wrong one.
- **Order the steps of a routine.** The player has to find the correct sequence of the steps of a daily routine (e.g., getting dressed, etc.) via touch or physical interaction. The screen displays empty placeholders (Fig. 3), in a continuous order, one for each step. In the touch-enabled mode, the player selects a step and touches an empty placeholder; in the board-game mode, she has to place the respective physical cards in the correct order on the board. The player can ask for help at any time in order to evaluate her progress. If help is requested at the beginning of a game, the system suggests a possible first step for that routine. In case the trainer deems it necessary, the correct solution is displayed and the player is urged to reproduce that sequence, hence supporting learning through mimicking.
- **Quizzes: Hazardous & Social Behaviors.** Two exercises in the form of quizzes allow the player to select the correct out of two behaviors, one of which is hazardous or socially inappropriate (Fig. 4). If help is needed, the system shows a hint regarding the negative consequences of the "wrong" behavior.
- **Analytics.** The system features a mechanism to assist trainers in deciding on-the-fly which game to launch depending on the player's progress. The analytics' dashboards have been designed to speed up this process by displaying rich information regarding performance trends, objects that seem to trouble the child, number of helps asked, etc.

Design Process & Preliminary Evaluation

The design process [7] was based on the principles of user-centered design involving multiple iterations for each step. Requirements elicitation has been carried out through questionnaires and interviews with 12 RC trainers with expertise in various domains (i.e., speech therapy, psychology, nursing, occupational therapy and pediatrics) in order to identify the characteristics and needs of the target audience, whereas the functionality has been consolidated through extended focus groups. High-fidelity prototypes were produced and evaluated by the trainers to receive preliminary feedback regarding the interaction paradigm and the overall design. Finally, before its in-vivo installation in the RC, it was important to ensure that the system is as flawless and usable as possible; to this end, the game was evaluated by 8 children without disabilities (2 girls and 6 boys), aging from 3.5 to 9 years old, so as to better match the cognitive age of the target audience.

The experiment revealed a high success rate of 86%. It is important to note that the majority of the partial success marks were caused by content comprehension problems and not by interaction problems. Still, there were zero failures, meaning that no child gave up on a game even when mistakes were made. This finding is supported by the two expert evaluators who reported that all the children, even the preschoolers, were able

Preliminary Evaluation: The goal was to identify any potential **usability problems** with the two interaction modes (physical vs digital), as well as to evaluate the overall **UX**, so as to eliminate major showstoppers before evaluating the system with the target audience.

Methodology: The user success rate [8] metric was used to measure total success. Each interaction was marked: a Success if the child completed the task with no help, Partial Success if the facilitator provided hints, and Failure if the child gave up on a task. An observation grid form was used to capture the number of wrong actions, random actions, and errors during each game, as well as any comments.

Figure 5: The facilitator introduces a task to a child

to switch between the two interaction modes with ease and understood what was expected of them to do in each game with minimal instructions given. Analysis of the recorded wrong actions indicated that some illustrations were not easily perceived, while elaboration on users' comments revealed their answers were influenced by their own habits and household arrangements. The later remains to be evaluated with the target users since the content was determined by the RC according to their needs and practices. Finally, almost all children wanted to continue playing even after the end of the session, meaning that the game kept the children engaged and amused.

Conclusions and Future Work

The game was highly appreciated via the preliminary evaluation; however, a full-scale evaluation experiment is being planned, including the students of the Rehabilitation Centre. The goal will be not only to assess the usability of the proposed environment, but also its actual impact in the educational process.

Practical Considerations

A touch-enabled PC with a CUDA-capable GPU (necessary for Computer-Vision algorithms) is required. Firstly, the board must be securely mounted on the table and then the vision algorithms must be calibrated based on its physical boundaries, to ensure the physical-to-digital translation of cards' position.

Acknowledgements

The authors would like to thank the Rehabilitation Centre for Children with Disabilities in Heraklion, Crete. The game content was imported through an editor implemented by E. Poutouris and N. Louloudakis; the analytics dashboards were designed by A. Ntagianta.

References

1. Robert L. Schalock, et al. 2010. Intellectual disability: Definition, classification, and systems of supports. American Association on Intellectual and Developmental Disabilities. 444 North Capitol Street NW Suite 846, Washington, DC 20001.
2. Michael L. Wehmeyer, et al. 2004. Technology use by students with intellectual disabilities: An overview. In Journal of Special Education Technology 19, 4: 7-21.
3. Linda C. Mechling. 2007. Assistive technology as a self-management tool for prompting students with intellectual disabilities to initiate and complete daily tasks: A literature review. In Education and Training in Developmental Disabilities, 252-269.
4. Segal, Ayelet. 2011. Do Gestural Interfaces Promote Thinking? Embodied Interaction: Congruent Gestures and Direct Touch Promote Performance in Math. ProQuest LLC. 789 East Eisenhower Parkway, PO Box 1346, Ann Arbor, MI 48106, 2011.
5. Montessori, Maria. 1948. The discovery of the child. Aakar books, 2004.
6. Price, Sara, and Yvonne Rogers. 2004. "Let's get physical: The learning benefits of interacting in digitally augmented physical spaces." Computers & Education 43.1: 137-151.
7. Ntoa, Stavroula, et al. 2015. "Analysis and Design of Three Multimodal Interactive Systems to Support the Everyday Needs of Children with Cognitive Impairments." International Conference on Universal Access in Human-Computer Interaction. Springer International Publishing.
8. Nielsen Norman Group: https://www.nngroup.com/articles/success-rate-the-simplest-usability-metric/

SAM: The School Attachment Monitor

Dong-Bach Vo[1]
Maki Rooksby[2]
Mohammad Tayarani[1]
Rui Huan[1]
Alessandro Vinciarelli[1]
Helen Minnis[2]
Stephen A. Brewster[1]

[1]Glasgow Interactive Systems Group
School of Computing Science
University of Glasgow, UK
{first.last}@glasgow.ac.uk
http://mig.dcs.gla.ac.uk

[2]Adverse Childhood Experiences Lab
Institute of Health and Wellbeing
University of Glasgow, UK
{first.last}@glasgow.ac.uk

IDC '17, June 27-30, 2017, Stanford, CA, USA

ACM ISBN 978-1-4503-4921-5/17/06.
http://dx.doi.org/10.1145/3078072.3091977

Abstract

Secure Attachment relationships have been shown to minimise social and behavioural problems in children and boosts resilience to risks later in life such as antisocial behaviour, heart pathologies, and suicide. Attachment assessment is an expensive and time-consuming process that is not often performed. The School Attachment Monitor (SAM) automates Attachment assessment to support expert assessors. It uses doll-play activities with the dolls augmented with sensors and the child's play recorded with cameras to provide data for assessment. Social signal processing tools are then used to analyse the data and to automatically categorize Attachment patterns. This paper presents the current SAM interactive prototype.

Author Keywords

Child Attachment; Attachment Assessment; Child Psychiatry; Automation; Social Signal Processing; Tangible Interaction; Child Computer Interaction

ACM Classification Keywords

H.5.0. Information interfaces and presentation (e.g., HCI): General.

Introduction

Attachment is the natural tendency of children to seek and to maintain the physical proximity with their care givers which provides protection and nurtures physical and psychological wellbeing. While it is a primitively-

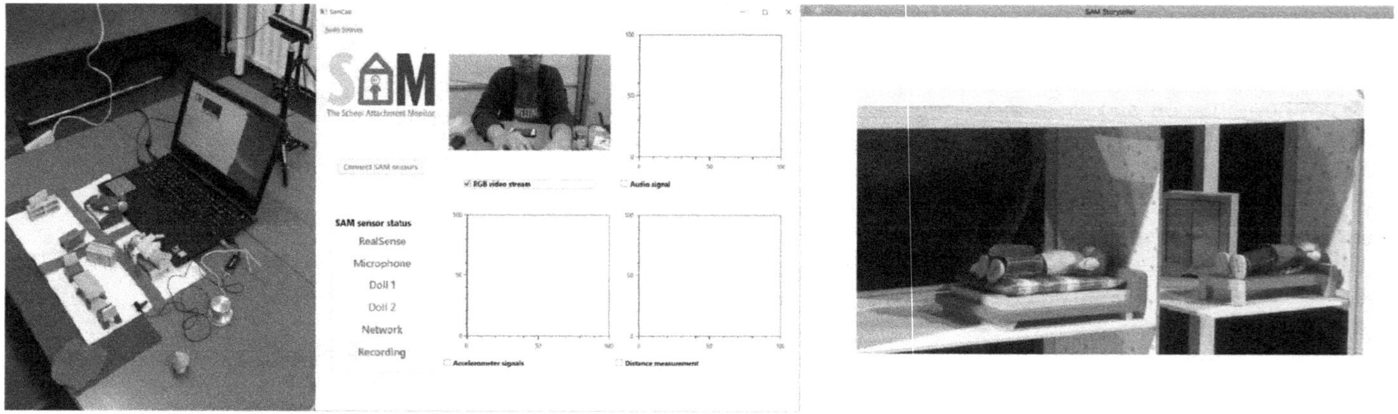

Figure 1: From left to right, SAM setup, SAM data collection application and sensor monitoring, SAM administration application.

motivated process to ensure survival of the species across humans and the animal kingdom, insecure attachment may reflect inconsistency, absence or hostility in the quality of care their young receives [1].

Secure Attachment can nurture confidence and sense of self-worth in children. Research suggests that it also provides the child with resilience against risk of suicide, social and emotional problems or even heart pathologies [2]. Early identification of Attachment misalignments would therefore minimise these risks to the individuals thereby also ameliorating the societal costs. Unfortunately, administrating and coding Attachment evaluations is costly, time consuming and requires highly-trained assessors [4]. This limits the number of children that can be assessed and referred for treatment. Automating Attachment evaluations would facilitate population screening and allow health care professionals (i.e. expert assessors) to prioritise their expertise for those in need of intervention. Our vision is that our School Attachment Monitor (SAM) will address this unmet need and provide the tool to make automatic Attachment classification possible.

SAM is designed to reflect methodology and principles of the MCAST [3], the gold standard for measuring Attachment in children aged 4-8 years. The MCAST is designed to assign a child of school age to one of the four possible Attachment conditions that can be observed: *interpersonal (secure) strategy*, *non-interpersonal (avoidant) strategy*, *ambivalent interpersonal strategy* and *disorganized strategy*. During MCAST, assessors show story vignettes to a child which portray mildly stressful situations (e.g., falling over and hurting a knee). The child is then asked to act out and tell the rest of the story using dolls that each represent the child and a caregiver. The way the child completes the story and their behaviour during the test provides the cues to assess their Attachment status. For example,

Figure 2: Smart dolls given to children during the SAM assessment. At the top of the figure from left to right: a Tinyduino computer, an inertial sensors module and a Bluetooth low energy module.

To equip the dolls with computers, their body was replaced with a small 3D-printed empty case. Thanks to this modification, the dolls can host a small Arduino computer powered with a cell coin battery, and a set of stackable modules to enable inertial sensing and wireless communication with the SAM data collection application.

the trained assessors rate on Attachment-related behaviour, narrative coherence, disorganized phenomena (if any), state of mind and the psychological motivation of the characters and any other elements relevant to the story.

SAM: The School Attachment Monitor

In this paper, we outline the design of SAM. One of the objectives of SAM is to provide a tool to allow a non-expert to administer an Attachment assessment (based on MCAST) and automatically categorize the Attachment status of the child. SAM is made of three components: one to collect data, one to administer the test, and another to process the data to make an Attachment classification. This paper discusses the first two parts. SAM is based around a laptop so it is easily portable and can be taken into schools for assessments.

The first application collects data when the child is telling a story (Figure 1, centre). Tracking the movements of the dolls is difficult given the wide range of ways in which children may play with them. We overcome this by using a novel combination of tangible dolls with embedded sensors and depth camera tracking so that the child being assessed can handle and play with dolls as they would in MCAST, without the technology interfering their play behaviour. An Intel Realsense SR300 camera (http://j.mp/RealSenseTech) is used to record RGB and depth data depicting the face and the hands when the child tells the story using the dolls. The small size of the SR300 sensor allows ease of transport. A lapel microphone worn by the child records their speech. Our initial designs used the microphone in the RealSense and the laptop but were not robust to the variety of noises that occurred during the school day. Finally, a Bluetooth inertial measurement unit is embedded in a 3D printed case inside each doll (Figure 2) to provide orientation and acceleration data from the dolls for classification. Having the sensors in the dolls allows us to track movements even if the depth camera cannot see them; for example, they may for example be obscured by the child's hands or hidden under the table during play.

Several challenges had to be overcome to create a functional prototype. Recording the data coming from all the sensors at the same time was difficult. For instance, recording high definition RGB and depth data at the same time requires a significant amount of storage, bandwidth and computing power. Our final approach, which operates in real time, relies on running simultaneously FFMPEG (https://ffmpeg.org) on the GPU to compress and encode the RGB video stream, and an LZ4 based algorithm on the CPU to compress depth data. An SSD drive copes with the high demand for data bandwidth and storage. A Bluetooth Low Energy stack and a mechanism to synchronize the inertial measurements with the other data streams was developed and deployed on a Tinyduino (https://tinycircuits.com) fitted inside each doll (Figure 2).

The second software component delivers the story vignettes to the child and engages them in acting out the stories with the dolls. Implemented using Unity, it has been designed as a game. The application starts by playing a video sequence where a professional actress introduces the task and what is expected from the child. She/He is then prompted to set up the play area according to the story that is about to be told.

Following a workshop run with young children to investigate how they could interact with SAM, a "smart" push button was included in the setup. For example, when the child has finished setting up the playground up and are ready to listen to the story stem, they press the button. Another use is to notify the system when the child's story is complete. While carrying different actions, it simplifies the interaction with the system.

SAM Demonstration

In this demonstration, we will exhibit two components of SAM: the data collection and the story delivery. The attendees of IDC will be able to experience SAM as an administrator by monitoring all the sensors the system is using to collect data from the children's stories and by examining the different types of data that are being collected. They will also be able to experience SAM as a child who is being receiving the attachment assessment by watching the vignettes and completing the stories with the dolls.

Practical Consideration

Work on SAM is ongoing. An adult is still required to introduce the application to children and to explain how and when to use the SAM interactive inputs. Our current work focuses on investigating new ways to support and teach young children how to interact with the system in order to reduce adult supervision. Progress from this research will be integrated to the SAM prototype for the demonstration.

SAM development has already reached an important milestone. The current prototype has been evaluated and used to collect data from 30 children in primary schools.

SAM is the first attempt at automating Attachment assessments. It has the potential to screen Attachment across the population and identifying the children with disorganised family attachment that need attention. We believe that our research will improve significantly population health and wellbeing.

Acknowledgements

This research was funded by EPSRC grant EP/M025055/1.

References

1. John Bowlby. 1988. A secure Base. Routheldge.
2. Maxia Dong, Wayne H. Giles, Vincent J. Felitti, Shanta R. Dube, Janice E. Williams, Daniel P. Chapman and Roberta F. Anda. 2004. Insights into causal pathways for ischemic heart disease. *Circulation*, *110*(13), 1761-1766. https://doi.org/10.1161/01.CIR.0000143074.54995.7F
3. Jonathan Green, Charlie Stanley, Vicky Smith, & Ruth Goldwyn. 2000. A new method of evaluating Attachment representations in young school-age children: The Manchester Child Attachment Story Task. *Attachment & Human Development*, *2*(1), 48-70.

   http://dx.doi.org/10.1080/146167300361318
4. Helen Minnis, Reuben Millward, Claire Sinclair, Eilis Kennedy, Anne Greig, Kate Towlson, Waren Read and Johathan Hill. 2006. The Computerized MacArthur Story Stem Battery. *International journal of methods in psychiatric research*, *15*(4), 207-214. http://dx.doi.org/10.1002/mpr.198

Close the Circuit 'N Play the Electrons: Learning Electricity with an Augmented Circuit Exhibit

Elham Beheshti
Northwestern University
Evanston, IL 60208, USA
beheshti@u.northwestern.edu

David Kim
Northwestern University
Evanston, IL 60208, USA

Gabrielle Ecanow
Northwestern University
Evanston, IL 60208, USA

Michael Horn
Northwestern University
Evanston, IL 60208, USA
michael-horn@northwestern.edu

IDC '17, June 27-30, 2017, Stanford, CA, USA

ACM ISBN 978-1-4503-4921-5/17/06.
http://dx.doi.org/10.1145/3078072.3091978

Abstract

In this demo, we present *Spark*, an augmented circuit exhibit that enables visitors to make circuits using a set of tangible components and observe a simulation of electrons flowing through the circuit. Our goal is to use multiple representations of a circuit to help convey basic concepts of current and resistance. In *Spark,* the electron simulation and tangible circuit components are coupled using augmented reality techniques. We developed our system through a three-year iterative design process. We tested earlier versions of the design at a science museum with parent-child dyads and found that having access to the electron simulation could benefit children to better understand the concepts of electricity. We also observed that coupling the electron simulation through augmented reality can significantly enhance the learning benefits of the exhibit.

Author Keywords

Electrical circuits; multiple representations; augmented reality; agent-based modeling; design; interactive surfaces; tangible interaction; museum learning.

ACM Classification Keywords

H.5.2 Information Interfaces and Presentation: User Interfaces - Interaction styles

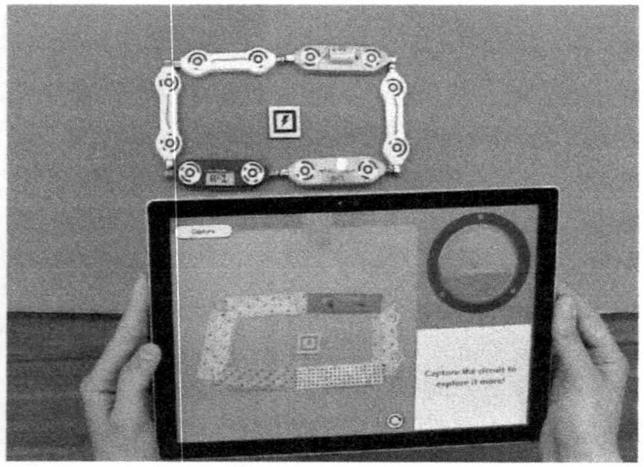

Figure 1. A demonstration of *Spark* Exhibit.

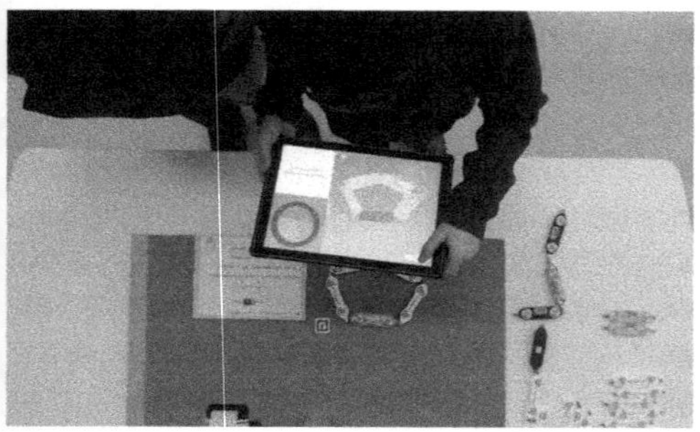

Figure 2. A parent-child dyad using the *Spark* Exhibit.

Introduction

In this demo, we present the design of *Spark*, an augmented circuit exhibit for science museums. *Spark* combines a physical circuit kit with a 3D visualization of current flow inspired by Sengupta and Wilensky's agent-based representation of electrical concepts [11]. Visitors can make circuits by connecting circuit components such as wires, batteries, resistors, and lightbulbs. They can then explore a simulation of electrons moving through the various components of their circuit. We used augmented reality techniques to display the simulation on a tablet computer that visitors hold above their circuit. This creates the illusion of peering inside the circuit (Figure 1). The primary goal of our design is to enhance children's understanding of electrical current and resistance by enabling them to develop meaningful connections between the electron simulation and the circuit components.

Related Work

There are several computational environments and activities that allow children to investigate simple circuits. Examples include the Circuit Construction Kit from the PhET project, which simulates the behavior of simple circuits [5]; and LightUp [4], which uses augmented reality to project a simple representation of current flow on top of an image of the physical circuit. NIELS [11] is an example of an agent-based modeling environment that shows how electrical concepts such as current and resistance emerge from the interactions between electrons and ions in a conductive material. NIELS directly inspired the design of electron simulation in *Spark*.

Contribution

Understanding the flow of current in electrical circuits can be challenging for learners of all ages. Research in Learning Sciences has documented a variety of mental models that novices rely on as they struggle with concepts like resistance and current (e.g. [6]). One promising strategy to help learners understand circuits is to provide dynamic visual representations of electrical concepts [11]. The primary goal of our design is to improve children's understanding by enabling them interact with two representations of a circuit: a collection of tangible components and a 3D visualization that shows the flow of current inside the circuit components (Figure 2). Our findings have implications for design of interactive exhibit environments.

Learning with Multiple Representations

Prior research suggests that using multiple representations can improve learning but that they are difficult to design and that learners might fail to gain from multiple representations if they are not carefully designed [1]. We use AR in our design to *dynamically link* the circuit components with the electron simulation to support an effective translation between the representations. Our findings from testing earlier versions of the exhibit offer insight on affordances of using augment reality in interactive exhibits.

Interaction with Tangibles

We are also interested in studying the effects of working with physical circuit components (tangibles) on visitors learning and interaction. Research has shown that physical manipulatives can support science learning [9]. Recent museum studies also suggest that physical manipulative are more inviting than their virtual counterparts [7,8]. The results of this study will

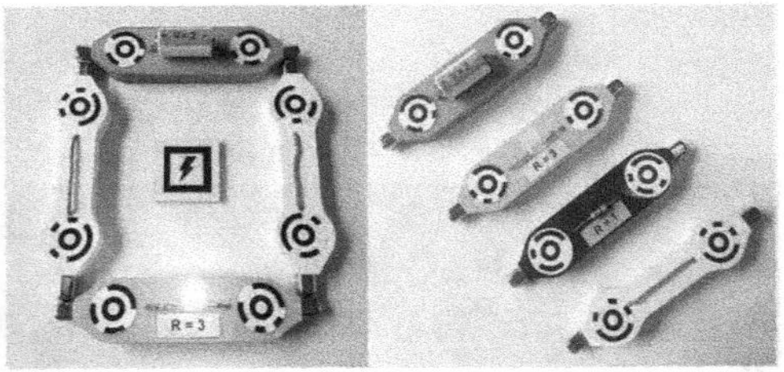

Figure 3. The physical circuit components in *Spark*.

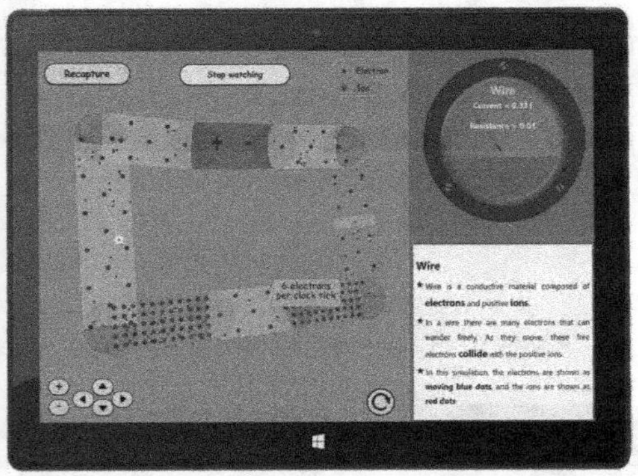

Figure 4. The electron model display in *Spark*. The blue dots are moving electrons and the red dots represent ions in conductive materials. Resistors have higher ion densities than wires.

shed light on advantages and disadvantages of using tangibles in interactive exhibits.

Design of spark

Through a three-year iterative design process [2,3], we developed an interactive exhibit that enables visitors to construct circuits and then see a simulation of electrons moving through the various components. The system consists of two main components (Figure 1): a tangible circuit kit and an agent-based model of current flow.

Circuit Kit

The design of physical components is inspired by the work of Chan and colleagues on LightUp [4]. Similar to LightUp, the electronic components of the circuit are attached to each other with magnetic connectors. To detect the circuit components and render the corresponding electron simulation of circuit, we use TopCode markers [12] on both ends of each component (see Figure 3).

Electron Model Display

We developed a 3D visualization of current flow using Three.js [13], a browser-based JavaScript library based on WebGL. *Spark* electron model is inspired by NIELS simulation environment [10] and is based on Drude's free electron theory in which electrical current and resistance can be thought of as phenomena that emerge from simple kinetic interactions between electrons and ions in the conductive materials. A Microsoft Surface Pro 4 tracks an AR Toolkit [14] marker to display the electron simulation.

On the tablet display (Figure 4), visitors can tap on a "watch an electron" button to track the movement of a random electron through the circuit. Visitors can also tap on a component to see its electrical measures, a textual description about the component, and also a counter that shows the "electrons per clock tick" rate. This measure indicates how many electrons pass by the cross section of the component over a certain time, which is directly proportional to the measure of current in that component. Finally, visitors can zoom and pan the display using direct touch interaction or buttons in a toolbar.

Audience

We designed *Spark* to be used as an interactive exhibit in informal learning environments. The exhibit is intended to serve novices of any age to learn about electricity and electrical circuits. However, we consider children between the ages of 10 and 14 years old as our target users.

Evaluation

We evaluated the earlier versions of *Spark* at the Museum of Science and Industry in Chicago. Our goal was to investigate different ways to link the circuit with the electron simulation to support an effective translation between the representations. In one version of the exhibit (Figure 5), the simulation is displayed alongside a digital representation of circuit on the same multi-touch tabletop display. In another version (Figure 6), we used AR to display the simulation on a tablet computer that visitors hold above the tabletop display. We recruited parent-child dyads to evaluate these two versions of our design. We also included a control condition in which families could create and test circuits on a tabletop screen, but without the electron model. Our findings show that children gain from using the electron model, with children performing better in the AR condition. Moreover, our analysis suggests that

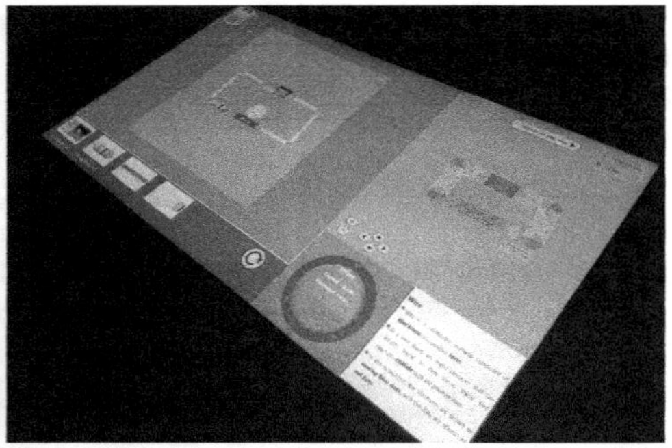

Figure 5. A single-display version of *Spark*.

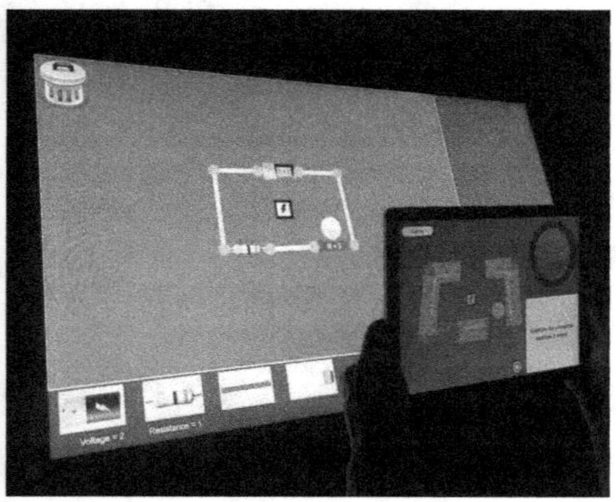

Figure 6. An AR version of *Spark*.

children in the AR condition were more likely to attend to the electron simulation and the behavior of electrons moving in the circuit.

Acknowledgements

We thank the Museum of Science and Industry in Chicago, and its Manager of Evaluation and Research, Aaron Price, for their valuable help and allowing us to conduct this study in their facilities. Thanks to Uri Wilensky and Anne Marie Piper who provided us with insightful comments. We also thank the members of TIDAL lab and CCL lab at Northwestern University.

References

1. Shaaron Ainsworth. 2006. DeFT: A conceptual framework for considering learning with multiple representations. *Learning and Instruction* 16, 3: 183–198.
2. E. Beheshti, A. Aljuhani, and M.S. Horn. 2014. Electrons to light bulbs: Understanding electricity with a multi-level simulation environment. In *2014 IEEE Frontiers in Education Conference (FIE)*, 1–8.
3. Elham Beheshti, Mmachi Obiorah, and Michael S. Horn. 2015. "Let's Dive into It!": Learning Electricity with Multiple Representations. In *Proceedings of the 14th International Conference on Interaction Design and Children* (IDC '15), 263–266.
4. Joshua Chan, Tarun Pondicherry, and Paulo Blikstein. 2013. LightUp: An Augmented, Learning Platform for Electronics. In *Proceedings of the 12th International Conference on Interaction Design and Children* (IDC '13), 491–494.
5. N. D. Finkelstein, W. K. Adams, C. J. Keller, P. B. Kohl, K. K. Perkins, N. S. Podolefsky, S. Reid, and R. LeMaster. 2005. When learning about the real world is better done virtually: A study of substituting computer simulations for laboratory equipment. *Physical Review Special Topics - Physics Education Research* 1, 1: 10103.
6. Tina A Grotzer and Margot Sudbury. 2000. Moving Beyond Underlying Linear Causal Models of Electrical Circuits. In *annual meeting of the National Association of Research in Science Teaching*, New Orleans, LA.
7. Michael S. Horn, R. Jordan Crouser, and Marina U. Bers. 2011. Tangible interaction and learning: the case for a hybrid approach. *Personal and Ubiquitous Computing* 16, 4: 379–389.
8. Joyce Ma, Lisa Sindorf, Isaac Liao, and Jennifer Frazier. 2015. Using a Tangible Versus a Multi-touch Graphical User Interface to Support Data Exploration at a Museum Exhibit. In *Proc. of the Tangible, Embedded, and Embodied Interaction* (TEI '15), 33–40.
9. Taylor Martin and Daniel L. Schwartz. 2005. Physically Distributed Learning: Adapting and Reinterpreting Physical Environments in the Development of Fraction Concepts. *Cognitive Science* 29, 4: 587–625.
10. Pratim Sengupta. 2009. *Designing across Ages: Multi-Agent-Based Models and Learning Electricity*. ProQuest LLC.
11. Pratim Sengupta and Uri Wilensky. 2009. Learning Electricity with NIELS: Thinking with Electrons and Thinking in Levels. *Journal of Computers for Mathematical Learning* 14, 1: 21–50.
12. *TopCode library*. Retrieved from http://users.eecs.northwestern.edu/~mhorn/topcodes/
13. *Three.js library*. Retrieved from http://threejs.org/
14. *JSARToolKit library*. Retrieved from https://github.com/artoolkit/jsartoolkit5

Revisiting *Turtles* and *Termites*: an Open-ended Interactive Physical Game with Multiple Robots

Pauline Gourlet
Paragraphe C3U, Université Paris 8
& EnsadLab, Paris, France
pauline.gourlet@gmail.com

Mathieu Le Goc
Mechanical Engineering,
Shape Lab, Stanford, USA
mlegoc@stanford.edu

Sean Follmer
Mechanical Engineering,
Shape Lab, Stanford, USA
sean.follmer@gmail.com

IDC '17, June 27-30, 2017, Stanford, CA, USA

ACM ISBN 978-1-4503-4921-5/17/06.
http://dx.doi.org/10.1145/3078072.3091979

Abstract

We present a first prototype of an open-ended interactive physical game aiming at developing children's understanding of dynamic systems in a playful and embodied way. We use a swarm user interface, Zooids, developed by Le Goc et al., made of independent self-propelled elements that move collectively and react to user input. Papert promoted an active way of developing a computational literacy, through programming a turtle with LOGO, from which Resnick proposed StarLogo, a "multi-turtles" language to simulate complex systems behaviors. Our interface is positioned in between these two perspectives: it allows to physically interact with multiple "turtles", each having its own dynamic. Each Zooid can be assigned an action that will affect the system behavior. Based on this principle, our first prototype invites children to resolve situations by changing individual actions in a dynamic system.

Author Keywords

Computational Thinking; Game; Tangibles; System Thinking; Open-ended play

ACM Classification Keywords

H.5.m

Figure 1 – Picture of some Zooids, from the swarm user interface, developed by Le Goc [1].

Video:

https://www.youtube.com/watch?v=8Ik7V_QH5wk

Introduction

Dynamic systems and system thinking are hard to grasp. Research has shown that people's understanding of the dynamic behavior of systems is poor [4,8,11,12,15]. According to several researchers [4,16], these difficulties are due to a focus on short-term and causal reasoning, instead of acknowledging long-term and indirect consequences caused by time-delays and interconnectedness. We present an early and exploratory prototype of an open-ended interactive physical game allowing fun hands-on explorations of systems concepts, relying on the hypothesis that by making processes tangible, children will engage with systems' core concepts.

We use a swarm user interface, Zooids, developed by Le Goc [1] (see fig.1), made of independent self-propelled elements that move collectively and react to user input. This tangible interface handles both display and interaction: Zooids move on a tabletop and can be assigned specific actions. This can allow children to interact and program complex systems in a hands-on way. The interface helps bridge various approaches all rooted in constructionism theory [3,6]: it allows children to play in an embodied way while developing abstract concepts. It can also foster collaborative learning thanks to its tangible properties [14]. Because new physical elements can be added to the system, and new actions can be programmed and assigned to Zooids, the game has endless evolutive possibilities. This could engage children in creating new levels for which they would have to develop creative and innovative solutions based on systems principles.

Papert transformed our way of designing for learning. He exemplified his constructionist vision with the development of the LOGO language, embodied within turtle robot [6]. In a book untitled *Turtles, Termites and Traffic Jams* [8], Resnick pushes Papert's approach further and pleads for the design of decentralized systems, in which patterns are determined not by some central authority but by local interactions among many (parallel) components [5]. Resnick and his team built on Papert's work and developed StarLogo [9]: a screen-based "multi-turtles" program to simulate complex systems' behaviors. Our interface is positioned in between these two perspectives as it allows to physically interact with multiple "turtles", each having its own character and its own dynamic, that children can modify to affect the system. We have designed a series of figurines and "clothes" (see fig. 2), which, when placed on a Zooid, affect its behavior. Based on this interface, we designed a tangible open-ended game that invites children to resolve situations by programming individual actions within a dynamic system.

Related Work

Interfaces that explore system dynamics for learning are generally screen-based, such as StarLogo [9] and NetLogo [2,12]. However, some works attempt to combine GUIs and TUIs to develop system thinking, such as *Glowing Pathfinder Soup* [10], which involves sand landscapes and projected animations of animals. Others combine GUIs and gesture interfaces, such as *Connected World* [17], a gigantic interactive ecosystem. Tangible interfaces are more common to learn code or/and to write programming sequences. One of the first projects of that kind was developed in 1976 [7]; several others have followed since [5,18,19].

Figures 2 – Examples of figurines and clothes designed to suit and attribute functions to Zooids.

However, tangible interfaces that aim at developing system thinking while interacting with the physical world remain underexplored. To design our game prototype, we were inspired by *Lemmings* [20], a puzzle-platformer video game. Its objective is to guide a group of lemmings through a number of obstacles to a designated exit. To win, one must determine how to assign a limited number of eight different skills to specific lemmings that allow the selected lemming to alter the landscape, to affect the behavior of other lemmings, or to clear obstacles to create a safe passage for the rest of the lemmings. In addition, as our Zooids evolve in a physical world, we found another source of inspiration in Rube Goldberg's machines and other open-ended mechanical chains. These machines play with the physical properties of objects to create chains of events. Tseng et al. designed an open-ended kit to introduce children to such physical concepts, which was another source of inspiration [13].

Game Play

Our game is tabletop-based. Zooids are positioned on one side of the tabletop: at the entrance of the game terrain. At the other end is an exit, where one has to lead Zooids. Different physical obstacles made out of various materials (walls, ramps, dirt) are placed on the terrain. These block Zooids' path to the exit. The player has to find a way to clear the path for Zooids to access the exit (see fig.3). A default behavior is given to all Zooids: they go straight, unless stopped by an obstacle. Actions can be given to Zooids, individually when players put "clothes" on them. By changing the behavior of one Zooid, the trajectory of the other Zooids will be disturbed. Players succeed by effectively affecting the system, and leading the group of Zooids to the exit.

We have designed four characters that incarnate these actions. Each can be attributed to a Zooid by "dressing" it up (see fig. 2). These four characters are:

- The Bulldozer: gets rid of obstacles;
- The Builder: fills holes in the terrain;
- The Boy Scout: shows the path to others; and
- The Blocker: prevents others from going in the wrong direction.

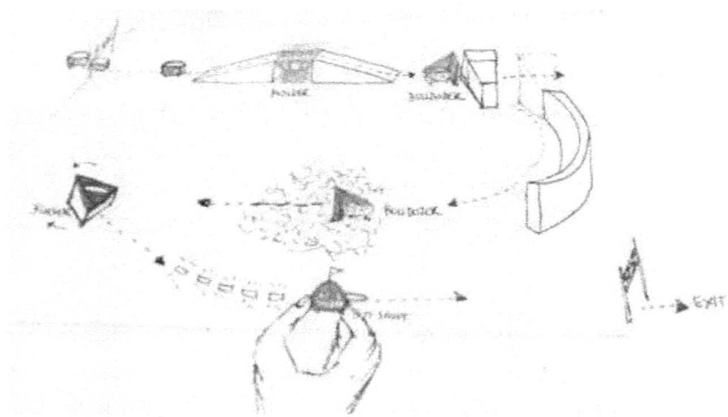

Figures 3 – Example of one terrain with obstacles and Zooids' path.

This first game level is an early iteration. Our aim is to trigger children's curiosity about system thinking and to gain deeper insights about how TUIs can help them grasp system concepts. We see a great agenda in using it during co-design sessions with children (age 5-10) to develop learning scenarios and refine our prototype.

Practical Considerations

We need one large table, one power plug with a power strip, and dark/low ambient light conditions for video projection.

References

1. M. Le Goc, L. Kim, A. Parsaei, J.-D. Fekete, P. Dragicevic, and S. Follmer. 2016. Zooids: Building Blocks for Swarm User Interfaces. 97–109.
2. Yu Guo, Aditi Wagh, Corey Brady, Sharona T. Levy, Michael S. Horn, and Uri Wilensky. 2016. Frogs to Think with: Improving Students' Computational Thinking and Understanding of Evolution in A Code-First Learning Environment. In *Proceedings of the The 15th International Conference on Interaction Design and Children* (IDC '16), 246–254.
3. Idit Harel, Seymour Papert, and Massachusetts Institute of Technology. Epistemology & Learning Research Group. 1991. *Constructionism*. Ablex Publishing Corporation.
4. Cindy E. Hmelo-Silver and Roger Azevedo. 2006. Understanding Complex Systems: Some Core Challenges. *Journal of the Learning Sciences* 15, 1: 53–61.
5. Michael S. Horn and Robert J. K. Jacob. 2006. Tangible Programming in the Classroom: A Practical Approach. In *CHI '06 Extended Abstracts on Human Factors in Computing Systems* (CHI EA '06), 869–874.
6. S. Papert. 1980. *Mindstorms: children, computers, and powerful ideas*. Basic Books, Inc, New York.
7. Radia Perlman. 1976. Using Computer Technology to Provide a Creative Learning Environment for Preschool Children.
8. Mitchel Resnick. 1994. *Turtles, Termites, and Traffic Jams: Explorations in Massively Parallel Microworlds*. MIT Press, Cambridge, MA, USA.
9. Mitchel Resnick. 1996. StarLogo: An Environment for Decentralized Modeling and Decentralized Thinking. In *Conference Companion on Human Factors in Computing Systems* (CHI '96), 11–12.
10. A. Rowe. 2010. Glowing Pathfinder Bugs. In *ACM SIGGRAPH 2010 Art Gallery*, 412–413.
11. J. D. Sterman. 1994. Learning in and about complex systems. *System Dynamics Review* 10, 2–3: 291–330.
12. Seth Tisue and Uri Wilensky. 2004. NetLogo: A simple environment for modeling complexity. In *in International Conference on Complex Systems*, 16–21.
13. T. Tseng, C. Bryant, and P. Blikstein. 2011. Mechanix: An Interactive Display for Exploring Engineering Design Through a Tangible Interface. In *Proceedings of the Fifth International Conference on Tangible, Embedded, and Embodied Interaction* (TEI '11), 265–266.
14. Oren Zuckerman and Ayelet Gal-Oz. 2013. To TUI or Not to TUI: Evaluating Performance and Preference in Tangible vs. Graphical User Interfaces. *Int. J. Hum.-Comput. Stud.* 71, 7–8: 803–820.
15. Oren Zuckerman and Mitchel Resnick. 2003. A Physical Interface for System Dynamics Simulation. In *CHI '03 Extended Abstracts on Human Factors in Computing Systems* (CHI EA '03), 810–811.
16. Oren Zuckerman and Mitchel Resnick. 2004. Hands-on Modeling and Simulation of Systems. In *Proceedings of the 2004 Conference on Interaction Design and Children: Building a Community* (IDC '04), 157–158.
17. Design I/O - CONNECTED WORLDS. Retrieved April 1, 2017 from http://design-io.com/projects/ConnectedWorlds/
18. Osmo | Play Beyond The Screen. https://www.playosmo.com/en/coding/
19. Cubetto: A robot teaching kids code & computer programming. *Primo Toys*. https://www.primotoys.com/
20. Lemmings – Games on Microsoft Store. *Microsoft Store*. https://www.microsoft.com/en-us/store/p/lemmings/9wzdncrfjcdm

Bear Abouts: Sharing Stories across the Physical and Digital

Becca Rose Glowacki
University of the West of England
Bristol, UK
Becca.glowacki@uwe.ac.uk

Figure 1: children aged 5-7 years using Bear Abouts.

IDC 2017, June 27–30, 2017, Stanford, CA, USA.
ACM ISBN 978-1-4503-4921-5/17/06.
DOI http://dx.doi.org/10.1145/3078072.3091980

Abstract
We have developed an interactive storytelling platform for mobile devices that encourages children to engage in story creation across both digital and physical spaces. In our pilot study we have found that when using Bear Abouts, children engage in open-ended creative activity with tablet devices, and they also re-tell and re-frame narratives with each other. The platform does not use external electronics hardware, and has the potential to be a low-cost option for tangible interactions. This paper provides context for the demo of the Bear Abouts platform.

Author Keywords
Creativity and Children; Tangible; Novel applications for children; Storytelling; Play; Mobile Devices.

ACM Classification Keywords
H.5.m. Information interfaces and presentation: Interaction design

Introduction
Recent reports show that younger children are mostly engaged in solitary activity when using mobile or tablet devices [1, 2, 3]. Rather than the viewing or playtime being a shared experience, in what is known as "joint media engagement" [4], the studies demonstrate that mobile media tend to be used by single participants. Addressing this type of use is important because children develop through social interactions, and joint engagement is integral to learning processes [4, 5].

We have identified two possibilities for exploring more social ways of engaging with digital media. These are

(1) through creative play with stories, and (2) through tangible interactions. We have developed a storytelling app called "Bear Abouts" that explores these possibilities with children.

The first possibility for a more social interaction is through creating stories, or sharing stories with others. Storytelling (i.e., creating and sharing stories) is a social activity [6, 7, 8]. Storytelling is also a method used to learn socially [6, 5]. The second possibility for exploring social engagement is through tangible interactions. Paul Dourish [9] explores the crossover between tangible and social interactions. He describes this intersection as "embodied" interaction. For Dourish, tangible interfaces encourage active participation between media participants in real space [8]. This encourages joint engagement and social interactions.

Related Work

The Bear Abouts app builds on prior work in embodied interaction and storytelling. There are a number of interactive devices that access and create stories using a combination of physical and digital environments. These tools expand on embodied interactions through tangible interfaces. *Storymat* [10] and *Animal Blocks* [11] were developed at the Gesture and Narrative Language group at the MIT Media Lab, and *Jabberstamp* [12] and *TOK* [13] combine multiple sensory experiences to develop interactive stories. In our work, we combine storytelling and embodied

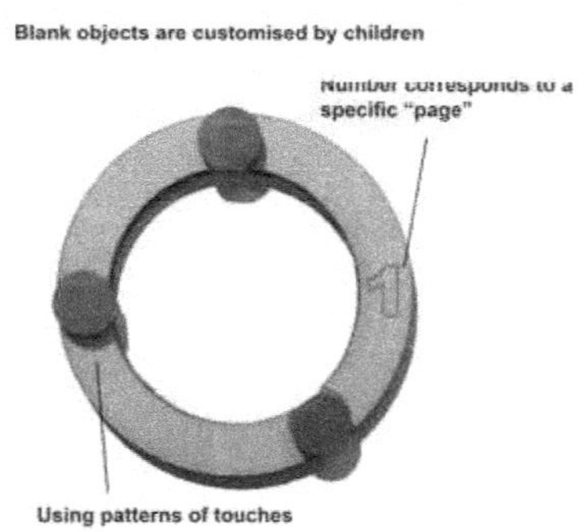

Figure 3: Blank story objects.

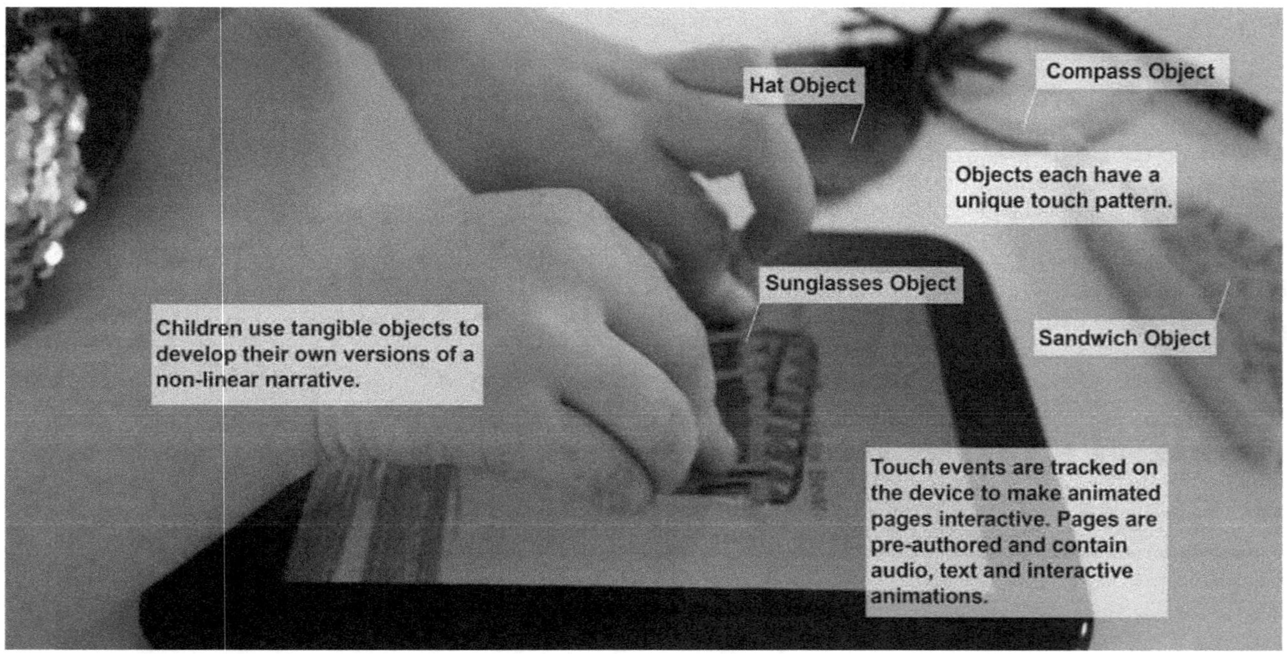

Figure 2: The current iteration of Bear Abouts (2017) uses custom patterns to connect paper objects with the storytelling app through capacitive touch.

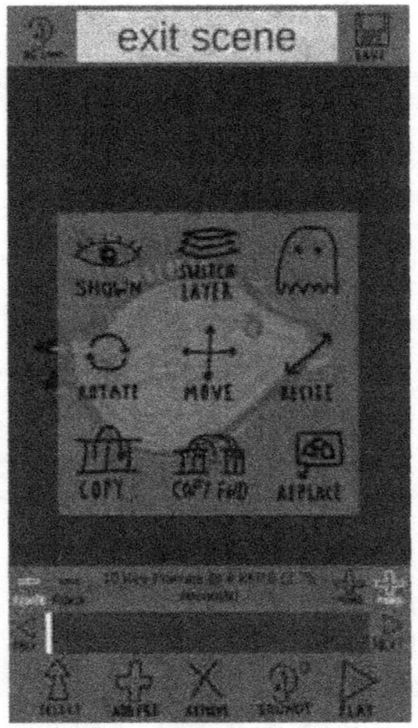

(a)

(b)

Figure 4: Bear Abouts story making platform. The story editor(a) and a collection of "pages" in a story (b).

interactions with mobile devices to create a platform that can be used without external electronic hardware, making it affordable for use in everyday or domestic environments.

Bear Abouts System

We have iterated the design over 2 years (2015-2017) to its current form (see figure 1). Bear Abouts is made up of physical objects and a digital platform (see figure 2). The platform recognizes a unique touch pattern on each object. The pattern is attached to paper objects with adhesive copper (see figure 3). The system uses machine learning to recognize each object (it can be calibrated to avoid variation error), and it recalls audio, text, and illustrations that are conceptually connected to the specific objects.

The initial design and development was focused on storytelling through physical artifacts, looking at non-linear narratives and the creative impact of allowing children to be the creators. Based on early user interactions, we developed the system so that people can add and edit their own stories, as well as re-tell other people's stories. Through our public tests we developed the platform to allow it to be a creation space, encouraging embodied interaction, story sharing, and story creation.

Doing it together

There are two methods of engaging with the current Bear Abouts system, (1) through connecting parts of a pre-made story, and (2) through developing an original story, and playing back.

In the first method (shown in figure 1 and 2), children develop narratives through piecing together elements of the story. In this version, each physical artifact is connected a "page" in the story. Pages are pre-made and include text, audio active animation that responds to the objects, and background animations that run on a loop. The order in which you place the objects on the screen determines the order of the narrative.

In a pilot study with 11 children aged 5-7 years, children worked together to develop narratives through arranging the connected objects to form a non-linear story. The Bear Abouts story is based on a migrant bear who has a bag of useful objects to aid him on his journey. Inside the bag are sunglasses, a sandwich, a compass, and a wooly hat (see figure 2). In the study, children developed their own narratives through determining the order in which they used the objects to help the bear. By doing so, the children developed verbal narratives together and when asked to recall their version of the stories, they used the objects as props to retell them. We found that children mostly used the device in groups, either taking it in turns to pass the objects between each other and sharing the storytelling between them; or by co-creating narratives together as they went along (see Table 1).

The second method to interact with the system is to develop your own narrative using our custom story-making platform and "blank" objects. The blank objects can be customized and are mapped to a "page." Children (or story-makers of any age) can add text, animations, illustrations, and audio to a page using the custom editor (see figure 4). When in "play" mode, a collection of pages (i.e., a story) can be played back using the customized objects, in a similar way to method (1).

Future considerations

This is a pilot study. Our preliminary research has involved tests with small groups of children and story-makers. We are currently carrying out further research into how children use the platform to read or listen to stories, as well as how they co-create with the platform. Future work on this can explore how a larger number of participants experience the platform.

A significant part of our design process has been concerned with developing sensors and software that connect paper with tablet devices without the use of external hardware. Now that we have stable systems,

Device usage	No. of Children
Use of device with another child through collaborative play	5
Use of device with another child through taking in turns	4
Use of device on their own	2

Table 1: Children's pattern of device usage with Bear Abouts, in study of 11 children aged 5-7 years.

our next step will be to iterate the design through further testing with children at libraries and homes in the UK; this research is planned to start in the summer of 2017.

Acknowledgements
We would like to thank the following people and organizations for their contribution or continued support in the development of Bear Abouts: Mark Wonnacott, Sarah Warden, Filton Ave Primary School, Pervasive Media Studio, Ursula Davies, Makerversity, Arts Council England, Innovate UK, Phill Tew, iSci, Ben Gwalchmai, Blythe Pepino, Martin Brown, Ideo (London), Natalie Freed

Practical Considerations
The demo is self-contained; the only provision needed would be power sockets to charge the mobile device.

References
1. Ofcom (2015) *Half of UK homes turn to tablets - in just five years*. Available at: https://www.ofcom.org.uk/about-ofcom/latest/media/media-releases/2015/five-years-of-tablets (Accessed: 25 February 2017).
2. Ofcom (2016) *Children's Media Lives –year 3 findings*. Available at: https://www.ofcom.org.uk/__data/assets/pdf_file/0015/94002/Childrens-Media-Lives-Year-3-report.pdf (Accessed: 25 February 2017).
3. Wartella, E. et al. (2016) *What kind of adults will our children become? The impact of growing up in a media-saturated world*, Journal of Children and Media, 10:1, pp. 13-20, DOI: 10.1080/17482798.2015.1124796
4. Takeuchi, L., & Stevens, R. (2011). The new coviewing: Designing for learning through joint media engagement. New York: The Joan Ganz Cooney Center at Sesame Workshop.
5. Vygotsky, L. S. (1978). Mind in society: The development of higher psychological processes. Cambridge, MA: Harvard University Press.
6. Liu, Chen-Chung et al. (2011) "An Enhanced Concept Map Approach To Improving Children's Storytelling Ability". *Computers & Education* 56.3 pp. 873-884.
7. Sylla, Cristina et al. (2015) "Investigating The Use Of Digital Manipulatives For Storytelling In Pre-School". International Journal of Child-Computer Interaction 6 pp.39-48.
8. Rainville, Kristin Nicole and Gordh, Bill. (2016) "Toward a Narrative Classroom: Storytelling, Media, and Literacy". *Young Children*
9. Dourish, P. (2001) Where the action is: The foundations of embodied interaction. Cambridge, MA: The MIT Press.
10. Ryokai, K & Cassell , J. (1999). StoryMat: A Play Space for Collaborative Storytelling. *CHI Late Breaking 1999*, pp. 272-273.
11. Ryokai, K. (2001) "Animal Blocks". *Gesture and Narrative Language Group, MIT Media Lab.* [Online]. [1 April 2017]. Available from: https://www.media.mit.edu/projects/animal-blocks/overview/
12. Raffle et al. (2007). Jabberstamp: embedding sound and voice in traditional drawings. *IDC 2007 Proceedings: Multimedia*, pp. 137-144.
13. Sylla, C., Coutinho, C., Branco, P. (2014). A Digital Manipulative for Embodied "Stage-Narrative" Creation. In *Entertainment Computing, Elsevier 5(4)*, pp. 495–507. doi:10.1016/j.entcom.2014.08.011

Energetic Alpha, Playful Handwriting Practice for Children

Gretchen Caldwell Rinnert
Kent State University
Kent, OH 44240, USA
grinnert@kent.edu

Joshua A. Talbott
Kent State University
Kent, OH 44240, USA
jtalbott@kent.edu

Marianne Martens
Kent State University
Kent, OH 44240, USA
mmarten3@kent.edu

Bryan Rinnert
3 Sight Photography
Kent, OH 44240, USA
brinnert@kent.edu

Aoife Mooney
Kent State University
Kent, OH 44240, USA
amooney2@kent.edu

IDC '17, June 27-30, 2017, Stanford, CA, USA

ACM ISBN 978-1-4503-4921-5/17/06.
http://dx.doi.org/10.1145/3078072.3091981

Abstract
Young children are enamored by screens, especially iPads and mobile devices. Apple's App Store offers close to 100,000 products aimed at young children. Many of the apps are poor quality and include in-app advertising, deficient navigation, or overly gamified elements that compete with content. "Extraneous animations, sound effects, and tangential games might be appealing to a child when activated but do not add to the child's understanding of the primary content because they disrupt the coherence of the learning experience and the child's engagement" (Hirsh-Pasek et al., 2015, p. 12). In an effort to create an educational but entertaining experience we developed an iPad application called Energetic Alpha. This interactive app teaches letter writing to children by using motion design and video content to educate and reward.

Author Keywords
Children; Design; Gamification; Handwriting; Learning; Motion Design; Writing

ACM Classification Keywords
Design; Human Factors

Introduction
Learning apps are widely popular among parents and children, but many are mediocre. Our design team

Figure 1: A screenshot from Energetic Alpha showing the main menu page (Rinnert, Martens, & Mooney 2017).

Figure 2: A screenshot from Energetic Alpha opening screen (Rinnert, Martens, & Mooney 2017).

received a seed grant to create a working prototype of an alphabet app for children between 4 and 7 years old called *Energetic Alpha. Energetic Alpha* teaches handwriting skills and offers rewards in the form of animations and videos. The design incorporates guidelines for creating diverse and inclusive media products developed by the Diversity in Apps Board (Seth, "Developing," 2016). Our primary goal is that the project will allow us to contribute to the research on creating, evaluating and defining what constitutes a high quality, inclusive, and educational app for young children.

Timely and Innovative

Much remains to be learned about how children interact with screens. Despite concerns around apps, there is also plenty of evidence that quality digital media formats can encourage learning—particularly in supporting different learning styles (Chiong et al 2012; NAEYC & Fred Rogers, 2012; Campaign for a Commercial Free Childhood CCFC, 2012; Crescenzi, Jewitt, & Price, 2014). *Energetic Alpha* is informed both by research and a commitment to inclusion. Work by Druin (2005) and Sanders (2008) on co-design and co-creation informs our product, along with user-studies with diverse children. *Energetic Alpha* uses design to engage preliterate children, by incorporating quality elements identified by librarians Campbell and Haines (2016), as well as guidelines on creating diverse and inclusive media products emphasized by the Diversity in Apps Board. Criticism around apps and screen time for the youngest children abounds. Yet "well-designed software affords children an appropriate level of control and agency depending on their age and experience, allowing them to proceed at their own pace and sustain their interest" (Hirsh-Pasek, Zosh, Golinkoff, Gray, Robb & Kaufman, 2015, p. 10).

Much research addresses the role of kinesthetic and multisensory learning experiences for young children. Chiong and DeLoache (2012) defined a *manipulative book* as one with interactive features that interest the child, and our app could be interpreted as such. While some children benefit from the kinesthetic and tactile experiences of manipulative books, interactive elements can also negatively increase the cognitive load of some children, distracting them from learning. In Chiong and DeLoache's (2012) study of children between 30-36 months, they found that while manipulative books did not positively affect learning, if manipulative elements were designed to focus children's attention on "the information to be learned," (p. 240) rather than away from this information, there appears to be some benefit to the learner (Chiong & DeLoache, 2013, p. 238). In our application, the interactive and manipulative elements are designed to enhance—and not distract—from the material to be learned.

Richardson (1997) found that the sequential and multisensory experience of the Montessori preschool approach had positive learning outcomes. "These provisions help the child develop prelinguistic and preliteracy skills that are among the requisites for the development of symbolic language spoken and written," (p. 255). *Energetic Alpha* also provides a sequential and multisensory approach for children learning to write, and the interaction and content are designed to highlight each other through interaction, sound, motion and repetition. Our application presents

Figure 3: A screenshot from Energetic Alpha showing the trace hint animation (Rinnert, Martens, & Mooney 2017).

Figure 4: A screenshot from Energetic Alpha showing the user testing session (Rinnert, Martens, & Mooney 2017).

a kinesthetic learning experience with a focused sequence of events.

As many children are growing up using screens from an early age, we seek to take advantage of these create a tool for playful letter writing practice. Handwriting has significant value and impacts student writing skills. "If children cannot form letters—or cannot form them with reasonable legibility and speed—they cannot translate the language in their minds into written text. Struggling with handwriting can lead to a self-fulfilling prophecy in which students avoid writing, come to think of themselves as not being able to write, and fall further and further behind their peers." (Graham, 2010) Many preschoolers flip and confuse similar letters, and write in reverse. Handwriting instruction focuses on teaching students quick, legible writing techniques so that they can focus on their ideas (Graham, 2010). Most children need to practice letter writing to correct these mistakes. Writing on paper alone cannot correct mistakes unless a tutor is present.

Methodology and Impact

Using our prototype, we conducted two user research sessions with children during the spring 2016 and winter of 2017. The first group included children in the target audience range: preliterate four-year-olds, 10 children, 5 girls and 5 boys, and 8 of those children were Caucasian and 2 were African American. The mean age was 6.8 years old. The children followed a task flow and were asked questions on a Likert scale, along with open ended questions regarding the content and subject matter of the videos. For example, a girl (age 7) wanted a unicorn in the app, while a boy (age 10) wanted more gamified elements. The first session established that our technology was in need of a complete redesign, and that error prevention and feedback needed to be implemented. We knew immediately that our slab serif typeface was confusing our young learners and we needed to bridge the gap between typography and handwriting in a fluid manner.

The second group included older children, who could provide more concrete feedback, consisting of 12 children, 8 girls and 4 boys. Of these children, 9 were Caucasian, and 3 were black. The mean age was 7.95 years old. Task booklets were used to guide the interviews, leading the children through the app in various stages. The app was presented without sound and motion to see how the children engaged with the interaction alone. Before sound elements were introduced children were given options on a variety of sound effects and elements and asked to select what they preferred. Before animation and video was introduced we offered them drawing tools and storyboards. We asked them what they would want to see if they correctly wrote a letter on the screen. The children were integral in selecting sounds, subject matter and visual aesthetics. Their insights and preferences were recorded in the task booklets. We have used their responses as we continue to develop new animations, videos and sounds.

Demo

The demo of *Energetic Alpha* shares the interface and the user experience. Videos are also used as hints for error feedback and as an incentive for continued play. Videos demonstrate a verb of the letter to help establish a mnemonic device, for example B=Build, M=Melting, and P=Popping. Each letter has a unique animation. Some are stop motion videos, and others are vector animations. The app is meant to grow with the child, allowing for customized use. A young child at 4-years old may have the settings at the most flexible level, allowing them to only touch the letter and it will unlock animations. While a child that is 7-years old may have the settings at the most advanced level and it will require precision and correct stroke order to proceed with game play. Our walkthrough will explain the user pathway, how a child would engage with the content and how a family member or teacher could encourage play and learning.

Technology

We have developed an app that engages the iPad as a practice writing surface that can track handwriting movements. The app uses the coordinates on the screen to help track stroke precision and order. The app breaks down the process of writing characters into a series of point values. These values coincide with device events based on user touch interaction. By converting the touch coordinates from the device to a universal format (X,Y: 0,0-1,1), we can program one dictionary set of points for each character. This enables us to use the same point values on many tablet sizes and quickly develop new letters, numbers, fonts, or graphics. In order to minimize the number of points we have to program for a particular font or letter, we leverage the boundaries of a PNG image alpha channel for any letter or graphic style to determine when a user draws "out of bounds" for the particular stroke shape. Our approach to the point programming involves breaking down each letter stroke into three parts: a finger touch down point, an appropriate number of finger tracing "fly-by" points (to ensure proper vector direction), and a finger lift up point. Each letter or character shape we want the user to mimic has a two-dimension ordered array of these stroke points for the number of strokes required to complete the letter. In addition to these hard-coded points, the app is also checking the user's current touch point value for opaque pixels on the letter character's PNG image layer (i.e. not scribbling out-of-bounds). Breaking down the letter tracing process into these sections, we are able to offer a sensitivity adjustment to the point bounds that can match the motor skills of the user and accommodate the inaccurate nature of finger or tablet based drawing. With this technical architecture in place, we are able to add the *Energetic Alpha* "game logic" to move the user through tracing a character. The interface recognizes errors and provides the user an animation hint to help them self-correct and get the writing task correct on the next try. Video elements are both embedded and use internet access to download larger files. The interactive elements are able to operate offline, but in order to view video content the user must be online.

Conclusion

Energetic Alpha is currently a fully functioning prototype, with the interface and user pathway complete. Our next steps include additional user testing, co-creation sessions and more formalized interviews with educators. We intend to release *Energetic Alpha* in Apple's App Store by the end of 2017. We expect that the project will generate future work as it has many transferable qualities.

Practical Considerations

We are prepared to share the demo with little to no additional technology provided. We will bring several iPads for our demonstration.

References

1. Chiong, C., & DeLoache, J.S. 2013. Learning the ABCs: What kinds of picture book facilitate young children's learning? *Journal of Early Childhood Literacy, 13*(2), 225-241. Retrieved May 3, 2017 from http://journals.sagepub.com/doi/abs/10.1177/1468798411430091
2. Chiong C., Ree, J., Takeuchi, L., and Erickson, I. 2012. Comparing parent-child co-reading on print, basic and enhanced e-Book platforms. New York, NY: The Joan Ganz Cooney Center.
3. Druin A. 2005. What children can teach us: Developing digital libraries for children with children. *The Library Quarterly,* 75, 1: 20-41.
4. Graham, S. 2010. Want to Improve Children's Writing? Don't Neglect Their Handwriting. *AMERICAN EDUCATOR*, V76(N1), 49-55. doi:http://www.aft.org/sites/default/files/periodicals/graham.pdf
5. Campbell, C., & Haines, C. (2016). *Becoming a media mentor: A guide for working with children and families*. Chicago, IL.: American Library Association.
6. Hirsh-Pasek, K., Zosh, J., Golinkoff, R.M., Gray, J.H., Robb, M. B., and Kaufman, J. 2015. Putting education in "educational" apps: Lessons from the science of learning. *Psychological Science in the Public Interest,* 16, 1: 3-31.
7. Richardson, S. O. 1997. The Montessori Preschool: Preparation for Writing and Reading. *Annals of Dyslexia*, 241-256. Retrieved May 5, 2017 from http://www.jstor.org/stable/23768103
8. Rinnert, G., Mooney, A. & Martens, M. Forthcoming, 2017. Energetic Alpha: Motion design as a cross disciplinary collaboration. *Kinetic Emergence.* (Eds.) R. Brian Stone and Leah Wahlin.
9. Sanders, E. 2008. Co-creation and the new landscapes of design. *CoDesign: International Journal of CoCreation in Design and the Arts* 4, 1: 5-18.
10. Seth, K. 2016. Developing children's media with diversity in mind. Retrieved March 30, 2017 from joanganzcooneycenter.org

Children Designing Videos: Tools, Pedagogical Models, and Best Practices for Digital Storytelling and Media-Making in the Classroom

Jari Multisilta
Tampere University of Tech.
Pohjoisranta 11C,
28101, Pori, Finland
jari.multisilta@tut.fi

Eric Hamilton
Pepperdine University
Malibu, CA, USA, 92603
eric.hamilton@pepperdine.edu

Hannele Niemi
University of Helsinki
Faculty of Behavioural Sciences
P.O. Box 9, FI-00014
University of Helsinki, Finland
hannele.niemi@helsinki.fi

IDC '17, June 27-30, 2017, Stanford, CA, USA

ACM ISBN 978-1-4503-4921-5/17/06.
http://dx.doi.org/10.1145/3078072.3091982

Abstract

Although video sharing is common among youth, schools are only beginning to apply digital videos and digital storytelling to formal learning. This paper presents pedagogical models, examples, best practices, and outcomes that illustrate how teachers and students design and use digital stories in knowledge creation in cross-cultural settings. The results are based on the empirical data and findings from several international pilot studies. On the one hand, working with digital video stories drove engagement. However, on the other hand, technical issues significantly lowered engagement. In addition, the video inquiry pedagogy supported inquiry learning. Students began to pose scientifically oriented questions and seek answers together.

Author Keywords

Video; storytelling; media-making; pedagogical models; STEM; children.

ACM Classification Keywords

K.3.1 Computer Uses in Education.

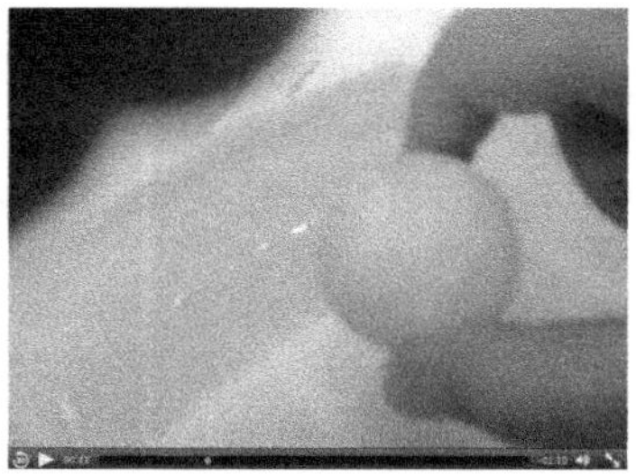

Figure 1: Examples of the topics in storytelling projects:
a) lab work documentary,
b) animal testing, and
c) recycling.

Introduction

Sharing photos and short videos with others has become increasingly popular among youth. For example, Khan Academy offers a large collection of educational videos, particularly on STEM subjects, available for free on the Internet. Although video sharing is common among youth, schools are only beginning to apply digital videos and digital storytelling to formal learning [1,2,3].

Digital video storytelling refers to learning activities that involve the creation and use of digital video to form a coherent narrative. In a learning context, digital storytelling involves both the creation and distribution of the content used in the learning process and interaction between the content users.

Digital video storytelling encompasses widely recognized 21st century skills [4]. By taking advantage of the creative potential of modern communication technologies, students can collaborate, explore their ideas, and become creators, producers, and active learning participants. Digital video storytelling can also motivate students, as it brings the technologies they use in their free time into the school environment.

This paper presents pedagogical models, methods, and outcomes of digital storytelling projects. The results are based on the empirical data and findings from several international pilot studies run by University of Helsinki, University of Pepperdine, and Stanford University.

Background

Hull [5] described digital storytelling as an alternative learning space that reflects youth culture and new media literacies. She argues that video storytelling can support conceptions of self, as it entails telling and sharing video stories that are meaningful to one's own learning. She found that digital storytelling can be a powerful form of self-representation for both children and adults, and that authoring video stories helps individuals develop agentive senses of self [6].

Another study [7] investigated how early childhood education teachers incorporated digital storytelling in their classrooms. They found that teachers considered digital storytelling as an alternative problem-based learning tool for enhancing young children's motivation. In addition, digital storytelling is one way teachers can adjust their practices to utilize technology and modern approaches to learning.

Digital videos can be used in the workplace, too. One study [8] examined how video storytelling has been used within the context of workplace learning. Video storytelling as a skill is useful not only at school but also after school and in working life. In fact, digital literacy is one of the most predominantly mentioned 21st century skills [4].

Learning with Digital Videos

Three different approaches were taken to using digital video in the classroom. The first approach was the global sharing pedagogy, which involved students sharing their digital stories globally and learning through collaboration on the videos [2]. The second approach was video inquiry learning, which aimed to provide approaches to learning that were based on the investigation of questions, scenarios, or problems using videos created and shared by students. The third approach featured aspects of the first two pedagogies and emphasized assistive and participatory teaching

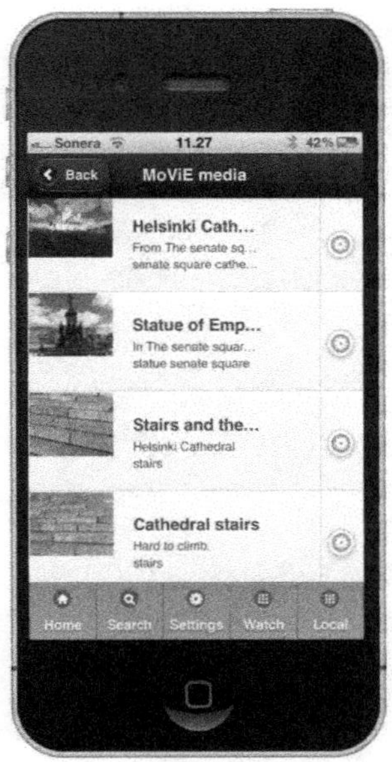

Figure 2: MoViE, Mobile Video Experience platform was used for creating video sories and for sharing videos with others.

through a network of Media-Making Clubs (MMCs) affiliated with US schools, the New York Hall of Science, and sites in Finland, Kenya, and Namibia. These MMCs have a mission to help others advance in STEM learning. More specifically, their purpose is to make digital artifacts (including videos, short subject films, games, computer programs, and specialized applications, such as interactive books) that represent, explain, and clarify STEM phenomena to others as successfully, creatively, and soundly as possible [9].

Global Sharing Pedagogy

The global sharing pedagogy (GSP) is a framework for designing and analyzing the learning activities and the learning process involved in co-creating video stories. learning is seen as the result of dialogical interactions between people, substances, and artifacts [1,2,3]. The primary objective of the GSP is to strengthen student engagement in learning and help them become active learners and knowledge creators.

Video Inquiry Learning

Inquiry learning is defined as "an approach to learning that involves a process of exploring the natural or material world, and that leads to asking questions, making discoveries, and rigorously testing those discoveries in the search for new understanding" [10]. Based on our experience, students found it difficult to develop arguments and reflect on what they saw in the video stories they and their peers produced. Argumentation, reflection, and commenting are important 21st century skills.

The video inquiry pedagogy was developed to help students learn the scientific discovery process, argumentation, and reflection. Inquiry learning supports the development of higher order thinking skills [11], i.e., problem-solving, critical thinking, creative thinking, and decision-making. In video inquiry learning, learners create video clips or video stories and start developing questions about the videos. They then discuss and search for answers to the questions together, drawing on the teacher and other available resources for support.

Tool

Many tools can be used for digital video storytelling. However, general tools, such as iMovie and YouTube, do not support specific pedagogical concepts. Therefore, the authors decided to develop a video storytelling platform that supports GSP, inquiry based learning and 21st century skills. The resulting platform, MoViE, has been used in international research projects in Finland, Greece, and California.

MoViE (Mobile Video Experience) enables users to record video clips using their mobile devices, upload the clips to the MoViE website, and create video stories using the clips that they and their collaborators have recorded. EdVisto (www.edvisto.com) is the current version of the MoViE. Currently EdVisto is used by the MMC network, in primary and secondary school settings, for both research and educational goals.

Discussion

Based on our studies, working with mobile videos both in the classroom and outside the classroom can provide an engaging experience. The engagement seems to combine both an emotional aspect, such as fun, and a commitment to hard work. In addition, group work, co-creation, and the MoViE platform were important factors for motivating students to learn and work with video stories. The lousy user experience, however, significantly lowered engagement.

Many of the video outputs from the pilot projects presented important messages and aimed to influence other viewers' opinions on topics like recycling, water, homelessness, and animal testing. Similar to [7], the students' own voices clearly shone through in the videos. Based on our data, we conclude that the creation and sharing of mobile video stories support the learning of 21st century skills. In addition, regarding video inquiry learning, we found that students began asking scientifically oriented questions as they conducted and filmed the experiment.

References

1. Niemi, H. & Multisilta, J. (2014) Global is Becoming Everywhere: Global Sharing Pedagogy. In Niemi, H., Multisilta, J., Lipponen, L. & Vivitsou, M. (eds.) (2014) *Finnish Innovations and Technologies in Schools: Towards New Ecosystems of Learning*. Rotterdam: Sense Publishers.
2. Niemi, H., Harju, V., Vivitsou, M., Viitanen, K., Multisilta, J. and Kuokkanen, A. (2014) Digital Storytelling for 21st-Century Skills in Virtual Learning Environments. *Creative Education*, **5**, 657-671.
3. Niemi, H. & Multisilta, J. (2015) Digital story telling promoting 21st century skills and students' engagement. Technology, Pedagogy and Education, Routledge.
4. Binkley, M., Erstad, O., Herman, J., Raizen, S., Ripley, M., Miller-Ricci, M., & Rumble, M. (2012) Defining 21st century skills. In P. Griffin, B. McGaw, & E. Care (Eds.), Assessment and teaching of twenty-first century skills (pp. 17–66). Dordrecht: Springer Science+Business Media BV.
5. Hull, G. A. (2003) At last: Youth culture and digital media: New literacies for new times. *Research in the Teaching of English*, *38*(2), 229-233.
6. Hull, G. A., & Katz, M. L. (2006) Crafting an agentive self: Case studies of digital storytelling. *Research in the Teaching of English*, 43-81.
7. Yuksel-Arslan, P., Yildirim, S., & Robin, B. R. (2016) A phenomenological study: teachers' experiences of using digital storytelling in early childhood education. *Educational Studies*, *42*(5), 427-445.
8. Katzeff, C., & Ware, V. (2006, October) Video storytelling as mediation of organizational learning. In *Proceedings of the 4th Nordic conference on Human-computer interaction: changing roles* (pp. 311-320). ACM.
9. Hamilton, E., Kapenda, L., Mbasu, Z., Miranda, H., Ngololo, E., Ogwel, J. C., ... & Stern, D. (2016) A Model and Research Agenda for Teacher and Student Collaboration Using Pen-Based Tablets in Digital Media Making in Sub-Saharan Africa. In *Revolutionizing Education with Digital Ink* (pp. 223-230). Springer International Publishing.
10. de Jong, T & van Joolingen W.R (2008) Model-Facilitated Learning. In Jonassen, D., Spector, M.J., Driscoll,M., Merrill,M.D. van Merrienboer, J (eds.) Handbook of Research on Educational Communications and Technology: A Project of the Association for Educational Communications and Technology. Routledge.
11. Lewis, A., & Smith, D. (1993) Defining higher order thinking. Theory into Practise. Vol 32, Issue 3. Taylor & Francis. 131-137.

Geometris: Designing Collaborative Mathematical Interactions For Children

Elena Durán-López
elena.duran@berkeley.edu

Leah F. Rosenbaum
leahr@berkeley.edu

Ganesh V. Iyer
ganesh.v@berkeley.edu

University of California, Berkeley
Berkeley, CA 94704, USA

IDC '17, June 27-30, 2017, Stanford, CA, USA

ACM ISBN 978-1-4503-4921-5/17/06.
http://dx.doi.org/10.1145/3078072.3091983.

Abstract
We present *Geometris*, a collaborative embodied geometry game for 6- to 11-year-old children. As shapes are projected onto the floor, players recreate those shapes on a 6x6 feet interactive mat. At the end of each level, a geometric pattern - the result of overlaying all created shapes - is displayed. Two dimensions of user interaction—mobility and division of labor—emerged during pilot gameplay sessions. We hypothesize that these interactions offer resources for children to learn geometry concepts as well as collaboration skills.

Author Keywords
Educational game; embodied learning; collaboration.

ACM Classification Keywords
H.5.2. User interfaces: interaction styles; K.3.1. Computer Uses in Education

Introduction
Mathematics is often portrayed as an abstract, solitary, and formulaic field. *Geometris*, an embodied and collaborative game, creates an environment in which young math learners can experience geometry as tangible and collaborative. The game enables physical movement as a means for thinking and talking about shapes. Its design requires players to work together to

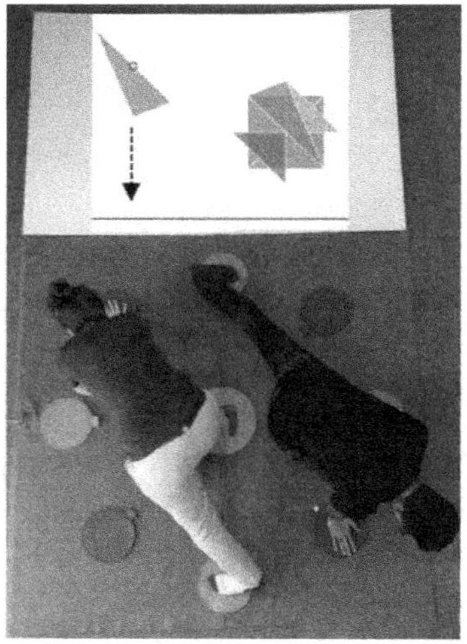

Figure 1: *Geometris* environment. Shapes descend on the projection area (top) toward the red horizontal line. Players recreate the shape with their bodies on the mat. Shapes that have been successfully created are shown in the bottom right corner of the projection area. The gray mat (bottom) contains 9 pressure-sensitive pads.

fulfill the provided challenges. Aligned with the idea of experiencing math in a different way, the score of the game features aesthetically pleasing geometric compositions rather than numerical scores often associated with high-stakes assessment.

The *Geometris* environment is composed of a 6x6 ft interactive mat and a 4x6 ft projection area [Fig. 1]. Two dimensional shapes are projected onto the floor near the mat, descending from the top of the projection area toward the red line at the bottom. Players work in groups to create the shapes on the mat by pressing only the pressure-sensitive pads that correspond to the vertices of the projected shape. To accomplish this task, children need to work together and coordinate their bodies. Each game level consists of 8 shapes and is scored by overlaying all successfully created shapes [Fig. 2]. Real-time feedback is provided both through an LED on each pad and in the projected image.

Related Work

Geometry is a fundamental pillar of mathematics [7]. The Common Core State Standards in mathematics for kindergarten to fifth grade include skills such as: comparing shapes by number of sides and corners, distinguishing identifying features (e.g. number of corners) from non-identifying features (e.g. size), and recognizing symmetry [6]. Spatial reasoning also poses particular challenges for older students as they study translations, rotations, and reflections of transformational geometry [2].

To address these challenges, some researchers emphasize the role of physical movement, arguing for embodied learning as an essential educational resource [1], with some math educators claiming that mathematical reasoning is rooted in bodily experiences [3].

Collaboration has also been identified as a critical skill for children. Specifically, working in dyads or small peer groups has been shown to facilitate children's learning and development [8]. The benefits of collaborative learning extend to mathematics, where research indicates that pair and small group work supports children in reasoning tasks [4]. We ground *Geometris* in these research findings, and through this game we aim to foster interactions that aid children to a) experience geometry in a new way, and b) develop collaboration skills.

Geometris interactions were inspired in part by existing games. We sought to recreate a sense of humorous frenzy in coordinating multiple players within a shared space as in Twister®. *Geometris*'s augmented mat is not unlike the traditional DanceDanceRevolution interface. In using elements of well-known games, we built on familiar game mechanics and user interfaces and add educational content to the experience.

Interaction Dimensions & Play Scenarios

We borrow Salen and Zimmerman schemas of rules and play when characterizing game design [5]. Rules define the essential structures of the game, and play captures the participants' experiences and social interactions with the game. *Geometris* has two rules: 1) players must create each shape before it reaches the red line at the bottom of the projection, and 2) for a shape to be validated, players must activate only the pads corresponding to the vertices of the shape. Nevertheless, the play - the way users interact with the

Figure 2: *Geometris* Level 1. :h triangle is projected, one at ime, for players to reconstruct on the mat. The prominent purple dot corresponds to mat's central circle and serves as a visual anchor, helping players map the projected shape onto : mat. The level concludes with a composition (bottom right) formed by overlaying all successfully created shapes.

Level 2 and 3 incorporate other kinds of shapes.

game - can be modulated by emphasizing different dimensions of the game.

Geometris play can be modulated along two dimensions: division of labor and mobility. By division of labor (DoL), we mean the distribution of resources and responsibilities among players. By mobility, we refer to whether or not players move around the mat.

In balanced DoL play, all children view the projection and share equal responsibility for creating the shapes on the mat. By contrast, unbalanced DoL play requires two distinct roles. "Guides" can see the prompted shapes but are instructed not to use the mat. Remaining players can access the mat but cannot see the prompted shapes and thus rely on the guide's instructions to construct each shape.

Balanced DoL play gives all players access to the same resources and responsibilities. In pilot tests, players negotiated those resources and responsibilities with different results. Some pairs spoke freely, sharing their thinking and directing each other; other pairs spoke little and gave directions through gestures. Consequently, this kind of play may be influenced by social comfort and power dynamics.

Unbalanced DoL play relies on verbal communication and is conducive to surfacing language about shapes and space. For example, geometric shape names (triangles, trapezoids, etc.) could emerge as a tool that streamlines communication and enhances performance, motivating players to learn these terms. However, resources are not equally distributed among players. If players do not rotate through roles, they may not have access to the same learning resources.

Play also varies along the dimension of mobility. In mobile play, players move freely around the mat, activating any pads they deem necessary. Children playing an immobile version of the game may not move around and instead are responsible for the 1-3 pads in their immediate vicinity. A sitting position facilitates immobile play, as it hinders gross body movement.

Mobile play facilitates a full-body experience of the shapes as players move, reorient, and stretch their bodies to create shapes. However, in this kind of play, children can occupy more than their "fair share" of the mat, even completing shapes without their peers' contribution. Again, collaboration is contingent on players' social relations and power dynamics.

While immobile play reduces the embodied experience of each shape, it distributes shape-creation over all players, prompting communication among them. It also presents an additional spatial reasoning task during a balanced DoL play scenario. When players are oriented differently relative to the projection, some must mentally rotate the projected shape before deciding whether or not to activate their pad [Fig 3, quad. II].

Figure 3 illustrates the plane in which these two dimensions coexist. Play scenarios can be located in one of these four quadrants. For example, in QI (unbalanced DoL play, immobile play) the projection area is located where only the guide can see it. Remaining players sit on the floor around the mat and follow the guide's instructions. In contrast, in QIII (balanced DoL play, mobile play), all players see the projection and move freely around the mat.

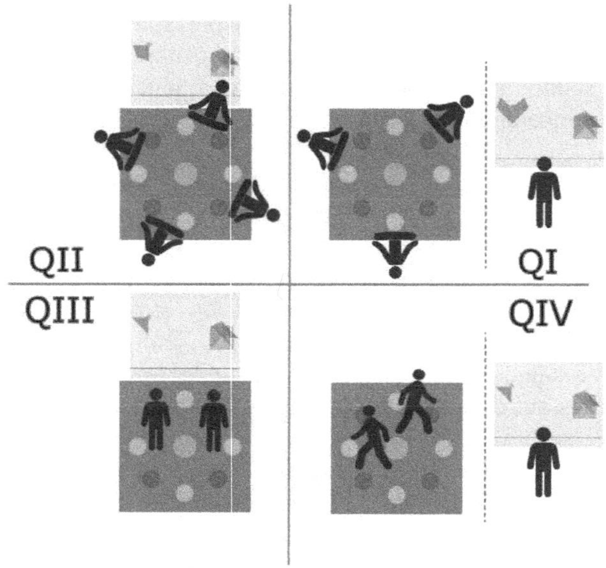

Figure 3: Four quadrants of *Geometris* play. QI: unbalanced DoL, immobile. QII: balanced DoL, immobile. QIII: balanced DoL, mobile. QIV: unbalanced DoL, mobile. Icon credits to Bradley Avison, Antonio Cozar, and Chiara Rossi of The Noun Project.

Conclusions and Future Directions

We are currently planning user studies with children to evaluate the play scenarios suggested above and to study the geometry and collaboration skills children develop through gameplay. We also plan to address needs raised through pilot testing, namely using non-skid material for the mat and allowing players to control the shapes' speed, perhaps with a knob.

We created *Geometris* to provide children with an experience of geometry as tangible, intimate, and collaborative. Preliminary work surfaced division of labor and mobility as central dimensions of gameplay. We seek to continue adapting *Geometris* to suit the physical, social, and developmental needs of young mathematics learners.

Acknowledgements

We thank Dr. Kimiko Ryokai and Noura Howell for their guidance in developing a *Geometris* prototype. We also thank CITRIS and the Barbara White Fund for their generous financial support.

References

1. Dor Abrahamson. 2014. Building educational activities for understanding. *Int. J. of Child-Computer Interaction* 2, 1: 1-16.
2. John Kirby and Douglas R. Boulter. 1999. Spatial ability and transformational geometry. *European Journal of Psychology of Education.* 14.2: 283
3. Ricardo Nemirovsky. 2003. Three conjectures concerning the relationship between body activity and understanding mathematics. In *Proc. PME 27*, 105-109.
4. Erin Phelps and William Damon. 1989. Problem solving with equals. *J. of Ed. Psych.*, 81, 4: 639.
5. Katie Salen and Eric Zimmerman. 2014. *Rules of play: Game design fundamentals*. MIT press.
6. Standards for Mathematical Practice. Retrieved December 13, 2016 from http://www.corestandards.org/Math/Practice/
7. Ian Thompson. 2003. *Enhancing primary mathematics teaching*. McGraw-Hill Education.
8. David Wood and Claire O'Malley. 1996. Collaborative learning between peers: An overview. *Educational Psychology in Practice 11*, 4: 4-9.

Forest Friends Demo: A Game-Exhibit to Promote Computer Science Concepts in Informal Spaces

Isaac Sung
University of Wisconsin–Madison
Madison, WI 53715, USA
cisung@wisc.edu

Matthew Berland
University of Wisconsin–Madison
Madison, WI 53715, USA
mberland@wisc.edu

IDC 2017, June 27–30, 2017, Stanford, CA, USA.
ACM ISBN 978-1-4503-4921-5/17/06.
http://dx.doi.org/10.1145/3078072.3091984

Abstract

Forest Friends is a strategic video game designed to introduce elements of computer science in an engaging and accessible way. The game includes artificial intelligence coding components that encourage participants to work with conditional statements. The research goal is to place the game in an informal learning environment to study the impact that it can have on young learners from diverse backgrounds.

Author Keywords

Computer science education; games; informal learning

ACM Classification Keywords

K.3.2 [Computers and education]: Computer and Information Science Education—Computer science education

Introduction

With computer science (CS) education on the horizon for many schools, it is crucial that children also gain access to informal learning environments where they can engage in computer science concepts outside of the classroom setting. Informal spaces can engage students in a way that formal classroom contexts cannot, and they can provide opportunities for learners to see programming concepts in action in a "real world" setting. Museums and public spaces can provide new contexts for young students to develop

Figure 1: Lobby of WID

identities of participation—that is, viewing CS as a feasible and aspirational interest or direction [2].

With *Forest Friends*, we aim to provide young middle school aged learners (ages 11–13) with an informal learning environment that will support social computational thinking skills. *Forest Friends* has two main goals: 1) to promote the understanding of computational thinking skills (e.g. abstraction, logical flow, conditional statements) and 2) to build identities of participation in computer science among young students. By creating an informal environment in which programming tasks are enjoyable, we can encourage students to further pursue computer science.

Related Work

Logo was one of the first educational programming languages developed specifically for children [6]. Other languages, such as Smalltalk and Scratch, were directly influenced by Papert's vision of a constructionist learning environment for kids [7]. These tinker-friendly languages have opened up the world of computer science to young learners around the world. Although these educational programming languages have been a major step forward for making computer science more accessible to all, there is still a need for more informal learning environments to engage students who may not normally find the topic applicable to their lives. By creating contexts where children enjoy using programming skills, we can reinforce their identities of participation in computer science and inspire those who may not have normally chosen the field. *Forest Friends* is not a "programming puzzle" game, as many other educational programming games can be. Rather, it requires an application of coding in order to advance your goals. It is open-ended, and there is no "right" answer to the programming section of the game.

Design Principles

The eventual goal of *Forest Friends* is to conduct research in a museum or other informal learning environment. One of the spaces that we are currently considering is the lobby area of the Wisconsin Instititues for Discovery (Figure 1). The lobby contains large touch screens that can be used to interact with various digital media. It would be an ideal location to place an interactive game because it is so freely accessible. On the first Saturday of each month, this space hosts a Saturday Science event which is free and open to all kids and families. With the goal of designing a game-exhibit in mind, Sue Allen's design framework for creating educational museum exhibits [1] seems appropriate to apply to *Forest Friends.*

Immediate apprehendability

Immediate apprehendability refers to the extent to which an exhibit's "purpose, scope, and properties" [1] can be understood immediately and with little to no cognitive effort. The UI and design of the game must be immediately understandable so that actions can be taken. This idea is similar to the concept of affordance [3, 5], but can be applied more generally to things such as labels and video game rules.

Physical interactivity

The ability to personally interact with an exhibit increases engagement and understanding [8]. The game will be interactive, but the five common pitfalls that Allen describes should be avoided.

Conceptual coherence

Conceptual coherence refers to the ability to impart abstract ideas and themes through exhibits. For *Forest Friends*, it will be an important challenge to make sure that users are learning the concepts of computer science that we intended. One method of applying this concept to this exhibit is by visually highlighting aspects of the game when it is running to create a clear connection between the code developed by the player and the actions in the game.

Diversity of learners
An important goal of this project is to promote identities in computer science for a diverse audience. The game must be designed in such a way that it is appealing to those who may not normally be attracted to computer science or programming topics.

Overview of Forest Friends

Forest Friends is a two-player resource strategy game where users will engage with concepts from computer programming, artificial intelligence (AI), experimentation/tinkering, and strategic planning. The game consists of two major sections: the main gameplay on the board, and the artificial intelligence "code cards" that act as a simple programming language to control some of your units on the board. In *Forest Friends*, each player will command their animals to secure territory and resources across the map in a fashion similar to the game *Risk*. The main gameplay resembles a board game as players move their units to outsmart opponents and control the board. At the heart of the gameplay are the code cards that players will use to "program" an AI ally (Figure 3). These code cards will enable players to easily discuss complex ideas that relate to computer science.

Each player begins the game with three different animal types that have strengths and weaknesses in a rock-paper-scissors like format. The players will directly control two out of the three types of animals, but one animal type will only be controlled by the code cards programmed by the user. As the game progresses, the player will see intended and unintended consequences of their code on the board, causing him or her to refine and re-test their scripts on the following turn. Each turn can last less than 30 seconds, and

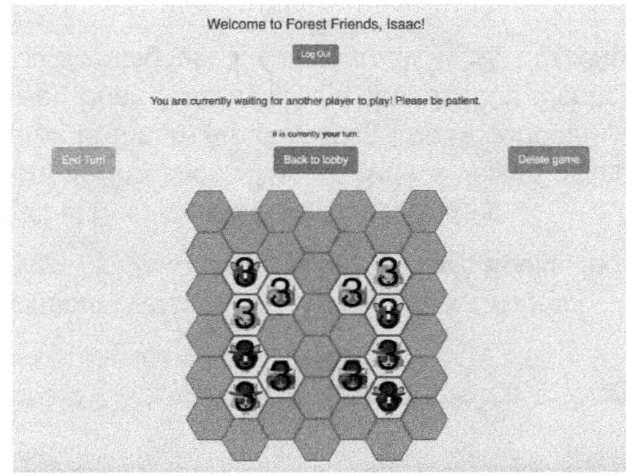

Figure 2: *Forest Friends* main board

the code is built incrementally through the cards. Players will also have to assess the changing board state, reexamine their strategy, and respond to the other player by changing their code. Successful expansion to new territory is determined by visible dice rolls that are based both on the unit type and quantity (more units means more dice). Even this concept of programmatic randomness is itself a complex concept hidden in many games that users play. Recent surveys by Pew Research Center [4] suggest that over 90% of underserved teens living in urban areas have played video games recently, and this game is designed to be a familiar experience for them.

Practical Considerations

This demo exhibit will require two tablets (or laptops) with web browsers and an internet connection. Touch screen interaction is preferred.

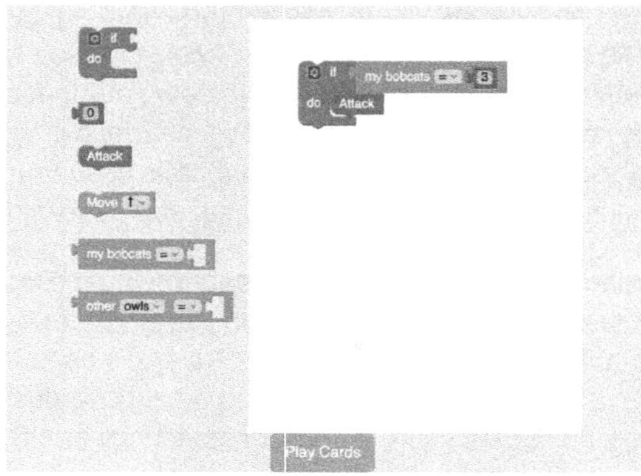

Figure 3: AI rule "cards." Currently implemented through Blockly, but in the future there will also be a card system.

Conclusion and Future Work

There are still many features to be added or completed before this game can be used in research. One major component is the AI coding system. Currently, it uses Blockly custom blocks; however, a system of "cards" that can be built incrementally would be much preferred. Future experiments could study the differences between the two methods of implementing the coding section of the game. Playtesting and iterating the game design is also needed. The current iteration also lacks a mechanism to make the code logic more visible to the players as they execute their code. Highlighting the code and the actions as they occur step-by-step would be one method of making the logic visible.

Once the game is ready for research, studies will be done to measure the impact of the game on children's attitudes towards computer science and programming. These measures and other learning gains—specifically their understanding of computational thinking skills and conditional statements—will be measured through pretests and posttests. Discourse data could also be gathered to study the interactions between participants during the game. We hope to launch this game-exhibit to science museums in various locations in order to reach a diverse audience.

REFERENCES

1. Sue Allen. 2004. Designs for learning: Studying science museum exhibits that do more than entertain. *Science Education* 88, SUPPL. 1 (2004).
2. Noah Weeth Feinstein and David Meshoulam. 2014. Science for what public? Addressing equity in American science museums and science centers. *Journal of Research in Science Teaching* 51, 3 (2014), 368–394.
3. James J Gibson. 1977. Perceiving, acting, and knowing: Toward an ecological psychology. *The Theory of Affordances* (1977), 67–82.
4. Amanda Lenhart and others. 2015. Teens, social media & technology overview 2015. *Pew Research Center* 9 (2015).
5. Donald A Norman. 1988. *The psychology of everyday things.* Basic books.
6. Seymour Papert. 1980. *Mindstorms: Children, computers, and powerful ideas.* Basic Books, Inc.
7. Mitchel Resnick, John Maloney, Andrés Monroy-Hernández, Natalie Rusk, Evelyn Eastmond, Karen Brennan, Amon Millner, Eric Rosenbaum, Jay Silver, Brian Silverman, and others. 2009. Scratch: programming for all. *Commun. ACM* 52, 11 (2009), 60–67.
8. Barbara P Schneider and Nicole Cheslock. 2003. *Measuring Results.* Coevolution Institute San Francisco, CA.

Knitting Visualizer: Connecting Craft and Code

Stephanie Yang
Columbia University Teachers College
New York, NY 10027, USA
syy2114@tc.columbia.edu

IDC '17, June 27-30, 2017, Stanford, CA, USA

ACM ISBN 978-1-4503-4921-5/17/06.
http://dx.doi.org/10.1145/3078072.3091985

Abstract
The Knitting Visualizer aims to highlight the relationship between craft and computation. This demo is targeted at amateur knitters who have a basic familiarity with programming and who would like to develop their own knitting patterns. The demo features two-way translation between Javascript code and a symbolic knitting chart with a preview of the physical product. Future work is planned to improve on this demo.

Author Keywords
knitting; programming languages; novice programming

ACM Classification Keywords
J.5 Computer applications: fine arts; K.3.2 Computer science education; K.8.1 Personal computing: freeware

Introduction
Margolis and Fisher [7] show that girls are typically not encouraged to pursue programming or other technical practices as frequently as boys, recreationally as well as formally, due to gender-based assumptions or unconscious biases. The activities girls are encouraged to pursue are those not considered technical, leading people to ignore any connections between the two. Knitting is one such activity. Despite assumptions that knitting and other craft practices are non-technical, there is a close relationship between craft culture and

technological culture both metaphorically and historically [2].

Buechley identifies multiple mathematical considerations central to producing some pieces of craftwork, knit or otherwise [3]. Others have highlighted the relationship between crafting and math or science [1]. Many scholars have also begun exploring ways to mix craftwork and electronics using microcontrollers and e-textiles [5,10]. These creative studies illustrate the applicability of traditional technology towards artistic and craft-based activities or vice versa, as well as the new possibilities for artifacts produced by using the two together. However, these mixed approaches tend to emphasize scientific concepts as a comparatively external design element. For example, both Kafai et al. [5] and Weibert et al. [10] consider the use of electronics as part of sewing projects and belcastro and Yackel [1] share knitting patterns that intentionally model mathematical designs. Few of these highlight the inherently procedural and computational aspect of the process of knitting itself, with or without electronic components. Craig et al. [4] explicitly describes the relationship between knitting pattern conventions and basic programming concepts.

Building on these relationships between craft and computing, the knitting visualizer seeks to highlight the computational aspect of knitting and use it to aid knitters in developing their own knitting patterns.

Demo Description

The knitting visualizer is intended as a constructionist environment [8,9] in which users are able to tinker with knitting patterns while using Javascript code to formalize or structure their work. The visualizer's intended use case is for knitters to use the code and manual edit features to create and tinker with custom knitting patterns. Some basic knitting knowledge is assumed on the part of the user.

Knitting patterns typically feature instructions on how to knit a particular piece. These instructions include written directions specifying what stitches to do in each row and/or symbolic charts specifying the same information visually. The visualizer allows the user to use Javascript code to generate a knitting pattern or use a knitting pattern to generate directions in code. Because the code is interpreted and generated based on basic functions analogous to existing knitting conventions (e.g., *knit(3)*, *purlRow()*), the generated code should be easily recognizable to any reader familiar with knitting stitches. In this way, the visualizer enables fluid two-way translation between written knitting specifications and the knitted pattern that would result from those specifications.

To encourage users to tinker with their patterns, the visualizer allows users to edit their patterns manually by modifying existing patterns stitch by stitch, or they may edit programmatically by writing and modifying Javascript code to generate full patterns. The site also includes options to resize the chart according to the user's specifications as well as a limited color palette with which to visualize multicolored patterns. Users may also toggle between "chart" view, a symbolic knitting chart, and "pattern" view, representing a rough visualization of what an item knit according to the user's specifications would look like. This is intended to help users quickly envision their patterns' end result without needing to spend significant amounts of time knitting test items (Figure 1).

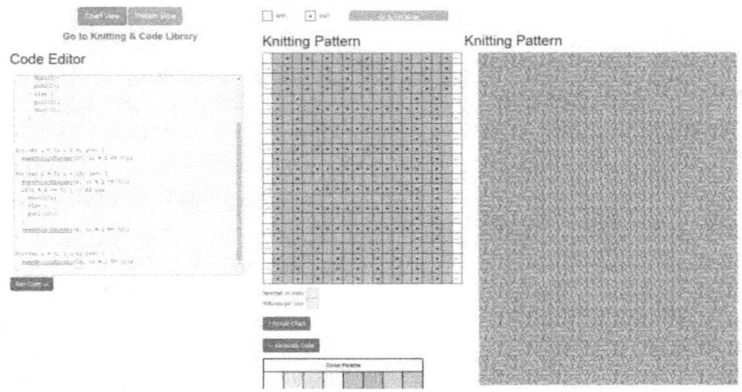

Figure 1: The current prototype version of the knitting visualizer, allowing two-way translation between Javascript code specifications for a knitting pattern and a symbolic chart pattern communicating equivalent specifications. The pattern view in this project allows a rough visual preview of what a knitted product made according to these instructions would look like.

A prototype version of this project has been developed and is currently hosted online at the following URL: http://www.columbia.edu/~syy2114/knitting-visualizer/

Limitations

Currently the prototype has several limitations. Some may be improved with time (e.g., error feedback, sparse reference library) but conceptually two major limitations stand out for this project that affect the relevance of this project to potential users.

First, this prototype is best used by an audience familiar with both Javascript code and the symbology of knitting charts, which is a specific subset of the overall target audience of amateur knitters.

Second, the scope of knitting patterns produced by the project is limited in comparison to the vast range of knitted products. The preview feature is a limiting factor here: the process of generating realistic visualizations of arbitrary knitting patterns is complex [6] and the designer's own amateur understanding of the physical nature of stitches and techniques additionally limits visualization. As a result, the prototype limits patterns to flat, fixed-width patterns achieved with knit and purl stitches only. While all knitting patterns generated within this project are technically possible to knit, the space of generable patterns represents only a subset of possible patterns.

Future Work

Further work on this project will address the first limitation, with a planned redesign of the coding portion so that users unfamiliar with Javascript or similar languages may instead use a programmatic but more symbolically familiar language grounded in knitting conventions in order to create knitting pattern specifications. Research is currently being conducted in order to determine what concepts may be most useful for such a language.

Although Javascript is used as the programming language in this application for convenience, a language more grounded in knitting practices would be more accessible to users unfamiliar with code. This would make the visualizer available to a wider audience, with the further goal of exploring how this project can be used to draw connections between craft and computation for amateur knitters. This could be especially helpful for girls and young women with crafting experience but little exposure to programming.

Practical Considerations
No special accommodations for this demo should be necessary other than a computer and a projector, as this project is hosted and available on the Internet.

Acknowledgements
I would like to thank my advisor, Dr. Nathan Holbert, for his support and encouragement throughout my work on this project.

References
1. sarah-marie belcastro and Carolyn Yackel. 2011. Crafting by Concepts: Fiber Arts and Mathematics. A.K. Peters Ltd., Natick, MA.
2. Jack Z. Bratich and Heidi M. Brush. 2011. Fabricating activism: Craft-work, popular culture, gender. Utopian studies 22 2: 233-260.
3. Buechley, L. Inclusive Maker Education: STEM is Everywhere. *FabLearn 2016*.
4. Michelle Craig, Sarah Petersen, and Andrew Petersen. 2012. Following a thread: knitting patterns and program tracing. In Proceedings of the 43rd ACM technical symposium on Computer Science Education (SIGCSE '12). ACM, New York, NY, USA, 233-238. http://dx.doi.org/10.1145/2157136.2157204
5. Yasmin B. Kafai, Eunkyoung Lee, Kristin Searle, Deborah Fields, Eliot Kaplan, and Debora Lui. 2014. A Crafts-Oriented Approach to Computing in High School: Introducing Computational Concepts, Practices, and Perspectives with Electronic Textiles. *Trans. Comput. Educ.* 14, 1, Article 1 (March 2014). http://dx.doi.org/10.1145/2576874
6. Jonathan M. Kaldor, Doug L. James, and Steve Marschner. 2008. Simulating knitted cloth at the yarn level. In *ACM SIGGRAPH 2008 papers* (SIGGRAPH '08). ACM, New York, NY, USA, Article 65. https://doi.org/10.1145/1399504.1360664
7. Allan Fisher and Jane Margolis. 2003. Unlocking the clubhouse: women in computing. SIGCSE Bull. 35, 1 (January 2003), .23-. http://dx.doi.org/10.1145/792548.611896
8. Seymour Papert. 1980. Mindstorms: Children, Computers, and Powerful Ideas. Basic Books, Inc., New York, NY, USA.
9. Seymour Papert and Idit Harel. 1991. Situating constructionism. *Constructionism* 36, 2: 1-11.
10. Anne Weibert, Andrea Marshall, Konstantin Aal, Kai Schubert, and Jennifer Rode. 2014. Sewing interest in E-textiles: analyzing making from a gendered perspective. In Proceedings of the 2014 conference on Designing interactive systems (DIS '14). ACM, New York, NY, USA, 15-24. http://dx.doi.org/10.1145/2598510.2600886

Cool Cities A Tangible User Interface for Thinking Critically about Climate Change

Sonia Doshi
Stanford University
doshisd@stanford.edu

Kimiya Hojjat
Stanford University
khojjat@stanford.edu

Anita Lin
Stanford University
anitalin@stanford.edu

Paulo Blikstein
Stanford University
paulob@stanford.edu

IDC '17, June 27-30, 2017, Stanford, CA, USA

ACM ISBN 978-1-4503-4921-5/17/06.
http://dx.doi.org/10.1145/3078072.3091986

Abstract
Understanding the relationship between human behavior and environmental impact is an important challenge for young learners. Children can benefit from learning experiences that enable them to actively consider and negotiate the complex tradeoffs that inform global issues. To address this challenge, we propose Cool Cities: a tangible user interface (TUI) game in which children aged 7-9 design environmentally friendly cities around different social and financial objectives. Learners place game pieces on the TUI to see their environmental and financial impact, which is reflected through a responsive display for learners to evaluate their decisions in real-time. We hope that by designing a constructivist learning experience in which learners practice the complex modeling and critical thinking needed for large-scale urban planning projects, they can better relate concepts of global warming to their lived experiences and discover powerful ideas for improving the world we live in.

Author Keywords
Tangible User Interfaces, Constructivism, Environmental Science Education, Negotiation, Peer-to-Peer Learning

ACM Classification Keywords
H.5.2 User Interfaces

Figure 1. One-dimensional representation of environmental impact, abstracted.

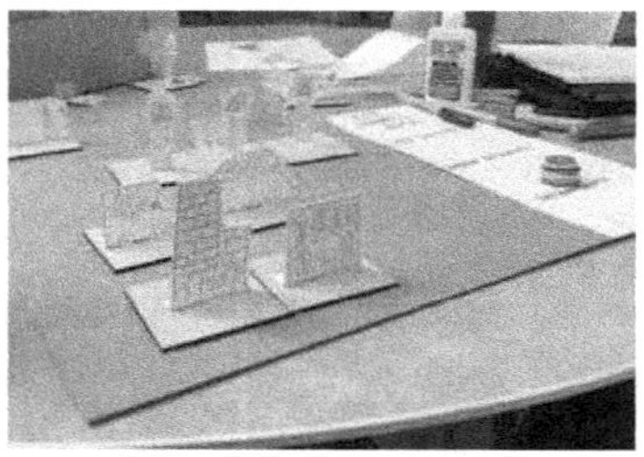

Figure 2. Three-dimensional representation of environmental impact, not abstracted (air quality, energy efficiency, and sustainability) with manual feedback.

1. INTRODUCTION

Despite increasing urgency around issues in environmental science education, students in the U.S. are largely under-informed about the complexity of climate change and how their day-to-day actions contribute to its effects [3]. We confront this knowledge-action gap with Cool Cities: a tangible learning experience that enables children to address tradeoffs between budgetary and environmental constraints. Together learners choose different physical elements of a city and negotiate a design based on various societal objectives. These elements communicate with the interface via programmed fiducials to display the resulting financial and environmental impact of their decisions. With a limited amount of resources (money and space), learners acting as city planners can engage in critical discourse and address these objectives creatively. Empowering kids to take on these important roles puts them face-to-face with the same types of challenges and gives them an opportunity to experiment with solutions.

2. BACKGROUND

Cool Cities provides a context where children can analyze and evaluate future possibilities of their environment in a concrete way. Several works informed the learning and design principles we applied. First, multiple perspectives reinforce the importance of teaching the complexities of environmental science to young children [4, 5]. Mochizuki and Bryan [5] emphasize how climate change highlights the relationships between environmental, social, and economic factors. Cool Cities provides a similar interdisciplinary environment for children to analyze these relationships. By interacting with digital artifacts that model the nuances of urban planning experiences, learners can start to develop concrete thought about abstract concepts related to environmental impact.

Secondly, interactive tabletops in particular facilitate joint attention and create a shared space in which learners can negotiate and manipulate artifacts collaboratively [1].

Furthermore, the TUI game externalizes the tensions involved in urban planning by providing a responsive system in which learners can immediately see and assess their decisions. In this regard, Cool Cities supports a grounded experience in which students sort and evaluate their options, gaining a deeper understanding of complex socio-environmental relationships.

Overall, learners can experiment with their understanding of the world and adapt their knowledge as they discover the changes needed for a new reality [6]. Such exploratory, agent-based learning environments can be empowering platforms for critical thinking, negotiation, and, we hope, behavior change. Further, exploring connections between real and modeled systems can catalyze inquiry toward deeper understanding of scientific phenomena [2]. By providing a framework for both physically and mentally constructing a fictitious city and its associated carbon emissions impact, Cool Cities fosters constructivist-learning experiences that could help children make more environmentally conscious choices.

3. DESIGN OVERVIEW & PRACTICAL CONSIDERATIONS

Figure 3. Current Version. TUI interface interacting with physical elements in play.

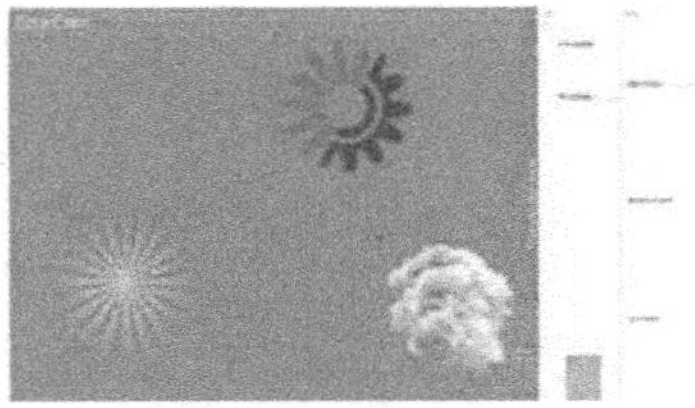

Figure 4. Current Version. Environmental impact is represented with two bar graphs: budget and carbon emissions, numerical values are abstracted. Other visual feedback includes temporal images, such as sunlight and smoke for certain elements, and neutral images for others.

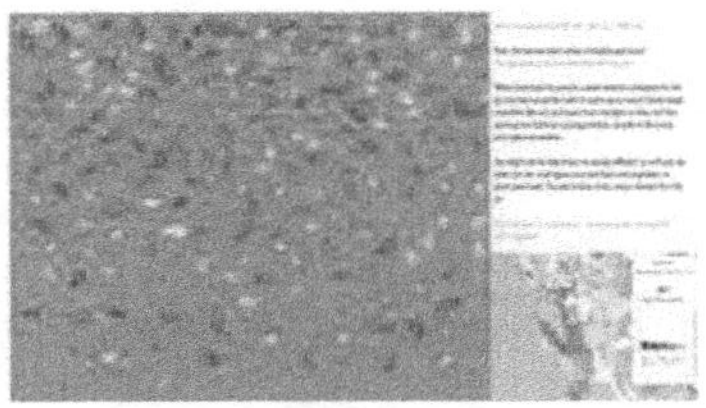

Figure 5. Current Version. Confetti and information panel displayed at the end of interaction.

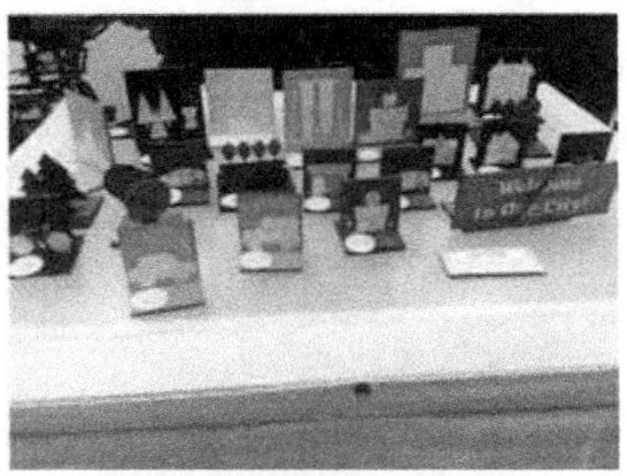

Figure 6. Current Version. City elements are laser cut and painted, with fiducials attached to the bottom.

Cool Cities is a multi-modal game experience built on the Processing language that uses an 18 by 24 inch TUI tabletop surface and laser-cut wooden game pieces (Figure 3). Each game piece represents a city element such as a building or park (Figure 6) and provides immediate visual feedback upon placement in the following ways: 1) a pair of responsive bar graphs fluctuating to changes in monetary allowance and carbon emissions, 2) images, such as smoke or sun rays, that appear directly under the element to provide more visual engagement between the physical components and the digital experience, and finally 3) a panel of information that compares the final design to a real city in the U.S. This final panel provides players with actionable insights for how they can transfer knowledge gained through their Cool Cities experience to their everyday lives.

4. DESIGN PROCESS

Cool Cities has gone through three major design iterations. Our first iteration (Figure 1) tested both the technical implementation of the experience, and the saliency of visual feedback to which users responded. We used an analog model for our second iteration to test the game play and interactive principles (Figure 2), which consisted of a cardboard interface with hand-drawn meters for air quality, energy efficiency, and sustainability. We tested this prototype with 3 children aged 7, 9, and 11 for conceptual clarity. Our most significant insights from these tests informed our decisions to include the following features in our third iteration:

- **Emphasis on Tradeoffs Between Monetary Impact and Carbon Emissions:** We wanted children to experiment with measurable outcomes that were intuitive and in tension with each other, in ways that the original environmental metrics were not to our users. In response, we included the monetary impact and carbon levels of their city visualized as two responsive bar graphs on the interface.
- **Responsive Visual Cues:** To provide more salient feedback about chosen elements, we programmed each game piece to display images representing positive, negative, and neutral impact when placed on the screen (Figure 4).
- **Peer Learning:** To encourage peer-to-peer learning and foster collaboration and negotiation skills, we included a character component. Learners take on one of two specific agent roles (mayor or environmental engineer) with an associated, and, often, conflicting objective (stay under budget, or maintain healthy carbon levels, respectively). Sometimes environmentally friendly choices can be expensive.
- **Focus Cards:** To anchor the players to a collective goal around their individual efforts as mayor or engineer, we included a series of citywide social objectives such as accommodating a large influx of tourists.
- **Real City Information:** To transfer knowledge to real-world experiences, we included real city information that correlated to their final design. For example, resulting cities with high carbon levels are compared to Houston, Texas, and learners are given suggestions for being environmentally conscious in their daily lives (Figure 5).

5. EVALUATION

We tested Cool Cities with a variety of adults and children in our age group at a learning technology exposition hosted by the Stanford Graduate School of Education. Two children, in particular, returned multiple times to play with Cool Cities and successfully negotiated the design of their cities against a variety of prompts. For example, when they were given the aforementioned tourist focus card, they debated which elements of their city they would need to remove in order to add an amusement park and keep their carbon emission levels low. High enthusiasm and successful performance from our target learners suggested how impactful Cool Cities could be as a learning tool for creative and collaborative problem solving in environmental education.

6. CONCLUSION & FUTURE WORK

Cool Cities enables children to explore tradeoffs between monetary and environmental impact. Constructing a city through peer-mediated interactions seems to encourage discourse around environmental tradeoffs, using the data produced by the system as a productive platform for argumentation. Future work may target additional or more complex tradeoffs. Subsequent iterations could also incorporate feedback around larger environmental trends. This could promote discourse about how environmental impact fluctuates over time and how human factors affect these changes. We could also scale the display of impact across multiple pieces that are placed together. We see Cool Cities as a system not environmental education, but as a platform for young learners to investigate social and natural phenomena with complex emergent behavior.

References

1. Wise, A. F., Antle, A. N., Warren, J., May, A., Fan, M. & Macaranas, A. (2015). What kind of world do you want to live in?: Positive interdependenceand collaborative processes in the land-use planning game "Youtopia." In Proceedings of the 11th International Conference on Computer Supported Learning (pp. 236-243). Gothenburg, Sweden: ICLS.

2. Paulo Blikstein. 2012. Bifocal modeling: a study on the learning outcomes of comparing physical and computational models linked in real time. In *Proceedings of the 14th ACM International Conference on Multimodal Interaction* (ICMI '12). ACM, New York, NY, USA, 257-264. DOI: http://dx.doi.org/10.1145/2388676.2388729

3. Richard J. Bord, Robert E. O'connor, and Ann Fisher. 2000. In what sense does the public need to understand global climate change? *Public Understanding of Science* 9, 3 (July 2000), 205–218. DOI:http://dx.doi.org/10.1088/0963-6625/9/3/301

4. Dana Fusco. 2001. Creating relevant science through urban planning and gardening. *Journal of Research in Science Teaching* 38, 8 (June 2001), 860–877. DOI:http://dx.doi.org/10.1002/tea.1036

5. Yoko Mochizuki and Audrey Bryan. 2015. Climate Change Education in the Context of Education for Sustainable Development: Rationale and Principles. *Journal of Education for Sustainable Development* 9, 1 (June 2015), 4–26. DOI:http://dx.doi.org/10.1177/0973408215569109

6. Seymour Papert. 1980. *Mindstorms: children, computers, and powerful ideas*, New York, NY: Basicbooks.

StringForce – A Forced Collaborative Interaction Game for Special Education

Wolmet Barendregt
University of Gothenburg
Göteborg, Sweden
wolmet.barendregt@gu.se

Eva Eriksson
Aarhus University, Aarhus, Denmark
Chalmers University of Technology, Göteborg, Sweden
evae@cc.au.dk

Peter Börjesson
University of Gothenburg &
Chalmers University of Technology
Göteborg, Sweden
peter.borjesson@gu.se

Olof Torgersson
University of Gothenburg &
Chalmers University of Technology
Göteborg, Sweden
olof.torgersson@gu.se

IDC '17, June 27-30, 2017, Stanford, CA, USA

ACM ISBN 978-1-4503-4921-5/17/06.
http://dx.doi.org/10.1145/3078072.3091987

Abstract

In this paper, we present the forced collaborative interaction game StringForce. StringForce is developed for a special education context to support training of collaboration skills, using readily available technologies and avoiding the creation of a "mobile bubble". In order to play StringForce two or four physically collocated tablets are required. These tablets are connected to form one large shared game area. The game can only be played by collaborating. StringForce extends previous work, both technologically and regarding social-emotional training. We believe StringForce to be an interesting demo for the IDC community, as it intertwines several relevant research fields, such as mobile interaction and collaborative gaming in the special education context.

Author Keywords

Forced Interaction; children, Child-Computer Interaction; special education; collaboration.

ACM Classification Keywords

H5.2. User Interfaces: Evaluation/methodology, User-centered design.

Introduction

The way we interact with computers has been revolutionized by the introduction of touch technology.

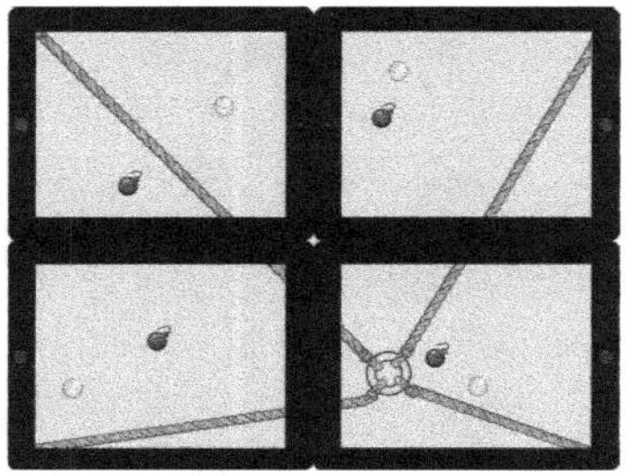

Figure 1: Four tablets arranged to create a large game board in StringForce.

1. People are co-located, letting them directly or indirectly notice each other's bodily presence.
2. There are easily noticed distinctions between those participating and those not participating.
3. Everybody involved focuses their attention upon the same thing or activity, and is aware that everybody else has the same focus.
4. All participants share a common emotion or mood related to the activity

Table 1: Collins' four necessary ingredients for interaction rituals [3, p.48]

Due to the direct and intuitive mode of interaction, **touch devices** can be used for diverse groups of users and the suitability of touch interaction for groups with intellectual disabilities (ID) has been noted in several studies, e.g. [10]. In contrast to regular computers they remove the need to use a mouse as a navigation device, which can provide challenges for people with cognitive and/or motor disabilities. Touch devices, e.g. tablets are therefore becoming increasingly popular in various educational settings, such as in Swedish compulsory school for children with learning disabilities. A variety of applications (or apps) are used both for training and leisure, such as Empatico to recognize emotions [5] and Minecraft to practice communication [12]. However, the vast majority of all apps developed for tablets are aimed at one user using the device alone, possibly communicating with others located somewhere else physically. There is a tendency that we are "Alone together" [15], each one enclosed in his or her **mobile bubble**.

Social relationships are of specific importance for children's mental health, as having friendships works as a protective factor against depression in children with communicative difficulties [2]. However, children with ID tend to have fewer and less intimate friendships compared to typically developing children [16], and the experience of social interaction with peers is not always enjoyable as exposure to bullying is also common among children with ID [3]. As a result, children with ID may have difficulties developing friendships and are often engaged in solitary play [7]. A possible solution is to engage children with ID in **playful collaborative activities** in which they can train their collaboration skills and get a sense of togetherness. Togetherness can be understood as the product of successful interaction rituals. According to Collins [3], who bases his work on Goffman [6] and Durkheim [4], a successful Interaction Ritual between people creates, among others, group solidarity and a sense of membership. On an individual level it creates a "feeling of confidence, elation, strength, enthusiasm, and initiative in taking action" [3, p. 49]. This kind of interaction is potentially useful for creating a bond between children. Collins states four necessary ingredients for these interaction rituals (see Table 1). Playing collaborative games, in contrast to competitive or solo games, is an activity that incorporates all these four ingredients as has been explored by Bergström [1]. Further, the **game rules** provide structure to the activity and thereby make it less difficult to understand than free play or unstructured everyday social interaction.

Large screen displays and tabletop computers, form a great platform for co-located collaborative games, as systems such as Tisch [8] point towards. Tabletop technologies have successfully been used to build applications to train social and emotional skills with autistic people [14], as they open up for a collective space where several users can share a screen.

However, as tabletop computers are still rather expensive, suggestions have also been made that tablets could, at a lower cost, encourage pro-social behavior through **sharing an interactive surface and passing the tablet to a partner** [10]. Since many special education schools already have access to tablets, this could be one viable way to create a technology to train collaborative skills.

Within the Computer Supported Cooperative Work area a well-known concept is single display groupware (SDG) systems, an interaction model where several persons have their own input devices but share a common output device [9]. However, an alternative is using the displays of several mobile phones or tablets to create one common game area. Related to this kind of collaborative activity is Collective Interaction [11, 13]. Collective Interaction puts focus on designing for **co-experiences among co-located people**. There are five key elements to consider when designing for Collective Interaction [13]:

1. The interaction itself invites for human-human interaction beyond what is in the interface – potentially deviating discussions from what is displayed
2. The spatial organization of people induces expectations of use
3. A shared goal is established on the basis of sharing responsibility and negotiating control of interaction
4. Establishing shared goal through negotiation is essential both in order to achieve the goal and in order to challenge it through e.g. teasing other participants.
5. The interaction may be asymmetrical, in the sense that people take on different roles, but the efforts of all participants are accounted for and valued in the use of the system.

Based on all elements discussed above, we have developed StringForce, a game with forced collaborative interaction.

StringForce

StringForce aims to provide children in special education with a way to practice collaboration in a rule-based co-located game, through touch-based interaction. Instead of using expensive tabletops it runs on technologies readily available in many special education schools. Based on interviews with teachers, the game forces the children to collaborate instead of allowing or encouraging collaboration.

In StringForce, two or four players use a tablet each, gathered in the same physical space to create a larger game area (see Figure 1). The players have to collaborate in moving a cursor connected to four strings to collect different items on the game board. There are also obstacles to avoid. When players progress through the game, both collectable items and obstacles move around to make the game more difficult. To clear a level, the players need to collect all items with the cursor and avoid the obstacles. The cursor is moved simultaneously by all players by either dragging or releasing their part of the string. The game requires the players to both create a common goal, i.e. the item to collect next, and to constantly communicate about how to reach that item.

StringForce utilizes Bluetooth for communication between devices and does not rely on a web-server. Instead, one of the tablets takes on the role of server, and manages message handling and updates between the other devices. During early tests of the setup procedure where one of the children had to start the game and invite others to participate, it was noted that the children struggled with the necessary steps to set up the game. They did not understand the order of the actions, and became competitive about being the one that hosted the game and invited others.

Therefore, an improved way to handle the setup of the game was designed. To counteract competition about being the one to host the game, the setup was

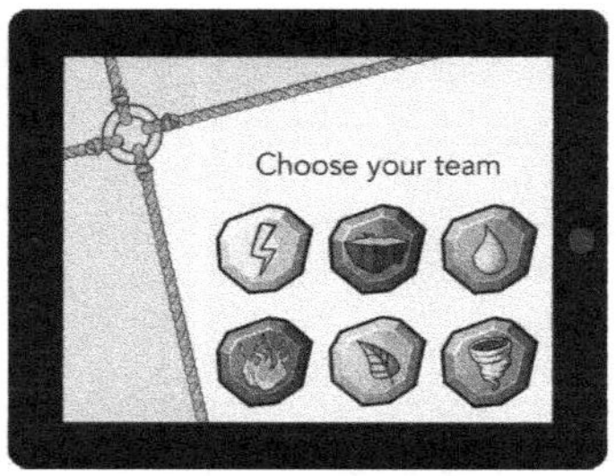

Figure 2: Start screen where players choose a team to play in.

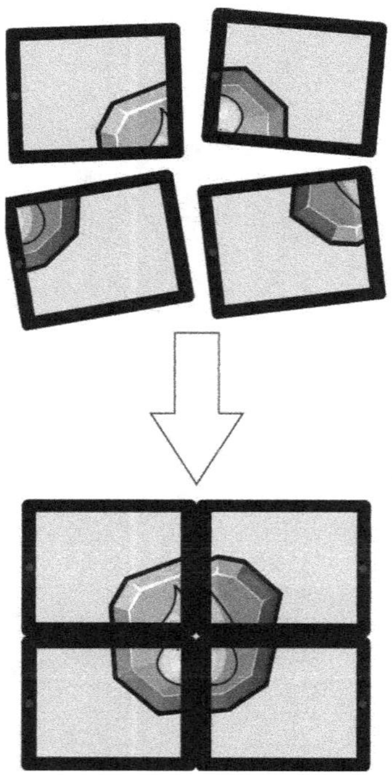

Figure 3: Setup screen where players solve a puzzle.

designed to hide which tablet acted as host, and moved the action of inviting others to the game. In the new version, children simply choose one of six teams to play in (see Figure 2), and the game assigns one of the tablets as server. The next part of the setup requires children to arrange the tablets in a correct way to build the game board. This is solved by asking the children to puzzle together an image showing the team they have chosen to play in (see Figure 3). A problem with the current solution is that the tablets' frames skew the image, making the puzzle harder to solve.

Practical Considerations

The demo consists of four iPads, so a table is needed where all four iPads can fit next to each other. Power outlets to charge the iPads would be preferable.

Acknowledgements

The work presented in this paper is a part of the Touch AT! project funded by the Marcus and Amalia Wallenberg Foundation under grant 2013.0063. We would like to thank Markus Norén Andersson and Sarar Innab for their programming excellence.

References

1. Karl Bergström. 2012. Playing for Togetherness - Designing for Interaction Rituals through Gaming Department of Applied Information Technology, Gothenburg University.
2. Catherine M. Cappadocia, Jonathan A. Weiss and D. Pepler. 2011. Bullying experiences among children and youth with autism spectrum disorders. J Autism Dev Disord, 42 (2). 266-277.
3. Randall Collins. 2004. Interaction ritual chains. Princeton University Press.
4. Emile Durkheim. 1912. The Elementary Forms of the Religious Life. Free Press.
5. Empaticus. 2013. www.empaticus.se.
6. Erving Goffman. 1961. Encounters: two studies in the sociology of interaction. Bobbs-Merrill.
7. Michael J. Guralnick. 2006. Peer relationships and the mental health of young children with intellectual delays. J. of Policy and Practice in Intellectual Disabilities, 3 (1). 49-56.
8. Ulf Hartelius, Johan Fröhlander, Staffan Björk. 2012. Tisch digital tools supporting board games Proceedings of the International Conference on the Foundations of Digital Games, ACM, Raleigh, North Carolina, 196-203.
9. Eva Hornecker, Paul Marshall, Sheep Dalton and Yvonne Rogers. 2008. Collaboration and interference: awareness with mice or touch input. in CSCW '08, ACM Press, 167-176.
10. Jean Pablo Hourcade, N.E. Bullock-Rest and T.E. Hansen. 2012. Multitouch tablet applications and activities to enhance the social skills of children with autism spectrum disorders. Personal Ubiquitous Comput, 16 (2). 157-168.
11. Peter G. Krogh and Marianne G. Petersen. 2008. Collective Interaction--Let's join forces. in COOP, 20-23.
12. Minecraft. 2016. www.minecraft.se.
13. Marianne G. Petersen, Peter G. Krogh, Morten B. Mortensen, Thomas Møller-Lassen and Ditte Hvas Mortensen. 2010. Collective interaction by design collective controllers for social navigation on digital photos. in 6th Nordic Conference on Human-Computer Interaction: Extending Boundaries (NordiCHI '10), ACM, 353-362.
14. Anne Marie Piper, Eileen O'Brien, Meredith Ringel Morris and Terry Winograd. 2006. SIDES: A Cooperative Tabletop Computer Game for Social Skills Development. In proceedings of CSCW '06, ACM Press, New York, New York, USA, 1-10.
15. Sherry Turkle. 2011. Alone Together: Why We Expect More from Technology and Less from Each Other. Basic Books, New York.
16. Amanda Webster and Mark Carter. 2007. Social relationships and friendship of children with developmental disabilities: implications for inclusive settings. A systematic review. J. of Intellecual & Developmental Disability, 32 (3). 200-213.

On Active Sharing and Responses to Joint Attention Bids by Children with Autism in a Loosely Coupled Collaborative Play Environment

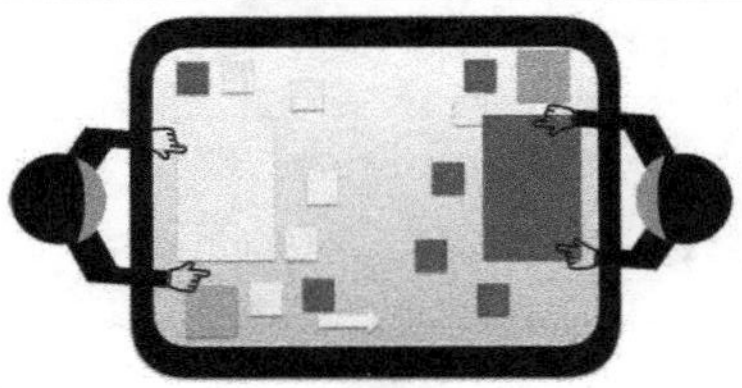

Figures 1: The basic illustration of the tabletop puzzle game.

Tiffany Y. Tang
Media Lab
Dept. of Computer Science
Wenzhou-Kean University
yatang@kean.edu

Aonan Guan
Media Lab
Dept. of Computer Science
Wenzhou-Kean University
guana@kean.edu

Pinata Winoto
Media Lab
Dept. of Computer Science
Wenzhou-Kean University
pwinoto@kean.edu

IDC '17, June 27-30, 2017, Stanford, CA, USA

ACM ISBN 978-1-4503-4921-5/17/06.
http://dx.doi.org/10.1145/3078072.3091988

Abstract

Social reputation management is essential in social interactions and believed to be mediated by the intrinsic motive to preserve and improve one's social reputation. Moreover, these activities are often only loosely structured. Prior studies revealed that children with autism spectrum disorder (ASD) are less sensitive to social reputation than their typically developing (TD) peers, which might explain their lack of reciprocity and desire to engage in social activities, despite that their brain functions that underpin social interaction remain intact with delayed development. Little is known about their reciprocity in loosely coupled collaboration environment where Free Play (FP, rather than Enforced Collaboration, or EC) is imposed. Our study in the long run aims at addressing this issue by engaging ASD children in a collaborative puzzle game where each child has a private work-space. The present study focuses on the design and development of such an application unfolded through a series of small-scale pilot studies with Chinese children at three different autism centers in the city. Preliminary qualitative and in-game quantitative results showed that their skills in reciprocity, active sharing aiming to completing their

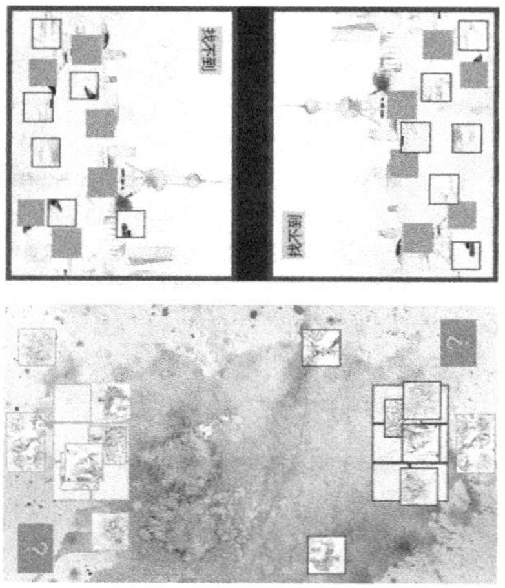

Figure 2: The system user interfaces; the top one (v2.0) includes colored border indicating ownership for each puzzle and workspace, a blue button can be pressed to seek help; the bottom one (v3.0) is the latest version where help button was replaced using a symbol since some ASD children cannot recognize words.

own task, (selective) initiating and responding to joint attention bids have satisfying been remedied and optimized in such a loosely structured play environment. There are two uniqueness of our study; one lies in the design of a loosely coupled collaborative play environment; another is to quantitatively measure some joint attention skills through children's behavioral actions.

Author Keywords

Autism; joint attention skills; reciprocity; collaboration; loosely structured play environment.

ACM Classification Keywords

H.5.m. Information interfaces and presentation (e.g., HCI): Miscellaneous.

Introduction and Background

Different from those collaborative games in [1, 2, 5, 7, 8, 10, 11, 13], ours provide each child with their private work-space. In this paper, we will describe the design and development of such an application unfolded through a series of small-scale pilot studies with Chinese children at three different autism centers in the city. The uniqueness of the game lies in its built-in automatic behavioral data collection which could provide insights on ASD children's performances and degree of reciprocity. Preliminary qualitative and in-game quantitative results on their skills in reciprocity and response to joint attention bids will be briefly discussed. To the best of our knowledge, such an application and study is one of the first of its kind in China.

The Development of a Loosely Coupled Collaborative Puzzle Game

In our previous work [13], two versions of the application were developed (referred to as v1.0). In order to accommodate teachers' and parents' feedbacks and in accordance with some key design patterns suggested in [9] for joint attention training and [4] for game design for ASD children, we delivered the revised version, v2.0 and v3.0 (see Figure 2). These two versions of the system had undergone two rounds of testing with both high-and low-functioning ASD children at two centers. Compared to v1.0 in [13], the most unique features of our game (referred to as v3.0) is a built-in game data collection module which can be used to assess the quantitative degree of reciprocity. Figure 3 shows these parameters.

Parameter	Application Output	Description	Notes
		Performance	
moveLX	LX move	the number of total moves for L player to put LX to the right place	
moveRX	RX move	the number of total moves for R player to put RX to the right place	
pcsLXSpan	pcsLXSpan	the time duration of L player to put LX to the right place	
pcsRXSpan	pcsRXSpan	the time duration of R player to put RX to the right place	
lXWrong	LX wrong at@ LY/RY	Piece LX was put at the wrong place (shown with correct position)	
rXWrong	RX wrong at@ LY/RY	Piece RX was put at the wrong place (shown with correct position)	
		Reciprocity	
askLGiveR	L helped R after being asked	The frequency of helps L player provided to the R player when being asked	
askRGiveL	R helped L after being asked	The frequency of helps R player provided to the L player when being asked	
notAskLGiveR	L helped R without being asked	The frequency of helps L player provided to the R player without being asked	active sharing
notAskRGiveL	R helped L without being asked	The frequency of helps R player provided to the L player without being asked	active sharing
lAskHelp	L Asked Help	The frequency of help-seeking by L player (by pressing the 'help' button)	
rAskHelp	R Asked Help	The frequency of help-seeking by R player (by pressing the 'help' button)	

Figure 3: In-game player behavioral data in the latest game

Since each player has 12 puzzle pieces, we label the pieces for left and right player as L1 (R1) to L12 (R12) respectively. X and Y represent the 2D index of each

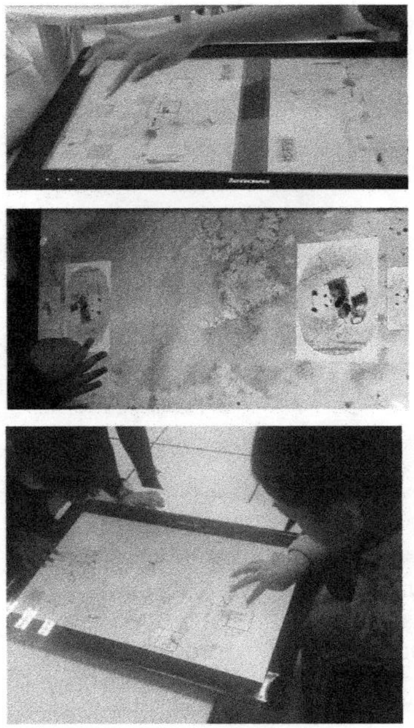

Figure 4: The top image shows a testing moment with the game (v2.0); while the middle captures a testing moment with the latest version of the game (v3.0) without the built-in data collection modules. The bottom one shows the game-playing moment where player actions were automatically recorded; both children and teachers were observed to provide physical, verbal and gestural prompts.

puzzle piece (see the bottom image in Figure 4 for the user interface of this version).

Findings and General Discussions

Due to space limitation, we report results obtained in the last pilot study with the system (v3.0).

Pilot Study Background and Participants

Three children joined our test; a girl of eight years old with HFASD and hyperactivity disorder (ADHD) (denoted as C1), a boy with HFASD of ten years old (denoted as C2), and a LFASD boy of nine years old (denoted as C3). The quantitative results were shown in Figure 5. In terms of overall performance, the HFASD boy (C2) scores the highest with relatively low error rate (19.7%) and much quicker average moving time (3644 ms) among the three. Both C1 and C3 sought comparable number of requests while C1 provided more proactive helps (helping without being asked). Overall, all children were able to provide proactive helps later in the game; but the child with LFASD (C3) responded less to joint attention bids than the other two.

Player	Levels played	Total moves	Avg.moving time (ms)	Error rate (%)	Number of help requests	Number of responses to help	Number of proactive helps
C1	6	92	9101	17.4%	12	0	8
C2	6	71	3644	19.7%	0	3	4
C3	3	69	6767	24.6%	11	0	2

Figure 5: Testing results (quantitative) in terms of reciprocity and general performance

General Discussions

The results of the present study is consistent with previous findings that some children with ASD are capable of engaging in some components of joint attention including looking in the direction of a point, without specific instruction or intervention [9]. Children were observed to be able to initialize bids for other individuals' joint attention by pointing to an object of interest so as to merely make request (i.e. proto-imperative behaviors, which are assumed to solicit another person's attention merely to request, not to "share an experience) (see the top and middle figures in Figure 4). This result is at odds with previous revelation that some children lack of abilities to initiate bids [6]. A plausible explanation lies in the context where our data was interpreted. That is, our assessment context is different from those in these previous studies in that children were not forced to engage in one activity; instead, they were offered separate workspace to engage in a social context (loosely coupled), yet at some points, they are expected to active share by proto-imperative pointing with a goal of not sharing an experience with others. Three children with LFASD were able to respond to joint attention bids by following another child or teachers' gestural and physical prompts.

Practical Considerations

The game requires a multitouch tabletop running Windows 8.1 or Windows 10. Ideally, the screen size should be larger than 19 inches for the best gameplay experience. Some commercial products that we have tested include Lenovo Horizon 2 and Lenovo Yoga Home 500 or 900.

Future Work

Our future work to be unfolded along this path is to carry out longevity studies to examine the full benefits of such a loosely structured play environment.

Acknowledgements

Financial support from Wenzhou-Kean University's Student Partnering with Faculty (SpF) Research Program (WKU201617005) is greatly acknowledged. We also appreciate children, parents and teachers at the Orange Wheat Field Children Support Center, Wenzhou Xinle Children Educational Development Center and Wenzhou Special Education School for participating in our study. Finally, thanks go to Ciara Haowei Yu for designing the puzzles and her efforts during the testing stages.

References

1. Alberto Battocchi, F Pianesi, Daniel Tomasini, Massimo Zancanaro, Gianluca Esposito, Paola Venuti, A Ben Sasson, Eynat Gal, Patrice L (Tamar) Weiss. 2009. Collaborative Puzzle Game: a tabletop interactive game for fostering collaboration in children with Autism Spectrum Disorders (ASD). In *Proc. of the ACM International Conference on Interactive Tabletops and Surfaces* (ITS'09), 197-204. http://doi.acm.org/10.1145/1731903.1731940
2. Ayelet Ben-Sasson, Liron Lamash, and Eynat Gal. 2012. To enforce or not to enforce? The use of collaborative interfaces to promote social skills in children with high functioning autism spectrum disorder. *Autism* 17, 5: 608–622.
3. Anne Deckers, Jeffrey Roelofs, Peter Muris, Mike Rinck. 2014. Desire for social interaction in children with autism spectrum disorders. *Research in Autism Spectrum Disorders* 8, 4: 449–453.
4. Susan Fletcher-Watson, Helen Pain, S. Hammond, A. Humphry, H. McConachie. 2016. Designing for young children with autism spectrum disorder: A case study of an iPad app. *Intl J of Child-Computer Interaction* 7:1-14.
5. Eynat Gal, Liron Lamash, Nirit Bauminger-Zviely, Massimo Zancanaro, Patrice L. (Tamar) Weiss. 2016. Using Multitouch Collaboration Technology to Enhance Social Interaction of Children with High-Functioning Autism. *Physical & Occupational Therapy in Pediatrics* 36, 1: 46-58.
6. Morton Ann Gernsbacher, Jennifer L. Stevenson, Suraiya Khandakar, H. Hill Goldsmith. 2008. Why Does Joint Attention Look Atypical in Autism? *Child Development and Perspective* 2, 1: 38-45.
7. Leonardo Giusti, Massimo Zancanaro, Eynat Gal, Patrice L. (Tamar) Weiss. 2011. Dimensions of collaboration on a tabletop interface for children with autism spectrum disorder. In *Proceedings of the SIGCHI Conference on Human Factors in Computing Systems* (CHI'11), 3295-3304, http://doi.acm.org/10.1145/1978942.1979431
8. Wooi Boon Goh, Wei Shou, Jacquelyn Tan, G.T. Jackson Lum. 2012. Interaction design patterns for multi-touch tabletop collaborative games. CHI '12 Extended Abstracts on Human Factors in Computing Systems (CHI'12), 141-150, http://doi.acm.org/10.1145/2212776.2212792
9. Megan P. Martins, Sandra L. Harris. 2006. Teaching Children with Autism to Respond to Joint Attention Initiations. *Child & Family Behavior Therapy* 28, 1: 51-68.
10. Anne Marie Piper, Eileen O'Brien, Meredith Ringel Morris, Terry Winograd. 2006. SIDES: a cooperative tabletop computer game for social skills development. In *Proc. of the 2006 20th conference on Computer supported cooperative work* (CSCW'06), 1-10, http://doi.acm.org/10.1145/1180875.1180877
11. Greis F. Mireya Silva, Alberto Raposo, Maryse Suplino. 2015. Exploring Collaboration Patterns in a Multitouch Game to Encourage Social Interaction and Collaboration Among Users with Autism Spectrum Disorder. *J. Computer Supported Cooperative Work*, 24:149–175.
12. Christina Whalen, Laura Schreibman. 2003. Joint attention training for children with autism using behavior modification procedures. *Journal of Child Psychology and Psychiatry* 44, 3: 456–468.
13. Pinata Winoto, Tiffany Y. Tang, Aonan Guan. 2016. I will Help You Pass the Puzzle Piece to Your Partner if This is What You Want Me to: The Design of Collaborative Puzzle Games to Train Chinese Children with Autism Spectrum Disorder Joint Attention Skills. In *Proc. of the 15th International Conference on Interaction Design and Children* (IDC'2016), 601-606. http://doi.acm.org/10.1145/2930674.2936012

DiMBI: An Interface to Connect People to Math's Big Ideas of Patterns and Relations

Ana Saavedra
Amy Shoemaker
Stanford University
Stanford, CA 94305, USA
anamar@stanford.edu
amyshoe@stanford.edu

Figure 1: The current version in upper portion of the TUI screen.

Abstract
Math education faces the challenge not only of *how* to teach math, but also of *what* math to teach. With the intention of promoting math's big ideas in formal and informal settings, we created DiMBI (Discovering Math's multimedia platform developed in Processing that uses reacTIVision to read users' interactions with selected tangible regular polygons (a triangle and a square). The corners of each polygon are linked with specific features that aim to promote transfer learning (colors and music). The features change as the user manipulates the objects through symmetric actions and permutation of corners. This is the first stage of our technology, which aims to bring big math ideas closer to the people, through more concrete interactions.

IDC '17, June 27-30, 2017, Stanford, CA, USA

ACM ISBN 978-1-4503-4921-5/17/06.
http://dx.doi.org/10.1145/3078072.3091989

Author Keywords
Mathematics education; pattern and music representation; tangible user interfaces; multimedia

Categories and Subject Descriptors
H.5.2 [Information Interfaces and Presentation]: User Interfaces. K.3.1 [Computers and Education]: Computer Uses in Education

Introduction
DiMBI provides a multimedia platform that allows students to weave together combinatorial patterns with music and color to provide a rich, personalizable experience of exploration. By combining physical manipulatives with virtual feedback we created an environment for students to reflect about and externalize their thinking processes [5].

DiMBI inhabits a unique niche that connects combinatorics (the study of *how many ways*) and abstract algebra (the study of epistemic structures, of what makes two structures identical, of ways to construct and re-present structures), while scaffolding freedom of exploration, discovery, and expression as students manipulate and create their own audio-visual experience.

Background
This project is driven by the notion that providing children multimedia tools to discover big ideas can re-empower both the big ideas and the children who re-discover them [5]. We focus

Learning Objectives

- *Pattern exploration*

  Students will gain familiarity with symmetries and permutations as manipulatable objects.

- *Rigid motion*

  Students will learn to generate symmetries through rotations and reflections of the square and triangle.

- *Isomorphism*

  Students will understand that permutation of elements (swapping polygon vertices) leads to a set of symmetries with identical structure.

- *Transfer/Creation*

  Students will be able to transfer the big idea of patterns into two parallel pattern-based elements: music and color, and will be able to create their own audio-visual experience by applying reflections, rotations, and permutations to the physical shapes.

on centering one of math's biggest ideas: patterns and relations. Developing a deep understanding of patterns and relations is foundational not only to mathematics, but also to computer science, physical science, and most forms of problem solving [3] and critical thinking.

Research on student engagement with patterns has identified that what students notice affects both what sorts of exploration and what type of thinking they are able to engage in [4]. Digital technologies provide the possibility of scaffolding what a student notices as they freely explore.

Tangibles
Incorporating tangible objects into multimedia educational environments can support student engagement in playful learning and can facilitate collaborative interaction with a concept [2, 6]. Tangible user interfaces have been used in math to support learning in a wide variety of topics. TanTab creates a multimedia environment for students to play with Tangrams and develop spacial reasoning skills [2]. Pattern blocks have been used to help children explore symmetry [8], but only with respect to axes, and with no connection to grouping or numeric representation of symmetries. Furthermore, these math technologies are confined to visual representations of the concepts at hand.

Multiple Representations
A powerful math technology should legitimate different forms of mathematical understanding via developing integrated, dynamic representations. In the case of patterns, the possibility for students to represent (with visual, auditory, and numeric representations) different forms of the same idea through the use of multimedia tools can also deepen their understanding. [7]

Math and Music
Bamburger has done substantial research on music education and the role of music as embodied mathematics [1]. However, to our knowledge, there have not been technologies developed using music to underscore mathematical patterns such as symmetries and permutations. The role of music in DiMBI is not only as an aid to gaining mathematical understanding, but also as means of expressing mathematical understanding that has been gained. Evidence of a student's deep understanding of a big idea is the appropriate transfer of that idea into different contexts. We thus see the musical element of DiMBI as a chance for students to concretely express their pattern discoveries as an auditory representation.

Design

DiMBI has been designed primarily for students from ages 10-14. Driving our design decisions are the four key learning objectives laid out at the left.

Design Principles
After choosing the core mathematical concepts, educational theories, and learning goals that sit at the heart of our project, we defined and applied the following three user principles.

1. *PHYSICAL INTERACTION.*
During the process of prototyping different DiMBI designs, we recognized the importance of having physical objects connected to a screen interface. A 10 year old participant said: *"I like this better than the computer because I can manipulate it."* Physical manipulation of an object to gain intuition remains a core part of DiMBI.

2. *ASSISTED FLEXIBILITY.*
One of the core characteristics of DiMBI is that it allows students to freely explore symmetries of rotations, reflections, and transpositions using pre-built polygons.

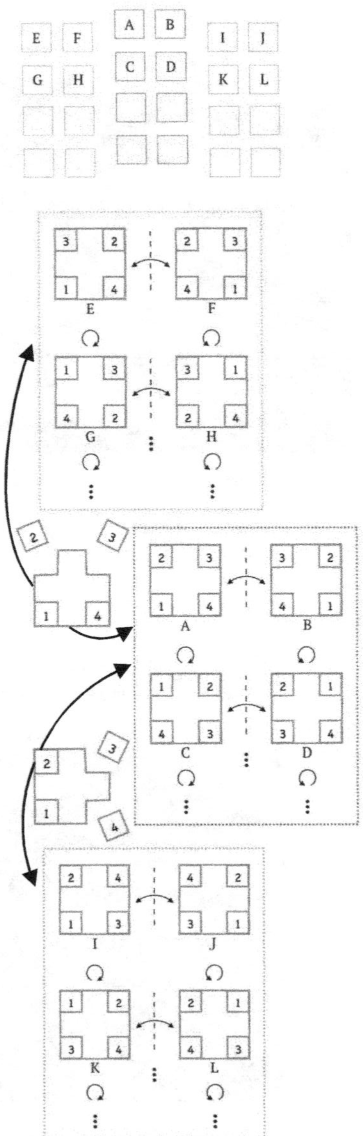

Figure 2: How manipulations (rotations, reflections, and corner transpositions) correspond to the squares in upper portion of the TUI screen.

Currently, there are two types of regular polygons in our design: triangle and square. Students have the flexibility to freely explore with the tool to better notice the symmetries and permutations, while having assistance from DiMBI to guarantee that learning objectives are accomplished. To ensure adherence to this principle, DiMBI has limited what types of interactions students can have with the technology (they are limited to *rigid motion symmetries* i.e., rotation and reflection, and to *permutations* i.e., taking off corners and swapping them). However, the symmetries they choose to place down, the order in which they create those symmetries, and the representations they notice (musical, color, numeric) are all up to the user.

3. *Concrete Knowledge Expression.*

With the intention of making the abstract ideas of symmetries and permutations more concrete, each polygon's corner is associated with a number (visible on the physical corner and on the corresponding location of virtual screen when the object is placed down) and with a unique percussive sound. When the polygon is set down, its nodes are played on a 12-beat measure, on a continuous loop. Applying a symmetry action or a permutation to the shape produces the associated sequence change in the numbers and sounds of the shape's corners.

The upper portion of the TUI screen (Figure 1) has six small triangles (arranged as 3x2) and three sets of eight small squares (arranges as 4x2).[1] Each of these four sections is associated with a set of polygon permutations closed under symmetry actions, with a hue, and with a musical instrument. By permuting corners, students can access different colors/instruments. By performing symmetric actions within a section, students can change the brightness and saturation of the hue along with the chord produced by the instrument. (See Figure 2 for a summary of sample manipulations.) The changes in musical tones and in hues help students to identify what happens when they change the positions of each of the corners, and to express their knowledge through creation of a desired compilation of chords and colors.

Hardware

The tangibles in DiMBI are laser cut wooden polygons whose corners have unique fiducials fastened to them. These corners can be a removed from the polygon, swapped with other vertices, and slid back into place, kept in position by a loose variation of the mortise-tenon joint. With this design, depicted in Figure 4, rotation and reflection of the objects are the easiest forms of manipulation. The user experiences a bit heavier cognitive load when manipulating vertices, to cue her attention. With this, we believe our design prompts the user to question whether this type of vertex manipulation (a permutation) might be fundamentally different from the other forms of manipulation (symmetry via rotation and reflection), which is then underscored by the corresponding change in color and instrument.

The TUI table incorporates a camera to read in the fiducials and a projector to create the tabletop images seen by the user, both incorporated beneath the tabletop.

Software

The virtual environment was created using Processing, a Java-based programming language. Our primary two reasons for selecting this open-source language were its strong built-in visualization environments and its compatibility with reacTIVision. The reacTIVision software uses a computer vision

[1]For the mathematical reader: these correspond to the dihedral group D_6 and the three isomorphic copies of D_8 within S_4.

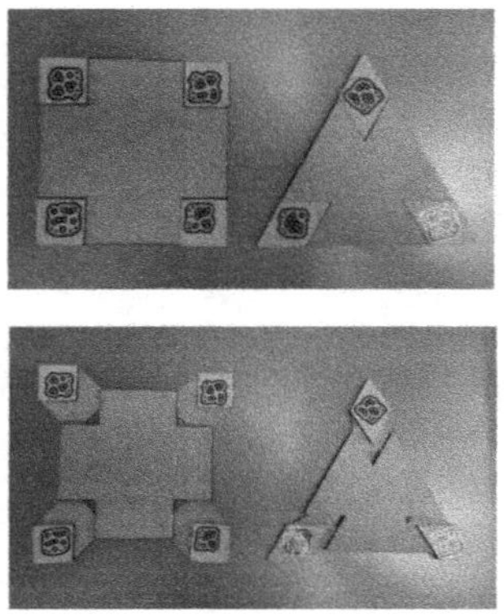

Figure 3: The current physical manipulatives used in DiMBI.

Figure 4: The current version of DiMBI.

algorithm to collect local information about each of the fiducials that enters the camera's scope.

Future Work

This first version of DiMBI promotes the successful accomplishment of the learning goals. In the short term, we plan to find other physical mechanisms similar to those within a Rubik's cube to promote our assisted flexibility principle. We believe this added structure might assist users in developing and testing meaningful schemata, thereby facilitating deeper understanding of the learning objectives. Once we have this mechanism, we plan to conduct user test sessions in formal and informal learning environments during three stages: interviews, think alouds, and focal groups. In the future, we hope to incorporate more freedom and personalization in choosing what audio and visuals are associated with each component of the interface. We also hope to incorporate a recording system in future iterations, so students can listen their thinking process used to arrive to different solutions. Additionally, future versions of DiMBI could usefully mediate a socially engaged and extrinsically motivated context. In a second phase, we plan to implement an interface that allows collaboration between pairs.

Conclusion

DiMBI was designed as an object-to-think-with, an "object in which there is an intersection of cultural presence, embedded knowledge, and the possibility for personal identification." [5] Through externalizing (via music, color, and physical manipulatives) the often abstract notions of permutations and symmetric actions, students are able to concretize the big idea of pattern generation. While the technology requires additional testing and further developments, it appears to be a promising tool for promoting big math ideas in informal or classroom settings.

Acknowledgements

We would like to thank Paulo Blikstein, Engin Bumbacher, Richard Davis and Chris Proctor for their guidance and support.

REFERENCES

1. J. Bamberger, A. diSessa. 2003. Music as Embodied Mathematics: A Study of Mutually Informing Affinity. *Journal of Computers for Mathematical Learning,* 8(2), 123-160.
2. P. Dillenbourg, M. Evans. 2011. Interactive tabletops in education. *Intl. Journal of Computer-Supported Collaborative Learning,* 6(4), 491–514.
3. R. Leikin, A. Berman, O. Zaslavsky. 2000. Applications of symmetry to problem solving. *Intl. Journal of Mathematical Education.* 31(6), 799-809. doi:10.1080/00207390050203315
4. J. Lobato, B. Rhodehamel. 2013. Students' Mathematical Noticing. *Journal for Research in Mathematics Education* 44(5), 809-850.
5. S. Papert. 1980. Mindstorms: Children, Computers, and Powerful Ideas. New York: Basic Books.
6. B. Schneider, P. Jermann, G. Zufferey, G., P. Dillenbourg. Benefits of a tangible interface for collaborative learning and interaction. *IEEE Transactions on Learning Technologies*, 99, 1–1.
7. J. van der Meij, T. de Jong. 2006. Supporting students' learning with multiple representations in a dynamic simulation-based learning environment. *Learning and Instruction, 16*(3), 199-212.
8. S. Yonemoto, T. Yotsumoto, R. Taniguchi. 2006. A Tangible Interface for Hands-on Learning. *Tenth Intl. Conference on Information Visualisation (IV'06),* 535-538. doi: 10.1109/IV.2006.13

Tuk Tuk: A Block-Based Programming Game

Chonnuttida Koracharkornradt
Stanford University
520 Galvez Mall, Room 102
CERAS Building
Stanford, California, 94305, USA
kchonnut@stanford.edu

IDC '17, June 27-30, 2017, Stanford, CA, USA

ACM ISBN 978-1-4503-4921-5/17/06.
http://dx.doi.org/10.1145/3078072.3091990

Abstract
Studying computer programming helps children develop computational thinking, a problem-solving methodology that can be transferred to solve everyday problems. Additionally, exposing children to an advanced computational concept of search algorithm allows them to see how different problem-solving techniques are designed to tackle more challenging tasks, and improve their ability to solve problems. We present a block-based programming game called Tuk Tuk for children in kindergarten level (junior version), and elementary and middle school level (standard version). With Tuk Tuk, learners create a computer program in a block-based language to control a car to complete a given task, earn money, reach the next level, and unlock new coding blocks. By completing each task, learners will learn important computational concepts and algorithms, a basis of computational thinking, such as conditionals, iterations, depth-first search (DFS) and breadth-first search (BFS).

Author Keywords
Block-Based Programming; Game

ACM Classification Keywords
D.2.6 Programming Environments

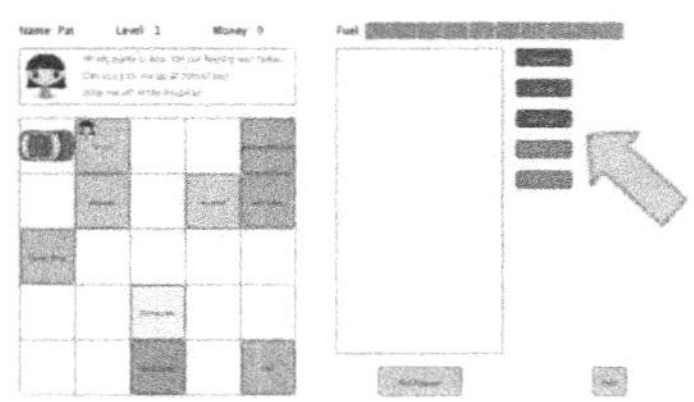

Figure 1: Learners use coding blocks to control a car in the standard version.

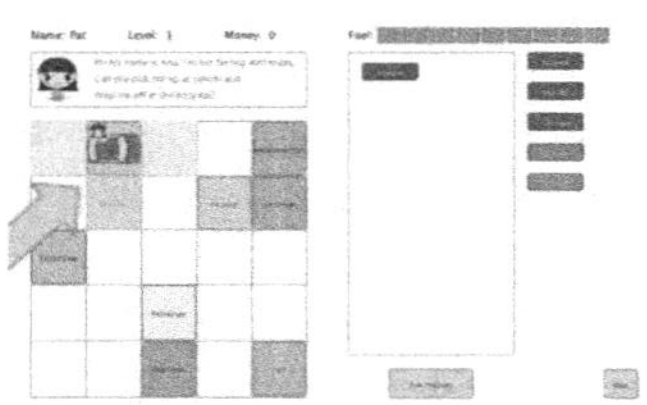

Figure 2: Learners move the car to control the car itself (programming-by-example) in the junior version.

Introduction
Studying computer programming helps children develop computational thinking [1]. We present a block-based programming game Tuk Tuk for beginners, specifically kindergarten students (junior version), and elementary and middle school students (standard version), which introduces basic computational concepts, a basis of computational thinking [1]. With Tuk Tuk, learners use coding blocks to control a car in the standard version (Figure 1), or simply move the car (programming-by-example) in the junior version (Figure 2). A chain of coding blocks, such as "pick up", "forward", and "drop off", forms a program to complete a given task after which the player earns money, reaches the next level, and unlocks new coding blocks.

While there are a number of programming platforms with a goal to encourage an understanding of basic computational concepts, our focus is on a concept that does not normally made available to children—the search algorithms i.e. depth-first search (DFS) and breadth-first search (BFS).

Related Work
In order to have children engage in a meaningful way with the learning process, the tools have to provide a low floor (easy to get started), and the designers have to selectively expose the foreground with respect to the learning goal and black box others [2]. Block-based programming language follows the pattern by blackboxing the syntax of programming, which results in an easy-to-use interface, and allows learners to jump into the central ideas of programming right away [3].

While several block-based programming platforms have been developed (e.g. Scratch, Snap), relatively few of these platforms present programming concepts in the game-based learning. Games have been used for educational purposes for a long time as they are not only fun, but also provide a competitive environment where students can compare their abilities and learn from others, which encourages engagement and motivates students in the learning process [4].

In order to teach young children programming concepts that are considered "too advanced" for their age, Topobo [5] uses programming-by-example concept where a child can program a robot by physically pushing and pulling the moving parts. Inspired by this approach, we develop a junior version of Tuk Tuk.

A more advanced programming concept of algorithms is incorporated into the game in order to allows children to see how different problem-solving techniques are designed to tackle the more challenging tasks, and improve children's ability to solve problems [6]. The car metaphor lends itself well to the path finding algorithms using in Google maps, in which DFS and BFS are the simplest graph search algorithms to learn.

Design
1) Design Overview
The main game screen consists of three sections. The "Game Status" section at the top left area of the screen shows player's name, level, money, and current task to be completed. The "Map" section at the bottom left area of the screen runs and displays the result of the program. The "Script" section at the right area of the screen shows the program being developed (Figure 3).

Tuk Tuk allows learners to program by using a block-based language or programming-by-example method,

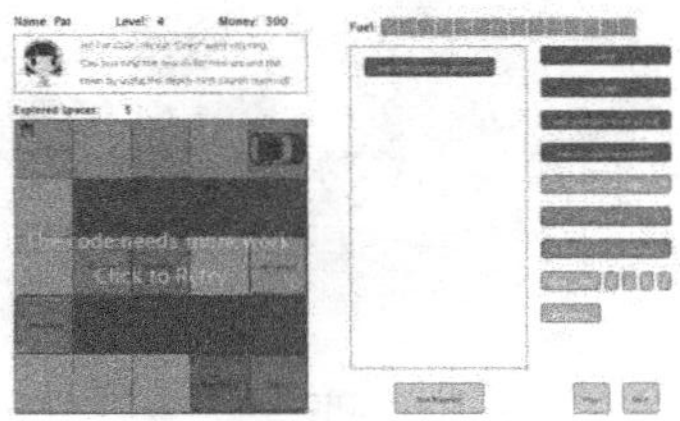

Figure 4: Sample of visual feedback and error message.

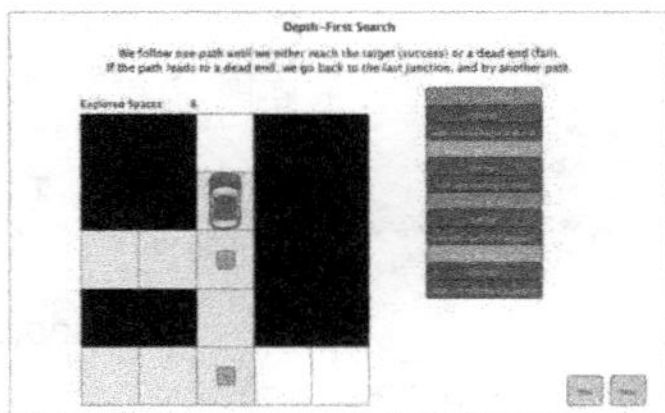

Figure 5: Introducing DFS.

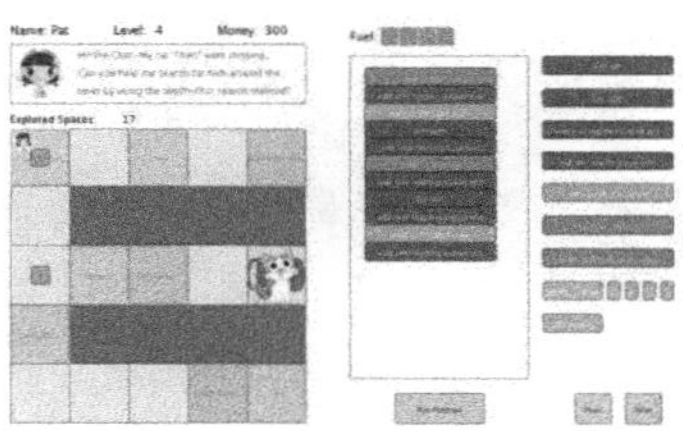

Figure 6: The cat will always appear at the last explored grid.

as well as implement DFS and BFS algorithms. There are multiple solutions to complete each task, and learners have to decide on how to solve the problem.

2) Core Mechanics ("What is possible?")
2.1) Coding Blocks
Tuk Tuk's coding blocks are represented as simple phrases so that learners can intuitively understand what each block does. The blocks are color-coded in order to help learners find blocks in the same category. The coding blocks are also easy to manipulate. Learners can click on a coding block in the palette to add it to the script, and click on a coding block in the script area to delete it from the script (Figure 3). Moreover, the coding blocks are designed to have embedded syntactical error correction. For example, learners can only insert the "else" block after the "if" block is used.

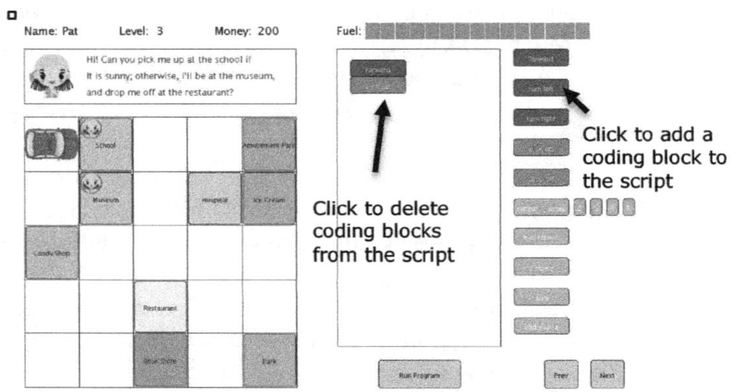

Figure 3: Main game screen layout.

2.2) Fuel Blocks
One fuel block is used for each coding block that learners add to the script. For each task, a limited numbers of fuel blocks are given in order to avoid too long script and encourage learners to think about how to solve the problems efficiently.

2.3) "Run Program" Button and Map Simulation Area
Tuk Tuk allows rapid iteration, the ability to add or delete blocks to a script and see the result quickly. Learners can run a program fragment at any time to see what it does. When the "Run Program" button is clicked, the "Map" section will simulate script execution. Learners can check whether the program do what it is intended to do, and if the program has an error, an error message will appear (Figure 4). These features help learners stay engaged in testing, debugging, and improving their program.

3) Built-in Pedagogy ("How what is possible is made available?")
Tuk Tuk introduces programming concepts as a game where learners obtain additional features when they progress to the next level.

At the beginning, learners only have "forward", "turn left", and "turn right" coding blocks (Figure 1). As they progress to level 2 and 3, "repeat" blocks and "if-else" blocks will be enabled, respectively (Figure 3). At level 4, there will be an instructional simulation of what DFS is, before the DFS coding blocks are enabled (Figure 5). Level 5 is similar to level 4, but focuses on BFS. The task for level 4 and 5 is to search for a cat lost in a town. We also design the solution in a way that the cat will always appear at the last explored grid (Figure 6) to make sure that the learners has utilized the algorithms properly. Next, level 6 and 7 allow learners to explore the differences and advantages of each search algorithm by giving them access to both DFS and BFS coding blocks. However, one algorithm is more

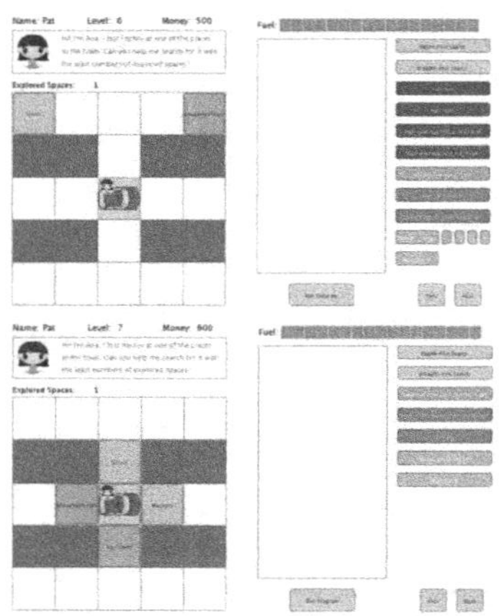

Figure 7: Explore the differences and advantages of each search algorithm.

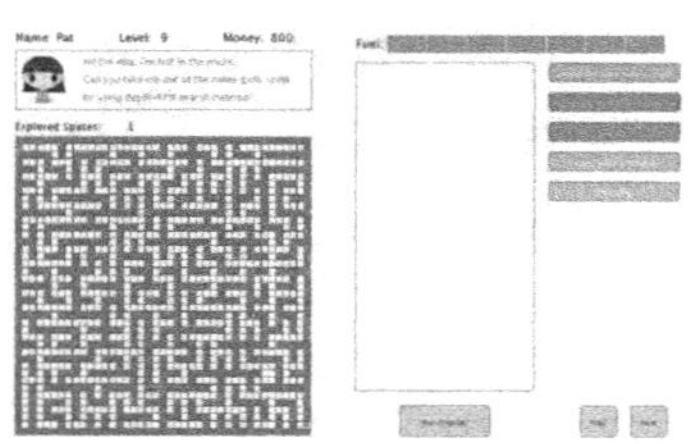

Figure 8: Complex Map.

Figure 9: Preliminary user testing.

preferable than another for a particular map. DFS is more suitable for level 6, and BFS is more suitable for level 7 (Figure 7). Level 8 is similar to level 4 and 5, but focuses on a compact version of DFS. At level 9 and 10, learners get to apply search algorithms to complex maps (Figure 8). The learners will discover the advantage of search algorithms as the last two levels are too large to direct the car to explore all spaces without the usage of search algorithms.

Preliminary User Testing
A 1-hour session interview was conducted with six- and eight-year-old girls (Figure 9). The interface interested the kids and the kids were eager to complete the task. They loved the designs, and immediately understood how to use coding blocks to control the car. In addition, we learned that the game mechanism works very well, i.e., the kids enjoyed the game, wanted to play it again, and had fun trying to beat each other. Finally, the learning goals were met. By completing level-2 task, children understood the concept of iterations as they managed to put the coding blocks inside the "repeat" block in order to make the car repeatedly perform sequence of actions. We hope that further user testing will confirm these initial findings and capture new ways to improve our design.

Conclusion and Future Work
Tuk Tuk is a block-based programming game that helps children develop computational thinking by learning computational concepts, especially search algorithms, through self-directed interfaces. Tuk Tuk can be easily downloaded online and is ready to use.

There are improvements that can be made on Tuk Tuk such as:

- Adding incentive to play the game e.g., learners can use money to decorate the car, or share their score online and see rankings.
- Introducing more advanced computational concepts such as artificial intelligence search techniques in games (e.g. chess, go, etc.) and allow learners to compete their created game agent, etc.

Acknowledgements
We would like to thank Paulo Blikstein, Assistant Professor at Stanford University, and our TAs for Beyond Bits and Atoms course, especially, Richard Davis, Engin Bumbacher, and Chris Proctor.

References
1. Kafai, Y., Burke, Q., & Resnick, M. (2014). *Connected Code: Why Children Need to Learn Programming*. MIT Press.
2. Papert, S. (1980). Mindstorms: Children, computers and powerful ideas. Basic Books, NY.
3. Resnick, Mitchel, John Maloney, Andres Monroy-Hernandez, Natalie Rusk, Evelyn Eastmond, and Karen Brennan. (2009). *Scratch: Programming for all*. Communications of the ACM 52 (11): 60-67.
4. Combefis, S., Beresnevicius G. & Dagiene, V. (2016). *Learning Programming through Games and Contests: Overview, Characterization, and Discussion*. Olympiads in Informatics Vol.10, 39-60.
5. Hayes Raffle and Cristobal Garcia. (2003). *Topobo for Tangible Learning*. MAS 712 Technological Tools for Learning.
6. Miller, B. and Ranum, D. (2011). *Problem Solving with Algorithms and Data Structures using Python: Second Edition*.

The Conference of the Birds: A Collaborative Storytelling Environment for Literacy Development

Fabio Campos
Stanford University
Stanford, CA 94305, USA
fabioc@stanford.edu

Ali Azhar
Stanford University
Stanford, CA 94305, USA
aazhar@stanford.edu

Paulo Blikstein
Stanford University
Stanford, CA 94305, USA
paulob@stanford.edu

IDC '17, June 27-30, 2017, Stanford, CA, USA

ACM ISBN 978-1-4503-4921-5/17/06.
http://dx.doi.org/10.1145/3078072.3091991

Abstract

Sociocultural theories of learning regard oral storytelling as a fundamental step towards literacy development. Collaborative play can lead to richer and sustained stories among children of young age.

We describe an interactive learning environment called The Conference of the Birds (CoB). By allowing two users to interact with the interface at the same time, the CoB allows children separated by physical or cultural distances to collaborate by creating narratives together. Through the CoB, children connect, cooperate and create joint stories, fostering the development of literacy, as well as collaboration and authorship skills.

In this paper we describe the principles, theories and design decisions that supported the creation of the CoB, and briefly discuss how kids can collaboratively create stories in a digital environment.

Author Keywords

Digital Storytelling; Literacy Development; Tangible Interaction; Collaborative Narratives;

ACM Classification Keywords

H.5.2 [**Information Interfaces and Presentation**]: User Interfaces—Input devices and strategies, interaction styles;

Figure 1: Pakistani kids playing with paper puppets.

Introduction

Stories have the power to embody our social and cultural contexts, and toys have the power to embody and augment those stories. Boys and girls from around the world imbue toys with personalities and create stories that combine imagination with aspects of their lives. What if children separated by distance could create stories together by sharing the same imaginary realm? How long, deep and rich would those stories be, and how much agency would users have compared to traditional storytelling media? Would this approach afford different outcomes if compared to physically playing together?

Aimed at children aged 4 to 7 – an age of intense make-believe play [7] – the CoB is an interactive narrative world that helps children develop negotiated stories. We named the platform after a homonymous Persian poem [1] in which a bird guides his colleagues on a journey of self-discovery.

The CoB was developed as a tangible user interface in which children manipulate physical props that are translated into digital birds. Each child visualizes their own bird as well as the other child's character, in a real time, interactive way. A meta-narrator introduces the poem's storyline and children develop their own chapters of the narrative using their tangible/digital objects and through joint storytelling and play. Aided by the constant interaction between the characters, we aim for longer and richer interactions between young learners.

This work is a first step to investigate the elements that are vital to allow children separated by distance or cultures to co-create sustained and richer narratives through digital storytelling systems.

Related Work

The CoB is designed to foster collaborative play and storytelling. In sociocultural research, oral storytelling and play are intrinsic to "outside-in" literacy skills which relate to the function and form of narratives. Decontextualized storytelling is a precursor to written literacy [8] and through our platform we seek to capitalize on children's' innate desire to tell stories.

Co-creating narratives and collaborating is a complex skill for young children. Toys augmented with interactive audiovisual capabilities have been shown to double the length of narratives. Yuill et. al [9] observed how children played as if "they were tied to a string" in such environments – a sign of cooperation in play.

Kurcikova [5] highlights the importance of personalization of elements as an enabler of greater agency, customized aesthetics and reciprocity in digital authorship and storytelling. Cassell's [3] work about Story Listening Systems lay four fundamental principles that allow these systems to be socio-culturally situated:

(a) **Playful Language** - Storytelling systems need to evoke playful language and use children's propensity to tell stories to bootstrap literacy. Playfulness is linked to creativity as it promotes divergent thinking [6].
(b) **Peer Play** - Storytelling systems need to encourage peer play and, most importantly, embody peers as playmates in the system [9], "*like an imaginary playmate with an active imagination*". [3]
(c) **Embodied Play** - Successful systems invite the kind of embodied play that children naturally engage in.
(d) **Meaningful Content** - Systems need to engage children in constructing meaningful content rather than constraining their stories. Aesthetics and personalization allow a closer relation with objects of play, increasing motivation and engagement. [5]

Other digital storytelling tools have paved the way for our work. StoryMat [3] supports collaborative storytelling among children who are not present at the same time or

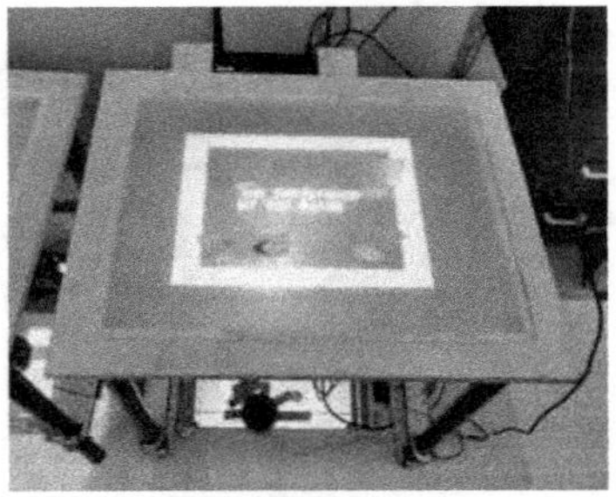

Figure 2: One of the two interactive low-cost tabletops.

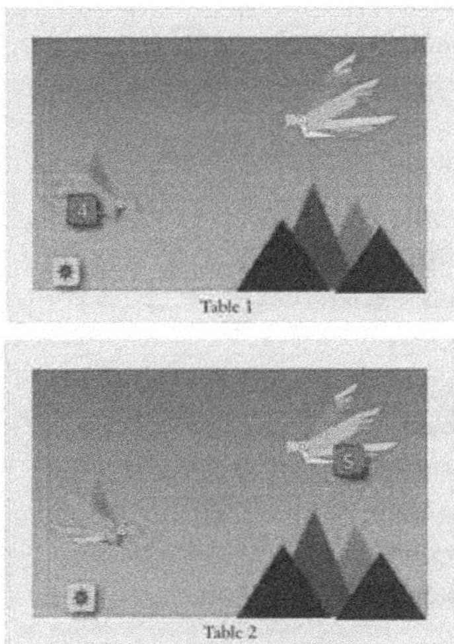

Figure 3: Optical fiducial codes are mapped into digital birds that move in real time. Fiducial #4 controls the parrot on both tables, and #5 controls the hawk. The sun piece changes the scene to daytime.

space. Research on Pagecraft [2] highlights the role of contextualized stories to support narrative development. The design for our project capitalizes on the frameworks developed in this body of research by providing an environment that combines personalization, collaboration and oral storytelling.

Design Elements

To define the current version of our storytelling environment, we conducted initial user testing over Skype with Pakistani children aged 5 to 7. To generate engagement through a shared object in the same attentional space, interviewers and children used paper bird puppets [Fig 1].

We drew several conclusions from this analogical prototype of the CoB. We found that to facilitate prolonged and rich storytelling, a narrative framework is needed: there needs to be a powerful and engaging context in which the story develops. We also observed that the personalization of story elements (i.e. naming a puppet and creating a background for it) was a fundamental element to generate greater engagement.

Based on these initial conclusions, and drawing from related theory and frameworks, we defined the main design features of the digital version of the CoB. The platform was designed using two low-cost, bottom-projected, custom made interactive tabletops. [Fig. 2] A system was developed to connect the two tabletops in real-time. The result was robust but designed with low-cost elements such as IKEA tables, acrylic mirrors, infrared LEDs and security cameras. Children manipulate tangible props with optical fiducial codes [Fig. 3] that are translated into birds by the system. Below we detail our most important design decisions and principles:

1. Narrative framework: We provided a story canvas, based on the original "The Conference of the Birds" poem, without limiting the narrative possibilities children can create. A meta narrator initiates the story, describing a meeting of birds in pursuit of a king. From this point on, children self-express and negotiate their own creations in a non-linear, open ended way. User-controlled alternating scenes help provide structure for the stories.

2. Personalization: Our user testing suggested that character personalization would be an important element, so children's first task is to create their own bird on the writable top surface of the interactive props.

3. Agency: To create more moments for joint dialogue and coordination, the system has two backdrops: day and night. Children alternate backdrops by getting "out" of the story for a moment, verbally coordinating with each other the scene change, and getting back in, leading to moments of meta-dialogue and to greater agency over the shared development of the stories.

4. Real-time reciprocity: Real-time reciprocity of movements is fundamental for weaving a negotiated story over the internet. Fiducial codes underneath the props track the movement of birds and map them onto both tables. Through interconnected server and client modules in the Processing programming language, users interact in real-time, creating a joint "puppet theatre".

5. Independent sounds and movement: Our user testing also suggested that having ambient sound and animated ambient objects lead to more creative storytelling. Our system includes sound elements in the background, as well as narrative elements such as rain, falling leaves, and non-player animated animals, providing subtle immersion into the tabletop world without diverting users' attention.

6. Recognizable cultural forms [4]: The use of tabletops naturally organize the play around it. Graphic and sound aesthetics resemble a video game, a recognizable format that automatically evokes interaction.

7. Physical movement: Instead of traditional screens (e.g. tablets), tabletop surfaces enable children to move around, as well as embodied play and collaboration.

Future Design Directions
We plan to improve the CoB so that it will allow us to further investigate the research questions mentioned in this paper. First, allowing users to control sounds would permit greater agency over narrative outcomes. To open new possibilities of self-expression, we plan to add new, customizable scenes, and user-defined semi-autonomous story elements (e.g. a flock of birds), as well as record and playback capabilities. We also plan to add further opportunities for negotiated interactions, such as players coordinating movements to change the backgrounds. We will work to assess the effects of our design elements over the richness of the narratives (e.g. increase in time, story elements, etc.). Finally, we envision extending the CoB to regular tablets and other digital devices to reduce hardware costs.

Conclusion
We presented The Conference of the Birds, a digital collaborative storytelling environment aimed at developing literacy. We aim to contribute to this field by demonstrating the roles of context, personalization and agency in the creation of more complex and sustained narratives. We seek to understand how children imagine, collaborate, and negotiate stories with peers that do not share the same physical space and the particular affordances of this approach.

Acknowledgements
This material is based upon work supported by Stanford's Lemann Center for Education Entrepreneurship and Innovation in Brazil and by the Transformative Learning Technologies Lab.

References
1. Farid Ud-Din Attar. 1984. The Conference of the Birds, transl. By Afkham Darbandi and Dick Davis.
2. Jim Budd, Krystina Madej, Jenna Stephens-Wells, Janice de Jong, Ehren Katzur and Laura Mulligan. 2007. PageCraft: learning in context a tangible interactive storytelling platform to support early narrative development for young children. In *Proceedings of the 6th international conference on Interaction design and children* (pp. 97-100). ACM. New York, NY. DOI:10.1145/1297277.1297296
3. Justine Cassell. 2004. Towards a model of technology and literacy development: Story listening systems. *Journal of Applied Developmental Psychology*, 25(1), 75-105. DOI: https://doi.org/10.1016/j.appdev.2003.11.003
4. Michael S. Horn. 2013. The role of cultural forms in tangible interaction design. In *Proceedings of the 7th International Conference on Tangible, Embedded and Embodied Interaction* (TEI '13). ACM, New York, NY. 117-124. DOI=http://dx.doi.org/10.1145/2460625.2460643
5. Natalia Kucirkova. 2016. Personalisation: A theoretical possibility to reinvigorate children's interest in storybook reading and facilitate greater book diversity. *Contemporary Issues in Early Childhood, 17(3)*, 304-316.
6. Sandra W. Russ and Astrida Seja Kaugars. 2001. Emotion in children's play and creative problem solving. *Creativity Research Journal, 13(2),* 211-219. http://dx.doi.org/10.1207/S15326934CRJ1302_8
7. Lev S. Vygotsky. 1967. Play and its role in the mental development of the child. *Soviet psychology, 5(3),* 6-18. DOI:10.2753/RPO1061-040505036
8. Graver J. Whitehurst and Christopher J. Lonigan. 1998. Child development and emergent literacy. Child development, 69(3), 848-872. DOI:10.1111/j.1467-8624.1998.tb06247.x
9. Nicola Yuill, Steve Hinske, Sophie E. Williams and Georgia Leith. 2014. How getting noticed helps getting on: successful attention capture doubles children's cooperative play. *Frontiers in psychology, 5.* DOI:10.3389/fpsyg.2014.00418

Sonification Blocks: A Block-Based Programming Environment For Embodied Data Sonification

Jack Atherton
Center for Computer Research in Music and Acoustics
Stanford University
Stanford, CA, USA
lja@ccrma.stanford.edu

Paulo Blikstein
Graduate School of Education
Stanford University
Stanford, CA, USA
paulob@stanford.edu

IDC '17, June 27-30, 2017, Stanford, CA, USA

ACM ISBN 978-1-4503-4921-5/17/06.
http://dx.doi.org/10.1145/3078072.3091992

Abstract
High school students often struggle to find the motivation to learn to program. Music can be a powerful motivator for these students, but existing tools that combine music production with programming often fail to meaningfully engage students with core computer science concepts. Sonification Blocks was created to shift the focus back toward big ideas in programming. Sonification Blocks is a programming language for data sonification, the process of creating audio algorithms and controlling them with streams of data. Its implementation as a block-based language with clear, interactive data visualizers allows high-school-aged learners to develop computational literacy. Furthermore, the act of manipulating sound parameters with data streams that are controlled through body motion may help connect learners with powerful ideas in programming and data science.

Author Keywords
computer science education; music; sonification; embodied cognition; constructionism

ACM Classification Keywords
K.3.2 [Computers and Education]: Computer and Information Science Education; H.5.5 [Information Interfaces and Presentation (e.g., HCI)]: Sound and Music Computing

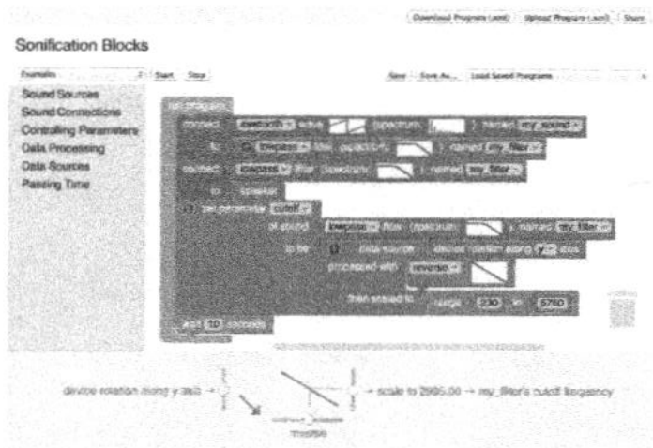

Figure 1: The Sonification Blocks workspace. Sonification Blocks is implemented in HTML, CSS, and JavaScript using Google Blockly and Web Audio [5, 8]. As such, it is cross-platform and free to use in any modern browser. Learners can save programs in the local browser storage, download and upload programs as XML files, and share web links that recreate their workspace when opened. These features allow learners to share their creations publicly and to easily collaborate with peers.

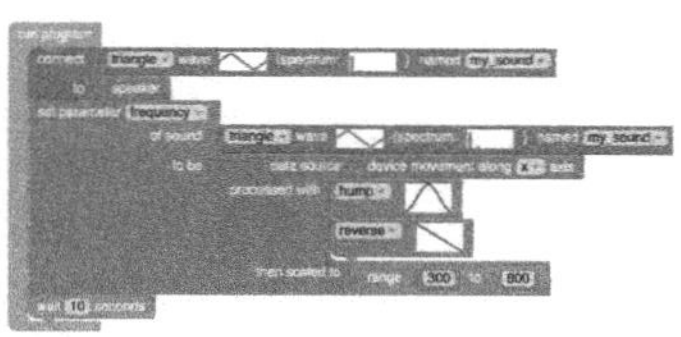

Figure 2: A program written in Sonification Blocks, sonifying the device's linear acceleration along the x axis by connecting it to the frequency of a triangle wave oscillator. Running this program also shows the live data processing visualization of Figure 5.

Introduction

Sonification Blocks (https://ccrma.stanford.edu/~lja/sonification/) is a web-based learning environment designed to introduce high-school-aged learners to introductory concepts in programming, data processing, and computer sound production. Data sonification is the act of controlling the parameters of an audio algorithm with values from a stream of data for the purpose of learning about the data. With Sonification Blocks, learners construct audio algorithms in a block-based programming language, controlling parameters of the sound by using sensors built into the device on which they program and by shaping the output of those sensors with a variety of "atomic" data processing functions (*atoms*). Our hope is that learners using Sonification Blocks will make progress toward two key components of computational literacy: object oriented thinking, especially in the domain of sound, and the processing and connection of flows of data.

Our work is grounded in the constructionist tradition, in that students learn by building and sharing personally meaningful sonifications [1]. Sonification Blocks also draws on ideas from embodied cognition in allowing the application of body-based cognition to a non-situated activity [10]. Playing a physical instrument is a situated activity, as musicians can feel their instrument's form and vibrations (the methods of generating sound) as they play. Audio programming divorces the thoughts associated with making sound from the production of sound, both in time (first write a program, then run it) and in physicality (the sound mechanism is hidden inside a device and is not controlled by bodily actions). The use of physical sensors for the control of sonification programs allows learners to apply bodily intuition for motion to the relatively non-situated task of audio programming, and the continual recompilation that occurs whenever the code is changed reconnects thought and audio output in time.

Background and Related Work

Introductory computer science students often struggle to stay motivated in text-only paradigms [7]. Some researchers have turned to music and audio programming as a motivator that works well across diversity of gender, race, and class [6, 7, 9]. A basic approach simply introduces the ability to play back or *trigger* audio files programmatically [2]. This ability is technically sufficient for some applications like games, but does not invite introspection about the act of sound generation itself. Tellingly, students who engage in sound triggering activities like making music videos engage less with core programming concepts like variables and control flow when compared to students creating games [2].

Two promising tools that use audio programming for computer science education are *EarSketch* and *BlockyTalky*. *EarSketch* is a "computational music remixing" library used to motivate high school students with no music background through a comprehensive computer science curriculum [6]. However, its lack of physical interaction via sensors or controllers prevents the use of bodily understanding during the music-making process. *BlockyTalky* is a block-based programming language and toolkit for creating sensor-controlled synthesizers that can communicate with each other over the internet [9]. These devices helped children aged 11–14 learn about advanced computer science topics, but long delays between sensor readings and audio output diminished students' ability to interpret how their programs were working. Also, the focus on creating music for a public performance led many students to mimic pop music rather than engaging with programming concepts.

In the realm of data science, the *Scratch Community Blocks* extension motivated children aged 11–15 to start building a data science literacy by allowing them to construct personally meaningful visualizations of data about the Scratch

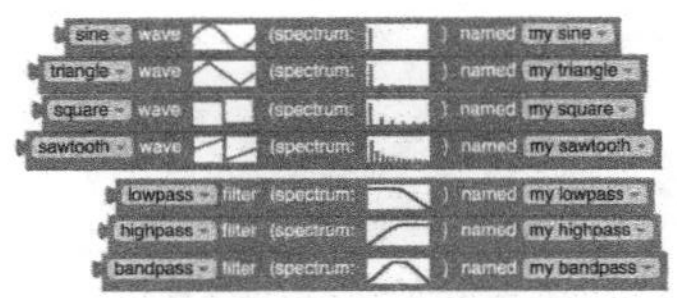

Figure 3: All variants of waveform blocks and effect blocks. Each of these blocks can be set to one of several sub-types, such as *triangle wave* or *lowpass filter*.

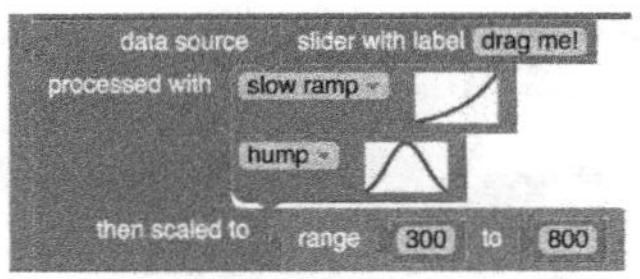

Figure 4: The data processing blocks. Here, a slider labeled "drag me" is fed through an exponential atom, followed by a gaussian atom, then scaled up. Figures 6 and 7 show the live updating graphs that are shown when this block is run.

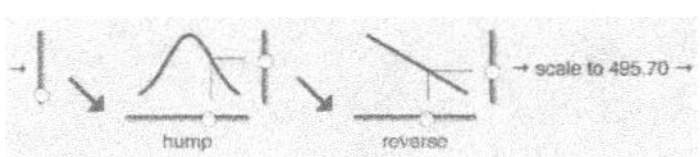

Figure 5: The visualization of a data processing chain. Here, a data stream is sent as an argument to two data processing atom functions composed together, then scaled up to a larger value. The sliders, graphs, and scaled value all update in real time, and each slider can be moved manually to determine its impact on the rest of the data processing chain and on the audio algorithm.

ecosystem [4]. However, it limited the notion of "data" to static information accessed through a database. Notably, users expected to be able to update visualizations in real time as the world changed, which was not possible due to the project's slow query times and caching system.

Design Overview

Sonification Blocks focuses on the activity of data sonification rather than the activity of making music. We were also intentional in choosing the layer of technical complexity to expose to students ("selective exposure," [3]). Data sonification allows users to engage with data in an immediate, time-varying way and to engage in programming sound without the distractions of composing or copying music. The top-level blocks of the language allow learners to connect audio objects to each other, to set parameters of those objects, and to pass time. Importantly, parameters can be set via the output of other audio objects and via the output of a data source, allowing complex audio signal chain configurations and enabling the sonification aspect of the language.

Audio Blocks

The two audio object blocks are the *waveform* and *effect* blocks (Figure 3). Each block shows the frequency domain representation of the underlying audio object so that its effect on the sound can be understood visually and aurally.

When one of these blocks is attached to a *set parameter* block, the parameter block updates its dropdown menu to show the parameters specific to the attached block. This behavior enables progress toward the set of learning goals that compose object-oriented thinking by instilling two notions: first, that objects have properties that are held in common with similar objects but not with all objects; second, that different object types belonging to the same larger category can be used interchangeably in some contexts.

Data Processing Blocks

The data blocks are linked together with the data processing chain block (Figure 4). This block can be used in the parameter block instead of a number or audio object. It takes a live data source, shapes it according to one or more data processing atoms, then scales the result to a specified range and sets the parameter with that value.

When a program is run, a live-updating chain of graphs and sliders representing the data processing flow of the program appears at the bottom of the page (Figure 5). Each slider can be moved manually to affect the rest of the chain, allowing debugging at a fine-grained level. If more than one data processing atom is linked together, the graph of composing each atom's function together is shown (Figure 6). This graph can be broken apart into the constituent atoms to observe the effect of each individually (Figure 7).

Sonification Blocks currently includes two kinds of data sources. Slider data sources let learners control the data flow by manually manipulating a slider located next to the visualizer chain, allowing them to explore the effect of each part of the chain at their own pace. Alternatively, when using a mobile device equipped with an accelerometer, learners can use the angular position, linear acceleration, or rotational acceleration of their device as a data source. Using accelerometer data sources allows learners to understand their audio algorithms in an embodied way by manipulating the algorithms with subtle hand and body movements.

Live Feedback

Changes in data sources propagate to parameters in the audio algorithm without any perceivable delay. This low latency allows learners to readily interpret the effect their gestures have on their audio algorithm. Also, a running audio algorithm is updated immediately whenever the underlying program is edited, affording quick back-and-forth testing.

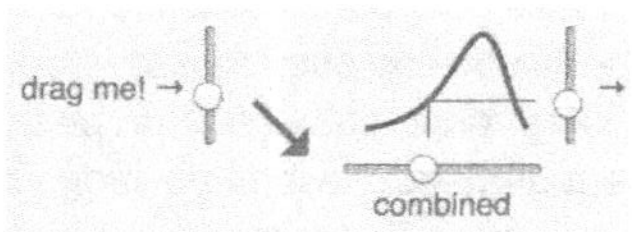

Figure 6: A combination graph, showing an exponential atom composed with a gaussian atom.

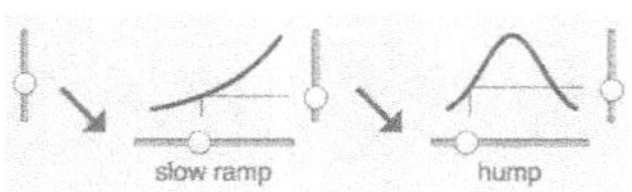

Figure 7: The individual atom component graphs, broken apart from the graph of Figure 6.

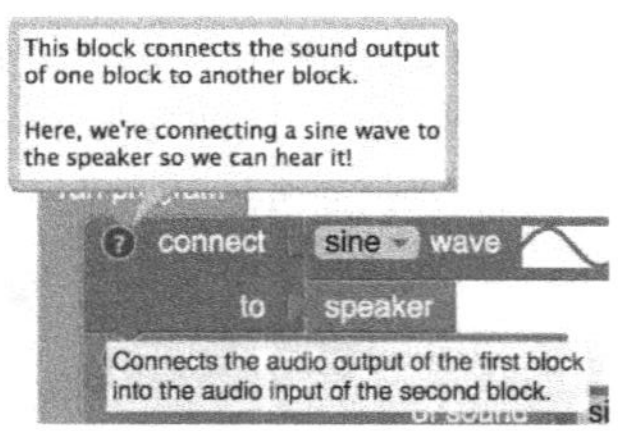

Figure 8: An example program comment (upper) and a mouse hover tooltip (lower).

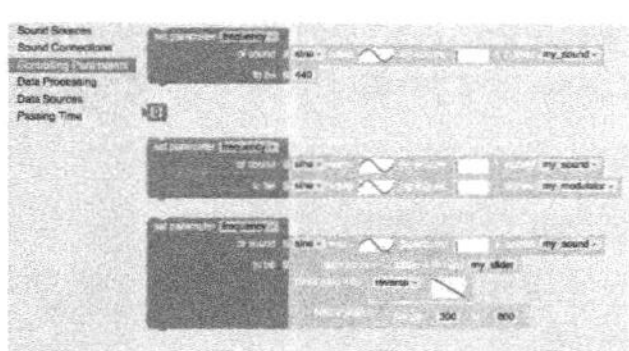

Figure 9: Shadow blocks in the toolbox, suggesting three different possible uses of the same block.

Scaffolding

Each block has a tooltip that explains what the block does whenever the cursor is hovered over it. Additionally, learners may load a number of example programs, which increase slowly through topic complexity and program length and have comments to explain how each unfamiliar block is used (Figure 8). Within the toolbox menus where learners find blocks for their programs, the inputs to complex blocks are filled out with potential configurations using *shadow* blocks. These blocks are lighter in color, suggesting a partial solution for how to use the parent blocks while also allowing learners to fill in the inputs with their own blocks. If a block can be used in multiple ways, it appears multiple times in the toolbox with different shadow inputs to encourage learners to explore all the options (Figure 9).

Conclusion

Sonification Blocks is a block-based programming language for data sonification. It allows learners to program audio synthesis algorithms and control them with streams of data, encountering big ideas in object-oriented thinking and computer music. Clear, interactive data visualizers show the effects of atomic data processors, allowing learners to start building a data science literacy. When using accelerometer data sources, learners can translate their bodily movements into sound for an embodied audio programming experience. Sonification Blocks provides a context and a language for exposing students to powerful ideas in both programming and sound synthesis.

Acknowledgments

We thank Richard Davis, Engin Bumbacher, and Chris Proctor for their invaluable feedback on early prototypes and on the manuscript. We also thank the Lemann Center at Stanford for its support.

References

[1] Edith Ackermann. 2001. Piaget's constructivism, Papert's constructionism: What's the difference?. In *Constructivism: Uses and Perspectives in Education.*

[2] Joel C. Adams and Andrew R. Webster. 2012. What do students learn about programming from game, music video, and storytelling projects?. In *Proceedings of the 43rd SIGCSE Technical Symposium.* 643–648.

[3] Paulo Blikstein. 2015. Computationally Enhanced Toolkits for Children: Historical Review and a Framework for Future Design. *Foundations and Trends in Human-Computer Interaction* 9, 1 (2015), 1–68.

[4] Sayamindu Dasgupta and Benjamin M. Hill. 2017. Scratch Community Blocks: Supporting Children as Data Scientists. *Preprint, arXiv:1702.00112* (2017).

[5] Google Developers. 2017. Blockly. (8 March 2017). Retrieved from https://developers.google.com/blockly/.

[6] Jason Freeman, Brian Magerko, Tom McKlin, and others. 2014. Engaging underrepresented groups in high school introductory computing through computational remixing with EarSketch. In *Proceedings of the 45th SIGCSE Technical Symposium.* 85–90.

[7] Mark Guzdial and Elliot Soloway. 2002. Teaching the Nintendo generation to program. *Commun. ACM* 45, 4 (2002), 17–21.

[8] Mozilla Developers Network. 2017. Web Audio API. (8 March 2017). Retrieved from https://developer.mozilla.org/en-US/docs/Web/API/Web_Audio_API.

[9] Benjamin R. Shapiro, Annie Kelly, Matthew Ahrens, and Rebecca Fiebrink. 2016. BlockyTalky: A Physical and Distributed Computer Music Toolkit for Kids. In *Proceedings of the 2016 International Conference on New Interfaces for Musical Expression (NIME16).*

[10] Margaret Wilson. 2002. Six views of embodied cognition. *Psychonomic bulletin & review* 9, 4 (2002).

BetaKit: Tinkering with Physical Programming

Cassia Fernandez
Universidade de São Paulo
São Paulo, SP, Brazil
cassia.fernandez@usp.br

Nathan Rabinovitch
Escola Alecrim
São Paulo, SP, Brazil
nathanrab@gmail.com

Roseli de Deus Lopes
Universidade de São Paulo
São Paulo, SP, Brazil
roseli.lopes@usp.br

IDC '17, June 27-30, 2017, Stanford, CA, USA

ACM ISBN 978-1-4503-4921-5/17/06.
http://dx.doi.org/10.1145/3078072.3099582

Abstract

Physical programming is becoming increasingly popular in schools, and many toolkits have been developed in the last years to introduce novices to the field. In this paper, we describe the development of a low cost physical programming toolkit suited for tinkering explorations and designed to be used with everyday materials. We present an overview of the design principles that guided the development of our kit and show projects created by elementary and middle school students.

Author Keywords

Robotics; Physical programming; Constructionism; Tinkering; Electronics Kits

ACM Classification Keywords

K.3.2 Computer and Information Science Education, H.5.2 User Interfaces

Introduction

Electronics and physical programming are important subjects in the maker field. Thereby, a growing number of toolkits have been designed in the last decades to allow children to explore computational concepts while building artifacts.

Figure 1. Some of the modules: buzzer, button and LED.

If those toolkits are to be used in educational settings like schools, a very important issue concerns to developing ways of engaging a greater number of students with diverse interests and backgrounds, since programming activities are commonly presented in gender-biased ways [1,7]. In this sense, the approaches and materials have to be carefully and intentionally chosen in order to allow a broader participation.

Background

Constructionism posits the importance of combining learners' engagement in personally meaningful projects with creating things that can be shared with others [3]. Grounded on this perspective, many researchers and educators have been developing activities, tools and approaches to support learning through making. In this section, we describe briefly the tinkering approach, which is connected to the goals that guided the development of the Betakit.

Tinkering is an experimental and exploratory way of interacting with materials, in which activities can be faced through diverse pathways and in levels of complexity related to personal interests [4,9]. Turkle and Papert [8] contrasted Levi-Strauss' idea of *bricolage* to more structured and planned approaches to programming: while planners value hierarchy and abstraction, *bricoleurs* prefer negotiation and rearrangement. What Papert called *bricolage* is connected to tinkering practices, and can be extended from programming to making in general. Given its playful and open-ended characteristics, tinkering can be a valuable approach to lower the barriers for participation in the physical programming field.

Design principles

Robotics and physical programming kits designed for children have been developed for many decades, from Papert's programmable turtles back in the 1970s and the LEGO-Logo platform in the 1980s, to the rich diversity of today's kits.

Although the great number of toolkits available, we didn't find any kit available in our country that would fit in our budget (since we wanted to use them in classroom settings), and with characteristics suited for tinkering explorations. So, we decided to make our own toolkit, and designed it to allow the creation of interactive objects integrating low cost materials that can be easily found - like cardboards, clothespins and screws - with sensors and actuators, through fast iteration processes.

The kit is based on an Arduino microcontroller, which is inside a wooden box with audio connectors outputs (Figure). We selected 12 pins to be exposed that were ready-to-use in the S4A environment (5 for inputs, 5 for outputs and 2 for servo motors), with each set of pins (inputs, outputs, motors) in one side of the box. The elements that we have been using so far are buttons, light sensors, proximity sensors, potentiometers, micro servo motors, LEDs, lasers and buzzers (Figure 1).

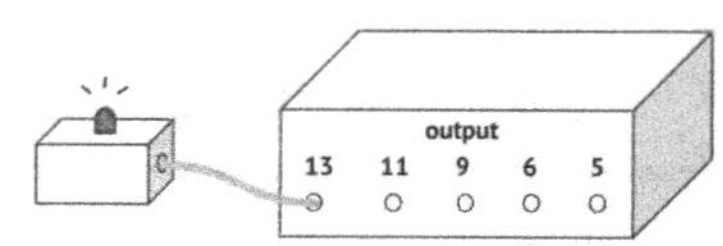

Figure 2. Representation of the microcontroller box connected to the LED module

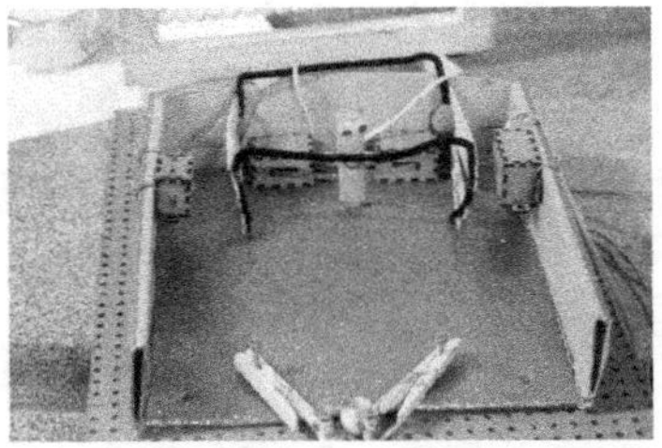

Figure 2. Soccer game created by middle school students

Figure 3. Pokemon created by middle school students

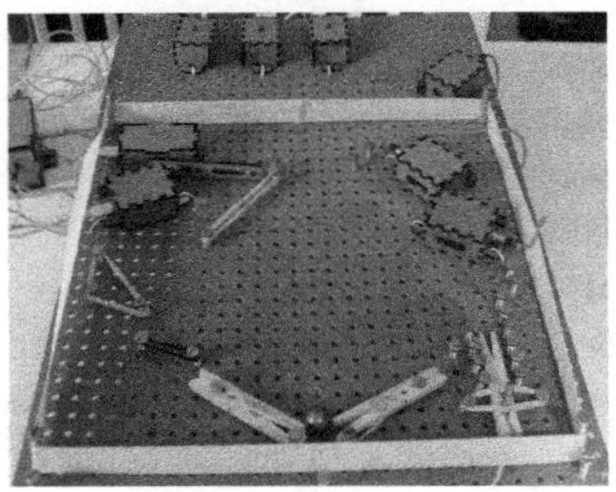

Figure 4. Pinball machine with BetaKit modules

The development of the kit intended to support low floors - an easy way to get started - and wide walls - ways to engage learners driven by diverse interests and learning styles - [5], with high levels of *tinkerability* [6]. Since we were concerned in offering an engaging and creative experience in introductory activities, we didn't focus on high ceilings. In the following sessions, we describe the characteristics of our toolkit that are connected to the ideas of *low floors* and *wide walls*.

Low floor
A shield on top of the Arduino makes possible to connect the modules to it through audio jacks (each one with its own ground and VCC), and everything is protected inside a wooden box where the pin numbers are engraved. The sensors and actuators are also inside small wooden boxes with audio connectors to reduce the chance of making mistakes when connecting the elements (Figure 1).

Blikstein [2] proposes the analytic construct of selective exposure (what is foregrounded and backgrounded in hardware and software design) for analyzing the usability (low floor) and power (high ceiling) of robotics toolkits and physical computing devices. According to this framework, there are eight common elements or concepts that can be exposed or hidden in computationally enhanced toolkits: resistors; understanding of Ohm's law; functionality of a breadboard; polarity; microcontroller pins; electrical connections; programming; and the idea of inputs and outputs.

Given our goals, we focused on high modularity to allow exploration of the building aspects, exposing kids only to the microcontroller pin numbers, electrical connections (with audio cables), programming, and to the distinction between inputs and outputs. We also chose to enclosure the electrical parts to reduce the debugging steps, enabling learners to focus on explorations with the materials through fast iteration.

In what concerns to embedded error, the audio connectors can be used in any position, so the kit communicate itself how the parts should be connected - and, due to its radial symmetry, the possibilities of wrong connections are reduced and the iteration process is faster.

Wide walls
When thinking about ways to offer means of expression for kids with diverse interests and learning styles, we experimented with a great range of materials searching for flexibility. The sensors and actuators in the kit were carefully chosen to allow multiple ways of interaction and to be low cost. The switches, for example, are easy to be pressed because of its shape, which allows the use of small balls and other non-heavy objects to press it. The light sensor combined with the laser is also flexible for building interactive projects, offering an easy way to check if something is in between them - even if separated by long distances. The light sensor itself can be used for a range of applications, acting as a tilt sensor or as a proximity detector, for example.

Another important aspect are the cables used to connect the modules with the microcontroller box. We chose to use one meter long audio cables, which affords the creation of structures in medium scale - so the projects don't have to be so small in consequence of the cable's size limitations as in other robotics kits. The long cables also allow more collaboration when

The modules have loops in two axes, so they can be easily attached to pegboards and cardboards.

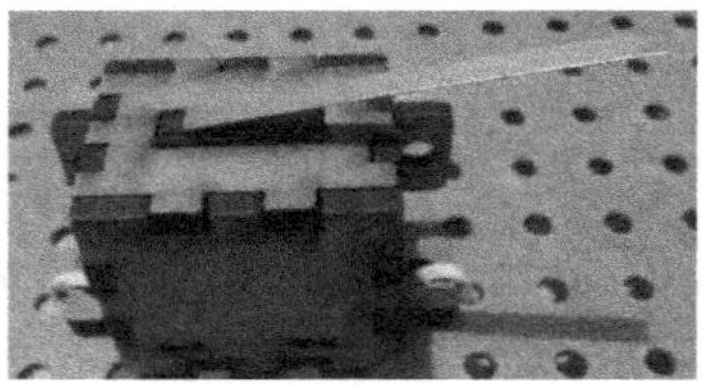

Figure 6. Button attached to a pegboard with coated wires

Figure 7. Elementary school kids experimenting with projects

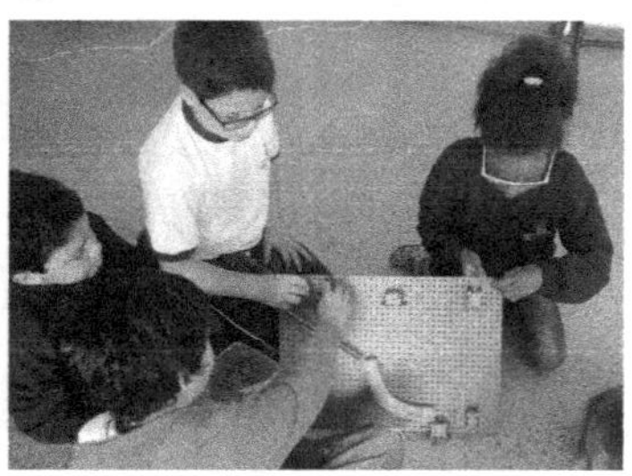

Figure 8. Kids building part of a Rube Goldberg Machine

working in projects, since can kids work together in different parts of bigger structures (Figure 5).

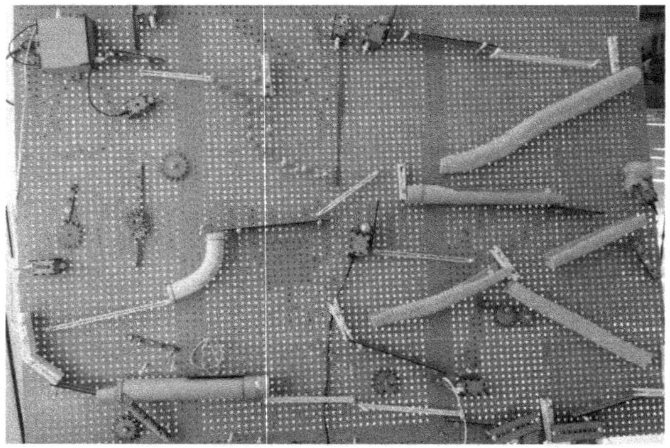

Figure 5. Rube Goldberg machine created with the BetaKit

The kit doesn't come with any mechanical parts for pedagogical reasons, encouraging kids to look at the environment around them to look for potentially useful materials for their creations. This practice can stimulate creativity in building with diverse ranges of resources and looking at everyday materials in new ways [4]. However, since some initial sort of resources can be useful to start explorations, we suggest the use of flexible elements suited for a great range of applications, such as coated wires for connecting the modules (Figure 6), screws, pegboards and cardboard boxes.

We used digital fabrication tools to make the wooden boxes for the first prototypes, which enabled constant refinements of the design. Laser cutting also makes the kits low-cost in small scales and allows anyone to cut and assemble the parts together, and to open the modules to fix problems.

Limitations

We also observed some limitations in the design of our toolkit. First, the sensors and actuators have to be connected through cables, which limits the extension of what kids can build, and can create some confusion when many cables are connected. Wireless communication devices could be a good improvement for the future, when their prices become lower. Also, the kit does not make explicit the differences between categories of parts (sensors, actuators and motors), which requires some initial tests for users being able to categorize the elements by themselves. These aspects are being explored for the next versions.

Future research

The BetaKit has been used in classrooms in four different schools and in informal learning spaces in São Paulo, Brazil. Elementary and middle school students create a great range of projects with our toolkit, including interactive art projects, tangible games (Figure 2, Figure 4), animals and characters (Figure 3, Figure 8), and Rube Goldberg Machines (Figure 8). Our initial observations of its use show us a promising field for allowing more tinkerability when learning physical programming.

In order to better understand new ways to keep improving the design of our toolkit, we intend to look closely at its use in diverse learning settings. We are also interested in ways to share the project documentation with a greater community, so other people can tinker with its design and applications.

References

1. Paulo Blikstein. 2013. Digital Fabrication and "Making" in Education: The Democratization of Invention. In *FabLabs: Of Machines, Makers and Inventors*, J. Walter-Herrmann and C. Büching (eds.). Transcript Publishers, Bielefeld, 1–21.
2. Paulo Blikstein. 2015. Computationally Enhanced Toolkits for Children: Historical Review and a Framework for Future Design. *Foundations and Trends® in Human–Computer Interaction* 9, 1: 1–68. https://doi.org/10.1561/1100000057'
3. Seymour Papert and Idit Harel. 1991. Situating constructionism. In *Constructionism*, Seymour Papert and Idit Harel (eds.). Ablex Publishing Corporation.
4. Mike Petrich, Karen Wilkinson, and Bronwyn Bevan. 2013. It Looks Like Fun, But Are They Learning? In *Design, Make, Play: Growing the next generation of STEM innovators*. Routledge, New York, 50–70.
5. Mitchel Resnick, Brad Myers, Kumiyo Nakakoji, Ben Shneiderman, Randy Pausch, Ted Selker, and Mike Eisenberg. 2005. *Design Principles for Tools to Support Creative Thinking*. Washington, DC.
6. Mitchel Resnick and Eric Rosenbaum. 2013. Designing for Tinkerability. In *Design, Make, Play: Growing the next generation of STEM innovators*. Routledge, New York, 163–181.
7. Natalie Rusk, Mitchel Resnick, Robbie Berg, and Margaret Pezalla-Granlund. 2008. New pathways into robotics: Strategies for broadening participation. *Journal of Science Education and Technology* 17, 1: 59–69. https://doi.org/10.1007/s10956-007-9082-2
8. Sherry Turkle and Seymour Papert. 1991. Epistemological Pluralism and the Revaluation of the Concrete. In *Constructionism*. Ablex Publishing Corporation, 161–191.
9. Shirin Vossoughi and Bronwyn Bevan. 2014. Making and Tinkering : A Review of the Literature. *National Research Council Committee on Out of School Time STEM*: 1–55.

Interaction Design and Autistic Children

Christopher Frauenberger,
Julia Makhaeva,
Katharina Spiel

Human-Computer Interaction Group
Institute for Design and Assessment of Technology
TU Wien (Vienna University of Technology), Austria

christopher.frauenberger@tuwien.ac.at
julia.makhaeva@tuwien.ac.at
katharina.spiel@tuwien.ac.at

IDC '17, June 27-30, 2017, Stanford, CA, USA
ACM 978-1-4503-4921-5/17/06.
http://dx.doi.org/10.1145/3078072.3081309

Abstract
With this workshop we aim to bring together researchers who explore interactive technologies in the context of autistic children. At a point at which considerable effort has been invested in this area and results are promising, but hardly conclusively convincing, we argue that it is time to critically reflect on our work. We do this by posing three provocative questions: 1) Are we trying to do the right thing? 2) Is it working? and 3) Does it matter? With all three questions we aim to kick-start a debate about the goals and intentions with which research is done in this area, how we define that technology is successful and how we can ensure that our research has real-world impact beyond the people involved directly.

Author Keywords
autism; children

ACM Classification Keywords
H.5.m [Information interfaces and presentation (e.g., HCI)]: Miscellaneous; See [http://acm.org/about/class/1998/]: for full list of ACM classifiers. This section is required.

Introduction
Autism is a neuro-developmental condition that manifests itself in many different ways. Its hallmark features are atypical social and communication skills as well as repetitive

thought patterns and behaviours. While its causes remain unclear, it is likely to be an interaction between genetic and environmental factors [2]. As diagnostic criteria are shifting and our understanding about autism improves, prevalence rates are on the rise with a currently estimated number of 1 in 68 children being on the spectrum [17].

Autistic children[1] often show an affinity to digital technology as they perceive it as a predictable, structured and save medium [16]. This has led to increasing attention in the research community on how to use digital technologies in interventions or as every-day supports in the lives of autistic children and their social environment.

The majority of work concerning children is aimed at scaffolding social skills development through interactive technologies. This includes, for example, using tangible user interfaces to increase social interactions during play [3], applications for touch screen devices such as tablets of phones [9], full-body interactions in augmented environments [14], virtual environments [1] or robotics [19]. Several meta-reviews have aimed to provide an overview of the current status of the field, which is commonly referred to as ASDTech. For example, Ploog et al. concludes that there is a lot of promise, but mixed evidence for the effectiveness of technology to enhance social, communication and language development in children [15]. Fletcher-Watson has compared the evidence behind the wide range of available apps for autism, calling for more rigour in methodology [4]. Kientz et al. possibly provide the most extensive overview of different kinds of interactive technologies for autism and the diverse contexts they are being used in [11].

Our own work in the field takes a critical stance towards normative assumptions. Building on the inspiring work by Mankoff et al. [13], we argue for shifting the starting point for technology design from mitigating deficits to creating positive experience that respond to desires and ideas that go beyond the mitigation of limitations that may associated with autism [6]. For the past 3 years, the OutsideTheBox project[2] has engaged autistic children to co-design interactive, smart objects that afford positive experiences through technologies and allows them to share that experience with their social peers. The process we employ is participatory throughout, providing scope for autistic children to shape the development of technology that is meaningful to them. Through multiple case studies, we have made methodological contributions to co-designing with autistic children [8, 12], theoretical contributions that critically reflect on our models of disability and how that reflects on the technologies we design [5] and with respect to rethinking the way we assess the experience of autistic children with technology [18].

With this work we aimed to highlight that technology can have diverse roles in the lives of autistic children and that designing and evaluating these technologies is situated, complex and multi-faceted. This raises methodological and theoretical challenges which we want to begin to address with this workshop.

Scope of the Workshop

With this workshop, we want to bring together the substantial number of researchers in our community who explore technology in the context of autism, to collectively reflect on the status of our efforts and engage in a critical discussion about future directions in this area. In a talk given by the first author as part of the Digital Bubbles Seminar Se-

[1] We are aware about the complex discussions surrounding person-first vs. label-first language; we opt for the latter, due to it being the predominantly self-chosen form of people on the spectrum [10].

[2] http://outsidethebox.at

ries[3], he posed three leading questions to facilitate such a reflective process, which this workshop aims to pick up on:

1. Are we trying to do the right thing?
2. Is it working?
3. Does it matter?

The first question aims to provoke researchers to take a step back and critically examine their goals and, inherently, their assumptions about what roles technology can have in the lives of autistic children. What are the intentions with which we design technology in this space telling us about our conception of autism? In a related workshop at CHI'16 [7], we explored a similar question which led to a healthy debate around empowerment, neuro-diversity, assistance and functional support.

Diversifying goals also means that evaluating technology becomes a lot more challenging. What is success? What does it mean to design technology that "affords positive experience" or supports the well-being of autistic children? How can we make statements about the impact of the technology we build that are both, scientifically rigorous **and** relevant within the messy life-worlds of autistic children?

Finally, the last question relates to how we can achieve impact that is sustainable and scalable. A lot of research rightly involves autistic children directly in developing technology and the heterogeneity of the target group means, that outcomes vary from case to case. How can we scale up or even transfer insights when solutions rely on being fitted to particular users and particular contexts?

[3] http://digitalbubbles.org.uk/

Schedule & Activities

We are proposing a full day workshop that combines input from the participants from within their contexts of research with focus group work for critical reflection. The proposed schedule is as follows:

9:00	Welcome & Introductions
9:10	Participant Input - Show & Tell
10:00	Focus Session: Are we doing the right thing?
11:00	**Coffee Break**
11:15	Focus Session: Is it working?
12:15	Quick Synopsis & Documentation in the plenum
12:30	**Lunch Break**
13:30	Focus Session: Does it matter?
14:30	**Coffee Break**
15:00	Synopsis and Discussion
16:00	Fresh Air Break
16:15	Plans for Dissemination
17:00	**Workshop end**

In the Participant Input session, we will ask participants to prepare 3 slides about their work, engaging with the workshop themes from in a reversed form: 1) Our goal is... 2) We know it is working, because... 3) It matters, because...

All focus sessions will follow the same format: there will be a 10 minutes presentation as a provocation to stimulate discussion before all participants split up in groups to discuss. Each group will be 4 to 8 people and moderated by one organiser (or a designated participant).

Organisers

All three organisers currently work on the OutsideTheBox project at the Human-Computer Interaction Group, Institute for Design and Assessment of Technology, TU Wien, Austria.

Christopher Frauenberger is principle investigator of OutsideTheBox. His research focuses on designing technology with and for marginalised user groups, such as those with disabilities and in particular with autistic children. He is committed to participatory design approaches and builds on theories and methods from diverse fields such as the action research, disability studies, philosophy of science, research ethics amongst others.

Julia Makhaeva is product designer, MA and specialises in social design, social interaction and conceptual work. She graduated from the University of Applied Sciences Dresden in Germany. Prior to joining OutsideTheBox, she was a social and product designer at morethanshelters in Berlin and Hamburg, a social enterprise that creates concepts and solutions for humanitarian needs. She is exploring how designers might empower stakeholders, particularly children, by means of participation and co-design. She is also interested in how smart materials and technologies could be used as tools for gaining and sharing knowledge.

Katharina Spiel uses humanistic theories to understand problems in human-computer interaction. Previous work dealt with gender construction in Italian western, blind players in text-based games and the novelty effect on gameplay experiences. Within OutsideTheBox the focus lies on understanding the experiences autistic children have with technologies and how autistic children can be directly included in evaluation.

Outcomes

As the main outcome, we plan to launch a special issue, preferably in the International Journal for Child Computer Interaction, which synthesises the main challenges that were identified. Furthermore, we aim to report more directly on what was discussed in a collective publication, for example in the ACM interactions magazine.

Call for Participants

This workshop aims to bring together researchers who explore interactive technologies in the context of autistic children. Our aim is to foster the relationships between researchers in this field and critically reflect on the current status of our efforts. We do this by posing three provocative questions:

1) Are we trying to do the right thing? 2) Is it working? 3) Does it matter?

We invite position papers (two to four pages, SIGCH Extended Abstract Format) which explore existing work through these questions. Submissions should include a brief overview of the research (past or planned), as well one paragraph reflection for each of the three questions. For more background, please see the full workshop proposal document on our webpage (below).

Position papers should be submitted by XXX 2017 (12pm PDT) via email to *christopher.frauenberger@tuwien.ac.at*. The selection process will ensure that high quality contributions from a range of different perspectives are invited to participate.

Additional resources, related literature and further practical information is available at the workshop's webpage: http://outsidethebox.at/en/idc17-workshop

At least one author of an accepted submission is required to attend the workshop, and participants must register for both the workshop and at least one day of the main conference.

Acknowledgements

This research is funded by the Austrian Science Fund (FWF): [P26281-N23] "OutsideTheBox - Rethinking Assistive Technologies with Children with Autism" project.

REFERENCES

1. S. Cobb, L. Beardon, R. Eastgate, T. Glover, S. Kerr, H. Neale, S. Parsons, S. Benford, E. Hopkins, P. Mitchell, G. Reynard, and J. Wilson. 2002. Applied Virtual Environments to Support Learning of Social Interaction Skills in Users With Aspergers Syndrome. *Digital Creativity* 13 (March 2002), 11–22(12). DOI: http://dx.doi.org/doi:10.1076/digc.13.1.11.3208
2. Marc Fakhoury. 2015. Autistic spectrum disorders: A review of clinical features, theories and diagnosis. *International Journal of Developmental Neuroscience* 43 (June 2015), 70–77. DOI:http://dx.doi.org/10.1016/j.ijdevneu.2015.04.003
3. William Farr, Nicola Yuill, and Hayes Raffle. 2010. Social benefits of a tangible user interface for children with Autistic Spectrum Conditions. *Autism* 14, 3 (2010), 237–252. DOI: http://dx.doi.org/10.1177/1362361310363280
4. Sue Fletcher-Watson. 2013. A Targeted Review of Computer-Assisted Learning for People with Autism Spectrum Disorder: Towards a Consistent Methodology. *Review Journal of Autism and Developmental Disorders* 1, 2 (Nov. 2013), 87–100. DOI:http://dx.doi.org/10.1007/s40489-013-0003-4
5. Christopher Frauenberger. 2015a. Disability and Technology - A Critical Realist Perspective. In *Proceedings of the 17th International ACM SIGACCESS Conference on Computers & Accessibility*. ACM Press, Lisbon, Portugal, 8. DOI: http://dx.doi.org/10.1145/2700648.2809851 Best Paper Nomination.
6. Christopher Frauenberger. 2015b. Rethinking Autism and Technology. *interactions* 22, 2 (Feb. 2015), 57–59. DOI:http://dx.doi.org/10.1145/2728604
7. Christopher Frauenberger, Judith Good, and Narcis Pares. 2016a. Autism and Technology: Beyond Assistance & Intervention. In *Proceedings of the 2016 CHI Conference Extended Abstracts on Human Factors in Computing Systems (CHI EA '16)*. ACM, New York, NY, USA, 3373–3378. DOI: http://dx.doi.org/10.1145/2851581.2856494
8. Christopher Frauenberger, Julia Makhaeva, and Katharina Spiel. 2016b. Designing Smart Objects with Autistic Children: Four Design Exposès. In *Proceedings of the 2016 CHI Conference on Human Factors in Computing Systems (CHI '16)*. ACM, New York, NY, USA, 130–139. DOI: http://dx.doi.org/10.1145/2858036.2858050 Honorable Mention (best 4% of submissions).
9. Juan Pablo Hourcade, Stacy R. Williams, Ellen A. Miller, Kelsey E. Huebner, and Lucas J. Liang. 2013. Evaluation of Tablet Apps to Encourage Social Interaction in Children with Autism Spectrum Disorders. In *Proceedings of the SIGCHI Conference on Human Factors in Computing Systems (CHI '13)*. ACM, New York, NY, USA, 3197–3206. DOI: http://dx.doi.org/10.1145/2470654.2466438

10. Lorcan Kenny, Caroline Hattersley, Bonnie Molins, Carole Buckley, Carol Povey, and Elizabeth Pellicano. 2015. Which terms should be used to describe autism? Perspectives from the UK autism community. *Autism* (July 2015). DOI: http://dx.doi.org/10.1177/1362361315588200
11. Julie A. Kientz, Matthew S. Goodwin, Gillian R. Hayes, and Gregory D. Abowd. 2013. Interactive Technologies for Autism. *Synthesis Lectures on Assistive, Rehabilitative, and Health-Preserving Technologies* 2, 2 (2013), 1–177. DOI:http://dx.doi.org/10.2200/S00533ED1V01Y201309ARH004
12. Julia Makhaeva, Christopher Frauenberger, and Katharina Spiel. 2016. Creating Creative Spaces for Co-Designing with Autistic Children – The concept of a “Handlungsspielraum”. In *Proceedings of the 14th Participatory Design Conference.* ACM Press, Aarhus, Denmark, 51–60. DOI: http://dx.doi.org/10.1145/2940299.2940306
13. Jennifer Mankoff, Gillian R. Hayes, and Devva Kasnitz. 2010. Disability studies as a source of critical inquiry for the field of assistive technology. In *Proceedings of the 12th international ACM SIGACCESS conference on Computers and accessibility (ASSETS '10).* ACM, Orlando, Florida, USA, 3–10. DOI: http://dx.doi.org/10.1145/1878803.1878807
14. Joan Mora-Guiard, Ciera Crowell, Narcis Pares, and Pamela Heaton. 2016. Lands of Fog: Helping Children with Autism in Social Interaction through a Full-Body Interactive Experience. ACM Press, 262–274. DOI: http://dx.doi.org/10.1145/2930674.2930695
15. Bertram O. Ploog, Alexa Scharf, DeShawn Nelson, and Patricia J. Brooks. 2013. Use of Computer-Assisted Technologies (CAT) to Enhance Social, Communicative, and Language Development in Children with Autism Spectrum Disorders. *Journal of Autism and Developmental Disorders* 43, 2 (Feb. 2013), 301–322. DOI: http://dx.doi.org/10.1007/s10803-012-1571-3
16. Sathiyaprakash Ramdoss, Wendy Machalicek, Mandy Rispoli, Austin Mulloy, Russell Lang, and Mark O'Reilly. 2012. Computer-based interventions to improve social and emotional skills in individuals with autism spectrum disorders: A systematic review. *Developmental Neurorehabilitation* 15, 2 (2012), 119–135. DOI: http://dx.doi.org/10.3109/17518423.2011.651655
17. Ginny Russell, Stephan Collishaw, Jean Golding, Susan E Kelly, and Tamsin Ford. 2015. Changes in diagnosis rates and behavioural traits of autism spectrum disorder over time. *British Journal of Psychiatry Open* 1, 2 (2015), 110–115. DOI: http://dx.doi.org/10.1192/bjpo.bp.115.000976
18. Katharina Spiel, Christopher Frauenberger, and Geraldine Fitzpatrick. 2017. Experiences of autistic children with technologies. *International Journal of Child-Computer Interaction* (Feb. 2017). DOI: http://dx.doi.org/10.1016/j.ijcci.2016.10.007
19. Joshua Wainer, Ester Ferrari, Kerstin Dautenhahn, and Ben Robins. 2010. The effectiveness of using a robotics class to foster collaboration among groups of children with autism in an exploratory study. *Personal Ubiquitous Comput.* 14, 5 (July 2010), 445–455. DOI: http://dx.doi.org/10.1007/s00779-009-0266-z

Playing Together: The Importance of Joint Engagement in the Design of Technology for Children

Catalina Naranjo-Bock
Google Inc.
1600 Amphitheater Parkway
Mountain View, CA, 94043 USA
catalinanb@google.com

Jennie Ito, Ph.D.
Google Inc.
1600 Amphitheater Parkway
Mountain View, CA, 94043 USA
jenniei@google.com

IDC '17, June 27-30, 2017, Stanford, CA, USA

ACM ISBN 978-1-4503-4921-5/17/06.
http://dx.doi.org/10.1145/3078072.3081310

Abstract
In the design of technology for children, many products focus on providing content that is both engaging and appropriate for children at a given age and developmental stage. However, less attention is paid to the *context* in which children tend to engage with digital products. When focusing on children age 13 and younger, context often includes social interaction with parents, caregivers, and friends, which provides many opportunities to design digital experiences that support co-play and joint media engagement (JME).

In this workshop, we will be discussing real world case studies, as well as theoretical approaches used by researchers, designers, and academics to design technology for children that includes and fosters co-play and JME experiences. Our discussion will be centered not only on understanding *what* are co-engagement experiences, but also *how* these are produced and *why* these are important for the child end user. The expected outcome of the workshop will be a set of principles, examples, and guidelines for digital media developers to consider when designing rich digital experiences that take into consideration not only the child, but the context for engagement as well.

Author Keywords: Joint media engagement; co-engagement; children; interaction design

ACM Classification Keywords
H.5.m. Information interfaces and presentation (e.g., HCI): Miscellaneous.

Introduction

Consider the following (fictional) scenarios:

Scenario 1:
Noah heard about the new Pokemon GO game from his friends at school and immediately downloaded it. As an 8-year-old, he uses his dad's old phone to play games after school or during the weekends. His aunt is visiting, and he asked her to download the game on her own phone so he could teach her how to use it, and catch Pokemons together while they are out spending time together.

Scenario 2:
Ana's 11-year-old daughter loves to play Candy Crush Saga and is constantly talking about it with her friends. Ana decided to download the game on her phone and start playing as an opportunity to bond and connect with her daughter. She sometimes asks her daughter for help, even if she doesn't really need it.

Scenario 3:
Sara often lets her 6-year-old son and 3-year-old daughter play games and watch videos on her old tablet while she cooks dinner. Her kids have to share the tablet so they take turns and often fight over who gets to play first or what to watch. A family friend told Sara about the game Sago Mini Doodlecast. When Sara's kids tried the app, they worked together on the drawings and enjoyed recording their voices. They were also excited to share what they made together with Sara.

Technology use by children comes in many different facets, which are often not by design. The scenarios above are examples of case studies we have come across during our own research and practice, and represent different ways in which parents and kids are using mobile games to enrich both their digital and real-life experiences. Suddenly, mobile games are not only a way for isolated users to spend free time, but become instruments for social bonding and keeping abreast of each other's interests [8]. In fact, recent research shows that playing digital games together is growing in popularity, particularly among families with children age 4-10 [14]. When games are shared with someone the child cares about, the experience of the game itself becomes much more enriching and memorable [9].

When developing media for children, these unexpected usage patterns and emerging relationships tend to be a novelty for the product makers, as these are generally not taken into account when developing the technology itself [12]. However, the topics of co-play, JME, and taking into account the context in which children use technology, are all recently emerging as vital considerations for the field (e.g., [3, 9-10, 12, 13-16]). This workshop aims to take an introspective look at these topics as it relates to the design of technology for children between the ages of 2 and 13 years.

In her book Screen Time, Lisa Guernsey, writes about the importance of considering the three Cs -- the individual *child, content, and context* -- when selecting, using, and developing digital media with and for young children [6]. In 2012, the Fred Rogers Center used Guernsey's three Cs to inform their Framework for Quality, which is meant to provide guidance for parents, educators, and media creators on the quality of digital media [5]. According to their framework, quality in digital media for young children should take into account the following:

> ***Child:*** *The distinct cognitive abilities, physical abilities, social-emotional needs, aptitudes, and interest of individual children, at different developmental stages should be considered.*
> ***Content:*** *The intent of the content should be clear -- to educate, introduce new information, develop particular skills, and/or entertain.*
> ***Context:*** *Especially for children age 5 and younger, the media product should encourage joint engagement. For older children, interactivity and engagement with the media product, including the engagement of children as creators of content should be a priority [5, pp. 1-2].*

Although the three Cs are the same in terms of their level of importance, *context* tends to be a more nebulous concept to grasp and to design for. What are some ways in which we can define *context* when designing for children of different ages, and why is this important? While this is one of the questions we wish to discuss further in the workshop, what we do know from decades of research on television and young children, as well as emerging research on children's use of digital media, is that context matters because:

> ***Relationships Matter***: *...young children learn best in the context of interactions and relationships with tuned-in, responsive, and caring adults.*
>
> ***Joint Engagement Matters***: *...adult/child interactions are key to language learning, and this is also true when using media with children. Reading a book or playing with an app leads to more learning when adults and children share the experience* [4, p. 27].

Using media together supports learning, so technology should be used to support and strengthen adult/child relationships and promote joint engagement [3-4, 12, 16].

When purposefully including context as a design parameter for the design of technology for children, product developers can aspire to not only create engaging games, toys, books, etc., but *meaningful experiences and connections* [12]. These experiences are joint media experiences, defined by Guersney and Levine as "when any two or more people -- parents and child, siblings, or peers -- are looking at the same media at the same time, are involved in the content together, and are prompted by what they are seeing to interact with each other and bring more meaning to what they are watching or doing" [7, pg. 171].

Over the last 5 years, field leaders from organizations such as The Joan Ganz Cooney Center, The Fred Rogers Center, and the TEC Center at Erikson Institute have produced a number of publications that provide insight into the context of conjoint technology usage and suggest various design strategies for encouraging co-engagement, including [1-17]:

- Think of experiences that parents and children can play or use together, or foster family teamwork.
- Provide suggestions for parents on how to play together.
- Create content that appeals and challenges kids and parents.
- Connect in-app learning to the real world
- Extend play beyond the screen.
- Appeal to multiple generations.
- Provide opportunities for users to grow through participation.
- Offer related real-world activities.
- Have content that revolves around children's existing interests, not prescribed topics.
- Consider the types of gameplay kids and adults enjoy the most
- Provide users with ways to assist and expand on the educational benefits of media.
- Enable co-creation.
- Allow for varying degrees of parental involvement.
- Encourage communication with family members, caregivers, or friends.
- Connect to real-life experiences.

These insights, as well as topics outlined in this paper will provide the starting point for a much more in-depth discussion regarding how to design for JME. During the workshop, we wish to expand on a) the meaning of JME, b) what constitutes successful implementations of these experiences on the design of technology for children, c) why are these important for children as end users, and d) best practices on how to implement them.

Topics of Discussion

The goal of this workshop is to bring together researchers, designers, academics, and media developers, who envision, design, create and study technologies for children. We would like to build a community to expand possible guidelines and design principles to foster co-engagement experiences on the design of technology for children.

- How should we design digital products for children that foster co-engagement experiences?
- How should we cater for the needs of multiple types of possible users?
- How do co-engagement experiences manifest within different ages and developmental stages?
- What are examples of successful co-engagement experiences and why?
- How do co-engagement experiences bring more meaning to technology products for children? Why are they important?

Workshop Outcomes

The outcome of the workshop will be a whitepaper and potentially a journal publication with a set of principles, best practices and case studies that should be considered when designing technology for children that foster co-engagement experiences.

Structure Of Workshop

This half day workshop will include activities centered on addressing the issues mentioned above. Select workshop attendees will present their research, design work, and/or selection of examples focusing on the topic of the workshop and the questions of interest. This will be followed by breakout sessions for attendees to discuss the open questions in small groups and share the learning with the entire group. After the breakout sessions, attendees will come together to discuss design principles and best practices for designing technologies for children that foster co-engagement experiences.

References

[1] Chiong, C. (2010). *Can video games promote intergenerational play and literacy learning?* New York: The Joan Ganz Cooney Center at Sesame Workshop.

[2] Chiong, C., & Shuler, C. (2010). *Learning: Is there an app for that? Investigations of young children's usage and learning with mobile devices and apps.* New York: The Joan Ganz CooneyCenter at Sesame Workshop.

[3] Donohue, C (Ed.). (2017). *Family Engagement in the Digital Age: Early Childhood Educators as Media Mentors.* New York: Routledge and Washington, DC: National Association for the Education of Young Children.

[4] Donohue, C (Ed.). (2015). *Technology and Digital Media in the Early Years: Tools for Teaching and Learning.* New York: Routledge and Washington, DC: National Association for the Education of Young Children.

[5] Fred Rogers Center for Early Learning and Children's Media at Saint Vincent College. (2012). *A framework for quality in digital media for children: Considerations for parents, educators, and media creators.* Latrobe, PA: Fred Rogers Center

[6] Guernsey, L. (2012). *Screen Time: How Electronic Media—From Baby Videos to Educational Software—Affects Your Young Child.* New York: Basic Books.

[7] Guernsey, L., & Levine, M. (2015). *Tap, Click, Read: Growing Readers in a World of Screens.* San Francisco, CA: Jossey-Bass.

[8] Ito, M., Baumer, S., Bittanti, M., boyd, d., Cody, R., Herr-Stephenson, B., ... Tripp, L. (2010). *Hanging Out, Messing Around, and Geeking Out: Kids Living and Learning with New Media.* Cambridge, MA: MIT Press.

[9] PlayScience. (2016). *Let's coplay. A developer's guide to family cooperative mobile play.* Retrieved from http://playsciencelab.com/new-developers-guide-mobile-family-co-play-playscience/

[10] Sobel, K., Bhattacharya, A., Hiniker, A., Lee, J. H., Kientz, J. A., & Yip, J. C. (2017). "It wasn't really about the Pokémon": Parents' perspectives on a location-based mobile game. In Proc. CHI 2017.

[11] Takeuchi, L., (2011). *Families matter: Designing media for a digital age.* New York: The Joan Ganz Cooney Center at Sesame Workshop.

[12] Takeuchi, L., & Stevens, R. (2011, December). *The new coviewing: Designing for learning through joint media engagement.* New York: The Joan Ganz Cooney Center at Sesame Workshop.

[13] The Joan Ganz Cooney Center. (2016, October). [Digital Games and Family Life: Exploring the games and titles kids and parents choose to play] [Infographic]. Retrieved from http://www.joanganzcooneycenter.org/wp-content/uploads/2016/10/jgcc_dgfl_2.pdf

[14] The Joan Ganz Cooney Center. (2017, January). [Digital Games and Family Life: Families play both board/card games and digital games together] [Infographic]. Retrieved from http://www.joanganzcooneycenter.org/wp-content/uploads/2017/01/JGCC-DGFL-4.pdf

[15] The Joan Ganz Cooney Center. (2016, December). [Digital Games and Family Life: When parents and kids play together] [Infographic]. Retrieved from http://www.joanganzcooneycenter.org/wp-content/uploads/2016/12/JGCC-DGFL-3.pdf

[16] The Joan Ganz Cooney Center (2014). *Family Time with Apps: A Guide to Using Apps with Your Kids.* Retrieved from www.joanganzcooneycenter.org/publication/family-time-with-apps/

[17] Vaala, S., Ly, A., & Levine, M.H. (2015). *Getting a read on the app stores: A market scan and analysis of children's literacy apps.* New York, NY: The Joan Ganz Cooney Center at Sesame Workshop.

Of Kittens and Kiddies: Reflections on Participatory Design with Small Animals and Small Humans

Yoram Chisik
Madeira Interactive Technologies
Institute (M-ITI)
Caminho da Penteada, Funchal
Portugal
ychisik@gmail.com

Clara Mancini
Department of Computing
The Open University
Walton Hall, Milton Keynes
United Kingdom
clara.mancini@open.ac.uk

IDC'17, June 27 - 30, 2017, Stanford, CA, USA.

ACM ISBN 978-1-4503-4921-5/17/06
http://dx.doi.org/10.1145/3078072.3081311.

Abstract
Participatory Design with children strives to broaden the perspective of and increase empathy in design for the needs and desires of children by giving children a voice in the design process. The exact nature of the role played by children in the design process (e.g. user, informant, co-designer) and how much voice they are actually given has been the subject of a long and heated debate in the IDC community. The emerging field of Animal Computer Interaction, which seeks to empower animals through the participatory design of user-centered technology, offers an interesting opportunity for a comparative analysis. Indeed, working with animals poses many of the challenges also posed by working with children, due to similarities with regards to cognitive capabilities or attention span at particular developmental stages, and with regards to the designer's ability to communicate with them. This workshop aims to bring together researchers from the fields of animal and child computer interaction to explore similarities and difference in the challenges they face, the methods they use and the lessons they have learnt, to date, with the objective of gaining a better understanding of these important aspects and setting an agenda for further collaboration and study between the two communities.

Author Keywords
Participatory Design; Animal Computer Interaction; ACI; Interaction Design with Children.

ACM Classification Keywords
H.5.2. User Interfaces (D.2.2, H.1.2, I.3.6): *User-centered design*.

Introduction
In the IDC community researchers do not presume to know what goes on inside a child's mind; instead, they seek and generate ideas through observation, interaction and collaboration with children in the field and the lab to create solutions that address needs and desires from the child perspective.

IDCers seek to empower, add value, and in general strive to broaden the perspective and increase the level of empathy in design for every aspect in the life of a child, by giving children a voice in the design process.

The degrees in which children can effectively express themselves and therefore effectively take part in a participatory design process varies greatly with age and according to developmental parameters. To compound matters, the meaning of what counts as participation, what is the exact nature of the role played by participants (e.g. user, informant, co-designer) and how much voice is actually given to them in the design process is the subject of an ongoing debate in the community [1,2,5,6].

The emerging field of Animal Computer Interaction (ACI) [3,4] seeks to extend the field of user centered design beyond the human species by exploring the interaction between animals and technology, and developing participatory frameworks and protocols for the design of technology intended for animals. In this respect ACI offers important opportunities for comparison and reflection on the theory and practice of participatory design. Indeed, working with animals poses many of the same challenges that designers encounter when working with children, having to account for the participants' specific cognitive capabilities at particular developmental stages, and contend with limited attention spans and communication barriers.

With this workshop we aim to bring together researchers from the fields of animal and child computer interaction, in order to contrast the challenges, they face, the methods they use and the lessons they have learnt so far. We believe the juxtaposition of animals and children to be potentially controversial but at the same time, and partly because of its controversy, we argue that it provides a unique lens through which we can examine core notions such as those of *participant* and *participation* beyond preconceptions surrounding distinctions of species or age. We propose that this juxtaposition will enable researchers to gain a better understanding of participatory design with children and animals as a practice and research approach, and of the values that participatory design brings to each of the research communities respectively as well as to the broader research and design community more broadly.

Aims and Goals
The workshop has the following main goals:

1. To build a community of researchers engaged in work related to interaction design with children,

animals or both, who are interested in comparing the two domains.

2. To share experiences of designing *for* and *with* animals and children, and identify similarities and differences in the process, with a focus on related challenges, so that individual insights can benefit the community's reflection on participatory design as a whole.

3. To identify opportunities, and develop an agenda, for further research and interdisciplinary collaborations.

4. To share the reflections of the workshop participants with the wider community, via the publication of a journal article or a journal special issue.

Overall, we expect that the workshop will constitute the basis for the development of a long-lasting working group devoted to the exploration of issues related to participatory design through the lens of animal and child computer interaction.

Format

The workshop's format will be that of a full day event, involving 10 to 25 participants. Participants will be recruited via direct invitation through the authors' extensive networks of contacts in the fields of both ACI and interaction design with children, as well as via a call for participation on relevant mailing lists and websites. In order to be invited to take part in the workshop, participants will be required to submit a short position paper about their work in either field, and their thoughts on the juxtaposition of participatory design with animals and children.

The workshop's day will be divided into five sessions: introductions, presentations, mapping, discussion and planning.

Introductions
The organizers will introduce their perspective on the workshop topic and invite the participants to briefly introduce themselves to the rest of the attendees.

Presentations
Through short presentations, participants will share their experiences with participatory design with either animals or children, or both, including research approaches, challenges faced and lessons learnt.

Mapping
Based on the content of the presentations, participants will engage in a mapping session moderated by the organizers and aiming to identify similarities and differences between participatory design with children, on the one hand, and participatory design with animals, on the other hand.

Discussion
The themes that will emerge during the mapping session, will be subsequently discussed in order to explore possible research topics and collaborations that participants and the wider community could explore going forward.

Planning
The day will end with a planning session during which participants will draw a plan of action, based on the outcome of the discussion session, for publication and potential future studies and collaborations

References

[1] Allison Druin. 2002. The role of children in the design of new technology. *Behaviour and Information Technology*, 21, 1–25.

[2] Tuck Wah Leong and Ole Sejer Iversen. 2015. Values-led Participatory Design as a Pursuit of Meaningful Alternatives. In *Proceedings of the Annual Meeting of the Australian Special Interest Group for Computer Human Interaction (OzCHI '15)*, Bernd Ploderer, Marcus Carter, Martin Gibbs, Wally Smith, and Frank Vetere (Eds.). ACM, New York, NY, USA, 314-323.

[3] Clara Mancini. 2017. Towards an animal-centred ethics for Animal–Computer Interaction. *International Journal of Human-Computer Studies*, 98 pp. 221–233.

[4] Clara Mancini. 2016. Animal-Computer Interaction: a Manifesto (2011) and sections from Towards an Animal-Centred Ethics for Animal-Computer Interaction (2016). In: Bastian, Michelle; Jones, Owain; Moore, Niamh and Roe, Emma Eds. *Participatory Research in More-than-Human Worlds*. Abingdon: Routledge, pp. 54–65.

[5] Michael Scaife, Yvonne Rogers, Frances Aldrich, and Matt Davies. 1997. Designing for or designing with? Informant design for interactive learning environments. In *Proceedings of the ACM SIGCHI Conference on Human factors in computing systems (CHI '97)*. ACM, New York, NY, USA, 343-350.

[6] Svetlana Yarosh, Iulian Radu, Seth Hunter, and Eric Rosenbaum. 2011. Examining values: an analysis of nine years of IDC research. In *Proceedings of the 10th International Conference on Interaction Design and Children (IDC '11)*. ACM, New York, NY, USA, 136-144.

Make2Learn with IoT: Engaging Children into Joyful Design and Making of Interactive Connected Objects

Monica Divitini, Michail N. Giannakos, Simone Mora, Sofia Papavlasopoulou
Norwegian University of Science and Technology
Sem Sælandsvei 7-9, 7491 Trondheim, Norway
{divitini, mihcailg, simonem, spapav}@ntnu.no

Ole Sejer Iversen
Participatory IT Center, Aarhus University
Aarhus, Denmark
oiversen@cs.au.dk

IDC '17, June 27-30, 2017, Stanford, CA, USA

ACM ISBN 978-1-4503-4921-5/17/06.
http://dx.doi.org/10.1145/3078072.3081312

Abstract

The Make2Learn workshop aims to explore the introduction in the learning processes of tools and methods for creative and joyful ideation, design and prototyping of Internet of Things (IoT) artifacts. Making IoT artefacts enable children to foster co-creativity and joy in learning processes and to construct knowledge; leading to STEM concepts. Making activities for IoT often have a broad perspective that includes not just digital fabrication, but also design thinking concepts such as problem elaboration, brainstorming, ideation and reflection. Make2learn aims to bring together a multidisciplinary group of experts for exploring how the intersection between the design, making, learning and IoT fields can accelerate the acquisition of 21st Century learning competences. During the workshop a set of tools and methods to engage children in ideation and prototyping of IoT artefacts will be demonstrated. Participants are also invited to bring and present their own tools. This will allow us to better understand and improve the value of Maker philosophy and the role of design and making IoT technologies to support teaching and learning.

Author Keywords
Maker movement; IoT; prototyping tools; ideation tools; learning technologies; constructionist.

ACM Classification Keywords
K.3.1 Computer-assisted instruction (CAI); H.5.m. Information interfaces and presentation (e.g., HCI): Miscellaneous.

Introduction
Making in education is growing enormously, with recent research initiatives including a special issue on digital fabrication [5] and the launch of the *FabLearn* [1] community, to mention few. At the same time, advances in the Internet of Things (IoT) is providing a set of methods and tools to enable and foster making activities via collaborative ideation and prototyping e.g. *Arduino IoT*[1], *LittleBits Cloud*[2], *Tiles Toolkit*[3].

The creative production of IoT artifacts can be linked to teaching new 21st-century and design literacy skills [2] via educational programmes that emphasize the development of problem solving, creative thinking sketching and reflection abilities in new hybrid learning environments "that combines digital fabrication, design thinking and collaborative ideation and innovation" [7]. Designing and prototyping IoT artifacts have the potential to make the symbolic and abstract manipulations involved in creative procedures more concrete and manageable for young students [3]; and to support making as a creative, joyful and problem-solving experience. For example, artifacts allow students to learn by iteratively testing, rebuilding their designs and working collaboratively. Further, by involving children in the design decisions they begin to develop technological fluency and the needed competences, in a joyful way. Finally, during the past decade, we have seen an increased appearance of environments and community spaces (e.g. Hackerspaces, Makerspaces, TechShops, and FabLabs) offering diverse opportunities for young students to facilitate learning through making.

However, there are a number of challenges in ensuring that procedures, tools and environments, embody appropriate progression and engender motivation and joy. For example, tools often serve specific, narrow tasks and are not designed to be used together. Tools are not always associated with a specific methodology, vice-versa methods don't always provide tools that can be easily used by practitioners and educators. Finally, there are factors that limit the adoption of tools and methods by educators, like difficulty to learn/use, lack of documentation and evidence-based best practises as well as limited learning activities utilizing those tools and methods. This workshop will attempt to address these key research challenges.

Precedent editions of the Make2Learn workshop has organized at the International Conference on Entertainment Computing (2015) and Interaction Design and Children Conference (2016). Information related to the PC members and conference proceedings

---

[1] Arduino IoT - https://create.arduino.cc/iot/

[2] Little Bits Cloud - http://littlebits.cc/cloud

[3] Tiles IoT Toolkit – http://tilestoolkit.io

Figure 1: Children using Tiles toolkit alternating ideation and coding activities

as well as the selected papers [4] and publications can be found at the workshop websites[4][5].

Objectives

Make2Learn with IoT aims to bring together researchers, educators, designers and developers who are interested in the exploration of making principles and supportive IoT technologies towards the acquisition of 21st Century learning competences. The workshop aims to provide an environment where participants will get opportunities to collaborate with others in their own and complementary research areas. Our objectives can be summarised in:

1. Accelerate research on Maker Movement by proposing ways to create greater interest and synergies among researchers, educators, students, policymakers, and industrial developers;
2. Understand how novel IoT technologies, methods and tools can be used to involve children in making interactive and connected artefacts;
3. Promote rigorous multidimensional and multidisciplinary methods and tools and implement rigorous experimentation strategies and metrics for in-depth longitudinal case studies.

Procedure

We invite participants to bring and present their own research related to learning, design and making tools; as well as about the respective procedure they use.

Works can be presented as short talks, videos, demos or hands-on sessions.

Then, we will use a card-based ideation tool for the IoT, Tiles Toolkit [6] (Figure 1), as a mean to facilitate discussion among participants. Tiles can be used to support ideation and design activities in multiple ways. Learning goals that can be achieved playing with Tiles include: building basic knowledge of the IoT, design thinking skills, development of communication and reflection skills, collaboration and teambuilding. Idea generated with the tool can be used as an input for guiding prototyping exploration with code, electronics and craftwork. Tiles will allow participants to formulate better understanding of several technical and practical aspects that could be valuable in designing effective making activities to foster joyful engagement and creativity in learning.

Dissemination activities, expected participants and practical information

Papers will be published online on the workshop website http://m2l-iot.webflow.io. All presentations will be made available to workshop participants. In addition, we aim to publish the extended versions of the workshop papers to a special issue (e.g., IJCCI).

Workshop intents to have 15-20 participants; with focused interaction among participants, so participants will have informed positions and access to the accepted papers. Papers will be reviewed by the workshop organizers. PC members with whom we have long collaboration will assist in promoting the workshop and reviewing the submitted papers.

[4] Make2Learn 2015 workshop - *http://make2learn.wix.com/icec2015*

[5] Make2Learn 2016 workshop - *http://www.idc2016.org/wp-content/uploads/2016/04/WS5.pdf*

References

1. Paulo Blikstein. 2013. Gears of Our Childhood: Constructionist Toolkits, Robotics, and Physical Computing, Past and Future. *Proceedings of the 12th International Conference on Interaction Design and Children*: 173–182.
2. Justine Cassell. 2004. Towards a model of technology and literacy development: Story listening systems. *Journal of Applied Developmental Psychology* 25, 1: 75–105.
3. Mihaly Csikszentmihalyi. 1996. *Creativity: Flow and the Psychology of Discovery and Invention*. Harper Collins.
4. Michail N Giannakos, Monica Divitini, Ole Sejer Iversen, and Pavlos Koulouris. 2015. Workshop of Making as a Pathway to Foster Joyful Engagement and Creativity in Learning (Make2Learn). *CEUR-WS* 1450.
5. Ole Sejer Iversen, Rachel Charlotte Smith, Paulo Blikstein, Eva-Sophie Katterfeldt, and Janet C Read. 2015. Digital fabrication in education: Expanding the research towards design and reflective practices. *International Journal of Child-Computer Interaction* 5: 1–2.
6. Simone Mora, Francesco Gianni, and Monica Divitini. 2017. Tiles: A Card-based Ideation Toolkit for the Internet of Things. *To Appear in Proceedings of Desigining Interactive Systems Conference DIS*: 1–12. http://doi.org/10.1145/3064663.3064699
7. Rachel Charlotte Smith, Ole Sejer Iversen, and Mikkel Hjorth. 2015. Design thinking for digital fabrication in education. *International Journal of Child-Computer Interaction* 5: 20–28.

Equity & Inclusivity at IDC

Kiley Sobel
University of Washington
Seattle, WA 98195, USA
ksobel@uw.edu

Carmen Gonzalez
University of Washington
Seattle, WA 98195, USA
cmgonzal@uw.edu

Julie A. Kientz
University of Washington
Seattle, WA 98195, USA
jkientz@uw.edu

Jason C. Yip
University of Washington
Seattle, WA 98195, USA
jcyip@uw.edu

Tamara L. Clegg
University of Maryland
College Park, MD 20742, USA
tclegg@umd.edu

Abstract

In this one-day workshop, we aim to bring together a community of researchers at the Interaction Design and Children (IDC) conference who will share how they already make or plan to make *equity*—promoting fairness by allocating more resources and opportunities to those who need it— and *inclusivity*— the inclusion and meaningful participation of people who might otherwise be excluded or marginalized— foundational to their research with children and families. By discussing theoretical and practice-based approaches, providing feedback on each other's research, and collectively identifying concerns and challenges in addressing equity and inclusivity when doing and assessing research in IDC, we intend to do twofold. First, we will build our understanding of how our approaches, designs, and/or methods may either be restricting or facilitating equitable access and participation of diverse children and their families. Second, we will work to establish and articulate approaches to our research that forefront equity and inclusivity, taking into account how intersecting identities affect how the children and families with whom we work have or do not have access to various sources of power.

IDC '17, June 27-30, 2017, Stanford, CA, USA

ACM ISBN 978-1-4503-4921-5/17/06.
http://dx.doi.org/10.1145/3078072.3081313

Author Keywords

Equity; inclusivity; inclusion; children; families.

ACM Classification Keywords

K.4.2. Computers and society: Social issues.

Introduction

Within the Interaction Design and Children (IDC) community, researchers have shown a strong commitment to designing for and with children and families from underrepresented and disenfranchised groups. This IDC research has spanned from studying, designing for, and co-designing with children with disabilities (e.g., [5,6,16,20,24]) and other minorities and marginalized youth (e.g., [3,7,17,22]), and has addressed issues of broadening participation (e.g., [14,26,27]).

In line with this deep commitment, three workshops were held at the 2008, 2009, and 2010 IDC conferences that emphasized the importance for our research community to consider the ways in which information and communication technologies affect the participation and inclusion of marginalized young people in various contexts (*Marginalized Young People: Inclusion Through ICT* [12], *Digital Technologies* and *Marginalized Youth: Reducing the Gap* [1], and *Digital Technologies and Marginalized Youth* [15]).

In subsequent years, workshops were organized at IDC that addressed other issues of marginality as well. In 2012, 2013, and 2014, three IDC workshops specifically highlighted the cross-section of technologies and children with disabilities (*Interactive Technologies for Children with Special Needs* [2], *Designing for and with Children with Special Needs in Multiple Settings* [21], and *Interaction Design with Children with Disabilities* [4,11]). Then, in 2015 and 2016, IDC workshops were run that examined the power differentials between adults and children during the design process (*Balancing the needs of children and adults in the design of technology for children* [19] and *Roles and Values of Children in Design* [18,23]).

Through our one-day workshop inspired by these past IDC workshops plus other CSCW and CHI panels and workshops on social justice and design [8,9] and feminist approaches [10,13,25], we aim to both reaffirm and build on our commitments in IDC to designing for and with children and families from marginalized communities.

During the workshop, participants will discuss how we can continue to make *equity*— promoting fairness by allocating more resources and opportunities to those who need it— and *inclusivity*— the inclusion and meaningful participation of people who might otherwise be excluded or marginalized— foundational to the work we do in IDC. These issues— equity and inclusivity— complement each other as we can use equitable practices and approaches to promote inclusion in our designs and methods. Then, rather than focusing on one type of technology (e.g., ICT), one group (e.g., children with disabilities), or one methodological approach (e.g., participatory design) like past workshops at IDC, we will combine these topics to update our understanding of equity and inclusivity within IDC research by taking an intersectional perspective to these issues. Taking an intersectional perspective means that we will examine how all of the intersecting identities (i.e., gender, race, class, ability, age, etc.) of the children and families with whom we work affect how they have or do not have access to various sources of power.

Main Topics

The theme of this workshop concerns both *equity* and *inclusivity* as they relate to the theoretical perspectives, methods, and designs we take up and produce through our IDC research. Initially, participants will discuss and give feedback on each other's current or planned research with children and/or families, which can be viewed through lenses of equity and inclusivity. Next, we will discuss theoretical and practice-based approaches that influence issues around equity and inclusivity—namely intersectionality, feminism, critical disability studies, critical pedagogy, and critical race theory—to explore ways they might be employed during our IDC research. Finally, we will collectively identify concerns, challenges, and goals in addressing issues of equity and inclusivity when doing and assessing research in IDC.

Workshop Goals

Through our generative discussions, we expect two main outcomes. First, we will build our understanding of how our approaches, designs, and/or methods may either be restricting or facilitating equitable access and participation of diverse children and their families. For example, we could analyze how our work's theoretical underpinnings, the artifacts we design and test, or our methodological decisions might draw on feminist theory by explicitly promoting gender equality in, for instance, middle school science, technology, engineering, and math (STEM) education. This could be by framing our work to promote more representation of girls in STEM, by designing technologies that aim to engage girls in science, or by recruiting more girls in co-design sessions. At the same time, we could also examine how we could better uptake other theories, like critical race theory, for this same research agenda to ground our understanding of how children's racial identities may also affect how they experience oppression, exclusion, and inequities in STEM education, which could be reflected in our approaches, designs, and methods as well.

Second, we will work to establish and articulate approaches to our research that forefront equity and inclusivity with an intersectional perspective. This may allow us to move forward in our research while taking into account the intersecting identities of the children and families with whom we work and how these identities affect their (dis)locations of power and privilege in interconnected ways.

Organizers

Kiley Sobel is a doctoral candidate and a National Science Foundation Graduate Research Fellow in the Department of Human Centered Design & Engineering at the University of Washington. She is interested in inclusive design, child-computer interaction, and assistive technology. She has worked as a teacher's assistant in various early childhood education classrooms and as a behavioral therapist for children with autism. Her primary research is in understanding how interactive technology might help increase opportunities for children with diverse abilities and needs to equally, actively, and meaningfully participate in the same setting. She is currently working on her dissertation to investigate the role of interactive technology during inclusive play, or play between children with and without disabilities.

Julie A. Kientz is an associate professor in the Department of Human Centered Design & Engineering at the University of Washington. Dr. Kientz's primary research areas are in the fields of Human-Computer Interaction, Ubiquitous Computing, Health Informatics, and Accessible Computing. Her research focuses on understanding and reducing the user burdens of interactive technologies for health and education through the design of future applications. She has designed, developed, and evaluated mobile, sensor, and social applications for parents of young children tracking developmental progress, individuals with visual impairments, special education teachers working with children with autism, designing health technologies for families, and designing new tools for inclusive education. Her primary research methods involve human-centered design, technology development, and a mix of qualitative and quantitative methods.

Tamara L. Clegg is an assistant professor in the College of Information Studies and the Department of Teaching and Learning, Policy and Leadership at the University of Maryland. Her work focuses on developing technology (e.g., social media, mobile apps, e-textiles, community displays) to support life-relevant learning where learners, particularly those from underrepresented groups in science, engage in science in the context of achieving personally relevant goals. She seeks to understand ways such learning environments and technologies support scientific disposition development. Tamara's work is funded by the National Science Foundation, the Institute of Museum and Library Studies, and Google.

Carmen Gonzalez is an assistant professor in the University of Washington's Department of Communication. She has conducted community-based and participatory research over the last 10 years, investigating the communication practices of immigrant and minority populations in the contexts of health promotion and civic engagement. In recent work, she examined how communication ecologies—networks of communication resources—impact health care among Latinas and how community assets can be leveraged to address health disparities. She has also examined how Latino families make decisions about adopting digital technologies and how these tools facilitate learning in home and school settings. At the UW, she continues to explore how technology shapes the lives of individuals and families, and develop strategies to promote technology as a tool for empowerment.

Jason C. Yip is an assistant professor at the Information School and adjunct assistant professor in Human Centered Design & Engineering at the University of Washington. He is also a senior research fellow at the Joan Ganz Cooney Center at Sesame Workshop. His research examines how technologies can support parents and children learning together. He is a co-principal investigator on a National Science Foundation Cyberlearning project on designing social media technologies to support neighborhoods learning science together from non-dominant communities. He is the director of KidsTeam UW, an intergenerational group of ethnically diverse children (ages 7 – 11) and researchers co-designing new technologies and learning activities for children, with children. Finally, Dr. Yip is the principal investigator of a Google Faculty Research Award project that examines how Latino children search and broker online information for their English-language learning parents.

References

1. Edith K. Ackermann, Françoise Decortis, Juan Pablo Hourcade, and Heidi Schelhowe. 2009. Digital technologies and marginalized youth: Reducing the gap. In *Proceedings of the 8th International Conference on Interaction Design and Children* (IDC '09). ACM, New York, NY, USA. Retrieved from http://homepage.divms.uiowa.edu/~hourcade/idc-workshop/index.html.

2. Meryl Alper, Juan Pablo Hourcade, and Shuli Gilutz. 2012. Interactive technologies for children with special needs. In *Proceedings of the 11th International Conference on Interaction Design and Children* (IDC '12). ACM, New York, NY, USA, 363-366. DOI= http://doi.acm.org/10.1145/2307096.2307169
3. Alissa N. Antle, Leslie Chesick, Aaron Levisohn, Srilekha Kirshnamachari Sridharan, and Perry Tan. 2015. Using neurofeedback to teach self-regulation to children living in poverty. In *Proceedings of the 14th International Conference on Interaction Design and Children* (IDC '15). ACM, New York, NY, USA, 119-128. DOI=http://dx.doi.org/10.1145/2771839.2771852
4. Wolmet Barendregt, Karin Slegers, Eva Ericsson, Olof Torgersson, Carl Heath, Robert Fohlín, Anders-Petter Andersson, and Tobias Sonne. 2014. Including children with disabilities in the design process. In *Proceedings of the 13th International Conference on Interaction Design and Children* (IDC '14). ACM, New York, NY, USA. Retrieved from http://idc2014.org/wp-content/uploads/2014/09/disability-design-process.pdf.
5. Arpita Bhattacharya, Mirko Gelsomini, Patricia Pérez-Fuster, Gregory D. Abowd, and Agata Rozga. 2015. Designing motion-based activities to engage students with autism in classroom settings. In *Proceedings of the 14th International Conference on Interaction Design and Children* (IDC '15). ACM, New York, NY, USA, 69-78. DOI=http://dx.doi.org/10.1145/2771839.2771847
6. Peter Börjesson, Wolmet Barendregt, Eva Eriksson, and Olof Torgersson. 2015. Designing technology for and with developmentally diverse children: a systematic literature review. In *Proceedings of the 14th International Conference on Interaction Design and Children* (IDC '15). ACM, New York, NY, USA, 79-88. DOI=http://dx.doi.org/10.1145/2771839.2771848
7. Karen E. Fisher, Katya Yefimova, and Eiad Yafi. 2016. Future's Butterflies: Co-Designing ICT Wayfaring Technology with Refugee Syrian Youth. In *Proceedings of the The 15th International Conference on Interaction Design and Children* (IDC '16). ACM, New York, NY, USA, 25-36. DOI: https://doi.org/10.1145/2930674.2930701
8. Sarah Fox, Mariam Asad, Katherine Lo, Jill P. Dimond, Lynn S. Dombrowski, and Shaowen Bardzell. 2016. Exploring Social Justice, Design, and HCI. In *Proceedings of the 2016 CHI Conference Extended Abstracts on Human Factors in Computing Systems* (CHI EA '16). ACM, New York, NY, USA, 3293-3300. DOI: https://doi.org/10.1145/2851581.2856465
9. Sarah Fox, Jill Dimond, Lilly Irani, Tad Hirsch, Michael Muller, and Shaowen Bardzell. 2017. Social Justice and Design: Power and oppression in collaborative systems. In *Companion of the 2017 ACM Conference on Computer Supported Cooperative Work and Social Computing* (CSCW '17 Companion). ACM, New York, NY, USA, 117-122. DOI: https://doi.org/10.1145/3022198.3022201
10. Sarah Fox, Amanda Menking, Stephanie Steinhardt, Anna Lauren Hoffmann, and Shaowen Bardzell. 2017. Imagining Intersectional Futures: Feminist approaches in CSCW. In *Companion of the 2017 ACM Conference on Computer Supported Cooperative Work and Social Computing* (CSCW '17 Companion). ACM, New York, NY, USA, 387-393. DOI: https://doi.org/10.1145/3022198.3022665
11. Christopher Frauenberger, Judith Good, and Jennifer Mankoff. 2014. Values and stances in interaction design for children with disabilities. In *Proceedings of the 13th International Conference on Interaction Design and Children* (IDC '14). ACM, New York, NY, USA. Retrieved from

http://idc2014.org/wp-content/uploads/2014/09/disability-value.pdf.

12. Franca Garzotto and Heidi Schelhowe. 2008. Marginalized young people: inclusion through ICT. In *Proceedings of the 7th international conference on Interaction design and children* (IDC '08). ACM, New York, NY, USA, 101-104. DOI=http://dx.doi.org/10.1145/1463689.1463730
13. Libby Hemphill, Ingrid Erickson, David Ribes, and Ines Mergel. 2014. Feminism and social media research. In *Proceedings of the companion publication of the 17th ACM conference on Computer supported cooperative work & social computing* (CSCW Companion '14). ACM, New York, NY, USA, 319-322. DOI=http://dx.doi.org/10.1145/2556420.2558864
14. Nathan Holbert. 2016. Bots for Tots: Building Inclusive Makerspaces by Leveraging "Ways of Knowing". In *Proceedings of the The 15th International Conference on Interaction Design and Children* (IDC '16). ACM, New York, NY, USA, 79-88. DOI: http://dx.doi.org/10.1145/2930674.2930718
15. Juan Pablo Hourcade, Natasha E. Bullock-Rest, and Heidi Schelhowe. 2010. Digital Technologies and Marginalized Youth. In *Proceedings of the 9th International Conference on Interaction Design and Children* (IDC '10). ACM, New York, NY, USA, 360-363. DOI=http://dx.doi.org/10.1145/1810543.1810614
16. Janio Jadan-Guerrero, Javier Jaen, María A. Carpio, and Luis A. Guerrero. 2015. Kiteracy: a kit of tangible objects to strengthen literacy skills in children with down syndrome. In *Proceedings of the 14th International Conference on Interaction Design and Children* (IDC '15). ACM, New York, NY, USA, 315-318. DOI=http://dx.doi.org/10.1145/2771839.2771905
17. Minal Jain and Pradeep Yammiyavar. 2015. Game based learning tool seeking peer support for empowering adolescent girls in rural Assam. In *Proceedings of the 14th International Conference on Interaction Design and Children* (IDC '15). ACM, New York, NY, USA, 275-278. DOI=http://dx.doi.org/10.1145/2771839.2771895
18. Monica Landoni, Elisa Rubegni, Emma Nicol, and Janet Read. 2016. How Many Roles Can Children Play?. In *Proceedings of the The 15th International Conference on Interaction Design and Children* (IDC '16). ACM, New York, NY, USA, 720-725. DOI: http://dx.doi.org/10.1145/2930674.2932222
19. Lettie Malan, Catalina Naranjo-Bock, and Tejinder K. Judge. 2015. Balancing the needs of children and adults in the design of technology for children. In *Proceedings of the 14th International Conference on Interaction Design and Children* (IDC '15). ACM, New York, NY, USA, 474-477. DOI=http://dx.doi.org/10.1145/2771839.2771927
20. Stefan Manojlovic, Laurens Boer, and Paula Sterkenburg. 2016. Playful interactive mirroring to support bonding between parents and children with Down Syndrome. In *Proceedings of the The 15th International Conference on Interaction Design and Children* (IDC '16). ACM, New York, NY, USA, 548-553. DOI: http://dx.doi.org/10.1145/2930674.2935987
21. Roisin McNaney, Madeline Balaam, Kevin Marshall, Abigail Durrant, Janet Read, Judith Good, Judy Robertson, and Gregory Abowd. 2013. Designing for and with children with special needs in multiple settings. In *Proceedings of the 12th International Conference on Interaction Design and Children* (IDC '13). ACM, New York, NY, USA, 603-605. DOI=http://dx.doi.org/10.1145/2485760.2485889
22. Ekaterina Muravevskaia, Fatemeh Tavassoli, and Christina Gardner-McCune. 2016. Developing children's cultural awareness and empathy through games and fairy tales. In *Proceedings of the The*

15th International Conference on Interaction Design and Children (IDC '16). ACM, New York, NY, USA, 701-706. DOI: http://dx.doi.org/10.1145/2930674.2935998

23. Helle Marie Skovbjerg, Tilde Bekker, and Wolmet Barendregt. 2016. Being Explicit about Underlying Values, Assumptions and Views when Designing for Children in the IDC Community. In *Proceedings of the The 15th International Conference on Interaction Design and Children* (IDC '16). ACM, New York, NY, USA, 713-719. DOI: http://dx.doi.org/10.1145/2930674.2932224
24. Kiley Sobel, Katie O'Leary, and Julie A. Kientz. 2015. Maximizing children's opportunities with inclusive play: considerations for interactive technology design. In *Proceedings of the 14th International Conference on Interaction Design and Children* (IDC '15). ACM, New York, NY, USA, 39-48. DOI=http://dx.doi.org/10.1145/2771839.2771844
25. Stephanie B. Steinhardt, Amanda Menking, Ingrid Erickson, Andrea Marshall, Asta Zelenkauskaite, and Jennifer Rode. 2015. Feminism and Feminist Approaches in Social Computing. In *Proceedings of the 18th ACM Conference Companion on Computer Supported Cooperative Work & Social Computing* (CSCW'15 Companion). ACM, New York, NY, USA, 303-308. DOI=http://dx.doi.org/10.1145/2685553.2685561
26. Greg Walsh, Craig Donahue, and Zachary Pease. 2016. Inclusive Co-Design within a Three-Dimensional Game Environment. In *Proceedings of the The 15th International Conference on Interaction Design and Children* (IDC 7'16). ACM, New York, NY, USA, 1-10. DOI: http://dx.doi.org.offcampus.lib.washington.edu/10.1145/2930674.2930721
27. Greg Walsh and Elizabeth Foss. 2015. A case for intergenerational distributed co-design: the online kidsteam example. In *Proceedings of the 14th International Conference on Interaction Design and Children* (IDC '15). ACM, New York, NY, USA, 99-108. DOI=http://dx.doi.org/10.1145/2771839.2771850

Analyzing Children's Contributions and Experiences in Co-design Activities: Synthesizing Productive Practices

Maarten Van Mechelen
Mintlab, KU Leuven – imec
Leuven, Belgium
Maarten.vanmechelen
@kuleuven.be

Marikken Høiseth
Department of Design
Faculty of Architecture & Design
NTNU, Trondheim, Norway
Marikken.hoiseth@ntnu.no

Gökçe Elif Baykal
Design, Technology & Society
PhD Program
Koç University, Istanbul, Turkey
Gbaykal13@ku.edu.tr

Fenne Van Doorn
Industrial Design Engineering
Studiolab, TU Delft
Delft, Netherlands
F.a.p.vandoorn@tudelft.nl

Asimina Vasalou
UCL Knowledge Lab
Institute of Education, UCL
London, UK
a.vasalou@ucl.ac.uk

Alice Schut
Science Education and
Communication, TU Delft
Delft, Netherlands
A.schut@tudelft.nl

IDC '17, June 27-30, 2017, Stanford, CA, USA

ACM ISBN 978-1-4503-4921-5/17/06.
http://dx.doi.org/10.1145/3078072.3081314

Abstract
Today, it has been broadly acknowledged in the CCI community that children are not only active learners and users of technology, but can also actively participate in the design process. However, it remains challenging to analyze children's experiences and creative contributions resulting from co-design activities (e.g. stories, paper prototypes, enacted ideas). This workshop will explore different ways to analyze children's (0 to 18 years) experiences and contributions in co-design activities, the perceived benefits and challenges of these approaches, and will serve as a venue for synthesizing productive practices that will move the CCI community forward.

Author Keywords
Participatory design; co-design; co-creation; children; design methods; data analysis

ACM Classification Keywords
H.5.m. Information interfaces and presentation (e.g., HCI): Miscellaneous

Introduction
Participatory Design (PD) is often described as a set of theories, practices and studies related to the design of technology, aiming to give those that will ultimately be

impacted by the technology a voice in its design [1][2]. Under the influence of PD, the role of children in design processes has changed tremendously [3]. Whereas children were initially involved passively as technology users, their role was gradually broadened to that of active participants using a variety of co-design techniques. Nevertheless, it has been acknowledged that it is not easy to involve children as design partners in open-ended, future-oriented work [4]. The particular challenge that will be addressed in this workshop is how to analyze children's experiences and creative contributions resulting from co-design activities. This challenge has been a topic of much debate in the Child Computer Interaction community.

Broadly speaking, a distinction can be made between researchers looking for inspiration in the form of useful design ideas (e.g., [5] [9] [7] [8]), and researchers that take a more interpretative stance by looking beyond the surface level of children's ideas to deduce insights and knowledge embedded in children's creative contributions (e.g., [9] [10] [11] [12]. In previous work, we used the terms *descriptive* and *knowledge* perspective to refer to this distinction [13]. Another way to think about this is in terms of co-design as a *practice* and *research through co-design* akin to research through design. If there is not yet a well-defined design problem, approaches that fall under the knowledge perspective may be more appropriate as they provide researchers with profound insights in what drives and motivates children. In later design stages, the descriptive perspective may be preferable as the focus will have shifted from *problem* to *solution* finding. At this point, researchers may be more interested in quickly developing one or more prototypes based on a descriptive analysis of children's ideas, focusing on functional elements (e.g. product features) and aesthetic characteristics [13]. The knowledge and descriptive perspective can be seen as the opposite ends of the same continuum.

Within the descriptive perspective, different approaches have been developed. An often used technique in Cooperative Inquiry [5] is to give participants a bag with materials to build low-tech prototypes. Each team then presents their prototypes to the other teams and an adult takes notes on the *big ideas* on a white board. Big ideas are the ideas that are most surprising, most repeated among groups and evoke most reaction from the whole team. These big ideas are then developed into working prototypes [6]. In turn, Read et al. [8] have looked for better ways to include and represent children's ideas and to help children understand how their contributions are used in the further design process. Their TRAck (tracking, representing and acknowledging) method encourages careful scrutiny of children's designs, and allows researchers to distill useful design ideas in a quantitative manner. With TRAck, a more inclusive PD process can be ensured, because the ideas that come through and are developed into working prototypes are those of the majority of children rather than those preferred by the designers [8].

Within the knowledge perspective, different types of knowledge have been revealed with co-design techniques. According to Sanders [14], the act of *making* in co-design activities enables participants to reflect upon their experiences and express *deeper levels of knowledge* that would not have surfaced without such concrete materials. With deeper levels of knowledge she refers to people's *tacit* and *latent* needs.

These needs cannot readily be expressed in words, as they relate to *silent knowledge* that is practiced in everyday life or to *future needs* that are difficult to identify in the present [15]. To unravel these deeper levels of knowledge, Sanders [15] focuses on the story that comes along with the design. The recurring themes in these stories are believed to reflect participants' tacit and latent needs and are used to inform design.

Other researchers have focused on using co-design techniques to elicit *values,* a particular kind of knowledge [16][17]. The concept of value has been used in psychology to explain the motivational basis of attitudes and behavior. Approaches that fit within this strand see the co-design process as a negotiation of values that participants bring to the table [18]. A core task for researchers is to mediate this process and facilitate dialogue between participants. Since not all values emerge by explicit means, careful observation and interpretation are required, also with regard to the artifacts that are being created. To this end, Van Mechelen et al. [13] developed the GLID method (Grounding, Listing, Identifying, Distilling). With GLID, verbal and material co-design outcomes are integrated in a multimodal analysis. The method aims to go beyond the surface level of ideas, by identifying children's values embedded in co-design outcomes.

Despite these valuable contributions in the field of CCI, some challenges remain, at least partly, unresolved. One such challenge is the risk for conformation bias. Taking a knowledge perspective to analyzing children's contributions implies a process of interpretation. Since interpretation is not value free, multiple and equally valid interpretations can co-exist. This increases the risk for confirmation bias and *ventriloquism* whereby the researchers' own views are stated as if they were articulated by the participants. Another challenge is the analysis of different semiotic resources in a coherent manner. A tendency in both the descriptive and knowledge perspective is to focus primarily on what participants say about their creations, neglecting other modes, such as the visual and tangible dimensions of the artifacts. Although this problem has recently been addressed by some researchers (e.g., [13][19]), it remains challenging to move away from this unilateral focus on the verbal explanation. These and other challenges will be addressed during the workshop.

Workshop Goals and Expected Outcomes

In this workshop, we reflect on the analysis of children's creative contributions and experiences in co-design activities. We intend to explore and map out the ways in which researchers and practitioners in the CCI community have approached this in academic and industry settings alike, and we will define and prioritize a future agenda. This will be fostered before, during and after the workshop through a number of forums. A dedicated website will serve as a portal for forming and discussing this agenda within and outside the workshop: www.codesignwithchildren.wordpress.com

References

1. M. J. Muller, "Participatory Design: The Third Space in HCI," in *The Human-computer Interaction Handbook*, J. A. Jacko and A. Sears, Eds. Hillsdale, NJ, USA: L. Erlbaum Associates Inc., 2002, pp. 1051–1068.
2. D. Schuler and A. Namioka, Eds., *Participatory Design: Principles and Practices*. Hillsdale, NY: L. Erlbaum Associates Inc., 1993.

3. J. C. Read and P. Markopoulos, "Child-computer interaction," *Int. J. Child-Comput. Interact.*, vol. 1, no. 1, pp. 2–6, 2013.
4. M. Scaife and Y. Rogers, "Kids as informants: telling us what we didn't know or confirming what we knew already?," in *The Design of Children's Technology: How We Design, What We Design, and Why.*, Morgan Kaufman, 1999.
5. A. Druin, "Cooperative Inquiry: Developing New Technologies for Children with Children," in *Proceedings of the SIGCHI Conference on Human Factors in Computing Systems*, NY, USA, 1999.
6. M. Guha, A. Druin, and J. Fails, "Cooperative Inquiry Revisited: Reflections of the Past and Guidelines for the Future of Intergenerational Co-design," *Int. J. Child-Comput. Interact.*, vol. Volume 1, no. Issue 1, pp. 14 – 23, 2013.
7. E. Mazzone, J. Read, and R. Beale, "Understanding Children's Contributions During Informant Design," in *Proceedings of the 22Nd British HCI Group Annual Conference on People and Computers: Culture, Creativity, Interaction - Volume 2*, Swinton, UK, 2008.
8. J. C. Read, D. Fitton, and M. Horton, "Giving Ideas an Equal Chance: Inclusion and Representation in Participatory Design with Children," in *Proceedings of the 2014 Conference on Interaction Design and Children*, NY, USA, 2014.
9. J. Derboven, M. Van Mechelen, and K. Slegers, "Multimodal Analysis in Participatory Design with Children: A Primary School Case Study," in *Proceedings of the 33rd Annual ACM Conference on Human Factors in Computing Systems*, NY, USA, 2015.
10. C. Frauenberger, J. Good, W. Keay-Bright, and H. Pain, "Interpreting Input from Children: A Designerly Approach," in *Proceedings of the SIGCHI Conference on Human Factors in Computing Systems*, NY, USA, 2012.
11. M. A. Gielen, "Exploring the child's mind – contextmapping research with children," *Digit. Creat.*, vol. 19, no. 3, pp. 174–184, 2008.
12. F. van Doorn, P. J. Stappers, and M. Gielen, "Design Research by Proxy: Using Children As Researchers to Gain Contextual Knowledge About User Experience.," in *Proceedings of the SIGCHI Conference on Human Factors in Computing Systems*, NY, USA, 2013.
13. M. Van Mechelen, J. Derboven, A. Laenen, D. Geerts, and V. Vanden Abeele, "The GLID method: Moving from design features to underlying values in co-design," *Int. J. Hum.-Comput. Stud.*, 2017.
14. E. B.-N. Sanders, "From User-Centered to Participatory Design Approaches," in *Design and the Social Sciences*, Oxford: Taylor & Francis Books Limited, 2002.
15. E. B.-N. Sanders, "Postdesign and Participatory Culture," presented at the Proceedings of the International Conference "Useful and Critical: The Position of Research in Design," Helsinki, 1999.
16. J. Halloran, E. Hornecker, M. Stringer, E. Harris, and G. Fitzpatrick, "The value of values: Resourcing co-design of ubiquitous computing," *CoDesign*, vol. 5, no. 4, pp. 245–273, 2009.
17. O. S. Iversen, K. Halskov, and T. W. Leong, "Rekindling Values in Participatory Design," in *Proceedings of the 11th Biennial Participatory Design Conference*, NY, USA, 2010.
18. C. Frauenberger, J. Good, G. Fitzpatrick, and O. S. Iversen, "In pursuit of rigour and accountability in participatory design," *Int. J. Hum.-Comput. Stud.*, vol. 74, pp. 93–106, 2015.
19. L. Malinverni, J. Mora-Guiard, and N. Pares, "Towards methods for evaluating and communicating participatory design: A multimodal approach," *Int. J. Hum.-Comput. Stud.*, 2016.

Learning by Making for STEM Success

Lynn Cominsky
Carolyn Peruta
Susan Wandling
Sonoma State University
Rohnert Park, CA 94928, USA
lynnc@universe.sonoma.edu
carolyn@universe.sonoma.edu
susan.wandling@sonoma.edu

Betsy McCarthy
Linlin Li
WestEd
Redwood City, CA 94063, USA
bmccart@wested.org
lli@wested.org

IDC '17, June 27-30, 2017, Stanford, CA, USA

ACM ISBN 978-1-4503-4921-5/17/06.
http://dx.doi.org/10.1145/3078072.3081315

Abstract
Sonoma State University's Learning by Making program, funded by the US Department of Education's Investing in Innovation program, has created a one-year course that is now approved as a college preparatory Science Laboratory course (Area D) by the UC/CSU Doorways process. An innovative hardware platform has been developed that has been optimized for use by students in high needs rural communities with low Internet bandwidth. All programming is done in the Logo language that supports experimental design, use of a variety of environmental and physical sensors, and analysis of the resulting data.

Author Keywords
STEM; NGSS; Logo; high-school curriculum; Making; experiments.

ACM Classification Keywords
K.3.0. Computers and Education; General.

Integrated Environmental and Biological Sciences: Curriculum Overview

The Learning by Making first-year course fuses mathematical skill-building and computational thinking applied to real-world scientific problems where solutions are constructed by students and instructors working together.

Students undertake personally relevant investigations in environmental science and biological sciences, using Logo, a programming language, to read sensors and to obtain and analyze data. They also develop and use models, construct explanations and arguments from experimental evidence, and report and communicate their results to peers and instructor.

Prerequisites:

Algebra I (Recommended)

Introduction

Learning by Making is a five-year curriculum development project that is funded through a grant to Sonoma State University from the US Department of Education's Investing in Innovation program. Our goal is to develop a high-school curriculum that is aligned with the Next Generation Science Standards (NGSS), integrating all four aspects of STEM (Science, Technology, Engineering and Mathematics). The project has four main objectives:

- Design and develop NGSS-aligned STEM curriculum
- Increase teacher's competence to implement the curriculum
- Offer new STEM course at six participating high schools
- Increase math and science proficiency scores

To date, the new STEM curriculum has been piloted, revised and redeployed to approximately 135 students each year. Evaluation of all aspects of the program has been conducted by external experts at WestEd.

Course Overview

There are eight units in the Integrated Environmental and Biological Sciences Curriculum. The course has been specifically developed to implement Next Generation Science Standards in the high school classroom. As such, Disciplinary Core Ideas are integrated with cross-cutting concepts and presented in the context of scientific and engineering design practices.

Course Alignment with NGSS

This course builds basic skills in electronics, programming, data acquisition and analysis, constructing explanations and making simple models. Units include simple experiments that are performed by the students. More in-depth experiments are constructed as the course progresses. For each major experiment, students are engaged in the complete life cycle of an experiment that spans all 8 NGSS goals as summarized below:

1. Asking questions (for science) and defining problems (for engineering) – All Units

2. Developing and using models - see units 2, 3, 4 , 5, 6, 7

3. Planning and carrying out investigations - see units 1, 3, 4, 5, 6, 7, 8

4. Analyzing and interpreting data - see units 3, 4, 5, 6, 7, 8

5. Using mathematics and computational thinking – All Units

6. Constructing explanations (for science) and designing solutions (for engineering) – All Units

7. Engaging in argument from evidence – All Units

8. Obtaining, evaluating, and communicating information – All Units

Unit Descriptions

Unit 1: Welcome to STEM

Introduction to the computer and keeping laboratory notes

The purpose of Unit 1 is to introduce students to the course and to set the stage for the three-dimensional learning strategies of the Next Generation Science Standards. The unit begins with four activities that

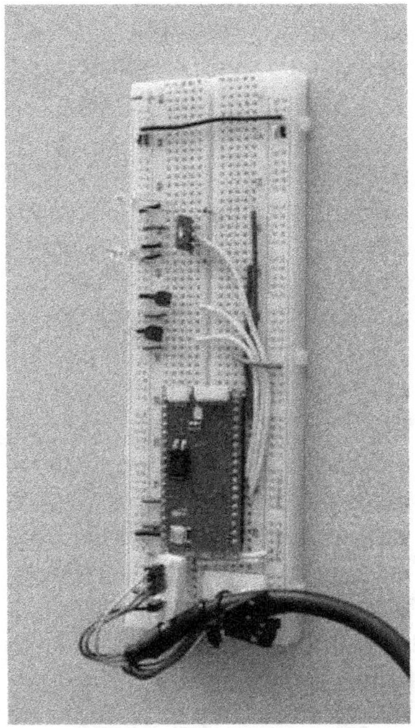

Figure 1: The Basic Board is the heart of the Learning by Making hardware setup. The Basic Board includes two temperature sensors and a light sensor. It is built by the students in Unit 4. The green circuit board was designed specifically for the Learning by Making project. The cable at the bottom connects to the computer.

emphasize the team building and effective communications skills necessary to carry out vital science and engineering practices. The teacher utilizes student-driven learning by facilitating group work with open ended prompts. In each activity students are presented with a problem, overall goal, specific design constraints, and strategic communication barriers. Students must use mathematical and computational thinking to construct explanations and design solutions for each problem. Students are then asked to reflect on the imposed communication barriers and problem solving strategies.

Unit 2: Turtle Logo
Computational Thinking and Geometric Explorations using Logo
The purpose of Unit 2 is to introduce students to the computer and computer programming language that they will be using throughout the course. Turtle Logo can be used to draw on the computer screen while demonstrating rudimentary computational thinking concepts such as looping and conditionals. Students create original Turtle Art using their own choice of shapes and colors. At least one loop must be included in their Turtle Logo program.

Unit 3: Go with the Electron Flow
Investigating Energy and Charge in Electronic Circuits
In Unit 3, students are introduced to breadboards and learn how to wire the power and ground for their own breadboards. They also learn how to use a digital multimeter to measure current, resistance and voltage, and build a simple analog circuit that uses a battery and a resistor. Students modify simple circuits, draw circuit schematics, make predictions for voltage values, measure the voltages and record and report the results. The unit includes series and parallel circuits.

Students also plan and carry out investigations around voltage, current, resistance; analyze and interpret the data from the readings; and draw conclusions about Ohm's law.

Unit 4: Let There Be Light
Designing Microcontroller Experiments
In Unit 4, students are introduced to the circuit boards that comprise the hardware platform for the Learning by Making experiments. They learn how to connect the boards to the computer and how to use them to acquire data from analog sensors. They also learn the basics of analog to digital and digital to analog conversion. Students then plan and carry out investigations into the relationship between light intensity and distance, analyzing graphs to determine this relationship. They also plan and carry out investigations into the linearity of their temperature and light sensors.

Unit 5: Getting Warm
Measuring Heat and Energy
In Unit 5, students learn how to analyze and display data using the Logo programming language. They also learn how to process measurements to increase signal to noise and to use simple statistics (mean, median, etc.), linear regressions and plotting and graphing techniques. Another important goal is to develop the procedures to calibrate a sensor so that output plots display physical units.

Unit 6: A Muddy Affair
Investigating Organism Growth in a Microbial Fuel Cell
In Unit 6, students pose questions and then plan and carry out investigations using microbial fuel cells. These investigations into organism growth use transparent containers, anode and cathode materials, a light source, heaters and temperature sensors. Students use

Figure 2: Microbial Fuel Cell with the Basic Board used in Unit 6

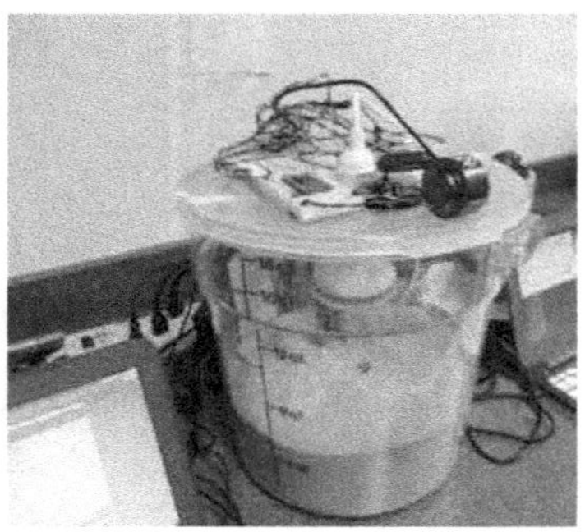

Figure 3: Heat Diffusion Experiment used in Unit 7

temperature data in a feedback loop to control a heater needed to optimize (or impair) the conditions for organism growth, which is measured by recording the voltage from the fuel cell. Students analyze and display the voltage data as the experiment runs through many days, thinking through the factors that have affected the organism growth rate. They then plan and carry out an additional investigation for which they will predict the organism growth rate.

Unit 7: As the World Warms
Investigating Heat Diffusion with Real World Extensions
In Unit 7, students learn about the heat diffusion experiment that uses a relay-controlled light bulb, a bucket of sand or other heat conducting material, and temperature sensors placed at specified depths. They modify the experiment by controlling the light on/off cycle, and read out the temperature sensor, while analyzing and displaying the data in real time as the experiment runs through many cycles. They also predict the behavior of the temperature sensor(s) prior to running the experiment.

Unit 8: Being a Maker
Creating Individualized Experiments
In Unit 8, students synthesize all the skills and practices that they have learned throughout the year. They design their own experiments that use the hardware, software, sensors, and data analysis techniques to test a hypothesis they have put forth.

Evaluation

WestEd, independent evaluator of the LbyM project, continues to observe teacher trainings and to review lesson plans in order to inform the design and implementation of the Learning by Making STEM curriculum and teacher training.

WestEd conducted a pilot assessment in May 2016 to determine the reliability of the instrument that will be used to assess improvements in mathematics and science proficency. The pilot assessment results indicated acceptable reliability (KR-20=0.76). Student scores on the pilot assessment ranged from 17% to 94% with an average percent correct score of 55.7%. Percent of science items correct ranged from 15% to 92% with an average percent correct score of 53.46%, and the percent of math items correct ranged from 11% to 100% with an average percent correct score of 59.70%. An item analysis did not suggest that there were certain topics on which students scored higher than others.

At the onset of the Fall 2016 semester, WestEd researchers started collecting demographic data for students enrolled in the course and for students in the comparison group. The assessment will be repeated at the end of the Spring 2017 semester.

Acknowledgements

We thank all the teachers in the Mendocino County high schools who have piloted the Learning by Making curriculum, and our partners at the Mendocino County Office of Education. Support for Learning by Making is provided by Investing in Innovation development grant U411C130090-13A from the US Department of Education. We also acknowledge support from Dr. Garrett Jernigan, Brian Silverman, Barry Silverman, Dr. Warren Wiscombe, Dr. Douglas B. Clarke, the Anderson Valley Educational Foundation, Sparkfun and Adafruit.

Feelbot: Reducing Use of Bad Words in Children through Wearable using Artificial Intelligence and Gamification

Ganesh Gaikwad
TATA Consultancy Services
Pune 411057, India
gaikwadgv@gmail.com

Abhishek Jain
TATA Consultancy Services
Pune 411057, India
abhishek.jain520@gmail.com

Abstract Author Keywords
Child psychology, Wearable, Chatbots, Gamification, Design, Voice recognition, intelligence, HCI, Fun, Behavior change.

Abstract
Feelbot is a cloud based self-learning system that helps children in reducing the use of bad words in their in-person and online communication. It can be used with existing wearable hardware such as wrist band, mobile phone or smart watch. It has a listening component that children can wear all the time. It gives real time alerts when the bad words are being used and also suggests better words to avoid the offense. The system is self-learning and uses cloud platform to analyze communication and create personalized game-challenges for a child. The real time support and the analytics can help a child in spotting and changing their undesirable language and motivates them towards developing mindful and kindful behavior through Gamification. The solution gives control to child for sharing the content and analytics to maintain privacy.

IDC '17, June 27-30, 2017, Stanford, CA, USA

ACM ISBN 978-1-4503-4921-5/17/06.
http://dx.doi.org/10.1145/3078072.3105876

ACM Classification Keywords
H.5.2 User Interfaces (D.2.2, H.1.2, I.3.6): User-centered design, Voice I/O, Natural language, Auditory (non-speech) feedback, Training, help, and documentation

Introduction
While children are growing physically, cognitively and psychologically, their behavior changes can be challenging for parents and school authorities at times. With the advent of social media, multimedia and digital platforms, children are getting connected with others

very quickly in person or virtually. Information exchange and social learning are increasing rapidly due to digital era. While using these channels, proper use of language is critical factor for the well-being of children in all their communication. Sometimes, children use bad words in their friend circle or among classmates without noticing the consequences and somewhere hurting others and themselves emotionally. However, the unique challenge here is how can one monitor their language real time, prevent offensive and bad words and inculcate desirable use of words. We are proposing a system that listens to in-person and online communication and alerts a child through wearable device(s). While using online channel, it can suggest options of better words and sentences to convey the message. The proposed system 'Feelbot' provides a way for children to interact freely in person and online with others and respect the feelings of others.

Background

Parenting experts suggest that child's use of bad words could have multiple underlying reasons. For example, Paty Wipfler [1] suggests that cursing for teenagers is just another way of exploring vocabulary. When children discover that cursing gets a reaction, they are likely to use it whenever they feel powerless. Seeking attention is also one of the reason to use bad words by children. Being and becoming upset in situations also leads children to lash out at another child verbally. Understanding psychological aspects of using bad words by children is an important factor in designing the solution to this problem.

Dr. B.J. Fogg [2] has proposed a behavior model framework to analyze any behavior. As per Fogg's model, three elements must converge at the same moment for a behavior to occur: Motivation, Ability, and Trigger. Dr. Fogg has also laid a guideline to design for a behavioral change [3]. As per this model, the design should aim at reducing the behavior of using bad words over time by reducing either of the motivation, ability or trigger. Similarly the positive behavior of using a better language can be achieved by changing motivation, ability or trigger. These behavior changes can be called as Grey Path and Purple Path respectively. The proposed system alerts a child at the time of trigger for using bad words and prevents the behavior (Grey Path). By suggesting alternatives for using better language at such situation, the system increases the ability towards a positive behavior (Purple Path).

System & architecture

Feelbot system is an integrated system comprising of multiple advanced technologies like wearables, internet of things, cloud platform and artificial intelligence. Overall system architecture of Feelbot is depicted in figure 1. It can be divided in to three generic modules, a. Observe b. Analyze and c. Respond.

Observe

The first most important job of Feelbot is to observe the child behavior. Observation is in the form of listening the words a child uses and his/her tone. The biometric information like heartbeat, expressions etc. is observed with the help of wearable devices like fitness band, watch, wearable tag, voice sensor, and biometric sensor. Such a wearable device can be Myle wearable [4, 5 and 6] or Fitness band presented in Figure 1 & 2.

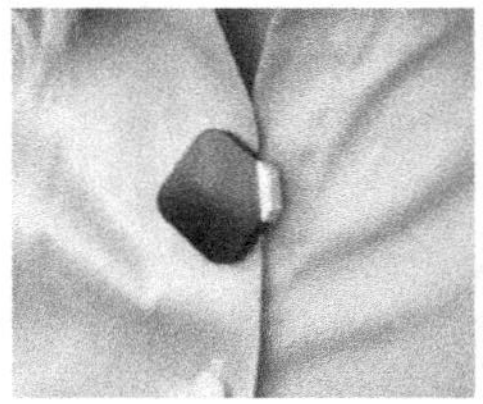

Figure 1: Myle (wearable device) for taking notes.

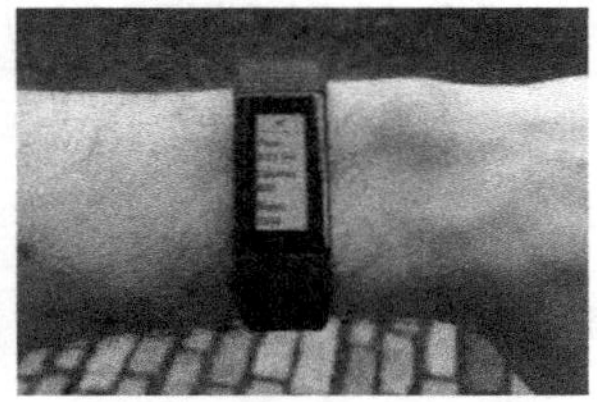

Figure 2: Fitness band for tracking biometric information and health.

In the context of online interaction, this observation will play an important role in tracking the kind of words and phrases a child is writing or sending to one or group. Smart keyboards can be integrated with social applications, desktop applications, messenger applications that can track the writing behavior of a child. This module observes and stores relevant information at the centralized cloud based intelligent platform. A child can refer to the same and can share it with others if required.

Analyze
Feelbot system has an intelligent sub-system which will work on analysis part. Analysis of language used by children is the prime factor. It also analyzes the mood of a child with the help of biometric information. This component uses the following factors to analyze the language used by a child:

- List of bad/hard words (prepared with the help of crowd sourced initiatives)
- Normal pitch of tone and variations in the tone with respect to mood. System can learn the behavior of a child and understand his/her mood via voice, tone and pitch. Researchers at MIT have prepared an artificially intelligent, wearable system [7] (figure 3) that can predict if a conversation is happy, sad, or neutral based on a person's speech patterns and vitals.

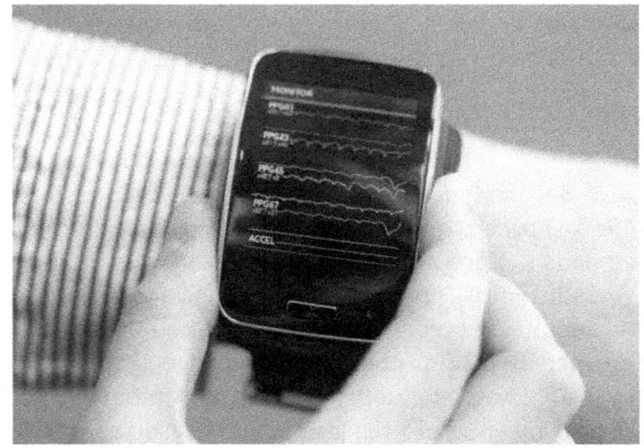

Figure 3: A Samsung Simband displays real-time results on conversational narrative and tone.

Post analysis of current behavior of child (in person/online) system will generate insights that will guide Feelbot to take actions (Responses).

Respond
This component is used for giving responses. Responses are the output that help child in preventing use of bad words with respect to the context. As per the analysis, Feelbot system can alert and notify children when they use bad words in interaction via signals/response on wearable (vibration, auditory response, visual response etc.). This can help them be aware of the triggers and change the behavior.

In harsh conditions, Feelbot can prompt humorous quotes which can help in changing mood of children and preventing them in becoming upset. If Feelbot senses a heated argument among children, it can show some tips (Figure 4) like breath deeply or be silent for 1 minute etc. This can take their temperament under control.

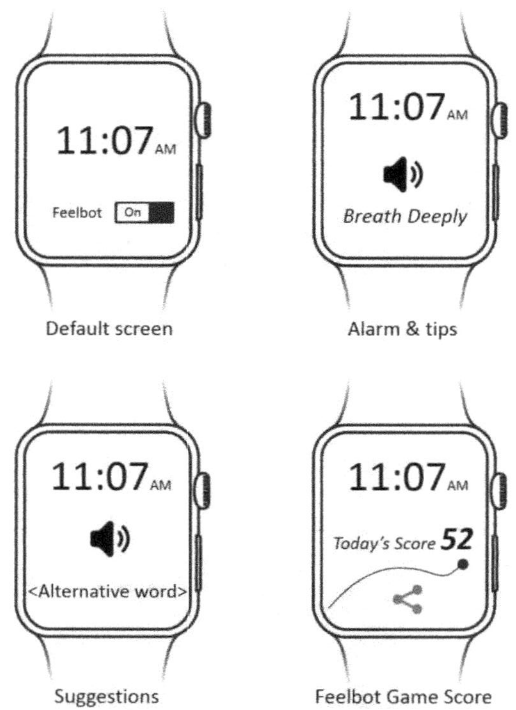

Figure 4: Wearable device on a child wrist; providing tips and alerts (visual/audio/vibration etc.)

While interacting online, Feelbot can filter and alert a child while sending bad or hurting message to others and also help him/her with some alternative phrases or words that will not hurt others' feelings.

Bringing Fun: Gamified strategy

Such a system should be acceptable by children. It can't be nagging and children should engage without a push. Hence the behavioral change for children should be supported with fun for better engagement and adoption. For bringing fun in overall Feelbot system Gamification mechanics can be implemented. Based upon analytics data at Feelbot system, a virtual gamified system can be proposed. Children, their classmates, teachers, parents, neighbors etc. can be included as players and teams in this game. Activities and behavior of child in real life can be simulated in virtual game where Gamification tactics can be integrated like scores (example: how many bad words you avoided or hearts you won today, how many appreciations you got this week etc.), challenges (example: not to loose temper when others send bad words), appreciation & awards, leaderboard (example: your ranking in class for the best behavior, fair communication etc.).

Discussion

Though many of the contemporary technologies seem to make this proposed system possible, we feel there has to be some motivation already to adopt this system. It can't be pushed by authorities or parents alone as a regulator. It depends on how we are able to intertwine it with the gadgets like smart watches children are already using.

Although the system helps children in improving behavior, it shouldn't be intrusive. It could be shut at will in a situation like sports where shouting is normal.

The words that system stores should be accessible to a child only and the score can be shared with others to respect their privacy.

Children are already getting too much of gadgets and technology. It is worthwhile to ponder if we are pushing more of it through this system. Can the same functionality be achieved through some transparent system that children don't even know it exists?

We feel there is a large potential to empower this system for other learning goals of children such as building strong vocabulary or improving speaking skills. It would be interesting to consider other positive uses of such a system.

References

1. Patty Wifler, Bad Words from Good Kids https://www.handinhandparenting.org/article/bad-words-from-good-kids/
2. Dr. B.J. Fogg's behavior model, http://www.behaviormodel.org/
3. Dr. B.J. Fogg's behavior grid, http://www.behaviorwizard.org/wp/behavior-grid/
4. "Your Wearable Smart Voice Recorder." Myle. N.p., n.d. 2017. http://getmyle.com/
5. "Senstone, Never Miss a Note Again." Kickstarter. N.p., n.d. 2017. https://www.kickstarter.com/projects/835264493/senstone-the-intelligent-wearable-voice-recorder
6. Stables, James. "Garmin Vivosmart HR Review." Wareable. N.p., 17 June 2016. Web. https://www.wareable.com/garmin/garmin-vivosmart-hr-plus-review
7. Adam Conner-Simons | Rachel Gordon | CSAIL. "Wearable AI System Can Detect a Conversation's Tone." MIT News. N.p., 01 Feb. 2017. http://news.mit.edu/2017/wearable-ai-can-detect-tone-conversation-0201

Promoting CARE: Changes via Awareness, Recognition and Experience

Monica Landoni
Anton Fedosov
Evangelos Niforatos
Faculty of Informatics
Università della Svizzera italiana
Via G Buffi 13
Lugano, 6900, Switzerland
monica.landoni@usi.ch
anton.fedosov@usi.ch
evangelos.niforatos@usi.ch

IDC '17, June 27-30, 2017, Stanford, CA, USA

ACM ISBN 978-1-4503-4921-5/17/06.
http://dx.doi.org/10.1145/3078072.3105877.

Abstract
We propose to design playful solutions to help young people better understand the consequences of their use of language in a community of peers. Our system, CARE, will analyse the content of their messages and extract the emotions they are charged with, both in terms of strength (arousal) and valence (negative or positive). Their effects will be translated visually in forms suitable for the different age groups. A positive reinforcement policy will be in place where good behaviour results in awards and popularity among a restricted circle of friends. Finally a simple and cheap wearable device will be offered to young persons willing to be alerted in case they get into an aggressive mood so to raise their awareness and help control themselves better.

Author Keywords
Behavioural, change; Empathy; Emotions; Playful, Experience; Design; Avatars; Synthetic, characters.

ACM Classification Keywords
H.5.m. Information interfaces and presentation (e.g., HCI): Miscellaneous.

Introduction

Here we present the system **CARE** (**C**hanging via **A**wareness, **R**ecognition and **E**xperience) to address Challenge 2: *Create mindful & kindful social support tools: tools to help young people be considerate of their own and others' feelings (in person or online).*

We believe this is a scenario where technology could be used to foster and support a behavioural change in young persons. Our system will filter messages before these are sent. It will automatically recognise hurtful content and flag a message as being negatively charged if it is above a certain threshold of acceptance, to be defined by the community of friends involved. It will highlight emotionally charged words/expressions, and let the young person intending to send that message choose whether he/she prefers the provided alternative wording right away, or watch the effect it will have on a virtual community of avatars that will react to offensive and abusive provocations. Thus, children will become aware of the damage they could cause to others and decide whether to change their message or not. CARE should not be prescriptive nor punitive in nature. Its purpose is to raise awareness in children by informing them about the consequences of using offensive language. In order to encourage good behaviour, the system will reward children who are using words with positive valence and ignore those who do not. These rewards will be visible via a Translucent Board (TB) to be shared among the small circle of friends inside which, children are exchanging messages. TB will be used to keep track of the children's behaviour in real life and while being visible to their peers, it will not be made public, thus ensuring privacy. Finally, we will design a tool to help children get a stronger sense of self-awareness of their mood, temperament and inclination towards angry interaction with their peers, in the shape of a wristband to provide visual clues of children's mood via colours and/or light based on the Empatica[1] design.

CARE will feature four main functions: (1) detection of hurtful messages; (2) representation of the effects of hurtful behaviour; (3) socially supported behavioural change; (4) recognition and awareness of current mood.

Detecting Hurtful Messages

This component will be a mobile app running on the child's personal device used for exchanging messages with his/her peers and perform the detection and filtering of unsuitable content produced by children. We propose to use advanced data mining approaches to detect hurtful content, adapted from those developed for bullying detection [1, 13, 15, 17], since there are many similarities between the two scenarios. We will start by filtering out messages according to a list of emotionally charged words divided according to their positive and negative valence. Our system will need to include new terms, specific lexicons/jargons, and language constructs used by young writers. Thus, we will rely on supervised approaches [5, 16, 17] to learn from examples and be able to detect hurtful elements also by taking into consideration the structure of the social networks being used by children as described by Huang et al in [11]. There is a growing body of literature on how to detect "offensive, abusive, aggressive and bullying content on social media" [3] and we will look there for the most suitable approach to help us detect hurtful content. This is a very complex

[1] See https://www.empatica.com/science

Figure 1: Nintendo's Tomodachi Life. The original image CC-BY 2.0 BagoGames on Flickr

Figure 2: Mii™ misbehaving. The original image CC-BY 2.0 BagoGames on Flickr

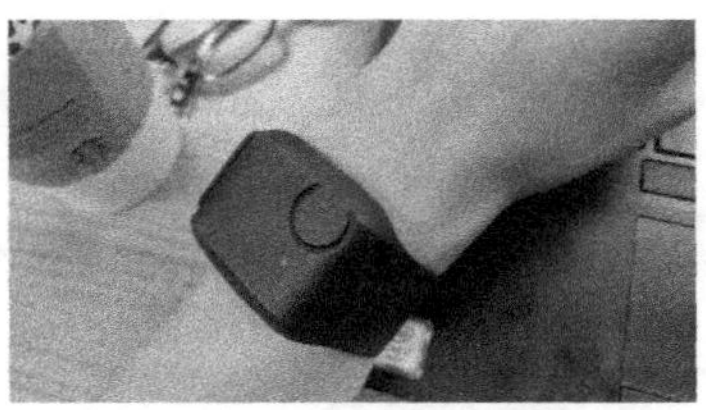

Figure 3: Empatica E4 wristband. Image CC-BY-ND 2.0 ih on Flickr

task since we will deal with ambiguity and misunderstanding on many levels, as described in this extract from the description of Challenge 2: "*... someone can say something as a joke and someone takes it bad and get bullied online*". The output of this component will be an articulated and rich model of the different forms that hurtful content can have, along with their implications and consequences. This will pave the way for their adequate virtual representation.

Representing the Effect of Hurtful Behavior in a Virtual Environment

We envisage at least two different solutions to be proposed to users according to their age group: (1) an emotional checker for older children, and (2) a game-like component for younger users.

Our emotional checker would work and behave like a spelling checker for emotionally charged expressions. These will be graphically highlighted with suitable colors to attract attention. Alternative non-hurtful expressions will be suggested to replace those found as inappropriate.

For the design of the game-like component we will build a Reflective User Interface [5] to "*...change the spread of hurtful online behavior*". This approach includes, among others, the use of notifications, delays in action and displays of consequences, all crucial elements of our design. Besides, we will investigate how to adapt and explore the design of synthetic characters together with dynamic narratives beyond the school scenario as in FearNot! [10]. Inspiration will also come from popular life-simulation games such as Tomodachi Life[2] where children can create Mii™ characters to be based on friends and family, see Figures 1 and 2. Children will be able to define characters, select possible scenarios and follow a narrative created by them dynamically. A richer virtual environment for them to experience the effects and consequences of hurtful behavior.

Socially Supported Behavioural Change: the Translucent Board

The Social Translucence (ST) framework [8] has been already successfully applied to the design of technology in changing behaviour in health scenarios [2]. Our Translucent Board (TB) will reward children for their good behaviour by making their merits visible to their peers. As it is of crucial importance to be able to maintain children's privacy, we propose to use the TB only among small circles of friends and assign nicknames to all participants. By providing good examples "*it would help them (other children) know what to say and what not to say to make friends, and relationships*" [taken from description of Challenge 2]. We will revisit the concepts of Behavior Chart and Hall of Fame with a game like approach and have synthetic characters/avatars as in the reflective interface described above to act in that space. We will design a reward mechanism to fit into the game narrative as an incentive for good behavior.

Recognition and Awareness of Current Mood

We aim to design a simple and cheap adaptation of the Empatica wristband as in Figure 3, and incorporate the data gathered by its sensors to provide the wearer with indication of his/her mood. Currently the E4 wristband is used for measuring stress, engagement, and excitement. By combining these measures within a model of behavior that focuses on anger, we will be

[2] http://www.nintendo.com/games/detail/tomodachi-life-3ds

able to provide wearers with visible feedback, e.g., changing color and/or showing a suitable emoji, of how calm or angry they are. The wristband would give out a signal to warn the child about his/her current emotional state and warn that his/her reactions are being affected by anger, as happens when "*I get upset or emotional my rational part of my brain shuts down ...*" [taken from description of Challenge 2]. This would in turn invite the child to pause and reflect on the suitability of the message/reaction he/she is going to issue and help him/her be mindful and in control.

Methodology

Children as Co-designers

We will explore all the solutions listed above by including in our design team a group of volunteering children, by following a widely adopted approach to design [6, 7]. In our past experiences [4], involving young people in the design of tools intended for them is beneficial in terms of creativity of proposed solutions and in the gathering of realistic and rich user requirements. We will define suitable activities and gather continuous feedback with similar tools as those described in [13].

Gender and Ethical Issues

As in [10], we expect boys and girls to react differently to the proposed solutions. We will make sure to include in our co-design team an equal number of both genders and plan for separate narratives and visual representation of virtual characters for fulfilling their different needs and preferences. Besides, we will make sure children's contribution is acknowledged and valued as much as that of adult members of the design team.

Measuring Changes

Setting up criteria and measures to evaluate how CARE has achieved its goals of encouraging positive changes in children, especially in the long term, will be a complex task. We plan to evaluate each of the new tools according to usability and quality of the user experience. We expect our co-designers to provide us with meaningful insights and act as fellow co-evaluators. In the description provided for Challenge 2, we read that children are aware and afraid of the long term effect of their misbehavior: "*if you post something bad it's hard to just get rid of it ... and your reputation can be ruined by one post*". We will expand on this observation and look for measures of how our intervention has made a difference in children's life from that perspective.

Conclusions

We have described the components of a system, CARE, as an answer to Challenge 2 posed by children from two schools in rural areas in *Ban Samkha* and *Nederland*. Our design is based on their anecdotes, insights and initial feedback, together with previous experiences working with children ages 8-12 in local schools and public libraries. The goal of our system is to raise children's awareness and help them avoid the regret of having said and/or written something hurtful. We propose to combine state of the art solutions for filtering messages and provide children with a game-like experience to help them reflect on the upcoming effect of their actions. Fun and engagement are at the core of the proposed system, designed to provide positive reinforcement and stop harm before it happens.

References

1. Al-garadi, Mohammed Ali, Kasturi Dewi Varathan, Sri Devi Ravana. 2016. Cybercrime Detection in Online Communications. *Computers in Human Behaviour*. 63(C). 433-443.
2. Caraban, A. Ferreria, M., J., Belim, V., Lyra, O. and Karapanos, E. (2014) SmartHolder: Sensing and raising Families Awareness of Tooth Brushing Habits. *Proceedings of the 13th International Conference on Interaction Design and Children - IDC '14.* ACM Press 341-344.
3. Chatzakou Despoina, Nicolas Kourtellis, Jeremy Blackburn, Emiliano De Cristofaro, Gianluca Stringhini and Athena Vakali. 2017. Measuring #GamerGate: A Tale of Hate, Sexism, and Bullying. 2017. *International WWW Conference*.
4. Colombo Luca and Monica Landoni. A diary study of children's user experience with EBooks using flow theory as framework. *Proceedings of the 13th International Conference on Interaction Design and Children - IDC '14.* ACM Press. 135-144
5. Dinakar, Karthik, Birago Jones, Catherine Havasi, Henry Lieberman and Rosalind Picard. 2012. "Common Sense Reasoning for Detection, Prevention, and Mitigation of Cyberbullying". *ACM Transaction on Interactive Intelligent System*. 2(3).
6. Druin, Allison. 1999. "Cooperative inquiry: developing new technologies for children with children." *Proceedings of the SIGCHI conference on Human Factors in Computing Systems*. ACM.
7. Druin, Allison. 2002. "The role of children in the design of new technology". *Behaviour and Information Technology* 21(1).
8. Erikson, T. and Kellogg, W. A. 2000. Social Translucence: An Approach to Designing Systems that Support Social Processes. *Transaction of Computer-Human Interaction*, 7(1). 59-83.
9. Hall, Lynne, Woods , Sarah , Dautenhahn , K , Sobral , D , Paiva , A , Wolke , D & Newall , L. 2004. "Designing empathic agents: adults versus kids'. Lecture Notes in Computer Science, vol 3220. 604-613.
10. Hall, Lynne, Susan Jones, Ana Paiva, Ruth Aylett. 2009. FearNot! Providing Children with Strategies to Cope with Bullying. ACM. *Proceedings of IDC 2009*.
11. Huang, Qianjia, Vivek K. Singh, Pradeep K. Atrey. 2014. Cyber Bullying Detection Using Social and Textual Analysis. *Proceedings of SAM'14*.
12. Mancilla-Caceres, JuanF. Eyal Amir, Dortohy Espelage. 2013. Adaptive Game for reducing Aggressive Behavior. ACM *IUI'13 Companion*.
13. Read, Janet, C. and Stuart MacFarlane. 2006. "Using the fun toolkit and other survey methods to gather opinions in child computer interaction". *Proceedings of the 2006 conference on Interaction design and children*, June 07-09, Tampere, Finland.
14. Raminhos Cátia. Ana Paula Cláudio, Maira Beatriz Carmo, Susa Carvalhosa, Maria de Jessu Candeias, Augusta Gaspar. 2015. A Serious Game-based Solution to prevent Bullying. ACM. *Proceedings of MoMM'2015*.
15. Vala Marco, João Dias, Ana Paiva. 2006. Mind the body: filling the gap between minds and bodies in synthetic characters. IVA'06. *Proceedings of the 6th International Conference on Intelligent Virtual Agents.*
16. Xu, Jun-Ming, Xiaoijn Zhu, Amy Bellmore. 2012. Fast Learning for Sentiment Analysis on Bullying. *Proceedings of WISDOM'12*.
17. Zhao Rui, Anna Zhou, Kezhi Mao, 2016. Automatic Detection of CyberBullying on Social Networks based on Bullying Features. ACM. *ICDNC 16.*

Author Index

www.ingramcontent.com/pod-product-compliance
Lightning Source LLC
LaVergne TN
LVHW080104011026
849160LV00013B/1026
* 9 7 8 1 4 5 0 3 5 5 9 1 9 *